Department of Economic and Social Affairs
Population Division

World Population Ageing 2007

United Nations
New York, 2007

DESA

The Department of Economic and Social Affairs of the United Nations Secretariat is a vital interface between global policies in the economic, social and environmental spheres and national action. The Department works in three main interlinked areas: (i) it compiles, generates and analyses a wide range of economic, social and environmental data and information on which States Members of the United Nations draw to review common problems and take stock of policy options; (ii) it facilitates the negotiations of Member States in many intergovernmental bodies on joint courses of action to address ongoing or emerging global challenges; and (iii) it advises interested Governments on the ways and means of translating policy frameworks developed in United Nations conferences and summits into programmes at the country level and, through technical assistance, helps build national capacities.

Note

ST/ESA/SER.A/260

ISBN 978-92-1-151432-2
Sales No. E.07.XIII.5

United Nations publication

Preface

As the proportion of the world's population in the older ages continues to increase, the need for improved information and analysis of demographic ageing increases. Knowledge is essential to assist policy makers to define, formulate and evaluate goals and programmes, and to raise public awareness and support for needed policy changes.

The Population Division of the Department of Economic and Social Affairs of the United Nations has long experience in the analysis of population ageing. In addition to preparing national estimates and projections of older populations, the Population Division has contributed to the analysis of the determinants and consequences of population ageing. The Population Division is the organizational unit of the Secretariat charged with monitoring progress towards the achievement of the goals set out in the Programme of Action of the International Conference on Population and Development, held in Cairo in 1994. The Programme of Action enunciated objectives and recommended actions concerning population ageing and older persons (United Nations, 1995).

The Population Division has also organized expert meetings on various aspects of population ageing. In 1997, for example, the Division convened a meeting on below-replacement fertility (United Nations, 2000); in 2000, two meetings on population ageing were organized: the first on the living arrangements of older persons (United Nations, 2001), and the second on policy responses to population ageing and population decline (United Nations, 2004). More recently, in 2005, the Population Division organized an expert group meeting on the social and economic implications of changing population age structures (United Nations, forthcoming).

In 1982, the United Nations adopted the International Plan of Action on Ageing at the first World Assembly on Ageing (United Nations, 1982). Then, in 1999 in its resolution 54/262, the General Assembly decided to convene the Second World Assembly on Ageing in 2002. The Second World Assembly adopted the Madrid International Plan of Action on Ageing, marking a turning point in how the world addresses the key challenge of building a society for all ages. The Plan focuses on three priority areas: older persons and development; advancing health and well-being into old age; and ensuring enabling and supportive environments.

This new edition of *World Population Ageing 1950-2050* updates the original report released in 2002 in conjunction with the Second World Assembly on Ageing, and incorporates new variables. As in the case of the original report, this new edition provides a description of global trends in population ageing and includes a series of indicators of the ageing process by development regions, major areas, regions and countries. It is intended to provide a solid demographic foundation for the follow-up activities of the Second World Assembly on Ageing.

Comments and suggestions on this report are welcome and may be addressed to Ms. Hania Zlotnik, Director, Population Division, Department of Economic and Social Affairs, United Nations Secretariat, New York, N.Y. 10017, fax number (212) 963-2147.

Sources, methods and classifications

Data on demographic trends used in the present report are taken from the 2004 Revision of the official United Nations world population estimates and projections (United Nations, 2005a). In addition, data on labour force participation were obtained from the International Labour Organization (International Labour Office, 2006); on illiteracy from the United Nations Educational, Scientific and Cultural Organization (UNESCO Institute for Statistics, 2006); on statutory pensionable age from the United States Social Security Administration (United States Social Security Administration, 2006); and on living arrangements and marital status from two recent United Nations publications (United Nations, 2005b and 2006).

The population estimates and projections, which are prepared biennially by the Population Division of the Department of Economic and Social Affairs of the United Nations Secretariat, provide the standard and consistent set of population figures that are used throughout the United Nations system as the basis for activities requiring population information. In the case of the 2004 Revision, standard demographic techniques were used to estimate the population by age and sex for the base year (2005) as well as trends in total fertility, life expectancy at birth, infant mortality and international migration up to 2004. The resulting estimates provided the basis from which the population projections follow.

The countries and areas identified as statistical units by the Statistics Division of the United Nations and covered by the above estimates and projections are grouped geographically into six major areas: Africa; Asia; Europe; Latin America and the Caribbean; Northern America; and Oceania. Those major areas are further divided geographically into 21 regions. In addition, the regions are summarized, for statistical convenience, into two general groups—more developed and less developed—on the basis of demographic and socio-economic characteristics. The less developed regions include all regions of Africa, Asia (excluding Japan), Latin America and the Caribbean, and Oceania (excluding Australia and New Zealand). The more developed regions include all other regions plus the three countries excluded from the less developed regions. See annex II for further detail.

Contents

Annex tables

Explanatory notes

Symbols of United Nations documents are composed of capital letters combined with figures.

The following symbols have been used in the tables throughout this report:

..   **Two dots** indicate that data are not available or are not separately reported.

—   **An em dash** indicates that the amount is nil or negligible.

-   **A hyphen** indicates that the item is not applicable.

−   **A minus sign** before a figure indicates a decrease.

.   **A point** is used to indicate decimals.

/   **A slash** indicates a crop year or financial year, for example, 1994/95.

-   **Use of a hyphen** between dates representing years, for example, 1990-1995, signifies the full period involved, including the beginning and end years.

Details and percentages in tables do not necessarily add to totals because of rounding.

Reference to **"dollars" ($)** indicates United States dollars, unless otherwise stated.

The term **"billion"** signifies a thousand million.

موجز تنفيذي

شكلت خطة عمل مدريد الدولية المتعلقة بالشيخوخة والإعلان السياسي اللذان اعتُمدا بالجمعية العالمية للشيخوخة في نيسان/أبريل ٢٠٠٢ [1] نقطة تحوّل في الطريقة التي يتصدى بها العالم للتحدّي الرئيسي المتمثل في بناء مجتمع لجميع الأعمار. وتركز الخطة على ثلاثة مجالات ذات أولوية: كبار السن والتنمية؛ والمحافظة على الصحة والرفاه حتى سن متقدمة؛ وضمان توافر بيئات مؤاتية وداعمة. وهي تشكل المرة الأولى التي تعتمد فيها الحكومات نهجاً شاملاً يربط بين مسائل الشيخوخة وغيرها من أُطر التنمية الاجتماعية والاقتصادية وحقوق الإنسان، وعلى الأخص الأُطر التي اتُفق عليها في مؤتمرات الأمم المتحدة ومؤتمرات قمتها التي انعقدت خلال تسعينات القرن العشرين.

وقد أيدت القضايا ذات الصلة بشيخوخة السكان وكبار السن دوراً بارزاً في المؤتمرات السكانية الدولية الكبرى الثلاثة التي نظمتها الأمم المتحدة خلال ربع القرن الماضي. فقد أقر المؤتمر الدولي للسكان والتنمية الذي عُقد عام ١٩٩٤، على سبيل المثال، بأن الأثر الاقتصادي والاجتماعي لشيخوخة السكان هو فرصة وتحدٍّ على حد سواء بالنسبة لكل المجتمعات [2]. وقد أعادت الإجراءات الأساسية لمواصلة تنفيذ برنامج عمل المؤتمر الدولي للسكان والتنمية، في الآونة الأخيرة، وهي إجراءات اعتمدتها الجمعية العامة في دورتها الاستثنائية الحادية والعشرين في ٢ تموز/يوليه ١٩٩٩، التأكيد على حاجة كل المجتمعات للتصدّي للعواقب الهامة لشيخوخة السكان في العقود القادمة [3]. وستركز لجنة الأمم المتحدة للسكان والتنمية أعمالها في عام ٢٠٠٧ على الهياكل المتغيّرة لأعمار السكان وآثارها على التنمية، وهو الموضوع الخاص لدورتها الأربعين.

ولشعبة السكان بالأمم المتحدة تاريخ عريق في دراسة شيخوخة السكان، بما في ذلك عن طريق تقدير وإسقاط حجم المجموعات السكانية الآخذة في الشيخوخة وخصائصها، ومن فحص محددات شيخوخة السكان وعواقبها. فطالما سعت شعبة السكان باستمرار إلى لفت انتباه الحكومات والمجتمع الدولي إلى شيخوخة السكان، وذلك من التقرير الرائد عن شيخوخة السكان الذي صدر عام ١٩٥٦ وركز في المقام الأول على شيخوخة السكان في البلدان الأكثر نمواً، إلى المخطط البياني الجداري للأمم المتحدة بشأن شيخوخة السكان الذي صدر عام ٢٠٠٦ [4].

وقررت لجنة الأمم المتحدة للتنمية الاجتماعية إجراء استعراض وتقييم كل خمس سنوات للتقدم المحرز في تنفيذ خطة عمل مدريد للشيخوخة. وعلاوة على ذلك، شددت الجمعية العامة على الحاجة

---

[1]   انظر: تقرير الجمعية العالمية الثانية للشيخوخة (منشورات الأمم المتحدة A/CONF.197/9، رقم المبيع: E.02.IV.4).

[2]   السكان والتنمية، المجلد ١: برنامج العمل الذي اعتُمد بالمؤتمر الدولي للسكان والتنمية، القاهرة، ٥ – ١٣ أيلول/ سبتمبر ١٩٩٤ (منشورات الأمم المتحدة، رقم المبيع: E.95.XIII.7).

[3]   استعراض وتقييم التقدم المحرز في تحقيق أهداف ومقاصد برنامج عمل المؤتمر الدولي للسكان والتنمية، تقرير عام ١٩٩٩ (منشورات الأمم المتحدة، رقم المبيع: E.99.XIII.16).

[4]   شيخوخة السكان وآثارها الاقتصادية والاجتماعية، دراسات سكانية، عدد ٢٦ (منشورات الأمم المتحدة، رقم المبيع: 1956.XIII. 6)؛ وشيخوخة السكان ٢٠٠٦ (منشورات الأمم المتحدة، رقم المبيع: E.06.XIII.2).

إلى بيانات سكانية مفصلة على أساس العمر والجنس. ويوفر هذا التقرير الأساس الديمغرافي لأنشطة متابعة الجمعية العالمية الثانية للشيخوخة. فهو يتناول عملية شيخوخة السكان في العالم ككل، وفي المناطق الأكثر نمواً والأقل نمواً، وفي المناطق والأقاليم الكبرى، بالإضافة إلى بلدان فردية. وتتوافر لمحات ديمغرافية تغطي الفترة من عام ١٩٥٠ إلى عام ٢٠٥٠ عن كل بلد، وتسلط الضوء على المؤشرات ذات الصلة بشيخوخة السكان.

وتؤكد محتويات هذا التقرير أربع نتائج هامة:

١ – شيخوخة السكان ظاهرة غير مسبوقة، وعملية لا نظير لها في تاريخ البشرية. فتشيخ بمجموعة سكانية حينما يصاحب ارتفاع نسبة كبار السن (أي من تبلغ أعمارهم ٦٠ عاماً فما فوق) انخفاضاً في نسبة الأطفال (الأشخاص دون سن ١٥ عاماً) ثم يصاحبها انخفاض في نسب الأشخاص في سن العمل (١٥ إلى ٥٩ عاماً). ويُتوقّع أن يفوق عدد كبار السن على مستوى العالم عدد الأطفال لأول مرة في عام ٢٠٤٧. أما في المناطق الأكثر نمواً، حيث شيخوخة السكان أكثر تقدماً بكثير، انخفض عدد الأطفال عن عدد كبار السن في عام ١٩٩٨.

٢ – شيخوخة السكان ظاهرة منتشرة، حيث إنها تكاد تؤثر في جميع بلدان العالم. وتنشأ شيخوخة السكان أساساً عن تراجع الخصوبة على نحو صار عالمياً تقريباً. ولما ينتج عن هذا من تباطؤ في نمو عدد الأطفال، تصاحبه زيادة مطردة في عدد كبار السن، تأثير مباشر على الإنصاف والتضامن داخل الأجيال وفيما بينها، وهما يشكلان البنيان الذي يقوم عليه المجتمع.

٣ – شيخوخة السكان ظاهرة عميقة ولها نتائج وآثار كبيرة على جميع مناحي الحياة البشرية. فسيكون لشيخوخة السكان في المجال الاقتصادي أثر على النمو الاقتصادي، والمدخرات، والاستثمار، والاستهلاك، وأسواق العمل، والمعاشات التقاعدية، والضرائب، والتحويلات بين الأجيال. وفي الميدان الاجتماعي، تؤثر شيخوخة السكان في تركيب الأسرة وترتيبات المعيشة، والطلب على المساكن، واتجاهات الهجرة، وعلم الأوبئة، والحاجة لخدمات الرعاية الصحية. أما في المجال السياسي، يمكن أن تحدد شيخوخة السكان أنماط التصويت والتمثيل السياسي.

الشكل ١

نسبة السكان في سن ٦٠ فما فوق: العالم، ١٩٥٠ – ٢٠٥٠

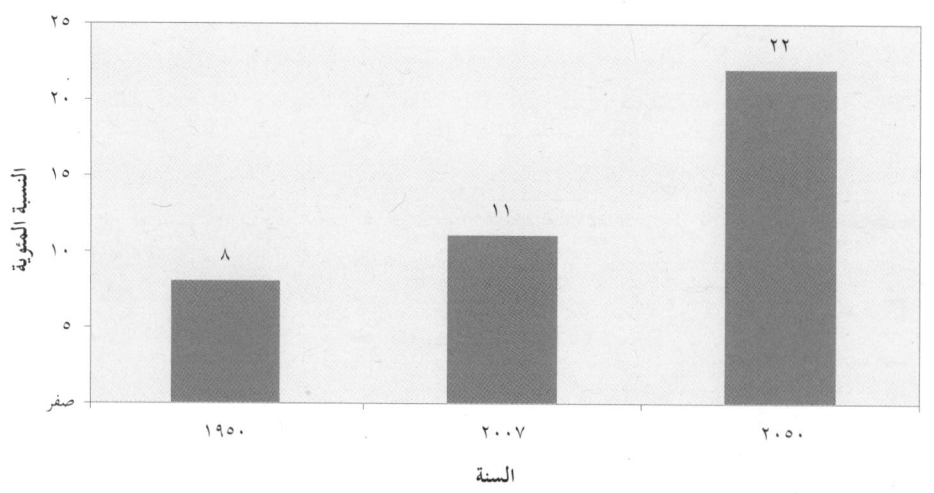

٤ - شيخوخة السكان ظاهرة مستمرة. فقد ظلت نسبة كبار السن منذ عام ١٩٥٠ في ازدياد مطرد، مرتفعة من ٨ في المائة في عام ١٩٥٠ إلى ١١ في المائة في عام ٢٠٠٧، ومن المتوقّع أن تصل إلى ٢٢ في المائة في عام ٢٠٥٠ (الشكل ١). وما دامت وفيات المسنين مستمرة في الانخفاض ومعدلات الخصوبة باقية على انخفاضها، ستستمر نسبة كبار السن في الارتفاع.

وفيما يلي أهم النتائج التي خلص إليها هذا التقرير:

- نظراً لأن من غير المحتمل أن ترتفع معدلات الخصوبة من جديد إلى المعدلات العالية التي كانت مألوفة في الماضي، فإن شيخوخة السكان لا رجعة فيها، كما أن من المرجح أن المجموعات السكانية الشابة المألوفة حتى وقت قريب ستصبح نادرة على مدى القرن الحادي والعشرين.

- وصل عدد السكان الذين تبلغ أعمارهم ٦٠ سنة فما فوق في عام ٢٠٠٠ إلى ٦٠٠ مليون نسمة، وهـو ثلاثة أضعاف عـددهم عام ١٩٥٠. وفي عام ٢٠٠٦، تجاوز عدد كبار السن الـ ٧٠٠ مليون نسمة. ومن المتوقّع أن يكون هناك بليونا مسنّ على قيد الحياة عـام ٢٠٥٠، مما يفيد ضمنياً بتضاعف عددهم مرة أخرى ثلاثة أضعاف على مدى ٥٠ عاماً.

- يتنامى عدد كبار السن عالمياً بمعدل ٢,٦ في المائة كل عام، وهذا أسرع بكثير من عدد السكان ككل الذي يزداد بنسبة ١,١ في المائة كل عام. ومن المتوقّع أن يستمر عدد كبار السن في النمو بصورة أسرع من عدد السكان في سائر المجموعات العمرية، وذلك حتى عام ٢٠٥٠ على الأقل. وسيتطلب مثل هذا النمو السريع إدخال تعديلات اقتصادية واجتماعية بعيدة المدى في أغلب البلدان.

- توجد فروق واضحة بين المناطق المتقدمة النمو والمناطق النامية من حيث عدد كبار السن ونسبتهم. فيبلغ حالياً عمر أكثر من خمس سكان المناطق الأكثر نمواً ٦٠ عاماً أو أكثر، ومن المتوقّع أن يكون قرابة ثلث سكان البلدان المتقدمة النمو من تلك الشريحة العمرية بحلول عام ٢٠٥٠. أما في المناطق الأقل نمواً، فسيتأثر كبار السن اليوم بما لا يزيد عن ٨ في المائة من السكان، غير أن من المتوقّع أن يمثلوا، بحلول عام ٢٠٥٠، خمس السكان، مما يفيد ضمنياً باحتمال وصول العالم النامي بحلول منتصف القرن إلى نفس المرحلة في عملية شيخوخة السكان التي وصلها بالفعل العالم المتقدم النمو.

- تزيد سرعة شيخوخة السكان في البلدان النامية عنها في البلدان المتقدمة النمو. ونتيجة لذلك، فإن الوقت المتاح أمام البلدان النامية للتكيّف مع عواقب شيخوخة السكان سيكون أقل. وبالإضافة إلى هذا، فإن شيخوخة السكان في البلدان النامية تحدث في مستويات من التنمية الاقتصادية الاجتماعية أدنى مما هي في البلدان المتقدمة النمو.

- يبلغ العمر الوسيط في العالم اليوم ٢٨ سنة، أي أن نصف سكان العالم تقل أعمارهم عن تلك السن، بينما تزيد أعمار النصف الآخر عنها. والبلد الذي توجد فيه أصغر المجموعات السكانية سناً هو أوغندا، حيث يبلغ العمر الوسيط ١٥ عاماً، أما البلد الذي توجد فيه أكبر المجموعات السكانية سناً فهو اليابان، التي يبلغ العمر الوسيط فيها ٤٣ عاماً. ومن المرجح أن يرتفع العمر الوسيط العالمي على مدى العقود الأربعة التالية عشر سنوات ليبلغ ٣٨ عاماً سنة ٢٠٥٠. ومن المرجح آنذاك أن تصبح بوروندي وأوغندا اللذين توجد فيهما أصغر المجموعات السكانية سناً، حيث يبلغ العمر الوسيط ٢٠ عاماً، بينما يُتوقع أن توجد أكبر المجموعات السكانية سناً في منطقة ماكاو الإدارية الخاصة في الصين وفي جمهورية كوريا، حيث يُتوقّع أن يصل العمر الوسيط إلى ٥٤ عاماً.

وبحموعة كبار السن ذاتها آخذة في الشيخوخة. فمن بين السكان البالغين من العمر ٦٠ عاماً أو أكثر، فإن أسرع المجموعات نمواً هم أكبر المسنين، أي الذين تبلغ أعمارهم ٨٠ عاماً فما فوق. فأعدادهم تزداد حالياً بنسبة ٣,٩ في المائة كل عام. ويستأثر الأشخاص الذين تبلغ أعمارهم ٨٠ عاماً فما فوق بحوالي ١ بين كل ٨ من كبار السن (٦٠ عاماً فما فوق). ومن المتوقّع أن ترتفع هذه النسبة بحلول عام ٢٠٥٠ لتصل إلى حوالي شخصين يبلغ عمرهما ٨٠ عاماً فما فوق بين كل ١٠ من كبار السن.

• تبيّن نسبة الدعم المحتمل، ألا وهو عدد من تتراوح أعمارهم بين ١٥ و٦٤ عاماً لكل مسنّ يبلغ عمره ٦٥ عاماً فما فوق، عدد العمال المحتملين الموجودين لكل مسنّ. ومع تقدم بحموعة سكانية ما في السن، تميل قيمة نسبة الدعم المحتمل إلى الانخفاض. فقد انخفضت نسبة الدعم المحتمل في الفترة بين عامي ١٩٥٠ و٢٠٠٧ من ١٢ عاملاً إلى ٩ عمال محتملين لكل شخص يبلغ عمره ٦٥ سنة فما فوق. ومن المتوقّع أن تواصل نسبة الدعم المحتمل انخفاضها بحلول عام ٢٠٥٠ لتصل إلى ٤ عمال محتملين لكل شخص يبلغ عمره ٦٥ سنة فما فوق (الشكل ٢). ولانخفاض نسب الدعم المحتمل آثار هامة على نظم الضمان الاجتماعي، لا سيما بالنسبة لنظم المعاشات التقاعدية التي تقوم على دفع الاستحقاقات أولاً بأول والتي تموّل بموجبها الضرائب المفروضة على رواتب العمال الحاليين معاشات المتقاعدين.

• ونظراً لأن النساء يعشن أكثر من الرجال، فإن النساء يشكلن أغلبية كبار السن. ويفوق حالياً عدد النساء عدد الرجال بحوالي ٧٠ مليون بين الأشخاص الذين تبلغ أعمارهم ٦٠ عاماً فما فوق. أما بالنسبة للذين تبلغ أعمارهم ٨٠ عاماً فما فوق، فيبلغ عدد النساء ضعفي عدد الرجال تقريباً، وبالنسبة للذين تبلغ أعمارهم مائة عام فما فوق، يتراوح عدد النساء بين أربعة وخمسة أضعاف عدد الرجال (الشكل ٣).

• عادة ما تعتل صحة كبار السن بتقدم العمر، مما يتسبب في زيادة الطلب على الرعاية طويلة الأجل مع تزايد عدد كبار السن. وتمثل نسبة دعم الوالدين، وهي نسبة السكان الذين تبلغ أعمارهم ٨٥ سنة فما فوق إلى السكان الذين تتراوح أعمارهم بين ٥٠ و٦٤ عاماً، مؤشراً

الشكل ٢

نسبة الدعم المحتمل: العالم، ١٩٥٠ – ٢٠٥٠

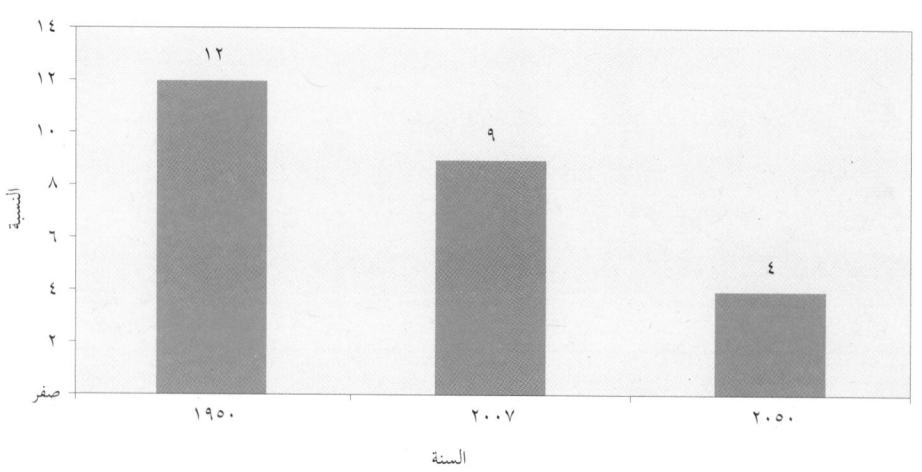

نسبة النساء بين الأشخاص الذين تتراوح أعمارهم بين ٤٠ و٥٩، و٦٠ فما فوق، و٨٠ فما فوق، و١٠٠ فما فوق: العالم، ٢٠٠٧

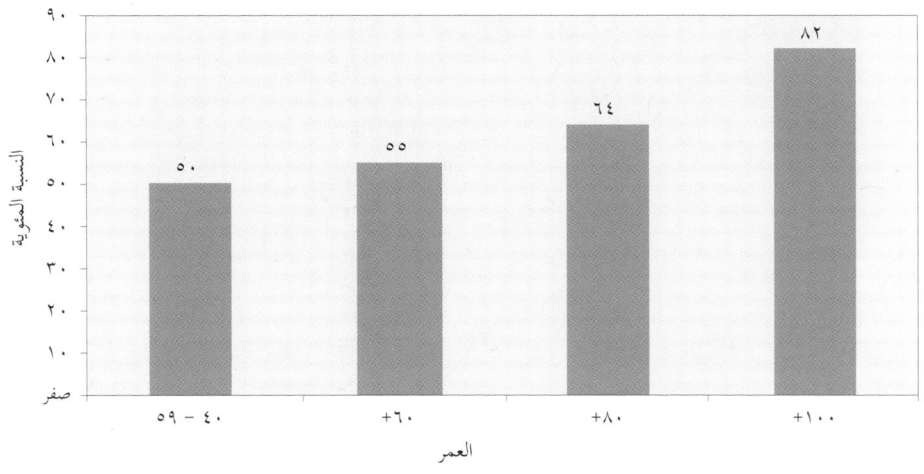

لمستوى الدعم الذي يمكن للأسر أن تقدمه لمسنّيها. وعلى مستوى العالم، كان هناك عام ١٩٥٠ أقل من شخصين يبلغ عمرهما ٨٥ سنة فما فوق لكل ١٠٠ شخص تتراوح أعمارهم بين ٥٠ و٦٤ عاماً. أما اليوم، فتتجاوز تلك النسبة بقليل ٤ أشخاص لكل ١٠٠ شخص، غير أن من المتوقّع أن تصل إلى ١٢ لكل ١٠٠ شخص بحلول عام ٢٠٥٠. ويعني هذا أن الأشخاص الذين تجاوزوا هم أنفسهم بكثير فترة منتصف العمر سيتضاعف احتمال اضطلاعهم بمسؤولية رعاية الأقارب الأكبر سناً ثلاث مرات عما هو عليه اليوم.

- كبار السن الذين يعيشون بمفردهم أكثر عرضة للعزلة الاجتماعية والحرمان الاقتصادي، ولذلك فقد يحتاجون إلى دعم خاص. وبسبب ارتفاع معدلات بقاء المسنّات على قيد الحياة وانخفاض النزعة لديهن إلى التزوج من جديد، فإنهن أكثر عرضة من المسنّين للعيش بمفردهن. وعلى مستوى العالم، تعيش نسبة تقدر بـ ١٩ في المائة من النساء اللاتي يبلغن من العمر ٦٠ عاماً فما فوق بمفردهن، بينما لا ينطبق هذا سوى على ٨ في المائة من الرجال من تلك الفئة العمرية.

- تتباين السن الفعلية للتقاعد بشكل كبير بين مختلف المجموعات السكانية. فيمكن لكبار السن في البلدان التي يرتفع فيها الدخل الفردي التقاعد في سن أصغر ومن ثم تتجه معدلات مشاركتهم في القوة العاملة إلى الانخفاض في الأعمار الأكبر. ومن ثم، فإن ١٣ في المائة فقط من الرجال الذين يبلغون من العمر ٦٥ عاماً فما فوق نشطون اقتصادياً في المناطق الأكثر نمواً، بينما ينتمي ٣٩ في المائة إلى القوة العاملة بالمناطق الأقل نمواً. والفارق مماثل بين النساء. ففي المناطق الأكثر نمواً، فإن ٧ في المائة من المسنّات نشطات اقتصادياً، مقارنة بـ ١٥ في المائة في المناطق الأقل نمواً. ويبقى كبار السن نشطين اقتصاديا لفترات أطول في المناطق الأقل نمواً بسبب التغطية المحدودة لبرامج المعاشات التقاعدية والدخول الصغيرة نسبياً التي توفرها.

- السن القانونية التي يمكن فيها الحصول على معاش تقاعدي كامل بشرط إتمام حد أدنى من الوقت في الإسهام في نظام المعاشات التقاعدية (أي سن التقاعد) هي ذاتها في معظم البلدان بالنسبة للنساء والرجال. إلاّ أن النساء في كثير من البلدان مؤهلات لتلقّي استحقاقات المعاش التقاعدي الكامل في أعمار أقل من أعمار الرجال، رغم توقّع أن تعيش النساء لفترات أطول من فترات الرجال بعد سن الستين. ويميل سن التقاعد بالنسبة للرجال والنساء لأن يكون أعلى في البلدان المتقدمة النمو عنه في البلدان النامية.

- لا تزال الأمية شائعة بين كبار السن في المناطق الأقل نمواً. ويُقدر حالياً أن أكثر من نصف الأشخاص الذين يبلغون من العمر ٦٥ عاماً فما فوق في البلدان النامية أميون. ولا يحظى سوى ما يقارب ثلث المسنّات وثلاثة أخماس المسنين في البلدان النامية بإلمام بسيط بالقراءة والكتابة. أما في المناطق الأكثر نمواً، فجميع المسنّين تقريباً ملمين بالقراءة والكتابة إلا في عدد قليل من البلدان.

إجمالاً، ونتيجة للانتقال من الخصوبة المرتفعة إلى الخصوبة المنخفضة وللتراجع المستمر في وفيات الراشدين، فإن سكان أغلب البلدان يتقدمون في العمر. وهذا التحوّل الديمغرافي غير المسبوق، الذي بدأ في العالم المتقدم النمو في القرن التاسع عشر، وظهر في فترة أقرب في البلدان النامية، آخذ بالفعل في تغيير كثير من المجتمعات. ويُتوقّع أن تتسارع عملية الشيخوخة في المستقبل القريب، لا سيما في البلدان النامية. ونظراً لأن الوقت المتاح أمام حكومات البلدان النامية للتكيف مع التغيّرات المرتبطة بشيخوخة السكان قصير نسبياً، من الضروري أن تبدأ في اتخاذ خطوات لمواجهة التحديات والاستفادة بأقصى درجة ممكنة من الفرص التي تجلبها شيخوخة السكان. ويقدم هذا التقرير الأساس الديمغرافي لمعرفة مدى شيخوخة السكان وعمقها اليوم وفي السنوات المقبلة في كل بلد من بلدان العالم.

执行摘要

2002年4月第二次老龄问题世界大会通过的《马德里老龄问题国际行动计划》和《政治宣言》,[1]标志着世界在迎接构建一个顾及所有年龄组的社会的重大挑战方面的一个转折点。《计划》着重于三大优先领域:老年人和发展;增进老年人的健康和福祉;并确保形成有利和支助性的环境。这是各国政府第一次采取综合办法,把老龄问题同社会经济发展和人权的其他框架联系起来,这特别是指1990年代联合国大型会议和首脑会议所商定的框架。

同人口老化和老年人有关的问题在联合国过去25年间所主办的三大国际人口会议上占有显要位置。例如,1994年国际人口与发展会议承认,人口老化的经济和社会影响对所有社会而言,既是机遇,也是挑战。[2]最近,为进一步执行1999年7月2日联大第二十一届特别会议通过的《国际人口与发展会议行动纲领》采取的重要行动重申所有社会必须处理今后几十年内人口老化带来的重大问题。[3]2007年,联合国人口与发展委员会将把工作重点放在不断变化的人口年龄结构及其对社会的影响方面,而这正是该委员会第四十届会议的特别主题。

联合国人口司长期以来就有研究人口老化的传统,包括估计和预测老化人口的规模和特征,并审查人口老化的决定因素和后果。从1956年首发人口老化问题报告(侧重于较发达国家的人口老化问题)到2006年发布联合国人口老化问题挂图,人口司一直争取让各国政府和国际社会注意人口老化问题。[4]

联合国社会发展委员会决定每五年对执行《马德里老龄问题行动计划》的进展情况进行审查和评价。此外,联大强调必须按年龄和性别对人口数据进行分类。本报告从人口学角度为第二次老龄问题世界大会的后续活动奠定基础。本报告把世界人口老化的进程视为整体,各区域(无论发达程度)、主要地区和区域以及个别国家都包括在内。提供了1950年至2050年期间每个国家的人口学数据,突出人口老化的相关指标。

本报告内容强调四大定论:

1. 人口老化是前所未有的,在人类历史上没有发生过类似的进程。老年人(即达到或超过60岁者)的比例增加,而少年儿童(15岁以下者)比例减少,

---

1　见第二次老龄问题世界大会报告(联合国出版物A/CONF.197/9,英文出售品编号E.02. IV.4)。

2　人口与发展,第一卷,国际人口与发展会议(1994年9月5至13日,开罗)通过的行动纲领(联合国出版物,英文出售品编号E.95.XIII.7)。

3　《审查和评价实现国际人口与发展会议行动纲领各项目标和目的的进展情况,1999年报告》,(联合国出版物,英文出售品编号E.99.XIII.16)。

4　The Ageing of Populations and its Economic and Social Implications, Population Studies, No. 26(联合国出版物,英文出售品编号1956.XIII.6);and Population Ageing 2006(联合国出版物,英文出售品编号E.06.XIII.2)。

而劳动适龄(15至59岁)人口比例也有下降，这样就形成人口老化。在世界范围内，2047年，老年人人数预期将首次超过儿童人数。在人口老化问题更突出的较发达区域，1998年，儿童人数就低于老年人人数。

2. 人口老化是渗透性的，它影响世界几乎所有国家。人口老化的原因，主要在于生育率下降这一近乎世界性的问题。由此造成儿童人数增长速度放慢，而老人人数持续增加，这对作为社会基础的代间、代内公平和团结产生了直接影响。

3. 人口老化是影响深远的问题，对人类生活所有方面都具有重大影响。在经济领域，人口老化将对经济增长、储蓄、投资、消费、劳动力市场、养恤金、税务和代间转移产生影响。在社会领域，人口老化影响到家庭组成和生活安排、住房需求、移徙趋势、流行病以及保健服务需求。在政治领域，人口老化可能会影响投票格局和政治代表性。

4. 人口老化是长期性的。1950年以来，老年人比例持续增加，从1950年的8％增加到2007年的11％，2050年预期将达到22％（图一）。只要老年人死亡率继续下降、生育率依然很低，老年人的比例将继续增加。

本报告主要定论如下：

• 生育率不大可能恢复到过去常见的高度，所以，人口老化是不可逆转的，直到最近都常见的青少年人口群在二十一世纪期间可能变得少见。

• 2000年，60岁或60岁以上人口有6亿人，比1950年增加了两倍。2006年，老年人口超过7亿。2050年，据预测将有20亿老年人存活，也就是说，他们的人数在50年间再度增加两倍。

• 全球而言，老年人人口以每年2.6％的速率增加，这比整体人口(每年增加1.1％)的增长率要高得多。至少直到2050年，老年人口预期将继续比其他年龄组增长更快。此类迅速增长将要求大多数国家在经济和社会方面作出重大调整。

图一
60岁及60岁以上人口比例：世界，1950-2050年

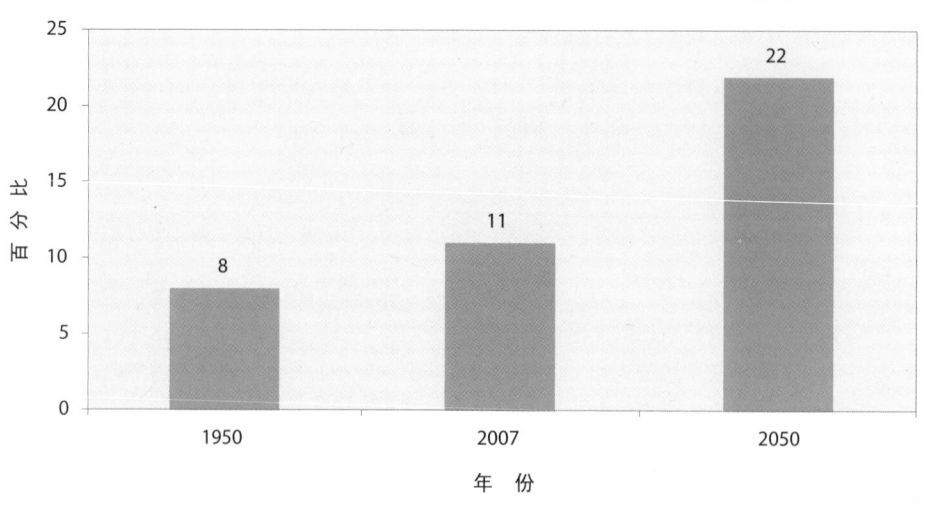

- 发达区域和发展中区域在老年人人数和比例方面存在明显差异。在较发达区域，超过五分之一的人口目前达到或超过60岁，据预测到2050年，发达国家近三分之一的人口属于该年龄组。在欠发达区域，老年人今天只占人口的8%，但到2050年，预期他们将占人口的五分之一，这意味着到本世纪中叶，发展中世界人口老化进程可能进入与目前发达世界所处阶段相同的阶段。

- 发展中国家人口老化的步伐比发达国家快。因此，发展中国家适应人口老化影响的时间相对较少。此外，相对于发达国家而言，发展中国家人口老化是在社会经济欠发达的情况下发生的。

- 今天，世界中位年龄为28岁，就是说，世界人口中有一半人低于这一年龄，而另一半则高于这一年龄。人口最年轻的国家是乌干达，其中位年龄为15岁，人口最老的是日本，其中位年龄为43岁。今后40年间，世界中位年龄可能会提高十岁，2050年达到38岁。届时，人口最年轻的国家可能是布隆迪和乌干达，中位年龄均为20岁，而最老的人口预期是在中国澳门特别行政区和大韩民国，其据预测中位年龄将均为54岁。

- 老年人口本身也在老化。在60岁及60岁以上者当中，增长最快的人口是最老的老人，也就是年届80或80岁以上者。目前，该年龄段人数在以每年3.9%的速度增长。今天，80或80岁以上者约占老年人（60或60岁以上）的1/8。到2050年，预期这一比例将增加到约有十分之二老年人达到或超过80岁。

- 可能供养比率，即65岁或65岁以上人口与15至64岁人口之间的比率，表明对于每一名老年人而言，有多少可能的劳动力。随着人口的老化，可能供养比率值往往下降。1950年至2007年间，可能供养比率从有一名65岁或65岁以上者就有12名可能的劳动力，减至9名可能的劳动力。据预测，到2050年，可能供养比率将再度下降到有一名老年人就有4名可能的劳动力（图二）。可能供养比率下降对社会保障制度，尤其是对现收现付养恤金制（即以在职工人的纳税支付退休人员的养恤金）产生重大影响。

图二
可能供养比率：世界，1950-2050年

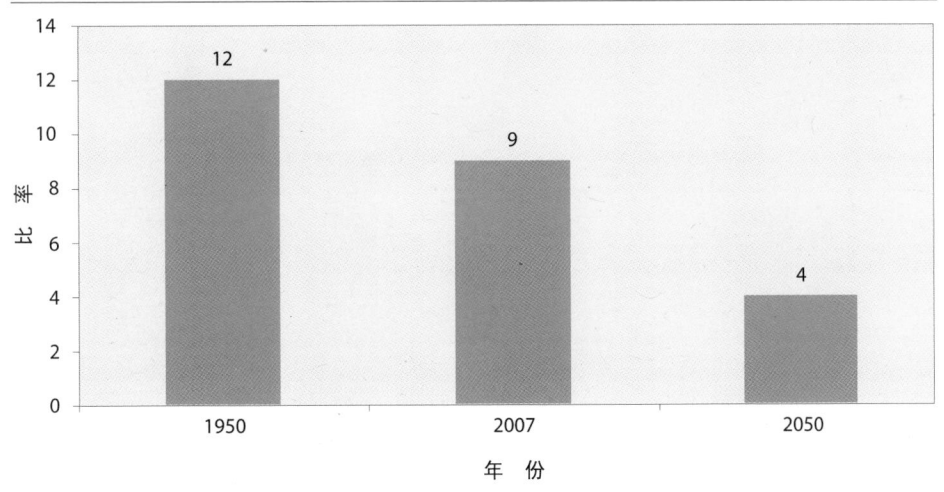

- 妇女比男子长寿，所以，老年人多为女性。目前，年届60或60岁以上者中，妇女比男性多出约7 000万人。年龄达到或超过80岁者中，女性人数几乎比男子多出一倍，而百岁老人中，女性人数约为男性人数的四至五倍(图三)。

- 随着年龄的增加，老年人的身体健康状况往往变坏，表明随着老年人数的增加，对长期看护的需求也有增加。抚养父母率，即85岁或85岁以上人口相对于50岁至64岁人口的比例，表明家庭能在多大程度上抚养其耆老。在全球范围内，1950年，相对于每100名50至64岁之间者，85岁或85岁以上者不到两人；今天，这一比率稍微高于4％，到2050年，预期达到12％。也就是说，那些本身已逾中年者要承担照料耆老亲属的可能性将比今天大两倍。

- 独居老者更有可能经历社会孤独和经济处境恶化，因而需要特别支助。老年妇女存活率较高，再婚倾向较低，因而她们比老年男子更有可能独居。在全球范围内，60或60岁以上的老妪中，有19％独居，而该年龄组只有8％的男子独居。

- 各国人口退休的有效年龄迥然相异。在人均收入高的国家，老年人可以较早退休，这样，老人参与劳动力程度就较低。因此，在较发达区域，65岁或65岁以上男子中，只有13％仍然积极参与经济活动，而欠发达区域的此类男子有39％仍然属于劳动力成员。女性也有类似的差别。在较发达区域，7％的老年妇女积极参与经济活动；在欠发达地区，这一比例为15％。在欠发达区域，老年人积极参加经济活动的时间较长，因为养恤金方案覆盖范围有限，所提供的收入也较低。

- 在多数国家，向养恤金制度缴款的起码期间届满后即能领取全额养恤金的法定年龄（可领养恤金年龄），男女都一样。然而，在许多国家，妇女在比男子低的年龄层次就能领取全额养恤金福利，而60岁以上妇女一般比男子长寿。在发达国家，可领养恤金年龄，不分男女，往往比发展中国家要高。

- 在欠发达区域的老年人中，文盲依然普遍。目前，在发展中国家，65岁或65岁以上的所有人中，估计超过半数为文盲。发展中国家只有约三分之

图三
40-59岁、60岁以上、80岁以上和百岁以上人口中女性比例：世界，2007年

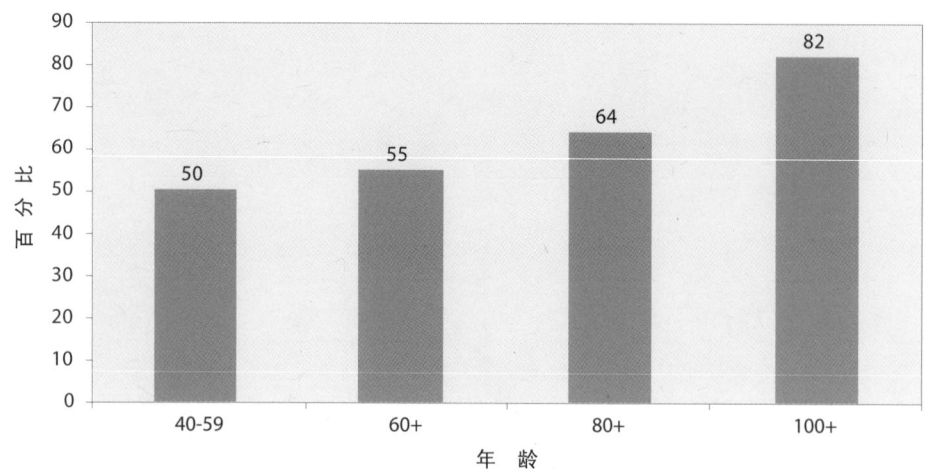

一的老年妇女和约五分之三的老年男子能基本识字、写字。在较发达区域，除少数国家外，老年人口普遍都识字。

简而言之，由于从高生育率向低生育率过渡，而成年人死亡率持续降低，因此，世界大多数国家正在出现人口老化。这一史无前例的人口变化十九世纪始于发达世界，最近也出现在发展中国家；它已经改变了许多社会。预期在最近的将来，老龄化进程将加快，尤其是在发展中国家。发展中国家政府要在较短时间内适应与人口老化有关的变化，因此，它们必须立即着手采取步骤，迎接这项挑战，并充分利用人口老化所带来的机会。本报告从人口学角度为确定今天及来年世界各国人口老化的程度和深度奠定基础。

Executive summary

The Madrid International Plan of Action on Ageing and the Political Declaration adopted at the Second World Assembly on Ageing in April 2002[1] marked a turning point in how the world addresses the key challenge of building a society for all ages. The Plan focuses on three priority areas: older persons and development; advancing health and well-being into old age; and ensuring enabling and supportive environments. It represents the first time Governments have adopted a comprehensive approach linking questions of ageing to other frameworks for social and economic development and human rights, most notably those agreed to at the United Nations conferences and summits of the 1990s.

Issues related to population ageing and older persons have played a prominent role in the three major international population conferences organized by the United Nations during the past quarter century. For example, the International Conference on Population and Development, held in 1994, recognized that the economic and social impact of population ageing is both an opportunity and a challenge to all societies.[2] More recently, the key actions for the further implementation of the Programme of Action of the International Conference on Population and Development, adopted by the General Assembly at its twenty-first special session on 2 July 1999, reiterated the need for all societies to address the significant consequences of population ageing in the coming decades.[3] In 2007, the United Nations Commission on Population and Development will focus its work on the changing age structures of populations and their implications for development, the special theme for its fortieth session.

The Population Division of the United Nations has a long tradition of studying population ageing, including by estimating and projecting the size and characteristics of ageing populations and by examining the determinants and consequences of population ageing. From the groundbreaking report on population ageing published in 1956, which focused mainly on population ageing in the more developed countries, to the United Nations wall chart on population ageing published in 2006, the Population Division has consistently sought to bring population ageing to the attention of Governments and the international community.[4]

The United Nations Commission on Social Development has decided to conduct every five years a review and appraisal of progress made in implementing the Madrid Plan of Action on Ageing. Furthermore, the General Assembly has stressed the need for population data disaggregated by age and sex. This report provides the demographic founda-

---

1   See *Report of the Second World Assembly on Ageing* (United Nations publication A/CONF.197/9, Sales No. E.02.IV.4).

2   *Population and Development*, vol. 1: *Programme of Action adopted at the International Conference on Population and Development, Cairo, 5-13 September 1994* (United Nations publication, Sales No. E.95.XIII.7).

3   *Review and Appraisal of the Progress Made in Achieving the Goals and Objectives of the Programme of Action of the International Conference on Population and Development, 1999 Report* (United Nations publication, Sales No. E.99.XIII.16).

4   *The Ageing of Populations and its Economic and Social Implications*, Population Studies, No. 26 (United Nations publication, Sales No. 1956. XIII.6); and *Population Ageing 2006* (United Nations publication, Sales No. E.06.XIII.2).

tion for the follow-up activities of the Second World Assembly on Ageing. It considers the process of population ageing for the world as a whole, for more and less developed regions, major areas and regions, as well as individual countries. Demographic profiles covering the period 1950 to 2050 are provided for each country, highlighting the relevant indicators of population ageing.

The contents of this report underscore four major findings:

1. Population ageing is unprecedented, a process without parallel in the history of humanity. A population ages when increases in the proportion of older persons (that is, those aged 60 years or over) are accompanied by reductions in the proportion of children (persons under age 15) and then by declines in the proportions of persons in the working ages (15 to 59). At the world level, the number of older persons is expected to exceed the number of children for the first time in 2047. In the more developed regions, where population ageing is far advanced, the number of children dropped below that of older persons in 1998.

2. Population ageing is pervasive since it is affecting nearly all the countries of the world. Population ageing results mainly from reductions of fertility that have become virtually universal. The resulting slowdown in the growth of the number of children coupled with the steady increase in the number of older persons has a direct bearing on both the intergenerational and intragenerational equity and solidarity that are the foundations of society.

3. Population ageing is profound, having major consequences and implications for all facets of human life. In the economic area, population ageing will have an impact on economic growth, savings, investment, consumption, labour markets, pensions, taxation and intergenerational transfers. In the social sphere, population ageing influences family composition and living arrangements, housing demand, migration trends, epidemiology and the need for health-care services. In the political arena, population ageing may shape voting patterns and political representation.

4. Population ageing is enduring. Since 1950 the proportion of older persons has been rising steadily, passing from 8 per cent in 1950 to 11 per cent in 2007, and is expected to reach 22 per cent in 2050 (figure I). As long as old age mortality continues to decline and fertility remains low, the proportion of older persons will continue to increase.

Figure I
Proportion of population 60 years or over: world, 1950-2050

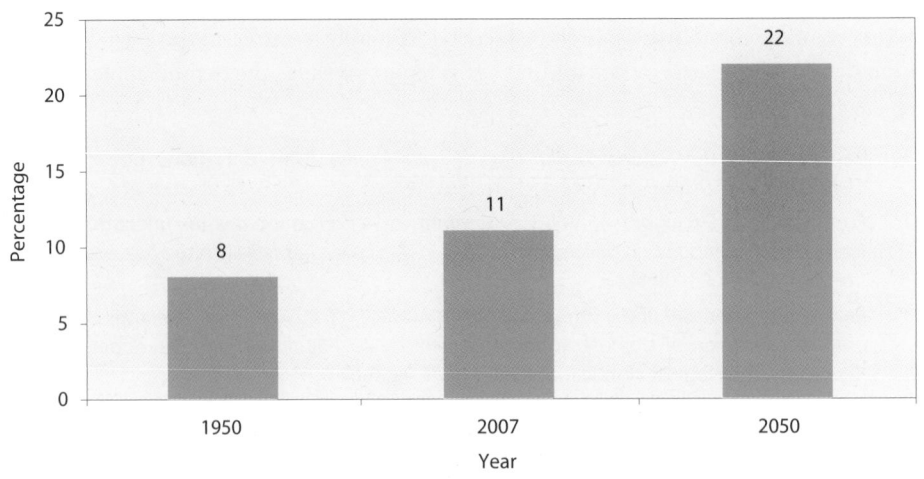

World Population Ageing 2007

The major findings of this report are the following:

- Because fertility levels are unlikely to rise again to the high levels common in the past, population ageing is irreversible and the young populations that were common until recently are likely to become rare over the course of the twenty-first century.

- In 2000, the population aged 60 years or over numbered 600 million, triple the number present in 1950. In 2006, the number of older persons had surpassed 700 million. By 2050, 2 billion older persons are projected to be alive, implying that their number will once again triple over a span of 50 years.

- Globally the population of older persons is growing at a rate of 2.6 per cent per year, considerably faster than the population as a whole which is increasing at 1.1 per cent annually. At least until 2050, the older population is expected to continue growing more rapidly than the population in other age groups. Such rapid growth will require far-reaching economic and social adjustments in most countries.

- Marked differences exist between developed and developing regions in the number and proportion of older persons. In the more developed regions, over a fifth of the population is currently aged 60 years or over and by 2050, nearly a third of the population in developed countries is projected to be in that age group. In the less developed regions, older persons account today for just 8 per cent of the population but by 2050 they are expected to account for a fifth of the population, implying that, by mid-century, the developing world is likely to reach the same stage in the process of population ageing that the developed world is already at.

- The pace of population ageing is faster in developing countries than in developed countries. Consequently, developing countries will have less time to adjust to the consequences of population ageing. Moreover, population ageing in developing countries is taking place at lower levels of socio-economic development than has been the case for developed countries.

- Today the median age for the world is 28 years, that is, half the world's population is below that age and the other half is above it. The country with the youngest population is Uganda, with a median age of 15 years, and the oldest is Japan, with a median age of 43 years. Over the next four decades, the world's median age will likely increase by ten years, to reach 38 years in 2050. At that time, the countries with the youngest populations will likely be Burundi and Uganda, with median ages of 20 years each, whereas the oldest populations are expected to be in Macao SAR China and in the Republic of Korea whose median ages are projected to be 54 years in each.

- The population of older persons is itself ageing. Among those aged 60 years or over, the fastest growing population is that of the oldest-old, that is, those aged 80 years or over. Their numbers are currently increasing at 3.9 per cent per year. Today, persons aged 80 years or over account for about 1 in every 8 older persons (60 or over). By 2050, this ratio is expected to increase to approximately 2 persons aged 80 or over among every 10 older persons.

- The potential support ratio (PSR), that is, the number of persons aged 15 to 64 per each older person aged 65 years or over, indicates how many potential workers there are per older person. As a population ages, the value of the potential support ratio tends to fall. Between 1950 and 2007, the potential support ratio declined from 12 to 9 potential workers per person aged 65 or over. By 2050, the potential support ratio is projected to drop further to reach 4 potential workers per older person (figure II). The reduction of potential support ratios has important implications for social security schemes, particularly for pay-as-you-go pension systems under which taxes on current workers pay the pensions of retirees.

Figure II
Potential support ratio (PSR): world, 1950-2050

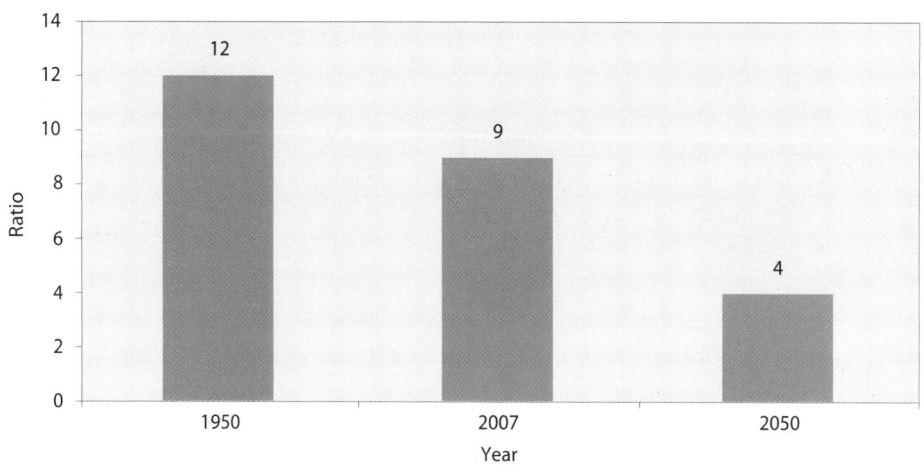

- Because women live longer than men, women constitute the majority of older persons. Currently, women outnumber men by about 70 million among those aged 60 years or over. Among those aged 80 years or over, women are nearly twice as numerous as men, and among centenarians women are between four and five times as numerous as men (figure III).

- The health of older persons typically deteriorates with increasing age, inducing greater demand for long-term care as the numbers of older persons increase. The parent support ratio, that is, the ratio of the population aged 85 or over to that aged 50 to 64, provides an indication of the level of support families may be able to provide to their oldest members. Globally, there were fewer than 2 persons aged 85 or over for every 100 persons aged 50 to 64 in 1950. Today, that ratio is slightly over 4 per 100 but it is projected to reach 12 per 100 by 2050. That is, persons who are themselves well past middle age will be three times more likely than they are today to be responsible for the care of older relatives.

- Older persons living alone are at greater risk of experiencing social isolation and economic deprivation, and may therefore require special support. Because of higher survivorship and lower propensities to remarry, older women are more likely than older men to live alone. Globally, an estimated 19 per cent of women aged 60 years or over live alone, whereas just 8 per cent of men in that age group do so.

- The effective age at retirement varies considerably among populations. In countries with high per capita incomes, older persons can retire earlier and thus tend to have lower labour force participation rates at older ages. Thus, just 13 per cent of men aged 65 years or over are economically active in the more developed regions, whereas 39 per cent are in the labour force of the less developed regions. The difference is similar among women. In the more developed regions, 7 per cent of older women are economically active, compared to 15 per cent in the less developed regions. Older persons remain economically active for longer in the less developed regions because of the limited coverage of pension programmes and the relatively small incomes they provide.

- In most countries the statutory age at which a full pension can be obtained provided a minimum period of contributions to the pension system is completed (i.e., the pensionable age) is the same for women and men. In many countries, however, women become eligible for full pension benefits at lower ages than men, even

Figure III
Proportion of women among persons aged 40-59, 60+, 80+ and 100+ years: world, 2007

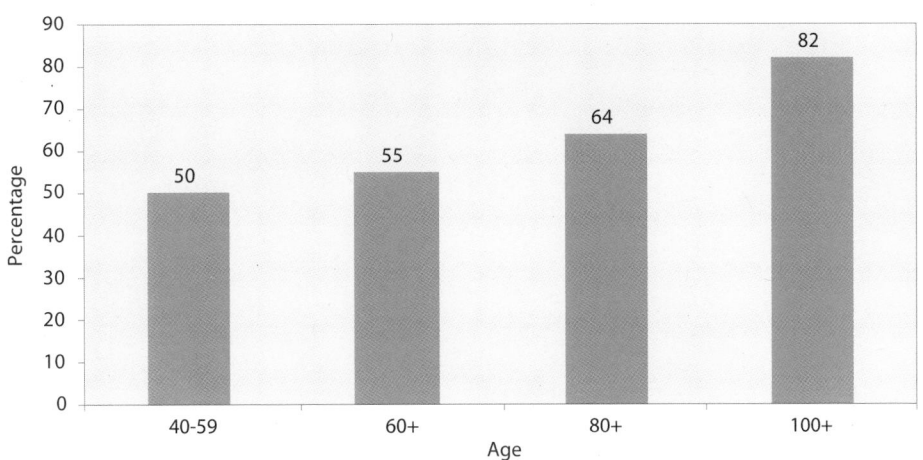

though women can expect to live longer than men after age 60. For both men and women, pensionable ages tend to be higher in developed than in developing countries.

- Illiteracy is still common among the older population of less developed regions. Currently, it is estimated that over half of all persons aged 65 or over in developing countries are illiterate. Only about a third of older women and about three fifths of older men in developing countries have basic reading and writing skills. In the more developed regions, literacy among the older population is nearly universal in all but a few countries.

In sum, as a result of the transition from high to low fertility and the continuous reduction of adult mortality, the population of most countries of the world is ageing. This unprecedented demographic change, which started in the developed world in the nineteenth century and is more recent in developing countries, is already transforming many societies. The ageing process is expected to accelerate in the near future, particularly in developing countries. Because they have a shorter time to adapt to the changes associated with population ageing, it is urgent that the Governments of developing countries begin taking steps to face the challenges and make the best of the opportunities that population ageing brings. This report provides the demographic basis for ascertaining the extent and depth of population ageing today and in the years to come in each country of the world.

Résumé

Le Plan d'action international de Madrid sur le vieillissement et la Déclaration politique adoptés à la deuxième Assemblée mondiale sur le vieillissement en avril 2002[1] ont marqué un tournant dans la façon dont le monde envisage la tâche ardue qu'est l'édification d'une société pour tous les âges. Le Plan d'action repose sur trois orientations prioritaires : les personnes âgées et le développement; la promotion de la santé et du bien-être jusque dans le troisième âge; et la création d'environnements porteurs et favorables. C'était la première fois que les gouvernements envisageaient les choses de façon globale, en reliant les questions du vieillissement à d'autres programmes de développement social et économique et de droits de l'homme, tout particulièrement ceux convenus aux conférences et réunions au sommet des Nations Unies des années 90.

Les questions relatives au vieillissement de la population et aux personnes âgées ont occupé une place de premier plan lors des trois grandes conférences internationales sur la population organisées par les Nations Unies au cours des 25 dernières années. Ainsi, la Conférence internationale sur la population et le développement, qui a eu lieu en 1994, a reconnu que l'incidence économique et sociale du vieillissement de la population constituait pour toutes les sociétés à la fois une chance et une gageure[2]. Plus récemment, dans les principales mesures pour la poursuite de l'application du Programme d'action de la Conférence internationale sur la population et le développement qu'elle a adoptées à sa vingt et unième session extraordinaire, le 2 juillet 1999, l'Assemblée générale a souligné à nouveau que toutes les sociétés devraient, notamment, s'interroger sur les répercussions importantes qu'aurait le vieillissement de la population dans les décennies à venir[3]. En 2007, la Commission de la population et du développement axera ses travaux sur l'évolution de la pyramide des âges des populations et ses effets sur le développement, thème spécial de sa quarantième session.

Cela fait longtemps que la Division de la population de l'ONU étudie la question du vieillissement de la population, notamment par des estimations et des projections des populations de personnes âgées et des études sur les déterminants et les conséquences du vieillissement de la population. Depuis le premier rapport sur le vieillissement de la population, datant de 1956, qui traitait surtout de la situation des pays développés, jusqu'à la première planche murale publiée par l'ONU en 1999, la Division de la population n'a cessé d'appeler l'attention de la communauté internationale sur la question du vieillissement de la population[4].

---

1   Voir *Rapport de la deuxième Assemblée mondiale sur le vieillissement* (publication des Nations Unies, A/CONF.197/9, numéro de vente : F.02.IV.4).

2   *Programme d'action adopté à la Conférence internationale sur la population et le développement, Le Caire, 5-13 septembre 1994, Population et développement,* vol. I (publication des Nations Unies, numéro de vente : F.95.XIII.7).

3   *Examen et évaluation des progrès accomplis dans la réalisation des buts et objectifs du Programme d'action de la Conférence internationale sur la population et le développement, Rapport 1999* (publication des Nations Unies, numéro de vente : F.99.XIII.16).

4   *The Aging of Populations and its Economic and Social Implications,* Études démographiques n° 26 (publication des Nations Unies, numéro de vente : 1956.XIII.6); et *Population Ageing 1999* (publication des Nations Unies, numéro de vente : E.99.XIII.11).

La Commission du développement social a décidé d'examiner et d'évaluer tous les cinq ans l'application du Plan d'action international de Madrid sur le vieillissement. L'Assemblée générale, pour sa part, a souligné la nécessité de disposer de données démographiques ventilées par âge et par sexe. Le présent rapport fournit les éléments démographiques nécessaires aux activités de suivi de la deuxième Assemblée mondiale sur le vieillissement. Le vieillissement de la population y est examiné aux niveaux du monde, des régions plus ou moins développées, des grandes régions et des pays. On y trouvera, pour chaque pays, les profils démographiques de 1950 à 2050, mettant en évidence les indicateurs du vieillissement de la population.

Quatre constatations se dégagent du présent rapport :

1. Le vieillissement de la population est un phénomène nouveau sans équivalent dans l'histoire de l'humanité. Une population vieillit lorsque l'augmentation de la proportion des personnes âgées (60 ans et plus) s'accompagne d'une diminution d'abord de la proportion des enfants (moins de 15 ans) puis de la proportion des personnes en âge de travailler (de 15 à 59 ans). Au niveau mondial, ce sera en principe en 2047 que le nombre des personnes âgées dépassera pour la première fois le nombre des enfants. Dans les régions développées où le vieillissement de la population est déjà à un stade avancé, le nombre des personnes âgées a surpassé le nombre des enfants en 1998.

2. Le vieillissement de la population est un phénomène très répandu, touchant pratiquement tous les pays. Il est principalement dû à une baisse de la fécondité qui se manifeste quasiment partout. Le ralentissement consécutif de l'accroissement du nombre d'enfants, conjugué à l'augmentation constante du nombre de personnes âgées influe directement sur l'équité et la solidarité intergénérations et intragénérations, sur lesquelles toute société se fonde.

3. Le vieillissement de la population est marquant et lourd de conséquences et d'incidences sur tous les aspects de la vie de l'homme. Sur le plan économique, le vieillissement de la population retentira sur la croissance économique, l'épargne, l'investissement, la consommation, les marchés du travail, les pensions, les impôts et les transferts entre générations. Sur le plan social, il modifie la composition de la famille et les modes de vie commune, la demande de logements, les tendances de la migration, l'épidémiologie et les besoins en matière de soins de santé. Sur

Graphique I

Proportion des personnes âgées de 60 ans et plus dans le monde, 1950-2050

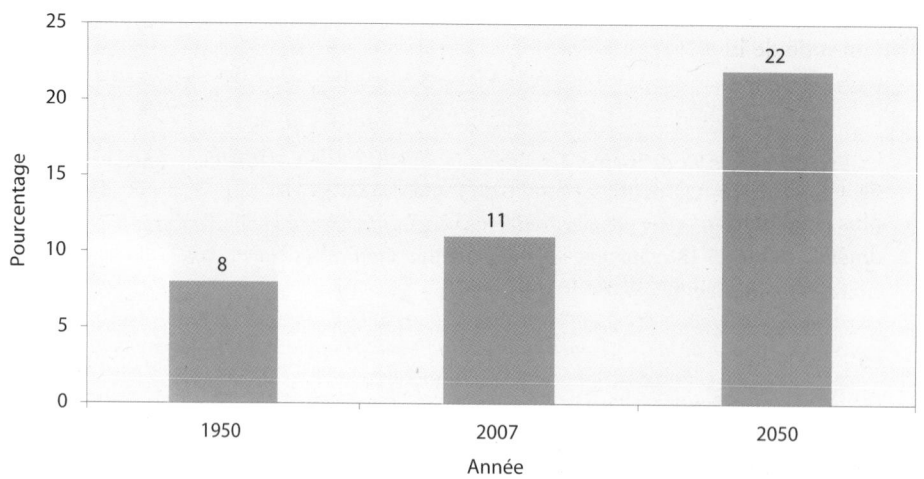

le plan politique, il peut déterminer la répartition des votes et la représentation politique.

4. Le vieillissement de la population est un phénomène durable. Depuis 1950, la proportion de personnes âgées ne cesse de croître, passant de 8 % en 1950 à 11 % en 2007; elle pourrait atteindre les 22 % en 2050 (graphique I). Tant que la mortalité sénile continue de régresser et que la fécondité demeure faible, la proportion de personnes âgées ne cessera d'augmenter.

Les principales conclusions du rapport sont les suivantes :

- Du fait que la fécondité ne retrouvera probablement pas les hauts niveaux d'antan, le vieillissement de la population est irréversible et les populations jeunes qui étaient courantes jusqu'à il y a peu deviendront sans doute rares au XXIe siècle;

- En 2000, le monde comptait 600 millions de personnes âgées de 60 ans et plus, soit trois fois plus qu'en 1950. En 2006, leur nombre a dépassé les 700 millions. Selon les projections, elles seront 2 milliards en 2050, c'est-à-dire que leur nombre aura encore triplé en l'espace de 50 ans;

- À l'échelle mondiale, le nombre des personnes âgées augmente de 2,6 % chaque année, c'est-à-dire beaucoup plus vite que la population dans son ensemble, dont le taux d'accroissement est de 1,1 % par an. Le nombre des personnes âgées doit en principe continuer d'augmenter plus rapidement que le nombre des personnes des autres tranches d'âge et ce au moins jusqu'à 2050. Face à une croissance aussi rapide, la plupart des pays devront faire d'importants ajustements économiques et sociaux;

- Il y a des différences marquées entre les régions développées et les régions en développement pour ce qui est du nombre et de la proportion des personnes âgées. Dans les régions développées, les personnes âgées de 60 ans et plus constituent plus d'un cinquième de la population et, en 2050, leur proportion par rapport à la population générale doit être de plus d'un tiers. Dans les régions moins avancées, les personnes âgées ne forment pour l'instant que 8 % de la population mais en 2050 leur proportion doit être d'un cinquième, ce qui veut dire que, au milieu du siècle, les pays en développement atteindront sans doute le stade de vieillissement démographique que connaissent en ce moment les pays en développement;

- Le vieillissement de la population étant plus rapide chez eux que dans les pays développés, les pays en développement auront moins de temps pour réagir. De plus, dans ces pays, le vieillissement de la population se produit à un niveau de développement socio-économique plus bas que celui que connaissaient les pays développés au moment où ils ont été touchés par ce phénomène;

- De nos jours, l'âge médian est de 28 ans dans le monde entier, ce qui veut dire que la moitié de la population mondiale a moins de 28 ans et l'autre moitié plus. Le pays à la population la plus jeune est l'Ouganda, l'âge médian y étant de 15 ans, et celui à la population la plus âgée est le Japon, où l'âge médian est de 43 ans. Au cours des 40 prochaines années, l'âge médian mondial augmentera probablement de 10 ans, passant à 38 ans en 2050. À ce moment-là, les pays à la population la plus jeune seront vraisemblablement le Burundi et l'Ouganda, où l'âge médian sera de 20 ans, tandis que les populations les plus vieilles seront probablement celle de Macao (région administrative spéciale de Chine) et celle de la République de Corée, avec un âge médian de 54 ans;

- La population de personnes âgées elle-même vieillit. Dans la tranche des 60 ans et plus, la catégorie dont l'accroissement est le plus rapide est celle des personnes très âgées, de 80 ans et plus. Leur nombre augmente actuellement au rythme de 3,9 % par an. De nos jours, une personne âgée (60 ans ou plus) sur huit a au moins 80 ans.

En 2050, cette proportion devrait encore augmenter et environ 2 personnes âgées sur 10 pourraient avoir au moins 80 ans;

- Le rapport actifs/inactifs, c'est-à-dire le nombre de personnes ayant entre 15 et 64 ans pour chaque personne âgée de 65 ans au moins, représente le nombre de travailleurs potentiels par personne âgée. Plus la population vieillit plus ce rapport baisse. Entre 1950 et 2007, il est passé de 12 à 9 travailleurs potentiels par personne de 65 ans ou plus. Selon les projections, il continuera à baisser pour n'être plus, en 2050, que de quatre travailleurs potentiels par personne âgée (graphique II). La diminution du rapport actifs/inactifs a d'importantes répercussions sur les régimes de sécurité sociale, en particulier sur les systèmes de retraite par répartition, dans lesquels les retraites sont financées par les cotisations des actifs.

- Vivant plus longtemps que les hommes, les femmes constituent la majorité des personnes âgées. Actuellement, il y a 70 millions de plus de femmes que d'hommes parmi les personnes de 60 ans et plus. Parmi les personnes âgées de 80 ans ou plus, il y a presque deux fois plus de femmes que d'hommes; parmi les centenaires, les femmes sont entre quatre et cinq fois plus nombreuses que les hommes (graphique III);

- La santé décline généralement avec l'âge, d'où l'accroissement de la demande de soins de longue durée à mesure que le nombre de personnes âgées augmente. Le ratio de dépendance par rapport à la génération suivante, c'est-à-dire le rapport entre le nombre de personnes de 85 ans et plus et le nombre de personnes ayant entre 50 et 64 ans, indique le niveau de soutien que les familles pourraient apporter aux plus âgés de leurs membres. À l'échelle mondiale, il y avait en 1950 moins de 2 personnes de 85 ans ou plus pour 100 personnes ayant entre 50 et 64 ans. Ce rapport, qui est actuellement d'un peu plus de 4 %, pourrait atteindre 12 % d'ici à 2050, ce qui veut dire que les personnes d'âge mûr et plus auront trois fois plus de chances qu'actuellement d'avoir à prendre en charge des parents âgés;

- Les personnes âgées vivant seules sont plus exposées à l'isolement social et aux privations et ont de ce fait besoin d'une aide spéciale. Ayant de plus grandes chances de survie et étant moins portées à se remarier, les femmes âgées ont une probabilité plus forte de devoir vivre seules que les hommes âgés. À l'échelle du monde, on estime que 19 % des femmes de 60 ans ou plus vivent seules, contre 8 % des hommes de la même tranche d'âge;

- L'âge réel de retraite varie considérablement d'une population à l'autre. Dans les pays ayant un revenu par habitant élevé, les personnes âgées peuvent partir plus

Graphique II
Rapport actifs/inactifs dans le monde, 1950-2050

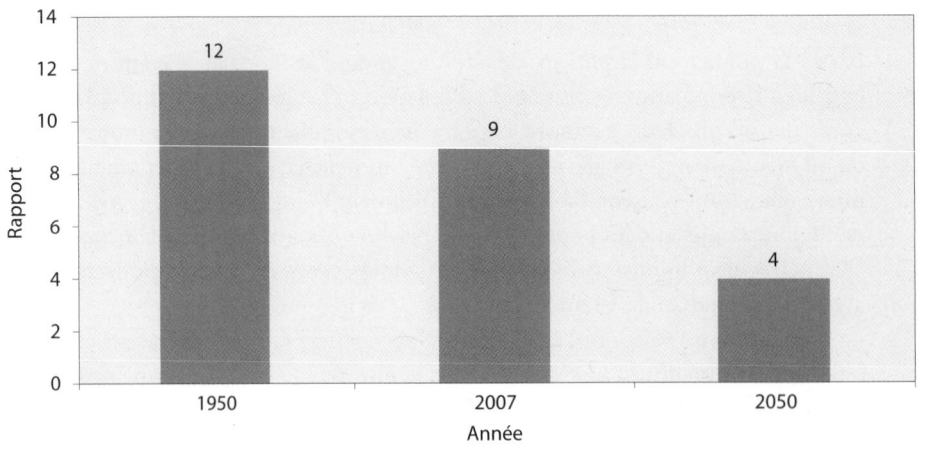

Graphique III
Proportion de femmes parmi les personnes âgées de 40 à 59 ans, de 60 ans et plus, de 80 ans et plus et de 100 ans et plus dans le monde, 2007

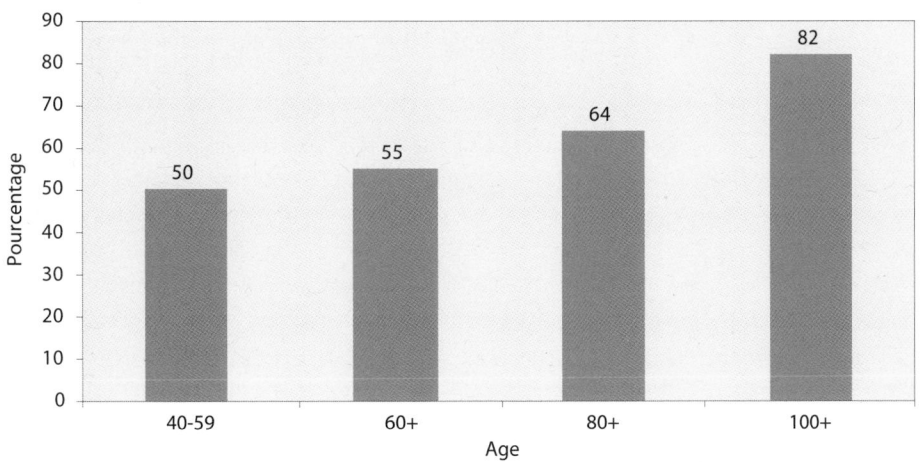

tôt à la retraite, de sorte que leur taux d'activité est généralement plus faible. Ainsi, dans les régions développées, parmi les hommes de 65 ans ou plus, 13 % seulement sont économiquement actifs, contre 39 % dans les régions moins avancées. Cette différence s'observe aussi chez les femmes. Dans les régions développées, 7 % des femmes âgées sont économiquement actives, contre 15 % dans les régions moins avancées. Les personnes âgées demeurent économiquement actives plus longtemps dans les pays moins avancés en raison de la couverture limitée des régimes de retraite et du revenu assez faible qu'ils offrent;

- Dans la plupart des pays, l'âge donnant droit à une pleine retraite sous réserve d'une période minimale de cotisation au régime de pension (c'est-à-dire l'âge de la retraite) est le même pour les femmes et les hommes. Dans beaucoup de pays, toutefois, les femmes peuvent partir à la retraite plus tôt que les hommes, même si elles peuvent s'attendre à vivre plus longtemps que les hommes après 60 ans. Pour les femmes comme pour les hommes, l'âge du départ à la retraite est souvent plus élevé dans les pays développés que dans les pays en développement;

- L'analphabétisme est encore répandu chez les personnes âgées dans les pays en développement. Actuellement, dans ces pays, on estime que plus de la moitié des personnes de 65 ans ou plus seraient analphabètes. Il n'y a qu'un tiers environ des femmes âgées et trois cinquièmes des hommes âgés qui sachent lire et écrire. Dans les régions développées, pratiquement toutes les personnes âgées savent lire et écrire, et ce, dans quasiment tous les pays.

Pour récapituler, on peut dire que la fécondité ayant chuté et la mortalité adulte ne cessant de diminuer, la population vieillit dans la plupart des pays. Cette mutation démographique sans précédent, apparue dans les pays développés au XIXe siècle, a gagné plus récemment les pays en développement; elle est en train de transformer nombre de sociétés. Le vieillissement de la population s'accélérera probablement dans un proche avenir, en particulier dans les pays en développement. Parce qu'ils ont moins de temps pour s'adapter aux problèmes liés au vieillissement de leur population, les gouvernements des pays en développement doivent commencer à prendre des mesures pour se préparer aux difficultés qu'il entraîne et en tirer avantage si possible. Les éléments présentés dans le rapport permettront d'évaluer l'étendue et la gravité de ce phénomène dans chaque pays du monde, dans sa forme actuelle et à venir.

Резюме

Мадридский международный план действий по проблемам старения и Политическая декларация, принятые на второй Всемирной ассамблее по проблемам старения в апреле 2002 года[1], перевернули представления международного сообщества о ключевой проблеме создания общества для людей всех возрастов. В Мадридском международном плане действий по проблемам старения указываются следующие три приоритетные направления деятельности: участие пожилых людей в развитии; обеспечение здравоохранения и благосостояния в пожилом возрасте; и обеспечение благоприятных и позитивных условий для людей всех возрастных групп. В этом документе правительства впервые применили комплексный подход, в соответствии с которым деятельность по вопросам старения была увязана с другими направлениями работы в области социально-экономического развития и защиты прав человека, согласованными в основном на конференциях и встречах на высшем уровне Организации Объединенных Наций в 90-е годы.

Вопросам старения населения и положения пожилых людей уделялось большое внимание на всех трех крупных международных конференциях по вопросам народонаселения, организованных Организацией Объединенных Наций за последние двадцать пять лет. Например, Международная конференция по народонаселению и развитию, проведенная в 1994 году, признала, что социально-экономические последствия демографического старения открывают перед всеми странами новые возможности и одновременно ставят перед ними новые задачи[2]. Позднее в «Основных направлениях деятельности по дальнейшему осуществлению Программы действий Международной конференции по народонаселению и развитию», принятых Генеральной Ассамблеей на ее двадцать первой специальной сессии 2 июля 1999 года, было вновь подчеркнуто, что в предстоящие десятилетия всем странам потребуется учитывать важные последствия старения населения[3]. В 2007 году Комиссия по народонаселению и развитию сосредоточит внимание на специальной теме своей сороковой сессии «Изменение возрастной структуры населения и его последствия для развития».

Отдел народонаселения Секретариата Организации Объединенных Наций давно занимается проблемой демографического старения, в частности оценкой и прогнозированием численности и состава стареющего населения и изучением причин и последствий старения населения. С момента опубликования своего исторического доклада о старении населения в 1956 году, в котором в основном рассматривался вопрос о демографическом старении в наиболее развитых странах, до выхода настенной диаграммы «Старение населения мира» в 2006 году Отдел народонасе-

---

1   См. Доклад второй Всемирной ассамблеи по проблемам старения (A/CONF.197/9, издание Организации Объединенных Наций, в продаже под № R.02.IV.4).

2   *Доклад Международной конференции по народонаселению и развитию, том 1: Программа действий Международной конференции по народонаселению и развитию, Каир, 5–13 сентября 1994 года* (издание Организации Объединенных Наций, в продаже под № R.95.XIII.7).

3   *Обзор и оценка прогресса, достигнутого в реализации целей и задач Программы действий Международной конференции по народонаселению и развитию, доклад за 1999 год* (издание Организации Объединенных Наций, в продаже под № R.99.XIII.16).

ления постоянно стремился привлечь внимание правительств и международного сообщества к проблеме демографического старения[4].

Комиссия Организации Объединенных Наций по народонаселению и развитию постановила раз в пять лет проводить обзор и оценку прогресса, достигнутого в реализации целей и задач Мадридского плана действий по проблемам старения. Кроме того, Генеральная Ассамблея обратила особое внимание на необходимость сбора демографических данных, дезагрегированных по возрастному и половому признакам. В настоящем докладе содержатся демографические данные, необходимые для проведения последующих мероприятий по осуществлению решений Всемирной ассамблеи по проблемам старения. В нем рассматривается процесс демографического старения во всем мире и в масштабах отдельных в большей или меньшей степени развитых регионов, крупных территорий и районов, а также стран. По всем странам приводятся данные о демографическом составе за период 1950–2050 годов вместе с важнейшими показателями демографического старения.

Настоящий доклад позволяет сделать четыре главных вывода.

1. Процесс демографического старения сейчас приобрел беспрецедентные масштабы, которые не имеют аналогов за всю историю человечества. Старение населения характеризуется увеличением процентной доли пожилых людей (т. е. лиц в возрасте 60 лет и старше) при сокращении процентной доли детей (т. е. лиц в возрасте до 15 лет), а также сокращением процентной доли населения трудоспособного возраста (от 15 до 59 лет). Ожидается, что в 2047 году число пожилых людей в мире превысит число детей. В наиболее развитых регионах, где старение населения происходит гораздо более быстрыми темпами, в 1998 году численность пожилых людей уже превысила численность детей.

2. Демографическое старение представляет собой широко распространенное явление, так как оно происходит практически во всех странах мира. Одной из главных причин старения населения является практически повсеместное снижение рождаемости. Вызываемое этим снижение темпов роста числа детей на фоне неуклонного увеличения численности пожилых лиц непосредственно отражается на представлениях о принципах справедливости и солидарности, которые имеют основополагающее значение в жизни общества, как среди представителей одного поколения, так и среди представителей разных поколений.

3. Старение населения — глубинный процесс, который сильно сказывается на всех сторонах жизни людей. В экономической сфере старение населения отражается на экономическом росте, накоплениях, инвестициях, потреблении, занятости, пенсионном обеспечении, налоговой политике и передаче накопленных знаний и опыта из поколения в поколение. В социальной сфере старение населения сказывается на составе семьи и условиях жизни, потребностях в жилье, миграционных тенденциях, эпидемиологической обстановке и потребностях в медицинской помощи. В политической сфере старение населения может влиять на результаты выборов и систему политического представительства.

4. Демографическое старение как тенденция носит долгосрочный характер. С 1950 года доля лиц старших возрастов непрерывно увеличивалась: с 8 процентов в 1950 году в 2007 году, по прогнозам, она должна достичь 11 процентов, а в 2050 году — 22 процентов (диаграмма I). Пока имеет место тенденция к снижению смертности в пожилом возрасте и сохраняются низкие показатели рождаемости, доля населения пожилого возраста будет продолжать увеличиваться.

---

4   *The Ageing of Populations and its Economic and Social Implications,* Population Studies, No. 26 (United Nations publication, Sales No. 1956.XIII.6); и *Population Ageing 2006* (United Nations publication, Sales No. E.06.XIII.2).

Доля населения в возрасте 60 лет и старше: в мире, 1950–2050 годы

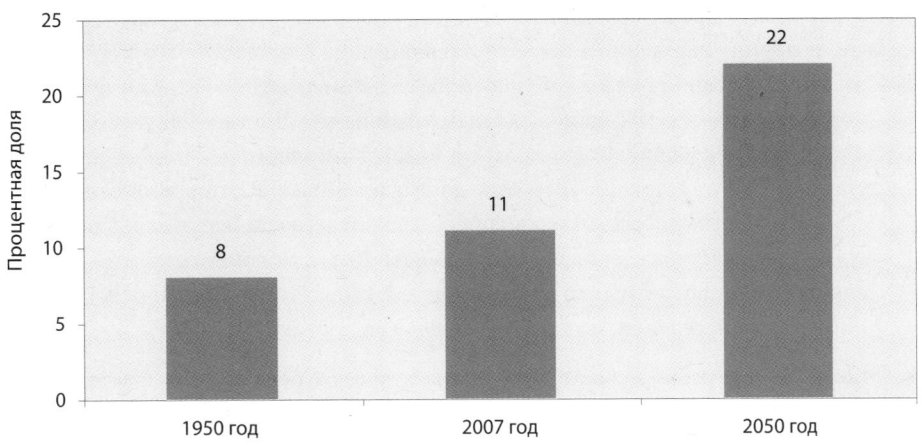

В свете положений настоящего доклада можно сделать следующие основные выводы:

• поскольку повышение показателей рождаемости до прежних высоких уровней, характерных в прошлом, маловероятно, процесс демографического старения носит необратимый характер и доля молодежи, которая до последнего времени составляла значительную часть населения, в XXI веке, судя по всему, пойдет на убыль;

• в 2000 году численность населения в возрасте 60 лет и старше составляла 600 миллионов человек, что в три раза больше, чем в 1950 году. В 2006 году число пожилых людей превысило 700 миллионов человек, и ожидается, что к 2050 году оно составит 2 миллиарда человек, т. е. опять утроится за 50 лет;

• в мировом масштабе темпы роста численности пожилого населения составляют 2,6 процента в год, т. е. значительно опережают темпы роста населения в целом, которые составляют 1,1 процента в год. Ожидается, что по крайней мере до 2050 года численность пожилого населения будет увеличиваться опережающими по сравнению с другими возрастными категориями темпами. Столь высокие темпы роста численности пожилого населения потребуют проведения глубоких социально-экономических преобразований в большинстве стран;

• между развитыми и развивающимися регионами существуют значительные различия с точки зрения численности и процентной доли пожилого населения. В настоящее время пятую часть населения наиболее развитых регионов составляют лица в возрасте 60 лет и старше, причем, согласно прогнозам, к 2050 году лица этой возрастной категории будут составлять почти треть населения развитых стран. В менее развитых регионах доля пожилых лиц в настоящее время составляет лишь 8 процентов, однако, согласно прогнозам, к 2050 году на нее будет приходиться пятая часть всего населения, а это значит, что к середине столетия развивающиеся страны могут достигнуть такого же этапа демографического старения, на котором развитые страны находятся в настоящее время;

• в развивающихся странах процесс старения населения идет быстрее, чем в развитых странах. Соответственно, у развивающихся стран будет меньше времени на адаптацию к его последствиям. Кроме того, процесс старения населения в развивающихся странах происходит на более низких уровнях социально-экономического развития, чем в развитых странах;

- в настоящее время средний возраст мирового населения составляет 28 лет, т. е. половину населения в мире составляют лица старше и половину — моложе 28 лет. Страной с самым молодым населением является Уганда, где средний возраст равняется 15 годам, а с самым пожилым — Япония, где он составляет 43 года. В следующие 40 лет средний возраст мирового населения, вероятно, увеличится на 10 лет и к 2050 году достигнет 38 лет. В это время странами с самым молодым населением, как представляется, будут Бурунди и Уганда, где средний возраст населения будет составлять 20 лет, а с самым старым — специальный административный район Китая Макао и Республика Корея, где средний возраст населения, по прогнозам, должен достигнуть 54 лет;

- пожилое население, в свою очередь, тоже стареет. Среди лиц в возрасте 60 лет и старше наиболее динамично увеличивается процентная доля населения самой старшей возрастной категории — лиц в возрасте 80 лет и старше. В настоящее время их численность ежегодно увеличивается на 3,9 процента. Среди лиц в возрасте 60 лет и старше сегодня каждому восьмому за 80. При этом ожидается, что к 2050 году из каждых десяти пожилых людей примерно двое будут старше 80 лет;

- коэффициент потенциальной поддержки (КПП), т. е. соотношение лиц в возрасте от 15 до 64 лет и лиц в возрасте 65 лет и старше, показывает сколько лиц трудоспособного возраста приходится на одного пожилого человека. По мере старения населения коэффициент потенциальной поддержки, как правило, снижается. За период с 1950 года по 2007 год коэффициент потенциальной поддержки сократился с 12 до 9 лиц трудоспособного возраста на одного человека в возрасте 65 лет и старше. Согласно прогнозам, к 2050 году коэффициент потенциальной поддержки должен еще больше снизиться и составит четыре человека трудоспособного возраста на одного пожилого человека (диаграмма II). Снижение коэффициентов потенциальной поддержки имеет важные последствия для механизмов социального обеспечения, в частности для пенсионных систем, в соответствии с которыми выплата пенсий производится за счет налогообложения работающих;

Диаграмма II
Коэффициент потенциальной поддержки (КПП): в мире, 1950–2050 годы

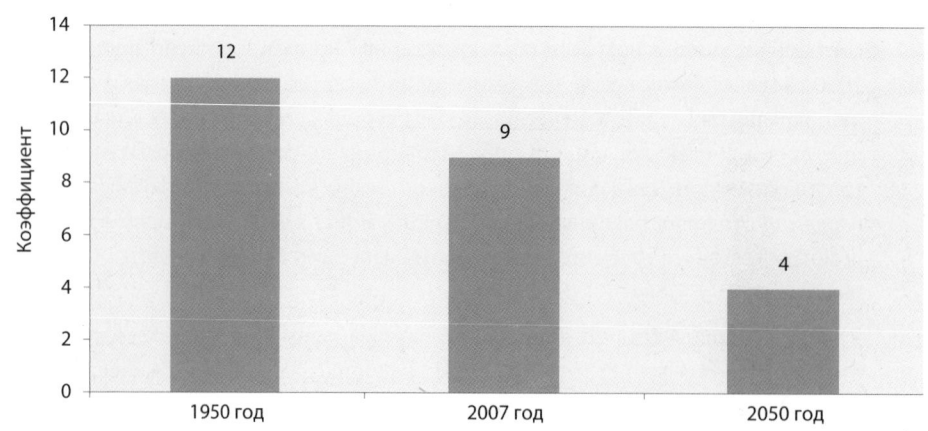

- среди лиц пожилого возраста преобладают женщины, так как у них продолжительность жизни больше, чем у мужчин. В настоящее время среди населения в возрасте 60 лет и старше женщин примерно на 70 миллионов человек больше, чем мужчин. Среди лиц в возрасте 80 лет и старше их почти в два раза больше, чем мужчин, а среди лиц в возрасте 100 лет и старше — в 4–5 раз (диаграмма III);

- здоровье пожилых лиц с возрастом как правило ухудшается, и по мере увеличения их численности увеличиваются и потребности в услугах по долгосрочному уходу за престарелыми. Коэффициент поддержки родителей, т.е. соотношение лиц в возрасте 85 лет и старше и лиц в возрасте от 50 до 64 лет, позволяет оценивать масштабы потенциальной поддержки, которую оказывают пожилым членам семьи их родственники. В 1950 году в мире насчитывалось менее 2 человек в возрасте 85 лет и старше на каждые 100 человек в возрасте от 50 до 64 лет. Сейчас этот показатель составляет чуть больше 4:100, а к 2050 году он, по прогнозам, достигнет 12:100. Это значит, что вероятность того, что нагрузка на лица, которые сами уже перешагнули рубеж среднего возраста, по выполнению обязанностей по уходу за своими престарелыми родственниками увеличится в три раза;

- одинокие пожилые люди сталкиваются с бóльшим риском подвергнуться социальной изоляции и экономическим лишениям и, соответственно, нуждаются в особой поддержке. В связи с более высокими показателями доживаемости и более низкой вероятностью повторного вступления в брак среди пожилых одиноких женщин больше, чем мужчин. В мировом масштабе доля одиноких среди женщин в возрасте 60 лет и старше составляет 19 процентов, а у мужчин этой возрастной группы соответствующий показатель равняется лишь 8 процентам;

- между разными группами населения имеются значительные различия и с точки зрения фактического возраста прекращения трудовой деятельности. В странах с высоким уровнем дохода на душу населения пожилые люди выходят на пенсию раньше и, таким образом, в этих странах отмечаются более низкие показатели участия пожилых на рынке труда. Так, в более развитых регионах доля мужчин в возрасте 65 лет и старше среди экономически активного населения составляет лишь 13 процентов, тогда как в менее развитых регионах она

Диаграмма III

Процентная доля женщин среди населения в возрасте 40–59 лет, 60 лет и старше, 80 лет и старше и 100 лет и старше: в мире, 2007 год

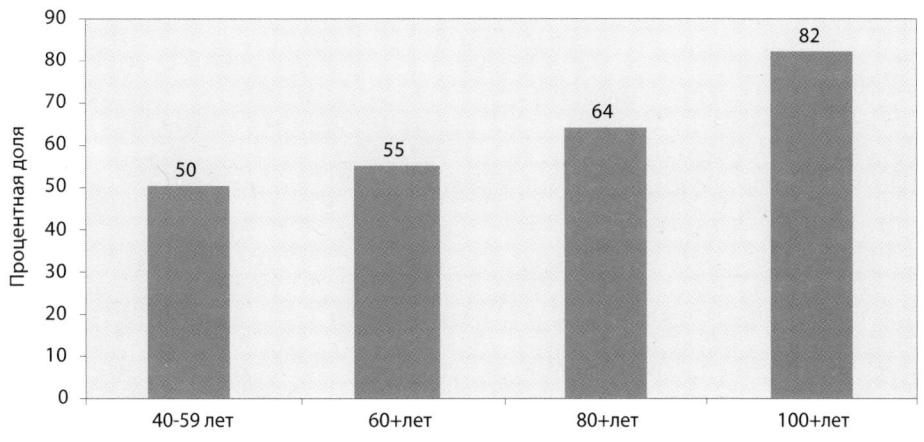

достигает 39 процентов. Аналогичные различия прослеживаются и среди женщин. В более развитых регионах доля пожилых женщин среди экономически активного населения составляет 7 процентов, а в менее развитых регионах — 15 процентов. В менее развитых регионах пожилые люди продолжают дольше трудиться в силу ограниченности охвата пенсионных программ и сравнительно небольшого размера пенсионных пособий;

- в большинстве стран возраст выхода на пенсию (так называемый пенсионный возраст), при наступлении которого пенсия выплачивается в полном размере при условии выработки минимального пенсионного стажа, установлен одинаковым для женщин и мужчин. Однако во многих странах женщины имеют право на полное пенсионное обеспечение в более молодом возрасте, чем мужчины, хотя показатели доживаемости у женщин после достижения возраста 60 лет выше, чем у мужчин. В развитых странах возраст выхода на пенсию как для мужчин, так и для женщин как правило выше, чем в развивающихся;

- в наименее развитых регионах по-прежнему остро стоит проблема неграмотности пожилого населения. Согласно оценкам, в настоящее время в развивающихся странах свыше половины населения в возрасте 65 лет и старше не владеют грамотой. Лишь примерно треть пожилых женщин и примерно три пятых пожилых мужчин в развивающихся странах имеют элементарные навыки чтения и письма. В более же развитых регионах, за исключением отдельных стран, практически все пожилые люди владеют грамотой.

Итак, в результате снижения показателей рождаемости и сохраняющейся тенденции к сокращению показателей смертности среди взрослого населения в большинстве стран мира наблюдается процесс демографического старения. Это беспрецедентное демографическое явление, которое охватило развитые страны в XIX веке и которое в последнее время распространилось на развивающиеся страны, уже трансформирует облик многих стран. Ожидается, что в ближайшем будущем процесс старения населения, особенно в развивающихся странах, ускорится. Поскольку у развивающихся стран будет меньше времени для адаптации к последствиям демографического старения, правительства этих стран должны немедленно принять меры, чтобы отреагировать на этот вызов и максимально эффективно использовать возможности, которые заключает в себе процесс демографического старения. Настоящий доклад обеспечивает демографическую базу для оценки глубины и остроты проблемы старения в каждой стране мира как в настоящее время, так и на предстоящие годы.

Resumen

El Plan de Acción Internacional de Madrid sobre el Envejecimiento y la Declaración Política aprobados en la Segunda Asamblea Mundial sobre el Envejecimiento en abril de 2002[1] constituyeron un punto de inflexión en la forma de plantear en todo el mundo el crucial problema de crear una sociedad para todas las edades. El Plan está centrado en tres esferas prioritarias: las personas de edad y el desarrollo; la promoción de la salud y el bienestar hasta la vejez; y la creción de un entorno propicio y favorable. En el Plan, los gobiernos adoptaron por primera vez un enfoque global en el que se vinculaban las cuestiones del envejecimiento con otros marcos para el desarrollo social y económico y los derechos humanos, principalmente los establecidos en las conferencias y reuniones en la cumbre de las Naciones Unidas de los años noventa.

Las cuestiones relacionadas con el envejecimiento de la población y las personas de edad han desempeñado un importante papel en las tres grandes conferencias internacionales sobre la población organizadas por las Naciones Unidas en el último cuarto de siglo. Por ejemplo, la Conferencia Internacional sobre la Población y el Desarrollo celebrada en 1994, señaló que los efectos económicos y sociales del envejecimiento de la población eran tanto una oportunidad como un reto para todas las sociedades[2]. Más recientemente, en las principales actividades organizadas para proseguir la aplicación del Programa de Acción de la Conferencia Internacional sobre la Población y el Desarrollo, aprobado por la Asamblea General en su vigésimo primer período extraordinario de sesiones el 2 de julio de 1999, se reiteró la necesidad de que todas las sociedades hicieran frente a las importantes consecuencias del envejecimiento de la población en las próximas décadas[3]. En 2007, la Comisión de Población y Desarrollo de las Naciones Unidas centrará su labor en el estudio de los cambios en las estructuras de las poblaciones y sus repercusiones en el desarrollo, que constituirá el tema especial de su 40° período de sesiones.

La División de Población de las Naciones Unidas cuenta con una larga tradición en el estudio del envejecimiento de la población, labor que comprende la preparación de estimaciones y proyecciones del tamaño y las características de las poblaciones de edad, y el examen de los factores determinantes y las consecuencias del envejecimiento de la población. Desde el innovador informe sobre el envejecimiento de la población de 1956, centrado principalmente en el envejecimiento de la población en los países más desarrollados, hasta el gráfico mural de las Naciones Unidas sobre el envejecimiento de la población publicado en 2006, la División de Población ha tratado sistemáticamente de señalar a la atención de los gobiernos y la comunidad internacional la cuestión del envejecimiento de la población[4].

---

1   Véase el *Informe de la Segunda Asamblea Mundial sobre el Envejecimiento* (publicación de las Naciones Unidas, A/CONF.197/9, número de venta: S.02.IV.4).

2   *Población y Desarrollo*, vol. 1: *Programa de Acción adoptado en la Conferencia Internacional sobre la Población y el Desarrollo, El Cairo, 5 a 13 de septiembre de 1994* (publicación de las Naciones Unidas, número de venta: S.95.XIII.7).

3   *Examen y evaluación de los progresos alcanzados en el logro de los objetivos del Programa de Acción de la Conferencia Internacional sobre la Población y el Desarrollo, Informe de 1999* (publicación de las Naciones Unidas, número de venta: S.99.XIII.16).

4   *The Ageing of Populations and its Economic and Social Implications*, Estudios de Población, No. 26 (publicación de las Naciones Unidas, número de venta: 1956.XIII.6), y *Population Ageing 2006* (publicación de las Naciones Unidas, número de venta: E.06.XIII.2).

La Comisión de Desarrollo Social de las Naciones Unidas ha decidido realizar cada cinco años un examen y evaluación de los avances en la aplicación del Plan de Acción de Madrid sobre el Envejecimiento. Además, la Asamblea General ha destacado la necesidad de contar con datos de población desglosados por edad y sexo. En el presente informe se sientan las bases demográficas de las actividades de seguimiento de la Segunda Asamblea Mundial sobre el Envejecimiento. En él se examina el proceso del envejecimiento de la población en todo el mundo, las regiones con distintos grados de desarrollo, las principales zonas y regiones, y en los distintos países. Se presentan perfiles demográficos del período 1950-2050 para cada país, en los que se ponen de relieve los indicadores relacionados con el envejecimiento de la población.

En el presente informe se destacan cuatro conclusiones principales:

1. El envejecimiento de la población es un proceso sin precedentes ni paralelo en la historia de la humanidad. La población envejece cuando aumenta el porcentaje de personas de edad (60 años o más) al tiempo que disminuyen el porcentaje de niños (menores de 15 años) y el de personas en edad de trabajar (de 15 a 59 años). Se prevé que, a nivel mundial, el número de personas de edad superará por primera vez el de jóvenes en 2047. En las zonas más desarrolladas, en las que el envejecimiento de la población está muy avanzado, el número de niños era menor que el de personas de edad en 1998.

2. El envejecimiento de la población, que afecta prácticamente a todos los países del mundo, se debe principalmente a las reducciones de la fertilidad, que se han hecho prácticamente universales. El fenómeno ha tenido como consecuencia una disminución en el aumento del número de niños, acompañado de un aumento constante en el número de personas de edad, e incide directamente en la equidad y la solidaridad intergeneracionales e intrageneracionales, que son los fundamentos de la sociedad.

3. El envejecimiento de la población es profundo y tiene importantes consecuencias y ramificaciones en todas las facetas de la vida humana. En lo económico, el envejecimiento de la población incidirá en el crecimiento económico, el ahorro, las inversiones, el consumo, los mercados de trabajo, las pensiones, la tributación y las transferencias intergeneracionales. En lo social, el envejecimiento de la población influye en las condiciones de vida y la composición de la familia, la demanda de vivienda, las tendencias de la migración, la epidemiología y los servicios de atención de la salud. En lo político, el envejecimiento de la población puede alterar los patrones de voto y la representación.

4. El envejecimiento de la población es permanente. Desde 1950 la proporción de personas de edad ha estado aumentando regularmente; pasó del 8% en 1950 al 11% en 2007 y se calcula que llegará al 22% en 2050 (gráfico 1). Mientras la mortalidad en la edad avanzada siga disminuyendo y la fertilidad se mantenga baja, la proporción de las personas de edad seguirá aumentando.

Las principales conclusiones de este informe son las siguientes:

- No es probable que los niveles de fertilidad vuelvan a alcanzar los altos niveles que eran habituales en épocas pasadas, el envejecimiento de la población es irreversible y las poblaciones jóvenes —tan comunes hasta hace poco— se irán haciendo más escasas durante el siglo XXI.

- En 2000 había 600 millones de personas de 60 años o más, tres veces más que en 1950, y en 2006 habían sobrepasado los 700 millones. Se calcula que para 2050, habrá 2.000 millones de personas de edad, lo que significa que, una vez más, este grupo de edad se habrá triplicado en un lapso de 50 años.

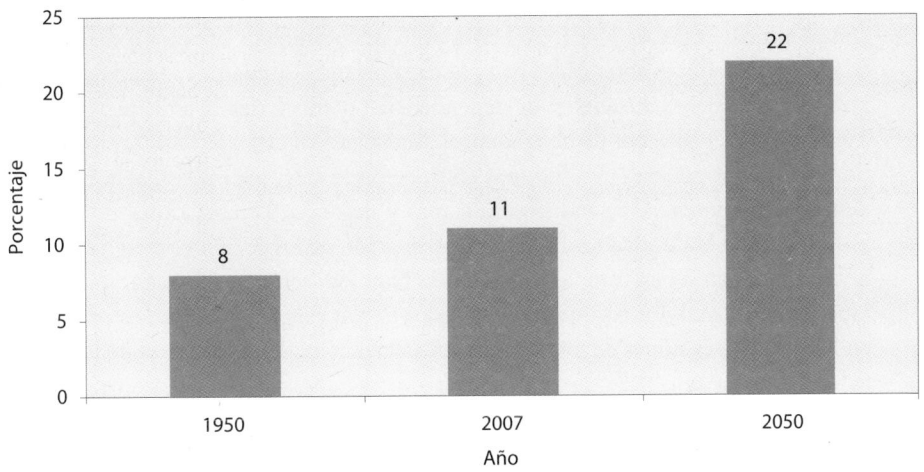

- A nivel mundial la población de personas de edad aumenta a razón del 2,6% por año, mucho más de prisa que la población total, que aumenta en 1,1% por año. Se calcula que, al menos hasta 2050, la población de edad seguirá aumentando con más rapidez que la población de los demás grupos de edad. Ese rápido crecimiento requerirá unos ajustes económicos y sociales de gran envergadura en la mayoría de los países.

- Se observan diferencias acusadas en el número y la proporción de personas de edad de las distintas regiones. En las más desarrolladas, más de una quinta parte de la población tiene 60 años o más, y hacia 2050 cerca de un tercio de la población de los países desarrollados se encontrará en ese grupo de edad. En las regiones menos desarrolladas, las personas de edad representan actualmente tan sólo el 8% de la población, pero se calcula que hacia 2050 representarán un quinto de la población, lo que significa que, a mediados de siglo, el mundo en desarrollo puede llegar al mismo estadio en el proceso de envejecimiento de la población que los países desarrollados en la actualidad.

- Como el ritmo de envejecimiento de la población es más rápido en los países en desarrollo que en los desarrollados, los países en desarrollo tendrán menos tiempo para adaptarse a las consecuencias del envejecimiento de la población. Además el crecimiento de la población en los países en desarrollo se produce a niveles de desarrollo socioeconómico más bajos que los que existían en su momento en los países desarrollados.

- Actualmente la mediana de edad en el mundo es de 28 años, es decir, la mitad de la población tiene menos de esa edad y la otra mitad tiene más. El país con la población más joven es Uganda, con una mediana de edad de 15 años, y la población más vieja es la del Japón, con una mediana de edad de 43 años. En las cuatro próximas décadas, la mediana de edad del mundo aumentará probablemente 10 años, con lo que alcanzará los 38 años en 2050. Para entonces, los países con las poblaciones más jóvenes serán probablemente Burundi y Uganda, con medianas de edad de 20 años cada uno, y Macao (RAE de China) y la República de Corea tendrán las poblaciones más viejas, con medianas de edad de 54 años en cada país.

- La población de personas de edad, a su vez, también está envejeciendo. Entre las personas de 60 años o más, la población que crece más rápidamente es la de los más mayores —de 80 años o más—, que aumenta actualmente a una tasa anual de 3,9%. En la actualidad, una de cada 8 personas de edad (de 60 años o más) tiene

80 años o más y se calcula que, hacia 2050, la proporción será de cerca de 2 personas de 80 años o más por cada 10 personas de edad.

- El cociente de dependencia potencial, es decir el número de personas con edades comprendidas entre los 15 y los 64 años por cada persona de 65 años o más, indica cuántos trabajadores potenciales hay por cada persona de edad. A medida de que la población envejece, el cociente de dependencia potencial tiende a disminuir. Entre 1950 y 2007, el cociente de dependencia potencial se redujo de 12 a 9 trabajadores potenciales por persona de 65 o más años. Se prevé que, para 2050, el cociente de dependencia potencial se reducirá aún más y llegará a 4 trabajadores potenciales por cada persona de edad (gráfico II). La reducción de los cocientes de dependencia potencial tienen repercusiones importantes para los regímenes de seguridad social, especialmente para los regímenes de pensiones con cargo a los ingresos corrientes, en los que las pensiones de los jubilados se pagan con las aportaciones de los trabajadores en activo.

- Como las mujeres viven más que los hombres, las mujeres son mayoría entre las personas de edad. En la actualidad hay unos 70 millones más de mujeres que de hombres con 60 años o más. Entre las personas de 80 años o más, hay cerca de 2 veces más mujeres que hombres, y entre los centenarios hay entre 4 y 5 veces más mujeres que hombres (gráfico III).

- La salud de las personas de edad suele deteriorarse con la edad, lo que se traduce en un incremento de la demanda de atención de largo plazo a medida que aumenta el número de las personas de más edad. El cociente de dependencia parental, es decir, el número de personas de 85 años o más respecto de la población de entre 50 y 64 años, da una idea del nivel de apoyo que las familias pueden brindar a sus miembros de más edad. En 1950 había en todo el mundo menos de dos personas de 85 años o más por cada 100 personas de 50 a 64 años. Actualmente la relación ha aumentado a algo más de 4 por cada 100, pero se proyecta que llegará a 12 por cada 100 en 2050; es decir, que las personas que hoy ya han pasado con creces la edad madura tendrán tres veces más probabilidades que en la actualidad de tener que atender a sus parientes mayores.

- Las personas de edad que viven solas corren más riesgo de sufrir aislamiento social y privaciones económicas, por lo que pueden requerir un apoyo especial. Debido a su mayor longevidad y a su menor propensión a volverse a casar, las mujeres de

Gráfico II

Cociente de dependencia potencial en el mundo, de 1950 a 2050

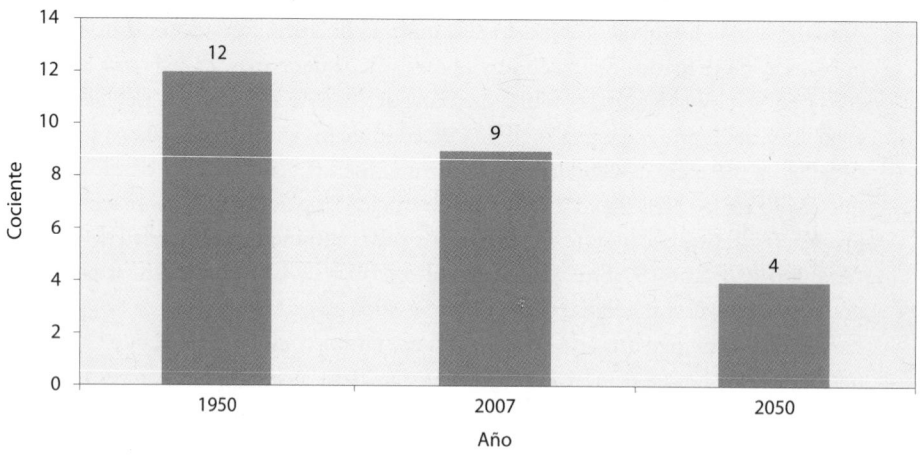

Porcentaje de mujeres entre los grupos de edad de 40 a 59 años, mayores de 60, mayores de 80 y mayores de 100 años en todo el mundo en 2007

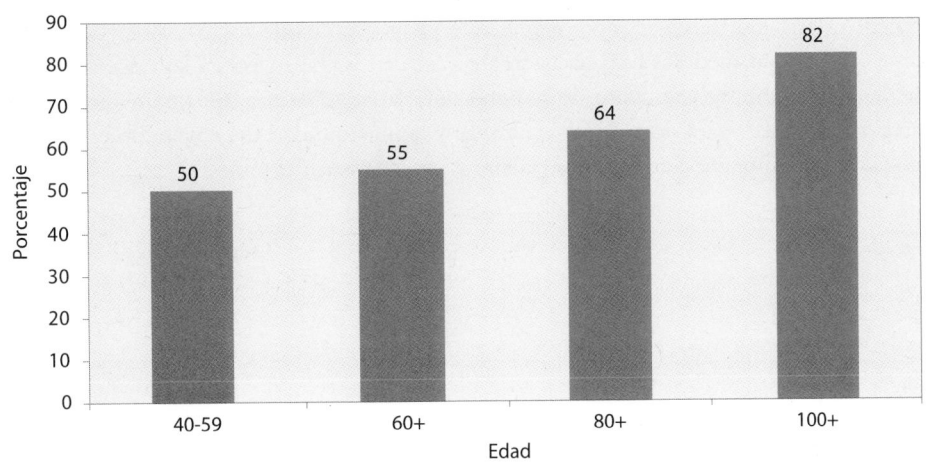

edad tienen más probabilidades que los hombres de vivir solas. Se calcula que, en todo el mundo, el 19% de las mujeres de 60 años o más viven solas, mientras que solamente el 8% de los hombres se encuentra en esa situación.

- La edad efectiva de jubilación varía considerablemente entre las poblaciones. En los países con altos ingresos per cápita, las personas de edad pueden jubilarse antes y, por consiguiente, tienden a participar menos en la fuerza de trabajo en las edades más avanzadas. Así pues, sólo el 13% de los hombres de 65 años o más son económicamente activos en las regiones más desarrolladas, mientras que en las menos desarrolladas el 39% de los hombres está en la fuerza de trabajo. La diferencia es similar entre las mujeres. En las regiones más desarrolladas, el 7% de las mujeres de edad son económicamente activas, frente al 15% en las regiones menos desarrolladas. Las personas de edad son económicamente activas durante más tiempo en las regiones menos desarrolladas debido a la limitada cobertura de los programas de pensiones y a la relativa exigüidad de los ingresos que proporcionan.

- En la mayoría de los países la edad reglamentaria para poder cobrar una pensión completa, siempre que se haya cotizado durante un período mínimo al régimen de pensiones, es decir, la edad mínima de jubilación es la misma para las mujeres que para los hombres. Sin embargo, en muchos países las mujeres pueden jubilarse con prestaciones completas a edades menores que los hombres, a pesar de que la esperanza de vida de las mujeres es mayor que la de los hombres después de los 60 años. Tanto para los hombres como para las mujeres, la edad de jubilación tiende a ser más alta en los países desarrollados que en los países en desarrollo.

- El analfabetismo es todavía común en la población de más edad de los países menos desarrollados. Actualmente se calcula que más de la mitad de las personas de 65 años o más de los países en desarrollo son analfabetas. Solamente alrededor de un tercio de las mujeres de edad y unas tres quintas partes de los hombres de edad de los países en desarrollo saben leer y escribir a nivel elemental. La población de edad está alfabetizada prácticamente en todos los países de las regiones más desarrolladas.

Resumiendo, debido a la transición de una fertilidad alta a una fertilidad baja y a la constante reducción de la mortalidad de los adultos, la población de la mayor parte de los países del mundo está envejeciendo. Este cambio demográfico sin precedentes, que comenzó en el mundo desarrollado en el siglo XIX y más recientemente en los países en desarrollo, ya está transformando muchas sociedades. Se prevé que el proceso de envejecimiento se acelerará en el futuro próximo, sobre todo en los países en desarrollo. Como estos países tienen menos tiempo para adaptarse a los cambios que conlleva el envejecimiento de la población, es apremiante que los gobiernos de los países en desarrollo empiecen a tomar medidas para hacer frente a esos retos y aprovechen las oportunidades que les ofrece el envejecimiento de la población. En el presente informe se sientan las bases demográficas para determinar el alcance y la profundidad del envejecimiento de la población actualmente y en los años próximos en cada país del mundo.

Introduction

The dynamics and consequences of population ageing

Population ageing—the process whereby older individuals account for a proportionally larger share of the total population—was a key demographic outcome of population trends during the twentieth century and will surely be the distinctive trait of populations during the twenty-first century. Starting first in the more developed countries, population ageing has now become apparent in much of the developing world and it will affect virtually all countries over the medium-term future, although its intensity and depth will vary considerably among countries.

The shift in age structure associated with population ageing has a profound impact on a broad range of economic, political and social processes. For example, concerns are growing about the long-term viability of intergenerational social support systems, which are crucial for the well-being of both the older and younger generations (Cliquet and Nizamuddin, 1999). Such concern is especially acute in societies where provision of care within the family becomes increasingly difficult as family size decreases and women, who are traditionally the main caregivers, engage in employment outside the home.

As people live longer, certain benefits, such as pensions, health care or old-age support, need to be paid over longer periods. Consequently, to remain sustainable, social security systems need to change (Creedy, 1998; Bravo, 1999). Increasing longevity may also result in rising medical costs and increasing demands for health services, since older people are typically more vulnerable to chronic diseases (de Jong-Gierveld and van Solinge, 1995; Holliday, 1999).

This report provides an overview of population ageing worldwide, focusing on five particularly relevant public policy issues. In dealing with each of these issues, attention is given to the course of the ageing process, which has not been the same in all countries. There has been considerable variation in the timing, levels and patterns of population ageing. Therefore, the assessment of trends is made on the basis of groups of countries, disaggregated according to development levels and major geographic areas.

The first chapter of this report focuses on the demographic determinants of population ageing. It examines the worldwide decline in fertility and mortality that underlies population ageing. The analysis is based on three indicators: the total fertility rate, life expectancy (at birth and at ages 60, 65 and 80), and the probability of survival (to ages 60, 65 and 80).

Especially at the earlier stages of the demographic transition, reductions in fertility are the primary determinants of the timing and extent of population ageing. However, as later stages of the transition are reached, reductions in mortality, particularly at older ages, contribute more to increasing the number of older persons and thus accelerating population ageing.

An important consequence of the reductions of fertility is a progressive reduction in the availability of kin on whom future generations of older persons may rely upon for support. This change may significantly impact on the well-being of older persons, especially in the less developed regions where social support for older persons is largely provided by the immediate family (Hoyert, 1991; Wolf, 1994). At the same time, improved chances of surviving to the older ages are likely to spur efforts to improve the health status of the older population and lead to reforms in pension and health systems.

The second chapter of this report focuses on the magnitude and speed of population ageing, examining regional differences in the progression of the ageing process through the analysis of the share and growth rate of number of older persons (i.e., those aged 60 years or over, 65 years or over, and 80 years or over).

As the impact of population ageing on socio-economic conditions may be amplified by the speed at which it occurs, it is important to consider not only the degree but also the pace of changes in the age structure. When the proportion of older persons in the total population increases rapidly over a short period, as is currently the case in some developed and developing countries, it becomes particularly difficult for the institutions to adapt and adjust.

The third chapter considers the changing balance between age groups and analyses changes in the relative size of the older and younger groups of the population from various perspectives. Six indicators are examined: the percentage of the population in broad age groups (0-14, 15-59 and 60 or over), the ageing index, the median age, various types of dependency ratios (total, youth and old-age), the potential support ratio and the parent support ratio.

When the proportion of older persons increases, the shares of other age groups change. The shifting weights of the various age groups tend to create social and political pressures that may result in changing patterns of resource allocation among generations, sometimes giving rise to intergenerational conflict (Walker, 1990; Jackson, 1998). Complementarities may also rise. Thus, as children account for a declining proportion of the population, there may be a reduction in the number of schools just as the increasing share of the older population begins to require more long-term care facilities. A commonly used measure to assess the potential impact of the changing age composition of populations is the ageing index, that is, the ratio of those aged 60 years or over to those under age 15 (children).

A decrease of the potential support ratio, which implies a rise in the old-age dependency ratio, indicates in most societies that an increasing number of beneficiaries of health and pension systems (that is, persons aged 65 years or over) have to be supported by a relatively smaller number of contributors (that is, persons of working age, usually between the ages of 15 and 64). Such a change is likely to pose heavier demands on the working-age population, whether in the form of higher taxes or other contributions, so as to maintain a stable flow of benefits to the older population. Even though there may also be a sharp decline in the youth dependency ratio, this reduction may not be sufficient to offset the increased costs related to an ageing population because the costs involved in supporting older persons are, in general, higher than those involved in supporting children and adolescents (United Nations, 1988; Baldacci and Lugaresi, 1997).

In most societies, support to the elderly is only partially provided through public resource transfers. The family remains an important source of support to older persons, especially in developing countries where social security systems often have a very restricted coverage (United Nations, 1994). Family support is particularly crucial in the case of very old persons, whose physical and economic needs are usually greater. The parent support ratio provides an indication of the overall demand on families to provide support for their oldest members. The continuing increase of this ratio implies that, increasingly, persons aged 50 to 64 will find themselves responsible for the care of one or more family members aged 85 years or over.

The fourth chapter of this report presents a demographic profile of the older population, drawing attention to two important features of the ageing process: the progressive ageing of the older population itself and its feminization. It also examines the significant gender differences with regard to marital status and living arrangements of older persons.

The rapid growth of the oldest groups among the older population is of special relevance in terms of public policy. In most parts of the world, the group aged 80 years or over is growing faster than any other age group and is expected to continue growing at very rapid rates until at least 2050. Although this group constitutes a small proportion of the total population, the number of persons involved is increasingly significant, especially in developing countries. Because health status typically declines with advancing age, higher numbers of oldest-old imply a growing demand for long-term care (Pollard, 1995; Crimmins, 1997).

The increasing female share of the older population is also relevant to public policy. Because mortality rates are usually higher among men than among women, even at older ages, the percentage female among the population by age group tends to increase with advancing age. In most countries, older women greatly outnumber older men. The implications of this gender imbalance for public support and planning can be significant because older women typically have less education, less work experience and less access to public assistance and other private income sources than older men (Higuchi, 1996; United Nations, 1999b). Older women are also more likely to be living without a spouse either because they are widowed or separated or because they never married. Hence, they are also more likely to live alone than older men. As a result, older women are less likely than older men to receive assistance from close relatives, including spouses. In most countries, the major concern about providing adequate support to the oldest-old centres primarily on the need of support by older women.

The fifth chapter focuses on the socio-economic characteristics of the older population, considering several dimensions that can greatly affect the well-being of older individuals: their labour force participation, the statutory pensionable age, and the literacy status of older persons.

Labour force participation among the older population is considerably higher in developing countries than in developed countries, mainly because of the lack of adequate pension and retirement programmes in most developing countries. Furthermore, in many developing countries there are still large concentrations of older workers in agriculture and in the informal sector, both of which are generally not covered by social security systems or pensions (International Labour Office, 2000). In terms of gender, labour force participation rates have dropped among older men and have risen among older women, resulting in a relatively high female share among the older work force.

Although lower levels of labour force participation at older ages are generally associated with higher levels of social security coverage, the decline in the labour force participation of older men in both developed and developing countries is likely to be related to factors such as a shortage of employment opportunities, skill obsolescence and deficient knowledge and training to keep abreast of new developments (Drury, 1994; Taylor and Walker, 1996).

Lastly, there appears to be general agreement that higher levels of educational attainment result in better health and economic status among older persons. Improvements in the educational attainment of older persons may also alleviate any cultural gap between generations that may have widened over the past century. In developing countries, in particular, illiteracy is still high at all ages but especially among older persons. Higher levels of literacy among younger generations are expected to improve their prospects as they age and thus result in a better quality of life for those reaching old age.

Annexes III and IV to this report present detailed statistics on population ageing, including estimates and projections of the number of older persons and all the summary indicators discussed in the report. Definitions for each indicator can be found in annex I. Indicators are presented for the world as a whole, for the major development groups, and for geographic major areas and regions, as well as for each country or area with at least 100,000 inhabitants in 2005, as presented in *World Population Prospects: The 2004 Revision* (United Nations, 2005a). For the composition of the geographic major areas or regions used, see annex II. Summary tables displaying selected indicators by region and country are presented in annex III. Profiles for regions and countries are also presented in annex IV.

Chapter I
Demographic determinants of population ageing

The process underlying global population ageing is known as the "demographic transition", a process whereby reductions in mortality, particularly at young ages, are followed by reductions in fertility. Decreasing fertility along with increasing life expectancy (figure 1) has reshaped the age structure of the population in most regions of the planet by shifting the relative weight of the population from younger to older groups. The role of international migration in changing age distributions has been far less important than that of fertility and mortality (Lesthaeghe, 2004; United Nations, 2005c).

A. Reductions in fertility

Decreasing fertility has been the primary cause of population ageing because, as fertility moves steadily to lower levels, people of reproductive age have fewer children relative to those of older generations, with the result that sustained fertility reductions eventually lead to a reduction of the proportion of children and young persons in a population and a corresponding increase of the proportions in older groups.

The reduction of fertility has been dramatic since 1950. At the world level, total fertility has dropped almost by half, from 5.0 children per woman in 1950-1955 to 2.7 in 2005-2010, and it is expected to keep on declining to reach 2.1 children per women in 2045-2050.

As a result of the sustained decline in fertility that occurred in developed countries during the twentieth century, total fertility in the more developed regions has dropped from an already low level of 2.8 children per woman in 1950-1955 to an extremely low level of 1.6 children per woman in 2005-2010. This level is well below that needed to

Fertility is well below replacement level in the more developed regions

Figure 1
Total fertility rate and life expectancy at birth: world, 1950-2050

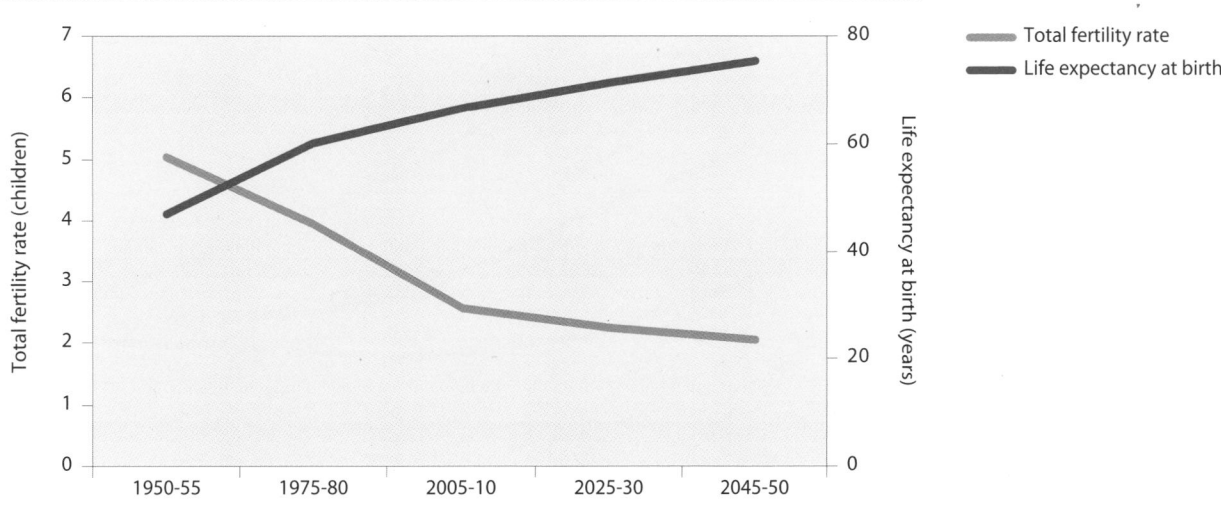

ensure the replacement of generations (about 2.1 children per woman). In fact, practically all developed countries are currently experiencing below-replacement fertility. In 14 developed countries total fertility is currently under 1.3 children per woman, levels that are unprecedented in human history.

Fertility decline in the less developed regions started later and has proceeded faster

Major fertility reductions in the less developed regions occurred, in general, during the last three decades of the twentieth century. From 1950-1955 to 2005-2010, the total fertility in the developing world dropped by almost 60 per cent, from 6.2 to 2.7 children per woman (figure 2).

However, great disparities persist. In the least developed countries, total fertility is now 4.7 children per woman. In particular, in Eastern Africa, Middle Africa and Western Africa, total fertility is still in excess of 5.2 children per woman. Yet, in Eastern Asia, South-eastern Asia, the Caribbean and South America, total fertility is currently 2.4 children per woman or less. In 33 developing countries, the total fertility rate is estimated to be already below replacement level.

Regional differences in fertility are expected to decrease

Since the transition towards lower fertility levels is expected to continue in developing countries and fertility levels in developed countries are expected to increase slightly, differences in fertility among regions are expected to decrease in the future. Total fertility in the less developed regions is expected to drop from the current 2.7 children per woman to 2.3 children per woman by 2025-2030, and to 2.1 by 2045-2050. Fertility in the more developed regions is projected to rise from the current 1.6 children per woman to 1.7 children per woman in 2025-2030 and 1.8 children per woman in 2045-2050. A particularly sharp reduction is expected for the least developed countries, where total fertility may reach 2.6 children per woman in 2045-2050, down from 4.7 children per woman in 2005-2010 and 3.5 children per woman in 2025-2030 (figure 2). These projected values for the least developed countries are contingent on the occurrence of major changes regarding desired family size and the use of contraception in those countries.

B. Reductions in mortality

As fertility levels drop, mortality has also continued to decline, especially at older ages. When fertility reaches low levels and remains low, reductions in mortality at older ages gain importance as a cause of population ageing. In developed countries, in particular,

Figure 2
Total fertility rate: world and development regions, 1950-2050

World
More developed regions
Less developed regions
Least developed countries

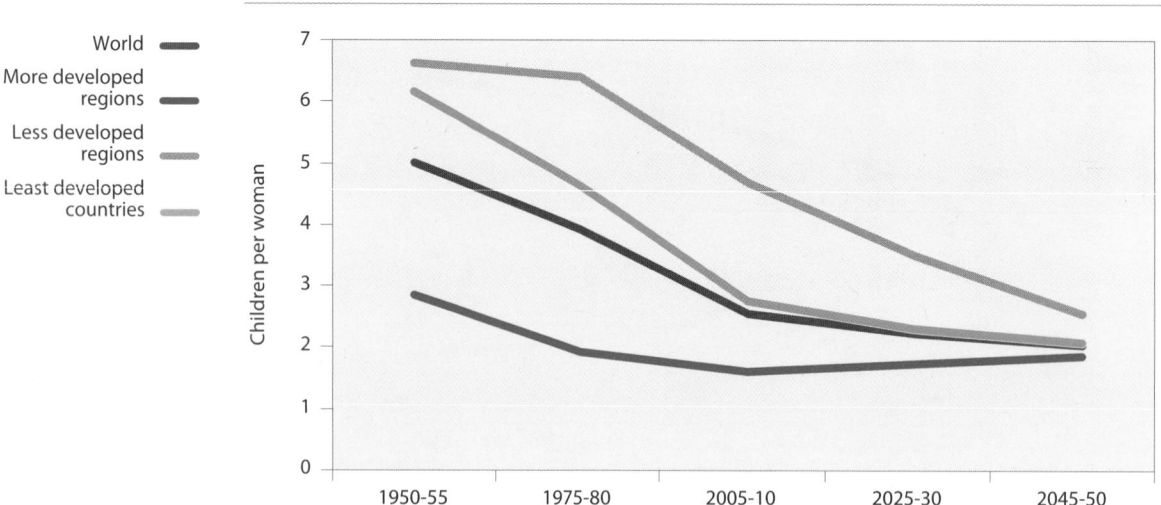

where low fertility has prevailed for at least two decades, increases in the proportion of the older population are now primarily caused by increasing survival to advanced ages (Grundy, 1996; National Research Council, 2001; United Nations, 2005c).

Since 1950, life expectancy at birth increased globally by 20 years, from 46.6 years in 1950-1955 to 66.5 years in 2005-2010 (figure 3). On average, the gain in life expectancy at birth was 23.5 years in the less developed regions and 10.1 years in the more developed regions (figure 3). Nevertheless, a considerable advantage still persists in favour of the latter. At current mortality rates an individual born in the more developed regions is now expected to outlive an individual born in the less developed regions by almost 12 years. If the individual is born in the group of least developed countries, this disadvantage doubles to almost 25 years.

People are living longer, but large variations remain

While in some developing countries or areas, such as Israel, Hong Kong Special Administrative Region (SAR) of China and Macao Special Administrative Region (SAR) of China, life expectancy at birth is currently higher than 80 years, in others, such as Botswana, Lesotho and Swaziland, it does not surpass 35 years. In many countries, especially those classified as least developed, low levels of life expectancy at birth are partly due to the spread of HIV. On average, life expectancy in the least developed countries lengthened by 16 years since 1960, substantially less than the average gain recorded by developing countries as a whole (figure 3).

Great variations in life expectancy exist within the less developed regions

Among developed countries, the range of variation in life expectancy is significantly narrower than among developing countries. Apart from a few countries in Eastern Europe where life expectancy at birth is currently between 65 and 69 years, the range in life expectancy among the rest of the developed countries is just 10 years in length: from 72 years in Romania to 82 years in Japan.

Over the next four decades, life expectancy at birth is projected to increase globally by about 9 years, to reach 75 years in 2045-2050 (figure 3). As mortality becomes more concentrated at older ages, the difference in life expectancy among regions will tend to decrease. By 2025-2030, life expectancy at birth is expected to reach, on average, about 80 years in the more developed regions and 70 years in the less developed regions. By 2045-2050 it is expected to have risen to 82 years in the more developed regions and to 74 years in the less developed regions. Thus, the gap between the two is expected to remain at about 8 years by 2045-2050, down from approximately 10 years in 2025-2030 and from almost 12 years at present.

Regional differences in life expectancy at birth are expected to decrease

Figure 3
Life expectancy at birth: world and development regions, 1950-2050

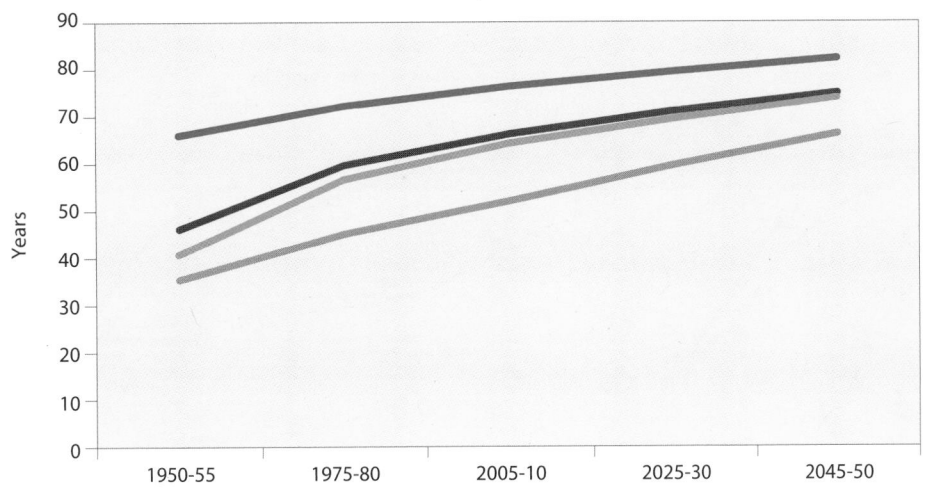

As a result of the generalized shift of mortality to older ages, the survival curve is expected gradually to approach an almost rectangular shape in all regions of the world (figure 4). Under current mortality conditions, almost 3 out of every 4 newborns in the world are expected to survive to age 60, and about 1 out of every 3 to age 80. Under the mortality conditions projected for the period 2045-2050, approximately 7 out of every 8 newborns would survive to age 60, and more than half would survive to age 80.

Not only are more people surviving to old age, but once there, they tend to live longer. Over the next four decades, global life expectancy at age 60 is expected to increase from 19.6 years in 2005-2010 to 22.4 years in 2045-2050 (a 14 per cent gain); from 16.0 to 18.5 years (by 16 per cent) at age 65, and from 7.7 to 9.0 years (by 17 per cent) at age 80 (figures 5 and 6). According to these figures, the higher the starting age, the higher the relative gain in life expectancy. The same holds for the more developed regions, whose average life expectancy at age 80 is projected to increase by 23 per cent over the next four decades as compared with 16 per cent at age 60 and 8 per cent at birth. Similarly, average life expectancy at age 80 in the less developed regions is expected to increase by 22 per cent as compared with 18 per cent at age 60 and 15 per cent at birth (figure 6).

In contrast, for the least developed countries, where mortality levels at young ages remain high, proportional improvements in life expectancy during the next four decades are expected to be higher at birth than at older ages.

Except for a small number of countries, where cultural factors have resulted in lower life expectancy for females than for males, reductions in mortality have been substantially

Figure 4
Projected survival curves: world and development regions: 2005-2010 and 2045-2050

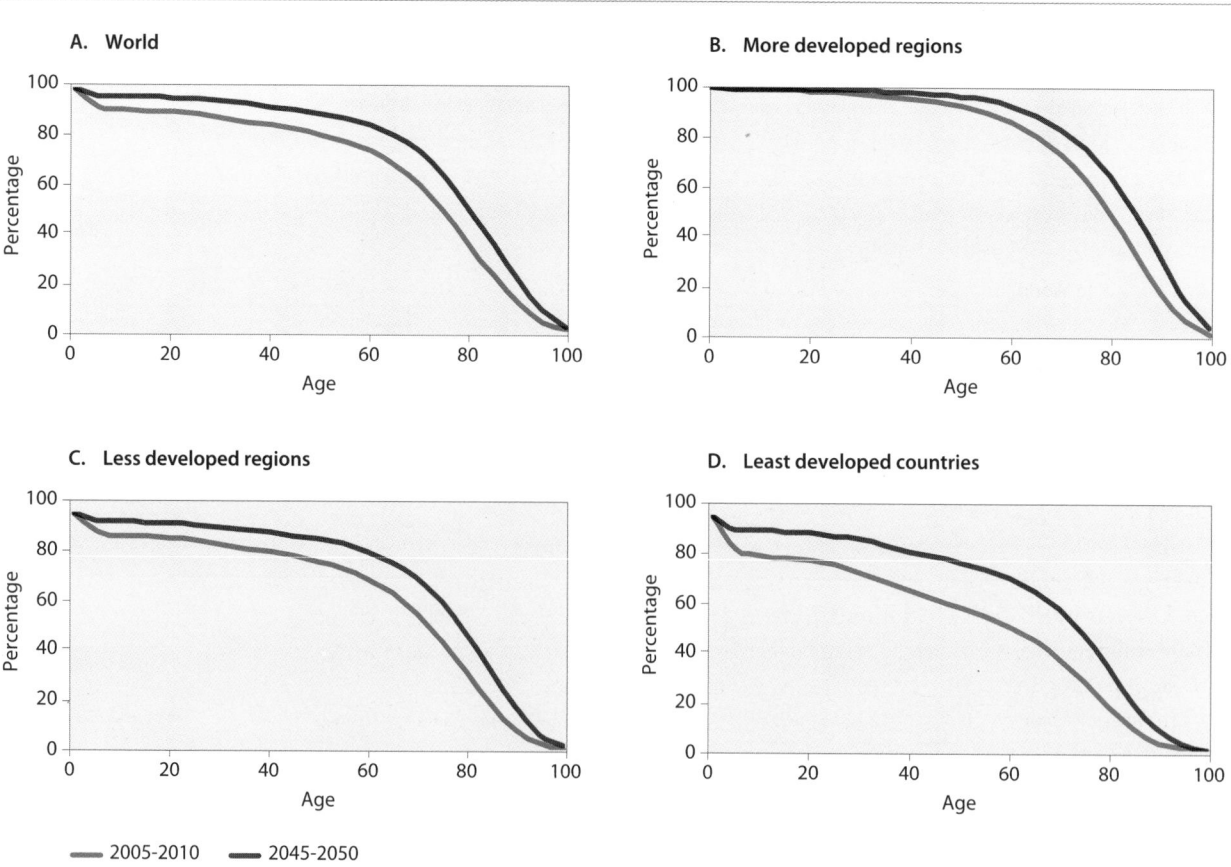

World Population Ageing 2007

Figure 5
Life expectancy at ages 60, 65 and 80: world, 2005-2050

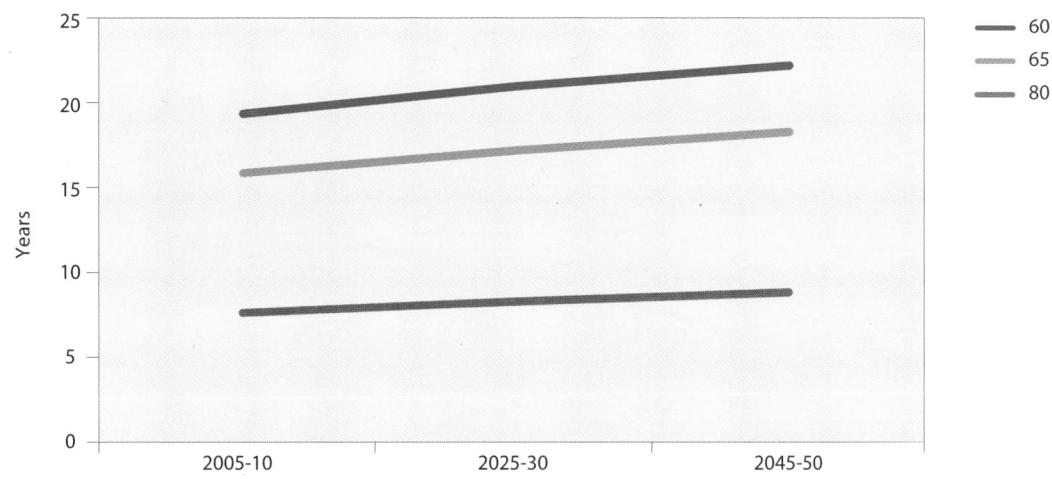

Figure 6
**Percentage increase in life expectancy at birth, at age 60 and at age 80
between 2005 and 2050: world and development regions**

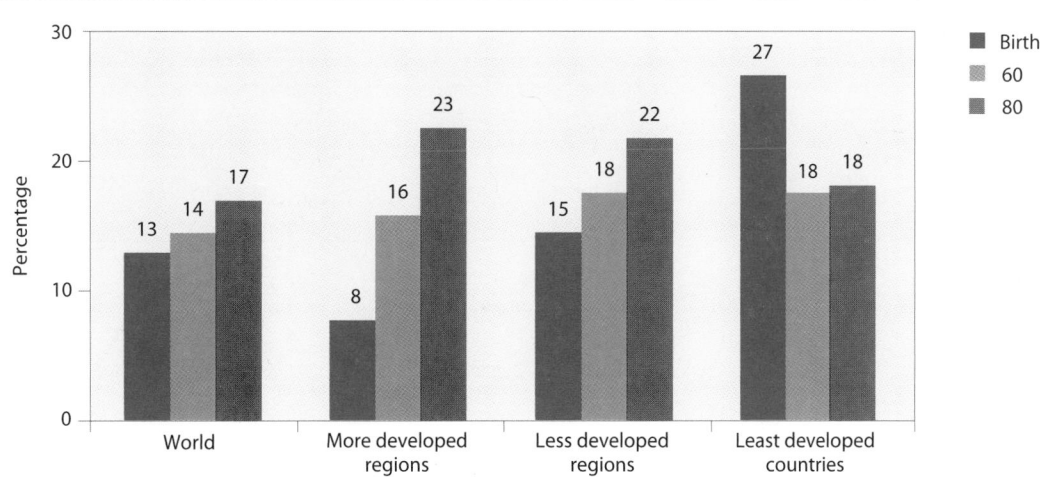

higher among females than males in practically all age groups. As a result, the female advantage in life expectancy at birth increased from 2.8 years in 1950-1955 to 4.4 years in 2005-2010 globally. By 2045-2050, the female to male difference in life expectancy at birth is expected to increase to 4.7 years at the world level (figure 7a).

In the more developed regions, where women currently outlive men by 7.3 years on average, the gender gap in life expectancy at birth is expected to narrow gradually to reach 5.9 years by 2045-2050 (figure 7b). In the less developed regions, where the female to male difference in life expectancy at birth has been stable, it is expected to continue increasing, passing from 3.5 years in 2005-2010 to 4.4 years by 2045-2050 (figure 7c).

In Japan, women have a life expectancy at birth of 86 years, the highest in the world. In 32 other countries, female life expectancy at birth now exceeds 82 years. These countries include the following seven developing countries or areas: Hong Kong SAR China, Israel, Macao SAR China, and the United Arab Emirates in Asia, as well as Guadeloupe, Martinique and the U.S. Virgin Islands in the Caribbean.

The female advantage in life expectancy at birth has widened; future trends are expected to follow different paths

Figure 7
**Male and female life expectancy at birth and gender gap:
world and development regions, 1950-2050**

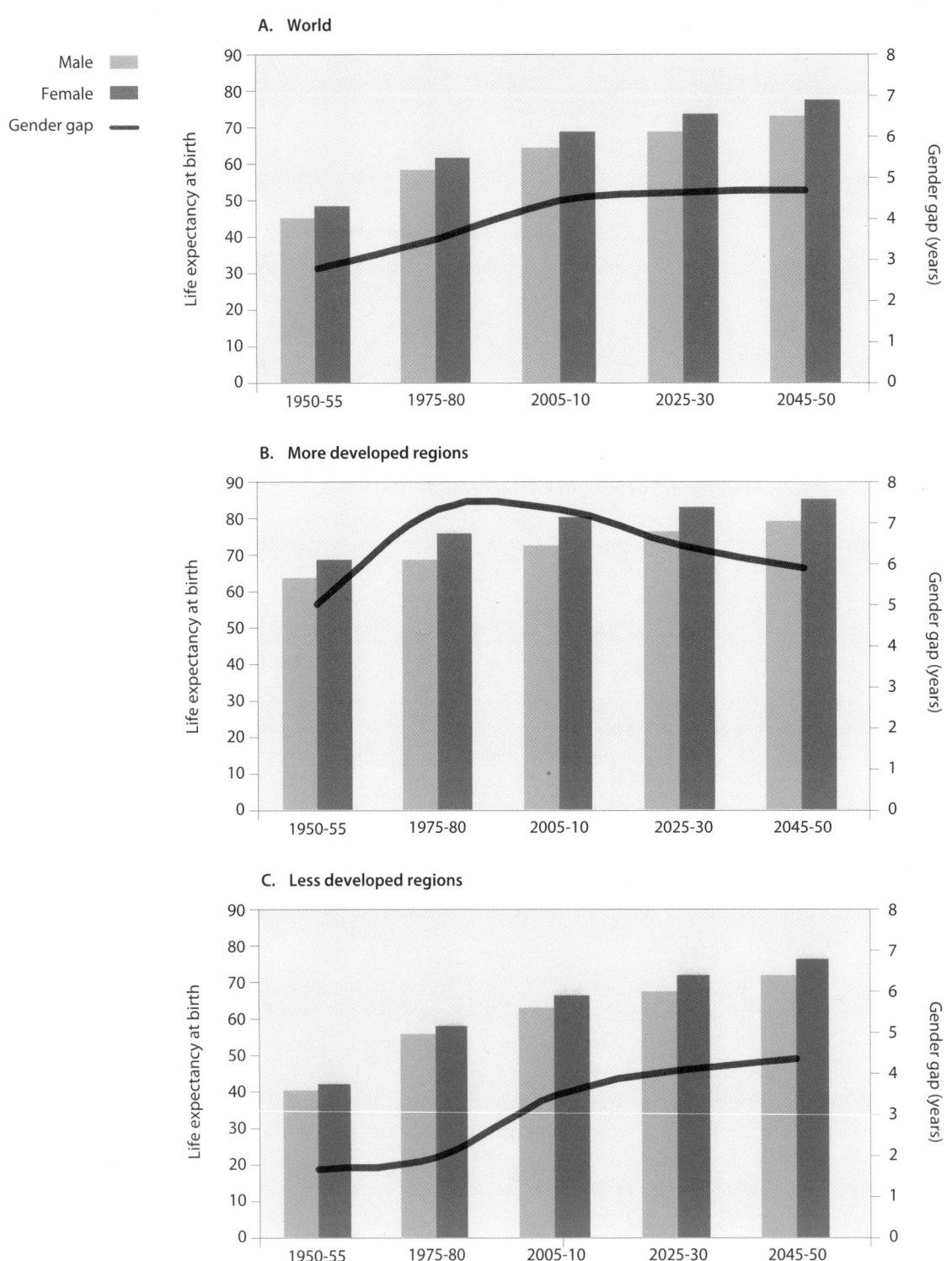

By 2045-2050, female life expectancy at birth is expected to surpass 92 years in Japan and 86 years in 28 other countries. Under the mortality conditions projected for the middle of this century, 59 per cent of the world's female newborns would survive to age 80 if they were subject during all their lives to the mortality projected for 2045-2050, up from 43 per cent under current mortality conditions. In 40 countries, including 16 developing countries, this proportion is projected to exceed 73 per cent. However, in 25 countries, mostly located in Eastern Africa and Western Africa, this proportion is expected to remain below 35 per cent even by 2050.

Chapter II
Magnitude and speed of population ageing

In 1950, there were 205 million persons aged 60 or over throughout the world (figure 8). At that time, only 3 countries had more than 10 million people aged 60 or over: China (42 million), India (20 million), and the United States of America (20 million). By 2007, the number of persons aged 60 or over had increased three and a half times to 705 million and there were 11 countries with more than 10 million people aged 60 or over, including China (152 million), India (92 million), the United States (52 million), Japan (36 million), the Russian Federation (24 million) and Germany (21 million). By 2050, the population aged 60 or over is projected to increase again nearly threefold to reach 2 billion (figure 8).

The number of older persons has more than tripled since 1950; it will almost triple again by 2050

Also by 2050, 32 countries are expected to have more than 10 million people aged 60 or over, including five countries with more than 50 million older people: China (432 million), India (330 million), the United States (104 million), Indonesia (67 million) and Brazil (63 million).

In 1950-1955, the average annual growth rate of the number of persons aged 60 years or over was only slightly higher than the rate of growth for the total population (both were around 1.8 per cent, as is shown in figure 9).

In 2005-2010, the growth rate of the older population at 2.6 per cent annually is more than twice that of the total population (1.1 per cent). Over the mid-term future, the difference between those two growth rates is expected to increase as the baby boom generation reaches age 60 in several parts of the world. By 2025-2030, projections indicate that the population aged 60 or over will be growing 3.7 times more rapidly than the total population (at an annual growth rate of 2.7 per cent compared to 0.7 per cent for the total population, as is shown in figure 9). Although the growth rate of the popu-

The older population is growing faster than the total population in practically all regions of the world and the difference in growth rates is increasing

Figure 8
Population aged 60 or over: world and development regions, 1950-2050

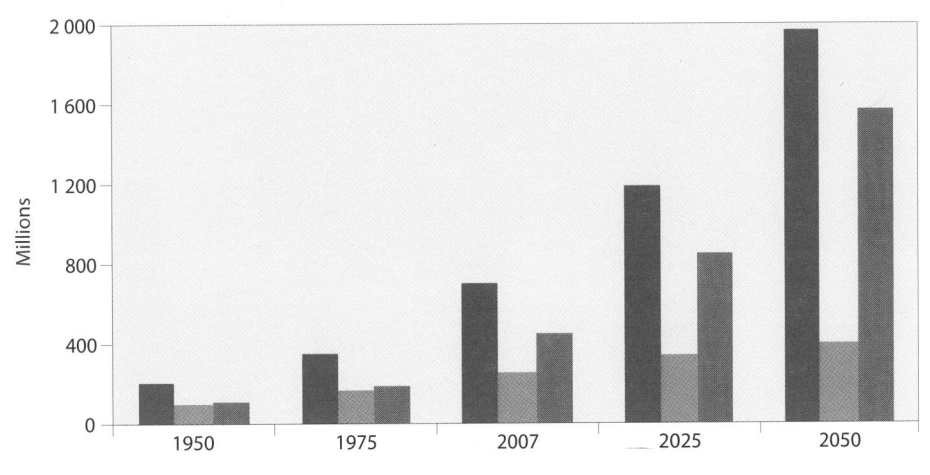

- ■ World
- ▨ More developed regions
- ■ Less developed regions

Figure 9
Average annual growth rate of total population and population aged 60 or over: world, 1950-2050

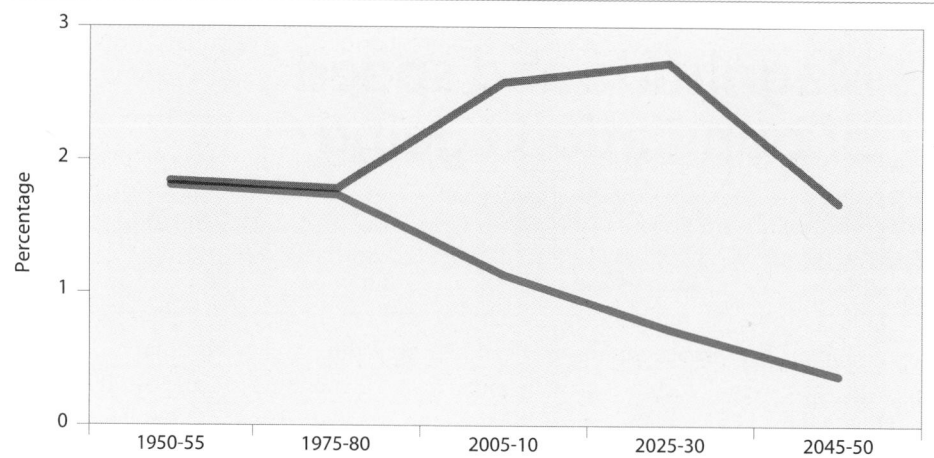

lation aged 60 or over is expected to decline to 1.7 per cent in 2045-2050, it will still be more than 4 times the growth rate of the total population at that time (0.4 per cent).

Since the older population has grown faster than the total population, the proportion of older persons relative to the rest of the population has increased considerably. At the global level, 8 per cent of the population was at least 60 years of age in 1950 (figure 10), and just over 5 per cent was at least 65 years of age. By 2007, those proportions had increased to 11 per cent and just under 8 per cent, respectively. By 2050, 22 per cent of the world population is projected to be 60 years or over, and just under 17 per cent will likely be 65 years or over.

Already by 1950, developed countries as a whole had a higher proportion of their population aged 60 years or over than developing countries (12 per cent vs. 6 per cent). Developed countries continue being at a more advanced stage of the demographic transition and have populations that are already showing strong signs of ageing. Furthermore, their populations are projected to remain considerably older than those of developing countries as a whole. Currently, 21 per cent of the population in the more developed regions is aged 60 years or over, whereas just about 8 per cent of that in the less developed

Figure 10
Proportion of population aged 60 or over: world and development regions, 1950-2050

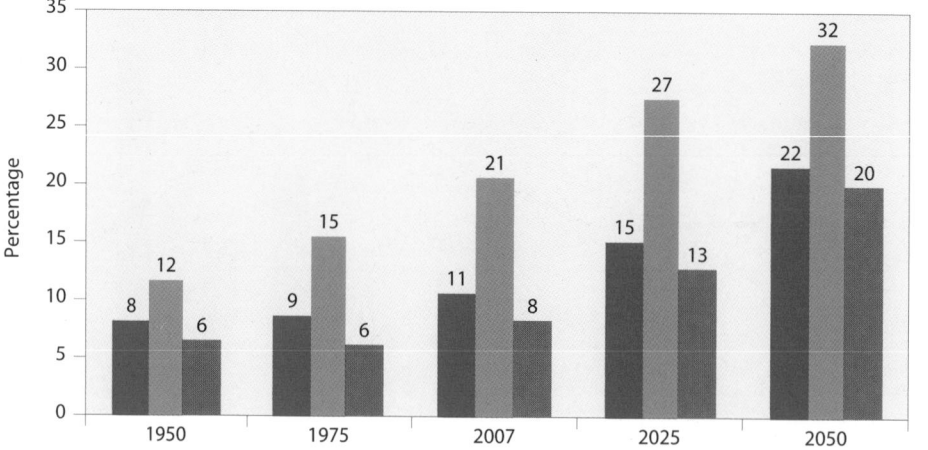

regions is in that age group (figure 10). By 2050, 32 per cent of the population of the more developed regions is projected to be 60 years or over, whereas the equivalent proportion will likely be 20 per cent in the less developed regions (figure 10). A large difference is also evident regarding the proportions aged 65 years or over which are projected to be 25 per cent in the more developed regions and 14 per cent in the less developed regions.

Europe is currently the major area with the highest proportions of older persons and is projected to remain so until 2050. About 35 per cent of the population of Europe is projected to be 60 years or over in 2050, up from 21 per cent in 2007. About 28 per cent is projected to be 65 or over, up from 16 per cent in 2007. In contrast, only 10 per cent of the population of Africa is projected to be 60 or over in 2050, up from 5 per cent in 2007. The proportion aged 65 or over in Africa is projected to rise from 3 per cent in 2007 to 7 per cent in 2050.

People aged 60 years or over currently constitute more than 25 per cent of the population of Germany, Italy and Japan, and there are 24 other countries with proportions of older persons ranging from 20 per cent to 25 per cent. By 2050, more than 40 per cent of the population is expected to be 60 years or older in six countries or areas: Macao SAR China, Italy, Japan, Martinique, the Republic of Korea and Slovenia. In addition to these countries, persons aged 60 or over will constitute more than 33 per cent of the population in another 28 countries, including six developing countries. In Italy, Japan, the Republic of Korea and Spain, 33 per cent of the population will be aged 65 years or over in 2050, and in 38 additional countries, including 11 developing countries, individuals aged 65 years or over will constitute between 25 per cent and 33 per cent of the population.

In contrast with the relatively slow process of population ageing experienced so far by most developed countries, the ageing process in the majority of developing countries is occurring at a faster pace and, therefore, over a shorter period. Furthermore, with the large populations that characterize many developing countries, large numbers of older persons live in those countries even if they constitute still relatively low proportions of the total population.

In 1950-1955, the average annual growth rate of the number of persons aged 60 years or over was practically the same in the more developed regions as in the less developed regions (close to 1.8 per cent, as shown in figure 11).

From that time on, the growth rates of the older population increased in the less developed regions but declined at first in the more developed regions, only to increase

Figure 11
**Average annual growth rate of population 60 or over:
world and development regions, 1950-2050**

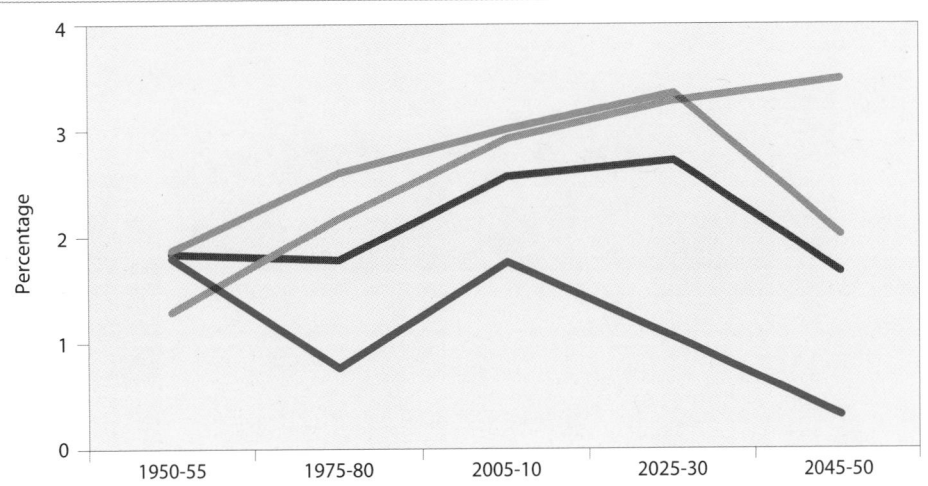

markedly in recent times. Currently, the average annual growth rate of the population aged 60 years or over is 3 per cent in the less developed regions and 1.8 per cent in the more developed regions (figure 11). By 2025-2030, this rate is expected to rise to 3.4 per cent in the less developed regions and to decrease to 1.1 per cent in the more developed regions. After 2030, the growth rate of the population aged 60 years or over is expected to decline in both the more developed regions and the less developed regions. Yet, by 2045-2050, the growth rate of the older population in the less developed regions is projected to be almost seven times as high as that in the more developed regions (2 per cent vs. 0.3 per cent).

In the least developed countries, the growth rate of the older population is projected to continue increasing at least until 2050. By 2045-2050, the population aged 60 years or over in the least developed countries is projected to be growing at a rate of 3.5 per cent per year, more than eleven times that of the more developed regions (0.3 per cent annually).

Although the proportion of older persons is higher in the more developed regions, their number is increasingly larger in the less developed regions. From 1950 to 2007, the number of persons aged 60 years or over increased globally by an average of 9 million persons per year. Sixty-nine per cent of that increase occurred in the less developed regions and 31 per cent in the more developed regions. As a result, the proportion of all persons aged 60 years or over living in the less developed regions rose from 54 per cent in 1950 to 64 per cent in 2007 (figure 12).

Over the next four decades, the concentration of older persons in the less developed regions will intensify. The number of people aged 60 years or over living in the less developed regions is expected to increase more than threefold, passing from 453 million in 2007 to 1.6 billion in 2050. In contrast, the number of older persons in the more developed regions is projected to increase by about 60 per cent, passing from 252 million in 2007 to 400 million in 2050. Consequently, by 2050 nearly 80 per cent of the world's older population is expected to live in developing countries (figure 12).

The older population will increasingly be concentrated in the less developed regions

Figure 12
Distribution of world population aged 60 or over by development regions, 1950-2050

More developed regions ■
Less developed regions ▨

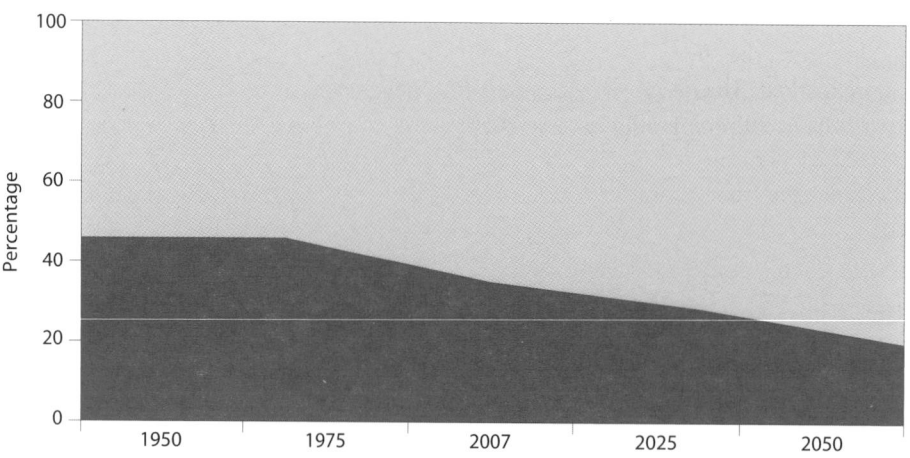

Chapter III

The changing balance among age groups

A. Distribution of the population by broad age groups

In most populations, the increasing proportions of older persons have been accompanied by steady reductions in the proportion of young persons. At the world level, the proportion of children (that is, persons under 15 years of age) dropped from 34 per cent in 1950 to 28 per cent in 2007 (figure 13a). By 2050, the proportion of children is projected to decline by almost one third and the proportion of persons aged 60 years or over (22 per cent) will, for the first time in history, exceed that of children (20 per cent). During 2007-2050, the proportion of persons whose ages range from 15 to 59 will change slightly, passing from 62 per cent in 2007 to 58 per cent in 2050.

> The balance between young and old is shifting in favour of the old throughout the world

In 2007, the proportion of persons aged 60 years or over in the more developed regions (21 per cent) is already higher than the proportion of children (17 per cent), as is shown in figure 13b. By 2050, the proportion of children is projected to decline slightly to 16 per cent, while the proportion of older persons is projected to reach 32 per cent. As the baby boom generations reach old age and there is a declining inflow of young people, the proportion of persons aged 15 to 59 in the more developed regions is also expected to decline substantially over the coming four decades, from 63 per cent in 2007 to 52 per cent in 2050.

> In the more developed regions, the proportion of older persons already exceeds that of children; by 2050 it will be double that of children

From 1950 to 2007, the proportion of people aged 60 years or over in the less developed regions increased only slightly, from 6 per cent to 8 per cent, while the proportion of children (persons under 15 years of age) declined from 38 per cent to 30 per cent (figure 13c).

> Changes in the age distribution of the less developed regions have been slow, but will accelerate over the coming decades

In future, the change in age distribution in the less developed regions is expected to be more marked. The proportion of older persons will increase by a factor of 2.5 to reach 20 per cent in 2050 and the proportion of children will fall by about a third to reach a projected 21 per cent. The share of the population aged 15 to 59 is projected to change slightly, passing from 62 per cent in 2007 to 59 per cent in 2050.

B. Ageing index

The ageing index is the ratio of the population aged 60 years or over to that under age 15. Between 1950 and 2007, the ageing index increased by more than half at the world level, passing from 24 older persons per 100 children to 39 per 100 (figure 14). Over the next four decades, the ageing index is projected almost to triple. By the year 2050, there will be 107 older persons for every 100 children in the world. As observed in the introduction to the present report, this trend may lead to compelling demands for changes in the way a society allocates resources among generations.

> The ageing index will triple by mid-century

In 2007, there are only 28 older persons per 100 children in the less developed regions but over the next decades this ratio is projected to increase markedly, reach-

> The ageing index is significantly higher in the more developed regions but will grow faster in the less developed regions

Figure 13
**Distribution of population by broad age groups:
world and development regions, 1950-2050**

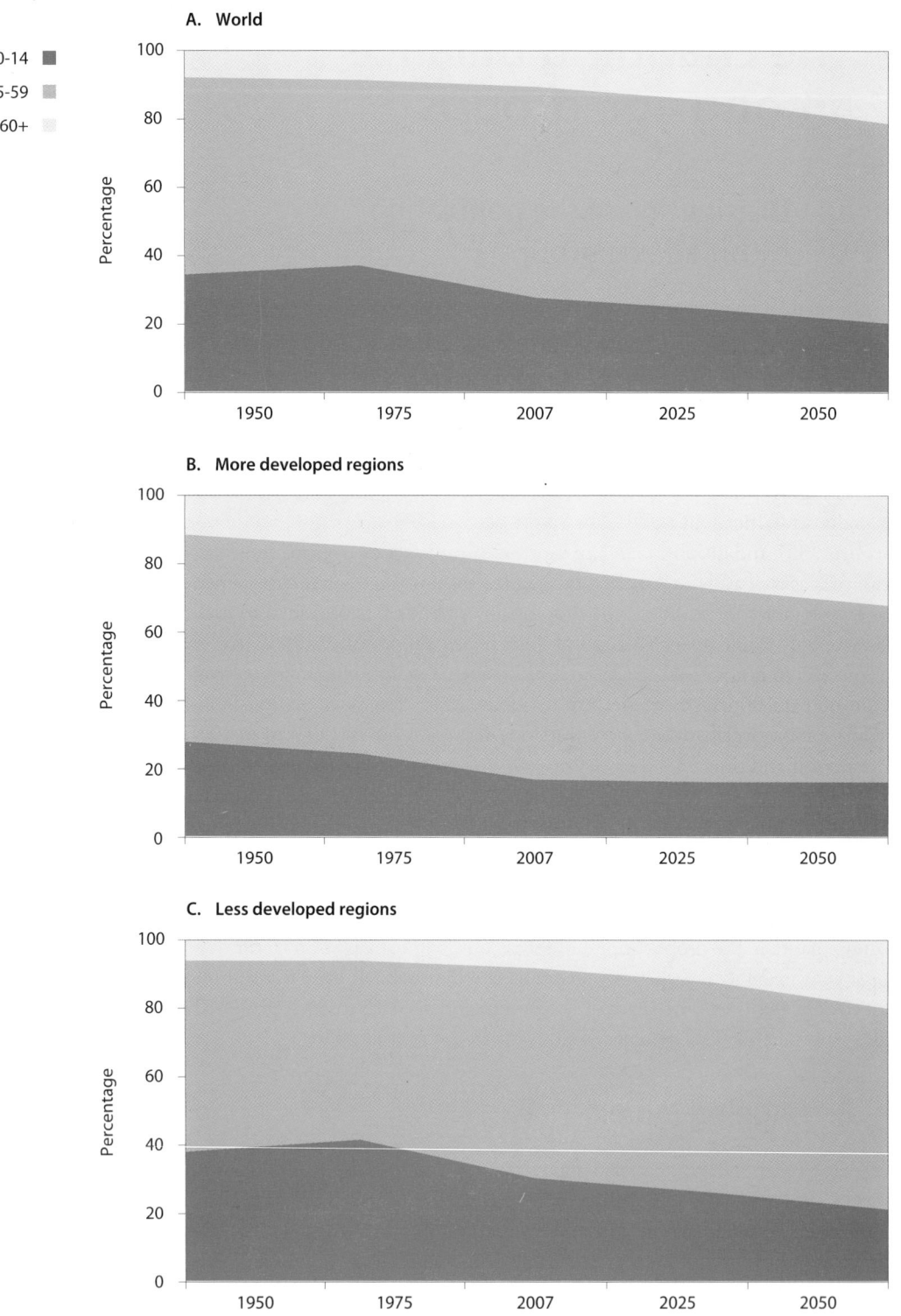

A. World

B. More developed regions

C. Less developed regions

0-14
15-59
60+

ing 96 per 100 in 2050 (figure 14). During 2007-2050 the ageing index in the more developed regions is projected to rise from 124 older persons per 100 children to 207 per 100.

Figure 14
Number of persons 60 or over per hundred children under 15: world and development regions, 1950-2050

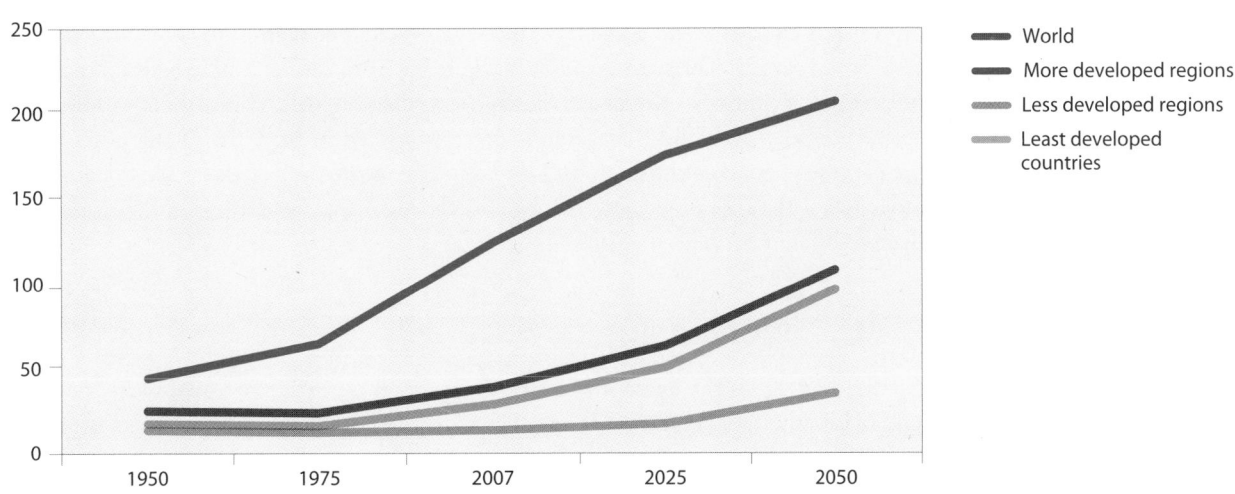

Currently, the ageing index in Europe, at 136 older persons per 100 children, is ten times that of Africa, which is still a low 13 older persons per 100 children (figure 15). Between 2007 and 2050, the ageing index is expected to rise significantly in all six major areas. Asia as well as Latin America and the Caribbean are expected to experience remarkable increases in their respective ageing indices, which are projected nearly to quadruple. However, the ageing index for Europe will remain the highest. By 2050, the ageing index is projected to range from a high of 230 older persons per 100 children in Europe to a low of 35 per 100 in Africa. That is, by mid-century, Europe will have almost two older persons for every child while Africa is likely to have still almost three children for every older person and thus remain the region with the youngest population.

In 2007, there are already 26 countries with an ageing index higher than 120 older persons per 100 children. With the exception of Japan, all of them are located in Europe. In six countries—Bulgaria, Germany, Greece, Italy, Japan and Latvia—the ageing index

Regional differentials in ageing indices are substantial

Disparities in the ageing index are even more marked at the country level

Figure 15
Number of persons 60 or over per hundred children under 15: major areas, 2007 and 2050

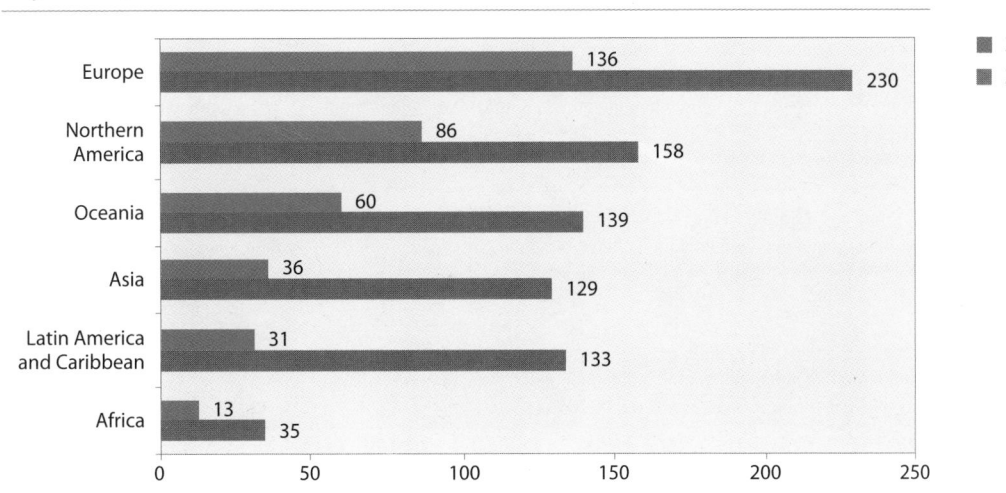

is higher than 160 older persons per 100 children. At the other end of the distribution, there are 20 countries, most located in Africa, with an ageing index lower than 10 older persons per 100 children.

By 2050, ten countries or areas are expected to have more than 3 persons aged 60 or over per child (i.e., their ageing indices will be higher than 300). These include five developing countries or areas, namely, Hong Kong SAR China, Macao SAR China, Martinique, the Republic of Korea and Singapore. In Macao SAR China, there will be nearly 4 older persons per child (its ageing index is projected to be 375). At the other end of the distribution, 18 countries, most located in Africa, are projected to have still an ageing index lower than 25 older persons per 100 children, that is, they will likely have more than 4 children per older person.

C. Median age

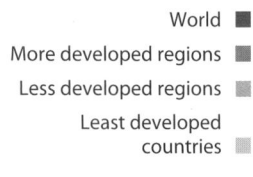

During 2007-2050, the median age of the world population is projected to increase by about 10 years

The median age in the more developed regions is 13 years higher than in the less developed regions and 20 years higher than in the least developed countries

The median age is the age that divides the population into two equal parts, one with ages below the median age and the other with ages above the median age. From 1950 to 2005, the median age of the world population increased only by 4 years, from nearly 24 years to nearly 28 years (figure 16). From 2005 to 2050, it is expected to increase by nearly 10 years. That is, in 2050, half of the world population is projected to be older than 38 years.

The median age of the population in the more developed regions was about 39 years in 2005, up from 29 years in 1950. In the less developed regions, the median age was 26 years in 2005, just 5 years higher than in 1950 when it was 21 years. In the least developed countries, the median age decreased from 1950 to 2005, from 20 years to 19 years, as a result of their continued high fertility (figure 16).

From 2005 to 2050, the median age of the population of the more developed regions is projected to reach an unprecedented level of 45 years. In the less developed regions, the median age will increase by more than 10 years to reach 37 years in 2050, a level approaching that currently observed in the more developed regions. During 2005-2050, the median age is also projected to increase significantly in the least developed countries, although its level in 2050 (27 years) will still be 10 years lower than that for the less developed regions as a whole.

Figure 16
Median age of the population: world and development regions, 1950-2050 (*years*)

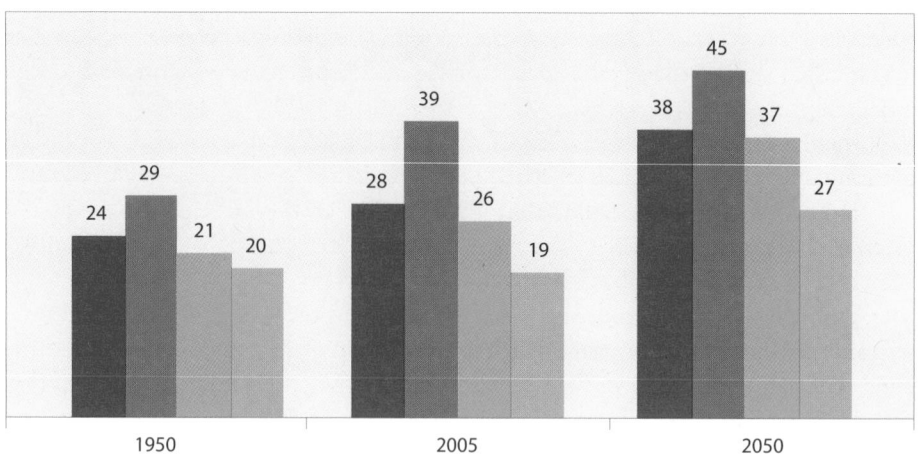

In 2005, the median age of Europe was 39 years, more than twice as high as the median age of 19 years in Africa. By 2050, the median age in Europe is projected to rise to 47, a level 20 years higher than that projected for Africa. At the country level, the median age in 2005 ranged from 15 years in Niger and Uganda to 43 years in Japan. Italy and Germany, with median ages of 42 years, follow and are in turn followed by eight European countries with median ages above 40.

The median age of Europe is double that of Africa

By 2050, the oldest populations are expected to be those of Macao SAR China and the Republic of Korea, where half the population is projected to be at least 54 years old. Martinique and Italy will come next, with median ages around 53 years. Thirteen other countries or areas, including six located in Eastern Europe, will also have populations where persons over 50 years of age will predominate. At the opposite extreme, in 17 countries, most located in Africa, persons under 25 years of age are expected to be the majority of the population.

D. Dependency ratio

The total dependency ratio is a commonly used measure of potential social support needs. It is calculated as the ratio of the number of children (persons under age 15) and older persons (persons aged 65 years or over) to the number of persons in the working ages (that is, those aged 15 to 64) expressed per 100 population. The interpretation of the ratio is based on the notion that all persons under 15 and those aged 65 or over are likely to be in some sense dependent on the population in the working ages. Those in the working ages are assumed to provide direct or indirect support to those in the dependent ages (Kinsella and Gist, 1995). Such support may be provided within the family, through religious or communal institutions, or through the State.

It must be recognized, however, that the dependency ratio provides at best only a rough approximation of the actual dependency burden in a society. Not all children and older persons require support, nor do all persons of working age provide direct or indirect support to children and older persons (Taeuber, 1992). In fact, evidence indicates that older persons in many societies are often providers of support to their adult children (Morgan, Schuster and Butler, 1991; Saad, 2001). Thus, although it is a useful indicator of trends in potential support needs, the dependency ratio and, more specifically, the old-age dependency ratio, should be interpreted with caution.

At the world level, the total dependency ratio increased from 65 in 1950 to 74 in 1975 (figure 17). This change was mainly due to the substantial increases in the proportion of children observed in most developing countries, which in turn resulted from declining infant and child mortality and continued high fertility. Then, as fertility dropped, the total dependency ratio also declined, to reach 54 in 2007. This decline in the total dependency ratio occurred despite the increasing proportion of older persons over the period. The tendency for the total dependency ratio to decrease is projected to continue at least until 2025. By that time, the total dependency ratio is projected to reach 53, but it will start increasing soon after to reach 58 in 2050, a level similar to that observed in 2000.

At the global level, the ratio between the "dependent" and the working age populations has decreased since 1950 but is expected to increase in the future

In the more developed regions, the increase in the total dependency ratio is expected to start earlier, so that it will likely rise from 47 in 2007 to 58 in 2025 and keep on rising to reach 71 in 2050.

Although the world's total dependency ratio is projected to change little between 2007 and 2050, the composition of the ratio will undergo important changes over the period. Currently, the child population accounts for the large majority of the world's dependent population. In the future, the contribution of the child component of the dependency ratio will become similar to that of the old-age component. This shift will

A profound shift is expected in the composition of the total dependency ratio

Figure 17

Total dependency ratio: world and development regions, 1950-2050

World

More developed regions

Less developed regions

Least developed
countries

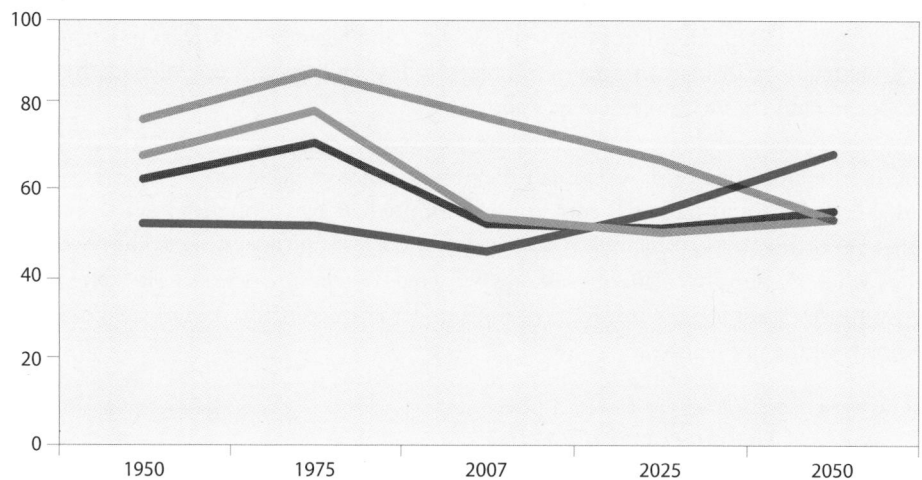

be the result of the combined effects of fertility reduction and increasing longevity. Currently, the old-age component contributes about 21 per cent of the world's total dependency ratio. By 2050, its share will more than double to reach 44 per cent (figure 18a).

In the more developed regions, where the share of older persons in the numerator of the dependency ratio is already large (48 per cent in 2007), the old-age component is projected to rise to 62 per cent by 2050 (figure 18b). In the less developed regions, the old-age component will still account for less than half (41 per cent) of the total dependency ratio by 2050 (figure 18c).

The old-age dependency ratio is the ratio of the population aged 65 or over to the population aged 15 to 64 expressed per 100 population. Although the current differences among major areas in the old-age dependency ratio are expected to persist until 2050, all major areas will experience remarkable increases in that ratio. From 2007 to 2050, the ratio of persons aged 65 or over to those of working age is projected to grow from 6 per 100 to 10 per 100 in Africa, from 10 to 27 in Asia, from 10 to 29 in Latin America and the Caribbean, from 16 to 31 in Oceania, from 19 to 34 in Northern America and from 23 to 48 in Europe (figure 19).

Currently, Japan has the world's highest old-age dependency ratio of 32 older persons per 100 persons of working age. It is followed closely by Italy and Germany, where the old-age dependency ratios are 31 and 29 respectively. Over the next four decades, the old-age dependency ratio is projected to increase substantially in most countries of the world. By 2050, Japan, with an old-age dependency ratio of 71, will still have the world's highest level of old-age dependency, followed by Italy (69) and Spain (66). In another 20 countries, most located in Europe, the old-age dependency ratio is projected to be higher than 50 older persons per 100 persons of working age. At the same time, in 36 countries or areas, most located in Africa, the population aged 65 years or over is expected to be less than one tenth the size of the working-age population.

The old-age dependency ratio will almost double in Africa, Northern America and Oceania; it will more than double in Europe, and almost triple in Asia as well as in Latin America and the Caribbean

The world's highest old-age dependency ratio will more than double in the next four decades

E. Potential support ratio

The potential support ratio is an alternative way of expressing the numerical relationship between those more likely to be economically productive and those more likely to be dependants. It is the inverse of the old-age dependency ratio, that is, the number of persons of working age (i.e., aged 15 to 64) per person aged 65 or over.

Figure 18
Composition of the total dependency ratio: world and development regions, 1950-2050

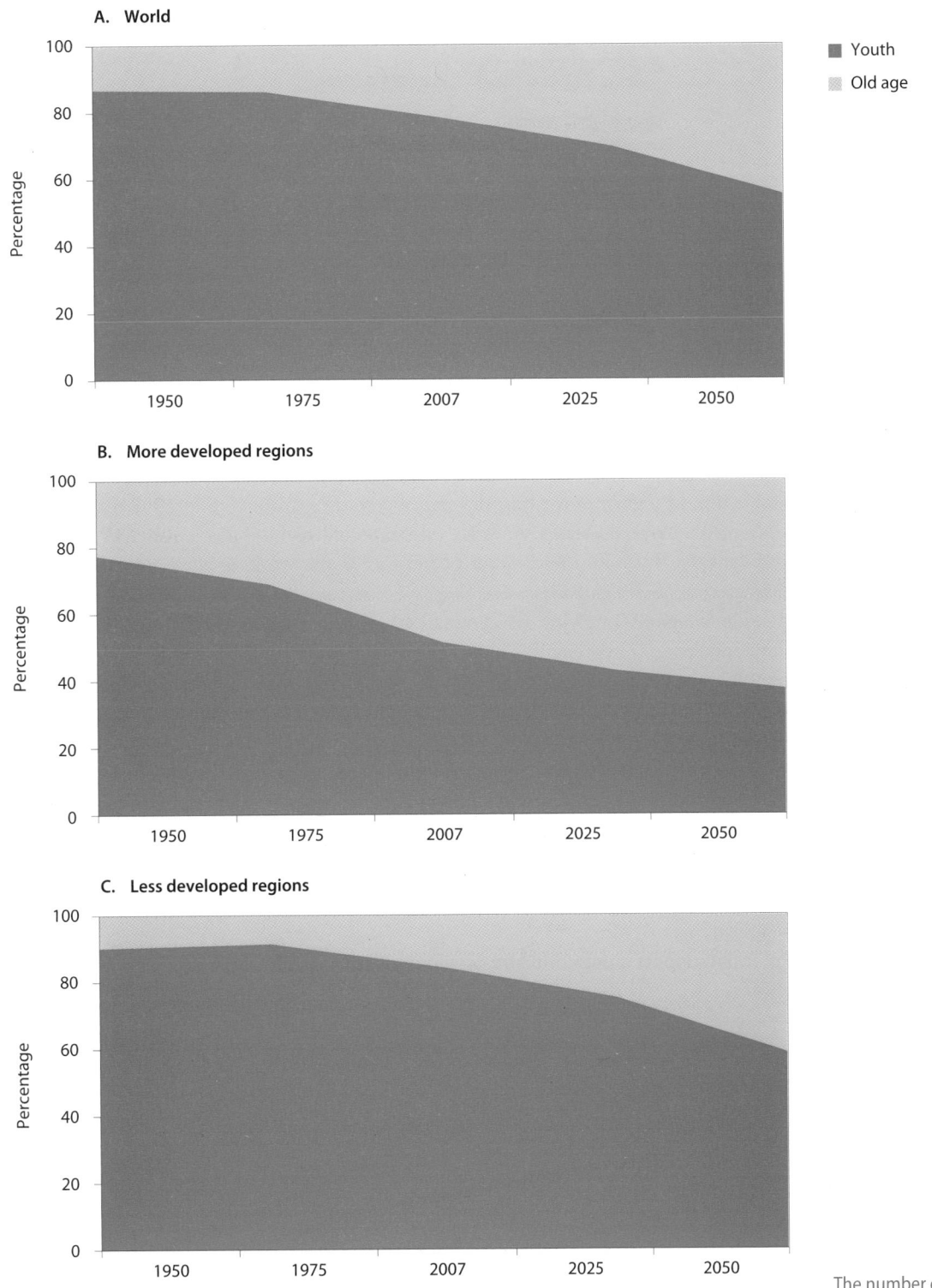

A. World

B. More developed regions

C. Less developed regions

Youth
Old age

Between 1950 and 2007, the ratio of people aged 15-64 to persons 65 or older decreased globally by 25 per cent, from 11.6 to 8.7. The decrease was particularly important in the more developed regions, where the ratio dropped by almost half, from 8.2

The number of working-age people per older person is expected to drop globally by more than 50 per cent over the next four decades

Figure 19

Old-age dependency ratio: major areas, 2007 and 2050

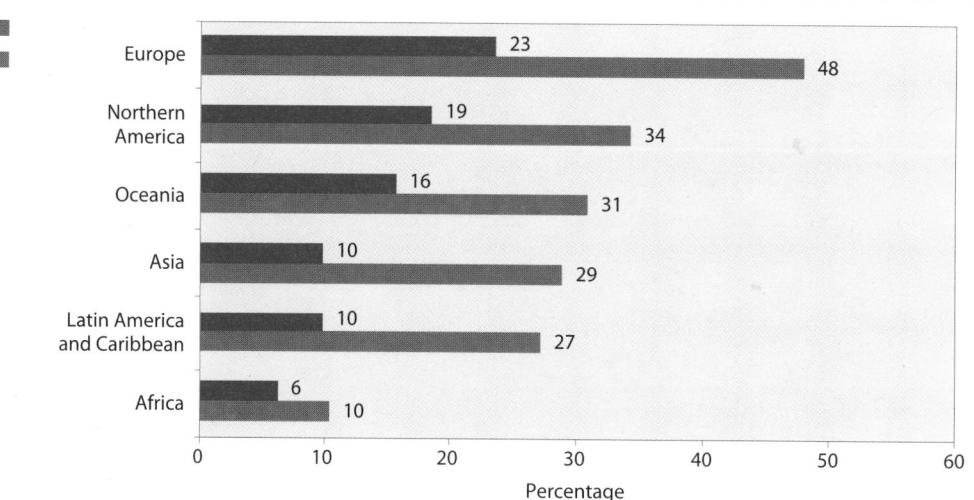

in 1950 to 4.4 in 2007. During this same period, the potential support ratio decreased by under 25 per cent in the less developed regions (from 14.9 in 1950 to 11.3 in 2007) and increased slightly in the least developed countries (from 16.8 in 1950 to 17 in 2007) (figure 20). Large decreases, however, are expected to take place over the first half of this century. By 2050, the number of persons in the working ages per older person is projected to be 3.9 globally, a decrease of 55 per cent relative to 2007; 2.3 in the more developed regions, implying a decrease of 49 per cent relative to 2007, and 4.4 in the less developed regions, representing a decrease of 61 per cent with respect to the level reached in 2007. The decline will be smallest in the least developed countries as a whole, amounting to 42 per cent and leading to a support ratio of 9.8 persons of working age per older person in 2050.

In Europe, there are 4.3 persons aged 15-64 per person aged 65 or over in 2007, the lowest potential support ratio among the major areas. Relatively low potential support ratios also characterize Northern America (5.4) and Oceania (6.4). In Asia, Latin America and the Caribbean, and Africa the potential support ratios are higher, at 10.1, 10.2 and 16.2, respectively (figure 21).

Currently, there are little more than 4 persons of working age per older person in Europe and by 2050 their number will have decreased to little more than 2

Figure 20
Potential support ratio: world and developing regions, 1950-2050

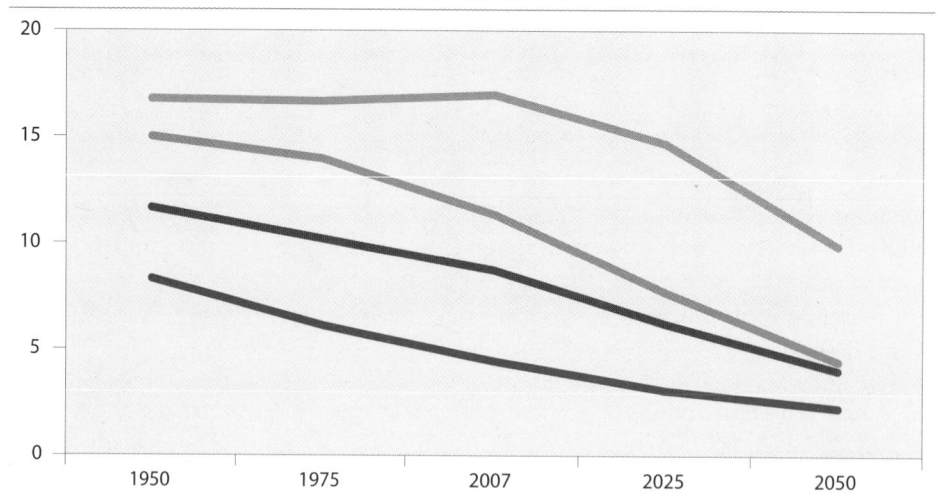

Figure 21
**Number of persons 15-64 per persons 65 or over: major areas,
2007 and 2050**

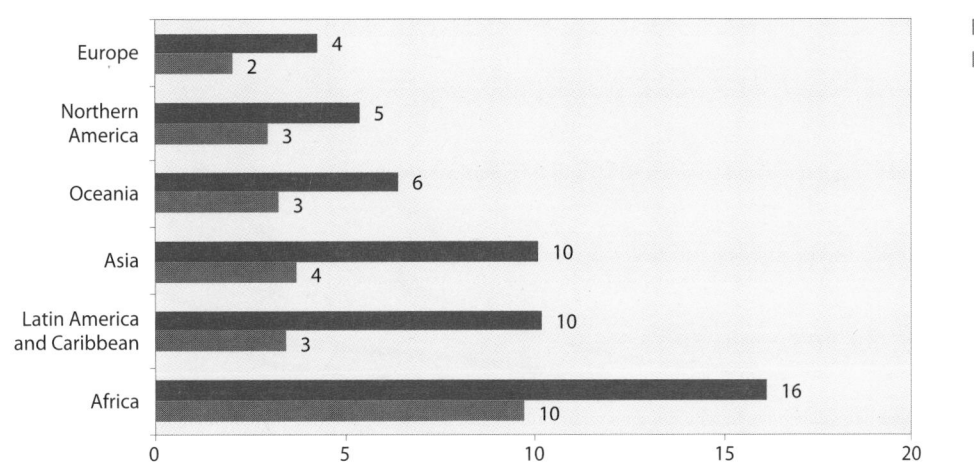

Over the next four decades, the potential support ratio is projected to drop substantially in all major areas, particularly in Asia and Latin America and the Caribbean. By 2050, that ratio is projected to drop to about 2 in Europe, to under 3 in Northern America, and to under 4 in each, Asia, Latin America and the Caribbean, and Oceania. In Africa, there will still be almost 10 persons of working age for every person aged 65 or over by 2050.

In 2007, the potential support ratio is under 5 in 31 European countries as well as in Georgia, Japan and Uruguay. In three of those countries, namely, Germany, Italy and Japan, the potential support ratio is under 3.5. At the same time, the potential support ratio is above 20 in 16 countries, most of which are located in Eastern Africa and Western Asia.

Important variations in the potential support ratio will remain at the country level

By 2050, the potential support ratio is projected to be below 3.5 in 82 countries and to remain above 20 in only two, Liberia and Swaziland. In 23 countries, including 7 developing countries, the potential support ratio is expected to decline to under 2 persons of working age for every older person. In Italy and Japan, the potential support ratio is expected to drop below 1.5. At the other extreme of the distribution, 22 countries are expected still to have potential support ratios above 12 by 2050.

F. Parent support ratio

The parent support ratio is the number of persons aged 85 years or over divided by the number aged 50 to 64 and expressed per 100 persons. This measure has been commonly used to assess the demands on families to provide support for their oldest members. It relates those aged 85 or over to their presumed offspring, who were born when the older persons were in their twenties and thirties. However, because the persons included in the numerator are not necessarily related by kinship ties to those in the denominator, the parent support ratio is only a rough indicator of changes expected in the family support system available for the very old (Kinsella and Taeuber, 1993).

Because people are living longer and thus are more likely to experience multiple chronic diseases, an increasing number of adults are expected to face the need to care for very old and sometimes frail relatives. An indicator of this trend is found in the parent support ratio. At the global level, there were fewer than 2 persons aged 85 or over per 100 persons aged 50-64 in 1950. By 2007, that ratio had more than doubled to reach 4.5 per 100, and by 2050 it is projected almost to triple (figure 22).

An increasing number of persons in their fifties and sixties will have surviving parents or other very old relatives

Figure 22
Parent support ratio: world and development regions, 1950-2050

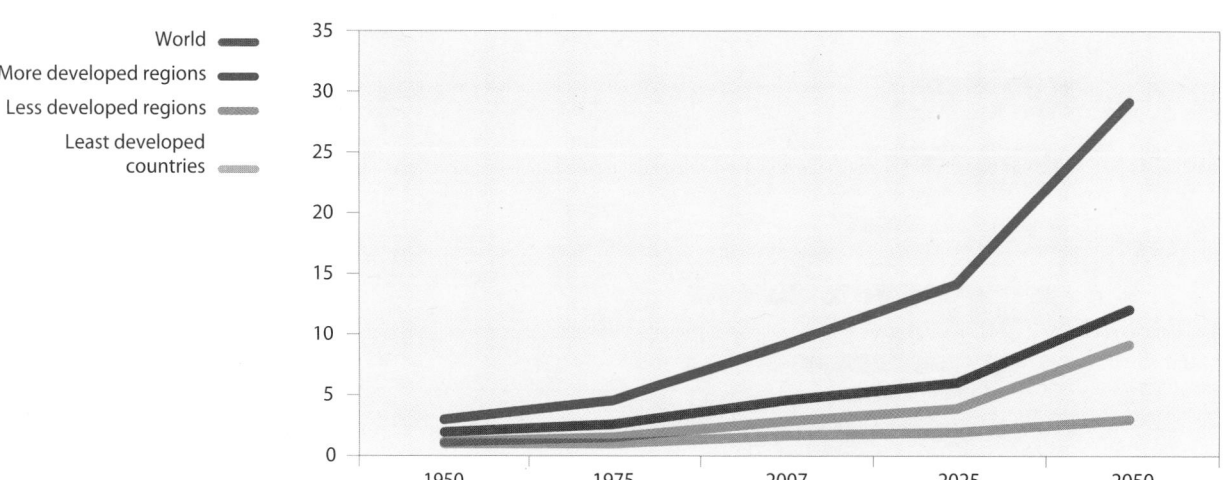

Remarkably high levels of the parent support ratio are projected in the more developed regions, particularly in Japan

In 2050, the parent support ratio in the more developed regions is projected to reach 29, up from 9 in 2007 (figure 22). With a parent support ratio of 13, Sweden currently has the world's highest such ratio in the world. By 2050, Japan is projected to have the world's highest parent support ratio, at 58 persons aged 85 or over per hundred persons aged 50-64. Also in 2050, the parent support ratio is expected to surpass 30 in another 18 countries or areas, most located in Europe.

The parent support ratio is projected to remain significantly lower in developing countries. In the less developed regions as a whole, it is projected to rise from 3 in 2007 to 9 in 2050. Thus, by 2050, there will still be more than 10 people aged 50-64 for every person aged 85 or over in the less developed regions as compared to fewer than 4 in the more developed regions.

Chapter IV
Demographic profile of the older population

A. Age composition

A notable aspect of the global ageing process is the progressive demographic ageing of the older population itself. In most countries, regardless of their geographic location or developmental stage, the population aged 80 or over is growing faster than any younger segment of the older population.

At the world level, the average annual growth rate of the number of persons aged 80 or over, 3.9 per cent per year, is currently 50 per cent higher than the growth rate of the population aged 60 or over, which averages 2.6 per cent per year (figure 23). Although the growth rates of both age groups are expected to decline over the next four decades, by 2045-2050 the growth rate of the population aged 80 or over, at 3.0 per cent per year, will still be almost double that of the population aged 60 or over, which is expected to be 1.7 per cent per year.

In 1950, 1 in 15 persons aged 60 or over was aged 80 or over but by 2007, that ratio had increased to 1 in 8, and by 2050 it is expected to increase further to reach nearly 1 in 5 (figure 24). The most remarkable increase is expected to occur in Japan where, in 2050, more than 1 in every 3 persons aged 60 or over will be at least 80 years old.

Persons aged 80 or over constitute today less than 2 per cent of the population but their share is projected to reach 4.3 per cent in 2050. Currently, the population aged 80 or over accounts for more than 5 per cent of the population in four countries: France, Italy, Japan and Sweden.

> Older populations are themselves ageing

> The number of persons aged 80 or over is increasing substantially

Figure 23
Average annual population growth rate at ages 60 or over, 65 or over and 80 or over: world, 1950-2050

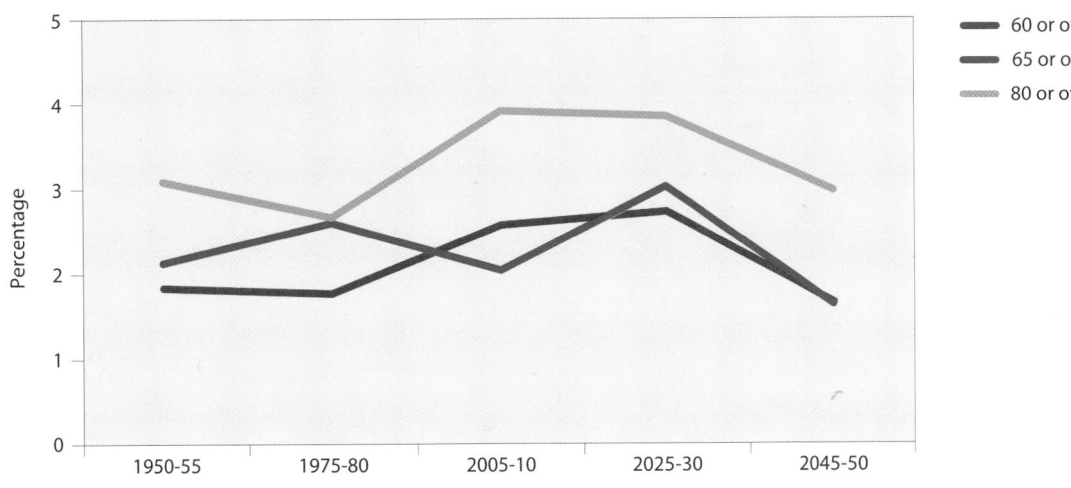

Legend:
— 60 or over
— 65 or over
— 80 or over

Figure 24
**Distribution of population aged 60 or over by age groups:
world, 1950-2050**

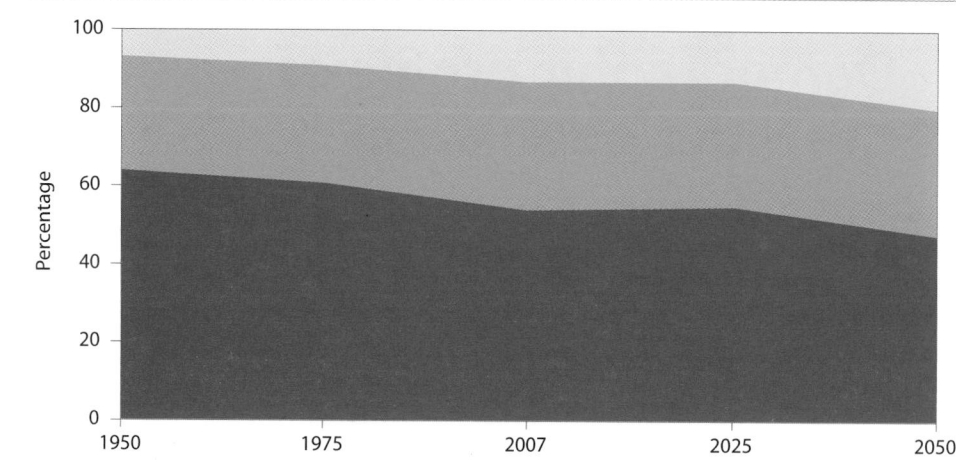

60-69
70-79
80+

In 1950, persons aged 80 or over numbered less than 14 million. By 2007 their number had risen to 94 million persons and it is expected nearly to quadruple by 2050, to reach 394 million (figure 25).

Currently, five countries account for 50 per cent of the population aged 80 or over. They are: China with 16 million, the United States with 11 million, India with 9 million, Japan with 7 million, and Germany with 4 million. In 2050, five countries will have more than 10 million people aged 80 or over: China with 101 million, India with 53 million, the United States with 29 million, Japan with 17 million and Brazil with 14 million. Together they will account for 54 per cent of the population aged 80 or over.

People aged 80 or over currently constitute almost 4 per cent of the population of Europe and more than 3 per cent of the population of Northern America. The proportion of persons aged 80 or over is considerably lower in the major areas of the developing world. Thus, they constitute 1.3 per cent of the population of Latin America and the Caribbean, 1 per cent of that of Asia and 0.4 per cent of that of Africa. Such regional differences are projected to persist until 2050.

Five countries are the home of half of the world's population aged 80 or over

The proportion of persons aged 80 or over is significantly higher in the more developed regions than in the less developed regions

Figure 25
Population aged 80 or over: world, 1950-2050

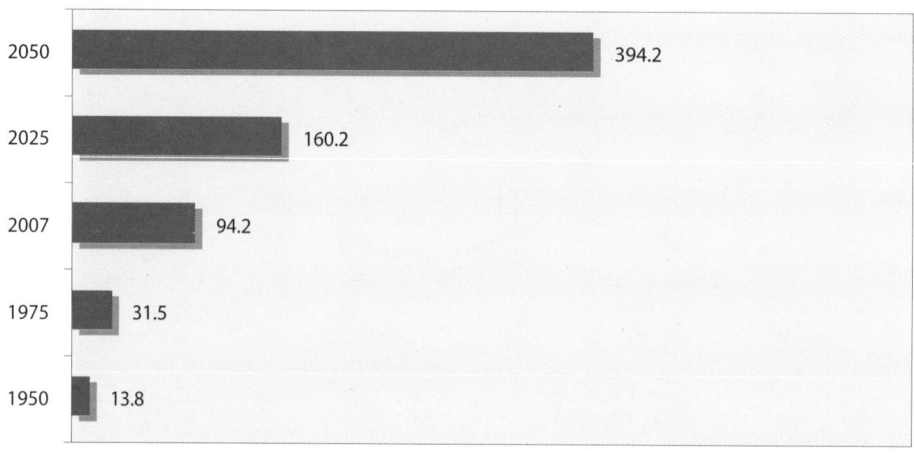

Millions

By mid-century, about 1 in every 10 individuals will be aged 80 years or over in the more developed regions, compared with about 1 in 30 in the less developed regions. In the least developed countries as a whole, only about 1 in every 100 persons is projected to be aged 80 or over in 2050. By then, 20 countries, most located in Europe, are projected to have at least 10 per cent of their population aged 80 years or over.

Currently, slightly more than half of all persons aged 80 years or over (51 per cent) live in the more developed regions (figure 26). In the course of the next four decades, however, the population aged 80 years or over is expected to grow significantly faster in the less developed regions. As a consequence, by 2025, 58 per cent of the population aged 80 or over will live in the less developed regions and by 2050 that proportion will rise to 71 per cent (figure 26).

Although the proportion of people who live to be a hundred is still very small, their number is growing rapidly. There are currently an estimated 310,000 centenarians in the world. By 2050 their number is projected to rise to 3.7 million, a twelvefold increase (figure 27). Currently, the great majority of centenarians (71 per cent) live in the more developed regions and, although that proportion is projected to decrease

Most people aged 80 years or over now live in the more developed regions but soon the majority will live in the less developed regions

By 2050, the number of centenarians is expected to increase twelve times

Figure 26
Distribution of world population aged 80 or over by development regions, 1950-2050

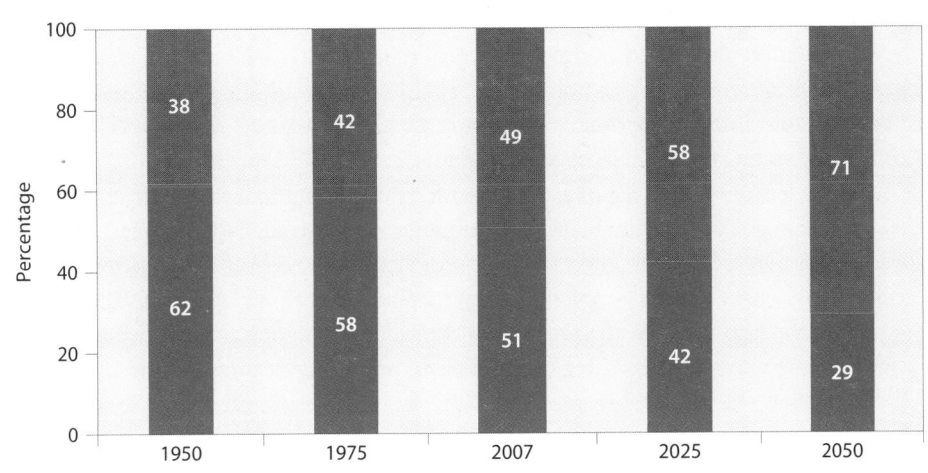

Figure 27
Distribution of world centenarians by development regions, 2007-2050

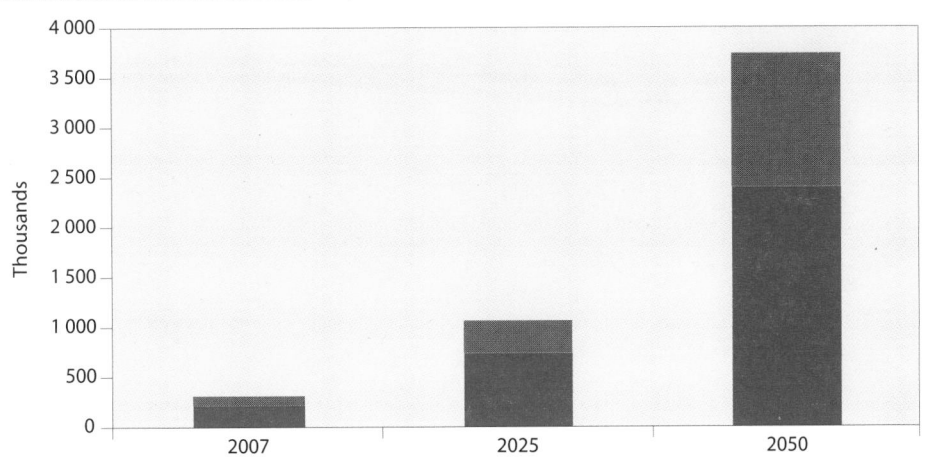

to 64 per cent by 2050, still by that time developed countries will be the home of the majority of centenarians on earth.

In the less developed regions, a significant increase in the number of centenarians is projected to occur during 2007-2050, when their numbers will rise from 91,000 to 1.3 million. Nevertheless, developing countries will continue having a smaller proportion of all centenarians than developed countries.

Within the more developed regions, Japan will experience a remarkable increase in the number of centenarians, which are projected to pass from less than 37,000 in 2007 to almost a million in 2050. Consequently, by mid-century Japan is expected to have the world's largest number and proportion of centenarians, since nearly 1 per cent of Japan's population will be aged 100 years or over.

B. Sex ratio of the older population

Women constitute a majority of the older population and their share of the older population increases with age

Because women's life expectancy is greater than that of men, they constitute a majority of the older population. At the global level, the sex ratio of the population aged 60 or over is 82 males per 100 females (figure 28). Thus, women aged 60 or over outnumber men of the same age by approximately 70 million. Assuming that past mortality trends will continue, by 2050 it is expected that there will be 85 men per 100 women aged 60 or over and 80 men per 100 women aged 65 or over. Among the population aged 80 or over, the sex ratio is projected to be 61 men per 100 women.

Sex ratios at older ages are significantly lower in the more developed regions than in the less developed regions

In the more developed regions, large gender differences in longevity translate into low sex ratios among the older population. In 2007, there are 73 men per 100 women among persons aged 60 or over in the more developed regions and just 47 men per 100 women among those aged 80 or over (figure 29).

In the less developed regions, older women outnumber older men by smaller margins because the sex differentials in life expectancy are generally smaller. Thus, there are currently 88 men per 100 women among persons aged 60 or over in the less developed regions and 66 men per 100 women among those aged 80 or over (figure 29).

Trends in sex ratios at older ages are expected to differ between the more developed and the less developed regions

Over the next decades, the sex ratio of the older population is projected to increase in most of the more developed regions as a result of a faster decline in mortality among older men than among older women. By 2050, the average sex ratio in the more devel-

Figure 28
Number of men per hundred women at ages 60 or over, 65 or over and 80 or over: world, 1950-2050

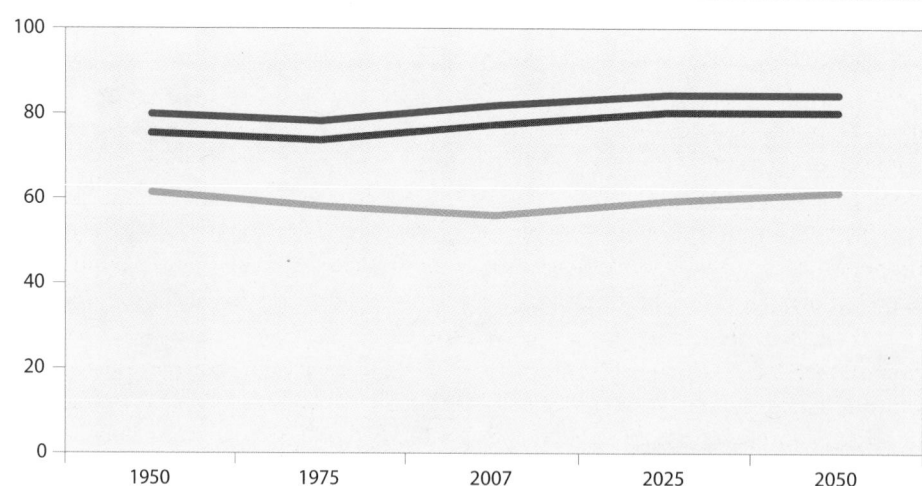

60 or over
65 or over
80 or over

Figure 29
**Number of men per hundred women at ages 60 or over and
80 or over: development regions, 1950-2050**

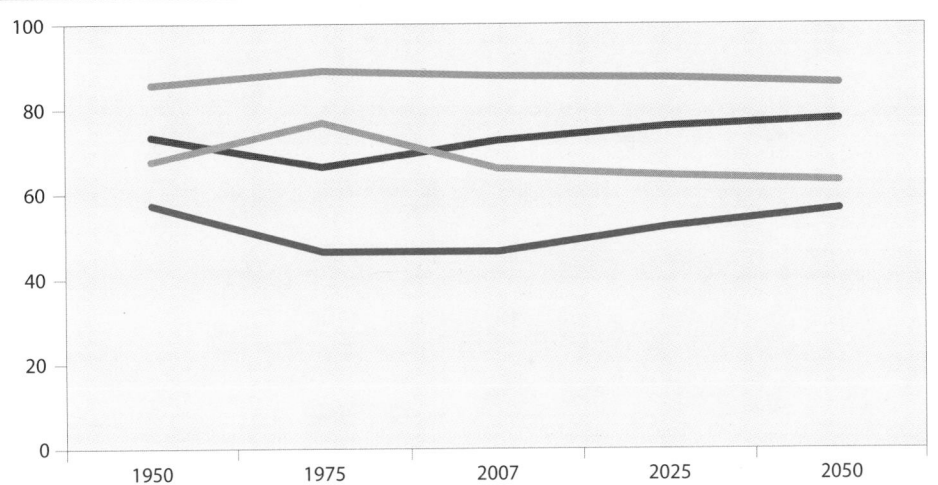

Legend:
- More developed regions (60 or over)
- More developed regions (80 or over)
- Less developed regions (60 or over)
- Less developed regions (80 or over)

oped regions is projected to be 78 men per 100 women among persons aged 60 or over and 57 men per 100 women among persons aged 80 or over, implying a significant increase with respect to the levels estimated for 2007 (73 among those aged 60 or over and 47 among those aged 80 or over), as is shown in figure 29.

In the less developed regions, mixed trends are projected over the next four decades. As a result, women are expected to constitute an increasing proportion of the older population in most developing countries. However, in several countries in Africa, the share of men in the population aged 60 or over is expected to increase. An increase is also expected in the share of men in the population aged 80 or over in several countries in Asia where the proportions of older persons are already relatively high. Consequently, the average sex ratio in the less developed regions in 2050 is projected to be 86 men per 100 women among persons aged 60 or over and 63 among those aged 80 or over, only slightly lower than the levels estimated for 2007, namely, 88 and 66 men per 100 women, respectively (figure 29).

As a result of the differing trends projected for the more developed and the less developed regions, the difference in the sex ratios of their populations aged 60 or over is expected to decrease from 15 points in 2007 to 8 points in 2050. During that period, the difference between the sex ratios of the population aged 80 or over in the more developed and the less developed regions is projected to decrease from 21 to 6 points.

Among the major areas, Europe has today the lowest sex ratio at older ages (69 men per 100 women among people aged 60 or over and 43 men per 100 women among persons aged 80 or over) owing both to its large sex differentials in life expectancy and to the effects of the Second World War. Asia, in contrast, has the highest sex ratio among persons aged 60 or over (88 men per 100 women), while Africa has the highest sex ratio among persons aged 80 or over (67 men per 100 women), as is shown in figure 30.

In several countries, most of which are located in Eastern Europe and Northern Europe, women currently outnumber men by more than 5 to 3 among the population aged 60 or over. In nine countries, the sex ratios at ages 60 or over are lower than 60 men per 100 women. In 13 countries, the sex ratio of the population aged 80 or over is below 40 men per 100 women. At the other extreme of the distribution, men outnumber women at older ages in several countries, most located in Western Asia. In 17 countries, the sex ratio of the population aged 60 or over surpasses 100 men per 100 women and in 6 countries, sex ratios higher than 100 are found among the population aged 80 or over.

Sex ratios at older ages vary greatly among major areas and countries

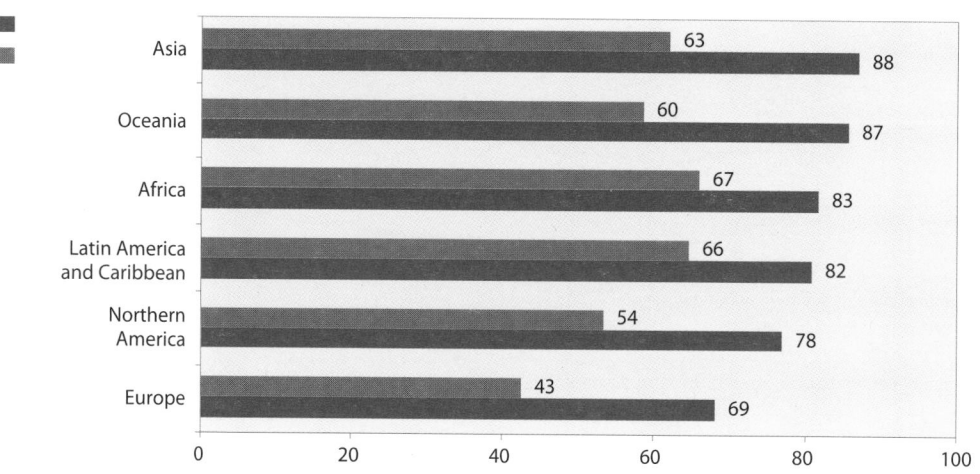

Figure 30
Number of men per hundred women at ages 60 or over and 80 or over: major areas, 2007

The range of variation of sex ratios at older ages is particularly wide among developing countries. While there are more older men than older women in Kuwait, Qatar, and the United Arab Emirates, countries such as Argentina, Kazakhstan and South Africa have a higher proportion of women at older ages than many European countries. However, the range of variation is expected to narrow over the next fourth decades.

C.   Marital status

The majority of older men are married but most older women are not

Marital status can strongly affect the emotional and economic well-being of older persons, particularly those with an illness or disability, as it determines living arrangements and the availability of caregivers. In general, older men are more likely to live with a spouse than older women because of a combination of factors, including the higher life expectancy of women, the tendency of men to marry women who are younger than they are, and the higher remarriage rates among older widowed men than among widowed women. The implication of such situation is that older men are more likely than older women to receive assistance from their spouses, especially when their health fails.

At the global level, an estimated 62 per cent of the population aged 60 years or over is married. There are marked differences between men and women. Among older women, 48 per cent are married and living with a spouse, while among older men the proportion married reaches 80 per cent. On average, there are only 31 older men without a spouse per 100 older women in the same situation.

The general pattern whereby older men are more likely to have a spouse than older women is observed in both the more developed and the less developed regions, where the corresponding figures are practically the same (figure 31). For the group of least developed countries, however, the proportion of men with spouses is higher than at the world level (85 per cent) and that of older women with spouses is lower than the world average (39 per cent).

The proportions of older men with spouses are considerably higher than those of older women with spouses in all major areas

The proportion of persons aged 60 or over who are still married varies from 57 per cent in Latin America and the Caribbean to 64 per cent in Asia. The gender gap in the percentage married among older persons is highest in Africa, where older men are more than twice as likely as older women to still have a spouse (85 per cent among older men versus 39 per cent among older women), and lowest in Northern America

Figure 31

Percentage currently married among population aged 60 or over by sex: world and development regions

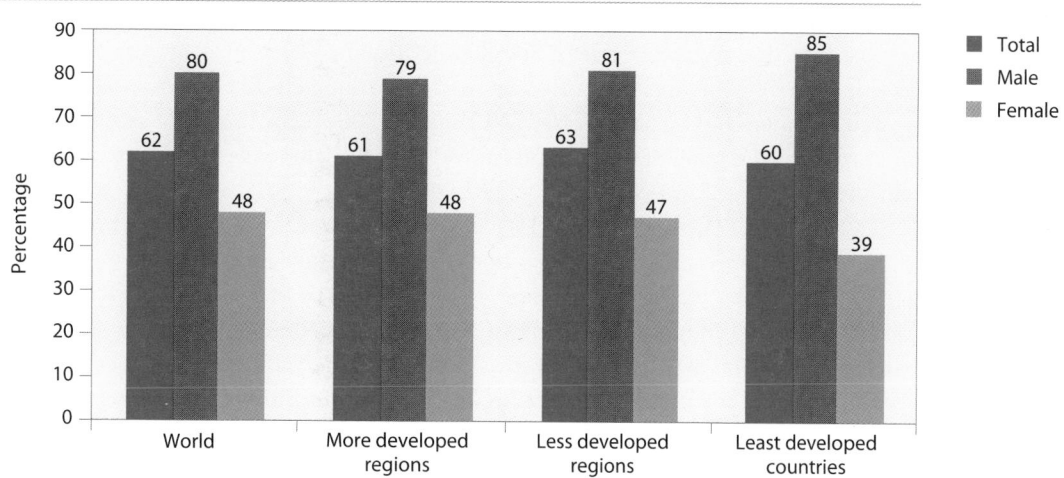

and Oceania, where the corresponding proportions are about 75 per cent among older men and 50 per cent among older women (figure 32).

The proportion still married among persons aged 60 or over ranges from 37 per cent in French Guiana to 78 per cent in Swaziland. In the majority of countries, more than half of older persons are still married. The few countries where that is not the case are located mostly in the Caribbean. At the high end of the distribution, there are seven countries in Africa and Asia where more than 70 per cent of the older population is still married. In no country did the proportion married among older women surpass that of older men, and in only one, French Guiana, were less than half of older men still married. The gender gap in the percentage married varies from 11 percentage points in Belize to 69 percentage points in Chad. In 20 countries, the gap is lower than 25 percentage points while in another 18, the gap is higher than 50 percentage points.

The proportions of older men and women who are still married varies considerably among countries

Figure 32

Percentage currently married among men and women aged 60 or over and gender gap: major areas

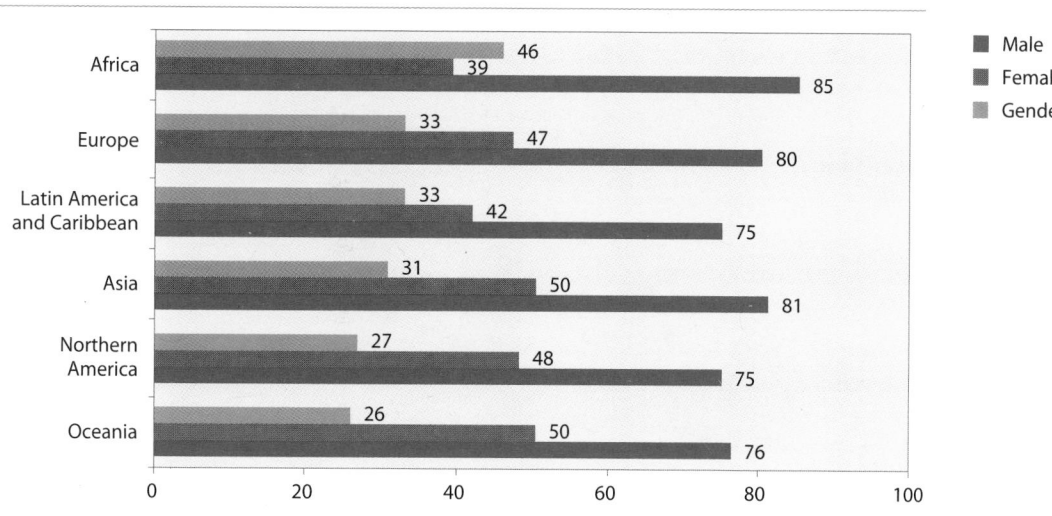

D. Living arrangements

About one out of every seven older persons, approximately 90 million people, live alone

Older persons living alone constitute a group that is of natural social and policy concern. Those living alone are more likely to need outside assistance in the case of illness or disability, are at greater risk of social isolation and, even in countries with well-developed systems of social security, are disproportionately likely—especially if they are older women—to be poor (Casey and Yamada, 2002). For the world as a whole, the proportion of the population aged 60 or over who live alone is estimated to be 14 per cent (figure 33).

Older persons are more likely to live alone in the more developed regions than in the less developed regions

On average, one out of every 14 persons aged 60 or over (7 per cent) lives alone in the less developed regions, whereas in the more developed regions, one out of every four (25 per cent) lives alone (figure 33). In Africa, Asia and Latin America and the Caribbean, the levels of solitary living among persons aged 60 or over range from 7 per cent to 9 per cent, whereas in Europe, Northern America and Oceania, they range between 25 per cent and 26 per cent (figure 34). Within Europe, the different regions show markedly different proportions of older persons living alone, ranging from 19 per cent to 24 per cent in Southern Europe and Eastern Europe, respectively, to 32 per cent and 34 per cent in Western Europe and Northern Europe, respectively.

At the country level, the proportion of older persons living alone varies considerably

Among the 134 countries or areas for which data are available, the proportion of the population aged 60 or over living alone ranges from less than 1 per cent in Bahrain in 1991 to almost 40 per cent in Denmark in 1994. In general, the proportion living alone is lowest in countries or areas of Africa and Asia and highest in Europe or in countries whose populations are mainly of European origin. Proportions of older persons living alone tend to be higher in Latin America and the Caribbean than in the other major areas of the developing world. However, there is considerable variation within regions and a few developing countries have values more typical of European countries. For instance, although the average proportion of older persons living alone is just 8 per cent in Africa, in Ghana, 22 per cent of older persons live alone. Several Caribbean countries and Israel also have more than 20 per cent of their older population living alone. Conversely, in about a quarter of all European countries the proportion of older persons living alone is below 20 per cent, with the lowest values, ranging from 10 per cent to 15 per cent, found in Malta, Spain and Serbia and Montenegro. In general, within Europe, Southern European countries display the lowest proportions of older persons living alone.

Figure 33
**Percentage of population aged 60 or over living alone by sex:
world and development regions**

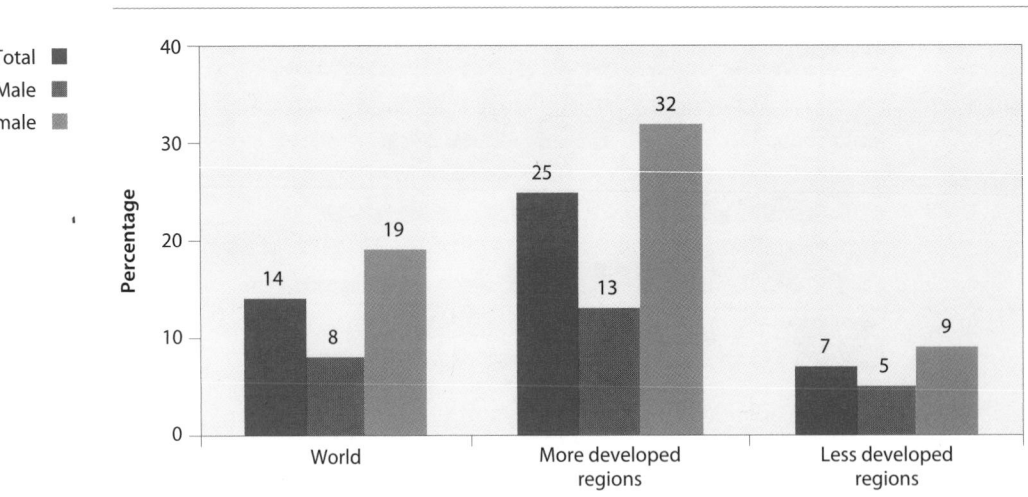

Figure 34

Percentage of population aged 60 or over living alone by sex: major areas

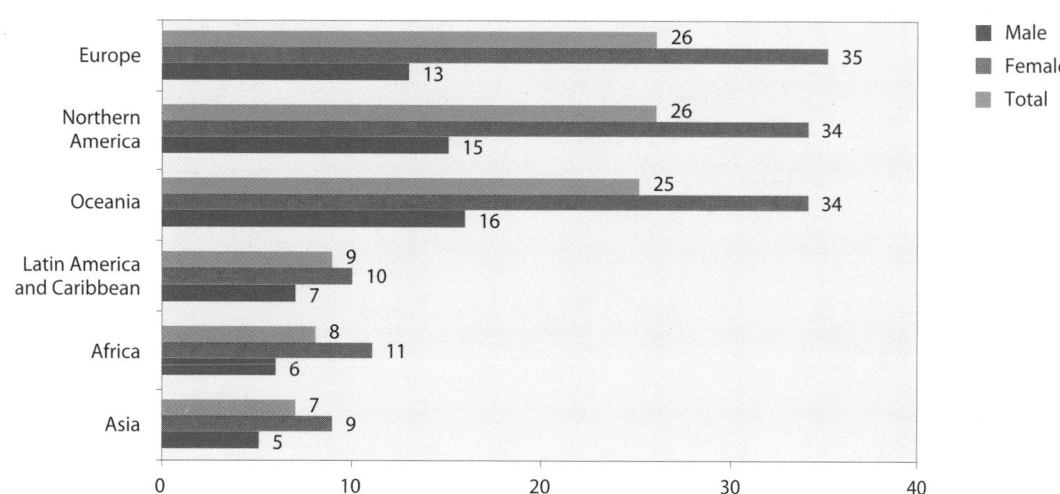

At the global level, the average proportion of women aged 60 or over living alone is 19 per cent, more than double the proportion of older men living alone (8 per cent). Gender differences are significantly larger in the more developed regions, where levels of solitary living are relatively higher than in the less developed regions (figure 33). More older women than older men live alone because older women are more likely to be widowed and hence less likely to be living with a spouse (figure 31). Among persons without spouses, however, older men are more likely than older women to live alone in most countries; that is, if a man survives to old age without a spouse, he often has a higher risk of living alone (United Nations, 2005b).

Older women are usually more likely than older men to live alone

The gender gap in solitary living is particularly high in Western Europe where the proportion of older women who live alone (43 per cent) is almost triple that of older men (15 per cent). In Africa and Asia, the proportion of older women living alone (11 per cent in Africa and 9 per cent in Asia) is about 80 per cent higher than among older men (6 per cent in Africa and 5 per cent in Asia). In Latin America and the Caribbean, 10 per cent of older women live alone, compared to just 7 per cent of older men (figure 34). Only in the Caribbean does a higher proportion of older men live alone than that of older women (10 per cent of older men compared to 9 per cent of older women).

Gender differences in solitary living vary greatly among both regions and countries

In most countries, the proportion of older persons living alone is higher among women than among men. The exceptions are mostly found in Central America and the Caribbean. The gender difference in the proportion of older persons living alone ranges from 6 percentage points in favour of men in Panama to 30.5 percentage points in favour of women in the Netherlands.

Chapter V
Socio-economic characteristics of the older population

A.   Illiteracy rates

The attainment of universal primary education has been a reality in most developed countries for a long time. As a result, literacy in these regions is assumed to be nearly universal even among the older population and most developed countries no longer gather information on this subject. However, some of the few developed countries having age-specific data on literacy, most of which are located in Eastern Europe and Southern Europe, still show high levels of illiteracy at older ages. In Malta, for instance, 28 per cent of persons aged 65 or over were illiterate in 1995. In Bosnia and Herzegovina, 17 per cent of the population aged 65 or over was illiterate in 2000 and the equivalent proportion was 18 per cent in TFYR Macedonia in 2002. Among the remaining developed countries having the required data, illiteracy levels among older persons vary from 0.4 per cent in Estonia in 2000 to 14 per cent in Serbia and Montenegro in 2003.

In developing countries, levels of educational attainment have generally improved over time, with the result that younger generations are better educated than older ones. However, even for younger generations, levels of educational attainment remain low in many developing countries. Combining the data available for 80 developing countries, it is estimated that, on average, 53 per cent of persons aged 65 or over living in developing countries are illiterate. With the exception of Costa Rica, the proportion of illiterate persons in the developing countries with data is higher among older women than among older men. It is estimated that, on average, 65 per cent of women and 42 per cent of men aged 65 years or over are illiterate in developing countries, a gap of 23 percentage points (figure 35).

In developed countries, literacy among the older population is nearly universal

In developing countries, illiteracy remains high among older people, especially among older women

Figure 35
**Estimated average illiterary rate at ages 65 or over by sex:
80 developing countries, 2007**

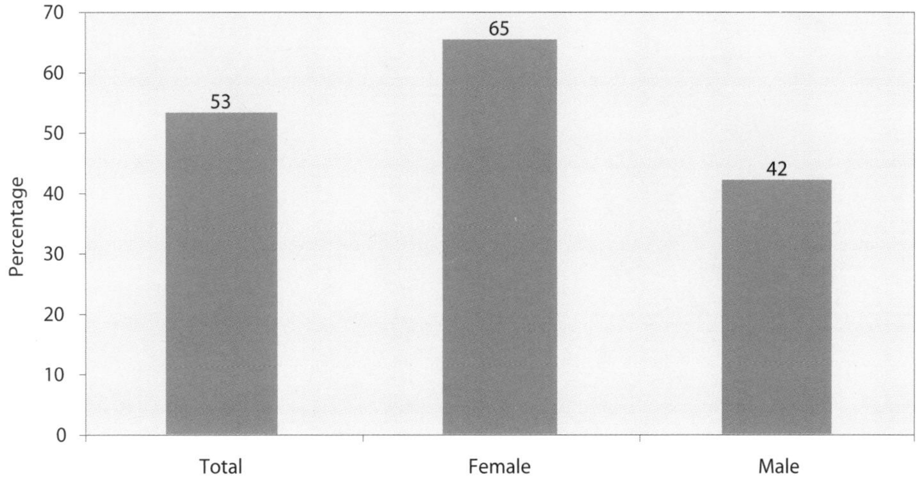

Data on illiteracy levels by age are available for 32 countries in Africa, 31 in Asia and 16 in Latin American and the Caribbean. On the basis of those data, it is estimated that, in Africa, 70 per cent of the population aged 65 or over is illiterate. The equivalent estimate is 58 per cent for Asia and 29 per cent for Latin American and the Caribbean (figure 36). That is, there are major differences in levels of illiteracy among the older population in the major areas of the developing world.

The estimated average level of illiteracy among women aged 65 or over in Africa is 84 per cent and it is 71 per cent in Asia, levels that are 27 to 28 percentage points higher than those estimated among older men (57 per cent in Africa and 43 per cent in Asia). In Latin America and the Caribbean the gender gap is just 5 percentage points, since the illiteracy level among older women is estimated at 31 per cent compared to 26 per cent among older men (figure 36).

There are huge differences in illiteracy levels among older persons in the developing countries having the required data. In some countries in Africa, such as Benin, Burkina Faso, Chad and Mali, over 90 per cent of persons aged 65 years or over were illiterate around 2000, with illiteracy levels being higher among older women (above 96 per cent) than among older men (above 87 per cent). At the other end of the distribution, in countries such as Armenia, Cuba and Tonga, less than 5 per cent of persons aged 65 or over are illiterate, though illiteracy still tends to be higher among older women than among older men. This wide range of variation is expected to decrease in the future as educational attainment continues to improve in most countries.

B.   Labour force participation

Older people today are as likely to participate in the labour force as they were in 1980: about 20 per cent of older persons are economically active worldwide. However, this stability over time masks important changes in labour force participation rates by sex. Among older men, the labour force participation rate decreased from 35 per cent in 1980 to 30 per cent in 2007, and is expected to decline further to 27 per cent by 2020. Among older women, the labour force participation rate has been increasing, passing from 10 per cent in 1980 to 12 per cent in 2007, and is projected to reach 14 per cent by 2020 (figure 37). By that time, the overall labour force participation rate of older persons is projected to decrease slightly from the current 20 per cent to 19 per cent.

Figure 36
Estimated average illiteracy rate at ages 65 or over by sex: major areas, 2007

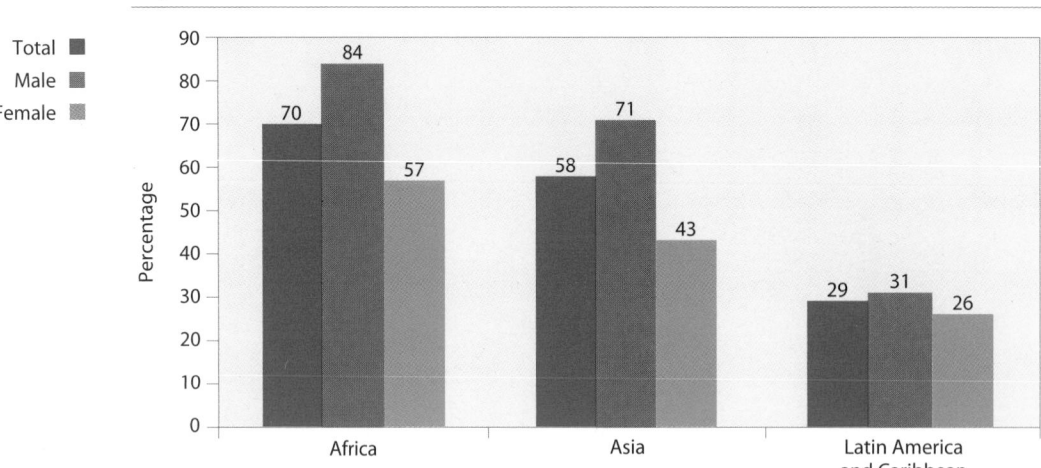

Figure 37
**Total, male and female labour force participation at ages 65 or over:
world, 1980-2020**

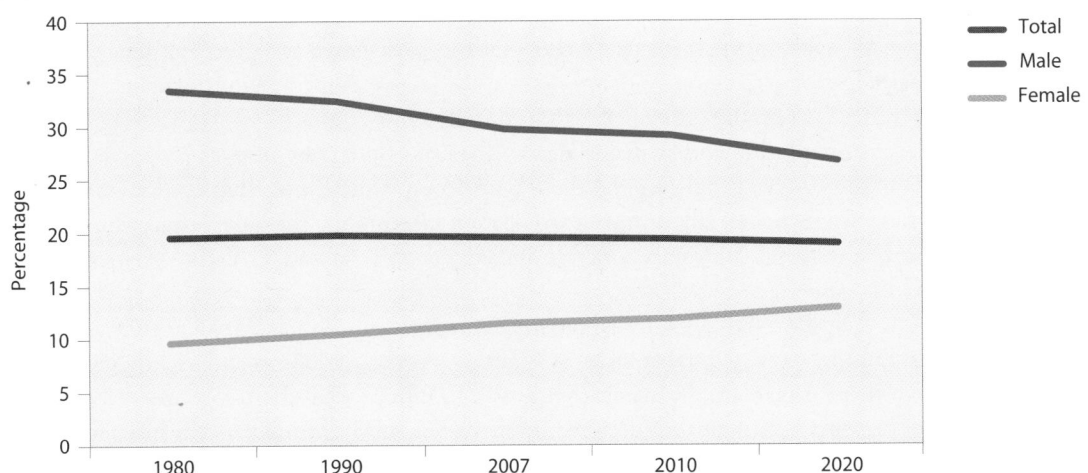

Traditionally, the proportion of older men who are economically active has been markedly higher than the proportion of older women. However, because labour force participation at older ages has dropped among men and risen among women, the female share of the older labour force has increased over the past decades, especially in the more developed regions. In 1980, women accounted for 37 per cent of the workers aged 65 or over in the more developed regions and 25 per cent of those in the less developed regions. By 2007, their share had increased to 43 per cent in the more developed regions and to 31 per cent in the less developed regions. At the global level, women's share of the older work force rose from 28 per cent in 1980 to 33 per cent in 2007 (figure 38).

Old-age support systems in the form of pension and retirement programmes are less prevalent in developing countries than in developed countries. Consequently, people are compelled to continue working into old age in developing countries for lack of alternative support, with the result that the labour force participation rates at older ages tend to be higher in developing countries than in developed countries. Thus, in 1980, the labour force participation rate among people aged 65 or over was about 28 per cent in the

The female share of the older work force is increasing

The labour force participation rates of older persons are higher in the less developed regions

Figure 38
**Distribution of economically active population aged 65 or over by sex:
world, 1980-2020**

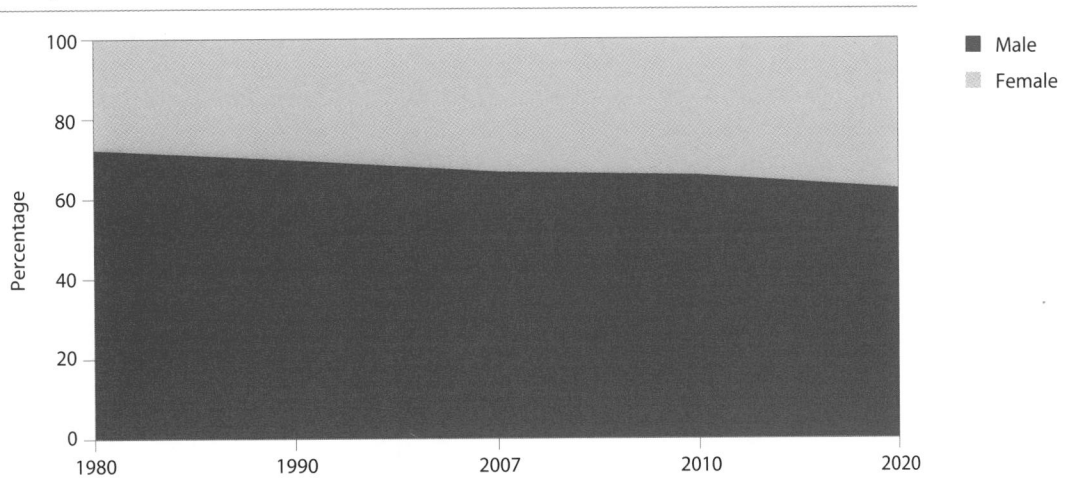

less developed regions and close to 10 per cent in the more developed regions. However, labour force participation rates at older ages have been declining and are currently 26 per cent in the less developed regions and 9 per cent in the more developed regions. By 2020, they are projected to decrease further in the less developed regions, to 24 per cent, and to remain stable in the more developed regions. As is shown in figure 39, the labour force participation rate among older persons in the less developed regions remained about triple that in the more developed regions during 1980-2020.

Among the world's major areas, Africa has by far the highest proportion of economically active people among those 65 or over, while Europe has the lowest. Between these two extremes, labour force participation rates among the older population are lower in Oceania and Northern America and higher in Asia and in Latin America and the Caribbean.

During 1980-2007, the labour force participation rate among older persons decreased in Europe, remained stable in Latin America and the Caribbean and slightly increased in Northern America and Oceania (figure 40). In Europe, the labour force participation rate of persons aged 65 or over declined by about one third, from 8 per cent in 1980 to 5 per cent in 2007. The reduction between 1980 and 2007 was about 10 per cent in Africa (from 45 per cent to 40 per cent) and Asia (from 27 per cent to 24 per cent). Over the same period, the participation rate increased by about 10 per cent in Oceania (from 9 per cent to 10 per cent), by almost 20 per cent in Northern America (from 12 per cent to 14 per cent), and remained practically constant at around 24 per cent in Latin America and the Caribbean. In most major areas, the labour force participation rates of older men declined while those of older women increased. However, the female labour force participation rate among the older population decreased slightly in Africa and Europe.

In at least 21 countries, fewer than 4 per cent of persons aged 65 or over are currently working. In four of them (France, Luxembourg, Réunion and Slovakia), the proportion of older persons in the labour force is lower than 1 per cent. At the other end of the distribution, over half of all persons aged 65 or over continue to work in at least 30 countries. In Mozambique, the labour force participation rate among older persons is particularly high, at more than 80 per cent.

Labour force participation rates among older men in 2007 range from less than 1.5 per cent in some European countries (France, Luxembourg and Slovakia) and in Réunion to more than 86 per cent in some African countries (e.g., Congo, Sierra Leone

The labour force participation rate among older persons is lowest in Europe and highest in Africa

In some countries, less than 1 per cent of the population aged 65 or over is in the labour force

Figure 39

Labour force participation of population aged 65 or over: development regions, 1980-2020

More developed regions ■
Less developed regions ■
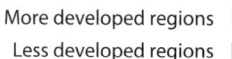

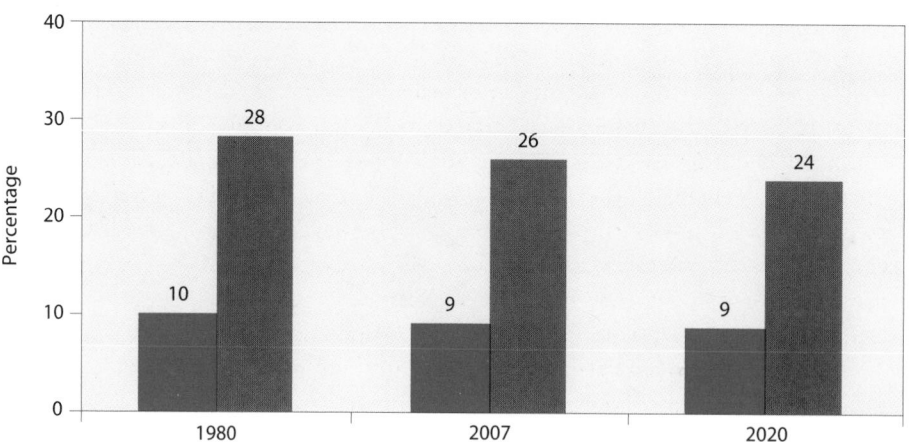

Figure 40
**Labour force participation of population aged 65 or over:
major areas, 1980 and 2007**

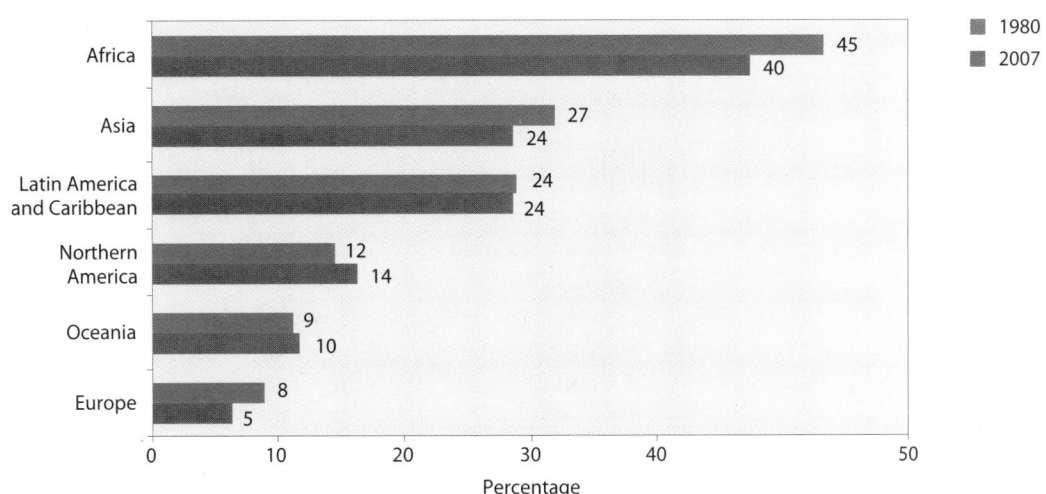

and Somalia). Among older women, labour force participation rates range from less than 0.5 per cent in Luxembourg and Réunion, to more than 70 per cent in Burundi, Malawi and Mozambique.

The labour force participation of older persons has declined in the majority of countries. In 15 countries, the participation rate of persons aged 65 or over has declined by more than 70 per cent since 1980 and in five of them the reduction has been over 80 per cent. The largest decrease was observed in Slovakia, where the labour force participation rate of older persons dropped from 11 per cent in 1980 to 0.8 per cent in 2007.

Some countries have experienced dramatic declines in the labour force participation of older people

In about a third of all countries, however, the reported labour force participation rates of older persons have increased since 1980. In four countries with economies in transition—Georgia, Kazakhstan, Kyrgyzstan and Romania—the participation rates more than tripled. In Romania, in particular, the labour force participation rate among those aged 65 or over increased more than sixfold, from 5 per cent in 1980 to 31 per cent in 2007.

C.   Statutory pensionable age

Although in some countries pension benefits are payable at any age after a certain period of employment, most commonly ranging from 30 to 40 years of continuous employment, qualifying for a benefit in most countries is conditional on both attaining a specified age and completing the specified period of contributions. In recent years, the minimum age required before a pension entitlement can be claimed has increased in several countries, mainly in response to the budgetary constraints arising from population ageing.

The statutory pensionable age is often higher for men than for women

In many countries, women become eligible for full pension benefits at lower ages than men, although women generally survive longer than men. Based on information for 159 countries, the statutory pensionable age as of 2006 was 65 years or higher for men in 31 per cent of the countries with data and for women in 18 per cent of the 159 countries. The pensionable age for men was lower than 60 years in 22 per cent of the countries with data and for women in 47 per cent of those countries (figure 41).

Although the norm has been for a difference of about 5 years between the pensionable age of men and women, there is an emerging trend toward equalizing the statutory pensionable age between the sexes. As of 2006, men and women had the same statutory

In most countries the pensionable age is the same for women as for men

Figure 41

Distribution of countries by statutory pensionable age of men and women: 2006 assessment (*N=159*)

Less than 60 years ■
Between 60 and 64 years ■
65 years or higher ■

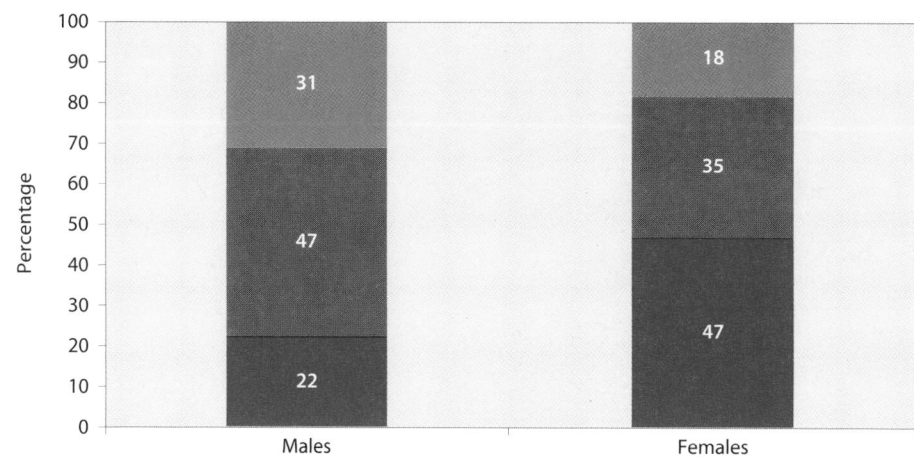

pensionable age in 60 per cent of countries with data available (figure 42). The same pensionable age for men and women was particularly common in the developing world where 65 per cent of the countries with information had the same pensionable age for both. In 56 per cent of developed countries, the pensionable age remained higher for men than for women.

Men become eligible for full pension benefits at age 65 or over in 61 per cent of developed countries, but the pensionable age is 65 or over in only about 20 per cent of developing countries (figure 43). In no developed country is the pensionable age for men lower than 60 years, whereas that is the case in almost 30 per cent of developing countries. For women, the pensionable age is 65 years or over in 39 per cent of developed countries and in only 11 per cent of developing countries (figure 43). In more than 40 per cent of developing countries the pensionable age for women is 55 years or lower, a situation that is similar in less than 5 per cent of developed countries. These differences reflect, to a certain extent, differences in life expectancy, which is lower in developing countries.

For both men and women, pensionable ages tend to be higher in developed countries than in developing countries

Figure 42
Percentage of countries for which the statutory pensionable age is either the same for both sexes or higher for men than for women: 2006 assessment

Same for men and women ■
Higher for men than for women ■

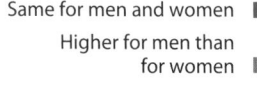

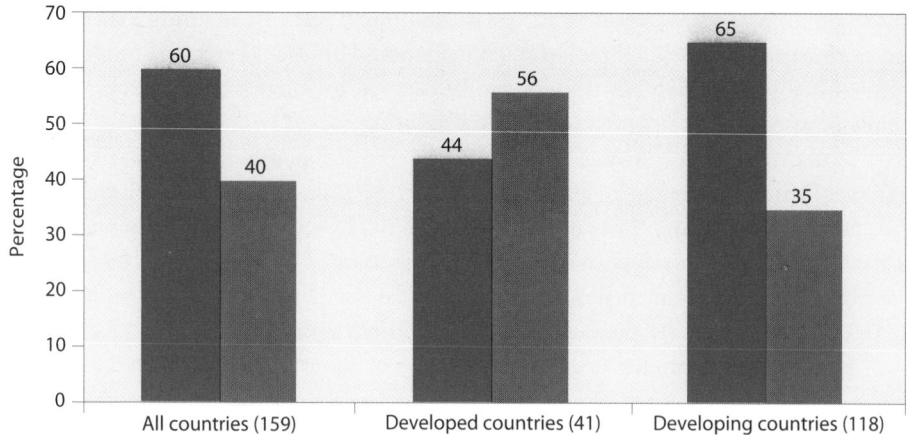

Figure 43
Percentage of countries for which the statutory pensionable age is 65 years or higher by sex: 2006 assessment

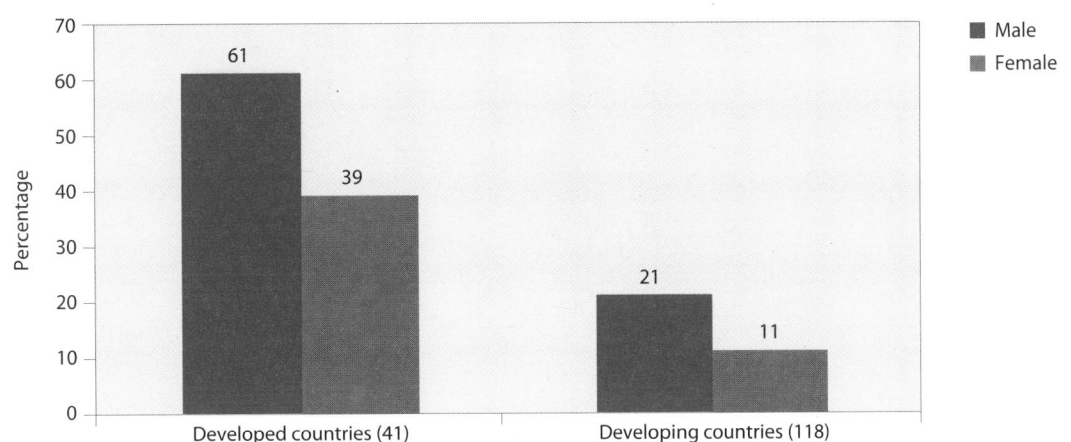

In 60 per cent of countries in Latin American and the Caribbean the statutory pensionable age for men is higher than 60 years, while only 7 per cent of countries in this major area have a pensionable age below 60 years (figure 44). In contrast, the pensionable age for men is below 60 years in 41 per cent of the countries in Africa, while it is higher than 60 years in just 12 per cent of African countries. In Asia, the proportion of countries with a pensionable age for men that is below 60 years is lower than the corresponding proportion in Africa but higher than that in Latin America and the Caribbean. In addition, the proportion of Asian countries with a pensionable age for men above 60 (32 per cent) is higher than the corresponding proportion in Africa and lower than that in Latin American and the Caribbean (figure 44).

Among developing countries, pensionable ages tend to be higher in Latin America and the Caribbean and lower in Africa

Figure 44
Distribution of countries by statutory pensionable age of men: major areas, 2006 assessment

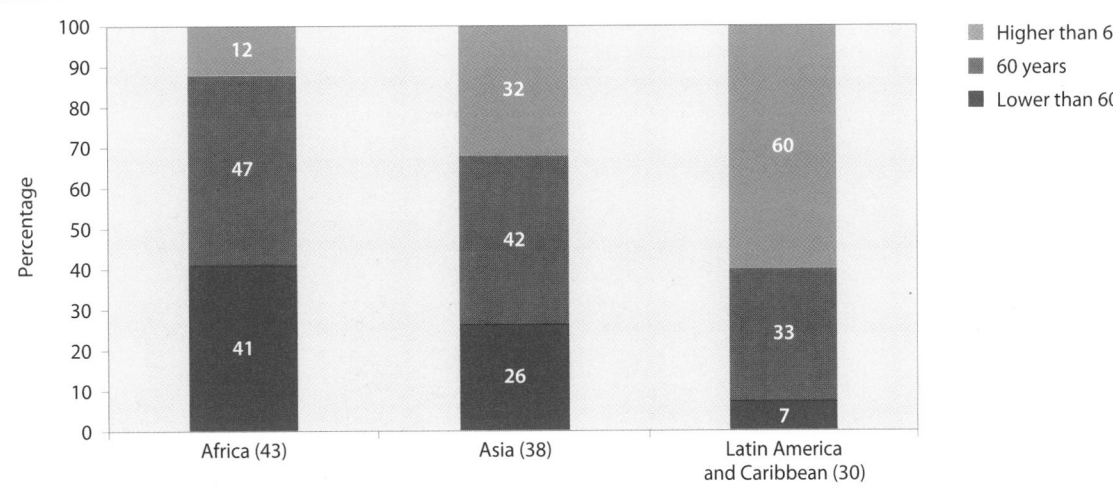

Chapter VI
Conclusion

Global population ageing is a by-product of the demographic transition in which both mortality and fertility decline from higher to lower levels. Currently, the total fertility rate is below the replacement level in practically all industrialized countries. In the less developed regions, the fertility decline started later and has proceeded faster than in the more developed regions. Yet, in all regions people are increasingly likely to survive to older ages, and once there they are tending to live longer, as the gains in life expectancy are relatively higher at older ages.

The older population is growing at a considerably faster rate than that of the world's total population. In absolute terms, the number of older persons has more than tripled since 1950 and will almost triple again by 2050. In relative terms, the percentage of older persons is projected to more than double worldwide by the middle of this century. However, notable differences exist between regions in the numbers and proportions at higher ages. Although the highest proportions of older persons are found in the more developed regions, this age group is growing considerably more rapidly in the less developed regions. As a consequence, the older population will be increasingly concentrated in the less developed regions.

The young-old balance is shifting throughout the world. In the more developed regions, the proportion of older persons already exceeds that of children, and by 2050 it is expected to be double that of children. In the less developed regions, age-distribution changes have been slow but will accelerate over the coming decades. Currently, the median age in the more developed regions is more than 13 years higher than in the less developed regions and almost 20 years higher than in the least developed countries.

An increase in the old-age dependency ratio indicates a situation in which an increasing number of potential beneficiaries of health and pension funds (mainly those aged 65 and over) are supported by a relatively smaller number of potential contributors (those in the economically active ages of 15-64). This trend tends to impose heavier demands on the working-age population (in the form of higher taxes and other contributions) in order to maintain a stable flow of benefits to the older groups. Even the sharp decline in youth dependency that has accompanied the increase in old-age dependency may not be enough to offset the increased costs, since the relative expense of supporting the old is, in general, higher than that of supporting the young.

The continuing increase of the parent support ratio implies that more and more frequently the young-old will find themselves responsible for the care of one or more very old family members. Parent support ratios are lower in the developing regions, where public institutions for the support of the very old tend to be less fully developed. However, the ratio is rising quite rapidly in the developing regions as well.

As the numbers and relative proportions of the older population increase, their demographic characteristics are also changing. For instance, the older population is itself undergoing a process of demographic ageing. At the global level, the most rapidly growing age group is that aged 80 and over. Although the oldest-old still constitute a small proportion of the total population, their numbers are becoming increasingly important, especially in the less developed regions.

In most countries, older women greatly outnumber older men. In many cases, the difference is so large that the concerns of the older population should in fact be viewed primarily as the concerns of older women. This is especially true in the case of the oldest-old populations, as the female share increases markedly with age.

Older men are much more likely to be married than are older women due to a combination of factors that include the higher female life expectancy, the tendency for men to marry slightly younger women, and the higher remarriage rates among older widowed men than women. As a consequence, older men are in general more likely than older women to receive assistance from a spouse, especially when health fails.

Because older women are less likely than older men to be married, mainly because of widowhood, a significantly higher proportion of older women than older men live alone, particularly in the more developed regions. Older women living alone constitute a group of special social and policy concern as they are at greater risk of social isolation and economic deprivation. It is worth noting, however, that among the unmarried, older men are more likely than older women to live alone in most countries.

Labour force participation of the older population has remained stable worldwide over the last decades and is considerably higher in the less developed than in the more developed regions. Nearly everywhere, however, the trend has been towards lower levels of economic activity among older men and higher levels among older women, thus increasing the female share of the older work force. Although lower levels of labour force participation at older ages are usually a sign of higher levels of social security coverage, they may also result from other factors, such as a shortage of employment opportunities and obsolescence of skills and knowledge.

Illiteracy remains high in the less developed regions among older people, especially women. Available evidence suggests that only slightly more than half of all persons 65 and older and less than 35 per cent of women in this age group are literate in those regions. This situation is of special concern as higher levels of education are generally associated with better health and economic status within the older population.

As the twentieth century drew to a close, population ageing and its social and economic consequences were drawing increased attention from policy makers worldwide. Currently, many countries, especially in the more developed regions, have already achieved population structures older than any ever seen in human history. In most cases, the ageing societies also experienced rapid economic growth during the second half of the twentieth century. While major shortcomings and unmet needs remained, most developed countries expanded and diversified their systems of social security and health care and, on the whole, the standard of living of the old as well as the young improved as populations aged. However, strains were building in those support systems, as the older population continued to grow more rapidly than that of younger adults and as earlier withdrawal from the labour force added to the demands on public pension systems.

The twenty-first century will witness even more rapid population ageing than did the century just past. Worldwide, the percentage of the population aged 60 years or over has increased by 3 points—from 8 to 11 per cent—since the middle of the twentieth century. Until the middle of the twenty-first century, that percentage is projected to increase by 11 points, to 22 per cent. By that time, the population of the less developed regions will have about the same percentage of persons aged 60 years or over as the current percentage in the more developed regions. The developing countries will reach that stage over a shorter period than that required by the more developed regions. In many cases, rapid population ageing will be taking place in countries where the level of economic development is still low. The challenge for the future is "to ensure that persons everywhere are able to age with security and dignity and to continue to participate in their societies as citizens with full rights" (United Nations, 2002, para. 10).

References

Baldacci, E. and S. Lugaresi (1997). Social Expenditure and Demographic Evolution: A Dynamic Approach. *Genus*, vol. 53, No. 1-2 (January-June).

Bravo, J. (1999). Fiscal Implications of Ageing Societies Regarding Public and Private Pension Systems. In *Population Ageing: Challenges for Policies and Programmes in Developed and Developing Countries*, R. Cliquet and M. Nizamuddin, eds. New York: United Nations Population Fund; and Brussels: Centrum voor Bevolkings-en Gezinsstudiën (CBGS).

Casey, B. and A. Yamada (2002). *Getting Older, Getting Poorer? A Study of the Earnings, Pensions, Assets and Living Arrangements of Older People in Nine Countries*. Labour Market and Social Policy Occasional Papers, No. 60. DEELSA/ELSA/WD (2002) 4. Paris: OECD.

Cliquet, R. and M. Nizamuddin, eds. (1999). *Population Ageing: Challenges for Policies and Programmes in Developed and Developing Countries*. New York: United Nations Population Fund; and Brussels: Centrum voor Bevolkings-en Gezinsstudiën (CBGS).

Creedy, J. (1998). *Pensions and Population Ageing: An Economic Analysis*. Cheltenham, United Kingdom; and Northampton, Massachusetts: Edward Elgar Publishing.

Crimmins, E. (1997). Trends in mortality, morbidity, and disability: what should we expect for the future of our ageing population. In *International Population Conference, Beijing, 1997*, vol. 1. Liège, Belgium: International Union for the Scientific Study of Population (IUSSP).

de Jong-Gierveld, J. and H. van Solinge (1995). *Ageing and Its Consequences for the Socio-Medical System*. Population Studies, No. 29. Strasbourg, France: Council of Europe Press.

Drury, E. (1994). Age discrimination against older workers in the European Union. In *Studies on the Four Pillars*. Geneva Papers on Risk and Insurance: Issues and Practice, No. 73.

Grundy, E. (1996). Population ageing in Europe. In *Europe's Population in the 1990s*, David Coleman, ed. New York: Oxford University Press.

Higuchi, K. (1996). Women in an ageing society. In *Added Years of Life in Asia: Current Situation and Future Challenges*. Asian Population Studies Series, No. 141. Bangkok: Economic Commission for Asia and the Pacific.

Holliday, R. (1999). Ageing in the 21st century. *The Lancet* (December), vol. 354, Supplement No. 4.

Hoyert, D. L. (1991). Financial and household exchanges between generations. *Research on Aging*, vol. 13, No. 2.

International Labour Office (2000). *World Labour Report 2000: Income Security and Social Protection in a Changing World*. Geneva.

_____ (2006). Economically active population estimates and projections: 1980-2020. Database on labour statistics—LABORSTA, available from http://laborsta.ilo.org (accessed 01 June 2006).

Jackson, W. A. (1998). *Political Economy of Population Ageing*. Cheltenham, United Kingdom; and Northampton, Massachusetts: Edward Elgar Publishing.

Kinsella, K. and Y. J. Gist (1995). *Older Workers, Retirement, and Pensions: A Comparative International Chartbook*. Washington, D.C.: United States Bureau of the Census (IPC/95-2RP).

Kinsella, K. and C. M. Taeuber (1993). *An Aging World II*. International Population Reports. Washington, D.C.: United States Bureau of the Census (P95/92-3).

Lesthaeghe, R. (2004). Europe's demographic issues: fertility, household formation and replacement migration. *Population Bulletin of the United Nations*, Special Issue Nos. 44/45 (Sales No. E.02.XIII.4).

Morgan, D. L., T. L. Schuster and E. W. Butler (1991). Role reversals in the exchange of social support. *Journal of Gerontology*, vol. 46, No. 5.

National Research Council (2001). *Preparing for an Aging World: The Case for Cross-National Research*. Panel on a Research Agenda and New Data for an Aging World, Committee on Population and Committee on National Statistics, Division of Behavioral and Social Sciences and Education. Washington, D.C.: National Academy Press.

Pollard, J. H. (1995). Long-term care in selected countries: demographic and insurance perspectives. *Zeitschrift für Bevölkerungswissenschaft*, vol. 20, No. 3.

Saad, P. M. (2001). Support transfers between elderly parents and adult children in two Brazilian settings (CD-ROM). Paper presented at the Twenty-fourth IUSSP General Population Conference, Salvador de Bahia, Brazil, 18-24 August 2001. Paris: International Union for the Scientific Study of Population.

Taeuber, C. M. (1992). *Sixty-five Plus in America*. Current Population Reports, Special Studies P23-178. Washington, D.C.: United States Bureau of the Census.

Taylor, P. E. and A. Walker (1996). Intergenerational relations in the labour market: the attitudes of employers and older workers. In *The New Generational Contract, Intergenerational Relations, Old Age and Welfare*, A. Walker, ed. London: University College London Press.

UNESCO Institute for Statistics (2006). Senior literacy rates by country and by gender for selected age cohorts. Special tabulation prepared on April 2006.

United Nations (1956). *The Aging of Populations and Its Economic and Social Implications*. Population Studies, No. 26. Sales No. 1956.XIII.6.

_____ (1982). *Report of the World Assembly on Aging, Vienna, 26 July to 6 August 1982*. Sales No. E.82.I.16.

_____ (1988). *Economic and Social Implications of Population Aging*. Proceedings of the International Symposium on Population Structure and Development, Tokyo, 10-12 September 1987. Sales No. E.90.XIII.18.

_____ (1994). *Ageing and the Family*. Proceedings of the United Nations International Conference on Ageing Populations in the Context of the Family, Kitakyushu, Japan, 15-19 October 1990. Sales No. E.94.XIII.4.

_____ (1995). *Programme of Action Adopted at the International Conference on Population and Development, Cairo, 5-13 September 1994*. Population and Development, vol. 1. Sales No. E.95.XIII.7.

_____ (1999a). *Review and Appraisal of the Progress Made in Achieving the Goals and Programme of Action of the International Conference on Population and Development, 1999 Report*. Sales No. E.99.XIII.16.

_____ (1999b). *Ageing in a Gendered World: Women's Issues and Identities*. International Research and Training Institute for the Advancement of Women (INSTRAW). Sales No. E.99.III.C.1.

_____ (2000). *Below-Replacement Fertility*. Population Bulletin of the United Nations. Special Issue Nos. 40/41. Sales No. E.99.XIII.13.

_____ (2001). *Population Ageing and Living Arrangements of Older Persons: Critical Issues and Policy Responses*. Population Bulletin of the United Nations, Special Issue Nos. 42/43. Sales No. E.01.XIII.16.

_____ (2002). *Report of the Second World Assembly on Ageing, Madrid, 8-12 April 2002*. Sales No. E.02.IV.4.

_____ (2004). *Policy Responses to Population Decline and Ageing*. Population Bulletin of the United Nations, Special Issue Nos. 44/45. Sales No. E.02.XIII.4.

_____ (2005a). *World Population Prospects: The 2004 Revision*, vol. I, *Comprehensive Tables*, Sales No. E.05.XIII.5; and vol. II, *Sex and Age Distribution of the World Population*, Sales No. E.05.XIII.6.

_____ (2005b). *Living Arrangements of Older Persons Around the World*. Sales No. E.05.XIII.9.

_____ (2005c). The diversity of changing population age structures in the world. Working paper, United Nations Expert Group Meeting on Social and Economic Implications of Changing Population Age Structures, Mexico City: 31 August–2 September 2005.

_____ (2006). *Population Ageing 2006*. Wallchart. Sales No. E.06.XIII.2.

_____ (forthcoming). Proceedings of the United Nations Expert Group Meeting on Social and Economic Implications of Changing Population Age Structures. Mexico City: 31 August–2 September 2005.

United States Social Security Administration (2006). Social Security Programs Throughout the World (Europe, September 2004; Asia and the Pacific, March 2005; Africa, September 2005; the Americas, March 2006) and International Updates, available from http://www.ssa.gov/policy/data_sub50.html (accessed June 2006).

Walker, A. (1990). The economic "burden" of ageing and the prospect of intergenerational conflict. *Ageing and Society*, vol. 10, No. 4 (December).

Wolf, D. A. (1994). The elderly and their kin: patterns of availability and access. In *Demography of Aging*, L. G. Martin and S. H. Preston, eds. Washington, D.C.: National Academy Press.

Annexes

Annex I
Definition of the indicators of population ageing

A.   Ageing index

The **ageing index** is calculated as the number of persons aged 60 years or over per hundred persons under age 15.

B.   Dependency ratio

The **total dependency ratio** is the number of persons under age 15 plus persons aged 65 or over per one hundred persons 15 to 64. It is the sum of the youth dependency ratio and the old-age dependency ratio.

The **youth dependency ratio** is the number of persons 0 to 14 years per one hundred persons 15 to 64 years.

The **old-age dependency ratio** is the number of persons aged 65 years or over per one hundred persons 15 to 64 years.

C.   Growth rate

A population's **growth rate** is the increase (or decrease) in the number of persons in the population during a certain period of time, expressed as a percentage of the population at the beginning of the time period. The **average annual growth rates** for all ages as well as for particular age groups are calculated on the assumption that growth is continuous.

D.   Illiteracy rate

The **illiteracy rate** of a particular age group indicates the proportion of persons in that group who cannot read with understanding and cannot write a short simple statement on their everyday life. National definitions of literacy may in some cases differ. A list of literacy definitions for different countries can be found at the UNESCO Institute for Statistics (UIS) website (http://stats.uis.unesco.org).

E.   Labour force participation

The **labour force participation rate** consists of the economically active population in a particular age group as a percentage of the total population of that same age group. The active population (or labour force) includes persons in paid or unpaid employment, members of the armed forces (including temporary members) and the unemployed (including first-time job-seekers.). This definition is the one adopted by the Thirteenth International Conference of Labour Statisticians (Geneva, 1982). National definitions may differ in some cases. For information on the differences in scope, definitions and methods of calculation used for the various national series, see International Labour Organization, Sources and Methods: Labour Statistics (formerly Statistical Sources and

Methods), vol. 2, Employment, Wages, Hours of Work and Labour Cost (Establishment Surveys), 2nd edition (Geneva, 1995); vol. 3, Economically Active Population, Employment, Unemployment and Hours of Work (Household Surveys), 2nd edition (Geneva, 1990); and vol. 4, Employment, Unemployment, Wages and Hours of Work (Administrative Records and Related Sources) (Geneva, 1989).

F. Life expectancy

Life expectancy at a specific age is the average number of additional years a person of that age could expect to live if current mortality levels observed for ages above that age were to continue for the rest of that person's life. In particular, life expectancy at birth is the average number of years a newborn would live if current age-specific mortality rates were to continue.

G. Median age

The **median age** of a population is the age that divides a population into two groups of the same size, such that half the total population is younger than this age, and the other half older.

H. Parent support ratio

The **parent support ratio** is the number of persons aged 85 years or over per one hundred persons aged 50 to 64 years.

I. Potential support ratio

The **potential support ratio** is the number of persons aged 15 to 64 per every person aged 65 or over.

J. Sex ratio

The **sex ratio** is calculated as the number of males per one hundred females in a population. The sex ratio may be calculated for a total population or for a specific age group.

K. Survival rate

The **survival rate** to a specific age X is the proportion of newborns in a given year who would be expected to survive at age X if current mortality trends were to continue for at least the next X years. Survival rates are derived from the life table, which is an analytic procedure designed to produce estimates of life expectancies and other measures of survivorship, based on prevailing age-specific death rates.

L. Total fertility rate

The **total fertility rate** is the average number of children a woman would bear over the course of her lifetime if current age-specific fertility rates remained constant throughout her childbearing years (normally between the ages of 15 and 49). The current total fertility rate is an indicator of the level of fertility at a given time.

Classification of major areas and regions

Africa

Eastern Africa	Middle Africa	Northern Africa	Western Africa
Burundi	Angola	Algeria	Benin
Comoros	Cameroon	Egypt	Burkina Faso
Djibouti	Central African	Libyan Arab	Cape Verde
Eritrea	Republic	Jamahiriya	Côte d'Ivoire
Ethiopia	Chad	Morocco	Gambia
Kenya	Congo	Sudan	Ghana
Madagascar	Democratic Republic	Tunisia	Guinea
Malawi	of the Congo	Western Sahara	Guinea-Bissau
Mauritius	Equatorial Guinea		Liberia
Mozambique	Gabon	**Southern Africa**	Mali
Réunion	Sao Tome and Principe		Mauritania
Rwanda		Botswana	Niger
Seychelles*		Lesotho	Nigeria
Somalia		Namibia	St. Helena*
Uganda		South Africa	Senegal
United Republic of		Swaziland	Sierra Leone
Tanzania			Togo
Zambia			
Zimbabwe			

Asia

Eastern Asia	South-central Asia	South-eastern Asia	Western Asia
China	Afghanistan	Brunei Darussalam	Armenia
China, Hong Kong SAR	Bangladesh	Cambodia	Azerbaijan
China, Macao SAR	Bhutan	East Timor	Bahrain
Democratic People's	India	Indonesia	Cyprus
Republic of Korea	Iran (Islamic	Lao People's	Georgia
Japan	Republic of)	Democratic	Iraq
Mongolia	Kazakhstan	Republic	Israel
Republic of Korea	Kyrgyzstan	Malaysia	Jordan
	Maldives	Myanmar	Kuwait
	Nepal	Philippines	Lebanon
	Pakistan	Singapore	Occupied
	Sri Lanka	Thailand	Palestinian
	Tajikistan	Viet Nam	Territory
	Turkmenistan		Oman
	Uzbekistan		Qatar
			Saudi Arabia
			Syrian Arab
			Republic
			Turkey
			United Arab Emirates
			Yemen

Europe

Eastern Europe
Belarus
Bulgaria
Czech Republic
Hungary
Poland
Republic of Moldova
Romania
Russian Federation
Slovakia
Ukraine

Northern Europe
Channel Islands
Denmark
Estonia
Faeroe Islands*
Finland
Iceland
Ireland
Isle of Man*
Latvia
Lithuania
Norway
Sweden
United Kingdom of
    Great Britain and
    Northern Ireland

Southern Europe
Albania
Andorra*
Bosnia and
    Herzegovina
Croatia
Gibraltar*
Greece
Holy See*
Italy
Malta
Portugal
San Marino*
Serbia and
    Montenegro
Slovenia
Spain
The former Yugoslav
    Republic of
    Macedonia

Western Europe
Austria
Belgium
France
Germany
Liechtenstein*
Luxembourg
Monaco*
Netherlands
Switzerland

Latin America and the Caribbean

Caribbean
Anguilla*
Antigua and Barbuda*
Aruba*
Bahamas
Barbados
British Virgin Islands*
Cayman Islands*
Cuba
Dominica*
Dominican Republic
Grenada*
Guadeloupe
Haiti
Jamaica
Martinique
Montserrat*
Netherlands Antilles
Puerto Rico
Saint Kitts and Nevis*
Saint Lucia
Saint Vincent and the
    Grenadines
Trinidad and Tobago
Turks and Caicos
    Islands*
United States Virgin
    Islands

Central America
Belize
Costa Rica
El Salvador
Guatemala
Honduras
Mexico
Nicaragua
Panama

South America
Argentina
Bolivia
Brazil
Chile
Colombia
Ecuador
Falkland Islands
    (Malvinas)*
French Guiana
Guyana
Paraguay
Peru
Suriname
Uruguay
Venezuela

Northern America

Bermuda*
Canada
Greenland*

St. Pierre and Miquelon*
United States of America

Oceania

Australia/New Zealand

Australia

New Zealand

Melanesia

Fiji

New Caledonia

Papua New Guinea

Solomon Islands

Vanuatu

Micronesia

Guam

Kiribati*

Marshall Islands*

Micronesia (Federated States of)

Nauru*

Northern Mariana Islands*

Palau*

Polynesia

American Samoa*

Cook Islands*

French Polynesia

Niue*

Pitcairn*

Samoa

Tokelau*

Tonga

Tuvalu*

Wallis and Futuna Islands*

List of least developed countries

Afghanistan

Angola

Bangladesh

Benin

Bhutan

Burkina Faso

Burundi

Cambodia

Cape Verde

Central African Republic

Chad

Comoros

Democratic Republic of the Congo

Democratic Republic of Timor-Leste

Djibouti

Equatorial Guinea

Eritrea

Ethiopia

Gambia

Guinea

Guinea-Bissau

Haiti

Kiribati

Lao People's Democratic Republic

Lesotho

Liberia

Madagascar

Malawi

Maldives

Mali

Mauritania

Mozambique

Myanmar

Nepal

Niger

Rwanda

Samoa

Sao Tome and Principe

Senegal

Sierra Leone

Solomon Islands

Somalia

Sudan

Togo

Tuvalu

Uganda

United Republic of Tanzania

Vanuatu

Yemen

Zambia

Note: Countries or areas with a population of less than 100,000 in 2005 are indicated by an asterisk (*). These countries or areas are included in the regional totals, but are not shown separately.

Annex III
Summary tables

Table A.III.1

Population aged 60 or over, 65 or over and 80 or over by sex (thousands): world, major areas and regions, 2007

Major areas and regions	60 or over			65 or over			80 or over		
	Total	Male	Female	Total	Male	Female	Total	Male	Female
World	1 409 635	317 734	387 083	990 251	216 070	279 055	188 348	33 728	60 446
More developed regions	504 051	106 132	145 894	377 601	76 218	112 582	95 745	15 262	32 611
Less developed regions	905 583	211 602	241 189	612 651	139 852	166 473	92 603	18 466	27 835
Least developed countries	81 489	18 665	22 079	52 021	11 746	14 265	6 036	1 271	1 747
Africa	100 112	22 694	27 362	64 966	14 430	18 053	7 667	1 540	2 294
Eastern Africa	28 090	6 352	7 693	18 097	4 032	5 017	2 146	439	634
Middle Africa	10 480	2 332	2 908	6 708	1 464	1 891	750	146	229
Northern Africa	27 299	6 258	7 391	18 375	4 116	5 071	2 346	482	692
Southern Africa	7 692	1 585	2 261	4 898	959	1 490	636	95	223
Western Africa	26 551	6 166	7 109	16 887	3 859	4 585	1 789	378	517
Asia	770 818	180 710	204 699	527 382	120 472	143 219	83 906	16 219	25 734
Eastern Asia	397 928	93 384	105 580	277 463	62 948	75 783	48 595	8 565	15 732
South-central Asia	250 518	59 398	65 861	167 244	39 051	44 571	24 228	5 394	6 720
South-eastern Asia	92 725	21 120	25 243	62 326	13 917	17 246	8 314	1 710	2 447
Western Asia	29 647	6 809	8 015	20 350	4 556	5 619	2 769	549	835
Europe	306 952	62 778	90 698	233 688	45 704	71 140	55 699	8 411	19 438
Eastern Europe	108 065	19 713	34 320	82 966	14 348	27 135	15 989	2 019	5 976
Northern Europe	41 830	9 192	11 724	30 714	6 480	8 877	8 544	1 438	2 834
Southern Europe	69 730	15 060	19 805	53 510	11 167	15 588	13 457	2 298	4 431
Western Europe	87 327	18 814	24 849	66 499	13 710	19 540	17 709	2 657	6 198
Latin America and the Caribbean	105 393	23 706	28 990	72 965	16 057	20 425	14 761	2 921	4 459
Caribbean	8 813	2 030	2 377	6 172	1 403	1 683	1 307	277	377
Central America	23 628	5 439	6 374	16 255	3 696	4 431	3 172	664	922
South America	72 952	16 237	20 239	50 539	10 959	14 311	10 282	1 981	3 160
Northern America	116 588	25 573	32 721	84 308	17 842	24 312	24 494	4 296	7 951
Oceania	9 772	2 273	2 613	6 942	1 565	1 906	1 821	340	570
Australia/New Zealand	8 866	2 046	2 387	6 382	1 427	1 764	1 757	325	553
Polynesia	105	25	27	70	17	19	11	2	4
Melanesia	720	183	178	438	110	109	45	11	12
Micronesia	81	19	21	52	12	14	7	2	2

Table A.III.2

Percentage of population aged 60 or over, 65 or over and 80 or over by sex: world, major areas and regions, 2007

Major areas and regions	60 or over			65 or over			80 or over		
	Total	Male	Female	Total	Male	Female	Total	Male	Female
World	10.7	9.6	11.8	7.5	6.5	8.5	1.4	1.0	1.8
More developed regions	20.7	18.0	23.3	15.5	12.9	18.0	3.9	2.6	5.2
Less developed regions	8.4	7.7	9.1	5.7	5.1	6.2	0.9	0.7	1.0
Least developed countries	5.1	4.7	5.6	3.3	2.9	3.6	0.4	0.3	0.4
Africa	5.3	4.8	5.8	3.4	3.1	3.8	0.4	0.3	0.5
Eastern Africa	4.7	4.2	5.1	3.0	2.7	3.3	0.4	0.3	0.4
Middle Africa	4.5	4.1	5.0	2.9	2.6	3.2	0.3	0.3	0.4
Northern Africa	6.9	6.3	7.5	4.6	4.1	5.2	0.6	0.5	0.7
Southern Africa	7.1	5.9	8.2	4.5	3.6	5.4	0.6	0.4	0.8
Western Africa	4.8	4.4	5.2	3.1	2.8	3.4	0.3	0.3	0.4
Asia	9.6	8.9	10.4	6.6	5.9	7.3	1.0	0.8	1.3
Eastern Asia	12.9	11.9	14.0	9.0	8.0	10.0	1.6	1.1	2.1
South-central Asia	7.5	7.0	8.1	5.0	4.6	5.5	0.7	0.6	0.8
South-eastern Asia	8.1	7.4	8.8	5.5	4.9	6.0	0.7	0.6	0.9
Western Asia	6.7	6.0	7.4	4.6	4.0	5.2	0.6	0.5	0.8
Europe	21.1	17.9	24.0	16.1	13.1	18.8	3.8	2.4	5.1
Eastern Europe	18.3	14.3	22.0	14.1	10.4	17.4	2.7	1.5	3.8
Northern Europe	21.7	19.5	23.8	15.9	13.7	18.0	4.4	3.1	5.8
Southern Europe	23.2	20.5	25.8	17.8	15.2	20.3	4.5	3.1	5.8
Western Europe	23.4	20.6	26.1	17.8	15.0	20.5	4.7	2.9	6.5
Latin America and the Caribbean	9.1	8.3	9.9	6.3	5.6	7.0	1.3	1.0	1.5
Caribbean	11.1	10.3	11.8	7.8	7.1	8.4	1.6	1.4	1.9
Central America	7.8	7.3	8.3	5.4	5.0	5.7	1.0	0.9	1.2
South America	9.5	8.5	10.4	6.6	5.8	7.3	1.3	1.0	1.6
Northern America	17.3	15.4	19.1	12.5	10.8	14.2	3.6	2.6	4.7
Oceania	14.4	13.5	15.4	10.3	9.3	11.2	2.7	2.0	3.4
Australia/New Zealand	18.0	16.8	19.1	12.9	11.7	14.1	3.6	2.7	4.4
Polynesia	7.8	7.4	8.3	5.3	4.8	5.7	0.8	0.6	1.1
Melanesia	4.5	4.5	4.6	2.8	2.7	2.8	0.3	0.3	0.3

Table A.III.3
Selected indicators on ageing: world, major areas and regions, 2007

Major areas and regions	Ageing index	Broad age groups (percentage)			Median age	Dependency ratios		
		0-14	15-59	60+		Total	Youth	Old-age
World	38.7	27.6	61.8	10.7	28.1	53.9	42.4	11.5
More developed regions	124.2	16.7	62.6	20.7	38.6	47.4	24.6	22.9
Less developed regions	28.0	30.0	61.6	8.4	25.6	55.5	46.7	8.8
Least developed countries	12.4	41.3	53.6	5.1	18.9	80.4	74.5	5.9
Africa	12.9	41.1	53.6	5.3	18.9	80.2	74.0	6.2
Eastern Africa	10.6	44.0	51.3	4.7	17.5	88.7	83.0	5.7
Middle Africa	9.9	45.9	49.6	4.5	16.8	95.4	89.7	5.7
Northern Africa	21.4	32.3	60.8	6.9	23.0	58.7	51.3	7.4
Southern Africa	21.5	33.0	59.9	7.1	23.0	60.0	52.8	7.2
Western Africa	11.0	43.7	51.5	4.8	17.6	87.7	81.9	5.7
Asia	35.8	27.0	63.4	9.6	27.7	50.5	40.6	9.9
Eastern Asia	65.1	19.8	67.2	12.9	33.5	40.5	27.9	12.7
South-central Asia	23.4	32.2	60.3	7.5	23.5	59.2	51.2	8.0
South-eastern Asia	28.4	28.7	63.2	8.1	25.7	51.8	43.5	8.3
Western Asia	20.1	33.1	60.2	6.7	23.6	60.6	53.2	7.3
Europe	136.2	15.5	63.4	21.1	39.0	46.1	22.6	23.5
Eastern Europe	123.4	14.9	66.8	18.3	37.5	40.8	20.9	19.8
Northern Europe	124.3	17.5	60.8	21.7	38.9	50.2	26.2	23.9
Southern Europe	155.6	14.9	61.9	23.2	39.8	48.7	22.2	26.5
Western Europe	147.3	15.9	60.7	23.4	40.7	50.9	24.0	26.9
Latin America and the Caribbean	31.3	29.2	61.6	9.1	25.9	55.1	45.3	9.8
Caribbean	40.8	27.1	61.8	11.1	28.0	53.6	41.7	11.9
Central America	24.6	31.7	60.5	7.8	24.0	58.9	50.4	8.5
South America	33.3	28.4	62.1	9.5	26.4	53.8	43.8	10.1
Northern America	86.1	20.1	62.6	17.3	36.3	48.4	29.8	18.6
Oceania	59.7	24.2	61.4	14.4	32.3	52.5	36.9	15.6
Australia/New Zealand	93.1	19.3	62.7	18.0	36.5	47.6	28.5	19.1
Polynesia	23.6	33.1	59.1	7.8	23.4	62.3	53.7	8.5
Melanesia	11.9	38.0	57.5	4.5	20.4	68.7	64.1	4.7
Micronesia	21.5	32.7	60.3	7.0	24.9	59.2	52.0	7.2

Potential support ratio	Parent support ratio	Sex ratios (per 100 women)			Growth rates (percentage)				Major areas and regions
		60+	65+	80+	Total	60+	65+	80+	
8.7	4.5	82.1	77.4	55.8	1.1	2.6	2.0	3.9	World
4.4	9.0	72.7	67.7	46.8	0.2	1.8	1.0	3.3	More developed regions
11.3	2.7	87.7	84.0	66.3	1.3	3.0	2.6	4.6	Less developed regions
17.0	1.6	84.5	82.3	72.8	2.3	2.9	3.0	3.8	Least developed countries
16.2	1.6	82.9	79.9	67.1	2.1	2.8	2.7	4.1	Africa
17.7	1.7	82.6	80.4	69.3	2.3	2.7	2.7	3.8	Eastern Africa
17.7	1.5	80.2	77.4	63.8	2.7	2.2	2.4	3.1	Middle Africa
13.6	1.9	84.7	81.2	69.6	1.7	3.2	2.5	5.2	Northern Africa
13.9	2.0	70.1	64.4	42.8	0.1	3.2	3.6	4.3	Southern Africa
17.4	1.3	86.7	84.2	73.2	2.3	2.5	2.8	3.5	Western Africa
10.1	3.1	88.3	84.1	63.0	1.1	3.0	2.6	4.7	Asia
7.9	3.8	88.4	83.1	54.4	0.5	3.1	2.4	4.8	Eastern Asia
12.5	2.6	90.2	87.6	80.3	1.5	2.8	2.7	4.5	South-central Asia
12.0	2.2	83.7	80.7	69.9	1.2	2.9	2.9	4.5	South-eastern Asia
13.6	2.1	84.9	81.1	65.8	1.9	2.7	2.2	6.0	Western Asia
4.3	8.1	69.2	64.2	43.3	−0.1	1.2	0.4	3.4	Europe
5.0	4.8	57.4	52.9	33.8	−0.5	0.6	−1.2	4.6	Eastern Europe
4.2	11.0	78.4	73.0	50.7	0.3	1.8	1.2	1.4	Northern Europe
3.8	9.9	76.0	71.6	51.9	0.2	1.4	1.0	4.2	Southern Europe
3.7	10.4	75.7	70.2	42.9	0.2	1.4	1.3	2.8	Western Europe
10.2	4.9	81.8	78.6	65.5	1.3	3.4	3.2	4.6	Latin America and the Caribbean
8.4	6.2	85.4	83.3	73.4	0.8	2.7	2.7	3.3	Caribbean
11.7	4.4	85.3	83.4	72.0	1.4	3.7	3.8	4.9	Central America
9.9	4.9	80.2	76.6	62.7	1.3	3.4	3.1	4.7	South America
5.4	9.8	78.2	73.4	54.0	0.9	2.6	1.8	1.7	Northern America
6.4	7.9	87.0	82.1	59.6	1.2	3.2	2.5	3.1	Oceania
5.2	9.0	85.7	80.8	58.8	1.0	3.2	2.5	3.1	Australia/New Zealand
11.7	3.1	93.9	89.3	58.9	0.9	2.5	3.0	3.5	Polynesia
21.5	1.2	102.9	100.5	95.7	1.7	3.3	2.7	2.8	Melanesia
13.9	1.8	89.3	84.6	71.3	1.6	4.7	3.2	3.9	Micronesia

Table A.III.4
Country ranking by percentage of population aged 60 or over, 2007

Country	60 or over	Rank	Country	60 or over	Rank
Japan	27.9	1	TFYR Macedonia	15.9	49
Italy	26.4	2	Ireland	15.5	50
Germany	25.3	3	Netherlands Antilles	14.9	51
Sweden	24.1	4	Republic of Korea	14.6	52
Greece	23.4	5	Guadeloupe	14.5	53
Austria	23.3	6	Armenia	14.4	54
Bulgaria	22.9	7	Argentina	14.1	55
Belgium	22.9	8	Republic of Moldova	13.9	56
Latvia	22.8	9	Israel	13.7	57
Portugal	22.8	10	Barbados	13.6	58
Switzerland	22.7	11	Singapore	13.5	59
Finland	22.6	12	Albania	12.4	60
Croatia	22.5	13	Chile	12.2	61
France	21.9	14	Dem. People's Rep. of Korea	11.8	62
Denmark	21.9	15	China, Macao SAR	11.5	63
Estonia	21.8	16	China	11.4	64
United Kingdom	21.8	17	Trinidad and Tobago	11.4	65
Spain	21.7	18	Sri Lanka	11.2	66
Hungary	21.3	19	Kazakhstan	11.1	67
Slovenia	21.2	20	Thailand	11.0	68
Czech Republic	21.1	21	Jamaica	10.3	69
Ukraine	21.0	22	Lebanon	10.3	70
Lithuania	20.9	23	Réunion	10.2	71
Norway	20.7	24	Mauritius	10.0	72
Channel Islands	20.1	25	Bahamas	9.8	73
Malta	20.1	26	Saint Lucia	9.7	74
Netherlands	20.1	27	New Caledonia	9.7	75
Bosnia and Herzegovina	19.9	28	Guam	9.4	76
Romania	19.5	29	Brazil	9.2	77
Serbia and Montenegro	18.8	30	Suriname	9.2	78
Canada	18.7	31	Panama	9.1	79
Luxembourg	18.4	32	Azerbaijan	9.1	80
Belarus	18.3	33	St. Vincent and the Grenadines	9.1	81
United States Virgin Islands	18.2	34	Tonga	8.9	82
Australia	18.1	35	Tunisia	8.8	83
Georgia	18.1	36	Costa Rica	8.7	84
Puerto Rico	17.5	37	Ecuador	8.6	85
Uruguay	17.5	38	Indonesia	8.5	86
Martinique	17.5	39	Mexico	8.2	87
Poland	17.4	40	Turkey	8.2	88
New Zealand	17.4	41	French Polynesia	8.2	89
Cyprus	17.4	42	India	8.1	90
United States of America	17.2	43	Venezuela	8.0	91
Russian Federation	17.1	44	Peru	8.0	92
Slovakia	16.8	45	Colombia	7.9	93
Iceland	16.4	46	Myanmar	7.9	94
China, Hong Kong SAR	16.1	47	El Salvador	7.8	95
Cuba	16.1	48	Guyana	7.7	96

Country	60 or over	Rank	Country	60 or over	Rank
Lesotho	7.6	97	Jordan	5.3	145
Kyrgyzstan	7.5	98	Mozambique	5.2	146
Viet Nam	7.4	99	Cape Verde	5.2	147
Malaysia	7.4	100	United Republic of Tanzania	5.2	148
Egypt	7.3	101	Tajikistan	5.0	149
South Africa	7.2	102	Nicaragua	5.0	150
Bhutan	7.1	103	Brunei Darussalam	5.0	151
Morocco	6.9	104	Maldives	5.0	152
French Guiana	6.9	105	Micronesia (Fed. States of)	5.0	153
Bolivia	6.9	106	Senegal	4.9	154
Libyan Arab Jamahiriya	6.9	107	Togo	4.9	155
Fiji	6.8	108	Timor-Leste	4.9	156
Algeria	6.6	109	Djibouti	4.9	157
Samoa	6.6	110	Bahrain	4.9	158
Iran (Islamic Republic of)	6.6	111	Madagascar	4.8	159
Dominican Republic	6.5	112	Syrian Arab Republic	4.8	160
Western Sahara	6.3	113	Nigeria	4.8	161
Philippines	6.3	114	Ethiopia	4.7	162
Guatemala	6.3	115	Malawi	4.7	163
Gabon	6.2	116	Zambia	4.7	164
Turkmenistan	6.1	117	Saudi Arabia	4.7	165
Gambia	6.1	118	Guinea-Bissau	4.6	166
Uzbekistan	6.1	119	Chad	4.6	167
Haiti	6.1	120	Iraq	4.5	168
Central African Republic	6.0	121	Congo	4.5	169
Belize	6.0	122	Occupied Palestinian Terr.	4.4	170
Pakistan	5.9	123	Comoros	4.4	171
Equatorial Guinea	5.9	124	Afghanistan	4.4	172
Nepal	5.9	125	Benin	4.4	173
Ghana	5.9	126	Oman	4.4	174
Cambodia	5.8	127	Dem. Rep. of the Congo	4.2	175
Sudan	5.8	128	Solomon Islands	4.2	176
Bangladesh	5.8	129	Burkina Faso	4.2	177
Honduras	5.7	130	Somalia	4.2	178
Guinea	5.7	131	Mali	4.1	179
Mongolia	5.7	132	Kenya	4.1	180
Paraguay	5.7	133	Burundi	4.1	181
Swaziland	5.7	134	Papua New Guinea	4.0	182
Cameroon	5.7	135	Eritrea	4.0	183
Zimbabwe	5.5	136	Rwanda	4.0	184
Botswana	5.5	137	Angola	3.9	185
Namibia	5.5	138	Uganda	3.8	186
Sierra Leone	5.5	139	Yemen	3.7	187
Sao Tome and Principe	5.4	140	Liberia	3.6	188
Côte d'Ivoire	5.4	141	Kuwait	3.4	189
Lao People's Dem. Republic	5.3	142	Niger	3.2	190
Vanuatu	5.3	143	Qatar	2.7	191
Mauritania	5.3	144	United Arab Emirates	1.7	192

Table A.III.5
Country ranking by median age, 2005

Country	Median age	Rank	Country	Median age	Rank
Japan	42.9	1	United States Virgin Islands	35.0	49
Italy	42.3	2	Barbados	34.7	50
Germany	42.1	3	TFYR Macedonia	34.2	51
Finland	40.9	4	Ireland	34.2	52
Switzerland	40.8	5	Iceland	34.1	53
Belgium	40.6	6	Guadeloupe	34.1	54
Croatia	40.6	7	Puerto Rico	33.3	55
Austria	40.6	8	Republic of Moldova	33.0	56
Bulgaria	40.6	9	China	32.6	57
Slovenia	40.2	10	Uruguay	32.1	58
Sweden	40.1	11	Armenia	31.7	59
Greece	39.7	12	Dem. People's Rep. of Korea	31.1	60
Channel Islands	39.7	13	Qatar	30.9	61
Denmark	39.5	14	Chile	30.6	62
Latvia	39.5	15	Thailand	30.5	63
Portugal	39.5	16	Mauritius	30.4	64
Netherlands	39.3	17	Bahrain	29.8	65
France	39.3	18	Sri Lanka	29.6	66
Czech Republic	39.0	19	Kuwait	29.5	67
Ukraine	39.0	20	Trinidad and Tobago	29.4	68
United Kingdom	39.0	21	Kazakhstan	29.4	69
China, Hong Kong SAR	38.9	22	Réunion	29.3	70
Estonia	38.9	23	United Arab Emirates	29.0	71
Hungary	38.8	24	Israel	28.9	72
Canada	38.6	25	Argentina	28.9	73
Spain	38.6	26	New Caledonia	28.4	74
Norway	38.2	27	Albania	28.3	75
Luxembourg	38.1	28	Guam	28.1	76
Malta	38.1	29	Bahamas	27.6	77
Bosnia and Herzegovina	38.0	30	Azerbaijan	27.5	78
Lithuania	37.8	31	French Polynesia	26.9	79
Belarus	37.8	32	Brazil	26.8	80
Singapore	37.5	33	Lebanon	26.8	81
Russian Federation	37.3	34	Tunisia	26.8	82
Romania	36.7	35	Indonesia	26.5	83
Australia	36.6	36	Turkey	26.3	84
China, Macao SAR	36.6	37	Brunei Darussalam	26.2	85
Poland	36.5	38	Costa Rica	26.1	86
Serbia and Montenegro	36.5	39	Panama	26.1	87
Martinique	36.4	40	Guyana	25.7	88
Netherlands Antilles	36.2	41	Saint Lucia	25.6	89
United States of America	36.1	42	Myanmar	25.5	90
New Zealand	35.8	43	Colombia	25.4	91
Slovakia	35.6	44	Suriname	25.1	92
Cuba	35.6	45	Mexico	25.0	93
Georgia	35.5	46	Jamaica	24.9	94
Cyprus	35.3	47	Viet Nam	24.9	95
Republic of Korea	35.1	48	Malaysia	24.7	96

Country	Median age	Rank	Country	Median age	Rank
Venezuela	24.7	97	Cape Verde	19.3	145
St. Vincent and the Grenadines	24.6	98	Lesotho	19.2	146
Fiji	24.5	99	Solomon Islands	19.2	147
India	24.3	100	Iraq	19.1	148
Morocco	24.2	101	Lao People's Dem. Republic	19.1	149
Peru	24.2	102	Maldives	18.9	150
Ecuador	24.0	103	Djibouti	18.9	151
French Guiana	24.0	104	Cameroon	18.8	152
Algeria	24.0	105	Zimbabwe	18.7	153
Libyan Arab Jamahiriya	23.9	106	Comoros	18.7	154
Kyrgyzstan	23.8	107	Namibia	18.6	155
Mongolia	23.7	108	Côte d'Ivoire	18.5	156
South Africa	23.5	109	Sierra Leone	18.4	157
Iran (Islamic Republic of)	23.4	110	Timor-Leste	18.4	158
Turkmenistan	23.3	111	Mauritania	18.4	159
Dominican Republic	23.3	112	United Republic of Tanzania	18.2	160
El Salvador	23.3	113	Senegal	18.2	161
Egypt	22.8	114	Swaziland	18.1	162
Western Sahara	22.7	115	Guatemala	18.1	163
Uzbekistan	22.6	116	Central African Republic	18.1	164
Oman	22.3	117	Guinea	18.0	165
Philippines	22.2	118	Kenya	17.9	166
Bangladesh	22.1	119	Togo	17.9	167
Tonga	21.8	120	Somalia	17.9	168
Saudi Arabia	21.6	121	Madagascar	17.8	169
Jordan	21.3	122	Mozambique	17.7	170
Belize	21.2	123	Benin	17.6	171
Bolivia	20.8	124	Equatorial Guinea	17.6	172
Paraguay	20.8	125	Nigeria	17.5	173
Syrian Arab Republic	20.6	126	Ethiopia	17.5	174
Cambodia	20.3	127	Rwanda	17.5	175
Sudan	20.1	128	Eritrea	17.4	176
Nepal	20.1	129	Occupied Palestinian Terr.	17.1	177
Bhutan	20.1	130	Burundi	17.0	178
Pakistan	20.0	131	Zambia	16.7	179
Haiti	20.0	132	Afghanistan	16.7	180
Botswana	19.9	133	Angola	16.6	181
Ghana	19.8	134	Yemen	16.5	182
Honduras	19.8	135	Liberia	16.3	183
Gambia	19.8	136	Congo	16.3	184
Nicaragua	19.7	137	Chad	16.3	185
Papua New Guinea	19.7	138	Malawi	16.3	186
Vanuatu	19.6	139	Dem. Rep. of the Congo	16.3	187
Micronesia (Fed. States of)	19.6	140	Burkina Faso	16.2	188
Sao Tome and Principe	19.6	141	Guinea-Bissau	16.2	189
Gabon	19.4	142	Mali	15.8	190
Samoa	19.4	143	Niger	15.5	191
Tajikistan	19.3	144	Uganda	14.8	192

Table A.III.6
Country ranking by ageing index, 2007

Country	Ageing index	Rank	Country	Ageing index	Rank
Japan	201.0	1	China, Macao SAR	79.7	49
Italy	189.8	2	United States Virgin Islands	79.5	50
Germany	182.3	3	Ireland	77.0	51
Bulgaria	172.5	4	Iceland	76.7	52
Greece	166.0	5	Armenia	74.9	53
Latvia	164.4	6	Singapore	74.8	54
Austria	156.1	7	Barbados	74.0	55
Slovenia	155.9	8	Uruguay	73.2	56
Czech Republic	150.7	9	Netherlands Antilles	68.3	57
Croatia	150.0	10	Guadeloupe	59.9	58
Ukraine	149.5	11	China	55.9	59
Spain	149.2	12	Trinidad and Tobago	54.9	60
Estonia	148.3	13	Argentina	54.8	61
Portugal	144.3	14	Chile	51.5	62
Switzerland	142.9	15	Kazakhstan	50.1	63
Sweden	142.8	16	Israel	49.7	64
Hungary	140.1	17	Dem. People's Rep. of Korea	49.1	65
Belgium	139.2	18	Albania	48.0	66
Lithuania	134.3	19	Sri Lanka	47.9	67
Finland	134.3	20	Thailand	47.5	68
Romania	130.3	21	Mauritius	42.0	69
Belarus	126.9	22	Azerbaijan	38.0	70
Channel Islands	126.3	23	Réunion	37.9	71
Bosnia and Herzegovina	125.5	24	Lebanon	37.2	72
United Kingdom	124.7	25	Tunisia	35.6	73
France	121.1	26	Bahamas	35.4	74
Malta	119.9	27	New Caledonia	35.4	75
Denmark	117.9	28	Saint Lucia	35.4	76
China, Hong Kong SAR	116.1	29	Jamaica	34.2	77
Russian Federation	114.0	30	Brazil	33.7	78
Netherlands	112.6	31	St. Vincent and the Grenadines	32.1	79
Poland	112.3	32	Costa Rica	31.9	80
Canada	110.3	33	Guam	31.9	81
Norway	108.0	34	Suriname	31.0	82
Slovakia	106.1	35	Indonesia	30.9	83
Serbia and Montenegro	105.4	36	Panama	30.6	84
Georgia	101.2	37	French Polynesia	30.2	85
Luxembourg	98.6	38	Turkey	28.6	86
Australia	95.0	39	Myanmar	28.1	87
Cyprus	91.8	40	Mexico	27.6	88
Cuba	87.4	41	Ecuador	27.3	89
TFYR Macedonia	85.5	42	Guyana	26.9	90
Martinique	84.3	43	Viet Nam	26.5	91
New Zealand	84.0	44	Venezuela	26.5	92
United States of America	83.9	45	Colombia	26.2	93
Republic of Korea	83.4	46	India	26.1	94
Republic of Moldova	81.6	47	Peru	25.7	95
Puerto Rico	81.1	48	Tonga	25.6	96

Country	Ageing index	Rank	Country	Ageing index	Rank
Kyrgyzstan	24.8	97	Syrian Arab Republic	13.3	145
Iran (Islamic Republic of)	24.5	98	Lao People's Dem. Republic	13.3	146
El Salvador	23.6	99	Nicaragua	13.3	147
Malaysia	23.5	100	Equatorial Guinea	13.2	148
Algeria	23.2	101	Guinea	13.2	149
Libyan Arab Jamahiriya	23.1	102	Côte d'Ivoire	13.0	150
Morocco	22.8	103	Oman	13.0	151
South Africa	22.4	104	Saudi Arabia	12.9	152
Egypt	22.2	105	Micronesia (Fed. States of)	12.8	153
Fiji	21.9	106	Sierra Leone	12.8	154
French Guiana	20.7	107	Maldives	12.6	155
Dominican Republic	20.4	108	Qatar	12.6	156
Turkmenistan	20.4	109	United Republic of Tanzania	12.4	157
Lesotho	20.1	110	Mauritania	12.3	158
Mongolia	19.6	111	Mozambique	12.0	159
Uzbekistan	19.3	112	Djibouti	12.0	160
Western Sahara	19.1	113	Timor-Leste	11.8	161
Bhutan	19.0	114	Senegal	11.8	162
Bahrain	18.7	115	Togo	11.4	163
Bolivia	18.5	116	Iraq	11.2	164
Philippines	18.5	117	Madagascar	11.1	165
Brunei Darussalam	17.4	118	Nigeria	11.0	166
Belize	17.0	119	Ethiopia	10.7	167
Bangladesh	16.7	120	Comoros	10.6	168
Haiti	16.5	121	Solomon Islands	10.5	169
Samoa	16.3	122	Zambia	10.3	170
Cambodia	16.2	123	Papua New Guinea	10.2	171
Gabon	15.9	124	Benin	10.0	172
Pakistan	15.8	125	Malawi	9.9	173
Paraguay	15.5	126	Occupied Palestinian Terr.	9.8	174
Nepal	15.5	127	Guinea-Bissau	9.7	175
Gambia	15.4	128	Chad	9.7	176
Ghana	15.4	129	Kenya	9.6	177
Honduras	15.0	130	Afghanistan	9.5	178
Sudan	15.0	131	Congo	9.4	179
Botswana	14.9	132	Somalia	9.4	180
Guatemala	14.7	133	Rwanda	9.3	181
Jordan	14.5	134	Burundi	9.2	182
Swaziland	14.3	135	Eritrea	9.0	183
Zimbabwe	14.2	136	Dem. Rep. of the Congo	8.9	184
Central African Republic	14.2	137	Burkina Faso	8.9	185
Kuwait	14.1	138	Mali	8.6	186
Cameroon	14.0	139	Angola	8.5	187
Sao Tome and Principe	13.9	140	Yemen	8.0	188
Namibia	13.8	141	United Arab Emirates	7.9	189
Vanuatu	13.6	142	Liberia	7.7	190
Cape Verde	13.5	143	Uganda	7.4	191
Tajikistan	13.4	144	Niger	6.6	192

Annex IV
Profiles of ageing

Table A.IV.1
Profiles of ageing by major area and region

World

Indicator	Age	1950	1975	2007	2025	2050
Population (thousands)						
Total	Total	2 519 469.8	4 073 739.8	6 615 852.1	7 905 239.3	9 075 902.8
	0-14	864 139.2	1 497 563.8	1 822 801.5	1 909 249.0	1 832 572.5
	15-59	1 449 967.8	2 226 438.0	4 088 233.1	4 803 387.5	5 275 177.2
	60-64	74 487.9	118 078.1	209 691.9	360 452.0	503 215.5
	65-69	56 547.9	94 333.5	170 854.5	290 322.9	430 577.7
	70-74	38 290.2	66 301.8	134 662.0	229 798.0	350 409.2
	75-79	22 256.7	39 573.6	95 435.1	151 811.1	289 726.8
	80-84			57 460.0	87 293.8	205 929.4
	85-89			25 272.0	47 127.4	116 979.6
	90-94	13 780.0	31 451.0	8 930.2	19 073.1	50 770.1
	95-99			2 201.0	5 666.2	16 806.2
	100+			310.7	1 058.1	3 738.6
Female	Total	1 262 368.4	2 026 880.2	3 291 804.8	3 944 539.4	4 552 428.4
	0-14	423 039.4	730 450.8	887 839.7	931 317.3	895 252.2
	15-59	725 228.5	1 100 062.4	2 016 881.7	2 365 832.0	2 590 752.5
	60-64	39 494.9	62 964.6	108 028.2	185 253.9	253 748.1
	65-69	31 371.2	51 828.8	90 473.9	152 022.0	222 127.7
	70-74	21 642.5	37 893.4	73 549.8	124 167.8	186 205.3
	75-79	13 049.0	23 781.2	54 585.5	85 350.8	160 119.9
	80-84			35 364.4	51 795.2	120 187.5
	85-89			16 716.7	30 199.4	73 368.4
	90-94	8 543.0	19 898.9	6 403.8	13 335.9	34 774.8
	95-99			1 707.6	4 375.2	12 757.2
	100+			253.4	889.9	3 134.9
Male	Total	1 257 101.4	2 046 859.7	3 324 047.2	3 960 699.9	4 523 474.4
	0-14	441 099.8	767 113.0	934 961.7	977 931.8	937 320.3
	15-59	724 739.4	1 126 375.6	2 071 351.4	2 437 555.5	2 684 424.7
	60-64	34 993.0	55 113.5	101 663.7	175 198.1	249 467.4
	65-69	25 176.7	42 504.7	80 380.6	138 301.0	208 450.0
	70-74	16 647.7	28 408.4	61 112.2	105 630.2	164 203.9
	75-79	9 207.7	15 792.5	40 849.6	66 460.3	129 607.0
	80-84			22 095.6	35 498.6	85 741.9
	85-89			8 555.3	16 928.0	43 611.2
	90-94	5 237.1	11 552.1	2 526.4	5 737.2	15 995.3
	95-99			493.4	1 291.0	4 048.9
	100+			57.3	168.2	603.7
Percentage in older ages						
Total	60+	8.2	8.6	10.7	15.1	21.7
	65+	5.2	5.7	7.5	10.5	16.1
	80+	0.5	0.8	1.4	2.0	4.3
Female	60+	9.0	9.7	11.8	16.4	23.4
	65+	5.9	6.6	8.5	11.7	17.9
	80+	0.7	1.0	1.8	2.6	5.4
Male	60+	7.3	7.5	9.6	13.8	19.9
	65+	4.5	4.8	6.5	9.3	14.4
	80+	0.4	0.6	1.0	1.5	3.3
Ageing index		23.8	23.4	38.7	62.5	107.4
Broad age groups (percentage)	0-14	34.3	36.8	27.6	24.2	20.2
	15-59	57.6	54.7	61.8	60.8	58.1
	60+	8.2	8.6	10.7	15.1	21.7
Median age (years)		23.9	22.4	28.1*	32.8	37.8
Dependency ratio	Total	65.3	73.8	53.9	53.1	57.1
	Youth	56.7	63.9	42.4	37.0	31.7
	Old Age	8.6	9.9	11.5	16.1	25.4
Potential support ratio		11.6	10.1	8.7	6.2	3.9
Parent support ratio		1.8	2.6	4.5	5.9	12.0
Sex ratio (per 100 women)	60+	80.0	78.1	82.1	84.2	84.6
	65+	75.4	73.7	77.4	80.1	80.3
	80+	61.3	58.1	55.8	59.3	61.4

* *Estimate refers to year 2005.*

Indicator	Age	1950-1955	1975-1980	2005-2010	2025-2030	2045-2050
Growth rate (percentage)	Total	1.8	1.7	1.1	0.7	0.4
	60+	1.8	1.8	2.6	2.7	1.7
	65+	2.1	2.6	2.0	3.0	1.6
	80+	3.1	2.7	3.9	3.8	3.0
Total fertility rate (per woman)		5.0	3.9	2.5	2.2	2.0
Life expectancy (years)						
Total	Birth	46.6	59.9	66.5	71.1	75.1
	60	..	..	19.6	21.2	22.4
	65	..	..	16.0	17.4	18.5
	80	..	..	7.7	8.5	9.0
Female	Birth	48.0	61.7	68.7	73.5	77.5
	60	..	..	21.2	23.0	24.3
	65	..	..	17.3	19.0	20.2
	80	..	..	8.3	9.2	9.9
Male	Birth	45.3	58.2	64.3	68.8	72.8
	60	..	..	17.9	19.4	20.5
	65	..	..	14.5	15.8	16.8
	80	..	..	6.8	7.4	7.9
Survival rate (percentage)						
Total	60	..	..	74.1	79.8	84.9
	65	..	..	68.5	75.0	80.5
	80	..	..	36.5	44.7	51.7
Female	60	..	..	77.1	82.3	86.9
	65	..	..	72.5	78.5	83.6
	80	..	..	43.2	51.8	58.9
Male	60	..	..	71.3	77.4	83.0
	65	..	..	64.5	71.5	77.6
	80	..	..	30.1	37.8	44.6

		1980	1990	2007	2010	2020
Labour force participation (percentage)						
Total	65+	19.6	19.8	19.5	19.4	19.0
Female	65+	9.5	10.4	11.5	11.9	12.8
Male	65+	33.5	32.5	29.8	29.1	26.8

Percentage married, age 60+				Percentage living alone, age 60+		
Total	Female	Male		Total	Female	Male
62.2	47.6	80.1		14.0	19.0	8.0

Statutory pensionable age (2006)				Percentage illiterate, age 65+		
	Female	Male		Total	Female	Male
	–	–		..	..	..

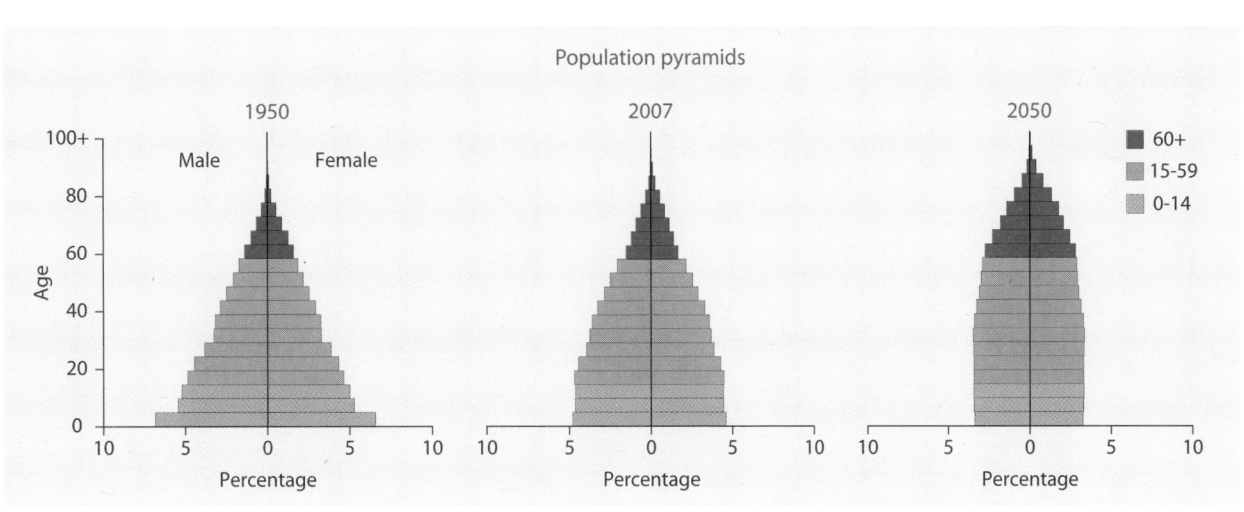

Population pyramids

United Nations Department of Economic and Social Affairs, Population Division

More developed regions

Indicator	Age	1950	1975	2007	2025	2050
Population (thousands)						
Total	Total	812 771.7	1 047 196.4	1 217 483.8	1 248 954.1	1 236 200.5
	0-14	222 314.4	253 657.3	202 990.3	195 886.1	193 420.2
	15-59	495 109.8	632 037.3	762 467.8	710 117.1	642 751.3
	60-64	31 313.8	48 995.7	63 225.5	82 652.7	79 291.1
	65-69	25 243.4	42 066.3	55 317.9	75 938.8	75 316.3
	70-74	18 562.7	31 514.3	47 146.7	64 849.2	68 313.2
	75-79	11 709.4	20 547.8	38 463.1	51 573.9	61 311.1
	80-84			27 408.7	32 760.4	49 654.8
	85-89			13 200.9	20 908.0	35 825.0
	90-94	8 518.1	18 377.8	5 500.1	9 967.7	19 812.2
	95-99			1 543.4	3 563.1	8 099.2
	100+			219.4	737.1	2 405.9
Female	Total	425 514.6	541 471.2	626 850.4	643 492.9	635 809.6
	0-14	109 405.1	123 934.2	98 884.3	95 378.4	94 166.1
	15-59	261 227.2	320 673.3	382 072.2	353 594.6	316 941.5
	60-64	17 436.4	27 819.4	33 311.9	43 310.5	40 557.2
	65-69	14 322.1	24 401.3	30 242.2	40 929.9	39 346.6
	70-74	10 739.9	19 029.9	26 754.8	36 076.9	36 695.6
	75-79	6 975.5	13 093.1	22 974.4	29 680.7	34 176.0
	80-84			17 829.0	19 952.6	29 169.0
	85-89			9 216.2	13 871.3	22 668.2
	90-94	5 408.3	12 520.1	4 131.9	7 205.5	13 771.7
	95-99			1 246.2	2 846.1	6 247.4
	100+			187.3	646.4	2 070.3
Male	Total	387 257.1	505 725.2	590 633.4	605 461.2	600 390.9
	0-14	112 909.3	129 723.1	104 106.0	100 507.7	99 254.1
	15-59	233 882.6	311 364.0	380 395.7	356 522.5	325 809.9
	60-64	13 877.4	21 176.2	29 913.6	39 342.2	38 734.0
	65-69	10 921.3	17 665.0	25 075.7	35 008.9	35 969.7
	70-74	7 822.8	12 484.5	20 391.9	28 772.3	31 617.6
	75-79	4 733.9	7 454.7	15 488.7	21 893.2	27 135.1
	80-84			9 579.7	12 807.8	20 485.8
	85-89			3 984.7	7 036.7	13 156.8
	90-94	3 109.8	5 857.7	1 368.3	2 762.3	6 040.6
	95-99			297.2	717.0	1 851.9
	100+			32.1	90.7	335.6
Percentage in older ages						
Total	60+	11.7	15.4	20.7	27.5	32.4
	65+	7.9	10.7	15.5	20.8	25.9
	80+	1.0	1.8	3.9	5.4	9.4
Female	60+	12.9	17.9	23.3	30.2	35.3
	65+	8.8	12.8	18.0	23.5	29.0
	80+	1.3	2.3	5.2	6.9	11.6
Male	60+	10.4	12.8	18.0	24.5	29.2
	65+	6.9	8.6	12.9	18.0	22.8
	80+	0.8	1.2	2.6	3.9	7.0
Ageing index		42.9	63.7	124.2	175.1	206.8
Broad age groups (percentage)	0-14	27.4	24.2	16.7	15.7	15.6
	15-59	60.9	60.4	62.6	56.9	52.0
	60+	11.7	15.4	20.7	27.5	32.4
Median age (years)		29.0	31.0	38.6*	43.1	45.5
Dependency ratio	Total	54.4	53.8	47.4	57.5	71.2
	Youth	42.2	37.2	24.6	24.7	26.8
	Old Age	12.2	16.5	22.9	32.8	44.4
Potential support ratio		8.2	6.1	4.4	3.0	2.3
Parent support ratio		2.9	4.4	9.0	14.1	29.1
Sex ratio (per 100 women)	60+	73.7	66.7	72.7	76.3	78.0
	65+	71.0	62.9	67.7	72.1	74.2
	80+	57.5	46.8	46.8	52.6	56.6

*   *Estimate refers to year 2005.*

Indicator	Age	1950-1955	1975-1980	2005-2010	2025-2030	2045-2050
Growth rate (percentage)	Total	1.2	0.7	0.2	0.0	−0.1
	60+	1.8	0.8	1.8	1.1	0.3
	65+	2.1	2.3	1.0	1.6	0.4
	80+	3.2	3.6	3.3	3.1	1.0
Total fertility rate (per woman)		2.8	1.9	1.6	1.7	1.8
Life expectancy (years)						
Total	Birth	66.1	72.3	76.2	79.5	82.1
	60	..	..	21.6	23.5	25.0
	65	..	..	17.8	19.5	20.9
	80	..	..	8.5	9.6	10.4
Female	Birth	68.5	75.9	79.9	82.7	85.0
	60	..	..	23.6	25.7	27.3
	65	..	..	19.5	21.4	23.0
	80	..	..	9.2	10.6	11.5
Male	Birth	63.5	68.6	72.6	76.3	79.1
	60	..	..	19.3	21.1	22.6
	65	..	..	15.7	17.3	18.7
	80	..	..	7.4	8.3	9.0
Survival rate (percentage)						
Total	60	..	..	86.2	90.1	92.9
	65	..	..	81.2	85.9	89.3
	80	..	..	49.9	58.2	65.1
Female	60	..	..	91.1	93.2	94.9
	65	..	..	87.5	90.2	92.5
	80	..	..	60.3	67.5	73.5
Male	60	..	..	81.3	87.0	90.8
	65	..	..	74.9	81.5	86.1
	80	..	..	39.5	48.6	56.4

		1980	1990	2007	2010	2020
Labour force participation (percentage)						
Total	65+	10.1	9.5	9.1	9.0	8.8
Female	65+	6.1	6.5	6.5	6.7	7.0
Male	65+	16.6	14.3	12.9	12.4	11.3

Percentage married, age 60+				Percentage living alone, age 60+		
Total	Female	Male		Total	Female	Male
61.0	48.0	79.3		..	..	..

Statutory pensionable age (2006)				Percentage illiterate, age 65+		
	Female	Male		Total	Female	Male
	–	–		..	..	..

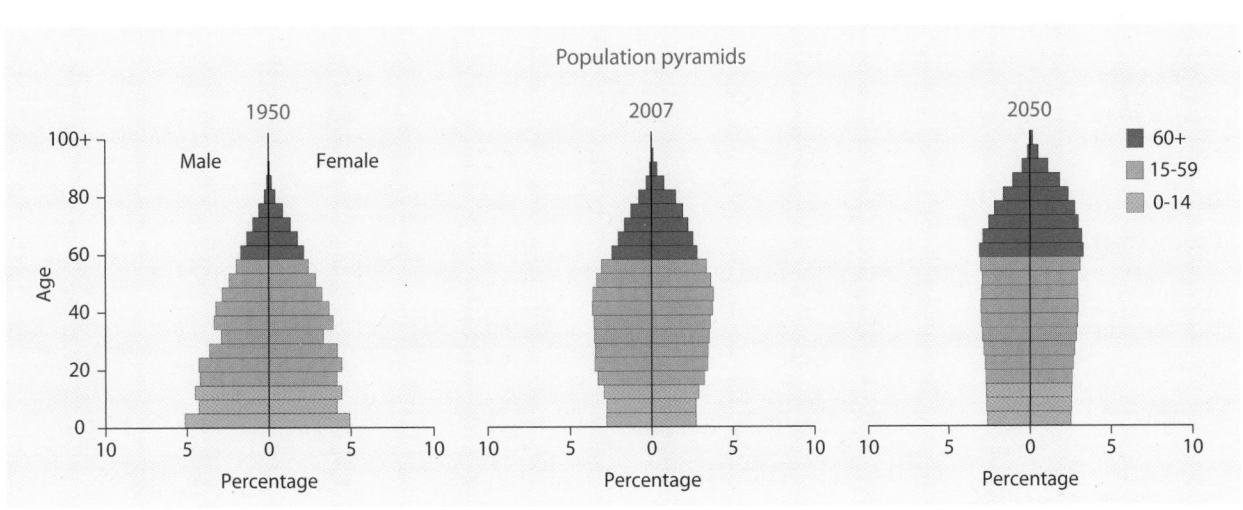

Population pyramids

1950   2007   2050

60+
15-59
0-14

Male   Female

Less developed regions

Indicator	Age	1950	1975	2007	2025	2050
Population (thousands)						
Total	Total	1 706 698.1	3 026 543.4	5 398 368.2	6 656 285.2	7 839 702.3
	0-14	641 824.8	1 243 906.6	1 619 811.2	1 713 362.9	1 639 152.2
	15-59	954 858.0	1 594 400.7	3 325 765.3	4 093 270.5	4 632 425.9
	60-64	43 174.1	69 082.4	146 466.4	277 799.3	423 924.3
	65-69	31 304.5	52 267.2	115 536.6	214 384.1	355 261.5
	70-74	19 727.5	34 787.5	87 515.3	164 948.8	282 096.0
	75-79	10 547.3	19 025.8	56 972.0	100 237.2	228 415.7
	80-84			30 051.3	54 533.5	156 274.6
	85-89			12 071.1	26 219.4	81 154.7
	90-94	5 261.9	13 073.2	3 430.1	9 105.3	30 957.9
	95-99			657.6	2 103.0	8 706.9
	100+			91.3	321.0	1 332.7
Female	Total	836 853.8	1 485 409.0	2 664 954.4	3 301 046.6	3 916 618.9
	0-14	313 634.3	606 516.6	788 955.4	835 938.8	801 086.0
	15-59	464 001.2	779 389.1	1 634 809.5	2 012 237.5	2 273 811.0
	60-64	22 058.5	35 145.2	74 716.3	141 943.4	213 190.9
	65-69	17 049.1	27 427.5	60 231.7	111 092.0	182 781.1
	70-74	10 902.5	18 863.6	46 794.9	88 091.0	149 509.7
	75-79	6 073.5	10 688.1	31 611.1	55 670.1	125 943.9
	80-84			17 535.5	31 842.6	91 018.4
	85-89			7 500.5	16 328.1	50 700.2
	90-94	3 134.7	7 378.8	2 271.9	6 130.4	21 003.1
	95-99			461.4	1 529.1	6 509.9
	100+			66.1	243.5	1 064.6
Male	Total	869 844.3	1 541 134.4	2 733 413.8	3 355 238.6	3 923 083.4
	0-14	328 190.5	637 389.9	830 855.8	877 424.1	838 066.2
	15-59	490 856.8	815 011.6	1 690 955.8	2 081 033.0	2 358 614.8
	60-64	21 115.6	33 937.2	71 750.1	135 855.9	210 733.4
	65-69	14 255.4	24 839.7	55 304.8	103 292.1	172 480.4
	70-74	8 824.9	15 923.9	40 720.4	76 857.8	132 586.3
	75-79	4 473.8	8 337.7	25 360.9	44 567.1	102 471.8
	80-84			12 515.9	22 690.8	65 256.1
	85-89			4 570.6	9 891.4	30 454.4
	90-94	2 127.3	5 694.4	1 158.1	2 974.9	9 954.7
	95-99			196.2	573.9	2 197.1
	100+			25.2	77.5	268.1
Percentage in older ages						
Total	60+	6.4	6.2	8.4	12.8	20.0
	65+	3.9	3.9	5.7	8.6	14.6
	80+	0.3	0.4	0.9	1.4	3.6
Female	60+	7.1	6.7	9.1	13.7	21.5
	65+	4.4	4.3	6.2	9.4	16.0
	80+	0.4	0.5	1.0	1.7	4.3
Male	60+	5.8	5.8	7.7	11.8	18.5
	65+	3.4	3.6	5.1	7.8	13.1
	80+	0.2	0.4	0.7	1.1	2.8
Ageing index		17.1	15.1	28.0	49.6	95.7
Broad age groups (percentage)	0-14	37.6	41.1	30.0	25.7	20.9
	15-59	55.9	52.7	61.6	61.5	59.1
	60+	6.4	6.2	8.4	12.8	20.0
Median age (years)		21.4	19.4	25.6*	30.8	36.6
Dependency ratio	Total	71.0	81.9	55.5	52.3	55.0
	Youth	64.3	74.8	46.7	39.2	32.4
	Old Age	6.7	7.2	8.8	13.1	22.6
Potential support ratio		14.9	14.0	11.3	7.6	4.4
Parent support ratio		1.0	1.5	2.7	3.8	9.1
Sex ratio (per 100 women)	60+	85.8	89.2	87.7	87.6	86.3
	65+	79.9	85.1	84.0	83.9	82.0
	80+	67.9	77.2	66.3	64.6	63.5

* *Estimate refers to year 2005.*

Indicator	Age	1950-1955	1975-1980	2005-2010	2025-2030	2045-2050
Growth rate (percentage)	Total	2.1	2.1	1.3	0.9	0.5
	60+	1.9	2.6	3.0	3.4	2.0
	65+	2.1	2.9	2.6	3.7	2.0
	80+	2.9	1.4	4.6	4.4	3.9
Total fertility rate (per woman)		6.2	4.6	2.7	2.3	2.1
Life expectancy (years)						
Total	Birth	41.1	56.9	64.6	69.6	74.0
	60	..	..	18.5	20.3	21.8
	65	..	..	15.0	16.6	17.9
	80	..	..	7.0	7.8	8.5
Female	Birth	42.0	57.9	66.4	71.7	76.2
	60	..	..	19.8	21.9	23.5
	65	..	..	16.0	17.9	19.4
	80	..	..	7.4	8.4	9.3
Male	Birth	40.3	55.9	62.9	67.6	71.8
	60	..	..	17.2	18.8	20.0
	65	..	..	13.9	15.2	16.3
	80	..	..	6.4	7.0	7.5
Survival rate (percentage)						
Total	60	..	..	72.1	78.4	83.9
	65	..	..	66.0	73.3	79.3
	80	..	..	32.3	41.4	49.2
Female	60	..	..	74.7	80.8	85.8
	65	..	..	69.6	76.7	82.3
	80	..	..	37.6	47.8	56.1
Male	60	..	..	69.7	76.2	82.0
	65	..	..	62.6	70.0	76.4
	80	..	..	27.2	35.2	42.4

		1980	1990	2007	2010	2020
Labour force participation (percentage)						
Total	65+	28.3	28.0	25.9	25.5	24.0
Female	65+	13.0	14.0	14.9	15.2	15.9
Male	65+	46.2	44.3	39.0	37.8	33.8

Percentage married, age 60+				Percentage living alone, age 60+		
Total	Female	Male		Total	Female	Male
62.9	47.3	80.5		..	..	..

Statutory pensionable age (2006)				Percentage illiterate, age 65+		
	Female	Male		Total	Female	Male
	–	–		..	..	..

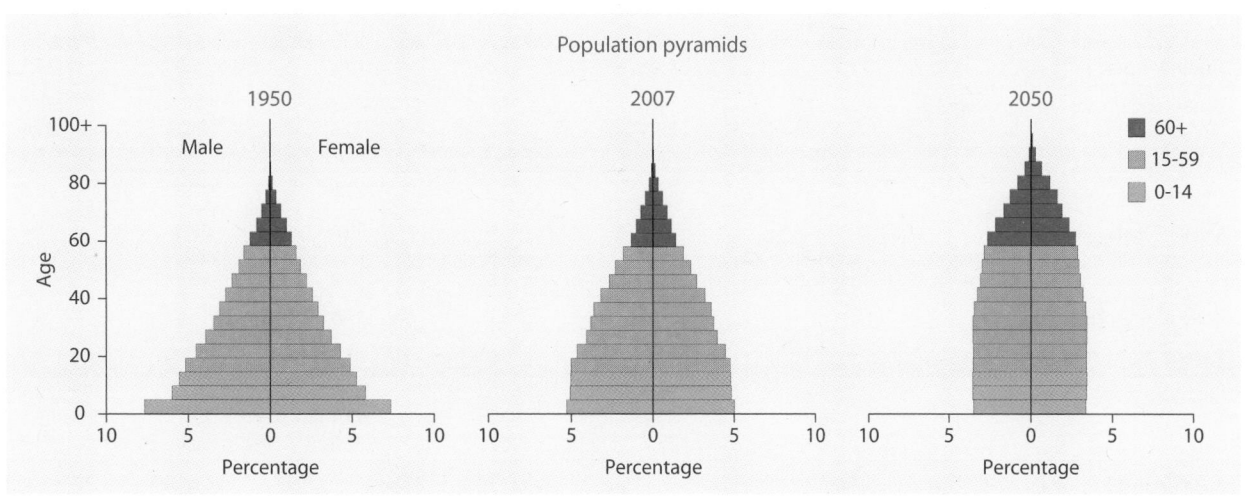

Population pyramids

United Nations Department of Economic and Social Affairs, Population Division

Least developed countries

Indicator	Age	1950	1975	2007	2025	2050
Population (thousands)						
Total	Total	200 789.1	355 869.5	795 647.3	1 167 460.5	1 735 368.0
	0-14	82 485.5	158 343.6	328 512.6	432 540.8	502 294.3
	15-59	107 388.2	179 401.9	426 390.2	662 425.6	1 061 882.6
	60-64	4 270.5	6 947.5	14 733.8	25 484.7	57 051.7
	65-69	3 069.5	5 198.7	10 981.2	19 382.5	44 796.6
	70-74	1 965.6	3 223.1	7 503.0	13 590.4	31 635.3
	75-79	1 063.1	1 788.9	4 508.7	8 143.3	20 595.8
	80-84			2 121.4	4 044.8	11 103.2
	85-89			718.0	1 443.4	4 529.8
	90-94	546.7	965.8	156.4	347.4	1 245.3
	95-99			20.4	52.8	212.8
	100+			1.6	4.8	20.7
Female	Total	99 808.8	177 498.8	397 290.4	581 420.7	865 352.3
	0-14	41 133.0	78 307.1	162 205.4	213 557.6	247 701.3
	15-59	52 874.5	89 767.3	213 005.8	328 740.7	527 118.4
	60-64	2 187.2	3 522.8	7 814.7	13 307.1	28 997.8
	65-69	1 620.9	2 683.1	5 914.5	10 337.6	23 181.7
	70-74	1 075.4	1 711.2	4 096.4	7 408.7	16 805.1
	75-79	604.5	964.7	2 507.0	4 588.6	11 345.4
	80-84			1 210.4	2 351.1	6 427.3
	85-89			424.7	869.9	2 783.5
	90-94	313.4	542.6	96.9	219.8	822.5
	95-99			13.6	35.9	153.1
	100+			1.2	3.6	16.3
Male	Total	100 980.3	178 370.7	398 356.9	586 039.8	870 015.8
	0-14	41 352.6	80 036.4	166 307.3	218 983.2	254 593.0
	15-59	54 513.7	89 634.6	213 384.5	333 685.0	534 764.2
	60-64	2 083.3	3 424.7	6 919.1	12 177.6	28 053.8
	65-69	1 448.6	2 515.6	5 066.7	9 044.9	21 614.9
	70-74	890.2	1 511.9	3 406.6	6 181.8	14 830.2
	75-79	458.7	824.2	2 001.6	3 554.6	9 250.4
	80-84			911.1	1 693.7	4 676.0
	85-89			293.3	573.5	1 746.3
	90-94	233.2	423.2	59.5	127.5	422.8
	95-99			6.8	16.8	59.7
	100+			0.4	1.2	4.4
Percentage in older ages						
Total	60+	5.4	5.1	5.1	6.2	9.9
	65+	3.3	3.1	3.3	4.0	6.6
	80+	0.3	0.3	0.4	0.5	1.0
Female	60+	5.8	5.3	5.6	6.7	10.5
	65+	3.6	3.3	3.6	4.4	7.1
	80+	0.3	0.3	0.4	0.6	1.2
Male	60+	5.1	4.9	4.7	5.7	9.3
	65+	3.0	3.0	2.9	3.6	6.0
	80+	0.2	0.2	0.3	0.4	0.8
Ageing index		13.2	11.4	12.4	16.8	34.1
Broad age groups (percentage)	0-14	41.1	44.5	41.3	37.0	28.9
	15-59	53.5	50.4	53.6	56.7	61.2
	60+	5.4	5.1	5.1	6.2	9.9
Median age (years)		19.6	17.7	18.9*	21.8	27.3
Dependency ratio	Total	79.8	91.0	80.4	69.7	55.1
	Youth	73.9	85.0	74.5	62.9	44.9
	Old Age	6.0	6.0	5.9	6.8	10.2
Potential support ratio		16.8	16.7	17.0	14.6	9.8
Parent support ratio		0.9	0.9	1.6	1.9	2.9
Sex ratio (per 100 women)	60+	88.2	92.3	84.5	85.3	89.1
	65+	83.9	89.4	82.3	82.1	85.5
	80+	74.4	78.0	72.8	69.3	67.7

*   *Estimate refers to year 2005.*

Indicator	Age	1950-1955	1975-1980	2005-2010	2025-2030	2045-2050
Growth rate (percentage)	Total	2.0	2.5	2.3	1.9	1.3
	60+	1.3	2.2	2.9	3.3	3.5
	65+	1.3	2.5	3.0	3.5	3.8
	80+	1.3	3.0	3.8	4.1	4.2
Total fertility rate (per woman)		6.6	6.4	4.7	3.5	2.6
Life expectancy (years)						
Total	Birth	36.1	45.9	52.5	59.9	66.5
	60	..	..	16.4	17.8	19.3
	65	..	..	13.1	14.3	15.5
	80	..	..	5.8	6.2	6.8
Female	Birth	36.8	46.9	53.4	61.1	68.2
	60	..	..	17.0	18.7	20.4
	65	..	..	13.6	15.0	16.4
	80	..	..	6.0	6.5	7.2
Male	Birth	35.4	44.9	51.5	58.6	64.9
	60	..	..	15.7	16.9	18.1
	65	..	..	12.5	13.6	14.5
	80	..	..	5.5	5.9	6.3
Survival rate (percentage)						
Total	60	..	..	52.5	63.4	73.1
	65	..	..	46.6	57.8	67.9
	80	..	..	18.5	26.7	35.6
Female	60	..	..	54.0	65.1	75.1
	65	..	..	48.7	60.2	70.8
	80	..	..	20.6	29.8	40.3
Male	60	..	..	51.0	61.7	71.2
	65	..	..	44.6	55.3	65.2
	80	..	..	16.3	23.5	31.0

			1990	2007	2010	2020
Labour force participation (percentage)						
Total	65+		54.3	52.5	45.2	44.5	43.0
Female	65+		37.7	38.4	30.9	30.6	30.4
Male	65+		72.7	68.9	62.6	61.5	58.4

Percentage married, age 60+				Percentage living alone, age 60+		
Total	Female	Male		Total	Female	Male
60.2	38.8	85.1		..	..	..

Statutory pensionable age (2006)				Percentage illiterate, age 65+		
	Female	Male		Total	Female	Male
	–	–		..	..	..

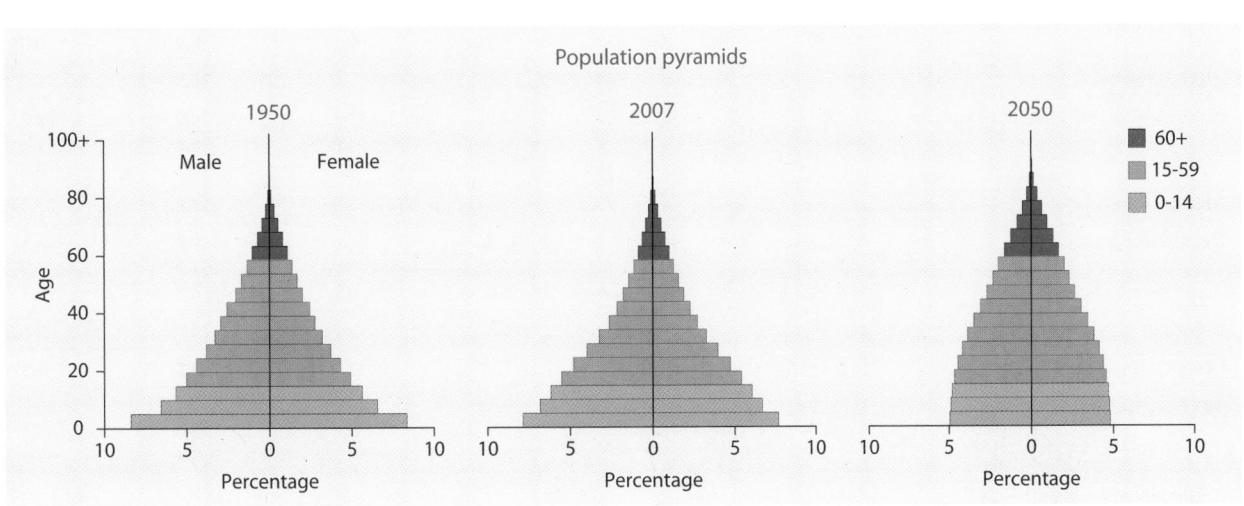

Population pyramids

Africa

Indicator	Age	1950	1975	2007	2025	2050
Population (thousands)						
Total	Total	224 068.0	415 824.0	945 345.6	1 344 491.1	1 936 951.8
	0-14	94 014.0	186 911.9	388 190.8	495 478.9	555 662.6
	15-59	118 222.3	208 110.4	507 098.9	763 254.1	1 188 405.3
	60-64	4 585.7	7 757.3	17 573.0	28 889.3	64 068.9
	65-69	3 327.0	5 783.0	13 408.2	22 872.4	50 415.4
	70-74	2 157.3	3 815.6	9 486.2	16 494.8	35 614.8
	75-79	1 165.0	2 182.5	5 754.6	10 019.5	22 715.7
	80-84			2 701.6	5 004.5	12 488.8
	85-89			912.3	1 927.7	5 544.6
	90-94	596.6	1 263.3	194.0	475.2	1 687.3
	95-99			24.1	69.0	316.9
	100+			1.8	5.6	31.6
Female	Total	113 224.0	209 106.5	472 743.8	668 540.4	963 426.3
	0-14	46 915.7	92 698.3	191 782.0	244 696.8	274 094.2
	15-59	59 764.0	105 120.9	253 599.7	377 109.8	588 268.1
	60-64	2 479.6	4 084.7	9 309.0	15 114.1	32 181.0
	65-69	1 828.3	3 115.6	7 261.5	12 257.0	25 750.6
	70-74	1 208.5	2 098.8	5 239.8	9 091.6	18 613.9
	75-79	673.5	1 240.1	3 258.1	5 711.3	12 348.4
	80-84			1 583.2	2 969.2	7 227.6
	85-89			562.5	1 214.3	3 491.5
	90-94	354.4	748.3	128.8	320.8	1 176.2
	95-99			17.7	51.0	247.7
	100+			1.5	4.6	27.1
Male	Total	110 844.0	206 717.5	472 601.7	675 950.6	973 525.5
	0-14	47 098.4	94 213.6	196 408.9	250 782.0	281 568.3
	15-59	58 458.3	102 989.5	253 499.2	386 144.4	600 137.2
	60-64	2 106.1	3 672.6	8 264.0	13 775.2	31 888.0
	65-69	1 498.6	2 667.4	6 146.8	10 615.4	24 664.8
	70-74	948.9	1 716.8	4 246.5	7 403.3	17 000.9
	75-79	491.4	942.4	2 496.5	4 308.2	10 367.2
	80-84			1 118.4	2 035.3	5 261.2
	85-89			349.8	713.5	2 053.1
	90-94	242.2	515.1	65.1	154.5	511.1
	95-99			6.4	17.9	69.2
	100+			0.3	1.0	4.4
Percentage in older ages						
Total	60+	5.3	5.0	5.3	6.4	10.0
	65+	3.2	3.1	3.4	4.2	6.7
	80+	0.3	0.3	0.4	0.6	1.0
Female	60+	5.8	5.4	5.8	7.0	10.5
	65+	3.6	3.4	3.8	4.7	7.1
	80+	0.3	0.4	0.5	0.7	1.3
Male	60+	4.8	4.6	4.8	5.8	9.4
	65+	2.9	2.8	3.1	3.7	6.2
	80+	0.2	0.2	0.3	0.4	0.8
Ageing index		12.6	11.1	12.9	17.3	34.7
Broad age groups (percentage)	0-14	42.0	44.9	41.1	36.9	28.7
	15-59	52.8	50.0	53.6	56.8	61.4
	60+	5.3	5.0	5.3	6.4	10.0
Median age (years)		19.0	17.4	18.9*	21.8	27.4
Dependency ratio	Total	82.5	92.6	80.2	69.7	54.7
	Youth	76.6	86.6	74.0	62.5	44.4
	Old Age	5.9	6.0	6.2	7.2	10.3
Potential support ratio		16.9	16.5	16.2	13.9	9.7
Parent support ratio		0.9	1.2	1.6	2.3	3.3
Sex ratio (per 100 women)	60+	80.8	84.3	82.9	83.5	90.9
	65+	78.3	81.1	79.9	79.9	87.0
	80+	68.4	68.8	67.1	64.1	64.9

*   *Estimate refers to year 2005.*

Indicator	Age	1950-1955	1975-1980	2005-2010	2025-2030	2045-2050
Growth rate (percentage)	Total	2.2	2.8	2.1	1.7	1.2
	60+	1.6	2.7	2.8	2.8	3.5
	65+	1.5	2.7	2.7	3.0	3.8
	80+	1.4	3.0	4.1	4.1	3.4
Total fertility rate (per woman)		6.7	6.6	4.7	3.4	2.5
Life expectancy (years)						
Total	Birth	38.4	48.7	49.9	58.0	65.4
	60	..	..	16.6	18.1	19.5
	65	..	..	13.3	14.6	15.8
	80	..	..	5.8	6.4	7.0
Female	Birth	39.7	50.2	50.6	59.0	67.0
	60	..	..	17.4	19.0	20.6
	65	..	..	13.9	15.4	16.7
	80	..	..	6.1	6.8	7.5
Male	Birth	37.1	47.1	49.3	56.9	63.8
	60	..	..	15.7	17.0	18.3
	65	..	..	12.6	13.6	14.7
	80	..	..	5.5	5.9	6.4
Survival rate (percentage)						
Total	60	..	..	46.8	58.8	70.0
	65	..	..	41.6	53.6	65.0
	80	..	..	17.0	25.5	34.7
Female	60	..	..	47.5	59.9	71.8
	65	..	..	42.9	55.5	67.6
	80	..	..	19.0	28.6	39.2
Male	60	..	..	46.0	57.7	68.3
	65	..	..	40.2	51.8	62.6
	80	..	..	14.9	22.2	30.4

		1980	1990	2007	2010	2020
Labour force participation (percentage)						
Total	65+	44.5	44.3	39.5	39.0	37.2
Female	65+	30.1	30.2	25.6	25.6	25.1
Male	65+	61.9	61.5	56.7	55.8	52.4

Percentage married, age 60+				Percentage living alone, age 60+		
Total	Female	Male		Total	Female	Male
60.0	38.8	85.4		8.0	11.0	6.0

Statutory pensionable age (2006)				Percentage illiterate, age 65+		
	Female	Male		Total	Female	Male
	–	–		..	..	..

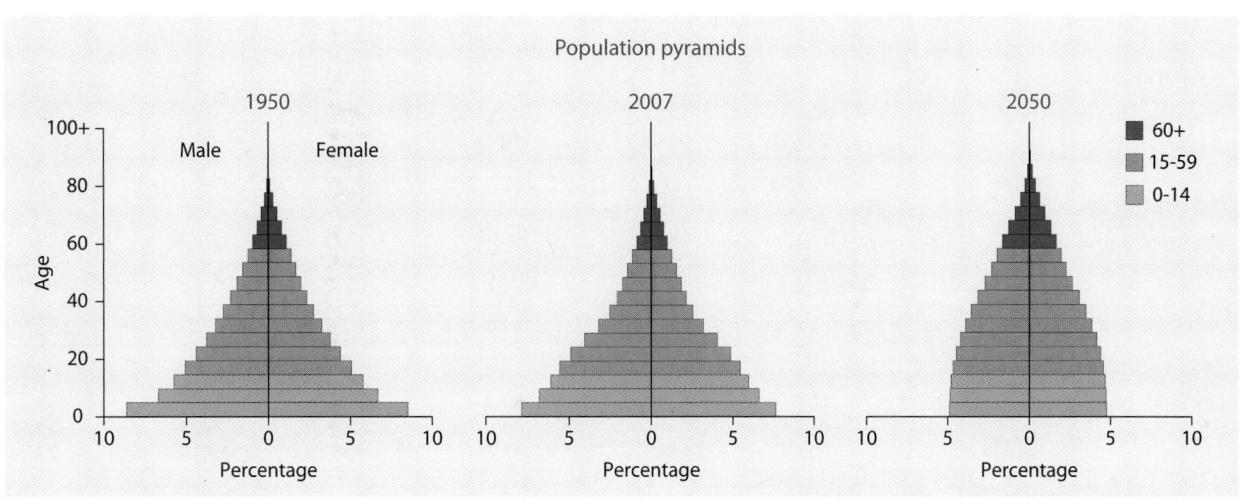

Population pyramids

Eastern Africa

Indicator	Age	1950	1975	2007	2025	2050
Population (thousands)						
Total	Total	64 986.2	125 811.5	301 527.7	447 683.2	678 715.7
	0-14	28 219.7	58 455.9	132 683.9	176 825.6	206 497.1
	15-59	33 643.2	61 702.1	154 798.7	247 874.8	417 203.4
	60-64	1 218.6	2 181.7	4 996.4	7 695.0	19 521.2
	65-69	889.7	1 578.0	3 751.0	6 085.7	14 552.6
	70-74	568.3	1 038.6	2 630.3	4 435.6	10 003.1
	75-79	302.4	558.6	1 594.7	2 746.6	6 065.6
	80-84			753.7	1 372.3	3 148.5
	85-89			257.3	504.6	1 300.1
	90-94	144.3	296.6	54.6	123.6	359.7
	95-99			6.7	17.9	59.2
	100+			0.5	1.5	5.3
Female	Total	32 914.0	63 622.4	151 639.6	223 342.2	338 574.3
	0-14	14 141.9	29 241.3	66 005.6	87 832.9	102 424.7
	15-59	17 022.0	31 309.6	77 941.2	122 951.0	207 690.8
	60-64	665.6	1 149.2	2 675.8	4 037.9	9 816.8
	65-69	497.1	845.8	2 037.6	3 296.0	7 402.3
	70-74	321.9	573.2	1 449.0	2 462.9	5 185.1
	75-79	177.8	322.2	896.7	1 560.5	3 242.6
	80-84			437.0	801.9	1 765.2
	85-89			156.1	306.0	772.6
	90-94	87.8	181.2	35.4	79.3	228.9
	95-99			4.8	12.5	41.0
	100+			0.4	1.2	4.1
Male	Total	32 072.2	62 189.0	149 888.1	224 341.0	340 141.4
	0-14	14 077.8	29 214.5	66 678.3	88 992.6	104 072.4
	15-59	16 621.2	30 392.5	76 857.5	124 923.9	209 512.6
	60-64	553.0	1 032.5	2 320.6	3 657.1	9 704.3
	65-69	392.6	732.3	1 713.4	2 789.7	7 150.3
	70-74	246.4	465.4	1 181.3	1 972.8	4 818.0
	75-79	124.6	236.4	698.0	1 186.1	2 822.9
	80-84			316.7	570.4	1 383.3
	85-89			101.2	198.5	527.5
	90-94	56.5	115.4	19.2	44.3	130.8
	95-99			1.9	5.4	18.2
	100+			0.1	0.3	1.2
Percentage in older ages						
Total	60+	4.8	4.5	4.7	5.1	8.1
	65+	2.9	2.8	3.0	3.4	5.2
	80+	0.2	0.2	0.4	0.5	0.7
Female	60+	5.3	4.8	5.1	5.6	8.4
	65+	3.3	3.0	3.3	3.8	5.5
	80+	0.3	0.3	0.4	0.5	0.8
Male	60+	4.3	4.2	4.2	4.6	7.8
	65+	2.6	2.5	2.7	3.0	5.0
	80+	0.2	0.2	0.3	0.4	0.6
Ageing index		11.1	9.7	10.6	13.0	26.6
Broad age groups (percentage)	0-14	43.4	46.5	44.0	39.5	30.4
	15-59	51.8	49.0	51.3	55.4	61.5
	60+	4.8	4.5	4.7	5.1	8.1
Median age (years)		18.2	16.7	17.5*	19.8	25.6
Dependency ratio	Total	86.4	96.9	88.7	75.2	55.4
	Youth	80.9	91.5	83.0	69.2	47.3
	Old Age	5.5	5.4	5.7	6.0	8.1
Potential support ratio		18.3	18.4	17.7	16.7	12.3
Parent support ratio		0.8	0.9	1.7	2.2	2.4
Sex ratio (per 100 women)	60+	78.5	84.1	82.6	83.0	93.3
	65+	75.6	80.6	80.4	79.4	90.4
	80+	64.3	63.7	69.3	68.2	73.3

* *Estimate refers to year 2005.*

Indicator	Age	1950-1955	1975-1980	2005-2010	2025-2030	2045-2050
Growth rate (percentage)	Total	2.3	3.0	2.3	1.9	1.4
	60+	1.5	3.1	2.7	2.6	4.1
	65+	1.5	3.2	2.7	2.7	4.2
	80+	2.2	4.1	3.8	3.8	3.2
Total fertility rate (per woman)		6.9	7.0	5.2	3.6	2.6
Life expectancy (years)						
Total	Birth	37.2	48.1	47.4	56.9	64.7
	60	..	..	16.3	17.6	18.9
	65	..	..	13.1	14.2	15.2
	80	..	..	5.8	6.2	6.6
Female	Birth	38.5	49.7	47.8	57.8	66.2
	60	..	..	17.0	18.3	19.7
	65	..	..	13.6	14.8	15.9
	80	..	..	6.0	6.4	6.9
Male	Birth	35.9	46.5	47.1	56.0	63.3
	60	..	..	15.6	16.8	18.0
	65	..	..	12.5	13.5	14.5
	80	..	..	5.5	5.9	6.3
Survival rate (percentage)						
Total	60	..	..	41.0	55.5	68.2
	65	..	..	36.2	50.2	63.0
	80	..	..	14.4	22.9	32.1
Female	60	..	..	41.1	56.5	70.0
	65	..	..	36.8	51.8	65.6
	80	..	..	15.7	25.2	35.8
Male	60	..	..	40.8	54.5	66.4
	65	..	..	35.4	48.6	60.5
	80	..	..	13.0	20.5	28.7

		1980	1990	2007	2010	2020
Labour force participation (percentage)						
Total	65+	59.7	59.6	56.2	55.6	53.9
Female	65+	48.2	47.9	44.2	44.1	43.7
Male	65+	73.6	73.9	71.2	70.1	66.7

Percentage married, age 60+				Percentage living alone, age 60+		
Total	Female	Male		Total	Female	Male
59.4	39.0	83.9		9.0	13.0	6.0

Statutory pensionable age (2006)				Percentage illiterate, age 65+		
	Female	Male		Total	Female	Male
	–	–		..	..	..

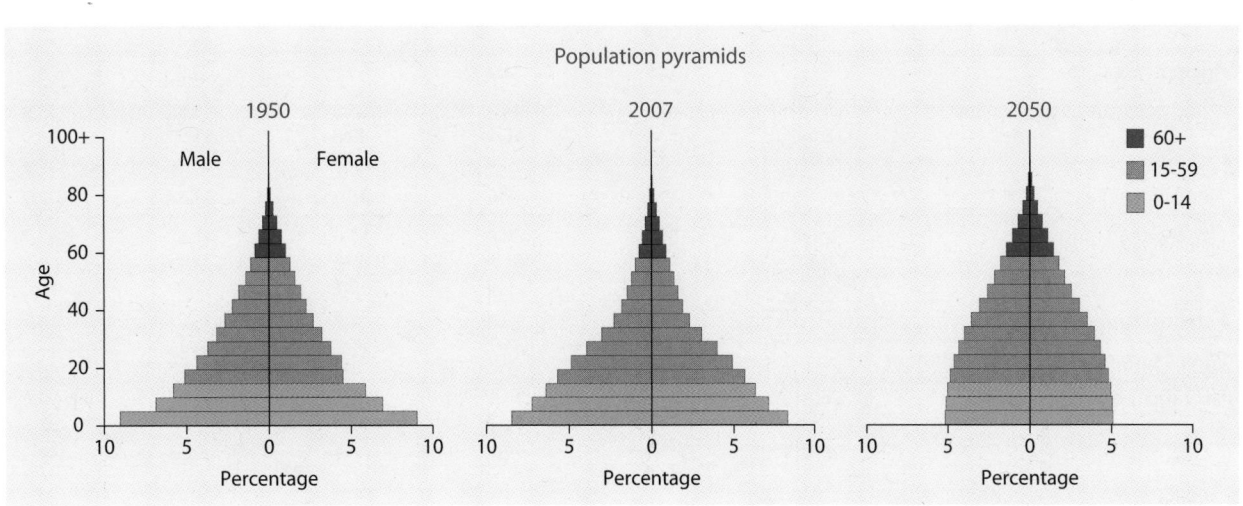

Population pyramids

Middle Africa

Indicator	Age	1950	1975	2007	2025	2050
Population (thousands)						
Total	Total	26 332.1	46 986.7	115 725.6	184 331.6	303 349.1
	0-14	10 829.9	21 066.5	53 142.2	80 707.3	102 851.3
	15-59	13 956.7	23 555.3	57 343.5	95 619.5	181 790.2
	60-64	549.0	907.1	1 885.7	2 801.9	6 772.7
	65-69	409.6	660.8	1 428.5	2 136.0	4 998.2
	70-74	284.0	430.7	976.1	1 501.3	3 394.2
	75-79	173.4	238.5	574.5	912.2	2 031.3
	80-84			266.2	452.3	1 010.2
	85-89			88.5	159.4	386.6
	90-94	129.6	127.7	18.2	36.4	98.5
	95-99			2.1	4.9	14.7
	100+			0.1	0.4	1.1
Female	Total	13 701.2	24 015.8	58 348.7	92 510.8	152 069.5
	0-14	5 498.6	10 546.5	26 530.2	40 282.9	51 175.5
	15-59	7 322.6	12 120.7	28 910.5	47 846.5	91 085.8
	60-64	307.8	502.6	1 017.4	1 477.2	3 454.5
	65-69	231.9	373.6	784.1	1 157.7	2 587.6
	70-74	163.1	249.7	546.8	833.1	1 791.8
	75-79	101.4	142.1	330.6	520.4	1 101.6
	80-84			159.0	266.5	569.4
	85-89			55.9	98.5	229.8
	90-94	75.7	80.7	12.4	24.1	62.6
	95-99			1.6	3.5	10.1
	100+			0.1	0.3	0.9
Male	Total	12 630.9	22 970.9	57 376.9	91 820.8	151 279.6
	0-14	5 331.3	10 520.0	26 612.0	40 424.4	51 675.8
	15-59	6 634.1	11 434.7	28 433.0	47 773.0	90 704.5
	60-64	241.2	404.5	868.3	1 324.7	3 318.3
	65-69	177.7	287.2	644.4	978.3	2 410.6
	70-74	120.9	181.1	429.3	668.2	1 602.4
	75-79	72.0	96.4	243.8	391.8	929.7
	80-84			107.2	185.8	440.7
	85-89			32.6	60.9	156.8
	90-94	53.9	47.0	5.8	12.3	35.9
	95-99			0.5	1.3	4.5
	100+			0.0	0.1	0.3
Percentage in older ages						
Total	60+	5.9	5.0	4.5	4.3	6.2
	65+	3.8	3.1	2.9	2.8	3.9
	80+	0.5	0.3	0.3	0.4	0.5
Female	60+	6.4	5.6	5.0	4.7	6.4
	65+	4.2	3.5	3.2	3.1	4.2
	80+	0.6	0.3	0.4	0.4	0.6
Male	60+	5.3	4.4	4.1	3.9	5.9
	65+	3.4	2.7	2.6	2.5	3.7
	80+	0.4	0.2	0.3	0.3	0.4
Ageing index		14.3	11.2	9.9	9.9	18.2
Broad age groups (percentage)	0-14	41.1	44.8	45.9	43.8	33.9
	15-59	53.0	50.1	49.6	51.9	59.9
	60+	5.9	5.0	4.5	4.3	6.2
Median age (years)		19.6	17.6	16.8*	17.9	22.9
Dependency ratio	Total	81.5	92.1	95.4	87.3	60.9
	Youth	74.7	86.1	89.7	82.0	54.5
	Old Age	6.9	6.0	5.7	5.3	6.3
Potential support ratio		14.6	16.8	17.7	18.9	15.8
Parent support ratio		1.7	0.9	1.5	1.8	1.9
Sex ratio (per 100 women)	60+	75.6	75.3	80.2	82.7	90.7
	65+	74.2	72.3	77.4	79.2	87.8
	80+	71.1	58.3	63.8	66.3	73.1

* *Estimate refers to year 2005.*

Indicator	Age	1950-1955	1975-1980	2005-2010	2025-2030	2045-2050
Growth rate (percentage)	Total	1.9	2.9	2.7	2.3	1.6
	60+	0.4	2.7	2.2	2.6	3.9
	65+	-0.4	2.8	2.4	2.6	4.0
	80+	-2.7	3.4	3.1	3.1	3.6
Total fertility rate (per woman)		6.0	6.6	6.1	4.5	2.9
Life expectancy (years)						
Total	Birth	36.2	46.3	44.5	51.8	59.7
	60	..	..	15.5	16.5	17.8
	65	..	..	12.5	13.3	14.3
	80	..	..	5.5	5.9	6.3
Female	Birth	37.8	48.0	45.5	53.0	61.2
	60	..	..	16.1	17.2	18.5
	65	..	..	12.9	13.8	14.9
	80	..	..	5.7	6.1	6.5
Male	Birth	34.6	44.6	43.5	50.2	58.2
	60	..	..	14.8	15.7	17.0
	65	..	..	11.9	12.6	13.7
	80	..	..	5.2	5.5	6.0
Survival rate (percentage)						
Total	60	..	..	39.1	49.0	61.0
	65	..	..	34.0	43.5	55.4
	80	..	..	12.3	17.8	25.7
Female	60	..	..	40.5	50.7	63.0
	65	..	..	35.7	45.6	58.0
	80	..	..	13.8	19.8	28.6
Male	60	..	..	37.7	46.8	59.0
	65	..	..	32.3	40.8	52.9
	80	..	..	10.8	15.2	22.9

		1980	1990	2007	2010	2020
Labour force participation (percentage)						
Total	65+	51.4	51.7	52.1	52.0	52.2
Female	65+	34.1	35.8	34.9	34.8	34.9
Male	65+	75.1	72.9	74.3	74.2	74.1

Percentage married, age 60+			Percentage living alone, age 60+		
Total	Female	Male	Total	Female	Male
54.2	32.9	80.9	10.0	12.0	8.0

Statutory pensionable age (2006)		Percentage illiterate, age 65+		
Female	Male	Total	Female	Male
–	–	..	..	..

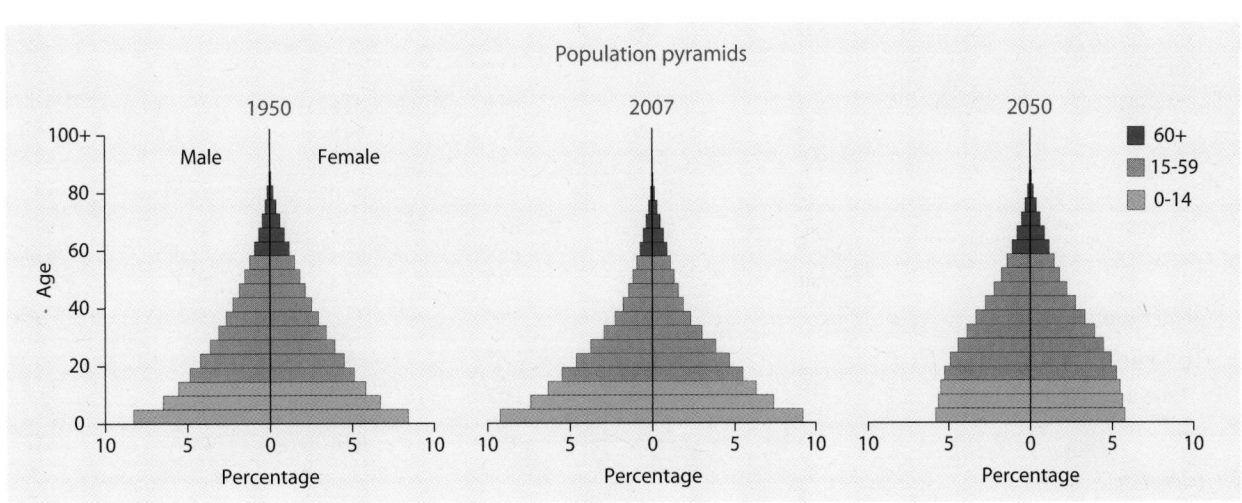

Population pyramids

Northern Africa

Indicator	Age	1950	1975	2007	2025	2050
Population (thousands)						
Total	Total	53 302.4	97 863.0	197 695.7	255 959.0	311 893.4
	0-14	21 984.7	43 150.1	63 913.8	69 173.0	64 288.9
	15-59	28 338.7	49 119.6	120 132.5	159 645.1	186 958.7
	60-64	1 135.0	1 920.7	4 462.1	9 132.0	17 276.9
	65-69	837.6	1 551.7	3 556.7	7 277.8	15 398.1
	70-74	556.2	1 059.1	2 720.5	5 223.8	11 802.6
	75-79	305.4	639.5	1 737.0	3 108.5	8 065.5
	80-84			825.9	1 536.0	4 788.5
	85-89			279.0	667.8	2 358.5
	90-94	144.8	422.2	60.3	169.5	783.3
	95-99			7.4	23.9	157.0
	100+			0.5	1.6	15.4
Female	Total	26 621.1	48 751.9	98 447.3	127 786.8	156 692.5
	0-14	10 919.8	21 128.5	31 311.2	33 857.7	31 392.4
	15-59	14 122.6	24 690.5	59 744.9	79 304.5	92 628.5
	60-64	589.8	979.0	2 320.2	4 743.9	8 774.5
	65-69	438.8	814.2	1 910.1	3 811.7	7 986.8
	70-74	298.5	560.0	1 492.1	2 820.6	6 274.9
	75-79	169.3	348.1	977.2	1 765.0	4 489.8
	80-84			478.8	916.3	2 866.0
	85-89			168.1	430.8	1 558.0
	90-94	82.4	231.6	38.9	117.0	577.9
	95-99			5.3	18.1	130.0
	100+			0.4	1.3	13.8
Male	Total	26 681.3	49 111.1	99 248.4	128 172.2	155 200.9
	0-14	11 064.8	22 021.6	32 602.6	35 315.3	32 896.5
	15-59	14 216.1	24 429.1	60 387.6	80 340.6	94 330.2
	60-64	545.3	941.7	2 141.9	4 388.1	8 502.4
	65-69	398.8	737.5	1 646.5	3 466.1	7 411.4
	70-74	257.7	499.1	1 228.3	2 403.2	5 527.7
	75-79	136.1	291.4	759.9	1 343.5	3 575.8
	80-84			347.0	619.7	1 922.5
	85-89			110.9	237.0	800.5
	90-94	62.4	190.6	21.4	52.5	205.4
	95-99			2.1	5.8	27.0
	100+			0.1	0.3	1.6
Percentage in older ages						
Total	60+	5.6	5.7	6.9	10.6	19.4
	65+	3.5	3.8	4.6	7.0	13.9
	80+	0.3	0.4	0.6	0.9	2.6
Female	60+	5.9	6.0	7.5	11.4	20.9
	65+	3.7	4.0	5.2	7.7	15.3
	80+	0.3	0.5	0.7	1.2	3.3
Male	60+	5.2	5.4	6.3	9.8	18.0
	65+	3.2	3.5	4.1	6.3	12.5
	80+	0.2	0.4	0.5	0.7	1.9
Ageing index		13.6	13.0	21.4	39.2	94.3
Broad age groups (percentage)	0-14	41.2	44.1	32.3	27.0	20.6
	15-59	53.2	50.2	60.8	62.4	59.9
	60+	5.6	5.7	6.9	10.6	19.4
Median age (years)		19.3	17.7	23.0*	28.9	36.1
Dependency ratio	Total	80.8	91.7	58.7	51.7	52.7
	Youth	74.6	84.5	51.3	41.0	31.5
	Old Age	6.3	7.2	7.4	10.7	21.2
Potential support ratio		16.0	13.9	13.6	9.4	4.7
Parent support ratio		0.9	1.9	1.9	2.6	6.2
Sex ratio (per 100 women)	60+	88.7	90.7	84.7	85.6	85.6
	65+	86.5	88.0	81.2	82.3	81.5
	80+	75.8	82.3	69.6	61.7	57.5

* *Estimate refers to year 2005.*

Indicator	Age	1950-1955	1975-1980	2005-2010	2025-2030	2045-2050
Growth rate (percentage)	Total	2.3	2.7	1.7	1.0	0.5
	60+	1.5	2.9	3.2	3.3	2.7
	65+	1.3	2.7	2.5	3.9	3.5
	80+	1.4	2.8	5.2	5.0	3.8
Total fertility rate (per woman)		6.8	6.1	2.9	2.3	2.0
Life expectancy (years)						
Total	Birth	42.0	54.2	68.4	73.1	76.8
	60	..	..	18.1	19.7	21.4
	65	..	..	14.4	15.9	17.4
	80	..	..	6.0	6.8	7.8
Female	Birth	43.2	55.5	70.3	75.2	79.0
	60	..	..	19.1	21.2	23.1
	65	..	..	15.2	17.1	18.9
	80	..	..	6.3	7.4	8.6
Male	Birth	40.9	52.9	66.5	71.0	74.5
	60	..	..	17.0	18.2	19.6
	65	..	..	13.5	14.5	15.7
	80	..	..	5.6	6.1	6.7
Survival rate (percentage)						
Total	60	..	..	78.5	84.8	89.1
	65	..	..	72.3	79.5	84.7
	80	..	..	34.0	43.2	51.7
Female	60	..	..	81.4	87.0	91.0
	65	..	..	76.2	82.9	87.6
	80	..	..	39.1	50.2	59.3
Male	60	..	..	75.8	82.6	87.3
	65	..	..	68.4	76.1	81.7
	80	..	..	29.0	36.4	44.0

		1980	1990	2007	2010	2020
Labour force participation (percentage)						
Total	65+	28.9	25.7	17.4	16.9	15.7
Female	65+	12.8	11.1	5.8	5.9	6.6
Male	65+	46.7	42.3	31.7	30.4	26.8

Percentage married, age 60+			Percentage living alone, age 60+		
Total	Female	Male	Total	Female	Male
61.0	37.4	88.5	8.0	12.0	4.0

Statutory pensionable age (2006)			Percentage illiterate, age 65+		
Female	Male		Total	Female	Male
–	–		..	..	..

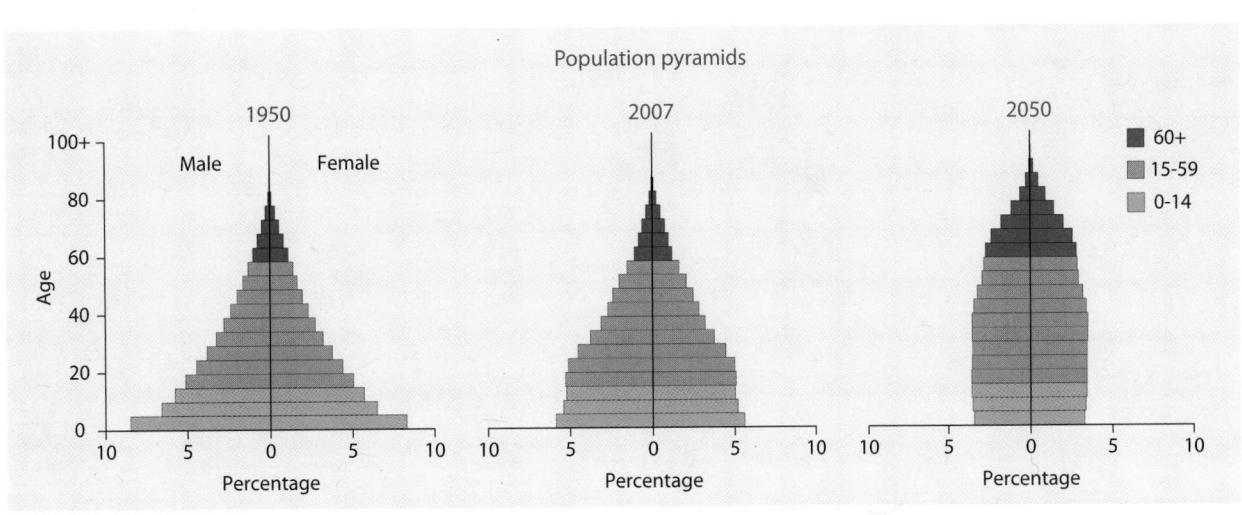

Population pyramids

United Nations Department of Economic and Social Affairs, Population Division

Southern Africa

Indicator	Age	1950	1975	2007	2025	2050
Population (thousands)						
Total	Total	15 624.2	29 301.8	54 334.6	55 136.5	56 004.2
	0-14	6 083.1	12 505.4	17 920.0	16 121.6	13 567.6
	15-59	8 601.1	15 281.8	32 568.5	32 941.7	35 493.1
	60-64	370.3	568.2	1 397.1	1 761.2	2 050.4
	65-69	263.5	416.8	1 027.7	1 571.4	1 602.9
	70-74	172.2	262.5	691.7	1 232.4	1 104.9
	75-79	89.8	153.8	411.6	795.8	867.4
	80-84			207.6	448.3	668.6
	85-89			83.8	192.0	413.0
	90-94	44.2	113.5	22.4	59.1	180.2
	95-99			3.8	11.5	48.9
	100+			0.4	1.3	6.9
Female	Total	7 877.0	14 764.8	27 647.8	27 331.4	27 456.3
	0-14	3 039.8	6 216.4	8 879.1	7 966.5	6 688.7
	15-59	4 304.5	7 666.7	16 507.4	15 701.0	17 084.9
	60-64	204.8	307.9	771.6	978.2	946.2
	65-69	148.2	239.7	591.9	918.1	753.0
	70-74	98.7	159.0	415.8	751.6	553.3
	75-79	53.5	98.1	259.3	511.2	498.0
	80-84			140.2	307.2	439.2
	85-89			61.4	140.6	300.9
	90-94	27.6	77.1	17.6	46.2	143.8
	95-99			3.1	9.6	42.1
	100+			0.3	1.2	6.3
Male	Total	7 747.2	14 537.0	26 686.8	27 805.1	28 547.9
	0-14	3 043.3	6 289.0	9 040.9	8 155.0	6 879.0
	15-59	4 296.7	7 615.0	16 061.1	17 240.8	18 408.3
	60-64	165.5	260.3	625.5	783.0	1 104.2
	65-69	115.3	177.1	435.9	653.3	849.9
	70-74	73.5	103.5	275.9	480.7	551.7
	75-79	36.3	55.7	152.3	284.6	369.4
	80-84			67.3	141.1	229.4
	85-89			22.4	51.5	112.1
	90-94	16.6	36.4	4.8	12.9	36.4
	95-99			0.6	1.9	6.8
	100+			0.0	0.1	0.6
Percentage in older ages						
Total	60+	6.0	5.2	7.1	11.0	12.4
	65+	3.6	3.2	4.5	7.8	8.7
	80+	0.3	0.4	0.6	1.3	2.4
Female	60+	6.8	6.0	8.2	13.4	13.4
	65+	4.2	3.9	5.4	9.8	10.0
	80+	0.3	0.5	0.8	1.8	3.4
Male	60+	5.3	4.4	5.9	8.7	11.4
	65+	3.1	2.6	3.6	5.8	7.6
	80+	0.2	0.3	0.4	0.7	1.4
Ageing index		15.5	12.1	21.5	37.7	51.2
Broad age groups (percentage)	0-14	38.9	42.7	33.0	29.2	24.2
	15-59	55.0	52.2	59.9	59.7	63.4
	60+	6.0	5.2	7.1	11.0	12.4
Median age (years)		20.7	18.5	23.0*	25.5	29.7
Dependency ratio	Total	74.2	84.9	60.0	58.9	49.2
	Youth	67.8	78.9	52.8	46.5	36.1
	Old Age	6.3	6.0	7.2	12.4	13.0
Potential support ratio		15.7	16.7	13.9	8.0	7.7
Parent support ratio		1.0	1.7	2.0	4.9	8.7
Sex ratio (per 100 women)	60+	76.4	71.8	70.1	65.8	88.5
	65+	73.7	64.9	64.4	60.6	78.8
	80+	60.3	47.2	42.8	41.1	41.3

*   Estimate refers to year 2005.

Indicator	Age	1950-1955	1975-1980	2005-2010	2025-2030	2045-2050
Growth rate (percentage)	Total	2.3	2.5	0.1	0.1	0.1
	60+	2.5	2.0	3.2	0.7	1.5
	65+	3.2	1.7	3.6	1.6	1.0
	80+	7.5	0.7	4.3	4.0	0.1
Total fertility rate (per woman)		6.5	5.1	2.7	2.2	1.9
Life expectancy (years)						
Total	Birth	44.7	55.4	43.0	50.8	59.1
	60	..	..	16.5	18.1	19.4
	65	..	..	13.6	15.1	16.1
	80	..	..	6.6	7.3	7.9
Female	Birth	45.8	58.5	42.6	49.9	59.9
	60	..	..	18.5	20.2	21.9
	65	..	..	15.3	16.7	18.2
	80	..	..	7.1	7.9	8.7
Male	Birth	43.6	52.5	43.3	51.3	58.3
	60	..	..	14.2	15.7	17.1
	65	..	..	11.6	12.8	14.0
	80	..	..	5.7	6.2	6.6
Survival rate (percentage)						
Total	60	..	..	25.8	35.9	50.9
	65	..	..	22.4	32.0	46.3
	80	..	..	9.5	15.8	25.0
Female	60	..	..	24.9	33.3	51.1
	65	..	..	22.5	30.6	47.9
	80	..	..	11.4	17.6	30.5
Male	60	..	..	26.4	38.1	50.9
	65	..	..	21.9	32.7	45.1
	80	..	..	7.0	12.5	19.9

		1980	1990	2007	2010	2020
Labour force participation (percentage)						
Total	65+	17.0	16.3	13.3	12.9	12.4
Female	65+	11.7	9.5	5.5	5.3	5.1
Male	65+	25.3	26.7	25.2	24.8	24.1

Percentage married, age 60+			Percentage living alone, age 60+		
Total	Female	Male	Total	Female	Male
59.8	46.5	78.3	8.0	8.0	8.0

Statutory pensionable age (2006)			Percentage illiterate, age 65+		
	Female	Male	Total	Female	Male
	–	–	..	..	..

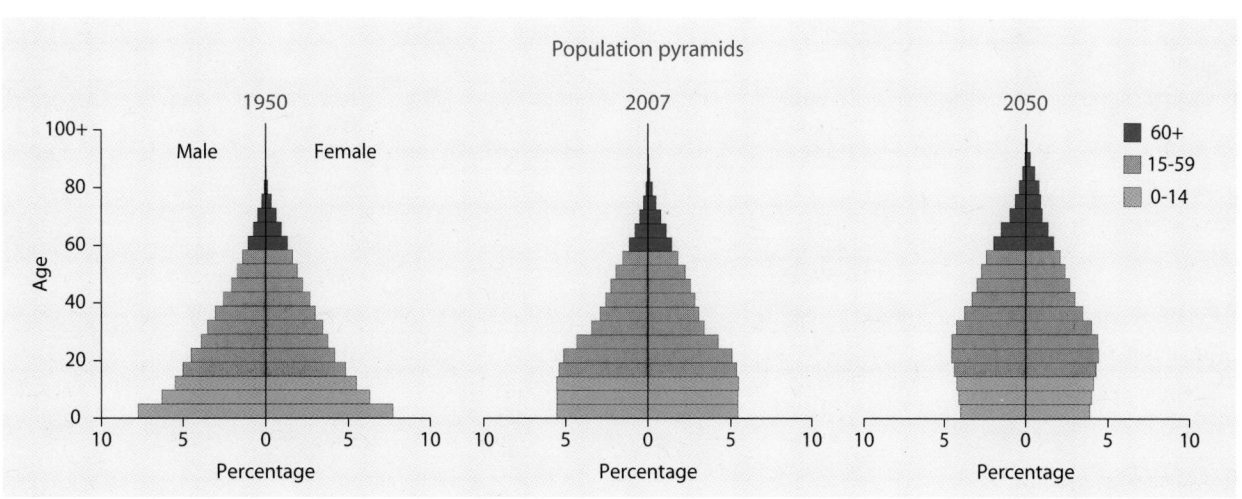

Population pyramids

1950   2007   2050

Male   Female

60+
15-59
0-14

Western Africa

Indicator	Age	1950	1975	2007	2025	2050
Population (thousands)						
Total	Total	63 823.1	115 861.1	276 061.9	401 380.8	586 989.3
	0-14	26 896.7	51 734.1	120 530.9	152 651.4	168 457.7
	15-59	33 682.6	58 451.6	142 255.7	227 172.9	366 959.8
	60-64	1 312.7	2 179.6	4 831.7	7 499.2	18 447.7
	65-69	926.6	1 575.7	3 644.3	5 801.4	13 863.5
	70-74	576.7	1 024.7	2 467.8	4 101.7	9 310.0
	75-79	294.0	592.1	1 436.8	2 456.4	5 685.8
	80-84			648.3	1 195.6	2 873.1
	85-89			203.6	403.9	1 086.3
	90-94	133.8	303.4	38.5	86.6	265.6
	95-99			4.2	10.8	37.2
	100+			0.3	0.7	2.7
Female	Total	32 110.6	57 951.6	136 660.4	197 569.2	288 633.7
	0-14	13 315.6	25 565.6	59 055.8	74 756.8	82 413.0
	15-59	16 992.3	29 333.4	70 495.7	111 306.8	179 778.1
	60-64	711.6	1 145.9	2 524.0	3 876.9	9 188.9
	65-69	512.3	842.3	1 937.8	3 073.5	7 020.9
	70-74	326.2	557.0	1 336.1	2 223.4	4 808.8
	75-79	171.6	329.5	794.3	1 354.2	3 016.5
	80-84			368.1	677.3	1 587.8
	85-89			121.0	238.3	630.1
	90-94	80.9	177.8	24.5	54.1	163.1
	95-99			2.9	7.3	24.5
	100+			0.2	0.6	2.0
Male	Total	31 712.5	57 909.5	139 401.5	203 811.6	298 355.7
	0-14	13 581.1	26 168.5	61 475.1	77 894.6	86 044.7
	15-59	16 690.2	29 118.2	71 760.0	115 866.2	187 181.7
	60-64	601.1	1 033.6	2 307.7	3 622.3	9 258.8
	65-69	414.2	733.3	1 706.6	2 727.9	6 842.6
	70-74	250.5	467.7	1 131.6	1 878.4	4 501.2
	75-79	122.5	262.7	642.5	1 102.2	2 669.4
	80-84			280.2	518.3	1 285.2
	85-89			82.6	165.5	456.2
	90-94	52.8	125.6	13.9	32.5	102.6
	95-99			1.2	3.5	12.6
	100+			0.1	0.2	0.7
Percentage in older ages						
Total	60+	5.1	4.9	4.8	5.4	8.8
	65+	3.0	3.0	3.1	3.5	5.6
	80+	0.2	0.3	0.3	0.4	0.7
Female	60+	5.6	5.3	5.2	5.8	9.2
	65+	3.4	3.3	3.4	3.9	6.0
	80+	0.3	0.3	0.4	0.5	0.8
Male	60+	4.5	4.5	4.4	4.9	8.4
	65+	2.6	2.7	2.8	3.2	5.3
	80+	0.2	0.2	0.3	0.4	0.6
Ageing index		12.1	11.0	11.0	14.1	30.6
Broad age groups (percentage)	0-14	42.1	44.7	43.7	38.0	28.7
	15-59	52.8	50.4	51.5	56.6	62.5
	60+	5.1	4.9	4.8	5.4	8.8
Median age (years)		18.9	17.6	17.6*	20.6	27.0
Dependency ratio	Total	82.4	91.1	87.7	71.0	52.3
	Youth	76.9	85.3	81.9	65.0	43.7
	Old Age	5.5	5.8	5.7	6.0	8.6
Potential support ratio		18.1	17.3	17.4	16.7	11.6
Parent support ratio		0.6	0.8	1.3	1.8	2.0
Sex ratio (per 100 women)	60+	79.9	85.9	86.7	87.4	95.0
	65+	77.0	83.4	84.2	84.3	92.0
	80+	65.3	70.6	73.2	73.6	77.1

* *Estimate refers to year 2005.*

Indicator	Age	1950-1955	1975-1980	2005-2010	2025-2030	2045-2050
Growth rate (percentage)	Total	2.2	2.8	2.3	1.8	1.3
	60+	2.1	2.5	2.5	2.8	4.0
	65+	2.0	2.4	2.8	2.9	4.3
	80+	2.0	2.9	3.5	3.5	3.7
Total fertility rate (per woman)		6.8	7.0	5.3	3.5	2.6
Life expectancy (years)						
Total	Birth	36.4	44.9	47.4	55.6	64.1
	60	..	..	15.8	17.1	18.4
	65	..	..	12.6	13.7	14.8
	80	..	..	5.4	5.9	6.3
Female	Birth	37.7	46.3	47.8	56.1	65.2
	60	..	..	16.3	17.7	19.2
	65	..	..	13.0	14.1	15.4
	80	..	..	5.6	6.0	6.5
Male	Birth	35.1	43.6	46.9	55.0	63.0
	60	..	..	15.2	16.4	17.7
	65	..	..	12.1	13.1	14.2
	80	..	..	5.2	5.6	6.0
Survival rate (percentage)						
Total	60	..	..	44.2	56.3	70.0
	65	..	..	38.9	50.7	64.5
	80	..	..	14.3	21.7	31.6
Female	60	..	..	44.9	57.1	71.5
	65	..	..	40.0	52.1	66.7
	80	..	..	15.6	23.6	34.7
Male	60	..	..	43.5	55.5	68.6
	65	..	..	37.7	49.3	62.4
	80	..	..	13.0	19.7	28.5

		1980	1990	2007	2010	2020
Labour force participation (percentage)						
Total	65+	49.5	51.1	48.1	47.6	46.9
Female	65+	32.6	33.6	30.1	29.9	29.9
Male	65+	69.8	72.0	69.6	68.7	67.1

Percentage married, age 60+				Percentage living alone, age 60+		
Total	Female	Male		Total	Female	Male
62.2	40.3	87.5		7.0	10.0	5.0

Statutory pensionable age (2006)			Percentage illiterate, age 65+		
Female	Male		Total	Female	Male
–	–		..	..	..

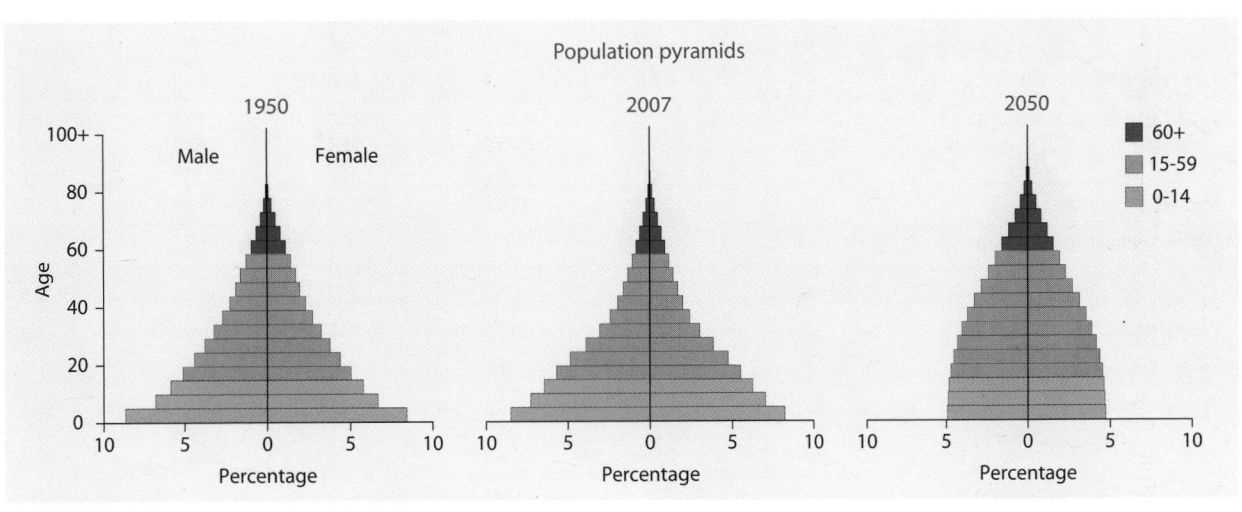

Population pyramids

Asia

Indicator	Age	1950	1975	2007	2025	2050
Population (thousands)						
Total	Total	1 396 254.1	2 395 218.0	3 995 674.0	4 728 131.3	5 217 202.1
	0-14	509 428.5	948 913.0	1 077 626.3	1 067 326.2	953 890.6
	15-59	792 311.9	1 287 035.5	2 532 638.5	2 954 533.2	3 032 074.5
	60-64	37 084.9	58 411.9	121 718.4	225 672.3	320 722.0
	65-69	27 017.9	44 302.3	96 881.8	174 151.4	270 656.3
	70-74	17 039.8	29 528.7	75 051.8	137 529.3	218 969.6
	75-79	8 995.6	15 872.9	49 804.1	85 622.0	185 970.6
	80-84			26 744.9	47 448.8	130 025.8
	85-89			11 046.2	23 850.5	67 719.4
	90-94	4 375.5	11 153.9	3 365.0	9 125.8	26 643.8
	95-99			704.7	2 434.8	8 566.6
	100+			92.3	437.1	1 962.9
Female	Total	681 394.2	1 169 264.1	1 961 447.9	2 337 316.9	2 604 357.8
	0-14	247 658.8	460 200.2	521 535.7	517 506.4	463 597.7
	15-59	382 852.3	624 822.4	1 235 213.3	1 445 239.8	1 479 726.8
	60-64	18 795.4	29 681.8	61 480.4	114 254.0	160 569.9
	65-69	14 757.9	23 226.3	50 072.1	89 236.7	138 737.5
	70-74	9 461.2	16 045.0	39 861.7	72 772.0	115 609.0
	75-79	5 224.8	8 958.2	27 550.6	47 185.1	102 124.3
	80-84			15 753.3	27 643.1	75 440.0
	85-89			7 047.2	14 940.2	42 204.5
	90-94	2 643.8	6 330.1	2 329.1	6 290.3	18 135.0
	95-99			530.5	1 874.5	6 532.2
	100+			74.0	374.8	1 680.8
Male	Total	714 859.9	1 225 954.0	2 034 226.0	2 390 814.4	2 612 844.3
	0-14	261 769.7	488 712.8	556 090.6	549 819.8	490 292.9
	15-59	409 459.6	662 213.1	1 297 425.2	1 509 293.4	1 552 347.7
	60-64	18 289.6	28 730.0	60 238.0	111 418.3	160 152.0
	65-69	12 260.0	21 076.0	46 809.8	84 914.7	131 918.8
	70-74	7 578.6	13 483.6	35 190.1	64 757.3	103 360.6
	75-79	3 770.7	6 914.7	22 253.4	38 436.8	83 846.3
	80-84			10 991.6	19 805.7	54 585.8
	85-89			3 999.0	8 910.3	25 515.0
	90-94	1 731.8	4 823.8	1 035.9	2 835.5	8 508.8
	95-99			174.2	560.3	2 034.4
	100+			18.3	62.3	282.1
Percentage in older ages						
Total	60+	6.8	6.6	9.6	14.9	23.6
	65+	4.1	4.2	6.6	10.2	17.5
	80+	0.3	0.5	1.0	1.8	4.5
Female	60+	7.5	7.2	10.4	16.0	25.4
	65+	4.7	4.7	7.3	11.1	19.2
	80+	0.4	0.5	1.3	2.2	5.5
Male	60+	6.1	6.1	8.9	13.9	21.8
	65+	3.5	3.8	5.9	9.2	15.7
	80+	0.2	0.4	0.8	1.3	3.5
Ageing index		18.6	16.8	35.8	66.2	129.1
Broad age groups (percentage)	0-14	36.5	39.6	27.0	22.6	18.3
	15-59	56.7	53.7	63.4	62.5	58.1
	60+	6.8	6.6	9.6	14.9	23.6
Median age (years)		22.0	20.3	27.7*	33.7	39.9
Dependency ratio	Total	68.3	78.0	50.5	48.7	55.6
	Youth	61.4	70.5	40.6	33.6	28.5
	Old Age	6.9	7.5	9.9	15.1	27.2
Potential support ratio		14.4	13.3	10.1	6.6	3.7
Parent support ratio		1.0	1.5	3.1	4.5	10.6
Sex ratio (per 100 women)	60+	85.7	89.1	88.3	88.6	86.3
	65+	79.0	84.9	84.1	84.6	81.9
	80+	65.5	76.2	63.0	62.9	63.1

*   *Estimate refers to year 2005.*

Indicator	Age	1950-1955	1975-1980	2005-2010	2025-2030	2045-2050
Growth rate (percentage)	Total	2.0	1.9	1.1	0.6	0.2
	60+	1.8	2.6	3.0	3.3	1.7
	65+	2.2	3.0	2.6	3.5	1.6
	80+	3.4	1.2	4.7	4.2	3.8
Total fertility rate (per woman)		5.9	4.2	2.3	2.0	1.9
Life expectancy (years)						
Total	Birth	41.4	58.6	68.8	73.5	77.2
	60	..	..	18.9	20.7	22.1
	65	..	..	15.4	16.9	18.1
	80	..	..	7.2	8.1	8.7
Female	Birth	42.2	59.3	70.8	75.9	79.5
	60	..	..	20.4	22.4	24.0
	65	..	..	16.6	18.4	19.8
	80	..	..	7.8	8.8	9.6
Male	Birth	40.7	57.8	66.8	71.3	75.0
	60	..	..	17.5	19.0	20.2
	65	..	..	14.1	15.4	16.4
	80	..	..	6.5	7.1	7.6
Survival rate (percentage)						
Total	60	..	..	78.9	84.7	89.4
	65	..	..	72.6	79.4	84.8
	80	..	..	36.6	45.6	53.3
Female	60	..	..	81.8	87.3	91.2
	65	..	..	76.6	83.2	87.8
	80	..	..	43.1	53.0	60.9
Male	60	..	..	76.2	82.2	87.6
	65	..	..	68.8	75.8	81.9
	80	..	..	30.6	38.6	46.0

		1980	1990	2007	2010	2020
Labour force participation (percentage)						
Total	65+	26.6	26.3	23.8	23.3	21.7
Female	65+	11.4	12.8	13.4	13.7	14.3
Male	65+	44.5	42.3	36.1	34.7	30.5

Percentage married, age 60+				Percentage living alone, age 60+		
Total	Female	Male		Total	Female	Male
64.5	49.7	81.1		7.0	9.0	5.0

Statutory pensionable age (2006)				Percentage illiterate, age 65+		
	Female	Male		Total	Female	Male
	–	–		..	..	..

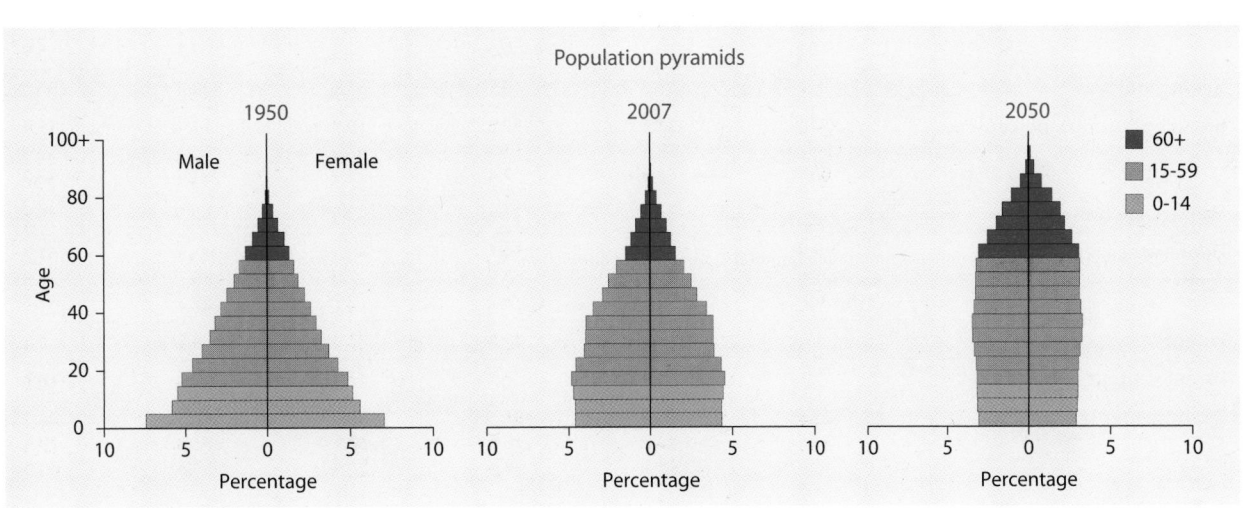

Population pyramids

Eastern Asia

Indicator	Age	1950	1975	2007	2025	2050
Population (thousands)						
Total	Total	670 984.9	1 096 726.2	1 540 865.1	1 651 971.1	1 586 703.9
	0-14	228 924.0	414 961.4	305 794.5	287 085.4	244 882.5
	15-59	392 301.7	600 912.7	1 036 106.6	1 010 746.2	834 865.2
	60-64	19 783.3	29 085.0	60 232.7	106 410.9	114 318.4
	65-69	14 873.0	22 211.2	48 160.2	81 003.0	94 985.6
	70-74	8 660.3	15 170.7	39 266.3	72 472.4	84 550.8
	75-79	4 433.5	7 856.5	27 007.1	46 326.5	87 201.8
	80-84			15 125.9	25 885.3	67 434.1
	85-89			6 545.4	13 956.8	36 015.2
	90-94	2 009.2	6 528.8	2 091.1	5 964.8	15 019.5
	95-99			471.5	1 768.4	5 839.6
	100+			63.7	351.4	1 591.3
Female	Total	325 303.0	534 995.3	754 425.0	815 908.3	792 791.7
	0-14	108 412.0	200 849.3	145 055.0	136 587.2	117 226.0
	15-59	189 262.7	289 600.5	503 789.7	490 456.8	400 473.7
	60-64	10 229.1	15 067.2	29 797.4	53 658.2	56 292.3
	65-69	8 157.9	12 102.0	24 335.5	41 169.3	48 086.0
	70-74	5 061.8	8 745.9	20 656.0	38 333.3	44 278.7
	75-79	2 794.9	4 779.0	15 059.0	25 430.3	47 748.4
	80-84			9 235.5	15 167.7	39 290.7
	85-89			4 463.0	8 991.7	22 784.6
	90-94	1 384.6	3 851.4	1 582.5	4 341.3	10 557.3
	95-99			393.7	1 452.2	4 642.5
	100+			57.5	320.2	1 411.4
Male	Total	345 681.9	561 731.0	786 440.1	836 062.8	793 912.2
	0-14	120 511.9	214 112.1	160 739.5	150 498.2	127 656.4
	15-59	203 038.9	311 312.2	532 316.9	520 289.4	434 391.5
	60-64	9 554.2	14 017.8	30 435.2	52 752.7	58 026.1
	65-69	6 715.2	10 109.2	23 824.7	39 833.7	46 899.6
	70-74	3 598.4	6 424.8	18 610.3	34 139.1	40 272.1
	75-79	1 638.6	3 077.5	11 948.1	20 896.1	39 453.3
	80-84			5 890.4	10 717.6	28 143.4
	85-89			2 082.3	4 965.1	13 230.6
	90-94	624.6	2 677.4	508.6	1 623.4	4 462.1
	95-99			77.8	316.2	1 197.1
	100+			6.3	31.2	180.0
Percentage in older ages						
Total	60+	7.4	7.4	12.9	21.4	32.0
	65+	4.5	4.7	9.0	15.0	24.7
	80+	0.3	0.6	1.6	2.9	7.9
Female	60+	8.5	8.3	14.0	23.1	34.7
	65+	5.3	5.5	10.0	16.6	27.6
	80+	0.4	0.7	2.1	3.7	9.9
Male	60+	6.4	6.5	11.9	19.8	29.2
	65+	3.6	4.0	8.0	13.5	21.9
	80+	0.2	0.5	1.1	2.1	5.9
Ageing index		21.7	19.5	65.1	123.4	207.0
Broad age groups (percentage)	0-14	34.1	37.8	19.8	17.4	15.4
	15-59	58.5	54.8	67.2	61.2	52.6
	60+	7.4	7.4	12.9	21.4	32.0
Median age (years)		23.5	21.6	33.5*	40.5	45.5
Dependency ratio	Total	62.8	74.1	40.5	47.9	67.2
	Youth	55.6	65.9	27.9	25.7	25.8
	Old Age	7.3	8.2	12.7	22.2	41.4
Potential support ratio		13.7	12.2	7.9	4.5	2.4
Parent support ratio		0.9	1.7	3.8	6.0	18.3
Sex ratio (per 100 women)	60+	80.1	81.5	88.4	87.5	84.3
	65+	72.3	75.6	83.1	83.2	79.5
	80+	45.1	69.5	54.4	58.3	60.0

* Estimate refers to year 2005.

Indicator	Age	1950-1955	1975-1980	2005-2010	2025-2030	2045-2050
Growth rate (percentage)	Total	1.8	1.4	0.5	0.0	−0.4
	60+	2.2	2.8	3.1	3.2	0.7
	65+	2.6	3.1	2.4	3.2	0.2
	80+	4.6	−1.0	4.8	4.5	3.8
Total fertility rate (per woman)		5.7	3.1	1.7	1.8	1.8
Life expectancy (years)						
Total	Birth	42.9	66.4	73.8	76.4	79.6
	60	..	..	20.0	21.7	23.1
	65	..	..	16.2	17.8	19.0
	80	..	..	7.6	8.7	9.2
Female	Birth	44.7	67.6	76.1	79.2	82.0
	60	..	..	22.0	23.9	25.2
	65	..	..	17.9	19.8	20.9
	80	..	..	8.4	9.7	10.3
Male	Birth	41.4	65.1	71.6	73.8	77.2
	60	..	..	18.1	19.6	21.0
	65	..	..	14.5	15.9	17.0
	80	..	..	6.5	7.3	7.8
Survival rate (percentage)						
Total	60	..	..	85.9	87.8	91.7
	65	..	..	80.3	83.1	87.8
	80	..	..	43.8	50.7	58.2
Female	60	..	..	88.3	90.3	93.3
	65	..	..	84.1	86.8	90.4
	80	..	..	52.4	59.5	66.1
Male	60	..	..	83.7	85.5	90.3
	65	..	..	76.7	79.6	85.4
	80	..	..	35.8	42.4	50.4

		1980	1990	2007	2010	2020
Labour force participation (percentage)						
Total	65+	18.3	20.4	18.0	17.4	15.9
Female	65+	7.2	9.9	11.3	11.7	12.6
Male	65+	33.0	33.5	26.0	24.2	19.8

Percentage married, age 60+			Percentage living alone, age 60+		
Total	Female	Male	Total	Female	Male
66.4	54.7	79.6	9.0	11.0	7.0

Statutory pensionable age (2006)			Percentage illiterate, age 65+		
	Female	Male	Total	Female	Male
	–	–	..	..	..

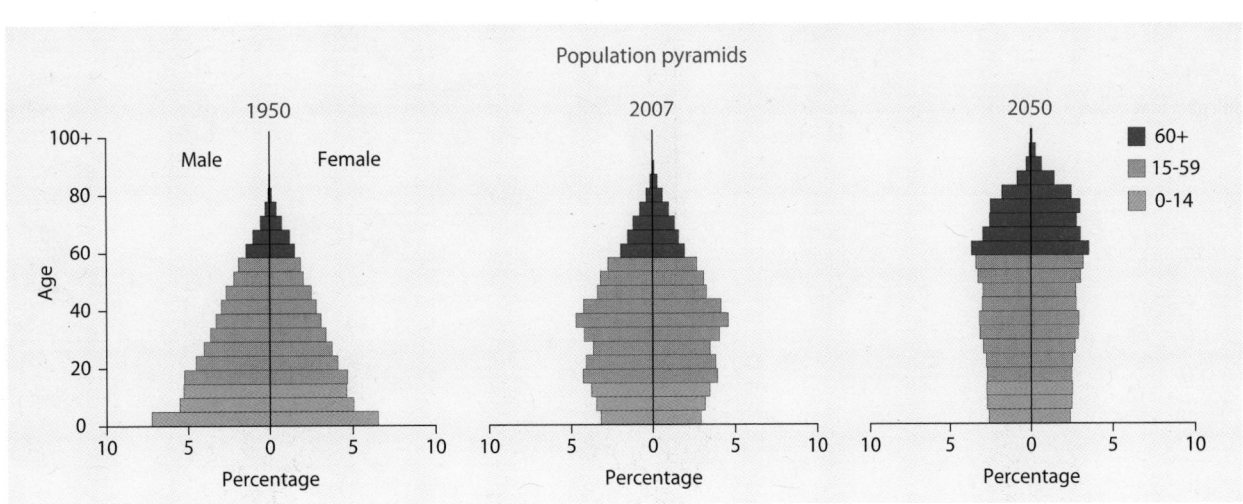

Population pyramids

1950   2007   2050

Male   Female

■ 60+
▨ 15-59
▢ 0-14

Age
Percentage

South-central Asia

Indicator	Age	1950	1975	2007	2025	2050
Population (thousands)						
Total	Total	496 092.1	876 101.8	1 661 857.1	2 098 693.8	2 495 028.2
	0-14	191 468.4	355 805.4	534 467.2	545 160.2	492 349.4
	15-59	274 257.7	466 642.4	1 002 130.8	1 320 886.0	1 521 660.6
	60-64	11 912.9	20 251.7	41 637.4	78 407.4	140 803.7
	65-69	8 234.8	15 159.3	32 649.4	61 169.1	117 530.6
	70-74	5 666.9	9 775.1	23 744.7	42 799.2	87 226.9
	75-79	3 029.0	5 449.0	15 113.8	26 171.7	64 052.3
	80-84			7 825.1	14 481.2	40 524.2
	85-89			3 146.0	6 769.8	20 829.9
	90-94	1 522.4	3 018.9	934.2	2 266.7	7 858.8
	95-99			184.0	510.9	1 913.9
	100+			24.6	71.6	277.9
Female	Total	241 097.5	423 861.7	812 607.7	1 033 991.2	1 241 918.5
	0-14	94 750.6	171 583.6	260 071.8	265 898.9	240 584.7
	15-59	130 914.0	225 874.9	486 674.7	646 553.9	746 917.2
	60-64	5 680.5	9 892.4	21 290.8	39 508.4	70 905.0
	65-69	4 497.6	7 433.4	17 084.0	31 282.0	60 431.4
	70-74	2 920.8	4 812.6	12 602.7	22 440.0	46 111.8
	75-79	1 568.7	2 745.3	8 164.1	14 355.1	35 068.0
	80-84			4 309.3	8 269.0	23 110.4
	85-89			1 763.4	3 980.8	12 431.6
	90-94	765.3	1 519.5	529.9	1 350.3	4 913.9
	95-99			103.4	309.3	1 254.4
	100+			13.6	43.5	190.1
Male	Total	254 994.6	452 240.2	849 249.4	1 064 702.6	1 253 109.6
	0-14	96 717.8	184 221.8	274 395.4	279 261.3	251 764.7
	15-59	143 343.7	240 767.5	515 456.1	674 332.1	774 743.4
	60-64	6 232.4	10 359.3	20 346.6	38 899.0	69 898.7
	65-69	3 737.2	7 725.9	15 565.4	29 887.0	57 099.2
	70-74	2 746.1	4 962.6	11 141.9	20 359.3	41 115.1
	75-79	1 460.3	2 703.7	6 949.7	11 816.6	28 984.2
	80-84			3 515.8	6 212.2	17 413.9
	85-89			1 382.6	2 789.0	8 398.2
	90-94	757.1	1 499.4	404.3	916.4	2 944.9
	95-99			80.6	201.6	659.5
	100+			11.0	28.1	87.8
Percentage in older ages						
Total	60+	6.1	6.1	7.5	11.1	19.3
	65+	3.7	3.8	5.0	7.3	13.6
	80+	0.3	0.3	0.7	1.1	2.9
Female	60+	6.4	6.2	8.1	11.8	20.5
	65+	4.0	3.9	5.5	7.9	14.8
	80+	0.3	0.4	0.8	1.3	3.4
Male	60+	5.9	6.0	7.0	10.4	18.1
	65+	3.4	3.7	4.6	6.8	12.5
	80+	0.3	0.3	0.6	1.0	2.4
Ageing index		15.9	15.1	23.4	42.7	97.7
Broad age groups (percentage)	0-14	38.6	40.6	32.2	26.0	19.7
	15-59	55.3	53.3	60.3	62.9	61.0
	60+	6.1	6.1	7.5	11.1	19.3
Median age (years)		20.7	19.6	23.5*	29.4	37.0
Dependency ratio	Total	73.4	79.9	59.2	50.0	50.1
	Youth	66.9	73.1	51.2	39.0	29.6
	Old Age	6.4	6.9	8.0	11.0	20.5
Potential support ratio		15.5	14.6	12.5	9.1	4.9
Parent support ratio		1.1	1.1	2.6	3.4	6.7
Sex ratio (per 100 women)	60+	96.8	103.2	90.2	91.4	89.1
	65+	89.2	102.3	87.6	88.0	85.4
	80+	98.9	98.7	80.3	72.7	70.4

* Estimate refers to year 2005.

Indicator	Age	1950-1955	1975-1980	2005-2010	2025-2030	2045-2050
Growth rate (percentage)	Total	2.0	2.2	1.5	0.9	0.5
	60+	1.6	2.6	2.8	3.3	2.7
	65+	1.8	2.9	2.7	3.7	3.0
	80+	2.1	3.5	4.5	4.0	3.7
Total fertility rate (per woman)		6.1	5.1	2.9	2.1	1.9
Life expectancy (years)						
Total	Birth	39.6	52.9	64.7	70.9	75.3
	60	..	..	17.7	19.6	21.2
	65	..	..	14.4	16.0	17.3
	80	..	..	6.9	7.5	8.2
Female	Birth	39.0	52.7	66.3	72.8	77.4
	60	..	..	18.7	20.8	22.8
	65	..	..	15.1	16.9	18.7
	80	..	..	7.1	7.9	8.8
Male	Birth	40.1	53.0	63.2	69.1	73.3
	60	..	..	16.8	18.4	19.7
	65	..	..	13.6	14.9	16.0
	80	..	..	6.6	7.2	7.6
Survival rate (percentage)						
Total	60	..	..	72.9	81.7	87.5
	65	..	..	65.7	75.6	82.4
	80	..	..	30.0	40.4	49.2
Female	60	..	..	76.1	84.4	89.5
	65	..	..	69.8	79.5	85.6
	80	..	..	34.5	46.4	56.2
Male	60	..	..	69.9	79.2	85.5
	65	..	..	61.9	72.0	79.3
	80	..	..	25.7	34.8	42.7

		1980	1990	2007	2010	2020
Labour force participation (percentage)						
Total	65+	36.8	33.8	29.1	28.6	27.0
Female	65+	14.7	14.3	12.1	12.1	12.2
Male	65+	58.7	54.3	48.6	47.6	44.0

Percentage married, age 60+			Percentage living alone, age 60+		
Total	Female	Male	Total	Female	Male
62.6	44.4	82.3	4.0	6.0	2.0

Statutory pensionable age (2006)			Percentage illiterate, age 65+		
	Female	Male	Total	Female	Male
	–	–	..	..	..

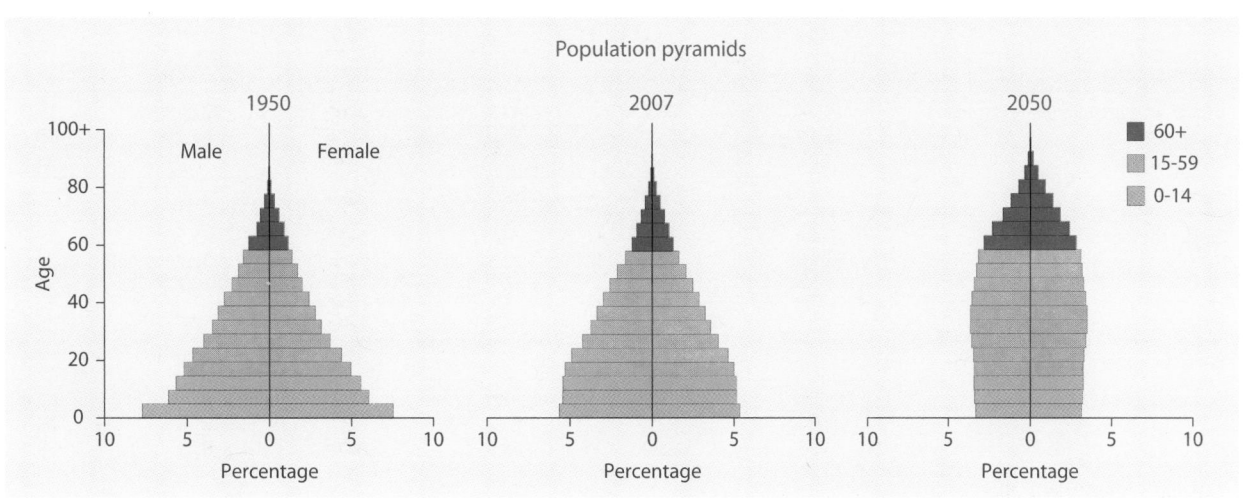

Population pyramids

1950   2007   2050

Male Female

■ 60+
▨ 15-59
▨ 0-14

South-eastern Asia

Indicator	Age	1950	1975	2007	2025	2050
Population (thousands)						
Total	Total	178 072.9	321 293.2	570 169.6	678 347.5	752 253.9
	0-14	69 243.6	135 336.0	163 515.8	152 607.8	135 503.6
	15-59	98 093.6	167 680.5	360 291.2	436 192.9	441 791.2
	60-64	3 983.8	6 855.5	15 199.8	30 154.8	46 394.6
	65-69	2 986.1	5 110.3	12 226.7	24 022.4	41 651.6
	70-74	1 996.9	3 348.5	9 077.2	16 843.3	33 941.4
	75-79	1 142.7	1 848.3	5 701.7*	9 957.1	25 147.6
	80-84			2 821.1	5 428.3	16 270.7
	85-89			1 043.2	2 347.9	8 037.1
	90-94	626.2	1 114.2	254.7	671.4	2 832.0
	95-99			35.5	111.5	614.6
	100+			2.7	10.0	69.5
Female	Total	89 342.1	160 551.1	285 873.9	340 790.7	379 926.8
	0-14	34 768.0	66 841.2	80 257.5	74 678.1	66 155.5
	15-59	48 797.2	83 934.4	180 373.9	217 746.0	218 397.2
	60-64	2 094.7	3 557.3	7 996.4	15 705.3	23 708.0
	65-69	1 604.6	2 704.8	6 580.8	12 691.9	21 775.1
	70-74	1 079.5	1 816.9	5 000.2	9 109.7	18 280.9
	75-79	636.5	1 033.1	3 217.8	5 630.1	14 151.1
	80-84			1 634.8	3 220.0	9 718.2
	85-89			626.7	1 472.9	5 190.5
	90-94	361.6	663.4	160.2	448.9	2 010.3
	95-99			23.6	80.2	481.2
	100+			1.9	7.7	58.8
Male	Total	88 730.8	160 742.1	284 295.7	337 556.8	372 327.1
	0-14	34 475.6	68 494.7	83 258.3	77 929.7	69 348.2
	15-59	49 296.4	83 746.1	179 917.4	218 446.9	223 394.0
	60-64	1 889.1	3 298.2	7 203.4	14 449.5	22 686.6
	65-69	1 381.5	2 405.5	5 646.0	11 330.5	19 876.5
	70-74	917.4	1 531.6	4 076.9	7 733.6	15 660.4
	75-79	506.3	815.2	2 483.9	4 327.0	10 996.5
	80-84			1 186.3	2 208.4	6 552.6
	85-89			416.5	875.0	2 846.6
	90-94	264.5	450.9	94.5	222.5	821.7
	95-99			11.9	31.4	133.3
	100+			0.8	2.3	10.7
Percentage in older ages						
Total	60+	6.0	5.7	8.1	13.2	23.3
	65+	3.8	3.6	5.5	8.8	17.1
	80+	0.4	0.3	0.7	1.3	3.7
Female	60+	6.5	6.1	8.8	14.2	25.1
	65+	4.1	3.9	6.0	9.6	18.9
	80+	0.4	0.4	0.9	1.5	4.6
Male	60+	5.6	5.3	7.4	12.2	21.4
	65+	3.5	3.2	4.9	7.9	15.3
	80+	0.3	0.3	0.6	1.0	2.8
Ageing index		15.5	13.5	28.4	58.7	129.1
Broad age groups (percentage)	0-14	38.9	42.1	28.7	22.5	18.0
	15-59	55.1	52.2	63.2	64.3	58.7
	60+	6.0	5.7	8.1	13.2	23.3
Median age (years)		20.5	18.7	25.7*	32.7	40.0
Dependency ratio	Total	74.4	84.1	51.8	45.5	54.1
	Youth	67.8	77.5	43.5	32.7	27.8
	Old Age	6.6	6.5	8.3	12.7	26.3
Potential support ratio		15.1	15.3	12.0	7.9	3.8
Parent support ratio		1.2	1.2	2.2	2.9	8.0
Sex ratio (per 100 women)	60+	85.8	87.0	83.7	85.1	83.4
	65+	83.4	83.7	80.7	81.8	79.4
	80+	73.2	68.0	69.9	63.9	59.4

* *Estimate refers to year 2005.*

Indicator	Age	1950-1955	1975-1980	2005-2010	2025-2030	2045-2050
Growth rate (percentage)	Total	2.1	2.2	1.2	0.7	0.2
	60+	1.0	2.4	2.9	3.5	1.9
	65+	1.0	2.9	2.9	3.9	2.4
	80+	1.9	3.1	4.5	3.9	3.9
Total fertility rate (per woman)		6.0	4.9	2.3	1.9	1.9
Life expectancy (years)						
Total	Birth	41.0	54.8	69.0	73.9	77.4
	60	..	..	18.1	19.7	21.4
	65	..	..	14.5	15.9	17.4
	80	..	..	6.3	7.0	8.0
Female	Birth	42.1	56.6	71.3	76.0	79.7
	60	..	..	19.0	21.0	23.1
	65	..	..	15.2	16.9	18.9
	80	..	..	6.6	7.4	8.7
Male	Birth	39.9	53.2	66.9	71.8	75.2
	60	..	..	17.0	18.3	19.7
	65	..	..	13.6	14.7	15.8
	80	..	..	6.0	6.4	6.9
Survival rate (percentage)						
Total	60	..	..	78.9	86.0	90.3
	65	..	..	72.3	80.4	85.7
	80	..	..	34.1	43.6	52.3
Female	60	..	..	82.5	88.6	92.1
	65	..	..	76.8	84.1	88.6
	80	..	..	39.3	50.0	59.6
Male	60	..	..	75.5	83.5	88.5
	65	..	..	67.9	76.8	82.8
	80	..	..	29.0	37.1	44.8

		1980	1990	2007	2010	2020
Labour force participation (percentage)						
Total	65+	35.7	35.9	35.6	35.5	34.1
Female	65+	22.2	23.9	26.1	26.8	27.5
Male	65+	51.8	50.4	47.4	46.4	42.3

Percentage married, age 60+			Percentage living alone, age 60+		
Total	Female	Male	Total	Female	Male
60.8	42.2	82.7	6.0	9.0	3.0

Statutory pensionable age (2006)		Percentage illiterate, age 65+		
Female	Male	Total	Female	Male
–	–	..	..	..

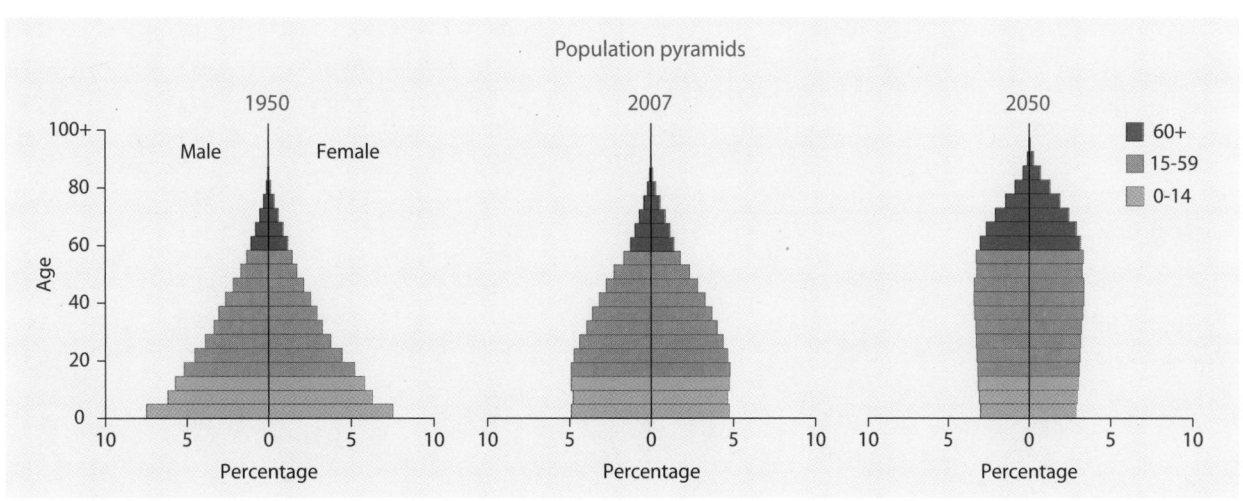

Population pyramids

1950   2007   2050

■ 60+
■ 15-59
■ 0-14

Male   Female

Age — Percentage

Western Asia

Indicator	Age	1950	1975	2007	2025	2050
Population (thousands)						
Total	Total	51 104.2	101 096.7	222 782.1	299 118.9	383 216.1
	0-14	19 792.5	42 810.2	73 848.7	82 472.7	81 155.2
	15-59	27 658.9	51 799.9	134 109.8	186 708.2	233 757.5
	60-64	1 404.9	2 219.7	4 648.5	10 699.3	19 205.2
	65-69	924.0	1 821.5	3 845.5	7 956.9	16 488.5
	70-74	715.7	1 234.4	2 963.6	5 414.4	13 250.5
	75-79	390.3	719.1	1 981.5	3 166.7	9 569.0
	80-84			972.7	1 653.9	5 796.8
	85-89			311.6	776.0	2 837.3
	90-94	217.8	491.9	85.0	222.9	933.6
	95-99			13.7	44.0	198.6
	100+			1.3	4.1	24.1
Female	Total	25 651.6	49 856.0	108 541.3	146 626.7	189 720.8
	0-14	9 728.2	20 926.0	36 151.3	40 342.2	39 631.5
	15-59	13 878.4	25 412.6	64 375.0	90 483.1	113 938.6
	60-64	791.0	1 164.9	2 395.8	5 382.1	9 664.7
	65-69	497.8	986.1	2 071.8	4 093.5	8 445.0
	70-74	399.1	669.7	1 602.7	2 889.0	6 937.6
	75-79	224.8	400.9	1 109.7	1 769.6	5 156.8
	80-84			573.6	986.4	3 320.8
	85-89			194.1	494.8	1 797.7
	90-94	132.2	295.9	56.5	149.7	653.5
	95-99			9.8	32.8	154.1
	100+			1.0	3.4	20.5
Male	Total	25 452.6	51 240.7	114 240.8	152 492.2	193 495.4
	0-14	10 064.3	21 884.2	37 697.4	42 130.5	41 523.6
	15-59	13 780.5	26 387.3	69 734.9	96 225.0	119 818.8
	60-64	613.9	1 054.8	2 252.7	5 317.2	9 540.6
	65-69	426.2	835.4	1 773.7	3 863.4	8 043.4
	70-74	316.6	564.7	1 360.9	2 525.3	6 313.0
	75-79	165.6	318.2	871.8	1 397.1	4 412.2
	80-84			399.1	667.5	2 476.0
	85-89			117.5	281.2	1 039.5
	90-94	85.5	196.0	28.5	73.2	280.1
	95-99			4.0	11.1	44.5
	100+			0.3	0.7	3.6
Percentage in older ages						
Total	60+	7.1	6.4	6.7	10.0	17.8
	65+	4.4	4.2	4.6	6.4	12.8
	80+	0.4	0.5	0.6	0.9	2.6
Female	60+	8.0	7.1	7.4	10.8	19.1
	65+	4.9	4.7	5.2	7.1	14.0
	80+	0.5	0.6	0.8	1.1	3.1
Male	60+	6.3	5.8	6.0	9.3	16.6
	65+	3.9	3.7	4.0	5.8	11.7
	80+	0.3	0.4	0.5	0.7	2.0
Ageing index		18.5	15.2	20.1	36.3	84.2
Broad age groups (percentage)	0-14	38.7	42.3	33.1	27.6	21.2
	15-59	54.1	51.2	60.2	62.4	61.0
	60+	7.1	6.4	6.7	10.0	17.8
Median age (years)		20.4	18.8	23.6*	28.5	35.3
Dependency ratio	Total	75.8	87.1	60.6	51.5	51.5
	Youth	68.1	79.2	53.2	41.8	32.1
	Old Age	7.7	7.9	7.3	9.7	19.4
Potential support ratio		12.9	12.7	13.6	10.3	5.2
Parent support ratio		1.5	2.3	2.1	2.7	6.3
Sex ratio (per 100 women)	60+	78.6	84.4	84.9	89.5	88.9
	65+	79.3	81.4	81.1	84.6	85.4
	80+	64.7	66.2	65.8	62.0	64.6

* Estimate refers to year 2005.

Indicator	Age	1950-1955	1975-1980	2005-2010	2025-2030	2045-2050
Growth rate (percentage)	Total	2.7	2.8	1.9	1.3	0.7
	60+	1.7	1.5	2.7	3.9	2.6
	65+	2.6	2.9	2.2	4.7	2.9
	80+	4.0	7.3	6.0	4.1	4.4
Total fertility rate (per woman)		6.5	5.4	3.1	2.4	2.0
Life expectancy (years)						
Total	Birth	45.2	60.1	69.2	74.8	77.9
	60	..	..	18.1	19.8	21.5
	65	..	..	14.5	16.0	17.5
	80	..	..	6.4	7.1	8.0
Female	Birth	46.7	62.1	71.4	77.2	80.2
	60	..	..	19.3	21.3	23.3
	65	..	..	15.4	17.2	19.1
	80	..	..	6.7	7.6	8.7
Male	Birth	43.7	58.3	67.2	72.6	75.6
	60	..	..	16.9	18.2	19.7
	65	..	..	13.5	14.6	15.9
	80	..	..	5.9	6.4	7.0
Survival rate (percentage)						
Total	60	..	..	80.0	87.7	91.0
	65	..	..	73.4	82.1	86.4
	80	..	..	34.5	44.7	52.9
Female	60	..	..	83.3	90.5	93.0
	65	..	..	77.9	86.3	89.7
	80	..	..	40.5	52.3	61.0
Male	60	..	..	77.0	85.2	89.1
	65	..	..	69.2	78.3	83.2
	80	..	..	28.9	37.5	45.3

		1980	1990	2007	2010	2020
Labour force participation (percentage)						
Total	65+	23.4	18.1	21.7	21.4	20.7
Female	65+	13.3	8.3	12.7	13.0	13.4
Male	65+	36.6	30.6	32.7	31.9	29.5

Percentage married, age 60+			Percentage living alone, age 60+		
Total	Female	Male	Total	Female	Male
66.0	49.0	86.3	9.0	14.0	5.0

Statutory pensionable age (2006)			Percentage illiterate, age 65+		
	Female	Male	Total	Female	Male
	–	–	..	..	..

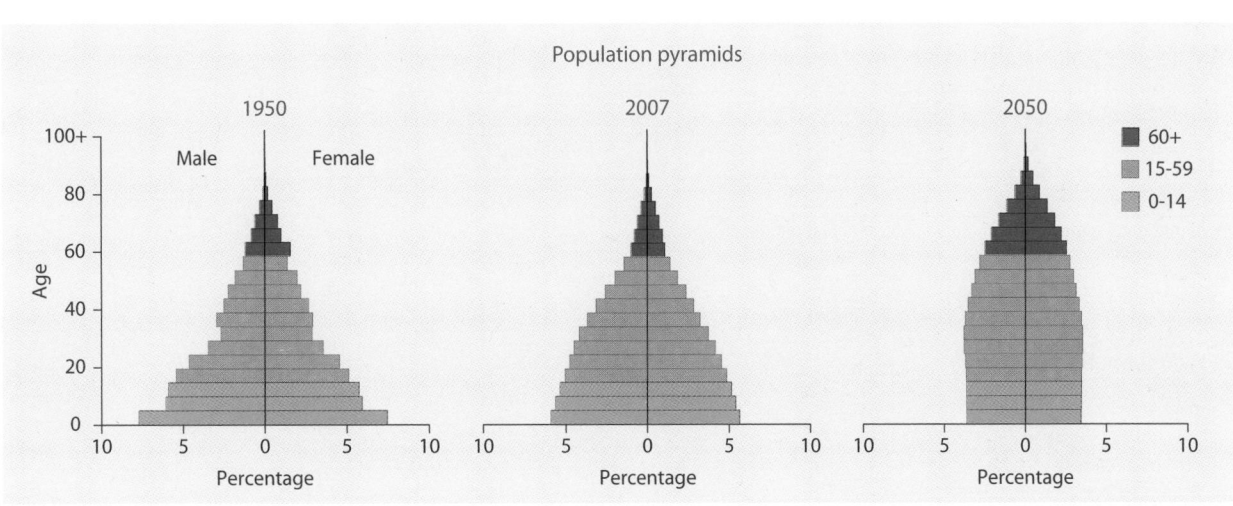

Population pyramids

1950   2007   2050

■ 60+
■ 15-59
■ 0-14

Europe

Indicator	Age	1950	1975	2007	2025	2050
Population (thousands)						
Total	Total	547 404.8	675 548.0	727 658.8	707 234.6	653 323.5
	0-14	143 240.9	160 349.9	112 689.4	104 124.2	98 111.2
	15-59	337 815.9	404 345.6	461 493.3	405 222.8	329 838.9
	60-64	21 388.1	33 585.4	36 631.9	49 366.6	45 239.3
	65-69	17 217.8	29 260.8	34 780.3	45 010.3	43 321.6
	70-74	13 194.2	22 203.3	30 069.3	37 613.4	39 257.9
	75-79	8 470.9	13 930.6	24 145.3	28 722.1	34 790.3
	80-84			16 916.8	17 970.9	28 234.3
	85-89			7 188.4	12 054.4	19 722.5
	90-94	6 077.0	11 872.6	2 876.9	5 212.2	10 254.6
	95-99			779.5	1 666.2	3 702.8
	100+			87.8	271.5	850.0
Female	Total	292 084.8	352 854.4	377 702.0	367 618.9	338 853.6
	0-14	70 613.7	78 350.4	54 869.4	50 656.9	47 708.5
	15-59	181 952.8	206 487.1	232 134.9	202 742.2	162 753.9
	60-64	12 399.2	19 580.5	19 557.8	26 213.7	23 381.7
	65-69	10 094.5	17 357.1	19 401.3	24 721.3	22 987.6
	70-74	7 851.8	13 723.1	17 466.0	21 464.5	21 533.3
	75-79	5 187.0	9 092.1	14 834.6	16 971.6	19 847.1
	80-84			11 372.2	11 229.6	16 956.6
	85-89			5 166.4	8 214.9	12 786.8
	90-94	3 985.9	8 264.1	2 198.0	3 831.0	7 287.7
	95-99			628.8	1 337.8	2 888.5
	100+			72.6	235.2	721.9
Male	Total	255 320.0	322 693.6	349 956.7	339 615.7	314 469.8
	0-14	72 627.2	81 999.5	57 819.9	53 467.4	50 402.7
	15-59	155 863.2	197 858.5	229 358.4	202 480.5	167 085.0
	60-64	8 988.9	14 004.9	17 074.1	23 152.8	21 857.6
	65-69	7 123.3	11 903.7	15 379.0	20 288.9	20 334.0
	70-74	5 342.3	8 480.2	12 603.3	16 148.9	17 724.7
	75-79	3 283.9	4 838.5	9 310.7	11 750.5	14 943.2
	80-84			5 544.7	6 741.3	11 277.8
	85-89			2 022.0	3 839.5	6 935.6
	90-94	2 091.2	3 608.4	678.9	1 381.2	2 966.9
	95-99			150.7	328.4	814.3
	100+			15.1	36.2	128.1
Percentage in older ages						
Total	60+	12.1	16.4	21.1	28.0	34.5
	65+	8.2	11.4	16.1	21.0	27.6
	80+	1.1	1.8	3.8	5.3	9.6
Female	60+	13.5	19.3	24.0	31.1	37.9
	65+	9.3	13.7	18.8	23.9	31.0
	80+	1.4	2.3	5.1	6.8	12.0
Male	60+	10.5	13.3	17.9	24.6	30.8
	65+	7.0	8.9	13.1	17.8	23.9
	80+	0.8	1.1	2.4	3.6	7.0
Ageing index		46.3	69.1	136.2	190.0	229.7
Broad age groups (percentage)	0-14	26.2	23.7	15.5	14.7	15.0
	15-59	61.7	59.9	63.4	57.3	50.5
	60+	12.1	16.4	21.1	28.0	34.5
Median age (years)		29.7	32.1	39.0*	44.4	47.1
Dependency ratio	Total	52.4	54.3	46.1	55.6	74.2
	Youth	39.9	36.6	22.6	22.9	26.2
	Old Age	12.5	17.6	23.5	32.7	48.0
Potential support ratio		8.0	5.7	4.3	3.1	2.1
Parent support ratio		3.0	4.3	8.1	12.9	27.9
Sex ratio (per 100 women)	60+	67.9	63.0	69.2	73.3	75.5
	65+	65.8	59.5	64.2	68.8	71.5
	80+	52.5	43.7	43.3	49.6	54.4

* Estimate refers to year 2005.

Indicator	Age	1950-1955	1975-1980	2005-2010	2025-2030	2045-2050
Growth rate (percentage)	Total	1.0	0.5	–0.1	–0.3	–0.4
	60+	1.5	0.0	1.2	1.0	0.2
	65+	1.8	2.0	0.4	1.5	0.3
	80+	2.7	3.5	3.4	2.4	1.2
Total fertility rate (per woman)		2.7	2.0	1.4	1.7	1.8
Life expectancy (years)						
Total	Birth	65.6	71.5	74.3	77.8	80.6
	60	..	..	20.6	22.4	24.1
	65	..	..	16.9	18.5	20.1
	80	..	..	8.0	9.0	9.9
Female	Birth	67.9	75.2	78.4	81.1	83.6
	60	..	..	22.6	24.6	26.3
	65	..	..	18.5	20.3	22.0
	80	..	..	8.5	9.8	10.9
Male	Birth	62.9	67.6	70.2	74.4	77.5
	60	..	..	18.2	20.0	21.6
	65	..	..	14.8	16.4	17.8
	80	..	..	7.0	7.8	8.6
Survival rate (percentage)						
Total	60	..	..	83.4	88.1	91.4
	65	..	..	77.9	83.5	87.3
	80	..	..	45.0	53.7	61.0
Female	60	..	..	89.9	91.9	93.8
	65	..	..	86.0	88.8	91.1
	80	..	..	56.3	63.8	70.2
Male	60	..	..	77.1	84.3	88.9
	65	..	..	69.9	78.2	83.4
	80	..	..	33.9	43.3	51.6

		1980	1990	2007	2010	2020
Labour force participation (percentage)						
Total	65+	7.5	6.5	5.3	5.1	4.8
Female	65+	4.6	4.5	3.9	3.9	3.9
Male	65+	12.5	9.8	7.4	7.0	6.3

Percentage married, age 60+			Percentage living alone, age 60+		
Total	Female	Male	Total	Female	Male
60.1	46.9	79.5	26.0	35.0	13.0

Statutory pensionable age (2006)	·		Percentage illiterate, age 65+		
	Female	Male	Total	Female	Male
	–	–	..	..	..

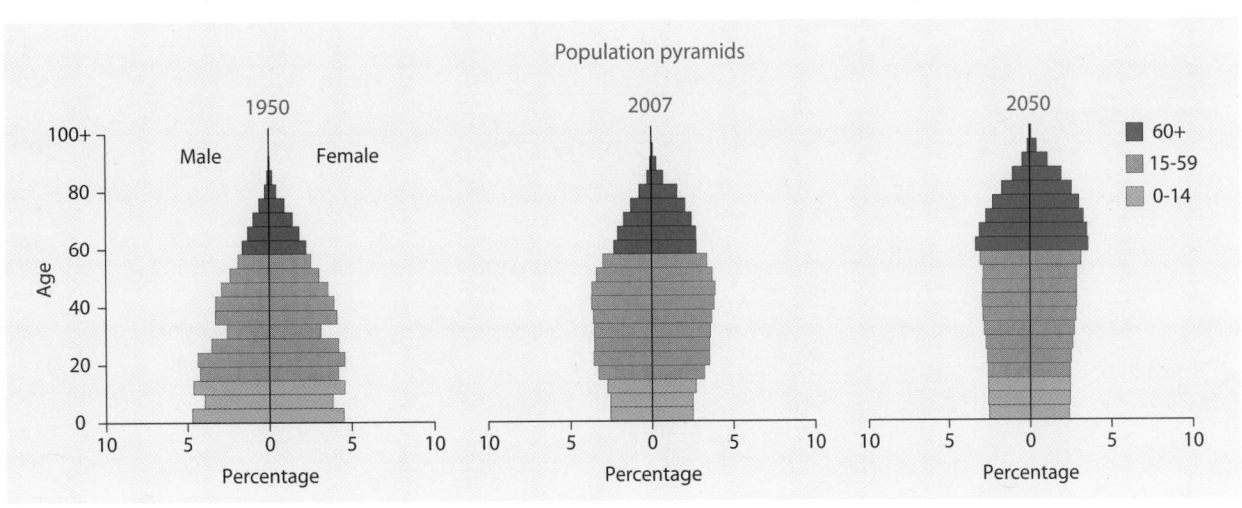

Population pyramids

1950   2007   2050

■ 60+
■ 15-59
■ 0-14

Eastern Europe

Indicator	Age	1950	1975	2007	2025	2050
Population (thousands)						
Total	Total	220 198.7	285 700.3	294 510.2	267 149.1	223 538.7
	0-14	61 915.0	67 118.0	43 803.9	39 111.2	33 415.2
	15-59	136 814.1	177 312.2	196 673.9	160 194.8	113 058.7
	60-64	7 121.4	13 756.2	12 549.3	17 548.3	18 623.0
	65-69	5 509.7	11 135.1	13 384.8	17 455.2	17 457.7
	70-74	4 095.2	7 952.5	11 327.6	14 250.7	14 589.7
	75-79	2 689.8	4 608.1	8 776.2	9 181.5	11 098.5
	80-84			5 400.8	4 560.9	7 300.4
	85-89			1 782.0	3 420.4	4 798.1
	90-94	2 053.5	3 818.2	655.6	1 098.4	2 402.5
	95-99			142.6	298.1	698.7
	100+			13.3	29.7	96.3
Female	Total	121 761.8	152 286.5	156 305.6	142 892.8	118 900.0
	0-14	30 711.5	32 879.2	21 343.8	19 029.8	16 239.1
	15-59	77 098.4	92 360.9	100 642.2	81 627.4	56 197.9
	60-64	4 400.7	8 616.6	7 184.7	9 953.8	10 006.1
	65-69	3 507.2	7 116.0	8 106.8	10 348.3	9 795.3
	70-74	2 699.0	5 338.4	7 170.2	8 892.6	8 617.7
	75-79	1 848.5	3 186.0	5 882.2	6 059.9	6 957.8
	80-84			3 942.7	3 222.5	4 924.9
	85-89			1 383.8	2 600.4	3 542.3
	90-94	1 496.6	2 789.4	523.3	881.0	1 927.6
	95-99			115.4	251.4	604.0
	100+			10.4	25.8	87.4
Male	Total	98 436.9	133 413.7	138 204.5	124 256.3	104 638.7
	0-14	31 203.5	34 238.8	22 460.1	20 081.4	17 176.2
	15-59	59 715.7	84 951.3	96 031.7	78 567.3	56 860.8
	60-64	2 720.7	5 139.6	5 364.7	7 594.5	8 616.9
	65-69	2 002.5	4 019.1	5 278.0	7 107.0	7 662.4
	70-74	1 396.2	2 614.1	4 157.4	5 358.1	5 972.0
	75-79	841.3	1 422.1	2 894.0	3 121.6	4 140.7
	80-84			1 458.1	1 338.4	2 375.5
	85-89			398.2	820.0	1 255.8
	90-94	557.0	1 028.8	132.3	217.4	474.9
	95-99			27.2	46.7	94.8
	100+			2.9	3.9	8.9
Percentage in older ages						
Total	60+	9.8	14.4	18.3	25.4	34.5
	65+	6.5	9.6	14.1	18.8	26.1
	80+	0.9	1.3	2.7	3.5	6.8
Female	60+	11.5	17.8	22.0	29.6	39.1
	65+	7.8	12.1	17.4	22.6	30.7
	80+	1.2	1.8	3.8	4.9	9.3
Male	60+	7.6	10.7	14.3	20.6	29.2
	65+	4.9	6.8	10.4	14.5	21.0
	80+	0.6	0.8	1.5	2.0	4.0
Ageing index		34.7	61.5	123.4	173.5	230.6
Broad age groups (percentage)	0-14	28.1	23.5	14.9	14.6	14.9
	15-59	62.1	62.1	66.8	60.0	50.6
	60+	9.8	14.4	18.3	25.4	34.5
Median age (years)		26.4	31.2	37.5*	43.0	47.2
Dependency ratio	Total	53.0	49.5	40.8	50.3	69.8
	Youth	43.0	35.1	20.9	22.0	25.4
	Old Age	10.0	14.4	19.8	28.3	44.4
Potential support ratio		10.0	6.9	5.0	3.5	2.3
Parent support ratio		3.1	3.5	4.8	9.1	17.5
Sex ratio (per 100 women)	60+	53.9	52.6	57.4	60.6	65.9
	65+	50.2	49.3	52.9	55.8	60.3
	80+	37.2	36.9	33.8	34.8	38.0

* *Estimate refers to year 2005.*

Indicator	Age	1950-1955	1975-1980	2005-2010	2025-2030	2045-2050
Growth rate (percentage)	Total	1.5	0.6	−0.5	−0.7	−0.8
	60+	1.7	0.1	0.6	0.1	0.6
	65+	2.1	2.9	−1.2	0.9	0.9
	80+	2.2	3.0	4.6	2.6	−0.5
Total fertility rate (per woman)		2.9	2.1	1.3	1.6	1.8
Life expectancy (years)						
Total	Birth	64.2	69.5	68.1	72.1	75.4
	60	..	..	17.8	19.5	21.1
	65	..	..	14.5	16.0	17.5
	80	..	..	6.8	7.6	8.4
Female	Birth	67.0	73.9	73.8	76.3	78.8
	60	..	..	19.9	21.8	23.5
	65	..	..	16.1	17.9	19.4
	80	..	..	7.1	8.2	9.1
Male	Birth	60.6	64.6	62.7	67.8	71.8
	60	..	..	15.0	16.6	18.3
	65	..	..	12.2	13.5	14.9
	80	..	..	5.9	6.4	6.9
Survival rate (percentage)						
Total	60	..	..	73.3	80.2	85.0
	65	..	..	65.9	73.6	79.4
	80	..	..	30.9	39.8	47.7
Female	60	..	..	84.5	86.6	89.0
	65	..	..	79.2	82.2	85.4
	80	..	..	43.6	51.7	58.8
Male	60	..	..	62.7	73.6	80.9
	65	..	..	53.2	64.7	73.2
	80	..	..	18.7	27.1	35.8

		1980	1990	2007	2010	2020
Labour force participation (percentage)						
Total	65+	8.6	9.1	6.8	6.4	5.6
Female	65+	5.3	6.8	5.4	5.3	4.9
Male	65+	15.6	14.3	9.4	8.7	6.9

Percentage married, age 60+				Percentage living alone, age 60+		
Total	Female	Male		Total	Female	Male
60.4	46.9	83.4		24.0	31.0	11.0

Statutory pensionable age (2006)				Percentage illiterate, age 65+		
	Female	Male		Total	Female	Male
	–	–		..	..	..

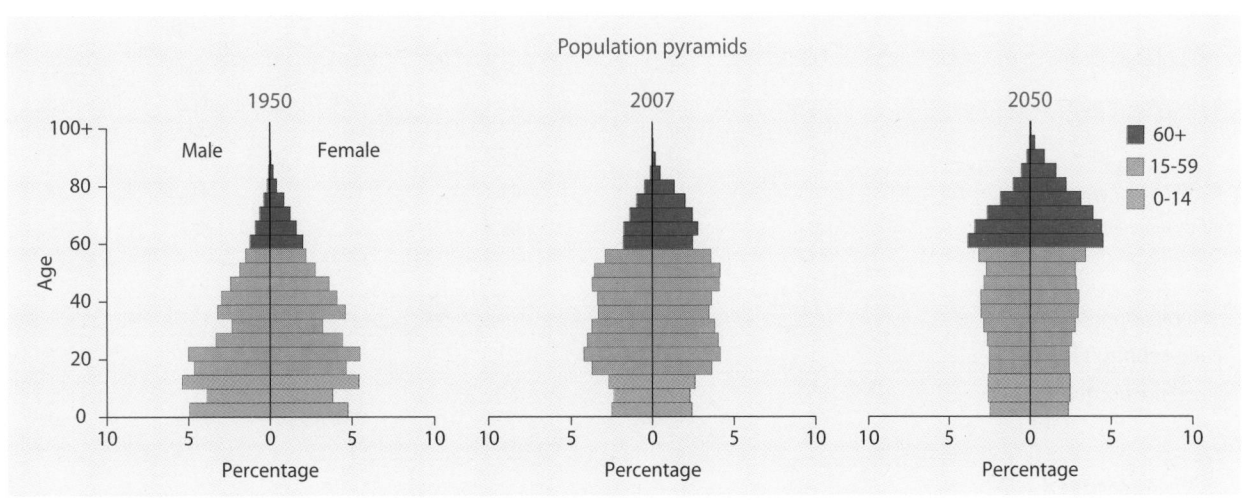

Population pyramids

Northern Europe

Indicator	Age	1950	1975	2007	2025	2050
Population (thousands)						
Total	Total	77 293.4	88 211.2	96 361.1	101 674.0	105 601.8
	0-14	18 317.0	20 542.5	16 830.0	17 060.6	17 066.5
	15-59	47 472.5	50 877.4	58 615.9	57 414.7	56 618.8
	60-64	3 541.7	4 836.3	5 558.2	6 722.9	6 638.0
	65-69	2 983.4	4 319.9	4 380.0	5 729.9	5 868.5
	70-74	2 330.3	3 371.5	3 660.1	4 837.8	5 188.3
	75-79	1 522.6	2 232.0	3 045.1	4 460.9	4 823.5
	80-84			2 306.8	2 807.8	4 256.9
	85-89			1 279.9	1 593.7	2 957.1
	90-94	1 125.9	2 031.6	524.3	746.2	1 491.8
	95-99			141.4	251.2	550.7
	100+			19.5	48.2	141.7
Female	Total	39 818.5	45 192.3	49 234.7	51 761.8	53 626.3
	0-14	8 977.7	10 007.0	8 205.4	8 326.5	8 326.0
	15-59	24 277.9	25 377.8	29 305.7	28 503.2	27 926.5
	60-64	1 961.5	2 590.3	2 846.2	3 461.0	3 306.7
	65-69	1 679.3	2 392.5	2 294.7	2 987.2	2 961.1
	70-74	1 328.5	1 987.8	1 989.5	2 590.7	2 701.7
	75-79	886.6	1 431.7	1 759.1	2 468.8	2 630.6
	80-84			1 442.5	1 650.8	2 448.1
	85-89			869.5	1 016.3	1 813.5
	90-94	707.0	1 405.2	390.8	522.0	993.4
	95-99			114.4	194.5	404.1
	100+			17.0	41.0	114.7
Male	Total	37 474.9	43 018.8	47 126.4	49 912.2	51 975.5
	0-14	9 339.3	10 535.6	8 624.6	8 734.1	8 740.5
	15-59	23 194.6	25 499.5	29 310.2	28 911.5	28 692.3
	60-64	1 580.2	2 246.0	2 712.0	3 261.9	3 331.3
	65-69	1 304.1	1 927.4	2 085.3	2 742.7	2 907.4
	70-74	1 001.8	1 383.7	1 670.6	2 247.1	2 486.6
	75-79	636.0	800.3	1 286.0	1 992.1	2 192.9
	80-84			864.3	1 157.0	1 808.8
	85-89			410.4	577.4	1 143.6
	90-94	418.9	626.4	133.5	224.2	498.4
	95-99			26.9	56.8	146.6
	100+			2.5	7.3	27.0
Percentage in older ages						
Total	60+	14.9	19.0	21.7	26.8	30.2
	65+	10.3	13.6	15.9	20.1	23.9
	80+	1.5	2.3	4.4	5.4	8.9
Female	60+	16.5	21.7	23.8	28.8	32.4
	65+	11.6	16.0	18.0	22.2	26.2
	80+	1.8	3.1	5.8	6.6	10.8
Male	60+	13.2	16.2	19.5	24.6	28.0
	65+	9.0	11.0	13.7	18.0	21.6
	80+	1.1	1.5	3.1	4.1	7.0
Ageing index		62.8	81.7	124.3	159.4	187.0
Broad age groups (percentage)	0-14	23.7	23.3	17.5	16.8	16.2
	15-59	61.4	57.7	60.8	56.5	53.6
	60+	14.9	19.0	21.7	26.8	30.2
Median age (years)		33.4	33.4	38.9*	41.9	43.7
Dependency ratio	Total	51.5	58.3	50.2	58.5	66.9
	Youth	35.9	36.9	26.2	26.6	27.0
	Old Age	15.6	21.5	23.9	31.9	40.0
Potential support ratio		6.4	4.7	4.2	3.1	2.5
Parent support ratio		3.6	5.2	11.0	13.1	26.1
Sex ratio (per 100 women)	60+	75.3	71.2	78.4	82.1	83.7
	65+	73.0	65.6	73.0	78.5	79.7
	80+	59.2	44.6	50.7	59.1	62.8

* Estimate refers to year 2005.

Indicator	Age	1950-1955	1975-1980	2005-2010	2025-2030	2045-2050
Growth rate (percentage)	Total	0.4	0.2	0.3	0.3	0.1
	60+	1.1	0.6	1.8	1.3	0.6
	65+	1.3	1.6	1.2	1.7	0.3
	80+	2.5	3.2	1.4	3.7	1.7
Total fertility rate (per woman)		2.3	1.8	1.7	1.8	1.8
Life expectancy (years)						
Total	Birth	69.2	73.1	78.7	81.3	83.5
	60	..	..	21.9	23.7	25.3
	65	..	..	17.9	19.6	21.1
	80	..	..	8.4	9.4	10.3
Female	Birth	71.5	76.2	81.2	83.6	85.6
	60	..	..	23.8	25.6	27.3
	65	..	..	19.6	21.3	22.8
	80	..	..	9.1	10.3	11.3
Male	Birth	66.8	69.9	76.0	78.9	81.3
	60	..	..	19.9	21.7	23.3
	65	..	..	16.1	17.7	19.2
	80	..	..	7.3	8.2	9.1
Survival rate (percentage)						
Total	60	..	..	91.2	93.7	95.4
	65	..	..	86.6	90.0	92.4
	80	..	..	54.3	62.0	68.2
Female	60	..	..	93.4	95.1	96.3
	65	..	..	90.0	92.3	94.1
	80	..	..	62.9	69.7	75.0
Male	60	..	..	88.9	92.3	94.5
	65	..	..	83.2	87.7	90.8
	80	..	..	45.4	54.1	61.3

		1980	1990	2007	2010	2020
Labour force participation (percentage)						
Total	65+	7.9	7.1	6.5	6.7	7.0
Female	65+	4.6	4.5	4.2	4.4	4.7
Male	65+	12.8	11.1	9.6	9.8	10.0

Percentage married, age 60+			Percentage living alone, age 60+		
Total	Female	Male	Total	Female	Male
60.2	49.6	74.4	34.0	44.0	21.0

Statutory pensionable age (2006)			Percentage illiterate, age 65+		
	Female	Male	Total	Female	Male
	–	–	..	..	..

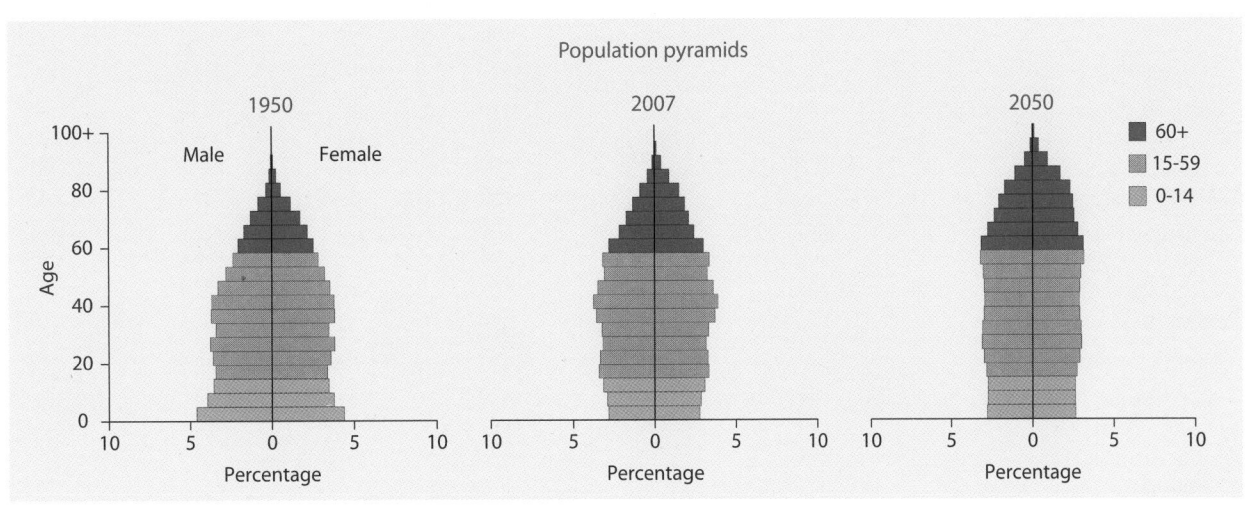

Population pyramids

United Nations Department of Economic and Social Affairs, Population Division

Southern Europe

Indicator	Age	1950	1975	2007	2025	2050
Population (thousands)						
Total	Total	108 996.3	132 471.9	150 196.1	148 865.6	138 715.6
	0-14	30 136.0	34 253.8	22 403.8	19 786.3	19 365.3
	15-59	66 575.0	77 795.8	92 927.1	84 171.3	65 846.5
	60-64	3 983.5	6 216.2	8 110.3	10 906.4	8 410.8
	65-69	3 141.2	5 406.3	7 301.2	9 559.9	9 143.9
	70-74	2 434.2	4 031.5	6 919.8	8 022.5	9 788.9
	75-79	1 576.6	2 564.0	5 805.3	6 711.4	9 384.4
	80-84			4 018.1	4 569.8	7 533.6
	85-89			1 802.8	3 012.3	5 190.3
	90-94	1 149.8	2 204.5	710.1	1 553.8	2 747.4
	95-99			181.9	497.1	1 038.3
	100+			15.5	74.8	266.4
Female	Total	56 121.9	67 812.1	76 782.6	76 025.4	70 987.9
	0-14	14 799.5	16 696.3	10 867.9	9 577.0	9 372.9
	15-59	34 363.4	39 498.4	46 109.4	41 407.4	32 088.6
	60-64	2 210.2	3 360.2	4 217.5	5 584.5	4 202.1
	65-69	1 747.8	2 968.7	3 914.3	5 009.6	4 646.0
	70-74	1 379.5	2 310.8	3 846.8	4 331.7	5 103.0
	75-79	915.5	1 557.0	3 396.2	3 794.9	5 081.7
	80-84			2 526.1	2 760.9	4 327.2
	85-89			1 231.3	1 978.5	3 238.1
	90-94	705.9	1 420.7	519.6	1 120.3	1 897.1
	95-99			141.1	395.2	800.7
	100+			12.6	65.4	230.6
Male	Total	52 874.4	64 659.8	73 413.5	72 840.1	67 727.7
	0-14	15 336.5	17 557.5	11 536.0	10 209.4	9 992.5
	15-59	32 211.7	38 297.4	46 817.8	42 763.8	33 757.9
	60-64	1 773.3	2 856.0	3 892.9	5 321.9	4 208.6
	65-69	1 393.4	2 437.6	3 386.9	4 550.4	4 497.9
	70-74	1 054.7	1 720.7	3 073.0	3 690.8	4 685.9
	75-79	661.0	1 006.9	2 409.1	2 916.4	4 302.7
	80-84			1 492.0	1 808.9	3 206.4
	85-89			571.6	1 033.8	1 952.1
	90-94	443.9	783.8	190.5	433.5	850.3
	95-99			40.8	101.9	237.6
	100+			2.9	9.4	35.8
Percentage in older ages						
Total	60+	11.3	15.4	23.2	30.2	38.6
	65+	7.6	10.7	17.8	22.8	32.5
	80+	1.1	1.7	4.5	6.5	12.1
Female	60+	12.4	17.1	25.8	32.9	41.6
	65+	8.5	12.2	20.3	25.6	35.7
	80+	1.3	2.1	5.8	8.3	14.8
Male	60+	10.1	13.6	20.5	27.3	35.4
	65+	6.7	9.2	15.2	20.0	29.2
	80+	0.8	1.2	3.1	4.7	9.3
Ageing index		40.8	59.6	155.6	227.0	276.3
Broad age groups (percentage)	0-14	27.6	25.9	14.9	13.3	14.0
	15-59	61.1	58.7	61.9	56.5	47.5
	60+	11.3	15.4	23.2	30.2	38.6
Median age (years)		27.6	31.2	39.8*	47.5	50.1
Dependency ratio	Total	54.5	57.7	48.7	56.6	86.8
	Youth	42.7	40.8	22.2	20.8	26.1
	Old Age	11.8	16.9	26.5	35.8	60.7
Potential support ratio		8.5	5.9	3.8	2.8	1.6
Parent support ratio		2.8	4.0	9.9	14.9	37.9
Sex ratio (per 100 women)	60+	76.5	75.8	76.0	79.3	81.2
	65+	74.8	72.0	71.6	74.8	78.1
	80+	62.9	55.2	51.9	53.6	59.9

* *Estimate refers to year 2005.*

Indicator	Age	1950-1955	1975-1980	2005-2010	2025-2030	2045-2050
Growth rate (percentage)	Total	0.8	0.8	0.2	−0.2	−0.4
	60+	1.3	0.7	1.4	1.5	−0.4
	65+	1.6	2.3	1.0	1.7	0.0
	80+	1.8	2.7	4.2	2.1	2.1
Total fertility rate (per woman)		2.7	2.2	1.4	1.6	1.8
Life expectancy (years)						
Total	Birth	63.3	73.0	79.1	81.5	83.7
	60	..	..	22.5	24.2	25.8
	65	..	..	18.5	20.0	21.6
	80	..	..	8.5	9.6	10.6
Female	Birth	65.2	76.0	82.2	84.6	86.7
	60	..	..	24.7	26.5	28.3
	65	..	..	20.3	22.0	23.8
	80	..	..	9.3	10.6	11.9
Male	Birth	61.5	70.0	75.9	78.5	80.7
	60	..	..	20.1	21.7	23.3
	65	..	..	16.3	17.7	19.2
	80	..	..	7.4	8.2	9.1
Survival rate (percentage)						
Total	60	..	..	91.2	93.4	94.8
	65	..	..	87.1	90.1	92.0
	80	..	..	57.0	63.6	69.4
Female	60	..	..	94.3	95.7	96.6
	65	..	..	91.6	93.5	94.7
	80	..	..	67.4	73.1	78.0
Male	60	..	..	88.3	91.2	93.1
	65	..	..	82.7	86.7	89.2
	80	..	..	46.4	54.0	60.8

		1980	1990	2007	2010	2020
Labour force participation (percentage)						
Total	65+	9.4	5.8	5.7	5.5	5.3
Female	65+	5.5	3.8	4.1	4.1	4.2
Male	65+	14.9	8.6	8.0	7.6	6.9

Percentage married, age 60+				Percentage living alone, age 60+		
Total	Female	Male		Total	Female	Male
62.4	48.2	81.1		19.0	26.0	9.0

Statutory pensionable age (2006)				Percentage illiterate, age 65+		
	Female	Male		Total	Female	Male
	–	–		..	..	..

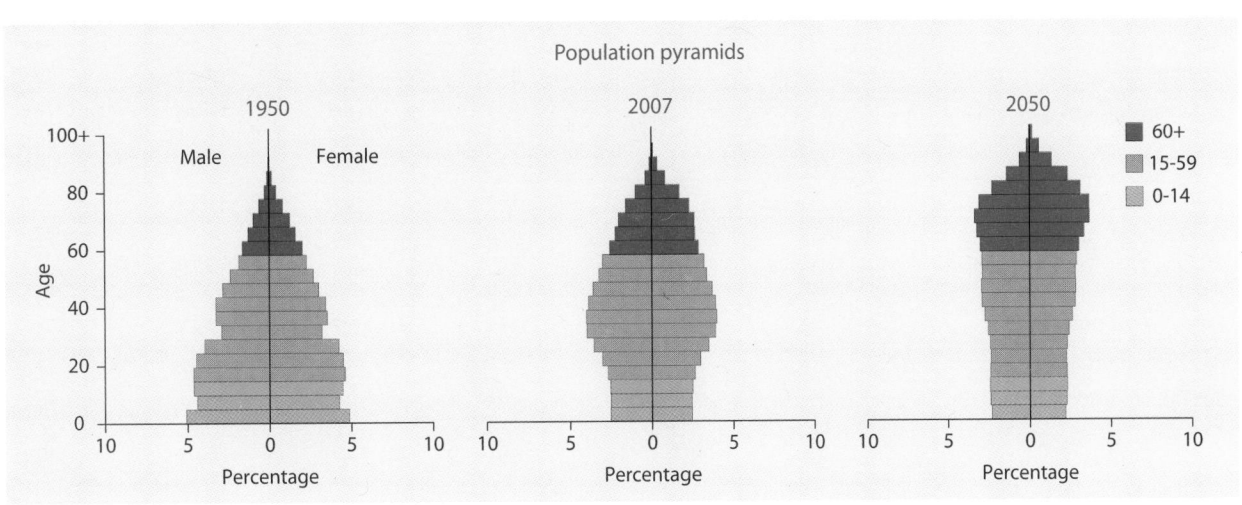

Population pyramids

United Nations Department of Economic and Social Affairs, Population Division

Western Europe

Indicator	Age	1950	1975	2007	2025	2050
Population (thousands)						
Total	Total	140 916.4	169 164.7	186 591.4	189 545.9	185 467.3
	0-14	32 872.9	38 435.5	29 651.5	28 166.1	28 264.1
	15-59	86 954.3	98 360.2	113 276.4	103 442.0	94 315.0
	60-64	6 741.4	8 776.8	10 414.0	14 189.0	11 567.5
	65-69	5 583.5	8 399.5	9 714.2	12 265.2	10 851.5
	70-74	4 334.5	6 847.9	8 161.8	10 502.5	9 691.0
	75-79	2 682.0	4 526.6	6 518.7	8 368.5	9 484.0
	80-84			5 191.1	6 032.3	9 143.5
	85-89			2 323.6	4 028.1	6 777.0
	90-94	1 747.8	3 818.2	986.9	1 813.7	3 612.9
	95-99			313.6	619.7	1 415.2
	100+			39.5	118.8	345.6
Female	Total	74 382.6	87 563.5	95 379.1	96 938.8	95 339.4
	0-14	16 124.9	18 767.9	14 452.4	13 723.6	13 770.6
	15-59	46 213.1	49 249.9	56 077.6	51 204.2	46 541.0
	60-64	3 826.8	5 013.5	5 309.4	7 214.5	5 866.8
	65-69	3 160.2	4 879.9	5 085.5	6 376.3	5 585.2
	70-74	2 444.8	4 086.1	4 459.5	5 649.5	5 111.0
	75-79	1 536.4	2 917.4	3 797.1	4 648.0	5 177.1
	80-84			3 460.8	3 595.4	5 256.4
	85-89			1 681.8	2 619.7	4 192.9
	90-94	1 076.4	2 648.8	764.4	1 307.7	2 469.6
	95-99			257.9	496.7	1 079.8
	100+			32.7	103.1	289.2
Male	Total	66 533.9	81 601.2	91 212.3	92 607.1	90 127.9
	0-14	16 748.0	19 667.6	15 199.2	14 442.5	14 493.6
	15-59	40 741.2	49 110.2	57 198.8	52 237.8	47 774.0
	60-64	2 914.7	3 763.3	5 104.6	6 974.5	5 700.8
	65-69	2 423.3	3 519.7	4 628.8	5 888.9	5 266.4
	70-74	1 889.7	2 761.8	3 702.3	4 853.0	4 580.1
	75-79	1 145.6	1 609.2	2 721.5	3 720.5	4 306.9
	80-84			1 730.2	2 437.0	3 887.1
	85-89			641.7	1 408.3	2 584.2
	90-94	671.4	1 169.4	222.5	506.1	1 143.3
	95-99			55.7	123.0	335.3
	100+			6.9	15.7	56.4
Percentage in older ages						
Total	60+	15.0	19.1	23.4	30.6	33.9
	65+	10.2	13.9	17.8	23.1	27.7
	80+	1.2	2.3	4.7	6.7	11.5
Female	60+	16.2	22.3	26.1	33.0	36.7
	65+	11.0	16.6	20.5	25.6	30.6
	80+	1.4	3.0	6.5	8.4	13.9
Male	60+	13.6	15.7	20.6	28.0	30.9
	65+	9.2	11.1	15.0	20.5	24.6
	80+	1.0	1.4	2.9	4.8	8.9
Ageing index		64.2	84.2	147.3	205.7	222.5
Broad age groups (percentage)	0-14	23.3	22.7	15.9	14.9	15.2
	15-59	61.7	58.1	60.7	54.6	50.9
	60+	15.0	19.1	23.4	30.6	33.9
Median age (years)		34.6	33.5	40.7*	45.4	46.6
Dependency ratio	Total	50.4	57.9	50.9	61.1	75.2
	Youth	35.1	35.9	24.0	23.9	26.7
	Old Age	15.3	22.0	26.9	37.2	48.5
Potential support ratio		6.5	4.5	3.7	2.7	2.1
Parent support ratio		2.7	5.2	10.4	16.2	35.8
Sex ratio (per 100 women)	60+	75.1	65.6	75.7	81.0	79.5
	65+	74.6	62.3	70.2	76.4	76.0
	80+	62.4	44.1	42.9	55.3	60.3

* *Estimate refers to year 2005.*

Indicator	Age	1950-1955	1975-1980	2005-2010	2025-2030	2045-2050
Growth rate (percentage)	Total	0.7	0.2	0.2	0.0	−0.2
	60+	1.7	−0.8	1.4	1.3	0.0
	65+	1.9	1.1	1.3	1.9	−0.1
	80+	3.9	4.6	2.8	2.0	1.4
Total fertility rate (per woman)		2.4	1.6	1.6	1.7	1.9
Life expectancy (years)						
Total	Birth	67.6	73.1	79.6	82.0	84.1
	60	..	..	22.8	24.5	26.1
	65	..	..	18.7	20.3	21.8
	80	..	..	8.8	9.7	10.7
Female	Birth	69.9	76.5	82.6	85.0	87.0
	60	..	..	25.0	26.8	28.5
	65	..	..	20.7	22.4	24.0
	80	..	..	9.5	10.8	12.0
Male	Birth	65.1	69.6	76.5	79.1	81.2
	60	..	..	20.3	22.1	23.7
	65	..	..	16.5	18.1	19.6
	80	..	..	7.5	8.4	9.2
Survival rate (percentage)						
Total	60	..	..	91.6	93.7	95.1
	65	..	..	87.4	90.4	92.5
	80	..	..	58.1	65.2	70.7
Female	60	..	..	94.2	95.7	96.8
	65	..	..	91.4	93.5	95.0
	80	..	..	68.5	74.4	78.8
Male	60	..	..	89.1	91.7	93.5
	65	..	..	83.4	87.3	89.9
	80	..	..	47.5	55.9	62.5

		1980	1990	2007	2010	2020
Labour force participation (percentage)						
Total	65+	4.6	3.1	2.5	2.5	2.5
Female	65+	3.0	2.0	1.6	1.7	1.9
Male	65+	7.2	5.0	3.7	3.7	3.4

Percentage married, age 60+			Percentage living alone, age 60+		
Total	Female	Male	Total	Female	Male
57.8	44.7	76.0	32.0	43.0	15.0

Statutory pensionable age (2006)			Percentage illiterate, age 65+		
	Female	Male	Total	Female	Male
	–	–	..	..	..

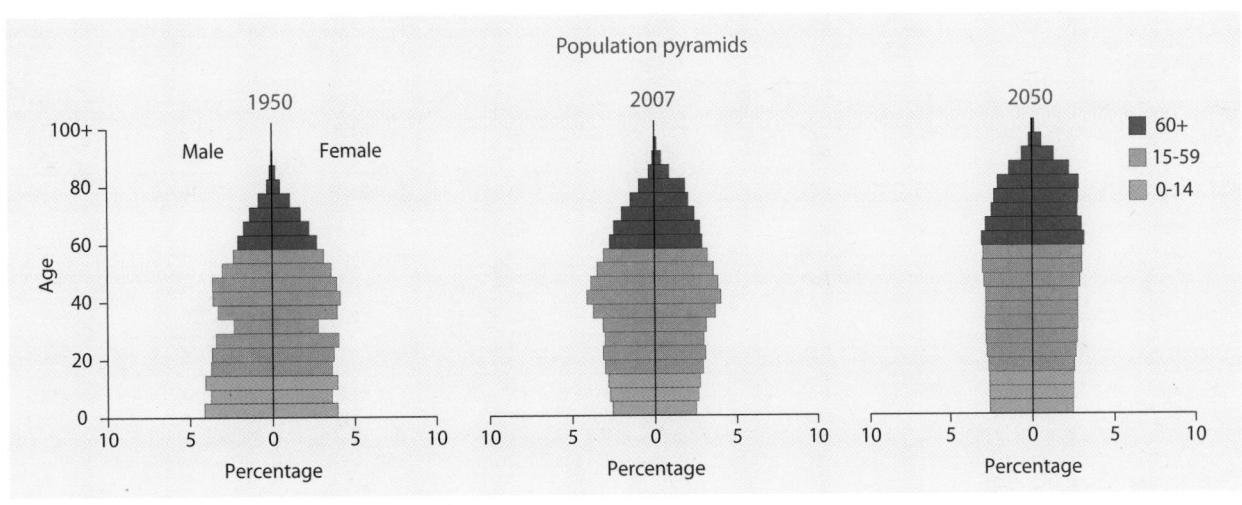

Population pyramids

Latin America and the Caribbean

Indicator	Age	1950	1975	2007	2025	2050
Population (thousands)						
Total	Total	167 321.0	322 448.6	576 489.1	696 541.3	782 902.8
	0-14	66 934.6	133 210.4	168 387.8	162 629.8	141 403.2
	15-59	90 427.7	168 211.4	355 404.7	433 238.5	452 847.2
	60-64	3 756.5	7 094.5	16 214.0	30 574.4	44 935.4
	65-69	2 696.0	5 558.1	12 648.6	24 234.2	40 817.3
	70-74	1 790.4	3 966.9	9 574.5	18 458.8	34 886.2
	75-79	1 059.7	2 575.8	6 879.1	12 688.1	27 665.2
	80-84			4 276.9	7 850.2	19 947.8
	85-89			2 103.8	4 345.5	12 500.6
	90-94	656.1	1 831.5	773.5	1 841.1	5 741.1
	95-99			192.1	566.2	1 824.0
	100+			33.9	114.3	334.8
Female	Total	83 594.0	161 453.0	291 974.8	353 892.2	399 908.8
	0-14	33 124.2	65 866.7	82 654.6	79 622.7	69 149.8
	15-59	45 154.0	84 396.0	180 330.2	218 360.1	225 897.3
	60-64	1 955.8	3 670.7	8 565.0	16 287.8	23 346.5
	65-69	1 423.2	2 923.5	6 789.3	13 141.6	21 648.0
	70-74	966.1	2 118.0	5 273.2	10 220.5	19 080.4
	75-79	588.4	1 422.5	3 903.6	7 235.0	15 711.5
	80-84			2 512.9	4 639.1	11 857.8
	85-89			1 293.2	2 697.6	7 840.3
	90-94	382.3	1 055.6	499.7	1 213.0	3 837.1
	95-99			130.0	394.5	1 297.7
	100+			23.2	80.3	242.5
Male	Total	83 727.0	160 995.6	284 514.2	342 649.1	382 994.0
	0-14	33 810.4	67 343.6	85 733.2	83 007.1	72 253.5
	15-59	45 273.8	83 815.4	175 074.6	214 878.5	226 950.0
	60-64	1 800.6	3 423.8	7 648.9	14 286.6	21 588.9
	65-69	1 272.8	2 634.7	5 859.4	11 092.6	19 169.3
	70-74	824.3	1 848.9	4 301.3	8 238.3	15 805.8
	75-79	471.3	1 153.2	2 975.5	5 453.1	11 953.8
	80-84			1 764.0	3 211.2	8 089.9
	85-89			810.7	1 647.9	4 660.2
	90-94	273.8	775.9	273.8	628.2	1 904.0
	95-99			62.1	171.7	526.3
	100+			10.7	34.0	92.3
Percentage in older ages						
Total	60+	6.0	6.5	9.1	14.5	24.1
	65+	3.7	4.3	6.3	10.1	18.4
	80+	0.4	0.6	1.3	2.1	5.2
Female	60+	6.4	6.9	9.9	15.8	26.2
	65+	4.0	4.7	7.0	11.2	20.4
	80+	0.5	0.7	1.5	2.6	6.3
Male	60+	5.5	6.1	8.3	13.1	21.9
	65+	3.4	4.0	5.6	8.9	16.2
	80+	0.3	0.5	1.0	1.7	4.0
Ageing index		14.9	15.8	31.3	61.9	133.4
Broad age groups (percentage)	0-14	40.0	41.3	29.2	23.3	18.1
	15-59	54.0	52.2	61.6	62.2	57.8
	60+	6.0	6.5	9.1	14.5	24.1
Median age (years)		20.2	19.3	25.9*	32.3	39.9
Dependency ratio	Total	77.7	83.9	55.1	50.2	57.3
	Youth	71.1	76.0	45.3	35.1	28.4
	Old Age	6.6	7.9	9.8	15.1	28.9
Potential support ratio		15.2	12.6	10.2	6.6	3.5
Parent support ratio		1.5	2.2	4.9	6.5	14.3
Sex ratio (per 100 women)	60+	87.3	87.9	81.8	80.1	79.9
	65+	84.6	85.3	78.6	76.9	76.3
	80+	71.6	73.5	65.5	63.1	60.9

*   *Estimate refers to year 2005.*

Indicator	Age	1950-1955	1975-1980	2005-2010	2025-2030	2045-2050
Growth rate (percentage)	Total	2.7	2.3	1.3	0.7	0.2
	60+	3.0	2.6	3.4	3.2	1.8
	65+	3.1	2.9	3.2	3.7	2.1
	80+	3.2	4.4	4.6	4.3	3.1
Total fertility rate (per woman)		5.9	4.5	2.4	2.0	1.9
Life expectancy (years)						
Total	Birth	51.4	63.0	72.9	76.8	79.5
	60	..	..	21.2	23.0	24.2
	65	..	..	17.5	19.1	20.2
	80	..	..	8.6	9.4	9.9
Female	Birth	53.1	65.7	76.1	79.9	82.5
	60	..	..	22.6	24.6	26.1
	65	..	..	18.7	20.6	21.9
	80	..	..	9.1	10.1	10.7
Male	Birth	49.7	60.5	69.8	73.7	76.4
	60	..	..	19.6	21.1	22.1
	65	..	..	16.2	17.5	18.3
	80	..	..	7.9	8.5	8.9
Survival rate (percentage)						
Total	60	..	..	81.2	85.9	89.1
	65	..	..	75.7	81.3	85.1
	80	..	..	45.6	54.3	60.4
Female	60	..	..	85.8	89.6	92.2
	65	..	..	81.2	86.0	89.3
	80	..	..	53.1	62.2	68.9
Male	60	..	..	76.7	82.2	86.0
	65	..	..	70.3	76.7	81.0
	80	..	..	38.1	46.1	51.7

		1980	1990	2007	2010	2020
Labour force participation (percentage)						
Total	65+	24.1	22.2	23.9	23.7	23.2
Female	65+	9.7	9.5	14.1	14.7	16.6
Male	65+	41.1	37.8	36.4	35.1	31.6

Percentage married, age 60+			Percentage living alone, age 60+		
Total	Female	Male	Total	Female	Male
57.1	42.3	75.0	9.0	10.0	7.0

Statutory pensionable age (2006)			Percentage illiterate, age 65+		
Female	Male		Total	Female	Male
–	–		..	..	..

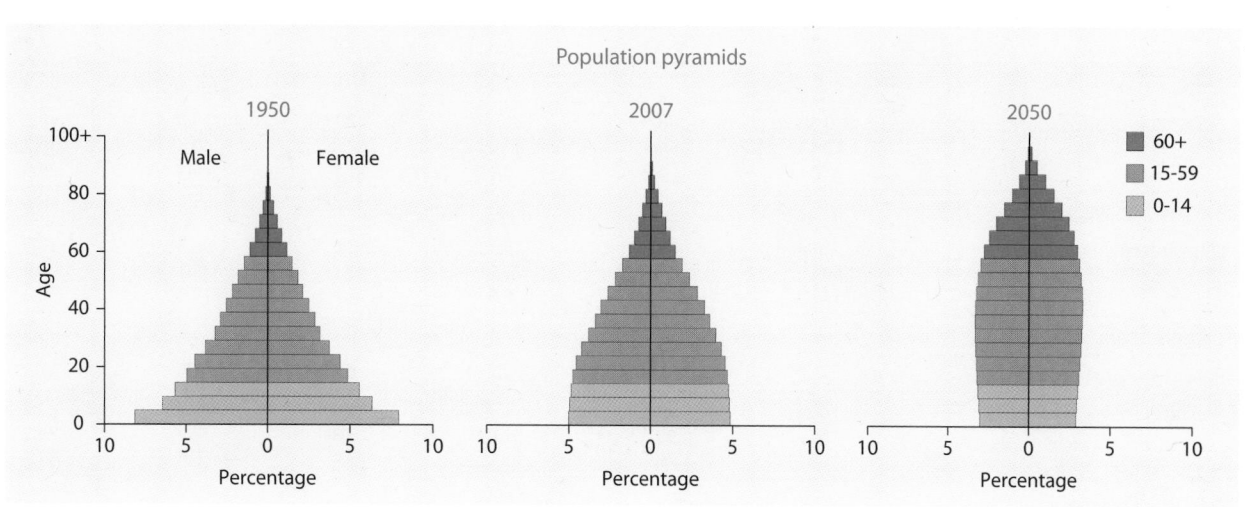

Population pyramids

Caribbean

Indicator	Age	1950	1975	2007	2025	2050
Population (thousands)						
Total	Total	17 027.3	27 120.5	39 786.0	44 663.1	46 438.4
	0-14	6 574.4	10 832.6	10 797.5	10 293.6	8 625.7
	15-59	9 283.0	14 093.3	24 582.1	27 053.6	26 315.6
	60-64	408.7	721.7	1 320.6	2 236.4	2 719.2
	65-69	312.3	580.1	1 058.4	1 612.8	2 338.9
	70-74	223.0	438.3	793.6	1 300.9	1 877.1
	75-79	141.0	261.5	580.4	981.6	1 763.0
	80-84			361.9	639.0	1 387.0
	85-89			191.2	351.3	897.9
	90-94	84.8	192.9	77.6	143.3	366.1
	95-99			19.6	43.2	123.2
	100+			3.1	7.5	24.6
Female	Total	8 453.8	13 590.9	20 057.3	22 508.7	23 384.3
	0-14	3 272.8	5 348.8	5 293.0	5 035.2	4 212.2
	15-59	4 592.0	7 134.4	12 387.6	13 447.3	12 926.0
	60-64	199.9	360.0	693.4	1 175.8	1 375.1
	65-69	154.3	292.3	558.7	867.2	1 203.8
	70-74	113.0	216.1	428.5	713.9	995.8
	75-79	74.2	134.0	319.1	555.3	971.7
	80-84			202.6	371.7	799.8
	85-89			111.6	214.2	550.6
	90-94	47.6	105.4	47.7	93.3	243.3
	95-99			12.8	29.6	87.7
	100+			2.1	5.4	18.4
Male	Total	8 573.6	13 529.6	19 728.8	22 154.5	23 054.1
	0-14	3 301.6	5 483.9	5 504.4	5 258.4	4 413.5
	15-59	4 691.1	6 959.0	12 194.5	13 606.3	13 389.6
	60-64	208.8	361.7	627.1	1 060.7	1 344.1
	65-69	158.1	287.8	499.7	745.6	1 135.1
	70-74	110.0	222.2	365.1	587.0	881.3
	75-79	66.8	127.5	261.4	426.4	791.3
	80-84			159.3	267.3	587.2
	85-89			79.6	137.1	347.3
	90-94	37.2	87.5	29.9	50.0	122.8
	95-99			6.8	13.6	35.4
	100+			1.0	2.1	6.2
Percentage in older ages						
Total	60+	6.9	8.1	11.1	16.4	24.8
	65+	4.5	5.4	7.8	11.4	18.9
	80+	0.5	0.7	1.6	2.7	6.0
Female	60+	7.0	8.2	11.8	17.9	26.7
	65+	4.6	5.5	8.4	12.7	20.8
	80+	0.6	0.8	1.9	3.2	7.3
Male	60+	6.8	8.0	10.3	14.8	22.8
	65+	4.3	5.4	7.1	10.1	16.9
	80+	0.4	0.6	1.4	2.1	4.8
Ageing index		17.8	20.3	40.8	71.1	133.3
Broad age groups (percentage)	0-14	38.6	39.9	27.1	23.0	18.6
	15-59	54.5	52.0	61.8	60.6	56.7
	60+	6.9	8.1	11.1	16.4	24.8
Median age (years)		21.4	20.3	28.0*	33.8	39.8
Dependency ratio	Total	75.7	83.1	53.6	52.5	59.9
	Youth	67.8	73.1	41.7	35.1	29.7
	Old Age	7.9	9.9	11.9	17.3	30.2
Potential support ratio		12.7	10.1	8.4	5.8	3.3
Parent support ratio		1.9	2.7	6.2	7.5	17.3
Sex ratio (per 100 women)	60+	98.6	98.1	85.4	81.7	84.1
	65+	95.6	97.0	83.3	78.2	80.2
	80+	78.1	83.0	73.4	65.8	64.7

* Estimate refers to year 2005.

Indicator	Age	1950-1955	1975-1980	2005-2010	2025-2030	2045-2050
Growth rate (percentage)	Total	1.8	1.5	0.8	0.4	–0.1
	60+	2.0	2.7	2.7	2.8	1.4
	65+	2.0	3.4	2.7	3.6	1.3
	80+	4.4	6.5	3.3	3.7	3.1
Total fertility rate (per woman)		5.2	3.6	2.4	2.1	1.9
Life expectancy (years)						
Total	Birth	52.2	64.5	68.7	73.2	76.9
	60	..	..	21.0	22.9	23.9
	65	..	..	17.4	19.0	20.0
	80	..	..	8.4	9.2	9.8
Female	Birth	53.6	66.5	70.9	75.2	79.0
	60	..	..	22.3	24.4	25.7
	65	..	..	18.5	20.3	21.5
	80	..	..	8.9	9.9	10.6
Male	Birth	50.9	62.7	66.5	71.1	74.8
	60	..	..	19.7	21.2	22.1
	65	..	..	16.1	17.4	18.3
	80	..	..	7.7	8.4	8.8
Survival rate (percentage)						
Total	60	..	..	74.6	79.8	84.7
	65	..	..	69.6	75.7	80.8
	80	..	..	41.5	50.1	56.5
Female	60	..	..	77.4	81.7	86.3
	65	..	..	73.1	78.4	83.2
	80	..	..	47.1	56.2	63.0
Male	60	..	..	71.8	77.9	83.2
	65	..	..	66.0	73.0	78.3
	80	..	..	35.9	43.8	50.0

		1980	1990	2007	2010	2020
Labour force participation (percentage)						
Total	65+	23.6	20.4	17.4	17.2	17.1
Female	65+	11.8	9.8	8.2	8.5	10.4
Male	65+	36.1	32.2	28.4	27.6	25.6

Percentage married, age 60+			Percentage living alone, age 60+		
Total	Female	Male	Total	Female	Male
54.6	42.3	68.5	10.0	9.0	10.0

Statutory pensionable age (2006)			Percentage illiterate, age 65+		
	Female	Male	Total	Female	Male
	–	–	..	..	..

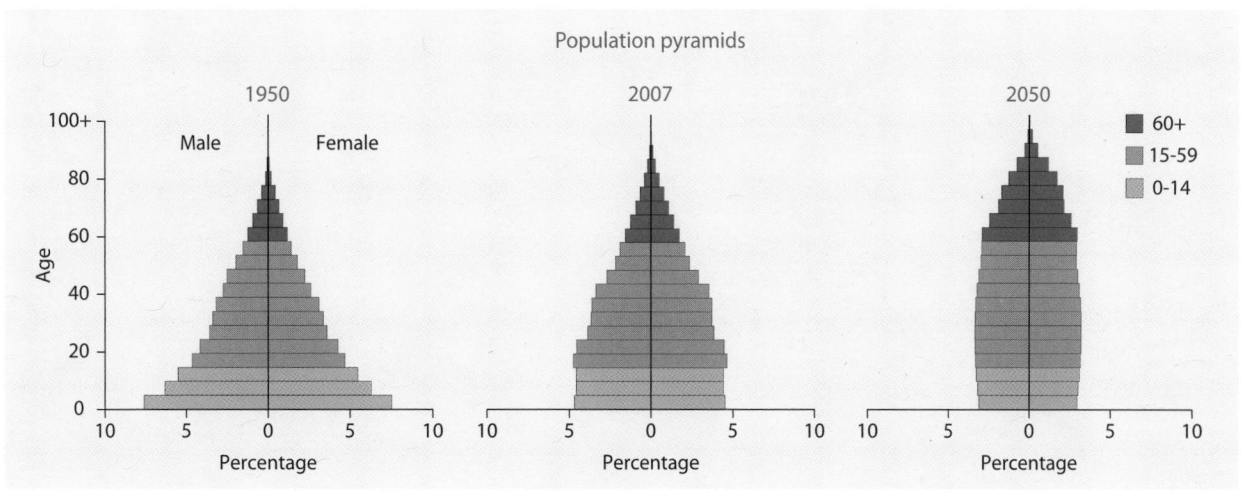

Population pyramids

1950   2007   2050

60+
15-59
0-14

Male   Female

Age — Percentage

Central America

Indicator	Age	1950	1975	2007	2025	2050
Population (thousands)						
Total	Total	37 298.9	79 154.9	151 267.4	185 678.4	209 556.9
	0-14	15 781.4	36 708.0	47 958.6	44 799.0	37 606.5
	15-59	19 086.2	38 131.0	91 494.9	117 125.3	121 202.4
	60-64	911.5	1 331.2	3 686.6	7 184.7	12 129.5
	65-69	659.2	1 085.1	2 852.6	5 751.9	10 729.4
	70-74	433.3	825.6	2 159.2	4 325.4	9 676.5
	75-79	265.8	574.6	1 529.6	2 993.8	7 985.9
	80-84			953.6	1 919.2	5 326.3
	85-89			449.3	1 032.8	3 058.5
	90-94	161.5	499.3	148.4	425.4	1 384.4
	95-99			31.4	107.8	400.8
	100+			3.1	13.0	56.6
Female	Total	18 621.5	39 617.4	77 066.5	94 926.6	107 768.1
	0-14	7 765.9	18 121.7	23 597.2	21 940.7	18 398.4
	15-59	9 551.7	19 178.3	47 094.8	59 889.8	61 197.8
	60-64	479.9	694.9	1 943.3	3 876.7	6 368.9
	65-69	352.1	577.8	1 511.8	3 123.3	5 737.1
	70-74	234.5	446.2	1 160.6	2 368.8	5 298.9
	75-79	146.1	316.6	836.8	1 667.7	4 511.4
	80-84			537.8	1 094.2	3 145.3
	85-89			265.5	612.6	1 887.5
	90-94	91.4	281.8	94.1	268.9	903.2
	95-99			22.1	74.1	278.9
	100+			2.5	9.7	40.7
Male	Total	18 677.4	39 537.5	74 200.9	90 751.7	101 788.9
	0-14	8 015.5	18 586.3	24 361.4	22 858.3	19 208.1
	15-59	9 534.6	18 952.7	44 400.0	57 235.5	60 004.6
	60-64	431.5	636.4	1 743.3	3 308.0	5 760.6
	65-69	307.1	507.3	1 340.8	2 628.6	4 992.3
	70-74	198.9	379.4	998.7	1 956.5	4 377.5
	75-79	119.7	258.0	692.8	1 326.2	3 474.5
	80-84			415.9	825.0	2 181.0
	85-89			183.9	420.2	1 171.0
	90-94	70.1	217.5	54.3	156.5	481.3
	95-99			9.2	33.7	121.9
	100+			0.7	3.3	16.0
Percentage in older ages						
Total	60+	6.5	5.5	7.8	12.8	24.2
	65+	4.1	3.8	5.4	8.9	18.4
	80+	0.4	0.6	1.0	1.9	4.9
Female	60+	7.0	5.8	8.3	13.8	26.1
	65+	4.4	4.1	5.7	9.7	20.2
	80+	0.5	0.7	1.2	2.2	5.8
Male	60+	6.0	5.1	7.3	11.7	22.2
	65+	3.7	3.4	5.0	8.1	16.5
	80+	0.4	0.6	0.9	1.6	3.9
Ageing index		15.4	11.8	24.6	53.0	134.9
Broad age groups (percentage)	0-14	42.3	46.4	31.7	24.1	17.9
	15-59	51.2	48.2	60.5	63.1	57.8
	60+	6.5	5.5	7.8	12.8	24.2
Median age (years)		18.9	16.7	24.0*	31.4	40.5
Dependency ratio	Total	86.5	100.6	58.9	49.4	57.2
	Youth	78.9	93.0	50.4	36.0	28.2
	Old Age	7.6	7.6	8.5	13.3	29.0
Potential support ratio		13.2	13.2	11.7	7.5	3.5
Parent support ratio		1.5	3.5	4.4	5.8	12.5
Sex ratio (per 100 women)	60+	86.5	86.2	85.3	81.4	80.1
	65+	84.4	84.0	83.4	79.7	77.1
	80+	76.7	77.2	72.0	69.9	63.5

* *Estimate refers to year 2005.*

Indicator	Age	1950-1955	1975-1980	2005-2010	2025-2030	2045-2050
Growth rate (percentage)	Total	2.7	2.7	1.4	0.8	0.2
	60+	2.5	2.0	3.7	3.8	2.0
	65+	3.0	2.1	3.8	3.9	2.2
	80+	3.3	3.3	4.9	4.3	4.0
Total fertility rate (per woman)		6.9	5.5	2.4	2.0	1.9
Life expectancy (years)						
Total	Birth	49.1	63.5	74.8	78.3	80.3
	60	..	..	21.9	23.5	24.5
	65	..	..	18.1	19.6	20.4
	80	..	..	8.5	9.3	9.8
Female	Birth	50.7	66.5	77.4	80.8	82.8
	60	..	..	22.9	24.9	26.0
	65	..	..	19.0	20.8	21.8
	80	..	..	8.9	9.9	10.5
Male	Birth	47.6	60.5	72.2	75.7	77.7
	60	..	..	20.8	22.0	22.7
	65	..	..	17.1	18.2	18.8
	80	..	..	7.9	8.6	8.9
Survival rate (percentage)						
Total	60	..	..	84.2	88.1	90.3
	65	..	..	79.3	84.1	86.6
	80	..	..	50.6	58.3	62.6
Female	60	..	..	87.8	91.0	92.8
	65	..	..	83.6	87.7	89.9
	80	..	..	56.3	64.8	69.5
Male	60	..	..	80.4	85.1	87.8
	65	..	..	74.9	80.3	83.3
	80	..	..	44.9	51.5	55.3

		1980	1990	2007	2010	2020
Labour force participation (percentage)						
Total	65+	37.0	32.5	27.2	25.5	20.8
Female	65+	16.5	13.7	13.8	13.8	14.0
Male	65+	61.6	55.2	43.3	39.7	29.2

Percentage married, age 60+				Percentage living alone, age 60+		
Total	Female	Male		Total	Female	Male
59.1	44.2	76.5		8.0	9.0	7.0

Statutory pensionable age (2006)				Percentage illiterate, age 65+		
	Female	Male		Total	Female	Male
	–	–		..	..	..

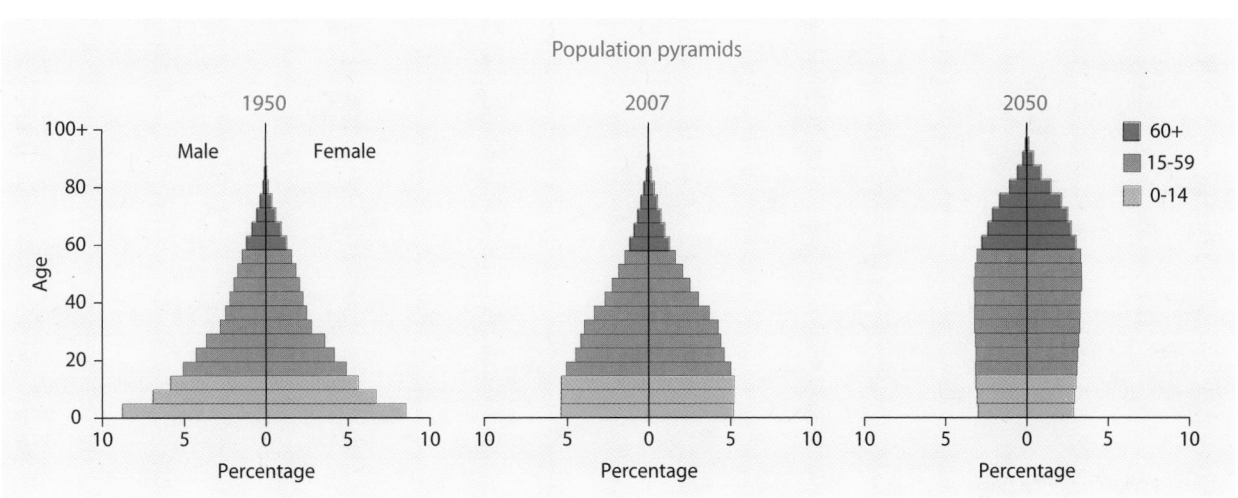

Population pyramids

1950   2007   2050

Male   Female

■ 60+
■ 15-59
▨ 0-14

South America

Indicator	Age	1950	1975	2007	2025	2050
Population (thousands)						
Total	Total	112 994.8	216 173.2	385 435.6	466 199.8	526 907.5
	0-14	44 578.8	85 669.7	109 631.7	107 537.3	95 171.0
	15-59	62 058.5	115 987.1	239 327.7	289 059.6	305 329.2
	60-64	2 436.4	5 041.5	11 206.8	21 153.3	30 086.7
	65-69	1 724.5	3 892.9	8 737.6	16 869.5	27 749.0
	70-74	1 134.1	2 703.0	6 621.7	12 832.5	23 332.6
	75-79	652.9	1 739.7	4 769.0	8 712.6	17 916.3
	80-84			2 961.4	5 292.1	13 234.5
	85-89			1 463.3	2 961.4	8 544.1
	90-94	409.8	1 139.3	547.6	1 272.4	3 990.5
	95-99			141.1	415.3	1 300.1
	100+			27.7	93.8	253.6
Female	Total	56 518.8	108 244.6	194 851.0	236 456.9	268 756.4
	0-14	22 085.5	42 396.2	53 764.3	52 646.8	46 539.1
	15-59	31 010.3	58 083.3	120 847.7	145 023.0	151 773.5
	60-64	1 276.0	2 615.8	5 928.3	11 235.4	15 602.5
	65-69	916.8	2 053.4	4 718.7	9 151.1	14 707.1
	70-74	618.7	1 455.6	3 684.2	7 137.8	12 785.7
	75-79	368.1	971.9	2 747.7	5 012.1	10 228.4
	80-84			1 772.6	3 173.2	7 912.8
	85-89			916.1	1 870.8	5 402.2
	90-94	243.3	668.4	357.9	850.8	2 690.6
	95-99			95.0	290.8	931.0
	100+			18.6	65.2	183.4
Male	Total	56 476.1	107 928.6	190 584.6	229 742.9	258 151.1
	0-14	22 493.2	43 273.5	55 867.4	54 890.4	48 631.9
	15-59	31 048.1	57 903.8	118 480.0	144 036.7	153 555.7
	60-64	1 160.3	2 425.7	5 278.5	9 917.9	14 484.2
	65-69	807.6	1 839.5	4 018.9	7 718.4	13 041.8
	70-74	515.4	1 247.4	2 937.6	5 694.7	10 546.9
	75-79	284.8	767.8	2 021.3	3 700.5	7 687.9
	80-84			1 188.8	2 118.9	5 321.6
	85-89			547.2	1 090.6	3 141.9
	90-94	166.5	470.9	189.7	421.6	1 299.9
	95-99			46.1	124.5	369.0
	100+			9.1	28.6	70.2
Percentage in older ages						
Total	60+	5.6	6.7	9.5	14.9	24.0
	65+	3.5	4.4	6.6	10.4	18.3
	80+	0.4	0.5	1.3	2.2	5.2
Female	60+	6.1	7.2	10.4	16.4	26.2
	65+	3.8	4.8	7.3	11.7	20.4
	80+	0.4	0.6	1.6	2.6	6.4
Male	60+	5.2	6.3	8.5	13.4	21.7
	65+	3.1	4.0	5.8	9.1	16.1
	80+	0.3	0.4	1.0	1.6	4.0
Ageing index		14.3	16.9	33.3	64.7	132.8
Broad age groups (percentage)	0-14	39.5	39.6	28.4	23.1	18.1
	15-59	54.9	53.7	62.1	62.0	57.9
	60+	5.6	6.7	9.5	14.9	24.0
Median age (years)		20.5	20.1	26.4*	32.6	39.7
Dependency ratio	Total	75.2	78.6	53.8	50.3	57.1
	Youth	69.1	70.8	43.8	34.7	28.4
	Old Age	6.1	7.8	10.1	15.6	28.7
Potential support ratio		16.4	12.8	9.9	6.4	3.5
Parent support ratio		1.4	1.8	4.9	6.7	14.9
Sex ratio (per 100 women)	60+	85.7	86.9	80.2	79.4	79.4
	65+	82.6	84.0	76.6	75.8	75.6
	80+	68.4	70.5	62.7	60.5	59.6

* *Estimate refers to year 2005.*

Indicator	Age	1950-1955	1975-1980	2005-2010	2025-2030	2045-2050
Growth rate (percentage)	Total	2.8	2.3	1.3	0.7	0.3
	60+	3.4	2.7	3.4	3.0	1.8
	65+	3.4	3.2	3.1	3.7	2.2
	80+	3.0	4.6	4.7	4.4	2.8
Total fertility rate (per woman)		5.7	4.3	2.4	2.0	1.9
Life expectancy (years)						
Total	Birth	52.0	62.6	72.7	76.6	79.4
	60	..	..	21.0	22.8	24.1
	65	..	..	17.4	19.0	20.1
	80	..	..	8.6	9.4	9.9
Female	Birth	53.8	65.3	76.2	79.9	82.7
	60	..	..	22.6	24.6	26.2
	65	..	..	18.7	20.5	21.9
	80	..	..	9.1	10.1	10.8
Male	Birth	50.3	60.1	69.3	73.2	76.0
	60	..	..	19.3	20.8	21.9
	65	..	..	15.9	17.3	18.1
	80	..	..	7.9	8.5	8.8
Survival rate (percentage)						
Total	60	..	..	80.9	85.6	89.0
	65	..	..	75.2	80.8	84.9
	80	..	..	44.4	53.2	59.8
Female	60	..	..	85.9	89.8	92.5
	65	..	..	81.2	86.0	89.6
	80	..	..	52.8	61.9	69.1
Male	60	..	..	75.9	81.5	85.6
	65	..	..	69.2	75.6	80.4
	80	..	..	36.2	44.5	50.4

		1980	1990	2007	2010	2020
Labour force participation (percentage)						
Total	65+	20.3	19.4	23.6	23.9	24.6
Female	65+	7.4	8.2	14.9	15.8	18.1
Male	65+	35.8	33.3	35.0	34.5	33.1

Percentage married, age 60+			Percentage living alone, age 60+		
Total	Female	Male	Total	Female	Male
56.8	41.7	75.4	9.0	11.0	7.0

Statutory pensionable age (2006)			Percentage illiterate, age 65+		
Female	Male		Total	Female	Male
–	–		..	..	..

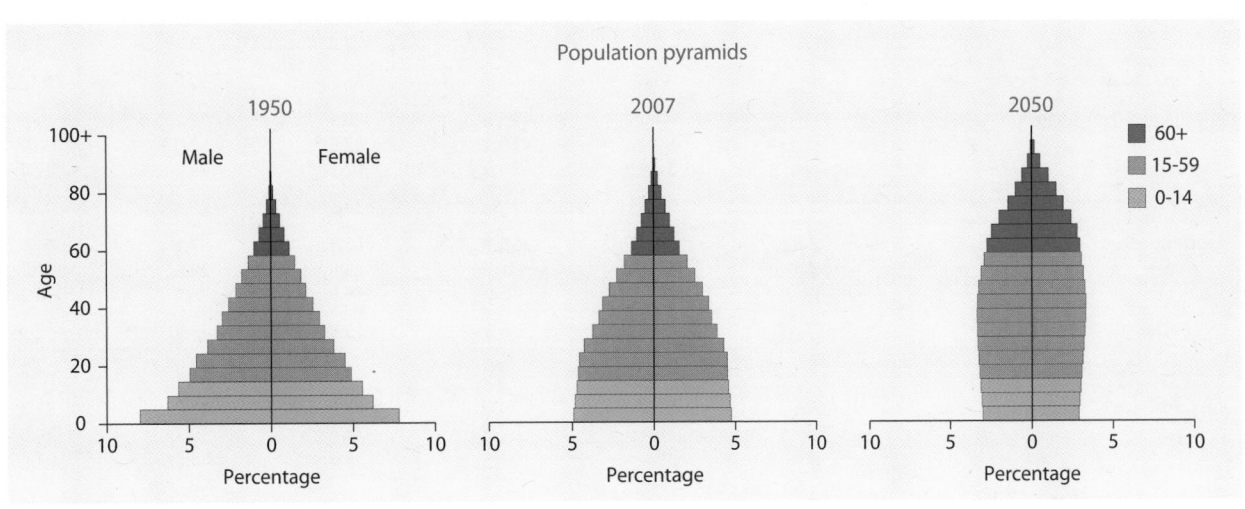

Population pyramids

1950   Male   Female
2007
2050

■ 60+
■ 15-59
▨ 0-14

Age   100+ 80 60 40 20 0

Percentage

Northern America

Indicator	Age	1950	1975	2007	2025	2050
Population (thousands)						
Total	Total	171 614.9	243 416.8	336 831.0	388 032.4	437 950.3
	0-14	46 696.5	61 515.2	67 719.0	71 090.4	74 951.0
	15-59	103 629.9	146 434.7	210 818.0	223 132.1	244 885.4
	60-64	7 188.7	10 468.3	16 140.0	23 801.0	25 551.2
	65-69	5 904.6	8 838.0	12 073.3	22 170.2	22 980.1
	70-74	3 844.6	6 358.5	9 655.5	18 158.0	19 699.2
	75-79	2 400.5	4 732.9	8 178.2	13 555.5	16 869.2
	80-84			6 318.7	8 282.6	13 858.2
	85-89			3 748.0	4 539.9	10 537.0
	90-94	1 950.1	5 069.2	1 615.3	2 228.9	5 918.5
	95-99			474.2	859.5	2 192.4
	100+			91.0	214.1	508.1
Female	Total	85 783.8	123 641.0	170 974.7	196 737.2	222 035.3
	0-14	22 861.5	30 080.4	33 019.5	34 658.4	36 546.7
	15-59	51 824.5	73 221.8	105 233.7	110 533.7	120 832.6
	60-64	3 621.2	5 554.9	8 409.3	12 276.5	12 932.7
	65-69	3 069.6	4 892.3	6 413.3	11 682.7	11 802.5
	70-74	2 015.1	3 669.1	5 278.7	9 802.5	10 334.7
	75-79	1 285.5	2 897.1	4 669.6	7 595.9	9 147.2
	80-84			3 847.6	4 898.6	7 915.1
	85-89			2 470.7	2 884.5	6 462.9
	90-94	1 106.4	3 325.4	1 173.0	1 555.1	3 992.6
	95-99			380.4	666.4	1 645.1
	100+			79.0	183.0	423.1
Male	Total	85 831.1	119 775.7	165 856.4	191 295.2	215 915.0
	0-14	23 835.1	31 434.8	34 699.4	36 432.1	38 404.4
	15-59	51 805.4	73 212.9	105 584.3	112 598.4	124 052.8
	60-64	3 567.5	4 913.4	7 730.7	11 524.6	12 618.5
	65-69	2 835.0	3 945.7	5 660.0	10 487.4	11 177.6
	70-74	1 829.5	2 689.4	4 376.8	8 355.5	9 364.5
	75-79	1 115.0	1 835.9	3 508.6	5 959.6	7 722.0
	80-84			2 471.1	3 384.1	5 943.1
	85-89			1 277.3	1 655.5	4 074.1
	90-94	843.7	1 743.8	442.2	673.8	1 925.9
	95-99			93.8	193.1	547.3
	100+			12.0	31.1	85.0
Percentage in older ages						
Total	60+	12.4	14.6	17.3	24.2	27.0
	65+	8.2	10.3	12.5	18.0	21.1
	80+	1.1	2.1	3.6	4.2	7.5
Female	60+	12.9	16.4	19.1	26.2	29.1
	65+	8.7	12.0	14.2	20.0	23.3
	80+	1.3	2.7	4.7	5.2	9.2
Male	60+	11.9	12.6	15.4	22.1	24.8
	65+	7.7	8.5	10.8	16.1	18.9
	80+	1.0	1.5	2.6	3.1	5.8
Ageing index		45.6	57.7	86.1	132.0	157.6
Broad age groups (percentage)	0-14	27.2	25.3	20.1	18.3	17.1
	15-59	60.4	60.2	62.6	57.5	55.9
	60+	12.4	14.6	17.3	24.2	27.0
Median age (years)		29.8	28.7	36.3*	38.8	41.5
Dependency ratio	Total	54.9	55.1	48.4	57.1	61.9
	Youth	42.1	39.2	29.8	28.8	27.7
	Old Age	12.7	15.9	18.6	28.4	34.2
Potential support ratio		7.9	6.3	5.4	3.5	2.9
Parent support ratio		3.2	5.6	9.8	11.4	24.2
Sex ratio (per 100 women)	60+	91.8	74.4	78.2	82.0	82.7
	65+	88.6	69.1	73.4	78.3	79.0
	80+	76.2	52.4	54.0	58.3	61.5

* Estimate refers to year 2005.

Indicator	Age	1950-1955	1975-1980	2005-2010	2025-2030	2045-2050
Growth rate (percentage)	Total	1.7	1.0	0.9	0.6	0.4
	60+	2.5	2.1	2.6	1.4	0.9
	65+	2.9	2.4	1.8	2.3	0.7
	80+	4.1	3.0	1.7	4.3	0.6
Total fertility rate (per woman)		3.5	1.8	2.0	1.8	1.9
Life expectancy (years)						
Total	Birth	68.8	73.3	78.2	80.5	82.7
	60	..	..	22.4	23.9	25.3
	65	..	..	18.5	19.8	21.1
	80	..	..	9.0	9.7	10.4
Female	Birth	71.9	77.3	80.8	83.1	85.2
	60	..	..	24.3	25.8	27.2
	65	..	..	20.2	21.6	22.9
	80	..	..	9.9	10.7	11.5
Male	Birth	66.1	69.6	75.5	77.9	80.2
	60	..	..	20.3	21.8	23.3
	65	..	..	16.6	17.9	19.2
	80	..	..	7.7	8.4	9.0
Survival rate (percentage)						
Total	60	..	..	89.2	91.6	93.8
	65	..	..	84.3	87.7	90.7
	80	..	..	54.2	60.8	67.0
Female	60	..	..	91.7	93.7	95.4
	65	..	..	87.9	90.6	93.0
	80	..	..	62.3	68.4	73.9
Male	60	..	..	86.8	89.6	92.2
	65	..	..	80.8	84.7	88.3
	80	..	..	45.8	53.0	59.9

		1980	1990	2007	2010	2020
Labour force participation (percentage)						
Total	65+	12.1	11.3	13.6	14.0	14.6
Female	65+	7.8	8.2	10.0	10.4	11.1
Male	65+	18.5	15.8	18.5	18.8	19.1

Percentage married, age 60+			Percentage living alone, age 60+		
Total	Female	Male	Total	Female	Male
59.9	48.1	75.2	26.0	34.0	15.0

Statutory pensionable age (2006)			Percentage illiterate, age 65+		
	Female	Male	Total	Female	Male
	–	–	..	..	..

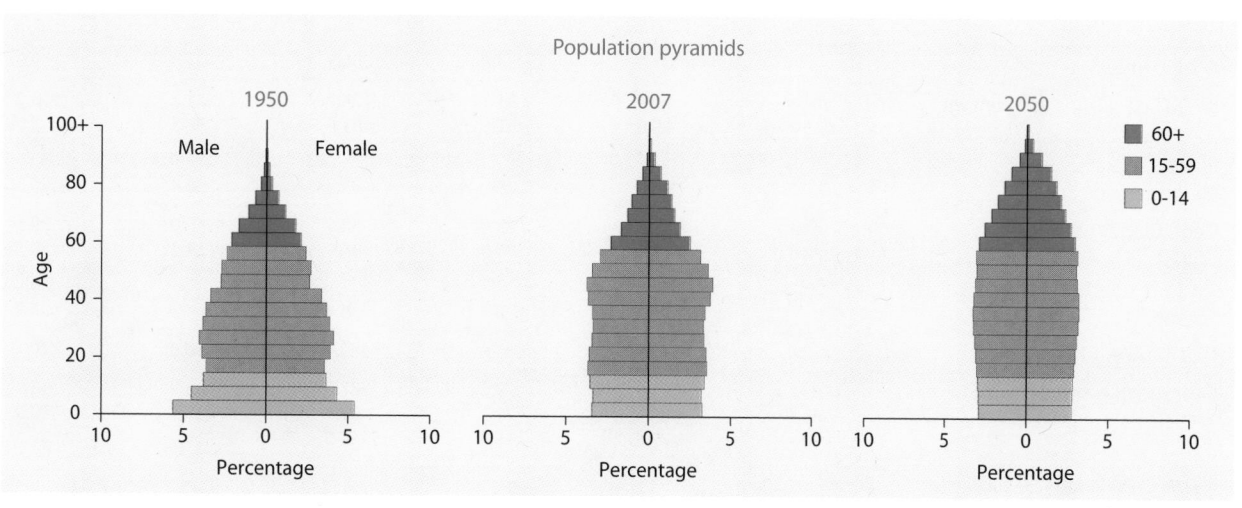

Population pyramids

1950   2007   2050

Male   Female

- 60+
- 15-59
- 0-14

Oceania

Indicator	Age	1950	1975	2007	2025	2050
Population (thousands)						
Total	Total	12 807.0	21 284.4	33 853.7	40 808.7	47 572.4
	0-14	3 824.6	6 663.5	8 188.2	8 599.5	8 553.8
	15-59	7 560.0	12 300.5	20 779.7	24 006.8	27 125.9
	60-64	484.0	760.8	1 414.6	2 148.4	2 698.7
	65-69	384.7	591.3	1 062.2	1 884.6	2 387.1
	70-74	264.0	428.9	824.6	1 543.6	1 981.5
	75-79	165.0	278.9	673.9	1 203.9	1 715.8
	80-84			501.2	736.7	1 374.5
	85-89			273.4	409.3	955.6
	90-94	124.7	260.5	105.5	189.8	524.8
	95-99			26.4	70.5	203.4
	100+			4.0	15.5	51.2
Female	Total	6 287.5	10 561.1	16 961.5	20 433.9	23 846.6
	0-14	1 865.5	3 254.8	3 978.6	4 176.0	4 155.3
	15-59	3 680.9	6 014.3	10 369.9	11 846.5	13 273.8
	60-64	243.7	392.0	706.7	1 107.8	1 336.3
	65-69	197.7	314.1	536.6	982.6	1 201.5
	70-74	139.7	239.4	430.4	816.7	1 034.0
	75-79	89.7	171.2	368.9	651.9	941.4
	80-84			295.3	415.6	790.3
	85-89			176.8	248.0	582.4
	90-94	70.2	175.4	75.0	125.7	346.1
	95-99			20.1	51.0	146.0
	100+			3.2	12.0	39.5
Male	Total	6 519.4	10 723.3	16 892.2	20 374.8	23 725.7
	0-14	1 959.1	3 408.8	4 209.7	4 423.5	4 398.5
	15-59	3 879.1	6 286.2	10 409.8	12 160.3	13 852.1
	60-64	240.3	368.8	707.9	1 040.6	1 362.4
	65-69	187.0	277.2	525.7	902.0	1 185.6
	70-74	124.2	189.5	394.2	726.9	947.5
	75-79	75.3	107.7	305.0	552.0	774.4
	80-84			205.8	321.1	584.2
	85-89			96.5	161.4	373.2
	90-94	54.5	85.1	30.5	64.1	178.7
	95-99			6.2	19.5	57.4
	100+			0.8	3.5	11.8
Percentage in older ages						
Total	60+	11.1	10.9	14.4	20.1	25.0
	65+	7.3	7.3	10.3	14.8	19.3
	80+	1.0	1.2	2.7	3.5	6.5
Female	60+	11.8	12.2	15.4	21.6	26.9
	65+	7.9	8.5	11.2	16.2	21.3
	80+	1.1	1.7	3.4	4.2	8.0
Male	60+	10.5	9.6	13.5	18.6	23.1
	65+	6.8	6.2	9.3	13.5	17.3
	80+	0.8	0.8	2.0	2.8	5.1
Ageing index		37.2	34.8	59.7	95.4	139.0
Broad age groups (percentage)	0-14	29.9	31.3	24.2	21.1	18.0
	15-59	59.0	57.8	61.4	58.8	57.0
	60+	11.1	10.9	14.4	20.1	25.0
Median age (years)		28.0	25.6	32.3*	36.4	40.5
Dependency ratio	Total	59.2	63.0	52.5	56.0	59.5
	Youth	47.5	51.0	36.9	32.9	28.7
	Old Age	11.7	11.9	15.6	23.1	30.8
Potential support ratio		8.6	8.4	6.4	4.3	3.2
Parent support ratio		2.9	3.6	7.9	10.0	20.1
Sex ratio (per 100 women)	60+	91.9	79.6	87.0	85.9	85.3
	65+	88.7	73.3	82.1	83.3	80.9
	80+	77.6	48.6	59.6	66.8	63.3

Estimate refers to year 2005.

Indicator	Age	1950-1955	1975-1980	2005-2010	2025-2030	2045-2050
Growth rate (percentage)	Total	2.1	1.5	1.2	0.8	0.4
	60+	1.7	2.7	3.2	2.1	1.3
	65+	2.3	3.3	2.5	2.6	1.2
	80+	2.8	3.6	3.1	4.6	1.7
Total fertility rate (per woman)		3.9	2.8	2.2	2.1	1.9
Life expectancy (years)						
Total	Birth	60.4	67.4	75.1	78.6	81.2
	60	..	..	22.6	24.0	24.9
	65	..	..	18.7	20.0	20.8
	80	..	..	9.0	9.8	10.5
Female	Birth	62.9	70.3	77.3	80.7	83.4
	60	..	..	24.5	25.9	26.9
	65	..	..	20.4	21.7	22.6
	80	..	..	9.8	10.8	11.6
Male	Birth	58.1	64.6	73.0	76.6	78.9
	60	..	..	20.6	22.0	22.8
	65	..	..	16.9	18.2	18.9
	80	..	..	8.0	8.7	9.3
Survival rate (percentage)						
Total	60	..	..	84.8	88.6	91.6
	65	..	..	80.4	84.5	87.8
	80	..	..	52.5	59.1	63.2
Female	60	..	..	86.4	89.8	92.8
	65	..	..	83.0	86.6	89.9
	80	..	..	60.1	66.0	70.0
Male	60	..	..	83.2	87.3	90.4
	65	..	..	77.9	82.3	85.7
	80	..	..	45.1	52.1	56.3

		1990	2007	2010	2020
Labour force participation (percentage)					
Total	65+	9.3	8.1	9.8	10.0	10.3
Female	65+	5.1	4.1	6.0	6.2	6.7
Male	65+	14.9	13.3	14.5	14.5	14.6

Percentage married, age 60+			Percentage living alone, age 60+		
Total	Female	Male	Total	Female	Male
61.9	49.9	76.0	25.0	34.0	16.0

Statutory pensionable age (2006)			Percentage illiterate, age 65+		
Female	Male		Total	Female	Male
–	–		..	..	..

Population pyramids

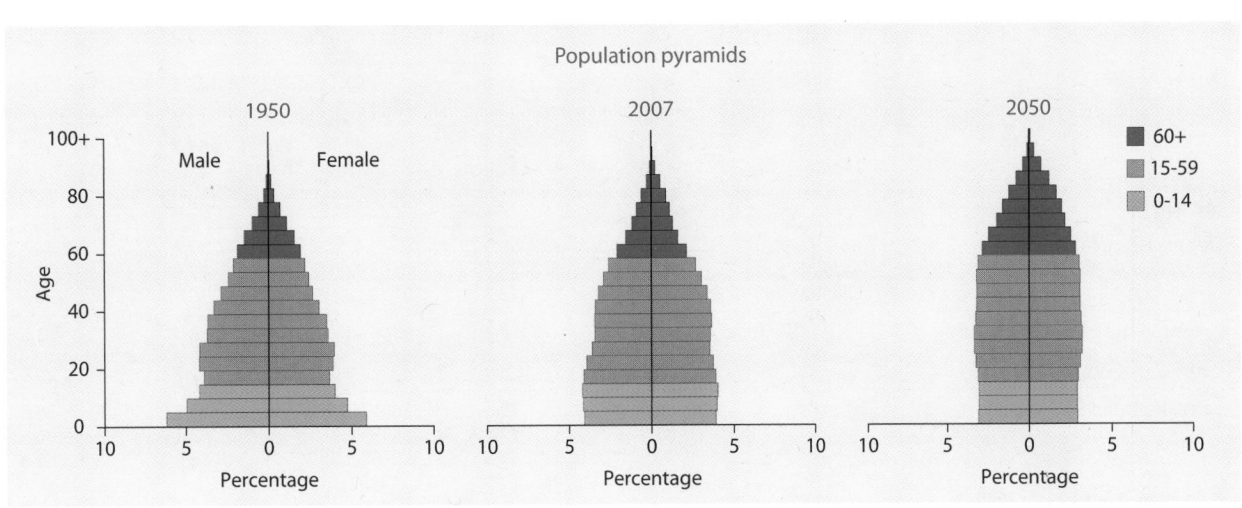

Australia/New Zealand

Indicator	Age	1950	1975	2007	2025	2050
Population (thousands)						
Total	Total	10 127.0	16 707.6	24 668.6	28 868.4	32 729.2
	0-14	2 734.0	4 683.2	4 763.2	5 102.1	5 290.0
	15-59	6 119.0	9 890.1	15 472.4	16 505.7	17 645.0
	60-64	435.0	684.0	1 241.9	1 778.0	2 022.0
	65-69	342.0	540.5	938.4	1 631.2	1 854.3
	70-74	234.0	397.5	744.5	1 382.2	1 605.8
	75-79	148.0	262.2	629.6	1 112.8	1 452.7
	80-84			479.9	694.2	1 221.2
	85-89			265.1	391.9	885.8
	90-94	115.0	250.1	103.5	185.2	502.9
	95-99			26.1	69.6	198.8
	100+			4.0	15.4	50.6
Female	Total	5 024.0	8 331.8	12 491.8	14 602.1	16 556.1
	0-14	1 339.0	2 286.4	2 320.1	2 485.7	2 576.5
	15-59	3 012.0	4 849.4	7 784.6	8 205.3	8 673.3
	60-64	221.0	354.0	622.7	917.5	1 007.0
	65-69	178.0	287.9	475.7	849.9	932.9
	70-74	126.0	222.6	389.7	730.4	831.2
	75-79	82.0	161.9	345.8	600.8	789.7
	80-84			284.1	390.7	697.1
	85-89			172.2	237.0	536.7
	90-94	66.0	169.6	73.8	122.6	330.5
	95-99			20.0	50.3	142.4
	100+			3.2	11.9	38.9
Male	Total	5 103.0	8 375.9	12 176.7	14 266.3	16 173.1
	0-14	1 395.0	2 396.9	2 443.2	2 616.4	2 713.5
	15-59	3 107.0	5 040.6	7 687.8	8 300.5	8 971.7
	60-64	214.0	330.0	619.2	860.5	1 015.0
	65-69	164.0	252.6	462.7	781.2	921.5
	70-74	108.0	174.9	354.7	651.8	774.6
	75-79	66.0	100.3	283.8	512.1	663.0
	80-84			195.8	303.5	524.1
	85-89			92.9	154.9	349.1
	90-94	49.0	80.5	29.7	62.6	172.4
	95-99			6.1	19.3	56.4
	100+			0.8	3.5	11.7
Percentage in older ages						
Total	60+	12.6	12.8	18.0	25.2	29.9
	65+	8.3	8.7	12.9	19.0	23.7
	80+	1.1	1.5	3.6	4.7	8.7
Female	60+	13.4	14.4	19.1	26.8	32.1
	65+	9.0	10.1	14.1	20.5	26.0
	80+	1.3	2.0	4.4	5.6	10.5
Male	60+	11.8	11.2	16.8	23.5	27.7
	65+	7.6	7.3	11.7	17.4	21.5
	80+	1.0	1.0	2.7	3.8	6.9
Ageing index		46.6	45.6	93.1	142.3	185.1
Broad age groups (percentage)	0-14	27.0	28.0	19.3	17.7	16.2
	15-59	60.4	59.2	62.7	57.2	53.9
	60+	12.6	12.8	18.0	25.2	29.9
Median age (years)		30.2	27.7	36.5*	40.6	43.7
Dependency ratio	Total	54.5	58.0	47.6	57.9	66.4
	Youth	41.7	44.3	28.5	27.9	26.9
	Old Age	12.8	13.7	19.1	30.0	39.5
Potential support ratio		7.8	7.3	5.2	3.3	2.5
Parent support ratio		3.1	3.9	9.0	12.2	26.8
Sex ratio (per 100 women)	60+	89.3	78.5	85.7	85.6	84.6
	65+	85.6	72.2	80.8	83.1	80.8
	80+	74.2	47.5	58.8	66.9	63.8

* *Estimate refers to year 2005.*

Indicator	Age	1950-1955	1975-1980	2005-2010	2025-2030	2045-2050
Growth rate (percentage)	Total	2.3	1.2	1.0	0.7	0.4
	60+	2.1	2.7	3.2	1.8	0.9
	65+	2.8	3.3	2.5	2.3	0.9
	80+	2.8	3.7	3.1	4.6	1.5
Total fertility rate (per woman)		3.3	2.1	1.8	1.9	1.9
Life expectancy (years)						
Total	Birth	69.6	73.3	80.8	83.1	85.0
	60	..	..	23.7	25.2	26.6
	65	..	..	19.5	20.9	22.2
	80	..	..	9.2	10.1	11.0
Female	Birth	72.3	76.8	83.2	85.4	87.2
	60	..	..	25.5	27.2	28.6
	65	..	..	21.2	22.7	24.1
	80	..	..	10.0	11.1	12.1
Male	Birth	67.0	70.0	78.3	80.8	82.6
	60	..	..	21.7	23.2	24.5
	65	..	..	17.7	19.0	20.2
	80	..	..	8.1	8.9	9.6
Survival rate (percentage)						
Total	60	..	..	92.9	94.9	96.1
	65	..	..	89.3	91.9	93.7
	80	..	..	61.9	68.0	72.7
Female	60	..	..	94.5	95.9	96.9
	65	..	..	91.8	93.8	95.1
	80	..	..	70.0	75.1	79.2
Male	60	..	..	91.2	93.8	95.3
	65	..	..	86.7	90.1	92.2
	80	..	..	53.8	60.7	66.0

		1980	1990	2007	2010	2020
Labour force participation (percentage)						
Total	65+	6.9	5.2	7.2	7.4	7.6
Female	65+	3.2	2.5	4.0	4.2	4.4
Male	65+	12.0	8.8	11.2	11.3	11.5

Percentage married, age 60+			Percentage living alone, age 60+		
Total	Female	Male	Total	Female	Male
..	..	..	..	..	..

Statutory pensionable age (2006)		Percentage illiterate, age 65+		
Female	Male	Total	Female	Male
–	–	..	..	..

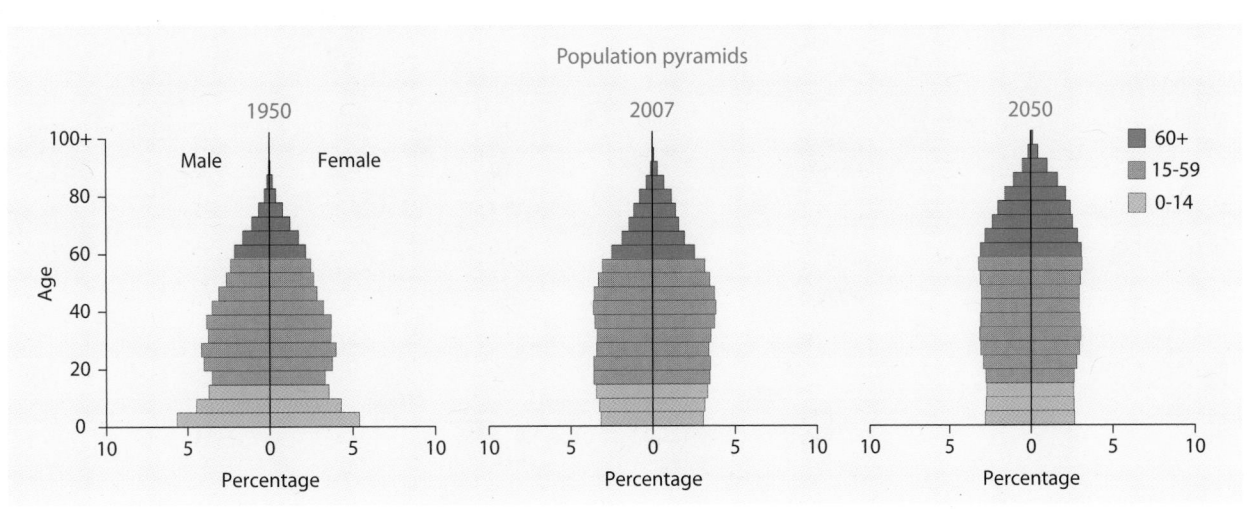

Population pyramids

Melanesia

Indicator	Age	1950	1975	2007	2025	2050
Population (thousands)						
Total	Total	2 289.4	3 864.8	7 941.2	10 460.7	13 231.2
	0-14	926.0	1 669.6	3 015.7	3 110.7	2 943.4
	15-59	1 233.0	2 041.3	4 565.3	6 602.0	8 523.8
	60-64	42.5	64.2	141.4	303.7	585.7
	65-69	38.2	42.3	100.3	203.3	458.8
	70-74	26.6	25.8	62.7	125.1	319.7
	75-79	15.0	13.5	33.3	69.4	215.8
	80-84			15.2	30.9	116.1
	85-89			5.7	12.1	50.1
	90-94	8.1	8.1	1.4	2.9	14.6
	95-99			0.2	0.5	2.8
	100+			0.0	0.1	0.3
Female	Total	1 082.4	1 883.7	3 858.0	5 097.9	6 481.7
	0-14	447.0	816.8	1 459.7	1 502.2	1 423.1
	15-59	576.3	987.2	2 220.8	3 197.8	4 128.9
	60-64	19.4	31.9	68.4	156.6	283.8
	65-69	17.5	21.9	49.2	107.1	230.5
	70-74	12.1	13.9	31.5	67.2	173.0
	75-79	6.7	7.5	17.0	39.1	125.4
	80-84			7.7	18.1	71.3
	85-89			2.9	7.5	32.9
	90-94	3.4	4.5	0.7	1.9	10.4
	95-99			0.1	0.3	2.2
	100+			0.0	0.0	0.3
Male	Total	1 207.0	1 981.1	4 083.2	5 362.8	6 749.5
	0-14	479.1	852.8	1 556.0	1 608.5	1 520.4
	15-59	656.7	1 054.0	2 344.5	3 404.2	4 394.9
	60-64	23.0	32.4	73.0	147.2	302.0
	65-69	20.6	20.4	51.1	96.1	228.3
	70-74	14.6	11.9	31.2	57.9	146.7
	75-79	8.3	6.0	16.3	30.3	90.4
	80-84			7.5	12.9	44.8
	85-89			2.8	4.6	17.2
	90-94	4.7	3.6	0.7	1.0	4.2
	95-99			0.1	0.1	0.6
	100+			0.0	0.0	0.1
Percentage in older ages						
Total	60+	5.7	4.0	4.5	7.2	13.3
	65+	3.8	2.3	2.8	4.2	8.9
	80+	0.4	0.2	0.3	0.4	1.4
Female	60+	5.5	4.2	4.6	7.8	14.3
	65+	3.7	2.5	2.8	4.7	10.0
	80+	0.3	0.2	0.3	0.5	1.8
Male	60+	5.9	3.7	4.5	6.5	12.4
	65+	4.0	2.1	2.7	3.8	7.9
	80+	0.4	0.2	0.3	0.3	1.0
Ageing index		14.1	9.2	11.9	24.0	59.9
Broad age groups (percentage)	0-14	40.4	43.2	38.0	29.7	22.2
	15-59	53.9	52.8	57.5	63.1	64.4
	60+	5.7	4.0	4.5	7.2	13.3
Median age (years)		19.7	18.1	20.4*	26.0	32.9
Dependency ratio	Total	79.5	83.6	68.7	51.5	45.2
	Youth	72.6	79.3	64.1	45.0	32.3
	Old Age	6.9	4.3	4.7	6.4	12.9
Potential support ratio		14.5	23.5	21.5	15.5	7.7
Parent support ratio		1.3	0.9	1.2	1.3	3.0
Sex ratio (per 100 women)	60+	120.6	93.2	102.9	88.0	89.7
	65+	121.7	87.6	100.5	84.1	82.4
	80+	140.1	81.0	95.7	66.8	57.2

*   *Estimate refers to year 2005.*

Indicator	Age	1950-1955	1975-1980	2005-2010	2025-2030	2045-2050
Growth rate (percentage)	Total	1.6	2.4	1.7	1.3	0.7
	60+	−2.8	2.5	3.3	4.0	3.0
	65+	−3.0	2.7	2.7	4.8	3.3
	80+	2.5	2.5	2.8	5.4	4.8
Total fertility rate (per woman)		6.3	5.6	3.5	2.5	2.0
Life expectancy (years)						
Total	Birth	37.4	50.3	59.5	66.1	71.2
	60	..	..	14.4	16.3	18.1
	65	..	..	11.6	13.2	14.8
	80	..	..	5.6	6.4	7.1
Female	Birth	38.5	51.5	60.5	67.3	72.9
	60	..	..	15.8	17.7	19.8
	65	..	..	12.8	14.4	16.1
	80	..	..	6.1	6.8	7.7
Male	Birth	36.5	49.2	58.7	64.9	69.6
	60	..	..	13.3	14.9	16.5
	65	..	..	10.7	12.0	13.3
	80	..	..	5.2	5.8	6.3
Survival rate (percentage)						
Total	60	..	..	62.1	73.4	81.7
	65	..	..	52.4	64.3	73.9
	80	..	..	16.7	25.7	35.2
Female	60	..	..	63.8	75.0	83.6
	65	..	..	55.4	67.3	77.3
	80	..	..	21.0	31.0	42.0
Male	60	..	..	60.5	71.8	80.0
	65	..	..	49.6	61.4	70.8
	80	..	..	13.2	20.6	28.6

		1980	1990	2007	2010	2020
Labour force participation (percentage)						
Total	65+	46.2	48.4	45.3	44.8	44.4
Female	65+	38.8	35.5	36.6	36.4	36.9
Male	65+	54.7	56.6	53.9	53.5	52.9

Percentage married, age 60+				Percentage living alone, age 60+		
Total	Female	Male		Total	Female	Male
..	..	..		..	..	..

Statutory pensionable age (2006)				Percentage illiterate, age 65+		
	Female	Male		Total	Female	Male
	–	–		..	..	..

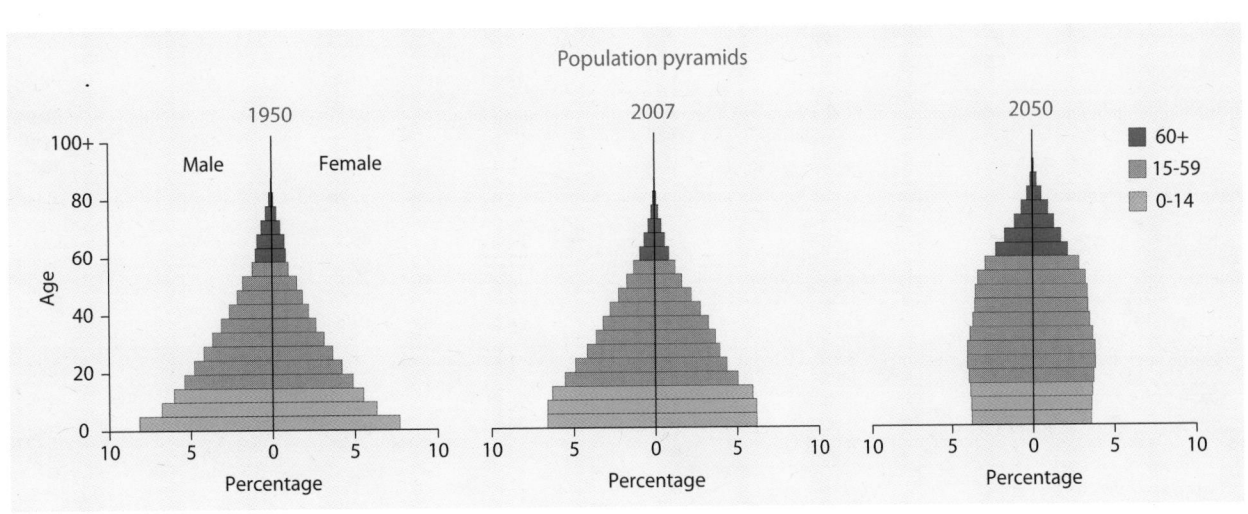

Population pyramids

1950 · Male · Female
2007
2050
60+
15-59
0-14

Micronesia

Indicator	Age	1950	1975	2007	2025	2050
Population (thousands)						
Total	Total	148.1	266.7	575.4	723.9	849.1
	0-14	52.5	112.8	187.9	194.4	177.1
	15-59	87.7	140.2	347.1	435.0	508.8
	60-64	2.6	5.1	14.3	32.3	44.0
	65-69	2.0	3.7	10.0	25.3	37.4
	70-74	1.5	2.5	7.7	18.1	27.4
	75-79	1.0	1.5	4.8	11.0	22.8
	80-84			2.5	5.0	17.8
	85-89			0.9	2.2	9.5
	90-94	0.9	1.0	0.2	0.6	3.5
	95-99			0.0	0.1	0.8
	100+			0.0	0.0	0.1
Female	Total	63.0	128.7	285.4	362.6	429.6
	0-14	25.6	55.2	91.6	94.8	86.3
	15-59	33.2	66.4	172.5	217.2	253.0
	60-64	1.3	2.5	7.2	16.7	22.6
	65-69	1.0	1.9	5.2	13.3	19.8
	70-74	0.8	1.3	4.2	9.7	14.9
	75-79	0.5	0.8	2.6	6.1	12.9
	80-84			1.4	3.0	10.6
	85-89			0.6	1.4	6.2
	90-94	0.5	0.6	0.1	0.4	2.5
	95-99			0.0	0.1	0.6
	100+			0.0	0.0	0.1
Male	Total	85.1	138.0	290.0	361.3	419.4
	0-14	26.8	57.6	96.3	99.6	90.8
	15-59	54.4	73.8	174.6	217.8	255.8
	60-64	1.3	2.5	7.1	15.6	21.4
	65-69	1.0	1.8	4.8	12.1	17.6
	70-74	0.7	1.2	3.5	8.4	12.4
	75-79	0.5	0.7	2.1	4.9	9.9
	80-84			1.1	2.0	7.2
	85-89			0.4	0.7	3.3
	90-94	0.4	0.4	0.1	0.2	1.0
	95-99			0.0	0.0	0.1
	100+			0.0	0.0	0.0
Percentage in older ages						
Total	60+	5.4	5.1	7.0	13.1	19.2
	65+	3.6	3.2	4.5	8.6	14.0
	80+	0.6	0.4	0.6	1.1	3.7
Female	60+	6.6	5.5	7.5	14.0	21.0
	65+	4.5	3.5	5.0	9.4	15.8
	80+	0.8	0.5	0.7	1.4	4.7
Male	60+	4.5	4.8	6.6	12.1	17.4
	65+	3.0	3.0	4.1	7.8	12.3
	80+	0.5	0.3	0.5	0.8	2.8
Ageing index		15.2	12.1	21.5	48.6	92.2
Broad age groups (percentage)	0-14	35.4	42.3	32.7	26.9	20.9
	15-59	59.2	52.6	60.3	60.1	59.9
	60+	5.4	5.1	7.0	13.1	19.2
Median age (years)		21.1	18.6	24.9*	29.1	36.1
Dependency ratio	Total	64.1	83.6	59.2	54.9	53.6
	Youth	58.1	77.7	52.0	41.6	32.0
	Old Age	6.0	5.9	7.2	13.3	21.6
Potential support ratio		16.8	16.9	13.9	7.5	4.6
Parent support ratio		2.7	1.5	1.8	2.7	9.8
Sex ratio (per 100 women)	60+	93.0	93.7	89.3	86.7	80.6
	65+	90.1	89.9	84.6	83.3	76.0
	80+	84.3	71.7	71.3	59.8	57.8

* *Estimate refers to year 2005.*

Indicator	Age	1950-1955	1975-1980	2005-2010	2025-2030	2045-2050
Growth rate (percentage)	Total	2.0	2.4	1.6	0.9	0.4
	60+	0.7	2.9	4.7	3.6	1.9
	65+	0.2	2.8	3.2	4.4	1.9
	80+	−2.6	4.7	3.9	7.1	3.7
Total fertility rate (per woman)		6.3	4.9	3.2	2.4	2.0
Life expectancy (years)						
Total	Birth	53.1	63.2	72.0	76.0	79.0
	60	..	..	18.8	20.4	22.2
	65	..	..	15.1	16.5	18.1
	80	..	..	6.3	7.3	8.3
Female	Birth	54.7	65.0	74.3	78.4	81.3
	60	..	..	20.1	22.1	24.0
	65	..	..	16.2	18.0	19.7
	80	..	..	6.7	7.9	9.1
Male	Birth	51.9	61.6	69.8	73.6	76.5
	60	..	..	17.5	18.7	20.1
	65	..	..	14.0	15.0	16.3
	80	..	..	5.8	6.4	7.1
Survival rate (percentage)						
Total	60	..	..	83.7	88.9	92.0
	65	..	..	77.4	83.6	87.6
	80	..	..	39.4	48.0	56.2
Female	60	..	..	86.7	91.3	93.7
	65	..	..	81.7	87.3	90.5
	80	..	..	46.3	56.1	64.0
Male	60	..	..	80.8	86.5	90.2
	65	..	..	73.4	80.0	84.6
	80	..	..	33.0	40.1	47.8

		1980	1990	2007	2010	2020
Labour force participation (percentage)						
Total	65+	51.7	48.0	44.1	43.7	43.3
Female	65+	42.6	38.8	34.7	34.5	34.4
Male	65+	62.0	57.8	55.1	54.6	53.9

Percentage married, age 60+			Percentage living alone, age 60+		
Total	Female	Male	Total	Female	Male
..	..	..	..	..	..

Statutory pensionable age (2006)			Percentage illiterate, age 65+		
	Female	Male	Total	Female	Male
	–	–	..	..	..

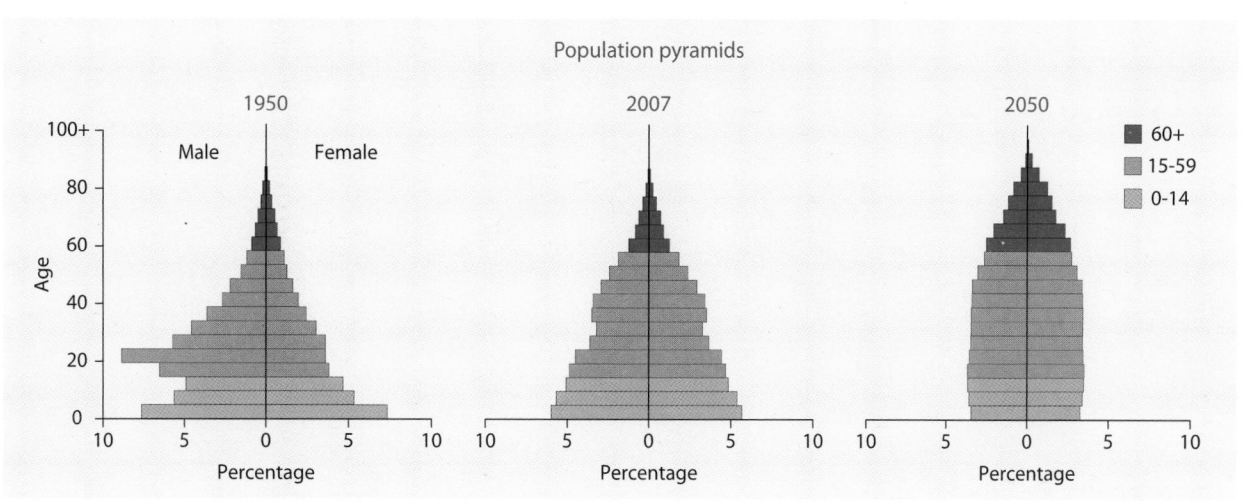

Population pyramids

Polynesia

Indicator	Age	1950	1975	2007	2025	2050
Population (thousands)						
Total	Total	242.4	445.4	668.5	755.7	762.9
	0-14	112.1	197.9	221.4	192.2	143.3
	15-59	120.3	229.0	394.9	464.1	448.2
	60-64	3.9	7.5	17.2	34.4	46.9
	65-69	2.5	4.8	13.5	24.8	36.6
	70-74	1.8	3.2	9.7	18.3	28.6
	75-79	1.0	1.7	6.2	10.7	24.5
	80-84			3.5	6.6	19.3
	85-89			1.6	3.2	10.3
	90-94	0.8	1.4	0.4	1.1	3.9
	95-99			0.1	0.3	1.1
	100+			0.0	0.0	0.2
Female	Total	118.2	217.0	326.3	371.3	379.2
	0-14	53.9	96.4	107.2	93.2	69.5
	15-59	59.4	111.2	192.1	226.3	218.6
	60-64	1.9	3.7	8.4	17.1	22.9
	65-69	1.2	2.4	6.5	12.3	18.4
	70-74	0.9	1.7	5.0	9.5	14.8
	75-79	0.5	1.0	3.5	5.9	13.4
	80-84			2.1	3.9	11.2
	85-89			1.1	2.0	6.6
	90-94	0.4	0.8	0.3	0.8	2.8
	95-99			0.1	0.2	0.9
	100+			0.0	0.0	0.1
Male	Total	124.3	228.3	342.2	384.4	383.7
	0-14	58.1	101.5	114.1	99.0	73.8
	15-59	60.9	117.7	202.8	237.8	229.6
	60-64	2.0	3.9	8.7	17.3	24.0
	65-69	1.4	2.4	7.0	12.5	18.2
	70-74	0.9	1.5	4.7	8.7	13.8
	75-79	0.5	0.7	2.7	4.8	11.1
	80-84			1.4	2.8	8.1
	85-89			0.6	1.1	3.7
	90-94	0.4	0.6	0.1	0.3	1.1
	95-99			0.0	0.0	0.2
	100+			0.0	0.0	0.0
Percentage in older ages						
Total	60+	4.1	4.2	7.8	13.1	22.5
	65+	2.5	2.5	5.3	8.6	16.3
	80+	0.3	0.3	0.8	1.5	4.5
Female	60+	4.1	4.3	8.3	13.9	24.0
	65+	2.5	2.6	5.7	9.3	18.0
	80+	0.3	0.3	1.1	1.9	5.7
Male	60+	4.2	4.0	7.4	12.4	20.9
	65+	2.6	2.3	4.8	7.9	14.7
	80+	0.3	0.3	0.6	1.1	3.4
Ageing index		8.9	9.4	23.6	51.7	119.5
Broad age groups (percentage)	0-14	46.2	44.4	33.1	25.4	18.8
	15-59	49.6	51.4	59.1	61.4	58.8
	60+	4.1	4.2	7.8	13.1	22.5
Median age (years)		16.9	17.4	23.4*	30.0	39.4
Dependency ratio	Total	95.1	88.3	62.3	51.6	54.1
	Youth	90.2	83.7	53.7	38.6	28.9
	Old Age	4.9	4.6	8.5	13.0	25.1
Potential support ratio		20.4	21.5	11.7	7.7	4.0
Parent support ratio		1.6	1.5	3.1	3.9	10.2
Sex ratio (per 100 women)	60+	107.0	96.7	93.9	92.1	88.1
	65+	109.5	91.4	89.3	87.6	82.4
	80+	95.6	82.5	58.9	61.3	60.5

* Estimate refers to year 2005.

Indicator	Age	1950-1955	1975-1980	2005-2010	2025-2030	2045-2050
Growth rate (percentage)	Total	2.6	1.4	0.9	0.4	−0.3
	60+	0.5	3.0	2.5	3.7	2.0
	65+	1.5	3.7	3.0	4.2	1.5
	80+	−1.0	2.1	3.5	3.2	4.3
Total fertility rate (per woman)		6.7	4.7	3.0	2.2	2.0
Life expectancy (years)						
Total	Birth	50.3	62.2	72.9	76.4	79.2
	60	..	..	18.5	20.4	22.2
	65	..	..	15.0	16.6	18.2
	80	..	..	7.1	7.9	8.7
Female	Birth	52.4	64.9	75.7	79.1	81.8
	60	..	..	20.5	22.6	24.4
	65	..	..	16.7	18.6	20.2
	80	..	..	7.8	8.8	9.8
Male	Birth	48.6	60.0	70.5	73.9	76.7
	60	..	..	16.7	18.2	20.0
	65	..	..	13.4	14.7	16.2
	80	..	..	6.1	6.7	7.4
Survival rate (percentage)						
Total	60	..	..	84.8	89.4	92.1
	65	..	..	77.6	83.5	87.5
	80	..	..	37.9	47.1	55.3
Female	60	..	..	88.0	91.5	93.7
	65	..	..	82.4	87.3	90.4
	80	..	..	47.1	56.9	64.4
Male	60	..	..	81.9	87.4	90.6
	65	..	..	73.1	80.0	84.7
	80	..	..	29.9	38.2	46.7

		1980	1990	2007	2010	2020
Labour force participation (percentage)						
Total	65+	22.0	17.8	17.2	16.7	15.3
Female	65+	9.5	6.4	8.4	8.5	8.6
Male	65+	36.0	30.1	26.8	25.8	22.8

Percentage married, age 60+			Percentage living alone, age 60+		
Total	Female	Male	Total	Female	Male
..	..	..	..	..	..

Statutory pensionable age (2006)		Percentage illiterate, age 65+		
Female	Male	Total	Female	Male
–	–	..	..	..

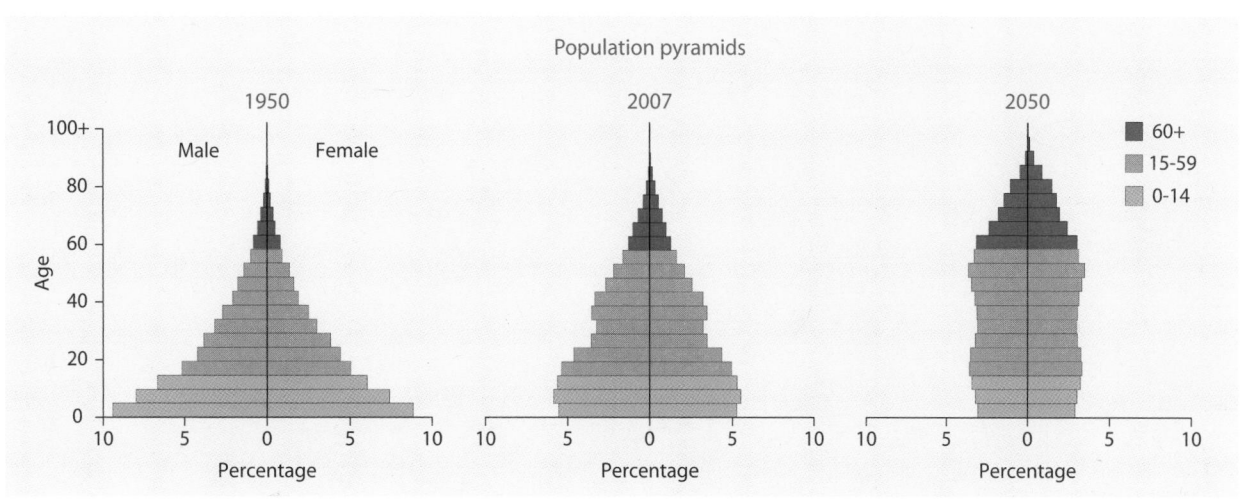

Population pyramids

Annex IV
Profiles of ageing

Table A.IV.2
Profiles of ageing by country or area

Afghanistan

Indicator	Age	1950	1975	2007	2025	2050
Population (thousands)						
Total	Total	8 151.5	14 319.3	32 254.4	55 442.6	97 324.4
	0-14	3 476.3	6 301.0	14 923.4	24 191.1	32 216.3
	15-59	4 307.1	7 342.0	15 918.3	28 820.2	58 854.8
	60-64	158.2	278.4	547.4	934.7	2 343.8
	65-69	108.1	196.3	399.2	675.4	1 709.3
	70-74	63.1	120.3	259.5	439.5	1 144.0
	75-79	28.4	58.5	138.5	249.0	665.2
	80-84			53.4	102.1	292.9
	85-89			12.9	26.5	83.7
	90-94	10.2	22.8	1.7	3.8	13.2
	95-99			0.1	0.3	1.0
	100+			0.0	0.0	0.0
Female	Total	3 931.6	6 910.3	15 617.9	26 861.6	47 223.5
	0-14	1 682.3	3 048.4	7 227.6	11 703.0	15 576.6
	15-59	2 065.9	3 523.1	7 675.9	13 923.2	28 460.3
	60-64	78.6	138.3	272.5	466.2	1 167.4
	65-69	54.1	98.5	201.3	341.7	864.6
	70-74	31.6	60.8	132.5	225.6	589.3
	75-79	14.1	29.7	71.8	130.2	350.7
	80-84			28.2	54.6	158.9
	85-89			7.0	14.6	47.1
	90-94	5.0	11.5	1.0	2.2	7.9
	95-99			0.1	0.2	0.7
	100+			0.0	0.0	0.0
Male	Total	4 219.8	7 409.0	16 636.5	28 581.0	50 100.9
	0-14	1 794.0	3 252.6	7 695.8	12 488.1	16 639.7
	15-59	2 241.2	3 819.0	8 242.4	14 896.9	30 394.5
	60-64	79.5	140.1	275.0	468.5	1 176.4
	65-69	54.0	97.8	197.9	333.7	844.7
	70-74	31.5	59.5	126.9	213.9	554.7
	75-79	14.3	28.8	66.6	118.8	314.5
	80-84			25.2	47.5	134.1
	85-89			5.9	11.9	36.6
	90-94	5.2	11.3	0.7	1.6	5.4
	95-99			0.0	0.1	0.4
	100+			0.0	0.0	0.0
Percentage in older ages						
Total	60+	4.5	4.7	4.4	4.4	6.4
	65+	2.6	2.8	2.7	2.7	4.0
	80+	0.1	0.2	0.2	0.2	0.4
Female	60+	4.7	4.9	4.6	4.6	6.7
	65+	2.7	2.9	2.8	2.9	4.3
	80+	0.1	0.2	0.2	0.3	0.5
Male	60+	4.4	4.6	4.2	4.2	6.1
	65+	2.5	2.7	2.5	2.5	3.8
	80+	0.1	0.2	0.2	0.2	0.4
Ageing index		10.6	10.7	9.5	10.1	19.4
Broad age groups (percentage)	0-14	42.6	44.0	46.3	43.6	33.1
	15-59	52.8	51.3	49.4	52.0	60.5
	60+	4.5	4.7	4.4	4.4	6.4
Median age (years)		18.6	18.0	16.7*	18.0	23.4
Dependency ratio	Total	82.6	87.9	95.9	86.3	59.0
	Youth	77.9	82.7	90.6	81.3	52.6
	Old Age	4.7	5.2	5.3	5.0	6.4
Potential support ratio		21.3	19.2	19.0	19.9	15.7
Parent support ratio		0.3	0.4	0.7	0.8	1.1
Sex ratio (per 100 women)	60+	100.6	99.6	97.7	96.8	96.2
	65+	100.3	98.4	95.8	94.6	93.6
	80+	105.4	97.9	88.0	85.4	82.2

* Estimate refers to year 2005.

Indicator	Age	1950-1955	1975-1980	2005-2010	2025-2030	2045-2050
Growth rate (percentage)	Total	1.9	1.2	3.5	2.7	1.8
	60+	2.0	1.4	3.2	3.5	4.1
	65+	2.0	1.6	3.3	3.6	4.1
	80+	1.7	3.0	3.8	4.0	4.7
Total fertility rate (per woman)		7.7	7.7	7.1	5.2	3.1
Life expectancy (years)						
Total	Birth	31.9	42.1	47.7	55.3	62.8
	60	..	..	14.8	15.9	17.2
	65	..	..	11.6	12.5	13.6
	80	..	..	4.5	5.0	5.3
Female	Birth	31.6	42.2	47.9	55.7	63.4
	60	..	..	15.2	16.5	17.9
	65	..	..	11.9	12.9	14.1
	80	..	..	4.7	5.1	5.5
Male	Birth	32.1	42.1	47.4	54.9	62.1
	60	..	..	14.4	15.4	16.5
	65	..	..	11.3	12.1	13.1
	80	..	..	4.4	4.8	5.1
Survival rate (percentage)						
Total	60	..	..	50.2	61.1	71.9
	65	..	..	43.8	54.6	65.7
	80	..	..	13.7	20.1	28.2
Female	60	..	..	51.4	62.3	73.4
	65	..	..	45.4	56.5	68.0
	80	..	..	14.9	22.0	31.1
Male	60	..	..	49.1	59.9	70.5
	65	..	..	42.2	52.8	63.5
	80	..	..	12.5	18.2	25.4

		1980	1990	2007	2010	2020
Labour force participation (percentage)						
Total	65+	38.5	40.5	43.0	43.2	43.3
Female	65+	17.5	19.0	21.3	21.5	21.7
Male	65+	60.0	62.8	65.6	65.8	66.0

Percentage married, age 60+			Percentage living alone, age 60+		
Total	Female	Male	Total	Female	Male
60.3	38.0	83.0	..	..	..

Statutory pensionable age (2006)			Percentage illiterate, age 65+ (2000)		
	Female	Male	Total	Female	Male
	55	60	80.9	96.8	74.5

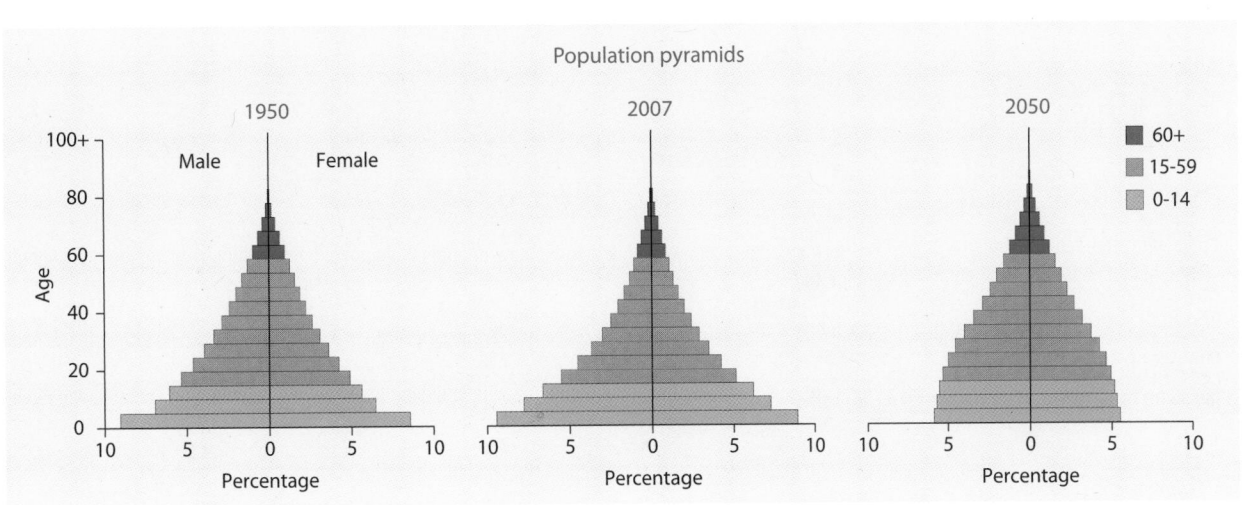

Population pyramids

Albania

Indicator	Age	1950	1975	2007	2025	2050
Population (thousands)						
Total	Total	1 215.0	2 400.8	3 163.3	3 483.7	3 458.1
	0-14	472.8	958.4	815.6	760.4	591.2
	15-59	619.8	1 277.3	1 955.9	2 075.4	1 951.5
	60-64	37.4	57.0	118.2	192.6	249.5
	65-69	32.5	42.4	103.9	177.2	208.8
	70-74	24.6	29.5	78.9	121.2	150.5
	75-79	16.5	20.7	50.7	81.1	121.9
	80-84			28.3	47.3	96.8
	85-89			9.3	21.7	58.1
	90-94	11.3	15.6	2.1	5.7	24.1
	95-99			0.2	1.0	5.1
	100+			0.0	0.1	0.6
Female	Total	603.2	1 186.7	1 596.3	1 770.8	1 764.4
	0-14	232.9	467.4	395.1	367.3	285.3
	15-59	308.0	631.9	991.4	1 047.0	952.5
	60-64	19.2	29.4	58.5	99.4	125.8
	65-69	16.5	22.0	52.4	92.2	112.4
	70-74	12.5	15.5	40.4	65.0	86.1
	75-79	8.4	11.4	29.6	46.5	73.0
	80-84			19.5	30.7	62.4
	85-89			7.3	16.6	41.6
	90-94	5.7	9.1	1.9	5.1	19.9
	95-99			0.2	1.0	4.7
	100+			0.0	0.1	0.6
Male	Total	611.8	1 214.1	1 566.9	1 712.9	1 693.7
	0-14	239.9	491.0	420.5	393.1	305.9
	15-59	311.8	645.4	964.5	1 028.4	999.0
	60-64	18.3	27.6	59.7	93.2	123.7
	65-69	16.0	20.3	51.6	85.0	96.4
	70-74	12.1	14.0	38.5	56.2	64.4
	75-79	8.2	9.3	21.1	34.7	48.9
	80-84			8.9	16.6	34.4
	85-89			2.0	5.1	16.4
	90-94	5.6	6.5	0.2	0.6	4.2
	95-99			0.0	0.0	0.4
	100+			0.0	0.0	0.0
Percentage in older ages						
Total	60+	10.1	6.9	12.4	18.6	26.5
	65+	7.0	4.5	8.6	13.1	19.3
	80+	0.9	0.6	1.3	2.2	5.3
Female	60+	10.3	7.4	13.1	20.1	29.8
	65+	7.1	4.9	9.5	14.5	22.7
	80+	1.0	0.8	1.8	3.0	7.3
Male	60+	9.8	6.4	11.6	17.0	23.0
	65+	6.8	4.1	7.8	11.6	15.7
	80+	0.9	0.5	0.7	1.3	3.3
Ageing index		25.9	17.2	48.0	85.2	154.8
Broad age groups (percentage)	0-14	38.9	39.9	25.8	21.8	17.1
	15-59	51.0	53.2	61.8	59.6	56.4
	60+	10.1	6.9	12.4	18.6	26.5
Median age (years)		20.6	19.5	28.3*	34.6	42.0
Dependency ratio	Total	84.9	79.9	52.5	53.6	57.1
	Youth	71.9	71.8	39.3	33.5	26.9
	Old Age	12.9	8.1	13.2	20.1	30.3
Potential support ratio		7.7	12.3	7.6	5.0	3.3
Parent support ratio		2.7	2.8	2.7	5.1	12.0
Sex ratio (per 100 women)	60+	96.5	88.9	86.7	81.8	73.8
	65+	97.0	86.4	80.8	77.1	66.1
	80+	96.9	71.8	38.2	42.0	42.9

* *Estimate refers to year 2005.*

Indicator	Age	1950-1955	1975-1980	2005-2010	2025-2030	2045-2050
Growth rate (percentage)	Total	2.5	2.1	0.5	0.2	–0.2
	60+	–0.8	4.3	2.3	1.8	2.0
	65+	0.6	5.1	2.4	2.8	1.7
	80+	1.3	5.4	3.9	3.1	1.7
Total fertility rate (per woman)		5.6	4.2	2.2	1.9	1.9
Life expectancy (years)						
Total	Birth	55.2	68.9	74.4	77.6	80.2
	60	..	..	19.3	20.8	22.8
	65	..	..	15.2	16.6	18.5
	80	..	..	6.2	7.1	8.3
Female	Birth	56.1	71.2	77.4	80.3	82.7
	60	..	..	21.6	23.3	25.0
	65	..	..	17.3	18.9	20.6
	80	..	..	7.1	8.3	9.5
Male	Birth	54.4	66.8	71.7	74.9	77.4
	60	..	..	17.1	18.2	20.1
	65	..	..	13.1	14.2	16.0
	80	..	..	4.6	5.3	6.5
Survival rate (percentage)						
Total	60	..	..	89.4	92.7	94.1
	65	..	..	84.7	88.6	90.7
	80	..	..	43.4	51.3	59.8
Female	60	..	..	91.7	93.8	95.2
	65	..	..	88.3	90.9	92.7
	80	..	..	55.3	62.7	68.9
Male	60	..	..	87.3	91.3	93.0
	65	..	..	81.2	86.0	88.7
	80	..	..	32.7	40.0	49.4

		1980	1990	2007	2010	2020
Labour force participation (percentage)						
Total	65+	23.4	19.1	15.5	15.1	14.7
Female	65+	7.5	6.1	9.0	9.9	12.6
Male	65+	43.4	36.2	23.5	21.6	17.4

Percentage married, age 60+				Percentage living alone, age 60+		
Total	Female	Male		Total	Female	Male
67.2	50.0	87.0		..	..	..

Statutory pensionable age (2006)				Percentage illiterate, age 65+ (2000)		
	Female	Male		Total	Female	Male
	60	65		7.3	10.3	3.8

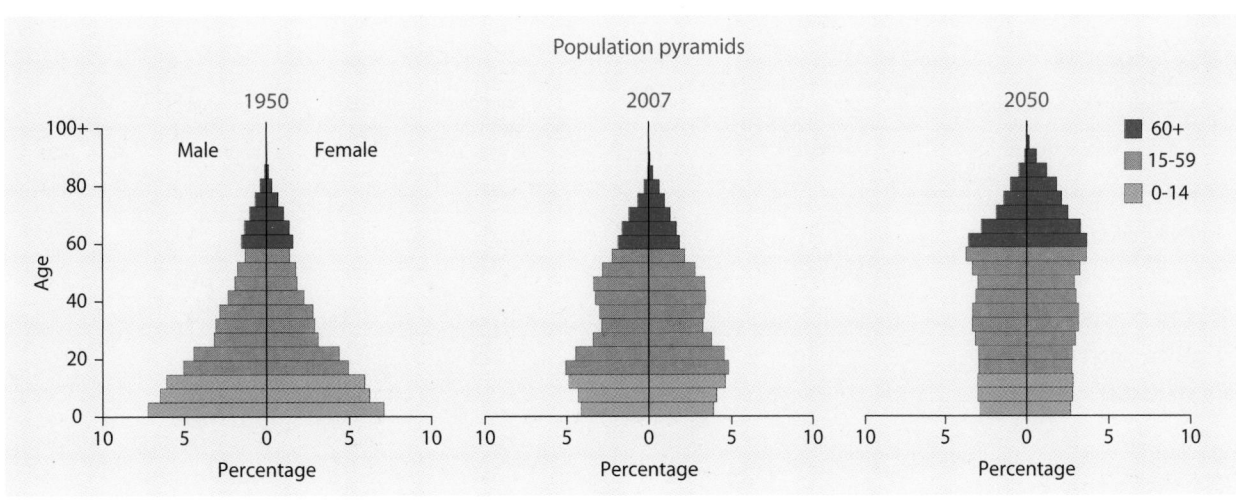

Population pyramids

Algeria

Indicator	Age	1950	1975	2007	2025	2050
Population (thousands)						
Total	Total	8 753.0	16 018.2	33 861.3	42 870.9	49 500.1
	0-14	3 512.9	7 626.6	9 583.7	10 511.0	9 001.5
	15-59	4 643.8	7 416.9	22 053.6	27 618.9	28 469.9
	60-64	213.4	304.9	667.3	1 715.7	3 310.0
	65-69	166.2	265.5	566.2	1 223.0	3 069.5
	70-74	121.6	183.1	475.5	898.0	2 347.5
	75-79	64.1	119.2	297.0	493.5	1 638.2
	80-84			144.2	250.2	1 007.5
	85-89			56.8	120.6	476.0
	90-94	31.1	102.0	14.4	34.4	145.8
	95-99			2.4	5.0	31.2
	100+			0.2	0.4	3.2
Female	Total	4 288.0	8 116.9	16 774.4	21 258.1	24 754.9
	0-14	1 756.6	3 741.1	4 685.3	5 140.5	4 391.8
	15-59	2 227.3	3 848.1	10 880.9	13 627.1	14 007.7
	60-64	107.5	161.6	352.2	860.5	1 654.6
	65-69	82.6	141.1	301.7	620.9	1 555.8
	70-74	63.3	99.0	253.4	468.3	1 222.0
	75-79	33.8	67.1	164.2	281.0	890.2
	80-84			86.0	149.7	586.2
	85-89			37.5	79.9	308.2
	90-94	16.9	58.9	11.0	25.5	108.8
	95-99			2.1	4.3	26.7
	100+			0.2	0.4	3.0
Male	Total	4 465.0	7 901.3	17 086.9	21 612.8	24 745.3
	0-14	1 756.3	3 885.5	4 898.4	5 370.5	4 609.7
	15-59	2 416.5	3 568.8	11 172.7	13 991.8	14 462.2
	60-64	105.9	143.3	315.1	855.3	1 655.4
	65-69	83.6	124.3	264.5	602.1	1 513.7
	70-74	58.3	84.1	222.1	429.7	1 125.5
	75-79	30.3	52.0	132.8	212.5	748.0
	80-84			58.3	100.5	421.2
	85-89			19.3	40.7	167.9
	90-94	14.3	43.1	3.4	9.0	37.0
	95-99			0.3	0.7	4.5
	100+			0.0	0.0	0.2
Percentage in older ages						
Total	60+	6.8	6.1	6.6	11.1	24.3
	65+	4.4	4.2	4.6	7.1	17.6
	80+	0.4	0.6	0.6	1.0	3.4
Female	60+	7.1	6.5	7.2	11.7	25.7
	65+	4.6	4.5	5.1	7.7	19.0
	80+	0.4	0.7	0.8	1.2	4.2
Male	60+	6.5	5.7	5.9	10.4	22.9
	65+	4.2	3.8	4.1	6.5	16.2
	80+	0.3	0.5	0.5	0.7	2.5
Ageing index		17.0	12.8	23.2	45.1	133.6
Broad age groups (percentage)	0-14	40.1	47.6	28.3	24.5	18.2
	15-59	53.1	46.3	65.1	64.4	57.5
	60+	6.8	6.1	6.6	11.1	24.3
Median age (years)		19.9	16.2	24.0*	32.3	39.4
Dependency ratio	Total	80.2	107.4	49.0	46.1	55.8
	Youth	72.3	98.8	42.2	35.8	28.3
	Old Age	7.9	8.7	6.9	10.3	27.4
Potential support ratio		12.7	11.5	14.6	9.7	3.6
Parent support ratio		1.2	3.7	2.5	2.5	7.0
Sex ratio (per 100 women)	60+	96.1	84.7	84.1	90.4	89.3
	65+	94.8	82.9	81.8	85.6	85.5
	80+	84.4	73.2	59.5	58.1	61.1

* *Estimate refers to year 2005.*

Indicator	Age	1950-1955	1975-1980	2005-2010	2025-2030	2045-2050
Growth rate (percentage)	Total	2.1	3.2	1.5	0.8	0.4
	60+	0.9	2.6	2.8	4.5	2.7
	65+	0.7	2.4	2.0	5.0	3.7
	80+	0.5	3.0	3.9	4.4	5.2
Total fertility rate (per woman)		7.3	7.2	2.4	2.0	1.9
Life expectancy (years)						
Total	Birth	43.1	58.0	72.3	76.2	79.0
	60	..	..	18.8	20.3	22.0
	65	..	..	15.0	16.3	17.9
	80	..	..	6.4	7.0	8.0
Female	Birth	44.2	59.0	73.7	78.0	80.9
	60	..	..	19.9	21.8	23.8
	65	..	..	16.0	17.7	19.5
	80	..	..	6.9	7.8	9.0
Male	Birth	42.1	57.0	70.9	74.4	77.0
	60	..	..	17.7	18.7	20.2
	65	..	..	14.0	14.8	16.2
	80	..	..	5.6	6.0	6.8
Survival rate (percentage)						
Total	60	..	..	84.8	90.0	92.6
	65	..	..	79.0	85.1	88.6
	80	..	..	39.6	48.0	56.0
Female	60	..	..	86.1	91.2	93.5
	65	..	..	80.8	87.2	90.3
	80	..	..	44.5	54.8	63.1
Male	60	..	..	83.6	88.8	91.7
	65	..	..	77.1	83.0	86.8
	80	..	..	34.8	41.4	49.0

		1980	1990	2007	2010	2020
Labour force participation (percentage)						
Total	65+	17.4	16.2	15.6	15.6	15.7
Female	65+	9.2	7.6	6.2	6.1	6.0
Male	65+	26.7	26.6	27.1	27.2	27.2

Percentage married, age 60+			Percentage living alone, age 60+		
Total	Female	Male	Total	Female	Male
62.6	40.0	89.0	..	..	..

Statutory pensionable age (2006)			Percentage illiterate, age 65+ (2000)		
	Female	Male	Total	Female	Male
	55	60	85.3	94.6	76.6

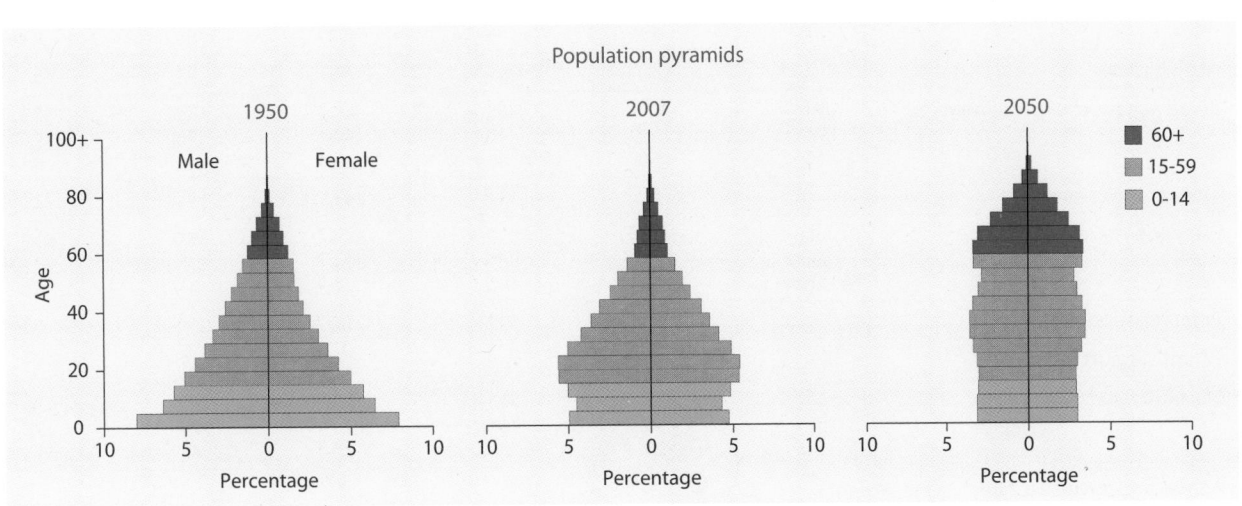

Population pyramids

Angola

Indicator	Age	1950	1975	2007	2025	2050
Population (thousands)						
Total	Total	4 147.5	6 812.7	16 867.3	26 829.5	43 501.3
	0-14	1 708.4	3 149.5	7 787.0	11 693.1	14 762.6
	15-59	2 233.5	3 356.2	8 421.1	13 999.7	26 068.2
	60-64	78.2	124.4	246.1	426.3	996.4
	65-69	58.3	88.2	183.7	314.2	715.3
	70-74	38.3	54.6	121.7	209.0	476.9
	75-79	19.5	27.7	68.1	112.8	279.4
	80-84			29.2	52.8	138.0
	85-89			8.6	17.4	50.8
	90-94	11.3	12.2	1.5	3.7	12.0
	95-99			0.2	0.4	1.6
	100+			0.0	0.0	0.1
Female	Total	2 113.0	3 465.8	8 547.0	13 563.0	21 975.6
	0-14	858.2	1 582.6	3 902.6	5 862.7	7 369.9
	15-59	1 140.2	1 712.8	4 280.6	7 071.1	13 177.4
	60-64	42.7	67.2	132.4	229.1	518.0
	65-69	32.3	48.6	100.3	172.7	377.5
	70-74	21.8	30.8	67.8	117.5	257.2
	75-79	11.2	16.2	39.1	64.7	155.3
	80-84			17.5	31.4	80.1
	85-89			5.5	10.9	31.2
	90-94	6.6	7.6	1.1	2.5	7.9
	95-99			0.1	0.3	1.2
	100+			0.0	0.0	0.1
Male	Total	2 034.5	3 346.9	8 320.3	13 266.5	21 525.6
	0-14	850.2	1 566.9	3 884.4	5 830.4	7 392.7
	15-59	1 093.2	1 643.4	4 140.6	6 928.6	12 890.8
	60-64	35.5	57.2	113.7	197.2	478.3
	65-69	26.0	39.5	83.3	141.5	337.9
	70-74	16.5	23.8	53.9	91.5	219.8
	75-79	8.3	11.5	29.0	48.1	124.1
	80-84			11.7	21.4	57.9
	85-89			3.1	6.5	19.6
	90-94	4.7	4.6	0.5	1.2	4.1
	95-99			0.0	0.1	0.5
	100+			0.0	0.0	0.0
Percentage in older ages						
Total	60+	5.0	4.5	3.9	4.2	6.1
	65+	3.1	2.7	2.4	2.6	3.8
	80+	0.3	0.2	0.2	0.3	0.5
Female	60+	5.4	4.9	4.3	4.6	6.5
	65+	3.4	3.0	2.7	2.9	4.1
	80+	0.3	0.2	0.3	0.3	0.5
Male	60+	4.5	4.1	3.5	3.8	5.8
	65+	2.7	2.4	2.2	2.3	3.5
	80+	0.2	0.1	0.2	0.2	0.4
Ageing index		12.0	9.8	8.5	9.7	18.1
Broad age groups (percentage)	0-14	41.2	46.2	46.2	43.6	33.9
	15-59	53.9	49.3	49.9	52.2	59.9
	60+	5.0	4.5	3.9	4.2	6.1
Median age (years)		19.4	16.8	16.6*	17.9	22.9
Dependency ratio	Total	79.4	95.7	94.6	86.0	60.7
	Youth	73.9	90.5	89.8	81.1	54.5
	Old Age	5.5	5.2	4.8	4.9	6.2
Potential support ratio		18.1	19.1	21.0	20.3	16.2
Parent support ratio		1.1	0.5	1.0	1.3	1.7
Sex ratio (per 100 women)	60+	79.4	80.1	81.1	80.7	87.0
	65+	77.2	76.9	78.4	77.6	83.9
	80+	71.2	60.2	63.4	64.6	68.2

* Estimate refers to year 2005.

Indicator	Age	1950-1955	1975-1980	2005-2010	2025-2030	2045-2050
Growth rate (percentage)	Total	1.8	2.8	2.8	2.3	1.6
	60+	0.7	2.5	2.5	3.0	3.9
	65+	−0.6	2.7	2.7	3.3	3.9
	80+	−2.9	3.9	3.8	3.3	3.8
Total fertility rate (per woman)		7.0	7.2	6.4	4.6	3.0
Life expectancy (years)						
Total	Birth	30.0	39.5	41.9	49.5	57.4
	60	..	..	14.8	15.9	17.2
	65	..	..	11.8	12.7	13.8
	80	..	..	5.2	5.6	6.1
Female	Birth	31.5	41.1	43.4	51.2	59.3
	60	..	..	15.4	16.5	17.9
	65	..	..	12.3	13.2	14.4
	80	..	..	5.4	5.8	6.3
Male	Birth	28.6	37.9	40.5	47.8	55.6
	60	..	..	14.1	15.1	16.4
	65	..	..	11.3	12.1	13.2
	80	..	..	4.9	5.3	5.7
Survival rate (percentage)						
Total	60	..	..	37.0	46.8	58.4
	65	..	..	31.7	41.1	52.5
	80	..	..	10.4	15.5	22.9
Female	60	..	..	39.2	49.3	61.1
	65	..	..	34.1	43.9	55.7
	80	..	..	12.0	17.7	25.8
Male	60	..	..	34.8	44.4	55.8
	65	..	..	29.3	38.3	49.5
	80	..	..	8.7	13.3	19.9

		1980	1990	2007	2010	2020
Labour force participation (percentage)						
Total	65+	55.1	54.0	54.4	54.3	54.2
Female	65+	37.5	39.6	37.3	37.1	37.0
Male	65+	77.8	72.4	76.2	76.2	76.3

Percentage married, age 60+			Percentage living alone, age 60+		
Total	Female	Male	Total	Female	Male
60.6	44.0	81.0	..	..	..

Statutory pensionable age (2006)		Percentage illiterate, age 65+ (2000)		
Female	Male	Total	Female	Male
..	..	66.4	81.0	52.4

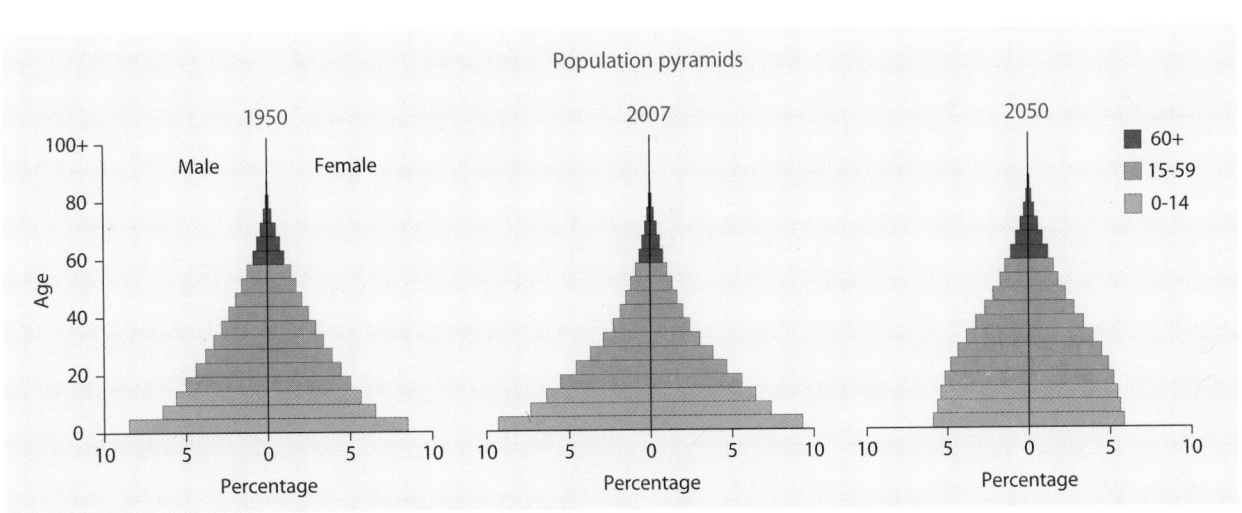

Population pyramids

1950   2007   2050

Male   Female

60+
15-59
0-14

Argentina

Indicator	Age	1950	1975	2007	2025	2050
Population (thousands)						
Total	Total	17 150.3	26 049.4	39 531.1	46 114.7	51 382.4
	0-14	5 235.4	7 611.1	10 210.6	10 141.4	9 129.9
	15-59	10 707.7	15 467.2	23 727.0	28 099.8	29 485.9
	60-64	485.8	996.7	1 515.3	2 017.7	3 016.5
	65-69	328.9	799.4	1 254.3	1 772.7	2 726.0
	70-74	201.2	574.7	1 044.2	1 502.5	2 520.1
	75-79	109.5	360.9	830.2	1 130.5	1 829.8
	80-84			549.5	750.2	1 276.9
	85-89			279.3	432.9	823.8
	90-94	81.7	239.3	98.8	198.8	413.4
	95-99			20.1	59.5	137.8
	100+			1.8	8.7	22.2
Female	Total	8 323.4	13 045.8	20 200.4	23 551.6	26 330.9
	0-14	2 575.4	3 750.0	5 019.5	4 979.3	4 481.5
	15-59	5 153.4	7 694.1	11 934.6	14 019.7	14 634.9
	60-64	226.1	521.6	804.8	1 065.5	1 556.6
	65-69	159.0	424.9	688.1	975.6	1 446.6
	70-74	102.2	310.0	601.1	854.5	1 388.5
	75-79	58.5	202.3	505.0	676.1	1 059.2
	80-84			357.3	477.2	787.0
	85-89			196.9	298.9	549.3
	90-94	48.8	142.8	75.2	149.3	301.6
	95-99			16.3	48.2	107.9
	100+			1.5	7.3	17.8
Male	Total	8 827.0	13 003.6	19 330.7	22 563.1	25 051.5
	0-14	2 660.0	3 861.1	5 191.1	5 162.2	4 648.4
	15-59	5 554.3	7 773.1	11 792.4	14 080.1	14 851.0
	60-64	259.7	475.1	710.4	952.2	1 459.9
	65-69	170.0	374.5	566.2	797.1	1 279.4
	70-74	99.0	264.6	443.1	648.0	1 131.6
	75-79	51.0	158.7	325.3	454.4	770.6
	80-84			192.2	273.0	489.9
	85-89			82.4	134.1	274.5
	90-94	32.9	96.5	23.5	49.5	111.8
	95-99			3.8	11.3	29.9
	100+			0.3	1.3	4.4
Percentage in older ages						
Total	60+	7.0	11.4	14.1	17.1	24.8
	65+	4.2	7.6	10.3	12.7	19.0
	80+	0.5	0.9	2.4	3.1	5.2
Female	60+	7.1	12.3	16.1	19.3	27.4
	65+	4.4	8.3	12.1	14.8	21.5
	80+	0.6	1.1	3.2	4.2	6.7
Male	60+	6.9	10.5	12.1	14.7	22.2
	65+	4.0	6.9	8.5	10.5	16.3
	80+	0.4	0.7	1.6	2.1	3.6
Ageing index		23.1	39.0	54.8	77.6	139.8
Broad age groups (percentage)	0-14	30.5	29.2	25.8	22.0	17.8
	15-59	62.4	59.4	60.0	60.9	57.4
	60+	7.0	11.4	14.1	17.1	24.8
Median age (years)		25.7	27.3	28.9*	34.0	40.3
Dependency ratio	Total	53.2	58.2	56.6	53.1	58.1
	Youth	46.8	46.2	40.5	33.7	28.1
	Old Age	6.4	12.0	16.2	19.4	30.0
Potential support ratio		15.5	8.3	6.2	5.1	3.3
Parent support ratio		1.6	1.9	7.5	10.2	14.7
Sex ratio (per 100 women)	60+	103.0	85.5	72.3	72.9	77.0
	65+	95.8	82.8	67.0	67.9	72.3
	80+	67.5	67.5	46.7	47.8	51.6

* Estimate refers to year 2005.

Indicator	Age	1950-1955	1975-1980	2005-2010	2025-2030	2045-2050
Growth rate (percentage)	Total	2.0	1.5	1.0	0.6	0.3
	60+	4.2	2.4	1.8	1.7	1.7
	65+	4.8	2.9	1.7	1.9	1.9
	80+	2.8	4.4	3.5	2.8	1.9
Total fertility rate (per woman)		3.2	3.4	2.3	1.9	1.9
Life expectancy (years)						
Total	Birth	62.5	68.5	75.3	78.5	80.7
	60	..	..	20.9	22.8	24.2
	65	..	..	17.2	19.0	20.2
	80	..	..	8.2	9.1	9.8
Female	Birth	65.1	71.9	79.1	82.2	84.5
	60	..	..	23.3	25.4	26.8
	65	..	..	19.2	21.1	22.5
	80	..	..	9.0	10.1	10.8
Male	Birth	60.4	65.3	71.6	74.7	77.0
	60	..	..	18.2	20.0	21.4
	65	..	..	14.8	16.4	17.6
	80	..	..	6.9	7.8	8.4
Survival rate (percentage)						
Total	60	..	..	85.8	89.2	91.4
	65	..	..	80.0	84.5	87.4
	80	..	..	47.4	56.2	62.2
Female	60	..	..	90.1	92.9	94.7
	65	..	..	86.1	89.9	92.3
	80	..	..	58.9	67.8	73.7
Male	60	..	..	81.4	85.5	88.2
	65	..	..	73.8	79.1	82.7
	80	..	..	35.7	44.2	50.5

		1980	1990	2007	2010	2020
Labour force participation (percentage)						
Total	65+	9.6	15.8	19.6	20.5	22.7
Female	65+	3.2	8.2	13.2	14.6	18.3
Male	65+	17.9	26.3	29.2	29.2	29.1

Percentage married, age 60+			Percentage living alone, age 60+ (1980)		
Total	Female	Male	Total	Female	Male
56.0	42.0	75.0	10.9	12.9	8.2

Statutory pensionable age (2006)			Percentage illiterate, age 65+ (2000)		
	Female	Male	Total	Female	Male
	60	65	6.2	6.5	5.7

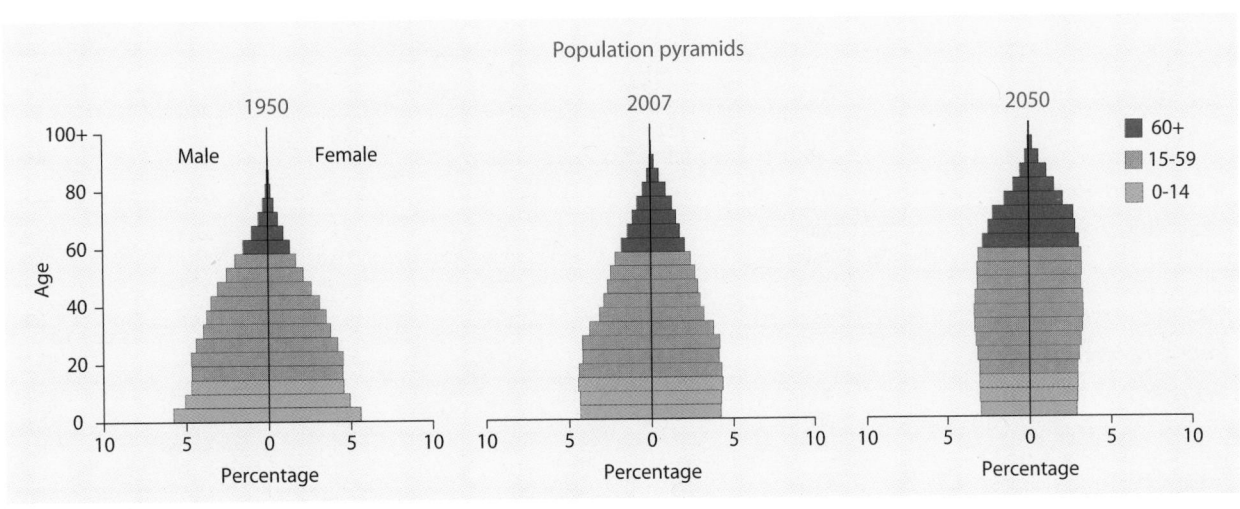

Population pyramids

United Nations Department of Economic and Social Affairs, Population Division

Armenia

Indicator	Age	1950	1975	2007	2025	2050
Population (thousands)						
Total	Total	1 353.5	2 825.7	2 999.2	2 907.7	2 506.0
	0-14	450.2	970.3	576.4	499.9	386.6
	15-59	737.0	1 619.4	1 991.1	1 750.5	1 286.8
	60-64	53.5	71.7	73.8	199.9	242.7
	65-69	42.3	62.9	112.7	187.4	196.9
	70-74	33.1	46.3	104.0	124.4	135.9
	75-79	21.2	25.4	80.5	63.8	90.8
	80-84			43.2	30.4	70.1
	85-89			11.5	35.9	60.0
	90-94	16.3	29.6	4.6	11.5	28.4
	95-99			1.3	3.6	6.9
	100+			0.2	0.3	0.9
Female	Total	711.3	1 446.8	1 604.9	1 567.7	1 349.3
	0-14	232.1	473.7	269.6	241.6	188.0
	15-59	387.7	830.6	1 076.5	918.8	649.8
	60-64	27.5	43.3	43.0	119.9	132.9
	65-69	22.6	37.8	66.0	112.8	114.5
	70-74	18.7	28.3	60.9	77.6	86.1
	75-79	12.6	14.9	47.9	40.8	59.4
	80-84			28.1	20.4	48.0
	85-89			8.4	24.6	42.9
	90-94	10.1	18.2	3.5	8.2	21.4
	95-99			0.9	2.7	5.6
	100+			0.1	0.3	0.7
Male	Total	642.2	1 378.9	1 394.3	1 340.0	1 156.7
	0-14	218.0	496.7	306.8	258.3	198.5
	15-59	349.3	788.8	914.6	831.7	636.9
	60-64	25.9	28.4	30.7	80.1	109.8
	65-69	19.8	25.1	46.7	74.7	82.5
	70-74	14.4	18.0	43.2	46.8	49.8
	75-79	8.5	10.6	32.6	22.9	31.4
	80-84			15.1	9.9	22.1
	85-89			3.0	11.3	17.1
	90-94	6.2	11.4	1.2	3.4	7.0
	95-99			0.3	0.9	1.3
	100+			0.0	0.1	0.1
Percentage in older ages						
Total	60+	12.3	8.3	14.4	22.6	33.2
	65+	8.3	5.8	11.9	15.7	23.5
	80+	1.2	1.0	2.0	2.8	6.6
Female	60+	12.9	9.8	16.1	26.0	37.9
	65+	9.0	6.9	13.4	18.3	28.1
	80+	1.4	1.3	2.6	3.6	8.8
Male	60+	11.7	6.8	12.4	18.7	27.8
	65+	7.6	4.7	10.2	12.7	18.3
	80+	1.0	0.8	1.4	1.9	4.1
Ageing index		37.0	24.3	74.9	131.5	215.4
Broad age groups (percentage)	0-14	33.3	34.3	19.2	17.2	15.4
	15-59	54.4	57.3	66.4	60.2	51.3
	60+	12.3	8.3	14.4	22.6	33.2
Median age (years)		22.4	21.9	31.7*	38.9	47.6
Dependency ratio	Total	71.2	67.1	45.2	49.1	63.8
	Youth	57.0	57.4	27.9	25.6	25.3
	Old Age	14.3	9.7	17.3	23.4	38.6
Potential support ratio		7.0	10.3	5.8	4.3	2.6
Parent support ratio		4.6	6.5	4.2	10.3	15.9
Sex ratio (per 100 women)	60+	81.8	65.6	66.8	61.4	62.8
	65+	76.4	65.6	65.9	59.1	55.8
	80+	60.8	62.8	47.9	45.4	40.2

* *Estimate refers to year 2005.*

Armenia

Indicator	Age	1950-1955	1975-1980	2005-2010	2025-2030	2045-2050
Growth rate (percentage)	Total	2.9	1.8	−0.2	−0.5	−0.8
	60+	−0.7	0.1	0.0	0.3	2.1
	65+	1.8	2.4	−1.9	2.8	1.9
	80+	2.4	0.9	9.7	0.3	−1.7
Total fertility rate (per woman)		4.5	2.5	1.4	1.6	1.9
Life expectancy (years)						
Total	Birth	62.8	70.6	72.0	75.0	77.4
	60	..	..	18.8	20.4	21.7
	65	..	..	15.4	16.8	18.0
	80	..	..	7.3	8.0	8.6
Female	Birth	65.9	73.5	75.1	77.8	80.0
	60	..	..	20.4	22.0	23.4
	65	..	..	16.6	18.0	19.3
	80	..	..	7.7	8.5	9.2
Male	Birth	59.7	67.3	68.4	71.6	74.3
	60	..	..	16.8	18.2	19.4
	65	..	..	13.8	14.9	15.9
	80	..	..	6.7	7.1	7.5
Survival rate (percentage)						
Total	60	..	..	82.8	86.7	89.3
	65	..	..	75.6	80.7	84.0
	80	..	..	38.6	46.3	52.4
Female	60	..	..	87.9	90.5	92.5
	65	..	..	82.4	86.0	88.6
	80	..	..	47.2	54.3	60.2
Male	60	..	..	76.8	82.1	86.1
	65	..	..	67.5	73.9	79.0
	80	..	..	29.3	36.2	42.6

		1980	1990	2007	2010	2020
Labour force participation (percentage)						
Total	65+	9.1	30.8	16.0	15.0	13.9
Female	65+	4.1	25.1	9.1	8.3	7.2
Male	65+	17.2	40.5	26.4	25.7	25.1

Percentage married, age 60+				Percentage living alone, age 60+ (2000)		
Total	Female	Male		Total	Female	Male
61.0	43.0	86.0		8.7	12.1	3.8

Statutory pensionable age (2006)				Percentage illiterate, age 65+ (2000)		
	Female	Male		Total	Female	Male
	59.5	63		3.2	4.5	1.3

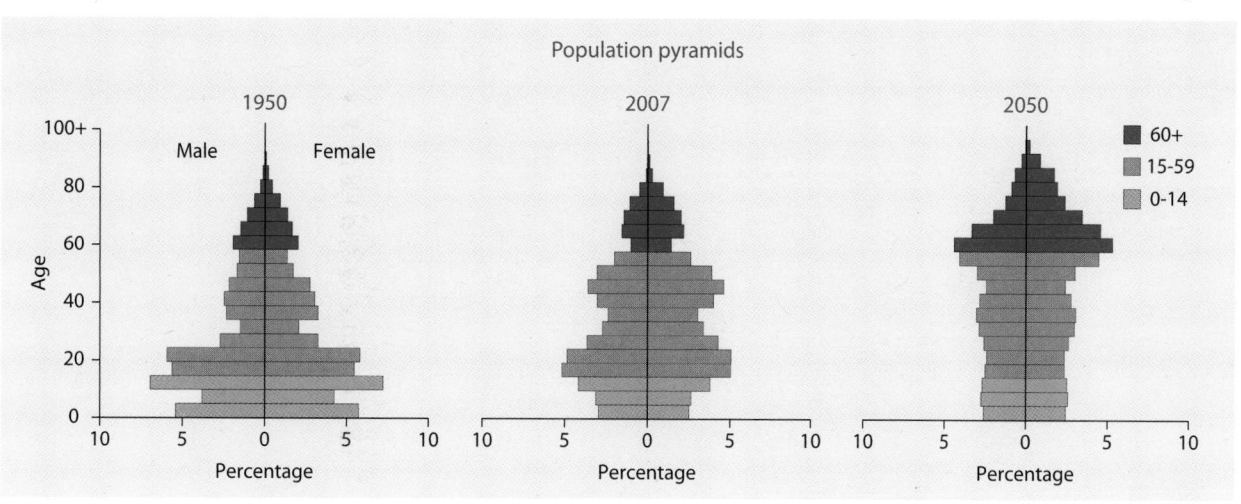

Population pyramids

Australia

Indicator	Age	1950	1975	2007	2025	2050
Population (thousands)						
Total	Total	8 219.0	13 624.5	20 575.9	24 329.0	27 939.6
	0-14	2 179.0	3 758.4	3 913.7	4 291.3	4 521.5
	15-59	5 016.0	8 124.0	12 942.6	13 928.8	15 062.2
	60-64	356.0	559.8	1 042.4	1 481.8	1 714.8
	65-69	273.0	439.7	785.8	1 370.7	1 592.6
	70-74	182.0	322.3	624.5	1 170.1	1 384.6
	75-79	119.0	214.7	529.4	938.7	1 246.4
	80-84			403.7	587.2	1 033.4
	85-89			222.7	330.3	743.4
	90-94	94.0	205.6	86.1	157.3	426.3
	95-99			21.6	59.5	170.6
	100+			3.4	13.4	43.9
Female	Total	4 075.0	6 787.0	10 412.2	12 303.9	14 142.4
	0-14	1 067.0	1 833.1	1 907.8	2 092.0	2 203.5
	15-59	2 464.0	3 976.9	6 501.5	6 922.2	7 415.8
	60-64	181.0	289.3	522.1	762.9	855.0
	65-69	143.0	234.4	397.5	713.5	802.0
	70-74	99.0	180.5	327.1	618.3	715.1
	75-79	67.0	133.0	291.8	507.0	674.5
	80-84			239.3	330.3	588.5
	85-89			144.4	199.7	450.7
	90-94	54.0	139.8	61.4	104.5	280.9
	95-99			16.6	43.1	122.6
	100+			2.7	10.4	33.8
Male	Total	4 144.0	6 837.5	10 163.8	12 025.1	13 797.2
	0-14	1 112.0	1 925.4	2 005.9	2 199.3	2 317.9
	15-59	2 552.0	4 147.1	6 441.2	7 006.6	7 646.4
	60-64	175.0	270.5	520.4	718.8	859.8
	65-69	130.0	205.3	388.3	657.2	790.6
	70-74	83.0	141.9	297.3	551.8	669.5
	75-79	52.0	81.6	237.6	431.8	571.9
	80-84			164.4	256.9	444.8
	85-89			78.3	130.6	292.8
	90-94	40.0	65.8	24.7	52.8	145.4
	95-99			5.1	16.3	48.0
	100+			0.7	3.0	10.0
Percentage in older ages						
Total	60+	12.5	12.8	18.1	25.1	29.9
	65+	8.1	8.7	13.0	19.0	23.8
	80+	1.1	1.5	3.6	4.7	8.7
Female	60+	13.3	14.4	19.2	26.7	32.0
	65+	8.9	10.1	14.2	20.5	25.9
	80+	1.3	2.1	4.5	5.6	10.4
Male	60+	11.6	11.2	16.9	23.4	27.8
	65+	7.4	7.2	11.8	17.5	21.5
	80+	1.0	1.0	2.7	3.8	6.8
Ageing index		47.0	46.4	95.0	142.4	184.8
Broad age groups (percentage)	0-14	26.5	27.6	19.0	17.6	16.2
	15-59	61.0	59.6	62.9	57.3	53.9
	60+	12.5	12.8	18.1	25.1	29.9
Median age (years)		30.4	28.0	36.6*	40.8	43.6
Dependency ratio	Total	53.0	56.9	47.1	57.9	66.5
	Youth	40.6	43.3	28.0	27.8	27.0
	Old Age	12.4	13.6	19.1	30.0	39.6
Potential support ratio		8.0	7.3	5.2	3.3	2.5
Parent support ratio		3.1	3.9	9.0	12.2	26.7
Sex ratio (per 100 women)	60+	88.2	78.3	85.7	85.7	84.7
	65+	84.0	71.9	80.8	83.1	81.1
	80+	74.1	47.0	58.8	66.8	63.7

* *Estimate refers to year 2005.*

Indicator	Age	1950-1955	1975-1980	2005-2010	2025-2030	2045-2050
Growth rate (percentage)	Total	2.3	1.4	1.0	0.7	0.4
	60+	2.2	2.8	3.2	1.9	1.0
	65+	2.9	3.4	2.5	2.3	1.0
	80+	2.3	3.7	3.2	4.6	1.5
Total fertility rate (per woman)		3.2	2.1	1.8	1.9	1.9
Life expectancy (years)						
Total	Birth	69.6	73.5	81.0	83.2	84.8
	60	..	..	23.8	25.3	26.4
	65	..	..	19.6	21.0	22.0
	80	..	..	9.2	10.1	10.8
Female	Birth	72.4	77.0	83.4	85.5	87.4
	60	..	..	25.7	27.3	28.7
	65	..	..	21.3	22.8	24.2
	80	..	..	10.0	11.1	12.1
Male	Birth	66.9	70.1	78.5	80.8	82.7
	60	..	..	21.8	23.2	24.5
	65	..	..	17.8	19.1	20.2
	80	..	..	8.1	8.9	9.6
Survival rate (percentage)						
Total	60	..	..	93.1	94.9	96.1
	65	..	..	89.5	92.1	93.6
	80	..	..	62.4	68.4	72.2
Female	60	..	..	94.7	96.1	97.0
	65	..	..	92.1	94.0	95.3
	80	..	..	70.7	75.6	79.6
Male	60	..	..	91.4	93.8	95.3
	65	..	..	87.0	90.1	92.3
	80	..	..	54.2	60.9	66.1

		1980	1990	2007	2010	2020
Labour force participation (percentage)						
Total	65+	6.3	4.9	6.3	6.4	6.6
Female	65+	2.9	2.3	3.2	3.3	3.5
Male	65+	11.1	8.5	10.1	10.1	10.2

Percentage married, age 60+			Percentage living alone, age 60+		
Total	Female	Male	Total	Female	Male
61.8	50.0	76.0	..	..	..

Statutory pensionable age (2006)			Percentage illiterate, age 65+		
Female	Male		Total	Female	Male
62.5	65		..	..	..

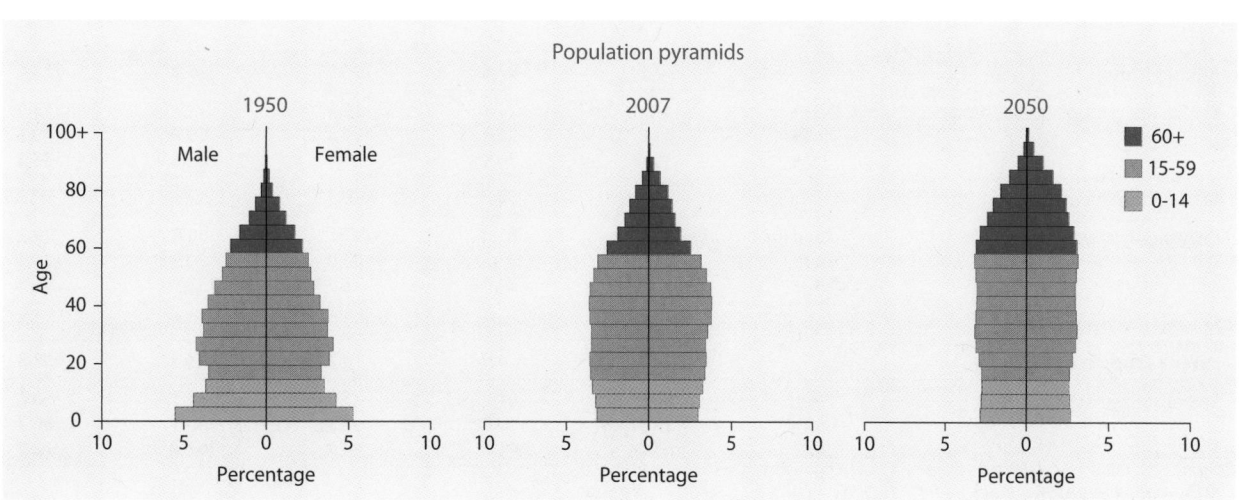

Population pyramids

1950   2007   2050

Male Female

60+
15-59
0-14

Austria

Indicator	Age	1950	1975	2007	2025	2050
Population (thousands)						
Total	Total	6 935.0	7 578.9	8 217.6	8 338.7	8 073.0
	0-14	1 581.0	1 760.7	1 225.5	1 107.1	1 094.3
	15-59	4 284.0	4 275.8	5 079.6	4 641.7	3 976.0
	60-64	351.0	415.3	485.5	678.0	525.7
	65-69	288.0	401.5	437.6	554.0	515.1
	70-74	218.0	331.4	334.4	431.9	454.0
	75-79	132.0	218.9	271.4	360.0	465.6
	80-84			228.9	293.0	462.4
	85-89			102.5	172.7	337.4
	90-94	81.0	175.3	40.9	72.5	169.3
	95-99			10.3	23.8	58.9
	100+			0.9	4.3	14.5
Female	Total	3 719.0	3 998.1	4 190.0	4 167.8	3 975.7
	0-14	776.0	861.8	597.0	539.0	532.7
	15-59	2 325.0	2 183.8	2 499.8	2 239.8	1 867.6
	60-64	201.0	243.4	248.5	334.8	248.7
	65-69	165.0	238.8	230.4	280.0	251.5
	70-74	126.0	202.2	184.5	226.7	227.7
	75-79	77.0	143.9	160.5	196.9	244.7
	80-84			154.0	170.8	250.6
	85-89			74.9	107.8	193.5
	90-94	49.0	124.1	31.3	49.9	106.0
	95-99			8.3	18.3	41.3
	100+			0.8	3.7	11.4
Male	Total	3 216.0	3 580.8	4 027.6	4 171.0	4 097.3
	0-14	805.0	898.9	628.5	568.1	561.6
	15-59	1 959.0	2 092.0	2 579.8	2 401.9	2 108.4
	60-64	150.0	171.9	237.0	343.1	277.0
	65-69	123.0	162.7	207.2	273.9	263.6
	70-74	92.0	129.2	149.9	205.2	226.3
	75-79	55.0	75.0	111.0	163.1	220.9
	80-84			75.0	122.2	211.8
	85-89			27.7	64.8	143.9
	90-94	32.0	51.1	9.6	22.5	63.2
	95-99			1.9	5.4	17.6
	100+			0.2	0.6	3.1
Percentage in older ages						
Total	60+	15.4	20.4	23.3	31.1	37.2
	65+	10.4	14.9	17.4	22.9	30.7
	80+	1.2	2.3	4.7	6.8	12.9
Female	60+	16.6	23.8	26.1	33.3	39.6
	65+	11.2	17.7	20.2	25.3	33.4
	80+	1.3	3.1	6.4	8.4	15.2
Male	60+	14.1	16.5	20.3	28.8	34.8
	65+	9.4	11.7	14.5	20.6	28.1
	80+	1.0	1.4	2.8	5.2	10.7
Ageing index		67.7	87.6	156.1	233.9	274.4
Broad age groups (percentage)	0-14	22.8	23.2	14.9	13.3	13.6
	15-59	61.8	56.4	61.8	55.7	49.2
	60+	15.4	20.4	23.3	31.1	37.2
Median age (years)		35.8	33.8	40.6*	47.1	50.0
Dependency ratio	Total	49.6	61.6	47.7	56.8	79.3
	Youth	34.1	37.5	22.0	20.8	24.3
	Old Age	15.5	24.0	25.6	35.9	55.0
Potential support ratio		6.4	4.2	3.9	2.8	1.8
Parent support ratio		2.3	4.9	10.2	13.9	37.3
Sex ratio (per 100 women)	60+	73.1	61.9	75.0	86.5	90.6
	65+	72.4	59.0	68.9	81.4	86.7
	80+	65.3	41.2	42.4	61.5	72.9

* *Estimate refers to year 2005.*

Indicator	Age	1950-1955	1975-1980	2005-2010	2025-2030	2045-2050
Growth rate (percentage)	Total	0.0	–0.1	0.1	0.0	–0.2
	60+	1.4	–1.3	1.3	1.9	0.0
	65+	1.7	0.6	2.0	2.5	0.1
	80+	4.2	3.0	2.5	1.8	2.4
Total fertility rate (per woman)		2.1	1.6	1.4	1.7	1.9
Life expectancy (years)						
Total	Birth	65.9	72.2	79.7	82.4	84.8
	60	..	..	22.8	24.8	26.7
	65	..	..	18.7	20.5	22.3
	80	..	..	8.6	9.8	11.0
Female	Birth	68.4	75.6	82.4	84.9	87.1
	60	..	..	24.7	26.7	28.5
	65	..	..	20.3	22.2	24.0
	80	..	..	9.1	10.6	12.0
Male	Birth	63.2	68.5	76.9	80.0	82.7
	60	..	..	20.6	22.9	24.9
	65	..	..	16.7	18.8	20.6
	80	..	..	7.6	8.7	9.9
Survival rate (percentage)						
Total	60	..	..	91.8	94.1	95.6
	65	..	..	87.8	91.0	93.2
	80	..	..	58.8	66.6	72.9
Female	60	..	..	94.4	95.9	96.9
	65	..	..	91.7	93.7	95.2
	80	..	..	68.3	74.4	79.2
Male	60	..	..	89.3	92.5	94.5
	65	..	..	84.0	88.5	91.5
	80	..	..	49.0	59.0	66.9

		1980	1990	2007	2010	2020
Labour force participation (percentage)						
Total	65+	2.3	1.5	2.7	2.7	2.6
Female	65+	1.5	1.1	1.9	1.9	1.9
Male	65+	3.7	2.2	3.9	3.8	3.4

Percentage married, age 60+				Percentage living alone, age 60+ (1995)		
Total	Female	Male		Total	Female	Male
53.7	37.0	78.0		30.7	42.0	12.9

Statutory pensionable age (2006)				Percentage illiterate, age 65+		
	Female	Male		Total	Female	Male
	60	65		..	..	..

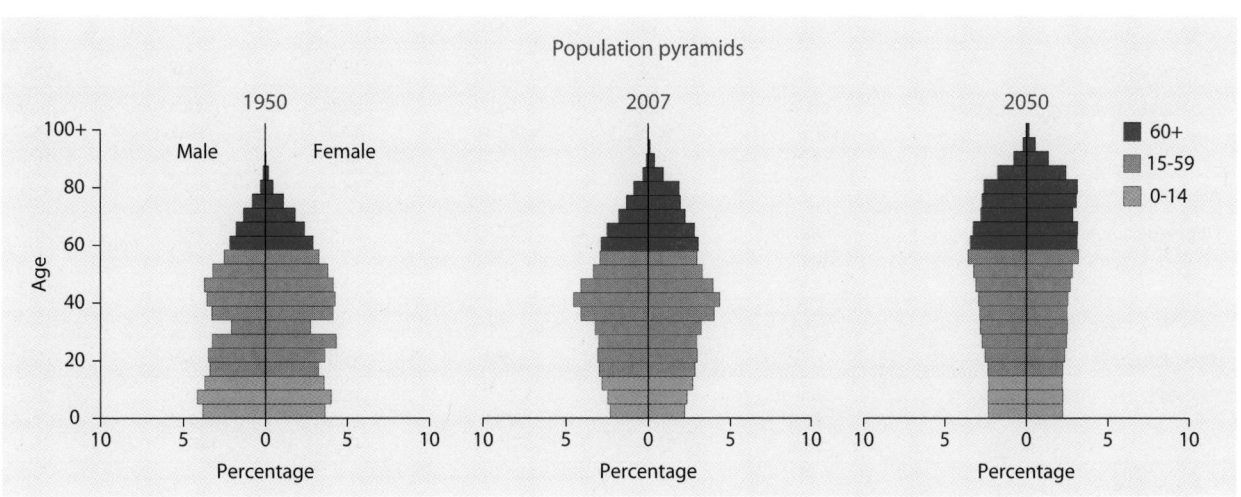

Population pyramids

1950 Male Female
2007
2050

Legend: 60+ · 15-59 · 0-14

Age axis: 100+, 80, 60, 40, 20, 0
Percentage axis: 10, 5, 0, 5, 10

Azerbaijan

Indicator	Age	1950	1975	2007	2025	2050
Population (thousands)						
Total	Total	2 896.0	5 689.0	8 535.7	9 596.5	9 630.6
	0-14	936.9	2 277.4	2 042.8	1 989.9	1 626.6
	15-59	1 637.5	2 963.7	5 716.5	6 023.5	5 412.5
	60-64	122.5	131.7	163.5	589.4	755.1
	65-69	88.0	114.2	207.6	446.7	585.4
	70-74	56.9	82.0	193.8	264.3	417.3
	75-79	31.5	53.0	129.7	112.2	328.1
	80-84			55.6	74.7	250.8
	85-89			17.1	63.2	170.7
	90-94	22.6	67.1	7.5	25.3	66.8
	95-99			1.5	6.5	15.2
	100+			0.3	0.8	1.9
Female	Total	1 532.5	2 914.8	4 396.6	4 988.0	5 044.1
	0-14	480.5	1 114.9	981.1	967.4	790.5
	15-59	875.1	1 514.3	2 960.8	3 089.7	2 715.0
	60-64	65.1	81.6	89.9	333.0	402.0
	65-69	48.9	73.3	118.8	254.9	326.9
	70-74	31.6	53.1	112.5	156.1	251.0
	75-79	17.7	34.1	77.2	69.3	205.9
	80-84			36.1	48.9	170.1
	85-89			12.7	44.1	119.1
	90-94	13.5	43.5	5.9	18.6	49.7
	95-99			1.3	5.2	12.3
	100+			0.2	0.7	1.7
Male	Total	1 363.5	2 774.2	4 139.1	4 608.5	4 586.5
	0-14	456.5	1 162.5	1 061.7	1 022.5	836.1
	15-59	762.4	1 449.3	2 755.7	2 933.8	2 697.5
	60-64	57.4	50.0	73.6	256.3	353.1
	65-69	39.1	40.9	88.7	191.8	258.5
	70-74	25.3	28.9	81.3	108.1	166.4
	75-79	13.7	18.9	52.5	43.0	122.2
	80-84			19.4	25.8	80.8
	85-89			4.4	19.1	51.6
	90-94	9.1	23.6	1.5	6.7	17.1
	95-99			0.3	1.3	2.9
	100+			0.0	0.1	0.2
Percentage in older ages						
Total	60+	11.1	7.9	9.1	16.5	26.9
	65+	6.9	5.6	7.2	10.4	19.1
	80+	0.8	1.2	1.0	1.8	5.2
Female	60+	11.5	9.8	10.3	18.7	30.5
	65+	7.3	7.0	8.3	12.0	22.5
	80+	0.9	1.5	1.3	2.4	7.0
Male	60+	10.6	5.9	7.8	14.2	23.0
	65+	6.4	4.0	6.0	8.6	15.3
	80+	0.7	0.9	0.6	1.1	3.3
Ageing index		34.3	19.7	38.0	79.6	159.3
Broad age groups (percentage)	0-14	32.4	40.0	23.9	20.7	16.9
	15-59	56.5	52.1	67.0	62.8	56.2
	60+	11.1	7.9	9.1	16.5	26.9
Median age (years)		22.8	19.1	27.5*	35.6	42.1
Dependency ratio	Total	64.5	83.8	45.2	45.1	56.1
	Youth	53.2	73.6	34.7	30.1	26.4
	Old Age	11.3	10.2	10.4	15.0	29.8
Potential support ratio		8.8	9.8	9.6	6.7	3.4
Parent support ratio		2.9	8.6	3.0	5.6	12.1
Sex ratio (per 100 women)	60+	81.7	56.9	70.8	70.1	68.4
	65+	78.0	55.1	68.0	66.2	61.6
	80+	67.3	54.3	45.7	45.1	43.3

* *Estimate refers to year 2005.*

Indicator	Age	1950-1955	1975-1980	2005-2010	2025-2030	2045-2050
Growth rate (percentage)	Total	2.8	1.6	0.8	0.2	−0.2
	60+	0.7	−0.4	0.5	2.8	2.2
	65+	4.5	1.2	0.4	5.3	1.8
	80+	5.6	1.9	10.7	−0.9	1.6
Total fertility rate (per woman)		5.5	3.6	1.9	1.9	1.9
Life expectancy (years)						
Total	Birth	58.0	65.2	67.5	71.4	74.5
	60	..	..	19.2	20.3	21.3
	65	..	..	15.9	16.8	17.6
	80	..	..	7.8	8.1	8.6
Female	Birth	61.5	68.7	71.2	75.2	77.6
	60	..	..	21.1	22.3	23.2
	65	..	..	17.3	18.4	19.1
	80	..	..	8.3	8.8	9.2
Male	Birth	54.4	61.2	63.8	67.4	71.2
	60	..	..	16.9	17.8	19.0
	65	..	..	14.0	14.7	15.6
	80	..	..	6.7	7.0	7.4
Survival rate (percentage)						
Total	60	..	..	76.1	81.5	85.5
	65	..	..	69.2	75.4	79.9
	80	..	..	36.3	42.8	48.4
Female	60	..	..	81.9	86.9	89.3
	65	..	..	76.9	82.5	85.4
	80	..	..	45.5	52.6	57.1
Male	60	..	..	70.1	75.8	81.6
	65	..	..	61.3	67.6	74.2
	80	..	..	27.1	32.2	38.7

		1980	1990	2007	2010	2020
Labour force participation (percentage)						
Total	65+	10.9	10.7	12.5	11.3	9.6
Female	65+	7.5	7.3	9.5	9.4	9.4
Male	65+	17.4	17.0	16.9	14.2	9.9

Percentage married, age 60+			Percentage living alone, age 60+		
Total	Female	Male	Total	Female	Male
63.5	46.0	87.0	..	..	..

Statutory pensionable age (2006)		Percentage illiterate, age 65+ (1999)		
Female	Male	Total	Female	Male
57	62	9.7	13.3	4.4

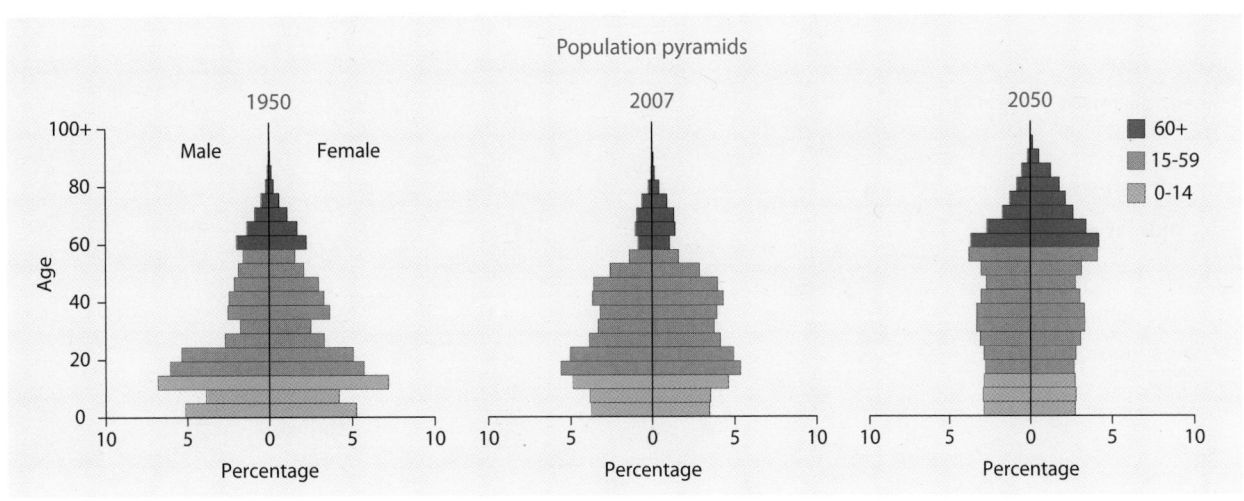

Population pyramids

Bahamas

Indicator	Age	1950	1975	2007	2025	2050
Population (thousands)						
Total	Total	79.1	188.9	331.6	403.5	465.8
	0-14	31.0	77.8	91.5	89.0	83.0
	15-59	42.8	99.9	207.7	247.6	264.3
	60-64	1.7	3.9	10.4	21.3	25.5
	65-69	1.4	3.1	8.3	16.4	24.6
	70-74	1.0	1.8	5.8	11.5	20.1
	75-79	0.7	1.1	3.8	7.9	18.2
	80-84			2.2	5.4	13.7
	85-89			1.2	2.9	9.7
	90-94	0.4	1.1	0.5	1.2	4.7
	95-99			0.1	0.3	1.6
	100+			0.0	0.1	0.4
Female	Total	42.4	96.2	170.4	209.5	244.3
	0-14	15.5	38.7	45.0	43.6	40.7
	15-59	23.8	51.1	107.3	127.8	135.4
	60-64	1.0	2.2	5.6	11.3	13.4
	65-69	0.8	1.7	4.5	9.0	13.2
	70-74	0.6	1.1	3.2	6.5	11.1
	75-79	0.4	0.7	2.2	4.7	10.5
	80-84			1.4	3.4	8.5
	85-89			0.8	2.0	6.4
	90-94	0.3	0.8	0.3	0.9	3.5
	95-99			0.1	0.3	1.3
	100+			0.0	0.0	0.3
Male	Total	36.7	92.7	161.2	193.9	221.5
	0-14	15.5	39.1	46.5	45.3	42.3
	15-59	19.0	48.9	100.4	119.9	129.0
	60-64	0.8	1.8	4.9	10.0	12.0
	65-69	0.6	1.3	3.8	7.3	11.4
	70-74	0.4	0.7	2.6	5.0	9.0
	75-79	0.3	0.4	1.6	3.2	7.7
	80-84			0.8	2.0	5.3
	85-89			0.4	0.9	3.2
	90-94	0.2	0.4	0.2	0.3	1.2
	95-99			0.0	0.1	0.3
	100+			0.0	0.0	0.1
Percentage in older ages						
Total	60+	6.6	5.9	9.8	16.6	25.4
	65+	4.4	3.8	6.6	11.3	20.0
	80+	0.6	0.6	1.2	2.5	6.5
Female	60+	7.2	6.7	10.6	18.2	27.9
	65+	4.8	4.4	7.3	12.8	22.4
	80+	0.7	0.8	1.5	3.2	8.2
Male	60+	6.1	5.0	8.9	14.8	22.7
	65+	4.0	3.1	5.9	9.7	17.3
	80+	0.5	0.4	0.9	1.7	4.5
Ageing index		16.9	14.2	35.4	75.2	142.9
Broad age groups (percentage)	0-14	39.2	41.2	27.6	22.0	17.8
	15-59	54.1	52.9	62.6	61.4	56.7
	60+	6.6	5.9	9.8	16.6	25.4
Median age (years)		20.7	19.3	27.6*	33.7	40.7
Dependency ratio	Total	77.6	81.8	52.0	50.0	60.7
	Youth	69.7	74.9	41.9	33.1	28.6
	Old Age	7.9	6.9	10.1	17.0	32.1
Potential support ratio		12.7	14.5	9.9	5.9	3.1
Parent support ratio		2.3	3.2	4.8	6.5	19.5
Sex ratio (per 100 women)	60+	73.3	72.6	79.4	75.4	73.6
	65+	71.6	68.3	75.8	70.1	69.7
	80+	58.9	53.2	59.3	50.4	50.4

* Estimate refers to year 2005.

Indicator	Age	1950-1955	1975-1980	2005-2010	2025-2030	2045-2050
Growth rate (percentage)	Total	2.3	2.1	1.3	0.8	0.4
	60+	1.7	3.5	3.5	3.3	1.4
	65+	1.8	4.0	4.3	4.5	1.9
	80+	2.6	1.9	4.2	4.2	3.2
Total fertility rate (per woman)		4.1	3.2	2.2	1.9	1.9
Life expectancy (years)						
Total	Birth	59.8	67.2	72.1	78.0	82.0
	60	..	..	21.4	23.9	25.6
	65	..	..	17.7	19.9	21.4
	80	..	..	8.7	9.9	10.8
Female	Birth	61.2	71.1	75.3	80.8	85.0
	60	..	..	23.5	26.6	28.2
	65	..	..	19.5	22.3	23.9
	80	..	..	9.2	11.0	12.1
Male	Birth	58.3	63.4	69.0	74.8	78.6
	60	..	..	19.1	20.8	22.5
	65	..	..	15.8	17.0	18.6
	80	..	..	7.9	8.2	8.9
Survival rate (percentage)						
Total	60	..	..	77.6	86.1	91.5
	65	..	..	72.4	82.2	88.1
	80	..	..	44.2	56.8	65.3
Female	60	..	..	81.6	87.7	93.1
	65	..	..	77.8	85.3	90.8
	80	..	..	53.7	66.6	74.5
Male	60	..	..	73.5	84.4	89.7
	65	..	..	66.8	78.9	85.1
	80	..	..	34.8	45.9	55.1

		1980	1990	2007	2010	2020
Labour force participation (percentage)						
Total	65+	30.7	22.7	21.6	21.6	21.2
Female	65+	24.0	16.5	12.6	12.6	12.5
Male	65+	39.9	31.0	33.4	33.5	33.5

Percentage married, age 60+			Percentage living alone, age 60+		
Total	Female	Male	Total	Female	Male
49.1	34.0	68.0	..	..	..

Statutory pensionable age (2006)			Percentage illiterate, age 65+		
	Female	Male	Total	Female	Male
	65	65	..	..	..

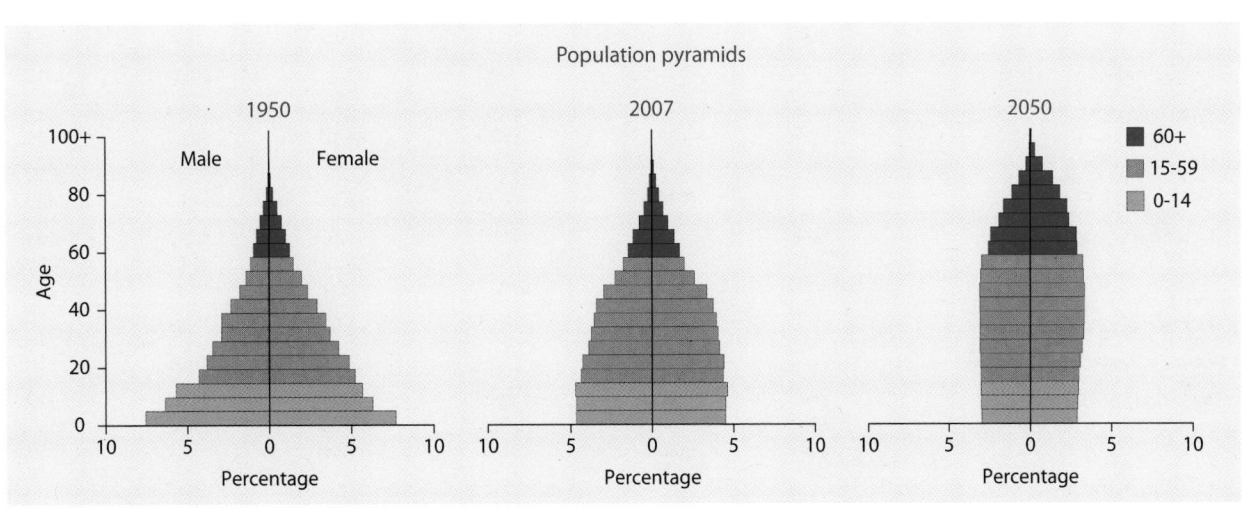

Population pyramids

United Nations Department of Economic and Social Affairs, Population Division

Bahrain

Indicator	Age	1950	1975	2007	2025	2050
Population (thousands)						
Total	Total	115.6	271.9	751.3	964.6	1 154.9
	0-14	48.9	117.0	195.8	180.8	188.6
	15-59	61.4	145.3	519.0	638.2	699.5
	60-64	2.0	3.6	13.4	57.0	66.2
	65-69	1.5	2.7	8.7	42.0	53.5
	70-74	1.0	1.7	6.7	26.3	44.4
	75-79	0.6	1.1	4.5	12.6	42.1
	80-84			2.3	4.7	34.3
	85-89			0.8	2.3	18.6
	90-94	0.3	0.7	0.2	0.7	6.4
	95-99			0.0	0.1	1.2
	100+			0.0	0.0	0.1
Female	Total	53.5	122.8	324.5	425.9	530.3
	0-14	24.0	57.2	95.7	88.1	92.0
	15-59	26.8	61.1	211.3	279.0	313.0
	60-64	1.0	1.6	5.6	23.6	30.0
	65-69	0.7	1.2	4.5	16.4	25.7
	70-74	0.5	0.8	3.4	9.4	21.6
	75-79	0.3	0.6	2.3	4.9	18.6
	80-84			1.2	2.6	15.7
	85-89			0.4	1.4	9.5
	90-94	0.2	0.4	0.1	0.4	3.5
	95-99			0.0	0.1	0.7
	100+			0.0	0.0	0.1
Male	Total	62.1	149.1	426.9	538.7	624.6
	0-14	24.9	59.8	100.1	92.7	96.6
	15-59	34.6	84.1	307.7	359.1	386.5
	60-64	1.0	2.0	7.8	33.4	36.2
	65-69	0.7	1.5	4.1	25.6	27.9
	70-74	0.5	0.9	3.3	16.9	22.7
	75-79	0.3	0.5	2.2	7.7	23.5
	80-84			1.1	2.1	18.6
	85-89			0.4	0.9	9.1
	90-94	0.1	0.3	0.1	0.2	3.0
	95-99			0.0	0.0	0.5
	100+			0.0	0.0	0.0
Percentage in older ages						
Total	60+	4.6	3.6	4.9	15.1	23.1
	65+	2.9	2.3	3.1	9.2	17.4
	80+	0.3	0.3	0.4	0.8	5.2
Female	60+	5.1	3.7	5.4	13.8	23.6
	65+	3.3	2.4	3.7	8.2	18.0
	80+	0.3	0.3	0.5	1.1	5.6
Male	60+	4.2	3.5	4.5	16.1	22.7
	65+	2.5	2.1	2.6	9.9	16.9
	80+	0.2	0.2	0.4	0.6	5.0
Ageing index		10.9	8.3	18.7	80.6	141.5
Broad age groups (percentage)	0-14	42.3	43.0	26.1	18.7	16.3
	15-59	53.1	53.4	69.1	66.2	60.6
	60+	4.6	3.6	4.9	15.1	23.1
Median age (years)		18.9	17.7	29.8*	34.8	40.6
Dependency ratio	Total	82.4	82.7	41.1	38.8	50.8
	Youth	77.2	78.6	36.8	26.0	24.6
	Old Age	5.2	4.1	4.3	12.8	26.2
Potential support ratio		19.1	24.3	23.0	7.8	3.8
Parent support ratio		1.2	1.2	1.2	1.6	11.7
Sex ratio (per 100 women)	60+	94.4	116.1	109.2	148.0	112.8
	65+	90.9	107.8	94.9	152.4	110.4
	80+	80.0	84.4	98.1	73.7	105.7

Indicator	Age	1950-1955	1975-1980	2005-2010	2025-2030	2045-2050
Growth rate (percentage)	Total	2.9	4.9	1.7	1.0	0.4
	60+	2.3	4.1	6.8	5.1	1.5
	65+	2.5	3.4	3.4	6.8	0.9
	80+	3.3	5.7	6.6	9.8	4.7
Total fertility rate (per woman)		7.0	5.2	2.3	1.9	1.9
Life expectancy (years)						
Total	Birth	50.9	65.6	75.1	77.9	80.3
	60	..	..	19.3	21.0	22.9
	65	..	..	15.5	17.0	18.7
	80	..	..	6.6	7.6	8.6
Female	Birth	52.5	67.8	76.7	79.9	82.4
	60	..	..	20.5	22.8	24.7
	65	..	..	16.5	18.6	20.3
	80	..	..	7.0	8.3	9.5
Male	Birth	49.6	63.9	73.9	76.6	78.8
	60	..	..	18.3	19.9	21.6
	65	..	..	14.6	16.0	17.5
	80	..	..	6.3	7.0	7.9
Survival rate (percentage)						
Total	60	..	..	88.5	91.8	93.6
	65	..	..	82.6	87.0	89.8
	80	..	..	43.6	51.5	59.8
Female	60	..	..	90.4	93.1	94.7
	65	..	..	85.8	89.6	91.9
	80	..	..	49.5	59.6	66.8
Male	60	..	..	87.5	90.8	92.6
	65	..	..	80.7	85.3	88.2
	80	..	..	38.7	46.9	54.5

		1980	1990	2007	2010	2020
Labour force participation (percentage)						
Total	65+	24.8	20.1	19.0	19.1	23.4
Female	65+	0.5	0.6	0.6	0.6	0.6
Male	65+	46.7	36.9	38.3	38.3	38.4

Percentage married, age 60+			Percentage living alone, age 60+ (1991)		
Total	Female	Male	Total	Female	Male
65.0	42.0	87.0	0.7	0.9	0.6

Statutory pensionable age (2006)			Percentage illiterate, age 65+		
	Female	Male	Total	Female	Male
	55	60	..	..	..

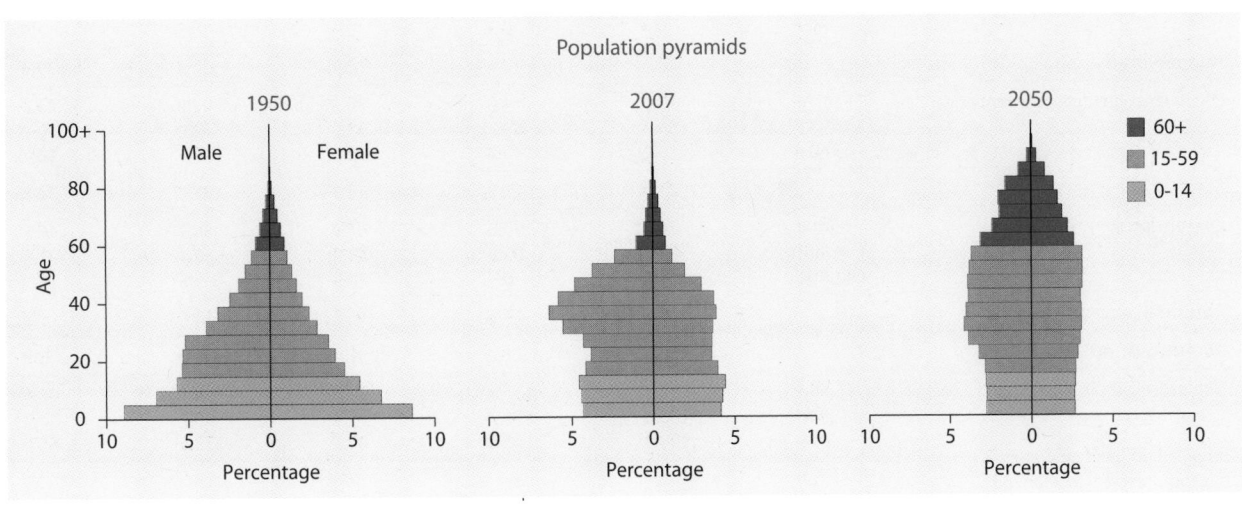

Population pyramids

United Nations Department of Economic and Social Affairs, Population Division

Bangladesh

Indicator	Age	1950	1975	2007	2025	2050
Population (thousands)						
Total	Total	41 782.9	73 178.2	147 059.1	193 751.8	242 937.3
	0-14	15 719.1	32 180.4	50 790.2	54 144.5	51 265.0
	15-59	23 493.1	36 780.0	87 773.8	122 070.1	151 000.5
	60-64	1 056.6	1 574.7	3 031.5	6 500.4	12 431.7
	65-69	730.1	1 312.8	2 319.5	4 781.5	10 552.9
	70-74	444.8	691.3	1 589.6	3 261.1	7 761.5
	75-79	239.1	414.6	945.6	1 736.7	5 330.7
	80-84			432.8	873.5	3 004.1
	85-89			140.7	307.4	1 229.4
	90-94	100.0	224.2	31.1	67.9	313.7
	95-99			4.1	8.2	45.1
	100+			0.2	0.5	2.8
Female	Total	19 556.0	35 188.3	71 991.5	95 600.3	121 476.5
	0-14	7 860.5	15 627.5	24 819.0	26 540.9	25 112.6
	15-59	10 484.8	17 660.3	42 759.5	60 023.1	74 781.2
	60-64	456.6	681.1	1 560.5	3 248.4	6 295.8
	65-69	340.1	595.7	1 207.9	2 423.0	5 443.5
	70-74	229.8	325.9	826.9	1 686.1	4 123.7
	75-79	134.1	191.3	493.0	955.5	2 942.4
	80-84			228.7	497.0	1 754.7
	85-89			76.4	179.9	771.3
	90-94	50.0	106.6	17.1	40.7	214.9
	95-99			2.4	5.2	33.9
	100+			0.2	0.3	2.3
Male	Total	22 226.9	37 989.9	75 067.6	98 151.5	121 460.8
	0-14	7 858.6	16 552.9	25 971.2	27 603.6	26 152.4
	15-59	13 008.3	19 119.8	45 014.3	62 047.0	76 219.3
	60-64	600.0	893.7	1 471.0	3 252.0	6 135.9
	65-69	390.0	717.2	1 111.6	2 358.5	5 109.4
	70-74	215.0	365.4	762.7	1 575.0	3 637.7
	75-79	105.0	223.3	452.6	781.2	2 388.3
	80-84			204.2	376.4	1 249.3
	85-89			64.3	127.4	458.1
	90-94	50.0	117.6	14.0	27.2	98.8
	95-99			1.7	3.0	11.2
	100+			0.1	0.2	0.5
Percentage in older ages						
Total	60+	6.2	5.8	5.8	9.1	16.7
	65+	3.6	3.6	3.7	5.7	11.6
	80+	0.2	0.3	0.4	0.6	1.9
Female	60+	6.2	5.4	6.1	9.5	17.8
	65+	3.9	3.5	4.0	6.1	12.6
	80+	0.3	0.3	0.5	0.8	2.3
Male	60+	6.1	6.1	5.4	8.7	15.7
	65+	3.4	3.7	3.5	5.3	10.7
	80+	0.2	0.3	0.4	0.5	1.5
Ageing index		16.4	13.1	16.7	32.4	79.3
Broad age groups (percentage)	0-14	37.6	44.0	34.5	27.9	21.1
	15-59	56.2	50.3	59.7	63.0	62.2
	60+	6.2	5.8	5.8	9.1	16.7
Median age (years)		21.6	17.8	22.1*	27.6	34.8
Dependency ratio	Total	70.2	90.8	61.9	50.7	48.6
	Youth	64.0	83.9	55.9	42.1	31.4
	Old Age	6.2	6.9	6.0	8.6	17.3
Potential support ratio		16.2	14.5	16.6	11.6	5.8
Parent support ratio		0.6	1.0	1.4	1.6	3.8
Sex ratio (per 100 women)	60+	112.3	121.9	92.5	94.1	88.4
	65+	100.8	116.7	91.5	90.7	84.7
	80+	100.0	110.4	87.5	73.9	65.5

* *Estimate refers to year 2005.*

Indicator	Age	1950-1955	1975-1980	2005-2010	2025-2030	2045-2050
Growth rate (percentage)	Total	1.9	2.3	1.8	1.2	0.6
	60+	1.7	1.0	3.0	3.9	2.8
	65+	2.0	2.0	3.2	4.4	3.4
	80+	4.4	3.0	4.1	3.9	4.9
Total fertility rate (per woman)		6.7	5.6	3.0	2.3	1.9
Life expectancy (years)						
Total	Birth	37.5	46.9	64.8	71.6	75.8
	60	..	..	16.5	18.0	19.8
	65	..	..	13.2	14.3	15.9
	80	..	..	5.6	6.0	6.9
Female	Birth	36.7	46.8	65.8	73.4	77.8
	60	..	..	17.3	18.9	21.3
	65	..	..	13.8	15.1	17.2
	80	..	..	5.9	6.3	7.5
Male	Birth	38.3	47.1	63.8	70.0	73.8
	60	..	..	15.8	17.0	18.2
	65	..	..	12.6	13.5	14.5
	80	..	..	5.4	5.8	6.1
Survival rate (percentage)						
Total	60	..	..	72.7	83.7	89.4
	65	..	..	65.0	76.9	83.9
	80	..	..	26.2	35.8	45.7
Female	60	..	..	74.3	86.2	91.4
	65	..	..	67.5	80.5	87.1
	80	..	..	29.4	40.8	53.1
Male	60	..	..	71.2	81.3	87.6
	65	..	..	62.6	73.5	80.8
	80	..	..	23.1	31.1	38.6

		1980	1990	2007	2010	2020
Labour force participation (percentage)						
Total	65+	57.9	54.6	30.0	28.8	28.0
Female	65+	37.1	42.4	11.3	10.3	9.5
Male	65+	75.5	65.9	50.5	49.4	48.7

Percentage married, age 60+			Percentage living alone, age 60+ (2000)		
Total	Female	Male	Total	Female	Male
68.7	43.0	95.0	1.8	3.3	0.6

Statutory pensionable age (2006)			Percentage illiterate, age 65+		
	Female	Male	Total	Female	Male
	57	57	..	..	..

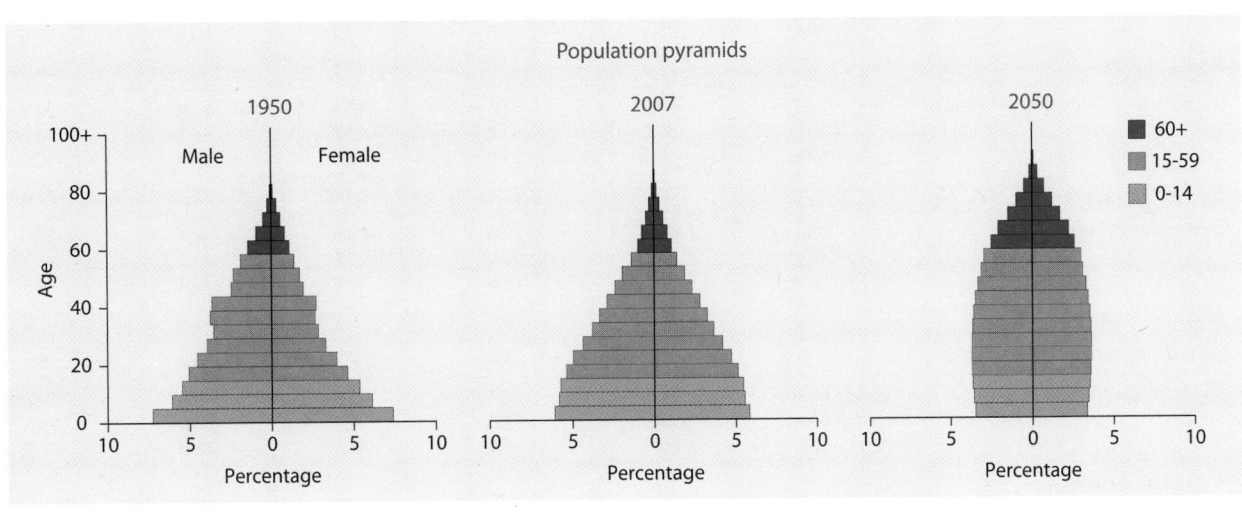

Population pyramids

1950 Male Female

2007

2050

■ 60+
■ 15-59
■ 0-14

Age — 100+, 80, 60, 40, 20, 0 — Percentage — 10, 5, 0, 5, 10

Barbados

Indicator	Age	1950	1975	2007	2025	2050
Population (thousands)						
Total	Total	211.0	245.6	270.9	278.4	255.3
	0-14	70.0	77.3	49.8	42.8	37.5
	15-59	123.0	134.9	184.3	165.2	126.2
	60-64	6.0	9.3	10.0	21.2	17.3
	65-69	4.0	10.6	7.5	18.4	17.3
	70-74	3.4	6.9	6.3	13.6	15.5
	75-79	2.7	3.8	5.6	8.9	15.9
	80-84			4.0	4.5	12.0
	85-89			2.3	2.5	8.3
	90-94	1.9	2.9	0.9	1.1	4.0
	95-99			0.2	0.4	1.2
	100+			0.0	0.1	0.2
Female	Total	114.0	128.1	139.8	142.6	131.5
	0-14	35.0	37.8	24.5	21.0	18.4
	15-59	66.0	71.6	92.8	82.4	62.2
	60-64	4.0	4.6	5.4	10.9	8.7
	65-69	3.0	5.8	4.4	9.8	8.9
	70-74	2.5	3.7	3.8	7.5	8.2
	75-79	2.0	2.8	3.6	5.1	8.8
	80-84			2.7	2.9	7.0
	85-89			1.6	1.8	5.3
	90-94	1.5	1.8	0.8	0.9	2.8
	95-99			0.2	0.3	0.9
	100+			0.0	0.1	0.2
Male	Total	97.0	117.5	131.1	135.8	123.7
	0-14	35.0	39.5	25.3	21.7	19.1
	15-59	57.0	63.3	91.5	82.8	64.0
	60-64	2.0	4.6	4.5	10.3	8.6
	65-69	1.0	4.8	3.1	8.6	8.4
	70-74	0.9	3.2	2.5	6.1	7.3
	75-79	0.7	1.1	2.0	3.7	7.0
	80-84			1.3	1.6	5.0
	85-89			0.6	0.7	3.1
	90-94	0.4	1.1	0.2	0.2	1.2
	95-99			0.0	0.0	0.2
	100+			0.0	0.0	0.0
Percentage in older ages						
Total	60+	8.5	13.6	13.6	25.3	35.9
	65+	5.7	9.9	9.9	17.7	29.1
	80+	0.9	1.2	2.7	3.0	10.0
Female	60+	11.4	14.6	16.1	27.5	38.7
	65+	7.9	11.0	12.2	19.8	32.1
	80+	1.3	1.4	3.8	4.1	12.3
Male	60+	5.2	12.5	10.9	23.0	32.9
	65+	3.1	8.6	7.5	15.4	26.0
	80+	0.5	0.9	1.7	1.9	7.6
Ageing index		25.7	43.3	74.0	164.7	244.6
Broad age groups (percentage)	0-14	33.2	31.5	18.4	15.4	14.7
	15-59	58.3	54.9	68.0	59.3	49.4
	60+	8.5	13.6	13.6	25.3	35.9
Median age (years)		24.6	23.7	34.7*	43.4	48.3
Dependency ratio	Total	63.6	70.4	39.4	49.4	77.9
	Youth	54.3	53.6	25.6	22.9	26.1
	Old Age	9.3	16.8	13.8	26.4	51.8
Potential support ratio		10.8	6.0	7.2	3.8	1.9
Parent support ratio		3.1	3.6	7.9	6.2	28.4
Sex ratio (per 100 women)	60+	38.5	78.7	63.8	79.8	80.0
	65+	33.3	72.0	57.7	74.0	76.3
	80+	29.9	57.6	41.4	42.9	57.9

Estimate refers to year 2005.

Indicator	Age	1950-1955	1975-1980	2005-2010	2025-2030	2045-2050
Growth rate (percentage)	Total	1.5	0.3	0.2	–0.1	–0.6
	60+	3.6	1.0	2.3	2.4	–0.1
	65+	5.0	1.6	0.3	3.7	0.2
	80+	9.3	8.0	0.7	5.6	1.7
Total fertility rate (per woman)		4.7	2.2	1.5	1.8	1.9
Life expectancy (years)						
Total	Birth	57.5	71.4	76.4	79.2	81.4
	60	..	..	21.2	22.8	24.3
	65	..	..	17.2	18.7	20.1
	80	..	..	7.7	8.8	9.6
Female	Birth	59.5	73.9	79.2	81.7	83.9
	60	..	..	23.0	24.8	26.4
	65	..	..	18.8	20.5	22.0
	80	..	..	8.5	9.7	10.7
Male	Birth	55.0	68.7	73.1	76.4	78.9
	60	..	..	18.8	20.5	22.1
	65	..	..	15.0	16.6	18.0
	80	..	..	6.3	7.3	8.2
Survival rate (percentage)						
Total	60	..	..	87.9	90.9	92.9
	65	..	..	83.3	86.9	89.6
	80	..	..	50.1	57.4	63.7
Female	60	..	..	91.1	92.8	94.2
	65	..	..	87.7	89.9	91.8
	80	..	..	58.9	65.7	71.3
Male	60	..	..	84.6	88.9	91.6
	65	..	..	78.6	83.9	87.4
	80	..	..	39.6	48.6	55.9

		1980	1990	2007	2010	2020
Labour force participation (percentage)						
Total	65+	12.7	7.6	3.3	3.2	2.9
Female	65+	8.5	3.7	2.8	2.8	2.8
Male	65+	19.0	13.8	4.2	3.8	3.1

Percentage married, age 60+			Percentage living alone, age 60+ (1980)		
Total	Female	Male	Total	Female	Male
41.6	32.0	57.0	22.6	21.8	23.7

Statutory pensionable age (2006)			Percentage illiterate, age 65+		
	Female	Male	Total	Female	Male
	65	65	..	..	..

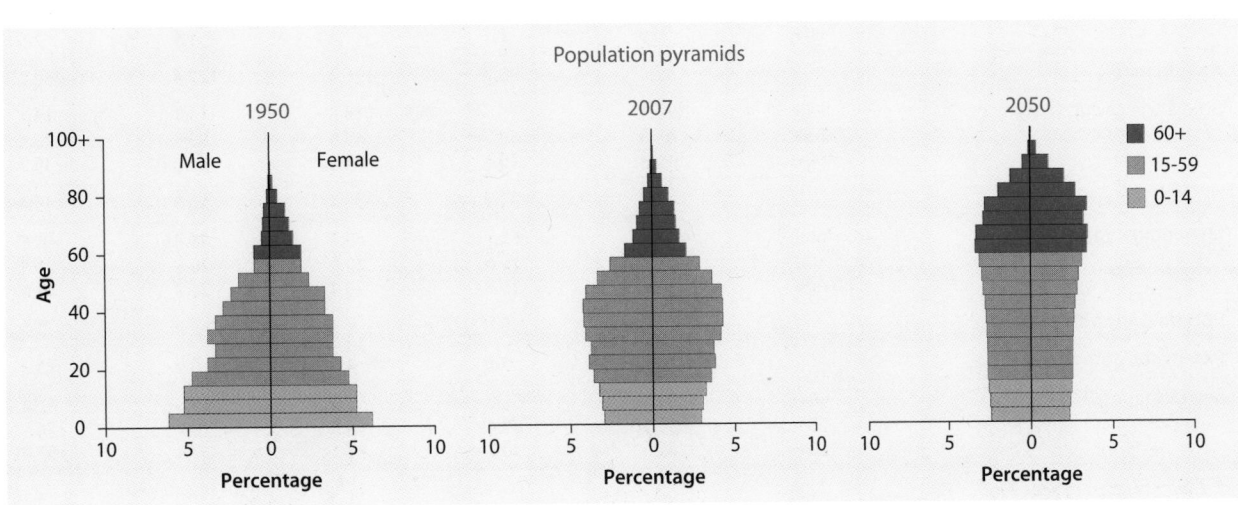

Population pyramids

United Nations Department of Economic and Social Affairs, Population Division

Belarus

Indicator	Age	1950	1975	2007	2025	2050
Population (thousands)						
Total	Total	7 745.0	9 367.0	9 645.2	8 635.4	7 017.0
	0-14	2 044.7	2 393.7	1 390.3	1 215.7	989.3
	15-59	4 726.6	5 640.2	6 490.9	5 263.1	3 548.4
	60-64	307.1	398.4	365.6	637.9	667.1
	65-69	252.0	349.0	434.1	570.0	584.8
	70-74	188.1	263.9	389.5	439.4	434.9
	75-79	127.1	155.9	312.6	229.2	335.0
	80-84			186.9	136.5	218.6
	85-89			51.5	100.8	154.9
	90-94	99.4	165.7	18.8	33.5	65.7
	95-99			4.5	8.5	16.6
	100+			0.5	0.8	1.8
Female	Total	4 321.0	5 039.9	5 144.5	4 644.8	3 793.8
	0-14	1 033.2	1 171.7	676.3	590.8	480.1
	15-59	2 677.2	2 983.3	3 315.5	2 683.1	1 786.6
	60-64	183.0	259.4	211.1	363.1	362.4
	65-69	152.7	227.8	270.4	346.8	332.4
	70-74	119.4	175.4	253.5	286.1	265.9
	75-79	85.7	104.4	216.4	158.4	220.6
	80-84			140.5	101.7	155.9
	85-89			41.2	79.5	119.1
	90-94	69.7	117.8	15.4	27.4	54.6
	95-99			3.7	7.3	14.6
	100+			0.4	0.7	1.6
Male	Total	3 424.0	4 327.1	4 500.7	3 990.6	3 223.2
	0-14	1 011.5	1 222.0	714.0	624.8	509.2
	15-59	2 049.4	2 656.9	3 175.4	2 579.9	1 761.8
	60-64	124.0	139.0	154.4	274.9	304.7
	65-69	99.2	121.2	163.8	223.2	252.4
	70-74	68.7	88.6	136.0	153.4	169.0
	75-79	41.4	51.5	96.1	70.8	114.3
	80-84			46.4	34.8	62.7
	85-89			10.3	21.3	35.8
	90-94	29.7	48.0	3.4	6.1	11.1
	95-99			0.8	1.3	2.0
	100+			0.1	0.1	0.2
Percentage in older ages						
Total	60+	12.6	14.2	18.3	25.0	35.3
	65+	8.6	10.0	14.5	17.6	25.8
	80+	1.3	1.8	2.7	3.2	6.5
Female	60+	14.1	17.6	22.4	29.5	40.3
	65+	9.9	12.4	18.3	21.7	30.7
	80+	1.6	2.3	3.9	4.7	9.1
Male	60+	10.6	10.4	13.6	19.7	29.5
	65+	7.0	7.1	10.2	12.8	20.1
	80+	0.9	1.1	1.4	1.6	3.5
Ageing index		47.6	55.7	126.9	177.4	250.6
Broad age groups (percentage)	0-14	26.4	25.6	14.4	14.1	14.1
	15-59	61.0	60.2	67.3	60.9	50.6
	60+	12.6	14.2	18.3	25.0	35.3
Median age (years)		27.2	30.5	37.8*	42.8	48.4
Dependency ratio	Total	53.9	55.1	40.7	46.3	66.5
	Youth	40.6	39.6	20.3	20.6	23.5
	Old Age	13.2	15.5	20.4	25.7	43.0
Potential support ratio		7.6	6.5	4.9	3.9	2.3
Parent support ratio		3.8	5.7	4.6	7.9	15.2
Sex ratio (per 100 women)	60+	59.5	50.7	53.0	57.3	62.4
	65+	55.9	49.4	48.5	50.7	55.6
	80+	42.6	40.7	30.3	29.4	32.3

* Estimate refers to year 2005.

Indicator	Age	1950-1955	1975-1980	2005-2010	2025-2030	2045-2050
Growth rate (percentage)	Total	0.2	0.6	−0.6	−0.8	−0.9
	60+	−0.5	−0.1	−0.9	0.1	1.0
	65+	0.4	2.1	−1.7	1.8	1.1
	80+	1.3	1.9	5.4	−0.3	−1.0
Total fertility rate (per woman)		2.6	2.1	1.2	1.5	1.7
Life expectancy (years)						
Total	Birth	65.9	71.1	68.7	72.0	75.2
	60	..	..	17.2	18.6	20.1
	65	..	..	14.1	15.3	16.6
	80	..	..	6.5	7.2	7.9
Female	Birth	70.0	75.5	74.5	77.0	79.4
	60	..	..	19.5	21.1	22.7
	65	..	..	15.8	17.2	18.6
	80	..	..	6.8	7.7	8.6
Male	Birth	61.1	65.8	63.1	66.9	70.8
	60	..	..	14.1	15.4	16.9
	65	..	..	11.6	12.5	13.8
	80	..	..	5.6	6.0	6.5
Survival rate (percentage)						
Total	60	..	..	74.5	80.6	86.0
	65	..	..	66.0	72.9	79.4
	80	..	..	29.6	37.0	44.7
Female	60	..	..	86.1	89.3	91.7
	65	..	..	80.2	84.4	87.7
	80	..	..	43.1	50.7	57.8
Male	60	..	..	63.4	72.0	80.3
	65	..	..	52.3	61.6	71.1
	80	..	..	16.6	22.6	30.6

		1980	1990	2007	2010	2020
Labour force participation (percentage)						
Total	65+	6.0	7.4	1.7	1.5	1.2
Female	65+	4.5	4.9	1.2	1.2	1.2
Male	65+	9.1	13.2	2.6	2.1	1.3

Percentage married, age 60+			Percentage living alone, age 60+		
Total	Female	Male	Total	Female	Male
54.0	39.0	81.0	..	..	..

Statutory pensionable age (2006)			Percentage illiterate, age 65+ (1999)		
Female	Male		Total	Female	Male
55	60		1.6	2.2	0.4

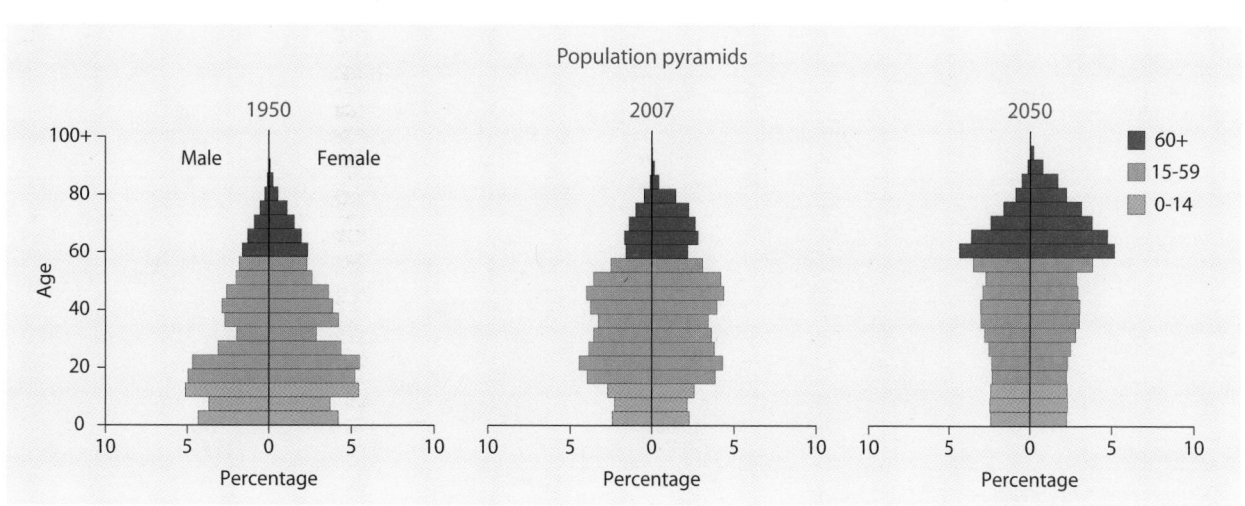

Population pyramids

United Nations Department of Economic and Social Affairs, Population Division   161

Belgium

Indicator	Age	1950	1975	2007	2025	2050
Population (thousands)						
Total	Total	8 639.0	9 800.7	10 453.5	10 590.3	10 301.7
	0-14	1 805.0	2 177.4	1 722.4	1 608.8	1 570.9
	15-59	5 455.0	5 746.0	6 332.9	5 793.0	5 298.3
	60-64	424.0	512.5	553.8	765.2	625.6
	65-69	366.0	474.4	474.8	698.2	597.6
	70-74	282.0	395.8	463.7	591.0	562.3
	75-79	182.0	269.0	394.6	488.1	534.8
	80-84			302.3	296.7	471.4
	85-89			135.7	202.0	356.4
	90-94	125.0	225.6	54.9	106.1	194.9
	95-99			16.3	35.0	72.6
	100+			1.9	6.3	17.0
Female	Total	4 386.0	5 002.0	5 322.5	5 371.1	5 241.4
	0-14	890.0	1 063.3	843.0	787.1	768.6
	15-59	2 741.0	2 851.6	3 117.5	2 846.8	2 602.2
	60-64	227.0	273.3	281.2	383.4	310.4
	65-69	197.0	264.7	249.4	356.9	300.5
	70-74	154.0	232.7	254.8	311.1	290.3
	75-79	102.0	167.5	231.4	269.1	286.2
	80-84			192.5	175.5	265.1
	85-89			94.8	131.1	217.3
	90-94	75.0	149.0	42.5	76.4	131.6
	95-99			13.8	28.2	55.0
	100+			1.7	5.5	14.4
Male	Total	4 253.0	4 798.7	5 131.0	5 219.3	5 060.4
	0-14	915.0	1 114.1	879.4	821.7	802.3
	15-59	2 714.0	2 894.5	3 215.5	2 946.2	2 696.2
	60-64	197.0	239.2	272.7	381.8	315.2
	65-69	169.0	209.7	225.4	341.3	297.1
	70-74	128.0	163.1	208.9	279.9	272.0
	75-79	80.0	101.5	163.2	219.0	248.6
	80-84			109.8	121.1	206.3
	85-89			41.0	70.9	139.1
	90-94	50.0	76.6	12.4	29.7	63.4
	95-99			2.5	6.9	17.6
	100+			0.2	0.8	2.6
Percentage in older ages						
Total	60+	16.0	19.2	22.9	30.1	33.3
	65+	11.1	13.9	17.6	22.9	27.2
	80+	1.4	2.3	4.9	6.1	10.8
Female	60+	17.2	21.7	25.6	32.3	35.7
	65+	12.0	16.3	20.3	25.2	29.8
	80+	1.7	3.0	6.5	7.8	13.0
Male	60+	14.7	16.5	20.2	27.8	30.9
	65+	10.0	11.5	14.9	20.5	24.6
	80+	1.2	1.6	3.2	4.4	8.5
Ageing index		76.4	86.2	139.2	198.2	218.5
Broad age groups (percentage)	0-14	20.9	22.2	16.5	15.2	15.2
	15-59	63.1	58.6	60.6	54.7	51.4
	60+	16.0	19.2	22.9	30.1	33.3
Median age (years)		35.6	34.1	40.6*	44.9	46.3
Dependency ratio	Total	46.9	56.6	51.8	61.5	73.9
	Youth	30.7	34.8	25.0	24.5	26.5
	Old Age	16.2	21.8	26.8	37.0	47.4
Potential support ratio		6.2	4.6	3.7	2.7	2.1
Parent support ratio		3.0	5.1	10.6	15.8	33.9
Sex ratio (per 100 women)	60+	82.6	72.7	76.1	83.5	83.5
	65+	80.9	67.7	70.6	79.0	79.9
	80+	66.7	51.4	48.1	55.1	62.8

* Estimate refers to year 2005.

Indicator	Age	1950-1955	1975-1980	2005-2010	2025-2030	2045-2050
Growth rate (percentage)	Total	0.5	0.1	0.1	0.0	−0.2
	60+	1.4	−0.5	1.6	1.1	−0.1
	65+	1.4	0.7	0.5	1.7	−0.2
	80+	3.5	3.4	3.1	2.9	0.9
Total fertility rate (per woman)		2.3	1.7	1.7	1.8	1.9
Life expectancy (years)						
Total	Birth	67.5	72.4	79.6	81.8	83.8
	60	..	..	22.9	24.4	25.9
	65	..	..	18.8	20.2	21.6
	80	..	..	8.7	9.6	10.6
Female	Birth	70.2	75.7	82.7	84.7	86.7
	60	..	..	25.2	26.7	28.2
	65	..	..	20.8	22.2	23.7
	80	..	..	9.6	10.6	11.8
Male	Birth	65.0	69.1	76.4	79.0	81.1
	60	..	..	20.3	22.1	23.6
	65	..	..	16.4	18.1	19.4
	80	..	..	7.3	8.3	9.1
Survival rate (percentage)						
Total	60	..	..	91.4	93.5	94.9
	65	..	..	87.5	90.3	92.3
	80	..	..	58.5	64.8	70.1
Female	60	..	..	94.0	95.4	96.5
	65	..	..	91.3	93.2	94.7
	80	..	..	69.0	73.8	78.2
Male	60	..	..	89.0	91.7	93.4
	65	..	..	83.8	87.5	89.9
	80	..	..	47.7	56.0	62.1

		1980	1990	2007	2010	2020
Labour force participation (percentage)						
Total	65+	1.8	1.1	1.5	1.5	1.6
Female	65+	1.0	0.6	0.8	0.8	0.8
Male	65+	3.1	1.9	2.4	2.5	2.7

Percentage married, age 60+			Percentage living alone, age 60+ (1994)		
Total	Female	Male	Total	Female	Male
59.9	48.0	76.0	29.3	38.9	16.2

Statutory pensionable age (2006)			Percentage illiterate, age 65+		
	Female	Male	Total	Female	Male
	63	65	..	..	..

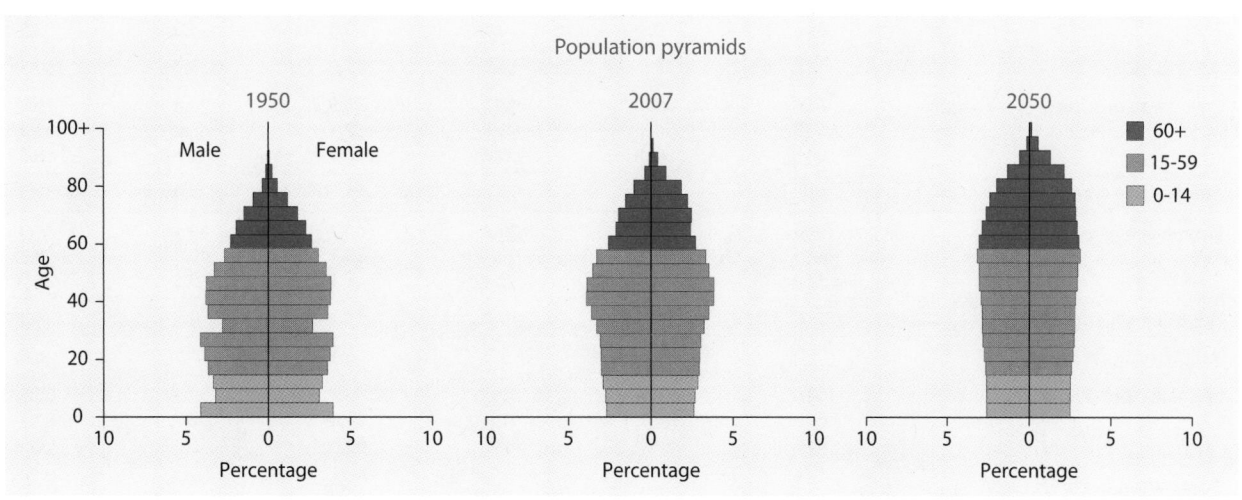

Population pyramids

United Nations Department of Economic and Social Affairs, Population Division

Belize

Indicator	Age	1950	1975	2007	2025	2050
Population (thousands)						
Total	Total	68.9	133.7	280.4	366.3	442.1
	0-14	26.6	63.0	99.7	98.0	85.3
	15-59	38.2	61.6	163.8	233.3	271.3
	60-64	1.6	3.1	4.9	11.7	23.6
	65-69	1.2	2.4	3.9	8.9	20.3
	70-74	0.7	1.7	3.2	6.2	16.0
	75-79	0.4	1.1	2.3	4.0	11.7
	80-84			1.5	2.2	7.5
	85-89			0.7	1.3	4.2
	90-94	0.3	0.9	0.3	0.5	1.7
	95-99			0.1	0.1	0.5
	100+			0.0	0.0	0.1
Female	Total	35.2	66.8	139.0	183.4	223.5
	0-14	13.5	31.0	49.2	48.4	42.1
	15-59	19.6	31.0	81.4	116.7	135.3
	60-64	0.8	1.6	2.4	6.1	12.1
	65-69	0.6	1.2	1.9	4.5	10.6
	70-74	0.4	0.8	1.6	3.1	8.5
	75-79	0.2	0.6	1.2	2.1	6.5
	80-84			0.8	1.2	4.3
	85-89			0.4	0.7	2.6
	90-94	0.1	0.5	0.1	0.3	1.1
	95-99			0.0	0.1	0.3
	100+			0.0	0.0	0.1
Male	Total	33.7	67.0	141.4	183.0	218.6
	0-14	13.1	32.0	50.5	49.6	43.1
	15-59	18.7	30.6	82.4	116.5	136.0
	60-64	0.8	1.4	2.5	5.6	11.5
	65-69	0.6	1.2	2.0	4.4	9.7
	70-74	0.3	0.8	1.6	3.0	7.5
	75-79	0.2	0.5	1.2	1.9	5.2
	80-84			0.7	1.0	3.2
	85-89			0.3	0.6	1.6
	90-94	0.1	0.4	0.1	0.2	0.6
	95-99			0.0	0.0	0.1
	100+			0.0	0.0	0.0
Percentage in older ages						
Total	60+	6.0	6.8	6.0	9.6	19.3
	65+	3.6	4.5	4.3	6.4	14.0
	80+	0.4	0.7	0.9	1.1	3.1
Female	60+	6.1	7.2	6.1	9.9	20.6
	65+	3.7	4.7	4.3	6.6	15.2
	80+	0.4	0.7	1.0	1.3	3.7
Male	60+	5.9	6.5	6.0	9.2	18.0
	65+	3.5	4.3	4.2	6.1	12.8
	80+	0.3	0.6	0.8	1.0	2.5
Ageing index		15.5	14.5	17.0	35.7	100.3
Broad age groups (percentage)	0-14	38.6	47.1	35.5	26.8	19.3
	15-59	55.5	46.1	58.4	63.7	61.4
	60+	6.0	6.8	6.0	9.6	19.3
Median age (years)		20.8	16.2	21.2*	28.0	37.3
Dependency ratio	Total	73.0	106.7	66.2	49.5	49.9
	Youth	66.7	97.3	59.1	40.0	28.9
	Old Age	6.3	9.4	7.1	9.5	21.0
Potential support ratio		15.9	10.7	14.1	10.5	4.8
Parent support ratio		1.6	3.2	5.1	4.5	8.0
Sex ratio (per 100 women)	60+	92.3	90.6	100.7	92.6	85.5
	65+	91.0	91.9	99.4	92.8	82.2
	80+	88.1	82.0	84.8	81.2	66.3

* *Estimate refers to year 2005.*

Indicator	Age	1950-1955	1975-1980	2005-2010	2025-2030	2045-2050
Growth rate (percentage)	Total	3.0	1.5	1.9	1.0	0.5
	60+	3.6	0.5	3.2	4.1	2.9
	65+	4.1	1.8	2.1	4.6	3.4
	80+	5.0	9.4	3.4	4.4	4.1
Total fertility rate (per woman)		6.7	6.2	2.8	2.0	1.9
Life expectancy (years)						
Total	Birth	57.7	69.7	71.7	74.0	78.0
	60	..	..	21.2	22.2	23.2
	65	..	..	17.4	18.3	19.2
	80	..	..	8.1	8.6	9.2
Female	Birth	58.3	70.6	74.1	76.5	80.4
	60	..	..	22.3	23.5	24.7
	65	..	..	18.3	19.5	20.6
	80	..	..	8.6	9.3	10.0
Male	Birth	57.1	68.9	69.5	71.6	75.6
	60	..	..	20.2	20.9	21.5
	65	..	..	16.5	17.1	17.7
	80	..	..	7.6	7.9	8.2
Survival rate (percentage)						
Total	60	..	..	79.9	82.3	88.3
	65	..	..	75.2	78.0	84.1
	80	..	..	45.4	49.9	56.8
Female	60	..	..	83.4	85.4	90.6
	65	..	..	79.4	81.8	87.2
	80	..	..	51.0	56.1	63.3
Male	60	..	..	76.5	79.2	86.0
	65	..	..	71.2	74.2	81.1
	80	..	..	40.5	44.0	50.2

		1980	1990	2007	2010	2020
Labour force participation (percentage)						
Total	65+	31.2	29.8	29.8	29.6	29.3
Female	65+	7.4	9.7	11.8	11.8	11.9
Male	65+	57.2	50.9	47.9	47.8	47.6

Percentage married, age 60+			Percentage living alone, age 60+ (1980)		
Total	Female	Male	Total	Female	Male
53.6	48.0	59.0	13.4	11.2	15.6

Statutory pensionable age (2006)			Percentage illiterate, age 65+		
Female	Male		Total	Female	Male
65	65		..	..	..

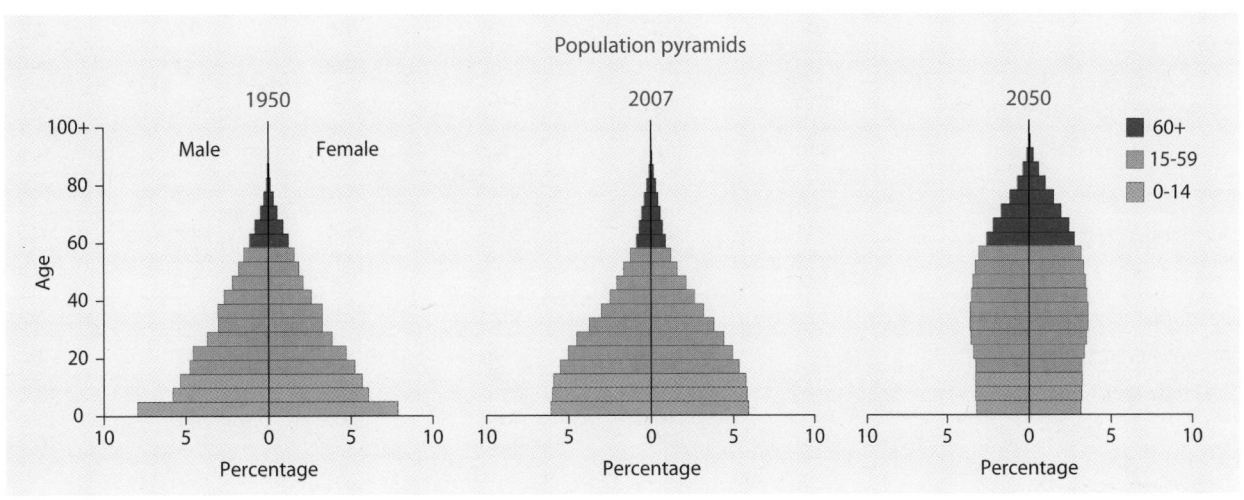

Population pyramids

1950   2007   2050

Male   Female

60+
15-59
0-14

Age / Percentage

Benin

Indicator	Age	1950	1975	2007	2025	2050
Population (thousands)						
Total	Total	2 004.9	3 212.2	8 971.0	14 254.1	22 122.6
	0-14	725.3	1 424.8	3 920.7	5 448.4	6 197.1
	15-59	1 006.8	1 602.6	4 657.9	8 006.0	13 812.4
	60-64	95.6	61.2	147.1	278.4	725.2
	65-69	77.2	47.4	107.3	225.9	581.3
	70-74	53.5	34.4	71.8	155.1	386.3
	75-79	30.5	23.6	41.5	88.4	244.4
	80-84			18.4	38.3	123.8
	85-89			5.3	11.5	42.5
	90-94	16.0	18.2	0.8	1.9	8.8
	95-99			0.1	0.2	0.8
	100+			0.0	0.0	0.0
Female	Total	1 043.8	1 645.4	4 440.8	7 030.1	10 920.0
	0-14	376.0	705.9	1 925.8	2 673.2	3 034.0
	15-59	520.0	836.1	2 291.3	3 929.6	6 791.9
	60-64	51.8	33.2	81.3	141.3	365.1
	65-69	41.1	26.0	60.6	118.3	297.1
	70-74	28.8	19.3	41.9	83.9	201.1
	75-79	17.1	14.0	24.8	51.7	130.5
	80-84			11.2	23.3	68.9
	85-89			3.4	7.4	25.1
	90-94	9.0	10.8	0.6	1.3	5.6
	95-99			0.0	0.1	0.6
	100+			0.0	0.0	0.0
Male	Total	961.1	1 566.9	4 530.2	7 223.9	11 202.7
	0-14	349.2	718.9	1 994.9	2 775.2	3 163.1
	15-59	486.8	766.5	2 366.6	4 076.4	7 020.4
	60-64	43.9	27.9	65.8	137.1	360.1
	65-69	36.1	21.5	46.8	107.6	284.2
	70-74	24.7	15.1	30.0	71.2	185.2
	75-79	13.5	9.6	16.7	36.7	113.9
	80-84			7.2	15.0	54.8
	85-89			2.0	4.1	17.4
	90-94	7.0	7.3	0.3	0.6	3.2
	95-99			0.0	0.0	0.2
	100+			0.0	0.0	0.0
Percentage in older ages						
Total	60+	13.6	5.8	4.4	5.6	9.6
	65+	8.8	3.8	2.7	3.7	6.3
	80+	0.8	0.6	0.3	0.4	0.8
Female	60+	14.2	6.3	5.0	6.1	10.0
	65+	9.2	4.3	3.2	4.1	6.7
	80+	0.9	0.7	0.3	0.5	0.9
Male	60+	13.0	5.2	3.7	5.2	9.1
	65+	8.5	3.4	2.3	3.3	5.9
	80+	0.7	0.5	0.2	0.3	0.7
Ageing index		37.6	13.0	10.0	14.7	34.1
Broad age groups (percentage)	0-14	36.2	44.4	43.7	38.2	28.0
	15-59	50.2	49.9	51.9	56.2	62.4
	60+	13.6	5.8	4.4	5.6	9.6
Median age (years)		23.7	17.6	17.6*	20.5	27.5
Dependency ratio	Total	81.9	93.1	86.7	72.1	52.2
	Youth	65.8	85.6	81.6	65.8	42.6
	Old Age	16.1	7.4	5.1	6.3	9.5
Potential support ratio		6.2	13.5	19.6	15.9	10.5
Parent support ratio		1.2	1.8	1.0	1.3	2.0
Sex ratio (per 100 women)	60+	84.7	78.9	75.4	87.1	93.1
	65+	84.7	76.4	72.3	82.3	90.4
	80+	77.6	67.8	62.2	61.6	75.5

* Estimate refers to year 2005.

Indicator	Age	1950-1955	1975-1980	2005-2010	2025-2030	2045-2050
Growth rate (percentage)	Total	1.2	2.9	3.0	2.1	1.4
	60+	−0.4	1.0	3.9	3.5	4.1
	65+	−0.4	0.2	3.5	3.6	4.7
	80+	−0.7	−2.1	3.6	5.5	4.3
Total fertility rate (per woman)		6.8	7.1	5.4	3.5	2.5
Life expectancy (years)						
Total	Birth	38.2	49.2	55.9	64.0	70.6
	60	..	..	16.6	18.0	19.5
	65	..	..	13.1	14.3	15.5
	80	..	..	5.2	5.6	6.1
Female	Birth	39.4	50.9	56.6	65.2	71.7
	60	..	..	17.3	18.8	20.4
	65	..	..	13.6	14.9	16.3
	80	..	..	5.4	5.8	6.4
Male	Birth	37.0	47.4	55.1	62.9	69.5
	60	..	..	15.8	17.1	18.6
	65	..	..	12.4	13.5	14.8
	80	..	..	4.9	5.3	5.8
Survival rate (percentage)						
Total	60	..	..	59.6	71.8	81.8
	65	..	..	53.8	66.2	77.1
	80	..	..	21.4	31.0	41.6
Female	60	..	..	60.9	73.6	83.2
	65	..	..	55.9	69.0	79.5
	80	..	..	23.9	34.8	46.1
Male	60	..	..	58.1	70.1	80.4
	65	..	..	51.6	63.6	74.8
	80	..	..	18.7	27.2	37.3

		1980	1990	2007	2010	2020
Labour force participation (percentage)						
Total	65+	57.0	59.2	53.5	53.2	53.7
Female	65+	36.8	41.2	35.0	34.6	34.3
Male	65+	83.6	83.9	79.1	78.7	78.4

Percentage married, age 60+			Percentage living alone, age 60+ (2001)		
Total	Female	Male	Total	Female	Male
50.3	30.0	78.0	10.3	11.7	9.0

Statutory pensionable age (2006)		Percentage illiterate, age 65+ (2002)		
Female	Male	Total	Female	Male
55	55	92.0	96.2	87.0

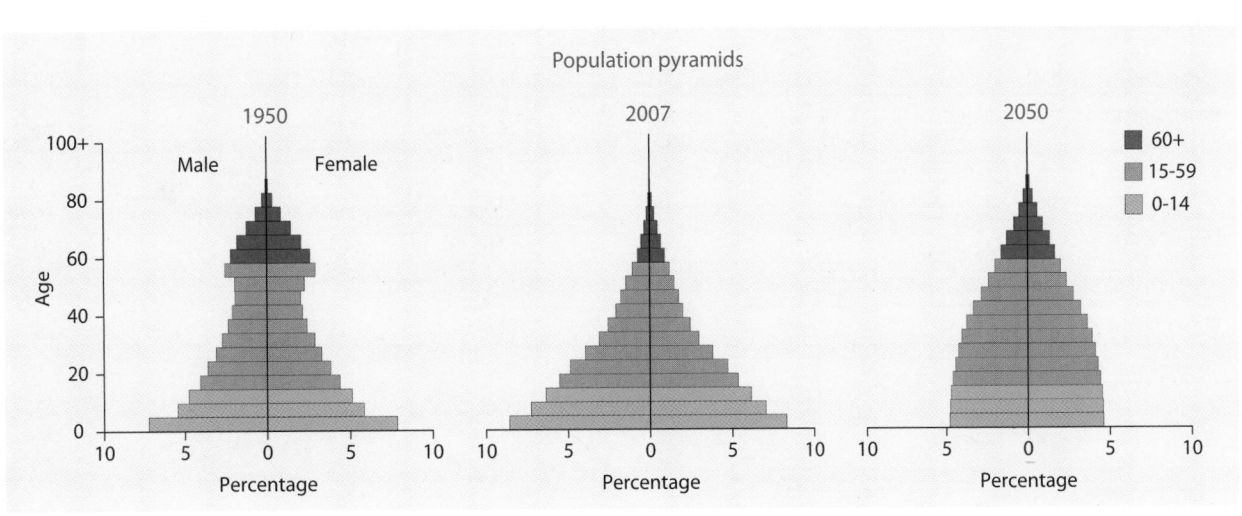

Population pyramids

United Nations Department of Economic and Social Affairs, Population Division

Bhutan

Indicator	Age	1950	1975	2007	2025	2050
Population (thousands)						
Total	Total	733.7	1 161.4	2 260.2	3 209.1	4 392.8
	0-14	299.9	476.0	843.7	1 015.6	1 032.3
	15-59	395.7	620.9	1 256.0	1 937.2	2 714.3
	60-64	15.4	25.2	54.3	80.4	212.0
	65-69	10.9	18.2	42.3	64.2	167.2
	70-74	6.8	11.7	30.5	48.0	120.5
	75-79	3.4	6.3	19.2	34.3	76.8
	80-84			9.7	19.1	42.9
	85-89			3.5	7.9	19.5
	90-94	1.7	3.2	0.8	2.1	6.1
	95-99			0.1	0.3	1.1
	100+			0.0	0.0	0.1
Female	Total	363.8	575.0	1 115.0	1 583.5	2 172.6
	0-14	147.7	233.8	412.9	496.6	504.3
	15-59	196.0	307.4	618.6	954.7	1 337.6
	60-64	8.0	13.0	27.6	40.4	106.4
	65-69	5.7	9.5	21.8	32.8	84.8
	70-74	3.6	6.2	16.0	24.9	61.8
	75-79	1.9	3.4	10.3	18.1	39.8
	80-84			5.3	10.3	22.7
	85-89			2.0	4.4	10.7
	90-94	1.0	1.8	0.5	1.2	3.6
	95-99			0.1	0.2	0.7
	100+			0.0	0.0	0.1
Male	Total	369.9	586.4	1 145.2	1 625.6	2 220.2
	0-14	152.2	242.2	430.8	519.0	528.0
	15-59	199.7	313.5	637.4	982.5	1 376.6
	60-64	7.4	12.2	26.6	40.0	105.5
	65-69	5.2	8.7	20.5	31.4	82.4
	70-74	3.2	5.5	14.5	23.1	58.8
	75-79	1.6	2.9	8.9	16.2	37.0
	80-84			4.4	8.8	20.1
	85-89			1.5	3.5	8.8
	90-94	0.7	1.4	0.3	0.9	2.6
	95-99			0.0	0.1	0.4
	100+			0.0	0.0	0.0
Percentage in older ages						
Total	60+	5.2	5.6	7.1	8.0	14.7
	65+	3.1	3.4	4.7	5.5	9.9
	80+	0.2	0.3	0.6	0.9	1.6
Female	60+	5.5	5.9	7.5	8.3	15.2
	65+	3.3	3.6	5.0	5.8	10.3
	80+	0.3	0.3	0.7	1.0	1.7
Male	60+	4.9	5.2	6.7	7.6	14.2
	65+	2.9	3.1	4.4	5.2	9.5
	80+	0.2	0.2	0.5	0.8	1.4
Ageing index		12.7	13.6	19.0	25.2	62.6
Broad age groups (percentage)	0-14	40.9	41.0	37.3	31.6	23.5
	15-59	53.9	53.5	55.6	60.4	61.8
	60+	5.2	5.6	7.1	8.0	14.7
Median age (years)		19.5	19.6	20.1*	25.0	32.3
Dependency ratio	Total	78.5	79.8	72.5	59.1	50.1
	Youth	73.0	73.7	64.4	50.3	35.3
	Old Age	5.5	6.1	8.1	8.7	14.8
Potential support ratio		18.1	16.4	12.3	11.5	6.7
Parent support ratio		0.7	0.8	2.3	3.4	3.9
Sex ratio (per 100 women)	60+	89.6	90.5	92.0	93.9	95.4
	65+	87.3	88.2	89.9	91.7	93.7
	80+	73.6	75.7	80.2	83.4	84.3

* Estimate refers to year 2005.

Indicator	Age	1950-1955	1975-1980	2005-2010	2025-2030	2045-2050
Growth rate (percentage)	Total	1.6	2.1	2.2	1.5	1.0
	60+	1.7	2.5	3.0	2.8	4.1
	65+	1.7	2.6	3.2	2.7	4.4
	80+	1.4	3.6	4.7	3.5	4.0
Total fertility rate (per woman)		5.9	5.9	3.8	2.6	2.1
Life expectancy (years)						
Total	Birth	35.3	43.3	64.9	71.7	75.8
	60	..	..	18.0	19.4	21.0
	65	..	..	14.4	15.6	17.0
	80	..	..	6.3	6.8	7.5
Female	Birth	36.1	44.1	66.1	73.1	77.2
	60	..	..	18.5	20.0	21.7
	65	..	..	14.9	16.0	17.6
	80	..	..	6.5	6.9	7.8
Male	Birth	34.5	42.5	63.6	70.4	74.5
	60	..	..	17.4	18.9	20.2
	65	..	..	14.0	15.2	16.4
	80	..	..	6.1	6.6	7.1
Survival rate (percentage)						
Total	60	..	..	72.3	82.4	88.0
	65	..	..	66.1	76.9	83.3
	80	..	..	31.0	40.9	49.7
Female	60	..	..	74.5	84.5	89.7
	65	..	..	68.7	79.5	85.6
	80	..	..	33.7	44.0	53.3
Male	60	..	..	70.3	80.4	86.4
	65	..	..	63.6	74.4	81.2
	80	..	..	28.4	37.9	46.2

		1980	1990	2007	2010	2020
Labour force participation (percentage)						
Total	65+	33.0	34.3	41.9	43.6	47.6
Female	65+	14.4	15.0	25.7	28.8	36.3
Male	65+	54.1	55.9	60.0	60.0	60.0

Percentage married, age 60+			Percentage living alone, age 60+		
Total	Female	Male	Total	Female	Male
54.8	42.0	73.0	..	..	..

Statutory pensionable age (2006)		Percentage illiterate, age 65+		
Female	Male	Total	Female	Male
..	..	..	..	..

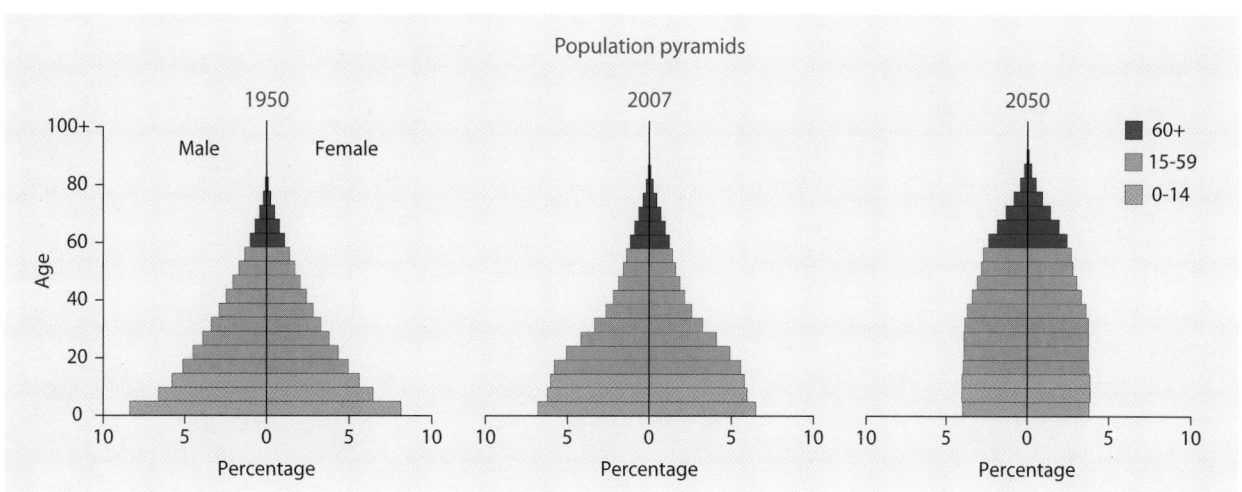

Population pyramids

1950   2007   2050

Male   Female

60+
15-59
0-14

Age

Percentage

Bolivia

Indicator	Age	1950	1975	2007	2025	2050
Population (thousands)						
Total	Total	2 713.6	4 758.9	9 524.6	12 368.5	14 908.1
	0-14	1 123.3	2 048.1	3 544.6	3 569.2	2 977.5
	15-59	1 438.0	2 446.7	5 324.8	7 625.1	9 321.1
	60-64	57.4	100.3	215.2	369.0	741.3
	65-69	41.9	74.1	168.6	297.7	605.8
	70-74	28.7	49.0	126.7	222.0	480.6
	75-79	16.3	26.9	84.6	149.9	366.9
	80-84	⎫		41.9	81.8	228.6
	85-89	⎪		14.4	38.2	120.8
	90-94	⎬ 7.8	13.7	3.4	12.5	49.6
	95-99	⎪		0.4	2.8	13.5
	100+	⎭		0.0	0.4	2.5
Female	Total	1 360.5	2 414.3	4 777.0	6 190.0	7 478.2
	0-14	557.3	1 023.5	1 737.9	1 748.0	1 454.6
	15-59	721.8	1 248.7	2 681.1	3 798.0	4 607.6
	60-64	30.1	52.7	113.8	194.1	379.4
	65-69	22.3	39.6	90.6	159.7	316.8
	70-74	15.5	26.6	69.7	122.6	259.3
	75-79	9.0	15.1	47.8	85.1	205.9
	80-84	⎫		24.5	48.1	134.5
	85-89	⎪		8.9	23.7	75.2
	90-94	⎬ 4.5	8.0	2.3	8.4	33.1
	95-99	⎪		0.3	2.0	9.8
	100+	⎭		0.0	0.3	2.0
Male	Total	1 353.2	2 344.6	4 747.6	6 178.5	7 430.0
	0-14	566.1	1 024.6	1 806.7	1 821.2	1 523.0
	15-59	716.2	1 198.0	2 643.7	3 827.1	4 713.4
	60-64	27.4	47.6	101.4	174.9	361.9
	65-69	19.6	34.6	77.9	138.0	288.9
	70-74	13.2	22.3	56.9	99.4	221.4
	75-79	7.3	11.8	36.8	64.8	161.0
	80-84	⎫		17.4	33.7	94.2
	85-89	⎪		5.5	14.5	45.6
	90-94	⎬ 3.4	5.7	1.1	4.1	16.5
	95-99	⎪		0.1	0.7	3.7
	100+	⎭		0.0	0.1	0.6
Percentage in older ages						
Total	60+	5.6	5.5	6.9	9.5	17.5
	65+	3.5	3.4	4.6	6.5	12.5
	80+	0.3	0.3	0.6	1.1	2.8
Female	60+	6.0	5.9	7.5	10.4	18.9
	65+	3.8	3.7	5.1	7.3	13.9
	80+	0.3	0.3	0.8	1.3	3.4
Male	60+	5.2	5.2	6.3	8.6	16.1
	65+	3.2	3.2	4.1	5.8	11.2
	80+	0.2	0.2	0.5	0.9	2.2
Ageing index		13.6	12.9	18.5	32.9	87.6
Broad age groups (percentage)	0-14	41.4	43.0	37.2	28.9	20.0
	15-59	53.0	51.4	55.9	61.6	62.5
	60+	5.6	5.5	6.9	9.5	17.5
Median age (years)		19.2	18.3	20.8*	26.4	35.9
Dependency ratio	Total	81.5	86.8	71.9	54.7	48.2
	Youth	75.1	80.4	64.0	44.6	29.6
	Old Age	6.3	6.4	7.9	10.1	18.6
Potential support ratio		15.8	15.6	12.6	9.9	5.4
Parent support ratio		0.8	0.9	2.2	3.9	7.2
Sex ratio (per 100 women)	60+	87.1	85.9	83.0	82.3	84.3
	65+	84.9	83.3	80.2	79.0	80.2
	80+	75.7	70.9	67.1	64.3	63.0

* *Estimate refers to year 2005.*

Indicator	Age	1950-1955	1975-1980	2005-2010	2025-2030	2045-2050
Growth rate (percentage)	Total	2.0	2.4	1.8	1.0	0.5
	60+	1.6	2.1	3.1	3.3	3.0
	65+	1.2	2.9	2.8	3.4	3.1
	80+	1.8	4.2	5.9	4.9	4.2
Total fertility rate (per woman)		6.8	5.8	3.5	2.3	1.9
Life expectancy (years)						
Total	Birth	40.4	50.0	65.6	71.7	76.5
	60	..	..	18.4	20.7	22.8
	65	..	..	14.8	16.9	18.8
	80	..	..	6.4	7.8	8.9
Female	Birth	42.5	52.1	67.7	74.0	79.0
	60	..	..	19.4	22.0	24.5
	65	..	..	15.6	18.0	20.3
	80	..	..	6.7	8.3	9.6
Male	Birth	38.5	48.0	63.4	69.4	74.0
	60	..	..	17.4	19.3	21.0
	65	..	..	13.9	15.6	17.2
	80	..	..	6.0	7.1	8.0
Survival rate (percentage)						
Total	60	..	..	71.9	80.1	86.0
	65	..	..	66.3	75.2	81.9
	80	..	..	32.1	43.5	54.1
Female	60	..	..	75.2	82.9	88.6
	65	..	..	70.2	79.0	85.5
	80	..	..	36.7	49.7	61.7
Male	60	..	..	68.7	77.2	83.5
	65	..	..	62.3	71.4	78.4
	80	..	..	27.3	37.2	46.4

		1980	1990	2007	2010	2020
Labour force participation (percentage)						
Total	65+	50.2	43.5	60.1	60.7	60.8
Female	65+	26.3	32.2	40.9	40.9	40.9
Male	65+	78.9	57.1	84.0	85.4	86.0

Percentage married, age 60+			Percentage living alone, age 60+ (1998)		
Total	Female	Male	Total	Female	Male
59.7	47.0	75.0	13.2	14.4	11.7

Statutory pensionable age (2006)			Percentage illiterate, age 65+ (2001)		
	Female	Male	Total	Female	Male
	65	65	51.9	66.3	34.5

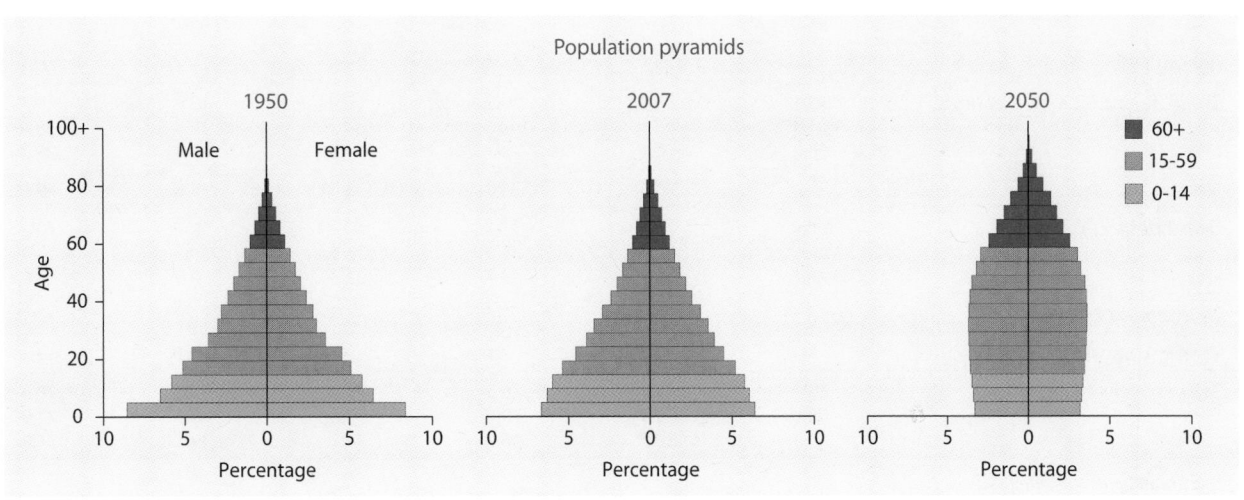

Population pyramids

Bosnia and Herzegovina

Indicator	Age	1950	1975	2007	2025	2050
Population (thousands)						
Total	Total	2 661.3	3 747.1	3 919.7	3 741.0	3 170.5
	0-14	1 006.2	1 156.6	622.1	509.2	434.8
	15-59	1 493.4	2 286.4	2 516.7	2 206.7	1 605.0
	60-64	55.2	98.2	201.7	269.3	249.8
	65-69	36.5	91.7	216.4	239.5	234.1
	70-74	34.3	59.5	182.6	205.0	214.7
	75-79	22.1	35.9	112.2	137.8	178.5
	80-84			50.8	90.0	127.5
	85-89			12.0	59.6	79.9
	90-94	13.6	18.8	3.9	19.5	34.5
	95-99			1.0	3.9	10.1
	100+			0.1	0.4	1.6
Female	Total	1 376.7	1 905.0	2 017.7	1 926.2	1 625.6
	0-14	500.7	563.7	302.2	245.8	209.7
	15-59	780.3	1 169.0	1 266.9	1 095.8	782.1
	60-64	31.5	57.4	109.5	141.9	127.1
	65-69	20.8	49.6	121.0	129.7	122.3
	70-74	21.0	32.3	104.4	114.8	116.0
	75-79	13.8	21.0	67.4	81.8	101.3
	80-84			33.9	57.6	78.2
	85-89			8.7	41.0	53.5
	90-94	8.6	12.0	2.8	14.4	25.6
	95-99			0.7	3.2	8.2
	100+			0.1	0.3	1.4
Male	Total	1 284.6	1 842.1	1 902.0	1 814.8	1 544.9
	0-14	505.5	592.9	319.9	263.4	225.0
	15-59	713.1	1 117.4	1 249.8	1 110.9	822.9
	60-64	23.7	40.8	92.2	127.4	122.7
	65-69	15.7	42.1	95.4	109.8	111.7
	70-74	13.3	27.2	78.2	90.2	98.7
	75-79	8.3	14.9	44.8	56.0	77.2
	80-84			16.9	32.4	49.3
	85-89			3.3	18.7	26.4
	90-94	5.0	6.8	1.1	5.1	8.9
	95-99			0.3	0.8	1.9
	100+			0.0	0.1	0.2
Percentage in older ages						
Total	60+	6.1	8.1	19.9	27.4	35.7
	65+	4.0	5.5	14.8	20.2	27.8
	80+	0.5	0.5	1.7	4.6	8.0
Female	60+	7.0	9.0	22.2	30.4	39.0
	65+	4.7	6.0	16.8	23.0	31.2
	80+	0.6	0.6	2.3	6.0	10.3
Male	60+	5.1	7.2	17.5	24.3	32.2
	65+	3.3	4.9	12.6	17.3	24.2
	80+	0.4	0.4	1.1	3.1	5.6
Ageing index		16.1	26.3	125.5	201.3	260.1
Broad age groups (percentage)	0-14	37.8	30.9	15.9	13.6	13.7
	15-59	56.1	61.0	64.2	59.0	50.6
	60+	6.1	8.1	19.9	27.4	35.7
Median age (years)		20.0	24.0	38.0*	44.8	49.5
Dependency ratio	Total	71.9	57.1	44.2	51.1	70.9
	Youth	65.0	48.5	22.9	20.6	23.4
	Old Age	6.9	8.6	21.3	30.5	47.5
Potential support ratio		14.5	11.6	4.7	3.3	2.1
Parent support ratio		2.0	2.1	2.4	10.2	18.4
Sex ratio (per 100 women)	60+	69.0	76.5	74.1	75.3	78.4
	65+	65.9	79.2	70.8	70.7	73.9
	80+	58.2	56.7	46.7	49.1	51.9

* Estimate refers to year 2005.

Indicator	Age	1950-1955	1975-1980	2005-2010	2025-2030	2045-2050
Growth rate (percentage)	Total	2.0	0.9	0.1	–0.6	–0.7
	60+	0.3	0.6	2.0	0.6	0.2
	65+	0.3	2.9	2.2	1.2	0.2
	80+	1.2	6.7	10.9	0.6	0.8
Total fertility rate (per woman)		4.8	2.2	1.3	1.5	1.8
Life expectancy (years)						
Total	Birth	53.7	69.8	74.9	77.0	79.0
	60	..	..	19.4	20.5	21.9
	65	..	..	15.7	16.7	18.0
	80	..	..	7.2	7.7	8.4
Female	Birth	54.8	72.1	77.5	79.5	81.5
	60	..	..	21.0	22.4	23.9
	65	..	..	17.0	18.3	19.7
	80	..	..	7.6	8.4	9.3
Male	Birth	52.6	67.4	72.1	74.4	76.4
	60	..	..	17.5	18.5	19.8
	65	..	..	14.1	14.9	16.0
	80	..	..	6.4	6.6	7.2
Survival rate (percentage)						
Total	60	..	..	87.4	90.2	92.0
	65	..	..	81.1	84.6	87.4
	80	..	..	42.6	48.5	54.7
Female	60	..	..	91.1	92.7	94.1
	65	..	..	86.3	88.7	90.8
	80	..	..	51.0	57.4	63.6
Male	60	..	..	83.8	87.6	90.0
	65	..	..	75.8	80.5	84.0
	80	..	..	33.8	39.3	45.7

		1980	1990	2007	2010	2020
Labour force participation (percentage)						
Total	65+	12.0	11.8	6.0	5.8	5.8
Female	65+	7.3	7.6	5.8	5.8	5.8
Male	65+	18.4	18.6	6.3	5.9	5.8

Percentage married, age 60+			Percentage living alone, age 60+		
Total	Female	Male	Total	Female	Male
..	..	..	..	..	..

Statutory pensionable age (2006)			Percentage illiterate, age 65+ (2000)		
	Female	Male	Total	Female	Male
	..	..	16.8	27.4	4.7

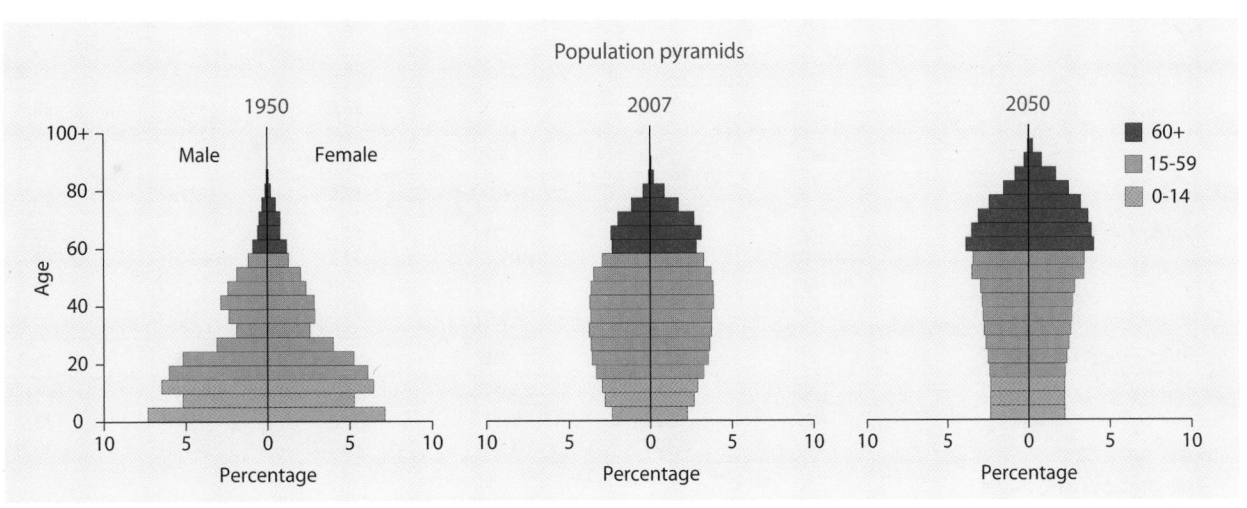

Population pyramids

Botswana

Indicator	Age	1950	1975	2007	2025	2050
Population (thousands)						
Total	Total	448.8	884.6	1 753.1	1 655.0	1 657.5
	0-14	199.6	432.7	648.3	567.3	471.7
	15-59	219.1	415.1	1 007.9	955.6	1 073.3
	60-64	10.9	11.6	34.1	30.9	41.2
	65-69	8.7	9.1	26.2	34.3	28.0
	70-74	5.9	7.9	18.0	30.9	14.8
	75-79	3.0	4.5	10.3	20.2	10.3
	80-84			5.8	10.6	8.6
	85-89			2.1	4.2	6.2
	90-94	1.6	3.7	0.4	0.9	2.8
	95-99			0.0	0.1	0.6
	100+			0.0	0.0	0.1
Female	Total	235.2	456.3	888.2	797.2	784.9
	0-14	99.7	215.6	321.6	281.0	232.8
	15-59	116.3	220.4	509.0	438.9	507.7
	60-64	6.9	6.3	19.3	16.6	14.2
	65-69	5.5	4.7	15.4	19.7	9.1
	70-74	3.8	4.2	11.1	18.4	4.9
	75-79	2.0	2.5	6.6	12.4	4.4
	80-84			3.7	6.8	4.9
	85-89			1.4	2.8	4.2
	90-94	1.1	2.4	0.3	0.7	2.1
	95-99			0.0	0.1	0.5
	100+			0.0	0.0	0.0
Male	Total	213.6	428.3	864.9	857.8	872.6
	0-14	99.9	217.1	326.8	286.2	238.9
	15-59	102.8	194.6	498.9	516.7	565.6
	60-64	4.1	5.3	14.8	14.3	27.0
	65-69	3.2	4.4	10.8	14.6	18.9
	70-74	2.1	3.7	6.9	12.5	9.9
	75-79	1.0	2.0	3.7	7.9	5.8
	80-84			2.1	3.9	3.8
	85-89			0.7	1.4	2.0
	90-94	0.5	1.2	0.1	0.3	0.6
	95-99			0.0	0.0	0.1
	100+			0.0	0.0	0.0
Percentage in older ages						
Total	60+	6.7	4.2	5.5	8.0	6.8
	65+	4.3	2.9	3.6	6.1	4.3
	80+	0.4	0.4	0.5	1.0	1.1
Female	60+	8.2	4.4	6.5	9.7	5.7
	65+	5.3	3.0	4.3	7.6	3.8
	80+	0.5	0.5	0.6	1.3	1.5
Male	60+	5.1	3.9	4.5	6.4	7.8
	65+	3.2	2.6	2.8	4.7	4.7
	80+	0.2	0.3	0.3	0.6	0.7
Ageing index		15.1	8.5	14.9	23.3	23.9
Broad age groups (percentage)	0-14	44.5	48.9	37.0	34.3	28.5
	15-59	48.8	46.9	57.5	57.7	64.8
	60+	6.7	4.2	5.5	8.0	6.8
Median age (years)		17.6	15.5	19.9*	22.0	25.7
Dependency ratio	Total	95.1	107.3	68.2	67.8	48.7
	Youth	86.8	101.4	62.2	57.5	42.3
	Old Age	8.4	5.9	6.0	10.3	6.4
Potential support ratio		12.0	16.9	16.6	9.7	15.6
Parent support ratio		1.4	2.3	1.8	6.6	6.0
Sex ratio (per 100 women)	60+	56.7	82.0	68.1	71.0	153.6
	65+	55.2	81.3	63.6	66.7	136.4
	80+	48.7	51.4	55.1	53.6	55.1

* Estimate refers to year 2005.

Indicator	Age	1950-1955	1975-1980	2005-2010	2025-2030	2045-2050
Growth rate (percentage)	Total	2.6	3.4	−0.4	−0.2	0.2
	60+	1.3	2.1	3.2	−1.8	3.0
	65+	2.1	1.1	3.2	−0.5	1.6
	80+	3.3	0.3	2.1	3.9	−4.2
Total fertility rate (per woman)		6.7	6.4	2.9	2.3	1.9
Life expectancy (years)						
Total	Birth	47.6	60.0	33.9	44.0	53.8
	60	..	..	16.8	17.5	18.7
	65	..	..	13.8	14.7	15.5
	80	..	..	6.0	6.5	7.0
Female	Birth	49.5	61.7	32.7	41.0	53.2
	60	..	..	17.8	18.6	20.9
	65	..	..	14.6	15.6	17.2
	80	..	..	6.2	6.8	7.7
Male	Birth	45.6	58.1	35.0	46.4	54.6
	60	..	..	15.4	16.2	17.4
	65	..	..	12.8	13.5	14.3
	80	..	..	5.6	5.9	6.1
Survival rate (percentage)						
Total	60	..	..	10.7	19.2	37.9
	65	..	..	9.3	16.8	34.2
	80	..	..	4.1	8.2	17.8
Female	60	..	..	9.1	13.2	35.6
	65	..	..	8.2	11.7	33.2
	80	..	..	3.9	6.3	20.1
Male	60	..	..	12.2	24.6	40.3
	65	..	..	10.4	21.1	35.7
	80	..	..	4.0	8.9	16.8

		1980	1990	2007	2010	2020
Labour force participation (percentage)						
Total	65+	52.5	40.3	33.6	34.2	35.2
Female	65+	36.0	25.0	24.9	27.3	32.6
Male	65+	73.0	61.9	47.2	44.8	39.1

Percentage married, age 60+				Percentage living alone, age 60+		
Total	Female	Male		Total	Female	Male
53.0	37.0	77.0		..	..	..

Statutory pensionable age (2006)				Percentage illiterate, age 65+ (2003)		
	Female	Male		Total	Female	Male
	65	65		69.1	73.2	63.7

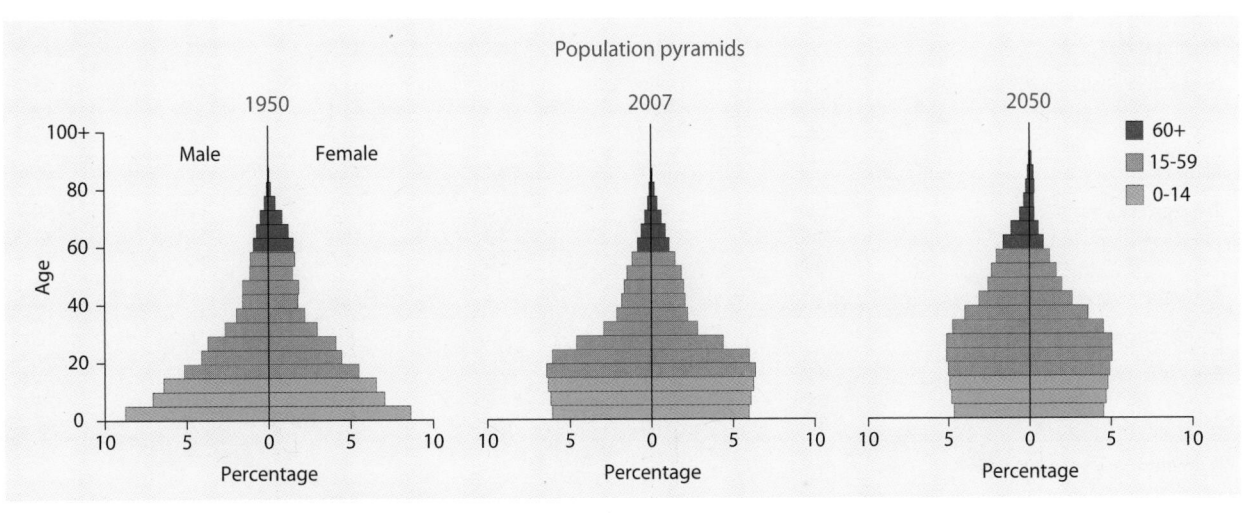

Population pyramids

Brazil

Indicator	Age	1950	1975	2007	2025	2050
Population (thousands)						
Total	Total	53 974.7	108 124.4	191 341.4	227 929.7	253 105.3
	0-14	22 432.0	43 588.1	52 450.6	50 642.3	44 861.0
	15-59	28 915.5	58 038.2	121 206.5	142 139.0	144 936.9
	60-64	1 021.6	2 293.9	5 491.2	10 823.4	14 614.6
	65-69	723.1	1 737.3	4 310.1	8 539.9	14 150.5
	70-74	462.6	1 183.0	3 188.7	6 407.5	11 666.1
	75-79	267.1	797.1	2 238.9	4 297.1	8 887.5
	80-84			1 384.1	2 574.3	6 582.2
	85-89			694.1	1 518.1	4 402.4
	90-94	152.7	486.9	278.9	670.7	2 112.3
	95-99			80.3	250.3	732.0
	100+			17.9	67.1	159.8
Female	Total	27 198.7	54 164.3	97 105.8	116 252.0	129 882.6
	0-14	11 146.0	21 656.9	25 730.9	24 797.0	21 932.7
	15-59	14 602.5	29 083.4	61 576.1	71 759.1	72 261.1
	60-64	560.4	1 176.3	2 936.1	5 821.5	7 651.0
	65-69	393.3	903.3	2 346.5	4 676.8	7 571.5
	70-74	256.2	628.9	1 777.0	3 589.1	6 479.6
	75-79	151.0	438.2	1 281.2	2 480.1	5 152.4
	80-84			811.7	1 539.5	3 985.3
	85-89			416.4	944.2	2 802.8
	90-94	89.3	277.3	169.9	433.6	1 418.9
	95-99			49.2	167.0	515.8
	100+			10.7	44.1	111.5
Male	Total	26 776.0	53 960.2	94 235.6	111 677.7	123 222.7
	0-14	11 286.0	21 931.2	26 719.7	25 845.3	22 928.3
	15-59	14 313.1	28 954.8	59 630.4	70 380.0	72 675.8
	60-64	461.2	1 117.6	2 555.1	5 001.8	6 963.5
	65-69	329.8	834.1	1 963.6	3 863.1	6 578.9
	70-74	206.5	554.1	1 411.7	2 818.3	5 186.6
	75-79	116.1	358.9	957.7	1 817.1	3 735.1
	80-84			572.4	1 034.7	2 596.9
	85-89			277.7	573.9	1 599.6
	90-94	63.4	209.6	109.0	237.1	693.4
	95-99			31.2	83.3	216.3
	100+			7.2	23.0	48.3
Percentage in older ages						
Total	60+	4.9	6.0	9.2	15.4	25.0
	65+	3.0	3.9	6.4	10.7	19.2
	80+	0.3	0.5	1.3	2.2	5.5
Female	60+	5.3	6.3	10.1	16.9	27.5
	65+	3.3	4.1	7.1	11.9	21.6
	80+	0.3	0.5	1.5	2.7	6.8
Male	60+	4.4	5.7	8.4	13.8	22.4
	65+	2.7	3.6	5.7	9.4	16.8
	80+	0.2	0.4	1.1	1.7	4.2
Ageing index		11.7	14.9	33.7	69.4	141.1
Broad age groups (percentage)	0-14	41.6	40.3	27.4	22.2	17.7
	15-59	53.6	53.7	63.3	62.4	57.3
	60+	4.9	6.0	9.2	15.4	25.0
Median age (years)		19.2	19.4	26.8*	33.4	40.3
Dependency ratio	Total	80.3	79.2	51.0	49.0	58.6
	Youth	74.9	72.2	41.4	33.1	28.1
	Old Age	5.4	7.0	9.6	15.9	30.5
Potential support ratio		18.6	14.4	10.4	6.3	3.3
Parent support ratio		1.2	1.7	4.8	7.0	16.5
Sex ratio (per 100 women)	60+	81.2	89.8	80.5	78.5	77.4
	65+	80.4	87.1	77.7	75.3	73.7
	80+	71.0	75.6	68.4	62.4	58.3

* Estimate refers to year 2005.

Indicator	Age	1950-1955	1975-1980	2005-2010	2025-2030	2045-2050
Growth rate (percentage)	Total	3.1	2.4	1.3	0.7	0.2
	60+	3.8	2.9	3.6	2.9	1.6
	65+	3.8	3.5	3.3	3.8	2.3
	80+	4.0	5.1	5.3	4.4	2.7
Total fertility rate (per woman)		6.2	4.3	2.2	1.9	1.9
Life expectancy (years)						
Total	Birth	50.9	61.5	71.9	76.2	79.2
	60	..	..	21.0	22.8	24.2
	65	..	..	17.6	19.1	20.3
	80	..	..	9.1	9.7	10.2
Female	Birth	52.6	63.9	75.7	79.8	82.7
	60	..	..	22.5	24.6	26.2
	65	..	..	18.8	20.6	22.0
	80	..	..	9.6	10.4	11.0
Male	Birth	48.7	59.2	68.2	72.6	75.7
	60	..	..	19.4	20.9	21.9
	65	..	..	16.2	17.4	18.2
	80	..	..	8.5	8.9	9.1
Survival rate (percentage)						
Total	60	..	..	78.7	84.3	88.2
	65	..	..	72.7	79.3	84.0
	80	..	..	42.6	51.8	59.0
Female	60	..	..	84.7	89.0	92.2
	65	..	..	79.6	85.0	89.1
	80	..	..	50.8	60.6	68.5
Male	60	..	..	72.8	79.6	84.4
	65	..	..	65.9	73.5	79.0
	80	..	..	34.7	43.0	49.3

		1980	1990	2007	2010	2020
Labour force participation (percentage)						
Total	65+	19.7	18.2	22.9	22.7	22.3
Female	65+	5.6	5.3	14.2	14.7	16.5
Male	65+	35.6	33.5	34.0	33.1	30.0

Percentage married, age 60+			Percentage living alone, age 60+ (1996)		
Total	Female	Male	Total	Female	Male
58.3	42.0	78.0	8.8	11.7	5.3

Statutory pensionable age (2006)			Percentage illiterate, age 65+ (2004)		
	Female	Male	Total	Female	Male
	60	65	34.2	36.4	31.4

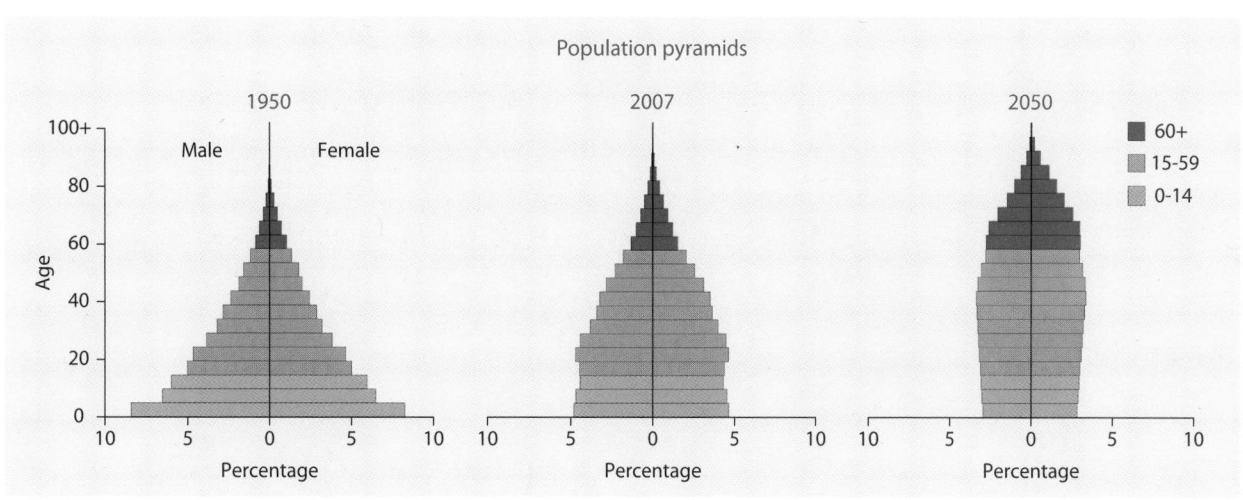

Population pyramids

United Nations Department of Economic and Social Affairs, Population Division

Brunei Darussalam

Indicator	Age	1950	1975	2007	2025	2050
Population (thousands)						
Total	Total	48.0	160.8	390.0	526.3	680.6
	0-14	17.5	64.5	112.3	116.5	126.8
	15-59	26.9	87.3	258.2	350.8	417.4
	60-64	1.3	3.3	7.0	19.0	35.7
	65-69	1.0	2.4	4.7	17.4	31.4
	70-74	0.7	1.6	3.8	12.1	26.7
	75-79	0.4	1.0	2.4	6.3	19.4
	80-84			1.1	2.5	13.3
	85-89			0.4	1.2	6.3
	90-94	0.4	0.7	0.1	0.5	2.8
	95-99			0.0	0.1	0.7
	100+			0.0	0.0	0.1
Female	Total	23.3	77.8	188.4	258.6	342.3
	0-14	8.4	31.4	54.1	56.0	61.0
	15-59	13.0	41.9	125.6	176.4	208.4
	60-64	0.7	1.6	2.6	8.7	17.9
	65-69	0.5	1.2	1.8	7.4	16.1
	70-74	0.4	0.8	1.9	5.0	14.0
	75-79	0.2	0.5	1.2	2.6	10.5
	80-84			0.6	1.2	7.8
	85-89			0.3	0.7	3.9
	90-94	0.2	0.4	0.1	0.4	2.0
	95-99			0.0	0.1	0.6
	100+			0.0	0.0	0.1
Male	Total	24.7	83.0	201.7	267.7	338.3
	0-14	9.1	33.1	58.3	60.5	65.8
	15-59	13.9	45.4	132.6	174.4	209.0
	60-64	0.6	1.7	4.4	10.3	17.9
	65-69	0.5	1.2	2.8	10.0	15.2
	70-74	0.3	0.8	1.9	7.1	12.7
	75-79	0.2	0.5	1.1	3.6	8.9
	80-84			0.5	1.3	5.5
	85-89			0.1	0.4	2.4
	90-94	0.2	0.3	0.0	0.1	0.8
	95-99			0.0	0.0	0.1
	100+			0.0	0.0	0.0
Percentage in older ages						
Total	60+	7.6	5.6	5.0	11.2	20.0
	65+	4.9	3.5	3.2	7.6	14.8
	80+	0.7	0.4	0.4	0.8	3.4
Female	60+	8.2	5.8	4.6	10.1	21.3
	65+	5.4	3.7	3.2	6.8	16.1
	80+	0.8	0.5	0.6	0.9	4.2
Male	60+	7.0	5.4	5.4	12.3	18.8
	65+	4.4	3.4	3.2	8.4	13.5
	80+	0.6	0.4	0.3	0.7	2.6
Ageing index		20.8	13.9	17.4	50.6	107.6
Broad age groups (percentage)	0-14	36.4	40.1	28.8	22.1	18.6
	15-59	56.0	54.3	66.2	66.7	61.3
	60+	7.6	5.6	5.0	11.2	20.0
Median age (years)		22.4	19.8	26.2*	31.5	37.4
Dependency ratio	Total	70.4	77.5	47.1	42.3	50.2
	Youth	62.1	71.2	42.4	31.5	28.0
	Old Age	8.3	6.3	4.7	10.8	22.2
Potential support ratio		12.0	15.9	21.1	9.3	4.5
Parent support ratio		2.3	1.5	1.6	2.4	8.3
Sex ratio (per 100 women)	60+	90.3	99.9	125.3	125.2	87.1
	65+	87.2	96.4	106.9	128.5	83.0
	80+	82.1	74.2	56.4	75.4	61.6

Estimate refers to year 2005.

Indicator	Age	1950-1955	1975-1980	2005-2010	2025-2030	2045-2050
Growth rate (percentage)	Total	5.6	3.7	2.1	1.3	0.8
	60+	3.8	−1.6	6.0	4.5	2.5
	65+	3.5	−0.6	3.6	4.4	2.8
	80+	−3.5	3.8	5.3	8.4	5.0
Total fertility rate (per woman)		7.0	4.4	2.3	1.9	1.9
Life expectancy (years)						
Total	Birth	60.4	69.7	77.1	79.1	81.1
	60	..	..	20.1	21.6	23.3
	65	..	..	16.0	17.4	19.0
	80	..	..	7.0	7.8	8.8
Female	Birth	61.1	71.4	79.7	82.0	83.7
	60	..	..	22.4	24.2	25.6
	65	..	..	18.3	20.0	21.3
	80	..	..	8.6	9.6	10.4
Male	Birth	59.6	68.1	75.0	77.0	78.7
	60	..	..	18.3	19.8	21.2
	65	..	..	14.2	15.6	16.9
	80	..	..	5.2	6.3	7.1
Survival rate (percentage)						
Total	60	..	..	91.8	93.4	94.4
	65	..	..	87.3	89.7	91.3
	80	..	..	47.4	54.2	61.6
Female	60	..	..	93.1	94.6	95.5
	65	..	..	88.9	91.2	92.7
	80	..	..	56.9	64.3	69.4
Male	60	..	..	90.7	92.3	93.4
	65	..	..	85.9	88.2	89.8
	80	..	..	39.4	47.1	53.6

		1980	1990	2007	2010	2020
Labour force participation (percentage)						
Total	65+	31.0	19.6	12.6	11.9	9.3
Female	65+	6.4	4.3	2.7	2.6	2.6
Male	65+	53.4	34.0	21.8	19.9	14.3

Percentage married, age 60+				Percentage living alone, age 60+		
Total	Female	Male		Total	Female	Male
67.0	50.0	83.0		..	..	..

Statutory pensionable age (2006)				Percentage illiterate, age 65+ (2001)		
	Female	Male		Total	Female	Male
	55	55		62.4	80.3	43.7

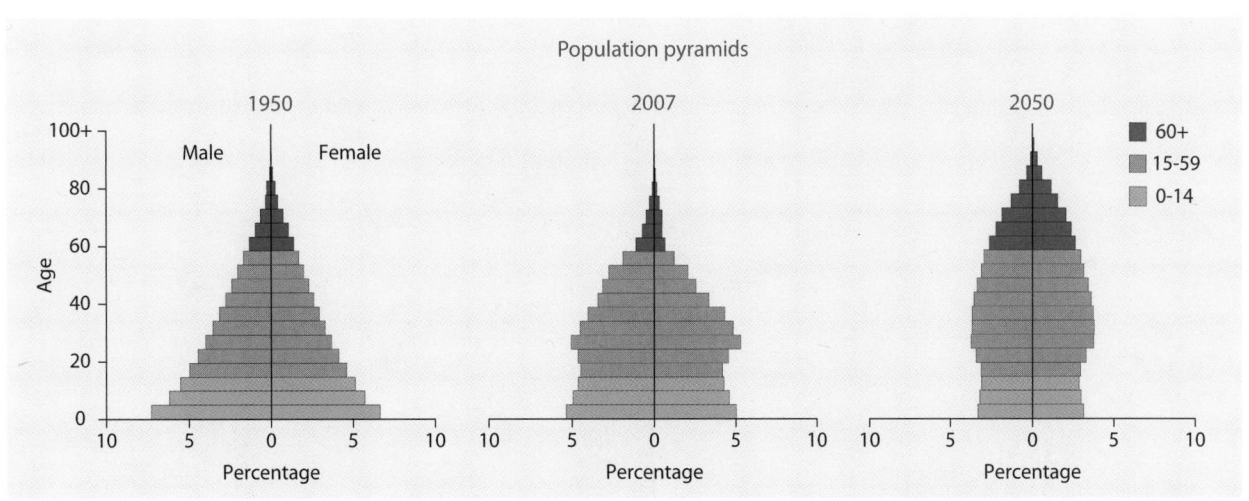

Population pyramids

Bulgaria

Indicator	Age	1950	1975	2007	2025	2050
Population (thousands)						
Total	Total	7 251.0	8 720.7	7 615.7	6 552.4	5 064.7
	0-14	1 942.0	1 919.8	1 013.3	807.9	651.5
	15-59	4 572.0	5 396.5	4 854.7	3 896.6	2 449.9
	60-64	249.0	451.4	462.5	442.6	432.1
	65-69	208.0	389.3	384.6	431.9	419.1
	70-74	146.2	279.9	368.1	389.0	405.8
	75-79	84.2	161.4	287.7	303.4	316.4
	80-84			177.3	164.5	204.6
	85-89			52.0	81.1	116.8
	90-94	49.7	122.4	13.2	29.5	51.6
	95-99			2.2	5.4	14.5
	100+			0.2	0.5	2.2
Female	Total	3 627.0	4 366.9	3 932.8	3 400.6	2 625.1
	0-14	954.0	933.1	493.0	392.5	316.1
	15-59	2 273.0	2 688.4	2 431.8	1 926.9	1 198.6
	60-64	138.0	229.6	250.2	234.7	219.9
	65-69	110.0	203.5	214.7	239.2	217.9
	70-74	78.2	149.8	211.8	225.5	220.5
	75-79	45.8	90.1	172.5	186.4	183.3
	80-84			112.8	108.4	129.2
	85-89			35.0	58.4	82.7
	90-94	28.0	72.4	9.3	23.5	41.7
	95-99			1.7	4.7	13.1
	100+			0.1	0.5	2.1
Male	Total	3 624.0	4 353.8	3 682.9	3 151.8	2 439.6
	0-14	988.0	986.7	520.3	415.4	335.4
	15-59	2 299.0	2 708.1	2 422.9	1 969.7	1 251.4
	60-64	111.0	221.8	212.2	207.9	212.2
	65-69	98.0	185.9	169.9	192.7	201.2
	70-74	68.0	130.1	156.3	163.5	185.3
	75-79	38.4	71.3	115.3	117.0	133.1
	80-84			64.6	56.1	75.5
	85-89			17.0	22.7	34.1
	90-94	21.7	49.9	3.9	6.0	9.9
	95-99			0.5	0.7	1.4
	100+			0.0	0.0	0.1
Percentage in older ages						
Total	60+	10.2	16.1	22.9	28.2	38.8
	65+	6.7	10.9	16.9	21.4	30.2
	80+	0.7	1.4	3.2	4.3	7.7
Female	60+	11.0	17.1	25.6	31.8	42.3
	65+	7.2	11.8	19.3	24.9	33.9
	80+	0.8	1.7	4.0	5.8	10.2
Male	60+	9.3	15.1	20.1	24.3	35.0
	65+	6.2	10.0	14.3	17.7	26.3
	80+	0.6	1.1	2.3	2.7	5.0
Ageing index		38.0	73.2	172.5	228.7	301.3
Broad age groups (percentage)	0-14	26.8	22.0	13.3	12.3	12.9
	15-59	63.1	61.9	63.7	59.5	48.4
	60+	10.2	16.1	22.9	28.2	38.8
Median age (years)		27.3	34.0	40.6*	46.1	51.2
Dependency ratio	Total	50.4	49.1	43.2	51.0	75.7
	Youth	40.3	32.8	19.1	18.6	22.6
	Old Age	10.1	16.3	24.2	32.4	53.1
Potential support ratio		9.9	6.1	4.1	3.1	1.9
Parent support ratio		1.8	3.1	4.3	8.1	17.3
Sex ratio (per 100 women)	60+	84.3	88.4	73.4	70.9	76.8
	65+	86.3	84.8	69.6	66.0	71.9
	80+	77.4	68.9	54.1	43.7	45.0

* Estimate refers to year 2005.

Indicator	Age	1950-1955	1975-1980	2005-2010	2025-2030	2045-2050
Growth rate (percentage)	Total	0.7	0.3	−0.7	−1.0	−1.1
	60+	1.6	−0.2	0.6	−0.1	0.1
	65+	2.6	2.0	−0.3	0.0	0.3
	80+	5.5	2.6	3.0	2.8	0.6
Total fertility rate (per woman)		2.5	2.2	1.2	1.5	1.8
Life expectancy (years)						
Total	Birth	64.1	71.0	73.0	76.0	78.8
	60	..	..	18.3	19.9	21.7
	65	..	..	14.7	16.1	17.7
	80	..	..	6.2	7.1	8.1
Female	Birth	66.1	73.6	76.3	79.0	81.6
	60	..	..	20.1	22.0	24.0
	65	..	..	16.1	17.8	19.7
	80	..	..	6.7	7.8	9.1
Male	Birth	62.2	68.5	69.8	73.0	75.9
	60	..	..	16.3	17.5	19.3
	65	..	..	13.0	14.0	15.5
	80	..	..	5.4	5.8	6.6
Survival rate (percentage)						
Total	60	..	..	84.8	89.0	92.0
	65	..	..	78.0	83.3	87.4
	80	..	..	37.7	45.9	54.4
Female	60	..	..	90.3	92.5	94.4
	65	..	..	85.6	88.7	91.3
	80	..	..	47.9	56.4	64.5
Male	60	..	..	79.3	85.6	89.7
	65	..	..	70.5	77.9	83.6
	80	..	..	27.9	35.1	44.1

		1980	1990	2007	2010	2020
Labour force participation (percentage)						
Total	65+	10.7	7.3	1.9	1.9	1.8
Female	65+	3.9	3.5	1.3	1.4	1.5
Male	65+	18.8	12.2	2.7	2.6	2.2

Percentage married, age 60+			Percentage living alone, age 60+ (1992)		
Total	Female	Male	Total	Female	Male
64.7	53.0	80.0	19.0	24.8	11.9

Statutory pensionable age (2006)		Percentage illiterate, age 65+ (2001)		
Female	Male	Total	Female	Male
57.5	62	3.8	5.0	2.3

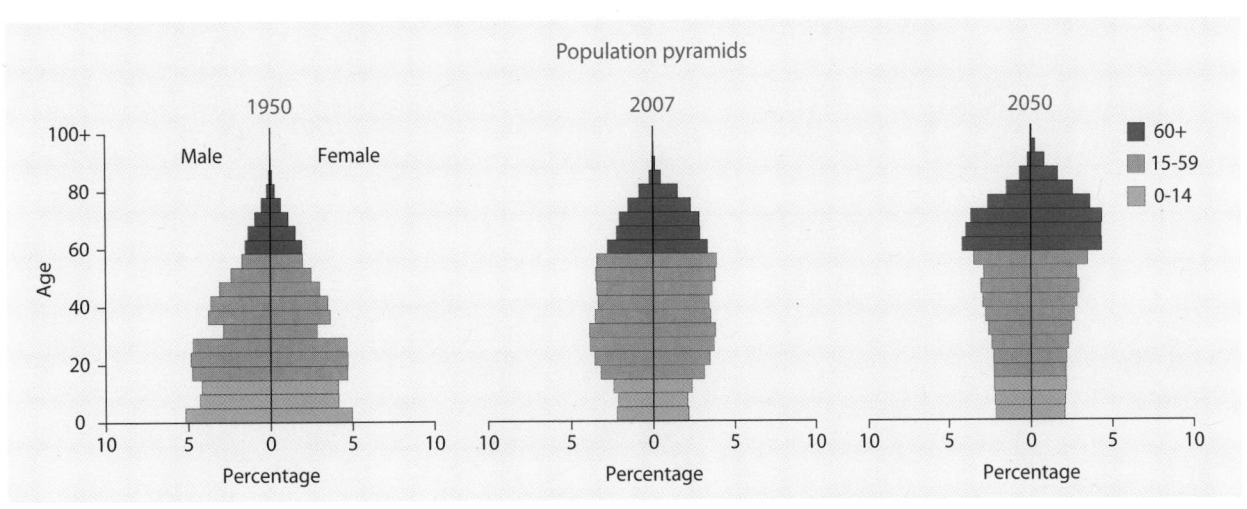

Population pyramids

Burkina Faso

Indicator	Age	1950	1975	2007	2025	2050
Population (thousands)						
Total	Total	3 860.6	5 947.3	14 042.3	23 162.5	39 093.2
	0-14	1 653.2	2 684.2	6 578.0	9 964.8	12 556.2
	15-59	2 033.8	2 918.5	6 879.4	12 329.0	23 904.8
	60-64	63.8	132.1	211.6	314.0	968.2
	65-69	50.2	96.0	156.1	229.1	692.1
	70-74	33.9	67.2	109.4	156.6	483.9
	75-79	17.6	36.9	66.6	106.0	311.3
	80-84			30.7	46.8	130.9
	85-89			9.0	13.7	38.3
	90-94	8.2	12.6	1.4	2.3	6.8
	95-99			0.1	0.2	0.6
	100+			0.0	0.0	0.0
Female	Total	1 737.3	2 898.1	6 974.7	11 439.7	19 291.7
	0-14	720.4	1 328.8	3 238.4	4 903.3	6 171.0
	15-59	919.3	1 408.1	3 428.6	6 048.9	11 747.1
	60-64	34.5	61.3	102.1	168.5	487.2
	65-69	28.2	44.9	83.1	131.5	355.7
	70-74	19.3	30.5	60.5	95.6	254.9
	75-79	10.5	17.4	38.3	55.4	170.3
	80-84			17.7	26.4	75.9
	85-89			5.2	8.5	24.3
	90-94	5.0	7.0	0.8	1.5	4.8
	95-99			0.1	0.1	0.5
	100+			0.0	0.0	0.0
Male	Total	2 123.3	3 049.3	7 067.6	11 722.7	19 801.5
	0-14	932.8	1 355.4	3 339.6	5 061.4	6 385.2
	15-59	1 114.5	1 510.4	3 450.7	6 280.1	12 157.7
	60-64	29.3	70.8	109.5	145.5	481.0
	65-69	22.0	51.0	73.0	97.6	336.4
	70-74	14.6	36.7	48.9	61.0	229.0
	75-79	7.1	19.5	28.3	50.6	141.0
	80-84			13.0	20.4	55.0
	85-89			3.8	5.2	14.0
	90-94	3.2	5.5	0.6	0.8	2.0
	95-99			0.0	0.1	0.1
	100+			0.0	0.0	0.0
Percentage in older ages						
Total	60+	4.5	5.8	4.2	3.8	6.7
	65+	2.8	3.6	2.7	2.4	4.3
	80+	0.2	0.2	0.3	0.3	0.5
Female	60+	5.6	5.6	4.4	4.3	7.1
	65+	3.6	3.4	2.9	2.8	4.6
	80+	0.3	0.2	0.3	0.3	0.5
Male	60+	3.6	6.0	3.9	3.3	6.4
	65+	2.2	3.7	2.4	2.0	3.9
	80+	0.1	0.2	0.2	0.2	0.4
Ageing index		10.5	12.8	8.9	8.7	21.0
Broad age groups (percentage)	0-14	42.8	45.1	46.8	43.0	32.1
	15-59	52.7	49.1	49.0	53.2	61.1
	60+	4.5	5.8	4.2	3.8	6.7
Median age (years)		18.4	17.4	16.2*	18.1	24.1
Dependency ratio	Total	84.1	95.0	98.0	83.2	57.2
	Youth	78.8	88.0	92.8	78.8	50.5
	Old Age	5.2	7.0	5.3	4.4	6.7
Potential support ratio		19.1	14.3	19.0	22.8	14.9
Parent support ratio		0.6	0.6	1.4	1.2	1.2
Sex ratio (per 100 women)	60+	77.9	113.8	90.1	78.2	91.6
	65+	74.2	112.9	81.6	73.9	87.7
	80+	62.9	78.6	73.6	72.6	67.5

* Estimate refers to year 2005.

Indicator	Age	1950-1955	1975-1980	2005-2010	2025-2030	2045-2050
Growth rate (percentage)	Total	1.3	2.0	2.9	2.5	1.7
	60+	0.7	2.1	2.3	3.9	4.5
	65+	0.5	2.6	1.9	3.2	4.4
	80+	0.7	7.0	1.8	3.8	6.0
Total fertility rate (per woman)		6.3	7.8	6.3	4.5	2.9
Life expectancy (years)						
Total	Birth	36.3	45.9	49.3	57.4	65.6
	60	..	..	15.7	16.9	18.4
	65	..	..	12.4	13.4	14.6
	80	..	..	4.9	5.3	5.8
Female	Birth	37.7	47.3	49.5	58.4	67.1
	60	..	..	16.1	17.8	19.4
	65	..	..	12.6	14.0	15.4
	80	..	..	5.0	5.5	6.0
Male	Birth	35.0	44.6	48.5	56.4	64.1
	60	..	..	15.0	16.0	17.3
	65	..	..	11.8	12.7	13.8
	80	..	..	4.7	5.0	5.4
Survival rate (percentage)						
Total	60	..	..	48.7	60.2	73.5
	65	..	..	43.1	54.6	68.2
	80	..	..	15.4	23.0	33.3
Female	60	..	..	49.0	61.7	75.7
	65	..	..	44.1	56.9	71.5
	80	..	..	16.2	25.8	38.2
Male	60	..	..	47.1	58.8	71.5
	65	..	..	41.0	52.3	65.2
	80	..	..	13.4	19.6	28.7

		1980	1990	2007	2010	2020
Labour force participation (percentage)						
Total	65+	62.1	61.1	58.6	58.1	55.8
Female	65+	41.8	43.5	46.6	46.8	47.6
Male	65+	80.5	79.2	73.2	71.6	66.1

Percentage married, age 60+			Percentage living alone, age 60+ (1999)		
Total	Female	Male	Total	Female	Male
60.0	37.0	87.0	2.3	2.4	2.3

Statutory pensionable age (2006)		Percentage illiterate, age 65+ (2003)		
Female	Male	Total	Female	Male
55	55	95.2	98.9	92.1

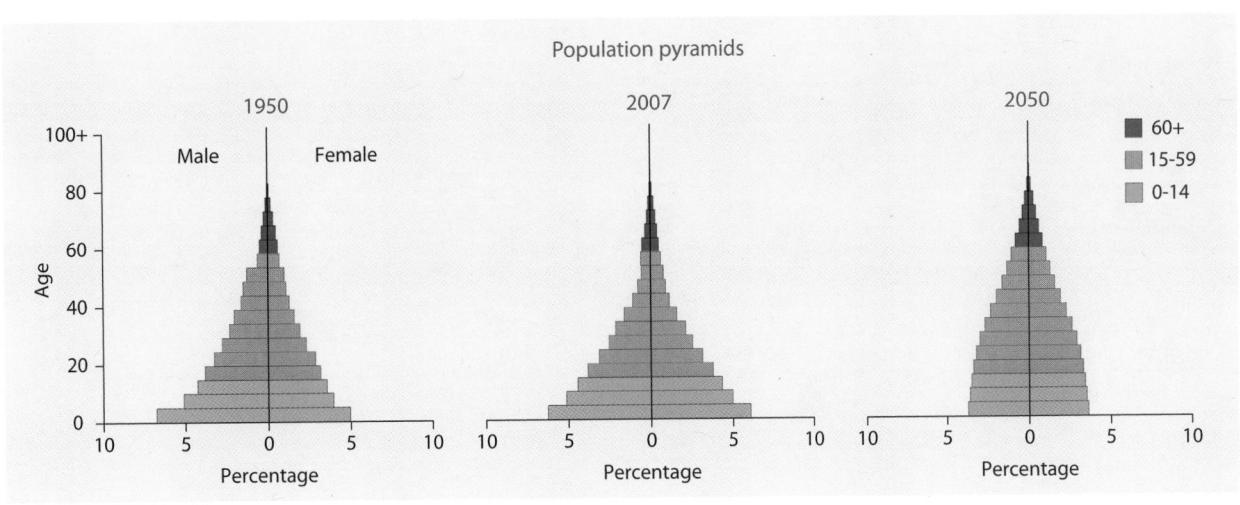

Population pyramids

Burundi

Indicator	Age	1950	1975	2007	2025	2050
Population (thousands)						
Total	Total	2 456.3	3 680.4	8 140.8	14 003.4	25 811.8
	0-14	1 004.2	1 674.5	3 607.7	6 495.9	9 938.8
	15-59	1 324.4	1 802.9	4 201.1	6 911.9	14 424.2
	60-64	48.1	76.5	116.0	201.6	542.9
	65-69	36.4	57.3	87.9	167.6	407.6
	70-74	23.8	38.1	61.5	120.9	250.0
	75-79	13.1	21.2	38.3	62.0	139.1
	80-84			19.5	29.9	69.9
	85-89			7.1	10.7	29.6
	90-94	6.3	9.9	1.6	2.6	8.4
	95-99			0.2	0.4	1.3
	100+			0.0	0.0	0.1
Female	Total	1 280.1	1 918.6	4 154.7	7 057.0	12 955.6
	0-14	512.6	837.9	1 801.0	3 244.3	4 951.2
	15-59	695.9	961.5	2 152.5	3 472.3	7 239.0
	60-64	26.6	43.9	68.4	109.9	277.5
	65-69	20.5	33.5	52.9	94.2	212.1
	70-74	13.4	22.6	37.7	70.0	133.6
	75-79	7.4	12.9	23.9	37.9	77.1
	80-84			12.4	19.1	40.5
	85-89			4.7	7.2	18.2
	90-94	3.7	6.3	1.1	1.8	5.5
	95-99			0.1	0.3	0.9
	100+			0.0	0.0	0.1
Male	Total	1 176.2	1 761.8	3 986.1	6 946.5	12 856.1
	0-14	491.6	836.6	1 806.7	3 251.6	4 987.5
	15-59	628.5	841.4	2 048.7	3 439.6	7 185.1
	60-64	21.5	32.6	47.7	91.7	265.4
	65-69	15.9	23.8	35.1	73.4	195.5
	70-74	10.4	15.5	23.8	50.9	116.4
	75-79	5.7	8.3	14.4	24.1	62.1
	80-84			7.0	10.8	29.4
	85-89			2.4	3.6	11.4
	90-94	2.6	3.6	0.5	0.8	2.9
	95-99			0.0	0.1	0.4
	100+			0.0	0.0	0.0
Percentage in older ages						
Total	60+	5.2	5.5	4.1	4.3	5.6
	65+	3.2	3.4	2.7	2.8	3.5
	80+	0.3	0.3	0.3	0.3	0.4
Female	60+	5.6	6.2	4.8	4.8	5.9
	65+	3.5	3.9	3.2	3.3	3.8
	80+	0.3	0.3	0.4	0.4	0.5
Male	60+	4.8	4.8	3.3	3.7	5.3
	65+	2.9	2.9	2.1	2.4	3.3
	80+	0.2	0.2	0.2	0.2	0.3
Ageing index		12.7	12.1	9.2	9.2	14.6
Broad age groups (percentage)	0-14	40.9	45.5	44.3	46.4	38.5
	15-59	53.9	49.0	51.6	49.4	55.9
	60+	5.2	5.5	4.1	4.3	5.6
Median age (years)		19.5	17.0	17.0*	16.6	20.3
Dependency ratio	Total	79.0	95.8	88.6	96.9	72.5
	Youth	73.2	89.1	83.6	91.3	66.4
	Old Age	5.8	6.7	5.0	5.5	6.1
Potential support ratio		17.2	14.9	20.0	18.1	16.5
Parent support ratio		0.9	0.9	1.7	1.9	2.1
Sex ratio (per 100 women)	60+	78.4	70.3	65.0	75.0	89.3
	65+	76.9	68.0	62.5	71.0	85.7
	80+	70.3	57.1	53.8	53.6	67.6

* Estimate refers to year 2005.

Burundi

Indicator	Age	1950-1955	1975-1980	2005-2010	2025-2030	2045-2050
Growth rate (percentage)	Total	1.8	2.3	3.7	2.6	2.1
	60+	1.0	2.0	2.9	2.1	4.6
	65+	1.1	2.4	2.6	2.6	5.3
	80+	1.8	4.3	2.4	3.7	2.1
Total fertility rate (per woman)		6.8	6.8	6.8	5.4	3.5
Life expectancy (years)						
Total	Birth	39.0	46.1	45.6	53.1	61.0
	60	..	..	15.9	16.8	18.1
	65	..	..	12.7	13.6	14.6
	80	..	..	5.6	6.0	6.4
Female	Birth	40.6	47.6	46.5	54.4	62.7
	60	..	..	16.4	17.5	18.9
	65	..	..	13.1	14.1	15.2
	80	..	..	5.8	6.2	6.6
Male	Birth	37.5	44.4	44.5	51.7	59.4
	60	..	..	15.1	16.0	17.3
	65	..	..	12.1	12.9	13.9
	80	..	..	5.3	5.6	6.1
Survival rate (percentage)						
Total	60	..	..	39.7	50.0	62.4
	65	..	..	34.8	44.5	56.9
	80	..	..	13.2	18.8	27.2
Female	60	..	..	41.0	51.6	64.5
	65	..	..	36.3	46.6	59.6
	80	..	..	14.5	20.9	30.3
Male	60	..	..	38.2	48.4	60.3
	65	..	..	32.9	42.4	54.2
	80	..	..	11.4	16.5	24.1

		1980	1990	2007	2010	2020
Labour force participation (percentage)						
Total	65+	76.0	75.9	79.7	79.7	79.6
Female	65+	72.3	73.9	76.4	76.2	75.6
Male	65+	81.5	78.8	85.1	85.3	85.4

Percentage married, age 60+			Percentage living alone, age 60+		
Total	Female	Male	Total	Female	Male
59.3	40.0	90.0	..	..	..

Statutory pensionable age (2006)			Percentage illiterate, age 65+ (2000)		
	Female	Male	Total	Female	Male
	60	60	81.4	90.4	73.3

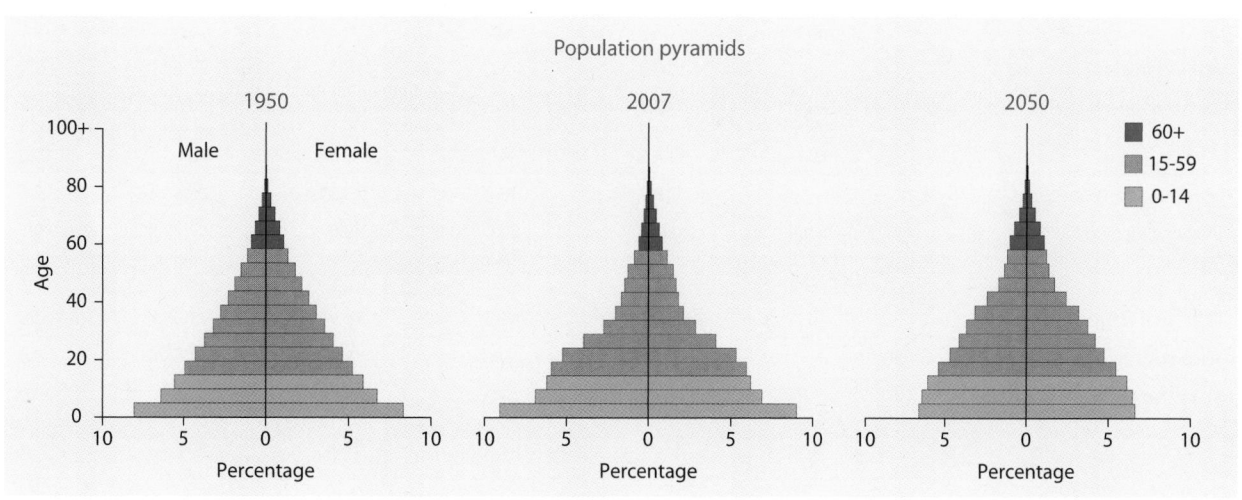

Population pyramids

United Nations Department of Economic and Social Affairs, Population Division

185

Cambodia

Indicator	Age	1950	1975	2007	2025	2050
Population (thousands)						
Total	Total	4 345.8	7 097.8	14 638.1	19 992.8	25 971.7
	0-14	1 834.7	2 999.1	5 270.1	6 191.4	5 985.7
	15-59	2 313.7	3 768.0	8 511.8	12 094.9	16 081.0
	60-64	79.8	132.2	331.6	586.2	1 340.6
	65-69	53.3	92.9	227.2	456.9	1 210.9
	70-74	35.0	58.8	152.2	326.7	480.1
	75-79	19.5	31.4	93.7	205.6	458.4
	80-84			38.6	97.7	277.0
	85-89			11.1	27.7	111.1
	90-94	9.8	15.4	1.7	5.2	24.3
	95-99			0.1	0.5	2.5
	100+			0.0	0.0	0.1
Female	Total	2 173.0	3 545.4	7 552.5	10 179.5	13 093.0
	0-14	910.3	1 485.2	2 589.5	3 031.6	2 929.8
	15-59	1 154.7	1 879.6	4 422.8	6 117.7	7 981.4
	60-64	42.5	70.0	197.5	341.7	704.9
	65-69	29.4	50.4	141.9	272.6	657.6
	70-74	19.5	32.8	101.1	197.9	274.7
	75-79	10.9	18.1	64.1	129.4	272.1
	80-84			27.2	64.5	176.6
	85-89			7.3	19.7	76.0
	90-94	5.7	9.3	1.1	4.0	17.9
	95-99			0.1	0.4	2.0
	100+			0.0	0.0	0.1
Male	Total	2 172.8	3 552.4	7 085.5	9 813.4	12 878.8
	0-14	924.4	1 513.9	2 680.6	3 159.9	3 055.9
	15-59	1 159.0	1 888.3	4 089.0	5 977.2	8 099.7
	60-64	37.3	62.2	134.1	244.5	635.7
	65-69	23.9	42.5	85.3	184.3	553.3
	70-74	15.5	26.0	51.2	128.8	205.4
	75-79	8.6	13.3	29.6	76.2	186.3
	80-84			11.4	33.2	100.4
	85-89			3.8	8.0	35.0
	90-94	4.1	6.1	0.6	1.2	6.4
	95-99			0.0	0.1	0.5
	100+			0.0	0.0	0.0
Percentage in older ages						
Total	60+	4.5	4.7	5.8	8.5	15.0
	65+	2.7	2.8	3.6	5.6	9.9
	80+	0.2	0.2	0.4	0.7	1.6
Female	60+	5.0	5.1	7.2	10.1	16.7
	65+	3.0	3.1	4.5	6.8	11.3
	80+	0.3	0.3	0.5	0.9	2.1
Male	60+	4.1	4.2	4.5	6.9	13.4
	65+	2.4	2.5	2.6	4.4	8.4
	80+	0.2	0.2	0.2	0.4	1.1
Ageing index		10.8	11.0	16.2	27.6	65.2
Broad age groups (percentage)	0-14	42.2	42.3	36.0	31.0	23.0
	15-59	53.2	53.1	58.1	60.5	61.9
	60+	4.5	4.7	5.8	8.5	15.0
Median age (years)		18.7	18.7	20.3*	25.4	32.6
Dependency ratio	Total	81.6	82.0	65.5	57.7	49.1
	Youth	76.7	76.9	59.6	48.8	34.4
	Old Age	4.9	5.1	5.9	8.8	14.7
Potential support ratio		20.4	19.6	16.9	11.3	6.8
Parent support ratio		0.7	0.6	1.0	1.6	3.3
Sex ratio (per 100 women)	60+	82.8	83.2	58.5	65.6	79.0
	65+	79.5	79.5	53.1	62.7	73.6
	80+	71.9	65.9	44.3	48.1	52.2

* *Estimate refers to year 2005.*

Indicator	Age	1950-1955	1975-1980	2005-2010	2025-2030	2045-2050
Growth rate (percentage)	Total	2.2	–1.4	2.0	1.3	0.8
	60+	2.0	–0.5	4.1	3.2	4.2
	65+	2.0	–1.2	4.5	3.8	6.3
	80+	1.6	–7.2	5.7	5.5	3.8
Total fertility rate (per woman)		6.3	4.7	3.7	2.6	2.1
Life expectancy (years)						
Total	Birth	39.4	31.2	58.0	66.0	71.1
	60	..	..	17.2	18.9	20.3
	65	..	..	13.6	15.0	16.3
	80	..	..	5.4	5.9	6.5
Female	Birth	40.8	32.5	61.3	68.2	73.4
	60	..	..	18.0	19.8	21.5
	65	..	..	14.1	15.7	17.2
	80	..	..	5.5	6.2	6.9
Male	Birth	38.1	30.0	54.6	63.5	68.7
	60	..	..	16.0	17.6	19.0
	65	..	..	12.7	14.0	15.1
	80	..	..	5.0	5.5	5.9
Survival rate (percentage)						
Total	60	..	..	61.8	73.4	80.5
	65	..	..	56.4	68.5	76.4
	80	..	..	24.2	35.1	44.2
Female	60	..	..	68.8	77.6	84.1
	65	..	..	63.8	73.6	80.9
	80	..	..	29.3	40.5	50.6
Male	60	..	..	54.5	69.0	77.1
	65	..	..	48.5	63.1	71.9
	80	..	..	18.2	28.8	37.3

		1980	1990	2007	2010	2020
Labour force participation (percentage)						
Total	65+	33.6	31.8	30.3	30.5	30.9
Female	65+	21.0	21.8	23.8	24.3	26.1
Male	65+	48.6	46.7	42.6	41.8	38.8

Percentage married, age 60+				Percentage living alone, age 60+		
Total	Female	Male		Total	Female	Male
57.2	43.0	83.0		..	..	..

Statutory pensionable age (2006)			Percentage illiterate, age 65+ (2004)		
Female	Male		Total	Female	Male
..	..		61.9	84.3	28.6

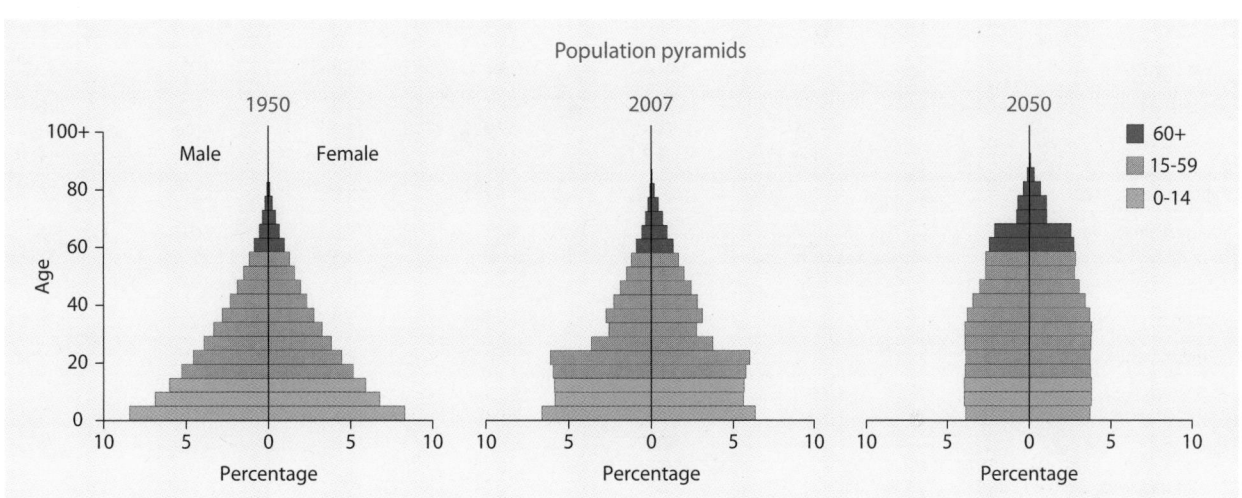

Population pyramids

Cameroon

Indicator	Age	1950	1975	2007	2025	2050
Population (thousands)						
Total	Total	4 466.5	7 563.2	16 874.4	21 619.7	26 891.5
	0-14	1 770.7	3 282.9	6 818.0	7 193.3	6 832.3
	15-59	2 440.1	3 847.5	9 098.8	13 050.2	17 076.4
	60-64	100.8	163.4	329.9	459.3	1 047.1
	65-69	72.5	120.9	256.5	357.0	799.8
	70-74	46.1	80.2	181.4	262.6	541.1
	75-79	24.4	44.8	111.4	168.0	327.7
	80-84			54.4	87.5	173.7
	85-89			19.2	32.7	71.1
	90-94	11.9	23.4	4.2	7.9	19.0
	95-99			0.5	1.1	3.0
	100+			0.0	0.1	0.3
Female	Total	2 277.3	3 835.5	8 472.4	10 788.9	13 393.0
	0-14	890.7	1 639.9	3 388.6	3 576.3	3 394.9
	15-59	1 245.5	1 958.1	4 564.8	6 466.4	8 466.3
	60-64	54.4	87.3	175.0	240.7	522.6
	65-69	39.9	65.8	137.6	191.9	405.1
	70-74	25.7	44.6	98.7	144.1	278.5
	75-79	14.1	25.6	61.9	94.0	173.4
	80-84			31.2	50.2	96.4
	85-89			11.6	19.5	41.6
	90-94	7.1	14.2	2.7	5.0	11.8
	95-99			0.4	0.8	2.0
	100+			0.0	0.1	0.2
Male	Total	2 189.2	3 727.7	8 402.0	10 830.8	13 498.5
	0-14	880.1	1 643.0	3 429.5	3 617.0	3 437.4
	15-59	1 194.6	1 889.4	4 534.1	6 583.8	8 610.0
	60-64	46.4	76.1	154.9	218.6	524.5
	65-69	32.6	55.1	118.9	165.1	394.7
	70-74	20.4	35.7	82.7	118.5	262.6
	75-79	10.3	19.2	49.5	73.9	154.3
	80-84			23.2	37.4	77.3
	85-89			7.6	13.2	29.5
	90-94	4.8	9.3	1.5	2.9	7.2
	95-99			0.1	0.3	1.0
	100+			0.0	0.0	0.1
Percentage in older ages						
Total	60+	5.7	5.7	5.7	6.4	11.1
	65+	3.5	3.6	3.7	4.2	7.2
	80+	0.3	0.3	0.5	0.6	1.0
Female	60+	6.2	6.2	6.1	6.9	11.4
	65+	3.8	3.9	4.1	4.7	7.5
	80+	0.3	0.4	0.5	0.7	1.1
Male	60+	5.2	5.2	5.2	5.8	10.7
	65+	3.1	3.2	3.4	3.8	6.9
	80+	0.2	0.2	0.4	0.5	0.9
Ageing index		14.4	13.2	14.0	19.1	43.7
Broad age groups (percentage)	0-14	39.6	43.4	40.4	33.3	25.4
	15-59	54.6	50.9	53.9	60.4	63.5
	60+	5.7	5.7	5.7	6.4	11.1
Median age (years)		20.3	18.5	18.8*	23.1	29.5
Dependency ratio	Total	75.8	88.6	79.0	60.0	48.4
	Youth	69.7	81.8	72.3	53.2	37.7
	Old Age	6.1	6.7	6.7	6.8	10.7
Potential support ratio		16.4	14.9	15.0	14.7	9.4
Parent support ratio		0.7	0.9	2.0	2.4	2.5
Sex ratio (per 100 women)	60+	81.1	82.3	84.5	84.4	94.7
	65+	78.5	79.5	82.4	81.4	91.8
	80+	68.2	65.3	70.8	71.3	75.6

* Estimate refers to year 2005.

Indicator	Age	1950-1955	1975-1980	2005-2010	2025-2030	2045-2050
Growth rate (percentage)	Total	1.6	2.9	1.6	1.1	0.7
	60+	1.5	2.8	2.0	2.2	3.7
	65+	1.5	3.0	2.2	2.3	4.0
	80+	1.5	4.1	2.7	2.7	3.1
Total fertility rate (per woman)		5.7	6.4	4.1	2.7	2.2
Life expectancy (years)						
Total	Birth	36.0	48.4	46.3	53.9	61.0
	60	..	..	16.0	17.0	18.3
	65	..	..	12.9	13.7	14.8
	80	..	..	5.7	6.0	6.5
Female	Birth	37.5	49.9	46.7	54.5	62.0
	60	..	..	16.6	17.6	19.0
	65	..	..	13.3	14.2	15.4
	80	..	..	5.9	6.2	6.7
Male	Birth	34.5	46.9	45.8	53.1	60.1
	60	..	..	15.4	16.3	17.6
	65	..	..	12.4	13.2	14.2
	80	..	..	5.4	5.8	6.2
Survival rate (percentage)						
Total	60	..	..	39.6	50.5	61.3
	65	..	..	34.7	45.1	56.1
	80	..	..	13.4	19.5	27.4
Female	60	..	..	40.0	50.9	62.2
	65	..	..	35.6	46.1	57.6
	80	..	..	14.5	20.9	29.8
Male	60	..	..	39.1	49.8	60.5
	65	..	..	33.8	43.9	54.5
	80	..	..	12.2	17.7	25.0

		1980	1990	2007	2010	2020
Labour force participation (percentage)						
Total	65+	40.2	41.9	38.6	38.3	37.9
Female	65+	25.6	26.7	20.2	19.8	19.4
Male	65+	58.5	60.7	61.0	60.8	60.7

Percentage married, age 60+

Total	Female	Male
51.4	28.0	79.0

Percentage living alone, age 60+ (1998)

Total	Female	Male
8.3	8.6	8.0

Statutory pensionable age (2006)

Female	Male
60	60

Percentage illiterate, age 65+

Total	Female	Male
..	..	..

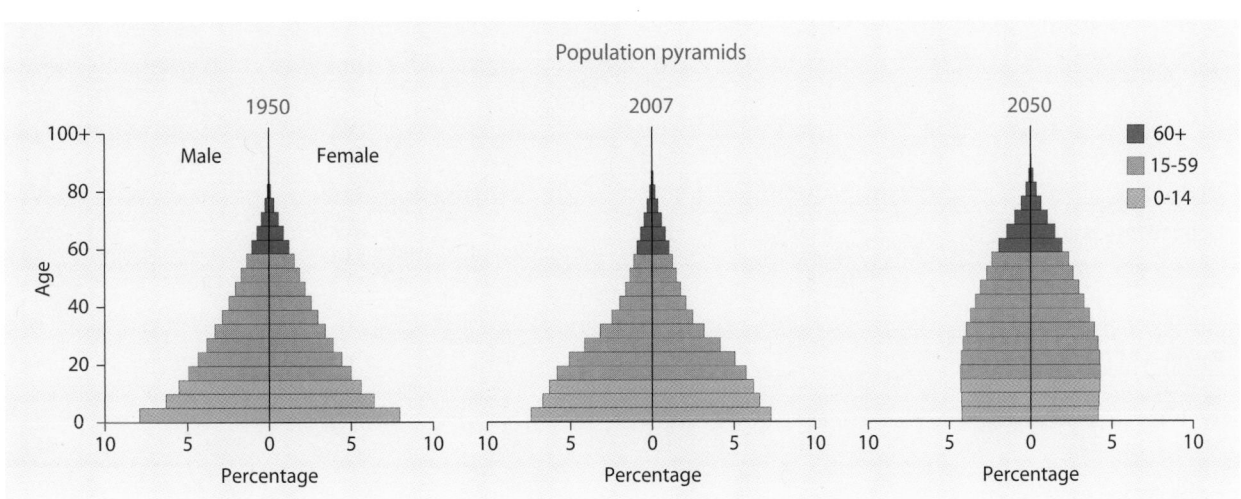
Population pyramids

Canada

Indicator	Age	1950	1975	2007	2025	2050
Population (thousands)						
Total	Total	13 737.0	23 142.3	32 852.2	37 796.9	42 844.3
	0-14	4 077.0	6 057.1	5 556.8	5 817.2	6 742.3
	15-59	8 104.0	14 228.5	21 164.6	21 377.3	22 456.2
	60-64	502.0	899.0	1 706.6	2 686.8	2 656.4
	65-69	418.0	700.9	1 275.5	2 449.3	2 499.1
	70-74	303.0	524.3	1 056.7	2 003.4	2 251.2
	75-79	184.0	353.9	879.1	1 555.1	1 960.1
	80-84			655.2	963.3	1 674.9
	85-89			362.5	546.6	1 399.1
	90-94	149.0	378.6	150.0	279.0	812.1
	95-99			39.7	99.1	317.0
	100+			5.5	20.0	75.9
Female	Total	6 768.0	11 562.5	16 563.5	19 039.5	21 639.8
	0-14	2 000.0	2 955.6	2 705.4	2 831.7	3 281.9
	15-59	4 013.0	7 047.7	10 495.8	10 541.7	11 040.9
	60-64	239.0	463.7	869.3	1 354.9	1 327.7
	65-69	197.0	369.8	660.3	1 257.9	1 261.9
	70-74	147.0	286.3	560.6	1 054.8	1 153.6
	75-79	92.0	206.6	490.8	843.6	1 035.2
	80-84			397.6	547.7	922.6
	85-89			239.8	332.4	816.6
	90-94	80.0	232.9	108.0	184.7	515.9
	95-99			31.3	73.5	223.6
	100+			4.7	16.6	59.9
Male	Total	6 969.0	11 579.7	16 288.7	18 757.4	21 204.5
	0-14	2 077.0	3 101.5	2 851.4	2 985.4	3 460.4
	15-59	4 091.0	7 180.8	10 668.9	10 835.6	11 415.3
	60-64	263.0	435.3	837.3	1 331.8	1 328.7
	65-69	221.0	331.1	615.1	1 191.3	1 237.1
	70-74	156.0	238.0	496.1	948.6	1 097.7
	75-79	92.0	147.3	388.3	711.5	924.9
	80-84			257.7	415.6	752.3
	85-89			122.7	214.1	582.5
	90-94	69.0	145.7	42.0	94.3	296.2
	95-99			8.4	25.6	93.4
	100+			0.8	3.4	16.0
Percentage in older ages						
Total	60+	11.3	12.3	18.7	28.1	31.8
	65+	7.7	8.5	13.5	20.9	25.6
	80+	1.1	1.6	3.7	5.0	10.0
Female	60+	11.2	13.5	20.3	29.8	33.8
	65+	7.6	9.5	15.1	22.6	27.7
	80+	1.2	2.0	4.7	6.1	11.7
Male	60+	11.5	11.2	17.0	26.3	29.8
	65+	7.7	7.4	11.9	19.2	23.6
	80+	1.0	1.3	2.6	4.0	8.2
Ageing index		38.2	47.2	110.3	182.3	202.4
Broad age groups (percentage)	0-14	29.7	26.2	16.9	15.4	15.7
	15-59	59.0	61.5	64.4	56.6	52.4
	60+	11.3	12.3	18.7	28.1	31.8
Median age (years)		27.7	27.4	38.6*	43.1	45.2
Dependency ratio	Total	59.6	53.0	43.6	57.1	70.6
	Youth	47.4	40.0	24.3	24.2	26.8
	Old Age	12.2	12.9	19.3	32.9	43.8
Potential support ratio		8.2	7.7	5.2	3.0	2.3
Parent support ratio		3.3	5.2	8.9	12.6	32.5
Sex ratio (per 100 women)	60+	106.1	83.2	82.3	87.1	86.5
	65+	104.3	78.7	77.5	83.6	83.5
	80+	86.3	62.6	55.2	65.2	68.6

* *Estimate refers to year 2005.*

Indicator	Age	1950-1955	1975-1980	2005-2010	2025-2030	2045-2050
Growth rate (percentage)	Total	2.7	1.2	0.9	0.7	0.4
	60+	2.3	2.6	3.2	1.6	0.7
	65+	2.9	3.3	2.4	2.7	0.7
	80+	3.2	2.9	3.1	4.8	0.8
Total fertility rate (per woman)		3.7	1.7	1.5	1.7	1.9
Life expectancy (years)						
Total	Birth	69.0	74.2	80.7	83.1	85.3
	60	..	..	23.6	25.4	27.1
	65	..	..	19.5	21.1	22.7
	80	..	..	9.3	10.3	11.3
Female	Birth	71.5	78.1	83.1	85.4	87.6
	60	..	..	25.4	27.2	29.0
	65	..	..	21.1	22.8	24.5
	80	..	..	10.1	11.2	12.4
Male	Birth	66.7	70.5	78.2	80.8	83.0
	60	..	..	21.6	23.5	25.2
	65	..	..	17.7	19.3	20.9
	80	..	..	8.1	9.1	10.1
Survival rate (percentage)						
Total	60	..	..	92.6	94.5	95.9
	65	..	..	88.8	91.6	93.6
	80	..	..	61.2	68.2	73.9
Female	60	..	..	94.4	95.9	97.0
	65	..	..	91.4	93.7	95.3
	80	..	..	68.9	74.9	79.9
Male	60	..	..	90.9	93.2	94.7
	65	..	..	86.2	89.5	91.8
	80	..	..	53.3	61.4	67.8

		1980	1990	2007	2010	2020
Labour force participation (percentage)						
Total	65+	8.0	6.7	6.5	6.6	6.9
Female	65+	4.0	3.7	3.6	3.7	3.9
Male	65+	13.4	10.9	10.2	10.3	10.6

Percentage married, age 60+			Percentage living alone, age 60+ (1991)		
Total	Female	Male	Total	Female	Male
61.4	49.0	77.0	24.4	32.9	13.7

Statutory pensionable age (2006)			Percentage illiterate, age 65+		
	Female	Male	Total	Female	Male
	65	65	..	..	..

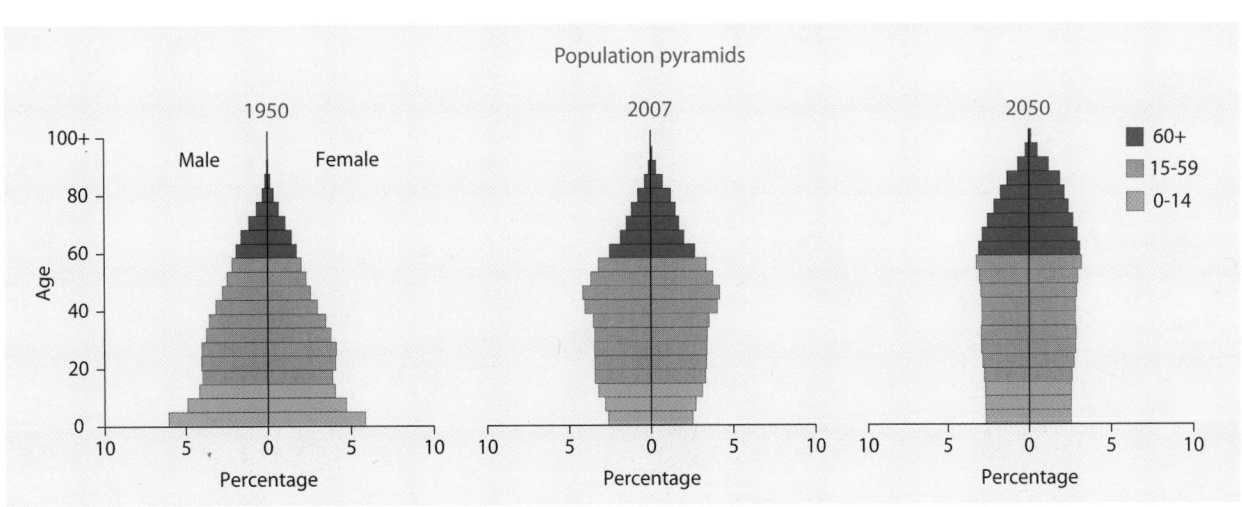

Population pyramids

1950   Male   Female   2007   2050

Legend: 60+, 15-59, 0-14

Cape Verde

Indicator	Age	1950	1975	2007	2025	2050
Population (thousands)						
Total	Total	146.1	277.8	530.4	749.8	1 001.8
	0-14	50.0	130.0	204.1	233.1	225.1
	15-59	86.6	125.2	298.7	462.0	612.8
	60-64	3.6	7.5	5.9	22.2	52.2
	65-69	2.2	5.6	7.3	14.4	43.0
	70-74	1.8	4.3	6.9	9.1	29.9
	75-79	1.3	3.7	4.7	4.1	18.0
	80-84			1.9	2.5	12.4
	85-89			0.7	1.8	6.0
	90-94	0.6	1.5	0.2	0.5	1.9
	95-99			0.0	0.1	0.4
	100+			0.0	0.0	0.0
Female	Total	79.8	148.0	275.2	382.8	508.3
	0-14	25.5	65.7	101.7	115.6	111.1
	15-59	47.7	69.3	155.4	233.4	305.8
	60-64	2.5	4.1	3.8	12.0	27.0
	65-69	1.5	3.1	4.9	9.1	22.8
	70-74	1.3	2.5	4.5	6.2	16.9
	75-79	0.9	2.4	3.0	2.8	10.6
	80-84			1.3	1.9	7.9
	85-89			0.5	1.4	4.3
	90-94	0.5	0.9	0.2	0.4	1.6
	95-99			0.0	0.1	0.4
	100+			0.0	0.0	0.0
Male	Total	66.3	129.9	255.2	367.0	493.6
	0-14	24.5	64.3	102.4	117.5	114.1
	15-59	38.9	56.0	143.3	228.6	307.0
	60-64	1.1	3.4	2.1	10.2	25.2
	65-69	0.8	2.5	2.4	5.2	20.3
	70-74	0.6	1.8	2.4	2.9	13.0
	75-79	0.4	1.3	1.7	1.3	7.5
	80-84			0.7	0.6	4.5
	85-89			0.2	0.4	1.7
	90-94	0.1	0.6	0.1	0.1	0.3
	95-99			0.0	0.0	0.0
	100+			0.0	0.0	0.0
Percentage in older ages						
Total	60+	6.5	8.1	5.2	7.3	16.4
	65+	4.0	5.4	4.1	4.3	11.1
	80+	0.4	0.6	0.5	0.7	2.1
Female	60+	8.3	8.8	6.6	8.8	18.0
	65+	5.1	6.0	5.2	5.7	12.7
	80+	0.6	0.6	0.7	1.0	2.8
Male	60+	4.5	7.4	3.7	5.7	14.7
	65+	2.8	4.8	2.9	2.9	9.6
	80+	0.1	0.5	0.4	0.3	1.3
Ageing index		19.1	17.4	13.5	23.4	72.8
Broad age groups (percentage)	0-14	34.2	46.8	38.5	31.1	22.5
	15-59	59.2	45.1	56.3	61.6	61.2
	60+	6.5	8.1	5.2	7.3	16.4
Median age (years)		21.4	16.3	19.3*	25.0	33.7
Dependency ratio	Total	62.0	109.3	74.2	54.8	50.7
	Youth	55.5	97.9	67.0	48.1	33.9
	Old Age	6.6	11.4	7.2	6.7	16.8
Potential support ratio		15.2	8.8	14.0	14.9	6.0
Parent support ratio		1.5	1.9	3.3	3.1	5.1
Sex ratio (per 100 women)	60+	45.0	73.8	52.6	61.7	79.2
	65+	45.2	70.2	51.9	48.6	73.3
	80+	16.6	73.5	53.2	31.0	45.9

* Estimate refers to year 2005.

Indicator	Age	1950-1955	1975-1980	2005-2010	2025-2030	2045-2050
Growth rate (percentage)	Total	3.0	0.8	2.2	1.5	0.8
	60+	3.6	1.1	−0.2	5.2	4.0
	65+	4.4	3.2	−0.6	6.6	4.7
	80+	6.2	4.8	6.2	0.1	5.3
Total fertility rate (per woman)		6.6	6.8	3.4	2.4	2.0
Life expectancy (years)						
Total	Birth	48.7	60.1	71.7	75.9	78.6
	60	..	..	18.3	20.2	21.7
	65	..	..	14.6	16.4	17.6
	80	..	..	6.1	7.2	8.1
Female	Birth	50.0	61.5	74.4	78.5	81.2
	60	..	..	19.3	21.8	23.8
	65	..	..	15.3	17.6	19.5
	80	..	..	6.4	7.8	9.0
Male	Birth	47.0	58.5	68.3	72.7	75.7
	60	..	..	16.6	17.8	19.2
	65	..	..	13.2	14.2	15.3
	80	..	..	5.6	6.0	6.5
Survival rate (percentage)						
Total	60	..	..	83.6	88.9	92.1
	65	..	..	77.2	83.3	87.5
	80	..	..	37.0	47.2	54.0
Female	60	..	..	87.8	91.9	93.9
	65	..	..	82.4	87.9	90.8
	80	..	..	43.0	55.1	63.5
Male	60	..	..	78.5	85.8	90.1
	65	..	..	70.4	78.7	84.2
	80	..	..	28.6	36.2	43.8

		1980	1990	2007	2010	2020
Labour force participation (percentage)						
Total	65+	31.2	31.5	19.2	17.1	11.3
Female	65+	10.4	11.8	6.6	6.6	6.6
Male	65+	59.2	59.4	43.6	38.6	21.6

Percentage married, age 60+			Percentage living alone, age 60+		
Total	Female	Male	Total	Female	Male
52.6	37.0	79.0	..	..	..

Statutory pensionable age (2006)			Percentage illiterate, age 65+		
	Female	Male	Total	Female	Male
	..	65	..	..	..

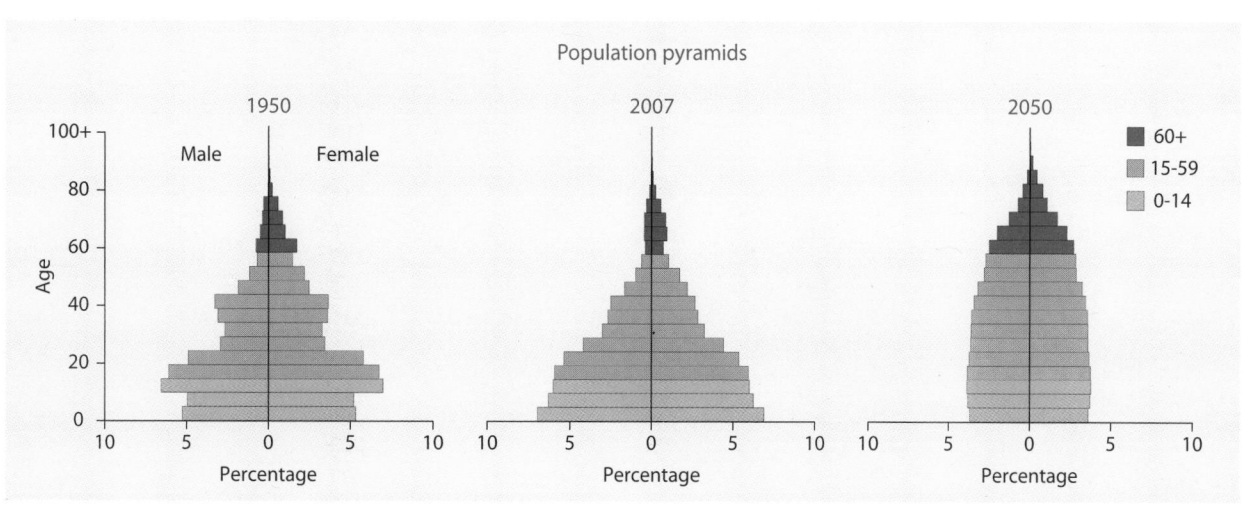

Population pyramids

Central African Republic

Indicator	Age	1950	1975	2007	2025	2050
Population (thousands)						
Total	Total	1 314.2	2 059.6	4 150.6	5 269.4	6 747.4
	0-14	473.9	853.3	1 768.3	1 986.2	1 963.7
	15-59	739.7	1 071.2	2 131.7	2 970.6	4 259.0
	60-64	36.9	49.9	81.6	91.5	191.1
	65-69	28.8	37.6	66.9	81.7	136.3
	70-74	19.2	25.3	49.0	65.2	92.6
	75-79	10.5	14.4	30.9	40.4	54.6
	80-84			15.3	22.3	30.7
	85-89			5.5	8.8	14.2
	90-94	5.2	7.8	1.2	2.2	4.4
	95-99			0.2	0.3	0.8
	100+			0.0	0.0	0.1
Female	Total	685.3	1 071.7	2 122.2	2 658.4	3 413.6
	0-14	243.8	432.3	888.2	996.6	981.1
	15-59	387.1	562.1	1 089.9	1 481.8	2 158.2
	60-64	20.0	28.0	45.8	49.9	97.1
	65-69	15.3	21.3	37.9	46.5	69.8
	70-74	10.4	14.6	28.2	38.1	48.1
	75-79	5.9	8.5	18.2	24.4	29.3
	80-84			9.4	13.8	17.6
	85-89			3.6	5.6	8.8
	90-94	2.9	5.0	0.9	1.5	3.0
	95-99			0.1	0.2	0.6
	100+			0.0	0.0	0.1
Male	Total	628.8	987.9	2 028.4	2 611.0	3 333.8
	0-14	230.1	421.1	880.1	989.6	982.6
	15-59	352.6	509.1	1 041.8	1 488.8	2 100.8
	60-64	16.9	22.0	35.8	41.7	94.0
	65-69	13.5	16.3	29.0	35.3	66.5
	70-74	8.8	10.7	20.8	27.1	44.5
	75-79	4.6	5.9	12.7	16.0	25.3
	80-84			5.9	8.5	13.1
	85-89			1.9	3.1	5.4
	90-94	2.3	2.9	0.4	0.7	1.5
	95-99			0.0	0.1	0.2
	100+			0.0	0.0	0.0
Percentage in older ages						
Total	60+	7.7	6.6	6.0	5.9	7.8
	65+	4.8	4.1	4.1	4.2	4.9
	80+	0.4	0.4	0.5	0.6	0.7
Female	60+	7.9	7.2	6.8	6.8	8.0
	65+	5.0	4.6	4.6	4.9	5.2
	80+	0.4	0.5	0.7	0.8	0.9
Male	60+	7.3	5.8	5.2	5.1	7.5
	65+	4.6	3.6	3.5	3.5	4.7
	80+	0.4	0.3	0.4	0.5	0.6
Ageing index		21.2	15.8	14.2	15.7	26.7
Broad age groups (percentage)	0-14	36.1	41.4	42.6	37.7	29.1
	15-59	56.3	52.0	51.4	56.4	63.1
	60+	7.7	6.6	6.0	5.9	7.8
Median age (years)		22.6	19.3	18.1*	20.5	26.0
Dependency ratio	Total	69.2	83.7	87.5	72.1	51.6
	Youth	61.0	76.1	79.9	64.9	44.1
	Old Age	8.2	7.6	7.6	7.2	7.5
Potential support ratio		12.2	13.2	13.1	13.9	13.3
Parent support ratio		0.9	1.1	2.3	3.6	2.6
Sex ratio (per 100 women)	60+	84.8	74.6	73.9	73.6	91.3
	65+	84.7	72.4	71.9	69.8	88.2
	80+	77.7	57.8	58.9	58.6	67.0

* Estimate refers to year 2005.

Indicator	Age	1950-1955	1975-1980	2005-2010	2025-2030	2045-2050
Growth rate (percentage)	Total	1.4	2.5	1.4	1.1	0.9
	60+	0.0	2.1	1.2	0.5	3.9
	65+	0.2	2.3	1.5	0.8	3.5
	80+	1.2	3.4	2.6	1.8	0.6
Total fertility rate (per woman)		5.5	5.9	4.6	3.0	2.3
Life expectancy (years)						
Total	Birth	35.5	46.8	39.5	48.0	57.0
	60	..	..	15.9	17.0	18.2
	65	..	..	12.8	13.8	14.8
	80	..	..	5.7	6.1	6.5
Female	Birth	38.0	49.5	40.0	49.3	59.3
	60	..	..	16.6	17.8	19.2
	65	..	..	13.4	14.4	15.5
	80	..	..	5.9	6.3	6.7
Male	Birth	33.0	44.1	39.0	46.7	54.8
	60	..	..	15.0	16.0	17.3
	65	..	..	12.1	13.0	14.0
	80	..	..	5.3	5.7	6.2
Survival rate (percentage)						
Total	60	..	..	26.1	37.7	52.1
	65	..	..	22.7	33.5	47.5
	80	..	..	8.7	14.5	23.1
Female	60	..	..	26.1	39.1	55.7
	65	..	..	23.1	35.4	51.6
	80	..	..	9.6	16.5	27.1
Male	60	..	..	25.9	36.3	48.8
	65	..	..	22.1	31.7	43.6
	80	..	..	7.7	12.5	19.6

		1980	1990	2007	2010	2020
Labour force participation (percentage)						
Total	65+	70.7	72.7	73.0	73.0	72.9
Female	65+	62.9	65.4	64.3	64.3	64.2
Male	65+	81.5	83.1	85.1	85.2	85.5

Percentage married, age 60+			Percentage living alone, age 60+ (1995)		
Total	Female	Male	Total	Female	Male
52.9	37.0	74.0	12.5	16.3	8.6

Statutory pensionable age (2006)			Percentage illiterate, age 65+ (2000)		
	Female	Male	Total	Female	Male
	50	55	86.8	96.7	78.9

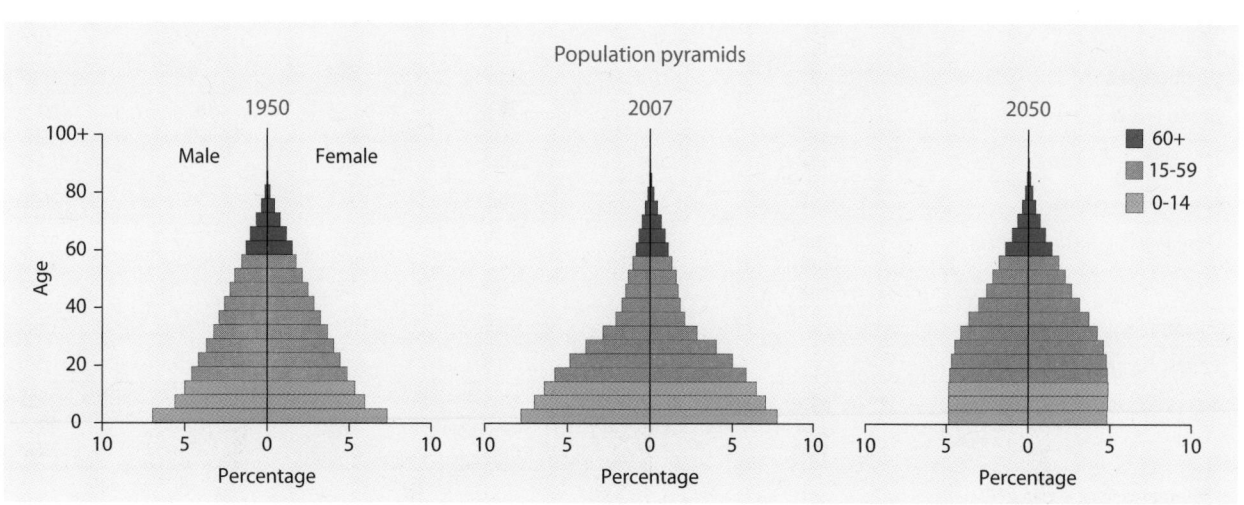

Population pyramids

Chad

Indicator	Age	1950	1975	2007	2025	2050
Population (thousands)						
Total	Total	2 657.8	4 184.9	10 302.8	17 189.0	31 496.8
	0-14	1 000.5	1 822.7	4 877.6	8 008.6	11 647.6
	15-59	1 475.6	2 121.9	4 953.7	8 491.5	18 236.0
	60-64	67.3	91.9	164.0	239.7	590.7
	65-69	52.1	68.1	128.3	185.3	427.1
	70-74	34.5	44.0	89.8	131.2	289.0
	75-79	18.8	24.5	53.8	76.3	175.7
	80-84			25.3	38.8	87.5
	85-89			8.4	13.9	33.3
	90-94	9.1	11.8	1.7	3.2	8.6
	95-99			0.2	0.4	1.3
	100+			0.0	0.0	0.1
Female	Total	1 356.1	2 129.1	5 200.4	8 628.8	15 774.6
	0-14	504.2	914.1	2 436.5	3 993.8	5 791.1
	15-59	754.0	1 082.2	2 504.7	4 258.4	9 135.4
	60-64	36.2	49.3	87.9	126.8	302.5
	65-69	27.6	37.6	69.7	100.4	222.1
	70-74	18.5	24.4	49.6	72.6	152.9
	75-79	10.5	14.2	30.5	43.3	95.2
	80-84			14.9	22.7	49.3
	85-89			5.2	8.5	19.8
	90-94	5.1	7.2	1.1	2.1	5.4
	95-99			0.1	0.3	0.9
	100+			0.0	0.0	0.1
Male	Total	1 301.7	2 055.8	5 102.4	8 560.2	15 722.2
	0-14	496.3	908.6	2 441.1	4 014.9	5 856.5
	15-59	721.6	1 039.7	2 449.0	4 233.1	9 100.5
	60-64	31.1	42.6	76.2	112.9	288.2
	65-69	24.5	30.5	58.6	84.9	205.1
	70-74	15.9	19.5	40.2	58.6	136.1
	75-79	8.3	10.2	23.3	33.1	80.5
	80-84			10.3	16.2	38.2
	85-89			3.2	5.4	13.6
	90-94	4.0	4.6	0.6	1.1	3.1
	95-99			0.0	0.1	0.4
	100+			0.0	0.0	0.0
Percentage in older ages						
Total	60+	6.8	5.7	4.6	4.0	5.1
	65+	4.3	3.5	3.0	2.6	3.2
	80+	0.3	0.3	0.3	0.3	0.4
Female	60+	7.2	6.2	5.0	4.4	5.4
	65+	4.5	3.9	3.3	2.9	3.5
	80+	0.4	0.3	0.4	0.4	0.5
Male	60+	6.4	5.2	4.2	3.6	4.9
	65+	4.0	3.2	2.7	2.3	3.0
	80+	0.3	0.2	0.3	0.3	0.4
Ageing index		18.2	13.2	9.7	8.6	13.9
Broad age groups (percentage)	0-14	37.6	43.6	47.3	46.6	37.0
	15-59	55.5	50.7	48.1	49.4	57.9
	60+	6.8	5.7	4.6	4.0	5.1
Median age (years)		21.5	18.3	16.3*	16.5	21.0
Dependency ratio	Total	72.3	89.0	101.3	96.9	67.3
	Youth	64.8	82.3	95.3	91.7	61.9
	Old Age	7.4	6.7	6.0	5.1	5.4
Potential support ratio		13.5	14.9	16.6	19.4	18.4
Parent support ratio		0.8	0.8	1.6	1.9	1.8
Sex ratio (per 100 women)	60+	85.7	81.0	81.9	82.9	90.2
	65+	85.4	77.8	79.5	79.8	87.4
	80+	77.8	64.5	65.8	67.8	73.4

* *Estimate refers to year 2005.*

Indicator	Age	1950-1955	1975-1980	2005-2010	2025-2030	2045-2050
Growth rate (percentage)	Total	1.4	2.0	2.7	2.8	2.0
	60+	–0.3	1.6	1.4	2.6	4.1
	65+	–0.2	1.7	1.6	2.6	4.0
	80+	0.3	3.1	2.3	2.6	3.7
Total fertility rate (per woman)		5.8	6.7	6.7	5.2	3.3
Life expectancy (years)						
Total	Birth	33.0	42.6	44.3	52.5	60.7
	60	..	..	15.4	16.6	17.9
	65	..	..	12.3	13.3	14.4
	80	..	..	5.4	5.9	6.3
Female	Birth	34.3	44.3	45.4	53.8	62.2
	60	..	..	15.9	17.2	18.6
	65	..	..	12.8	13.8	14.9
	80	..	..	5.7	6.1	6.5
Male	Birth	31.7	41.0	43.3	51.3	59.2
	60	..	..	14.7	15.9	17.1
	65	..	..	11.8	12.8	13.8
	80	..	..	5.1	5.6	6.0
Survival rate (percentage)						
Total	60	..	..	39.0	50.5	63.0
	65	..	..	33.8	44.8	57.3
	80	..	..	12.0	18.4	26.7
Female	60	..	..	40.4	52.2	65.1
	65	..	..	35.5	47.0	60.0
	80	..	..	13.5	20.4	29.7
Male	60	..	..	37.6	48.8	60.9
	65	..	..	32.1	42.7	54.7
	80	..	..	10.5	16.3	23.9

		1980	1990	2007	2010	2020
Labour force participation (percentage)						
Total	65+	67.8	68.2	69.9	69.9	69.7
Female	65+	52.4	55.3	60.1	61.1	64.2
Male	65+	87.5	84.5	82.3	81.0	76.6

Percentage married, age 60+			Percentage living alone, age 60+ (1997)		
Total	Female	Male	Total	Female	Male
47.1	16.0	85.0	11.2	17.8	5.0

Statutory pensionable age (2006)			Percentage illiterate, age 65+ (2000)		
	Female	Male	Total	Female	Male
	55	55	93.5	99.8	89.2

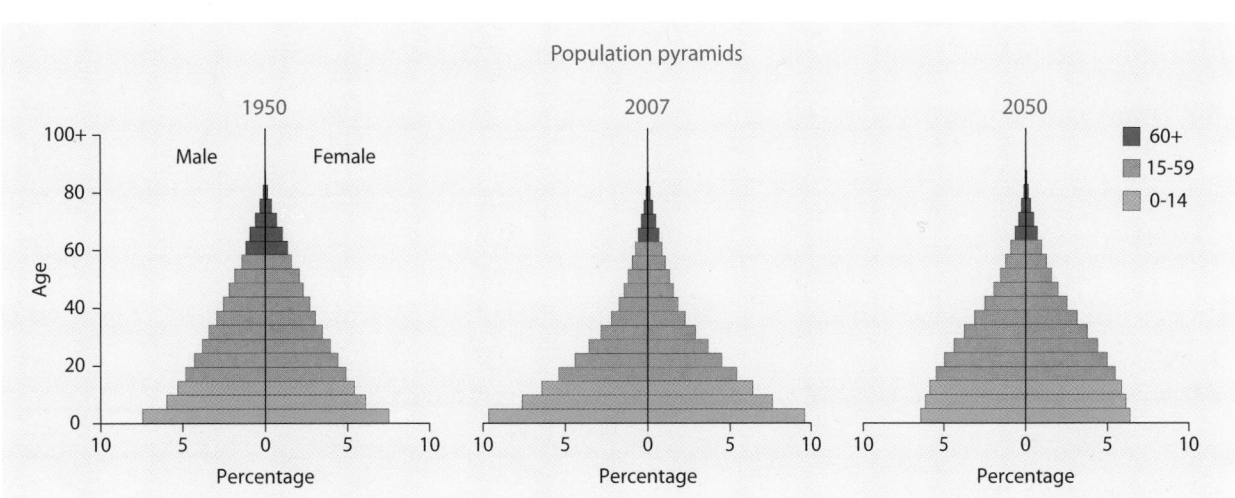

Population pyramids

Channel Islands

Indicator	Age	1950	1975	2007	2025	2050
Population (thousands)						
Total	Total	102.2	127.3	150.5	160.7	171.2
	0-14	21.8	25.7	24.0	24.1	27.4
	15-59	62.8	75.7	96.2	92.1	92.5
	60-64	5.1	7.3	8.4	12.0	10.4
	65-69	4.5	6.5	6.5	9.7	8.6
	70-74	3.6	5.1	5.5	7.8	7.7
	75-79	2.4	3.5	4.4	7.2	7.8
	80-84			3.2	4.0	7.8
	85-89			1.7	2.4	5.4
	90-94	2.0	3.5	0.6	1.0	2.6
	95-99			0.1	0.3	0.9
	100+			0.0	0.0	0.2
Female	Total	53.1	65.7	76.7	81.8	86.9
	0-14	10.7	12.6	11.6	11.7	13.2
	15-59	32.2	38.0	48.7	46.2	45.6
	60-64	2.9	3.9	4.3	6.2	5.2
	65-69	2.5	3.5	3.3	5.0	4.3
	70-74	2.0	3.0	2.9	4.1	4.0
	75-79	1.4	2.2	2.5	3.9	4.2
	80-84			2.0	2.3	4.5
	85-89			1.1	1.5	3.3
	90-94	1.3	2.5	0.4	0.7	1.7
	95-99			0.1	0.2	0.7
	100+			0.0	0.0	0.2
Male	Total	49.1	61.6	73.8	78.9	84.3
	0-14	11.2	13.1	12.4	12.4	14.1
	15-59	30.6	37.7	47.5	45.9	46.9
	60-64	2.2	3.4	4.1	5.8	5.1
	65-69	2.0	3.0	3.2	4.7	4.3
	70-74	1.5	2.1	2.6	3.7	3.7
	75-79	1.0	1.3	1.9	3.3	3.6
	80-84			1.3	1.7	3.3
	85-89			0.5	0.9	2.1
	90-94	0.7	1.0	0.1	0.3	0.9
	95-99			0.0	0.1	0.2
	100+			0.0	0.0	0.0
Percentage in older ages						
Total	60+	17.2	20.3	20.1	27.7	30.0
	65+	12.2	14.6	14.6	20.2	23.9
	80+	2.0	2.8	3.7	4.8	9.9
Female	60+	19.2	23.0	21.5	29.3	32.3
	65+	13.8	17.1	16.0	21.7	26.3
	80+	2.5	3.8	4.7	5.8	11.9
Male	60+	15.0	17.5	18.7	26.0	27.6
	65+	10.6	11.9	13.1	18.7	21.5
	80+	1.5	1.6	2.6	3.8	7.7
Ageing index		80.5	100.9	126.3	184.8	187.6
Broad age groups (percentage)	0-14	21.4	20.2	15.9	15.0	16.0
	15-59	61.4	59.5	63.9	57.3	54.0
	60+	17.2	20.3	20.1	27.7	30.0
Median age (years)		35.7	34.6	39.7*	43.4	43.6
Dependency ratio	Total	50.6	53.3	43.9	54.4	66.4
	Youth	32.2	30.9	22.9	23.1	26.6
	Old Age	18.4	22.4	21.0	31.2	39.8
Potential support ratio		5.4	4.5	4.8	3.2	2.5
Parent support ratio		4.3	6.9	8.1	10.6	28.6
Sex ratio (per 100 women)	60+	71.9	71.1	83.8	85.8	82.8
	65+	71.2	65.2	79.0	83.0	79.2
	80+	53.4	39.7	53.3	62.8	63.0

* *Estimate refers to year 2005.*

Indicator	Age	1950-1955	1975-1980	2005-2010	2025-2030	2045-2050
Growth rate (percentage)	Total	0.7	0.3	0.3	0.4	0.2
	60+	1.7	0.2	2.5	1.9	0.3
	65+	1.6	1.2	0.9	2.5	−0.2
	80+	2.8	2.0	1.4	5.1	2.2
Total fertility rate (per woman)		2.1	1.5	1.4	1.7	1.9
Life expectancy (years)						
Total	Birth	70.6	73.1	79.0	81.6	83.8
	60	..	..	21.5	23.7	25.5
	65	..	..	17.4	19.4	21.2
	80	..	..	7.6	9.0	10.2
Female	Birth	73.7	76.9	81.5	84.1	86.4
	60	..	..	23.4	25.7	27.8
	65	..	..	19.1	21.3	23.2
	80	..	..	8.3	10.0	11.4
Male	Birth	67.4	69.3	76.6	79.2	81.5
	60	..	..	19.5	21.6	23.6
	65	..	..	15.6	17.5	19.3
	80	..	..	6.6	7.8	9.0
Survival rate (percentage)						
Total	60	..	..	93.2	94.7	95.7
	65	..	..	89.1	91.5	93.1
	80	..	..	54.8	63.4	69.7
Female	60	..	..	95.1	96.1	96.9
	65	..	..	92.3	93.9	95.1
	80	..	..	64.2	71.7	77.4
Male	60	..	..	91.4	93.3	94.7
	65	..	..	85.9	89.1	91.3
	80	..	..	45.7	55.2	62.9

		1980	1990	2007	2010	2020
Labour force participation (percentage)						
Total	65+	10.7	8.9	6.5	6.2	5.6
Female	65+	8.5	7.0	5.5	5.5	5.5
Male	65+	14.1	11.8	7.8	7.0	5.8

Percentage married, age 60+			Percentage living alone, age 60+		
Total	Female	Male	Total	Female	Male
..	..	..	..	..	..

Statutory pensionable age (2006)			Percentage illiterate, age 65+		
	Female	Male	Total	Female	Male
	..	..	..	..	..

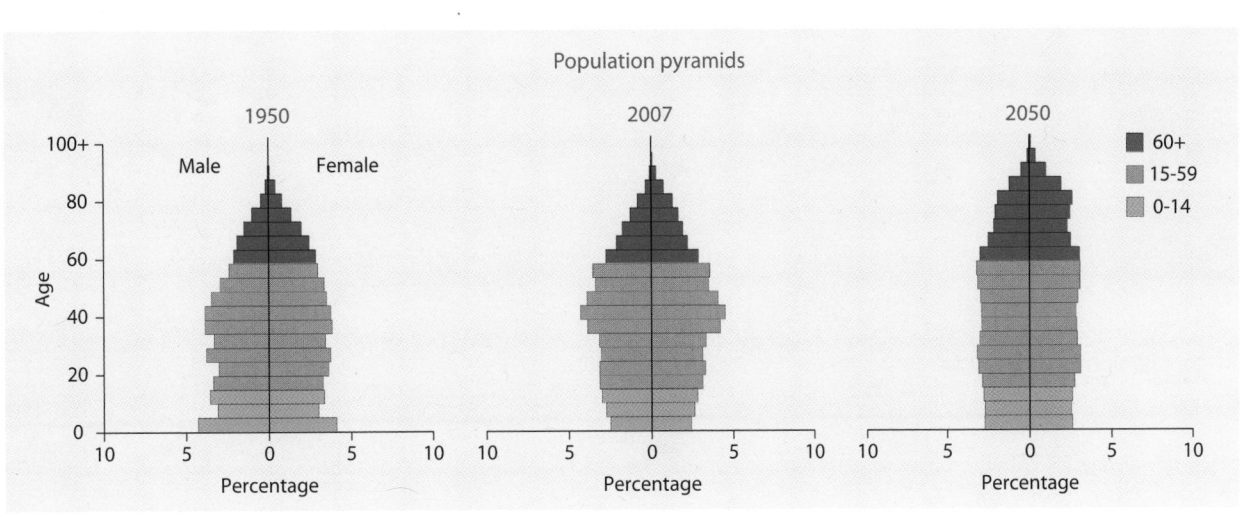

Population pyramids

Chile

Indicator	Age	1950	1975	2007	2025	2050
Population (thousands)						
Total	Total	6 081.9	10 413.2	16 634.8	19 266.2	20 657.5
	0-14	2 233.0	3 850.7	3 946.7	3 746.3	3 408.4
	15-59	3 432.2	5 748.4	10 655.6	11 599.5	11 329.8
	60-64	157.8	262.0	615.8	1 156.9	1 350.7
	65-69	108.8	218.1	471.5	949.0	1 160.4
	70-74	78.3	152.5	361.2	688.4	949.6
	75-79	43.5	101.1	273.7	495.7	884.6
	80-84			172.0	332.8	717.1
	85-89			91.5	179.7	516.6
	90-94	28.3	80.5	36.2	85.4	250.5
	95-99			9.4	27.5	76.3
	100+			1.4	5.0	13.4
Female	Total	3 069.5	5 276.5	8 406.1	9 764.6	10 567.4
	0-14	1 105.8	1 904.4	1 937.7	1 838.3	1 672.2
	15-59	1 738.5	2 913.2	5 326.5	5 775.8	5 618.4
	60-64	82.0	142.7	323.6	599.1	690.7
	65-69	58.0	120.9	254.1	500.9	604.9
	70-74	43.2	86.5	202.6	374.1	509.8
	75-79	24.9	59.0	161.0	281.0	494.6
	80-84			106.6	199.0	421.8
	85-89			60.5	114.2	323.1
	90-94	17.2	49.7	25.4	58.3	167.8
	95-99			6.9	20.0	54.6
	100+			1.0	3.7	9.6
Male	Total	3 012.5	5 136.8	8 228.7	9 501.7	10 090.1
	0-14	1 127.2	1 946.3	2 009.0	1 908.0	1 736.2
	15-59	1 693.7	2 835.1	5 329.1	5 823.6	5 711.4
	60-64	75.8	119.3	292.1	557.8	659.9
	65-69	50.8	97.2	217.3	448.1	555.5
	70-74	35.1	66.0	158.6	314.3	439.8
	75-79	18.7	42.1	112.7	214.7	390.1
	80-84			65.4	133.8	295.3
	85-89			31.0	65.5	193.5
	90-94	11.2	30.8	10.8	27.0	82.7
	95-99			2.5	7.5	21.7
	100+			0.3	1.3	3.8
Percentage in older ages						
Total	60+	6.9	7.8	12.2	20.3	28.7
	65+	4.3	5.3	8.5	14.3	22.1
	80+	0.5	0.8	1.9	3.3	7.6
Female	60+	7.3	8.7	13.6	22.0	31.0
	65+	4.7	6.0	9.7	15.9	24.5
	80+	0.6	0.9	2.4	4.0	9.2
Male	60+	6.4	6.9	10.8	18.6	26.2
	65+	3.8	4.6	7.3	12.8	19.6
	80+	0.4	0.6	1.3	2.5	5.9
Ageing index		18.7	21.1	51.5	104.6	173.7
Broad age groups (percentage)	0-14	36.7	37.0	23.7	19.4	16.5
	15-59	56.4	55.2	64.1	60.2	54.8
	60+	6.9	7.8	12.2	20.3	28.7
Median age (years)		22.2	21.0	30.6*	37.0	43.1
Dependency ratio	Total	69.4	73.3	47.6	51.0	62.9
	Youth	62.2	64.1	35.0	29.4	26.9
	Old Age	7.2	9.2	12.6	21.7	36.0
Potential support ratio		13.9	10.9	8.0	4.6	2.8
Parent support ratio		1.7	2.9	6.0	8.4	21.1
Sex ratio (per 100 women)	60+	85.1	77.5	78.0	82.3	80.6
	65+	80.9	74.7	73.1	78.1	76.7
	80+	65.0	61.9	54.8	59.5	61.1

*   *Estimate refers to year 2005.*

Indicator	Age	1950-1955	1975-1980	2005-2010	2025-2030	2045-2050
Growth rate (percentage)	Total	2.1	1.4	1.0	0.5	0.1
	60+	3.3	2.2	3.5	2.6	1.3
	65+	3.3	2.3	3.6	3.7	1.1
	80+	3.9	3.5	4.9	3.9	2.0
Total fertility rate (per woman)		5.0	2.8	1.9	1.9	1.9
Life expectancy (years)						
Total	Birth	54.7	67.1	78.6	80.7	82.2
	60	..	..	22.8	24.1	25.0
	65	..	..	18.9	20.1	20.9
	80	..	..	9.2	9.8	10.2
Female	Birth	56.7	70.3	81.5	83.9	85.4
	60	..	..	24.5	26.2	27.3
	65	..	..	20.4	21.9	22.9
	80	..	..	9.9	10.6	11.2
Male	Birth	52.9	63.8	75.5	77.6	79.0
	60	..	..	20.7	21.9	22.7
	65	..	..	17.1	18.1	18.7
	80	..	..	8.3	8.7	9.0
Survival rate (percentage)						
Total	60	..	..	89.4	91.6	92.9
	65	..	..	84.8	87.6	89.4
	80	..	..	55.6	61.7	65.8
Female	60	..	..	92.8	94.5	95.5
	65	..	..	89.3	91.8	93.3
	80	..	..	64.2	71.1	75.6
Male	60	..	..	86.1	88.7	90.2
	65	..	..	80.2	83.5	85.6
	80	..	..	46.6	52.3	56.1

		1980	1990	2007	2010	2020
Labour force participation (percentage)						
Total	65+	15.5	15.1	8.8	7.2	5.9
Female	65+	6.2	5.4	6.0	5.9	5.9
Male	65+	28.2	28.9	12.7	8.9	6.0

Percentage married, age 60+			Percentage living alone, age 60+ (1992)		
Total	Female	Male	Total	Female	Male
55.5	43.0	72.0	8.8	9.2	8.2

Statutory pensionable age (2006)			Percentage illiterate, age 65+ (2002)		
	Female	Male	Total	Female	Male
	60	65	14.7	14.8	14.4

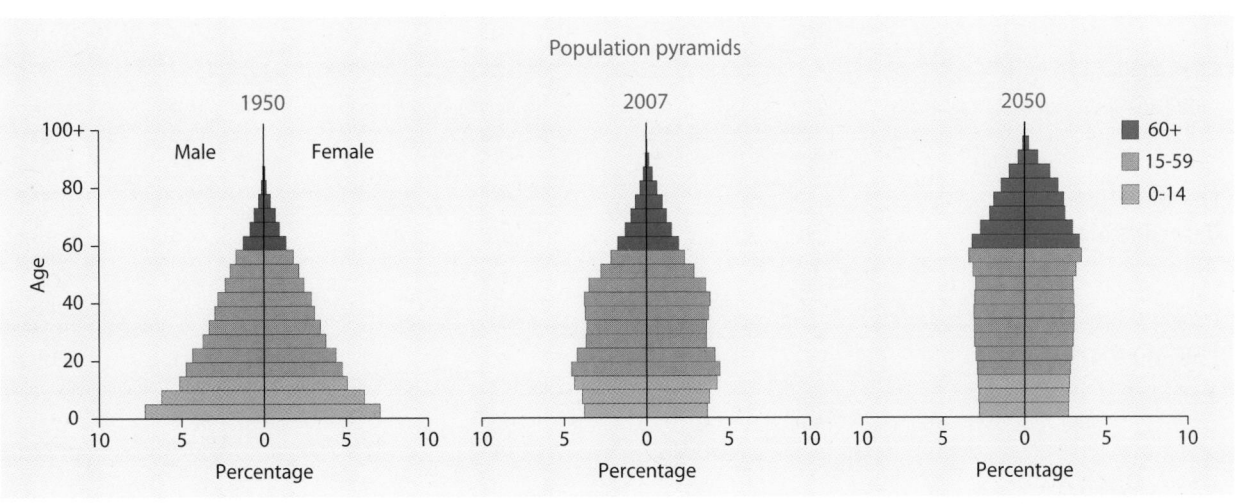

Population pyramids

China

Indicator	Age	1950	1975	2007	2025	2050
Population (thousands)						
Total	Total	554 760.0	927 807.6	1 331 355.9	1 441 426.1	1 392 306.7
	0-14	186 047.3	366 377.6	272 241.6	258 472.6	218 421.7
	15-59	327 140.5	497 095.2	907 049.7	892 968.7	742 352.6
	60-64	16 720.8	23 504.5	47 532.3	92 716.5	102 429.9
	65-69	12 569.1	17 833.2	37 713.3	68 660.7	82 370.2
	70-74	7 121.4	12 024.7	30 428.7	61 418.2	71 912.8
	75-79	3 602.2	5 867.6	20 175.2	35 629.4	74 269.0
	80-84			10 694.5	18 449.3	57 429.8
	85-89			4 219.9	9 086.8	28 794.5
	90-94	1 558.7	5 104.8	1 087.5	3 234.6	10 475.2
	95-99			188.5	692.2	3 372.4
	100+			24.8	97.0	478.7
Female	Total	266 559.8	449 956.3	647 926.0	707 728.5	691 834.3
	0-14	87 336.8	177 187.3	128 771.6	122 637.9	104 330.0
	15-59	156 169.5	237 503.2	439 869.3	432 360.9	355 052.3
	60-64	8 637.9	12 044.7	23 267.2	46 625.6	50 340.5
	65-69	6 876.1	9 711.9	18 823.3	34 711.2	41 622.9
	70-74	4 164.4	6 979.4	15 815.2	32 412.8	37 642.1
	75-79	2 287.7	3 603.9	11 122.8	19 459.9	40 667.0
	80-84			6 424.4	10 714.4	33 465.6
	85-89			2 827.4	5 803.8	18 224.6
	90-94	1 087.4	2 925.8	820.7	2 344.6	7 368.9
	95-99			161.1	569.4	2 697.8
	100+			23.1	87.8	422.8
Male	Total	288 200.2	477 851.4	683 429.9	733 697.6	700 472.4
	0-14	98 710.5	189 190.3	143 470.0	135 834.7	114 091.7
	15-59	170 971.0	259 592.0	467 180.3	460 607.7	387 300.3
	60-64	8 082.9	11 459.8	24 265.1	46 090.9	52 089.4
	65-69	5 693.0	8 121.4	18 890.0	33 949.5	40 747.3
	70-74	2 957.0	5 045.3	14 613.5	29 005.4	34 270.8
	75-79	1 314.5	2 263.6	9 052.4	16 169.5	33 602.0
	80-84			4 270.1	7 734.9	23 964.2
	85-89			1 392.5	3 282.9	10 569.9
	90-94	471.3	2 179.0	266.7	889.9	3 106.4
	95-99			27.4	122.8	674.6
	100+			1.8	9.1	55.9
Percentage in older ages						
Total	60+	7.5	6.9	11.4	20.1	31.0
	65+	4.5	4.4	7.9	13.7	23.6
	80+	0.3	0.6	1.2	2.2	7.2
Female	60+	8.6	7.8	12.2	21.6	33.6
	65+	5.4	5.2	8.6	15.0	26.3
	80+	0.4	0.7	1.6	2.8	9.0
Male	60+	6.4	6.1	10.6	18.7	28.4
	65+	3.6	3.7	7.1	12.4	21.0
	80+	0.2	0.5	0.9	1.6	5.5
Ageing index		22.3	17.6	55.9	112.2	197.6
Broad age groups (percentage)	0-14	33.5	39.5	20.4	17.9	15.7
	15-59	59.0	53.6	68.1	62.0	53.3
	60+	7.5	6.9	11.4	20.1	31.0
Median age (years)		23.9	20.6	32.6*	39.5	44.8
Dependency ratio	Total	61.3	78.2	39.5	46.2	64.8
	Youth	54.1	70.4	28.5	26.2	25.9
	Old Age	7.2	7.8	11.0	20.0	39.0
Potential support ratio		13.8	12.8	9.1	5.0	2.6
Parent support ratio		0.8	1.6	2.8	4.1	15.2
Sex ratio (per 100 women)	60+	80.3	82.4	91.8	89.9	85.6
	65+	72.4	75.8	86.6	85.9	80.7
	80+	43.3	74.5	58.1	61.7	61.7

*   *Estimate refers to year 2005.*

Indicator	Age	1950-1955	1975-1980	2005-2010	2025-2030	2045-2050
Growth rate (percentage)	Total	1.9	1.5	0.6	0.1	−0.4
	60+	2.1	2.8	3.2	3.6	0.9
	65+	2.5	3.0	2.3	3.6	0.2
	80+	3.9	−3.3	4.6	5.0	4.5
Total fertility rate (per woman)		6.2	3.3	1.7	1.9	1.9
Life expectancy (years)						
Total	Birth	40.7	65.4	72.6	75.3	78.7
	60	..	..	19.0	20.8	22.4
	65	..	..	15.2	16.9	18.3
	80	..	..	6.8	7.7	8.6
Female	Birth	42.3	66.3	74.6	77.7	80.9
	60	..	..	20.7	22.7	24.3
	65	..	..	16.7	18.5	20.0
	80	..	..	7.5	8.6	9.6
Male	Birth	39.3	64.4	70.8	73.0	76.6
	60	..	..	17.3	19.0	20.5
	65	..	..	13.8	15.2	16.6
	80	..	..	6.0	6.7	7.4
Survival rate (percentage)						
Total	60	..	..	85.3	87.1	91.4
	65	..	..	79.3	82.2	87.3
	80	..	..	39.9	47.8	56.1
Female	60	..	..	87.6	89.6	92.8
	65	..	..	82.9	85.9	89.7
	80	..	..	47.8	56.1	63.6
Male	60	..	..	83.3	84.9	90.0
	65	..	..	75.9	78.8	85.0
	80	..	..	32.8	40.1	48.7

		1980	1990	2007	2010	2020
Labour force participation (percentage)						
Total	65+	16.0	19.3	16.8	16.2	14.9
Female	65+	4.7	8.0	9.7	10.0	11.1
Male	65+	30.6	32.7	25.0	23.4	19.4

Percentage married, age 60+			Percentage living alone, age 60+ (1990)		
Total	Female	Male	Total	Female	Male
66.5	56.0	78.0	8.1	..	..

Statutory pensionable age (2006)			Percentage illiterate, age 65+		
	Female	Male	Total	Female	Male
	60	60	..	..	..

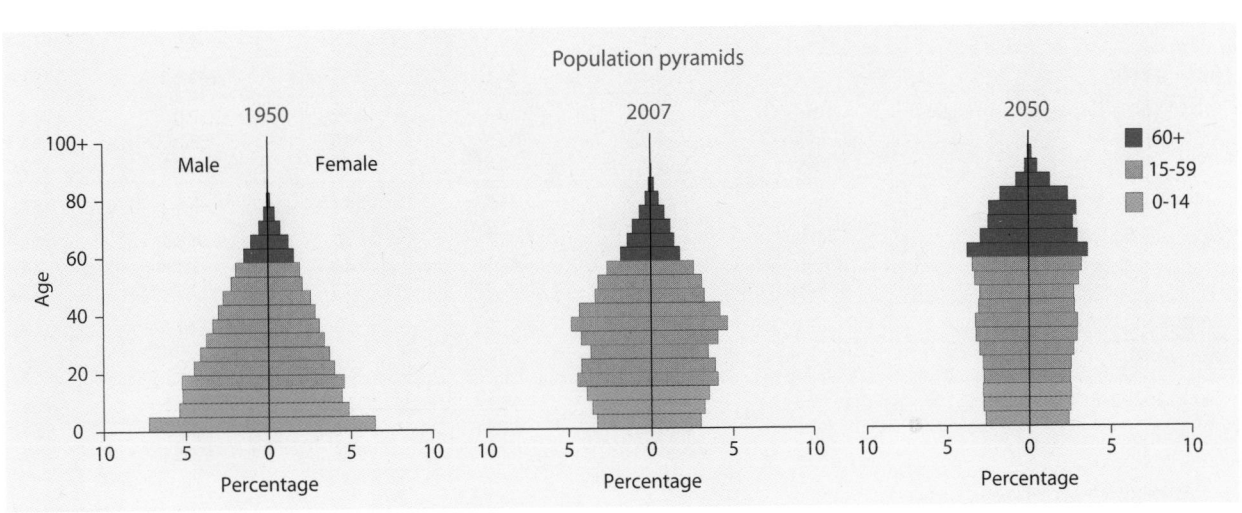

Population pyramids

China, Hong Kong Special Administrative Region

Indicator	Age	1950	1975	2007	2025	2050
Population (thousands)						
Total	Total	1 974.0	4 395.8	7 194.1	8 362.4	9 234.6
	0-14	599.2	1 334.2	999.2	1 006.1	1 149.0
	15-59	1 301.6	2 673.0	5 034.6	4 851.5	4 508.8
	60-64	23.9	151.1	290.7	703.7	597.7
	65-69	19.6	98.0	229.3	633.2	625.3
	70-74	15.5	68.4	228.7	465.8	594.3
	75-79	8.5	40.9	187.7	320.0	540.4
	80-84			124.4	161.0	456.8
	85-89			66.2	119.3	401.8
	90-94	5.7	30.2	26.2	69.3	243.3
	95-99			6.1	26.6	94.1
	100+			0.9	6.0	23.0
Female	Total	959.8	2 146.9	3 818.6	4 474.1	4 980.9
	0-14	281.8	651.0	493.9	494.2	563.4
	15-59	625.9	1 266.6	2 715.9	2 588.2	2 299.0
	60-64	15.8	77.0	142.7	394.9	313.8
	65-69	13.6	56.0	111.9	344.3	340.6
	70-74	12.0	44.6	115.6	251.8	341.5
	75-79	6.5	28.3	100.5	172.7	325.1
	80-84			72.4	88.9	286.7
	85-89			42.0	70.2	260.0
	90-94	4.2	23.4	18.2	45.0	164.3
	95-99			4.7	19.2	68.6
	100+			0.8	4.7	17.9
Male	Total	1 014.2	2 248.9	3 375.5	3 888.3	4 253.7
	0-14	317.4	683.2	505.3	511.9	585.6
	15-59	675.7	1 406.4	2 318.8	2 263.3	2 209.8
	60-64	8.1	74.1	148.0	308.8	283.9
	65-69	6.0	42.0	117.4	288.9	284.7
	70-74	3.5	23.8	113.1	214.0	252.9
	75-79	2.0	12.6	87.2	147.3	215.2
	80-84			52.0	72.1	170.2
	85-89			24.2	49.0	141.8
	90-94	1.5	6.8	8.1	24.3	79.0
	95-99			1.4	7.4	25.5
	100+			0.2	1.3	5.0
Percentage in older ages						
Total	60+	3.7	8.8	16.1	30.0	38.7
	65+	2.5	5.4	12.1	21.5	32.3
	80+	0.3	0.7	3.1	4.6	13.2
Female	60+	5.4	10.7	15.9	31.1	42.5
	65+	3.8	7.1	12.2	22.3	36.2
	80+	0.4	1.1	3.6	5.1	16.0
Male	60+	2.1	7.1	16.3	28.6	34.3
	65+	1.3	3.8	12.0	20.7	27.6
	80+	0.1	0.3	2.5	4.0	9.9
Ageing index		12.2	29.1	116.1	249.0	311.3
Broad age groups (percentage)	0-14	30.4	30.4	13.9	12.0	12.4
	15-59	65.9	60.8	70.0	58.0	48.8
	60+	3.7	8.8	16.1	30.0	38.7
Median age (years)		23.7	23.9	38.9*	46.8	51.0
Dependency ratio	Total	48.9	55.7	35.1	50.5	80.8
	Youth	45.2	47.2	18.8	18.1	22.5
	Old Age	3.7	8.4	16.3	32.4	58.3
Potential support ratio		26.9	11.9	6.1	3.1	1.7
Parent support ratio		1.6	1.0	7.5	11.2	43.6
Sex ratio (per 100 women)	60+	40.5	69.5	90.6	80.0	68.8
	65+	35.8	55.9	86.6	80.7	65.1
	80+	35.7	29.0	62.1	67.6	52.9

* Estimate refers to year 2005.

Indicator	Age	1950-1955	1975-1980	2005-2010	2025-2030	2045-2050
Growth rate (percentage)	Total	4.6	2.7	1.0	0.6	0.2
	60+	6.9	5.3	3.9	2.4	0.4
	65+	4.5	6.3	1.8	4.0	0.8
	80+	4.7	5.9	5.6	5.4	1.6
Total fertility rate (per woman)		4.4	2.3	1.0	1.2	1.5
Life expectancy (years)						
Total	Birth	61.1	73.6	82.2	84.6	86.9
	60	..	..	24.5	26.4	28.4
	65	..	..	20.3	22.1	24.0
	80	..	..	9.9	10.9	12.2
Female	Birth	64.9	76.8	85.1	87.4	89.5
	60	..	..	26.8	28.7	30.6
	65	..	..	22.3	24.2	26.0
	80	..	..	10.8	12.2	13.5
Male	Birth	57.2	70.5	79.3	81.6	83.7
	60	..	..	22.3	24.0	25.7
	65	..	..	18.3	19.8	21.4
	80	..	..	8.6	9.5	10.5
Survival rate (percentage)						
Total	60	..	..	94.1	95.6	96.5
	65	..	..	90.8	93.1	94.5
	80	..	..	64.6	71.6	77.3
Female	60	..	..	96.2	97.1	97.8
	65	..	..	94.0	95.4	96.4
	80	..	..	74.1	79.3	83.7
Male	60	..	..	91.8	93.7	95.1
	65	..	..	87.3	90.2	92.4
	80	..	..	55.7	62.9	69.3

		1980	1990	2007	2010	2020
Labour force participation (percentage)						
Total	65+	20.2	12.6	4.1	3.5	2.3
Female	65+	11.8	5.9	1.7	1.6	1.6
Male	65+	32.7	21.2	6.8	5.6	3.2

Percentage married, age 60+			Percentage living alone, age 60+ (1996)		
Total	Female	Male	Total	Female	Male
66.3	52.0	82.0	10.8	10.8	10.8

Statutory pensionable age (2006)			Percentage illiterate, age 65+		
	Female	Male	Total	Female	Male
	65	65	..	..	..

Population pyramids

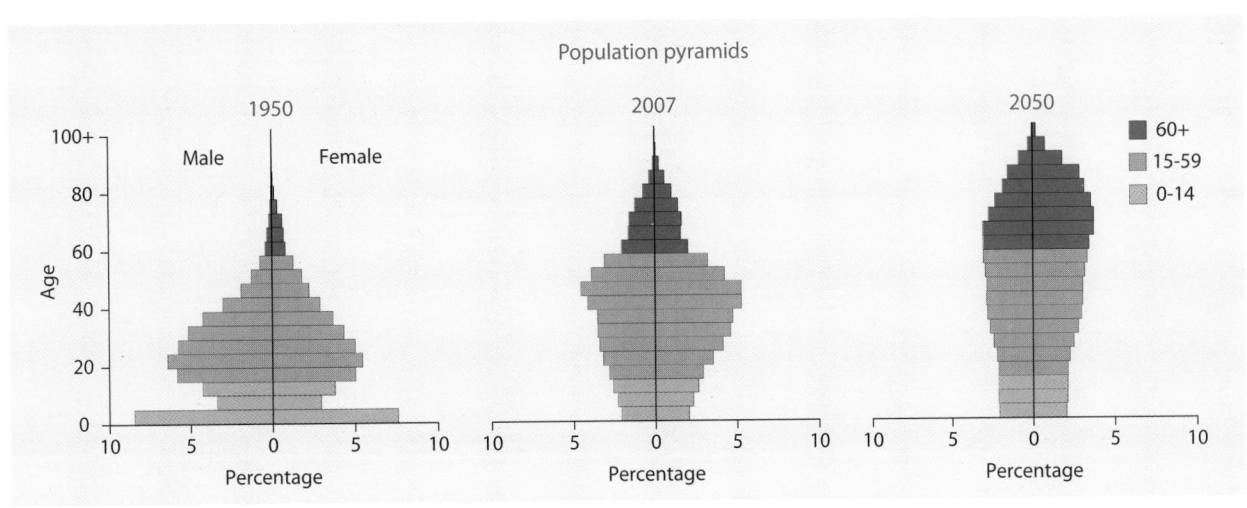

China, Macao Special Administrative Region

Indicator	Age	1950	1975	2007	2025	2050
Population (thousands)						
Total	Total	190.5	253.0	466.4	522.6	519.6
	0-14	54.6	74.7	67.2	62.9	57.1
	15-59	126.7	156.9	345.5	306.9	248.3
	60-64	3.2	7.2	17.1	43.6	47.3
	65-69	2.3	6.1	10.1	43.4	39.9
	70-74	1.7	3.9	8.8	31.6	29.6
	75-79	1.1	2.6	8.0	18.8	28.8
	80-84			5.5	8.1	27.3
	85-89			2.8	4.1	22.3
	90-94	0.8	1.6	1.0	2.2	13.7
	95-99			0.2	0.8	4.5
	100+			0.0	0.1	0.7
Female	Total	90.1	123.6	242.3	275.6	281.4
	0-14	25.6	36.4	32.9	30.7	27.9
	15-59	58.6	75.3	181.5	165.1	130.3
	60-64	1.9	3.7	7.7	24.5	24.4
	65-69	1.5	3.3	4.7	22.3	21.6
	70-74	1.2	2.4	4.5	15.4	17.0
	75-79	0.7	1.6	4.6	9.0	16.9
	80-84			3.5	4.1	17.5
	85-89			2.0	2.3	13.9
	90-94	0.5	1.0	0.7	1.5	8.4
	95-99			0.2	0.6	2.9
	100+			0.0	0.1	0.5
Male	Total	100.4	129.3	224.1	247.0	238.2
	0-14	29.0	38.3	34.4	32.2	29.2
	15-59	68.1	81.6	164.1	141.9	118.1
	60-64	1.3	3.5	9.4	19.1	22.9
	65-69	0.8	2.7	5.4	21.1	18.3
	70-74	0.5	1.5	4.2	16.2	12.7
	75-79	0.3	1.0	3.4	9.8	11.9
	80-84			2.0	4.0	9.7
	85-89			0.9	1.8	8.4
	90-94	0.3	0.5	0.2	0.7	5.3
	95-99			0.0	0.2	1.6
	100+			0.0	0.0	0.2
Percentage in older ages						
Total	60+	4.8	8.5	11.5	29.2	41.2
	65+	3.1	5.6	7.8	20.9	32.1
	80+	0.4	0.6	2.1	2.9	13.2
Female	60+	6.5	9.7	11.5	29.0	43.8
	65+	4.4	6.7	8.4	20.1	35.1
	80+	0.6	0.8	2.7	3.1	15.4
Male	60+	3.3	7.3	11.5	29.5	38.2
	65+	2.0	4.5	7.2	21.8	28.6
	80+	0.3	0.4	1.4	2.7	10.6
Ageing index		16.8	28.7	79.7	242.8	375.3
Broad age groups (percentage)	0-14	28.7	29.5	14.4	12.0	11.0
	15-59	66.5	62.0	74.1	58.7	47.8
	60+	4.8	8.5	11.5	29.2	41.2
Median age (years)		25.3	22.2	36.6*	45.0	54.4
Dependency ratio	Total	46.6	54.2	28.6	49.1	75.8
	Youth	42.1	45.5	18.5	17.9	19.3
	Old Age	4.6	8.7	10.1	31.2	56.4
Potential support ratio		21.9	11.6	9.9	3.2	1.8
Parent support ratio		1.6	1.8	4.6	6.1	33.9
Sex ratio (per 100 women)	60+	56.0	78.1	91.8	91.3	73.8
	65+	51.0	70.3	80.1	97.3	68.8
	80+	53.3	51.5	49.3	77.8	58.1

* *Estimate refers to year 2005.*

Indicator	Age	1950-1955	1975-1980	2005-2010	2025-2030	2045-2050
Growth rate (percentage)	Total	–1.0	–0.1	0.7	0.3	–0.2
	60+	4.1	5.7	5.7	2.6	1.3
	65+	2.8	6.1	2.6	4.2	0.9
	80+	–0.5	15.0	4.8	9.0	1.1
Total fertility rate (per woman)		5.0	2.0	0.9	1.2	1.5
Life expectancy (years)						
Total	Birth	54.0	69.5	80.7	83.2	85.4
	60	..	..	23.2	25.2	27.0
	65	..	..	19.1	20.8	22.6
	80	..	..	8.9	10.0	11.2
Female	Birth	56.5	72.1	82.7	85.0	86.9
	60	..	..	24.9	26.8	28.3
	65	..	..	20.6	22.4	23.8
	80	..	..	9.7	10.9	12.0
Male	Birth	51.5	67.0	78.6	81.4	83.6
	60	..	..	21.4	23.6	25.4
	65	..	..	17.3	19.4	21.1
	80	..	..	7.7	9.0	10.1
Survival rate (percentage)						
Total	60	..	..	93.7	95.4	96.2
	65	..	..	89.9	92.6	94.0
	80	..	..	60.6	68.4	74.3
Female	60	..	..	94.8	96.1	96.9
	65	..	..	92.0	93.9	95.0
	80	..	..	67.5	73.8	78.2
Male	60	..	..	92.6	94.4	95.6
	65	..	..	88.0	91.0	92.9
	80	..	..	53.8	62.9	69.3

		1980	1990	2007	2010	2020
Labour force participation (percentage)						
Total	65+	19.2	13.0	8.9	8.8	8.8
Female	65+	8.7	5.2	4.0	3.8	3.5
Male	65+	35.4	24.6	15.0	14.6	14.0

Percentage married, age 60+			Percentage living alone, age 60+ (1991)		
Total	Female	Male	Total	Female	Male
65.6	51.0	84.0	10.4	10.2	10.7

Statutory pensionable age (2006)			Percentage illiterate, age 65+ (2001)		
	Female	Male	Total	Female	Male
	..	..	43.8	60.5	20.3

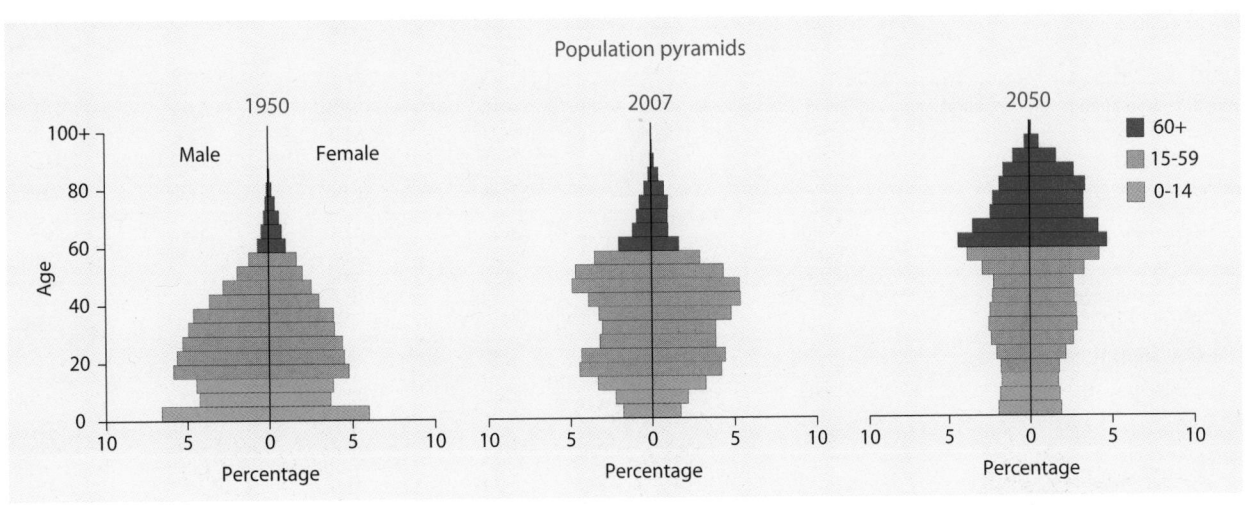

Population pyramids

Colombia

Indicator	Age	1950	1975	2007	2025	2050
Population (thousands)						
Total	Total	12 568.4	25 381.0	46 952.0	57 738.0	65 679.2
	0-14	5 358.4	11 013.7	14 144.4	13 761.0	11 913.6
	15-59	6 584.0	12 947.0	29 105.0	35 938.8	38 442.8
	60-64	230.5	507.3	1 225.9	2 653.5	3 626.9
	65-69	168.2	384.2	880.9	2 047.5	3 248.7
	70-74	115.0	266.2	646.8	1 503.0	2 811.9
	75-79	71.0	154.7	447.5	943.8	2 189.7
	80-84			280.5	507.5	1 721.9
	85-89			141.7	246.8	1 049.6
	90-94	41.3	107.9	56.5	99.1	478.8
	95-99			17.5	29.5	160.1
	100+			5.2	7.4	35.0
Female	Total	6 348.9	12 758.0	23 749.8	29 238.7	33 369.3
	0-14	2 659.1	5 428.3	6 920.7	6 723.3	5 819.6
	15-59	3 325.9	6 557.3	14 782.3	18 002.1	19 109.3
	60-64	129.1	266.6	649.5	1 420.6	1 865.7
	65-69	98.4	205.9	473.9	1 123.6	1 701.4
	70-74	67.8	144.8	359.1	851.5	1 515.3
	75-79	42.8	89.8	256.2	552.8	1 229.2
	80-84			165.5	308.4	1 011.6
	85-89			87.7	159.6	651.5
	90-94	25.8	65.3	37.7	68.8	320.4
	95-99			12.9	22.0	117.2
	100+			4.3	5.9	28.0
Male	Total	6 219.5	12 623.0	23 202.2	28 499.4	32 309.9
	0-14	2 699.4	5 585.4	7 223.7	7 037.7	6 094.0
	15-59	3 258.1	6 389.7	14 322.7	17 936.7	19 333.5
	60-64	101.3	240.7	576.4	1 232.9	1 761.2
	65-69	69.8	178.3	407.0	923.9	1 547.3
	70-74	47.2	121.5	287.7	651.5	1 296.6
	75-79	28.3	64.8	191.4	391.0	960.5
	80-84			115.0	199.1	710.3
	85-89			54.1	87.3	398.2
	90-94	15.5	42.6	18.8	30.4	158.4
	95-99			4.6	7.5	42.9
	100+			0.9	1.5	7.1
Percentage in older ages						
Total	60+	5.0	5.6	7.9	13.9	23.3
	65+	3.1	3.6	5.3	9.3	17.8
	80+	0.3	0.4	1.1	1.5	5.2
Female	60+	5.7	6.1	8.6	15.4	25.3
	65+	3.7	4.0	5.9	10.6	19.7
	80+	0.4	0.5	1.3	1.9	6.4
Male	60+	4.2	5.1	7.1	12.4	21.3
	65+	2.6	3.2	4.7	8.0	15.9
	80+	0.2	0.3	0.8	1.1	4.1
Ageing index		11.7	12.9	26.2	58.4	128.6
Broad age groups (percentage)	0-14	42.6	43.4	30.1	23.8	18.1
	15-59	52.4	51.0	62.0	62.2	58.5
	60+	5.0	5.6	7.9	13.9	23.3
Median age (years)		18.7	17.9	25.4*	31.5	39.3
Dependency ratio	Total	84.4	88.6	54.8	49.6	56.1
	Youth	78.6	81.9	46.6	35.7	28.3
	Old Age	5.8	6.8	8.2	14.0	27.8
Potential support ratio		17.2	14.7	12.2	7.2	3.6
Parent support ratio		1.2	1.9	4.3	4.3	14.4
Sex ratio (per 100 women)	60+	72.0	83.9	80.9	78.1	81.5
	65+	68.5	80.5	77.2	74.1	77.9
	80+	60.2	65.3	62.7	57.7	61.9

* *Estimate refers to year 2005.*

Indicator	Age	1950-1955	1975-1980	2005-2010	2025-2030	2045-2050
Growth rate (percentage)	Total	2.9	2.3	1.4	0.8	0.3
	60+	2.7	2.8	4.1	3.9	1.7
	65+	2.0	3.4	3.3	4.7	1.9
	80+	1.5	5.4	3.1	6.8	3.7
Total fertility rate (per woman)		6.8	4.3	2.5	2.0	1.9
Life expectancy (years)						
Total	Birth	50.6	63.8	73.3	76.4	79.2
	60	..	..	20.5	22.8	24.1
	65	..	..	16.8	18.9	20.1
	80	..	..	8.3	9.5	10.0
Female	Birth	52.3	66.0	76.3	79.6	82.5
	60	..	..	22.0	24.1	25.9
	65	..	..	18.1	20.1	21.7
	80	..	..	9.0	10.2	10.8
Male	Birth	49.0	61.6	70.3	73.2	76.0
	60	..	..	18.9	21.2	22.1
	65	..	..	15.4	17.5	18.3
	80	..	..	7.4	8.6	8.9
Survival rate (percentage)						
Total	60	..	..	83.5	86.0	89.2
	65	..	..	77.8	81.3	85.3
	80	..	..	43.8	52.8	59.7
Female	60	..	..	87.3	90.1	92.7
	65	..	..	82.5	86.1	89.6
	80	..	..	50.9	59.6	67.9
Male	60	..	..	79.6	81.9	85.8
	65	..	..	73.0	76.6	81.0
	80	..	..	36.7	45.7	51.4

		1980	1990	2007	2010	2020
Labour force participation (percentage)						
Total	65+	25.5	14.2	16.2	17.2	19.1
Female	65+	16.7	6.7	10.9	12.7	16.3
Male	65+	36.4	23.6	23.1	23.0	22.9

Percentage married, age 60+			Percentage living alone, age 60+ (2000)		
Total	Female	Male	Total	Female	Male
54.7	39.0	74.0	7.1	7.4	6.7

Statutory pensionable age (2006)		Percentage illiterate, age 65+ (2004)		
Female	Male	Total	Female	Male
55	60	25.0	27.1	22.4

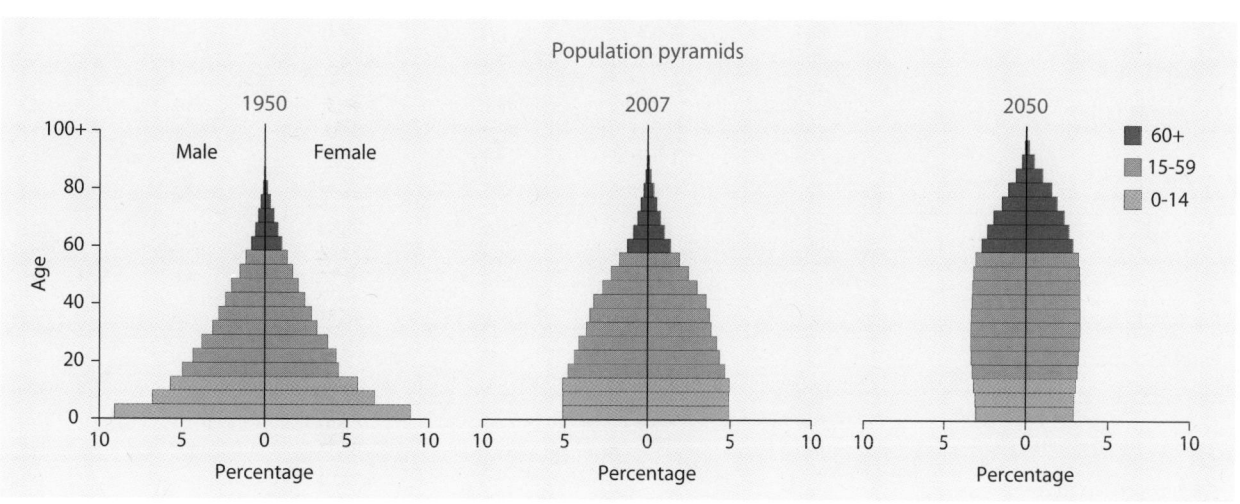

Population pyramids

Comoros

Indicator	Age	1950	1975	2007	2025	2050
Population (thousands)						
Total	Total	172.7	317.5	840.9	1 242.4	1 780.9
	0-14	75.1	151.5	349.4	413.5	441.5
	15-59	88.3	153.1	454.5	753.8	1 118.1
	60-64	3.3	5.1	14.1	28.5	70.6
	65-69	2.6	3.6	9.9	19.9	60.7
	70-74	1.8	2.3	6.6	13.0	41.9
	75-79	1.0	1.3	3.9	8.2	26.6
	80-84			1.8	3.9	14.2
	85-89			0.6	1.3	5.6
	90-94	0.5	0.8	0.1	0.3	1.4
	95-99			0.0	0.0	0.2
	100+			0.0	0.0	0.0
Female	Total	87.5	159.3	418.9	619.0	890.5
	0-14	37.8	75.0	172.1	203.4	216.1
	15-59	44.8	77.0	226.6	375.2	554.1
	60-64	1.7	2.7	7.5	14.8	36.3
	65-69	1.4	2.0	5.3	10.6	32.0
	70-74	1.0	1.3	3.7	7.1	23.0
	75-79	0.6	0.7	2.3	4.7	15.3
	80-84			1.1	2.3	8.7
	85-89			0.4	0.8	3.7
	90-94	0.3	0.5	0.1	0.2	1.1
	95-99			0.0	0.0	0.2
	100+			0.0	0.0	0.0
Male	Total	85.2	158.3	421.9	623.4	890.4
	0-14	37.4	76.4	177.3	210.1	225.4
	15-59	43.5	76.0	227.9	378.6	564.0
	60-64	1.6	2.3	6.6	13.7	34.2
	65-69	1.2	1.6	4.6	9.3	28.6
	70-74	0.8	1.0	3.0	5.9	19.0
	75-79	0.5	0.5	1.6	3.5	11.3
	80-84			0.7	1.6	5.5
	85-89			0.2	0.5	1.9
	90-94	0.2	0.3	0.0	0.1	0.4
	95-99			0.0	0.0	0.0
	100+			0.0	0.0	0.0
Percentage in older ages						
Total	60+	5.4	4.1	4.4	6.0	12.4
	65+	3.4	2.5	2.7	3.8	8.5
	80+	0.3	0.2	0.3	0.4	1.2
Female	60+	5.7	4.5	4.8	6.5	13.5
	65+	3.7	2.8	3.1	4.2	9.4
	80+	0.3	0.3	0.4	0.5	1.5
Male	60+	5.1	3.7	4.0	5.6	11.3
	65+	3.2	2.2	2.4	3.3	7.5
	80+	0.3	0.2	0.2	0.3	0.9
Ageing index		12.3	8.6	10.6	18.2	50.1
Broad age groups (percentage)	0-14	43.5	47.7	41.5	33.3	24.8
	15-59	51.1	48.2	54.0	60.7	62.8
	60+	5.4	4.1	4.4	6.0	12.4
Median age (years)		18.2	16.1	18.7*	23.2	30.7
Dependency ratio	Total	88.5	100.8	79.5	58.8	49.8
	Youth	82.0	95.8	74.6	52.9	37.1
	Old Age	6.5	5.0	4.9	6.0	12.7
Potential support ratio		15.4	19.9	20.4	16.8	7.9
Parent support ratio		1.2	1.0	1.3	1.4	2.9
Sex ratio (per 100 women)	60+	86.9	80.5	82.6	85.5	83.9
	65+	85.0	77.3	79.0	81.2	79.5
	80+	78.5	65.1	63.1	64.4	56.9

* Estimate refers to year 2005.

Indicator	Age	1950-1955	1975-1980	2005-2010	2025-2030	2045-2050
Growth rate (percentage)	Total	2.3	3.9	2.6	1.8	1.1
	60+	0.7	3.5	3.8	4.6	3.5
	65+	0.4	3.5	3.8	4.7	4.7
	80+	2.3	3.4	4.2	5.1	6.0
Total fertility rate (per woman)		6.3	7.1	4.3	2.8	2.2
Life expectancy (years)						
Total	Birth	40.7	50.9	65.2	71.9	75.9
	60	..	..	16.7	18.1	20.0
	65	..	..	13.3	14.4	16.1
	80	..	..	5.7	6.1	7.0
Female	Birth	42.0	53.0	67.4	74.4	78.4
	60	..	..	17.6	19.3	21.7
	65	..	..	14.0	15.3	17.6
	80	..	..	5.9	6.4	7.8
Male	Birth	39.5	49.0	63.0	69.4	73.4
	60	..	..	15.6	16.9	18.1
	65	..	..	12.5	13.4	14.4
	80	..	..	5.4	5.7	6.1
Survival rate (percentage)						
Total	60	..	..	73.2	84.0	89.4
	65	..	..	65.6	77.3	83.9
	80	..	..	26.8	36.5	46.4
Female	60	..	..	76.9	87.7	91.8
	65	..	..	70.2	82.3	87.8
	80	..	..	31.3	42.9	55.0
Male	60	..	..	69.8	80.5	87.0
	65	..	..	61.2	72.5	80.1
	80	..	..	22.3	30.3	37.8

		1980	1990	2007	2010	2020
Labour force participation (percentage)						
Total	65+	56.6	55.1	50.6	50.5	50.6
Female	65+	37.6	35.4	24.4	24.1	23.8
Male	65+	81.3	80.8	83.8	83.8	83.8

Percentage married, age 60+				Percentage living alone, age 60+ (1996)		
Total	Female	Male		Total	Female	Male
60.9	41.0	85.0		1.5	1.8	1.1

Statutory pensionable age (2006)				Percentage illiterate, age 65+		
	Female	Male		Total	Female	Male
	..	..		..	..	..

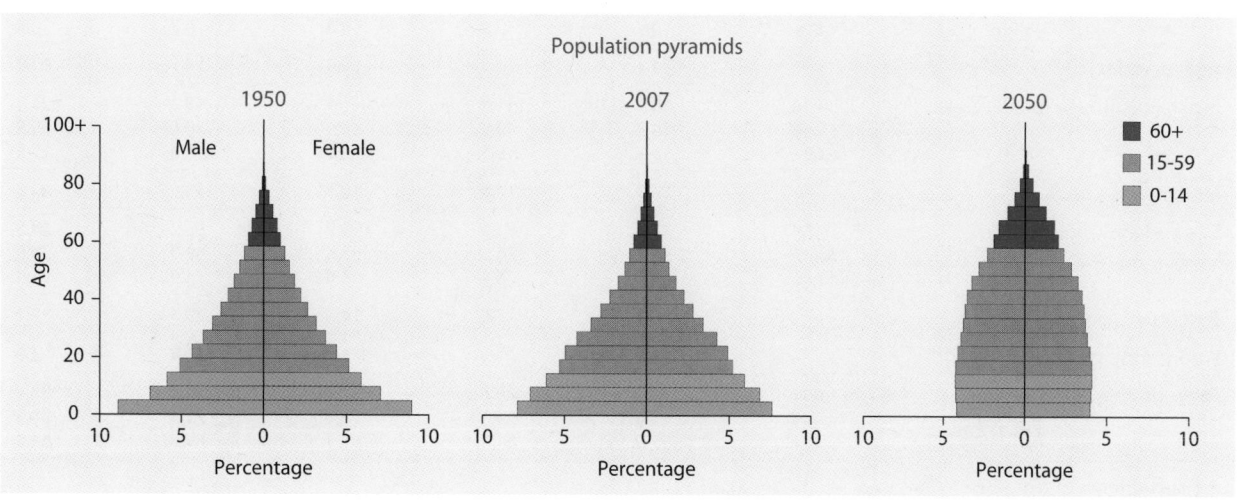

Population pyramids

United Nations Department of Economic and Social Affairs, Population Division

Congo

Indicator	Age	1950	1975	2007	2025	2050
Population (thousands)						
Total	Total	807.7	1 543.6	4 237.7	7 404.0	13 720.9
	0-14	323.9	692.5	2 009.3	3 383.6	4 865.0
	15-59	437.9	769.1	2 039.4	3 732.2	8 126.0
	60-64	17.9	30.7	67.0	99.2	267.0
	65-69	13.0	22.6	50.5	75.5	192.4
	70-74	8.3	15.2	35.4	54.3	132.8
	75-79	4.5	8.7	21.5	34.7	82.0
	80-84			10.3	17.0	38.5
	85-89			3.5	6.0	13.6
	90-94	2.3	4.9	0.7	1.4	3.2
	95-99			0.1	0.2	0.4
	100+			0.0	0.0	0.0
Female	Total	410.9	784.6	2 134.5	3 709.1	6 858.7
	0-14	162.7	346.9	1 002.1	1 687.2	2 416.9
	15-59	223.0	391.6	1 027.0	1 860.4	4 052.9
	60-64	9.6	16.6	36.1	52.7	136.2
	65-69	7.1	12.6	27.8	41.9	100.6
	70-74	4.6	8.7	19.9	31.2	72.0
	75-79	2.6	5.2	12.5	20.5	46.3
	80-84			6.2	10.4	22.8
	85-89			2.3	3.8	8.6
	90-94	1.4	3.1	0.5	0.9	2.1
	95-99			0.1	0.1	0.3
	100+			0.0	0.0	0.0
Male	Total	396.8	759.0	2 103.2	3 694.9	6 862.2
	0-14	161.2	345.6	1 007.2	1 696.4	2 448.1
	15-59	214.9	377.4	1 012.4	1 871.8	4 073.1
	60-64	8.3	14.0	30.8	46.5	130.8
	65-69	5.9	10.1	22.7	33.6	91.8
	70-74	3.7	6.5	15.4	23.1	60.8
	75-79	1.9	3.6	9.0	14.2	35.8
	80-84			4.0	6.6	15.7
	85-89			1.3	2.2	5.0
	90-94	0.9	1.9	0.2	0.4	1.0
	95-99			0.0	0.0	0.1
	100+			0.0	0.0	0.0
Percentage in older ages						
Total	60+	5.7	5.3	4.5	3.9	5.3
	65+	3.5	3.3	2.9	2.6	3.4
	80+	0.3	0.3	0.3	0.3	0.4
Female	60+	6.1	5.9	4.9	4.4	5.7
	65+	3.8	3.8	3.2	2.9	3.7
	80+	0.3	0.4	0.4	0.4	0.5
Male	60+	5.2	4.7	4.0	3.4	5.0
	65+	3.1	2.9	2.5	2.2	3.1
	80+	0.2	0.2	0.3	0.3	0.3
Ageing index		14.2	11.9	9.4	8.5	15.0
Broad age groups (percentage)	0-14	40.1	44.9	47.4	45.7	35.5
	15-59	54.2	49.8	48.1	50.4	59.2
	60+	5.7	5.3	4.5	3.9	5.3
Median age (years)		20.0	17.6	16.3*	16.9	21.9
Dependency ratio	Total	77.2	93.0	101.2	93.2	63.5
	Youth	71.1	86.6	95.4	88.3	58.0
	Old Age	6.2	6.4	5.8	4.9	5.5
Potential support ratio		16.3	15.6	17.3	20.3	18.1
Parent support ratio		0.9	1.1	1.8	1.9	1.6
Sex ratio (per 100 women)	60+	82.0	78.2	79.2	78.5	87.7
	65+	79.4	74.6	76.1	73.8	83.2
	80+	67.9	61.0	61.7	61.2	64.5

* Estimate refers to year 2005.

Indicator	Age	1950-1955	1975-1980	2005-2010	2025-2030	2045-2050
Growth rate (percentage)	Total	2.0	3.1	2.9	2.9	2.1
	60+	1.8	2.7	2.3	3.0	4.2
	65+	1.9	2.8	2.3	2.6	4.1
	80+	2.7	3.3	2.7	3.2	4.1
Total fertility rate (per woman)		5.7	6.3	6.3	4.7	3.0
Life expectancy (years)						
Total	Birth	42.1	55.7	53.5	60.5	67.2
	60	..	..	16.0	16.9	18.0
	65	..	..	12.9	13.6	14.4
	80	..	..	5.6	5.8	6.1
Female	Birth	44.5	57.9	54.8	61.9	69.0
	60	..	..	16.9	17.9	19.2
	65	..	..	13.5	14.3	15.3
	80	..	..	5.8	6.0	6.4
Male	Birth	39.8	53.6	52.2	59.0	65.5
	60	..	..	15.0	15.8	16.7
	65	..	..	12.1	12.6	13.4
	80	..	..	5.3	5.5	5.7
Survival rate (percentage)						
Total	60	..	..	50.3	61.0	73.0
	65	..	..	44.3	54.7	66.9
	80	..	..	17.1	23.2	31.4
Female	60	..	..	52.2	62.8	75.2
	65	..	..	46.9	57.5	70.4
	80	..	..	19.8	26.7	36.6
Male	60	..	..	48.3	59.2	70.9
	65	..	..	41.5	51.9	63.5
	80	..	..	14.2	19.5	26.3

		1980	1990	2007	2010	2020
Labour force participation (percentage)						
Total	65+	63.4	65.1	72.8	73.1	73.4
Female	65+	57.9	58.7	60.2	60.2	60.3
Male	65+	70.8	73.7	89.3	90.1	91.1

Percentage married, age 60+				Percentage living alone, age 60+		
Total	Female	Male		Total	Female	Male
56.7	38.0	80.0		..	..	..

Statutory pensionable age (2006)			Percentage illiterate, age 65+		
Female	Male		Total	Female	Male
55	55		..	..	..

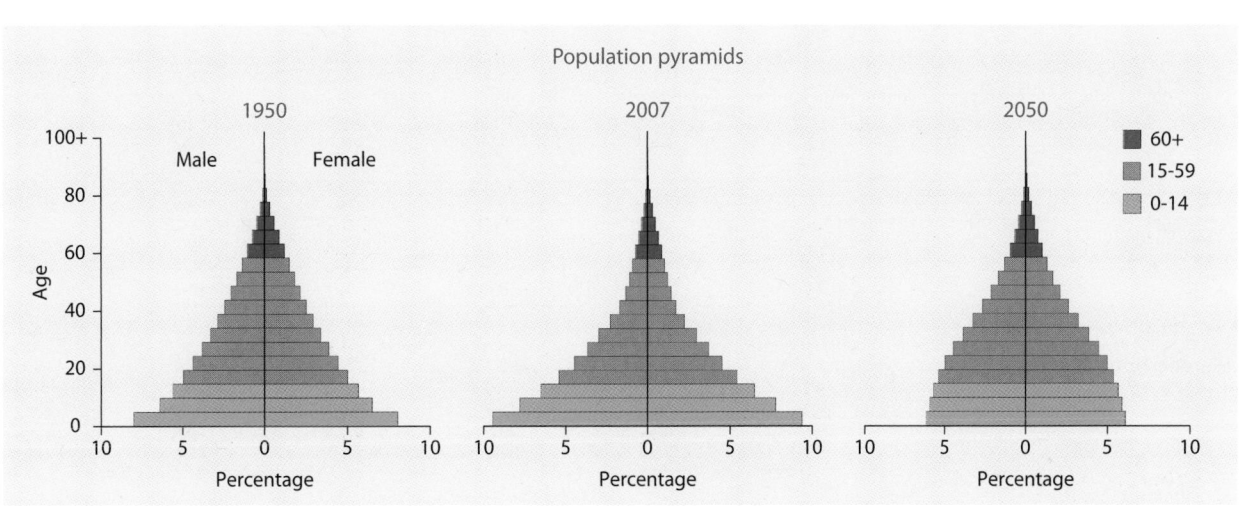

Population pyramids

United Nations Department of Economic and Social Affairs, Population Division

Costa Rica

Indicator	Age	1950	1975	2007	2025	2050
Population (thousands)						
Total	Total	966.0	2 050.9	4 467.6	5 549.3	6 426.0
	0-14	371.6	848.6	1 215.5	1 155.7	1 088.9
	15-59	520.7	1 061.0	2 865.0	3 504.6	3 635.0
	60-64	27.0	46.1	117.5	280.2	421.7
	65-69	20.0	35.9	89.9	224.2	367.4
	70-74	13.5	26.5	68.4	160.3	298.0
	75-79	8.0	18.4	51.0	104.1	226.3
	80-84			31.7	63.1	185.8
	85-89			18.7	35.6	124.9
	90-94	5.2	14.4	7.8	15.7	58.1
	95-99			1.9	5.0	17.1
	100+			0.3	0.9	2.7
Female	Total	473.1	1 011.5	2 197.4	2 743.5	3 211.4
	0-14	183.5	416.9	591.3	563.6	530.9
	15-59	250.7	524.2	1 402.2	1 716.6	1 778.9
	60-64	14.0	22.0	59.8	140.0	210.9
	65-69	10.7	17.4	46.4	113.4	187.0
	70-74	7.1	13.3	36.1	83.5	155.3
	75-79	4.3	9.7	27.5	56.3	122.0
	80-84			17.6	35.6	103.8
	85-89			10.6	20.9	73.3
	90-94	2.8	8.0	4.6	9.7	36.2
	95-99			1.1	3.2	11.4
	100+			0.2	0.6	1.8
Male	Total	492.9	1 039.4	2 270.3	2 805.8	3 214.6
	0-14	188.1	431.7	624.2	592.0	558.0
	15-59	270.0	536.7	1 462.8	1 788.0	1 856.1
	60-64	13.0	24.1	57.7	140.2	210.8
	65-69	9.3	18.5	43.5	110.8	180.5
	70-74	6.5	13.2	32.3	76.8	142.7
	75-79	3.7	8.7	23.5	47.8	104.3
	80-84			14.1	27.4	82.0
	85-89			8.0	14.6	51.6
	90-94	2.4	6.5	3.2	5.9	21.9
	95-99			0.7	1.8	5.7
	100+			0.1	0.3	0.9
Percentage in older ages						
Total	60+	7.6	6.9	8.7	16.0	26.5
	65+	4.8	4.6	6.0	11.0	19.9
	80+	0.5	0.7	1.3	2.2	6.0
Female	60+	8.2	7.0	9.3	16.9	28.1
	65+	5.3	4.8	6.6	11.8	21.5
	80+	0.6	0.8	1.6	2.6	7.1
Male	60+	7.1	6.8	8.1	15.2	24.9
	65+	4.4	4.5	5.5	10.2	18.3
	80+	0.5	0.6	1.2	1.8	5.0
Ageing index		19.8	16.7	31.9	76.9	156.3
Broad age groups (percentage)	0-14	38.5	41.4	27.2	20.8	16.9
	15-59	53.9	51.7	64.1	63.2	56.6
	60+	7.6	6.9	8.7	16.0	26.5
Median age (years)		21.6	18.7	26.1*	34.4	41.8
Dependency ratio	Total	76.4	85.3	49.8	46.6	58.4
	Youth	67.9	76.7	40.8	30.5	26.8
	Old Age	8.5	8.6	9.0	16.1	31.6
Potential support ratio		11.7	11.6	11.1	6.2	3.2
Parent support ratio		1.9	3.1	5.8	6.4	16.1
Sex ratio (per 100 women)	60+	89.8	100.9	89.9	91.9	88.8
	65+	88.2	96.9	87.1	88.4	85.4
	80+	86.4	81.2	76.9	71.6	71.6

* Estimate refers to year 2005.

Indicator	Age	1950-1955	1975-1980	2005-2010	2025-2030	2045-2050
Growth rate (percentage)	Total	3.1	2.7	1.5	0.9	0.3
	60+	2.5	3.3	4.0	3.5	2.2
	65+	2.9	3.1	3.5	4.6	2.3
	80+	3.6	4.2	4.3	4.9	2.8
Total fertility rate (per woman)		6.7	3.8	2.1	1.9	1.9
Life expectancy (years)						
Total	Birth	57.2	70.7	78.7	80.8	82.0
	60	..	..	23.0	24.3	25.0
	65	..	..	19.0	20.2	20.8
	80	..	..	9.1	9.8	10.1
Female	Birth	58.5	73.0	81.2	83.3	84.7
	60	..	..	24.5	26.0	26.9
	65	..	..	20.3	21.7	22.5
	80	..	..	9.7	10.4	10.9
Male	Birth	56.0	68.7	76.4	78.4	79.5
	60	..	..	21.6	22.5	23.1
	65	..	..	17.8	18.6	19.1
	80	..	..	8.6	9.0	9.2
Survival rate (percentage)						
Total	60	..	..	89.7	91.7	92.9
	65	..	..	85.4	88.1	89.5
	80	..	..	56.7	62.6	65.9
Female	60	..	..	92.5	94.1	95.0
	65	..	..	89.2	91.4	92.7
	80	..	..	64.2	70.3	74.0
Male	60	..	..	87.2	89.5	90.8
	65	..	..	82.1	84.9	86.5
	80	..	..	50.2	55.2	58.1

		1980	1990	2007	2010	2020
Labour force participation (percentage)						
Total	65+	23.8	18.1	18.7	18.6	18.7
Female	65+	3.7	3.5	6.7	6.7	6.7
Male	65+	44.5	33.7	32.4	32.4	32.5

Percentage married, age 60+			Percentage living alone, age 60+ (1984)		
Total	Female	Male	Total	Female	Male
57.3	44.0	72.0	7.8	8.0	7.5

Statutory pensionable age (2006)			Percentage illiterate, age 65+ (2000)		
	Female	Male	Total	Female	Male
	59	61	17.4	17.0	17.8

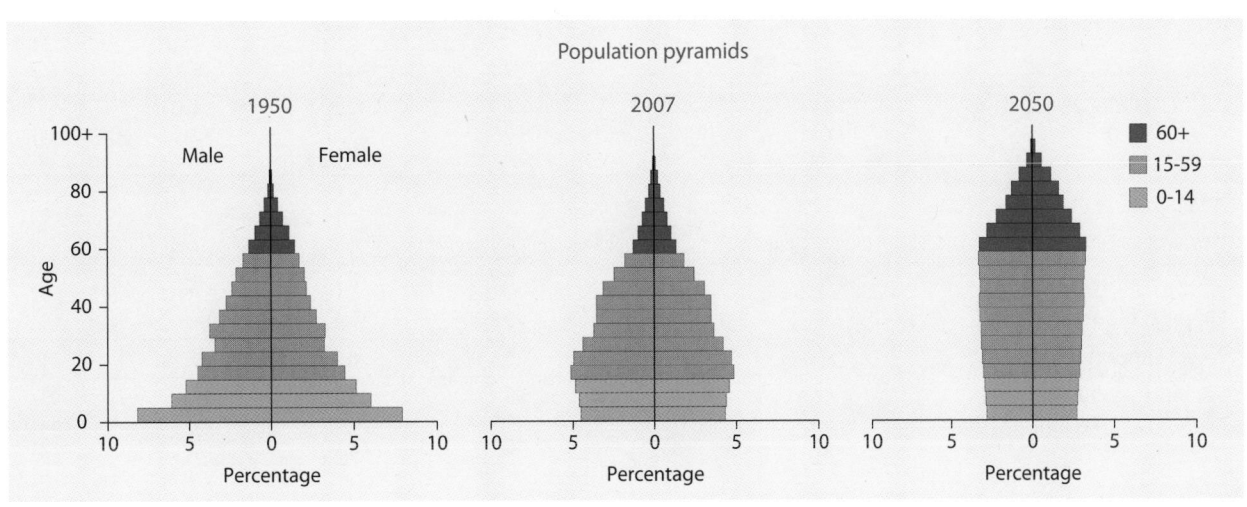

Population pyramids

Côte d'Ivoire

Indicator	Age	1950	1975	2007	2025	2050
Population (thousands)						
Total	Total	2 504.9	6 592.2	18 769.7	25 114.4	33 958.9
	0-14	1 078.8	2 962.7	7 727.0	8 646.2	8 651.5
	15-59	1 325.8	3 350.3	10 037.2	14 910.2	21 776.9
	60-64	42.3	112.7	372.5	503.7	1 296.4
	65-69	28.5	79.0	285.3	428.0	976.2
	70-74	17.0	49.7	189.9	321.8	628.0
	75-79	8.5	25.9	103.6	187.8	373.1
	80-84			41.7	87.0	178.4
	85-89			10.8	25.4	63.9
	90-94	3.9	11.8	1.5	4.0	13.2
	95-99			0.1	0.3	1.3
	100+			0.0	0.0	0.1
Female	Total	1 235.2	3 194.3	9 242.1	12 458.6	16 960.7
	0-14	528.0	1 483.1	3 862.4	4 317.2	4 309.0
	15-59	652.4	1 570.5	4 899.1	7 355.3	10 822.1
	60-64	22.4	55.1	172.3	247.5	651.4
	65-69	15.5	39.7	134.7	214.5	499.2
	70-74	9.5	25.7	92.1	164.5	328.7
	75-79	4.9	13.8	52.3	96.4	201.6
	80-84			22.1	46.4	100.7
	85-89			6.1	14.2	38.4
	90-94	2.4	6.3	0.9	2.4	8.6
	95-99			0.1	0.2	0.9
	100+			0.0	0.0	0.0
Male	Total	1 269.7	3 397.9	9 527.6	12 655.8	16 998.2
	0-14	550.8	1 479.6	3 864.7	4 329.1	4 342.6
	15-59	673.4	1 779.8	5 138.2	7 554.8	10 954.7
	60-64	19.8	57.6	200.2	256.2	645.0
	65-69	13.0	39.3	150.6	213.5	476.9
	70-74	7.5	24.0	97.8	157.4	299.3
	75-79	3.6	12.1	51.3	91.4	171.5
	80-84			19.5	40.6	77.7
	85-89			4.7	11.1	25.4
	90-94	1.6	5.5	0.6	1.6	4.7
	95-99			0.0	0.1	0.4
	100+			0.0	0.0	0.0
Percentage in older ages						
Total	60+	4.0	4.2	5.4	6.2	10.4
	65+	2.3	2.5	3.4	4.2	6.6
	80+	0.2	0.2	0.3	0.5	0.8
Female	60+	4.4	4.4	5.2	6.3	10.8
	65+	2.6	2.7	3.3	4.3	6.9
	80+	0.2	0.2	0.3	0.5	0.9
Male	60+	3.6	4.1	5.5	6.1	10.0
	65+	2.0	2.4	3.4	4.1	6.2
	80+	0.1	0.2	0.3	0.4	0.6
Ageing index		9.3	9.4	13.0	18.0	40.8
Broad age groups (percentage)	0-14	43.1	44.9	41.2	34.4	25.5
	15-59	52.9	50.8	53.5	59.4	64.1
	60+	4.0	4.2	5.4	6.2	10.4
Median age (years)		18.3	17.6	18.5*	22.5	29.5
Dependency ratio	Total	83.1	90.4	80.3	62.9	47.2
	Youth	78.9	85.6	74.2	56.1	37.5
	Old Age	4.2	4.8	6.1	6.8	9.7
Potential support ratio		23.6	20.8	16.4	14.6	10.3
Parent support ratio		0.5	0.6	0.9	1.6	1.7
Sex ratio (per 100 women)	60+	82.9	98.4	109.2	98.2	93.0
	65+	79.2	94.5	105.3	95.7	89.6
	80+	65.6	88.1	85.1	84.6	72.8

Estimate refers to year 2005.

Indicator	Age	1950-1955	1975-1980	2005-2010	2025-2030	2045-2050
Growth rate (percentage)	Total	3.4	4.7	1.7	1.4	1.1
	60+	3.7	4.7	2.7	1.7	4.5
	65+	3.6	4.8	3.1	1.9	4.9
	80+	2.6	5.9	4.3	3.5	2.6
Total fertility rate (per woman)		7.0	7.4	4.5	2.8	2.2
Life expectancy (years)						
Total	Birth	40.5	52.4	46.2	55.4	65.8
	60	..	..	15.6	17.0	18.6
	65	..	..	12.3	13.5	14.8
	80	..	..	4.9	5.3	5.8
Female	Birth	41.9	54.2	47.0	56.3	67.5
	60	..	..	16.5	18.0	19.8
	65	..	..	13.0	14.2	15.7
	80	..	..	5.2	5.6	6.2
Male	Birth	39.1	50.7	45.6	54.6	64.1
	60	..	..	14.8	16.0	17.4
	65	..	..	11.7	12.7	13.9
	80	..	..	4.7	5.0	5.4
Survival rate (percentage)						
Total	60	..	..	41.5	55.0	73.2
	65	..	..	36.7	49.8	68.1
	80	..	..	13.0	21.1	34.0
Female	60	..	..	42.5	56.0	75.5
	65	..	..	38.4	51.8	71.5
	80	..	..	15.0	24.2	39.4
Male	60	..	..	40.6	54.1	71.1
	65	..	..	35.2	48.1	64.9
	80	..	..	11.3	18.3	29.0

		1980	1990	2007	2010	2020
Labour force participation (percentage)						
Total	65+	46.1	49.4	48.7	48.7	48.0
Female	65+	22.5	24.4	17.6	17.6	17.6
Male	65+	70.1	73.5	78.3	78.5	78.7

Percentage married, age 60+			Percentage living alone, age 60+ (1999)		
Total	Female	Male	Total	Female	Male
58.1	34.0	80.0	4.0	2.9	5.0

Statutory pensionable age (2006)			Percentage illiterate, age 65+ (2000)		
	Female	Male	Total	Female	Male
	55	55	88.9	96.3	82.7

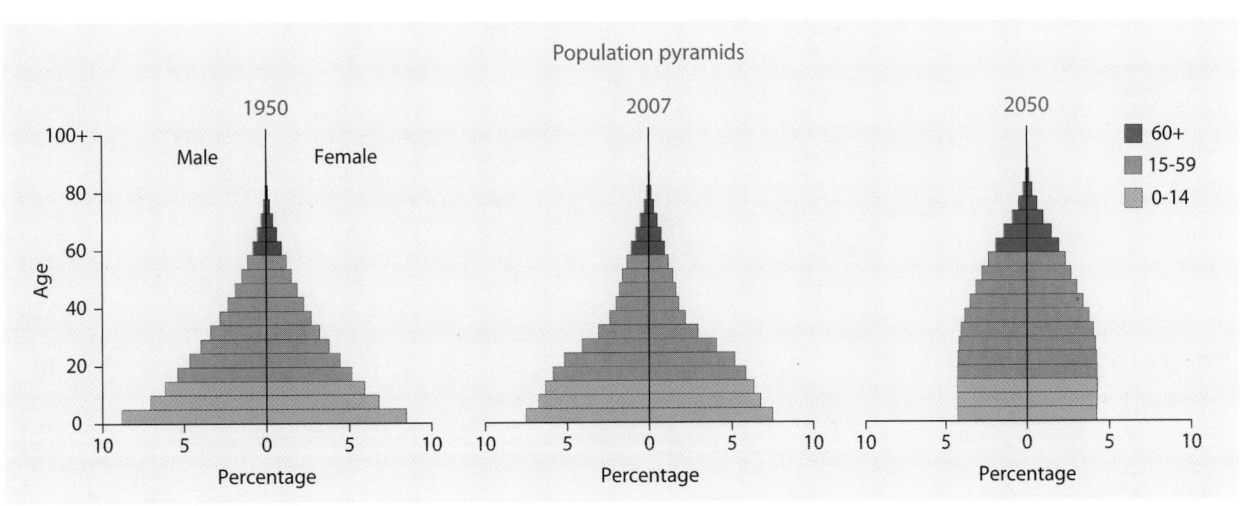

Population pyramids

Croatia

Indicator	Age	1950	1975	2007	2025	2050
Population (thousands)						
Total	Total	3 850.3	4 263.3	4 555.2	4 270.9	3 685.6
	0-14	1 030.3	916.6	684.6	599.2	531.4
	15-59	2 383.8	2 685.8	2 843.5	2 409.0	1 842.1
	60-64	132.7	191.5	236.8	301.4	260.3
	65-69	111.2	193.1	232.7	293.4	272.1
	70-74	85.5	138.9	232.9	257.8	248.4
	75-79	62.0	86.5	173.9	188.8	200.5
	80-84			102.1	105.1	153.0
	85-89			36.0	75.3	104.5
	90-94	44.8	50.9	9.9	32.1	52.9
	95-99			2.5	7.8	17.2
	100+			0.3	0.9	3.0
Female	Total	2 015.9	2 202.1	2 362.6	2 208.4	1 895.8
	0-14	508.8	448.3	333.2	291.1	258.1
	15-59	1 256.5	1 360.7	1 417.9	1 194.5	902.6
	60-64	76.4	110.3	127.1	158.1	132.4
	65-69	62.3	111.1	130.5	158.1	141.3
	70-74	48.0	82.3	137.3	142.8	133.5
	75-79	36.5	54.6	109.1	111.8	113.7
	80-84			71.5	67.9	92.6
	85-89			26.7	52.5	68.2
	90-94	27.4	34.8	7.2	24.4	37.7
	95-99			1.9	6.4	13.3
	100+			0.2	0.8	2.5
Male	Total	1 834.4	2 061.2	2 192.6	2 062.5	1 789.8
	0-14	521.5	468.3	351.4	308.1	273.3
	15-59	1 127.3	1 325.1	1 425.5	1 214.5	939.5
	60-64	56.3	81.2	109.7	143.4	127.9
	65-69	48.9	82.0	102.2	135.3	130.9
	70-74	37.5	56.6	95.6	115.1	114.9
	75-79	25.5	31.9	64.8	77.0	86.8
	80-84			30.7	37.2	60.5
	85-89			9.3	22.8	36.4
	90-94	17.4	16.1	2.7	7.7	15.3
	95-99			0.6	1.4	3.9
	100+			0.1	0.1	0.5
Percentage in older ages						
Total	60+	11.3	15.5	22.5	29.6	35.6
	65+	7.9	11.0	17.3	22.5	28.5
	80+	1.2	1.2	3.3	5.2	9.0
Female	60+	12.4	17.9	25.9	32.7	38.8
	65+	8.6	12.8	20.5	25.6	31.8
	80+	1.4	1.6	4.5	6.9	11.3
Male	60+	10.1	13.0	19.0	26.2	32.2
	65+	7.0	9.1	14.0	19.2	25.1
	80+	0.9	0.8	2.0	3.4	6.5
Ageing index		42.3	72.1	150.0	210.7	246.9
Broad age groups (percentage)	0-14	26.8	21.5	15.0	14.0	14.4
	15-59	61.9	63.0	62.4	56.4	50.0
	60+	11.3	15.5	22.5	29.6	35.6
Median age (years)		27.9	33.1	40.6*	45.4	48.8
Dependency ratio	Total	53.0	48.2	47.9	57.6	75.3
	Youth	40.9	31.9	22.2	22.1	25.3
	Old Age	12.1	16.3	25.7	35.5	50.0
Potential support ratio		8.3	6.1	3.9	2.8	2.0
Parent support ratio		3.0	2.7	5.4	13.1	24.0
Sex ratio (per 100 women)	60+	74.1	68.1	68.0	74.7	78.5
	65+	74.2	66.0	63.2	70.2	74.5
	80+	63.5	46.3	40.4	45.5	54.4

* *Estimate refers to year 2005.*

Croatia

Indicator	Age	1950-1955	1975-1980	2005-2010	2025-2030	2045-2050
Growth rate (percentage)	Total	0.6	0.5	−0.1	−0.5	−0.6
	60+	−0.2	−0.4	1.3	0.3	−0.2
	65+	−0.5	1.7	0.1	0.9	0.2
	80+	−1.1	4.6	5.6	2.2	0.0
Total fertility rate (per woman)		2.8	2.0	1.3	1.6	1.9
Life expectancy (years)						
Total	Birth	61.2	70.7	75.7	78.5	80.6
	60	..	..	19.9	21.7	23.1
	65	..	..	16.1	17.8	19.0
	80	..	..	7.2	8.3	9.0
Female	Birth	63.2	74.1	79.2	81.6	83.3
	60	..	..	21.9	23.9	25.2
	65	..	..	17.7	19.6	20.8
	80	..	..	7.7	9.0	9.8
Male	Birth	59.0	67.1	72.3	75.4	77.8
	60	..	..	17.5	19.4	20.9
	65	..	..	14.1	15.7	17.0
	80	..	..	6.3	7.1	7.9
Survival rate (percentage)						
Total	60	..	..	88.0	91.2	93.1
	65	..	..	82.1	86.5	89.2
	80	..	..	45.2	53.8	59.8
Female	60	..	..	92.8	94.4	95.4
	65	..	..	89.0	91.4	92.7
	80	..	..	56.2	64.2	68.9
Male	60	..	..	83.4	88.0	91.0
	65	..	..	75.4	81.6	85.7
	80	..	..	33.8	43.2	50.6

		1980	1990	2007	2010	2020
Labour force participation (percentage)						
Total	65+	20.9	11.2	4.2	3.9	3.5
Female	65+	10.8	7.8	3.5	3.4	3.4
Male	65+	36.7	17.5	5.2	4.6	3.7

Percentage married, age 60+			Percentage living alone, age 60+		
Total	Female	Male	Total	Female	Male
56.8	41.0	80.0	..	..	..

Statutory pensionable age (2006)			Percentage illiterate, age 65+ (2001)		
	Female	Male	Total	Female	Male
	58	63	6.9	9.9	2.1

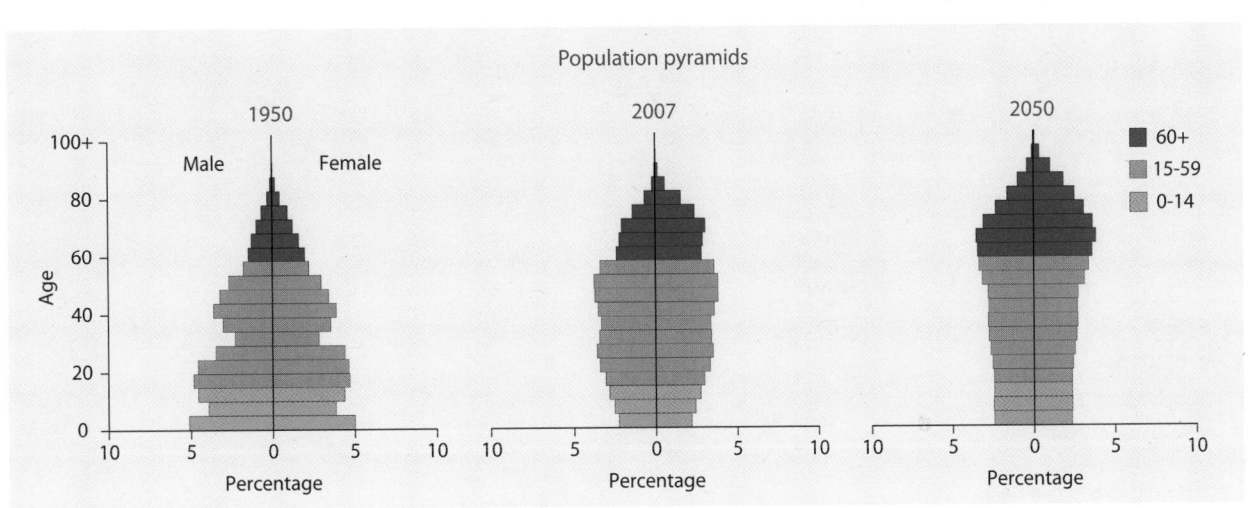

Population pyramids

Cuba

Indicator	Age	1950	1975	2007	2025	2050
Population (thousands)						
Total	Total	5 850.4	9 250.6	11 317.1	11 348.3	9 749.0
	0-14	2 094.8	3 455.2	2 080.0	1 716.5	1 322.3
	15-59	3 328.6	4 868.2	7 418.6	6 666.9	4 749.5
	60-64	142.9	292.7	524.9	918.3	680.3
	65-69	113.9	242.0	440.2	555.3	556.4
	70-74	83.5	196.6	323.8	514.9	520.6
	75-79	53.2	117.5	240.8	419.6	699.1
	80-84			154.8	293.5	606.6
	85-89			87.6	171.9	410.2
	90-94	33.4	78.4	37.0	68.2	142.7
	95-99			8.4	20.5	52.1
	100+			0.9	2.8	9.2
Female	Total	2 797.0	4 556.5	5 654.5	5 676.9	4 881.5
	0-14	1 048.3	1 696.5	1 014.4	833.2	641.3
	15-59	1 566.2	2 424.6	3 682.0	3 264.6	2 294.3
	60-64	59.8	141.7	271.2	467.7	337.1
	65-69	47.0	115.9	227.2	289.2	278.1
	70-74	35.1	87.0	170.4	273.5	265.8
	75-79	23.0	53.3	129.2	230.1	370.8
	80-84			83.8	163.8	331.9
	85-89			49.0	99.1	236.6
	90-94	17.5	37.5	21.7	41.2	86.9
	95-99			5.1	12.8	33.1
	100+			0.5	1.7	5.6
Male	Total	3 053.4	4 694.1	5 662.6	5 671.4	4 867.5
	0-14	1 046.5	1 758.7	1 065.6	883.2	681.0
	15-59	1 762.3	2 443.6	3 736.6	3 402.3	2 455.1
	60-64	83.1	151.0	253.7	450.6	343.2
	65-69	66.9	126.1	213.0	266.1	278.3
	70-74	48.4	109.6	153.5	241.4	254.8
	75-79	30.3	64.2	111.6	189.5	328.3
	80-84			71.1	129.7	274.7
	85-89			38.6	72.8	173.6
	90-94	15.9	40.9	15.3	27.0	55.8
	95-99			3.3	7.7	19.0
	100+			0.4	1.1	3.6
Percentage in older ages						
Total	60+	7.3	10.0	16.1	26.1	37.7
	65+	4.9	6.9	11.4	18.0	30.7
	80+	0.6	0.8	2.6	4.9	12.5
Female	60+	6.5	9.6	16.9	27.8	39.9
	65+	4.4	6.4	12.1	19.6	33.0
	80+	0.6	0.8	2.8	5.6	14.2
Male	60+	8.0	10.5	15.2	24.4	35.6
	65+	5.3	7.3	10.7	16.5	28.5
	80+	0.5	0.9	2.3	4.2	10.8
Ageing index		20.4	26.8	87.4	172.7	278.1
Broad age groups (percentage)	0-14	35.8	37.4	18.4	15.1	13.6
	15-59	56.9	52.6	65.6	58.7	48.7
	60+	7.3	10.0	16.1	26.1	37.7
Median age (years)		23.3	22.7	35.6*	44.2	49.9
Dependency ratio	Total	68.5	79.2	42.5	49.6	79.5
	Youth	60.3	66.9	26.2	22.6	24.4
	Old Age	8.2	12.3	16.3	27.0	55.2
Potential support ratio		12.2	8.1	6.1	3.7	1.8
Parent support ratio		2.0	2.5	7.6	9.2	32.9
Sex ratio (per 100 women)	60+	134.1	113.0	89.8	87.8	89.0
	65+	131.7	116.1	88.3	84.2	86.3
	80+	91.1	109.2	80.4	74.8	75.9

* *Estimate refers to year 2005.*

Indicator	Age	1950-1955	1975-1980	2005-2010	2025-2030	2045-2050
Growth rate (percentage)	Total	1.8	0.8	0.2	–0.3	–0.9
	60+	2.2	2.4	2.8	3.0	–0.2
	65+	1.6	3.1	3.0	3.9	–0.8
	80+	2.3	6.7	3.4	3.3	3.4
Total fertility rate (per woman)		4.1	2.1	1.6	1.7	1.8
Life expectancy (years)						
Total	Birth	59.3	72.6	78.6	81.3	82.5
	60	..	..	22.5	24.2	25.0
	65	..	..	18.5	20.1	20.8
	80	..	..	8.7	9.6	10.0
Female	Birth	61.3	74.3	80.3	83.0	84.2
	60	..	..	23.6	25.5	26.4
	65	..	..	19.5	21.3	22.1
	80	..	..	9.1	10.1	10.6
Male	Birth	57.7	71.1	76.8	79.5	80.7
	60	..	..	21.3	22.8	23.5
	65	..	..	17.5	18.9	19.5
	80	..	..	8.2	9.0	9.4
Survival rate (percentage)						
Total	60	..	..	89.7	92.3	93.4
	65	..	..	85.1	88.6	90.0
	80	..	..	55.8	63.3	66.4
Female	60	..	..	91.6	93.8	94.7
	65	..	..	87.8	90.8	92.1
	80	..	..	61.3	69.1	72.5
Male	60	..	..	87.7	90.9	92.2
	65	..	..	82.4	86.4	88.0
	80	..	..	50.4	57.5	60.6

		1980	1990	2007	2010	2020
Labour force participation (percentage)						
Total	65+	12.1	10.7	9.0	8.7	8.1
Female	65+	2.1	1.8	2.0	2.2	3.5
Male	65+	21.4	19.8	16.9	16.1	13.5

Percentage married, age 60+			Percentage living alone, age 60+ (1981)		
Total	Female	Male	Total	Female	Male
57.0	46.0	69.0	9.3	8.5	10.1

Statutory pensionable age (2006)			Percentage illiterate, age 65+ (2002)		
	Female	Male	Total	Female	Male
	55	60	0.8	0.8	0.8

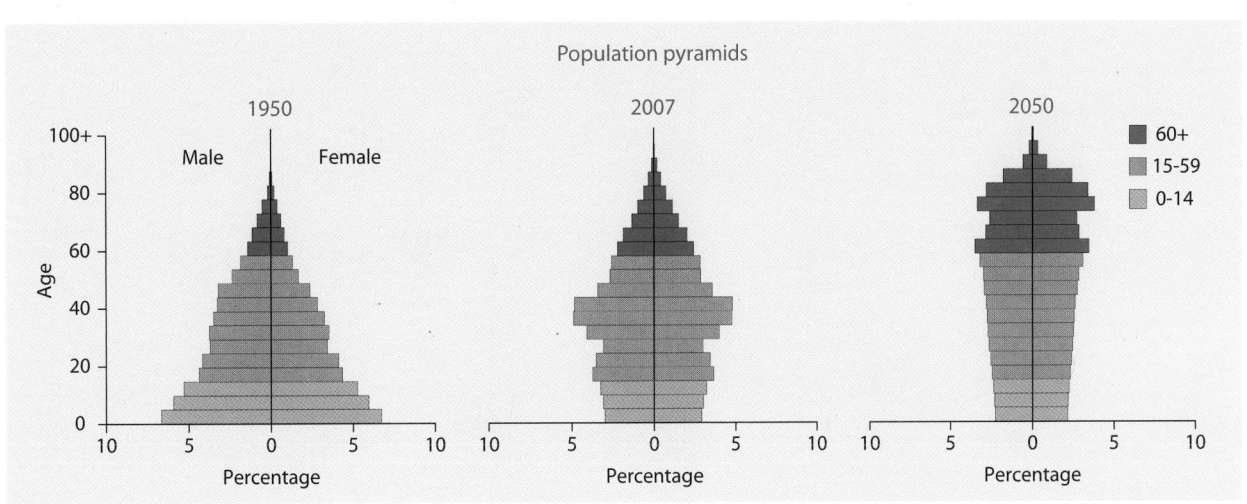

Population pyramids

Cyprus

Indicator	Age	1950	1975	2007	2025	2050
Population (thousands)						
Total	Total	494.0	609.2	853.8	1 013.8	1 174.4
	0-14	170.4	157.9	161.4	172.7	186.4
	15-59	278.7	366.7	544.1	605.3	638.9
	60-64	15.2	24.7	42.2	60.4	79.6
	65-69	12.0	22.7	33.9	56.2	74.0
	70-74	9.4	16.5	27.4	44.3	62.4
	75-79	5.3	9.5	21.1	34.4	48.9
	80-84			14.1	22.8	39.5
	85-89			6.9	11.6	26.3
	90-94	3.0	11.3	2.1	4.6	13.4
	95-99			0.4	1.2	4.2
	100+			0.0	0.2	0.8
Female	Total	250.4	306.3	438.7	518.4	596.6
	0-14	83.3	76.9	78.8	83.6	90.1
	15-59	144.0	184.3	279.3	304.9	314.5
	60-64	7.8	13.0	21.8	32.2	39.7
	65-69	6.0	12.3	17.8	29.8	37.5
	70-74	4.9	8.6	14.9	23.7	33.2
	75-79	2.8	5.6	12.0	19.1	27.8
	80-84			8.2	13.3	23.7
	85-89			4.2	7.4	16.8
	90-94	1.6	5.6	1.4	3.3	9.4
	95-99			0.3	0.9	3.3
	100+			0.0	0.1	0.7
Male	Total	243.6	302.9	415.1	495.5	577.8
	0-14	87.1	81.0	82.7	89.2	96.2
	15-59	134.7	182.4	264.8	300.4	324.4
	60-64	7.5	11.7	20.4	28.2	39.9
	65-69	5.9	10.4	16.1	26.4	36.5
	70-74	4.5	7.8	12.6	20.6	29.2
	75-79	2.5	3.9	9.1	15.3	21.1
	80-84			5.9	9.6	15.8
	85-89			2.7	4.2	9.6
	90-94	1.4	5.7	0.7	1.3	4.1
	95-99			0.1	0.2	0.9
	100+			0.0	0.0	0.1
Percentage in older ages						
Total	60+	9.1	13.9	17.4	23.3	29.7
	65+	6.0	9.8	12.4	17.3	23.0
	80+	0.6	1.9	2.8	4.0	7.2
Female	60+	9.2	14.7	18.4	25.0	32.2
	65+	6.1	10.5	13.4	18.8	25.5
	80+	0.6	1.8	3.2	4.8	9.0
Male	60+	9.0	13.1	16.3	21.4	27.2
	65+	5.9	9.2	11.4	15.7	20.3
	80+	0.6	1.9	2.3	3.1	5.3
Ageing index		26.4	53.7	91.8	136.5	187.3
Broad age groups (percentage)	0-14	34.5	25.9	18.9	17.0	15.9
	15-59	56.4	60.2	63.7	59.7	54.4
	60+	9.1	13.9	17.4	23.3	29.7
Median age (years)		23.7	27.1	35.3*	40.2	44.1
Dependency ratio	Total	68.1	55.7	45.6	52.3	63.5
	Youth	58.0	40.3	27.5	25.9	25.9
	Old Age	10.1	15.3	18.1	26.3	37.5
Potential support ratio		9.9	6.5	5.5	3.8	2.7
Parent support ratio		1.8	5.1	6.5	9.5	19.1
Sex ratio (per 100 women)	60+	94.7	87.8	83.9	81.6	81.8
	65+	93.9	86.8	80.3	79.6	77.0
	80+	88.2	101.8	67.0	61.7	56.6

* *Estimate refers to year 2005.*

Indicator	Age	1950-1955	1975-1980	2005-2010	2025-2030	2045-2050
Growth rate (percentage)	Total	1.4	0.1	1.1	0.7	0.5
	60+	3.0	0.2	2.6	1.8	1.5
	65+	3.7	0.9	2.6	2.3	1.7
	80+	5.4	−2.2	2.6	3.6	1.8
Total fertility rate (per woman)		3.7	2.3	1.6	1.8	1.9
Life expectancy (years)						
Total	Birth	67.0	73.7	79.2	81.4	83.4
	60	..	..	22.2	23.8	25.3
	65	..	..	18.0	19.5	20.9
	80	..	..	7.7	8.8	9.9
Female	Birth	69.0	75.5	81.6	83.8	85.7
	60	..	..	23.7	25.6	27.2
	65	..	..	19.4	21.1	22.7
	80	..	..	8.3	9.7	11.0
Male	Birth	65.1	72.0	76.7	78.9	80.9
	60	..	..	20.5	21.8	23.1
	65	..	..	16.5	17.7	18.9
	80	..	..	6.9	7.7	8.5
Survival rate (percentage)						
Total	60	..	..	92.4	94.2	95.5
	65	..	..	88.7	91.1	92.8
	80	..	..	58.1	64.1	69.3
Female	60	..	..	94.9	95.9	96.7
	65	..	..	92.1	93.6	94.8
	80	..	..	66.1	71.8	76.3
Male	60	..	..	89.8	92.3	94.2
	65	..	..	85.2	88.4	90.8
	80	..	..	49.9	56.0	61.7

		1980	1990	2007	2010	2020
Labour force participation (percentage)						
Total	65+	22.7	15.2	7.9	6.6	4.5
Female	65+	11.7	8.7	4.1	4.0	4.0
Male	65+	36.0	23.1	12.6	9.8	5.2

Percentage married, age 60+			Percentage living alone, age 60+ (1992)		
Total	Female	Male	Total	Female	Male
68.2	55.0	84.0	14.0	18.0	9.3

Statutory pensionable age (2006)		Percentage illiterate, age 65+ (2001)		
Female	Male	Total	Female	Male
65	65	16.4	25.0	5.8

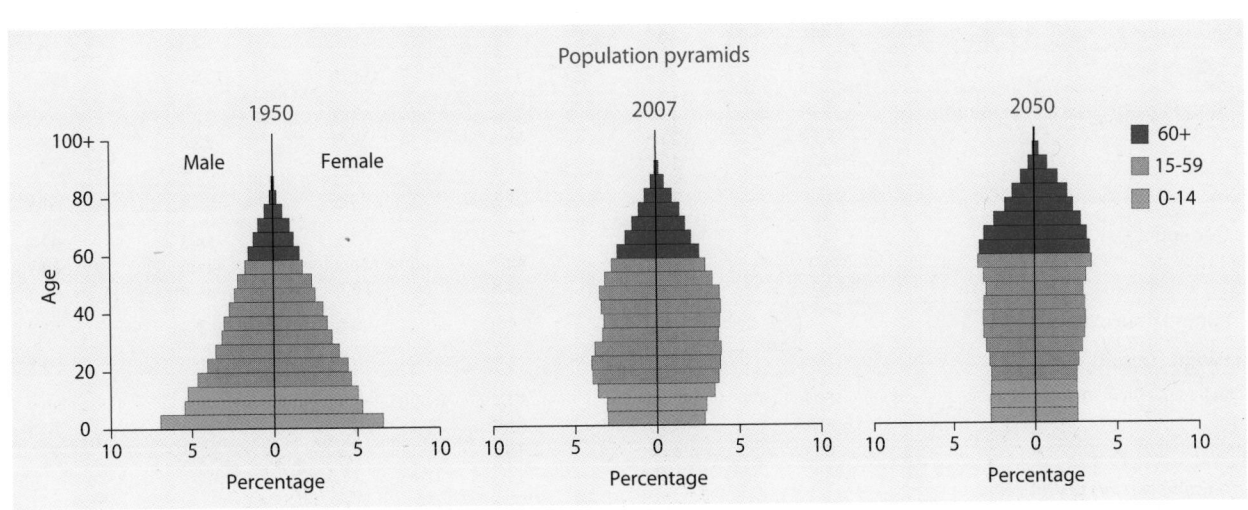

Population pyramids

United Nations Department of Economic and Social Affairs, Population Division

Czech Republic

Indicator	Age	1950	1975	2007	2025	2050
Population (thousands)						
Total	Total	8 925.1	9 997.4	10 198.0	9 752.7	8 452.1
	0-14	2 146.9	2 228.4	1 430.6	1 256.9	1 116.0
	15-59	5 667.5	5 935.6	6 610.8	5 697.0	4 010.7
	60-64	372.7	545.8	662.7	623.2	624.8
	65-69	297.1	512.3	461.1	593.6	632.2
	70-74	217.7	373.3	374.5	604.8	718.1
	75-79	135.5	227.8	318.6	500.8	590.6
	80-84			231.5	286.8	367.2
	85-89			80.0	125.9	231.1
	90-94	87.6	174.2	24.1	51.1	114.1
	95-99			4.0	11.7	40.9
	100+			0.1	0.9	6.4
Female	Total	4 585.0	5 140.1	5 233.8	5 016.1	4 354.7
	0-14	1 055.9	1 088.9	697.0	612.2	543.6
	15-59	2 899.6	2 986.9	3 277.0	2 804.2	1 964.4
	60-64	208.1	296.3	350.9	319.6	314.6
	65-69	167.4	284.7	254.7	316.1	325.2
	70-74	124.0	217.9	218.4	338.4	382.0
	75-79	77.7	141.7	198.8	298.2	329.6
	80-84			157.1	185.5	219.5
	85-89			58.2	90.1	151.7
	90-94	52.2	123.7	18.3	40.6	84.1
	95-99			3.2	10.3	34.0
	100+			0.1	0.9	5.9
Male	Total	4 340.2	4 857.3	4 964.2	4 736.6	4 097.4
	0-14	1 091.0	1 139.5	733.5	644.7	572.4
	15-59	2 768.0	2 948.7	3 333.8	2 892.8	2 046.4
	60-64	164.6	249.5	311.8	303.6	310.2
	65-69	129.7	227.6	206.3	277.5	307.1
	70-74	93.7	155.4	156.1	266.4	336.1
	75-79	57.8	86.1	119.7	202.6	261.0
	80-84			74.4	101.3	147.7
	85-89			21.8	35.8	79.4
	90-94	35.3	50.5	5.8	10.5	29.9
	95-99			0.8	1.5	6.9
	100+			0.0	0.0	0.5
Percentage in older ages						
Total	60+	12.4	18.3	21.1	28.7	39.3
	65+	8.3	12.9	14.6	22.3	32.0
	80+	1.0	1.7	3.3	4.9	9.0
Female	60+	13.7	20.7	24.1	31.9	42.4
	65+	9.2	14.9	17.4	25.5	35.2
	80+	1.1	2.4	4.5	6.5	11.4
Male	60+	11.1	15.8	18.1	25.3	36.1
	65+	7.3	10.7	11.8	18.9	28.5
	80+	0.8	1.0	2.1	3.1	6.5
Ageing index		51.7	82.3	150.7	222.7	298.0
Broad age groups (percentage)	0-14	24.1	22.3	14.0	12.9	13.2
	15-59	63.5	59.4	64.8	58.4	47.5
	60+	12.4	18.3	21.1	28.7	39.3
Median age (years)		32.7	32.6	39.0*	46.6	51.6
Dependency ratio	Total	47.8	54.2	40.2	54.3	82.3
	Youth	35.5	34.4	19.7	19.9	24.1
	Old Age	12.2	19.9	20.5	34.4	58.3
Potential support ratio		8.2	5.0	4.9	2.9	1.7
Parent support ratio		2.1	3.2	4.9	9.0	23.5
Sex ratio (per 100 women)	60+	76.4	72.3	71.2	75.0	80.1
	65+	75.1	67.7	64.4	70.0	76.3
	80+	67.6	40.8	43.4	45.6	53.4

* Estimate refers to year 2005.

Indicator	Age	1950-1955	1975-1980	2005-2010	2025-2030	2045-2050
Growth rate (percentage)	Total	0.8	0.6	−0.1	−0.5	−0.6
	60+	1.1	−1.2	2.6	0.5	0.0
	65+	0.9	1.3	1.9	0.6	0.3
	80+	3.6	2.1	3.1	5.1	0.8
Total fertility rate (per woman)		2.7	2.3	1.2	1.5	1.8
Life expectancy (years)						
Total	Birth	67.4	70.6	76.2	79.0	81.2
	60	..	..	19.9	21.8	23.5
	65	..	..	16.1	17.8	19.4
	80	..	..	7.1	8.1	9.2
Female	Birth	70.3	74.1	79.4	81.9	84.1
	60	..	..	22.0	24.0	25.8
	65	..	..	17.8	19.8	21.5
	80	..	..	7.6	9.0	10.2
Male	Birth	64.5	67.1	73.0	76.0	78.3
	60	..	..	17.5	19.2	21.1
	65	..	..	14.0	15.5	17.1
	80	..	..	6.1	6.8	7.7
Survival rate (percentage)						
Total	60	..	..	89.0	92.1	93.8
	65	..	..	83.1	87.4	90.0
	80	..	..	46.4	54.8	61.8
Female	60	..	..	92.9	94.6	95.8
	65	..	..	89.0	91.6	93.3
	80	..	..	57.4	65.5	71.5
Male	60	..	..	85.2	89.6	91.8
	65	..	..	77.2	83.2	86.8
	80	..	..	34.8	43.9	52.2

		1980	1990	2007	2010	2020
Labour force participation (percentage)						
Total	65+	11.7	8.2	3.3	3.1	2.5
Female	65+	7.2	5.2	2.1	2.1	2.1
Male	65+	18.8	13.3	5.2	4.5	3.1

Percentage married, age 60+				Percentage living alone, age 60+ (1991)		
Total	Female	Male		Total	Female	Male
55.8	40.0	79.0		33.6	44.2	17.4

Statutory pensionable age (2006)				Percentage illiterate, age 65+		
	Female	Male		Total	Female	Male
	59-60	61.6		..	..	..

Population pyramids

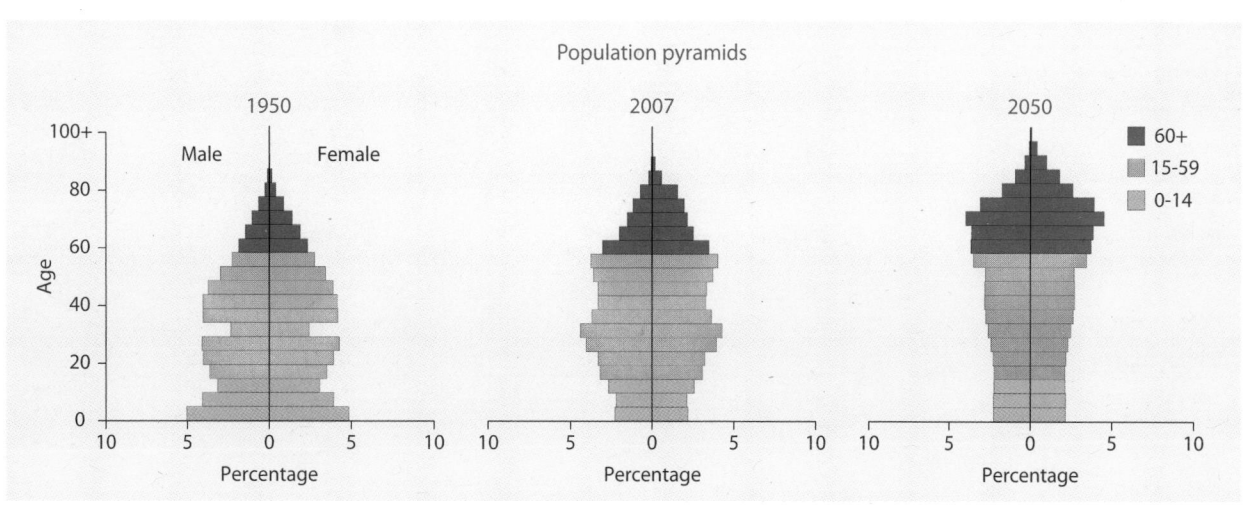

Democratic People's Republic of Korea

Indicator	Age	1950	1975	2007	2025	2050
Population (thousands)						
Total	Total	10 815.5	16 017.5	22 670.2	24 118.0	24 192.1
	0-14	4 404.8	6 114.5	5 449.7	4 832.5	4 202.1
	15-59	5 812.1	8 967.3	14 542.1	15 611.0	14 368.5
	60-64	263.9	356.3	1 014.1	1 288.0	1 511.9
	65-69	180.8	251.3	777.1	978.6	1 254.3
	70-74	82.5	159.4	467.0	483.5	944.2
	75-79	47.0	96.5	237.9	481.9	915.6
	80-84			118.4	286.6	627.9
	85-89			46.9	120.0	260.0
	90-94	24.3	72.2	14.1	30.0	90.2
	95-99			2.7	5.4	14.4
	100+			0.3	0.6	3.0
Female	Total	5 352.5	7 894.7	11 362.9	12 200.4	12 349.3
	0-14	2 162.0	2 978.9	2 669.9	2 362.4	2 049.7
	15-59	2 859.1	4 399.1	7 183.2	7 742.8	7 097.1
	60-64	136.0	182.4	538.0	674.6	779.8
	65-69	103.1	135.0	429.7	535.5	670.7
	70-74	48.9	90.9	269.7	280.4	531.0
	75-79	28.2	59.6	147.9	297.7	549.2
	80-84			78.8	193.4	405.7
	85-89			32.9	85.8	182.5
	90-94	15.2	48.7	10.5	23.0	69.0
	95-99			2.1	4.4	12.0
	100+			0.2	0.5	2.7
Male	Total	5 462.9	8 122.8	11 307.3	11 917.6	11 842.8
	0-14	2 242.8	3 135.7	2 779.8	2 470.1	2 152.3
	15-59	2 953.0	4 568.1	7 358.9	7 868.2	7 271.4
	60-64	127.9	173.9	476.1	613.4	732.1
	65-69	77.7	116.3	347.4	443.2	583.5
	70-74	33.6	68.4	197.3	203.1	413.2
	75-79	18.8	36.9	90.0	184.2	366.4
	80-84			39.6	93.2	222.3
	85-89			14.0	34.1	77.5
	90-94	9.1	23.5	3.6	7.0	21.2
	95-99			0.5	1.0	2.5
	100+			0.0	0.1	0.3
Percentage in older ages						
Total	60+	5.5	5.8	11.8	15.2	23.2
	65+	3.1	3.6	7.3	9.9	17.0
	80+	0.2	0.5	0.8	1.8	4.1
Female	60+	6.2	6.5	13.3	17.2	25.9
	65+	3.7	4.2	8.6	11.6	19.6
	80+	0.3	0.6	1.1	2.5	5.4
Male	60+	4.9	5.2	10.3	13.3	20.4
	65+	2.5	3.0	6.1	8.1	14.2
	80+	0.2	0.3	0.5	1.1	2.7
Ageing index		13.6	15.3	49.1	76.0	133.8
Broad age groups (percentage)	0-14	40.7	38.2	24.0	20.0	17.4
	15-59	53.7	56.0	64.1	64.7	59.4
	60+	5.5	5.8	11.8	15.2	23.2
Median age (years)		19.5	21.6	31.1*	35.5	40.5
Dependency ratio	Total	78.0	71.8	45.7	42.7	52.3
	Youth	72.5	65.6	35.0	28.6	26.5
	Old Age	5.5	6.2	10.7	14.1	25.9
Potential support ratio		18.2	16.1	9.3	7.1	3.9
Parent support ratio		0.8	1.7	2.1	3.2	7.3
Sex ratio (per 100 women)	60+	80.6	81.1	77.4	75.4	75.5
	65+	71.3	73.4	71.3	68.0	69.6
	80+	59.9	48.3	46.4	44.1	48.2

* *Estimate refers to year 2005.*

Indicator	Age	1950-1955	1975-1980	2005-2010	2025-2030	2045-2050
Growth rate (percentage)	Total	−0.9	1.4	0.4	0.2	−0.1
	60+	1.3	2.9	2.5	3.7	0.9
	65+	2.4	3.7	3.8	3.0	0.7
	80+	1.9	3.3	2.8	2.8	5.6
Total fertility rate (per woman)		3.3	2.8	1.9	1.9	1.9
Life expectancy (years)						
Total	Birth	49.0	66.9	64.5	70.1	73.8
	60	..	..	15.7	17.5	19.2
	65	..	..	12.7	14.3	15.6
	80	..	..	6.2	6.9	7.5
Female	Birth	49.9	69.6	67.5	73.0	76.5
	60	..	..	17.5	19.5	21.3
	65	..	..	14.2	15.9	17.5
	80	..	..	6.7	7.5	8.2
Male	Birth	48.0	64.4	61.7	67.3	71.1
	60	..	..	13.7	15.4	16.9
	65	..	..	11.0	12.3	13.6
	80	..	..	5.4	5.9	6.4
Survival rate (percentage)						
Total	60	..	..	70.5	80.0	85.7
	65	..	..	60.9	71.6	78.6
	80	..	..	22.8	32.5	40.8
Female	60	..	..	75.5	83.9	88.5
	65	..	..	67.6	77.5	83.3
	80	..	..	30.6	41.8	50.6
Male	60	..	..	65.8	76.2	82.9
	65	..	..	54.5	65.9	73.9
	80	..	..	15.4	23.3	31.0

		1980	1990	2007	2010	2020
Labour force participation (percentage)						
Total	65+	35.9	25.6	45.2	45.5	46.1
Female	65+	23.7	14.0	38.5	39.0	39.9
Male	65+	52.3	41.3	54.6	54.8	55.4

Percentage married, age 60+			Percentage living alone, age 60+ (1990)		
Total	Female	Male	Total	Female	Male
..	..	..	4.6	8.7	0.3

Statutory pensionable age (2006)			Percentage illiterate, age 65+		
	Female	Male	Total	Female	Male
	..	..	..	..	..

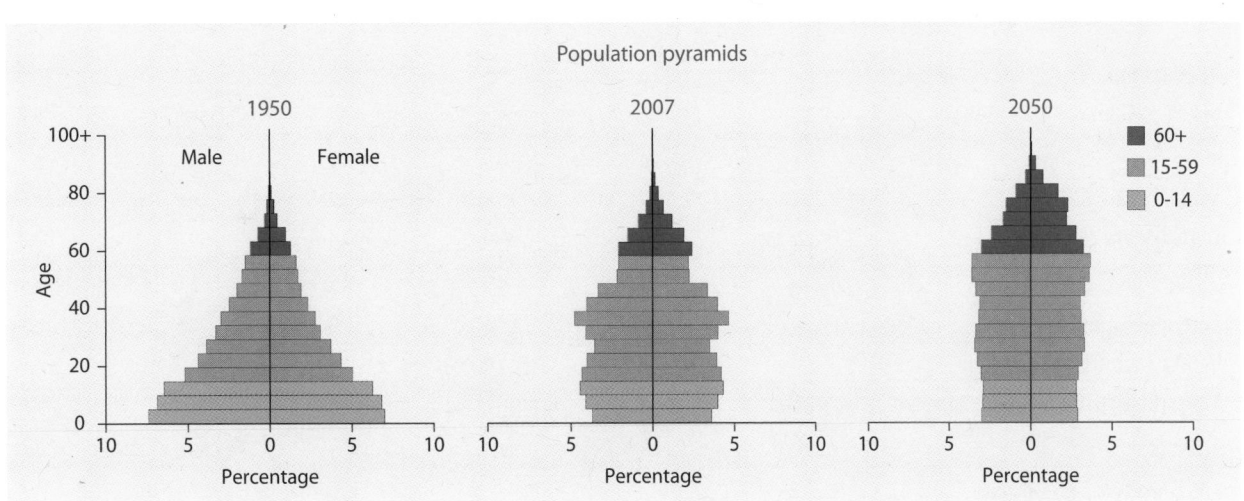

Population pyramids

Democratic Republic of the Congo

Indicator	Age	1950	1975	2007	2025	2050
Population (thousands)						
Total	Total	12 183.7	23 911.8	61 173.7	103 223.7	177 271.0
	0-14	5 322.5	10 920.4	29 025.1	47 444.6	61 744.5
	15-59	6 181.7	11 905.2	29 564.8	51 776.3	105 701.2
	60-64	218.5	418.8	957.4	1 422.5	3 563.6
	65-69	164.6	301.2	711.0	1 070.7	2 638.3
	70-74	123.5	195.8	474.2	738.7	1 796.5
	75-79	87.6	108.8	271.3	455.8	1 066.7
	80-84			121.9	221.0	514.7
	85-89			39.2	75.3	190.7
	90-94	85.3	61.7	7.8	16.5	47.4
	95-99			0.9	2.1	6.8
	100+			0.1	0.1	0.5
Female	Total	6 476.6	12 266.0	30 807.9	51 776.5	88 816.6
	0-14	2 723.4	5 458.5	14 487.5	23 672.1	30 708.8
	15-59	3 348.2	6 167.5	14 873.2	25 922.3	52 953.1
	60-64	129.3	239.3	519.8	745.6	1 822.0
	65-69	98.8	175.7	394.1	577.2	1 369.0
	70-74	74.4	117.8	268.8	408.0	950.0
	75-79	52.6	67.0	158.5	260.5	577.9
	80-84			74.2	131.1	288.1
	85-89			25.4	47.1	112.5
	90-94	50.0	40.2	5.5	11.1	30.0
	95-99			0.7	1.6	4.7
	100+			0.1	0.1	0.4
Male	Total	5 707.1	11 645.8	30 365.8	51 447.3	88 454.4
	0-14	2 599.1	5 461.9	14 537.6	23 772.5	31 035.7
	15-59	2 833.5	5 737.6	14 691.6	25 854.1	52 748.0
	60-64	89.3	179.5	437.6	677.0	1 741.6
	65-69	65.8	125.5	316.9	493.6	1 269.3
	70-74	49.1	78.0	205.3	330.8	846.6
	75-79	35.1	41.8	112.7	195.3	488.8
	80-84			47.7	89.9	226.6
	85-89			13.8	28.2	78.2
	90-94	35.4	21.5	2.3	5.4	17.4
	95-99			0.2	0.5	2.1
	100+			0.0	0.0	0.1
Percentage in older ages						
Total	60+	5.6	4.5	4.2	3.9	5.5
	65+	3.8	2.8	2.7	2.5	3.5
	80+	0.7	0.3	0.3	0.3	0.4
Female	60+	6.3	5.2	4.7	4.2	5.8
	65+	4.3	3.3	3.0	2.8	3.8
	80+	0.8	0.3	0.3	0.4	0.5
Male	60+	4.8	3.8	3.7	3.5	5.3
	65+	3.2	2.3	2.3	2.2	3.3
	80+	0.6	0.2	0.2	0.2	0.4
Ageing index		12.8	9.9	8.9	8.4	15.9
Broad age groups (percentage)	0-14	43.7	45.7	47.4	46.0	34.8
	15-59	50.7	49.8	48.3	50.2	59.6
	60+	5.6	4.5	4.2	3.9	5.5
Median age (years)		18.1	17.1	16.3*	16.8	22.1
Dependency ratio	Total	90.4	94.0	100.4	94.0	62.2
	Youth	83.2	88.6	95.1	89.2	56.5
	Old Age	7.2	5.4	5.3	4.9	5.7
Potential support ratio		13.9	18.5	18.8	20.6	17.4
Parent support ratio		2.8	1.0	1.3	1.7	1.8
Sex ratio (per 100 women)	60+	67.8	69.7	78.5	83.4	90.6
	65+	67.2	66.6	75.4	79.6	87.9
	80+	70.8	53.5	60.5	65.0	74.5

* *Estimate refers to year 2005.*

Indicator	Age	1950-1955	1975-1980	2005-2010	2025-2030	2045-2050
Growth rate (percentage)	Total	2.2	3.2	3.1	2.6	1.7
	60+	0.1	3.1	2.5	2.9	3.9
	65+	−1.3	3.1	2.8	2.7	4.1
	80+	−4.4	3.1	3.3	3.3	4.0
Total fertility rate (per woman)		6.0	6.6	6.7	4.9	3.0
Life expectancy (years)						
Total	Birth	39.1	47.8	44.7	51.6	59.5
	60	..	..	15.4	16.4	17.7
	65	..	..	12.3	13.2	14.3
	80	..	..	5.4	5.8	6.2
Female	Birth	40.6	49.4	45.8	52.9	60.9
	60	..	..	15.9	17.0	18.4
	65	..	..	12.7	13.7	14.8
	80	..	..	5.6	6.0	6.5
Male	Birth	37.5	46.2	43.6	50.4	58.1
	60	..	..	14.7	15.7	17.0
	65	..	..	11.8	12.6	13.7
	80	..	..	5.1	5.5	6.0
Survival rate (percentage)						
Total	60	..	..	40.0	49.2	60.9
	65	..	..	34.7	43.6	55.2
	80	..	..	12.3	17.5	25.4
Female	60	..	..	41.6	51.0	62.9
	65	..	..	36.6	45.8	57.8
	80	..	..	13.8	19.6	28.2
Male	60	..	..	38.5	47.5	58.9
	65	..	..	32.8	41.5	52.7
	80	..	..	10.8	15.5	22.7

		1980	1990	2007	2010	2020
Labour force participation (percentage)						
Total	65+	49.1	48.9	50.1	50.2	50.8
Female	65+	28.3	29.9	30.3	30.3	30.4
Male	65+	79.7	75.8	76.3	76.4	76.9

Percentage married, age 60+				Percentage living alone, age 60+		
Total	Female	Male		Total	Female	Male
54.9	34.0	82.0		..	..	..

Statutory pensionable age (2006)				Percentage illiterate, age 65+ (2001)		
	Female	Male		Total	Female	Male
	60	65		63.9	91.5	38.5

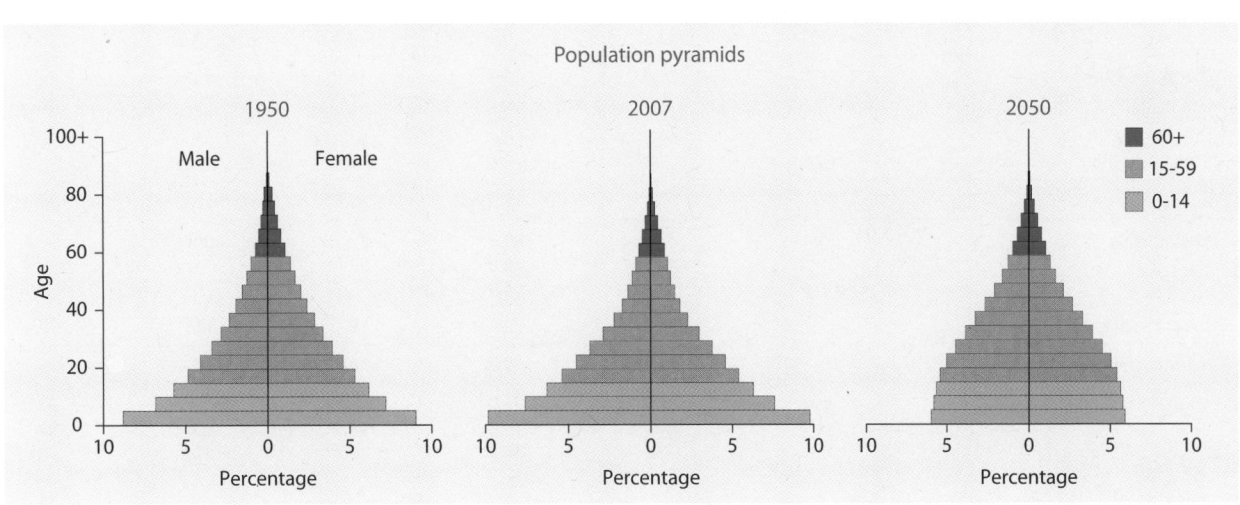

Population pyramids

Democratic Republic of Timor-Leste

Indicator	Age	1950	1975	2007	2025	2050
Population (thousands)						
Total	Total	433.4	672.4	1 067.9	1 938.2	3 265.0
	0-14	175.7	282.5	440.6	799.6	1 017.3
	15-59	233.5	359.6	575.2	1 029.6	1 969.9
	60-64	9.7	12.1	21.0	41.9	110.1
	65-69	6.9	8.3	15.1	30.4	83.8
	70-74	4.4	5.8	8.6	18.6	38.3
	75-79	2.2	2.8	4.8	10.8	24.5
	80-84			2.0	5.3	13.6
	85-89			0.6	1.6	5.9
	90-94	1.0	1.3	0.1	0.3	1.3
	95-99			0.0	0.0	0.1
	100+			0.0	0.0	0.0
Female	Total	214.0	330.4	517.2	951.2	1 614.2
	0-14	86.7	138.6	216.0	391.8	498.9
	15-59	113.8	176.1	274.6	502.7	971.9
	60-64	5.3	5.9	10.8	21.4	56.6
	65-69	3.8	4.0	7.4	15.5	43.5
	70-74	2.5	3.3	4.4	9.5	19.0
	75-79	1.3	1.7	2.6	6.2	12.3
	80-84			1.0	2.9	7.7
	85-89			0.3	0.9	3.5
	90-94	0.6	0.8	0.1	0.2	0.8
	95-99			0.0	0.0	0.1
	100+			0.0	0.0	0.0
Male	Total	219.4	342.0	550.7	987.0	1 650.7
	0-14	89.0	143.9	224.6	407.8	518.4
	15-59	119.7	183.5	300.6	526.9	998.0
	60-64	4.4	6.2	10.1	20.5	53.5
	65-69	3.1	4.3	7.7	14.9	40.3
	70-74	1.9	2.5	4.2	9.0	19.4
	75-79	0.9	1.1	2.2	4.6	12.2
	80-84			0.9	2.4	6.0
	85-89			0.2	0.7	2.4
	90-94	0.4	0.5	0.0	0.1	0.5
	95-99			0.0	0.0	0.1
	100+			0.0	0.0	0.0
Percentage in older ages						
Total	60+	5.6	4.5	4.9	5.6	8.5
	65+	3.3	2.7	2.9	3.5	5.1
	80+	0.2	0.2	0.2	0.4	0.6
Female	60+	6.3	4.8	5.1	6.0	8.9
	65+	3.8	3.0	3.1	3.7	5.4
	80+	0.3	0.2	0.3	0.4	0.7
Male	60+	4.9	4.3	4.6	5.3	8.1
	65+	2.9	2.5	2.8	3.2	4.9
	80+	0.2	0.1	0.2	0.3	0.5
Ageing index		13.8	10.7	11.8	13.6	27.3
Broad age groups (percentage)	0-14	40.5	42.0	41.3	41.3	31.2
	15-59	53.9	53.5	53.9	53.1	60.3
	60+	5.6	4.5	4.9	5.6	8.5
Median age (years)		19.6	18.9	18.4*	18.4	25.4
Dependency ratio	Total	78.2	80.9	79.1	80.9	57.0
	Youth	72.2	76.0	73.9	74.6	48.9
	Old Age	6.0	4.9	5.2	6.3	8.1
Potential support ratio		16.8	20.4	19.1	16.0	12.4
Parent support ratio		0.7	0.8	0.8	1.4	2.4
Sex ratio (per 100 women)	60+	79.3	93.0	95.7	92.3	93.6
	65+	76.8	85.8	96.9	89.9	93.1
	80+	66.6	63.1	85.7	79.6	73.4

* *Estimate refers to year 2005.*

Indicator	Age	1950-1955	1975-1980	2005-2010	2025-2030	2045-2050
Growth rate (percentage)	Total	1.3	−2.9	5.5	2.3	1.7
	60+	−2.4	−6.2	4.5	2.7	5.4
	65+	0.0	−5.2	5.7	4.3	6.8
	80+	0.0	−8.5	8.6	4.0	2.1
Total fertility rate (per woman)		6.4	4.3	7.2	4.2	2.6
Life expectancy (years)						
Total	Birth	30.0	31.2	57.7	66.7	72.8
	60	..	..	15.5	16.9	18.3
	65	..	..	12.4	13.4	14.6
	80	..	..	5.4	5.7	6.2
Female	Birth	30.4	32.5	58.9	68.5	75.0
	60	..	..	16.3	17.8	19.4
	65	..	..	13.0	14.1	15.5
	80	..	..	5.6	6.0	6.4
Male	Birth	29.6	30.0	56.6	65.1	70.7
	60	..	..	14.8	16.0	17.2
	65	..	..	11.8	12.7	13.7
	80	..	..	5.2	5.5	5.8
Survival rate (percentage)						
Total	60	..	..	61.6	75.7	85.6
	65	..	..	53.8	68.1	79.1
	80	..	..	19.3	28.4	37.9
Female	60	..	..	63.8	78.5	88.6
	65	..	..	56.7	72.0	83.4
	80	..	..	22.1	32.7	44.2
Male	60	..	..	59.5	73.3	82.6
	65	..	..	51.1	64.7	75.0
	80	..	..	16.8	24.5	32.5

		1980	1990	2007	2010	2020
Labour force participation (percentage)						
Total	65+	32.8	59.1	31.5	29.9	29.0
Female	65+	16.8	49.9	14.3	13.4	13.2
Male	65+	50.9	67.7	49.2	47.3	46.7

Percentage married, age 60+			Percentage living alone, age 60+		
Total	Female	Male	Total	Female	Male
..	..	..	..	..	..

Statutory pensionable age (2006)			Percentage illiterate, age 65+		
Female	Male		Total	Female	Male
..	..		..	..	..

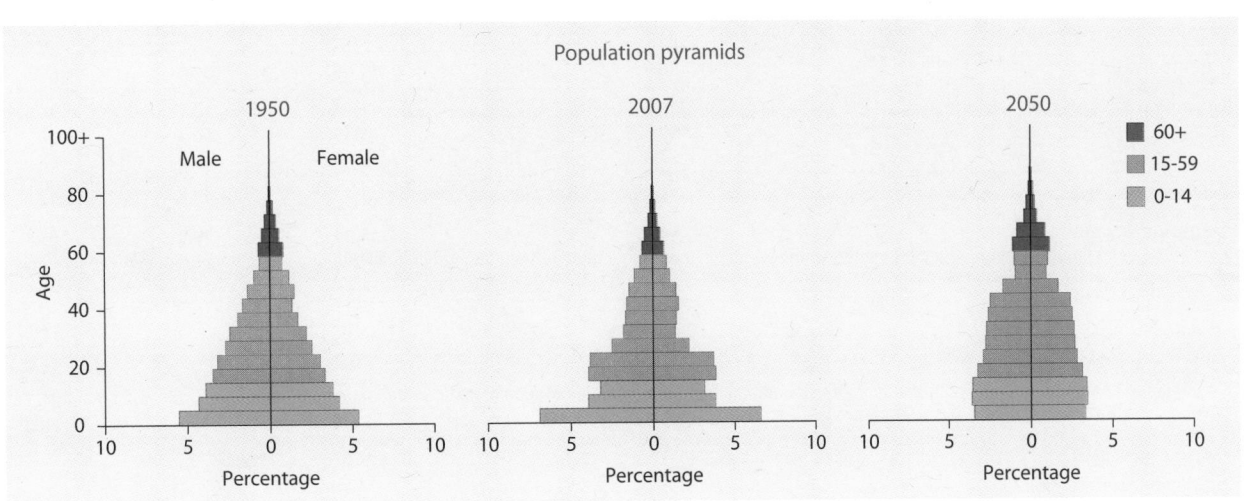

Population pyramids

Denmark

Indicator	Age	1950	1975	2007	2025	2050
Population (thousands)						
Total	Total	4 271.0	5 059.9	5 461.2	5 690.5	5 851.2
	0-14	1 124.0	1 143.4	1 013.8	950.9	975.3
	15-59	2 575.0	2 969.2	3 252.0	3 193.1	3 227.5
	60-64	182.0	269.6	352.0	378.0	317.2
	65-69	151.0	238.6	263.9	322.7	276.3
	70-74	115.0	186.1	194.6	280.7	286.3
	75-79	72.0	131.2	155.1	255.8	277.1
	80-84			121.1	171.9	228.6
	85-89			71.4	86.9	154.4
	90-94	52.0	121.5	29.3	37.1	75.4
	95-99			7.2	11.4	26.9
	100+			0.8	2.0	6.2
Female	Total	2 153.0	2 554.3	2 757.2	2 876.2	2 968.6
	0-14	551.0	558.3	492.9	461.7	473.4
	15-59	1 301.0	1 469.5	1 604.0	1 578.2	1 588.1
	60-64	95.0	140.4	176.5	188.5	159.3
	65-69	79.0	128.5	135.7	164.2	141.8
	70-74	60.0	105.2	105.0	147.2	150.4
	75-79	38.0	77.8	89.1	140.3	151.4
	80-84			76.3	101.6	131.3
	85-89			49.2	56.8	95.8
	90-94	29.0	74.7	21.8	26.9	51.6
	95-99			5.8	9.1	20.4
	100+			0.7	1.7	5.2
Male	Total	2 118.0	2 505.5	2 704.0	2 814.3	2 882.6
	0-14	573.0	585.2	520.9	489.2	501.9
	15-59	1 274.0	1 499.7	1 648.0	1 614.9	1 639.5
	60-64	87.0	129.3	175.4	189.4	157.9
	65-69	72.0	110.1	128.2	158.5	134.5
	70-74	55.0	81.0	89.7	133.5	135.9
	75-79	34.0	53.5	66.0	115.5	125.7
	80-84			44.7	70.3	97.4
	85-89			22.2	30.1	58.6
	90-94	23.0	46.8	7.4	10.2	23.9
	95-99			1.4	2.3	6.5
	100+			0.1	0.3	1.0
Percentage in older ages						
Total	60+	13.4	18.7	21.9	27.2	28.2
	65+	9.1	13.4	15.4	20.5	22.8
	80+	1.2	2.4	4.2	5.4	8.4
Female	60+	14.0	20.6	23.9	29.1	30.6
	65+	9.6	15.1	17.5	22.5	25.2
	80+	1.3	2.9	5.6	6.8	10.2
Male	60+	12.8	16.8	19.8	25.2	25.7
	65+	8.7	11.6	13.3	18.5	20.2
	80+	1.1	1.9	2.8	4.0	6.5
Ageing index		50.9	82.8	117.9	162.6	169.0
Broad age groups (percentage)	0-14	26.3	22.6	18.6	16.7	16.7
	15-59	60.3	58.7	59.5	56.1	55.2
	60+	13.4	18.7	21.9	27.2	28.2
Median age (years)		31.8	33.0	39.5*	42.3	42.8
Dependency ratio	Total	54.9	56.2	51.5	59.3	65.1
	Youth	40.8	35.3	28.1	26.6	27.5
	Old Age	14.1	20.9	23.4	32.7	37.6
Potential support ratio		7.1	4.8	4.3	3.1	2.7
Parent support ratio		3.3	5.3	10.0	11.8	24.6
Sex ratio (per 100 women)	60+	90.0	79.9	81.0	84.9	81.7
	65+	89.3	75.4	74.3	80.4	78.0
	80+	79.3	62.6	49.3	57.7	61.6

* *Estimate refers to year 2005.*

Denmark

Indicator	Age	1950-1955	1975-1980	2005-2010	2025-2030	2045-2050
Growth rate (percentage)	Total	0.8	0.2	0.3	0.2	0.1
	60+	2.0	1.0	2.1	1.1	−0.2
	65+	2.1	1.7	2.0	1.4	−0.6
	80+	3.5	3.9	0.4	3.6	1.5
Total fertility rate (per woman)		2.6	1.7	1.8	1.9	1.9
Life expectancy (years)						
Total	Birth	71.0	74.2	77.8	80.2	82.3
	60	..	..	21.2	22.9	24.4
	65	..	..	17.4	18.9	20.3
	80	..	..	8.2	9.0	9.9
Female	Birth	72.4	77.3	80.1	82.5	84.6
	60	..	..	23.0	24.8	26.4
	65	..	..	19.0	20.6	22.1
	80	..	..	9.0	10.0	10.9
Male	Birth	69.6	71.2	75.5	77.9	80.0
	60	..	..	19.4	20.9	22.4
	65	..	..	15.7	17.0	18.3
	80	..	..	7.1	7.8	8.6
Survival rate (percentage)						
Total	60	..	..	90.4	92.8	94.5
	65	..	..	85.1	88.5	91.0
	80	..	..	51.4	58.6	64.8
Female	60	..	..	92.3	94.3	95.6
	65	..	..	88.0	90.9	93.0
	80	..	..	59.1	66.4	72.1
Male	60	..	..	88.5	91.3	93.4
	65	..	..	82.2	86.2	89.1
	80	..	..	43.5	50.9	57.4

		1980	1990	2007	2010	2020
Labour force participation (percentage)						
Total	65+	7.7	7.4	3.6	3.7	3.9
Female	65+	3.8	3.4	3.2	3.6	4.4
Male	65+	13.1	13.0	4.1	3.8	3.2

Percentage married, age 60+			Percentage living alone, age 60+ (1994)		
Total	Female	Male	Total	Female	Male
55.3	44.0	70.0	39.1	50.0	24.7

Statutory pensionable age (2006)			Percentage illiterate, age 65+		
Female	Male		Total	Female	Male
65	65		..	..	..

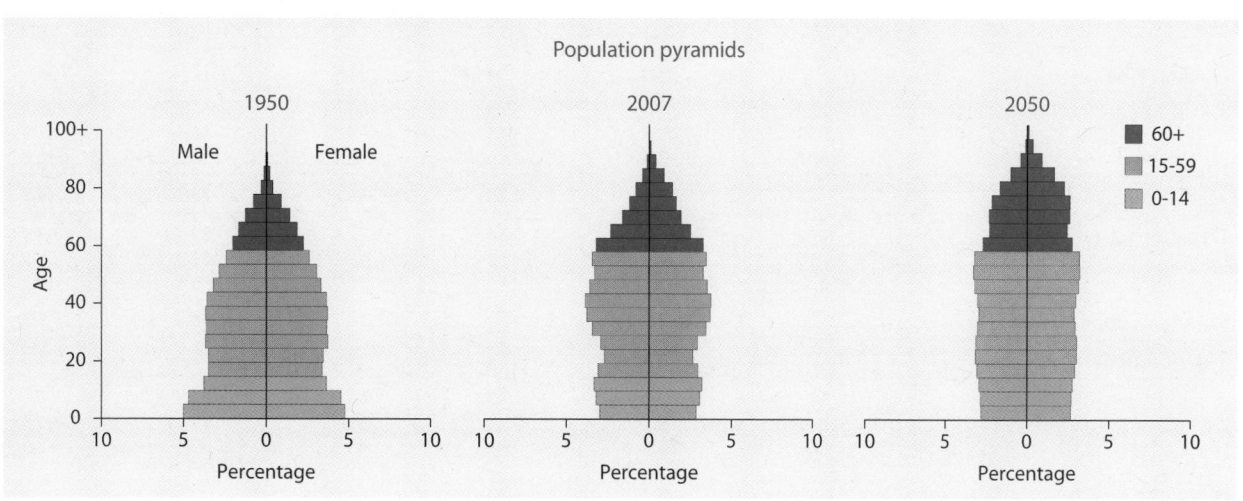

Population pyramids

Djibouti

Indicator	Age	1950	1975	2007	2025	2050
Population (thousands)						
Total	Total	62.0	223.9	820.2	1 107.0	1 547.2
	0-14	29.0	102.8	334.2	367.8	392.6
	15-59	30.8	113.0	446.0	669.0	988.3
	60-64	0.9	3.4	15.8	26.1	59.6
	65-69	0.6	2.3	11.0	18.7	44.1
	70-74	0.4	1.4	7.0	12.5	30.2
	75-79	0.2	0.7	3.9	7.8	18.8
	80-84			1.7	3.6	9.5
	85-89			0.5	1.1	3.3
	90-94	0.1	0.3	0.1	0.2	0.7
	95-99			0.0	0.0	0.1
	100+			0.0	0.0	0.0
Female	Total	31.2	112.7	409.9	551.5	772.7
	0-14	14.5	51.3	165.6	181.8	193.8
	15-59	15.6	56.9	222.6	331.8	491.0
	60-64	0.5	1.8	8.3	13.6	30.4
	65-69	0.3	1.3	5.9	10.0	22.9
	70-74	0.2	0.8	3.9	6.9	16.1
	75-79	0.1	0.4	2.2	4.4	10.4
	80-84			1.0	2.1	5.5
	85-89			0.3	0.7	2.0
	90-94	0.0	0.2	0.1	0.2	0.5
	95-99			0.0	0.0	0.1
	100+			0.0	0.0	0.0
Male	Total	30.8	111.2	410.2	555.5	774.5
	0-14	14.6	51.5	168.6	186.0	198.7
	15-59	15.3	56.1	223.4	337.3	497.3
	60-64	0.4	1.5	7.5	12.5	29.3
	65-69	0.3	1.0	5.1	8.7	21.2
	70-74	0.2	0.6	3.1	5.6	14.1
	75-79	0.1	0.3	1.6	3.4	8.4
	80-84			0.7	1.5	4.0
	85-89			0.2	0.4	1.3
	90-94	0.0	0.1	0.0	0.1	0.3
	95-99			0.0	0.0	0.0
	100+			0.0	0.0	0.0
Percentage in older ages						
Total	60+	3.4	3.6	4.9	6.3	10.8
	65+	2.0	2.1	2.9	4.0	6.9
	80+	0.1	0.2	0.3	0.4	0.9
Female	60+	3.8	4.0	5.3	6.9	11.4
	65+	2.2	2.4	3.3	4.4	7.4
	80+	0.2	0.2	0.3	0.5	1.0
Male	60+	3.1	3.2	4.4	5.8	10.1
	65+	1.8	1.9	2.6	3.5	6.4
	80+	0.1	0.1	0.2	0.4	0.7
Ageing index		7.4	7.9	12.0	19.1	42.4
Broad age groups (percentage)	0-14	46.8	45.9	40.7	33.2	25.4
	15-59	49.8	50.5	54.4	60.4	63.9
	60+	3.4	3.6	4.9	6.3	10.8
Median age (years)		16.5	17.0	18.9*	23.3	29.9
Dependency ratio	Total	95.2	92.4	77.6	59.3	47.6
	Youth	91.4	88.3	72.4	52.9	37.5
	Old Age	3.9	4.1	5.2	6.3	10.2
Potential support ratio		25.9	24.4	19.1	15.8	9.8
Parent support ratio		0.5	0.6	1.0	1.4	1.9
Sex ratio (per 100 women)	60+	82.3	79.3	84.0	84.9	89.4
	65+	79.1	75.9	80.0	81.0	85.6
	80+	64.6	62.4	63.8	67.1	68.9

* *Estimate refers to year 2005.*

Indicator	Age	1950-1955	1975-1980	2005-2010	2025-2030	2045-2050
Growth rate (percentage)	Total	2.5	8.4	1.6	1.6	1.1
	60+	2.6	9.0	3.2	3.5	3.7
	65+	2.6	9.1	3.5	3.6	3.6
	80+	2.8	9.7	3.9	4.4	4.2
Total fertility rate (per woman)		7.8	6.8	4.5	2.9	2.2
Life expectancy (years)						
Total	Birth	34.8	46.5	53.9	62.5	69.1
	60	..	..	15.6	16.6	17.5
	65	..	..	12.5	13.2	14.0
	80	..	..	5.4	5.7	6.0
Female	Birth	36.4	48.0	55.0	64.0	71.0
	60	..	..	16.3	17.4	18.5
	65	..	..	13.0	13.9	14.8
	80	..	..	5.6	5.9	6.2
Male	Birth	33.3	45.1	52.8	61.0	67.2
	60	..	..	14.8	15.6	16.5
	65	..	..	11.8	12.5	13.2
	80	..	..	5.2	5.4	5.6
Survival rate (percentage)						
Total	60	..	..	53.7	67.4	78.7
	65	..	..	46.9	60.2	71.7
	80	..	..	17.0	24.4	32.2
Female	60	..	..	55.3	69.5	81.5
	65	..	..	49.1	63.3	75.6
	80	..	..	19.4	27.9	37.2
Male	60	..	..	52.2	65.3	76.0
	65	..	..	44.6	57.3	67.9
	80	..	..	14.6	20.9	27.4

		1980	1990	2007	2010	2020
Labour force participation (percentage)						
Total	65+	41.3	41.3	39.3	39.3	39.2
Female	65+	27.8	25.4	21.2	21.1	20.9
Male	65+	59.0	62.0	61.9	61.9	61.9

Percentage married, age 60+			Percentage living alone, age 60+		
Total	Female	Male	Total	Female	Male
..	..	..	..	..	..

Statutory pensionable age (2006)			Percentage illiterate, age 65+		
	Female	Male	Total	Female	Male
	..	..	..	..	..

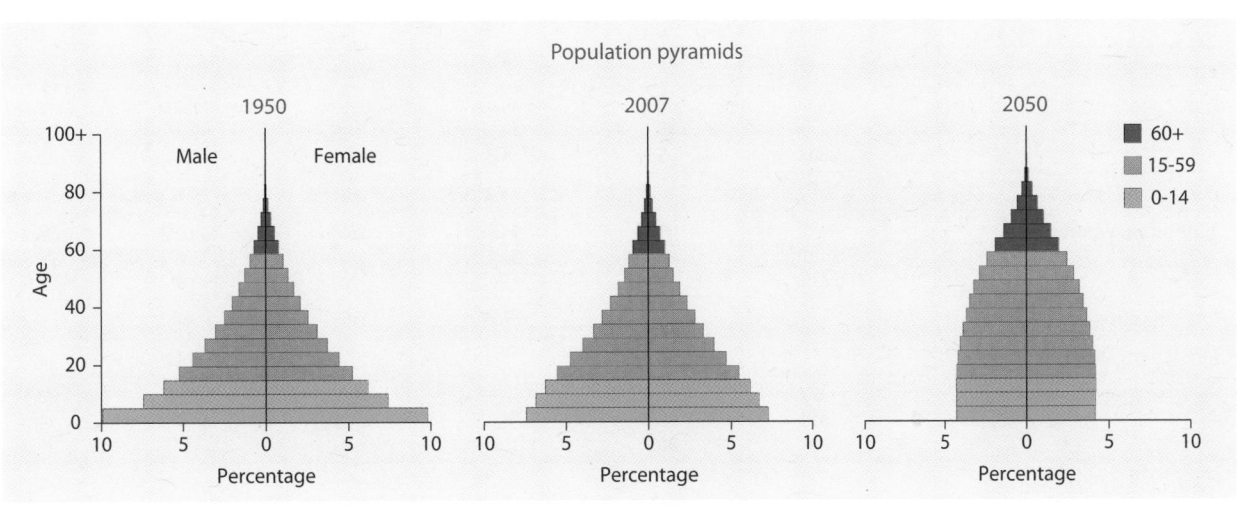

Population pyramids

United Nations Department of Economic and Social Affairs, Population Division

Dominican Republic

Indicator	Age	1950	1975	2007	2025	2050
Population (thousands)						
Total	Total	2 353.0	5 058.5	9 147.6	11 174.2	12 668.1
	0-14	1 047.6	2 308.7	2 925.1	2 907.0	2 456.0
	15-59	1 183.4	2 516.4	5 625.0	7 011.4	7 564.7
	60-64	46.2	85.0	203.7	436.2	696.2
	65-69	34.1	61.7	152.0	325.6	613.0
	70-74	22.7	43.9	108.8	221.1	465.3
	75-79	12.3	26.5	75.1	142.6	365.5
	80-84			37.4	78.1	267.7
	85-89			15.1	36.9	155.9
	90-94	6.7	16.3	4.6	12.3	64.1
	95-99			0.8	2.7	17.1
	100+			0.1	0.2	2.7
Female	Total	1 153.7	2 495.7	4 535.7	5 582.3	6 374.6
	0-14	518.9	1 137.9	1 435.2	1 423.3	1 200.8
	15-59	573.7	1 242.5	2 795.2	3 488.3	3 727.8
	60-64	22.9	39.9	102.6	227.4	356.8
	65-69	16.9	29.8	77.1	171.1	320.9
	70-74	11.5	22.3	56.2	117.8	250.9
	75-79	6.3	14.3	39.0	78.4	206.0
	80-84			19.4	44.5	158.0
	85-89			8.0	22.0	96.8
	90-94	3.5	9.0	2.5	7.7	42.5
	95-99			0.5	1.7	12.2
	100+			0.1	0.2	2.0
Male	Total	1 199.3	2 562.8	4 611.9	5 591.9	6 293.5
	0-14	528.7	1 170.8	1 489.9	1 483.8	1 255.2
	15-59	609.8	1 273.9	2 829.8	3 523.1	3 836.8
	60-64	23.3	45.1	101.1	208.8	339.4
	65-69	17.2	31.9	74.9	154.5	292.0
	70-74	11.2	21.6	52.6	103.3	214.4
	75-79	6.0	12.1	36.1	64.2	159.5
	80-84			18.0	33.6	109.8
	85-89			7.1	14.9	59.1
	90-94	3.1	7.3	2.1	4.6	21.7
	95-99			0.3	1.0	4.9
	100+			0.0	0.1	0.7
Percentage in older ages						
Total	60+	5.2	4.6	6.5	11.2	20.9
	65+	3.2	2.9	4.3	7.3	15.4
	80+	0.3	0.3	0.6	1.2	4.0
Female	60+	5.3	4.6	6.7	12.0	22.7
	65+	3.3	3.0	4.5	7.9	17.1
	80+	0.3	0.4	0.7	1.4	4.9
Male	60+	5.1	4.6	6.3	10.5	19.1
	65+	3.1	2.8	4.1	6.7	13.7
	80+	0.3	0.3	0.6	1.0	3.1
Ageing index		11.6	10.1	20.4	43.2	107.8
Broad age groups (percentage)	0-14	44.5	45.6	32.0	26.0	19.4
	15-59	50.3	49.7	61.5	62.7	59.7
	60+	5.2	4.6	6.5	11.2	20.9
Median age (years)		17.7	16.9	23.3*	29.2	37.1
Dependency ratio	Total	91.4	94.5	56.9	50.0	53.4
	Youth	85.2	88.7	50.2	39.0	29.7
	Old Age	6.2	5.7	6.8	11.0	23.6
Potential support ratio		16.2	17.5	14.8	9.1	4.2
Parent support ratio		1.2	1.5	2.5	3.4	11.0
Sex ratio (per 100 women)	60+	99.7	102.5	95.7	87.2	83.1
	65+	98.5	96.8	94.2	84.9	79.2
	80+	88.7	81.8	90.3	71.2	63.0

*   *Estimate refers to year 2005.*

Indicator	Age	1950-1955	1975-1980	2005-2010	2025-2030	2045-2050
Growth rate (percentage)	Total	3.0	2.5	1.4	0.8	0.2
	60+	2.3	2.7	3.7	4.0	2.3
	65+	2.4	3.1	3.4	4.9	2.8
	80+	3.4	3.3	6.6	6.2	4.1
Total fertility rate (per woman)		7.4	4.7	2.6	2.1	1.9
Life expectancy (years)						
Total	Birth	45.9	61.9	68.6	73.8	77.7
	60	..	..	19.4	21.7	23.2
	65	..	..	15.8	17.9	19.3
	80	..	..	7.3	8.7	9.4
Female	Birth	47.2	63.7	72.3	77.2	80.9
	60	..	..	20.8	23.4	25.2
	65	..	..	16.9	19.4	21.0
	80	..	..	7.7	9.3	10.2
Male	Birth	44.7	60.2	65.4	70.7	74.6
	60	..	..	18.1	19.9	21.2
	65	..	..	14.8	16.4	17.5
	80	..	..	6.8	7.9	8.4
Survival rate (percentage)						
Total	60	..	..	75.7	82.4	87.4
	65	..	..	69.9	77.4	83.1
	80	..	..	37.3	47.9	56.2
Female	60	..	..	81.9	86.9	91.0
	65	..	..	77.1	83.0	87.8
	80	..	..	45.2	56.5	65.1
Male	60	..	..	70.0	78.0	84.0
	65	..	..	63.4	71.9	78.5
	80	..	..	30.5	39.9	47.4

		1980	1990	2007	2010	2020
Labour force participation (percentage)						
Total	65+	42.8	37.3	33.2	33.5	35.2
Female	65+	10.3	10.9	16.6	19.0	27.2
Male	65+	75.2	62.9	50.9	49.3	44.4

Percentage married, age 60+			Percentage living alone, age 60+ (1999)		
Total	Female	Male	Total	Female	Male
55.5	38.0	73.0	6.1	5.9	6.4

Statutory pensionable age (2006)		Percentage illiterate, age 65+ (2002)		
Female	Male	Total	Female	Male
60	60	36.2	39.2	33.1

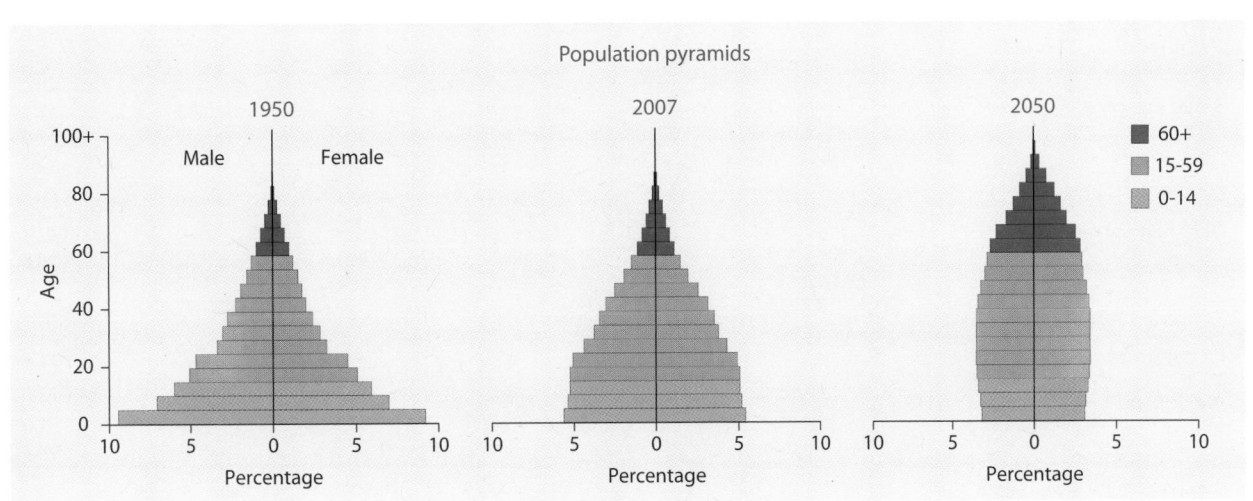

Population pyramids

Ecuador

Indicator	Age	1950	1975	2007	2025	2050
Population (thousands)						
Total	Total	3 387.4	6 907.2	13 610.7	16 819.3	19 213.9
	0-14	1 338.2	3 026.0	4 295.5	4 116.7	3 524.5
	15-59	1 773.5	3 458.8	8 143.0	10 410.8	11 262.3
	60-64	95.7	142.9	344.0	660.6	1 081.6
	65-69	76.7	107.7	279.6	543.3	955.7
	70-74	53.6	79.4	218.4	434.6	802.1
	75-79	30.5	52.1	158.8	289.9	645.6
	80-84			100.8	194.1	474.9
	85-89			50.9	112.6	291.7
	90-94	19.2	40.3	17.0	45.7	134.0
	95-99			2.7	10.2	38.0
	100+			0.1	0.7	3.6
Female	Total	1 703.7	3 435.9	6 788.7	8 429.0	9 707.8
	0-14	661.2	1 492.1	2 105.5	2 012.9	1 720.8
	15-59	891.3	1 720.0	4 065.1	5 195.7	5 581.6
	60-64	50.6	73.4	176.3	340.6	557.0
	65-69	41.7	56.2	145.1	283.5	501.6
	70-74	30.0	42.5	115.3	230.8	430.5
	75-79	17.6	28.5	85.2	156.9	356.1
	80-84			55.1	108.1	271.5
	85-89			28.9	65.2	174.7
	90-94	11.4	23.2	10.3	28.1	85.4
	95-99			1.8	6.8	26.1
	100+			0.1	0.5	2.5
Male	Total	1 683.6	3 471.3	6 822.0	8 390.2	9 506.2
	0-14	677.0	1 533.8	2 190.0	2 103.8	1 803.7
	15-59	882.2	1 738.8	4 077.9	5 215.1	5 680.7
	60-64	45.2	69.6	167.7	320.0	524.5
	65-69	35.1	51.5	134.4	259.8	454.1
	70-74	23.6	36.8	103.2	203.9	371.6
	75-79	12.9	23.7	73.6	133.0	289.5
	80-84			45.7	86.1	203.4
	85-89			22.0	47.4	117.0
	90-94	7.7	17.1	6.7	17.6	48.6
	95-99			0.9	3.4	12.0
	100+			0.0	0.2	1.1
Percentage in older ages						
Total	60+	8.1	6.1	8.6	13.6	23.0
	65+	5.3	4.0	6.1	9.7	17.4
	80+	0.6	0.6	1.3	2.2	4.9
Female	60+	8.9	6.5	9.1	14.5	24.8
	65+	5.9	4.4	6.5	10.4	19.0
	80+	0.7	0.7	1.4	2.5	5.8
Male	60+	7.4	5.7	8.1	12.8	21.3
	65+	4.7	3.7	5.7	9.0	15.8
	80+	0.5	0.5	1.1	1.8	4.0
Ageing index		20.6	14.0	27.3	55.7	125.6
Broad age groups (percentage)	0-14	39.5	43.8	31.6	24.5	18.3
	15-59	52.4	50.1	59.8	61.9	58.6
	60+	8.1	6.1	8.6	13.6	23.0
Median age (years)		20.6	17.9	24.0*	30.6	39.1
Dependency ratio	Total	81.2	91.8	60.4	51.9	55.7
	Youth	71.6	84.0	50.6	37.2	28.6
	Old Age	9.6	7.8	9.8	14.7	27.1
Potential support ratio		10.4	12.9	10.2	6.8	3.7
Parent support ratio		1.7	2.5	5.1	7.3	13.4
Sex ratio (per 100 women)	60+	82.2	88.8	89.7	87.8	84.1
	65+	78.6	85.8	87.5	85.4	81.0
	80+	67.6	73.6	78.2	74.1	68.2

* *Estimate refers to year 2005.*

Indicator	Age	1950-1955	1975-1980	2005-2010	2025-2030	2045-2050
Growth rate (percentage)	Total	2.6	2.8	1.4	0.8	0.3
	60+	1.0	2.2	3.5	3.2	2.1
	65+	1.3	2.7	3.6	3.5	2.3
	80+	1.1	2.7	5.1	3.7	3.1
Total fertility rate (per woman)		6.7	5.4	2.6	2.0	1.9
Life expectancy (years)						
Total	Birth	48.4	61.3	75.0	77.9	80.0
	60	..	..	22.9	23.9	24.7
	65	..	..	19.1	19.9	20.6
	80	..	..	8.8	9.4	9.8
Female	Birth	49.6	63.1	78.0	80.9	83.0
	60	..	..	24.1	25.4	26.4
	65	..	..	20.0	21.2	22.2
	80	..	..	9.2	10.0	10.6
Male	Birth	47.1	59.6	72.1	75.0	77.1
	60	..	..	21.8	22.3	22.8
	65	..	..	18.1	18.5	18.9
	80	..	..	8.3	8.7	8.9
Survival rate (percentage)						
Total	60	..	..	83.0	86.6	89.4
	65	..	..	78.6	82.6	85.7
	80	..	..	54.2	59.0	63.0
Female	60	..	..	87.3	90.3	92.4
	65	..	..	83.6	87.1	89.7
	80	..	..	60.9	66.5	71.2
Male	60	..	..	78.9	83.0	86.4
	65	..	..	73.9	78.2	81.8
	80	..	..	47.9	51.7	55.0

		1980	1990	2007	2010	2020
Labour force participation (percentage)						
Total	65+	41.6	42.8	31.3	30.5	28.5
Female	65+	12.4	19.0	19.9	20.2	21.1
Male	65+	75.3	69.9	44.3	42.3	37.0

Percentage married, age 60+			Percentage living alone, age 60+ (1990)		
Total	Female	Male	Total	Female	Male
57.5	48.0	68.0	9.0	9.2	8.7

Statutory pensionable age (2006)			Percentage illiterate, age 65+ (2001)		
	Female	Male	Total	Female	Male
	55	55	26.9	30.6	23.0

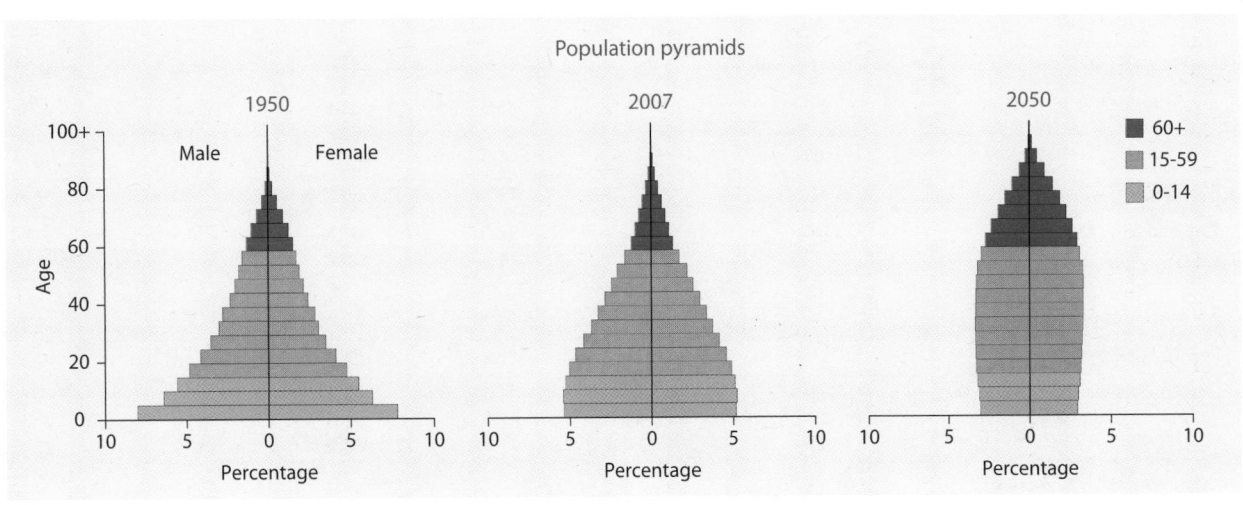

Population pyramids

Egypt

Indicator	Age	1950	1975	2007	2025	2050
Population (thousands)						
Total	Total	21 834.0	39 295.3	76 853.3	101 092.4	125 915.9
	0-14	8 663.9	16 074.9	25 401.6	27 919.4	26 297.0
	15-59	12 047.6	20 706.6	45 816.0	62 044.5	75 932.0
	60-64	475.1	876.6	1 902.6	3 608.2	6 960.1
	65-69	328.2	697.2	1 464.1	3 014.1	6 059.3
	70-74	193.9	499.0	1 112.1	2 207.8	4 578.7
	75-79	89.5	285.8	700.7	1 335.2	3 012.0
	80-84			332.3	637.8	1 755.4
	85-89			103.0	257.3	935.2
	90-94	35.9	155.2	19.0	60.8	318.6
	95-99			1.9	7.1	62.2
	100+			0.1	0.4	5.5
Female	Total	10 977.4	19 478.0	38 345.0	50 728.0	63 638.7
	0-14	4 293.5	7 825.5	12 443.0	13 657.8	12 823.8
	15-59	6 069.6	10 296.9	22 852.2	31 031.8	37 835.2
	60-64	254.5	460.5	981.1	1 882.3	3 578.5
	65-69	179.4	372.4	776.2	1 581.4	3 203.1
	70-74	108.3	272.3	620.5	1 211.1	2 472.4
	75-79	51.2	160.1	402.1	768.7	1 706.4
	80-84			195.0	382.6	1 086.9
	85-89			62.2	165.4	634.4
	90-94	20.9	90.3	11.6	41.8	240.2
	95-99			1.2	5.1	52.7
	100+			0.1	0.3	5.0
Male	Total	10 856.6	19 817.3	38 508.3	50 364.3	62 277.2
	0-14	4 370.4	8 249.4	12 958.6	14 261.6	13 473.1
	15-59	5 978.0	10 409.6	22 963.9	31 012.7	38 096.8
	60-64	220.6	416.1	921.6	1 725.9	3 381.6
	65-69	148.9	324.8	687.9	1 432.7	2 856.3
	70-74	85.6	226.7	491.6	996.7	2 106.3
	75-79	38.2	125.8	298.6	566.5	1 305.5
	80-84			137.2	255.2	668.5
	85-89			40.8	91.9	300.8
	90-94	14.9	64.9	7.3	19.0	78.3
	95-99			0.7	2.0	9.5
	100+			0.0	0.1	0.5
Percentage in older ages						
Total	60+	5.1	6.4	7.3	11.0	18.8
	65+	3.0	4.2	4.9	7.4	13.3
	80+	0.2	0.4	0.6	1.0	2.4
Female	60+	5.6	7.0	8.0	11.9	20.4
	65+	3.3	4.6	5.4	8.2	14.8
	80+	0.2	0.5	0.7	1.2	3.2
Male	60+	4.7	5.8	6.7	10.1	17.2
	65+	2.6	3.7	4.3	6.7	11.8
	80+	0.1	0.3	0.5	0.7	1.7
Ageing index		13.0	15.6	22.2	39.9	90.1
Broad age groups (percentage)	0-14	39.7	40.9	33.1	27.6	20.9
	15-59	55.2	52.7	59.6	61.4	60.3
	60+	5.1	6.4	7.3	11.0	18.8
Median age (years)		20.0	19.1	22.8*	28.1	35.7
Dependency ratio	Total	74.4	82.1	61.1	54.0	51.9
	Youth	69.2	74.5	53.2	42.5	31.7
	Old Age	5.2	7.6	7.8	11.5	20.2
Potential support ratio		19.3	13.2	12.8	8.7	5.0
Parent support ratio		0.5	1.2	1.6	2.6	6.2
Sex ratio (per 100 women)	60+	82.7	85.4	84.8	84.3	82.5
	65+	79.9	82.9	80.4	80.9	77.9
	80+	71.3	71.9	68.9	61.9	52.4

* *Estimate refers to year 2005.*

Indicator	Age	1950-1955	1975-1980	2005-2010	2025-2030	2045-2050
Growth rate (percentage)	Total	2.5	2.2	1.8	1.1	0.6
	60+	2.7	1.3	3.5	2.5	3.0
	65+	2.9	1.2	2.7	3.5	3.7
	80+	3.3	2.7	5.0	5.7	2.6
Total fertility rate (per woman)		6.6	5.5	3.0	2.3	1.9
Life expectancy (years)						
Total	Birth	42.4	54.0	71.2	75.5	78.4
	60	..	..	17.9	19.7	21.5
	65	..	..	14.2	15.8	17.4
	80	..	..	5.7	6.7	7.8
Female	Birth	43.6	55.3	73.5	77.9	80.8
	60	..	..	19.0	21.3	23.4
	65	..	..	15.0	17.2	19.1
	80	..	..	5.9	7.2	8.6
Male	Birth	41.2	52.9	68.9	73.1	76.0
	60	..	..	16.7	18.0	19.4
	65	..	..	13.3	14.3	15.6
	80	..	..	5.5	5.9	6.6
Survival rate (percentage)						
Total	60	..	..	83.5	89.1	92.1
	65	..	..	76.9	83.7	87.7
	80	..	..	35.6	45.4	54.0
Female	60	..	..	87.2	91.9	93.9
	65	..	..	82.1	88.0	90.9
	80	..	..	41.7	53.9	62.7
Male	60	..	..	79.9	86.4	90.3
	65	..	..	71.8	79.4	84.4
	80	..	..	29.5	37.2	45.0

		1980	1990	2007	2010	2020
Labour force participation (percentage)						
Total	65+	31.9	25.7	9.4	8.5	7.5
Female	65+	14.7	12.7	2.8	3.2	5.0
Male	65+	52.7	41.5	17.5	15.1	10.7

Percentage married, age 60+			Percentage living alone, age 60+ (2000)		
Total	Female	Male	Total	Female	Male
57.7	33.0	87.0	8.3	13.1	3.9

Statutory pensionable age (2006)		Percentage illiterate, age 65+ (2005)		
Female	Male	Total	Female	Male
60	60	54.0	76.2	27.8

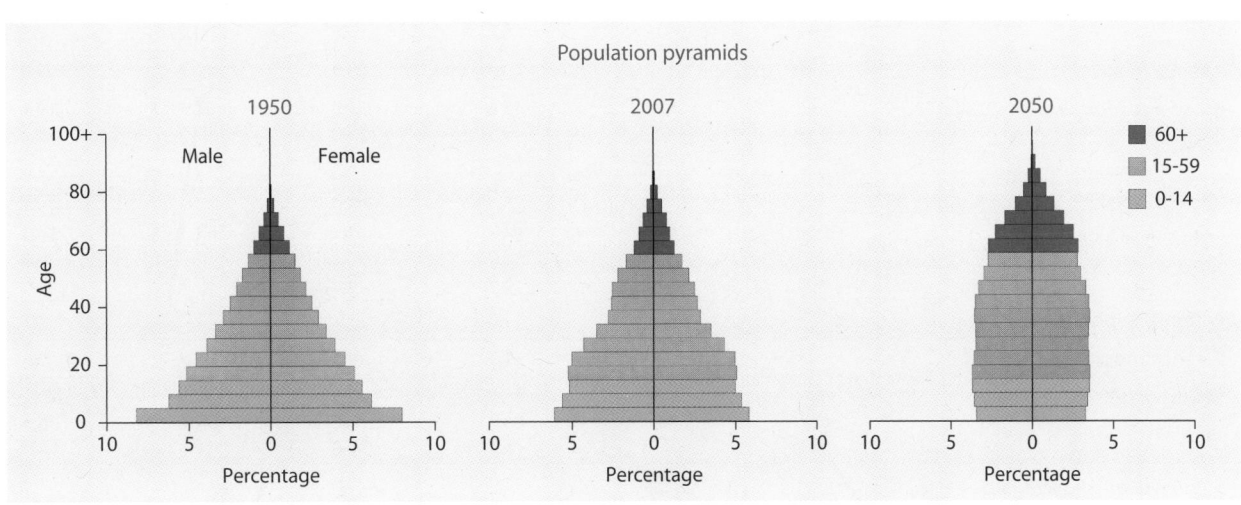

Population pyramids

United Nations Department of Economic and Social Affairs, Population Division

El Salvador

Indicator	Age	1950	1975	2007	2025	2050
Population (thousands)						
Total	Total	1 950.6	4 119.5	7 115.6	9 052.5	10 822.9
	0-14	839.9	1 878.8	2 363.1	2 360.9	2 087.4
	15-59	1 017.6	2 045.8	4 195.5	5 724.8	6 460.0
	60-64	32.9	70.3	167.8	283.5	554.2
	65-69	25.0	55.8	131.5	232.7	502.6
	70-74	17.1	36.9	106.2	176.6	476.5
	75-79	11.1	20.6	76.4	129.3	348.5
	80-84			45.2	77.8	213.8
	85-89			21.9	42.9	111.5
	90-94	7.0	11.4	6.7	18.3	51.0
	95-99			1.2	4.9	15.0
	100+			0.1	0.7	2.5
Female	Total	975.9	2 049.4	3 616.5	4 591.2	5 499.9
	0-14	415.3	926.2	1 157.9	1 154.4	1 020.1
	15-59	511.6	1 019.0	2 148.3	2 878.2	3 209.5
	60-64	17.0	36.7	89.4	160.0	287.2
	65-69	13.0	29.7	70.9	131.9	265.5
	70-74	9.0	20.0	58.7	100.2	259.4
	75-79	6.0	11.4	43.8	74.9	200.0
	80-84			27.3	47.0	133.2
	85-89			14.3	27.7	75.1
	90-94	4.0	6.5	4.8	12.8	36.6
	95-99			1.0	3.7	11.5
	100+			0.1	0.6	1.9
Male	Total	974.7	2 070.1	3 499.1	4 461.2	5 323.0
	0-14	424.6	952.7	1 205.2	1 206.5	1 067.4
	15-59	506.0	1 026.8	2 047.2	2 846.6	3 250.4
	60-64	15.9	33.6	78.4	123.6	267.0
	65-69	12.0	26.1	60.6	100.9	237.1
	70-74	8.1	16.9	47.5	76.4	217.1
	75-79	5.1	9.2	32.6	54.4	148.5
	80-84			17.9	30.9	80.6
	85-89			7.6	15.2	36.4
	90-94	3.0	4.8	1.9	5.5	14.4
	95-99			0.2	1.1	3.6
	100+			0.0	0.1	0.5
Percentage in older ages						
Total	60+	4.8	4.7	7.8	10.7	21.0
	65+	3.1	3.0	5.5	7.5	15.9
	80+	0.4	0.3	1.1	1.6	3.6
Female	60+	5.0	5.1	8.6	12.2	23.1
	65+	3.3	3.3	6.1	8.7	17.9
	80+	0.4	0.3	1.3	2.0	4.7
Male	60+	4.5	4.4	7.1	9.1	18.9
	65+	2.9	2.8	4.8	6.4	13.9
	80+	0.3	0.2	0.8	1.2	2.5
Ageing index		11.1	10.4	23.6	40.9	109.0
Broad age groups (percentage)	0-14	43.1	45.6	33.2	26.1	19.3
	15-59	52.2	49.7	59.0	63.2	59.7
	60+	4.8	4.7	7.8	10.7	21.0
Median age (years)		18.3	17.0	23.3*	29.1	37.5
Dependency ratio	Total	85.7	94.7	63.1	50.7	54.3
	Youth	80.0	88.8	54.2	39.3	29.8
	Old Age	5.7	5.9	8.9	11.4	24.5
Potential support ratio		17.5	17.0	11.2	8.8	4.1
Parent support ratio		1.4	1.1	4.7	5.7	9.6
Sex ratio (per 100 women)	60+	89.9	86.8	79.5	73.1	79.1
	65+	88.0	84.3	76.2	71.4	75.1
	80+	75.0	73.8	58.3	57.6	52.4

* Estimate refers to year 2005.

Indicator	Age	1950-1955	1975-1980	2005-2010	2025-2030	2045-2050
Growth rate (percentage)	Total	2.6	2.1	1.6	1.0	0.4
	60+	0.9	3.7	3.1	3.8	2.2
	65+	0.4	3.4	2.7	3.2	2.7
	80+	−0.5	4.7	4.8	4.1	4.7
Total fertility rate (per woman)		6.5	5.6	2.7	2.2	1.9
Life expectancy (years)						
Total	Birth	45.3	56.7	71.9	75.9	78.8
	60	..	..	20.7	22.5	23.8
	65	..	..	17.1	18.6	19.8
	80	..	..	8.0	8.9	9.7
Female	Birth	46.5	62.0	74.9	79.0	82.0
	60	..	..	22.3	24.2	25.9
	65	..	..	18.4	20.2	21.6
	80	..	..	8.7	9.7	10.5
Male	Birth	44.1	52.1	68.8	72.6	75.5
	60	..	..	19.1	20.4	21.5
	65	..	..	15.5	16.7	17.7
	80	..	..	7.1	7.8	8.4
Survival rate (percentage)						
Total	60	..	..	79.7	84.6	88.3
	65	..	..	74.2	80.0	84.2
	80	..	..	43.7	52.1	58.8
Female	60	..	..	83.9	88.4	91.6
	65	..	..	79.2	84.7	88.6
	80	..	..	51.2	60.4	67.9
Male	60	..	..	75.2	80.8	85.0
	65	..	..	69.0	75.1	79.9
	80	..	..	36.0	43.1	49.3

		1980	1990	2007	2010	2020
Labour force participation (percentage)						
Total	65+	37.7	34.6	23.9	21.5	16.9
Female	65+	17.3	21.5	16.0	15.8	15.5
Male	65+	63.1	51.3	34.2	29.0	18.9

Percentage married, age 60+				Percentage living alone, age 60+ (1992)		
Total	Female	Male		Total	Female	Male
52.2	38.0	70.0		7.2	6.2	8.4

Statutory pensionable age (2006)			Percentage illiterate, age 65+		
Female	Male		Total	Female	Male
55	60		..	..	..

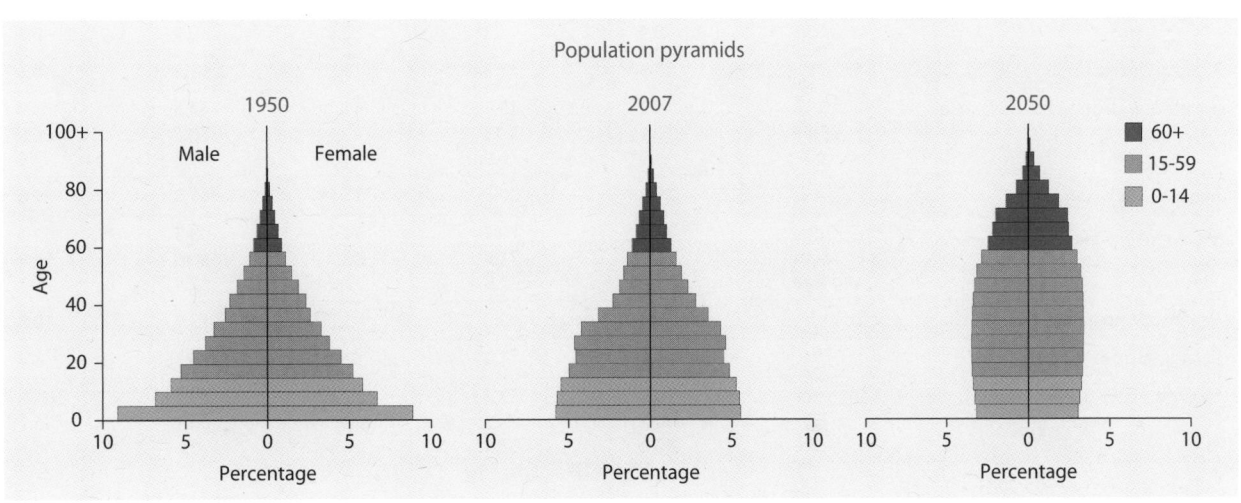

Population pyramids

Equatorial Guinea

Indicator	Age	1950	1975	2007	2025	2050
Population (thousands)						
Total	Total	225.5	227.6	526.7	762.2	1 146.3
	0-14	77.2	90.8	235.2	339.0	401.6
	15-59	128.4	121.1	260.4	381.4	688.0
	60-64	7.3	5.8	10.4	12.6	19.1
	65-69	5.7	4.3	8.3	10.9	13.8
	70-74	3.8	2.9	6.0	8.9	9.8
	75-79	2.1	1.7	3.7	5.3	7.0
	80-84			1.8	2.8	4.4
	85-89			0.6	1.1	2.0
	90-94	1.1	1.0	0.1	0.3	0.6
	95-99			0.0	0.0	0.1
	100+			0.0	0.0	0.0
Female	Total	114.7	115.9	265.6	378.2	569.7
	0-14	39.1	45.5	117.2	168.4	199.4
	15-59	65.1	61.9	131.4	187.0	342.0
	60-64	3.8	3.1	5.6	6.6	9.2
	65-69	2.9	2.4	4.5	5.9	6.7
	70-74	2.0	1.6	3.3	4.9	4.9
	75-79	1.1	0.9	2.1	3.0	3.7
	80-84			1.0	1.6	2.4
	85-89			0.4	0.6	1.1
	90-94	0.6	0.6	0.1	0.2	0.4
	95-99			0.0	0.0	0.1
	100+			0.0	0.0	0.0
Male	Total	110.9	111.7	261.1	384.0	576.6
	0-14	38.1	45.3	118.1	170.6	202.3
	15-59	63.3	59.2	129.0	194.4	346.0
	60-64	3.4	2.7	4.8	5.9	9.9
	65-69	2.8	2.0	3.8	5.0	7.1
	70-74	1.8	1.3	2.7	4.0	4.9
	75-79	1.0	0.8	1.6	2.3	3.4
	80-84			0.7	1.2	2.0
	85-89			0.2	0.4	0.8
	90-94	0.5	0.4	0.0	0.1	0.2
	95-99			0.0	0.0	0.0
	100+			0.0	0.0	0.0
Percentage in older ages						
Total	60+	8.9	6.9	5.9	5.5	4.9
	65+	5.6	4.4	3.9	3.8	3.3
	80+	0.5	0.4	0.5	0.6	0.6
Female	60+	9.1	7.4	6.4	6.0	5.0
	65+	5.8	4.8	4.3	4.3	3.4
	80+	0.5	0.5	0.6	0.7	0.7
Male	60+	8.6	6.4	5.4	4.9	4.9
	65+	5.4	4.0	3.5	3.4	3.2
	80+	0.4	0.4	0.4	0.5	0.5
Ageing index		25.9	17.3	13.2	12.3	14.1
Broad age groups (percentage)	0-14	34.2	39.9	44.7	44.5	35.0
	15-59	56.9	53.2	49.4	50.0	60.0
	60+	8.9	6.9	5.9	5.5	4.9
Median age (years)		23.8	20.2	17.6*	17.3	21.8
Dependency ratio	Total	66.3	79.4	94.5	93.5	62.1
	Youth	56.9	71.5	86.9	86.0	56.8
	Old Age	9.4	7.8	7.6	7.4	5.3
Potential support ratio		10.7	12.8	13.1	13.5	18.8
Parent support ratio		1.0	1.4	2.0	3.3	3.4
Sex ratio (per 100 women)	60+	90.5	83.2	82.3	83.1	100.0
	65+	90.5	80.5	80.7	80.3	96.2
	80+	80.0	67.8	67.2	70.7	76.5

* *Estimate refers to year 2005.*

Indicator	Age	1950-1955	1975-1980	2005-2010	2025-2030	2045-2050
Growth rate (percentage)	Total	1.1	−0.7	2.2	1.9	1.4
	60+	−0.2	−1.2	1.6	1.0	2.5
	65+	−0.2	−1.4	1.9	1.2	1.7
	80+	0.2	−1.1	3.0	2.3	1.2
Total fertility rate (per woman)		5.5	5.7	5.9	4.2	2.8
Life expectancy (years)						
Total	Birth	34.5	42.0	41.2	46.0	55.1
	60	..	..	15.8	17.1	18.1
	65	..	..	12.7	13.9	14.7
	80	..	..	5.6	6.1	6.5
Female	Birth	36.0	43.6	41.6	45.9	56.5
	60	..	..	16.5	17.7	18.8
	65	..	..	13.2	14.3	15.2
	80	..	..	5.9	6.3	6.7
Male	Birth	33.0	40.5	41.4	46.0	53.9
	60	..	..	15.4	16.5	17.4
	65	..	..	12.4	13.3	14.2
	80	..	..	5.4	5.9	6.3
Survival rate (percentage)						
Total	60	..	..	30.3	32.9	47.6
	65	..	..	26.5	29.4	43.2
	80	..	..	10.0	12.9	20.9
Female	60	..	..	30.7	32.2	49.9
	65	..	..	27.2	29.2	46.0
	80	..	..	11.0	13.5	23.4
Male	60	..	..	31.2	33.5	45.5
	65	..	..	27.0	29.6	40.7
	80	..	..	9.7	12.2	18.7

		1980	1990	2007	2010	2020
Labour force participation (percentage)						
Total	65+	37.1	38.5	40.5	40.2	40.2
Female	65+	23.7	27.6	32.8	34.0	37.5
Male	65+	53.8	52.2	50.0	48.0	43.5

Percentage married, age 60+				Percentage living alone, age 60+		
Total	Female	Male		Total	Female	Male
50.8	29.0	77.0		..	..	..

Statutory pensionable age (2006)				Percentage illiterate, age 65+ (2000)		
Female	Male			Total	Female	Male
60	60			47.8	77.6	27.5

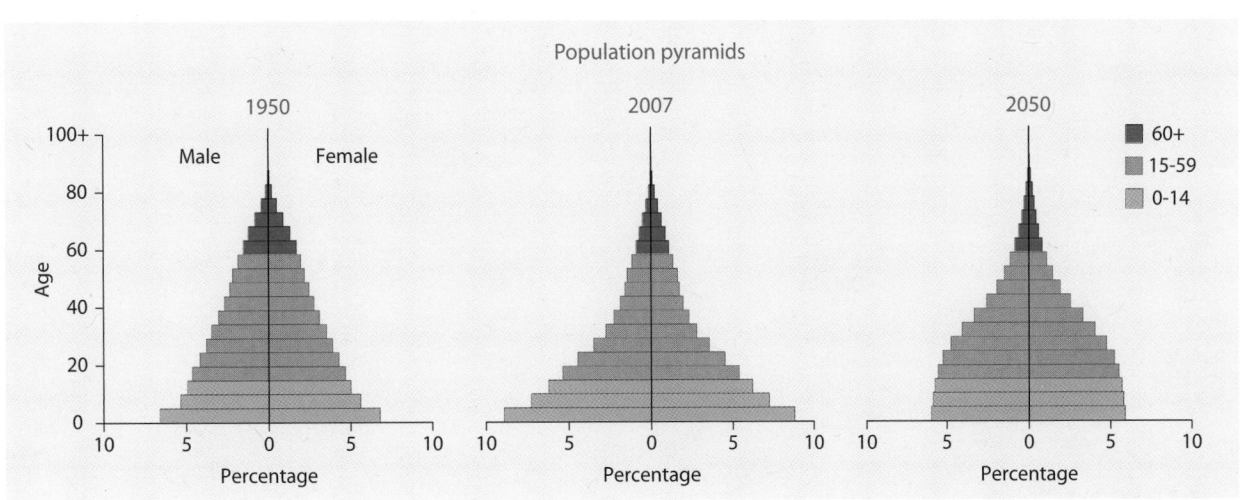

Population pyramids

Eritrea

Indicator	Age	1950	1975	2007	2025	2050
Population (thousands)						
Total	Total	1 140.1	2 088.7	4 708.1	7 351.6	11 228.7
	0-14	516.2	930.8	2 095.3	2 815.0	3 199.8
	15-59	565.4	1 070.1	2 424.4	4 229.4	7 083.8
	60-64	21.8	34.7	77.4	107.3	333.9
	65-69	16.6	24.3	51.6	81.5	253.9
	70-74	11.1	15.5	30.3	56.8	179.6
	75-79	6.1	8.7	17.2	35.8	104.9
	80-84			8.1	17.8	47.4
	85-89			2.8	6.1	17.9
	90-94	2.9	4.6	0.7	1.6	6.0
	95-99			0.1	0.3	1.3
	100+			0.0	0.0	0.2
Female	Total	575.2	1 053.7	2 392.8	3 692.9	5 615.6
	0-14	254.4	465.9	1 038.8	1 389.6	1 576.2
	15-59	288.0	539.1	1 241.5	2 114.2	3 508.7
	60-64	12.1	18.7	44.4	59.3	174.7
	65-69	9.2	13.3	30.1	50.1	138.5
	70-74	6.3	8.8	18.6	37.2	103.0
	75-79	3.5	5.1	11.2	24.1	64.2
	80-84			5.6	12.5	31.4
	85-89			2.0	4.5	12.9
	90-94	1.7	2.8	0.5	1.2	4.8
	95-99			0.1	0.2	1.1
	100+			0.0	0.0	0.1
Male	Total	564.9	1 035.0	2 315.3	3 658.7	5 613.1
	0-14	261.8	464.9	1 056.6	1 425.5	1 623.5
	15-59	277.4	531.0	1 182.9	2 115.3	3 575.2
	60-64	9.7	16.0	33.0	47.9	159.2
	65-69	7.4	11.0	21.5	31.4	115.5
	70-74	4.8	6.7	11.8	19.6	76.6
	75-79	2.6	3.6	6.0	11.7	40.7
	80-84			2.5	5.3	16.1
	85-89			0.8	1.6	5.0
	90-94	1.2	1.8	0.2	0.4	1.2
	95-99			0.0	0.1	0.2
	100+			0.0	0.0	0.0
Percentage in older ages						
Total	60+	5.1	4.2	4.0	4.2	8.4
	65+	3.2	2.5	2.4	2.7	5.4
	80+	0.3	0.2	0.3	0.4	0.6
Female	60+	5.7	4.6	4.7	5.1	9.5
	65+	3.6	2.8	2.8	3.5	6.3
	80+	0.3	0.3	0.3	0.5	0.9
Male	60+	4.5	3.8	3.3	3.2	7.4
	65+	2.8	2.2	1.9	1.9	4.5
	80+	0.2	0.2	0.2	0.2	0.4
Ageing index		11.3	9.4	9.0	10.9	29.5
Broad age groups (percentage)	0-14	45.3	44.6	44.5	38.3	28.5
	15-59	49.6	51.2	51.5	57.5	63.1
	60+	5.1	4.2	4.0	4.2	8.4
Median age (years)		17.3	17.6	17.4*	20.3	27.0
Dependency ratio	Total	94.2	89.1	88.2	69.5	51.4
	Youth	87.9	84.3	83.8	64.9	43.1
	Old Age	6.2	4.8	4.4	4.6	8.2
Potential support ratio		16.0	20.8	22.5	21.7	12.1
Parent support ratio		1.0	0.9	1.3	1.6	1.9
Sex ratio (per 100 women)	60+	78.4	80.3	67.4	62.3	78.1
	65+	77.3	77.0	62.9	53.9	71.7
	80+	70.6	64.5	42.9	39.4	44.5

* Estimate refers to year 2005.

Indicator	Age	1950-1955	1975-1980	2005-2010	2025-2030	2045-2050
Growth rate (percentage)	Total	2.0	2.6	3.1	2.0	1.4
	60+	0.6	9.3	3.6	3.7	4.0
	65+	0.6	11.0	4.2	2.7	4.6
	80+	2.0	21.2	4.0	4.8	5.5
Total fertility rate (per woman)		7.0	6.5	5.0	3.2	2.4
Life expectancy (years)						
Total	Birth	35.9	44.9	56.0	63.6	69.1
	60	..	..	14.5	16.4	18.1
	65	..	..	11.8	13.4	14.7
	80	..	..	5.8	6.5	7.1
Female	Birth	37.5	46.9	57.8	65.3	71.1
	60	..	..	15.9	18.0	20.0
	65	..	..	12.9	14.7	16.3
	80	..	..	6.2	6.9	7.6
Male	Birth	34.4	43.1	54.1	61.6	67.1
	60	..	..	12.7	14.4	15.9
	65	..	..	10.2	11.5	12.8
	80	..	..	5.1	5.6	6.1
Survival rate (percentage)						
Total	60	..	..	54.0	66.9	76.7
	65	..	..	45.2	58.5	69.2
	80	..	..	14.7	24.1	32.9
Female	60	..	..	57.0	69.6	78.8
	65	..	..	49.4	62.8	73.1
	80	..	..	19.2	29.9	40.7
Male	60	..	..	50.3	64.2	74.5
	65	..	..	40.3	54.1	65.2
	80	..	..	9.8	16.9	24.8

		1980	1990	2007	2010	2020
Labour force participation (percentage)						
Total	65+	52.1	50.7	44.9	44.4	42.8
Female	65+	26.3	29.1	25.2	25.0	24.7
Male	65+	81.1	81.0	76.1	75.9	75.6

Percentage married, age 60+			Percentage living alone, age 60+		
Total	Female	Male	Total	Female	Male
..	..	..	..	..	..

Statutory pensionable age (2006)		Percentage illiterate, age 65+		
Female	Male	Total	Female	Male
..	..	..	..	..

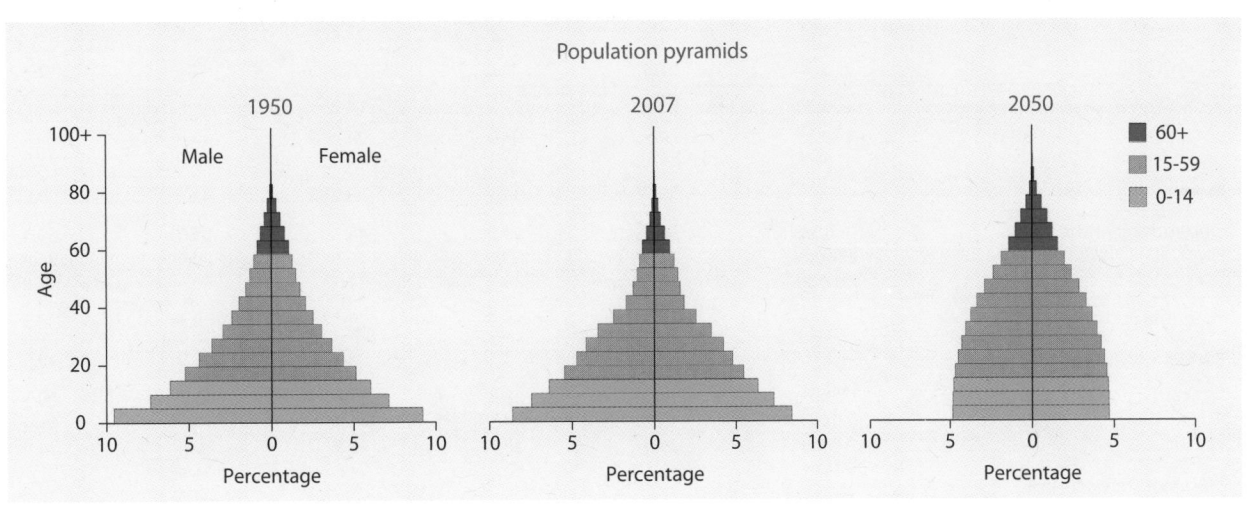

Population pyramids

Estonia

Indicator	Age	1950	1975	2007	2025	2050
Population (thousands)						
Total	Total	1 101.0	1 432.0	1 320.5	1 247.8	1 119.3
	0-14	281.5	312.0	194.3	197.1	176.7
	15-59	656.5	874.6	838.1	726.1	566.6
	60-64	46.3	70.9	67.8	79.0	93.3
	65-69	40.1	62.1	67.7	74.6	82.7
	70-74	32.9	50.5	59.4	63.1	66.0
	75-79	24.0	32.8	46.8	46.9	54.6
	80-84	⎫		29.8	29.7	37.3
	85-89	⎪		10.8	20.6	24.9
	90-94	⎬ 19.7	29.0	4.4	8.1	12.4
	95-99	⎪		1.1	2.3	4.0
	100+	⎭		0.1	0.3	0.7
Female	Total	631.5	771.3	713.6	668.9	587.8
	0-14	136.6	152.3	94.5	96.1	86.0
	15-59	382.9	454.0	431.5	364.6	278.4
	60-64	30.7	44.2	39.6	44.7	48.3
	65-69	27.1	40.3	41.6	44.5	44.7
	70-74	22.4	34.1	38.1	40.0	37.6
	75-79	17.1	23.9	32.0	31.8	33.7
	80-84	⎫		22.8	21.7	25.5
	85-89	⎪		8.8	16.3	19.0
	90-94	⎬ 14.7	22.4	3.7	6.9	10.5
	95-99	⎪		1.0	2.1	3.6
	100+	⎭		0.1	0.3	0.7
Male	Total	469.5	660.7	606.9	578.9	531.5
	0-14	144.9	159.7	99.7	101.1	90.7
	15-59	273.6	420.6	406.6	361.5	288.2
	60-64	15.5	26.7	28.2	34.3	45.0
	65-69	13.1	21.7	26.1	30.1	38.0
	70-74	10.5	16.4	21.3	23.1	28.5
	75-79	6.8	8.9	14.8	15.1	20.9
	80-84	⎫		7.1	8.0	11.8
	85-89	⎪		2.1	4.2	6.0
	90-94	⎬ 5.1	6.7	0.8	1.2	1.9
	95-99	⎪		0.2	0.2	0.3
	100+	⎭		0.0	0.0	0.0
Percentage in older ages						
Total	60+	14.8	17.1	21.8	26.0	33.6
	65+	10.6	12.2	16.7	19.7	25.3
	80+	1.8	2.0	3.5	4.9	7.1
Female	60+	17.7	21.4	26.3	31.1	38.0
	65+	12.9	15.7	20.7	24.5	29.8
	80+	2.3	2.9	5.1	7.1	10.1
Male	60+	10.9	12.2	16.6	20.1	28.7
	65+	7.5	8.1	11.9	14.2	20.2
	80+	1.1	1.0	1.7	2.4	3.8
Ageing index		57.9	78.6	148.3	164.6	212.8
Broad age groups (percentage)	0-14	25.6	21.8	14.7	15.8	15.8
	15-59	59.6	61.1	63.5	58.2	50.6
	60+	14.8	17.1	21.8	26.0	33.6
Median age (years)		29.9	34.1	38.9*	42.7	45.6
Dependency ratio	Total	56.7	51.5	45.8	55.0	69.6
	Youth	40.1	33.0	21.4	24.5	26.8
	Old Age	16.6	18.5	24.3	30.5	42.8
Potential support ratio		6.0	5.4	4.1	3.3	2.3
Parent support ratio		4.8	5.1	6.8	12.9	19.0
Sex ratio (per 100 women)	60+	45.5	48.8	53.6	55.8	68.3
	65+	43.6	44.5	48.9	50.1	61.4
	80+	34.6	29.7	27.9	29.0	34.0

* *Estimate refers to year 2005.*

Indicator	Age	1950-1955	1975-1980	2005-2010	2025-2030	2045-2050
Growth rate (percentage)	Total	1.0	0.6	−0.3	−0.4	−0.5
	60+	0.8	−0.8	0.4	0.1	1.0
	65+	0.7	1.1	0.0	0.6	1.1
	80+	1.3	1.6	4.3	1.1	0.0
Total fertility rate (per woman)		2.1	2.1	1.4	1.7	1.9
Life expectancy (years)						
Total	Birth	65.6	69.8	72.6	76.5	78.9
	60	..	..	19.1	20.9	22.1
	65	..	..	15.7	17.2	18.3
	80	..	..	7.4	8.2	8.8
Female	Birth	68.3	74.4	77.9	80.7	82.5
	60	..	..	21.7	23.6	24.9
	65	..	..	17.7	19.5	20.6
	80	..	..	8.0	9.0	9.8
Male	Birth	61.7	64.5	67.0	71.9	75.1
	60	..	..	15.6	17.3	18.9
	65	..	..	12.8	14.0	15.3
	80	..	..	6.0	6.3	6.8
Survival rate (percentage)						
Total	60	..	..	80.9	87.5	91.0
	65	..	..	73.7	81.6	86.0
	80	..	..	39.0	48.6	54.8
Female	60	..	..	90.0	92.7	94.1
	65	..	..	85.5	89.2	91.1
	80	..	..	53.8	62.0	66.9
Male	60	..	..	71.5	82.3	87.9
	65	..	..	61.3	73.6	81.0
	80	..	..	23.4	33.0	41.6

		1980	1990	2007	2010	2020
Labour force participation (percentage)						
Total	65+	11.6	16.1	14.0	14.0	14.2
Female	65+	9.3	13.5	13.5	13.8	14.3
Male	65+	16.8	22.1	15.0	14.5	13.9

Percentage married, age 60+

	Female	Male
Total		
47.6	32.0	76.0

Percentage living alone, age 60+ (1989)

Total	Female	Male
29.6	36.4	15.5

Statutory pensionable age (2006)

Female	Male
59	63

Percentage illiterate, age 65+ (2000)

Total	Female	Male
0.4	0.5	0.3

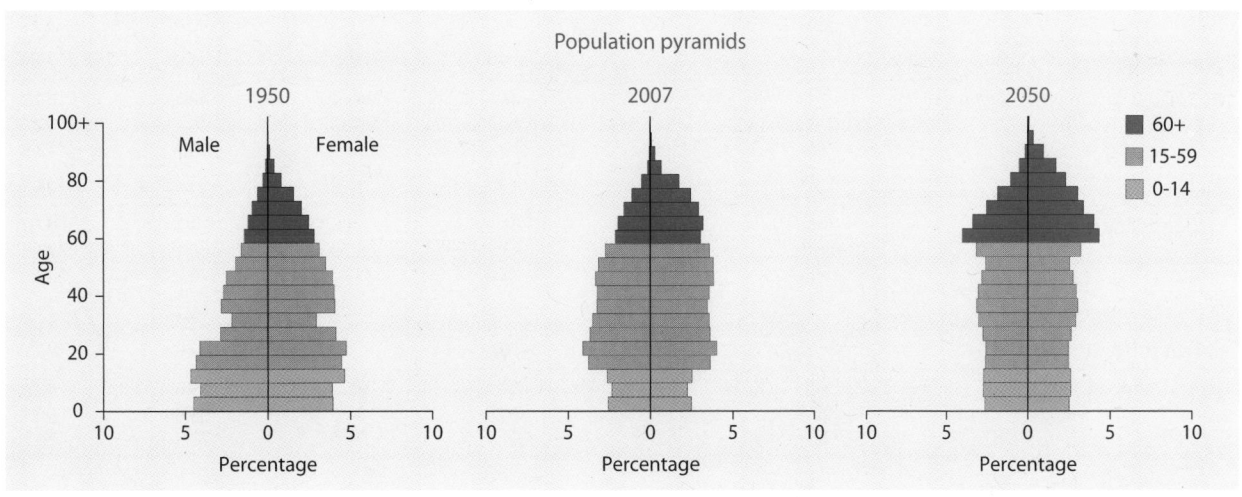

Population pyramids

Ethiopia

Indicator	Age	1950	1975	2007	2025	2050
Population (thousands)						
Total	Total	18 433.9	34 114.2	81 176.4	118 353.6	170 190.4
	0-14	8 135.4	15 515.7	35 674.3	45 430.1	48 824.2
	15-59	9 413.9	17 087.1	41 668.4	66 425.1	106 749.6
	60-64	333.6	598.9	1 414.2	2 262.4	5 150.4
	65-69	254.0	429.9	1 043.8	1 716.8	3 776.5
	70-74	167.1	277.6	702.6	1 220.5	2 635.2
	75-79	88.7	133.2	409.2	755.4	1 676.4
	80-84			188.3	374.4	899.2
	85-89			61.8	133.6	366.5
	90-94	41.3	71.8	12.3	30.9	96.4
	95-99			1.4	4.1	14.9
	100+			0.1	0.3	1.2
Female	Total	9 302.6	17 192.7	40 775.7	59 121.6	84 886.7
	0-14	4 040.4	7 759.3	17 745.1	22 548.0	24 221.0
	15-59	4 749.0	8 614.5	20 974.8	33 073.1	53 092.0
	60-64	189.2	313.6	740.6	1 186.1	2 593.4
	65-69	147.9	228.5	555.8	919.9	1 928.5
	70-74	97.1	151.8	379.7	666.3	1 373.3
	75-79	53.7	79.6	225.8	415.7	896.9
	80-84			107.5	211.5	499.0
	85-89			37.3	78.6	212.7
	90-94	25.4	45.5	8.0	19.3	59.2
	95-99			1.0	2.8	9.8
	100+			0.1	0.2	0.9
Male	Total	9 131.2	16 921.6	40 400.7	59 232.1	85 303.7
	0-14	4 095.0	7 756.4	17 929.2	22 882.1	24 603.1
	15-59	4 664.9	8 472.7	20 693.6	33 352.1	53 657.6
	60-64	144.4	285.3	673.6	1 076.3	2 557.0
	65-69	106.1	201.4	488.0	796.9	1 848.0
	70-74	70.0	125.8	322.9	554.3	1 261.9
	75-79	35.0	53.7	183.4	339.6	779.5
	80-84			80.8	162.8	400.3
	85-89			24.5	55.0	153.8
	90-94	15.9	26.3	4.3	11.6	37.2
	95-99			0.4	1.3	5.0
	100+			0.0	0.1	0.3
Percentage in older ages						
Total	60+	4.8	4.4	4.7	5.5	8.6
	65+	3.0	2.7	3.0	3.6	5.6
	80+	0.2	0.2	0.3	0.5	0.8
Female	60+	5.5	4.8	5.0	5.9	8.9
	65+	3.5	2.9	3.2	3.9	5.9
	80+	0.3	0.3	0.4	0.5	0.9
Male	60+	4.1	4.1	4.4	5.1	8.3
	65+	2.5	2.4	2.7	3.2	5.3
	80+	0.2	0.2	0.3	0.4	0.7
Ageing index		10.9	9.7	10.7	14.3	29.9
Broad age groups (percentage)	0-14	44.1	45.5	43.9	38.4	28.7
	15-59	51.1	50.1	51.3	56.1	62.7
	60+	4.8	4.4	4.7	5.5	8.6
Median age (years)		17.9	17.2	17.5*	20.4	26.8
Dependency ratio	Total	89.1	92.9	88.4	72.3	52.1
	Youth	83.5	87.7	82.8	66.1	43.6
	Old Age	5.7	5.2	5.6	6.2	8.5
Potential support ratio		17.7	19.4	17.8	16.2	11.8
Parent support ratio		0.8	0.8	1.4	2.0	2.4
Sex ratio (per 100 women)	60+	72.3	84.6	86.5	85.6	93.0
	65+	70.0	80.6	84.0	83.0	90.1
	80+	62.5	57.9	71.6	73.9	76.3

* Estimate refers to year 2005.

Indicator	Age	1950-1955	1975-1980	2005-2010	2025-2030	2045-2050
Growth rate (percentage)	Total	2.1	1.7	2.3	1.7	1.2
	60+	0.5	1.8	3.0	2.8	3.8
	65+	0.3	2.0	3.2	3.1	3.6
	80+	1.3	1.7	4.0	4.0	3.5
Total fertility rate (per woman)		7.1	6.8	5.4	3.5	2.5
Life expectancy (years)						
Total	Birth	34.1	44.5	48.5	56.3	64.1
	60	..	..	16.1	17.3	18.6
	65	..	..	12.9	14.0	15.0
	80	..	..	5.7	6.1	6.5
Female	Birth	35.4	46.0	49.4	57.1	65.4
	60	..	..	16.6	17.9	19.3
	65	..	..	13.3	14.4	15.5
	80	..	..	5.9	6.3	6.7
Male	Birth	32.8	43.1	47.7	55.5	62.8
	60	..	..	15.4	16.7	17.9
	65	..	..	12.4	13.4	14.4
	80	..	..	5.4	5.9	6.3
Survival rate (percentage)						
Total	60	..	..	44.9	55.3	67.8
	65	..	..	39.5	49.8	62.4
	80	..	..	15.2	22.1	31.1
Female	60	..	..	46.2	56.3	69.5
	65	..	..	41.2	51.3	64.7
	80	..	..	16.8	24.0	34.0
Male	60	..	..	43.5	54.3	66.2
	65	..	..	37.8	48.3	60.2
	80	..	..	13.6	20.2	28.2

		1980	1990	2007	2010	2020
Labour force participation (percentage)						
Total	65+	44.3	45.3	42.0	40.9	36.6
Female	65+	27.3	27.7	26.2	26.1	26.1
Male	65+	64.9	66.5	60.9	58.6	49.3

Percentage married, age 60+			Percentage living alone, age 60+ (2000)		
Total	Female	Male	Total	Female	Male
57.5	32.0	87.0	5.0	8.6	1.6

Statutory pensionable age (2006)			Percentage illiterate, age 65+		
Female	Male		Total	Female	Male
60	60		..	..	..

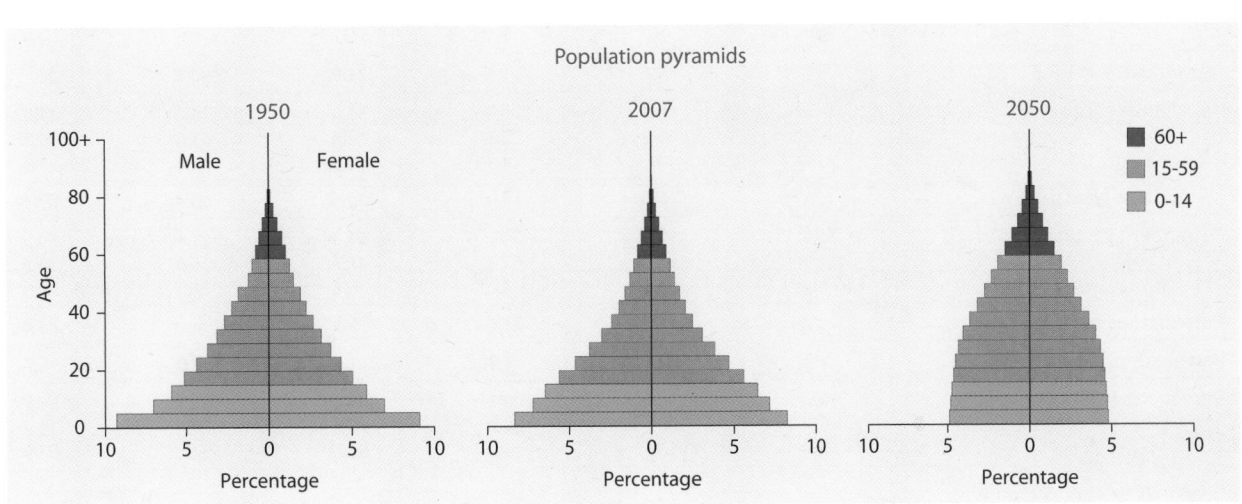

Population pyramids

Fiji

Indicator	Age	1950	1975	2007	2025	2050
Population (thousands)						
Total	Total	289.0	576.0	860.7	938.6	934.4
	0-14	135.0	229.6	266.4	227.1	167.0
	15-59	141.0	320.6	535.9	597.1	566.8
	60-64	5.0	10.5	23.1	40.9	54.2
	65-69	3.0	6.4	15.9	32.2	52.4
	70-74	2.3	4.5	9.9	20.3	40.3
	75-79	1.4	2.6	5.7	12.4	25.4
	80-84			2.5	5.9	16.1
	85-89			1.1	2.2	8.6
	90-94	1.3	1.8	0.2	0.5	2.9
	95-99			0.0	0.1	0.5
	100+			0.0	0.0	0.1
Female	Total	138.0	284.7	423.4	462.8	463.6
	0-14	67.0	112.7	129.4	110.2	81.0
	15-59	67.0	159.6	262.3	289.7	273.9
	60-64	2.0	5.0	12.0	21.2	26.8
	65-69	1.0	3.1	8.5	17.1	26.9
	70-74	0.6	2.2	5.5	11.4	21.8
	75-79	0.2	1.3	3.3	7.4	14.5
	80-84			1.5	3.8	10.1
	85-89			0.7	1.5	5.9
	90-94	0.2	0.8	0.1	0.4	2.2
	95-99			0.0	0.1	0.4
	100+			0.0	0.0	0.0
Male	Total	151.0	291.3	437.4	475.8	470.8
	0-14	68.0	116.9	137.0	116.8	86.0
	15-59	74.0	161.0	273.7	307.4	292.9
	60-64	3.0	5.5	11.1	19.7	27.4
	65-69	2.0	3.3	7.3	15.1	25.5
	70-74	1.7	2.3	4.4	8.9	18.6
	75-79	1.2	1.3	2.4	4.9	10.9
	80-84			1.0	2.1	6.0
	85-89			0.4	0.7	2.6
	90-94	1.1	1.0	0.1	0.1	0.7
	95-99			0.0	0.0	0.1
	100+			0.0	0.0	0.0
Percentage in older ages						
Total	60+	4.5	4.5	6.8	12.2	21.5
	65+	2.8	2.7	4.1	7.8	15.7
	80+	0.4	0.3	0.4	0.9	3.0
Female	60+	2.9	4.4	7.5	13.6	23.5
	65+	1.4	2.6	4.6	9.0	17.7
	80+	0.1	0.3	0.6	1.2	4.0
Male	60+	6.0	4.6	6.1	10.8	19.5
	65+	4.0	2.7	3.6	6.7	13.7
	80+	0.7	0.3	0.3	0.6	2.0
Ageing index		9.6	11.2	21.9	50.4	120.1
Broad age groups (percentage)	0-14	46.7	39.9	31.0	24.2	17.9
	15-59	48.8	55.7	62.3	63.6	60.7
	60+	4.5	4.5	6.8	12.2	21.5
Median age (years)		16.6	19.0	24.5*	30.9	39.4
Dependency ratio	Total	97.9	74.0	54.0	47.1	50.5
	Youth	92.5	69.3	47.7	35.6	26.9
	Old Age	5.5	4.6	6.3	11.5	23.6
Potential support ratio		18.3	21.6	15.9	8.7	4.2
Parent support ratio		2.1	1.3	1.4	2.0	6.7
Sex ratio (per 100 women)	60+	225.2	108.1	84.1	82.1	84.5
	65+	300.5	106.8	79.3	76.6	78.7
	80+	555.1	125.2	62.5	52.2	50.6

* Estimate refers to year 2005.

Indicator	Age	1950-1955	1975-1980	2005-2010	2025-2030	2045-2050
Growth rate (percentage)	Total	3.0	1.9	0.7	0.3	–0.3
	60+	1.5	2.3	3.8	2.3	1.6
	65+	4.5	3.0	3.7	3.6	2.8
	80+	7.6	0.6	3.5	5.4	2.6
Total fertility rate (per woman)		6.6	4.0	2.7	2.2	1.9
Life expectancy (years)						
Total	Birth	52.5	62.7	68.7	72.1	76.0
	60	..	..	15.9	17.6	19.8
	65	..	..	12.8	14.2	16.1
	80	..	..	5.8	6.5	7.6
Female	Birth	54.9	65.0	71.0	74.5	78.5
	60	..	..	17.4	19.3	21.9
	65	..	..	14.0	15.6	17.9
	80	..	..	6.1	7.0	8.3
Male	Birth	50.8	60.8	66.5	69.7	73.6
	60	..	..	14.4	15.7	17.7
	65	..	..	11.5	12.6	14.2
	80	..	..	5.2	5.7	6.5
Survival rate (percentage)						
Total	60	..	..	78.3	83.8	89.1
	65	..	..	68.8	75.7	82.8
	80	..	..	26.2	34.3	45.2
Female	60	..	..	82.0	87.1	91.3
	65	..	..	74.1	80.7	86.6
	80	..	..	33.2	42.8	54.7
Male	60	..	..	74.8	80.8	87.2
	65	..	..	63.8	70.9	79.2
	80	..	..	19.6	26.0	36.1

		1980	1990	2007	2010	2020
Labour force participation (percentage)						
Total	65+	23.5	22.8	20.9	20.7	20.2
Female	65+	5.9	5.9	6.1	6.1	6.3
Male	65+	40.6	40.6	39.5	39.3	38.5

Percentage married, age 60+			Percentage living alone, age 60+ (1985)		
Total	Female	Male	Total	Female	Male
58.9	44.0	76.0	2.0	2.4	1.5

Statutory pensionable age (2006)			Percentage illiterate, age 65+		
	Female	Male	Total	Female	Male
	55	55	..	..	..

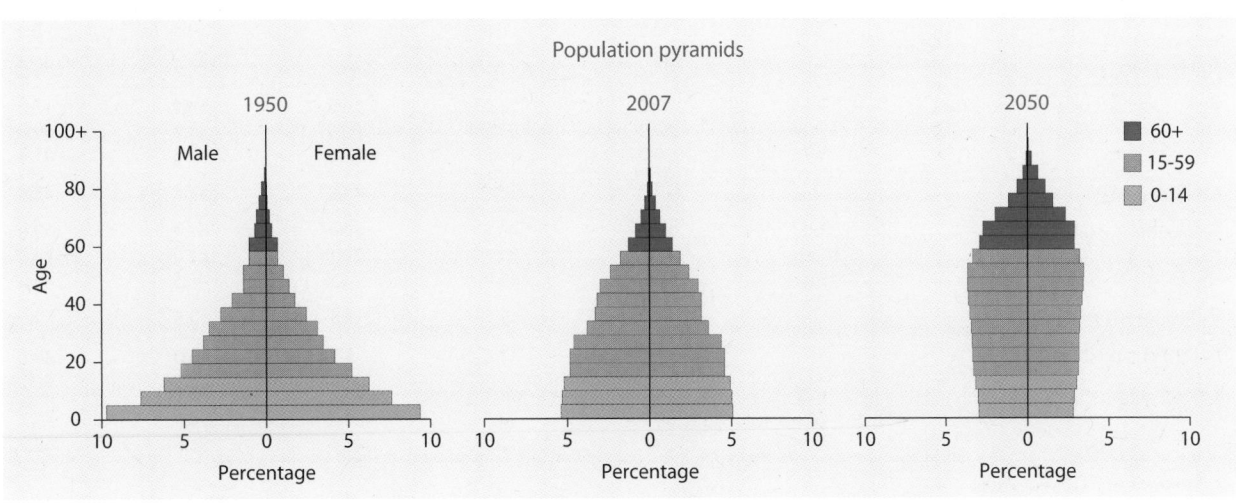

Population pyramids

1950   2007   2050

Male   Female

■ 60+
■ 15-59
■ 0-14

Age · Percentage

Finland

Indicator	Age	1950	1975	2007	2025	2050
Population (thousands)						
Total	Total	4 009.0	4 711.4	5 273.8	5 444.3	5 329.0
	0-14	1 202.0	1 037.1	887.0	877.3	818.7
	15-59	2 400.0	2 942.8	3 195.4	2 892.4	2 770.7
	60-64	140.0	231.4	334.8	359.2	323.0
	65-69	109.0	204.0	248.1	345.2	320.8
	70-74	78.0	144.2	209.6	332.3	294.8
	75-79	50.0	89.7	176.2	305.8	243.4
	80-84			128.2	170.2	227.5
	85-89			64.0	99.6	174.3
	90-94	30.0	62.2	24.6	45.4	101.7
	95-99			5.4	14.7	43.3
	100+			0.4	2.2	10.7
Female	Total	2 093.0	2 433.5	2 688.7	2 760.9	2 686.7
	0-14	589.0	507.6	434.3	429.3	400.5
	15-59	1 256.0	1 477.3	1 572.1	1 411.0	1 342.1
	60-64	81.0	133.0	170.7	181.6	158.8
	65-69	66.0	121.5	131.7	178.5	160.3
	70-74	49.0	90.4	116.9	177.4	151.3
	75-79	32.0	59.7	105.6	170.2	129.9
	80-84			85.6	101.6	128.7
	85-89			47.4	65.1	106.0
	90-94	20.0	43.8	19.5	32.7	67.9
	95-99			4.5	11.7	32.2
	100+			0.4	2.0	8.9
Male	Total	1 916.0	2 278.0	2 585.1	2 683.4	2 642.4
	0-14	613.0	529.5	452.7	448.1	418.2
	15-59	1 144.0	1 465.4	1 623.4	1 481.4	1 428.5
	60-64	59.0	98.4	164.1	177.6	164.2
	65-69	43.0	82.5	116.4	166.7	160.5
	70-74	29.0	53.8	92.8	154.9	143.5
	75-79	18.0	30.0	70.6	135.6	113.5
	80-84			42.6	68.7	98.8
	85-89			16.6	34.5	68.3
	90-94	10.0	18.4	5.0	12.7	33.8
	95-99			0.9	2.9	11.1
	100+			0.1	0.2	1.8
Percentage in older ages						
Total	60+	10.2	15.5	22.6	30.8	32.6
	65+	6.7	10.6	16.2	24.2	26.6
	80+	0.7	1.3	4.2	6.1	10.5
Female	60+	11.8	18.4	25.4	33.3	35.1
	65+	8.0	13.0	19.0	26.8	29.2
	80+	1.0	1.8	5.9	7.7	12.8
Male	60+	8.3	12.4	19.7	28.1	30.1
	65+	5.2	8.1	13.3	21.5	23.9
	80+	0.5	0.8	2.5	4.4	8.1
Ageing index		33.9	70.5	134.3	190.9	212.5
Broad age groups (percentage)	0-14	30.0	22.0	16.8	16.1	15.4
	15-59	59.9	62.5	60.6	53.1	52.0
	60+	10.2	15.5	22.6	30.8	32.6
Median age (years)		27.7	30.7	40.9*	44.1	45.6
Dependency ratio	Total	57.8	48.4	49.4	67.4	72.3
	Youth	47.3	32.7	25.1	27.0	26.5
	Old Age	10.5	15.8	24.3	40.5	45.8
Potential support ratio		9.5	6.3	4.1	2.5	2.2
Parent support ratio		2.1	2.6	8.3	16.0	33.6
Sex ratio (per 100 women)	60+	64.1	63.1	74.6	81.9	84.3
	65+	59.9	58.5	67.4	78.0	80.4
	80+	50.0	42.0	41.4	55.9	62.2

* *Estimate refers to year 2005.*

Indicator	Age	1950-1955	1975-1980	2005-2010	2025-2030	2045-2050
Growth rate (percentage)	Total	1.1	0.3	0.2	0.0	–0.1
	60+	1.5	1.3	3.2	0.6	0.0
	65+	1.7	2.7	1.8	1.1	0.2
	80+	1.9	6.9	3.1	5.3	0.2
Total fertility rate (per woman)		3.0	1.7	1.7	1.9	1.9
Life expectancy (years)						
Total	Birth	66.5	72.4	79.3	82.1	84.6
	60	..	..	22.5	24.4	26.3
	65	..	..	18.4	20.2	21.9
	80	..	..	8.4	9.6	10.8
Female	Birth	69.6	76.6	82.4	84.9	87.1
	60	..	..	24.6	26.6	28.4
	65	..	..	20.2	22.1	23.9
	80	..	..	9.1	10.5	11.9
Male	Birth	63.2	68.0	76.0	79.4	82.1
	60	..	..	20.0	22.1	24.0
	65	..	..	16.2	18.0	19.8
	80	..	..	7.2	8.3	9.4
Survival rate (percentage)						
Total	60	..	..	91.3	94.2	95.9
	65	..	..	87.3	91.0	93.4
	80	..	..	57.0	65.1	71.6
Female	60	..	..	94.5	96.0	97.0
	65	..	..	91.9	93.9	95.3
	80	..	..	67.8	74.1	79.1
Male	60	..	..	88.3	92.4	94.9
	65	..	..	82.8	88.1	91.6
	80	..	..	46.0	56.0	64.3

		1980	1990	2007	2010	2020
Labour force participation (percentage)						
Total	65+	9.7	5.5	3.9	4.0	4.3
Female	65+	5.6	3.4	1.6	1.6	1.6
Male	65+	17.0	9.3	7.3	7.5	7.7

Percentage married, age 60+				Percentage living alone, age 60+ (2000)		
Total	Female	Male		Total	Female	Male
52.8	41.0	70.0		35.2	45.3	21.0

Statutory pensionable age (2006)				Percentage illiterate, age 65+		
	Female	Male		Total	Female	Male
	65	65		..	..	..

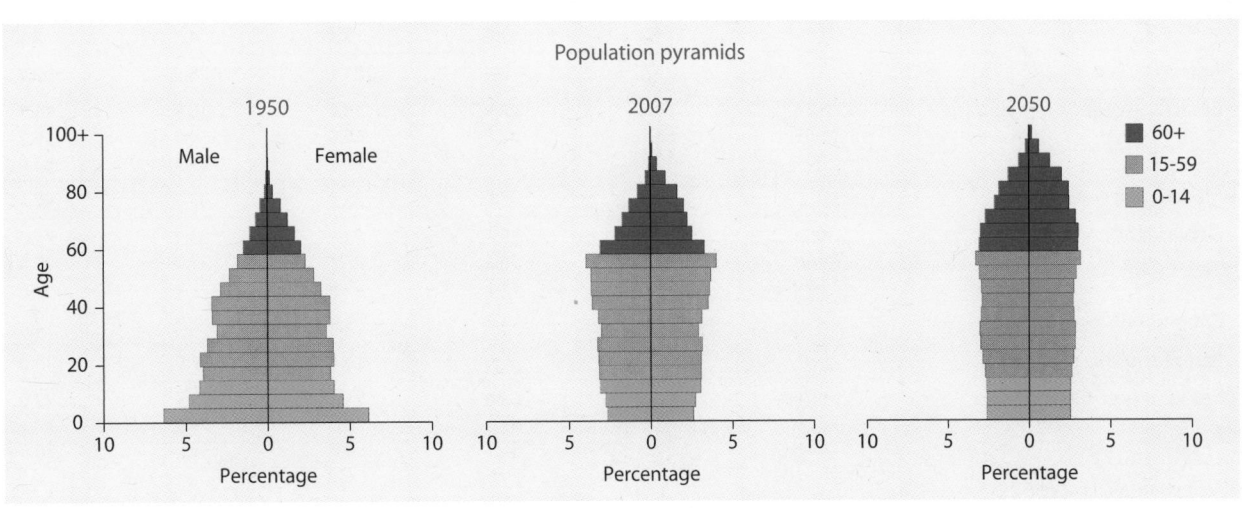

Population pyramids

United Nations Department of Economic and Social Affairs, Population Division

France

Indicator	Age	1950	1975	2007	2025	2050
Population (thousands)						
Total	Total	41 828.7	52 699.2	60 940.4	63 407.1	63 116.0
	0-14	9 498.0	12 594.5	11 021.9	10 449.5	9 936.0
	15-59	25 540.6	30 477.6	36 573.9	34 548.8	32 339.6
	60-64	2 028.5	2 526.0	3 223.5	4 098.1	3 726.9
	65-69	1 751.9	2 390.8	2 460.0	3 845.2	3 629.6
	70-74	1 376.1	2 016.4	2 429.3	3 521.4	3 356.8
	75-79	935.1	1 394.5	2 171.1	3 133.2	3 263.8
	80-84			1 742.9	1 725.1	2 777.6
	85-89			826.6	1 155.1	2 123.5
	90-94	698.5	1 299.3	354.3	651.3	1 262.9
	95-99			119.2	233.6	549.3
	100+			17.7	45.7	150.0
Female	Total	21 723.4	26 892.1	31 253.1	32 494.2	32 363.4
	0-14	4 679.4	6 158.4	5 376.5	5 094.9	4 844.4
	15-59	12 986.9	15 036.5	18 274.4	17 087.1	15 870.9
	60-64	1 180.6	1 357.9	1 650.0	2 128.3	1 873.6
	65-69	1 038.3	1 329.9	1 295.8	2 039.8	1 851.6
	70-74	811.8	1 179.8	1 343.2	1 916.4	1 755.0
	75-79	565.3	890.9	1 273.3	1 758.4	1 789.4
	80-84			1 101.7	1 024.8	1 615.9
	85-89			564.1	750.2	1 334.2
	90-94	461.0	938.7	264.6	470.3	877.5
	95-99			95.4	185.6	424.6
	100+			14.2	38.4	126.2
Male	Total	20 105.3	25 807.1	29 687.3	30 912.9	30 752.6
	0-14	4 818.6	6 436.2	5 645.4	5 354.6	5 091.5
	15-59	12 553.6	15 441.1	18 299.5	17 461.7	16 468.7
	60-64	847.9	1 168.1	1 573.5	1 969.8	1 853.3
	65-69	713.6	1 060.8	1 164.3	1 805.4	1 778.0
	70-74	564.2	836.6	1 086.0	1 605.0	1 601.7
	75-79	369.8	503.6	897.7	1 374.9	1 474.4
	80-84			641.2	700.3	1 161.6
	85-89			262.6	404.9	789.3
	90-94	237.5	360.7	89.8	181.0	385.5
	95-99			23.9	48.0	124.7
	100+			3.4	7.3	23.8
Percentage in older ages						
Total	60+	16.2	18.3	21.9	29.0	33.0
	65+	11.4	13.5	16.6	22.6	27.1
	80+	1.7	2.5	5.0	6.0	10.9
Female	60+	18.7	21.2	24.3	31.7	36.0
	65+	13.2	16.1	19.0	25.2	30.2
	80+	2.1	3.5	6.5	7.6	13.5
Male	60+	13.6	15.2	19.3	26.2	29.9
	65+	9.4	10.7	14.0	19.8	23.9
	80+	1.2	1.4	3.4	4.3	8.1
Ageing index		71.5	76.4	121.1	176.2	209.7
Broad age groups (percentage)	0-14	22.7	23.9	18.1	16.5	15.7
	15-59	61.1	57.8	60.0	54.5	51.2
	60+	16.2	18.3	21.9	29.0	33.0
Median age (years)		34.5	31.6	39.3*	43.3	45.5
Dependency ratio	Total	51.7	59.7	53.1	64.1	75.0
	Youth	34.5	38.2	27.7	27.0	27.5
	Old Age	17.3	21.5	25.4	37.0	47.4
Potential support ratio		5.8	4.6	3.9	2.7	2.1
Parent support ratio		3.7	6.5	11.4	17.0	37.0
Sex ratio (per 100 women)	60+	67.4	69.0	75.5	78.5	78.9
	65+	65.5	63.6	70.0	74.9	75.1
	80+	51.5	38.4	50.0	54.3	56.8

* *Estimate refers to year 2005.*

Indicator	Age	1950-1955	1975-1980	2005-2010	2025-2030	2045-2050
Growth rate (percentage)	Total	0.8	0.4	0.3	0.1	–0.1
	60+	0.8	–0.7	2.4	1.1	0.1
	65+	1.1	1.2	0.7	1.5	0.1
	80+	2.1	4.9	2.8	4.5	0.8
Total fertility rate (per woman)		2.7	1.9	1.9	1.9	1.9
Life expectancy (years)						
Total	Birth	66.6	73.7	80.0	82.5	84.7
	60	..	..	23.5	25.2	26.8
	65	..	..	19.5	21.0	22.5
	80	..	..	9.1	10.1	11.2
Female	Birth	69.5	77.8	83.5	85.8	88.0
	60	..	..	26.0	27.6	29.4
	65	..	..	21.6	23.2	24.8
	80	..	..	10.0	11.3	12.6
Male	Birth	63.7	69.7	76.5	79.2	81.5
	60	..	..	20.9	22.6	24.2
	65	..	..	17.1	18.6	20.0
	80	..	..	7.8	8.6	9.5
Survival rate (percentage)						
Total	60	..	..	91.0	93.4	95.1
	65	..	..	87.0	90.2	92.6
	80	..	..	60.7	67.0	72.5
Female	60	..	..	94.2	95.9	97.1
	65	..	..	91.7	93.9	95.5
	80	..	..	71.8	76.8	81.1
Male	60	..	..	87.8	90.9	93.1
	65	..	..	82.3	86.5	89.7
	80	..	..	49.3	57.0	63.7

		1980	1990	2007	2010	2020
Labour force participation (percentage)						
Total	65+	5.3	2.4	0.9	0.8	0.7
Female	65+	3.4	1.5	0.7	0.6	0.6
Male	65+	8.4	3.7	1.3	1.1	0.8

Percentage married, age 60+			Percentage living alone, age 60+ (1994)		
Total	Female	Male	Total	Female	Male
59.7	47.0	77.0	28.7	38.4	15.1

Statutory pensionable age (2006)			Percentage illiterate, age 65+		
Female	Male		Total	Female	Male
60	60		..	..	..

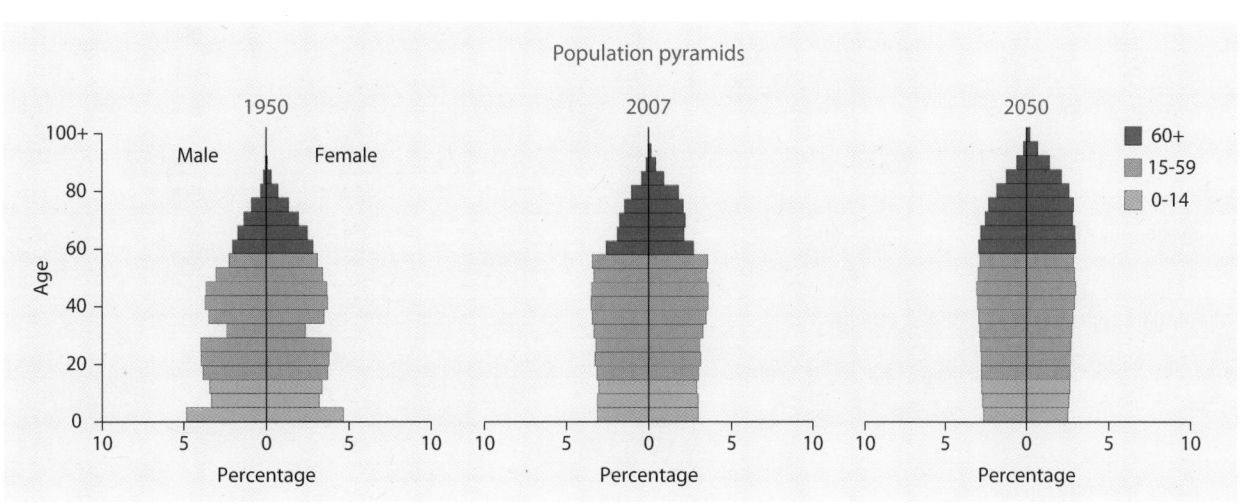

Population pyramids

United Nations Department of Economic and Social Affairs, Population Division

French Guiana

Indicator	Age	1950	1975	2007	2025	2050
Population (thousands)						
Total	Total	25.5	56.0	195.9	276.0	358.7
	0-14	7.8	21.7	65.2	70.6	67.4
	15-59	15.4	30.3	117.3	168.6	221.5
	60-64	0.8	1.4	5.2	12.6	18.5
	65-69	0.7	1.0	3.5	9.5	16.0
	70-74	0.4	0.8	2.3	7.1	11.1
	75-79	0.2	0.4	1.3	4.3	9.6
	80-84			0.8	2.2	7.8
	85-89			0.3	0.9	4.6
	90-94	0.1	0.4	0.1	0.3	1.7
	95-99			0.0	0.1	0.5
	100+			0.0	0.0	0.1
Female	Total	12.3	27.9	95.5	136.4	179.3
	0-14	4.0	10.8	31.9	34.5	32.9
	15-59	7.1	15.0	56.9	82.9	109.1
	60-64	0.4	0.7	2.4	6.5	9.1
	65-69	0.3	0.5	1.7	4.6	7.9
	70-74	0.2	0.4	1.1	3.6	5.3
	75-79	0.1	0.2	0.7	2.2	5.4
	80-84			0.5	1.2	4.9
	85-89			0.2	0.6	3.0
	90-94	0.1	0.3	0.1	0.2	1.2
	95-99			0.0	0.0	0.4
	100+			0.0	0.0	0.1
Male	Total	13.2	28.0	100.5	139.7	179.4
	0-14	3.8	10.9	33.2	36.1	34.5
	15-59	8.3	15.3	60.4	85.7	112.4
	60-64	0.4	0.7	2.8	6.1	9.4
	65-69	0.3	0.5	1.8	4.9	8.0
	70-74	0.2	0.4	1.1	3.5	5.8
	75-79	0.1	0.1	0.6	2.0	4.2
	80-84			0.3	0.9	2.9
	85-89			0.1	0.3	1.6
	90-94	0.1	0.2	0.0	0.1	0.5
	95-99			0.0	0.0	0.1
	100+			0.0	0.0	0.0
Percentage in older ages						
Total	60+	8.8	7.1	6.9	13.3	19.5
	65+	5.5	4.6	4.2	8.8	14.3
	80+	0.6	0.8	0.6	1.2	4.1
Female	60+	9.1	7.5	7.0	13.9	20.8
	65+	5.7	5.2	4.5	9.2	15.8
	80+	0.7	1.0	0.8	1.5	5.4
Male	60+	8.6	6.6	6.8	12.8	18.1
	65+	5.3	4.1	4.0	8.4	12.9
	80+	0.5	0.6	0.5	0.9	2.8
Ageing index		28.7	18.3	20.7	52.2	103.7
Broad age groups (percentage)	0-14	30.7	38.7	33.3	25.6	18.8
	15-59	60.5	54.2	59.9	61.1	61.7
	60+	8.8	7.1	6.9	13.3	19.5
Median age (years)		26.6	20.8	24.0*	29.8	37.6
Dependency ratio	Total	56.7	76.6	60.0	52.3	49.5
	Youth	48.1	68.4	53.2	38.9	28.1
	Old Age	8.6	8.2	6.8	13.4	21.4
Potential support ratio		11.6	12.2	14.8	7.5	4.7
Parent support ratio		1.6	3.5	2.0	3.0	10.4
Sex ratio (per 100 women)	60+	101.9	88.5	103.1	94.2	87.1
	65+	100.9	80.1	94.2	93.8	81.9
	80+	69.3	53.2	60.7	63.4	53.2

*   *Estimate refers to year 2005.*

Indicator	Age	1950-1955	1975-1980	2005-2010	2025-2030	2045-2050
Growth rate (percentage)	Total	2.3	4.0	2.2	1.4	0.8
	60+	2.1	3.8	6.0	3.9	2.3
	65+	3.4	4.1	5.7	5.0	2.5
	80+	4.4	4.7	3.2	7.4	3.9
Total fertility rate (per woman)		5.0	3.3	3.0	2.1	1.9
Life expectancy (years)						
Total	Birth	53.3	66.5	76.0	78.9	81.2
	60	..	..	20.0	21.8	23.6
	65	..	..	16.2	17.7	19.4
	80	..	..	7.2	8.1	9.2
Female	Birth	56.9	70.5	79.2	81.8	83.9
	60	..	..	22.3	24.2	25.9
	65	..	..	18.1	19.9	21.5
	80	..	..	8.1	9.3	10.3
Male	Birth	50.3	63.1	73.4	76.2	78.5
	60	..	..	18.1	19.6	21.3
	65	..	..	14.4	15.7	17.3
	80	..	..	6.1	6.7	7.7
Survival rate (percentage)						
Total	60	..	..	89.5	92.5	94.0
	65	..	..	84.0	88.2	90.4
	80	..	..	46.5	54.9	62.2
Female	60	..	..	92.5	94.3	95.5
	65	..	..	88.7	91.3	93.0
	80	..	..	57.3	65.1	71.0
Male	60	..	..	87.0	90.6	92.5
	65	..	..	80.1	85.0	87.9
	80	..	..	37.7	45.7	53.5

		1980	1990	2007	2010	2020
Labour force participation (percentage)						
Total	65+	13.0	8.9	9.3	9.6	9.7
Female	65+	6.9	4.7	6.8	7.7	8.8
Male	65+	20.2	13.7	11.9	11.5	10.6

Percentage married, age 60+			Percentage living alone, age 60+ (1982)		
Total	Female	Male	Total	Female	Male
37.5	29.0	46.0	29.6	27.6	31.7

Statutory pensionable age (2006)		Percentage illiterate, age 65+		
Female	Male	Total	Female	Male
..	..	..	..	..

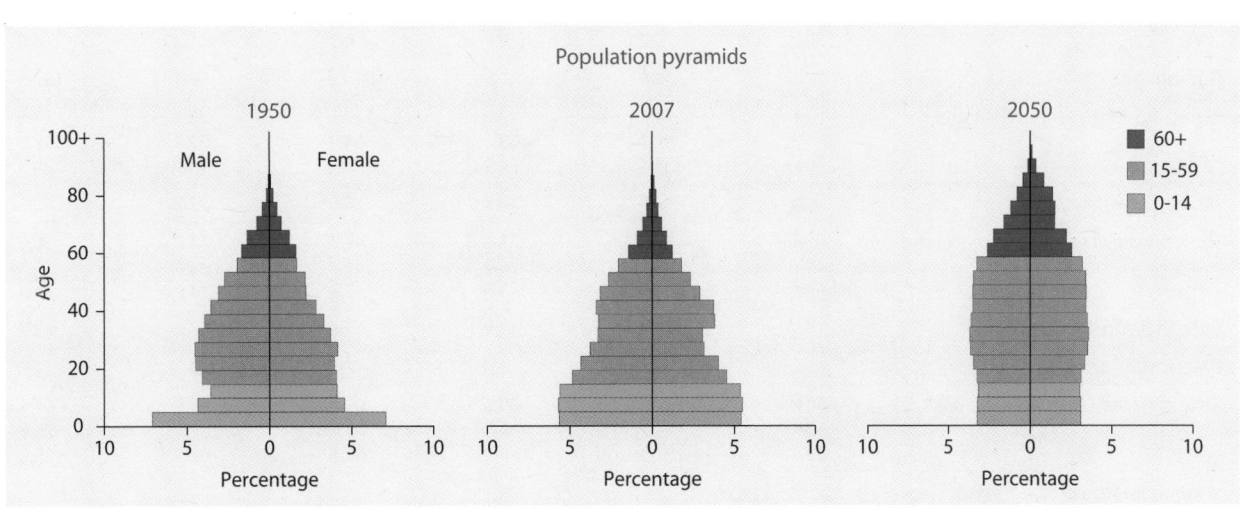

Population pyramids

United Nations Department of Economic and Social Affairs, Population Division

French Polynesia

Indicator	Age	1950	1975	2007	2025	2050
Population (thousands)						
Total	Total	60.7	129.8	263.9	321.2	359.9
	0-14	27.1	54.6	71.5	72.0	64.2
	15-59	31.0	69.0	170.9	201.5	207.4
	60-64	1.1	2.5	7.6	16.7	24.8
	65-69	0.7	1.7	5.8	12.0	18.8
	70-74	0.5	1.0	4.0	9.2	14.3
	75-79	0.2	0.4	2.4	4.9	12.4
	80-84			1.2	3.1	10.0
	85-89			0.5	1.3	5.3
	90-94	0.1	0.6	0.1	0.5	2.0
	95-99			0.0	0.1	0.6
	100+			0.0	0.0	0.1
Female	Total	29.6	62.1	129.1	159.1	180.7
	0-14	13.3	26.9	34.8	35.1	31.3
	15-59	15.1	32.1	83.5	99.1	101.5
	60-64	0.5	1.2	3.6	8.4	12.4
	65-69	0.3	0.8	2.8	6.0	9.9
	70-74	0.2	0.5	2.0	4.8	7.6
	75-79	0.1	0.2	1.3	2.6	6.8
	80-84			0.7	1.8	5.8
	85-89			0.3	0.8	3.5
	90-94	0.1	0.3	0.1	0.3	1.4
	95-99			0.0	0.1	0.5
	100+			0.0	0.0	0.1
Male	Total	31.1	67.7	134.8	162.1	179.2
	0-14	13.8	27.6	36.7	36.9	32.9
	15-59	15.9	36.8	87.4	102.4	105.9
	60-64	0.6	1.3	4.0	8.4	12.4
	65-69	0.4	0.9	3.0	6.0	8.9
	70-74	0.3	0.5	2.0	4.4	6.8
	75-79	0.1	0.2	1.1	2.2	5.6
	80-84			0.5	1.3	4.2
	85-89			0.1	0.5	1.9
	90-94	0.1	0.3	0.0	0.1	0.6
	95-99			0.0	0.0	0.1
	100+			0.0	0.0	0.0
Percentage in older ages						
Total	60+	4.4	4.9	8.2	14.9	24.5
	65+	2.6	2.9	5.3	9.7	17.6
	80+	0.2	0.5	0.7	1.5	5.0
Female	60+	3.9	4.8	8.4	15.6	26.5
	65+	2.4	2.9	5.6	10.4	19.6
	80+	0.2	0.5	0.9	1.9	6.2
Male	60+	4.8	4.9	8.0	14.1	22.6
	65+	2.8	2.9	5.0	9.0	15.6
	80+	0.2	0.5	0.5	1.2	3.8
Ageing index		9.8	11.5	30.2	66.3	137.6
Broad age groups (percentage)	0-14	44.6	42.0	27.1	22.4	17.8
	15-59	51.1	53.1	64.8	62.7	57.6
	60+	4.4	4.9	8.2	14.9	24.5
Median age (years)		17.8	18.7	26.9*	33.7	40.1
Dependency ratio	Total	89.2	81.6	47.9	47.2	55.0
	Youth	84.4	76.3	40.0	33.0	27.6
	Old Age	4.9	5.3	7.8	14.2	27.3
Potential support ratio		20.5	18.9	12.8	7.0	3.7
Parent support ratio		0.8	2.0	2.0	3.3	11.4
Sex ratio (per 100 women)	60+	129.9	109.2	99.0	91.9	84.4
	65+	124.2	108.6	92.6	88.1	79.0
	80+	101.5	111.7	56.7	62.9	59.7

* Estimate refers to year 2005.

Indicator	Age	1950-1955	1975-1980	2005-2010	2025-2030	2045-2050
Growth rate (percentage)	Total	2.7	3.0	1.3	0.7	0.2
	60+	2.7	2.7	3.5	4.1	2.4
	65+	2.7	3.3	4.7	4.7	1.7
	80+	2.9	−1.3	5.0	3.8	4.6
Total fertility rate (per woman)		6.0	4.2	2.3	1.9	1.9
Life expectancy (years)						
Total	Birth	48.9	62.4	74.1	77.4	79.9
	60	..	..	18.7	20.7	22.6
	65	..	..	15.1	16.9	18.6
	80	..	..	7.1	8.0	8.9
Female	Birth	50.0	64.9	76.8	80.0	82.4
	60	..	..	20.6	22.9	24.8
	65	..	..	16.8	18.8	20.5
	80	..	..	7.9	9.0	10.0
Male	Birth	48.0	60.5	71.7	75.0	77.5
	60	..	..	17.0	18.6	20.5
	65	..	..	13.5	14.9	16.6
	80	..	..	6.0	6.7	7.5
Survival rate (percentage)						
Total	60	..	..	86.6	90.7	92.9
	65	..	..	79.6	85.2	88.6
	80	..	..	39.1	49.0	57.4
Female	60	..	..	89.6	92.6	94.4
	65	..	..	84.1	88.5	91.2
	80	..	..	48.1	58.3	65.7
Male	60	..	..	83.8	88.9	91.4
	65	..	..	75.6	82.0	86.1
	80	..	..	31.6	40.4	49.2

		1980	1990	2007	2010	2020
Labour force participation (percentage)						
Total	65+	8.7	8.2	8.2	8.2	8.0
Female	65+	5.0	5.2	5.2	5.2	5.2
Male	65+	12.3	11.6	11.4	11.4	11.2

Percentage married, age 60+			Percentage living alone, age 60+		
Total	Female	Male	Total	Female	Male
55.4	45.0	66.0	..	..	..

Statutory pensionable age (2006)		Percentage illiterate, age 65+		
Female	Male	Total	Female	Male
..	..	..	..	..

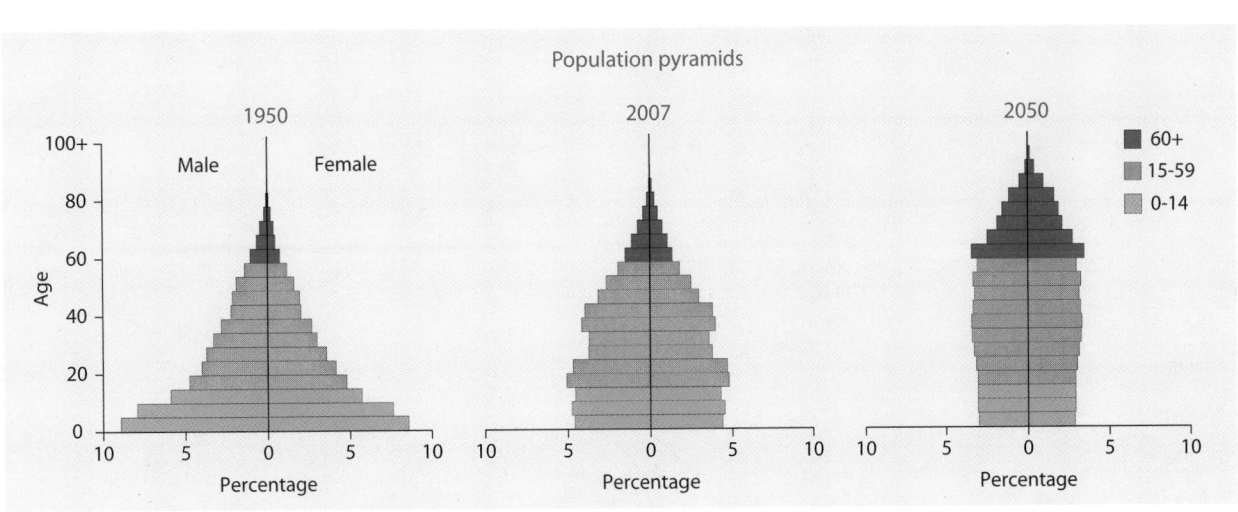

Population pyramids

United Nations Department of Economic and Social Affairs, Population Division

Gabon

Indicator	Age	1950	1975	2007	2025	2050
Population (thousands)						
Total	Total	469.0	601.2	1 428.9	1 809.0	2 278.8
	0-14	133.1	215.8	557.8	589.6	568.0
	15-59	283.1	324.7	782.6	1 075.3	1 452.7
	60-64	18.6	20.4	27.2	45.7	83.8
	65-69	14.6	16.4	20.9	37.2	61.2
	70-74	10.2	11.9	16.6	28.9	45.7
	75-79	5.9	7.3	12.5	17.6	33.2
	80-84			7.3	9.4	20.5
	85-89			3.1	3.9	10.0
	90-94	3.5	4.5	0.8	1.2	3.1
	95-99			0.1	0.2	0.6
	100+			0.0	0.0	0.0
Female	Total	240.5	306.3	716.4	895.1	1 119.3
	0-14	66.8	108.0	276.2	291.7	280.8
	15-59	144.5	165.0	392.9	528.4	709.5
	60-64	10.0	10.9	13.5	23.1	39.6
	65-69	8.0	8.9	10.9	19.3	29.6
	70-74	5.7	6.6	9.3	15.2	23.0
	75-79	3.4	4.2	7.0	9.3	17.8
	80-84			4.1	5.0	11.3
	85-89			1.8	2.2	5.6
	90-94	2.1	2.7	0.5	0.8	1.9
	95-99			0.1	0.1	0.4
	100+			0.0	0.0	0.0
Male	Total	228.5	294.8	712.5	913.9	1 159.5
	0-14	66.3	107.8	281.6	297.9	287.2
	15-59	138.6	159.7	389.6	546.8	743.3
	60-64	8.6	9.5	13.6	22.6	44.2
	65-69	6.7	7.5	10.1	17.9	31.6
	70-74	4.5	5.3	7.3	13.7	22.7
	75-79	2.5	3.2	5.4	8.3	15.4
	80-84			3.2	4.4	9.2
	85-89			1.3	1.7	4.4
	90-94	1.3	1.8	0.3	0.5	1.3
	95-99			0.0	0.1	0.2
	100+			0.0	0.0	0.0
Percentage in older ages						
Total	60+	11.3	10.1	6.2	8.0	11.3
	65+	7.3	6.7	4.3	5.4	7.6
	80+	0.7	0.8	0.8	0.8	1.5
Female	60+	12.1	10.9	6.6	8.4	11.5
	65+	8.0	7.3	4.7	5.8	8.0
	80+	0.9	0.9	0.9	0.9	1.7
Male	60+	10.3	9.3	5.8	7.6	11.1
	65+	6.6	6.0	3.9	5.1	7.3
	80+	0.6	0.6	0.7	0.7	1.3
Ageing index		39.7	28.1	15.9	24.4	45.4
Broad age groups (percentage)	0-14	28.4	35.9	39.0	32.6	24.9
	15-59	60.4	54.0	54.8	59.4	63.7
	60+	11.3	10.1	6.2	8.0	11.3
Median age (years)		28.4	23.3	19.4*	23.6	29.8
Dependency ratio	Total	55.5	74.2	76.5	61.4	48.3
	Youth	44.1	62.5	68.9	52.6	37.0
	Old Age	11.3	11.7	7.6	8.8	11.3
Potential support ratio		8.8	8.6	13.2	11.4	8.8
Parent support ratio		1.4	1.8	3.7	3.4	4.4
Sex ratio (per 100 women)	60+	81.1	82.2	87.3	92.2	100.0
	65+	78.4	79.5	81.9	89.7	94.9
	80+	62.9	65.5	73.9	81.4	78.8

* Estimate refers to year 2005.

Indicator	Age	1950-1955	1975-1980	2005-2010	2025-2030	2045-2050
Growth rate (percentage)	Total	0.3	2.9	1.6	1.1	0.8
	60+	−0.1	1.3	1.9	2.2	3.2
	65+	−0.1	1.6	1.2	2.8	2.5
	80+	−0.3	2.8	1.8	3.5	2.4
Total fertility rate (per woman)		4.0	5.5	3.5	2.5	2.1
Life expectancy (years)						
Total	Birth	37.0	52.8	53.3	58.9	68.0
	60	..	..	17.9	19.0	20.2
	65	..	..	14.4	15.4	16.4
	80	..	..	6.3	6.7	7.2
Female	Birth	38.6	54.4	53.6	58.3	68.3
	60	..	..	18.5	19.6	21.0
	65	..	..	14.9	15.9	17.1
	80	..	..	6.5	6.9	7.5
Male	Birth	35.5	51.2	53.1	59.5	67.6
	60	..	..	17.3	18.4	19.4
	65	..	..	13.9	14.9	15.8
	80	..	..	6.1	6.5	6.9
Survival rate (percentage)						
Total	60	..	..	48.3	53.0	70.8
	65	..	..	43.9	48.8	66.3
	80	..	..	20.6	25.4	37.8
Female	60	..	..	48.5	50.9	70.3
	65	..	..	44.6	47.4	66.6
	80	..	..	21.9	25.8	39.9
Male	60	..	..	48.2	54.9	71.2
	65	..	..	43.3	50.0	66.0
	80	..	..	19.2	24.8	35.6

		1980	1990	2007	2010	2020
Labour force participation (percentage)						
Total	65+	41.2	46.8	45.0	45.3	45.9
Female	65+	27.4	35.1	31.0	31.0	31.0
Male	65+	58.3	61.0	62.1	62.2	62.5

Percentage married, age 60+			Percentage living alone, age 60+ (2000)		
Total	Female	Male	Total	Female	Male
57.4	42.0	76.0	11.0	9.9	12.3

Statutory pensionable age (2006)			Percentage illiterate, age 65+		
	Female	Male	Total	Female	Male
	55	55	..	..	..

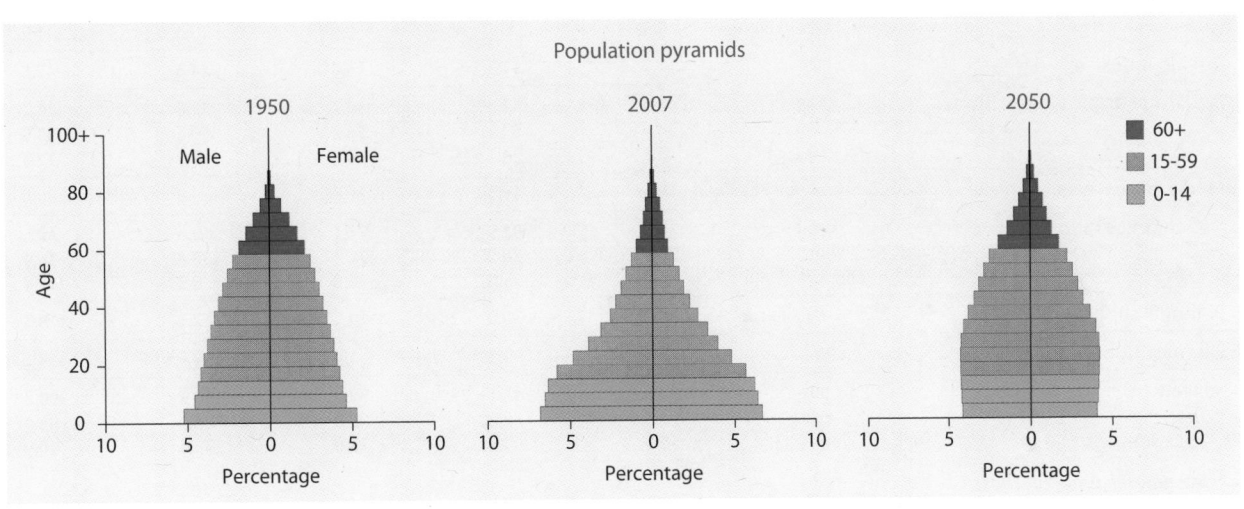

Population pyramids

United Nations Department of Economic and Social Affairs, Population Division

Gambia

Indicator	Age	1950	1975	2007	2025	2050
Population (thousands)						
Total	Total	293.7	555.0	1 594.0	2 254.2	3 106.2
	0-14	120.4	234.6	632.1	733.8	767.3
	15-59	159.2	294.4	864.4	1 342.1	1 957.1
	60-64	6.0	10.7	35.8	61.9	123.4
	65-69	4.1	7.4	26.8	46.5	96.3
	70-74	2.4	4.5	18.0	32.5	70.8
	75-79	1.1	2.3	10.3	21.1	48.1
	80-84			4.7	11.0	27.6
	85-89			1.5	4.1	11.8
	90-94	0.5	1.0	0.3	1.0	3.2
	95-99			0.0	0.1	0.5
	100+			0.0	0.0	0.0
Female	Total	150.7	282.9	803.3	1 130.6	1 555.8
	0-14	60.9	117.9	313.9	362.5	379.4
	15-59	81.8	150.7	437.5	673.6	976.3
	60-64	3.3	5.7	18.7	32.2	63.2
	65-69	2.3	4.0	14.1	24.5	50.0
	70-74	1.4	2.5	9.6	17.3	37.3
	75-79	0.7	1.3	5.6	11.4	25.8
	80-84			2.6	6.1	15.1
	85-89			0.9	2.4	6.6
	90-94	0.3	0.6	0.2	0.6	1.9
	95-99			0.0	0.1	0.3
	100+			0.0	0.0	0.0
Male	Total	143.0	272.0	790.7	1 123.7	1 550.3
	0-14	59.5	116.7	318.2	371.3	387.9
	15-59	77.4	143.7	427.0	668.5	980.8
	60-64	2.7	5.0	17.1	29.7	60.3
	65-69	1.8	3.4	12.6	22.1	46.3
	70-74	1.0	2.0	8.3	15.2	33.5
	75-79	0.5	1.0	4.7	9.7	22.3
	80-84			2.0	4.9	12.5
	85-89			0.6	1.8	5.2
	90-94	0.2	0.4	0.1	0.4	1.3
	95-99			0.0	0.0	0.2
	100+			0.0	0.0	0.0
Percentage in older ages						
Total	60+	4.8	4.7	6.1	7.9	12.3
	65+	2.8	2.7	3.9	5.2	8.3
	80+	0.2	0.2	0.4	0.7	1.4
Female	60+	5.3	5.0	6.5	8.4	12.9
	65+	3.1	3.0	4.1	5.5	8.8
	80+	0.2	0.2	0.5	0.8	1.5
Male	60+	4.3	4.3	5.8	7.5	11.7
	65+	2.4	2.5	3.6	4.8	7.8
	80+	0.1	0.2	0.4	0.6	1.2
Ageing index		11.7	11.1	15.4	24.3	49.8
Broad age groups (percentage)	0-14	41.0	42.3	39.7	32.6	24.7
	15-59	54.2	53.1	54.2	59.5	63.0
	60+	4.8	4.7	6.1	7.9	12.3
Median age (years)		19.5	19.3	19.8*	23.8	30.6
Dependency ratio	Total	77.8	81.9	77.1	60.6	49.3
	Youth	72.9	76.9	70.2	52.3	36.9
	Old Age	4.9	5.0	6.8	8.3	12.4
Potential support ratio		20.2	20.0	14.6	12.1	8.1
Parent support ratio		0.4	0.5	1.4	2.3	3.5
Sex ratio (per 100 women)	60+	77.6	82.1	87.9	88.7	90.8
	65+	74.5	79.2	85.8	86.9	88.6
	80+	55.5	66.3	75.0	78.6	80.0

* Estimate refers to year 2005.

Indicator	Age	1950-1955	1975-1980	2005-2010	2025-2030	2045-2050
Growth rate (percentage)	Total	1.4	3.2	2.3	1.6	1.0
	60+	1.4	3.5	3.6	3.2	3.1
	65+	1.4	3.7	4.1	3.6	3.1
	80+	1.0	4.7	5.5	4.1	3.6
Total fertility rate (per woman)		6.1	6.5	4.2	2.7	2.2
Life expectancy (years)						
Total	Birth	30.0	41.0	57.7	66.1	71.5
	60	..	..	17.0	18.4	19.4
	65	..	..	13.7	14.8	15.7
	80	..	..	6.0	6.5	6.8
Female	Birth	31.5	42.5	59.0	67.2	73.1
	60	..	..	17.6	18.9	20.0
	65	..	..	14.1	15.2	16.1
	80	..	..	6.2	6.6	7.0
Male	Birth	28.6	39.5	56.5	65.1	70.0
	60	..	..	16.4	17.9	18.8
	65	..	..	13.2	14.4	15.1
	80	..	..	5.7	6.3	6.6
Survival rate (percentage)						
Total	60	..	..	60.8	73.6	81.9
	65	..	..	54.6	67.7	76.3
	80	..	..	23.3	33.1	40.7
Female	60	..	..	62.8	75.3	84.2
	65	..	..	57.0	69.8	79.2
	80	..	..	25.6	35.5	44.2
Male	60	..	..	58.8	72.0	79.6
	65	..	..	52.2	65.6	73.5
	80	..	..	21.1	30.6	37.3

		1980	1990	2007	2010	2020
Labour force participation (percentage)						
Total	65+	60.5	60.7	58.5	58.4	58.5
Female	65+	49.0	49.7	42.7	42.4	42.2
Male	65+	74.8	73.9	76.9	77.1	77.3

Percentage married, age 60+			Percentage living alone, age 60+		
Total	Female	Male	Total	Female	Male
76.0	62.0	92.0	..	..	..

Statutory pensionable age (2006)		Percentage illiterate, age 65+		
Female	Male	Total	Female	Male
55	55	..	..	..

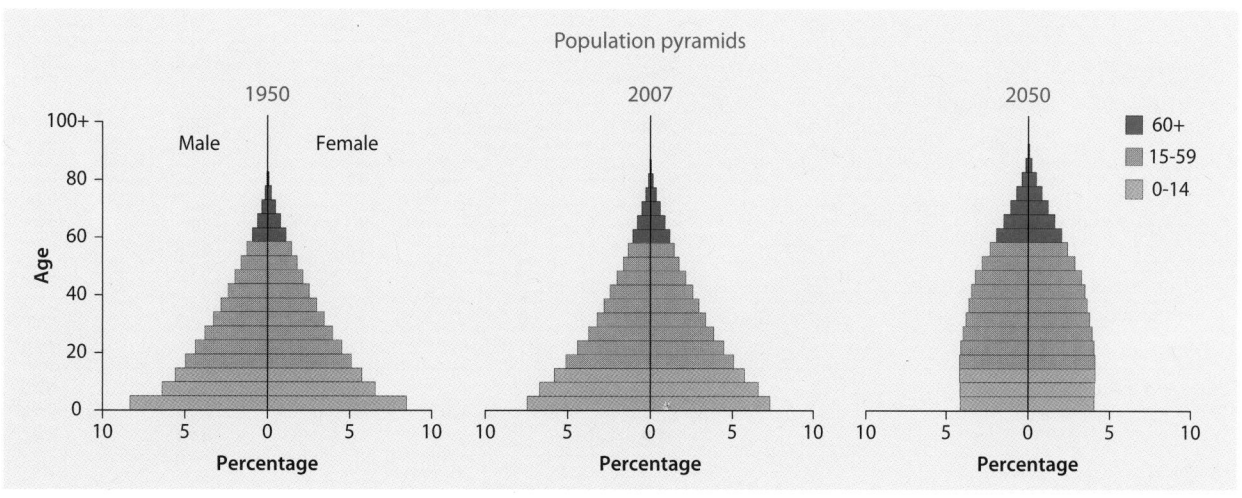

Population pyramids

United Nations Department of Economic and Social Affairs, Population Division

Georgia

Indicator	Age	1950	1975	2007	2025	2050
Population (thousands)						
Total	Total	3 527.0	4 908.0	4 395.8	3 916.9	2 984.6
	0-14	947.1	1 391.7	784.4	596.0	415.2
	15-59	2 054.2	2 906.7	2 817.4	2 317.9	1 492.2
	60-64	169.5	190.9	163.3	292.2	272.9
	65-69	138.8	155.3	207.4	256.3	229.3
	70-74	102.5	114.3	179.7	192.6	191.7
	75-79	64.8	67.4	136.1	122.9	153.3
	80-84			74.0	63.6	109.3
	85-89			22.8	54.6	79.1
	90-94	50.1	81.7	8.4	16.0	32.3
	95-99			2.0	4.5	8.1
	100+			0.3	0.4	1.1
Female	Total	1 897.8	2 602.5	2 321.6	2 074.6	1 578.8
	0-14	493.1	684.7	375.4	286.2	201.2
	15-59	1 105.0	1 533.7	1 470.1	1 184.6	735.1
	60-64	88.6	120.7	92.0	168.2	144.2
	65-69	78.2	97.6	118.5	147.3	128.2
	70-74	59.9	71.8	105.5	114.8	114.8
	75-79	40.0	41.8	83.6	76.9	94.7
	80-84			50.4	42.5	72.2
	85-89			17.6	38.3	56.4
	90-94	32.9	52.1	6.6	11.9	24.4
	95-99			1.6	3.5	6.6
	100+			0.2	0.4	1.0
Male	Total	1 629.2	2 305.5	2 074.2	1 842.3	1 405.8
	0-14	454.0	707.0	408.9	309.8	214.0
	15-59	949.2	1 372.9	1 347.4	1 133.2	757.1
	60-64	80.8	70.3	71.4	124.0	128.7
	65-69	60.6	57.7	88.9	109.0	101.1
	70-74	42.6	42.5	74.2	77.8	76.9
	75-79	24.8	25.6	52.6	46.0	58.6
	80-84			23.6	21.1	37.1
	85-89			5.2	16.3	22.7
	90-94	17.1	29.6	1.8	4.1	7.9
	95-99			0.4	0.9	1.5
	100+			0.1	0.1	0.2
Percentage in older ages						
Total	60+	14.9	12.4	18.1	25.6	36.1
	65+	10.1	8.5	14.3	18.1	26.9
	80+	1.4	1.7	2.4	3.6	7.7
Female	60+	15.8	14.8	20.5	29.1	40.7
	65+	11.1	10.1	16.5	21.0	31.6
	80+	1.7	2.0	3.3	4.7	10.2
Male	60+	13.9	9.8	15.3	21.7	30.9
	65+	8.9	6.7	11.9	14.9	21.8
	80+	1.1	1.3	1.5	2.3	4.9
Ageing index		55.5	43.8	101.2	168.3	259.4
Broad age groups (percentage)	0-14	26.9	28.4	17.8	15.2	13.9
	15-59	58.2	59.2	64.1	59.2	50.0
	60+	14.9	12.4	18.1	25.6	36.1
Median age (years)		27.3	28.3	35.5*	41.7	50.4
Dependency ratio	Total	58.6	58.4	47.5	50.1	69.1
	Youth	42.6	44.9	26.3	22.8	23.5
	Old Age	16.0	13.5	21.2	27.2	45.6
Potential support ratio		6.2	7.4	4.7	3.7	2.2
Parent support ratio		3.9	6.2	4.8	9.5	17.2
Sex ratio (per 100 women)	60+	75.4	58.7	66.8	66.1	67.6
	65+	68.7	59.0	64.2	63.2	61.4
	80+	52.0	56.8	40.6	44.1	43.2

* *Estimate refers to year 2005.*

Indicator	Age	1950-1955	1975-1980	2005-2010	2025-2030	2045-2050
Growth rate (percentage)	Total	1.7	0.7	−0.8	−0.8	−1.3
	60+	−0.1	0.3	0.1	0.3	0.7
	65+	1.9	2.0	−1.2	2.0	0.2
	80+	2.5	−0.4	6.9	0.9	−0.7
Total fertility rate (per woman)		3.0	2.4	1.4	1.6	1.8
Life expectancy (years)						
Total	Birth	60.6	69.6	71.0	73.8	76.4
	60	..	..	18.7	20.0	21.3
	65	..	..	15.0	16.2	17.4
	80	..	..	6.8	7.4	8.1
Female	Birth	64.4	73.2	74.8	77.3	79.6
	60	..	..	20.4	21.7	23.1
	65	..	..	16.4	17.6	18.9
	80	..	..	7.1	7.9	8.8
Male	Birth	56.8	65.6	67.1	70.0	73.1
	60	..	..	16.7	17.8	19.1
	65	..	..	13.3	14.3	15.4
	80	..	..	6.0	6.5	7.0
Survival rate (percentage)						
Total	60	..	..	81.8	85.5	88.6
	65	..	..	75.7	80.0	83.7
	80	..	..	37.5	43.9	50.5
Female	60	..	..	88.4	90.7	92.6
	65	..	..	83.6	86.5	89.0
	80	..	..	47.3	53.6	59.7
Male	60	..	..	75.0	80.0	84.7
	65	..	..	67.4	73.0	78.5
	80	..	..	27.4	33.2	40.2

		1980	1990	2007	2010	2020
Labour force participation (percentage)						
Total	65+	11.9	11.1	55.7	55.9	56.0
Female	65+	7.6	11.0	40.9	41.0	41.0
Male	65+	20.0	11.4	78.7	79.6	80.0

Percentage married, age 60+			Percentage living alone, age 60+		
Total	Female	Male	Total	Female	Male
56.6	38.0	84.0	..	..	..

Statutory pensionable age (2006)			Percentage illiterate, age 65+		
	Female	Male	Total	Female	Male
	60	65	..	..	..

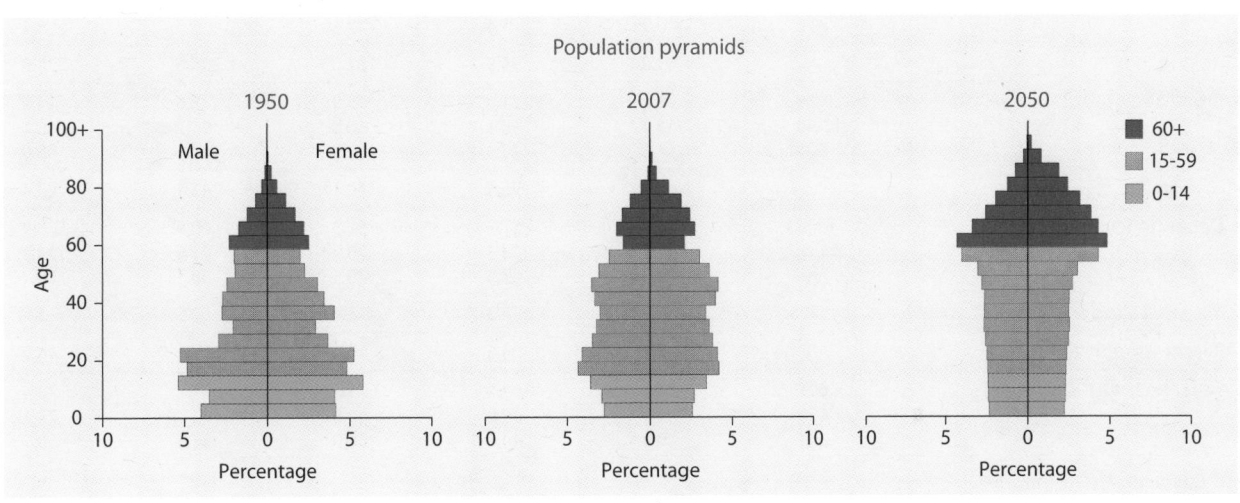

Population pyramids

United Nations Department of Economic and Social Affairs, Population Division

Germany

Indicator	Age	1950	1975	2007	2025	2050
Population (thousands)						
Total	Total	68 376.0	78 673.6	82 728.6	81 967.3	78 764.5
	0-14	15 854.0	16 931.1	11 486.7	11 163.6	11 731.0
	15-59	42 539.0	45 671.8	50 298.0	44 457.6	39 461.8
	60-64	3 338.0	4 397.5	4 735.2	6 786.7	5 196.2
	65-69	2 683.0	4 318.5	5 258.6	5 555.1	4 761.7
	70-74	2 080.0	3 449.5	4 045.4	4 614.2	4 073.5
	75-79	1 200.0	2 199.1	2 969.8	3 214.2	3 955.3
	80-84			2 389.8	2 980.3	4 248.1
	85-89			971.4	2 086.2	3 106.1
	90-94	682.0	1 706.0	420.7	791.8	1 538.9
	95-99			137.6	266.5	569.3
	100+			15.2	51.2	122.6
Female	Total	36 883.0	41 354.1	42 309.4	42 039.6	40 796.9
	0-14	7 761.0	8 256.5	5 589.7	5 431.6	5 708.0
	15-59	23 507.0	23 137.7	24 762.3	22 070.7	19 636.9
	60-64	1 903.0	2 645.4	2 411.0	3 429.9	2 670.8
	65-69	1 499.0	2 592.3	2 744.5	2 868.1	2 481.3
	70-74	1 149.0	2 090.7	2 191.7	2 478.9	2 175.9
	75-79	665.0	1 452.8	1 717.5	1 772.0	2 159.8
	80-84			1 676.9	1 788.2	2 446.8
	85-89			748.4	1 363.5	1 925.8
	90-94	399.0	1 178.8	338.4	574.0	1 053.6
	95-99			116.0	216.8	435.2
	100+			12.8	45.9	102.9
Male	Total	31 493.0	37 319.5	40 419.2	39 927.7	37 967.6
	0-14	8 093.0	8 674.6	5 897.0	5 732.0	6 023.1
	15-59	19 032.0	22 534.1	25 535.7	22 386.9	19 824.9
	60-64	1 435.0	1 752.1	2 324.2	3 356.8	2 525.4
	65-69	1 184.0	1 726.2	2 514.1	2 687.0	2 280.5
	70-74	931.0	1 358.8	1 853.6	2 135.2	1 897.7
	75-79	535.0	746.4	1 252.3	1 442.2	1 795.5
	80-84			712.9	1 192.1	1 801.3
	85-89			223.0	722.7	1 180.2
	90-94	283.0	527.2	82.3	217.8	485.3
	95-99			21.6	49.7	134.1
	100+			2.5	5.3	19.7
Percentage in older ages						
Total	60+	14.6	20.4	25.3	32.1	35.0
	65+	9.7	14.8	19.6	23.9	28.4
	80+	1.0	2.2	4.8	7.5	12.2
Female	60+	15.2	24.1	28.3	34.6	37.9
	65+	10.1	17.7	22.6	26.4	31.3
	80+	1.1	2.9	6.8	9.5	14.6
Male	60+	13.9	16.4	22.2	29.6	31.9
	65+	9.3	11.7	16.5	21.2	25.3
	80+	0.9	1.4	2.6	5.5	9.5
Ageing index		63.0	94.9	182.3	236.0	235.0
Broad age groups (percentage)	0-14	23.2	21.5	13.9	13.6	14.9
	15-59	62.2	58.1	60.8	54.2	50.1
	60+	14.6	20.4	25.3	32.1	35.0
Median age (years)		35.4	35.4	42.1*	47.1	47.4
Dependency ratio	Total	49.0	57.1	50.3	60.0	76.4
	Youth	34.6	33.8	20.9	21.8	26.3
	Old Age	14.5	23.3	29.5	38.2	50.1
Potential support ratio		6.9	4.3	3.4	2.6	2.0
Parent support ratio		2.1	4.6	10.0	17.1	36.2
Sex ratio (per 100 women)	60+	77.8	61.4	75.2	81.2	78.4
	65+	79.0	59.6	69.8	76.1	75.1
	80+	70.9	44.7	36.0	54.8	60.7

* Estimate refers to year 2005.

Indicator	Age	1950-1955	1975-1980	2005-2010	2025-2030	2045-2050
Growth rate (percentage)	Total	0.6	–0.1	0.0	–0.1	–0.2
	60+	2.1	–1.2	0.4	1.4	–0.1
	65+	2.5	0.9	1.7	2.0	–0.3
	80+	5.6	4.8	3.0	–0.4	1.8
Total fertility rate (per woman)		2.2	1.5	1.3	1.6	1.9
Life expectancy (years)						
Total	Birth	67.6	72.4	79.3	81.8	83.7
	60	..	..	22.3	24.2	25.7
	65	..	..	18.3	20.0	21.4
	80	..	..	8.6	9.5	10.5
Female	Birth	69.6	75.5	82.1	84.6	86.5
	60	..	..	24.5	26.4	28.0
	65	..	..	20.2	22.0	23.5
	80	..	..	9.3	10.6	11.7
Male	Birth	65.3	69.6	76.3	78.9	80.9
	60	..	..	19.9	21.8	23.3
	65	..	..	16.1	17.8	19.2
	80	..	..	7.2	8.2	9.0
Survival rate (percentage)						
Total	60	..	..	91.9	93.9	95.1
	65	..	..	87.4	90.4	92.3
	80	..	..	56.4	63.9	69.5
Female	60	..	..	94.2	95.7	96.6
	65	..	..	91.2	93.4	94.7
	80	..	..	66.5	73.0	77.4
Male	60	..	..	89.5	92.0	93.6
	65	..	..	83.6	87.4	89.8
	80	..	..	46.0	54.8	61.2

		1980	1990	2007	2010	2020
Labour force participation (percentage)						
Total	65+	4.5	3.1	2.9	3.0	3.0
Female	65+	3.2	2.0	1.8	1.9	1.9
Male	65+	6.8	5.3	4.5	4.5	4.5

Percentage married, age 60+			Percentage living alone, age 60+ (1994)		
Total	Female	Male	Total	Female	Male
56.2	43.0	75.0	33.6	45.5	15.1

Statutory pensionable age (2006)			Percentage illiterate, age 65+		
	Female	Male	Total	Female	Male
	65	65	..	..	..

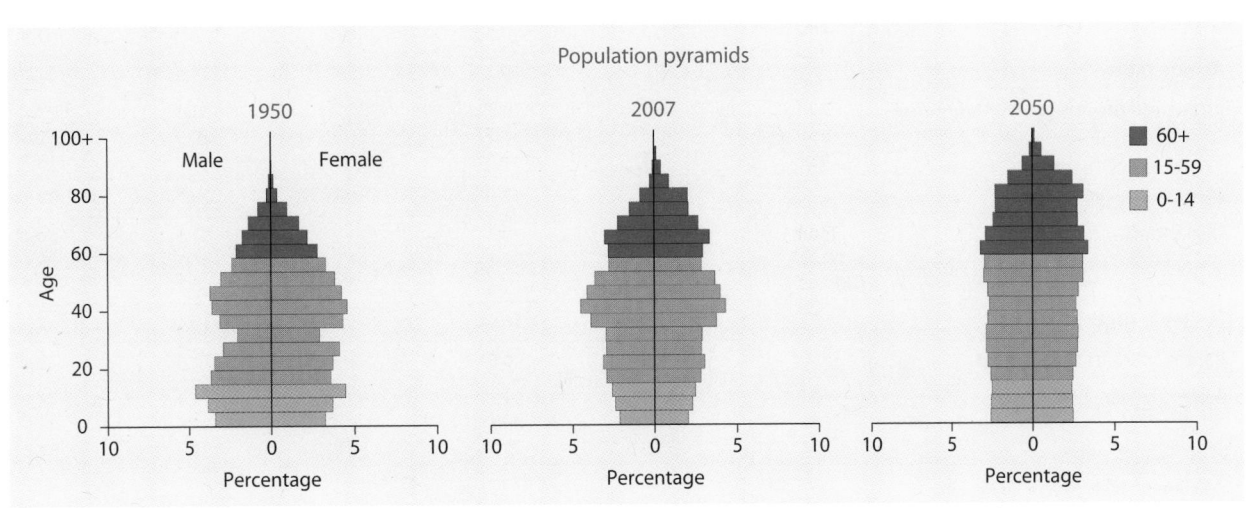

Population pyramids

Ghana

Indicator	Age	1950	1975	2007	2025	2050
Population (thousands)						
Total	Total	5 243.0	10 240.6	22 994.7	30 963.7	40 572.7
	0-14	2 365.3	4 573.6	8 772.7	9 728.5	9 618.6
	15-59	2 662.0	5 195.9	12 873.8	18 865.9	25 399.5
	60-64	86.6	180.9	480.0	785.8	1 815.4
	65-69	60.9	130.9	356.4	612.7	1 463.6
	70-74	38.4	85.4	248.8	440.2	1 022.5
	75-79	20.3	48.0	152.8	297.5	674.0
	80-84			75.9	154.8	365.8
	85-89			27.5	60.3	159.4
	90-94	9.6	25.8	6.1	15.5	45.7
	95-99			0.7	2.3	7.5
	100+			0.0	0.2	0.7
Female	Total	2 592.8	5 081.2	11 349.9	15 246.7	20 048.8
	0-14	1 157.3	2 254.2	4 288.4	4 764.9	4 716.3
	15-59	1 320.4	2 578.0	6 361.4	9 246.9	12 496.1
	60-64	45.0	93.3	244.2	399.4	903.6
	65-69	32.4	68.6	183.7	317.5	738.4
	70-74	20.9	45.7	130.0	232.1	523.9
	75-79	11.5	26.5	81.2	157.9	352.4
	80-84			41.3	83.9	197.1
	85-89			15.6	33.6	89.1
	90-94	5.2	15.0	3.7	9.0	26.8
	95-99			0.5	1.4	4.7
	100+			0.0	0.1	0.5
Male	Total	2 650.2	5 159.4	11 644.8	15 717.0	20 523.9
	0-14	1 207.9	2 319.5	4 484.3	4 963.6	4 902.3
	15-59	1 341.5	2 618.0	6 512.4	9 619.0	12 903.4
	60-64	41.6	87.5	235.9	386.4	911.8
	65-69	28.5	62.3	172.7	295.2	725.2
	70-74	17.5	39.7	118.8	208.1	498.6
	75-79	8.8	21.6	71.6	139.6	321.6
	80-84			34.6	71.0	168.7
	85-89			12.0	26.7	70.3
	90-94	4.4	10.9	2.4	6.4	18.9
	95-99			0.3	0.8	2.8
	100+			0.0	0.1	0.2
Percentage in older ages						
Total	60+	4.1	4.6	5.9	7.7	13.7
	65+	2.5	2.8	3.8	5.1	9.2
	80+	0.2	0.3	0.5	0.8	1.4
Female	60+	4.4	4.9	6.2	8.1	14.1
	65+	2.7	3.1	4.0	5.5	9.6
	80+	0.2	0.3	0.5	0.8	1.6
Male	60+	3.8	4.3	5.6	7.2	13.2
	65+	2.2	2.6	3.5	4.8	8.8
	80+	0.2	0.2	0.4	0.7	1.3
Ageing index		9.1	10.3	15.4	24.4	57.7
Broad age groups (percentage)	0-14	45.1	44.7	38.2	31.4	23.7
	15-59	50.8	50.7	56.0	60.9	62.6
	60+	4.1	4.6	5.9	7.7	13.7
Median age (years)		17.4	17.6	19.8*	24.7	31.7
Dependency ratio	Total	90.8	90.5	72.2	57.6	49.1
	Youth	86.1	85.1	65.7	49.5	35.3
	Old Age	4.7	5.4	6.5	8.1	13.7
Potential support ratio		21.3	18.5	15.4	12.4	7.3
Parent support ratio		0.8	0.9	1.9	2.6	3.4
Sex ratio (per 100 women)	60+	87.6	89.1	92.6	91.9	95.8
	65+	84.4	86.3	90.4	89.5	93.5
	80+	83.8	72.8	80.8	82.0	82.0

* Estimate refers to year 2005.

Indicator	Age	1950-1955	1975-1980	2005-2010	2025-2030	2045-2050
Growth rate (percentage)	Total	3.1	2.0	1.9	1.3	0.8
	60+	3.5	2.3	3.4	3.0	3.5
	65+	3.6	2.5	3.5	3.2	4.0
	80+	4.5	3.2	4.3	4.2	3.5
Total fertility rate (per woman)		6.7	6.7	3.8	2.6	2.1
Life expectancy (years)						
Total	Birth	43.1	51.8	58.0	65.5	71.3
	60	..	..	17.6	18.8	19.8
	65	..	..	14.2	15.1	16.0
	80	..	..	6.2	6.6	6.9
Female	Birth	44.6	53.2	58.5	66.6	72.9
	60	..	..	18.1	19.4	20.6
	65	..	..	14.5	15.6	16.6
	80	..	..	6.4	6.8	7.2
Male	Birth	41.8	50.4	57.4	64.4	69.8
	60	..	..	17.0	18.1	19.1
	65	..	..	13.7	14.6	15.4
	80	..	..	6.0	6.4	6.7
Survival rate (percentage)						
Total	60	..	..	59.0	70.4	80.3
	65	..	..	53.4	65.0	75.1
	80	..	..	24.3	32.9	41.3
Female	60	..	..	59.6	71.8	82.4
	65	..	..	54.5	67.0	78.0
	80	..	..	25.8	35.7	45.2
Male	60	..	..	58.1	69.1	78.2
	65	..	..	52.1	63.0	72.4
	80	..	..	22.4	30.3	37.7

		1980	1990	2007	2010	2020
Labour force participation (percentage)						
Total	65+	64.3	65.1	55.4	54.8	54.0
Female	65+	60.3	60.0	47.1	46.5	46.0
Male	65+	69.0	70.9	64.5	63.9	62.9

Percentage married, age 60+			Percentage living alone, age 60+ (1998)		
Total	Female	Male	Total	Female	Male
..	..	..	21.6	22.7	20.2

Statutory pensionable age (2006)		Percentage illiterate, age 65+ (2000)		
Female	Male	Total	Female	Male
60	60	70.5	79.4	61.6

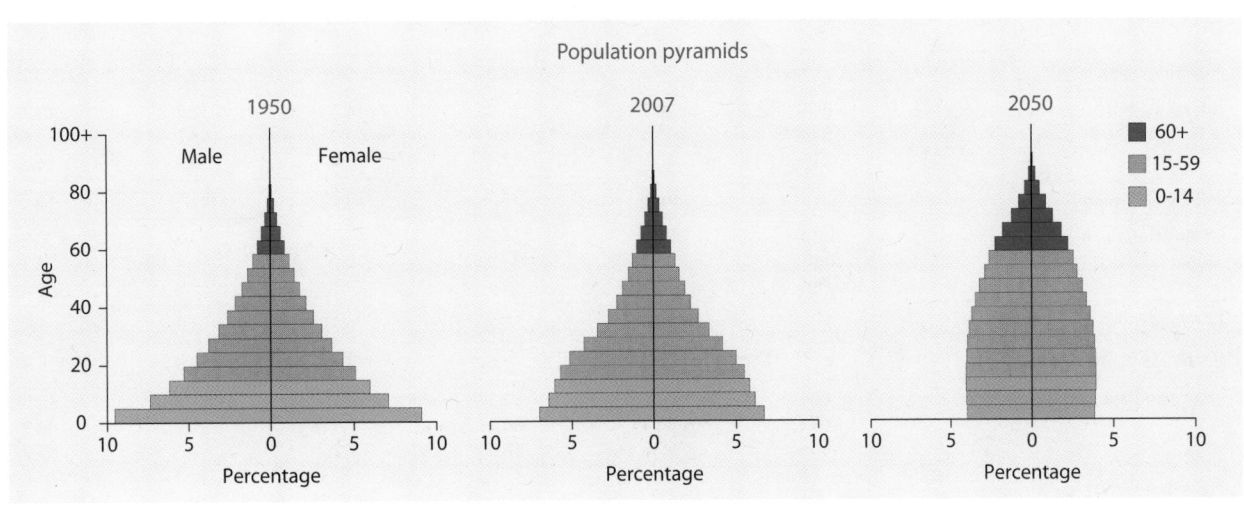

Population pyramids

United Nations Department of Economic and Social Affairs, Population Division

Greece

Indicator	Age	1950	1975	2007	2025	2050
Population (thousands)						
Total	Total	7 566.0	9 046.5	11 159.6	11 173.1	10 741.5
	0-14	2 168.0	2 160.5	1 574.4	1 420.5	1 466.3
	15-59	4 644.0	5 314.3	6 972.1	6 584.2	5 327.6
	60-64	240.0	465.1	571.2	755.1	699.8
	65-69	198.0	401.6	561.4	701.1	778.3
	70-74	147.0	315.5	559.9	586.7	783.5
	75-79	91.0	200.9	470.6	480.3	660.8
	80-84			272.0	296.1	510.2
	85-89			115.6	214.2	300.0
	90-94	78.0	188.6	47.4	100.5	153.3
	95-99			13.1	30.6	51.1
	100+			1.8	3.9	10.8
Female	Total	3 879.0	4 614.9	5 645.5	5 630.4	5 395.6
	0-14	1 058.0	1 046.9	765.0	690.3	712.4
	15-59	2 403.0	2 707.8	3 432.7	3 197.9	2 583.5
	60-64	133.0	245.7	297.6	388.4	343.4
	65-69	109.0	212.2	304.7	370.4	385.5
	70-74	80.0	173.4	309.4	315.6	399.6
	75-79	50.0	115.5	267.0	270.4	353.0
	80-84			160.1	175.4	291.3
	85-89			70.9	134.6	183.2
	90-94	46.0	113.4	29.1	64.5	100.2
	95-99			7.9	20.4	35.4
	100+			1.1	2.7	8.1
Male	Total	3 687.0	4 431.6	5 514.1	5 542.7	5 346.0
	0-14	1 110.0	1 113.6	809.4	730.2	753.9
	15-59	2 241.0	2 606.5	3 539.4	3 386.3	2 744.1
	60-64	107.0	219.4	273.6	366.7	356.4
	65-69	89.0	189.4	256.7	330.7	392.8
	70-74	67.0	142.1	250.5	271.1	383.9
	75-79	41.0	85.4	203.7	210.0	307.8
	80-84			112.0	120.7	219.0
	85-89			44.7	79.6	116.7
	90-94	32.0	75.2	18.3	36.0	53.1
	95-99			5.2	10.2	15.6
	100+			0.7	1.2	2.7
Percentage in older ages						
Total	60+	10.0	17.4	23.4	28.4	36.8
	65+	6.8	12.2	18.3	21.6	30.2
	80+	1.0	2.1	4.0	5.8	9.5
Female	60+	10.8	18.6	25.6	30.9	38.9
	65+	7.3	13.3	20.4	24.0	32.6
	80+	1.2	2.5	4.8	7.1	11.5
Male	60+	9.1	16.1	21.1	25.7	34.6
	65+	6.2	11.1	16.2	19.1	27.9
	80+	0.9	1.7	3.3	4.5	7.6
Ageing index		34.8	72.8	166.0	223.1	269.2
Broad age groups (percentage)	0-14	28.7	23.9	14.1	12.7	13.7
	15-59	61.4	58.7	62.5	58.9	49.6
	60+	10.0	17.4	23.4	28.4	36.8
Median age (years)		26.0	33.9	39.7*	46.5	49.3
Dependency ratio	Total	54.9	56.5	47.9	52.2	78.2
	Youth	44.4	37.4	20.9	19.4	24.3
	Old Age	10.5	19.1	27.1	32.9	53.9
Potential support ratio		9.5	5.2	3.7	3.0	1.9
Parent support ratio		3.3	5.8	8.9	13.8	25.4
Sex ratio (per 100 women)	60+	80.4	82.7	80.5	81.9	88.0
	65+	80.4	80.1	77.5	78.3	84.9
	80+	69.6	66.3	67.2	62.3	65.9

* *Estimate refers to year 2005.*

Indicator	Age	1950-1955	1975-1980	2005-2010	2025-2030	2045-2050
Growth rate (percentage)	Total	1.0	1.3	0.2	–0.1	–0.2
	60+	2.6	1.4	1.1	1.5	–0.2
	65+	2.9	2.7	0.3	1.2	0.5
	80+	3.1	3.6	5.5	1.6	2.2
Total fertility rate (per woman)		2.3	2.3	1.3	1.5	1.8
Life expectancy (years)						
Total	Birth	65.9	73.7	78.7	80.4	82.0
	60	..	..	22.1	23.2	24.3
	65	..	..	18.0	19.0	20.0
	80	..	..	8.0	8.8	9.5
Female	Birth	67.5	75.8	81.3	83.0	84.5
	60	..	..	23.7	25.0	26.2
	65	..	..	19.3	20.5	21.7
	80	..	..	8.4	9.3	10.2
Male	Birth	64.3	71.7	76.1	77.9	79.6
	60	..	..	20.4	21.4	22.4
	65	..	..	16.5	17.4	18.3
	80	..	..	7.6	8.1	8.6
Survival rate (percentage)						
Total	60	..	..	91.3	92.9	94.2
	65	..	..	87.3	89.4	91.0
	80	..	..	55.8	60.6	64.7
Female	60	..	..	94.4	95.3	96.1
	65	..	..	91.8	93.0	94.0
	80	..	..	64.6	69.1	73.0
Male	60	..	..	88.2	90.6	92.5
	65	..	..	82.9	85.9	88.3
	80	..	..	47.0	52.1	56.8

		1980	1990	2007	2010	2020
Labour force participation (percentage)						
Total	65+	12.1	7.7	4.0	3.6	2.8
Female	65+	6.9	4.5	2.4	2.3	2.3
Male	65+	18.6	11.8	6.1	5.2	3.4

Percentage married, age 60+			Percentage living alone, age 60+ (1994)		
Total	Female	Male	Total	Female	Male
66.3	51.0	85.0	18.3	26.1	8.9

Statutory pensionable age (2006)		Percentage illiterate, age 65+ (2001)		
Female	Male	Total	Female	Male
65	65	13.1	18.9	5.9

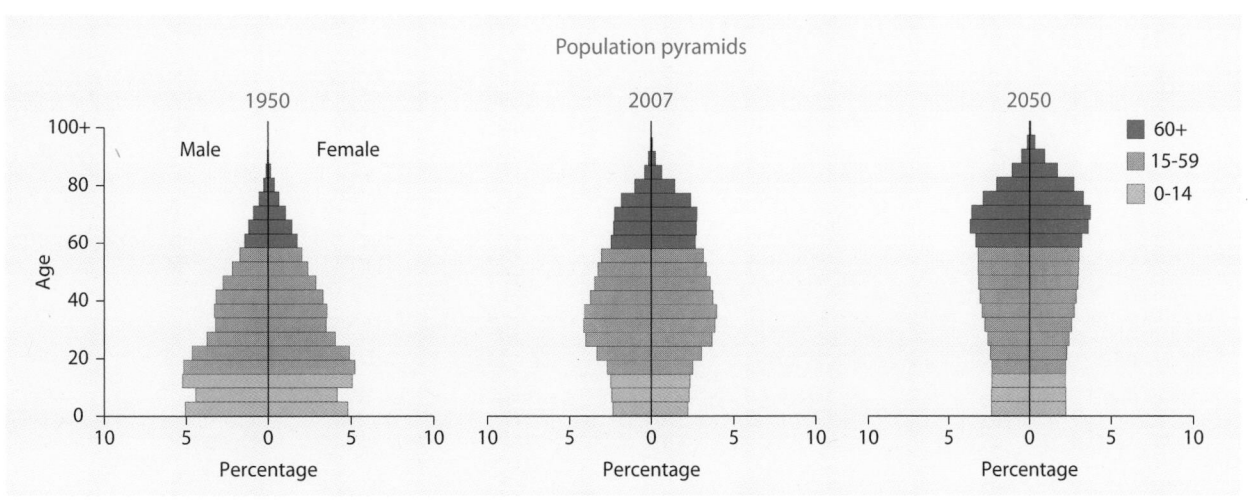

Population pyramids

Guadeloupe

Indicator	Age	1950	1975	2007	2025	2050
Population (thousands)						
Total	Total	210.0	328.5	454.6	487.1	474.1
	0-14	83.0	137.9	109.7	87.1	73.9
	15-59	113.0	162.0	279.2	281.5	243.2
	60-64	5.0	9.5	18.4	33.7	29.3
	65-69	3.0	7.2	14.4	27.5	25.3
	70-74	3.0	5.1	11.8	21.4	21.1
	75-79	2.0	3.3	9.1	15.9	28.3
	80-84			6.4	9.9	24.9
	85-89			3.6	5.9	16.1
	90-94	1.0	3.5	1.5	2.9	8.2
	95-99			0.5	1.0	3.1
	100+			0.1	0.2	0.7
Female	Total	109.0	167.8	235.5	255.0	251.9
	0-14	41.0	68.7	53.9	42.7	36.2
	15-59	59.0	83.0	144.8	146.5	125.1
	60-64	3.0	5.0	9.7	17.8	15.3
	65-69	2.0	3.9	7.7	14.4	13.6
	70-74	2.0	2.9	6.5	11.9	11.7
	75-79	1.0	2.0	5.3	9.0	16.5
	80-84			3.9	5.9	15.1
	85-89			2.3	3.7	10.0
	90-94	1.0	2.3	1.1	2.0	5.5
	95-99			0.4	0.8	2.3
	100+			0.1	0.2	0.6
Male	Total	101.0	160.7	219.1	232.0	222.2
	0-14	42.0	69.2	55.8	44.3	37.6
	15-59	54.0	79.0	134.4	135.0	118.1
	60-64	2.0	4.5	8.7	15.9	13.9
	65-69	1.0	3.3	6.7	13.1	11.7
	70-74	1.0	2.2	5.3	9.5	9.4
	75-79	1.0	1.3	3.8	6.8	11.8
	80-84			2.5	4.0	9.9
	85-89			1.3	2.2	6.1
	90-94	0.0	1.2	0.4	0.9	2.7
	95-99			0.1	0.2	0.8
	100+			0.0	0.0	0.1
Percentage in older ages						
Total	60+	6.7	8.7	14.5	24.3	33.1
	65+	4.3	5.8	10.4	17.4	26.9
	80+	0.5	1.1	2.7	4.1	11.2
Female	60+	8.3	9.6	15.7	25.8	36.0
	65+	5.5	6.6	11.6	18.8	29.9
	80+	0.9	1.4	3.3	5.0	13.3
Male	60+	5.0	7.8	13.2	22.7	29.9
	65+	3.0	5.0	9.2	15.8	23.6
	80+	0.0	0.7	2.0	3.2	8.8
Ageing index		16.9	20.7	59.9	136.1	212.6
Broad age groups (percentage)	0-14	39.5	42.0	24.1	17.9	15.6
	15-59	53.8	49.3	61.4	57.8	51.3
	60+	6.7	8.7	14.5	24.3	33.1
Median age (years)		20.9	18.5	34.1*	40.5	47.6
Dependency ratio	Total	78.0	91.5	52.8	54.5	74.0
	Youth	70.3	80.4	36.9	27.6	27.1
	Old Age	7.6	11.1	15.9	26.9	46.9
Potential support ratio		13.1	9.0	6.3	3.7	2.1
Parent support ratio		2.2	4.5	8.1	9.2	29.8
Sex ratio (per 100 women)	60+	55.6	77.6	78.1	80.1	73.4
	65+	50.0	72.1	73.8	76.6	69.9
	80+	0.0	52.2	55.2	58.0	58.6

* Estimate refers to year 2005.

Indicator	Age	1950-1955	1975-1980	2005-2010	2025-2030	2045-2050
Growth rate (percentage)	Total	2.3	–0.1	0.6	0.2	–0.4
	60+	2.7	2.9	3.1	3.1	0.2
	65+	4.0	3.6	2.5	3.5	–0.2
	80+	–2.0	3.2	3.0	4.2	3.4
Total fertility rate (per woman)		5.6	3.1	2.0	1.9	1.9
Life expectancy (years)						
Total	Birth	56.7	69.9	79.2	82.1	84.3
	60	..	..	23.1	24.8	26.3
	65	..	..	19.1	20.6	21.9
	80	..	..	9.3	10.1	10.9
Female	Birth	58.1	73.4	82.4	84.8	86.7
	60	..	..	25.2	26.9	28.3
	65	..	..	20.9	22.5	23.8
	80	..	..	10.2	11.1	12.0
Male	Birth	55.0	66.4	75.9	79.2	81.6
	60	..	..	20.9	22.6	23.9
	65	..	..	17.1	18.5	19.8
	80	..	..	8.0	8.8	9.5
Survival rate (percentage)						
Total	60	..	..	90.3	93.5	95.2
	65	..	..	86.2	90.2	92.5
	80	..	..	57.5	65.1	70.7
Female	60	..	..	93.6	95.4	96.5
	65	..	..	90.6	93.1	94.6
	80	..	..	66.7	72.9	77.5
Male	60	..	..	86.9	91.3	93.8
	65	..	..	81.5	87.0	90.2
	80	..	..	48.0	56.5	62.9

		1980	1990	2007	2010	2020
Labour force participation (percentage)						
Total	65+	3.5	3.2	3.4	3.4	3.4
Female	65+	3.3	3.2	4.0	4.1	4.1
Male	65+	3.8	3.2	2.5	2.5	2.4

Percentage married, age 60+				Percentage living alone, age 60+ (1990)		
Total	Female	Male		Total	Female	Male
48.2	36.0	64.0		22.6	..	..

Statutory pensionable age (2006)				Percentage illiterate, age 65+		
	Female	Male		Total	Female	Male
	..	..		..	..	..

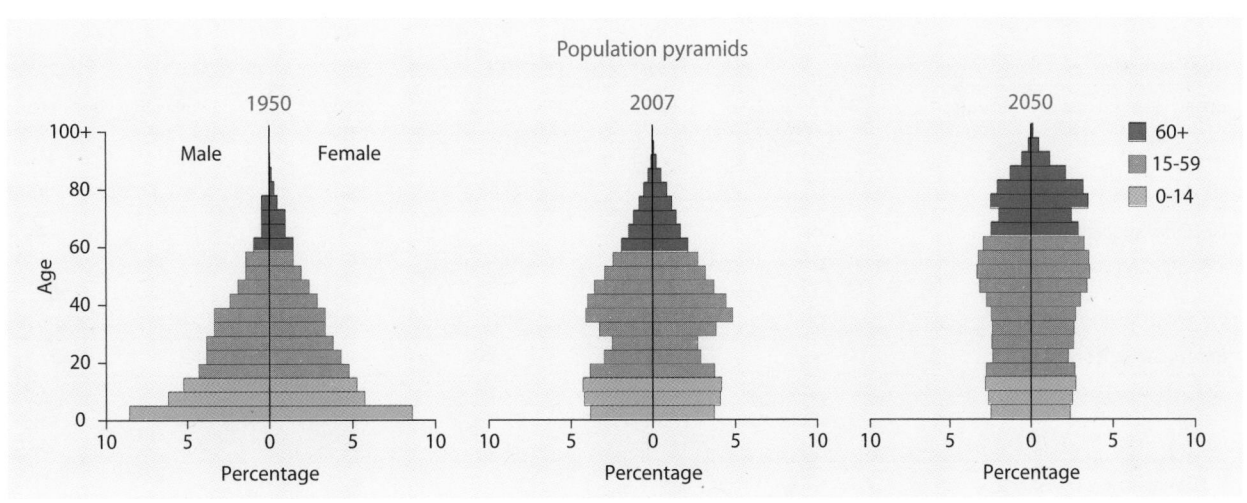

Population pyramids

1950   2007   2050

Male   Female

60+
15-59
0-14

Age

Percentage

Guam

Indicator	Age	1950	1975	2007	2025	2050
Population (thousands)						
Total	Total	59.7	95.4	174.9	217.2	253.5
	0-14	16.2	35.6	51.7	51.8	47.8
	15-59	42.2	56.1	106.7	130.1	151.5
	60-64	0.5	1.5	5.4	11.1	13.1
	65-69	0.3	1.0	4.1	9.3	10.8
	70-74	0.2	0.6	3.3	6.8	9.3
	75-79	0.2	0.3	2.3	4.6	8.7
	80-84			1.0	2.2	6.8
	85-89			0.3	1.0	3.8
	90-94	0.1	0.3	0.0	0.3	1.4
	95-99			0.0	0.0	0.3
	100+			0.0	0.0	0.0
Female	Total	19.2	44.0	85.9	107.5	126.4
	0-14	7.9	17.4	25.0	25.2	23.2
	15-59	10.6	24.8	52.3	63.7	73.9
	60-64	0.2	0.7	2.7	5.7	6.7
	65-69	0.2	0.5	2.2	4.6	5.5
	70-74	0.1	0.3	1.8	3.6	4.9
	75-79	0.1	0.2	1.2	2.6	4.7
	80-84			0.5	1.3	3.8
	85-89			0.2	0.7	2.4
	90-94	0.1	0.2	0.0	0.2	1.0
	95-99			0.0	0.0	0.3
	100+			0.0	0.0	0.0
Male	Total	40.5	51.4	89.0	109.7	127.1
	0-14	8.3	18.2	26.7	26.6	24.6
	15-59	31.6	31.4	54.4	66.5	77.6
	60-64	0.2	0.8	2.7	5.4	6.4
	65-69	0.2	0.5	1.9	4.7	5.2
	70-74	0.1	0.3	1.5	3.2	4.4
	75-79	0.1	0.1	1.0	2.0	4.0
	80-84			0.5	0.9	3.0
	85-89			0.1	0.3	1.4
	90-94	0.0	0.1	0.0	0.1	0.5
	95-99			0.0	0.0	0.1
	100+			0.0	0.0	0.0
Percentage in older ages						
Total	60+	2.2	3.8	9.4	16.2	21.4
	65+	1.3	2.3	6.3	11.1	16.2
	80+	0.2	0.3	0.8	1.6	4.9
Female	60+	3.7	4.2	10.1	17.4	23.2
	65+	2.4	2.6	6.9	12.0	17.9
	80+	0.3	0.4	0.8	2.0	5.9
Male	60+	1.4	3.5	8.8	15.1	19.6
	65+	0.8	2.0	5.7	10.2	14.6
	80+	0.1	0.2	0.7	1.2	3.8
Ageing index		8.0	10.2	31.9	68.0	113.4
Broad age groups (percentage)	0-14	27.1	37.3	29.6	23.9	18.9
	15-59	70.7	58.9	61.0	59.9	59.8
	60+	2.2	3.8	9.4	16.2	21.4
Median age (years)		22.8	21.2	28.1*	31.6	37.9
Dependency ratio	Total	39.8	65.6	56.0	53.8	54.0
	Youth	37.9	61.8	46.1	36.7	29.0
	Old Age	1.9	3.8	9.9	17.1	25.0
Potential support ratio		53.1	26.5	10.2	5.8	4.0
Parent support ratio		0.9	1.1	1.4	3.7	12.4
Sex ratio (per 100 women)	60+	82.4	97.1	90.0	89.0	85.0
	65+	73.1	87.3	86.0	86.6	81.8
	80+	56.9	61.7	89.1	60.6	65.4

* *Estimate refers to year 2005.*

Indicator	Age	1950-1955	1975-1980	2005-2010	2025-2030	2045-2050
Growth rate (percentage)	Total	1.1	2.2	1.4	0.9	0.4
	60+	3.5	6.1	4.5	3.3	1.2
	65+	3.2	6.4	3.3	3.9	0.7
	80+	4.9	5.4	8.8	6.5	3.4
Total fertility rate (per woman)		5.5	3.5	2.7	2.2	1.9
Life expectancy (years)						
Total	Birth	57.0	68.4	75.5	78.4	80.8
	60	..	..	19.7	21.4	23.2
	65	..	..	15.8	17.4	19.1
	80	..	..	6.2	7.4	8.6
Female	Birth	59.7	71.0	77.9	80.8	83.1
	60	..	..	21.0	23.2	25.1
	65	..	..	17.0	19.0	20.7
	80	..	..	6.5	8.0	9.4
Male	Birth	55.3	66.4	73.2	76.1	78.4
	60	..	..	18.3	19.6	21.4
	65	..	..	14.7	15.8	17.3
	80	..	..	6.0	6.6	7.5
Survival rate (percentage)						
Total	60	..	..	88.6	91.8	93.6
	65	..	..	82.8	87.3	90.0
	80	..	..	46.3	54.6	61.7
Female	60	..	..	91.7	94.0	95.3
	65	..	..	87.3	90.6	92.6
	80	..	..	54.4	63.6	69.9
Male	60	..	..	85.5	89.8	92.0
	65	..	..	78.5	84.1	87.4
	80	..	..	38.3	46.0	53.8

		1980	1990	2007	2010	2020
Labour force participation (percentage)						
Total	65+	51.7	48.0	44.1	43.7	43.3
Female	65+	42.6	38.8	34.7	34.5	34.4
Male	65+	62.0	57.8	55.1	54.6	53.9

Percentage married, age 60+			Percentage living alone, age 60+		
Total	Female	Male	Total	Female	Male
66.9	53.0	82.0	..	..	..

Statutory pensionable age (2006)		Percentage illiterate, age 65+		
Female	Male	Total	Female	Male
65	65	..	..	..

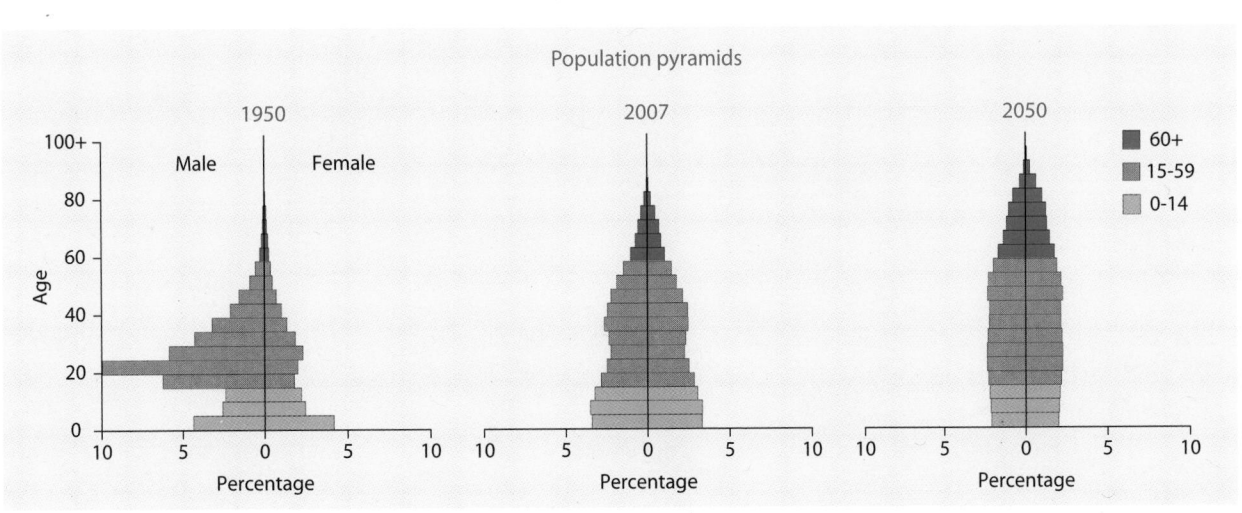

Population pyramids

1950   2007   2050

Legend: 60+, 15-59, 0-14

Guatemala

Indicator	Age	1950	1975	2007	2025	2050
Population (thousands)						
Total	Total	3 146.1	6 202.7	13 230.4	19 149.4	25 612.0
	0-14	1 403.0	2 780.8	5 642.6	6 655.2	5 823.3
	15-59	1 610.1	3 143.4	6 757.7	11 084.4	16 349.1
	60-64	53.5	102.6	253.2	401.8	1 014.0
	65-69	35.9	70.9	197.4	321.9	830.8
	70-74	23.0	52.5	161.7	268.4	621.5
	75-79	12.8	31.0	116.4	200.2	438.9
	80-84			66.3	119.3	282.7
	85-89			27.2	65.5	159.5
	90-94	7.7	21.5	6.9	26.5	68.9
	95-99			0.9	5.8	20.6
	100+			0.0	0.5	2.8
Female	Total	1 556.6	3 064.5	6 789.7	9 855.1	13 237.4
	0-14	691.2	1 367.9	2 786.8	3 272.1	2 855.5
	15-59	797.7	1 554.4	3 566.7	5 792.4	8 365.6
	60-64	27.1	51.5	131.7	227.8	559.7
	65-69	18.2	36.1	101.6	179.1	471.9
	70-74	11.7	27.1	84.4	147.5	367.2
	75-79	6.6	16.1	62.1	110.5	270.0
	80-84			36.0	66.4	179.0
	85-89			15.5	37.9	104.3
	90-94	4.2	11.6	4.3	16.7	47.2
	95-99			0.6	4.1	15.0
	100+			0.0	0.4	2.1
Male	Total	1 589.4	3 138.2	6 440.7	9 294.3	12 374.6
	0-14	711.8	1 412.9	2 855.9	3 383.0	2 967.9
	15-59	812.4	1 589.1	3 191.0	5 292.0	7 983.5
	60-64	26.5	51.1	121.6	174.0	454.3
	65-69	17.7	34.8	95.7	142.7	359.0
	70-74	11.3	25.4	77.3	120.9	254.3
	75-79	6.2	14.9	54.4	89.7	168.9
	80-84			30.2	52.8	103.7
	85-89			11.8	27.6	55.2
	90-94	3.5	9.9	2.7	9.7	21.8
	95-99			0.3	1.7	5.5
	100+			0.0	0.1	0.6
Percentage in older ages						
Total	60+	4.2	4.5	6.3	7.4	13.4
	65+	2.5	2.8	4.4	5.3	9.5
	80+	0.2	0.3	0.8	1.1	2.1
Female	60+	4.4	4.6	6.4	8.0	15.2
	65+	2.6	3.0	4.5	5.7	11.0
	80+	0.3	0.4	0.8	1.3	2.6
Male	60+	4.1	4.3	6.1	6.7	11.5
	65+	2.4	2.7	4.2	4.8	7.8
	80+	0.2	0.3	0.7	1.0	1.5
Ageing index		9.5	10.0	14.7	21.2	59.1
Broad age groups (percentage)	0-14	44.6	44.8	42.6	34.8	22.7
	15-59	51.2	50.7	51.1	57.9	63.8
	60+	4.2	4.5	6.3	7.4	13.4
Median age (years)		17.5	17.5	18.1*	22.3	31.9
Dependency ratio	Total	89.1	91.1	88.7	66.7	47.5
	Youth	84.3	85.7	80.5	57.9	33.5
	Old Age	4.8	5.4	8.2	8.8	14.0
Potential support ratio		20.9	18.5	12.2	11.4	7.2
Parent support ratio		1.1	1.8	3.7	6.4	6.8
Sex ratio (per 100 women)	60+	96.1	95.7	90.3	78.3	70.6
	65+	95.0	93.6	89.4	79.1	66.5
	80+	83.1	85.5	79.6	73.2	53.7

* *Estimate refers to year 2005.*

Indicator	Age	1950-1955	1975-1980	2005-2010	2025-2030	2045-2050
Growth rate (percentage)	Total	2.8	2.5	2.4	1.6	0.8
	60+	2.9	3.0	3.5	3.0	3.7
	65+	3.4	3.1	3.1	2.9	4.1
	80+	2.7	4.6	6.5	4.3	3.7
Total fertility rate (per woman)		7.0	6.2	4.2	2.6	1.8
Life expectancy (years)						
Total	Birth	42.0	55.9	68.5	74.0	77.8
	60	..	..	21.0	22.5	24.0
	65	..	..	17.3	18.7	20.0
	80	..	..	7.8	8.7	9.5
Female	Birth	42.3	57.3	72.1	77.4	81.1
	60	..	..	21.9	23.9	25.6
	65	..	..	18.1	19.8	21.4
	80	..	..	8.3	9.4	10.3
Male	Birth	41.8	54.3	64.9	70.4	74.1
	60	..	..	20.1	21.0	21.9
	65	..	..	16.5	17.3	18.1
	80	..	..	7.3	8.0	8.5
Survival rate (percentage)						
Total	60	..	..	73.2	81.0	86.1
	65	..	..	68.5	76.7	82.3
	80	..	..	41.9	50.8	58.5
Female	60	..	..	79.3	86.0	90.3
	65	..	..	74.9	82.2	87.3
	80	..	..	48.2	58.1	66.6
Male	60	..	..	66.8	75.6	81.8
	65	..	..	61.8	70.6	77.0
	80	..	..	35.7	43.1	49.1

		1980	1990	2007	2010	2020
Labour force participation (percentage)						
Total	65+	37.3	37.6	36.8	37.1	38.7
Female	65+	15.0	13.8	17.7	19.1	25.4
Male	65+	60.6	62.4	58.1	57.4	54.6

Percentage married, age 60+			Percentage living alone, age 60+ (1999)		
Total	Female	Male	Total	Female	Male
62.7	44.0	83.0	6.3	7.8	4.6

Statutory pensionable age (2006)		Percentage illiterate, age 65+ (2002)		
Female	Male	Total	Female	Male
63	63	59.4	65.4	53.3

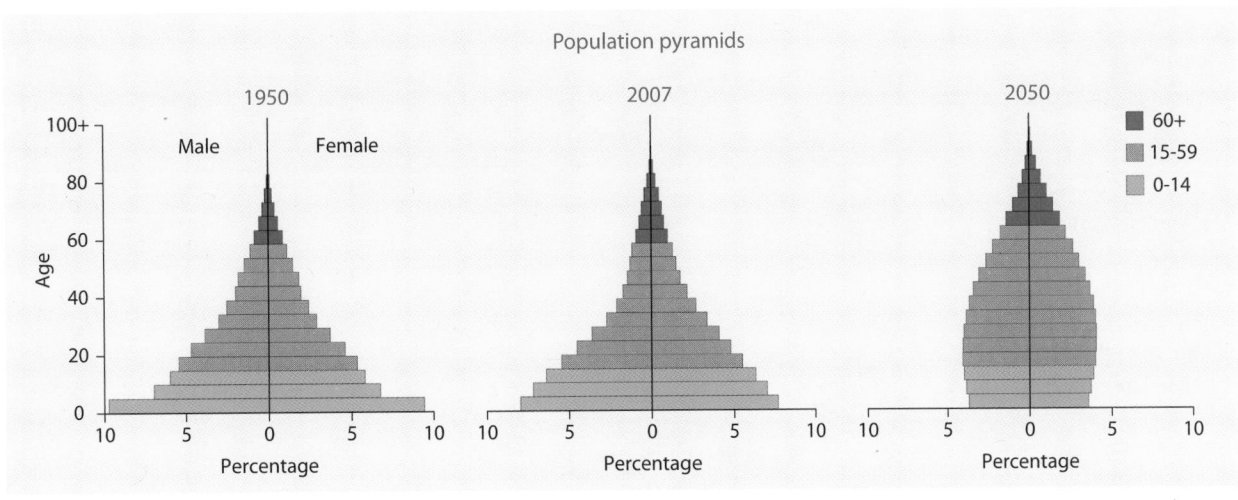

Population pyramids

Guinea

Indicator	Age	1950	1975	2007	2025	2050
Population (thousands)						
Total	Total	2 758.1	4 212.2	9 808.0	14 910.9	22 986.8
	0-14	1 168.8	1 785.4	4 259.3	5 795.1	6 600.0
	15-59	1 474.3	2 208.4	4 987.4	8 220.9	14 353.6
	60-64	50.8	90.8	209.8	308.4	671.0
	65-69	33.7	63.7	153.3	227.2	509.1
	70-74	19.0	38.7	104.8	163.2	383.2
	75-79	8.3	18.5	60.3	120.1	257.5
	80-84			25.5	55.9	147.0
	85-89			6.7	17.0	53.7
	90-94	3.2	6.8	0.9	2.9	10.7
	95-99			0.1	0.2	1.1
	100+			0.0	0.0	0.1
Female	Total	1 381.7	2 072.9	4 778.4	7 227.3	11 172.5
	0-14	577.3	868.5	2 063.4	2 810.1	3 211.0
	15-59	740.8	1 087.9	2 419.5	3 950.9	6 930.1
	60-64	27.5	47.7	107.4	154.9	325.3
	65-69	18.7	33.9	80.2	116.8	251.2
	70-74	10.8	20.9	56.0	85.8	194.8
	75-79	4.8	10.2	33.0	65.2	136.9
	80-84			14.4	31.6	82.9
	85-89			3.9	10.0	32.5
	90-94	1.9	3.8	0.6	1.8	7.0
	95-99			0.0	0.2	0.8
	100+			0.0	0.0	0.0
Male	Total	1 376.3	2 139.4	5 029.7	7 683.6	11 814.4
	0-14	591.5	916.9	2 195.8	2 984.9	3 389.0
	15-59	733.6	1 120.5	2 567.9	4 270.0	7 423.5
	60-64	23.3	43.2	102.4	153.5	345.7
	65-69	15.0	29.8	73.1	110.5	257.8
	70-74	8.3	17.8	48.9	77.4	188.5
	75-79	3.4	8.3	27.3	54.9	120.6
	80-84			11.1	24.2	64.1
	85-89			2.8	6.9	21.2
	90-94	1.2	3.0	0.3	1.1	3.7
	95-99			0.0	0.1	0.3
	100+			0.0	0.0	0.0
Percentage in older ages						
Total	60+	4.2	5.2	5.7	6.0	8.8
	65+	2.3	3.0	3.6	3.9	5.9
	80+	0.1	0.2	0.3	0.5	0.9
Female	60+	4.6	5.6	6.2	6.5	9.2
	65+	2.6	3.3	3.9	4.3	6.3
	80+	0.1	0.2	0.4	0.6	1.1
Male	60+	3.7	4.8	5.3	5.6	8.5
	65+	2.0	2.8	3.3	3.6	5.6
	80+	0.1	0.1	0.3	0.4	0.8
Ageing index		9.8	12.2	13.2	15.4	30.8
Broad age groups (percentage)	0-14	42.4	42.4	43.4	38.9	28.7
	15-59	53.5	52.4	50.8	55.1	62.4
	60+	4.2	5.2	5.7	6.0	8.8
Median age (years)		18.8	19.1	18.0*	20.1	26.8
Dependency ratio	Total	80.8	83.2	88.7	74.8	53.0
	Youth	76.6	77.7	82.0	67.9	43.9
	Old Age	4.2	5.6	6.8	6.9	9.1
Potential support ratio		23.8	18.0	14.8	14.5	11.0
Parent support ratio		0.3	0.3	1.1	1.8	2.5
Sex ratio (per 100 women)	60+	80.4	87.6	90.0	91.9	97.1
	65+	77.2	85.5	87.0	88.3	92.9
	80+	64.0	78.1	75.4	74.0	72.5

* *Estimate refers to year 2005.*

Indicator	Age	1950-1955	1975-1980	2005-2010	2025-2030	2045-2050
Growth rate (percentage)	Total	1.6	2.6	2.2	2.0	1.5
	60+	2.8	3.0	2.9	3.3	3.6
	65+	2.8	3.3	3.0	3.3	3.4
	80+	1.1	4.7	4.5	4.9	4.8
Total fertility rate (per woman)		5.8	6.9	5.5	3.6	2.5
Life expectancy (years)						
Total	Birth	33.1	41.4	54.4	62.0	70.3
	60	..	..	16.5	18.3	20.1
	65	..	..	13.0	14.6	16.1
	80	..	..	5.2	5.7	6.4
Female	Birth	33.4	41.8	54.5	62.4	71.7
	60	..	..	17.2	19.3	21.3
	65	..	..	13.5	15.3	17.1
	80	..	..	5.3	6.0	6.8
Male	Birth	32.7	41.0	54.2	61.6	69.0
	60	..	..	15.8	17.4	18.9
	65	..	..	12.5	13.9	15.1
	80	..	..	5.0	5.4	5.9
Survival rate (percentage)						
Total	60	..	..	56.4	65.6	79.2
	65	..	..	50.8	60.8	74.9
	80	..	..	20.1	29.6	42.6
Female	60	..	..	56.8	65.7	80.5
	65	..	..	52.0	61.9	77.4
	80	..	..	22.1	32.6	48.1
Male	60	..	..	55.9	65.5	78.0
	65	..	..	49.6	59.7	72.7
	80	..	..	18.2	26.6	37.5

		1980	1990	2007	2010	2020
Labour force participation (percentage)						
Total	65+	51.4	52.0	49.8	48.5	45.0
Female	65+	32.2	33.0	34.9	35.2	36.2
Male	65+	73.7	74.1	67.0	63.8	55.1

Percentage married, age 60+				Percentage living alone, age 60+ (1999)		
Total	Female	Male		Total	Female	Male
61.7	39.0	87.0		2.2	3.0	1.6

Statutory pensionable age (2006)			Percentage illiterate, age 65+ (2003)		
Female	Male		Total	Female	Male
55	55		89.3	97.6	83.9

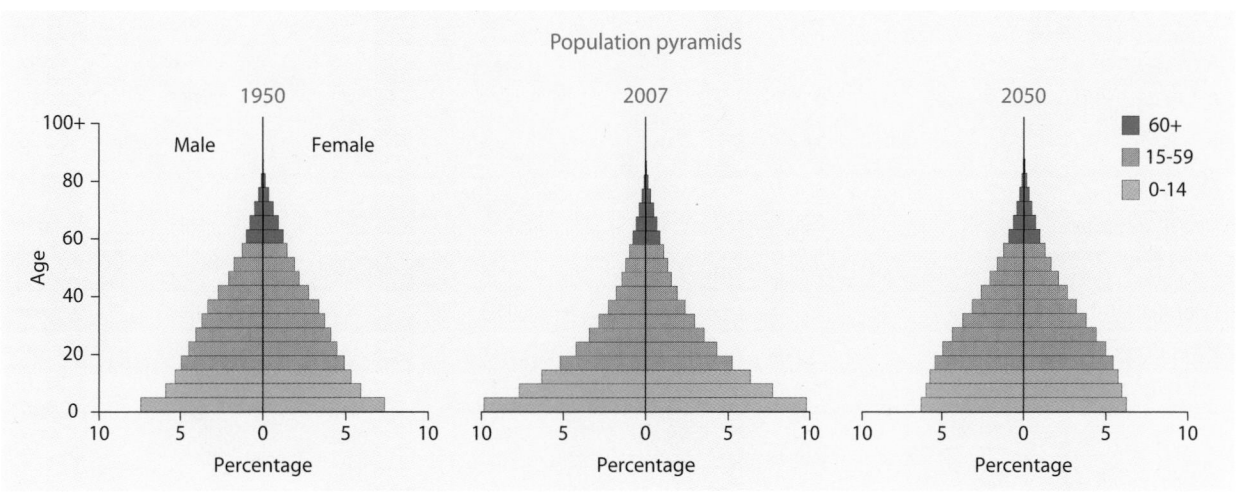

Population pyramids

Guinea-Bissau

Indicator	Age	1950	1975	2007	2025	2050
Population (thousands)						
Total	Total	504.8	650.8	1 681.6	2 874.9	5 312.0
	0-14	187.6	277.9	803.4	1 336.2	1 917.9
	15-59	287.3	334.7	800.3	1 421.2	3 118.4
	60-64	11.1	16.2	27.5	41.5	100.9
	65-69	8.6	10.9	21.2	30.9	72.1
	70-74	5.7	6.3	14.8	22.5	48.9
	75-79	3.0	3.3	8.8	13.1	31.0
	80-84			4.0	6.5	15.4
	85-89			1.3	2.3	5.8
	90-94	1.5	1.5	0.3	0.5	1.4
	95-99			0.0	0.1	0.2
	100+			0.0	0.0	0.0
Female	Total	255.2	330.7	850.3	1 446.0	2 668.0
	0-14	93.6	139.7	401.4	666.3	953.5
	15-59	145.1	170.0	406.5	715.5	1 568.4
	60-64	6.1	8.6	14.6	22.1	52.1
	65-69	4.7	5.9	11.4	16.8	37.7
	70-74	3.1	3.5	8.1	12.4	26.0
	75-79	1.7	1.9	4.9	7.3	17.0
	80-84			2.4	3.8	8.8
	85-89			0.8	1.4	3.4
	90-94	0.9	0.9	0.2	0.3	0.9
	95-99			0.0	0.1	0.1
	100+			0.0	0.0	0.0
Male	Total	249.6	320.2	831.3	1 428.9	2 643.9
	0-14	94.0	138.2	402.0	669.9	964.3
	15-59	142.2	164.7	393.8	705.7	1 550.0
	60-64	5.0	7.6	12.9	19.4	48.8
	65-69	3.9	5.0	9.8	14.1	34.4
	70-74	2.5	2.8	6.7	10.1	22.9
	75-79	1.3	1.4	3.8	5.8	14.0
	80-84			1.7	2.8	6.6
	85-89			0.5	0.9	2.3
	90-94	0.6	0.5	0.1	0.2	0.5
	95-99			0.0	0.0	0.1
	100+			0.0	0.0	0.0
Percentage in older ages						
Total	60+	5.9	5.9	4.6	4.1	5.2
	65+	3.7	3.4	3.0	2.6	3.3
	80+	0.3	0.2	0.3	0.3	0.4
Female	60+	6.5	6.3	5.0	4.4	5.5
	65+	4.1	3.7	3.3	2.9	3.5
	80+	0.3	0.3	0.4	0.4	0.5
Male	60+	5.4	5.4	4.3	3.7	4.9
	65+	3.4	3.0	2.7	2.4	3.1
	80+	0.2	0.2	0.3	0.3	0.4
Ageing index		15.9	13.7	9.7	8.8	14.4
Broad age groups (percentage)	0-14	37.2	42.7	47.8	46.5	36.1
	15-59	56.9	51.4	47.6	49.4	58.7
	60+	5.9	5.9	4.6	4.1	5.2
Median age (years)		21.7	19.0	16.2*	16.6	21.5
Dependency ratio	Total	69.2	85.5	103.1	96.5	65.0
	Youth	62.9	79.2	97.0	91.3	59.6
	Old Age	6.3	6.3	6.1	5.2	5.4
Potential support ratio		15.9	15.9	16.4	19.3	18.4
Parent support ratio		0.8	0.6	1.5	1.8	1.8
Sex ratio (per 100 women)	60+	81.6	82.7	83.7	83.0	88.7
	65+	81.3	79.1	81.1	80.5	86.0
	80+	70.0	59.6	66.6	69.6	72.0

* *Estimate refers to year 2005.*

Indicator	Age	1950-1955	1975-1980	2005-2010	2025-2030	2045-2050
Growth rate (percentage)	Total	0.9	4.0	2.9	2.9	2.1
	60+	−0.5	3.9	1.8	2.9	4.0
	65+	−0.7	4.8	2.0	2.8	3.8
	80+	−0.5	5.0	3.1	2.9	4.1
Total fertility rate (per woman)		5.6	7.1	7.1	5.3	3.2
Life expectancy (years)						
Total	Birth	32.5	37.5	45.5	54.4	63.2
	60	..	..	15.4	16.6	17.9
	65	..	..	12.4	13.3	14.4
	80	..	..	5.4	5.9	6.3
Female	Birth	34.0	39.0	46.7	56.0	65.2
	60	..	..	16.0	17.2	18.6
	65	..	..	12.8	13.8	14.9
	80	..	..	5.7	6.1	6.5
Male	Birth	31.1	36.0	44.2	53.0	61.3
	60	..	..	14.8	16.0	17.2
	65	..	..	11.8	12.8	13.8
	80	..	..	5.1	5.6	6.0
Survival rate (percentage)						
Total	60	..	..	41.7	54.9	69.0
	65	..	..	36.3	48.9	62.9
	80	..	..	12.9	20.1	29.4
Female	60	..	..	43.6	57.2	72.0
	65	..	..	38.4	51.6	66.4
	80	..	..	14.6	22.4	32.8
Male	60	..	..	39.7	52.6	66.1
	65	..	..	34.1	46.3	59.5
	80	..	..	11.3	17.7	26.0

		1980	1990	2007	2010	2020
Labour force participation (percentage)						
Total	65+	49.2	49.0	54.3	54.8	55.4
Female	65+	23.9	26.4	31.0	31.4	32.3
Male	65+	80.9	77.3	83.1	83.6	83.9

Percentage married, age 60+				Percentage living alone, age 60+		
Total	Female	Male		Total	Female	Male
..	..	..		..	..	..

Statutory pensionable age (2006)				Percentage illiterate, age 65+		
	Female	Male		Total	Female	Male
	..	..		..	..	..

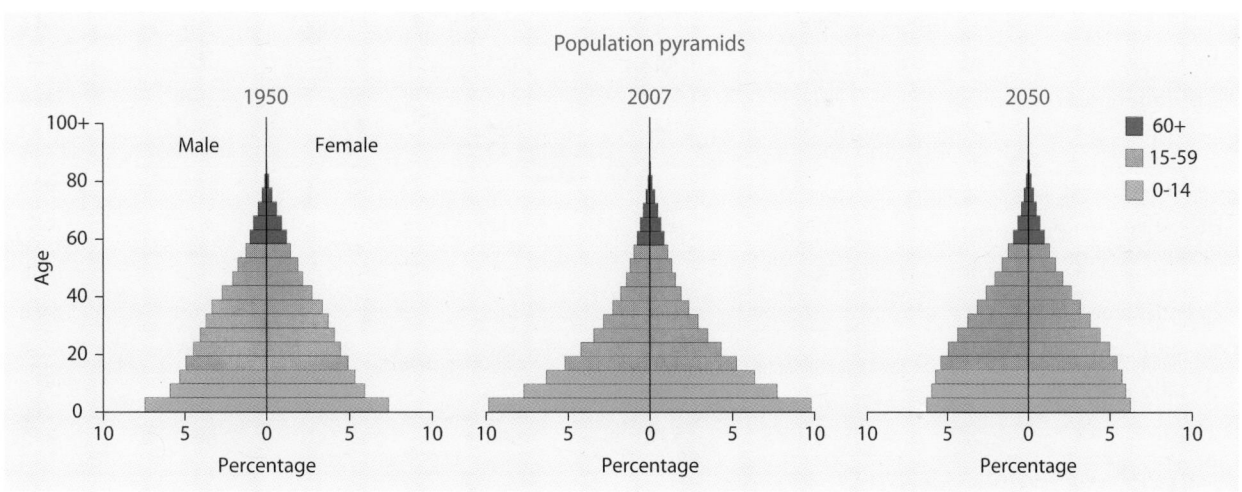

Population pyramids

Guyana

Indicator	Age	1950	1975	2007	2025	2050
Population (thousands)						
Total	Total	422.9	733.9	752.3	703.3	488.4
	0-14	173.7	323.8	216.1	139.9	65.0
	15-59	221.0	369.7	478.2	457.7	251.6
	60-64	9.0	13.1	18.4	34.7	32.9
	65-69	7.9	12.1	13.3	27.5	40.3
	70-74	5.7	6.9	10.5	19.2	36.3
	75-79	3.4	4.8	8.0	12.8	29.2
	80-84			4.9	6.8	18.0
	85-89			2.1	3.1	10.0
	90-94	2.2	3.5	0.7	1.2	4.0
	95-99			0.1	0.3	0.9
	100+			0.0	0.0	0.1
Female	Total	216.5	369.7	387.4	362.6	252.1
	0-14	90.3	161.3	106.6	68.6	31.7
	15-59	110.4	187.2	247.0	230.4	122.8
	60-64	4.5	6.5	10.4	20.1	16.8
	65-69	4.5	6.2	7.6	16.5	21.1
	70-74	3.4	3.6	6.1	11.4	20.1
	75-79	2.3	2.8	4.7	8.0	17.2
	80-84			3.0	4.5	11.4
	85-89			1.3	2.1	7.0
	90-94	1.1	2.2	0.5	0.9	3.0
	95-99			0.1	0.2	0.8
	100+			0.0	0.0	0.1
Male	Total	206.4	364.2	364.9	340.7	236.3
	0-14	83.4	162.6	109.5	71.3	33.3
	15-59	110.6	182.5	231.1	227.3	128.8
	60-64	4.5	6.6	7.9	14.6	16.1
	65-69	3.4	5.8	5.7	11.1	19.1
	70-74	2.3	3.3	4.4	7.8	16.2
	75-79	1.1	2.0	3.3	4.8	12.0
	80-84			2.0	2.3	6.6
	85-89			0.8	1.0	3.0
	90-94	1.1	1.3	0.2	0.3	1.0
	95-99			0.0	0.1	0.2
	100+			0.0	0.0	0.0
Percentage in older ages						
Total	60+	6.7	5.5	7.7	15.0	35.2
	65+	4.5	3.7	5.3	10.1	28.4
	80+	0.5	0.5	1.0	1.6	6.8
Female	60+	7.3	5.8	8.7	17.5	38.7
	65+	5.2	4.0	6.0	12.0	32.0
	80+	0.5	0.6	1.2	2.1	8.9
Male	60+	6.0	5.2	6.7	12.4	31.4
	65+	3.8	3.4	4.5	8.1	24.6
	80+	0.5	0.4	0.8	1.1	4.6
Ageing index		16.2	12.5	26.9	75.6	264.2
Broad age groups (percentage)	0-14	41.1	44.1	28.7	19.9	13.3
	15-59	52.3	50.4	63.6	65.1	51.5
	60+	6.7	5.5	7.7	15.0	35.2
Median age (years)		19.8	17.4	25.7*	35.0	49.6
Dependency ratio	Total	83.9	91.7	51.5	42.8	71.7
	Youth	75.5	84.6	43.5	28.4	22.9
	Old Age	8.3	7.1	8.0	14.4	48.8
Potential support ratio		12.0	14.1	12.5	6.9	2.0
Parent support ratio		2.4	2.0	3.9	3.7	14.7
Sex ratio (per 100 women)	60+	78.5	89.4	72.0	66.2	76.0
	65+	69.9	84.2	70.2	63.2	71.9
	80+	100.0	59.4	62.7	48.8	48.2

Estimate refers to year 2005.

Indicator	Age	1950-1955	1975-1980	2005-2010	2025-2030	2045-2050
Growth rate (percentage)	Total	2.8	0.7	0.0	–0.8	–2.3
	60+	–0.1	1.4	2.6	3.1	–0.2
	65+	–1.0	1.8	1.5	3.8	1.3
	80+	–0.9	3.4	2.5	5.0	2.9
Total fertility rate (per woman)		6.7	3.9	2.1	1.9	1.9
Life expectancy (years)						
Total	Birth	52.3	60.7	65.4	70.6	74.2
	60	..	..	18.4	20.3	21.3
	65	..	..	14.9	16.6	17.5
	80	..	..	7.0	7.8	8.4
Female	Birth	53.9	63.2	68.4	73.0	76.5
	60	..	..	19.8	21.9	23.1
	65	..	..	16.1	17.9	19.0
	80	..	..	7.4	8.3	9.0
Male	Birth	50.7	58.3	62.3	67.9	71.8
	60	..	..	16.7	18.3	19.3
	65	..	..	13.5	14.8	15.7
	80	..	..	6.4	6.9	7.3
Survival rate (percentage)						
Total	60	..	..	71.2	78.1	83.6
	65	..	..	64.9	72.8	78.6
	80	..	..	31.5	41.3	47.6
Female	60	..	..	75.7	80.9	85.6
	65	..	..	70.5	76.8	81.9
	80	..	..	38.4	48.4	55.1
Male	60	..	..	66.4	75.2	81.7
	65	..	..	58.8	68.4	75.4
	80	..	..	24.3	33.1	39.6

		1980	1990	2007	2010	2020
Labour force participation (percentage)						
Total	65+	24.6	23.5	19.9	19.6	19.3
Female	65+	14.6	12.9	10.3	10.2	10.1
Male	65+	35.9	36.0	33.6	33.5	33.2

Percentage married, age 60+				Percentage living alone, age 60+		
Total	Female	Male		Total	Female	Male
47.3	35.0	63.0		..	..	..

Statutory pensionable age (2006)				Percentage illiterate, age 65+		
	Female	Male		Total	Female	Male
	60	60		..	..	..

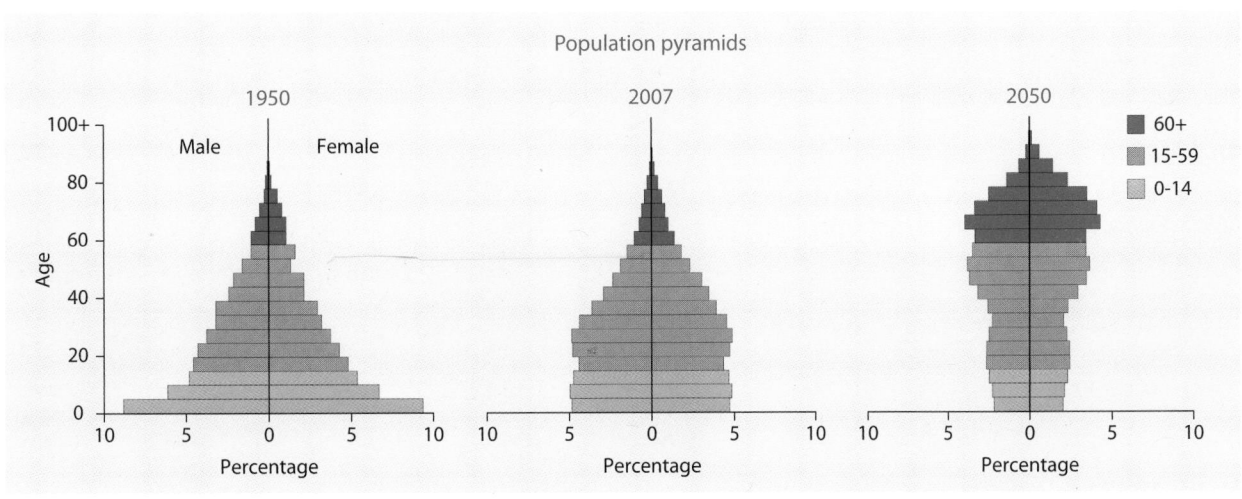

Population pyramids

United Nations Department of Economic and Social Affairs, Population Division

Haiti

Indicator	Age	1950	1975	2007	2025	2050
Population (thousands)						
Total	Total	3 260.8	4 919.7	8 773.1	10 868.0	12 996.0
	0-14	1 201.0	2 022.4	3 235.3	3 374.7	2 987.4
	15-59	1 792.2	2 553.1	5 004.3	6 672.6	7 967.8
	60-64	97.6	120.0	176.0	251.5	646.5
	65-69	73.3	93.1	138.2	199.2	514.5
	70-74	50.4	65.1	100.3	154.0	360.2
	75-79	28.5	39.2	63.3	105.3	236.4
	80-84			34.1	63.8	149.9
	85-89			15.2	31.5	82.8
	90-94	17.9	26.8	5.0	11.8	36.6
	95-99			1.2	3.0	11.6
	100+			0.2	0.6	2.2
Female	Total	1 674.6	2 509.8	4 444.3	5 444.5	6 465.7
	0-14	599.6	1 005.6	1 591.8	1 656.6	1 461.5
	15-59	927.9	1 318.3	2 554.9	3 319.8	3 927.0
	60-64	52.5	64.1	97.9	136.8	324.4
	65-69	40.0	50.2	76.5	112.9	262.0
	70-74	28.0	35.4	55.6	89.4	188.8
	75-79	16.1	21.4	35.4	61.9	129.1
	80-84			19.3	37.9	86.3
	85-89			8.9	19.2	51.6
	90-94	10.5	14.9	3.0	7.5	24.8
	95-99			0.7	2.1	8.5
	100+			0.2	0.4	1.7
Male	Total	1 586.2	2 409.8	4 328.8	5 423.5	6 530.3
	0-14	601.4	1 016.8	1 643.5	1 718.2	1 525.9
	15-59	864.3	1 234.8	2 449.4	3 352.9	4 040.8
	60-64	45.1	55.9	78.1	114.6	322.1
	65-69	33.2	42.8	61.6	86.3	252.6
	70-74	22.4	29.7	44.7	64.6	171.4
	75-79	12.4	17.7	27.9	43.4	107.2
	80-84			14.8	25.9	63.6
	85-89			6.3	12.3	31.2
	90-94	7.4	12.0	2.0	4.3	11.9
	95-99			0.4	1.0	3.2
	100+			0.1	0.2	0.5
Percentage in older ages						
Total	60+	8.2	7.0	6.1	7.6	15.7
	65+	5.2	4.6	4.1	5.2	10.7
	80+	0.5	0.5	0.6	1.0	2.2
Female	60+	8.8	7.4	6.7	8.6	16.7
	65+	5.6	4.9	4.5	6.1	11.6
	80+	0.6	0.6	0.7	1.2	2.7
Male	60+	7.6	6.6	5.5	6.5	14.8
	65+	4.8	4.2	3.6	4.4	9.8
	80+	0.5	0.5	0.5	0.8	1.7
Ageing index		22.3	17.0	16.5	24.3	68.3
Broad age groups (percentage)	0-14	36.8	41.1	36.9	31.1	23.0
	15-59	55.0	51.9	57.0	61.4	61.3
	60+	8.2	7.0	6.1	7.6	15.7
Median age (years)		22.4	19.3	20.0*	24.7	32.5
Dependency ratio	Total	72.5	84.0	69.4	57.0	50.9
	Youth	63.6	75.7	62.5	48.7	34.7
	Old Age	9.0	8.4	6.9	8.2	16.2
Potential support ratio		11.1	11.9	14.5	12.2	6.2
Parent support ratio		1.6	1.9	3.3	4.9	6.7
Sex ratio (per 100 women)	60+	81.9	85.0	79.3	75.3	89.5
	65+	79.7	83.9	79.1	71.8	85.2
	80+	70.0	80.6	73.5	64.8	63.8

* *Estimate refers to year 2005.*

Indicator	Age	1950-1955	1975-1980	2005-2010	2025-2030	2045-2050
Growth rate (percentage)	Total	1.5	2.1	1.4	0.9	0.5
	60+	1.1	1.0	2.1	2.8	4.1
	65+	1.3	1.1	2.4	2.8	4.6
	80+	1.2	1.5	3.3	3.8	3.8
Total fertility rate (per woman)		6.3	6.0	3.6	2.5	2.1
Life expectancy (years)						
Total	Birth	37.6	50.6	53.5	62.2	70.1
	60	..	..	17.2	20.2	22.6
	65	..	..	14.1	16.8	18.8
	80	..	..	7.0	8.3	9.3
Female	Birth	38.9	52.2	54.0	62.7	71.0
	60	..	..	17.7	21.1	24.0
	65	..	..	14.6	17.6	20.1
	80	..	..	7.3	8.8	10.0
Male	Birth	36.3	49.1	52.9	61.6	69.2
	60	..	..	16.5	19.1	21.0
	65	..	..	13.6	15.8	17.4
	80	..	..	6.7	7.7	8.5
Survival rate (percentage)						
Total	60	..	..	48.9	61.6	73.1
	65	..	..	43.2	56.5	68.7
	80	..	..	18.9	32.0	44.8
Female	60	..	..	49.3	61.4	73.0
	65	..	..	43.9	56.8	69.3
	80	..	..	20.2	34.1	48.7
Male	60	..	..	48.4	61.8	73.2
	65	..	..	42.2	56.1	68.0
	80	..	..	17.4	29.4	40.7

		1980	1990	2007	2010	2020
Labour force participation (percentage)						
Total	65+	55.6	52.4	47.6	47.2	46.0
Female	65+	41.7	36.7	25.1	24.7	24.1
Male	65+	72.1	71.2	76.0	76.1	76.1

Percentage married, age 60+			Percentage living alone, age 60+ (2000)		
Total	Female	Male	Total	Female	Male
54.7	43.0	69.0	8.5	8.6	8.3

Statutory pensionable age (2006)		Percentage illiterate, age 65+		
Female	Male	Total	Female	Male
55	55	..	..	..

Population pyramids

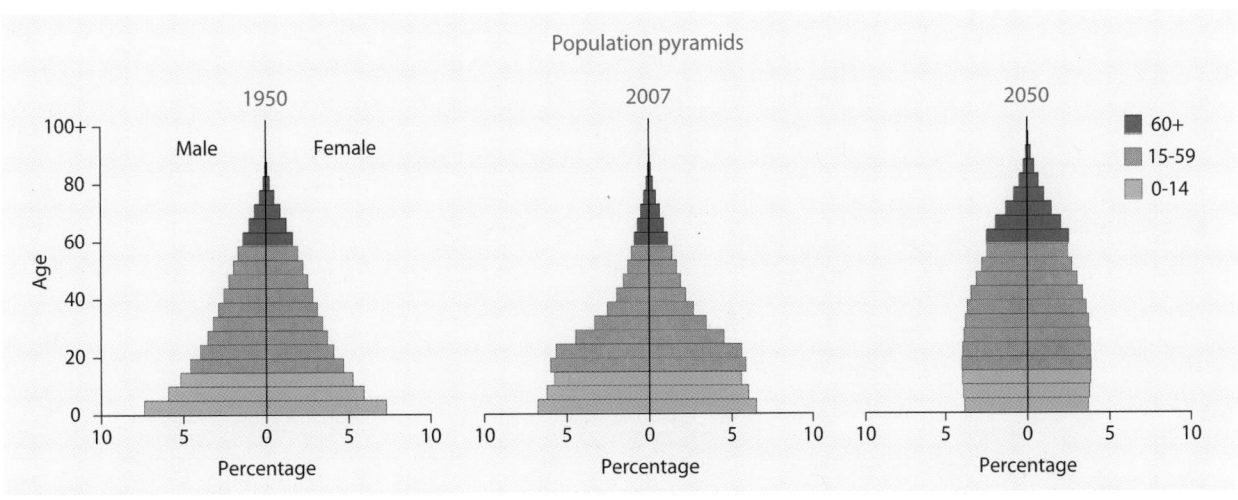

Honduras

Indicator	Age	1950	1975	2007	2025	2050
Population (thousands)						
Total	Total	1 379.8	3 016.0	7 520.7	10 238.5	12 776.0
	0-14	622.5	1 447.2	2 863.2	2 988.6	2 523.0
	15-59	703.1	1 443.6	4 226.6	6 366.9	7 995.4
	60-64	21.5	46.5	131.5	282.0	639.6
	65-69	14.9	34.8	107.0	216.1	530.7
	70-74	9.5	23.2	82.9	159.4	411.7
	75-79	5.4	13.5	55.7	102.8	297.2
	80-84			32.3	66.7	201.7
	85-89			15.9	37.4	113.9
	90-94	2.8	7.3	4.8	15.0	48.2
	95-99			0.7	3.3	13.1
	100+			0.0	0.3	1.5
Female	Total	685.1	1 500.8	3 729.3	5 073.5	6 352.5
	0-14	305.7	714.9	1 404.1	1 463.4	1 233.9
	15-59	350.1	719.2	2 095.0	3 136.5	3 922.5
	60-64	11.4	24.1	67.9	145.1	321.8
	65-69	8.1	18.4	56.1	113.3	271.6
	70-74	5.2	12.5	44.3	85.4	215.8
	75-79	3.1	7.5	30.5	56.7	161.4
	80-84			18.4	38.3	114.8
	85-89			9.5	22.6	69.1
	90-94	1.6	4.2	3.0	9.7	31.4
	95-99			0.5	2.3	9.2
	100+			0.0	0.2	1.0
Male	Total	694.7	1 515.2	3 791.3	5 165.0	6 423.5
	0-14	316.8	732.3	1 459.1	1 525.2	1 289.1
	15-59	353.0	724.4	2 131.5	3 230.4	4 072.9
	60-64	10.1	22.4	63.6	136.9	317.8
	65-69	6.9	16.4	50.9	102.8	259.2
	70-74	4.4	10.6	38.7	73.9	195.9
	75-79	2.4	6.0	25.2	46.2	135.8
	80-84			14.0	28.4	86.9
	85-89			6.4	14.8	44.8
	90-94	1.2	3.0	1.7	5.3	16.8
	95-99			0.2	1.0	3.9
	100+			0.0	0.1	0.4
Percentage in older ages						
Total	60+	3.9	4.2	5.7	8.6	17.7
	65+	2.4	2.6	4.0	5.9	12.7
	80+	0.2	0.2	0.7	1.2	3.0
Female	60+	4.3	4.4	6.2	9.3	18.8
	65+	2.6	2.8	4.4	6.5	13.8
	80+	0.2	0.3	0.8	1.4	3.6
Male	60+	3.6	3.9	5.3	7.9	16.5
	65+	2.1	2.4	3.6	5.3	11.6
	80+	0.2	0.2	0.6	1.0	2.4
Ageing index		8.7	8.7	15.0	29.5	89.5
Broad age groups (percentage)	0-14	45.1	48.0	38.1	29.2	19.7
	15-59	51.0	47.9	56.2	62.2	62.6
	60+	3.9	4.2	5.7	8.6	17.7
Median age (years)		17.2	15.9	19.8*	26.2	35.7
Dependency ratio	Total	90.4	102.4	72.6	54.0	48.0
	Youth	85.9	97.1	65.7	44.9	29.2
	Old Age	4.5	5.3	6.9	9.0	18.7
Potential support ratio		22.2	18.9	14.6	11.1	5.3
Parent support ratio		0.7	1.0	4.0	5.2	8.0
Sex ratio (per 100 women)	60+	85.0	87.6	87.2	86.4	88.8
	65+	82.2	84.5	84.5	82.9	85.1
	80+	73.8	71.5	71.1	67.6	67.8

* Estimate refers to year 2005.

Indicator	Age	1950-1955	1975-1980	2005-2010	2025-2030	2045-2050
Growth rate (percentage)	Total	3.1	3.4	2.1	1.2	0.6
	60+	2.7	3.7	3.4	4.0	3.4
	65+	2.8	3.9	3.6	4.2	3.7
	80+	3.0	6.1	5.3	3.7	4.4
Total fertility rate (per woman)		7.5	6.6	3.3	2.2	1.9
Life expectancy (years)						
Total	Birth	41.8	57.4	69.2	73.5	77.4
	60	..	..	21.4	22.8	24.0
	65	..	..	17.7	19.0	20.0
	80	..	..	8.3	9.0	9.6
Female	Birth	43.2	59.5	71.3	75.7	79.7
	60	..	..	22.7	24.4	25.8
	65	..	..	18.9	20.3	21.6
	80	..	..	8.8	9.7	10.4
Male	Birth	40.5	55.4	67.2	71.4	75.1
	60	..	..	20.1	21.2	22.2
	65	..	..	16.5	17.5	18.4
	80	..	..	7.7	8.2	8.7
Survival rate (percentage)						
Total	60	..	..	74.3	80.0	85.6
	65	..	..	69.4	75.6	81.8
	80	..	..	43.3	50.7	58.1
Female	60	..	..	76.8	82.1	87.4
	65	..	..	72.7	78.6	84.5
	80	..	..	48.9	57.0	65.1
Male	60	..	..	71.8	77.9	83.9
	65	..	..	66.3	72.7	79.1
	80	..	..	37.8	44.4	51.2

		1980	1990	2007	2010	2020
Labour force participation (percentage)						
Total	65+	34.7	34.4	40.7	41.2	42.0
Female	65+	15.8	14.2	20.3	21.0	22.3
Male	65+	57.0	57.8	64.9	65.3	65.8

Percentage married, age 60+			Percentage living alone, age 60+ (1988)		
Total	Female	Male	Total	Female	Male
58.1	44.0	74.0	5.6	5.3	5.9

Statutory pensionable age (2006)			Percentage illiterate, age 65+ (2001)		
	Female	Male	Total	Female	Male
	60	65	54.4	57.7	51.1

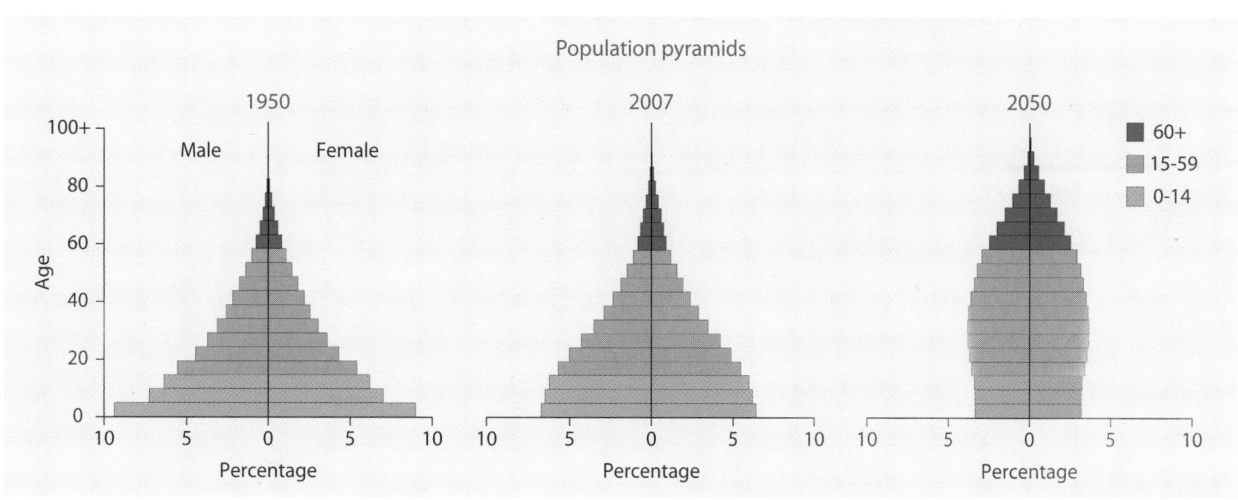

Population pyramids

United Nations Department of Economic and Social Affairs, Population Division

Hungary

Indicator	Age	1950	1975	2007	2025	2050
Population (thousands)						
Total	Total	9 338.0	10 531.8	10 044.6	9 435.9	8 262.3
	0-14	2 344.0	2 140.9	1 526.3	1 265.0	1 132.5
	15-59	5 937.0	6 463.8	6 379.1	5 620.1	4 140.4
	60-64	372.0	596.4	578.9	536.9	589.5
	65-69	305.0	515.7	479.5	588.1	577.6
	70-74	194.0	384.6	403.9	576.2	654.9
	75-79	113.0	253.0	327.8	395.6	513.7
	80-84			232.8	256.9	331.9
	85-89			86.4	133.4	183.0
	90-94	73.0	177.4	25.9	51.8	100.8
	95-99			3.7	11.0	33.6
	100+			0.1	0.8	4.3
Female	Total	4 848.0	5 423.0	5 264.3	4 938.1	4 297.8
	0-14	1 153.0	1 039.8	744.6	616.5	551.6
	15-59	3 098.0	3 273.9	3 199.1	2 778.1	2 031.2
	60-64	210.0	326.1	321.4	286.1	300.2
	65-69	172.0	288.3	284.0	329.5	303.0
	70-74	109.0	222.0	252.2	342.4	358.4
	75-79	63.0	155.4	214.4	251.2	298.4
	80-84			161.6	177.5	209.8
	85-89			63.7	102.4	129.6
	90-94	43.0	117.3	20.2	43.5	81.2
	95-99			3.1	10.1	30.4
	100+			0.1	0.8	4.2
Male	Total	4 490.0	5 108.8	4 780.2	4 497.8	3 964.5
	0-14	1 191.0	1 101.1	781.8	648.5	580.9
	15-59	2 839.0	3 189.9	3 180.0	2 842.0	2 109.2
	60-64	162.0	270.3	257.6	250.8	289.3
	65-69	133.0	227.4	195.5	258.6	274.6
	70-74	85.0	162.6	151.7	233.8	296.6
	75-79	50.0	97.6	113.4	144.4	215.4
	80-84			71.3	79.4	122.2
	85-89			22.7	31.1	53.4
	90-94	30.0	60.0	5.7	8.3	19.6
	95-99			0.6	0.9	3.3
	100+			0.0	0.0	0.1
Percentage in older ages						
Total	60+	11.3	18.3	21.3	27.0	36.2
	65+	7.3	12.6	15.5	21.3	29.0
	80+	0.8	1.7	3.5	4.8	7.9
Female	60+	12.3	20.5	25.1	31.3	39.9
	65+	8.0	14.4	19.0	25.5	32.9
	80+	0.9	2.2	4.7	6.8	10.6
Male	60+	10.2	16.0	17.1	22.4	32.1
	65+	6.6	10.7	11.7	16.8	24.8
	80+	0.7	1.2	2.1	2.7	5.0
Ageing index		45.1	90.0	140.1	201.6	264.0
Broad age groups (percentage)	0-14	25.1	20.3	15.2	13.4	13.7
	15-59	63.6	61.4	63.5	59.6	50.1
	60+	11.3	18.3	21.3	27.0	36.2
Median age (years)		29.9	34.2	38.8*	45.5	49.6
Dependency ratio	Total	48.0	49.2	44.4	53.3	74.7
	Youth	37.2	30.3	21.9	20.5	23.9
	Old Age	10.9	18.8	22.4	32.7	50.7
Potential support ratio		9.2	5.3	4.5	3.1	2.0
Parent support ratio		1.8	3.2	5.6	10.1	19.0
Sex ratio (per 100 women)	60+	77.1	73.7	62.0	65.3	74.3
	65+	77.0	69.9	56.1	60.2	69.6
	80+	69.8	51.2	40.3	35.8	43.6

* Estimate refers to year 2005.

Indicator	Age	1950-1955	1975-1980	2005-2010	2025-2030	2045-2050
Growth rate (percentage)	Total	1.0	0.3	−0.3	−0.5	−0.6
	60+	2.8	−0.9	1.1	0.5	0.0
	65+	3.3	1.6	1.0	−0.1	0.2
	80+	4.2	4.8	2.9	2.4	1.1
Total fertility rate (per woman)		2.7	2.1	1.3	1.5	1.8
Life expectancy (years)						
Total	Birth	63.7	69.5	73.8	77.3	79.7
	60	..	..	19.1	20.9	22.6
	65	..	..	15.7	17.2	18.7
	80	..	..	7.1	8.0	8.9
Female	Birth	65.8	72.8	77.7	80.7	83.0
	60	..	..	21.4	23.5	25.2
	65	..	..	17.5	19.3	20.9
	80	..	..	7.6	8.8	9.9
Male	Birth	61.5	66.3	69.8	73.7	76.4
	60	..	..	16.3	17.9	19.8
	65	..	..	13.2	14.4	16.0
	80	..	..	5.9	6.3	7.1
Survival rate (percentage)						
Total	60	..	..	83.8	89.3	92.0
	65	..	..	76.8	83.6	87.5
	80	..	..	41.0	49.9	57.4
Female	60	..	..	89.9	92.8	94.6
	65	..	..	85.3	89.2	91.7
	80	..	..	53.2	62.0	68.6
Male	60	..	..	77.8	85.8	89.5
	65	..	..	68.2	78.0	83.4
	80	..	..	28.0	37.0	46.1

		1980	1990	2007	2010	2020
Labour force participation (percentage)						
Total	65+	3.5	0.7	1.4	1.4	1.3
Female	65+	3.2	0.4	0.9	0.9	0.8
Male	65+	3.9	1.1	2.4	2.3	2.1

Percentage married, age 60+			Percentage living alone, age 60+ (1990)		
Total	Female	Male	Total	Female	Male
51.0	36.0	75.0	24.3	32.0	13.0

Statutory pensionable age (2006)		Percentage illiterate, age 65+		
Female	Male	Total	Female	Male
60	62	..	..	..

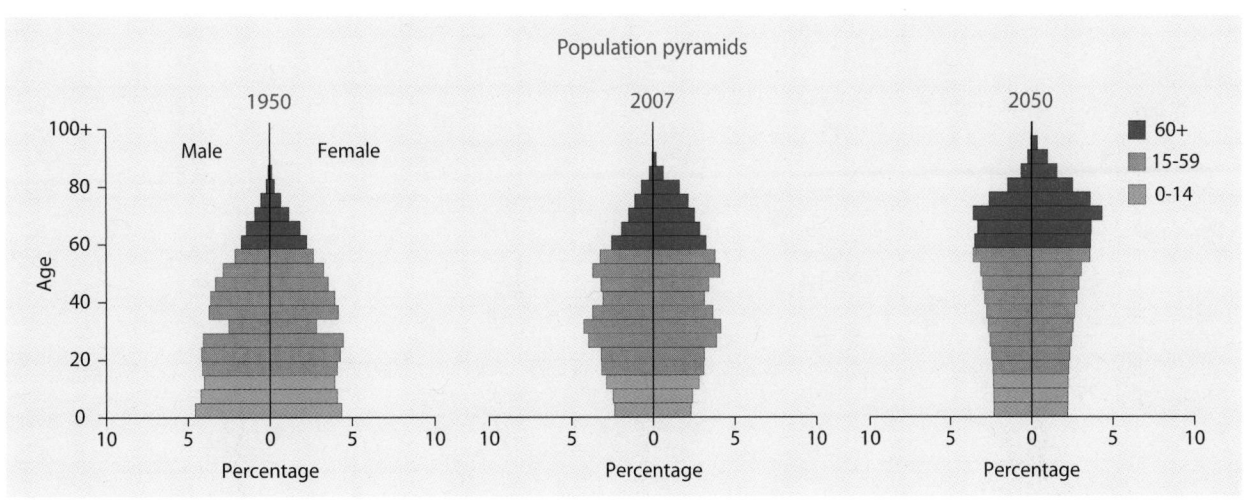

Population pyramids

United Nations Department of Economic and Social Affairs, Population Division

Iceland

Indicator	Age	1950	1975	2007	2025	2050
Population (thousands)						
Total	Total	143.0	218.0	299.7	340.2	370.1
	0-14	44.0	65.5	64.1	61.9	60.2
	15-59	84.0	124.8	186.5	195.7	196.9
	60-64	4.0	7.8	13.3	20.6	21.8
	65-69	4.0	6.5	9.8	19.2	20.9
	70-74	3.0	5.3	8.6	15.8	19.3
	75-79	2.0	4.1	7.6	12.0	17.0
	80-84			5.4	7.6	13.8
	85-89			2.9	4.1	10.8
	90-94	2.0	4.0	1.1	2.3	6.4
	95-99			0.3	0.8	2.5
	100+			0.0	0.2	0.6
Female	Total	72.0	107.9	149.9	170.9	187.8
	0-14	22.0	32.0	31.5	30.4	29.6
	15-59	42.0	61.0	92.2	97.4	98.3
	60-64	2.0	4.0	6.6	10.4	10.9
	65-69	2.0	3.4	5.0	9.7	10.6
	70-74	2.0	2.8	4.5	8.0	9.9
	75-79	1.0	2.3	4.2	6.2	8.9
	80-84			3.1	4.2	7.5
	85-89			1.8	2.5	6.2
	90-94	1.0	2.4	0.8	1.4	3.9
	95-99			0.2	0.5	1.7
	100+			0.0	0.1	0.4
Male	Total	71.0	110.2	149.8	169.3	182.3
	0-14	22.0	33.5	32.6	31.5	30.6
	15-59	42.0	63.8	94.3	98.3	98.6
	60-64	2.0	3.8	6.7	10.2	10.9
	65-69	2.0	3.1	4.8	9.5	10.3
	70-74	1.0	2.5	4.1	7.8	9.4
	75-79	1.0	1.8	3.5	5.8	8.1
	80-84			2.3	3.4	6.3
	85-89			1.1	1.7	4.6
	90-94	1.0	1.7	0.4	0.8	2.5
	95-99			0.1	0.2	0.8
	100+			0.0	0.0	0.2
Percentage in older ages						
Total	60+	10.5	12.7	16.4	24.3	30.5
	65+	7.7	9.2	12.0	18.2	24.7
	80+	1.4	1.9	3.3	4.4	9.2
Female	60+	11.1	13.8	17.5	25.2	31.9
	65+	8.3	10.1	13.1	19.1	26.1
	80+	1.4	2.2	3.9	5.1	10.5
Male	60+	9.9	11.7	15.3	23.3	29.1
	65+	7.0	8.3	10.8	17.3	23.1
	80+	1.4	1.5	2.6	3.6	7.9
Ageing index		34.1	42.3	76.7	133.2	187.9
Broad age groups (percentage)	0-14	30.8	30.1	21.4	18.2	16.3
	15-59	58.7	57.2	62.2	57.5	53.2
	60+	10.5	12.7	16.4	24.3	30.5
Median age (years)		26.5	25.4	34.1*	39.5	44.1
Dependency ratio	Total	62.5	64.5	50.0	57.2	69.3
	Youth	50.0	49.5	32.1	28.6	27.5
	Old Age	12.5	15.1	17.9	28.6	41.7
Potential support ratio		8.0	6.6	5.6	3.5	2.4
Parent support ratio		4.6	5.2	8.8	11.9	29.8
Sex ratio (per 100 women)	60+	87.6	86.2	87.3	91.5	88.6
	65+	83.4	83.6	82.6	89.4	86.0
	80+	100.6	69.3	66.1	70.4	72.8

* *Estimate refers to year 2005.*

Indicator	Age	1950-1955	1975-1980	2005-2010	2025-2030	2045-2050
Growth rate (percentage)	Total	2.0	0.9	0.8	0.5	0.2
	60+	2.5	2.1	2.8	1.8	0.8
	65+	0.0	2.4	2.1	2.6	0.9
	80+	0.0	4.7	3.4	4.5	1.3
Total fertility rate (per woman)		3.7	2.3	1.9	1.9	1.9
Life expectancy (years)						
Total	Birth	72.0	76.3	81.4	83.9	86.1
	60	..	..	23.7	25.6	27.4
	65	..	..	19.5	21.3	22.9
	80	..	..	9.0	10.2	11.4
Female	Birth	74.1	79.3	83.2	85.6	87.8
	60	..	..	25.2	27.1	29.0
	65	..	..	20.9	22.7	24.5
	80	..	..	9.7	11.0	12.3
Male	Birth	70.0	73.4	79.5	82.2	84.3
	60	..	..	22.2	24.0	25.7
	65	..	..	18.1	19.8	21.3
	80	..	..	8.2	9.3	10.3
Survival rate (percentage)						
Total	60	..	..	93.9	95.7	96.9
	65	..	..	90.3	93.0	94.7
	80	..	..	63.2	70.1	75.6
Female	60	..	..	95.0	96.3	97.3
	65	..	..	92.1	94.1	95.6
	80	..	..	69.7	75.6	80.4
Male	60	..	..	92.8	95.1	96.5
	65	..	..	88.6	91.9	93.9
	80	..	..	56.7	64.6	70.7

		1980	1990	2007	2010	2020
Labour force participation (percentage)						
Total	65+	28.8	27.1	17.4	17.0	16.7
Female	65+	18.9	18.4	9.8	9.5	9.3
Male	65+	40.9	37.9	26.7	26.0	25.1

Percentage married, age 60+				Percentage living alone, age 60+		
Total	Female	Male		Total	Female	Male
58.7	49.0	70.0		..	..	..

Statutory pensionable age (2006)				Percentage illiterate, age 65+		
	Female	Male		Total	Female	Male
	67	67		..	..	..

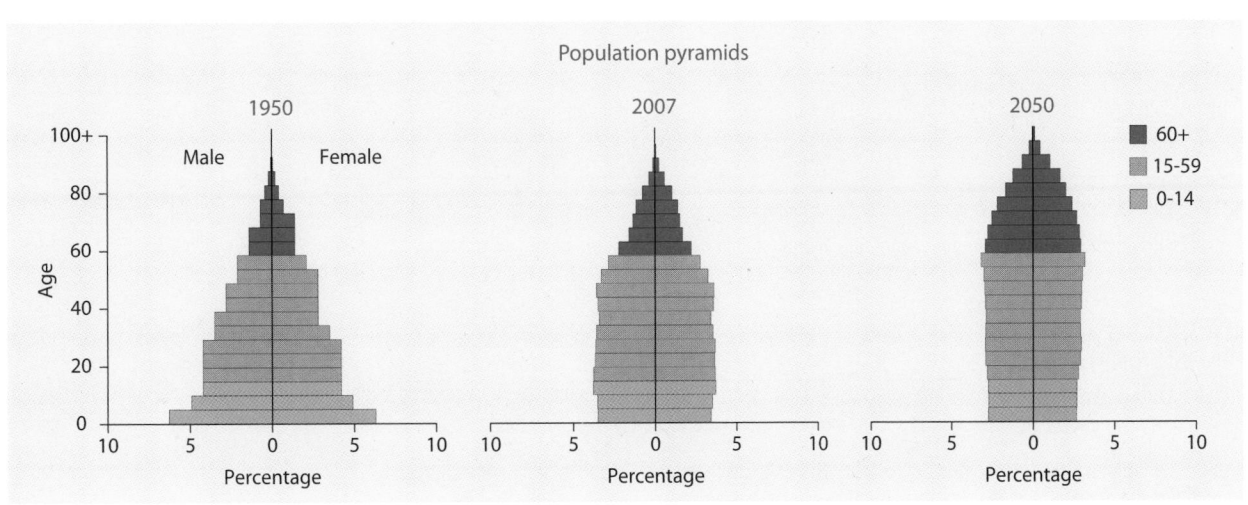

Population pyramids

India

Indicator	Age	1950	1975	2007	2025	2050
Population (thousands)						
Total	Total	357 560.8	620 700.8	1 135 613.8	1 395 496.4	1 592 704.0
	0-14	139 155.6	247 062.1	354 299.2	341 452.3	291 809.4
	15-59	198 307.0	335 149.7	688 876.1	885 898.5	971 211.9
	60-64	8 127.1	14 739.9	30 869.7	55 600.5	93 169.6
	65-69	5 338.7	10 890.2	23 965.2	43 698.1	78 519.0
	70-74	3 775.7	7 064.7	17 444.7	30 799.1	59 416.1
	75-79	1 934.3	3 874.4	11 011.5	19 456.9	45 662.8
	80-84			5 775.8	11 049.5	29 549.7
	85-89			2 451.3	5 225.4	15 501.7
	90-94	922.4	1 919.8	749.5	1 832.9	6 081.1
	95-99			150.9	420.8	1 544.9
	100+			19.9	62.3	237.7
Female	Total	174 255.2	299 249.7	553 966.1	687 270.1	793 641.0
	0-14	68 833.5	118 717.0	172 245.9	166 602.5	142 767.1
	15-59	94 838.5	161 718.5	333 190.4	433 002.6	476 546.3
	60-64	3 939.6	7 186.1	15 728.4	27 929.6	46 870.7
	65-69	3 151.7	5 300.5	12 522.8	22 291.1	40 354.4
	70-74	2 005.6	3 420.6	9 274.7	16 085.1	31 380.8
	75-79	1 020.7	1 956.7	5 944.4	10 634.5	24 931.8
	80-84			3 173.3	6 296.2	16 746.6
	85-89			1 370.8	3 055.7	9 148.8
	90-94	465.6	950.3	421.3	1 085.1	3 741.9
	95-99			83.4	250.4	992.6
	100+			10.6	37.2	159.9
Male	Total	183 305.6	321 451.1	581 647.8	708 226.4	799 063.0
	0-14	70 322.1	128 345.1	182 053.4	174 849.8	149 042.4
	15-59	103 468.5	173 431.2	355 685.7	452 895.9	494 665.6
	60-64	4 187.5	7 553.8	15 141.3	27 670.9	46 299.0
	65-69	2 187.0	5 589.7	11 442.4	21 407.0	38 164.6
	70-74	1 770.1	3 644.1	8 170.0	14 713.9	28 035.2
	75-79	913.6	1 917.7	5 067.1	8 822.4	20 730.9
	80-84			2 602.4	4 753.3	12 803.1
	85-89			1 080.5	2 169.8	6 352.9
	90-94	456.8	969.5	328.3	747.8	2 339.2
	95-99			67.5	170.4	552.3
	100+			9.3	25.1	77.8
Percentage in older ages						
Total	60+	5.6	6.2	8.1	12.0	20.7
	65+	3.3	3.8	5.4	8.1	14.8
	80+	0.3	0.3	0.8	1.3	3.3
Female	60+	6.1	6.3	8.8	12.8	22.0
	65+	3.8	3.9	5.9	8.7	16.1
	80+	0.3	0.3	0.9	1.6	3.9
Male	60+	5.2	6.1	7.5	11.4	19.4
	65+	2.9	3.8	4.9	7.5	13.6
	80+	0.2	0.3	0.7	1.1	2.8
Ageing index		14.4	15.6	26.1	49.2	113.0
Broad age groups (percentage)	0-14	38.9	39.8	31.2	24.5	18.3
	15-59	55.5	54.0	60.7	63.5	61.0
	60+	5.6	6.2	8.1	12.0	20.7
Median age (years)		20.4	20.0	24.3*	30.4	38.7
Dependency ratio	Total	73.2	77.4	57.8	48.2	49.6
	Youth	67.4	70.6	49.2	36.3	27.4
	Old Age	5.8	6.8	8.6	12.0	22.2
Potential support ratio		17.2	14.7	11.7	8.4	4.5
Parent support ratio		1.0	0.9	2.8	3.8	7.7
Sex ratio (per 100 women)	60+	89.9	104.6	90.5	91.8	89.1
	65+	80.2	104.2	87.7	88.4	85.6
	80+	98.1	102.0	80.8	73.3	71.9

* *Estimate refers to year 2005.*

Indicator	Age	1950-1955	1975-1980	2005-2010	2025-2030	2045-2050
Growth rate (percentage)	Total	2.0	2.1	1.4	0.8	0.3
	60+	2.0	2.9	2.8	3.2	2.4
	65+	2.1	3.2	2.8	3.6	2.6
	80+	1.4	4.1	4.3	3.9	3.7
Total fertility rate (per woman)		6.0	4.8	2.8	1.9	1.9
Life expectancy (years)						
Total	Birth	39.5	52.9	64.9	71.3	75.9
	60	..	..	17.9	19.7	21.4
	65	..	..	14.5	16.1	17.6
	80	..	..	7.1	7.7	8.4
Female	Birth	38.0	52.4	66.7	73.5	78.1
	60	..	..	18.9	21.1	23.1
	65	..	..	15.3	17.2	19.0
	80	..	..	7.3	8.1	9.1
Male	Birth	39.4	53.3	63.2	69.5	73.8
	60	..	..	16.9	18.6	19.9
	65	..	..	13.7	15.1	16.3
	80	..	..	6.8	7.4	7.9
Survival rate (percentage)						
Total	60	..	..	72.9	81.9	88.1
	65	..	..	65.7	75.8	83.0
	80	..	..	30.4	40.9	50.1
Female	60	..	..	76.6	85.0	90.2
	65	..	..	70.3	80.2	86.3
	80	..	..	35.2	47.6	57.5
Male	60	..	..	69.6	79.2	86.0
	65	..	..	61.5	72.1	79.7
	80	..	..	25.9	35.5	43.6

		1980	1990	2007	2010	2020
Labour force participation (percentage)						
Total	65+	37.0	33.7	29.6	29.0	27.3
Female	65+	13.9	13.1	11.7	11.6	11.6
Male	65+	59.6	55.2	50.1	49.0	45.1

Percentage married, age 60+			Percentage living alone, age 60+ (1999)		
Total	Female	Male	Total	Female	Male
61.8	44.0	81.0	3.3	5.0	1.8

Statutory pensionable age (2006)			Percentage illiterate, age 65+ (2001)		
	Female	Male	Total	Female	Male
	58	58	64.4	80.3	48.0

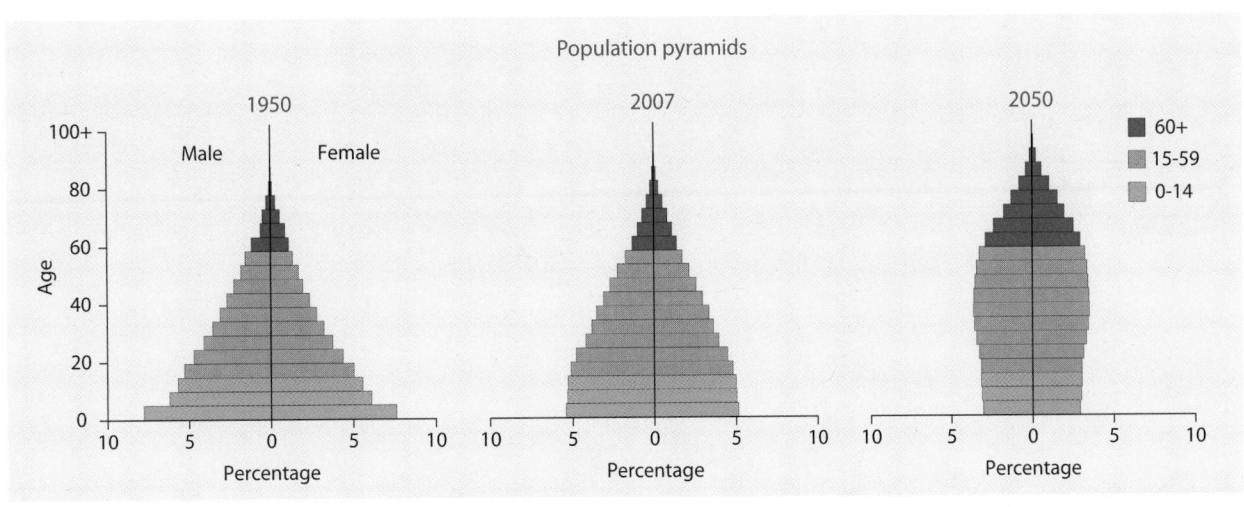

Population pyramids

Indonesia

Indicator	Age	1950	1975	2007	2025	2050
Population (thousands)						
Total	Total	79 538.0	134 394.6	228 121.3	263 746.2	284 639.6
	0-14	31 155.9	55 587.2	63 136.4	56 257.8	50 237.5
	15-59	43 429.3	71 553.3	145 498.0	172 896.1	167 047.5
	60-64	1 803.0	2 845.2	6 425.0	11 941.4	17 685.1
	65-69	1 388.6	2 074.7	5 377.6	9 519.3	16 546.2
	70-74	948.2	1 265.5	3 877.0	6 318.9	13 724.0
	75-79	537.5	657.7	2 324.9	3 719.1	9 907.2
	80-84			1 054.1	2 067.8	6 055.0
	85-89			343.6	814.6	2 549.4
	90-94	275.5	410.9	75.2	187.0	759.9
	95-99			8.9	22.9	118.5
	100+			0.5	1.3	9.3
Female	Total	40 082.9	67 113.7	114 263.6	132 267.9	144 045.3
	0-14	15 979.5	27 344.9	31 014.5	27 543.5	24 530.4
	15-59	21 552.7	35 896.7	72 533.7	86 325.7	82 699.5
	60-64	909.3	1 470.0	3 440.6	6 105.9	9 078.5
	65-69	719.2	1 099.8	2 928.2	4 947.7	8 714.7
	70-74	489.0	696.0	2 154.0	3 364.5	7 457.7
	75-79	285.9	367.1	1 319.4	2 116.2	5 613.4
	80-84			610.5	1 228.2	3 632.5
	85-89			208.0	499.7	1 664.2
	90-94	147.3	239.1	48.2	119.9	550.9
	95-99			6.1	15.5	95.4
	100+			0.4	1.0	8.2
Male	Total	39 455.1	67 281.0	113 857.7	131 478.3	140 594.3
	0-14	15 176.4	28 242.3	32 121.9	28 714.3	25 707.1
	15-59	21 876.6	35 656.6	72 964.3	86 570.3	84 347.9
	60-64	893.7	1 375.3	2 984.5	5 835.5	8 606.7
	65-69	669.4	974.9	2 449.4	4 571.6	7 831.5
	70-74	459.2	569.4	1 723.1	2 954.3	6 266.3
	75-79	251.6	290.7	1 005.4	1 602.9	4 293.8
	80-84			443.6	839.6	2 422.5
	85-89			135.6	314.9	885.2
	90-94	128.2	171.8	27.0	67.0	209.1
	95-99			2.8	7.4	23.1
	100+			0.1	0.4	1.1
Percentage in older ages						
Total	60+	6.2	5.4	8.5	13.1	23.7
	65+	4.0	3.3	5.7	8.6	17.4
	80+	0.3	0.3	0.6	1.2	3.3
Female	60+	6.4	5.8	9.4	13.9	25.6
	65+	4.1	3.6	6.4	9.3	19.3
	80+	0.4	0.4	0.8	1.4	4.1
Male	60+	6.1	5.0	7.7	12.3	21.7
	65+	3.8	3.0	5.1	7.9	15.6
	80+	0.3	0.3	0.5	0.9	2.5
Ageing index		15.9	13.0	30.9	61.5	134.1
Broad age groups (percentage)	0-14	39.2	41.4	27.7	21.3	17.6
	15-59	54.6	53.2	63.8	65.6	58.7
	60+	6.2	5.4	8.5	13.1	23.7
Median age (years)		20.0	19.1	26.5*	33.5	40.5
Dependency ratio	Total	75.8	80.6	50.2	42.7	54.1
	Youth	68.9	74.7	41.6	30.4	27.2
	Old Age	7.0	5.9	8.6	12.3	26.9
Potential support ratio		14.4	16.9	11.6	8.2	3.7
Parent support ratio		1.1	1.1	1.7	2.3	6.3
Sex ratio (per 100 women)	60+	94.2	87.3	81.9	88.0	83.0
	65+	91.9	83.5	79.5	84.3	79.1
	80+	87.0	71.8	69.8	65.9	59.5

* Estimate refers to year 2005.

Indicator	Age	1950-1955	1975-1980	2005-2010	2025-2030	2045-2050
Growth rate (percentage)	Total	1.7	2.2	1.1	0.5	0.1
	60+	0.0	2.5	2.4	3.6	1.6
	65+	0.0	3.3	2.9	3.6	2.3
	80+	1.7	2.2	5.2	2.4	4.8
Total fertility rate (per woman)		5.5	4.7	2.2	1.9	1.9
Life expectancy (years)						
Total	Birth	37.5	52.7	68.7	73.1	76.9
	60	..	..	17.3	18.4	20.4
	65	..	..	13.8	14.7	16.4
	80	..	..	5.8	6.2	7.2
Female	Birth	38.1	54.0	70.5	74.9	78.9
	60	..	..	18.1	19.4	22.1
	65	..	..	14.4	15.5	17.9
	80	..	..	6.1	6.4	8.0
Male	Birth	36.9	51.5	66.9	71.3	74.9
	60	..	..	16.3	17.4	18.6
	65	..	..	13.0	13.9	14.8
	80	..	..	5.6	5.9	6.2
Survival rate (percentage)						
Total	60	..	..	78.9	86.0	90.8
	65	..	..	71.6	79.6	85.7
	80	..	..	31.1	38.7	48.8
Female	60	..	..	81.6	88.4	92.2
	65	..	..	75.3	83.2	88.3
	80	..	..	35.5	43.9	56.4
Male	60	..	..	76.3	83.6	89.3
	65	..	..	67.9	76.0	82.9
	80	..	..	26.7	33.5	41.1

		1980	1990	2007	2010	2020
Labour force participation (percentage)						
Total	65+	39.1	39.3	41.7	42.6	44.4
Female	65+	23.0	25.0	29.8	31.4	34.3
Male	65+	58.2	56.3	56.6	56.7	56.7

Percentage married, age 60+			Percentage living alone, age 60+ (1997)		
Total	Female	Male	Total	Female	Male
57.9	36.0	84.0	7.3	11.9	2.4

Statutory pensionable age (2006)			Percentage illiterate, age 65+ (2004)		
	Female	Male	Total	Female	Male
	55	55	46.8	60.2	31.4

Population pyramids

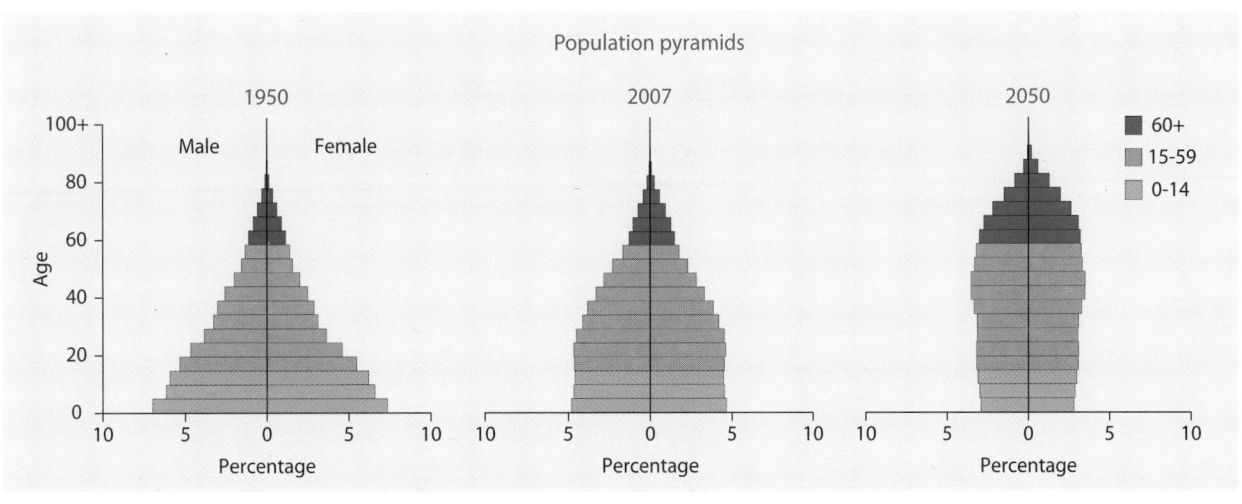

Iran (Islamic Republic of)

Indicator	Age	1950	1975	2007	2025	2050
Population (thousands)						
Total	Total	16 913.0	33 343.6	71 220.3	89 042.1	101 944.5
	0-14	6 611.0	14 836.6	19 085.3	20 763.7	18 182.0
	15-59	8 906.0	16 675.9	47 467.2	58 529.6	57 369.3
	60-64	493.0	658.1	1 462.3	3 327.2	7 907.6
	65-69	381.0	514.7	1 114.5	2 659.7	7 295.4
	70-74	271.0	353.1	941.8	1 898.5	4 976.5
	75-79	161.0	190.8	683.3	1 084.9	3 023.4
	80-84			344.5	505.5	1 860.9
	85-89			103.3	208.2	932.6
	90-94	90.0	114.3	16.6	57.1	322.9
	95-99			1.5	7.4	67.5
	100+			0.1	0.4	6.3
Female	Total	8 327.0	16 303.5	35 133.6	44 195.0	51 184.7
	0-14	3 276.0	7 194.2	9 304.3	10 141.4	8 868.0
	15-59	4 383.0	8 171.1	23 409.5	28 798.6	28 167.2
	60-64	236.0	331.3	795.2	1 687.5	3 980.2
	65-69	182.0	262.7	579.1	1 377.5	3 761.1
	70-74	128.0	182.0	476.6	1 056.3	2 649.4
	75-79	78.0	103.4	337.0	657.2	1 705.3
	80-84			169.0	307.4	1 129.6
	85-89			52.9	128.1	618.6
	90-94	44.0	58.8	9.2	35.9	241.7
	95-99			0.9	4.8	57.6
	100+			0.0	0.3	5.9
Male	Total	8 586.0	17 040.1	36 086.6	44 847.1	50 759.8
	0-14	3 335.0	7 642.4	9 781.0	10 622.2	9 314.0
	15-59	4 523.0	8 504.8	24 057.7	29 731.0	29 202.1
	60-64	257.0	326.8	667.1	1 639.7	3 927.4
	65-69	199.0	252.1	535.4	1 282.2	3 534.3
	70-74	143.0	171.1	465.3	842.3	2 327.1
	75-79	83.0	87.3	346.3	427.7	1 318.1
	80-84			175.5	198.1	731.3
	85-89			50.4	80.0	314.0
	90-94	46.0	55.5	7.4	21.2	81.2
	95-99			0.6	2.6	9.9
	100+			0.0	0.1	0.4
Percentage in older ages						
Total	60+	8.3	5.5	6.6	10.9	25.9
	65+	5.3	3.5	4.5	7.2	18.1
	80+	0.5	0.3	0.7	0.9	3.1
Female	60+	8.0	5.8	6.9	11.9	27.6
	65+	5.2	3.7	4.6	8.1	19.9
	80+	0.5	0.4	0.7	1.1	4.0
Male	60+	8.5	5.2	6.2	10.0	24.1
	65+	5.5	3.3	4.4	6.4	16.4
	80+	0.5	0.3	0.6	0.7	2.2
Ageing index		21.1	12.3	24.5	47.0	145.2
Broad age groups (percentage)	0-14	39.1	44.5	26.8	23.3	17.8
	15-59	52.7	50.0	66.6	65.7	56.3
	60+	8.3	5.5	6.6	10.9	25.9
Median age (years)		21.1	17.6	23.4*	33.3	40.6
Dependency ratio	Total	79.9	92.4	45.6	43.9	56.2
	Youth	70.3	85.6	39.0	33.6	27.9
	Old Age	9.6	6.8	6.6	10.4	28.3
Potential support ratio		10.4	14.8	15.3	9.6	3.5
Parent support ratio		1.4	1.1	1.9	2.3	6.4
Sex ratio (per 100 women)	60+	109.0	95.2	92.9	85.5	86.5
	65+	109.0	93.3	97.3	80.0	81.8
	80+	104.6	94.5	100.9	63.4	55.4

* Estimate refers to year 2005.

Indicator	Age	1950-1955	1975-1980	2005-2010	2025-2030	2045-2050
Growth rate (percentage)	Total	2.4	3.3	1.3	0.7	0.3
	60+	−0.2	3.0	2.7	3.7	3.6
	65+	0.4	2.2	1.3	4.3	5.1
	80+	0.8	2.1	5.1	6.3	4.1
Total fertility rate (per woman)		7.0	6.5	2.0	1.9	1.9
Life expectancy (years)						
Total	Birth	44.9	57.7	71.7	76.1	79.1
	60	..	..	18.0	20.0	22.0
	65	..	..	14.2	16.1	17.9
	80	..	..	5.8	6.9	8.1
Female	Birth	44.9	58.1	73.4	78.4	81.6
	60	..	..	19.0	21.7	24.1
	65	..	..	15.0	17.5	19.8
	80	..	..	5.9	7.5	9.0
Male	Birth	44.9	57.4	70.1	73.9	76.6
	60	..	..	17.0	18.2	19.8
	65	..	..	13.5	14.6	16.0
	80	..	..	5.6	6.0	6.8
Survival rate (percentage)						
Total	60	..	..	84.4	89.9	92.6
	65	..	..	78.0	84.6	88.4
	80	..	..	36.3	47.3	56.1
Female	60	..	..	87.2	92.3	94.5
	65	..	..	82.0	88.6	91.6
	80	..	..	41.6	55.7	65.2
Male	60	..	..	81.7	87.5	90.8
	65	..	..	73.8	80.7	85.3
	80	..	..	31.3	38.9	47.0

		1980	1990	2007	2010	2020
Labour force participation (percentage)						
Total	65+	29.1	33.8	32.4	31.7	30.0
Female	65+	6.4	7.5	10.4	10.5	10.6
Male	65+	53.6	58.2	55.0	55.0	54.8

Percentage married, age 60+				Percentage living alone, age 60+ (1996)		
Total	Female	Male		Total	Female	Male
71.6	50.0	92.0		9.0	15.1	3.7

Statutory pensionable age (2006)				Percentage illiterate, age 65+		
	Female	Male		Total	Female	Male
	60	65		..	..	..

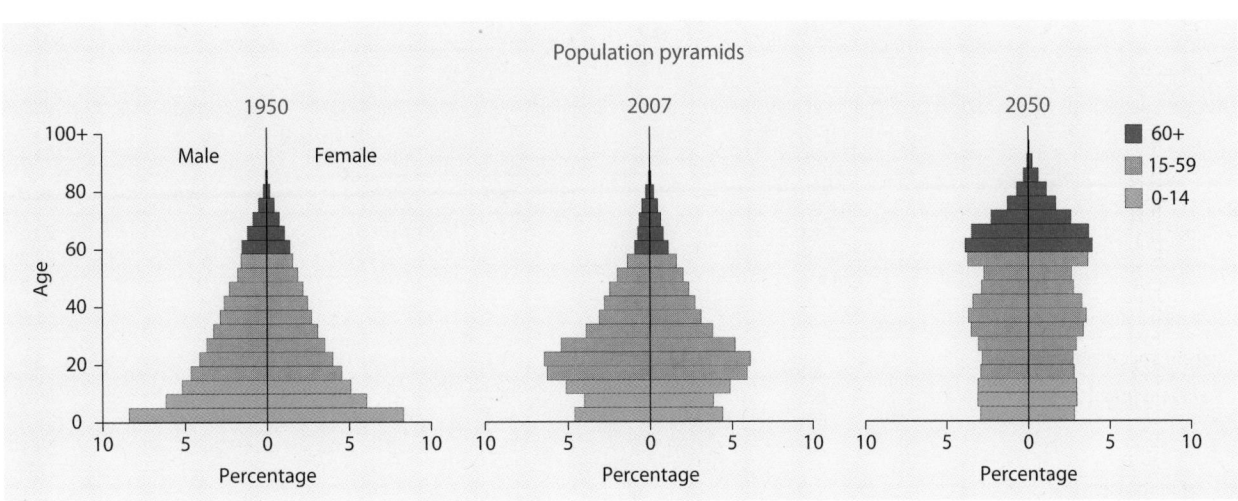

Population pyramids

1950 Male Female
2007
2050

Legend: 60+ / 15-59 / 0-14

Age / Percentage

Iraq

Indicator	Age	1950	1975	2007	2025	2050
Population (thousands)						
Total	Total	5 340.4	11 972.0	30 290.5	44 663.8	63 692.6
	0-14	2 165.0	5 734.0	12 187.1	14 561.0	15 459.3
	15-59	2 884.9	5 666.5	16 736.3	27 170.7	39 915.5
	60-64	108.6	215.2	503.4	1 163.5	2 705.7
	65-69	80.2	148.7	386.5	786.1	2 086.5
	70-74	60.6	110.4	236.4	517.7	1 595.0
	75-79	29.6	63.5	146.4	269.6	1 077.7
	80-84			68.3	143.7	572.5
	85-89			21.8	43.0	223.6
	90-94	11.4	33.8	4.0	7.6	50.2
	95-99			0.4	0.8	6.4
	100+			0.0	0.0	0.3
Female	Total	2 669.6	5 920.9	14 953.8	22 093.0	31 703.2
	0-14	1 075.4	2 807.4	5 980.4	7 124.3	7 548.1
	15-59	1 444.7	2 807.4	8 247.5	13 410.7	19 672.5
	60-64	55.5	112.3	259.9	599.5	1 382.5
	65-69	41.3	79.1	203.4	414.4	1 092.3
	70-74	30.8	59.9	127.3	280.3	863.3
	75-79	15.5	35.4	81.0	150.8	610.9
	80-84			38.8	82.7	346.1
	85-89			12.8	25.2	146.5
	90-94	6.2	19.5	2.5	4.5	35.8
	95-99			0.2	0.5	4.9
	100+			0.0	0.0	0.3
Male	Total	2 670.8	6 051.1	15 336.7	22 570.8	31 989.4
	0-14	1 089.6	2 926.6	6 206.7	7 436.7	7 911.3
	15-59	1 440.2	2 859.1	8 488.8	13 760.0	20 243.0
	60-64	53.0	102.9	243.5	564.1	1 323.2
	65-69	38.9	69.5	183.1	371.7	994.2
	70-74	29.8	50.5	109.1	237.3	731.7
	75-79	14.2	28.1	65.4	118.7	466.7
	80-84			29.5	61.1	226.5
	85-89			9.0	17.8	77.1
	90-94	5.2	14.3	1.6	3.1	14.3
	95-99			0.1	0.3	1.4
	100+			0.0	0.0	0.1
Percentage in older ages						
Total	60+	5.4	4.8	4.5	6.6	13.1
	65+	3.4	3.0	2.9	4.0	8.8
	80+	0.2	0.3	0.3	0.4	1.3
Female	60+	5.6	5.2	4.9	7.1	14.1
	65+	3.5	3.3	3.1	4.3	9.8
	80+	0.2	0.3	0.4	0.5	1.7
Male	60+	5.3	4.4	4.2	6.1	12.0
	65+	3.3	2.7	2.6	3.6	7.9
	80+	0.2	0.2	0.3	0.4	1.0
Ageing index		13.4	10.0	11.2	20.1	53.8
Broad age groups (percentage)	0-14	40.5	47.9	40.2	32.6	24.3
	15-59	54.0	47.3	55.3	60.8	62.7
	60+	5.4	4.8	4.5	6.6	13.1
Median age (years)		20.1	16.0	19.1*	24.0	31.2
Dependency ratio	Total	78.4	103.5	75.7	57.6	49.4
	Youth	72.3	97.5	70.7	51.4	36.3
	Old Age	6.1	6.1	5.0	6.2	13.2
Potential support ratio		16.5	16.5	20.0	16.0	7.6
Parent support ratio		0.8	1.1	1.3	1.1	2.9
Sex ratio (per 100 women)	60+	94.4	86.7	88.3	88.2	85.6
	65+	93.8	83.8	85.4	84.5	81.0
	80+	83.4	73.7	74.0	72.9	59.9

* *Estimate refers to year 2005.*

Indicator	Age	1950-1955	1975-1980	2005-2010	2025-2030	2045-2050
Growth rate (percentage)	Total	3.2	3.3	2.4	1.8	1.1
	60+	1.9	3.6	2.4	4.9	3.6
	65+	1.7	3.2	3.5	5.5	3.6
	80+	7.3	5.1	2.9	3.4	5.9
Total fertility rate (per woman)		7.3	6.8	4.2	2.8	2.2
Life expectancy (years)						
Total	Birth	45.3	60.3	61.0	72.1	76.0
	60	..	..	15.9	18.1	20.0
	65	..	..	12.5	14.4	16.0
	80	..	..	5.2	5.8	6.8
Female	Birth	46.2	61.4	62.5	74.3	78.3
	60	..	..	16.6	19.3	21.7
	65	..	..	13.0	15.2	17.5
	80	..	..	5.3	6.0	7.4
Male	Birth	44.5	59.4	59.5	70.0	73.8
	60	..	..	15.1	17.0	18.2
	65	..	..	12.0	13.5	14.5
	80	..	..	5.0	5.6	6.0
Survival rate (percentage)						
Total	60	..	..	68.2	84.8	89.8
	65	..	..	60.6	78.4	84.6
	80	..	..	22.3	37.2	46.9
Female	60	..	..	71.3	88.3	92.2
	65	..	..	64.5	83.4	88.5
	80	..	..	25.5	43.4	55.4
Male	60	..	..	65.3	81.6	87.5
	65	..	..	56.9	73.7	80.7
	80	..	..	19.2	31.2	38.8

		1980	1990	2007	2010	2020
Labour force participation (percentage)						
Total	65+	22.1	22.3	22.5	22.5	22.4
Female	65+	2.2	3.5	1.7	1.7	1.6
Male	65+	46.0	44.9	46.8	46.8	46.9

Percentage married, age 60+				Percentage living alone, age 60+		
Total	Female	Male		Total	Female	Male
68.2	50.0	89.0		..	..	..

Statutory pensionable age (2006)				Percentage illiterate, age 65+ (2000)		
	Female	Male		Total	Female	Male
	55	60		81.4	93.2	69.0

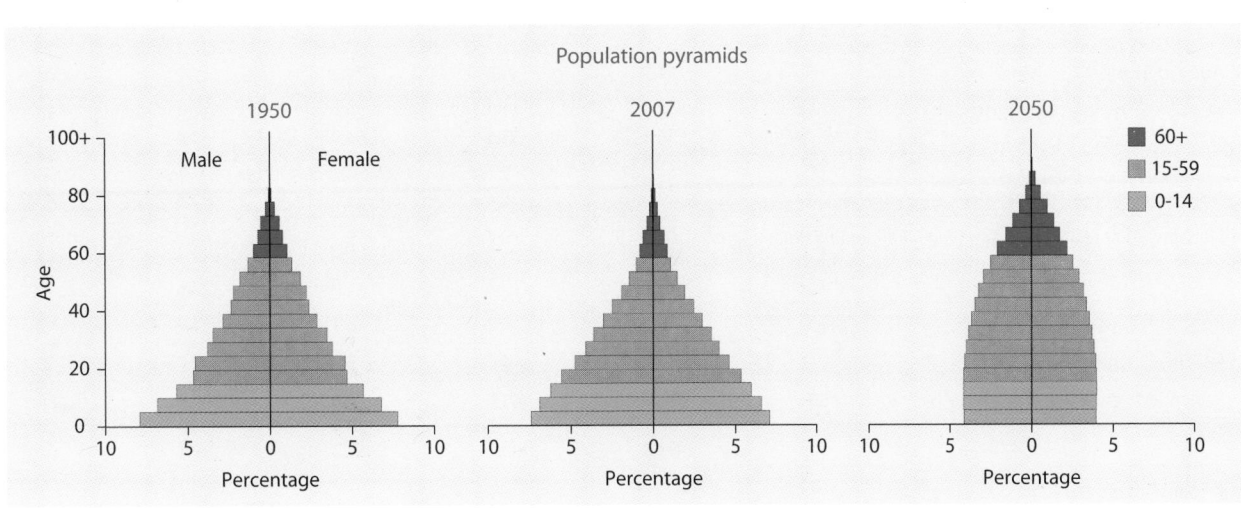

Population pyramids

Ireland

Indicator	Age	1950	1975	2007	2025	2050
Population (thousands)						
Total	Total	2 969.0	3 177.3	4 266.6	5 081.6	5 762.1
	0-14	858.0	991.9	857.8	883.3	890.8
	15-59	1 672.0	1 693.4	2 748.7	3 119.2	3 012.6
	60-64	122.0	142.3	193.0	298.9	365.6
	65-69	108.0	120.7	145.1	249.5	384.2
	70-74	100.0	99.6	117.8	199.9	355.9
	75-79	65.0	69.0	91.9	161.1	312.7
	80-84			63.6	92.4	222.5
	85-89			33.1	49.0	129.0
	90-94	44.0	60.4	12.7	21.0	62.6
	95-99			2.7	6.3	21.5
	100+			0.3	1.0	4.6
Female	Total	1 458.0	1 586.6	2 143.1	2 552.6	2 917.1
	0-14	420.0	484.9	418.0	429.5	433.1
	15-59	815.0	836.8	1 367.5	1 546.0	1 485.1
	60-64	61.0	71.7	95.7	151.0	181.8
	65-69	54.0	62.6	73.2	126.9	193.0
	70-74	51.0	53.8	61.8	104.9	185.8
	75-79	33.0	39.8	52.3	87.5	168.0
	80-84			40.0	54.1	126.7
	85-89			22.6	31.4	80.4
	90-94	24.0	36.9	9.4	15.1	42.9
	95-99			2.2	5.1	16.5
	100+			0.2	0.9	3.9
Male	Total	1 511.0	1 590.7	2 123.5	2 529.0	2 845.0
	0-14	438.0	506.9	439.8	453.8	457.8
	15-59	857.0	856.6	1 381.2	1 573.2	1 527.5
	60-64	61.0	70.7	97.2	147.9	183.8
	65-69	54.0	58.1	71.8	122.5	191.3
	70-74	49.0	45.8	55.9	95.1	170.1
	75-79	32.0	29.1	39.6	73.6	144.7
	80-84			23.6	38.3	95.9
	85-89			10.5	17.6	48.6
	90-94	20.0	23.5	3.3	5.9	19.7
	95-99			0.5	1.2	5.0
	100+			0.0	0.1	0.7
Percentage in older ages						
Total	60+	14.8	15.5	15.5	21.2	32.3
	65+	10.7	11.0	10.9	15.4	25.9
	80+	1.5	1.9	2.6	3.3	7.6
Female	60+	15.3	16.7	16.7	22.6	34.2
	65+	11.1	12.2	12.2	16.7	28.0
	80+	1.6	2.3	3.5	4.2	9.3
Male	60+	14.3	14.3	14.2	19.9	30.2
	65+	10.3	9.8	9.7	14.0	23.8
	80+	1.3	1.5	1.8	2.5	6.0
Ageing index		51.2	49.6	77.0	122.2	208.6
Broad age groups (percentage)	0-14	28.9	31.2	20.1	17.4	15.5
	15-59	56.3	53.3	64.4	61.4	52.3
	60+	14.8	15.5	15.5	21.2	32.3
Median age (years)		29.6	26.4	34.2*	41.6	45.8
Dependency ratio	Total	65.5	73.1	45.0	48.7	70.6
	Youth	47.8	54.0	29.2	25.8	26.4
	Old Age	17.7	19.0	15.9	22.8	44.2
Potential support ratio		5.7	5.2	6.3	4.4	2.3
Parent support ratio		3.7	4.6	7.2	7.2	20.4
Sex ratio (per 100 women)	60+	96.9	85.8	84.6	87.0	86.1
	65+	95.7	81.0	78.4	83.2	82.7
	80+	83.3	63.7	51.0	59.1	62.8

* *Estimate refers to year 2005.*

Indicator	Age	1950-1955	1975-1980	2005-2010	2025-2030	2045-2050
Growth rate (percentage)	Total	–0.3	1.4	1.3	0.6	0.3
	60+	–0.2	0.5	2.9	3.1	0.9
	65+	0.0	0.9	1.9	2.9	1.7
	80+	1.7	0.8	1.9	5.0	3.9
Total fertility rate (per woman)		3.4	3.5	1.9	1.9	1.9
Life expectancy (years)						
Total	Birth	66.9	72.0	78.5	81.1	83.5
	60	..	..	21.4	23.4	25.2
	65	..	..	17.4	19.2	20.9
	80	..	..	8.0	9.1	10.2
Female	Birth	68.2	74.6	81.1	83.7	86.1
	60	..	..	23.5	25.6	27.6
	65	..	..	19.3	21.3	23.1
	80	..	..	8.8	10.1	11.4
Male	Birth	65.7	69.6	75.9	78.6	81.0
	60	..	..	19.3	21.2	22.9
	65	..	..	15.4	17.1	18.7
	80	..	..	6.8	7.8	8.7
Survival rate (percentage)						
Total	60	..	..	92.1	94.2	95.7
	65	..	..	87.4	90.6	92.8
	80	..	..	53.1	61.4	68.2
Female	60	..	..	93.9	95.5	96.6
	65	..	..	90.6	92.9	94.6
	80	..	..	62.7	70.3	76.2
Male	60	..	..	90.2	92.9	94.7
	65	..	..	84.4	88.2	91.0
	80	..	..	43.8	52.6	60.2

		1980	1990	2007	2010	2020
Labour force participation (percentage)						
Total	65+	13.6	9.0	7.7	7.6	7.3
Female	65+	4.9	3.4	3.1	3.2	3.5
Male	65+	24.3	16.4	13.6	13.2	11.9

Percentage married, age 60+			Percentage living alone, age 60+ (1994)		
Total	Female	Male	Total	Female	Male
53.9	44.0	66.0	26.4	30.4	21.4

Statutory pensionable age (2006)			Percentage illiterate, age 65+		
	Female	Male	Total	Female	Male
	66	66	..	..	..

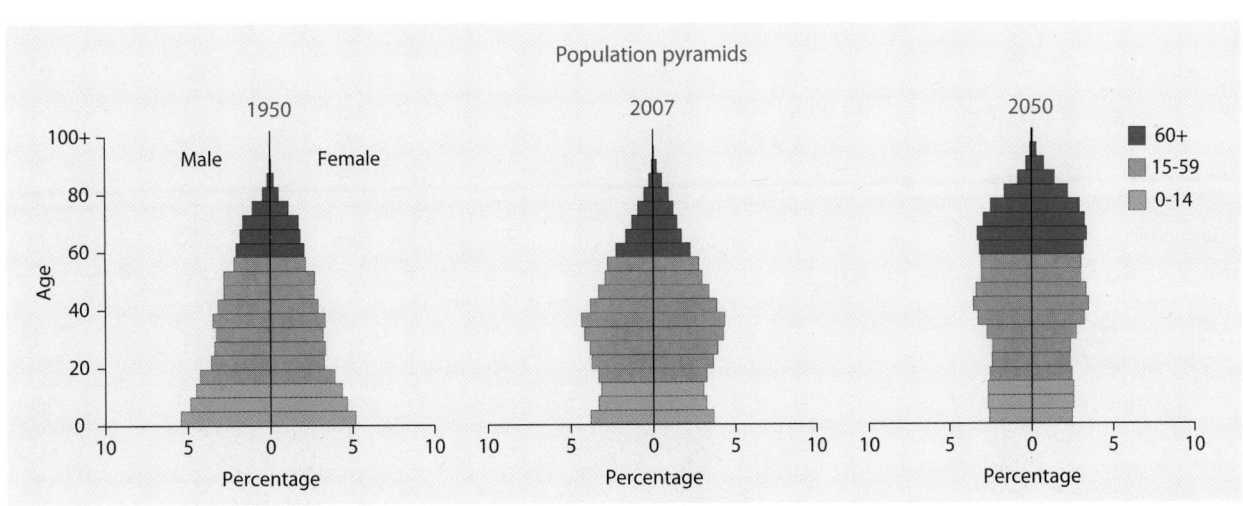

Population pyramids

Israel

Indicator	Age	1950	1975	2007	2025	2050
Population (thousands)						
Total	Total	1 258.0	3 358.3	6 967.4	8 734.2	10 403.3
	0-14	398.2	1 102.9	1 921.9	1 986.9	1 887.5
	15-59	781.1	1 859.2	4 089.6	5 150.2	5 954.5
	60-64	29.2	134.7	250.8	379.1	546.7
	65-69	21.2	110.2	196.5	355.2	514.0
	70-74	16.1	74.2	177.7	321.6	473.0
	75-79	8.3	45.1	145.6	258.1	399.6
	80-84			113.4	140.0	285.3
	85-89			53.6	91.8	192.2
	90-94	3.9	31.9	15.7	39.2	104.6
	95-99			2.4	10.9	38.9
	100+			0.1	1.2	7.0
Female	Total	611.2	1 675.8	3 517.5	4 371.2	5 178.0
	0-14	192.9	536.1	933.8	964.8	916.5
	15-59	377.0	935.3	2 046.1	2 532.8	2 908.3
	60-64	15.2	70.2	131.4	196.7	272.7
	65-69	11.3	55.4	106.0	188.2	258.2
	70-74	8.4	37.6	100.0	173.5	241.0
	75-79	4.4	24.0	85.9	143.1	210.9
	80-84			69.1	80.3	158.1
	85-89			33.2	56.3	112.6
	90-94	2.1	17.2	10.3	26.3	66.7
	95-99			1.7	8.1	27.5
	100+			0.1	1.0	5.6
Male	Total	646.8	1 682.5	3 449.9	4 363.0	5 225.3
	0-14	205.3	566.9	988.1	1 022.1	971.0
	15-59	404.1	924.0	2 043.5	2 617.4	3 046.1
	60-64	14.0	64.5	119.3	182.4	274.0
	65-69	9.9	54.8	90.6	167.0	255.8
	70-74	7.7	36.5	77.7	148.1	232.0
	75-79	3.9	21.1	59.6	115.0	188.8
	80-84			44.3	59.6	127.3
	85-89			20.4	35.5	79.6
	90-94	1.8	14.7	5.5	13.0	37.9
	95-99			0.8	2.8	11.4
	100+			0.0	0.2	1.4
Percentage in older ages						
Total	60+	6.3	11.8	13.7	18.3	24.6
	65+	3.9	7.8	10.1	13.9	19.4
	80+	0.3	0.9	2.7	3.2	6.0
Female	60+	6.8	12.2	15.3	20.0	26.1
	65+	4.3	8.0	11.5	15.5	20.9
	80+	0.3	1.0	3.2	3.9	7.2
Male	60+	5.8	11.4	12.1	16.6	23.1
	65+	3.6	7.6	8.7	12.4	17.9
	80+	0.3	0.9	2.1	2.5	4.9
Ageing index		19.8	35.9	49.7	80.4	135.7
Broad age groups (percentage)	0-14	31.7	32.8	27.6	22.7	18.1
	15-59	62.1	55.4	58.7	59.0	57.2
	60+	6.3	11.8	13.7	18.3	24.6
Median age (years)		25.5	24.0	28.9*	33.2	39.7
Dependency ratio	Total	55.3	68.4	60.5	58.0	60.0
	Youth	49.1	55.3	44.3	35.9	29.0
	Old Age	6.1	13.1	16.2	22.0	31.0
Potential support ratio		16.4	7.6	6.2	4.5	3.2
Parent support ratio		1.1	2.6	7.4	11.1	19.4
Sex ratio (per 100 women)	60+	90.2	93.8	77.8	82.8	89.3
	65+	89.0	94.7	73.6	80.0	86.5
	80+	83.2	85.3	62.1	64.6	69.5

* *Estimate refers to year 2005.*

Indicator	Age	1950-1955	1975-1980	2005-2010	2025-2030	2045-2050
Growth rate (percentage)	Total	6.6	2.3	1.7	0.9	0.5
	60+	9.1	2.2	3.7	2.0	1.5
	65+	10.0	4.3	1.9	2.1	1.7
	80+	11.2	7.7	3.9	5.4	1.8
Total fertility rate (per woman)		4.2	3.4	2.7	2.1	1.9
Life expectancy (years)						
Total	Birth	65.4	73.1	80.6	82.7	84.6
	60	..	..	23.4	25.0	26.4
	65	..	..	19.2	20.7	22.0
	80	..	..	8.6	9.7	10.7
Female	Birth	66.4	74.9	82.6	84.6	86.5
	60	..	..	24.6	26.3	28.0
	65	..	..	20.3	21.9	23.4
	80	..	..	9.0	10.3	11.5
Male	Birth	64.4	71.4	78.4	80.8	82.6
	60	..	..	21.9	23.5	24.9
	65	..	..	17.8	19.3	20.6
	80	..	..	8.0	8.9	9.7
Survival rate (percentage)						
Total	60	..	..	93.1	94.6	95.7
	65	..	..	89.6	91.8	93.3
	80	..	..	62.6	68.4	72.9
Female	60	..	..	95.0	96.1	96.8
	65	..	..	92.4	93.9	95.0
	80	..	..	69.0	74.1	78.2
Male	60	..	..	91.1	93.2	94.5
	65	..	..	86.7	89.7	91.7
	80	..	..	55.4	62.4	67.6

		1980	1990	2007	2010	2020
Labour force participation (percentage)						
Total	65+	16.6	12.6	8.0	7.5	6.3
Female	65+	6.6	6.4	4.4	4.3	4.2
Male	65+	27.9	20.2	12.8	11.8	9.0

Percentage married, age 60+			Percentage living alone, age 60+ (1995)		
Total	Female	Male	Total	Female	Male
61.2	46.0	81.0	24.0	33.7	11.8

Statutory pensionable age (2006)		Percentage illiterate, age 65+ (2004)		
Female	Male	Total	Female	Male
60	65	11.6	15.4	6.5

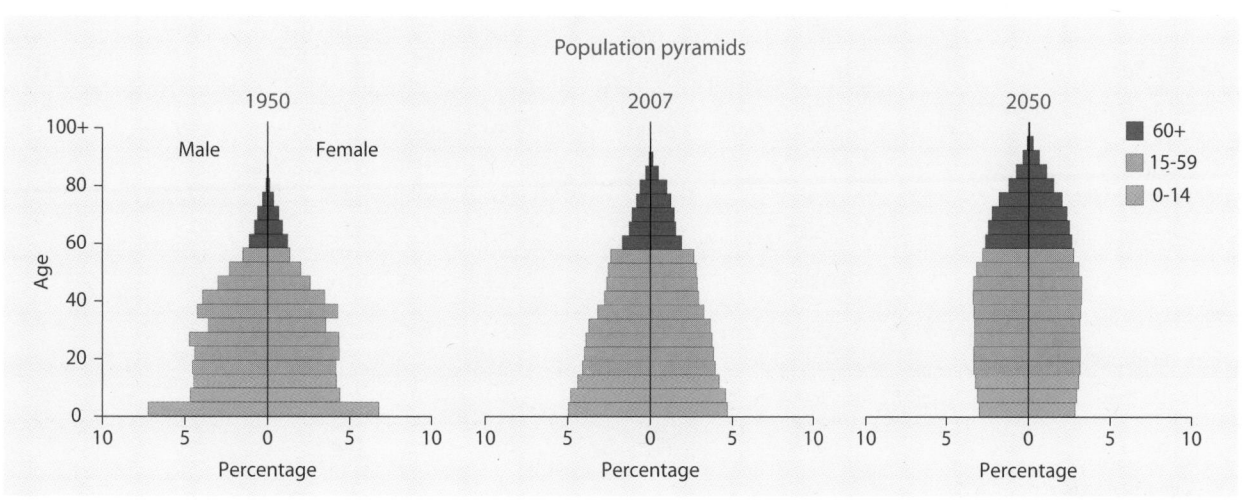

Population pyramids

United Nations Department of Economic and Social Affairs, Population Division

Italy

Indicator	Age	1950	1975	2007	2025	2050
Population (thousands)						
Total	Total	47 104.0	55 441.0	58 173.4	56 306.8	50 911.9
	0-14	12 397.2	13 436.7	8 089.2	6 707.4	6 683.9
	15-59	28 942.8	32 355.3	34 726.9	30 248.7	23 177.0
	60-64	1 874.3	2 970.8	3 469.4	4 509.2	2 960.8
	65-69	1 529.9	2 520.6	3 226.6	3 808.0	3 096.8
	70-74	1 119.0	1 868.1	2 970.3	3 303.3	3 457.0
	75-79	731.2	1 221.3	2 447.0	3 024.4	3 779.9
	80-84			1 880.7	2 103.6	3 344.5
	85-89			858.4	1 514.3	2 413.7
	90-94	509.6	1 068.2	381.6	770.0	1 300.7
	95-99			112.5	269.5	540.8
	100+			10.7	48.4	156.8
Female	Total	24 170.0	28 369.0	29 935.5	28 935.7	26 206.0
	0-14	6 068.2	6 554.7	3 924.7	3 252.7	3 241.3
	15-59	14 927.2	16 336.5	17 267.6	14 897.9	11 305.2
	60-64	1 040.4	1 582.7	1 793.9	2 299.5	1 476.7
	65-69	842.0	1 379.1	1 714.6	1 979.5	1 567.6
	70-74	604.3	1 071.5	1 644.2	1 770.3	1 790.4
	75-79	397.8	750.2	1 431.6	1 691.4	2 027.8
	80-84			1 189.2	1 255.1	1 896.8
	85-89			589.8	982.3	1 479.2
	90-94	290.1	694.4	281.6	551.2	878.6
	95-99			89.1	213.5	409.0
	100+			9.0	42.2	133.4
Male	Total	22 934.0	27 072.0	28 237.9	27 371.1	24 705.9
	0-14	6 329.0	6 882.1	4 164.5	3 454.6	3 442.6
	15-59	14 015.6	16 018.8	17 459.3	15 350.8	11 871.8
	60-64	833.9	1 388.1	1 675.5	2 209.7	1 484.1
	65-69	687.9	1 141.5	1 511.9	1 828.5	1 529.2
	70-74	514.7	796.6	1 326.1	1 533.0	1 666.6
	75-79	333.4	471.1	1 015.4	1 333.0	1 752.2
	80-84			691.5	848.5	1 447.8
	85-89			268.6	532.0	934.4
	90-94	219.6	373.9	100.0	218.8	422.1
	95-99			23.4	56.0	131.8
	100+			1.7	6.2	23.3
Percentage in older ages						
Total	60+	12.2	17.4	26.4	34.4	41.3
	65+	8.3	12.0	20.4	26.4	35.5
	80+	1.1	1.9	5.6	8.4	15.2
Female	60+	13.1	19.3	29.2	37.3	44.5
	65+	8.8	13.7	23.2	29.3	38.9
	80+	1.2	2.4	7.2	10.5	18.3
Male	60+	11.3	15.4	23.4	31.3	38.0
	65+	7.7	10.3	17.5	23.2	32.0
	80+	1.0	1.4	3.8	6.1	12.0
Ageing index		46.5	71.8	189.8	288.5	315.0
Broad age groups (percentage)	0-14	26.3	24.2	13.9	11.9	13.1
	15-59	61.4	58.4	59.7	53.7	45.5
	60+	12.2	17.4	26.4	34.4	41.3
Median age (years)		29.0	33.4	42.3*	50.5	52.5
Dependency ratio	Total	52.8	56.9	52.3	62.0	94.8
	Youth	40.2	38.0	21.2	19.3	25.6
	Old Age	12.6	18.9	31.1	42.7	69.2
Potential support ratio		7.9	5.3	3.2	2.3	1.4
Parent support ratio		2.8	4.3	12.2	18.9	50.0
Sex ratio (per 100 women)	60+	81.6	76.1	75.6	79.4	80.5
	65+	82.3	71.4	71.1	74.9	77.7
	80+	75.7	53.8	50.3	54.6	61.7

* *Estimate refers to year 2005.*

Indicator	Age	1950-1955	1975-1980	2005-2010	2025-2030	2045-2050
Growth rate (percentage)	Total	0.6	0.4	0.0	–0.3	–0.5
	60+	1.3	–0.1	1.6	1.5	–0.7
	65+	1.6	2.1	1.2	1.7	–0.6
	80+	2.4	3.0	3.6	2.2	2.2
Total fertility rate (per woman)		2.3	1.9	1.4	1.6	1.8
Life expectancy (years)						
Total	Birth	66.1	73.7	80.6	83.0	85.1
	60	..	..	23.5	25.2	27.0
	65	..	..	19.3	21.0	22.6
	80	..	..	9.0	10.1	11.3
Female	Birth	67.8	76.9	83.6	85.9	88.1
	60	..	..	25.7	27.6	29.4
	65	..	..	21.3	23.1	24.8
	80	..	..	9.9	11.3	12.6
Male	Birth	64.3	70.4	77.5	79.9	82.2
	60	..	..	21.0	22.8	24.5
	65	..	..	17.1	18.7	20.2
	80	..	..	7.7	8.6	9.6
Survival rate (percentage)						
Total	60	..	..	92.8	94.5	95.8
	65	..	..	89.1	91.6	93.4
	80	..	..	61.4	67.8	73.4
Female	60	..	..	95.1	96.4	97.3
	65	..	..	92.7	94.4	95.7
	80	..	..	71.3	76.7	81.2
Male	60	..	..	90.4	92.7	94.3
	65	..	..	85.5	88.8	91.2
	80	..	..	51.0	58.7	65.5

		1980	1990	2007	2010	2020
Labour force participation (percentage)						
Total	65+	5.8	3.3	3.1	3.0	2.6
Female	65+	3.5	2.1	1.5	1.5	1.5
Male	65+	9.0	5.1	5.4	5.0	4.0

Percentage married, age 60+			Percentage living alone, age 60+ (1994)		
Total	Female	Male	Total	Female	Male
61.5	47.0	81.0	22.6	31.9	10.0

Statutory pensionable age (2006)			Percentage illiterate, age 65+ (2001)		
	Female	Male	Total	Female	Male
	60	65	4.9	5.8	3.7

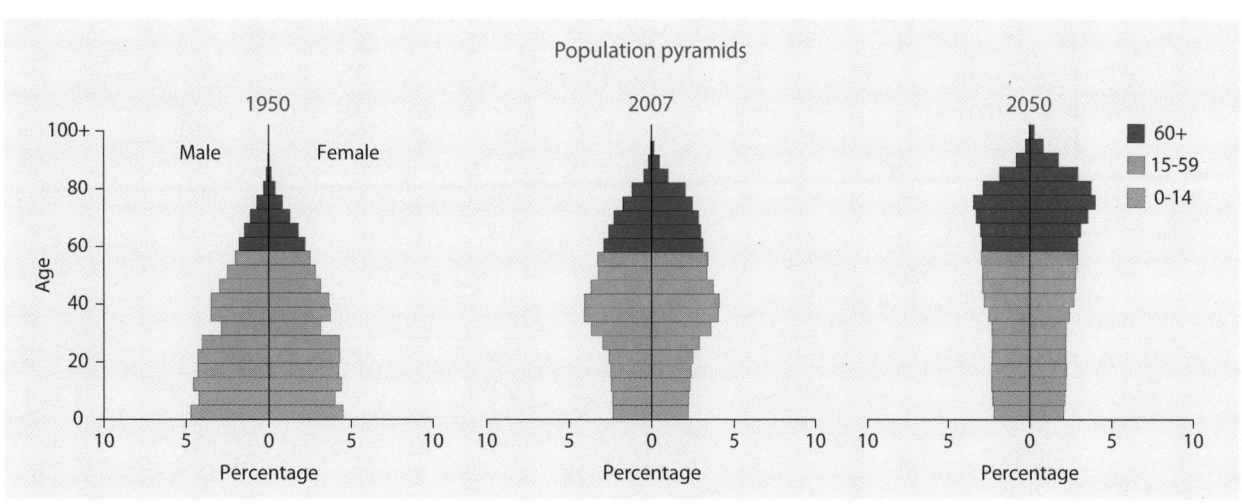

Population pyramids

1950 2007 2050

Male Female

60+ 15-59 0-14

Age Percentage

Jamaica

Indicator	Age	1950	1975	2007	2025	2050
Population (thousands)						
Total	Total	1 402.9	2 012.8	2 672.5	2 803.8	2 585.8
	0-14	505.5	910.4	807.9	684.5	478.2
	15-59	815.9	931.3	1 588.4	1 699.6	1 497.4
	60-64	27.4	54.3	73.0	129.9	153.0
	65-69	24.3	47.0	56.6	106.4	127.6
	70-74	17.6	33.0	49.9	69.2	94.1
	75-79	8.7	20.0	44.2	50.0	91.3
	80-84			27.9	33.2	73.2
	85-89			14.9	17.6	45.0
	90-94	3.5	16.7	7.0	9.6	19.9
	95-99			2.2	3.2	5.1
	100+			0.4	0.6	1.0
Female	Total	720.4	1 028.6	1 351.5	1 412.8	1 297.2
	0-14	252.2	451.5	394.3	334.1	233.2
	15-59	420.9	485.0	812.1	851.5	727.7
	60-64	15.3	27.8	35.9	71.8	77.8
	65-69	13.7	24.9	28.6	56.1	66.5
	70-74	10.6	17.6	27.5	35.9	51.9
	75-79	5.4	11.1	23.9	26.5	51.3
	80-84			14.6	17.8	43.5
	85-89			8.5	10.4	28.4
	90-94	2.3	10.7	4.4	6.2	12.8
	95-99			1.5	2.1	3.5
	100+			0.3	0.4	0.8
Male	Total	682.5	984.2	1 321.0	1 391.0	1 288.6
	0-14	253.3	459.0	413.5	350.4	245.0
	15-59	395.0	446.3	776.3	848.0	769.7
	60-64	12.1	26.6	37.2	58.1	75.2
	65-69	10.6	22.1	28.0	50.3	61.1
	70-74	7.0	15.4	22.4	33.3	42.2
	75-79	3.3	8.9	20.3	23.5	40.0
	80-84			13.4	15.4	29.7
	85-89			6.4	7.2	16.6
	90-94	1.2	6.0	2.6	3.4	7.1
	95-99			0.7	1.1	1.6
	100+			0.1	0.2	0.3
Percentage in older ages						
Total	60+	5.8	8.5	10.3	15.0	23.6
	65+	3.9	5.8	7.6	10.3	17.7
	80+	0.2	0.8	2.0	2.3	5.6
Female	60+	6.6	9.0	10.7	16.1	25.9
	65+	4.4	6.3	8.1	11.0	19.9
	80+	0.3	1.0	2.2	2.6	6.9
Male	60+	5.0	8.0	9.9	13.8	21.3
	65+	3.2	5.3	7.1	9.7	15.4
	80+	0.2	0.6	1.8	2.0	4.3
Ageing index		16.1	18.8	34.2	61.3	127.6
Broad age groups (percentage)	0-14	36.0	45.2	30.2	24.4	18.5
	15-59	58.2	46.3	59.4	60.6	57.9
	60+	5.8	8.5	10.3	15.0	23.6
Median age (years)		22.2	17.0	24.9*	30.7	39.3
Dependency ratio	Total	66.4	104.2	60.9	53.3	56.7
	Youth	59.9	92.4	48.6	37.4	29.0
	Old Age	6.4	11.8	12.2	15.8	27.7
Potential support ratio		15.6	8.4	8.2	6.3	3.6
Parent support ratio		1.1	3.0	9.1	7.4	14.1
Sex ratio (per 100 women)	60+	72.3	85.8	90.4	84.7	81.4
	65+	69.1	81.6	86.1	86.5	76.8
	80+	52.1	56.1	79.6	73.9	62.3

* Estimate refers to year 2005.

Indicator	Age	1950-1955	1975-1980	2005-2010	2025-2030	2045-2050
Growth rate (percentage)	Total	1.9	1.2	0.4	0.0	−0.6
	60+	3.4	3.0	1.2	2.6	1.3
	65+	3.2	4.1	1.0	3.3	1.0
	80+	12.4	12.4	2.7	2.0	2.7
Total fertility rate (per woman)		4.2	4.0	2.3	2.0	1.9
Life expectancy (years)						
Total	Birth	55.8	70.1	71.1	75.0	77.7
	60	..	..	21.0	21.9	22.9
	65	..	..	17.4	18.1	18.9
	80	..	..	8.4	8.7	9.2
Female	Birth	60.2	71.8	72.7	76.7	79.5
	60	..	..	21.9	23.0	24.1
	65	..	..	18.2	19.1	20.1
	80	..	..	8.9	9.3	9.8
Male	Birth	56.9	68.4	69.4	73.2	75.8
	60	..	..	20.0	20.7	21.5
	65	..	..	16.4	17.0	17.6
	80	..	..	7.9	8.0	8.3
Survival rate (percentage)						
Total	60	..	..	76.6	83.4	87.5
	65	..	..	71.1	78.4	83.0
	80	..	..	42.3	49.2	54.9
Female	60	..	..	78.6	85.2	89.2
	65	..	..	73.5	80.7	85.2
	80	..	..	46.5	54.0	60.0
Male	60	..	..	74.5	81.5	85.9
	65	..	..	68.7	76.0	80.8
	80	..	..	38.1	44.3	49.5

		1980	1990	2007	2010	2020
Labour force participation (percentage)						
Total	65+	46.4	37.1	26.6	26.0	25.1
Female	65+	30.4	23.6	13.8	13.1	12.3
Male	65+	65.3	53.6	41.4	40.7	39.6

Percentage married, age 60+			Percentage living alone, age 60+		
Total	Female	Male	Total	Female	Male
46.8	36.0	59.0	..	..	..

Statutory pensionable age (2006)			Percentage illiterate, age 65+		
Female	Male		Total	Female	Male
60	65		..	..	..

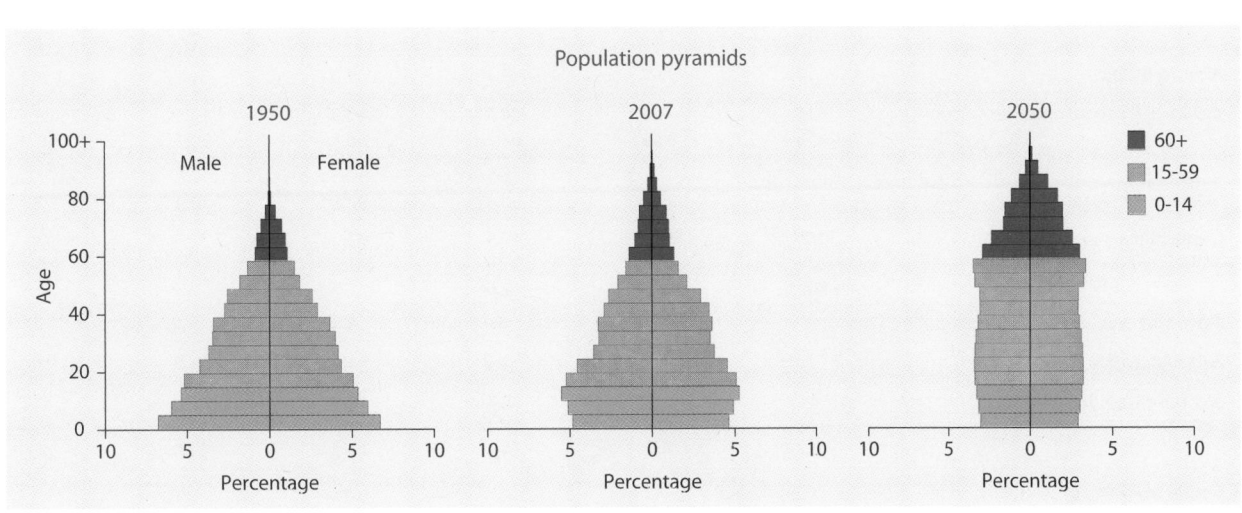

Population pyramids

United Nations Department of Economic and Social Affairs, Population Division

309

Japan

Indicator	Age	1950	1975	2007	2025	2050
Population (thousands)						
Total	Total	83 625.0	111 524.0	128 325.5	124 818.8	112 197.6
	0-14	29 643.0	27 109.0	17 818.7	15 569.3	15 068.0
	15-59	47 545.0	71 367.0	74 684.1	65 256.5	50 382.0
	60-64	2 302.0	4 258.0	9 211.8	7 707.1	6 478.7
	65-69	1 779.0	3 427.0	7 525.9	7 127.2	7 160.2
	70-74	1 290.0	2 555.0	6 677.5	7 695.5	7 750.3
	75-79	690.0	1 622.0	5 510.0	8 183.4	8 198.9
	80-84			3 693.2	5 812.6	6 341.1
	85-89			1 999.5	3 921.7	4 679.7
	90-94	376.0	1 186.0	904.5	2 341.4	3 136.3
	95-99			263.7	967.8	2 005.3
	100+			36.7	236.1	997.2
Female	Total	42 622.0	56 644.0	65 681.9	64 534.8	58 364.6
	0-14	14 591.0	13 217.0	8 675.3	7 577.5	7 334.5
	15-59	24 438.0	36 115.0	36 919.0	32 113.4	24 681.7
	60-64	1 195.0	2 330.0	4 722.2	3 902.8	3 235.8
	65-69	980.0	1 864.0	3 952.0	3 675.9	3 623.6
	70-74	747.0	1 415.0	3 620.5	4 079.4	3 996.4
	75-79	421.0	942.0	3 124.3	4 512.5	4 392.1
	80-84			2 325.2	3 433.7	3 600.2
	85-89			1 406.9	2 535.0	2 881.7
	90-94	250.0	761.0	687.0	1 696.7	2 160.8
	95-99			217.0	791.6	1 571.4
	100+			32.6	216.3	886.4
Male	Total	41 003.0	54 880.0	62 643.6	60 284.0	53 833.0
	0-14	15 052.0	13 892.0	9 143.4	7 991.8	7 733.5
	15-59	23 107.0	35 252.0	37 765.1	33 143.1	25 700.3
	60-64	1 107.0	1 928.0	4 489.6	3 804.3	3 242.9
	65-69	799.0	1 563.0	3 574.0	3 451.3	3 536.6
	70-74	543.0	1 140.0	3 057.0	3 616.1	3 753.9
	75-79	269.0	680.0	2 385.7	3 670.9	3 806.9
	80-84			1 368.1	2 379.0	2 740.9
	85-89			592.5	1 386.7	1 798.0
	90-94	126.0	425.0	217.5	644.7	975.4
	95-99			46.6	176.3	433.9
	100+			4.1	19.9	110.8
Percentage in older ages						
Total	60+	7.7	11.7	27.9	35.2	41.7
	65+	4.9	7.9	20.7	29.1	35.9
	80+	0.4	1.1	5.4	10.6	15.3
Female	60+	8.4	12.9	30.6	38.5	45.1
	65+	5.6	8.8	23.4	32.4	39.6
	80+	0.6	1.3	7.1	13.4	19.0
Male	60+	6.9	10.5	25.1	31.8	37.9
	65+	4.2	6.9	18.0	25.5	31.9
	80+	0.3	0.8	3.6	7.6	11.3
Ageing index		21.7	48.1	201.0	282.6	310.2
Broad age groups (percentage)	0-14	35.4	24.3	13.9	12.5	13.4
	15-59	56.9	64.0	58.2	52.3	44.9
	60+	7.7	11.7	27.9	35.2	41.7
Median age (years)		22.3	30.4	42.9*	50.0	52.3
Dependency ratio	Total	67.8	47.5	53.0	71.1	97.3
	Youth	59.5	35.8	21.2	21.3	26.5
	Old Age	8.3	11.6	31.7	49.7	70.8
Potential support ratio		12.1	8.6	3.2	2.0	1.4
Parent support ratio		1.6	2.6	11.7	28.7	57.8
Sex ratio (per 100 women)	60+	79.2	78.4	78.3	77.1	77.4
	65+	72.4	76.4	73.2	73.3	74.2
	80+	50.4	55.8	47.7	53.1	54.6

*   *Estimate refers to year 2005.*

Indicator	Age	1950-1955	1975-1980	2005-2010	2025-2030	2045-2050
Growth rate (percentage)	Total	1.4	0.9	0.1	−0.4	−0.5
	60+	2.4	2.8	2.8	0.6	−0.5
	65+	2.8	3.7	2.6	0.4	−0.2
	80+	6.3	6.0	5.3	3.4	0.8
Total fertility rate (per woman)		2.8	1.8	1.4	1.7	1.9
Life expectancy (years)						
Total	Birth	63.5	75.4	82.8	86.0	88.3
	60	..	..	25.4	27.8	29.7
	65	..	..	21.2	23.4	25.2
	80	..	..	10.3	11.9	13.2
Female	Birth	65.5	78.0	86.4	90.0	92.5
	60	..	..	28.1	31.1	33.3
	65	..	..	23.6	26.5	28.5
	80	..	..	11.6	13.8	15.4
Male	Birth	61.6	72.7	79.1	81.9	84.1
	60	..	..	22.3	24.4	26.1
	65	..	..	18.3	20.2	21.7
	80	..	..	8.4	9.5	10.6
Survival rate (percentage)						
Total	60	..	..	93.7	95.8	96.9
	65	..	..	90.6	93.5	95.2
	80	..	..	67.5	75.0	80.1
Female	60	..	..	96.1	97.8	98.5
	65	..	..	94.3	96.6	97.6
	80	..	..	78.2	84.9	88.8
Male	60	..	..	91.2	93.7	95.2
	65	..	..	86.8	90.4	92.6
	80	..	..	56.6	64.8	71.0

		1980	1990	2007	2010	2020
Labour force participation (percentage)						
Total	65+	26.3	24.4	18.7	17.3	14.2
Female	65+	15.5	16.2	13.0	13.0	13.0
Male	65+	41.0	36.5	26.5	23.2	15.9

Percentage married, age 60+			Percentage living alone, age 60+ (2000)		
Total	Female	Male	Total	Female	Male
67.3	53.0	86.0	12.7	..	..

Statutory pensionable age (2006)			Percentage illiterate, age 65+		
	Female	Male	Total	Female	Male
	65	65	..	..	..

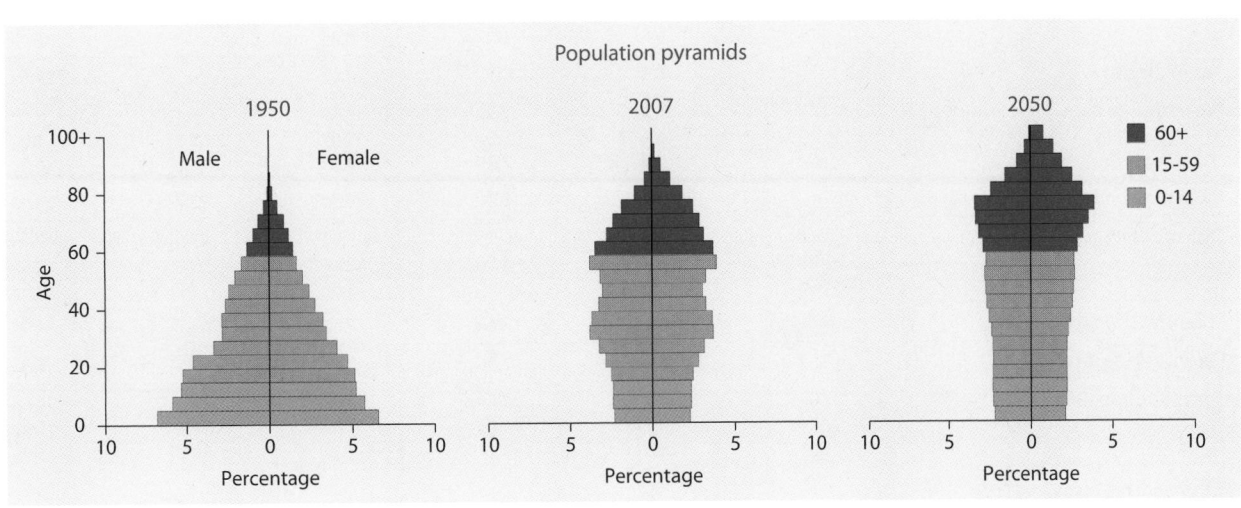

Population pyramids

Jordan

Indicator	Age	1950	1975	2007	2025	2050
Population (thousands)						
Total	Total	472.5	1 936.7	5 966.5	8 133.6	10 225.5
	0-14	216.0	914.0	2 168.5	2 200.3	1 958.8
	15-59	221.4	938.6	3 483.6	5 279.5	6 335.1
	60-64	12.2	29.1	112.2	254.7	527.3
	65-69	9.5	21.6	87.2	158.9	458.9
	70-74	7.4	16.4	59.0	100.9	374.9
	75-79	4.0	10.4	31.6	71.0	290.9
	80-84			15.8	42.9	175.7
	85-89			5.8	18.8	74.9
	90-94	2.0	6.7	2.2	5.7	22.9
	95-99			0.6	1.0	5.1
	100+			0.1	0.1	0.9
Female	Total	227.3	946.0	2 869.6	3 957.3	5 053.4
	0-14	103.0	449.2	1 058.3	1 074.9	955.5
	15-59	108.0	453.6	1 656.3	2 551.3	3 102.2
	60-64	5.6	14.9	54.8	121.8	263.4
	65-69	4.4	11.2	41.6	79.5	232.5
	70-74	3.5	8.2	29.4	52.3	191.8
	75-79	1.9	5.2	15.6	39.6	150.0
	80-84			8.7	23.1	93.5
	85-89			3.2	10.7	44.8
	90-94	0.9	3.7	1.2	3.4	15.3
	95-99			0.3	0.6	3.7
	100+			0.0	0.1	0.7
Male	Total	245.2	990.7	3 096.9	4 176.3	5 172.1
	0-14	112.9	464.8	1 110.2	1 125.4	1 003.3
	15-59	113.4	484.9	1 827.3	2 728.2	3 232.9
	60-64	6.6	14.2	57.4	132.9	263.9
	65-69	5.1	10.4	45.7	79.3	226.4
	70-74	3.9	8.2	29.6	48.6	183.1
	75-79	2.1	5.2	15.9	31.4	141.0
	80-84			7.1	19.8	82.2
	85-89			2.6	8.1	30.1
	90-94	1.1	3.0	1.0	2.3	7.6
	95-99			0.2	0.4	1.4
	100+			0.0	0.1	0.2
Percentage in older ages						
Total	60+	7.4	4.3	5.3	8.0	18.9
	65+	4.8	2.8	3.4	4.9	13.7
	80+	0.4	0.3	0.4	0.8	2.7
Female	60+	7.1	4.6	5.4	8.4	19.7
	65+	4.7	3.0	3.5	5.3	14.5
	80+	0.4	0.4	0.5	1.0	3.1
Male	60+	7.7	4.1	5.1	7.7	18.1
	65+	5.0	2.7	3.3	4.5	13.0
	80+	0.4	0.3	0.4	0.7	2.3
Ageing index		16.3	9.2	14.5	29.7	98.6
Broad age groups (percentage)	0-14	45.7	47.2	36.3	27.1	19.2
	15-59	46.9	48.5	58.4	64.9	62.0
	60+	7.4	4.3	5.3	8.0	18.9
Median age (years)		17.2	16.4	21.3*	27.7	37.0
Dependency ratio	Total	102.2	100.2	65.9	47.0	49.0
	Youth	92.4	94.5	60.3	39.8	28.5
	Old Age	9.8	5.7	5.6	7.2	20.5
Potential support ratio		10.2	17.6	17.8	13.9	4.9
Parent support ratio		1.6	2.1	2.2	2.3	5.6
Sex ratio (per 100 women)	60+	116.2	94.8	102.9	97.5	94.0
	65+	114.7	94.8	101.9	90.8	91.8
	80+	116.7	80.1	80.7	80.8	76.9

* Estimate refers to year 2005.

Indicator	Age	1950-1955	1975-1980	2005-2010	2025-2030	2045-2050
Growth rate (percentage)	Total	6.9	2.8	2.1	1.3	0.6
	60+	5.1	3.9	3.6	6.2	2.7
	65+	4.9	4.7	4.7	5.9	3.2
	80+	3.8	8.1	4.0	3.8	7.8
Total fertility rate (per woman)		7.4	7.4	3.1	2.1	1.9
Life expectancy (years)						
Total	Birth	43.2	61.1	72.5	76.3	79.0
	60	..	..	18.6	20.2	22.0
	65	..	..	15.0	16.4	18.0
	80	..	..	7.0	7.6	8.5
Female	Birth	46.5	63.0	74.2	78.3	81.1
	60	..	..	19.6	21.9	23.8
	65	..	..	15.8	17.8	19.6
	80	..	..	7.2	8.2	9.3
Male	Birth	42.2	59.4	71.0	74.5	77.1
	60	..	..	17.6	18.7	20.4
	65	..	..	14.2	15.1	16.5
	80	..	..	6.7	6.9	7.6
Survival rate (percentage)						
Total	60	..	..	83.9	89.3	92.1
	65	..	..	77.0	83.6	87.6
	80	..	..	37.6	46.9	55.0
Female	60	..	..	86.3	91.1	93.5
	65	..	..	80.4	86.7	90.0
	80	..	..	42.8	54.2	62.6
Male	60	..	..	81.8	87.7	90.8
	65	..	..	73.8	80.9	85.2
	80	..	..	33.1	40.2	48.2

		1980	1990	2007	2010	2020
Labour force participation (percentage)						
Total	65+	17.0	17.3	16.1	16.0	15.5
Female	65+	2.6	3.3	4.0	4.0	4.1
Male	65+	31.7	30.8	27.9	27.9	28.0

Percentage married, age 60+			Percentage living alone, age 60+ (1991)		
Total	Female	Male	Total	Female	Male
70.0	47.0	92.0	7.0	10.7	3.3

Statutory pensionable age (2006)			Percentage illiterate, age 65+ (2003)		
	Female	Male	Total	Female	Male
	55	60	58.5	82.5	36.7

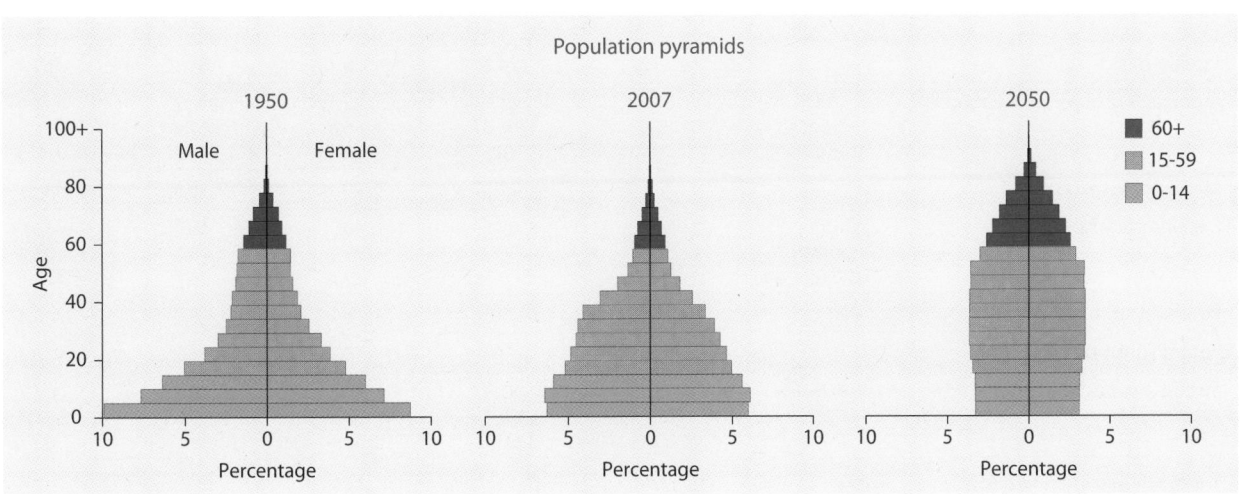

Population pyramids

Kazakhstan

Indicator	Age	1950	1975	2007	2025	2050
Population (thousands)						
Total	Total	6 703.0	14 136.0	14 802.5	14 773.6	13 085.8
	0-14	2 303.2	4 895.6	3 273.0	2 989.7	2 217.2
	15-59	3 716.8	8 033.1	9 891.0	9 246.3	7 268.8
	60-64	245.4	406.0	370.7	851.1	1 117.4
	65-69	179.6	316.4	506.1	674.0	816.5
	70-74	129.6	231.0	325.4	511.6	639.8
	75-79	76.5	129.7	240.7	224.4	465.3
	80-84			133.5	131.9	272.6
	85-89			38.0	111.3	193.0
	90-94	52.0	124.1	19.6	23.1	73.6
	95-99			4.0	9.2	19.5
	100+			0.5	0.9	2.1
Female	Total	3 459.2	7 319.8	7 723.4	7 787.5	6 935.2
	0-14	1 119.4	2 415.3	1 608.1	1 466.9	1 079.6
	15-59	1 986.6	4 109.7	5 086.6	4 739.8	3 669.7
	60-64	119.7	260.9	217.7	491.5	612.3
	65-69	90.9	207.4	303.6	406.7	467.6
	70-74	69.0	158.0	199.1	327.1	392.4
	75-79	42.9	85.9	159.4	150.0	300.4
	80-84			98.5	95.3	189.9
	85-89			30.4	83.6	145.4
	90-94	30.9	82.5	16.2	18.1	59.4
	95-99			3.4	7.7	16.7
	100+			0.4	0.8	1.8
Male	Total	3 243.8	6 816.2	7 079.1	6 986.1	6 150.6
	0-14	1 183.7	2 480.4	1 664.9	1 522.8	1 137.7
	15-59	1 730.2	3 923.4	4 804.4	4 506.5	3 599.1
	60-64	125.7	145.1	153.1	359.6	505.1
	65-69	88.7	108.9	202.5	267.3	348.9
	70-74	60.6	73.0	126.3	184.5	247.3
	75-79	33.6	43.8	81.3	74.4	164.9
	80-84			35.1	36.5	82.8
	85-89			7.6	27.7	47.6
	90-94	21.1	41.6	3.3	5.1	14.2
	95-99			0.6	1.5	2.8
	100+			0.1	0.1	0.2
Percentage in older ages						
Total	60+	10.2	8.5	11.1	17.2	27.5
	65+	6.5	5.7	8.6	11.4	19.0
	80+	0.8	0.9	1.3	1.9	4.3
Female	60+	10.2	10.9	13.3	20.3	31.5
	65+	6.8	7.3	10.5	14.0	22.7
	80+	0.9	1.1	1.9	2.6	6.0
Male	60+	10.2	6.1	8.6	13.7	23.0
	65+	6.3	3.9	6.5	8.5	14.8
	80+	0.7	0.6	0.7	1.0	2.4
Ageing index		29.7	24.7	50.1	84.9	162.4
Broad age groups (percentage)	0-14	34.4	34.6	22.1	20.2	16.9
	15-59	55.4	56.8	66.8	62.6	55.5
	60+	10.2	8.5	11.1	17.2	27.5
Median age (years)		23.2	22.3	29.4*	36.5	42.1
Dependency ratio	Total	69.2	67.5	44.2	46.3	56.0
	Youth	58.1	58.0	31.9	29.6	26.4
	Old Age	11.0	9.5	12.4	16.7	29.6
Potential support ratio		9.1	10.5	8.1	6.0	3.4
Parent support ratio		2.6	4.0	3.3	5.7	10.3
Sex ratio (per 100 women)	60+	93.4	51.9	59.3	60.5	64.7
	65+	87.4	50.1	56.3	54.8	57.7
	80+	68.5	50.4	31.4	34.5	35.7

* *Estimate refers to year 2005.*

Indicator	Age	1950-1955	1975-1980	2005-2010	2025-2030	2045-2050
Growth rate (percentage)	Total	3.5	1.1	0.0	−0.3	−0.7
	60+	1.4	0.3	−0.2	0.8	2.2
	65+	3.4	2.5	−0.8	3.1	1.4
	80+	3.9	2.7	8.0	−0.3	−0.5
Total fertility rate (per woman)		4.4	3.1	1.9	1.9	1.9
Life expectancy (years)						
Total	Birth	55.1	64.2	64.2	69.3	73.3
	60	..	..	17.2	18.7	19.9
	65	..	..	14.1	15.3	16.3
	80	..	..	6.9	7.3	7.9
Female	Birth	60.6	69.3	69.8	74.0	77.2
	60	..	..	19.3	20.8	22.2
	65	..	..	15.7	17.0	18.2
	80	..	..	7.3	7.9	8.5
Male	Birth	50.1	58.8	58.7	64.4	69.1
	60	..	..	14.4	15.8	16.9
	65	..	..	11.8	12.9	13.8
	80	..	..	5.8	6.2	6.5
Survival rate (percentage)						
Total	60	..	..	69.6	77.7	83.9
	65	..	..	61.5	70.4	77.2
	80	..	..	27.2	35.7	42.6
Female	60	..	..	79.7	85.5	89.3
	65	..	..	73.5	80.3	84.8
	80	..	..	38.8	47.4	54.3
Male	60	..	..	59.8	69.9	78.4
	65	..	..	49.8	60.3	69.5
	80	..	..	16.3	23.2	29.9

		1980	1990	2007	2010	2020
Labour force participation (percentage)						
Total	65+	4.3	4.9	14.6	14.8	15.0
Female	65+	1.9	3.1	11.8	12.2	12.4
Male	65+	9.6	9.2	19.5	19.7	19.8

Percentage married, age 60+			Percentage living alone, age 60+ (1999)		
Total	Female	Male	Total	Female	Male
53.6	37.0	80.0	15.9	21.3	7.5

Statutory pensionable age (2006)			Percentage illiterate, age 65+		
	Female	Male	Total	Female	Male
	58	63	..	..	..

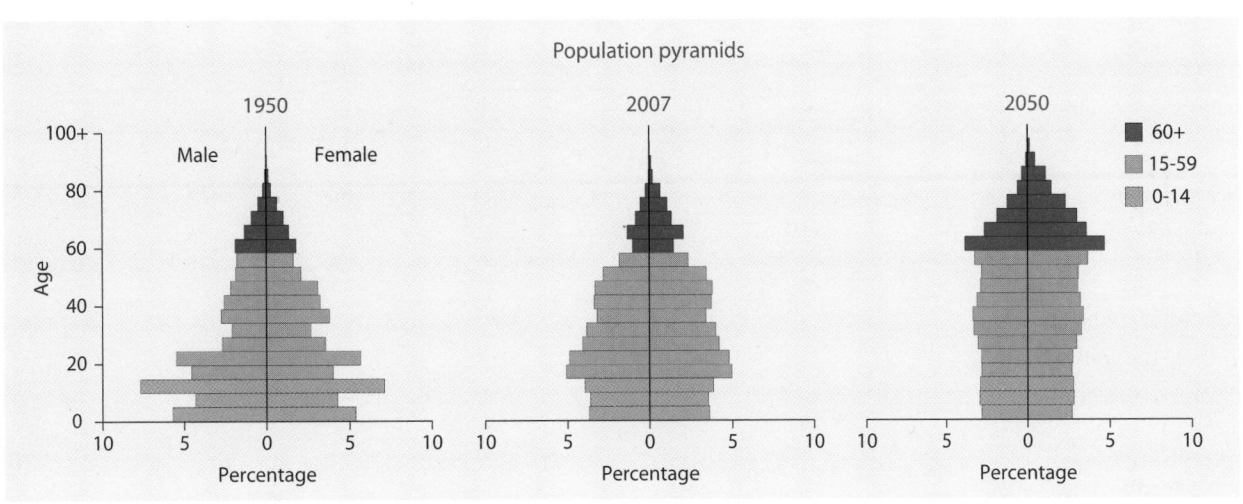

Population pyramids

Kenya

Indicator	Age	1950	1975	2007	2025	2050
Population (thousands)						
Total	Total	6 076.8	13 512.1	36 012.3	54 997.1	83 073.3
	0-14	2 416.8	6 717.5	15 410.0	20 835.1	23 282.9
	15-59	3 275.3	6 132.0	19 122.4	31 396.3	51 567.3
	60-64	146.2	228.8	485.7	936.3	3 003.7
	65-69	107.9	180.8	366.3	744.5	2 295.2
	70-74	68.7	128.5	296.2	543.9	1 473.9
	75-79	41.0	78.3	192.0	316.2	811.1
	80-84			94.4	143.3	407.5
	85-89			35.4	61.2	173.4
	90-94	21.0	46.1	8.6	17.6	49.6
	95-99			1.2	2.6	8.1
	100+			0.1	0.2	0.6
Female	Total	3 012.2	6 780.8	17 945.2	27 301.3	41 525.0
	0-14	1 205.5	3 359.2	7 656.4	10 367.2	11 573.5
	15-59	1 587.8	3 079.8	9 495.0	15 465.4	25 803.1
	60-64	78.4	111.2	256.7	472.4	1 510.5
	65-69	60.1	90.1	196.4	392.6	1 153.6
	70-74	40.1	68.7	159.8	296.5	734.0
	75-79	26.2	43.9	103.8	176.3	402.3
	80-84			51.3	82.0	213.6
	85-89			19.9	36.3	98.3
	90-94	14.2	27.9	5.1	10.9	30.3
	95-99			0.8	1.7	5.4
	100+			0.1	0.1	0.4
Male	Total	3 064.5	6 731.2	18 067.1	27 695.7	41 548.4
	0-14	1 211.2	3 358.2	7 753.6	10 467.9	11 709.4
	15-59	1 687.5	3 052.2	9 627.4	15 931.0	25 764.2
	60-64	67.8	117.6	229.0	463.9	1 493.2
	65-69	47.7	90.8	170.0	351.8	1 141.6
	70-74	28.6	59.9	136.4	247.4	739.9
	75-79	14.8	34.4	88.2	139.9	408.8
	80-84			43.1	61.3	193.9
	85-89			15.6	24.9	75.1
	90-94	6.8	18.2	3.5	6.7	19.3
	95-99			0.4	0.9	2.7
	100+			0.0	0.1	0.2
Percentage in older ages						
Total	60+	6.3	4.9	4.1	5.0	9.9
	65+	3.9	3.2	2.8	3.3	6.3
	80+	0.3	0.3	0.4	0.4	0.8
Female	60+	7.3	5.0	4.4	5.4	10.0
	65+	4.7	3.4	3.0	3.6	6.4
	80+	0.5	0.4	0.4	0.5	0.8
Male	60+	5.4	4.8	3.8	4.7	9.8
	65+	3.2	3.0	2.5	3.0	6.2
	80+	0.2	0.3	0.3	0.3	0.7
Ageing index		15.9	9.9	9.6	13.3	35.3
Broad age groups (percentage)	0-14	39.8	49.7	42.8	37.9	28.0
	15-59	53.9	45.4	53.1	57.1	62.1
	60+	6.3	4.9	4.1	5.0	9.9
Median age (years)		20.0	15.1	17.9*	20.4	27.6
Dependency ratio	Total	77.6	112.4	83.7	70.1	52.2
	Youth	70.6	105.6	78.6	64.4	42.7
	Old Age	7.0	6.8	5.1	5.7	9.6
Potential support ratio		14.3	14.7	19.7	17.7	10.5
Parent support ratio		1.1	1.5	2.1	2.3	2.3
Sex ratio (per 100 women)	60+	75.7	93.9	86.4	88.3	98.2
	65+	69.7	88.1	85.1	83.6	97.9
	80+	48.0	65.2	81.2	71.6	83.7

* Estimate refers to year 2005.

Indicator	Age	1950-1955	1975-1980	2005-2010	2025-2030	2045-2050
Growth rate (percentage)	Total	2.8	3.7	2.6	1.9	1.3
	60+	1.9	2.2	3.0	3.0	4.9
	65+	2.0	2.3	1.6	3.3	5.7
	80+	3.1	3.8	3.5	4.9	3.2
Total fertility rate (per woman)		7.5	7.6	5.0	3.2	2.4
Life expectancy (years)						
Total	Birth	42.3	56.2	50.3	63.6	69.3
	60	..	..	17.2	18.2	19.3
	65	..	..	13.9	14.7	15.5
	80	..	..	6.1	6.4	6.8
Female	Birth	44.1	58.2	49.4	65.1	71.2
	60	..	..	17.8	19.0	20.1
	65	..	..	14.4	15.3	16.2
	80	..	..	6.3	6.6	7.0
Male	Birth	40.5	54.2	51.1	62.1	67.5
	60	..	..	16.5	17.5	18.5
	65	..	..	13.3	14.0	14.9
	80	..	..	5.9	6.1	6.5
Survival rate (percentage)						
Total	60	..	..	43.3	68.1	77.3
	65	..	..	38.7	62.3	71.9
	80	..	..	17.0	30.1	37.9
Female	60	..	..	40.4	69.8	79.7
	65	..	..	36.6	64.7	75.0
	80	..	..	17.0	33.1	42.2
Male	60	..	..	46.0	66.6	75.1
	65	..	..	40.7	60.2	69.0
	80	..	..	16.7	27.1	34.0

		1980	1990	2007	2010	2020
Labour force participation (percentage)						
Total	65+	61.0	59.3	52.2	51.9	51.4
Female	65+	46.3	43.9	29.8	29.4	29.0
Male	65+	76.9	75.6	78.6	78.6	78.6

Percentage married, age 60+			Percentage living alone, age 60+ (1998)		
Total	Female	Male	Total	Female	Male
73.2	60.0	88.0	17.3	25.2	9.0

Statutory pensionable age (2006)			Percentage illiterate, age 65+ (2000)		
	Female	Male	Total	Female	Male
	55	55	67.0	80.1	56.0

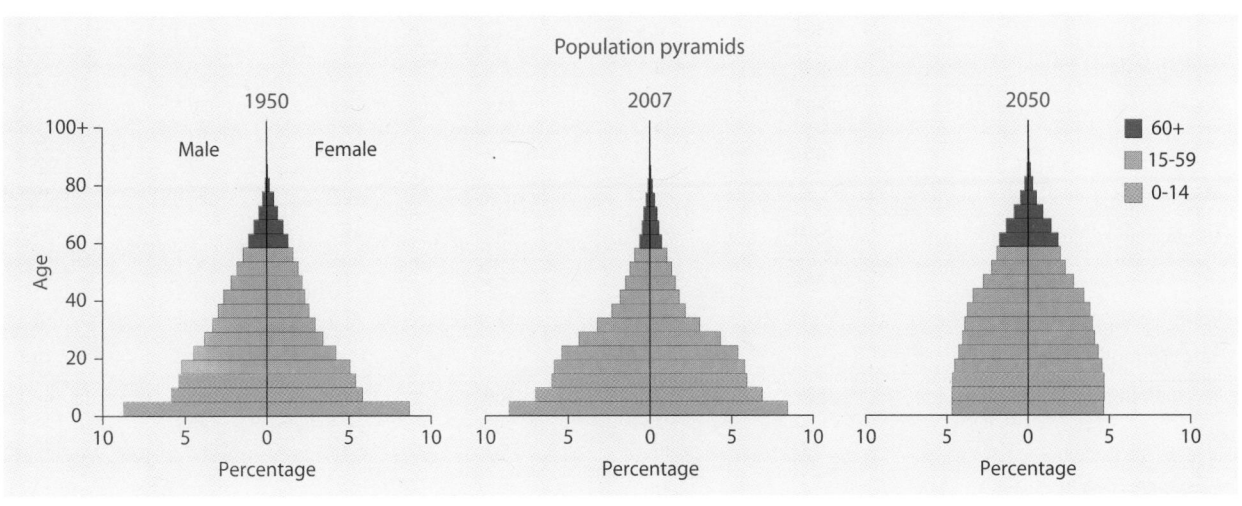

Population pyramids

Kuwait

Indicator	Age	1950	1975	2007	2025	2050
Population (thousands)						
Total	Total	152.3	1 006.6	2 839.3	4 001.6	5 279.2
	0-14	55.0	446.8	685.1	803.2	901.3
	15-59	90.5	533.5	2 058.0	2 790.7	3 098.1
	60-64	2.4	10.5	40.5	166.7	270.9
	65-69	2.2	6.1	26.8	115.4	275.4
	70-74	1.4	4.6	16.0	62.6	265.9
	75-79	0.6	2.6	7.5	35.2	226.8
	80-84			3.4	17.5	146.5
	85-89			1.4	7.6	63.7
	90-94	0.3	2.4	0.5	2.2	24.2
	95-99			0.1	0.5	5.5
	100+			0.0	0.1	0.9
Female	Total	61.8	456.0	1 147.1	1 693.6	2 362.7
	0-14	26.3	219.3	336.5	395.9	444.3
	15-59	32.2	223.8	771.4	1 142.3	1 390.3
	60-64	1.2	4.9	15.3	60.6	117.4
	65-69	1.1	3.0	10.5	42.3	116.4
	70-74	0.6	2.5	6.7	24.5	108.0
	75-79	0.3	1.4	3.5	14.3	84.0
	80-84			1.8	7.8	54.7
	85-89			0.8	4.0	29.7
	90-94	0.1	1.2	0.3	1.5	13.3
	95-99			0.1	0.4	3.8
	100+			0.0	0.1	0.8
Male	Total	90.5	550.5	1 692.2	2 308.0	2 916.5
	0-14	28.7	227.5	348.6	407.2	457.0
	15-59	58.3	309.7	1 286.6	1 648.4	1 707.7
	60-64	1.2	5.7	25.2	106.2	153.4
	65-69	1.1	3.1	16.3	73.1	159.0
	70-74	0.7	2.1	9.3	38.1	158.0
	75-79	0.3	1.3	4.0	20.9	142.7
	80-84			1.6	9.7	91.8
	85-89			0.5	3.6	34.0
	90-94	0.1	1.2	0.1	0.8	10.9
	95-99			0.0	0.1	1.7
	100+			0.0	0.0	0.2
Percentage in older ages						
Total	60+	4.5	2.6	3.4	10.2	24.2
	65+	2.9	1.6	2.0	6.0	19.1
	80+	0.2	0.2	0.2	0.7	4.6
Female	60+	5.4	2.8	3.4	9.2	22.4
	65+	3.6	1.8	2.1	5.6	17.4
	80+	0.2	0.3	0.3	0.8	4.3
Male	60+	3.8	2.4	3.4	10.9	25.8
	65+	2.5	1.4	1.9	6.3	20.5
	80+	0.1	0.2	0.1	0.6	4.8
Ageing index		12.4	5.9	14.1	50.8	142.0
Broad age groups (percentage)	0-14	36.1	44.4	24.1	20.1	17.1
	15-59	59.4	53.0	72.5	69.7	58.7
	60+	4.5	2.6	3.4	10.2	24.2
Median age (years)		21.5	18.2	29.5*	35.0	39.7
Dependency ratio	Total	64.1	85.0	35.3	35.3	56.7
	Youth	59.3	82.1	32.6	27.2	26.8
	Old Age	4.8	2.9	2.7	8.2	29.9
Potential support ratio		20.8	34.6	37.6	12.3	3.3
Parent support ratio		1.0	2.5	0.9	1.4	10.9
Sex ratio (per 100 women)	60+	103.0	102.8	145.8	162.4	142.3
	65+	102.2	94.8	133.8	154.2	145.7
	80+	87.6	93.1	72.9	102.7	135.6

* *Estimate refers to year 2005.*

Indicator	Age	1950-1955	1975-1980	2005-2010	2025-2030	2045-2050
Growth rate (percentage)	Total	5.4	6.2	2.5	1.4	0.8
	60+	5.9	3.5	7.7	8.0	1.6
	65+	8.0	4.0	7.9	7.8	2.4
	80+	17.0	0.7	7.0	8.2	8.6
Total fertility rate (per woman)		7.2	5.9	2.3	1.9	1.9
Life expectancy (years)						
Total	Birth	55.6	69.3	77.6	79.9	81.9
	60	..	..	20.9	22.5	24.1
	65	..	..	17.1	18.5	19.9
	80	..	..	8.0	8.8	9.5
Female	Birth	57.5	71.7	80.2	82.8	84.8
	60	..	..	23.0	25.0	26.6
	65	..	..	19.0	20.8	22.3
	80	..	..	9.5	10.4	11.2
Male	Birth	54.1	67.5	75.8	78.2	80.2
	60	..	..	19.3	21.1	22.7
	65	..	..	15.6	17.1	18.6
	80	..	..	6.6	7.6	8.5
Survival rate (percentage)						
Total	60	..	..	91.3	93.2	94.7
	65	..	..	85.6	88.7	91.2
	80	..	..	50.0	57.6	64.0
Female	60	..	..	93.2	94.8	95.9
	65	..	..	88.8	91.5	93.3
	80	..	..	58.1	66.1	72.0
Male	60	..	..	90.2	92.2	93.7
	65	..	..	83.7	87.1	89.6
	80	..	..	44.6	52.6	59.3

		1980	1990	2007	2010	2020
Labour force participation (percentage)						
Total	65+	7.4	8.4	9.1	8.3	6.2
Female	65+	0.9	0.6	0.6	0.7	0.7
Male	65+	14.1	15.8	15.5	13.8	9.9

Percentage married, age 60+			Percentage living alone, age 60+		
Total	Female	Male	Total	Female	Male
63.9	29.0	88.0	..	..	..

Statutory pensionable age (2006)			Percentage illiterate, age 65+ (2005)		
	Female	Male	Total	Female	Male
	50	50	48.5	69.0	30.7

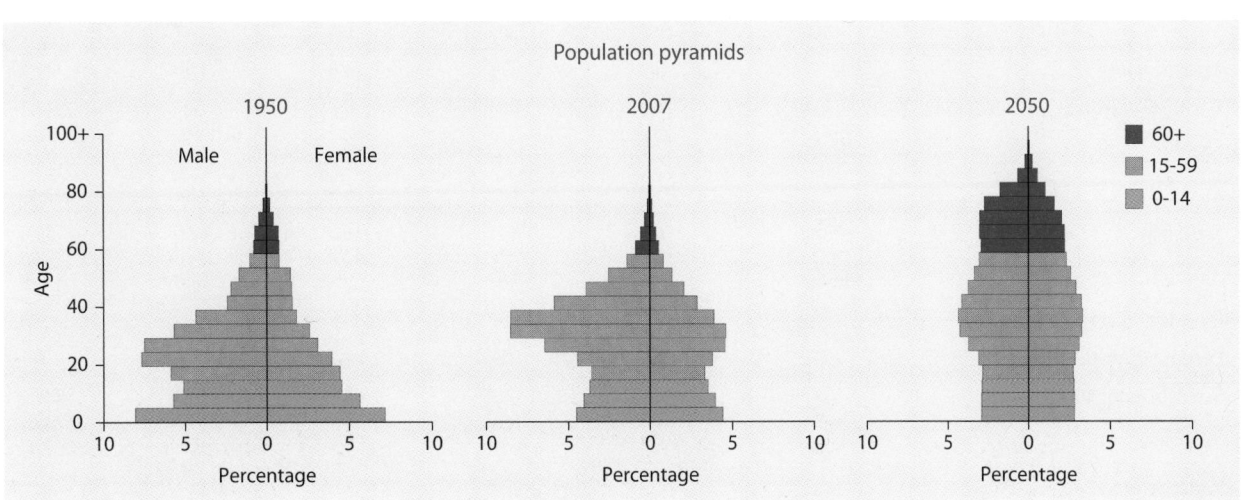

Population pyramids

Kyrgyzstan

Indicator	Age	1950	1975	2007	2025	2050
Population (thousands)						
Total	Total	1 740.0	3 299.0	5 385.9	6 282.4	6 663.8
	0-14	502.8	1 315.3	1 630.3	1 491.5	1 208.6
	15-59	1 020.3	1 704.2	3 351.2	4 018.6	3 974.0
	60-64	74.6	83.7	87.2	267.3	443.6
	65-69	58.5	68.7	101.3	216.8	351.7
	70-74	41.4	57.3	91.6	142.3	262.7
	75-79	25.4	34.7	69.1	75.2	196.0
	80-84			38.6	30.2	118.5
	85-89			11.9	28.8	73.3
	90-94	17.0	35.0	3.8	9.0	28.6
	95-99			0.8	2.4	6.2
	100+			0.1	0.2	0.6
Female	Total	911.2	1 705.2	2 733.5	3 194.4	3 404.0
	0-14	252.6	651.4	798.7	729.3	590.0
	15-59	546.2	875.1	1 693.5	2 013.1	1 966.9
	60-64	35.7	53.0	47.0	148.2	234.0
	65-69	29.7	44.7	56.7	123.3	192.1
	70-74	22.0	37.5	54.3	84.5	149.9
	75-79	14.7	21.7	43.5	47.4	118.5
	80-84			27.1	19.7	75.2
	85-89			9.2	20.3	50.9
	90-94	10.2	21.8	2.9	6.6	21.1
	95-99			0.6	1.8	4.8
	100+			0.1	0.1	0.5
Male	Total	828.8	1 593.8	2 652.4	3 088.0	3 259.8
	0-14	250.3	663.9	831.6	762.1	618.5
	15-59	474.1	829.1	1 657.7	2 005.5	2 007.1
	60-64	38.9	30.7	40.2	119.1	209.6
	65-69	28.7	24.0	44.6	93.5	159.6
	70-74	19.4	19.8	37.4	57.8	112.7
	75-79	10.6	13.1	25.5	27.8	77.5
	80-84			11.5	10.5	43.3
	85-89			2.7	8.6	22.3
	90-94	6.8	13.1	0.9	2.4	7.5
	95-99			0.2	0.6	1.4
	100+			0.1	0.1	0.2
Percentage in older ages						
Total	60+	12.5	8.5	7.5	12.3	22.2
	65+	8.2	5.9	5.9	8.0	15.6
	80+	1.0	1.1	1.0	1.1	3.4
Female	60+	12.3	10.5	8.8	14.1	24.9
	65+	8.4	7.4	7.1	9.5	18.0
	80+	1.1	1.3	1.5	1.5	4.5
Male	60+	12.6	6.3	6.1	10.4	19.5
	65+	7.9	4.4	4.6	6.5	13.0
	80+	0.8	0.8	0.6	0.7	2.3
Ageing index		43.1	21.2	24.8	51.8	122.6
Broad age groups (percentage)	0-14	28.9	39.9	30.3	23.7	18.1
	15-59	58.6	51.7	62.2	64.0	59.6
	60+	12.5	8.5	7.5	12.3	22.2
Median age (years)		25.3	19.5	23.8*	31.1	39.5
Dependency ratio	Total	58.9	84.5	56.6	46.6	50.8
	Youth	45.9	73.6	47.4	34.8	27.4
	Old Age	13.0	10.9	9.2	11.8	23.5
Potential support ratio		7.7	9.1	10.8	8.5	4.3
Parent support ratio		2.8	5.0	3.4	4.6	8.1
Sex ratio (per 100 women)	60+	92.9	56.4	67.6	70.9	74.9
	65+	85.5	55.7	63.2	66.3	69.3
	80+	66.0	60.1	38.5	45.8	49.0

* *Estimate refers to year 2005.*

Indicator	Age	1950-1955	1975-1980	2005-2010	2025-2030	2045-2050
Growth rate (percentage)	Total	1.8	1.9	1.1	0.5	0.0
	60+	−0.1	0.0	1.4	2.6	2.7
	65+	1.6	1.3	−1.3	4.3	2.6
	80+	2.5	2.1	7.6	3.4	1.7
Total fertility rate (per woman)		4.5	4.1	2.5	1.9	1.9
Life expectancy (years)						
Total	Birth	52.9	62.3	67.7	71.8	75.0
	60	..	..	18.6	19.9	21.1
	65	..	..	15.1	16.3	17.4
	80	..	..	7.1	7.6	8.2
Female	Birth	57.3	66.5	71.9	75.5	78.3
	60	..	..	20.5	21.8	23.1
	65	..	..	16.7	17.9	19.0
	80	..	..	7.4	8.1	8.8
Male	Birth	48.7	58.0	63.6	68.0	71.7
	60	..	..	16.3	17.6	18.9
	65	..	..	13.2	14.3	15.4
	80	..	..	6.3	6.8	7.3
Survival rate (percentage)						
Total	60	..	..	75.5	81.6	86.0
	65	..	..	68.8	75.6	80.7
	80	..	..	34.4	42.0	48.3
Female	60	..	..	82.6	87.1	90.1
	65	..	..	77.4	82.7	86.2
	80	..	..	45.2	52.4	58.3
Male	60	..	..	68.6	76.2	82.0
	65	..	..	60.4	68.6	75.2
	80	..	..	23.9	31.0	38.1

		1980	1990	2007	2010	2020
Labour force participation (percentage)						
Total	65+	4.0	5.7	21.6	23.3	25.5
Female	65+	2.4	3.5	16.2	17.9	20.0
Male	65+	7.2	10.3	30.1	31.9	34.0

Percentage married, age 60+			Percentage living alone, age 60+ (1997)		
Total	Female	Male	Total	Female	Male
56.4	39.0	82.0	9.3	12.2	5.3

Statutory pensionable age (2006)			Percentage illiterate, age 65+ (1999)		
	Female	Male	Total	Female	Male
	57	62	9.8	12.6	5.4

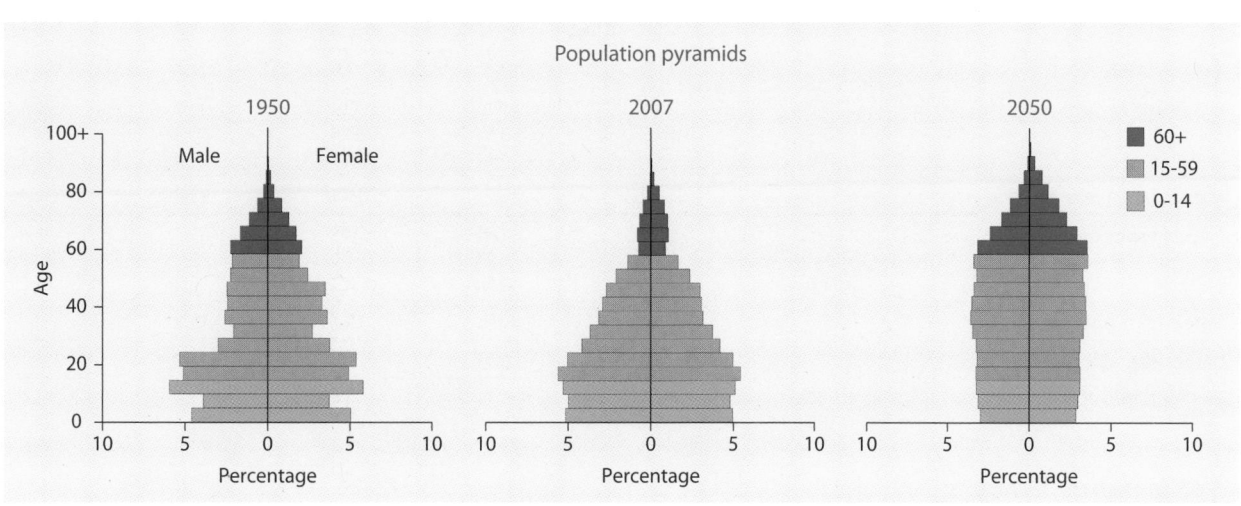

Population pyramids

Lao People's Democratic Republic

Indicator	Age	1950	1975	2007	2025	2050
Population (thousands)						
Total	Total	1 755.0	3 024.3	6 192.6	8 711.6	11 586.2
	0-14	735.1	1 273.1	2 482.3	2 851.6	2 614.5
	15-59	938.9	1 613.4	3 380.7	5 249.5	7 451.3
	60-64	31.5	57.1	107.2	217.8	515.7
	65-69	22.5	39.1	92.7	171.4	384.6
	70-74	14.4	24.7	60.1	105.4	279.8
	75-79	8.1	11.6	41.8	67.9	184.9
	80-84			19.2	30.1	100.4
	85-89			6.7	14.6	41.6
	90-94	4.5	5.3	1.7	2.8	11.8
	95-99			0.2	0.6	1.6
	100+			0.0	0.0	0.1
Female	Total	858.0	1 501.0	3 092.1	4 330.9	5 772.6
	0-14	358.5	631.2	1 218.2	1 397.0	1 282.9
	15-59	456.3	797.7	1 694.7	2 607.1	3 694.2
	60-64	16.2	29.2	58.1	114.2	262.3
	65-69	11.7	20.6	50.6	90.4	198.5
	70-74	8.1	13.0	32.3	57.0	147.0
	75-79	4.5	6.2	22.8	37.1	98.9
	80-84			10.5	17.6	56.7
	85-89			3.7	8.5	24.0
	90-94	2.7	3.1	1.1	1.7	7.0
	95-99			0.1	0.4	1.0
	100+			0.0	0.0	0.1
Male	Total	897.0	1 523.3	3 100.5	4 380.7	5 813.5
	0-14	376.6	641.9	1 264.1	1 454.6	1 331.6
	15-59	482.6	815.7	1 685.9	2 642.4	3 757.1
	60-64	15.3	27.9	49.1	103.6	253.4
	65-69	10.8	18.5	42.1	81.0	186.0
	70-74	6.3	11.7	27.9	48.4	132.8
	75-79	3.6	5.4	19.0	30.8	86.0
	80-84			8.7	12.5	43.6
	85-89			3.0	6.1	17.6
	90-94	1.8	2.2	0.7	1.1	4.7
	95-99			0.1	0.2	0.6
	100+			0.0	0.0	0.0
Percentage in older ages						
Total	60+	4.6	4.6	5.3	7.0	13.1
	65+	2.8	2.7	3.6	4.5	8.7
	80+	0.3	0.2	0.4	0.6	1.3
Female	60+	5.0	4.8	5.8	7.5	13.8
	65+	3.1	2.9	3.9	4.9	9.2
	80+	0.3	0.2	0.5	0.6	1.5
Male	60+	4.2	4.3	4.9	6.5	12.5
	65+	2.5	2.5	3.3	4.1	8.1
	80+	0.2	0.1	0.4	0.5	1.1
Ageing index		11.0	10.8	13.3	21.4	58.2
Broad age groups (percentage)	0-14	41.9	42.1	40.1	32.7	22.6
	15-59	53.5	53.3	54.6	60.3	64.3
	60+	4.6	4.6	5.3	7.0	13.1
Median age (years)		18.9	18.7	19.1*	23.8	32.1
Dependency ratio	Total	80.9	81.0	77.5	59.3	45.4
	Youth	75.8	76.2	71.2	52.2	32.8
	Old Age	5.1	4.8	6.4	7.2	12.6
Potential support ratio		19.6	20.7	15.7	13.9	7.9
Parent support ratio		1.0	0.6	1.9	2.2	3.1
Sex ratio (per 100 women)	60+	87.5	91.1	84.0	86.8	91.1
	65+	83.3	88.1	83.7	84.7	88.4
	80+	66.6	70.9	80.1	70.6	75.0

* Estimate refers to year 2005.

Indicator	Age	1950-1955	1975-1980	2005-2010	2025-2030	2045-2050
Growth rate (percentage)	Total	2.0	1.2	2.2	1.5	0.8
	60+	−0.1	2.0	2.7	3.6	3.8
	65+	1.1	2.1	1.2	4.0	3.6
	80+	−0.4	1.8	6.5	4.9	4.1
Total fertility rate (per woman)		6.2	6.7	4.3	2.6	1.9
Life expectancy (years)						
Total	Birth	37.8	43.5	56.5	65.9	72.2
	60	..	..	16.4	18.2	19.6
	65	..	..	13.1	14.6	15.7
	80	..	..	5.7	6.4	6.8
Female	Birth	39.2	45.0	57.7	67.6	74.3
	60	..	..	17.0	18.8	20.3
	65	..	..	13.6	15.1	16.3
	80	..	..	6.0	6.6	7.0
Male	Birth	36.5	42.1	55.3	64.3	70.1
	60	..	..	15.9	17.5	18.8
	65	..	..	12.7	14.1	15.1
	80	..	..	5.5	6.1	6.6
Survival rate (percentage)						
Total	60	..	..	60.0	73.8	83.0
	65	..	..	53.4	67.7	77.5
	80	..	..	21.3	32.4	41.7
Female	60	..	..	62.3	76.5	86.2
	65	..	..	56.0	70.9	81.4
	80	..	..	23.6	35.6	46.3
Male	60	..	..	57.7	71.2	80.0
	65	..	..	50.8	64.5	73.9
	80	..	..	19.1	29.1	37.4

		1980	1990	2007	2010	2020
Labour force participation (percentage)						
Total	65+	43.7	35.7	35.7	35.8	37.6
Female	65+	29.9	19.1	20.4	21.0	23.6
Male	65+	59.6	54.2	54.0	54.1	54.4

Percentage married, age 60+			Percentage living alone, age 60+		
Total	Female	Male	Total	Female	Male
..	..	..	..	..	..

Statutory pensionable age (2006)		Percentage illiterate, age 65+ (2001)		
Female	Male	Total	Female	Male
60	60	71.6	90.0	51.5

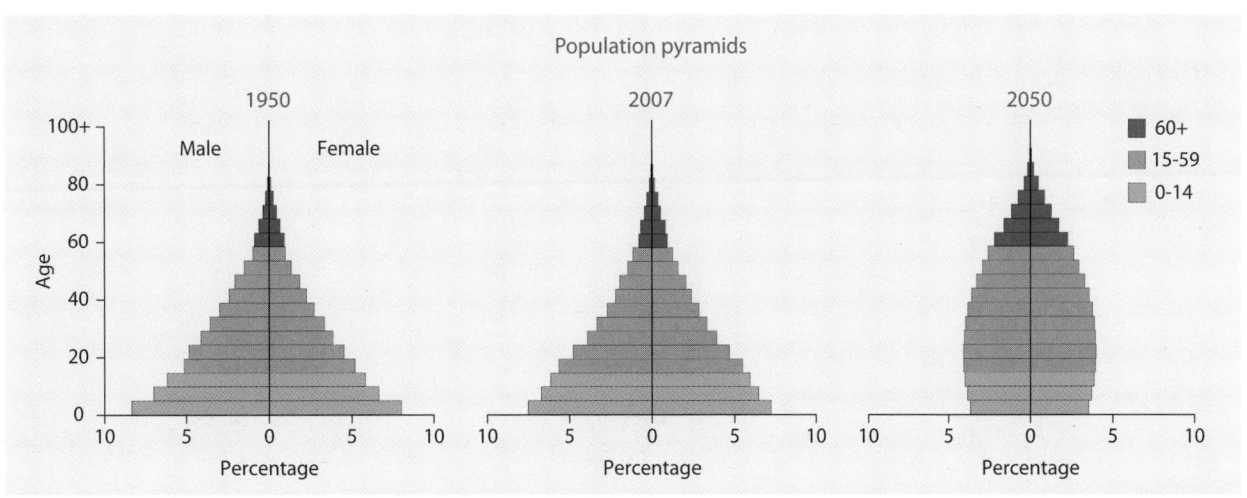

Population pyramids

Latvia

Indicator	Age	1950	1975	2007	2025	2050
Population (thousands)						
Total	Total	1 949.0	2 456.1	2 283.6	2 058.9	1 677.7
	0-14	493.6	518.1	316.8	290.6	231.3
	15-59	1 151.2	1 501.9	1 445.9	1 191.5	804.7
	60-64	86.4	123.8	123.4	144.6	154.0
	65-69	74.9	113.1	125.5	132.3	136.0
	70-74	60.6	90.1	103.3	103.1	108.5
	75-79	45.2	55.5	80.8	75.4	92.6
	80-84			52.7	57.0	66.4
	85-89			20.5	38.4	47.7
	90-94	37.1	53.7	9.7	17.3	25.0
	95-99			4.0	7.1	9.0
	100+			1.0	1.7	2.6
Female	Total	1 106.3	1 327.2	1 239.0	1 106.6	889.7
	0-14	243.2	253.1	154.3	141.3	112.4
	15-59	665.3	789.5	740.6	597.3	394.4
	60-64	54.5	76.3	71.6	80.3	79.3
	65-69	47.8	69.9	76.1	76.5	72.8
	70-74	39.4	58.7	66.3	63.4	61.3
	75-79	30.3	40.1	56.8	50.2	56.2
	80-84			42.0	41.8	44.6
	85-89			17.6	31.5	36.3
	90-94	25.9	39.7	8.9	15.7	21.5
	95-99			3.9	6.9	8.4
	100+			1.0	1.7	2.5
Male	Total	842.7	1 128.9	1 044.5	952.3	787.9
	0-14	250.4	265.0	162.5	149.3	118.9
	15-59	485.9	712.4	705.4	594.2	410.3
	60-64	31.9	47.5	51.7	64.3	74.7
	65-69	27.1	43.2	49.4	55.8	63.2
	70-74	21.2	31.3	37.0	39.7	47.2
	75-79	15.0	15.5	24.0	25.3	36.4
	80-84			10.7	15.1	21.7
	85-89			2.9	6.9	11.4
	90-94	11.2	14.0	0.8	1.6	3.5
	95-99			0.1	0.2	0.5
	100+			0.0	0.0	0.0
Percentage in older ages						
Total	60+	15.6	17.8	22.8	28.0	38.3
	65+	11.2	12.7	17.4	21.0	29.1
	80+	1.9	2.2	3.8	5.9	9.0
Female	60+	17.9	21.4	27.8	33.3	43.0
	65+	13.0	15.7	22.0	26.0	34.1
	80+	2.3	3.0	5.9	8.8	12.7
Male	60+	12.6	13.4	16.9	21.9	32.8
	65+	8.8	9.2	12.0	15.2	23.4
	80+	1.3	1.2	1.4	2.5	4.7
Ageing index		61.6	84.2	164.4	198.5	277.5
Broad age groups (percentage)	0-14	25.3	21.1	13.9	14.1	13.8
	15-59	59.1	61.1	63.3	57.9	48.0
	60+	15.6	17.8	22.8	28.0	38.3
Median age (years)		30.5	34.8	39.5*	44.3	50.5
Dependency ratio	Total	57.5	51.1	45.5	54.1	75.0
	Youth	39.9	31.9	20.2	21.7	24.1
	Old Age	17.6	19.2	25.3	32.4	50.9
Potential support ratio		5.7	5.2	3.9	3.1	2.0
Parent support ratio		5.5	6.0	8.6	15.0	23.5
Sex ratio (per 100 women)	60+	53.7	53.2	51.3	56.8	67.6
	65+	51.9	49.9	45.8	50.2	60.6
	80+	43.3	35.4	19.8	24.4	32.8

* Estimate refers to year 2005.

Indicator	Age	1950-1955	1975-1980	2005-2010	2025-2030	2045-2050
Growth rate (percentage)	Total	0.7	0.4	−0.5	−0.8	−0.9
	60+	0.1	−1.0	0.1	0.1	0.8
	65+	0.4	0.9	0.6	0.9	0.8
	80+	1.0	1.0	4.3	−0.2	0.0
Total fertility rate (per woman)		2.0	2.0	1.3	1.5	1.8
Life expectancy (years)						
Total	Birth	66.2	69.3	72.7	76.6	79.3
	60	..	..	19.6	21.2	22.6
	65	..	..	16.2	17.5	18.7
	80	..	..	8.2	8.8	9.3
Female	Birth	69.0	74.1	77.8	80.7	83.0
	60	..	..	22.3	24.1	25.6
	65	..	..	18.5	20.1	21.4
	80	..	..	9.2	10.0	10.7
Male	Birth	62.5	64.1	67.2	72.0	75.2
	60	..	..	15.7	17.5	19.0
	65	..	..	12.6	14.0	15.4
	80	..	..	5.4	6.2	6.8
Survival rate (percentage)						
Total	60	..	..	80.9	87.4	91.1
	65	..	..	74.0	81.6	86.2
	80	..	..	39.3	48.4	55.4
Female	60	..	..	88.6	91.8	94.0
	65	..	..	83.5	87.9	90.9
	80	..	..	53.1	61.3	67.7
Male	60	..	..	72.9	82.8	88.2
	65	..	..	63.9	74.9	81.5
	80	..	..	23.6	33.6	42.2

		1980	1990	2007	2010	2020
Labour force participation (percentage)						
Total	65+	15.4	14.5	9.2	9.3	9.5
Female	65+	12.1	11.6	6.4	6.3	5.9
Male	65+	22.3	21.2	15.2	15.8	17.2

Percentage married, age 60+			Percentage living alone, age 60+ (1989)		
Total	Female	Male	Total	Female	Male
51.6	40.0	74.0	24.0	29.3	13.2

Statutory pensionable age (2006)		Percentage illiterate, age 65+ (2000)		
Female	Male	Total	Female	Male
59.5	62	0.6	0.7	0.3

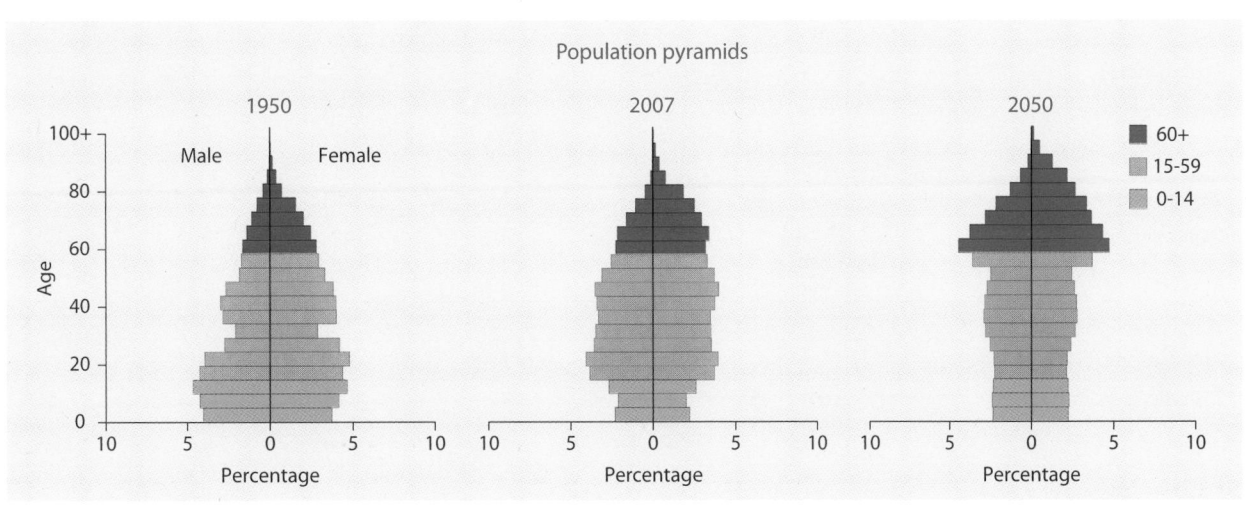

Population pyramids

United Nations Department of Economic and Social Affairs, Population Division

Lebanon

Indicator	Age	1950	1975	2007	2025	2050
Population (thousands)						
Total	Total	1 442.7	2 678.5	3 653.4	4 297.2	4 701.8
	0-14	493.6	1 076.0	1 013.7	959.0	830.5
	15-59	798.9	1 402.8	2 262.6	2 717.2	2 724.7
	60-64	45.1	68.7	106.5	203.2	287.8
	65-69	40.5	52.6	94.9	162.2	266.7
	70-74	31.5	37.2	80.7	112.4	218.9
	75-79	19.9	23.1	55.7	72.0	170.0
	80-84			28.0	42.4	113.7
	85-89			8.7	21.1	61.1
	90-94	13.2	18.2	2.4	6.6	22.8
	95-99			0.4	1.1	5.0
	100+			0.0	0.1	0.6
Female	Total	716.6	1 332.0	1 862.8	2 186.3	2 380.5
	0-14	246.6	529.3	497.3	469.1	405.3
	15-59	393.2	696.9	1 161.1	1 354.2	1 343.6
	60-64	22.8	35.1	57.6	113.2	145.9
	65-69	20.5	27.5	51.4	94.4	137.9
	70-74	16.1	20.0	43.2	66.4	116.8
	75-79	10.3	12.8	30.1	42.8	95.5
	80-84			15.4	26.6	70.0
	85-89			5.0	14.0	42.6
	90-94	7.1	10.5	1.5	4.7	17.9
	95-99			0.2	0.8	4.3
	100+			0.0	0.1	0.5
Male	Total	726.1	1 346.5	1 790.7	2 110.9	2 321.3
	0-14	247.0	546.7	516.4	489.9	425.2
	15-59	405.7	705.9	1 101.4	1 363.0	1 381.1
	60-64	22.4	33.6	48.9	90.0	141.9
	65-69	20.0	25.1	43.5	67.7	128.7
	70-74	15.4	17.2	37.5	46.0	102.1
	75-79	9.5	10.3	25.6	29.2	74.5
	80-84			12.6	15.8	43.7
	85-89			3.7	7.1	18.5
	90-94	6.1	7.7	0.9	1.9	4.9
	95-99			0.1	0.2	0.7
	100+			0.0	0.0	0.0
Percentage in older ages						
Total	60+	10.4	7.5	10.3	14.5	24.4
	65+	7.3	4.9	7.4	9.7	18.3
	80+	0.9	0.7	1.1	1.7	4.3
Female	60+	10.7	7.9	11.0	16.6	26.5
	65+	7.5	5.3	7.9	11.4	20.4
	80+	1.0	0.8	1.2	2.1	5.7
Male	60+	10.1	7.0	9.7	12.2	22.2
	65+	7.0	4.5	6.9	8.0	16.1
	80+	0.8	0.6	1.0	1.2	2.9
Ageing index		30.4	18.6	37.2	64.8	138.1
Broad age groups (percentage)	0-14	34.2	40.2	27.7	22.3	17.7
	15-59	55.4	52.4	61.9	63.2	58.0
	60+	10.4	7.5	10.3	14.5	24.4
Median age (years)		23.2	19.3	26.8*	33.2	40.5
Dependency ratio	Total	70.9	82.0	54.2	47.1	56.1
	Youth	58.5	73.1	42.8	32.8	27.6
	Old Age	12.4	8.9	11.4	14.3	28.5
Potential support ratio		8.0	11.2	8.8	7.0	3.5
Parent support ratio		2.8	2.9	2.8	4.1	9.7
Sex ratio (per 100 women)	60+	95.5	88.7	84.6	71.1	81.5
	65+	94.3	85.3	84.5	67.3	76.8
	80+	86.5	72.9	78.7	54.3	50.1

* *Estimate refers to year 2005.*

Indicator	Age	1950-1955	1975-1980	2005-2010	2025-2030	2045-2050
Growth rate (percentage)	Total	2.2	0.1	1.1	0.6	0.1
	60+	0.4	0.0	1.6	3.1	1.7
	65+	0.5	2.3	1.4	3.7	2.2
	80+	0.7	1.2	5.2	2.7	3.6
Total fertility rate (per woman)		5.7	4.3	2.2	1.9	1.9
Life expectancy (years)						
Total	Birth	55.9	66.6	73.1	76.8	79.4
	60	..	..	18.5	20.5	22.2
	65	..	..	14.7	16.5	18.2
	80	..	..	6.2	7.3	8.4
Female	Birth	57.7	69.0	75.3	79.0	81.6
	60	..	..	19.6	22.1	24.1
	65	..	..	15.7	18.0	19.8
	80	..	..	6.5	8.0	9.2
Male	Birth	54.3	64.4	70.9	74.4	77.0
	60	..	..	17.3	18.4	20.1
	65	..	..	13.8	14.7	16.2
	80	..	..	5.8	6.2	7.0
Survival rate (percentage)						
Total	60	..	..	86.0	90.4	92.8
	65	..	..	79.7	85.3	88.6
	80	..	..	38.9	49.0	56.7
Female	60	..	..	88.9	92.3	94.2
	65	..	..	83.8	88.5	91.1
	80	..	..	45.1	56.8	64.7
Male	60	..	..	82.8	88.5	91.3
	65	..	..	75.2	82.0	86.0
	80	..	..	32.7	39.9	48.3

		1980	1990	2007	2010	2020
Labour force participation (percentage)						
Total	65+	18.4	18.5	21.2	20.8	19.8
Female	65+	5.4	5.4	4.4	4.3	4.3
Male	65+	33.8	34.2	41.1	41.2	41.5

Percentage married, age 60+			Percentage living alone, age 60+		
Total	Female	Male	Total	Female	Male
64.6	45.0	86.0	..	..	..

Statutory pensionable age (2006)			Percentage illiterate, age 65+		
	Female	Male	Total	Female	Male
	64	64	..	..	..

Population pyramids

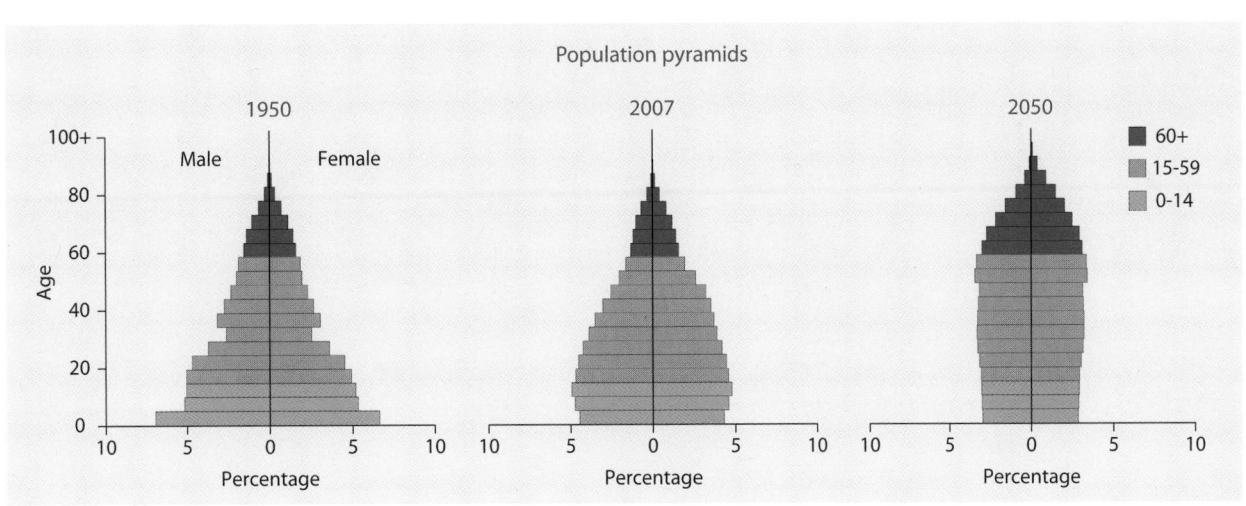

Lesotho

Indicator	Age	1950	1975	2007	2025	2050
Population (thousands)						
Total	Total	733.9	1 145.0	1 785.3	1 689.9	1 600.9
	0-14	298.5	507.2	676.5	605.7	473.1
	15-59	384.6	563.9	972.7	944.9	986.2
	60-64	18.0	26.2	40.5	32.3	50.6
	65-69	14.4	20.7	34.5	35.9	39.0
	70-74	9.8	14.0	28.5	30.6	22.4
	75-79	5.6	8.2	18.8	22.0	12.8
	80-84			9.5	11.9	8.6
	85-89			3.4	5.0	5.6
	90-94	3.0	5.0	0.7	1.3	2.1
	95-99			0.1	0.2	0.4
	100+			0.0	0.0	0.0
Female	Total	389.7	616.6	951.6	867.0	811.2
	0-14	151.9	253.3	335.9	300.5	234.2
	15-59	205.5	320.7	536.0	477.2	508.2
	60-64	11.2	14.8	24.1	20.0	22.3
	65-69	9.1	11.5	19.9	23.4	17.6
	70-74	6.3	7.9	16.1	20.0	10.6
	75-79	3.7	5.0	11.0	14.1	7.0
	80-84			5.8	7.7	5.5
	85-89			2.2	3.2	4.0
	90-94	2.0	3.3	0.5	0.9	1.6
	95-99			0.1	0.1	0.3
	100+			0.0	0.0	0.0
Male	Total	344.2	528.4	833.7	822.8	789.7
	0-14	146.6	253.9	340.5	305.1	238.9
	15-59	179.1	243.2	436.8	467.7	478.1
	60-64	6.8	11.3	16.5	12.3	28.3
	65-69	5.3	9.2	14.6	12.5	21.4
	70-74	3.5	6.0	12.4	10.6	11.8
	75-79	2.0	3.1	7.8	7.9	5.8
	80-84			3.7	4.2	3.2
	85-89			1.2	1.8	1.6
	90-94	0.9	1.6	0.2	0.4	0.5
	95-99			0.0	0.1	0.1
	100+			0.0	0.0	0.0
Percentage in older ages						
Total	60+	6.9	6.5	7.6	8.2	8.8
	65+	4.5	4.2	5.4	6.3	5.7
	80+	0.4	0.4	0.8	1.1	1.0
Female	60+	8.3	6.9	8.4	10.3	8.5
	65+	5.4	4.5	5.8	8.0	5.7
	80+	0.5	0.5	0.9	1.4	1.4
Male	60+	5.4	5.9	6.8	6.1	9.2
	65+	3.4	3.8	4.8	4.6	5.6
	80+	0.3	0.3	0.6	0.8	0.7
Ageing index		17.0	14.6	20.1	23.0	29.9
Broad age groups (percentage)	0-14	40.7	44.3	37.9	35.8	29.6
	15-59	52.4	49.2	54.5	55.9	61.6
	60+	6.9	6.5	7.6	8.2	8.8
Median age (years)		19.8	17.6	19.2*	21.1	25.1
Dependency ratio	Total	82.3	94.1	76.2	72.9	54.4
	Youth	74.1	86.0	66.8	62.0	45.6
	Old Age	8.1	8.1	9.4	10.9	8.8
Potential support ratio		12.3	12.4	10.6	9.1	11.4
Parent support ratio		1.3	1.4	2.9	7.9	4.7
Sex ratio (per 100 women)	60+	57.6	73.3	70.7	55.9	105.6
	65+	55.9	71.6	71.7	54.2	95.3
	80+	45.2	48.7	59.5	55.1	46.6

* *Estimate refers to year 2005.*

Indicator	Age	1950-1955	1975-1980	2005-2010	2025-2030	2045-2050
Growth rate (percentage)	Total	1.4	2.4	−0.3	−0.3	−0.1
	60+	0.8	2.2	0.8	−2.2	3.3
	65+	0.8	2.0	0.6	−1.1	3.5
	80+	2.3	2.0	2.7	1.7	−3.9
Total fertility rate (per woman)		5.8	5.7	3.3	2.4	2.0
Life expectancy (years)						
Total	Birth	42.1	51.7	34.3	43.9	52.9
	60	..	..	16.0	17.3	18.3
	65	..	..	13.1	14.1	15.0
	80	..	..	5.7	6.1	6.6
Female	Birth	43.4	53.2	34.2	42.7	53.2
	60	..	..	16.9	18.2	19.9
	65	..	..	13.8	14.8	16.2
	80	..	..	5.9	6.3	6.9
Male	Birth	40.4	50.0	34.2	45.2	52.9
	60	..	..	14.6	15.9	16.9
	65	..	..	12.1	13.0	13.8
	80	..	..	5.4	5.7	5.9
Survival rate (percentage)						
Total	60	..	..	11.9	23.6	38.9
	65	..	..	10.3	21.0	35.2
	80	..	..	4.1	9.6	17.6
Female	60	..	..	11.9	20.8	38.8
	65	..	..	10.5	18.9	36.1
	80	..	..	4.6	9.3	20.2
Male	60	..	..	11.1	26.4	39.5
	65	..	..	9.2	22.8	35.0
	80	..	..	3.2	9.1	15.3

		1980	1990	2007	2010	2020
Labour force participation (percentage)						
Total	65+	45.8	44.4	31.8	30.7	28.3
Female	65+	25.7	26.5	14.9	14.2	13.6
Male	65+	74.3	70.5	55.4	54.6	53.6

Percentage married, age 60+			Percentage living alone, age 60+		
Total	Female	Male	Total	Female	Male
58.8	42.0	81.0	..	..	..

Statutory pensionable age (2006)			Percentage illiterate, age 65+		
	Female	Male	Total	Female	Male
	..	..	..	..	..

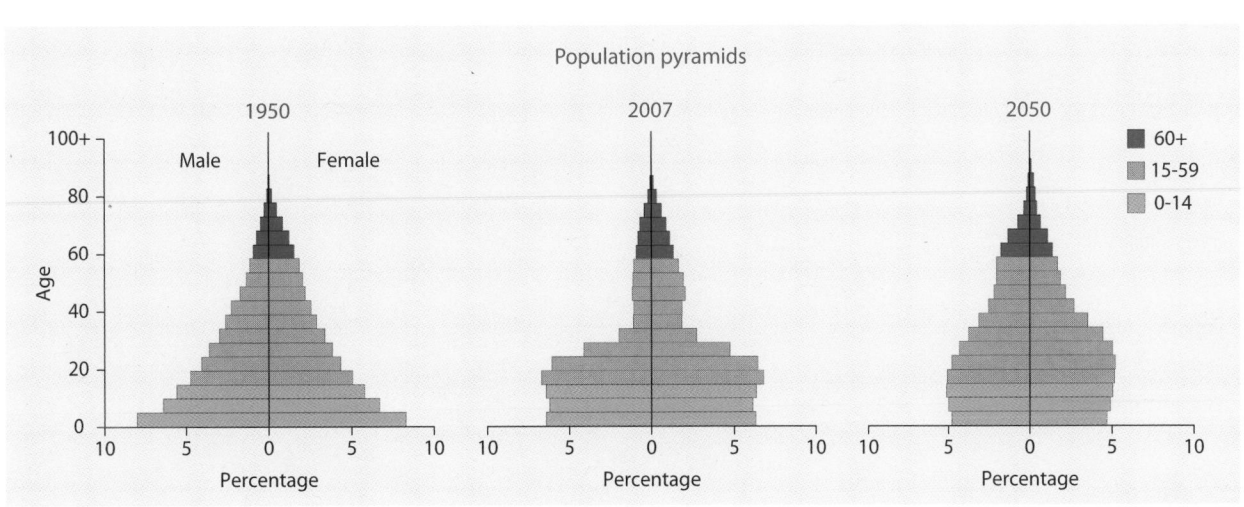

Population pyramids

Liberia

Indicator	Age	1950	1975	2007	2025	2050
Population (thousands)						
Total	Total	823.9	1 605.0	3 452.3	5 799.9	10 652.9
	0-14	341.8	734.7	1 634.4	2 685.6	3 944.7
	15-59	440.6	799.7	1 692.8	2 900.4	6 227.1
	60-64	16.7	27.9	48.7	79.8	187.5
	65-69	11.8	19.8	34.5	59.5	129.9
	70-74	7.4	12.6	22.3	39.9	83.0
	75-79	3.8	6.8	12.3	21.7	48.3
	80-84			5.3	9.5	22.7
	85-89			1.6	3.0	7.8
	90-94	1.8	3.5	0.3	0.6	1.7
	95-99			0.0	0.1	0.2
	100+			0.0	0.0	0.0
Female	Total	416.1	806.1	1 728.7	2 885.0	5 288.9
	0-14	170.4	365.5	813.8	1 335.5	1 955.9
	15-59	223.0	401.6	846.5	1 431.5	3 083.7
	60-64	8.9	15.0	25.8	42.5	93.6
	65-69	6.4	10.9	18.7	32.7	66.1
	70-74	4.1	7.1	12.4	22.5	43.7
	75-79	2.2	3.9	7.1	12.4	26.6
	80-84			3.1	5.6	13.3
	85-89			1.0	1.8	4.8
	90-94	1.1	2.1	0.2	0.4	1.1
	95-99			0.0	0.1	0.1
	100+			0.0	0.0	0.0
Male	Total	407.8	798.9	1 723.6	2 914.9	5 364.0
	0-14	171.4	369.2	820.6	1 350.2	1 988.8
	15-59	217.6	398.1	846.3	1 469.0	3 143.3
	60-64	7.8	12.9	22.9	37.2	94.0
	65-69	5.4	8.9	15.8	26.8	63.9
	70-74	3.3	5.5	10.0	17.4	39.4
	75-79	1.6	2.9	5.3	9.2	21.6
	80-84			2.1	3.8	9.4
	85-89			0.6	1.1	3.0
	90-94	0.7	1.4	0.1	0.2	0.6
	95-99			0.0	0.0	0.1
	100+			0.0	0.0	0.0
Percentage in older ages						
Total	60+	5.0	4.4	3.6	3.7	4.5
	65+	3.0	2.7	2.2	2.3	2.8
	80+	0.2	0.2	0.2	0.2	0.3
Female	60+	5.5	4.8	4.0	4.1	4.7
	65+	3.3	3.0	2.5	2.6	2.9
	80+	0.3	0.3	0.3	0.3	0.4
Male	60+	4.6	3.9	3.3	3.3	4.3
	65+	2.7	2.3	2.0	2.0	2.6
	80+	0.2	0.2	0.2	0.2	0.2
Ageing index		12.1	9.6	7.7	8.0	12.2
Broad age groups (percentage)	0-14	41.5	45.8	47.3	46.3	37.0
	15-59	53.5	49.8	49.0	50.0	58.5
	60+	5.0	4.4	3.6	3.7	4.5
Median age (years)		19.2	17.0	16.3*	16.6	20.9
Dependency ratio	Total	80.2	93.9	98.2	94.6	66.1
	Youth	74.7	88.8	93.9	90.1	61.5
	Old Age	5.4	5.2	4.4	4.5	4.6
Potential support ratio		18.4	19.4	22.8	22.2	21.8
Parent support ratio		0.7	0.8	1.0	1.2	1.3
Sex ratio (per 100 women)	60+	82.8	80.8	83.0	81.1	93.0
	65+	79.7	77.7	79.7	77.5	88.5
	80+	63.5	65.0	65.1	65.5	67.1

* Estimate refers to year 2005.

Indicator	Age	1950-1955	1975-1980	2005-2010	2025-2030	2045-2050
Growth rate (percentage)	Total	2.3	3.0	2.9	2.8	2.1
	60+	1.8	2.4	2.8	2.7	4.1
	65+	1.9	2.5	2.7	2.9	3.9
	80+	2.7	2.8	3.1	3.7	3.2
Total fertility rate (per woman)		6.5	6.9	6.8	5.2	3.3
Life expectancy (years)						
Total	Birth	38.5	43.4	42.5	50.6	60.6
	60	..	..	14.4	15.3	16.3
	65	..	..	11.6	12.3	13.1
	80	..	..	5.1	5.4	5.7
Female	Birth	40.0	44.7	43.1	51.2	61.7
	60	..	..	15.1	16.1	17.2
	65	..	..	12.1	12.9	13.7
	80	..	..	5.3	5.6	5.9
Male	Birth	37.0	42.8	41.9	50.1	59.5
	60	..	..	13.7	14.5	15.5
	65	..	..	11.0	11.7	12.4
	80	..	..	4.9	5.1	5.4
Survival rate (percentage)						
Total	60	..	..	35.6	46.5	63.6
	65	..	..	30.1	40.3	56.5
	80	..	..	9.5	14.3	22.4
Female	60	..	..	36.8	47.2	65.3
	65	..	..	31.7	41.7	59.1
	80	..	..	10.9	16.0	25.5
Male	60	..	..	34.3	45.8	62.1
	65	..	..	28.3	38.8	54.1
	80	..	..	8.1	12.4	19.5

		1980	1990	2007	2010	2020
Labour force participation (percentage)						
Total	65+	48.8	50.0	48.5	46.9	35.9
Female	65+	27.8	29.1	29.1	29.1	29.0
Male	65+	75.7	76.6	72.9	69.2	44.7

Percentage married, age 60+				Percentage living alone, age 60+		
Total	Female	Male		Total	Female	Male
59.6	46.0	76.0		..	..	..

Statutory pensionable age (2006)				Percentage illiterate, age 65+		
	Female	Male		Total	Female	Male
	60	60		..	..	..

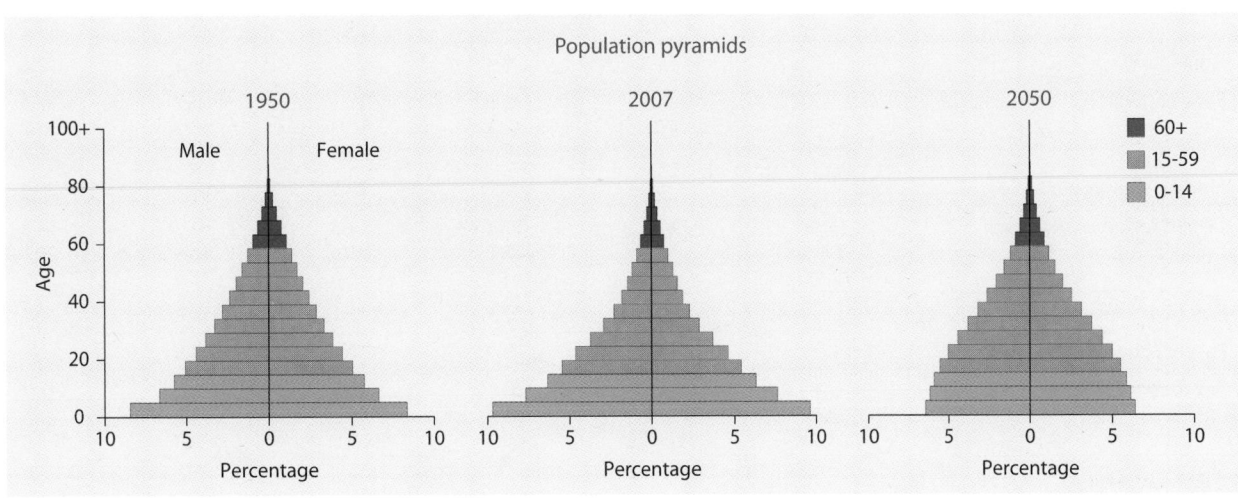

Population pyramids

Libyan Arab Jamahiriya

Indicator	Age	1950	1975	2007	2025	2050
Population (thousands)						
Total	Total	1 029.0	2 446.0	6 084.9	7 975.7	9 552.8
	0-14	431.2	1 126.1	1 807.3	1 967.2	1 772.2
	15-59	523.1	1 228.9	3 859.8	5 157.1	5 519.0
	60-64	26.1	36.2	153.8	262.9	572.9
	65-69	20.4	25.1	110.3	211.7	602.0
	70-74	15.5	16.0	74.3	163.1	440.4
	75-79	8.4	8.0	44.3	110.4	312.5
	80-84			22.6	62.2	187.5
	85-89			9.3	28.6	91.8
	90-94	4.3	5.7	2.7	9.9	40.2
	95-99			0.5	2.2	12.2
	100+			0.0	0.3	2.1
Female	Total	498.3	1 149.5	2 950.9	3 919.1	4 756.3
	0-14	210.6	550.9	882.1	959.1	864.5
	15-59	258.1	554.0	1 876.0	2 526.0	2 693.4
	60-64	10.6	17.2	67.1	130.8	285.2
	65-69	8.1	12.2	48.8	106.4	306.3
	70-74	6.2	8.1	34.1	82.2	230.9
	75-79	3.2	4.1	22.2	56.2	171.3
	80-84			12.7	33.3	108.9
	85-89			5.8	16.8	57.6
	90-94	1.5	3.0	1.8	6.5	27.6
	95-99			0.3	1.7	9.1
	100+			0.0	0.2	1.6
Male	Total	530.8	1 296.5	3 134.0	4 056.6	4 796.5
	0-14	220.6	575.2	925.1	1 008.1	907.8
	15-59	265.1	674.9	1 983.8	2 631.1	2 825.7
	60-64	15.5	19.0	86.8	132.1	287.8
	65-69	12.3	12.9	61.5	105.4	295.7
	70-74	9.3	7.9	40.2	80.9	209.5
	75-79	5.2	3.9	22.1	54.2	141.2
	80-84			9.9	28.9	78.7
	85-89			3.5	11.8	34.2
	90-94	2.8	2.7	0.9	3.5	12.6
	95-99			0.1	0.6	3.1
	100+			0.0	0.1	0.4
Percentage in older ages						
Total	60+	7.3	3.7	6.9	10.7	23.7
	65+	4.7	2.2	4.3	7.4	17.7
	80+	0.4	0.2	0.6	1.3	3.5
Female	60+	5.9	3.9	6.5	11.1	25.2
	65+	3.8	2.4	4.3	7.7	19.2
	80+	0.3	0.3	0.7	1.5	4.3
Male	60+	8.5	3.6	7.2	10.3	22.2
	65+	5.6	2.1	4.4	7.0	16.2
	80+	0.5	0.2	0.5	1.1	2.7
Ageing index		17.3	8.1	23.1	43.3	127.6
Broad age groups (percentage)	0-14	41.9	46.0	29.7	24.7	18.6
	15-59	50.8	50.2	63.4	64.7	57.8
	60+	7.3	3.7	6.9	10.7	23.7
Median age (years)		19.0	17.0	23.9*	31.1	39.3
Dependency ratio	Total	87.4	93.3	51.6	47.2	56.8
	Youth	78.5	89.0	45.0	36.3	29.1
	Old Age	8.8	4.3	6.6	10.9	27.7
Potential support ratio		11.3	23.1	15.2	9.2	3.6
Parent support ratio		1.4	1.0	2.1	3.8	8.8
Sex ratio (per 100 women)	60+	152.4	104.0	116.7	96.2	88.7
	65+	156.1	100.0	110.0	94.1	84.9
	80+	191.5	90.1	70.0	76.8	63.0

* Estimate refers to year 2005.

Indicator	Age	1950-1955	1975-1980	2005-2010	2025-2030	2045-2050
Growth rate (percentage)	Total	1.8	4.4	1.9	0.9	0.5
	60+	−0.1	4.4	4.7	4.1	2.5
	65+	−0.1	4.4	5.0	3.5	4.4
	80+	−0.9	0.7	6.3	5.5	5.2
Total fertility rate (per woman)		6.9	7.4	2.7	1.9	1.9
Life expectancy (years)						
Total	Birth	42.7	57.4	74.5	78.0	80.4
	60	..	..	19.3	21.4	23.2
	65	..	..	15.7	17.5	19.2
	80	..	..	7.6	8.4	9.3
Female	Birth	43.9	59.3	77.2	80.5	82.8
	60	..	..	21.6	23.7	25.3
	65	..	..	17.8	19.6	21.1
	80	..	..	8.4	9.4	10.3
Male	Birth	41.9	56.0	72.5	75.8	78.1
	60	..	..	17.6	19.4	21.1
	65	..	..	14.2	15.7	17.2
	80	..	..	6.7	7.4	8.0
Survival rate (percentage)						
Total	60	..	..	87.1	91.0	93.0
	65	..	..	80.1	85.7	88.9
	80	..	..	41.9	51.9	59.6
Female	60	..	..	89.3	92.4	94.3
	65	..	..	84.3	88.6	91.3
	80	..	..	52.2	61.2	67.7
Male	60	..	..	85.2	89.6	91.8
	65	..	..	76.8	82.9	86.6
	80	..	..	34.4	43.5	51.5

		1980	1990	2007	2010	2020
Labour force participation (percentage)						
Total	65+	21.7	22.3	24.3	24.2	23.5
Female	65+	4.7	4.5	4.2	4.1	4.1
Male	65+	38.9	40.0	42.5	42.6	42.7

Percentage married, age 60+				Percentage living alone, age 60+		
Total	Female	Male		Total	Female	Male
67.9	42.0	90.0		..	..	..

Statutory pensionable age (2006)				Percentage illiterate, age 65+		
	Female	Male		Total	Female	Male
	60	65		..	..	..

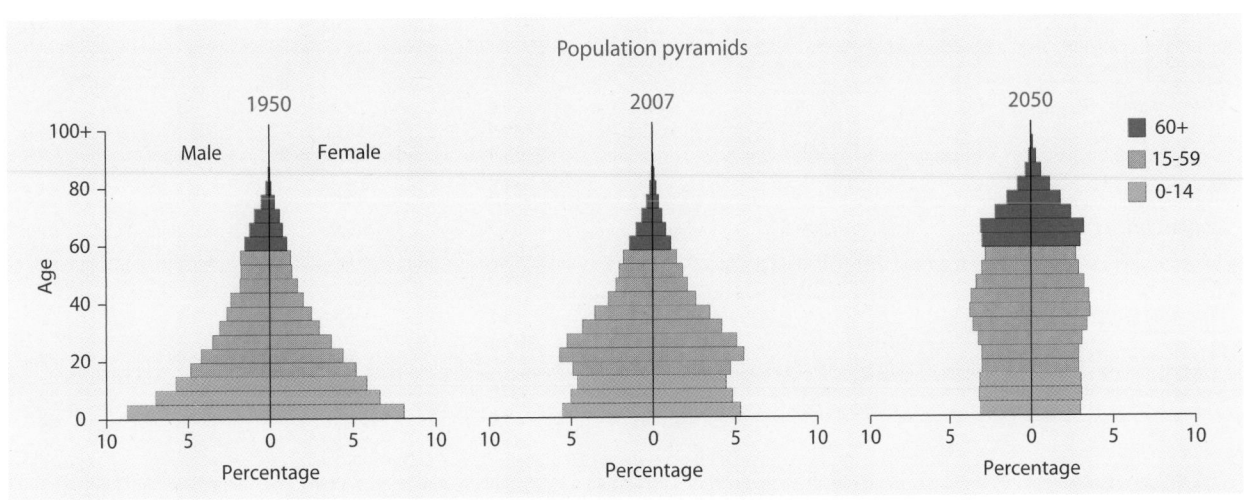

Population pyramids

Lithuania

Indicator	Age	1950	1975	2007	2025	2050
Population (thousands)						
Total	Total	2 567.4	3 301.6	3 403.0	3 129.5	2 564.6
	0-14	701.4	840.5	528.5	447.5	338.2
	15-59	1 524.7	1 962.3	2 164.7	1 834.3	1 254.0
	60-64	99.4	131.5	167.1	235.3	234.8
	65-69	84.9	139.3	165.0	195.9	198.0
	70-74	68.4	103.4	143.2	149.7	153.5
	75-79	49.3	64.4	117.4	100.7	144.3
	80-84			74.5	82.9	109.4
	85-89			28.2	51.4	81.3
	90-94	39.3	60.3	10.9	23.8	37.7
	95-99			3.3	7.1	11.4
	100+			0.4	0.8	1.9
Female	Total	1 409.4	1 747.0	1 817.3	1 668.3	1 363.2
	0-14	354.5	413.0	256.9	217.8	164.3
	15-59	841.0	1 029.6	1 106.2	922.0	615.5
	60-64	60.4	81.7	96.9	130.9	122.8
	65-69	52.2	77.3	100.2	114.3	106.6
	70-74	42.4	63.3	90.6	92.4	87.9
	75-79	32.1	42.0	79.6	66.7	88.9
	80-84			54.6	59.2	74.0
	85-89			21.2	39.1	60.2
	90-94	26.7	40.0	8.6	19.0	30.8
	95-99			2.4	6.1	10.2
	100+			0.2	0.7	1.8
Male	Total	1 158.0	1 554.7	1 585.7	1 461.2	1 201.4
	0-14	347.0	427.4	271.6	229.8	173.9
	15-59	683.7	932.6	1 058.4	912.3	638.5
	60-64	39.0	49.8	70.2	104.3	112.0
	65-69	32.6	62.1	64.8	81.6	91.4
	70-74	26.0	40.1	52.6	57.3	65.6
	75-79	17.1	22.4	37.8	34.0	55.3
	80-84			19.9	23.7	35.4
	85-89			7.0	12.4	21.1
	90-94	12.6	20.2	2.4	4.8	6.9
	95-99			0.9	1.0	1.2
	100+			0.1	0.1	0.1
Percentage in older ages						
Total	60+	13.3	15.1	20.9	27.1	37.9
	65+	9.4	11.1	15.9	19.6	28.8
	80+	1.5	1.8	3.4	5.3	9.4
Female	60+	15.2	17.4	25.0	31.7	42.8
	65+	10.9	12.7	19.7	23.8	33.8
	80+	1.9	2.3	4.8	7.4	13.0
Male	60+	11.0	12.5	16.1	21.8	32.4
	65+	7.6	9.3	11.7	14.7	23.1
	80+	1.1	1.3	1.9	2.9	5.4
Ageing index		48.6	59.4	134.3	189.4	287.6
Broad age groups (percentage)	0-14	27.3	25.5	15.5	14.3	13.2
	15-59	59.4	59.4	63.6	58.6	48.9
	60+	13.3	15.1	20.9	27.1	37.9
Median age (years)		27.8	31.3	37.8*	43.5	51.7
Dependency ratio	Total	58.1	57.7	45.9	51.2	72.3
	Youth	43.2	40.1	22.7	21.6	22.7
	Old Age	14.9	17.5	23.3	29.6	49.5
Potential support ratio		6.7	5.7	4.3	3.4	2.0
Parent support ratio		4.7	5.6	7.6	12.3	22.2
Sex ratio (per 100 women)	60+	59.5	64.0	56.3	60.4	66.7
	65+	57.5	65.0	51.9	54.0	60.2
	80+	47.0	50.5	34.8	33.8	36.6

* *Estimate refers to year 2005.*

Indicator	Age	1950-1955	1975-1980	2005-2010	2025-2030	2045-2050
Growth rate (percentage)	Total	0.5	0.7	−0.4	−0.7	−0.9
	60+	−0.3	−0.4	0.0	0.8	0.9
	65+	−0.3	1.0	0.8	1.9	0.5
	80+	0.2	2.8	5.2	−0.6	0.7
Total fertility rate (per woman)		2.7	2.1	1.3	1.5	1.8
Life expectancy (years)						
Total	Birth	64.9	70.8	73.3	77.0	79.6
	60	..	..	20.0	21.5	22.8
	65	..	..	16.4	17.7	18.9
	80	..	..	7.9	8.6	9.3
Female	Birth	67.8	75.4	78.6	81.3	83.5
	60	..	..	22.4	24.2	25.8
	65	..	..	18.3	20.0	21.4
	80	..	..	8.4	9.4	10.4
Male	Birth	61.5	66.0	67.8	72.4	75.5
	60	..	..	16.7	18.1	19.4
	65	..	..	13.7	14.7	15.7
	80	..	..	6.8	6.9	7.2
Survival rate (percentage)						
Total	60	..	..	81.4	87.7	91.3
	65	..	..	75.2	82.4	86.8
	80	..	..	41.5	50.1	56.8
Female	60	..	..	90.3	93.0	94.7
	65	..	..	86.3	89.8	92.1
	80	..	..	55.6	63.6	69.7
Male	60	..	..	72.5	82.4	88.0
	65	..	..	63.7	74.7	81.6
	80	..	..	26.5	35.2	42.9

		1980	1990	2007	2010	2020
Labour force participation (percentage)						
Total	65+	12.2	9.4	4.0	3.9	3.8
Female	65+	7.8	6.9	2.4	2.2	2.1
Male	65+	19.7	14.3	7.2	7.2	7.1

Percentage married, age 60+			Percentage living alone, age 60+ (1989)		
Total	Female	Male	Total	Female	Male
53.2	39.0	78.0	23.1	29.4	12.2

Statutory pensionable age (2006)			Percentage illiterate, age 65+ (2001)		
	Female	Male	Total	Female	Male
	59	62.5	0.7	0.7	0.6

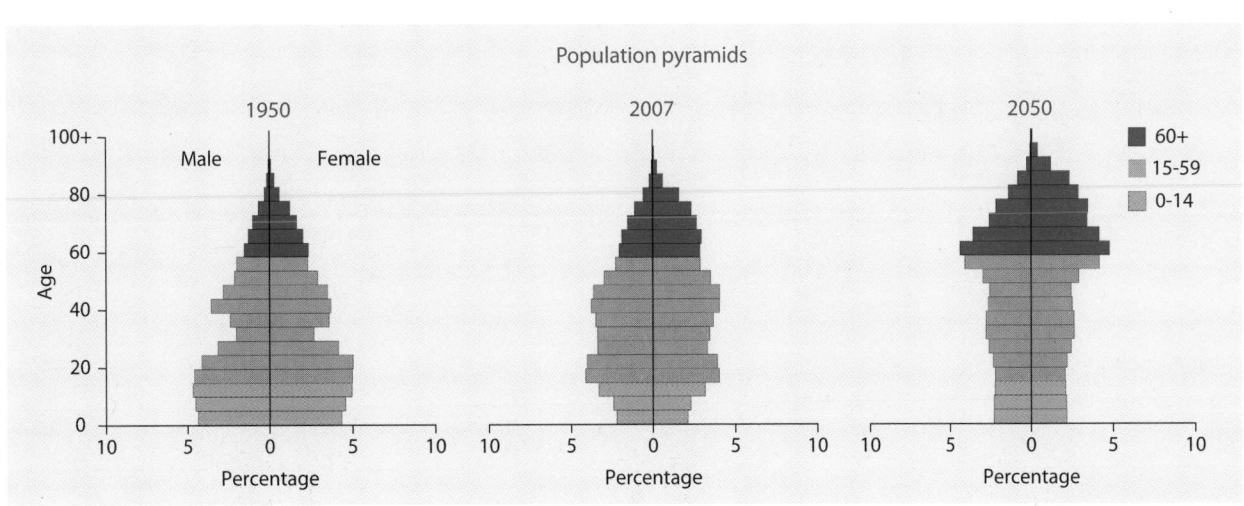

Population pyramids

1950 · 2007 · 2050

Male · Female

60+ · 15-59 · 0-14

Luxembourg

Indicator	Age	1950	1975	2007	2025	2050
Population (thousands)						
Total	Total	296.0	359.0	476.7	582.0	721.4
	0-14	59.0	77.4	89.1	98.4	119.8
	15-59	194.0	214.9	299.8	350.7	404.5
	60-64	14.0	19.8	22.3	37.6	41.0
	65-69	12.0	17.6	18.6	30.6	37.2
	70-74	8.1	13.3	16.3	23.6	35.3
	75-79	5.2	8.2	14.6	18.2	31.3
	80-84			9.4	11.0	25.1
	85-89			4.3	7.0	16.2
	90-94	3.7	7.7	1.9	3.4	7.8
	95-99			0.4	1.2	2.7
	100+			0.0	0.2	0.6
Female	Total	148.0	180.7	241.8	294.6	366.9
	0-14	29.0	37.6	43.3	47.8	58.2
	15-59	97.0	105.0	148.1	173.9	199.1
	60-64	7.0	10.7	11.2	18.8	20.7
	65-69	6.0	10.2	9.8	15.8	19.1
	70-74	4.2	7.6	9.1	12.6	18.9
	75-79	2.7	4.7	8.5	10.2	17.4
	80-84			6.4	6.8	14.7
	85-89			3.3	4.9	10.3
	90-94	2.0	4.9	1.6	2.7	5.7
	95-99			0.4	1.1	2.2
	100+			0.0	0.2	0.5
Male	Total	148.0	178.3	234.9	287.4	354.5
	0-14	30.0	39.7	45.7	50.5	61.6
	15-59	97.0	109.9	151.6	176.9	205.4
	60-64	7.0	9.1	11.1	18.8	20.3
	65-69	6.0	7.4	8.8	14.8	18.1
	70-74	3.9	5.6	7.2	11.0	16.3
	75-79	2.4	3.6	6.0	8.0	14.0
	80-84			3.0	4.3	10.3
	85-89			1.0	2.2	5.9
	90-94	1.7	2.9	0.3	0.7	2.2
	95-99			0.0	0.1	0.5
	100+			0.0	0.0	0.1
Percentage in older ages						
Total	60+	14.5	18.6	18.4	22.8	27.3
	65+	9.8	13.1	13.8	16.4	21.6
	80+	1.3	2.2	3.4	3.9	7.3
Female	60+	14.9	21.1	20.8	24.8	29.9
	65+	10.1	15.1	16.2	18.4	24.2
	80+	1.4	2.7	4.8	5.3	9.1
Male	60+	14.2	16.1	16.0	20.9	24.7
	65+	9.5	10.9	11.3	14.3	19.0
	80+	1.1	1.6	1.9	2.5	5.3
Ageing index		72.9	86.2	98.6	135.1	164.6
Broad age groups (percentage)	0-14	19.9	21.6	18.7	16.9	16.6
	15-59	65.5	59.9	62.9	60.3	56.1
	60+	14.5	18.6	18.4	22.8	27.3
Median age (years)		35.0	34.4	38.1*	41.3	42.9
Dependency ratio	Total	42.3	52.9	48.0	49.9	61.9
	Youth	28.4	33.0	27.7	25.3	26.9
	Old Age	13.9	20.0	20.4	24.5	35.1
Potential support ratio		7.2	5.0	4.9	4.1	2.9
Parent support ratio		2.7	4.6	8.2	9.7	20.2
Sex ratio (per 100 women)	60+	95.5	75.3	74.7	82.2	80.0
	65+	93.3	71.4	67.5	76.0	75.8
	80+	83.2	59.1	37.6	46.7	56.4

* *Estimate refers to year 2005.*

Indicator	Age	1950-1955	1975-1980	2005-2010	2025-2030	2045-2050
Growth rate (percentage)	Total	0.6	0.3	1.2	1.0	0.7
	60+	1.8	−0.8	1.8	2.6	0.9
	65+	2.0	1.0	1.1	2.9	0.9
	80+	4.9	−0.6	4.8	3.1	3.0
Total fertility rate (per woman)		2.0	1.5	1.7	1.8	1.9
Life expectancy (years)						
Total	Birth	65.9	71.7	79.1	81.7	83.7
	60	..	..	22.6	24.1	25.6
	65	..	..	18.4	19.9	21.2
	80	..	..	8.6	9.5	10.3
Female	Birth	68.9	75.3	82.2	84.5	86.5
	60	..	..	24.8	26.5	28.0
	65	..	..	20.5	22.1	23.5
	80	..	..	9.6	10.7	11.7
Male	Birth	63.1	68.2	75.9	78.8	80.8
	60	..	..	19.9	21.6	23.0
	65	..	..	15.9	17.5	18.7
	80	..	..	6.6	7.7	8.5
Survival rate (percentage)						
Total	60	..	..	91.2	93.8	95.3
	65	..	..	87.3	90.6	92.6
	80	..	..	56.7	63.8	69.2
Female	60	..	..	93.6	95.3	96.5
	65	..	..	90.8	93.0	94.6
	80	..	..	66.5	72.5	77.3
Male	60	..	..	88.9	92.3	94.1
	65	..	..	83.9	88.2	90.7
	80	..	..	46.4	54.8	60.8

		1980	1990	2007	2010	2020
Labour force participation (percentage)						
Total	65+	3.0	1.7	0.8	0.8	0.7
Female	65+	1.8	1.1	0.4	0.4	0.4
Male	65+	4.9	2.7	1.4	1.3	1.1

Percentage married, age 60+			Percentage living alone, age 60+		
Total	Female	Male	Total	Female	Male
55.8	41.0	76.0	..	..	..

Statutory pensionable age (2006)			Percentage illiterate, age 65+		
Female	Male		Total	Female	Male
65	65		..	..	..

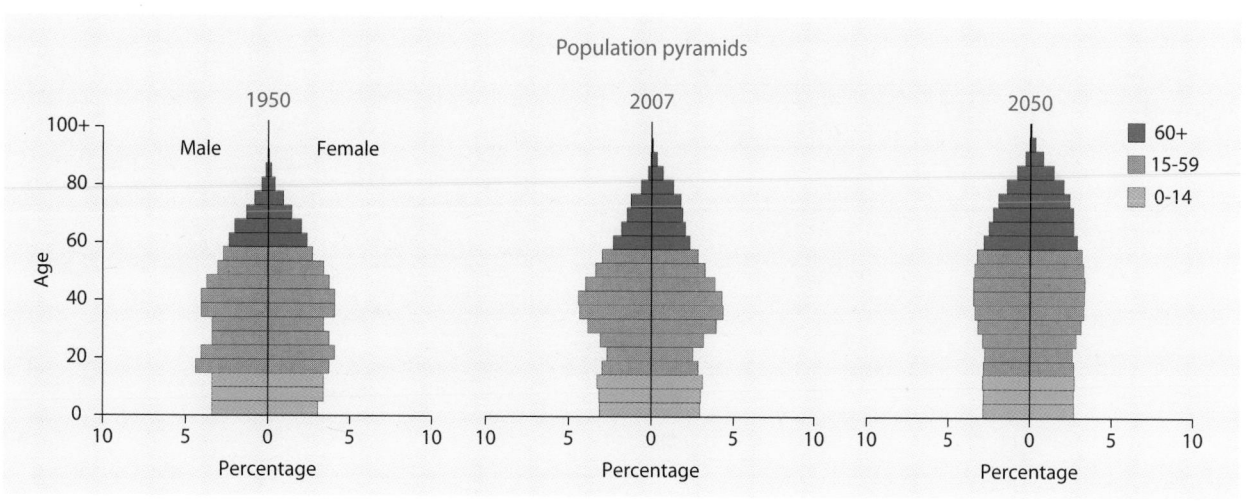

Population pyramids

Madagascar

Indicator	Age	1950	1975	2007	2025	2050
Population (thousands)						
Total	Total	4 229.6	7 909.1	19 608.9 ·	29 434.4	43 508.4
	0-14	1 767.3	3 561.2	8 540.4	10 855.7	12 039.9
	15-59	2 263.7	3 964.1	10 122.7	16 793.5	27 279.5
	60-64	82.4	148.4	326.8	630.3	1 410.9
	65-69	57.0	107.8	256.1	480.6	1 063.5
	70-74	34.4	70.2	179.1	336.3	775.7
	75-79	17.1	38.4	108.6	188.4	507.2
	80-84			52.4	100.0	279.8
	85-89			18.3	38.6	115.4
	90-94	7.7	19.1	3.9	9.6	31.3
	95-99			0.5	1.4	4.9
	100+			0.0	0.1	0.4
Female	Total	2 153.2	3 982.6	9 851.8	14 731.0	21 799.8
	0-14	896.5	1 776.1	4 257.7	5 377.7	5 969.3
	15-59	1 150.6	2 001.7	5 086.2	8 409.7	13 637.9
	60-64	43.7	77.6	171.8	325.8	720.5
	65-69	30.5	57.2	136.4	251.4	548.8
	70-74	18.5	37.9	96.8	178.0	407.7
	75-79	9.2	21.2	59.8	102.9	273.2
	80-84			29.6	56.2	154.6
	85-89			10.7	22.4	65.7
	90-94	4.2	11.0	2.4	5.9	18.6
	95-99			0.3	0.9	3.1
	100+			0.0	0.1	0.3
Male	Total	2 076.4	3 926.5	9 757.1	14 703.5	21 708.6
	0-14	870.8	1 785.0	4 282.7	5 477.9	6 070.6
	15-59	1 113.1	1 962.4	5 036.5	8 383.8	13 641.5
	60-64	38.7	70.8	155.1	304.5	690.3
	65-69	26.5	50.6	119.6	229.2	514.7
	70-74	15.9	32.3	82.3	158.3	367.9
	75-79	7.9	17.2	48.8	85.5	234.0
	80-84			22.9	43.8	125.2
	85-89			7.5	16.2	49.7
	90-94	3.5	8.1	1.4	3.7	12.7
	95-99			0.1	0.5	1.8
	100+			0.0	0.0	0.1
Percentage in older ages						
Total	60+	4.7	4.9	4.8	6.1	9.6
	65+	2.7	3.0	3.2	3.9	6.4
	80+	0.2	0.2	0.4	0.5	1.0
Female	60+	4.9	5.1	5.2	6.4	10.1
	65+	2.9	3.2	3.4	4.2	6.8
	80+	0.2	0.3	0.4	0.6	1.1
Male	60+	4.5	4.6	4.5	5.7	9.2
	65+	2.6	2.8	2.9	3.7	6.0
	80+	0.2	0.2	0.3	0.4	0.9
Ageing index		11.2	10.8	11.1	16.4	34.8
Broad age groups (percentage)	0-14	41.8	45.0	43.6	36.9	27.7
	15-59	53.5	50.1	51.6	57.1	62.7
	60+	4.7	4.9	4.8	6.1	9.6
Median age (years)		19.0	17.4	17.8*	21.2	27.8
Dependency ratio	Total	80.3	92.3	87.7	68.9	51.6
	Youth	75.3	86.6	81.7	62.3	42.0
	Old Age	5.0	5.7	5.9	6.6	9.7
Potential support ratio		20.2	17.5	16.9	15.1	10.3
Parent support ratio		0.6	0.8	1.7	2.1	2.8
Sex ratio (per 100 women)	60+	87.2	87.4	86.2	89.2	91.1
	65+	86.2	85.1	84.1	87.0	88.7
	80+	83.5	74.3	74.4	75.2	78.2

* Estimate refers to year 2005.

Indicator	Age	1950-1955	1975-1980	2005-2010	2025-2030	2045-2050
Growth rate (percentage)	Total	2.3	2.7	2.6	1.9	1.3
	60+	2.4	2.8	2.7	3.5	3.5
	65+	2.5	3.0	3.0	3.8	3.4
	80+	2.6	4.2	4.1	3.4	3.8
Total fertility rate (per woman)		6.8	6.6	4.9	3.1	2.4
Life expectancy (years)						
Total	Birth	36.7	46.9	56.2	63.0	69.3
	60	..	..	16.9	18.2	19.2
	65	..	..	13.6	14.6	15.5
	80	..	..	5.9	6.4	6.7
Female	Birth	37.0	47.9	57.4	64.3	71.1
	60	..	..	17.4	18.8	19.9
	65	..	..	14.0	15.1	16.0
	80	..	..	6.1	6.6	6.9
Male	Birth	36.4	45.9	55.0	61.7	67.6
	60	..	..	16.3	17.5	18.5
	65	..	..	13.1	14.1	14.9
	80	..	..	5.7	6.1	6.5
Survival rate (percentage)						
Total	60	..	..	58.0	67.4	77.5
	65	..	..	52.0	61.6	72.1
	80	..	..	21.9	29.5	37.8
Female	60	..	..	60.0	69.3	80.1
	65	..	..	54.4	64.1	75.3
	80	..	..	24.1	32.3	41.6
Male	60	..	..	56.0	65.5	75.1
	65	..	..	49.6	59.2	69.0
	80	..	..	19.8	26.8	34.1

		1980	1990	2007	2010	2020
Labour force participation (percentage)						
Total	65+	69.6	70.9	71.7	71.8	72.0
Female	65+	65.8	65.4	63.7	63.7	63.6
Male	65+	74.1	77.3	81.3	81.5	81.7

Percentage married, age 60+			Percentage living alone, age 60+ (1997)		
Total	Female	Male	Total	Female	Male
52.4	32.0	76.0	8.0	11.4	4.4

Statutory pensionable age (2006)		Percentage illiterate, age 65+ (2000)		
Female	Male	Total	Female	Male
55	60	53.4	69.0	39.4

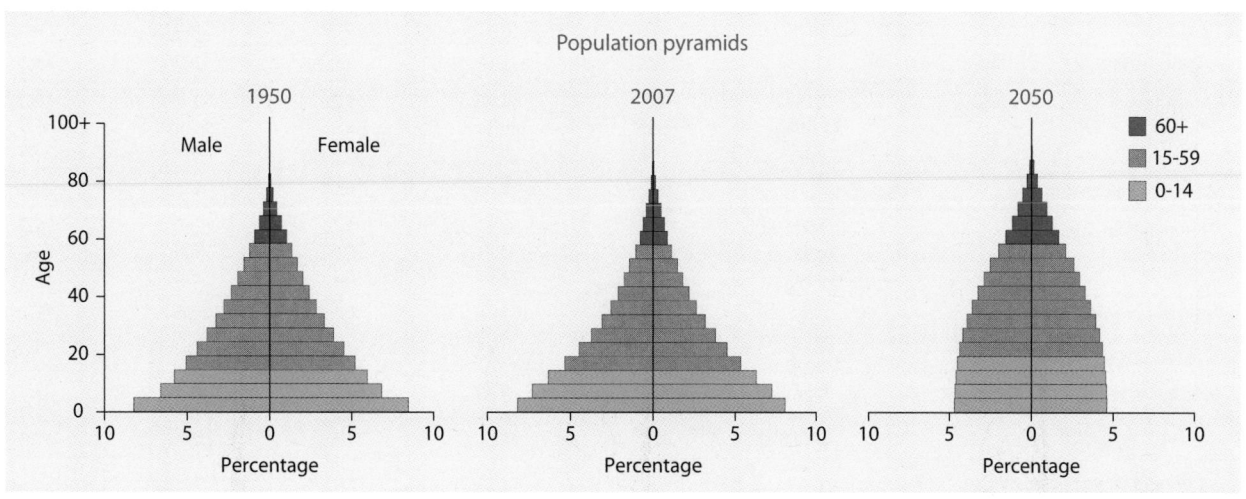

Population pyramids

Malawi

Indicator	Age	1950	1975	2007	2025	2050
Population (thousands)						
Total	Total	2 880.7	5 244.0	13 451.8	19 737.0	29 451.6
	0-14	1 316.5	2 477.3	6 354.5	8 372.6	9 490.9
	15-59	1 422.2	2 573.3	6 465.3	10 454.5	18 226.8
	60-64	53.8	80.2	225.4	283.9	593.9
	65-69	40.6	49.4	170.6	237.8	454.9
	70-74	26.7	35.5	120.1	184.1	337.6
	75-79	14.1	18.7	72.3	124.9	190.1
	80-84			32.5	57.5	105.6
	85-89			9.5	18.2	41.8
	90-94	6.8	9.5	1.5	3.1	9.1
	95-99			0.1	0.3	1.0
	100+			0.0	0.0	0.0
Female	Total	1 491.2	2 716.7	6 757.5	9 764.9	14 579.1
	0-14	675.1	1 267.7	3 152.2	4 144.7	4 698.2
	15-59	738.4	1 340.5	3 267.3	5 104.7	8 992.9
	60-64	29.0	44.3	119.2	154.4	290.7
	65-69	22.3	27.5	90.3	134.6	225.9
	70-74	14.6	20.1	63.6	106.5	170.6
	75-79	7.9	10.9	39.5	72.8	103.4
	80-84			18.7	34.0	63.1
	85-89			5.7	11.1	27.0
	90-94	3.9	5.7	1.0	2.0	6.4
	95-99			0.1	0.2	0.7
	100+			0.0	0.0	0.0
Male	Total	1 389.5	2 527.3	6 694.4	9 972.1	14 872.5
	0-14	641.4	1 209.7	3 202.3	4 228.0	4 792.7
	15-59	683.8	1 232.8	3 198.0	5 349.8	9 233.9
	60-64	24.8	35.9	106.2	129.5	303.1
	65-69	18.3	21.9	80.4	103.2	229.0
	70-74	12.1	15.4	56.5	77.6	166.9
	75-79	6.2	7.8	32.8	52.1	86.7
	80-84			13.8	23.5	42.4
	85-89			3.8	7.1	14.8
	90-94	2.9	3.8	0.6	1.1	2.7
	95-99			0.0	0.1	0.2
	100+			0.0	0.0	0.0
Percentage in older ages						
Total	60+	4.9	3.7	4.7	4.6	5.9
	65+	3.1	2.2	3.0	3.2	3.9
	80+	0.2	0.2	0.3	0.4	0.5
Female	60+	5.2	4.0	5.0	5.3	6.1
	65+	3.3	2.4	3.2	3.7	4.1
	80+	0.3	0.2	0.4	0.5	0.7
Male	60+	4.6	3.4	4.4	4.0	5.7
	65+	2.8	1.9	2.8	2.7	3.6
	80+	0.2	0.2	0.3	0.3	0.4
Ageing index		10.8	7.8	9.9	10.9	18.3
Broad age groups (percentage)	0-14	45.7	47.2	47.2	42.4	32.2
	15-59	49.4	49.1	48.1	53.0	61.9
	60+	4.9	3.7	4.7	4.6	5.9
Median age (years)		17.1	16.4	16.3*	18.3	23.7
Dependency ratio	Total	95.2	97.6	101.1	83.8	56.5
	Youth	89.2	93.4	95.0	78.0	50.4
	Old Age	6.0	4.3	6.1	5.8	6.1
Potential support ratio		16.7	23.5	16.5	17.2	16.5
Parent support ratio		0.7	0.6	1.3	2.2	2.0
Sex ratio (per 100 women)	60+	82.7	78.3	87.0	76.5	95.3
	65+	81.1	76.3	85.9	73.3	90.9
	80+	74.3	66.5	71.6	67.4	61.8

* Estimate refers to year 2005.

Indicator	Age	1950-1955	1975-1980	2005-2010	2025-2030	2045-2050
Growth rate (percentage)	Total	1.9	3.3	2.2	1.9	1.4
	60+	0.3	4.8	2.6	1.4	3.6
	65+	0.2	4.2	2.4	1.8	3.7
	80+	0.6	3.5	3.3	4.2	1.9
Total fertility rate (per woman)		6.8	7.6	5.7	3.7	2.6
Life expectancy (years)						
Total	Birth	36.3	43.8	41.1	50.4	58.9
	60	..	..	16.0	17.5	19.0
	65	..	..	12.8	14.0	15.2
	80	..	..	5.1	5.6	6.0
Female	Birth	36.7	44.6	40.6	50.3	60.3
	60	..	..	16.9	18.5	20.2
	65	..	..	13.4	14.7	16.2
	80	..	..	5.3	5.8	6.3
Male	Birth	35.8	43.0	41.6	50.3	57.7
	60	..	..	15.1	16.4	17.7
	65	..	..	12.1	13.2	14.2
	80	..	..	4.9	5.2	5.6
Survival rate (percentage)						
Total	60	..	..	28.5	41.3	55.6
	65	..	..	25.2	37.4	51.6
	80	..	..	9.6	17.1	27.0
Female	60	..	..	27.5	40.7	57.6
	65	..	..	24.8	37.7	54.6
	80	..	..	10.4	18.7	31.5
Male	60	..	..	29.4	41.7	53.8
	65	..	..	25.4	37.0	48.9
	80	..	..	8.8	15.1	23.0

		1980	1990	2007	2010	2020
Labour force participation (percentage)						
Total	65+	77.0	77.1	78.2	78.9	79.0
Female	65+	71.8	70.0	74.4	76.4	78.5
Male	65+	83.9	85.9	82.7	81.8	79.6

Percentage married, age 60+			Percentage living alone, age 60+ (2000)		
Total	Female	Male	Total	Female	Male
64.9	44.0	88.0	11.4	13.9	8.4

Statutory pensionable age (2006)		Percentage illiterate, age 65+ (1998)		
Female	Male	Total	Female	Male
..	..	64.3	78.7	48.0

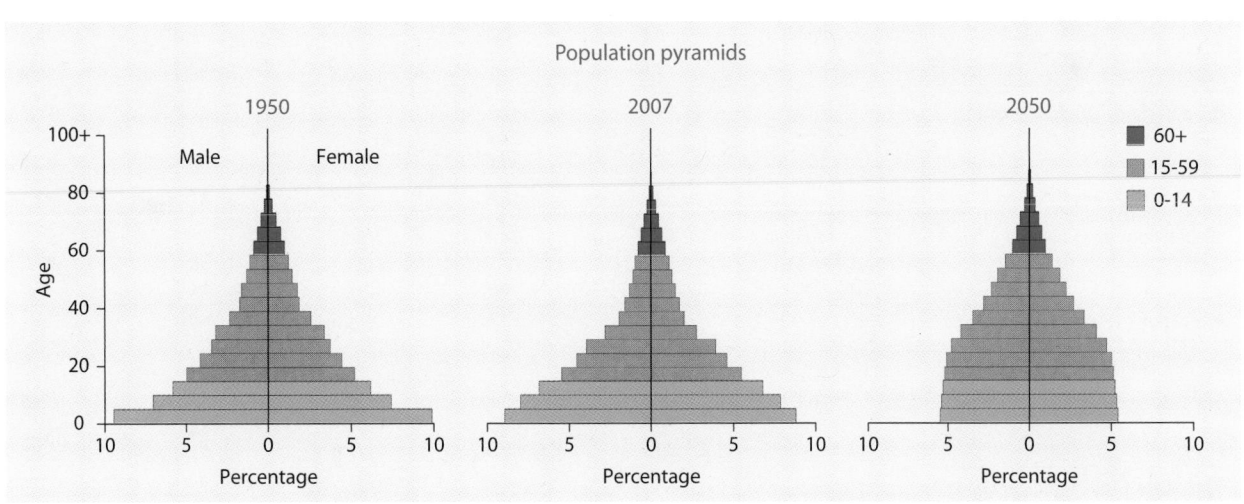

Population pyramids

United Nations Department of Economic and Social Affairs, Population Division

Malaysia

Indicator	Age	1950	1975	2007	2025	2050
Population (thousands)						
Total	Total	6 109.9	12 257.8	26 239.5	33 223.3	38 924.0
	0-14	2 498.8	5 159.8	8 226.4	7 844.2	7 076.0
	15-59	3 163.6	6 412.0	16 080.0	20 959.3	23 443.2
	60-64	138.6	228.8	682.4	1 465.7	2 121.2
	65-69	109.0	193.4	512.5	1 188.4	1 995.0
	70-74	97.9	114.7	352.8	835.5	1 579.9
	75-79	63.3	88.3	216.5	514.6	1 194.1
	80-84			107.1	249.4	803.3
	85-89			45.3	122.1	465.6
	90-94	38.7	60.8	13.6	35.6	190.6
	95-99			2.7	7.7	48.3
	100+			0.3	0.8	6.8
Female	Total	2 965.6	6 089.0	12 925.9	16 440.2	19 365.5
	0-14	1 242.5	2 545.7	4 003.3	3 809.7	3 435.0
	15-59	1 509.8	3 203.3	7 912.6	10 272.8	11 426.7
	60-64	66.6	111.6	339.8	749.2	1 054.6
	65-69	50.0	94.8	262.4	618.2	1 013.0
	70-74	46.4	54.3	188.9	448.2	829.7
	75-79	30.9	45.9	121.1	287.4	660.5
	80-84			61.6	146.1	473.1
	85-89			26.5	77.7	296.8
	90-94	19.4	33.4	8.0	24.6	133.3
	95-99			1.6	5.7	37.2
	100+			0.2	0.6	5.6
Male	Total	3 144.3	6 168.8	13 313.6	16 783.1	19 558.5
	0-14	1 256.3	2 614.1	4 223.1	4 034.5	3 641.1
	15-59	1 653.8	3 208.7	8 167.4	10 686.5	12 016.6
	60-64	72.0	117.2	342.6	716.5	1 066.6
	65-69	59.0	98.6	250.0	570.2	982.1
	70-74	51.5	60.4	163.9	387.3	750.2
	75-79	32.4	42.4	95.4	227.2	533.5
	80-84			45.5	103.3	330.2
	85-89			18.8	44.4	168.8
	90-94	19.3	27.4	5.6	11.0	57.3
	95-99			1.1	2.0	11.0
	100+			0.1	0.2	1.2
Percentage in older ages						
Total	60+	7.3	5.6	7.4	13.3	21.6
	65+	5.1	3.7	4.8	8.9	16.1
	80+	0.6	0.5	0.6	1.3	3.9
Female	60+	7.2	5.6	7.8	14.3	23.3
	65+	4.9	3.8	5.2	9.8	17.8
	80+	0.7	0.5	0.8	1.5	4.9
Male	60+	7.4	5.6	6.9	12.3	19.9
	65+	5.2	3.7	4.4	8.0	14.5
	80+	0.6	0.4	0.5	1.0	2.9
Ageing index		17.9	13.3	23.5	56.3	118.8
Broad age groups (percentage)	0-14	40.9	42.1	31.4	23.6	18.2
	15-59	51.8	52.3	61.3	63.1	60.2
	60+	7.3	5.6	7.4	13.3	21.6
Median age (years)		19.8	18.6	24.7*	31.1	39.3
Dependency ratio	Total	85.0	84.6	56.5	48.2	52.3
	Youth	75.7	77.7	49.1	35.0	27.7
	Old Age	9.4	6.9	7.5	13.2	24.6
Potential support ratio		10.7	14.5	13.4	7.6	4.1
Parent support ratio		2.7	2.6	2.1	3.4	9.6
Sex ratio (per 100 women)	60+	109.8	101.8	91.4	87.5	86.6
	65+	110.6	100.2	86.6	83.7	82.2
	80+	99.5	82.0	72.8	63.2	60.1

* *Estimate refers to year 2005.*

Indicator	Age	1950-1955	1975-1980	2005-2010	2025-2030	2045-2050
Growth rate (percentage)	Total	2.7	2.3	1.7	0.9	0.4
	60+	−1.4	2.7	4.7	3.2	1.9
	65+	−0.7	1.9	3.7	4.1	2.5
	80+	0.6	2.3	5.5	6.3	3.2
Total fertility rate (per woman)		6.8	4.2	2.6	1.9	1.9
Life expectancy (years)						
Total	Birth	48.4	65.2	74.1	77.4	79.9
	60	..	..	18.7	20.6	22.5
	65	..	..	15.0	16.7	18.5
	80	..	..	6.9	7.8	8.8
Female	Birth	50.0	67.1	76.5	79.8	82.3
	60	..	..	20.0	22.5	24.5
	65	..	..	16.1	18.4	20.2
	80	..	..	7.3	8.6	9.7
Male	Birth	47.0	63.5	71.9	75.1	77.6
	60	..	..	17.3	18.7	20.6
	65	..	..	13.9	15.0	16.7
	80	..	..	6.5	6.8	7.7
Survival rate (percentage)						
Total	60	..	..	87.1	91.1	93.1
	65	..	..	80.2	85.7	88.8
	80	..	..	39.5	49.1	57.4
Female	60	..	..	90.3	93.1	94.7
	65	..	..	85.0	89.1	91.5
	80	..	..	46.6	57.7	65.5
Male	60	..	..	84.0	89.2	91.5
	65	..	..	75.7	82.4	86.2
	80	..	..	32.9	40.7	49.4

		1980	1990	2007	2010	2020
Labour force participation (percentage)						
Total	65+	31.0	40.4	35.6	31.5	19.6
Female	65+	14.2	27.5	25.7	23.4	11.8
Male	65+	48.2	55.3	47.1	40.9	28.7

Percentage married, age 60+			Percentage living alone, age 60+ (1991)		
Total	Female	Male	Total	Female	Male
67.1	50.0	86.0	6.8	8.7	4.7

Statutory pensionable age (2006)		Percentage illiterate, age 65+ (2000)		
Female	Male	Total	Female	Male
55	55	55.7	69.5	39.8

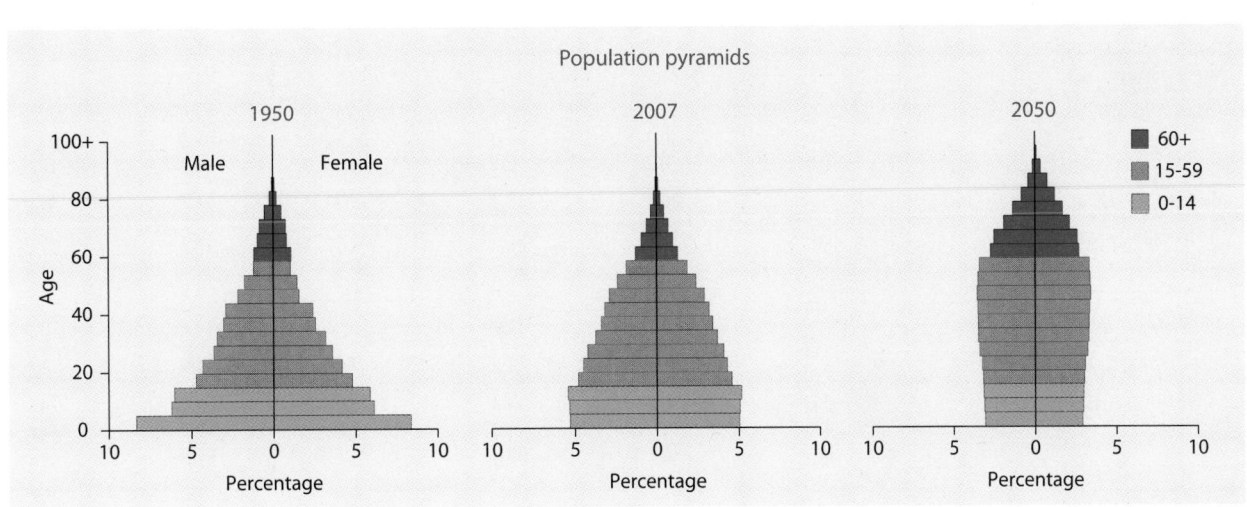

Population pyramids

Maldives

Indicator	Age	1950	1975	2007	2025	2050
Population (thousands)						
Total	Total	82.0	137.3	345.7	505.5	682.3
	0-14	27.1	57.4	136.7	159.4	143.9
	15-59	48.2	70.5	191.7	311.2	435.9
	60-64	2.5	3.4	5.4	12.7	34.3
	65-69	1.9	2.6	4.6	9.5	27.2
	70-74	1.2	1.8	3.4	6.8	18.3
	75-79	0.7	1.1	2.2	3.3	11.9
	80-84			1.1	1.8	6.6
	85-89			0.4	0.7	3.0
	90-94	0.5	0.6	0.1	0.2	0.9
	95-99			0.0	0.0	0.2
	100+			0.0	0.0	0.0
Female	Total	37.8	64.9	168.2	247.4	336.9
	0-14	12.8	27.7	66.5	78.2	70.7
	15-59	22.0	32.8	93.6	151.5	213.5
	60-64	1.2	1.6	2.6	6.1	17.0
	65-69	0.9	1.2	2.1	4.8	13.9
	70-74	0.6	0.9	1.6	3.6	9.4
	75-79	0.3	0.5	1.1	1.8	6.2
	80-84			0.5	0.9	3.7
	85-89			0.2	0.4	1.7
	90-94	0.2	0.3	0.0	0.1	0.6
	95-99			0.0	0.0	0.1
	100+			0.0	0.0	0.0
Male	Total	44.2	72.4	177.5	258.1	345.4
	0-14	14.3	29.7	70.3	81.1	73.2
	15-59	26.2	37.7	98.2	159.7	222.4
	60-64	1.4	1.8	2.8	6.6	17.3
	65-69	1.0	1.4	2.5	4.6	13.4
	70-74	0.7	0.9	1.8	3.2	8.9
	75-79	0.4	0.6	1.2	1.5	5.7
	80-84			0.6	0.9	3.0
	85-89			0.2	0.4	1.2
	90-94	0.3	0.3	0.0	0.1	0.3
	95-99			0.0	0.0	0.0
	100+			0.0	0.0	0.0
Percentage in older ages						
Total	60+	8.2	6.9	5.0	6.9	15.0
	65+	5.1	4.4	3.4	4.4	10.0
	80+	0.6	0.4	0.5	0.5	1.6
Female	60+	8.1	6.8	4.9	7.1	15.6
	65+	5.0	4.4	3.3	4.7	10.6
	80+	0.5	0.4	0.5	0.5	1.8
Male	60+	8.3	6.9	5.1	6.7	14.4
	65+	5.1	4.4	3.5	4.1	9.4
	80+	0.6	0.4	0.4	0.5	1.3
Ageing index		24.8	16.4	12.6	21.9	71.1
Broad age groups (percentage)	0-14	33.1	41.8	39.6	31.5	21.1
	15-59	58.8	51.3	55.5	61.6	63.9
	60+	8.2	6.9	5.0	6.9	15.0
Median age (years)		24.7	18.9	18.9*	24.8	34.0
Dependency ratio	Total	61.7	85.9	75.4	56.1	45.1
	Youth	53.4	77.7	69.4	49.2	30.6
	Old Age	8.2	8.2	6.0	6.9	14.5
Potential support ratio		12.1	12.2	16.6	14.6	6.9
Parent support ratio		1.3	1.2	1.9	1.9	3.4
Sex ratio (per 100 women)	60+	119.2	113.3	110.0	98.0	94.5
	65+	119.8	111.3	111.0	92.3	91.1
	80+	141.0	109.4	93.7	99.0	74.1

* *Estimate refers to year 2005.*

Indicator	Age	1950-1955	1975-1980	2005-2010	2025-2030	2045-2050
Growth rate (percentage)	Total	1.8	2.8	2.4	1.6	0.9
	60+	0.8	1.7	1.9	4.1	4.4
	65+	0.7	1.9	1.9	4.6	5.0
	80+	−2.7	3.0	4.3	3.3	4.9
Total fertility rate (per woman)		7.0	7.0	3.8	2.4	1.9
Life expectancy (years)						
Total	Birth	38.9	54.6	68.5	74.6	77.7
	60	..	..	17.2	19.0	20.9
	65	..	..	13.7	15.2	16.9
	80	..	..	5.8	6.4	7.5
Female	Birth	37.6	53.2	68.4	75.7	79.3
	60	..	..	17.7	19.9	22.3
	65	..	..	14.1	15.9	18.2
	80	..	..	5.9	6.7	8.1
Male	Birth	40.1	55.9	68.6	73.5	76.3
	60	..	..	16.7	18.1	19.6
	65	..	..	13.3	14.4	15.7
	80	..	..	5.7	6.1	6.8
Survival rate (percentage)						
Total	60	..	..	78.8	88.2	91.6
	65	..	..	71.5	82.2	86.9
	80	..	..	30.7	42.0	51.5
Female	60	..	..	78.4	89.3	92.5
	65	..	..	71.8	84.3	88.8
	80	..	..	32.6	46.4	57.6
Male	60	..	..	79.1	87.1	90.7
	65	..	..	71.0	80.2	85.0
	80	..	..	29.1	37.9	45.9

		1980	1990	2007	2010	2020
Labour force participation (percentage)						
Total	65+	32.7	32.9	41.7	42.5	42.0
Female	65+	16.5	13.1	32.5	35.4	39.7
Male	65+	47.2	51.6	50.0	49.0	44.5

Percentage married, age 60+			Percentage living alone, age 60+		
Total	Female	Male	Total	Female	Male
59.7	46.0	72.0	..	..	..

Statutory pensionable age (2006)		Percentage illiterate, age 65+ (2000)		
Female	Male	Total	Female	Male
..	..	10.0	10.7	9.5

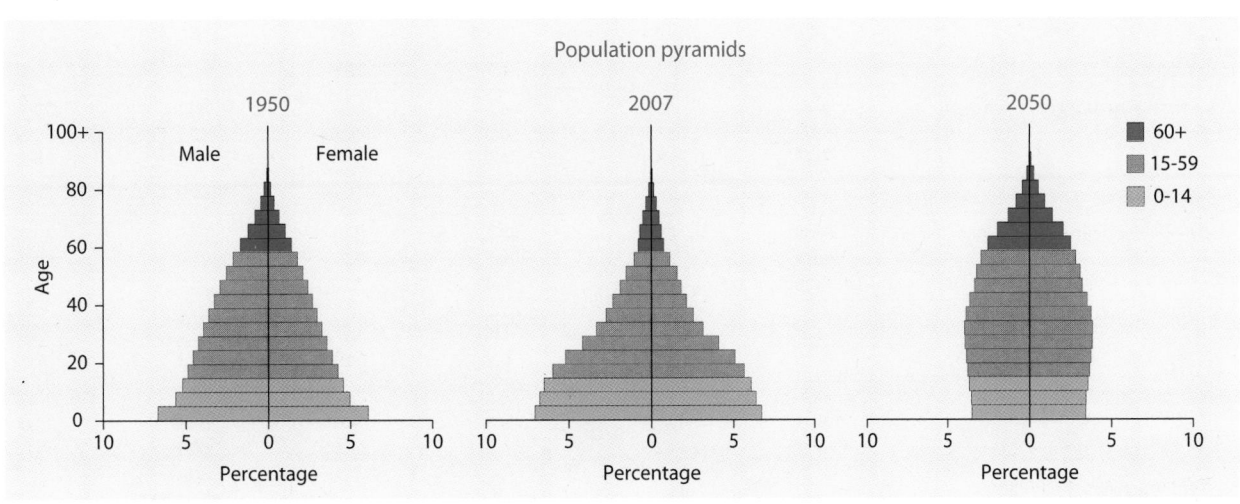

Population pyramids

Mali

Indicator	Age	1950	1975	2007	2025	2050
Population (thousands)						
Total	Total	3 449.2	6 211.3	14 324.7	24 031.0	41 975.6
	0-14	1 564.9	2 845.3	6 891.5	10 616.8	13 912.3
	15-59	1 768.1	3 117.1	6 842.5	12 546.9	25 433.3
	60-64	50.3	107.4	210.9	321.6	962.2
	65-69	33.2	72.9	165.8	233.8	732.2
	70-74	19.4	42.5	114.8	155.8	487.1
	75-79	9.3	19.4	65.2	95.9	284.3
	80-84			26.5	45.0	122.6
	85-89			6.6	13.0	35.2
	90-94	4.0	6.6	0.8	2.1	6.0
	95-99			0.0	0.2	0.5
	100+			0.0	0.0	0.0
Female	Total	1 724.6	3 106.7	7 179.2	11 928.6	20 761.2
	0-14	783.2	1 403.1	3 381.1	5 200.4	6 811.0
	15-59	888.0	1 570.4	3 461.0	6 228.3	12 537.8
	60-64	23.7	57.5	118.9	178.6	496.0
	65-69	15.3	39.2	94.4	134.1	387.2
	70-74	8.7	22.8	65.7	91.7	266.3
	75-79	4.0	10.3	37.9	57.9	162.0
	80-84			15.7	27.9	73.7
	85-89			4.0	8.3	22.6
	90-94	1.7	3.4	0.5	1.4	4.1
	95-99			0.0	0.1	0.4
	100+			0.0	0.0	0.0
Male	Total	1 724.6	3 104.5	7 145.5	12 102.5	21 214.5
	0-14	781.7	1 442.2	3 510.4	5 416.4	7 101.2
	15-59	880.1	1 546.7	3 381.5	6 318.6	12 895.5
	60-64	26.6	49.9	92.0	143.0	466.2
	65-69	17.9	33.6	71.4	99.7	345.0
	70-74	10.7	19.7	49.1	64.1	220.8
	75-79	5.2	9.1	27.4	38.1	122.3
	80-84			10.8	17.2	48.8
	85-89			2.6	4.7	12.6
	90-94	2.4	3.2	0.3	0.7	1.9
	95-99			0.0	0.0	0.1
	100+			0.0	0.0	0.0
Percentage in older ages						
Total	60+	3.4	4.0	4.1	3.6	6.3
	65+	1.9	2.3	2.7	2.3	4.0
	80+	0.1	0.1	0.2	0.3	0.4
Female	60+	3.1	4.3	4.7	4.2	6.8
	65+	1.7	2.4	3.0	2.7	4.4
	80+	0.1	0.1	0.3	0.3	0.5
Male	60+	3.6	3.7	3.5	3.0	5.7
	65+	2.1	2.1	2.3	1.9	3.5
	80+	0.1	0.1	0.2	0.2	0.3
Ageing index		7.4	8.7	8.6	8.2	18.9
Broad age groups (percentage)	0-14	45.4	45.8	48.1	44.2	33.1
	15-59	51.3	50.2	47.8	52.2	60.6
	60+	3.4	4.0	4.1	3.6	6.3
Median age (years)		17.2	17.0	15.8*	17.6	23.4
Dependency ratio	Total	89.7	92.6	103.1	86.7	59.0
	Youth	86.1	88.2	97.7	82.5	52.7
	Old Age	3.6	4.4	5.4	4.2	6.3
Potential support ratio		27.6	22.8	18.6	23.6	15.8
Parent support ratio		0.4	0.2	1.0	1.1	1.1
Sex ratio (per 100 women)	60+	117.6	86.8	75.2	73.5	86.2
	65+	121.7	86.8	74.1	69.9	82.0
	80+	142.9	94.5	67.9	60.1	63.0

* *Estimate refers to year 2005.*

Indicator	Age	1950-1955	1975-1980	2005-2010	2025-2030	2045-2050
Growth rate (percentage)	Total	2.2	2.3	2.9	2.6	1.8
	60+	2.4	3.0	1.6	3.8	4.4
	65+	2.0	3.3	2.0	3.3	4.9
	80+	−0.9	4.3	3.7	2.5	5.8
Total fertility rate (per woman)		7.1	7.6	6.6	4.8	3.1
Life expectancy (years)						
Total	Birth	31.8	39.8	49.3	57.6	65.6
	60	..	..	15.4	16.7	18.1
	65	..	..	12.0	13.1	14.3
	80	..	..	4.8	5.2	5.7
Female	Birth	32.4	40.6	49.9	58.4	66.9
	60	..	..	15.9	17.4	19.0
	65	..	..	12.4	13.7	15.0
	80	..	..	4.9	5.4	5.9
Male	Birth	31.2	39.1	48.6	56.8	64.2
	60	..	..	14.7	15.9	17.2
	65	..	..	11.6	12.5	13.6
	80	..	..	4.6	5.0	5.3
Survival rate (percentage)						
Total	60	..	..	50.8	62.9	75.1
	65	..	..	44.9	57.0	69.6
	80	..	..	15.1	22.9	32.8
Female	60	..	..	52.0	64.4	77.3
	65	..	..	46.7	59.2	72.7
	80	..	..	16.7	25.5	36.9
Male	60	..	..	49.2	61.3	73.0
	65	..	..	42.8	54.5	66.5
	80	..	..	13.3	20.0	28.6

		1980	1990	2007	2010	2020
Labour force participation (percentage)						
Total	65+	47.5	49.9	43.4	41.7	40.9
Female	65+	31.0	32.8	34.9	35.3	36.8
Male	65+	67.5	71.3	54.8	50.4	46.7

Percentage married, age 60+			Percentage living alone, age 60+ (2001)		
Total	Female	Male	Total	Female	Male
67.3	48.0	92.0	6.8	9.8	5.1

Statutory pensionable age (2006)			Percentage illiterate, age 65+ (1998)		
	Female	Male	Total	Female	Male
	58	58	92.8	97.4	88.8

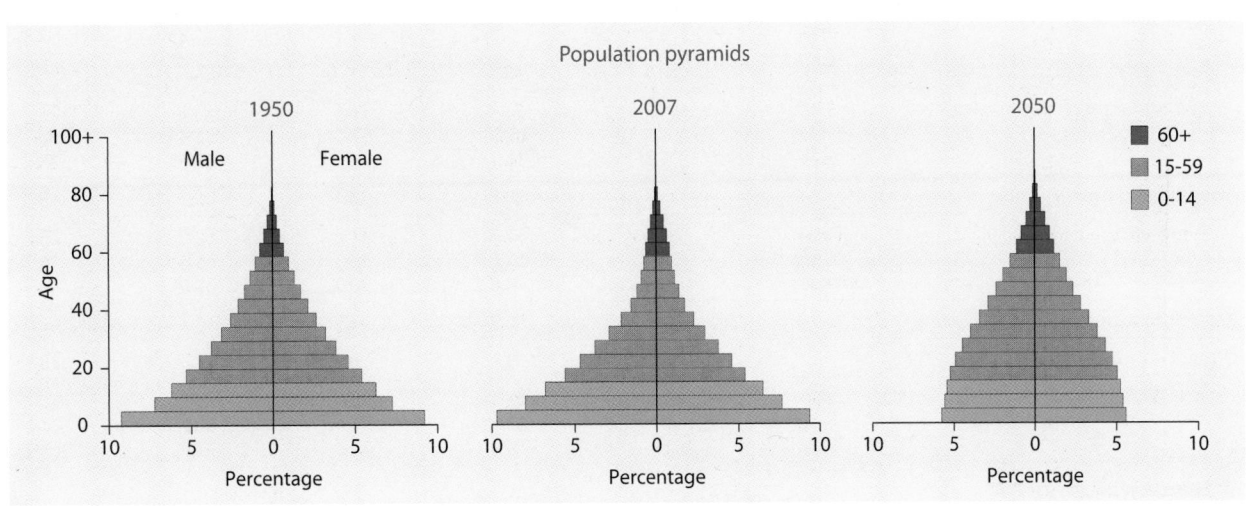

Population pyramids

Malta

Indicator	Age	1950	1975	2007	2025	2050
Population (thousands)						
Total	Total	312.0	304.2	405.3	431.5	428.3
	0-14	109.0	75.2	68.1	67.5	63.0
	15-59	174.0	189.1	255.6	239.1	214.4
	60-64	11.0	10.8	24.8	26.6	30.3
	65-69	7.0	11.6	17.8	28.3	30.0
	70-74	5.8	8.4	14.9	24.6	28.1
	75-79	3.3	4.9	11.3	22.5	22.5
	80-84			7.6	12.3	15.8
	85-89			3.6	6.6	12.6
	90-94	1.9	4.1	1.2	3.0	7.8
	95-99			0.3	0.9	2.9
	100+			0.0	0.2	0.8
Female	Total	158.0	157.3	204.2	216.6	215.3
	0-14	54.0	36.5	33.0	32.8	30.6
	15-59	88.0	99.3	125.3	116.6	104.5
	60-64	6.0	5.7	12.7	13.2	14.9
	65-69	4.0	6.1	9.5	14.4	15.0
	70-74	3.1	4.6	8.4	12.7	14.2
	75-79	1.8	2.8	6.7	12.2	11.7
	80-84			4.8	7.3	8.7
	85-89			2.5	4.4	7.5
	90-94	1.1	2.4	1.0	2.3	5.3
	95-99			0.3	0.7	2.3
	100+			0.0	0.1	0.7
Male	Total	154.0	146.9	201.1	214.9	213.0
	0-14	55.0	38.7	35.0	34.7	32.4
	15-59	86.0	89.8	130.3	122.5	109.9
	60-64	5.0	5.1	12.1	13.4	15.3
	65-69	3.0	5.6	8.4	14.0	15.0
	70-74	2.7	3.9	6.5	11.9	13.9
	75-79	1.5	2.2	4.5	10.3	10.8
	80-84			2.8	5.0	7.1
	85-89			1.1	2.2	5.1
	90-94	0.8	1.7	0.3	0.7	2.6
	95-99			0.0	0.1	0.7
	100+			0.0	0.0	0.1
Percentage in older ages						
Total	60+	9.3	13.1	20.1	28.9	35.2
	65+	5.8	9.6	14.0	22.8	28.2
	80+	0.6	1.4	3.2	5.3	9.3
Female	60+	10.1	13.7	22.5	31.0	37.2
	65+	6.3	10.1	16.2	24.9	30.3
	80+	0.7	1.5	4.2	6.8	11.3
Male	60+	8.4	12.5	17.8	26.8	33.2
	65+	5.2	9.0	11.8	20.6	26.0
	80+	0.5	1.2	2.1	3.8	7.3
Ageing index		26.6	53.1	119.9	184.9	239.4
Broad age groups (percentage)	0-14	34.9	24.7	16.8	15.6	14.7
	15-59	55.8	62.2	63.1	55.4	50.1
	60+	9.3	13.1	20.1	28.9	35.2
Median age (years)		23.7	28.8	38.1*	43.7	48.0
Dependency ratio	Total	68.6	52.2	44.5	62.4	75.0
	Youth	58.9	37.6	24.3	25.4	25.7
	Old Age	9.7	14.6	20.2	37.0	49.3
Potential support ratio		10.3	6.9	4.9	2.7	2.0
Parent support ratio		1.7	3.1	6.2	13.5	28.5
Sex ratio (per 100 women)	60+	81.3	85.3	78.0	85.7	88.1
	65+	80.0	83.8	71.4	81.8	84.8
	80+	77.4	70.3	49.0	54.9	63.7

* *Estimate refers to year 2005.*

Indicator	Age	1950-1955	1975-1980	2005-2010	2025-2030	2045-2050
Growth rate (percentage)	Total	0.1	1.3	0.4	0.1	−0.1
	60+	1.3	2.1	3.9	0.4	0.7
	65+	3.1	1.9	2.7	1.2	1.0
	80+	4.9	2.6	3.4	5.8	−0.4
Total fertility rate (per woman)		4.1	2.0	1.5	1.7	1.9
Life expectancy (years)						
Total	Birth	65.9	72.2	79.1	81.6	83.8
	60	..	..	21.9	23.9	25.7
	65	..	..	17.8	19.6	21.3
	80	..	..	8.1	9.3	10.4
Female	Birth	67.7	74.3	81.3	83.9	86.2
	60	..	..	23.7	25.8	27.8
	65	..	..	19.4	21.4	23.3
	80	..	..	9.0	10.4	11.6
Male	Birth	64.2	70.0	76.6	79.2	81.5
	60	..	..	19.9	21.8	23.7
	65	..	..	15.8	17.7	19.4
	80	..	..	6.6	7.8	8.9
Survival rate (percentage)						
Total	60	..	..	92.8	94.4	95.6
	65	..	..	88.6	91.2	93.0
	80	..	..	55.5	63.3	69.9
Female	60	..	..	94.2	95.6	96.7
	65	..	..	90.8	93.0	94.6
	80	..	..	62.9	70.6	76.5
Male	60	..	..	91.3	93.3	94.6
	65	..	..	86.4	89.3	91.5
	80	..	..	47.1	56.0	63.4

		1980	1990	2007	2010	2020
Labour force participation (percentage)						
Total	65+	7.4	4.0	2.0	1.7	1.1
Female	65+	2.5	1.1	0.5	0.5	0.5
Male	65+	13.3	7.9	4.1	3.4	1.9

Percentage married, age 60+			Percentage living alone, age 60+ (1980)		
Total	Female	Male	Total	Female	Male
49.5	37.0	66.0	10.5	..	..

Statutory pensionable age (2006)			Percentage illiterate, age 65+ (1995)		
	Female	Male	Total	Female	Male
	60	61	27.8	28.7	26.5

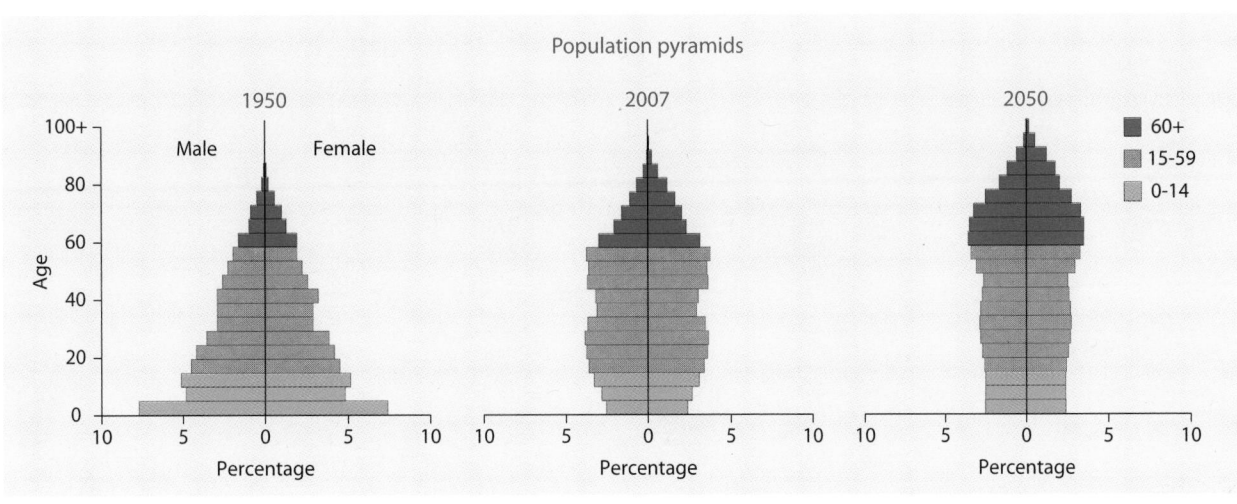

Population pyramids

Martinique

Indicator	Age	1950	1975	2007	2025	2050
Population (thousands)						
Total	Total	222.0	328.5	398.6	403.7	350.3
	0-14	83.0	132.3	82.6	64.7	44.3
	15-59	122.0	165.5	246.3	222.4	164.7
	60-64	5.4	10.2	17.4	32.8	25.8
	65-69	5.0	7.7	14.8	26.3	23.7
	70-74	3.3	5.6	13.0	20.4	18.9
	75-79	2.1	3.5	10.4	15.3	22.1
	80-84			7.3	10.0	21.9
	85-89			4.1	6.5	16.4
	90-94	1.2	3.7	1.8	3.5	8.4
	95-99			0.6	1.4	3.3
	100+			0.2	0.4	0.9
Female	Total	116.0	169.4	209.7	212.0	183.6
	0-14	42.0	66.0	40.6	31.7	21.7
	15-59	64.0	85.9	129.1	113.0	81.1
	60-64	3.0	5.4	9.5	18.0	13.2
	65-69	3.0	4.2	8.2	14.5	12.1
	70-74	2.1	3.2	7.3	11.8	10.1
	75-79	1.2	2.2	6.1	9.0	12.6
	80-84			4.5	6.1	13.4
	85-89			2.6	4.2	10.5
	90-94	0.7	2.5	1.3	2.4	5.8
	95-99			0.5	1.0	2.5
	100+			0.1	0.3	0.7
Male	Total	106.0	159.1	188.9	191.6	166.7
	0-14	41.0	66.3	42.0	33.0	22.6
	15-59	58.0	79.6	117.2	109.4	83.7
	60-64	2.4	4.8	7.9	14.9	12.6
	65-69	2.0	3.5	6.7	11.8	11.6
	70-74	1.2	2.4	5.7	8.6	8.8
	75-79	0.9	1.3	4.3	6.3	9.4
	80-84			2.8	3.9	8.5
	85-89			1.4	2.3	5.9
	90-94	0.5	1.2	0.6	1.1	2.6
	95-99			0.2	0.4	0.8
	100+			0.0	0.1	0.2
Percentage in older ages						
Total	60+	7.7	9.3	17.5	28.9	40.3
	65+	5.2	6.2	13.1	20.7	33.0
	80+	0.5	1.1	3.5	5.4	14.5
Female	60+	8.6	10.3	19.1	31.8	44.0
	65+	6.0	7.1	14.5	23.3	36.9
	80+	0.6	1.5	4.3	6.6	17.9
Male	60+	6.6	8.3	15.7	25.7	36.3
	65+	4.3	5.3	11.5	17.9	28.7
	80+	0.5	0.8	2.7	4.0	10.8
Ageing index		20.5	23.2	84.3	180.2	319.2
Broad age groups (percentage)	0-14	37.4	40.3	20.7	16.0	12.6
	15-59	55.0	50.4	61.8	55.1	47.0
	60+	7.7	9.3	17.5	28.9	40.3
Median age (years)		21.9	19.0	36.4*	44.2	53.0
Dependency ratio	Total	74.3	87.0	51.1	58.2	83.9
	Youth	65.1	75.3	31.3	25.3	23.2
	Old Age	9.1	11.7	19.8	32.8	60.6
Potential support ratio		11.0	8.6	5.0	3.0	1.6
Parent support ratio		2.3	3.4	10.4	12.6	39.8
Sex ratio (per 100 women)	60+	70.0	75.4	74.2	73.0	74.8
	65+	65.7	69.4	71.2	69.4	70.7
	80+	70.8	48.1	56.3	54.5	54.8

* *Estimate refers to year 2005.*

Indicator	Age	1950-1955	1975-1980	2005-2010	2025-2030	2045-2050
Growth rate (percentage)	Total	2.0	–0.1	0.3	–0.2	–0.9
	60+	0.1	3.6	2.4	2.4	0.2
	65+	0.9	4.7	1.8	3.4	0.0
	80+	10.3	6.3	3.4	3.1	2.4
Total fertility rate (per woman)		5.7	2.7	1.9	1.9	1.9
Life expectancy (years)						
Total	Birth	56.6	71.8	79.4	82.0	84.2
	60	..	..	23.2	24.9	26.5
	65	..	..	19.3	20.8	22.2
	80	..	..	9.6	10.4	11.2
Female	Birth	58.1	75.0	82.3	84.8	87.0
	60	..	..	25.3	27.0	28.6
	65	..	..	21.1	22.6	24.2
	80	..	..	10.5	11.3	12.3
Male	Birth	55.0	68.5	76.2	78.9	81.2
	60	..	..	20.8	22.5	24.1
	65	..	..	17.2	18.6	20.0
	80	..	..	8.4	9.1	9.8
Survival rate (percentage)						
Total	60	..	..	90.5	93.0	94.7
	65	..	..	86.0	89.5	91.9
	80	..	..	57.2	64.6	70.5
Female	60	..	..	93.1	95.1	96.5
	65	..	..	89.9	92.7	94.6
	80	..	..	66.2	72.7	78.2
Male	60	..	..	87.6	90.7	92.9
	65	..	..	81.6	85.9	89.2
	80	..	..	47.3	55.2	62.2

		1980	1990	2007	2010	2020
Labour force participation (percentage)						
Total	65+	4.5	3.3	3.7	3.7	3.7
Female	65+	3.5	2.4	3.5	3.6	3.7
Male	65+	6.0	4.6	4.0	3.9	3.8

Percentage married, age 60+			Percentage living alone, age 60+ (1990)		
Total	Female	Male	Total	Female	Male
48.2	37.0	63.0	21.7	..	..

Statutory pensionable age (2006)			Percentage illiterate, age 65+		
	Female	Male	Total	Female	Male
	..	..	..	..	..

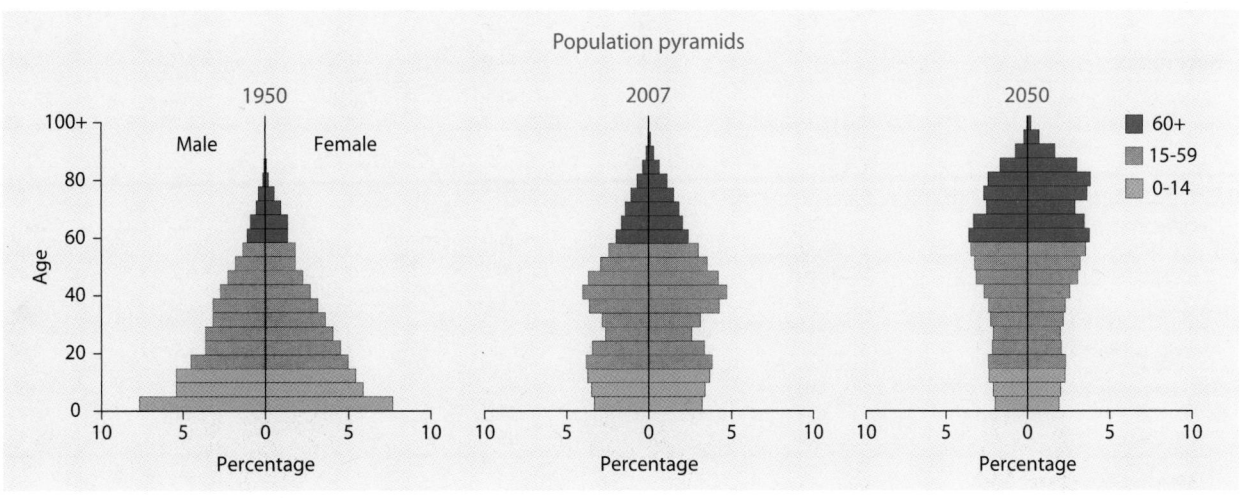

Population pyramids

Mauritania

Indicator	Age	1950	1975	2007	2025	2050
Population (thousands)						
Total	Total	825.0	1 423.3	3 247.4	4 972.8	7 496.9
	0-14	361.0	621.5	1 395.3	1 865.8	2 093.1
	15-59	433.0	733.4	1 680.8	2 821.2	4 675.9
	60-64	13.0	27.5	61.2	104.5	237.8
	65-69	9.0	19.4	46.4	75.4	189.1
	70-74	5.0	12.1	32.2	48.7	141.2
	75-79	3.0	6.3	19.1	32.8	90.0
	80-84			8.9	16.5	46.7
	85-89			2.9	6.1	17.9
	90-94	1.0	3.1	0.6	1.4	4.5
	95-99			0.1	0.2	0.6
	100+			0.0	0.0	0.1
Female	Total	403.0	718.0	1 640.0	2 500.9	3 761.0
	0-14	179.0	311.1	694.3	925.6	1 034.4
	15-59	211.0	371.7	852.1	1 419.4	2 343.1
	60-64	6.0	14.2	33.0	55.3	122.5
	65-69	4.0	10.1	25.3	40.8	98.5
	70-74	2.0	6.1	17.6	27.0	74.6
	75-79	1.0	3.2	10.5	18.5	48.6
	80-84			5.0	9.5	25.9
	85-89			1.7	3.7	10.3
	90-94	0.0	1.7	0.4	0.9	2.7
	95-99			0.1	0.1	0.4
	100+			0.0	0.0	0.0
Male	Total	422.0	705.2	1 607.4	2 471.9	3 735.9
	0-14	182.0	310.4	701.0	940.2	1 058.8
	15-59	222.0	361.7	828.7	1 401.8	2 332.8
	60-64	7.0	13.3	28.2	49.2	115.4
	65-69	5.0	9.3	21.1	34.6	90.6
	70-74	3.0	5.9	14.6	21.7	66.5
	75-79	2.0	3.1	8.6	14.3	41.4
	80-84			3.9	7.0	20.8
	85-89			1.2	2.5	7.6
	90-94	1.0	1.4	0.2	0.5	1.8
	95-99			0.0	0.1	0.2
	100+			0.0	0.0	0.0
Percentage in older ages						
Total	60+	3.8	4.8	5.3	5.7	9.7
	65+	2.2	2.9	3.4	3.6	6.5
	80+	0.1	0.2	0.4	0.5	0.9
Female	60+	3.2	4.9	5.7	6.2	10.2
	65+	1.7	2.9	3.7	4.0	6.9
	80+	0.0	0.2	0.4	0.6	1.0
Male	60+	4.3	4.7	4.8	5.3	9.2
	65+	2.6	2.8	3.1	3.3	6.1
	80+	0.2	0.2	0.3	0.4	0.8
Ageing index		8.6	11.0	12.3	15.3	34.8
Broad age groups (percentage)	0-14	43.8	43.7	43.0	37.5	27.9
	15-59	52.5	51.5	51.8	56.7	62.4
	60+	3.8	4.8	5.3	5.7	9.7
Median age (years)		18.0	18.2	18.4*	20.8	27.7
Dependency ratio	Total	85.0	87.1	86.4	70.0	52.6
	Youth	80.9	81.7	80.1	63.8	42.6
	Old Age	4.0	5.4	6.3	6.2	10.0
Potential support ratio		24.8	18.6	15.8	16.1	10.0
Parent support ratio		0.0	0.6	1.6	1.9	2.6
Sex ratio (per 100 women)	60+	138.5	93.8	83.0	83.3	89.8
	65+	157.1	93.6	81.6	80.2	87.7
	80+	0.0	85.2	73.4	70.4	77.4

* *Estimate refers to year 2005.*

Indicator	Age	1950-1955	1975-1980	2005-2010	2025-2030	2045-2050
Growth rate (percentage)	Total	1.7	2.4	2.7	2.0	1.3
	60+	3.1	3.1	2.6	3.9	3.3
	65+	2.3	3.5	2.7	3.8	3.6
	80+	6.1	4.7	4.1	3.7	5.0
Total fertility rate (per woman)		6.3	6.5	5.5	3.5	2.4
Life expectancy (years)						
Total	Birth	35.4	45.4	54.5	62.5	69.7
	60	..	..	16.1	17.5	19.0
	65	..	..	12.9	14.1	15.2
	80	..	..	5.6	6.1	6.6
Female	Birth	37.1	47.0	56.1	64.1	71.1
	60	..	..	16.7	18.1	19.5
	65	..	..	13.3	14.5	15.7
	80	..	..	5.9	6.3	6.8
Male	Birth	34.0	43.9	52.9	60.9	68.4
	60	..	..	15.5	16.9	18.4
	65	..	..	12.3	13.5	14.8
	80	..	..	5.3	5.9	6.4
Survival rate (percentage)						
Total	60	..	..	57.1	68.8	79.5
	65	..	..	50.5	62.4	73.7
	80	..	..	19.4	28.0	37.8
Female	60	..	..	59.9	71.5	81.7
	65	..	..	53.6	65.6	76.4
	80	..	..	21.9	31.0	40.8
Male	60	..	..	54.3	66.2	77.4
	65	..	..	47.3	59.3	71.1
	80	..	..	16.9	25.0	34.7

		1980	1990	2007	2010	2020
Labour force participation (percentage)						
Total	65+	44.0	45.1	41.1	40.9	40.5
Female	65+	24.5	24.3	22.9	22.8	22.6
Male	65+	65.7	69.4	63.4	63.2	63.1

Percentage married, age 60+			Percentage living alone, age 60+		
Total	Female	Male	Total	Female	Male
55.0	27.0	88.0	..	..	..

Statutory pensionable age (2006)			Percentage illiterate, age 65+		
Female	Male		Total	Female	Male
55	60		..	..	..

Population pyramids

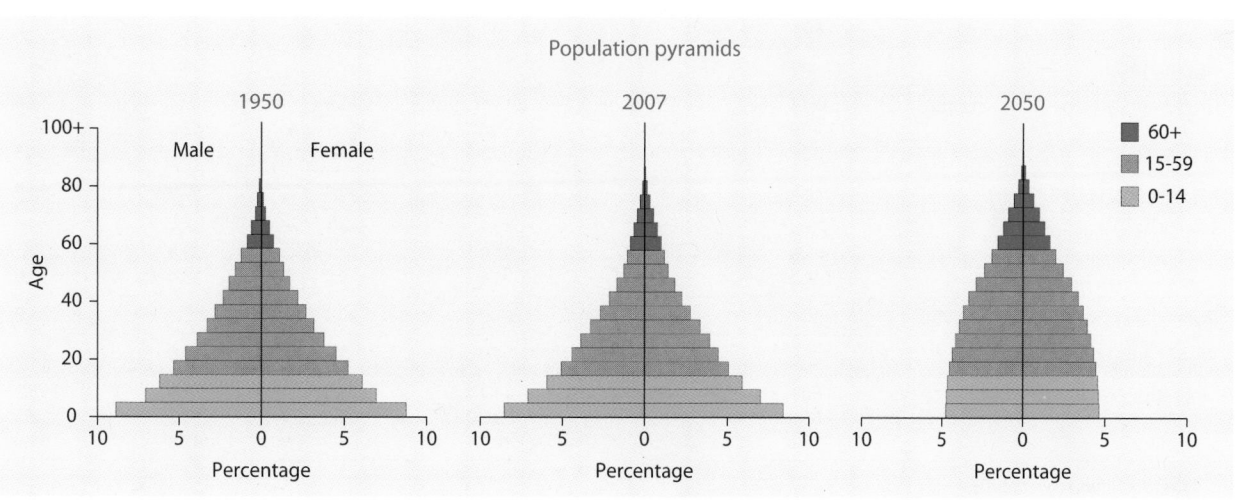

Mauritius

Indicator	Age	1950	1975	2007	2025	2050
Population (thousands)						
Total	Total	493.3	892.0	1 267.0	1 417.4	1 465.5
	0-14	222.7	353.9	302.1	274.6	248.5
	15-59	247.4	497.7	838.1	878.8	831.8
	60-64	8.5	15.9	41.1	86.4	83.9
	65-69	6.3	11.3	30.1	69.0	82.7
	70-74	4.2	7.0	22.0	51.0	79.0
	75-79	2.5	3.9	16.5	30.0	54.8
	80-84			10.6	15.6	42.1
	85-89			4.5	7.8	26.9
	90-94	1.7	2.2	1.5	3.1	11.6
	95-99			0.4	1.0	3.5
	100+			0.1	0.2	0.6
Female	Total	247.6	451.8	638.3	719.3	750.3
	0-14	110.8	174.4	148.4	134.6	121.7
	15-59	124.5	252.8	417.2	437.2	410.7
	60-64	4.4	9.1	22.1	45.0	43.3
	65-69	3.3	6.8	16.8	37.1	43.6
	70-74	2.3	4.5	12.7	28.7	43.5
	75-79	1.3	2.6	9.9	18.0	31.6
	80-84			6.7	10.0	25.8
	85-89			3.1	5.4	18.0
	90-94	0.9	1.6	1.1	2.3	8.6
	95-99			0.3	0.8	2.9
	100+			0.1	0.2	0.6
Male	Total	245.6	440.2	628.6	698.0	715.2
	0-14	111.9	179.5	153.7	139.9	126.8
	15-59	122.8	245.0	420.8	441.6	421.2
	60-64	4.1	6.8	19.0	41.4	40.6
	65-69	3.0	4.5	13.3	31.9	39.1
	70-74	1.9	2.5	9.4	22.3	35.5
	75-79	1.1	1.3	6.6	12.0	23.2
	80-84			3.9	5.5	16.3
	85-89			1.5	2.4	8.8
	90-94	0.7	0.6	0.4	0.8	3.0
	95-99			0.1	0.2	0.6
	100+			0.0	0.0	0.1
Percentage in older ages						
Total	60+	4.7	4.5	10.0	18.6	26.3
	65+	3.0	2.7	6.8	12.5	20.6
	80+	0.3	0.3	1.4	2.0	5.8
Female	60+	5.0	5.4	11.4	20.5	29.0
	65+	3.2	3.4	7.9	14.2	23.3
	80+	0.4	0.4	1.8	2.6	7.4
Male	60+	4.4	3.6	8.6	16.7	23.4
	65+	2.8	2.0	5.6	10.8	17.7
	80+	0.3	0.1	0.9	1.3	4.0
Ageing index		10.4	11.4	42.0	96.2	155.0
Broad age groups (percentage)	0-14	45.2	39.7	23.8	19.4	17.0
	15-59	50.1	55.8	66.1	62.0	56.8
	60+	4.7	4.5	10.0	18.6	26.3
Median age (years)		17.3	19.5	30.4*	36.9	42.0
Dependency ratio	Total	92.8	73.7	44.1	46.9	60.0
	Youth	87.0	68.9	34.4	28.4	27.1
	Old Age	5.7	4.8	9.8	18.4	32.9
Potential support ratio		17.5	21.0	10.3	5.4	3.0
Parent support ratio		1.7	1.0	3.6	4.6	15.3
Sex ratio (per 100 women)	60+	88.2	64.1	74.5	79.0	76.7
	65+	85.8	58.1	69.5	73.3	72.5
	80+	75.9	40.1	51.9	47.8	51.6

* *Estimate refers to year 2005.*

Indicator	Age	1950-1955	1975-1980	2005-2010	2025-2030	2045-2050
Growth rate (percentage)	Total	2.9	1.6	0.8	0.4	−0.1
	60+	0.9	6.6	3.5	2.5	0.5
	65+	0.6	7.1	2.4	3.8	1.0
	80+	−1.1	10.9	4.1	5.2	2.1
Total fertility rate (per woman)		6.3	3.1	1.9	1.9	1.9
Life expectancy (years)						
Total	Birth	51.0	65.1	73.0	76.0	78.8
	60	..	..	19.0	20.5	22.2
	65	..	..	15.6	16.9	18.3
	80	..	..	7.7	8.3	9.0
Female	Birth	52.3	67.6	76.3	79.0	81.7
	60	..	..	21.0	22.7	24.5
	65	..	..	17.2	18.7	20.3
	80	..	..	8.3	9.1	10.0
Male	Birth	49.7	62.4	69.7	73.0	75.9
	60	..	..	16.8	18.1	19.7
	65	..	..	13.7	14.7	16.0
	80	..	..	6.6	7.0	7.6
Survival rate (percentage)						
Total	60	..	..	83.0	87.6	91.0
	65	..	..	75.6	81.2	85.9
	80	..	..	38.6	46.2	54.2
Female	60	..	..	87.9	90.8	93.2
	65	..	..	82.2	86.3	89.7
	80	..	..	48.3	56.1	63.8
Male	60	..	..	78.3	84.3	88.8
	65	..	..	69.0	76.2	82.1
	80	..	..	29.1	36.3	44.5

		1980	1990	2007	2010	2020
Labour force participation (percentage)						
Total	65+	16.3	11.9	9.8	9.8	10.3
Female	65+	8.1	4.9	4.9	5.2	7.0
Male	65+	29.1	21.4	16.9	16.4	14.8

Percentage married, age 60+			Percentage living alone, age 60+		
Total	Female	Male	Total	Female	Male
53.3	33.0	80.0	..	..	..

Statutory pensionable age (2006)			Percentage illiterate, age 65+ (2000)		
Female	Male		Total	Female	Male
60	60		46.8	57.8	31.2

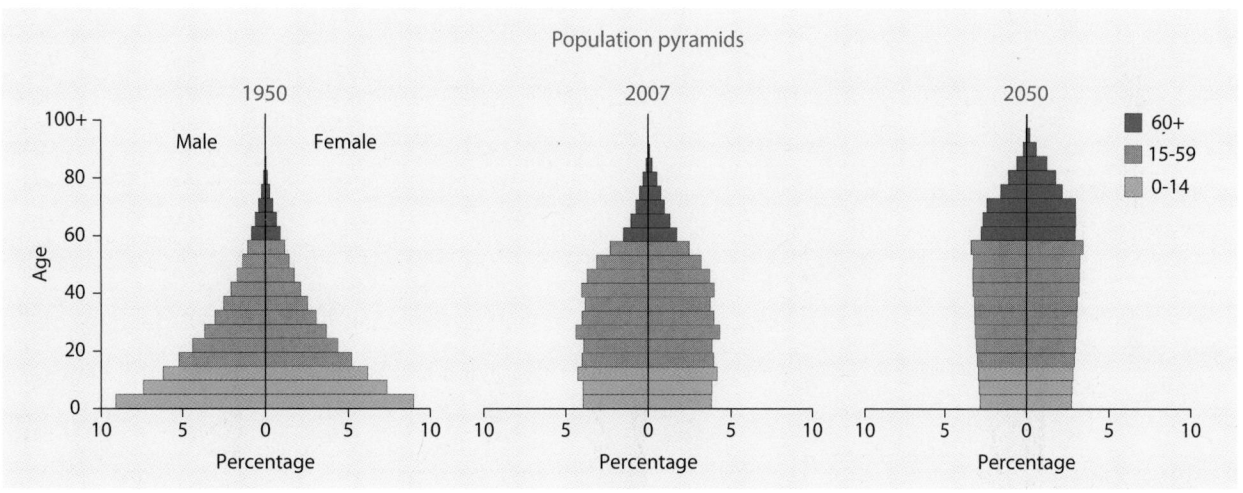

Population pyramids

Mexico

Indicator	Age	1950	1975	2007	2025	2050
Population (thousands)						
Total	Total	27 737.1	59 287.1	109 594.1	129 381.1	139 014.5
	0-14	11 643.7	27 692.3	32 621.2	28 327.6	23 229.2
	15-59	14 130.0	28 245.7	67 972.2	82 716.8	77 722.5
	60-64	731.6	982.8	2 823.1	5 533.2	8 691.9
	65-69	536.1	829.8	2 178.1	4 442.8	7 799.8
	70-74	349.8	645.8	1 629.2	3 327.1	7 316.1
	75-79	216.2	464.4	1 151.7	2 305.1	6 252.9
	80-84			730.7	1 498.3	4 160.0
	85-89			344.1	803.4	2 389.3
	90-94	129.7	426.2	115.6	331.8	1 090.8
	95-99			25.7	84.7	317.0
	100+			2.6	10.2	45.1
Female	Total	13 876.9	29 766.4	56 078.5	66 512.1	71 963.3
	0-14	5 726.1	13 682.4	16 062.1	13 867.4	11 364.0
	15-59	7 091.8	14 268.7	35 143.1	42 514.2	39 438.7
	60-64	387.4	518.5	1 495.7	2 993.2	4 574.8
	65-69	287.8	446.3	1 159.9	2 419.9	4 177.1
	70-74	190.6	352.0	878.6	1 827.4	4 006.0
	75-79	119.5	257.6	630.3	1 286.6	3 524.6
	80-84			411.8	854.1	2 450.6
	85-89			203.1	475.2	1 468.0
	90-94	73.7	241.0	73.4	208.5	707.9
	95-99			18.3	58.0	219.4
	100+			2.1	7.7	32.2
Male	Total	13 860.2	29 520.7	53 515.6	62 869.0	67 051.3
	0-14	5 917.5	14 010.0	16 559.1	14 460.2	11 865.2
	15-59	7 038.3	13 977.0	32 829.1	40 202.7	38 283.8
	60-64	344.2	464.4	1 327.4	2 540.1	4 117.1
	65-69	248.3	383.5	1 018.2	2 022.9	3 622.7
	70-74	159.2	293.8	750.6	1 499.7	3 310.1
	75-79	96.8	206.8	521.4	1 018.4	2 728.3
	80-84			318.9	644.2	1 709.4
	85-89			140.9	328.2	921.3
	90-94	56.0	185.2	42.2	123.3	383.0
	95-99			7.4	26.7	97.7
	100+			0.5	2.5	12.8
Percentage in older ages						
Total	60+	7.1	5.6	8.2	14.2	27.4
	65+	4.4	4.0	5.6	9.9	21.1
	80+	0.5	0.7	1.1	2.1	5.8
Female	60+	7.6	6.1	8.7	15.2	29.4
	65+	4.8	4.4	6.0	10.7	23.0
	80+	0.5	0.8	1.3	2.4	6.8
Male	60+	6.5	5.2	7.7	13.1	25.2
	65+	4.0	3.6	5.2	9.0	19.1
	80+	0.4	0.6	1.0	1.8	4.7
Ageing index		16.9	12.1	27.6	64.7	163.9
Broad age groups (percentage)	0-14	42.0	46.7	29.8	21.9	16.7
	15-59	50.9	47.6	62.0	63.9	55.9
	60+	7.1	5.6	8.2	14.2	27.4
Median age (years)		19.1	16.6	25.0*	33.4	43.0
Dependency ratio	Total	86.6	102.8	54.8	46.6	60.9
	Youth	78.3	94.7	46.1	32.1	26.9
	Old Age	8.3	8.1	8.7	14.5	34.0
Potential support ratio		12.1	12.4	11.5	6.9	2.9
Parent support ratio		1.5	4.2	4.4	5.8	14.0
Sex ratio (per 100 women)	60+	85.4	84.5	84.7	81.0	79.9
	65+	83.4	82.5	82.9	79.4	77.1
	80+	76.0	76.8	71.9	70.2	64.0

* *Estimate refers to year 2005.*

Indicator	Age	1950-1955	1975-1980	2005-2010	2025-2030	2045-2050
Growth rate (percentage)	Total	2.7	2.8	1.1	0.6	0.0
	60+	2.6	1.6	3.8	3.9	1.7
	65+	3.1	1.7	3.9	3.9	1.9
	80+	3.7	3.1	4.8	4.4	4.0
Total fertility rate (per woman)		6.9	5.4	2.1	1.9	1.9
Life expectancy (years)						
Total	Birth	50.6	65.1	76.2	79.6	81.3
	60	..	..	22.1	23.8	24.6
	65	..	..	18.2	19.7	20.5
	80	..	..	8.5	9.4	9.9
Female	Birth	52.5	68.3	78.6	81.9	83.5
	60	..	..	23.1	25.1	26.1
	65	..	..	19.1	20.9	21.8
	80	..	..	9.0	10.0	10.5
Male	Birth	48.9	62.1	73.7	77.2	78.9
	60	..	..	21.0	22.3	22.9
	65	..	..	17.3	18.4	19.0
	80	..	..	8.0	8.7	9.0
Survival rate (percentage)						
Total	60	..	..	86.4	90.2	91.9
	65	..	..	81.5	86.1	88.2
	80	..	..	52.6	60.4	64.1
Female	60	..	..	89.8	92.7	94.0
	65	..	..	85.5	89.4	91.1
	80	..	..	58.0	66.4	70.5
Male	60	..	..	82.7	87.5	89.7
	65	..	..	77.2	82.7	85.3
	80	..	..	47.0	53.8	57.2

		1980	1990	2007	2010	2020
Labour force participation (percentage)						
Total	65+	38.2	32.8	26.0	23.9	17.9
Female	65+	17.4	13.8	13.3	13.2	13.0
Male	65+	63.7	56.2	41.3	36.9	24.0

Percentage married, age 60+			Percentage living alone, age 60+ (2000)		
Total	Female	Male	Total	Female	Male
59.7	45.0	77.0	8.5	9.6	7.2

Statutory pensionable age (2006)			Percentage illiterate, age 65+ (2004)		
	Female	Male	Total	Female	Male
	65	65	34.4	36.7	31.8

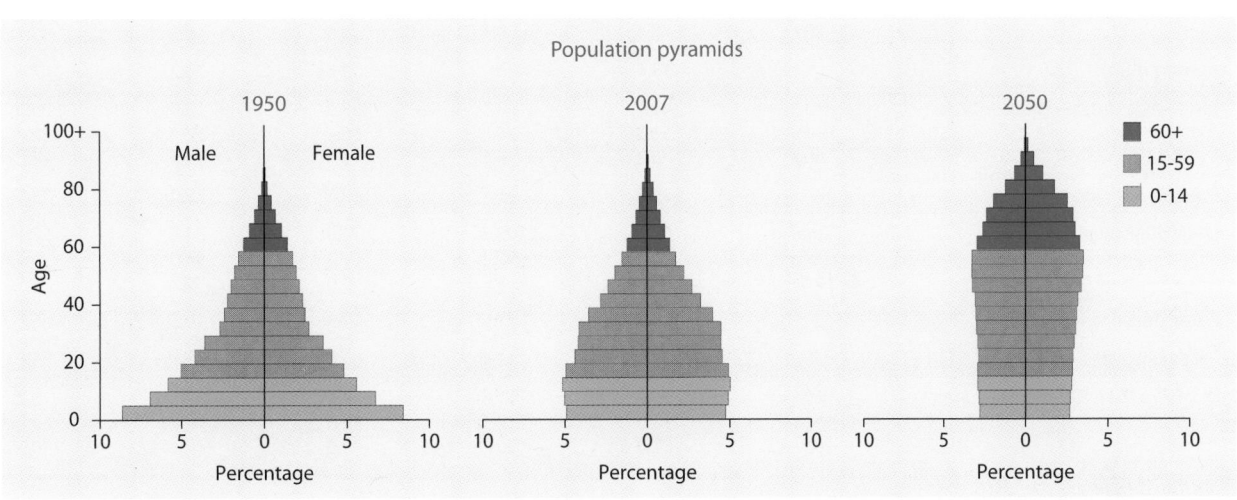

Population pyramids

United Nations Department of Economic and Social Affairs, Population Division

Micronesia (Federated States of)

Indicator	Age	1950	1975	2007	2025	2050
Population (thousands)						
Total	Total	32.0	63.1	111.9	116.6	98.6
	0-14	12.9	30.0	43.5	38.5	24.7
	15-59	17.1	29.1	62.8	67.3	57.2
	60-64	0.7	1.5	1.9	4.0	5.2
	65-69	0.5	1.1	1.2	3.0	4.7
	70-74	0.4	0.7	1.1	2.2	2.6
	75-79	0.2	0.5	0.6	1.1	1.9
	80-84			0.4	0.4	1.5
	85-89			0.2	0.2	0.7
	90-94	0.2	0.3	0.0	0.1	0.2
	95-99			0.0	0.0	0.0
	100+			0.0	0.0	0.0
Female	Total	15.5	30.5	55.7	59.3	52.2
	0-14	6.3	14.2	21.2	18.7	12.0
	15-59	8.2	14.3	31.4	34.7	30.4
	60-64	0.4	0.7	1.0	2.0	2.7
	65-69	0.3	0.5	0.7	1.7	2.7
	70-74	0.2	0.3	0.6	1.2	1.6
	75-79	0.1	0.2	0.4	0.7	1.2
	80-84			0.2	0.3	1.0
	85-89			0.1	0.1	0.4
	90-94	0.1	0.2	0.0	0.0	0.1
	95-99			0.0	0.0	0.0
	100+			0.0	0.0	0.0
Male	Total	16.5	32.6	56.2	57.3	46.3
	0-14	6.7	15.7	22.4	19.8	12.6
	15-59	8.8	14.7	31.3	32.6	26.8
	60-64	0.4	0.8	0.9	1.9	2.4
	65-69	0.3	0.6	0.5	1.3	2.0
	70-74	0.2	0.4	0.5	1.0	1.0
	75-79	0.1	0.3	0.3	0.5	0.7
	80-84			0.2	0.1	0.5
	85-89			0.1	0.1	0.2
	90-94	0.1	0.1	0.0	0.0	0.0
	95-99			0.0	0.0	0.0
	100+			0.0	0.0	0.0
Percentage in older ages						
Total	60+	6.3	6.5	5.0	9.3	17.0
	65+	4.1	4.2	3.2	5.9	11.7
	80+	0.5	0.5	0.6	0.5	2.4
Female	60+	6.6	6.3	5.6	10.0	18.8
	65+	4.3	4.1	3.7	6.6	13.6
	80+	0.6	0.5	0.7	0.7	3.0
Male	60+	6.0	6.6	4.4	8.6	14.9
	65+	3.8	4.3	2.8	5.2	9.6
	80+	0.4	0.4	0.5	0.3	1.7
Ageing index		15.6	13.7	12.8	28.2	67.8
Broad age groups (percentage)	0-14	40.4	47.5	38.9	33.0	25.0
	15-59	53.3	46.0	56.1	57.7	58.0
	60+	6.3	6.5	5.0	9.3	17.0
Median age (years)		19.8	16.1	19.6*	22.9	33.1
Dependency ratio	Total	80.1	106.8	72.9	63.7	58.1
	Youth	72.8	98.2	67.3	54.0	39.5
	Old Age	7.4	8.7	5.6	9.7	18.5
Potential support ratio		13.6	11.5	17.9	10.3	5.4
Parent support ratio		1.9	1.4	2.6	1.7	5.9
Sex ratio (per 100 women)	60+	96.7	111.8	79.9	83.1	70.2
	65+	93.8	112.5	76.0	76.7	62.9
	80+	82.0	90.2	70.6	49.2	50.9

*   *Estimate refers to year 2005.*

Indicator	Age	1950-1955	1975-1980	2005-2010	2025-2030	2045-2050
Growth rate (percentage)	Total	3.4	2.9	0.6	−0.3	−1.2
	60+	1.8	0.0	2.4	2.6	2.0
	65+	1.7	−0.3	−0.8	3.6	3.2
	80+	1.0	4.1	−4.8	8.0	3.2
Total fertility rate (per woman)		7.2	6.4	4.2	2.8	2.2
Life expectancy (years)						
Total	Birth	54.6	64.7	68.5	72.0	76.2
	60	..	..	17.2	18.1	20.0
	65	..	..	13.7	14.4	16.1
	80	..	..	5.8	6.1	6.9
Female	Birth	55.1	65.3	69.2	73.2	77.7
	60	..	..	17.9	18.9	21.3
	65	..	..	14.2	15.0	17.2
	80	..	..	6.0	6.3	7.5
Male	Birth	54.1	64.2	67.7	70.6	74.2
	60	..	..	16.5	17.2	18.4
	65	..	..	13.1	13.7	14.7
	80	..	..	5.7	5.8	6.1
Survival rate (percentage)						
Total	60	..	..	78.6	84.3	89.9
	65	..	..	71.2	77.6	84.5
	80	..	..	30.8	36.6	47.1
Female	60	..	..	79.7	85.9	91.3
	65	..	..	73.3	80.2	87.0
	80	..	..	33.7	40.5	52.8
Male	60	..	..	77.4	82.4	88.3
	65	..	..	69.2	74.8	81.7
	80	..	..	27.8	32.5	39.7

		1980	1990	2007	2010	2020
Labour force participation (percentage)						
Total	65+	..	..	..	..	..
Female	65+	..	..	..	..	..
Male	65+	..	..	..	..	..

Percentage married, age 60+			Percentage living alone, age 60+		
Total	Female	Male	Total	Female	Male
52.8	37.0	71.0	..	..	..

Statutory pensionable age (2006)		Percentage illiterate, age 65+		
Female	Male	Total	Female	Male
60	60	..	..	..

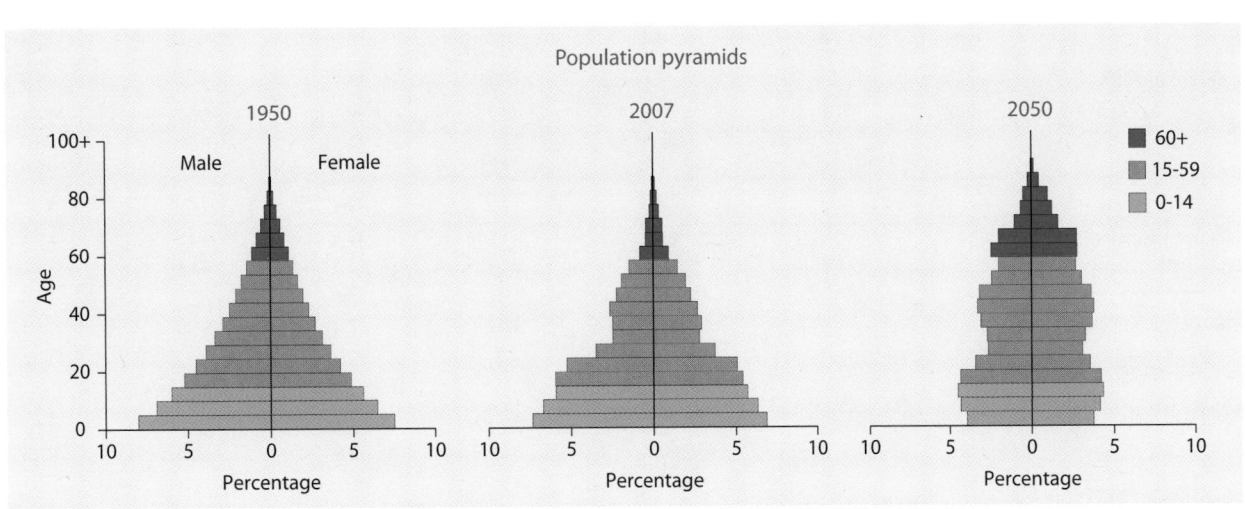

Population pyramids

Mongolia

Indicator	Age	1950	1975	2007	2025	2050
Population (thousands)						
Total	Total	761.3	1 447.4	2 711.5	3 266.5	3 624.8
	0-14	319.0	633.2	791.8	726.5	630.7
	15-59	400.7	745.6	1 764.5	2 196.5	2 131.2
	60-64	16.4	26.1	50.9	141.4	264.6
	65-69	11.8	18.4	40.2	95.3	205.8
	70-74	7.6	12.2	30.3	52.4	161.7
	75-79	4.0	7.1	19.0	28.1	115.8
	80-84			9.7	17.6	69.5
	85-89			4.0	6.7	34.3
	90-94	1.9	4.7	0.9	1.9	9.6
	95-99			0.1	0.2	1.4
	100+			0.0	0.0	0.1
Female	Total	388.5	724.1	1 353.2	1 629.6	1 819.7
	0-14	160.4	311.5	387.2	354.3	307.9
	15-59	204.6	374.4	881.3	1 088.5	1 046.2
	60-64	9.0	14.0	26.4	74.3	135.3
	65-69	6.6	10.2	21.1	51.3	107.5
	70-74	4.4	6.9	16.9	29.1	87.2
	75-79	2.4	4.2	11.0	16.1	64.6
	80-84			5.9	10.4	41.1
	85-89			2.7	4.2	22.0
	90-94	1.2	2.8	0.6	1.3	6.8
	95-99			0.1	0.2	1.1
	100+			0.0	0.0	0.1
Male	Total	372.8	723.3	1 358.3	1 636.9	1 805.1
	0-14	158.6	321.7	404.6	372.2	322.8
	15-59	196.1	371.3	883.2	1 108.0	1 085.0
	60-64	7.4	12.1	24.5	67.1	129.3
	65-69	5.2	8.2	19.1	44.0	98.3
	70-74	3.2	5.3	13.4	23.3	74.5
	75-79	1.6	2.9	8.0	11.9	51.3
	80-84			3.9	7.3	28.4
	85-89			1.4	2.5	12.3
	90-94	0.7	1.9	0.2	0.6	2.8
	95-99			0.0	0.1	0.3
	100+			0.0	0.0	0.0
Percentage in older ages						
Total	60+	5.5	4.7	5.7	10.5	23.8
	65+	3.3	2.9	3.8	6.2	16.5
	80+	0.2	0.3	0.5	0.8	3.2
Female	60+	6.1	5.3	6.3	11.5	25.6
	65+	3.8	3.3	4.3	6.9	18.2
	80+	0.3	0.4	0.7	1.0	3.9
Male	60+	4.9	4.2	5.2	9.6	22.0
	65+	2.9	2.5	3.4	5.5	14.8
	80+	0.2	0.3	0.4	0.6	2.4
Ageing index		13.1	10.8	19.6	47.3	136.8
Broad age groups (percentage)	0-14	41.9	43.7	29.2	22.2	17.4
	15-59	52.6	51.5	65.1	67.2	58.8
	60+	5.5	4.7	5.7	10.5	23.8
Median age (years)		19.0	18.0	23.7*	32.6	40.6
Dependency ratio	Total	82.5	87.5	49.4	39.7	51.3
	Youth	76.5	82.1	43.6	31.1	26.3
	Old Age	6.1	5.5	5.7	8.6	25.0
Potential support ratio		16.5	18.2	17.4	11.6	4.0
Parent support ratio		0.8	1.2	2.4	1.7	6.1
Sex ratio (per 100 women)	60+	76.9	79.6	83.2	83.9	85.3
	65+	73.3	75.9	78.8	79.7	81.1
	80+	60.7	65.8	58.9	65.0	61.7

*   *Estimate refers to year 2005.*

Indicator	Age	1950-1955	1975-1980	2005-2010	2025-2030	2045-2050
Growth rate (percentage)	Total	2.2	2.8	1.2	0.7	0.1
	60+	1.7	3.0	1.4	4.6	3.1
	65+	1.8	3.0	2.3	6.4	3.0
	80+	5.3	3.2	1.1	2.4	4.7
Total fertility rate (per woman)		6.0	6.6	2.2	1.9	1.9
Life expectancy (years)						
Total	Birth	42.2	55.5	65.9	71.9	75.9
	60	..	..	17.1	19.0	20.8
	65	..	..	13.8	15.4	17.0
	80	..	..	6.0	6.8	7.7
Female	Birth	43.5	57.0	67.7	73.6	78.0
	60	..	..	18.1	20.3	22.4
	65	..	..	14.6	16.4	18.3
	80	..	..	6.2	7.2	8.3
Male	Birth	41.0	54.0	63.9	70.1	73.9
	60	..	..	15.8	17.7	19.2
	65	..	..	12.8	14.3	15.6
	80	..	..	5.5	6.3	6.9
Survival rate (percentage)						
Total	60	..	..	74.2	83.2	88.4
	65	..	..	66.2	76.6	83.0
	80	..	..	29.4	40.2	49.4
Female	60	..	..	77.3	85.6	90.4
	65	..	..	70.5	80.2	86.3
	80	..	..	34.4	46.2	56.4
Male	60	..	..	70.8	80.9	86.5
	65	..	..	61.5	72.9	79.8
	80	..	..	23.8	34.3	42.4

		1980	1990	2007	2010	2020
Labour force participation (percentage)						
Total	65+	39.7	26.2	31.3	31.9	33.6
Female	65+	25.7	11.5	19.4	20.7	25.3
Male	65+	58.0	46.8	46.5	46.0	44.1

Percentage married, age 60+			Percentage living alone, age 60+		
Total	Female	Male	Total	Female	Male
50.1	33.0	71.0	..	..	..

Statutory pensionable age (2006)			Percentage illiterate, age 65+ (2000)		
	Female	Male	Total	Female	Male
	..	..	11.9	17.2	4.4

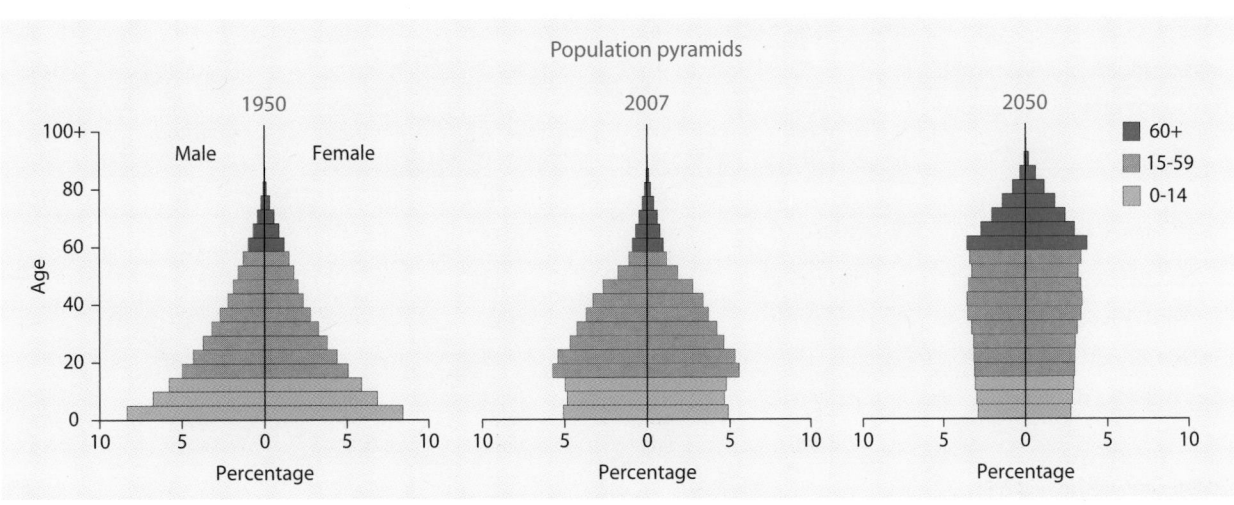

Population pyramids

Morocco

Indicator	Age	1950	1975	2007	2025	2050
Population (thousands)						
Total	Total	8 953.0	17 305.0	32 412.2	40 280.0	46 397.0
	0-14	3 973.9	8 163.8	9 851.7	10 110.7	8 885.2
	15-59	4 569.6	8 241.6	20 312.6	25 537.2	27 430.1
	60-64	152.6	266.3	683.5	1 582.3	2 695.2
	65-69	115.6	256.9	594.0	1 305.5	2 512.2
	70-74	84.2	162.3	455.3	874.4	2 013.2
	75-79	40.7	124.4	316.2	494.4	1 431.9
	80-84			141.2	233.8	855.6
	85-89			46.2	112.9	408.0
	90-94	16.5	89.7	10.4	25.0	138.1
	95-99			1.0	3.8	25.2
	100+			0.1	0.2	2.3
Female	Total	4 472.2	8 658.0	16 308.3	20 298.5	23 536.4
	0-14	1 974.6	4 013.0	4 842.7	4 962.1	4 338.8
	15-59	2 284.4	4 206.4	10 189.8	12 759.3	13 642.4
	60-64	78.6	123.0	371.9	856.3	1 383.5
	65-69	58.6	132.1	346.8	705.0	1 317.8
	70-74	44.8	79.4	260.2	482.0	1 089.9
	75-79	22.0	62.6	182.5	287.1	819.2
	80-84			81.4	148.3	525.5
	85-89			26.0	77.7	286.7
	90-94	9.1	41.5	6.3	17.5	108.4
	95-99			0.7	2.9	22.1
	100+			0.1	0.1	2.2
Male	Total	4 480.9	8 647.0	16 103.9	19 981.5	22 860.6
	0-14	1 999.3	4 150.8	5 009.0	5 148.5	4 546.4
	15-59	2 285.2	4 035.2	10 122.8	12 777.8	13 787.7
	60-64	74.0	143.3	311.6	726.1	1 311.8
	65-69	56.9	124.8	247.2	600.5	1 194.4
	70-74	39.4	82.9	195.1	392.4	923.3
	75-79	18.7	61.8	133.7	207.3	612.7
	80-84			59.8	85.5	330.1
	85-89			20.2	35.2	121.3
	90-94	7.3	48.2	4.1	7.4	29.7
	95-99			0.3	0.9	3.1
	100+			0.0	0.0	0.1
Percentage in older ages						
Total	60+	4.6	5.2	6.9	11.5	21.7
	65+	2.9	3.7	4.8	7.6	15.9
	80+	0.2	0.5	0.6	0.9	3.1
Female	60+	4.8	5.1	7.8	12.7	23.6
	65+	3.0	3.6	5.5	8.5	17.7
	80+	0.2	0.5	0.7	1.2	4.0
Male	60+	4.4	5.3	6.0	10.3	19.8
	65+	2.7	3.7	4.1	6.7	14.1
	80+	0.2	0.6	0.5	0.6	2.1
Ageing index		10.3	11.0	22.8	45.8	113.5
Broad age groups (percentage)	0-14	44.4	47.2	30.4	25.1	19.2
	15-59	51.0	47.6	62.7	63.4	59.1
	60+	4.6	5.2	6.9	11.5	21.7
Median age (years)		17.7	16.3	24.2*	30.6	37.9
Dependency ratio	Total	89.6	103.4	54.4	48.5	54.0
	Youth	84.2	96.0	46.9	37.3	29.5
	Old Age	5.4	7.4	7.5	11.2	24.5
Potential support ratio		18.4	13.4	13.4	8.9	4.1
Parent support ratio		0.7	3.5	1.9	2.4	6.9
Sex ratio (per 100 women)	60+	92.1	105.1	76.2	79.7	81.5
	65+	90.9	100.7	73.1	77.2	77.1
	80+	80.0	116.2	73.9	52.3	51.3

* *Estimate refers to year 2005.*

Indicator	Age	1950-1955	1975-1980	2005-2010	2025-2030	2045-2050
Growth rate (percentage)	Total	2.5	2.4	1.4	0.8	0.3
	60+	1.4	6.3	2.8	3.7	2.2
	65+	1.3	5.1	1.5	4.2	3.0
	80+	1.1	4.2	7.0	5.0	4.1
Total fertility rate (per woman)		7.2	5.9	2.6	2.1	1.9
Life expectancy (years)						
Total	Birth	42.9	55.6	71.0	75.4	78.4
	60	..	..	18.1	19.7	21.4
	65	..	..	14.4	15.8	17.4
	80	..	..	5.9	6.7	7.7
Female	Birth	43.9	57.5	73.3	77.8	80.7
	60	..	..	19.0	21.2	23.4
	65	..	..	15.1	17.1	19.1
	80	..	..	6.1	7.3	8.6
Male	Birth	41.9	54.1	68.8	73.0	75.9
	60	..	..	17.0	18.1	19.3
	65	..	..	13.5	14.3	15.4
	80	..	..	5.5	5.9	6.4
Survival rate (percentage)						
Total	60	..	..	83.3	89.2	92.3
	65	..	..	77.0	83.9	87.9
	80	..	..	36.2	45.4	53.6
Female	60	..	..	86.7	91.7	93.8
	65	..	..	81.4	87.7	90.6
	80	..	..	41.4	53.1	62.2
Male	60	..	..	80.0	86.6	90.7
	65	..	..	72.6	80.0	85.1
	80	..	..	30.6	37.6	44.7

		1980	1990	2007	2010	2020
Labour force participation (percentage)						
Total	65+	21.0	21.4	19.1	19.0	19.6
Female	65+	5.0	4.8	4.7	4.6	4.6
Male	65+	36.3	37.9	38.9	39.0	39.2

Percentage married, age 60+			Percentage living alone, age 60+ (1992)		
Total	Female	Male	Total	Female	Male
62.3	40.0	90.0	5.7	9.2	2.3

Statutory pensionable age (2006)			Percentage illiterate, age 65+ (2004)		
	Female	Male	Total	Female	Male
	60	60	86.2	96.6	75.0

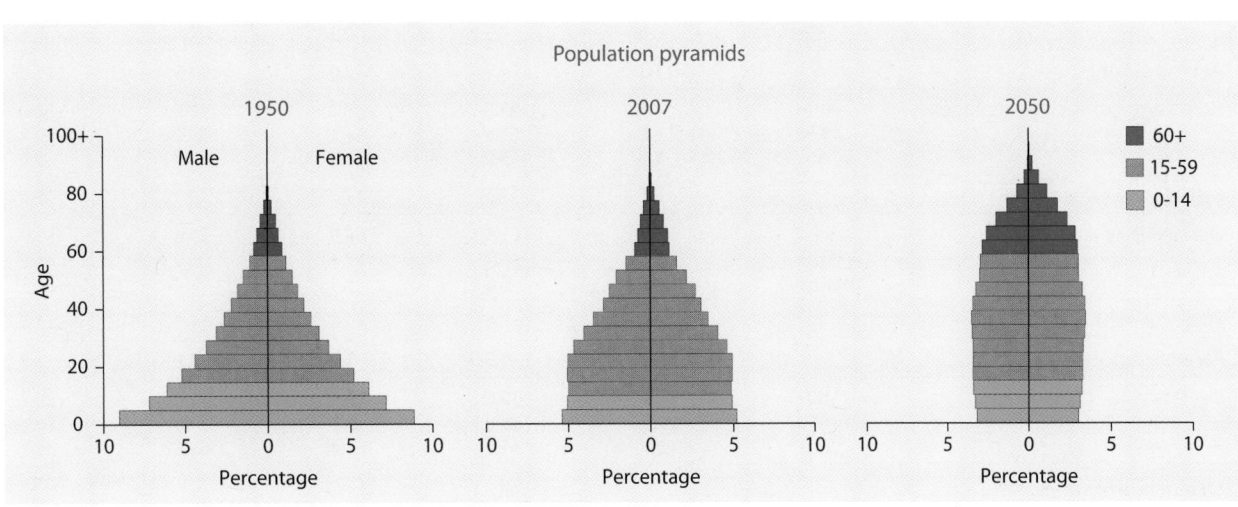

Population pyramids

Mozambique

Indicator	Age	1950	1975	2007	2025	2050
Population (thousands)						
Total	Total	6 442.1	10 569.3	20 522.5	27 555.7	37 604.4
	0-14	2 686.6	4 628.2	8 958.7	10 618.0	11 264.1
	15-59	3 452.3	5 416.0	10 487.2	15 370.5	23 469.3
	60-64	127.0	208.5	379.3	501.6	998.9
	65-69	87.7	149.5	290.6	410.2	733.3
	70-74	52.3	94.7	203.7	304.4	502.7
	75-79	25.2	49.5	122.7	197.8	337.8
	80-84			57.3	103.4	187.8
	85-89			18.8	38.8	82.6
	90-94	11.0	22.8	3.7	9.5	23.7
	95-99			0.4	1.3	3.8
	100+			0.0	0.1	0.3
Female	Total	3 293.5	5 396.8	10 554.2	13 860.0	18 844.8
	0-14	1 355.3	2 320.3	4 460.4	5 274.3	5 591.3
	15-59	1 768.7	2 784.1	5 480.1	7 694.8	11 737.8
	60-64	69.4	113.3	211.3	281.7	499.5
	65-69	48.8	82.7	165.0	229.9	367.9
	70-74	29.6	53.5	116.8	170.8	266.4
	75-79	14.8	28.8	71.5	114.6	197.4
	80-84			34.4	62.4	115.3
	85-89			11.8	24.2	51.2
	90-94	6.9	14.1	2.5	6.2	15.1
	95-99			0.3	0.9	2.6
	100+			0.0	0.1	0.2
Male	Total	3 148.6	5 172.5	9 968.3	13 695.7	18 759.6
	0-14	1 331.2	2 307.9	4 498.3	5 343.6	5 672.8
	15-59	1 683.6	2 631.9	5 007.2	7 675.7	11 731.5
	60-64	57.6	95.2	168.0	219.9	499.4
	65-69	39.0	66.8	125.7	180.3	365.4
	70-74	22.7	41.2	86.9	133.6	236.3
	75-79	10.4	20.7	51.1	83.2	140.4
	80-84			22.9	41.1	72.5
	85-89			6.9	14.7	31.4
	90-94	4.2	8.7	1.2	3.2	8.5
	95-99			0.1	0.4	1.2
	100+			0.0	0.0	0.1
Percentage in older ages						
Total	60+	4.7	5.0	5.2	5.7	7.6
	65+	2.7	3.0	3.4	3.9	5.0
	80+	0.2	0.2	0.4	0.6	0.8
Female	60+	5.1	5.4	5.8	6.4	8.0
	65+	3.0	3.3	3.8	4.4	5.4
	80+	0.2	0.3	0.5	0.7	1.0
Male	60+	4.2	4.5	4.6	4.9	7.2
	65+	2.4	2.7	3.0	3.3	4.6
	80+	0.1	0.2	0.3	0.4	0.6
Ageing index		11.3	11.3	12.0	14.8	25.5
Broad age groups (percentage)	0-14	41.7	43.8	43.7	38.5	30.0
	15-59	53.6	51.2	51.1	55.8	62.4
	60+	4.7	5.0	5.2	5.7	7.6
Median age (years)		19.1	18.1	17.7*	20.1	25.4
Dependency ratio	Total	80.0	87.9	88.9	73.6	53.7
	Youth	75.1	82.3	82.4	66.9	46.0
	Old Age	4.9	5.6	6.4	6.7	7.7
Potential support ratio		20.3	17.8	15.6	14.9	13.1
Parent support ratio		0.5	0.6	1.6	2.8	2.8
Sex ratio (per 100 women)	60+	79.0	79.6	75.4	75.9	89.4
	65+	76.2	76.8	73.3	74.9	84.2
	80+	60.6	61.9	63.4	63.4	61.7

* *Estimate refers to year 2005.*

Indicator	Age	1950-1955	1975-1980	2005-2010	2025-2030	2045-2050
Growth rate (percentage)	Total	1.5	2.6	1.8	1.4	1.1
	60+	1.5	2.7	2.3	1.7	3.5
	65+	1.5	2.9	2.6	2.0	3.2
	80+	0.8	4.3	4.2	3.1	2.1
Total fertility rate (per woman)		6.5	6.4	5.1	3.3	2.4
Life expectancy (years)						
Total	Birth	31.3	42.7	41.8	50.9	59.6
	60	..	..	16.0	17.3	18.6
	65	..	..	12.9	14.0	15.0
	80	..	..	5.7	6.2	6.6
Female	Birth	32.5	44.3	41.9	51.4	61.2
	60	..	..	16.6	17.9	19.3
	65	..	..	13.3	14.5	15.6
	80	..	..	5.9	6.4	6.8
Male	Birth	30.1	41.2	41.7	50.1	58.0
	60	..	..	15.3	16.5	17.7
	65	..	..	12.3	13.3	14.4
	80	..	..	5.4	5.9	6.3
Survival rate (percentage)						
Total	60	..	..	30.5	42.7	57.0
	65	..	..	26.6	38.3	52.1
	80	..	..	10.3	17.1	26.1
Female	60	..	..	30.4	43.1	59.4
	65	..	..	27.0	39.1	55.2
	80	..	..	11.1	18.4	29.2
Male	60	..	..	30.6	41.9	54.6
	65	..	..	26.3	36.9	49.3
	80	..	..	9.4	15.2	23.1

		1980	1990	2007	2010	2020
Labour force participation (percentage)						
Total	65+	84.4	86.7	82.0	81.3	79.8
Female	65+	78.5	82.5	79.2	79.2	79.2
Male	65+	92.1	92.5	85.9	84.1	80.5

Percentage married, age 60+			Percentage living alone, age 60+ (1997)		
Total	Female	Male	Total	Female	Male
56.0	34.0	85.0	14.3	18.1	11.0

Statutory pensionable age (2006)			Percentage illiterate, age 65+		
	Female	Male	Total	Female	Male
	55	55	..	..	..

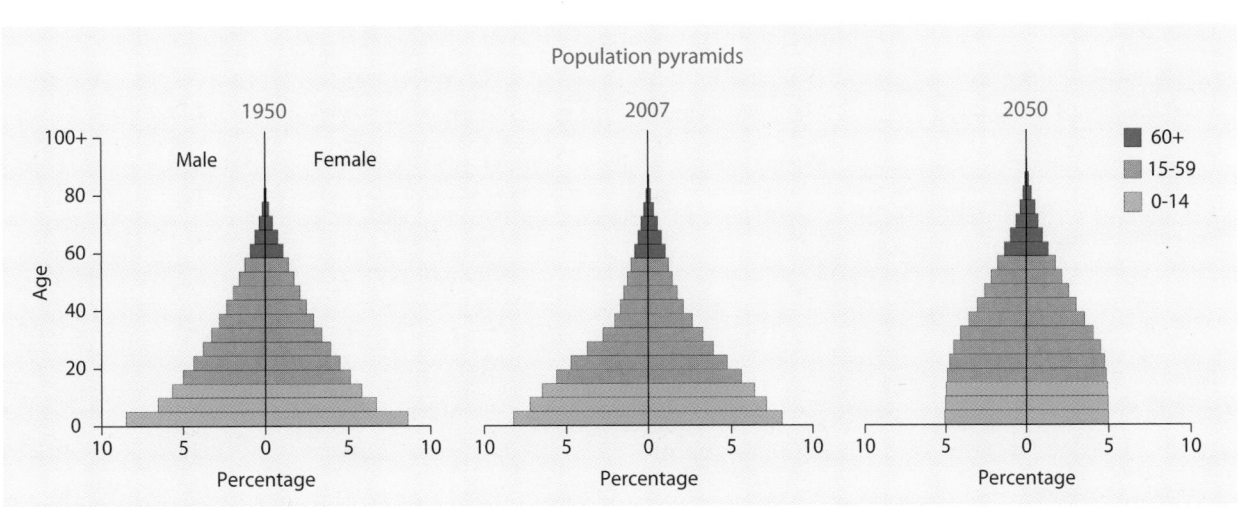

Population pyramids

United Nations Department of Economic and Social Affairs, Population Division

Myanmar

Indicator	Age	1950	1975	2007	2025	2050
Population (thousands)						
Total	Total	17 831.8	30 138.0	51 474.7	59 002.4	63 657.3
	0-14	6 738.4	12 311.2	14 418.5	12 564.1	10 902.3
	15-59	10 116.5	15 893.4	32 998.1	38 794.5	37 234.2
	60-64	398.5	705.5	1 423.5	2 473.6	4 134.2
	65-69	274.7	530.6	1 004.8	1 968.2	3 654.2
	70-74	170.2	364.2	698.5	1 458.6	3 045.4
	75-79	88.3	205.8	485.4	939.6	2 244.4
	80-84			282.1	504.3	1 401.0
	85-89			123.0	210.7	697.8
	90-94	45.2	127.2	34.5	70.6	268.0
	95-99			5.8	16.2	67.0
	100+			0.6	2.0	8.8
Female	Total	8 941.7	15 115.8	25 943.0	29 943.6	32 436.6
	0-14	3 346.6	6 119.4	7 113.6	6 180.3	5 351.6
	15-59	5 058.3	7 965.7	16 652.2	19 583.1	18 554.2
	60-64	212.5	367.5	744.5	1 314.5	2 146.3
	65-69	149.9	281.2	533.0	1 060.5	1 941.1
	70-74	95.4	196.3	376.3	803.0	1 668.7
	75-79	51.1	113.4	267.2	526.6	1 273.6
	80-84			159.4	291.6	828.2
	85-89			71.6	126.6	436.0
	90-94	28.0	72.2	21.0	44.8	180.3
	95-99			3.7	11.1	49.4
	100+			0.4	1.5	7.1
Male	Total	8 890.0	15 022.2	25 531.7	29 058.8	31 220.7
	0-14	3 391.8	6 191.7	7 304.9	6 383.8	5 550.6
	15-59	5 058.2	7 927.7	16 345.8	19 211.3	18 680.1
	60-64	186.1	338.0	679.0	1 159.1	1 987.9
	65-69	124.8	249.4	471.8	907.8	1 713.1
	70-74	74.8	167.9	322.2	655.6	1 376.7
	75-79	37.2	92.4	218.2	413.0	970.8
	80-84			122.7	212.7	572.8
	85-89			51.4	84.1	261.8
	90-94	17.2	55.0	13.5	25.8	87.7
	95-99			2.0	5.1	17.6
	100+			0.2	0.5	1.7
Percentage in older ages						
Total	60+	5.5	6.4	7.9	13.0	24.4
	65+	3.2	4.1	5.1	8.8	17.9
	80+	0.3	0.4	0.9	1.4	3.8
Female	60+	6.0	6.8	8.4	14.0	26.3
	65+	3.6	4.4	5.5	9.6	19.7
	80+	0.3	0.5	1.0	1.6	4.6
Male	60+	5.0	6.0	7.4	11.9	22.4
	65+	2.9	3.8	4.7	7.9	16.0
	80+	0.2	0.4	0.7	1.1	3.0
Ageing index		14.5	15.7	28.1	60.8	142.4
Broad age groups (percentage)	0-14	37.8	40.8	28.0	21.3	17.1
	15-59	56.7	52.7	64.1	65.8	58.5
	60+	5.5	6.4	7.9	13.0	24.4
Median age (years)		21.8	19.5	25.5*	33.5	41.2
Dependency ratio	Total	69.6	81.6	49.5	43.0	53.9
	Youth	64.1	74.2	41.9	30.4	26.4
	Old Age	5.5	7.4	7.7	12.5	27.5
Potential support ratio		18.2	13.5	13.1	8.0	3.6
Parent support ratio		0.9	1.4	2.9	3.2	7.9
Sex ratio (per 100 women)	60+	82.0	87.6	86.4	82.9	81.9
	65+	78.3	85.2	83.9	80.4	78.3
	80+	61.4	76.3	74.1	69.0	62.7

* *Estimate refers to year 2005.*

Indicator	Age	1950-1955	1975-1980	2005-2010	2025-2030	2045-2050
Growth rate (percentage)	Total	1.8	2.2	0.9	0.5	0.1
	60+	2.6	2.7	3.4	3.4	2.1
	65+	2.9	2.5	3.0	3.5	2.5
	80+	4.4	3.7	3.2	5.2	4.0
Total fertility rate (per woman)		6.0	5.3	2.1	1.9	1.9
Life expectancy (years)						
Total	Birth	36.8	50.5	61.8	69.6	74.7
	60	..	..	18.0	20.0	21.5
	65	..	..	14.6	16.3	17.7
	80	..	..	6.9	7.6	8.3
Female	Birth	38.1	52.6	64.8	72.3	77.2
	60	..	..	18.8	21.1	22.9
	65	..	..	15.3	17.2	18.8
	80	..	..	7.2	8.1	8.9
Male	Birth	35.5	48.5	58.9	67.0	72.1
	60	..	..	17.1	18.7	20.0
	65	..	..	13.9	15.2	16.3
	80	..	..	6.5	7.1	7.5
Survival rate (percentage)						
Total	60	..	..	66.7	78.3	85.3
	65	..	..	60.3	72.7	80.5
	80	..	..	28.4	40.3	49.5
Female	60	..	..	72.1	82.3	88.3
	65	..	..	66.2	77.5	84.3
	80	..	..	33.4	46.4	55.9
Male	60	..	..	61.5	74.3	82.5
	65	..	..	54.7	67.9	76.7
	80	..	..	23.7	34.2	42.9

		1980	1990	2007	2010	2020
Labour force participation (percentage)						
Total	65+	53.9	53.8	53.5	53.4	53.3
Female	65+	42.1	43.3	45.5	45.9	47.5
Male	65+	67.7	66.0	63.0	62.4	60.4

Percentage married, age 60+				Percentage living alone, age 60+ (1990)		
Total	Female	Male		Total	Female	Male
54.8	39.0	73.0		4.6	5.9	3.1

Statutory pensionable age (2006)				Percentage illiterate, age 65+ (2000)		
	Female	Male		Total	Female	Male
	..	..		24.9	35.1	11.7

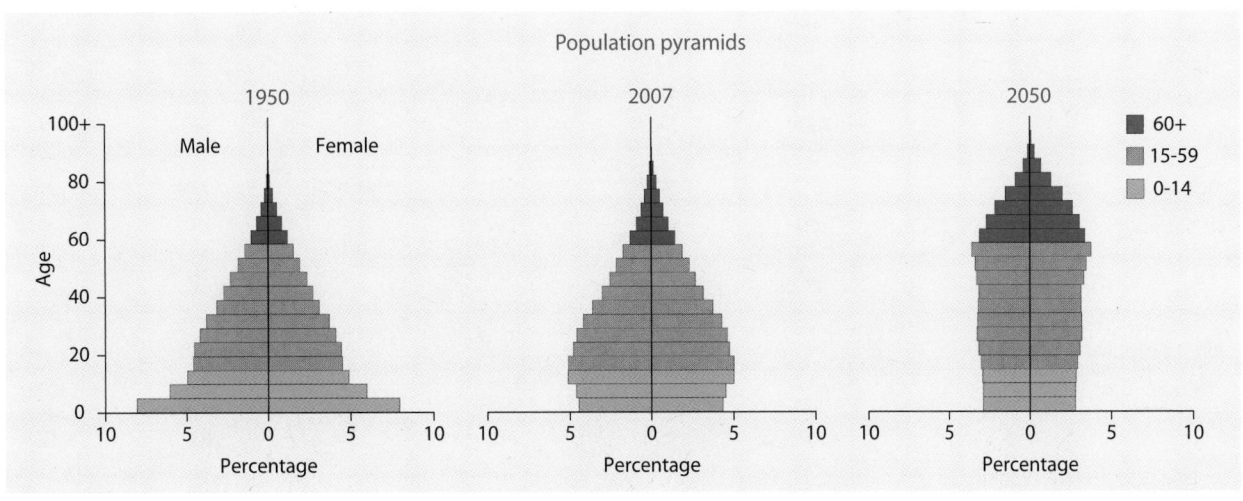

Population pyramids

Namibia

Indicator	Age	1950	1975	2007	2025	2050
Population (thousands)						
Total	Total	485.3	890.6	2 072.3	2 519.4	3 059.9
	0-14	188.1	389.2	828.2	860.3	802.7
	15-59	265.3	451.9	1 130.2	1 476.7	1 968.2
	60-64	12.0	18.4	39.1	57.2	103.9
	65-69	8.8	13.4	29.3	47.7	68.1
	70-74	6.4	9.4	21.0	35.9	45.0
	75-79	3.2	5.2	14.2	23.5	33.2
	80-84			7.2	12.3	22.5
	85-89			2.5	4.5	11.8
	90-94	1.6	3.0	0.5	1.1	3.8
	95-99			0.1	0.2	0.7
	100+			0.0	0.0	0.1
Female	Total	244.3	446.0	1 043.0	1 240.6	1 501.6
	0-14	92.5	193.4	410.5	426.6	397.0
	15-59	134.6	225.0	569.4	710.6	961.6
	60-64	6.6	10.0	21.2	30.7	48.1
	65-69	4.9	7.4	16.0	26.9	31.4
	70-74	3.3	5.3	11.7	21.0	21.3
	75-79	1.6	3.0	8.0	13.8	17.4
	80-84			4.2	7.4	13.4
	85-89			1.6	2.8	7.9
	90-94	0.8	1.9	0.4	0.7	2.8
	95-99			0.0	0.1	0.6
	100+			0.0	0.0	0.1
Male	Total	241.0	444.6	1 029.3	1 278.8	1 558.3
	0-14	95.6	195.9	417.7	433.7	405.8
	15-59	130.7	226.9	560.8	766.2	1 006.6
	60-64	5.4	8.4	17.9	26.5	55.8
	65-69	3.9	6.0	13.3	20.8	36.7
	70-74	3.1	4.0	9.3	14.9	23.7
	75-79	1.6	2.2	6.1	9.6	15.7
	80-84			3.0	4.9	9.1
	85-89			1.0	1.7	3.9
	90-94	0.8	1.2	0.2	0.4	0.9
	95-99			0.0	0.1	0.1
	100+			0.0	0.0	0.0
Percentage in older ages						
Total	60+	6.6	5.6	5.5	7.2	9.4
	65+	4.1	3.5	3.6	5.0	6.0
	80+	0.3	0.3	0.5	0.7	1.3
Female	60+	7.0	6.2	6.0	8.3	9.5
	65+	4.4	4.0	4.0	5.9	6.3
	80+	0.3	0.4	0.6	0.9	1.6
Male	60+	6.1	4.9	4.9	6.2	9.4
	65+	3.9	3.0	3.2	4.1	5.8
	80+	0.3	0.3	0.4	0.6	0.9
Ageing index		17.0	12.7	13.8	21.2	36.0
Broad age groups (percentage)	0-14	38.8	43.7	40.0	34.1	26.2
	15-59	54.7	50.7	54.5	58.6	64.3
	60+	6.6	5.6	5.5	7.2	9.4
Median age (years)		20.9	18.1	18.6*	23.1	28.1
Dependency ratio	Total	75.0	89.4	77.2	64.2	47.7
	Youth	67.8	82.8	70.8	56.1	38.7
	Old Age	7.2	6.6	6.4	8.2	8.9
Potential support ratio		13.9	15.1	15.6	12.3	11.2
Parent support ratio		1.0	1.2	2.1	3.2	4.0
Sex ratio (per 100 women)	60+	85.5	78.8	80.7	76.3	102.0
	65+	87.3	75.8	78.7	71.9	95.0
	80+	95.0	63.3	68.4	64.5	56.8

*   *Estimate refers to year 2005.*

Namibia

Indicator	Age	1950-1955	1975-1980	2005-2010	2025-2030	2045-2050
Growth rate (percentage)	Total	2.0	2.1	1.0	0.9	0.7
	60+	0.5	2.2	2.7	1.5	3.8
	65+	1.2	2.2	2.7	2.4	2.4
	80+	2.7	2.2	4.0	3.9	1.2
Total fertility rate (per woman)		6.0	6.5	3.5	2.5	2.1
Life expectancy (years)						
Total	Birth	41.7	56.5	45.9	55.5	62.2
	60	..	..	17.2	18.3	19.5
	65	..	..	13.9	14.9	15.9
	80	..	..	5.9	6.4	7.1
Female	Birth	42.6	57.5	45.1	54.6	62.9
	60	..	..	18.1	19.4	21.3
	65	..	..	14.6	15.8	17.4
	80	..	..	6.2	6.7	7.7
Male	Birth	40.8	55.3	46.6	56.0	61.5
	60	..	..	16.1	17.0	18.0
	65	..	..	13.1	13.8	14.6
	80	..	..	5.7	5.9	6.2
Survival rate (percentage)						
Total	60	..	..	31.3	43.7	56.9
	65	..	..	28.0	39.6	52.6
	80	..	..	12.4	19.8	28.7
Female	60	..	..	29.7	41.1	57.1
	65	..	..	27.1	38.0	53.9
	80	..	..	13.0	20.7	33.2
Male	60	..	..	32.6	46.0	56.9
	65	..	..	28.5	40.8	51.6
	80	..	..	11.4	18.0	24.8

		1980	1990	2007	2010	2020
Labour force participation (percentage)						
Total	65+	26.8	28.3	25.5	25.2	24.6
Female	65+	27.2	23.6	21.0	20.7	20.4
Male	65+	26.2	34.3	31.3	31.0	30.4

Percentage married, age 60+

	Total	Female	Male
	53.0	34.0	76.0

Percentage living alone, age 60+ (1992)

Total	Female	Male
4.2	3.9	4.6

Statutory pensionable age (2006)

Female	Male
60	60

Percentage illiterate, age 65+ (2001)

Total	Female	Male
46.0	53.1	36.0

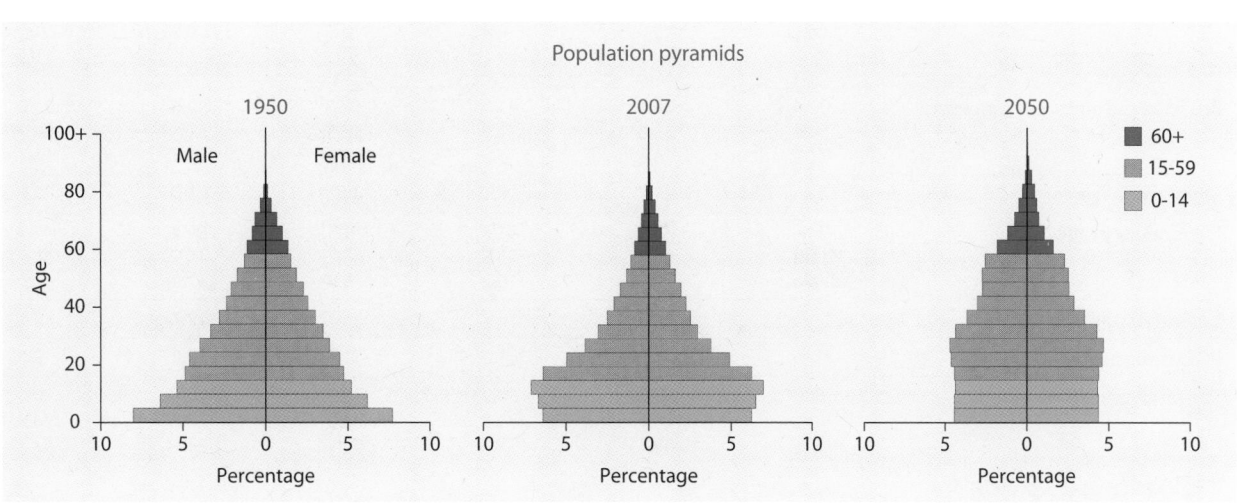

Population pyramids

Nepal

Indicator	Age	1950	1975	2007	2025	2050
Population (thousands)						
Total	Total	8 642.9	13 547.7	28 225.5	38 599.5	51 171.8
	0-14	3 315.8	5 627.2	10 720.0	11 803.0	11 676.6
	15-59	4 756.3	7 169.2	15 848.8	23 767.8	32 270.5
	60-64	215.9	287.9	600.5	1 071.8	2 377.4
	65-69	158.8	210.9	449.9	811.7	1 870.5
	70-74	104.8	137.1	305.7	570.1	1 357.3
	75-79	58.9	72.9	180.7	336.8	884.9
	80-84			84.8	166.0	482.8
	85-89			28.5	57.9	195.0
	90-94	32.4	42.5	5.9	12.7	49.5
	95-99			0.7	1.6	7.0
	100+			0.0	0.1	0.5
Female	Total	4 323.4	6 722.6	14 239.8	19 508.6	26 041.1
	0-14	1 644.0	2 731.9	5 212.8	5 763.6	5 709.8
	15-59	2 360.1	3 586.5	8 091.9	12 024.7	16 303.2
	60-64	114.6	151.6	330.4	600.4	1 249.9
	65-69	86.8	112.7	252.1	455.5	1 009.5
	70-74	59.7	74.7	175.0	320.7	764.0
	75-79	36.1	40.5	105.5	197.6	527.0
	80-84			50.5	100.4	306.1
	85-89			17.4	36.3	130.8
	90-94	22.2	24.7	3.8	8.3	35.1
	95-99			0.5	1.1	5.3
	100+			0.0	0.1	0.4
Male	Total	4 319.6	6 825.1	13 985.7	19 091.0	25 130.7
	0-14	1 671.9	2 895.3	5 507.2	6 039.4	5 966.8
	15-59	2 396.3	3 582.7	7 757.0	11 743.2	15 967.3
	60-64	101.4	136.3	270.1	471.4	1 127.5
	65-69	72.0	98.2	197.8	356.2	861.0
	70-74	45.0	62.4	130.6	249.4	593.3
	75-79	22.8	32.4	75.2	139.2	357.8
	80-84			34.3	65.6	176.7
	85-89			11.1	21.6	64.2
	90-94	10.2	17.8	2.2	4.4	14.4
	95-99			0.2	0.5	1.7
	100+			0.0	0.0	0.1
Percentage in older ages						
Total	60+	6.6	5.5	5.9	7.8	14.1
	65+	4.1	3.4	3.7	5.1	9.5
	80+	0.4	0.3	0.4	0.6	1.4
Female	60+	7.4	6.0	6.6	8.8	15.5
	65+	4.7	3.8	4.2	5.7	10.7
	80+	0.5	0.4	0.5	0.7	1.8
Male	60+	5.8	5.1	5.2	6.9	12.7
	65+	3.5	3.1	3.2	4.4	8.2
	80+	0.2	0.3	0.3	0.5	1.0
Ageing index		17.2	13.4	15.5	25.7	61.9
Broad age groups (percentage)	0-14	38.4	41.5	38.0	30.6	22.8
	15-59	55.0	52.9	56.2	61.6	63.1
	60+	6.6	5.5	5.9	7.8	14.1
Median age (years)		21.1	19.1	20.1*	25.5	32.7
Dependency ratio	Total	73.8	81.7	71.6	55.4	47.7
	Youth	66.7	75.5	65.2	47.5	33.7
	Old Age	7.1	6.2	6.4	7.9	14.0
Potential support ratio		14.0	16.1	15.6	12.7	7.1
Parent support ratio		1.0	1.0	1.5	1.8	3.0
Sex ratio (per 100 women)	60+	78.7	85.9	77.2	76.1	79.4
	65+	73.2	83.5	74.6	74.7	74.5
	80+	45.7	72.3	66.2	63.1	53.8

* *Estimate refers to year 2005.*

Indicator	Age	1950-1955	1975-1980	2005-2010	2025-2030	2045-2050
Growth rate (percentage)	Total	1.5	2.2	1.9	1.4	0.9
	60+	0.4	2.0	3.0	3.4	3.5
	65+	0.3	2.2	3.2	3.6	3.8
	80+	0.3	2.1	3.6	4.0	4.7
Total fertility rate (per woman)		6.1	5.7	3.3	2.4	2.0
Life expectancy (years)						
Total	Birth	36.2	46.7	63.6	71.0	75.4
	60	..	..	16.4	17.8	19.6
	65	..	..	13.1	14.2	15.7
	80	..	..	5.6	6.0	6.8
Female	Birth	35.5	46.5	64.1	72.4	77.2
	60	..	..	17.1	18.6	20.9
	65	..	..	13.6	14.8	16.8
	80	..	..	5.8	6.2	7.3
Male	Birth	36.7	47.0	63.0	69.5	73.4
	60	..	..	15.7	16.9	18.1
	65	..	..	12.5	13.4	14.4
	80	..	..	5.4	5.7	6.1
Survival rate (percentage)						
Total	60	..	..	70.9	82.6	88.9
	65	..	..	63.2	75.8	83.3
	80	..	..	25.1	34.8	44.8
Female	60	..	..	71.8	84.6	90.8
	65	..	..	64.9	78.7	86.4
	80	..	..	27.5	38.8	51.2
Male	60	..	..	69.8	80.5	87.0
	65	..	..	61.3	72.5	80.2
	80	..	..	22.3	30.3	37.8

		1980	1990	2007	2010	2020
Labour force participation (percentage)						
Total	65+	50.3	27.0	23.1	22.8	22.0
Female	65+	35.0	14.3	12.5	12.5	12.5
Male	65+	68.6	42.8	37.2	36.6	34.6

Percentage married, age 60+			Percentage living alone, age 60+ (2001)		
Total	Female	Male	Total	Female	Male
63.2	50.0	80.0	4.5	6.6	2.6

Statutory pensionable age (2006)			Percentage illiterate, age 65+ (2001)		
	Female	Male	Total	Female	Male
	55	55	84.0	95.8	72.5

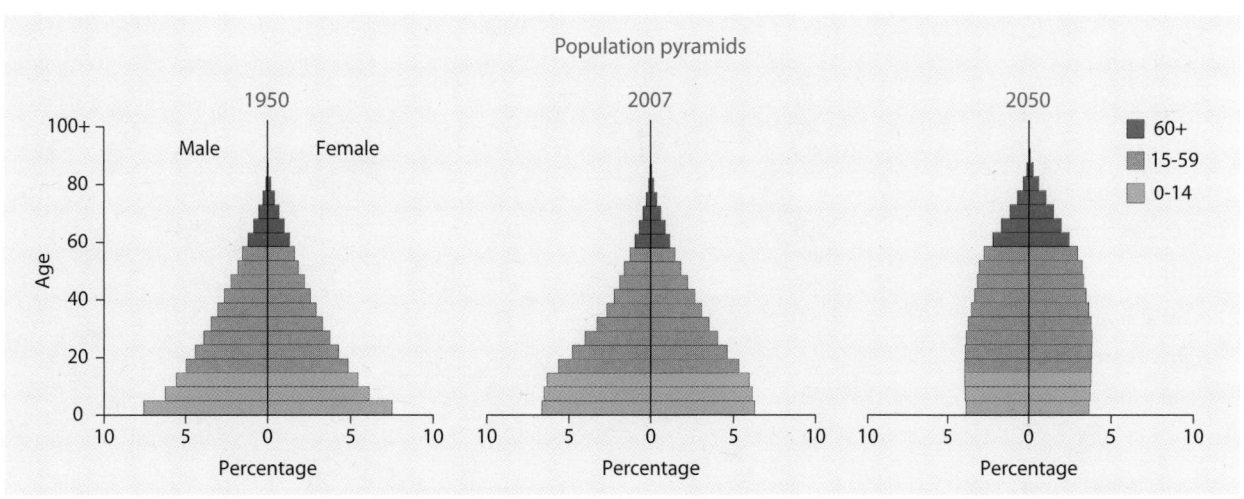

Population pyramids

1950 1950 2007 2050

Male Female

60+
15-59
0-14

Age · Percentage

Netherlands

Indicator	Age	1950	1975	2007	2025	2050
Population (thousands)						
Total	Total	10 114.0	13 666.3	16 429.0	17 177.9	17 139.4
	0-14	2 964.0	3 463.2	2 937.8	2 661.1	2 673.3
	15-59	5 991.0	8 135.6	10 182.9	9 596.2	9 096.0
	60-64	376.0	592.7	944.8	1 249.8	1 012.8
	65-69	305.0	511.0	706.1	1 086.1	910.7
	70-74	231.0	412.7	586.7	916.6	848.2
	75-79	145.0	280.2	464.4	800.2	872.0
	80-84			339.4	460.6	792.8
	85-89			180.0	254.9	542.8
	90-94	102.0	270.9	68.8	113.6	273.4
	95-99			16.3	33.4	96.1
	100+			1.8	5.5	21.5
Female	Total	5 073.0	6 862.1	8 269.9	8 658.6	8 683.6
	0-14	1 445.0	1 691.8	1 433.2	1 297.8	1 303.6
	15-59	3 026.0	4 006.4	4 997.9	4 698.2	4 442.9
	60-64	193.0	315.5	472.7	624.7	505.0
	65-69	157.0	284.0	363.4	557.4	460.8
	70-74	120.0	238.5	317.7	485.2	438.8
	75-79	76.0	160.3	271.3	442.5	471.5
	80-84			218.4	273.1	450.6
	85-89			127.4	166.2	334.1
	90-94	56.0	165.5	53.0	82.1	186.1
	95-99			13.4	26.7	72.5
	100+			1.5	4.7	17.8
Male	Total	5 041.0	6 804.2	8 159.1	8 519.3	8 455.8
	0-14	1 519.0	1 771.4	1 504.5	1 363.3	1 369.7
	15-59	2 965.0	4 129.2	5 185.0	4 898.0	4 653.1
	60-64	183.0	277.2	472.1	625.2	507.8
	65-69	148.0	227.0	342.7	528.7	449.9
	70-74	111.0	174.1	269.1	431.3	409.4
	75-79	69.0	119.8	193.1	357.7	400.5
	80-84			121.0	187.5	342.2
	85-89			52.6	88.8	208.7
	90-94	46.0	105.5	15.9	31.5	87.4
	95-99			2.9	6.7	23.5
	100+			0.3	0.8	3.7
Percentage in older ages						
Total	60+	11.5	15.1	20.1	28.6	31.3
	65+	7.7	10.8	14.4	21.4	25.4
	80+	1.0	2.0	3.7	5.1	10.1
Female	60+	11.9	17.0	22.2	30.8	33.8
	65+	8.1	12.4	16.5	23.5	28.0
	80+	1.1	2.4	5.0	6.4	12.2
Male	60+	11.0	13.3	18.0	26.5	28.8
	65+	7.4	9.2	12.2	19.2	22.8
	80+	0.9	1.6	2.4	3.7	7.9
Ageing index		39.1	59.7	112.6	184.9	200.9
Broad age groups (percentage)	0-14	29.3	25.3	17.9	15.5	15.6
	15-59	59.2	59.5	62.0	55.9	53.1
	60+	11.5	15.1	20.1	28.6	31.3
Median age (years)		28.0	29.4	39.3*	44.0	45.3
Dependency ratio	Total	58.9	56.6	47.6	58.4	69.5
	Youth	46.6	39.7	26.4	24.5	26.4
	Old Age	12.3	16.9	21.2	33.8	43.1
Potential support ratio		8.1	5.9	4.7	3.0	2.3
Parent support ratio		2.8	5.0	8.2	10.9	29.4
Sex ratio (per 100 women)	60+	92.5	77.6	79.9	84.8	82.8
	65+	91.4	73.8	73.0	80.1	79.2
	80+	82.1	63.7	46.6	57.0	62.7

* *Estimate refers to year 2005.*

Indicator	Age	1950-1955	1975-1980	2005-2010	2025-2030	2045-2050
Growth rate (percentage)	Total	1.2	0.7	0.4	0.1	−0.1
	60+	2.7	1.4	2.8	1.6	−0.2
	65+	2.8	2.0	1.8	2.1	−0.5
	80+	4.4	3.6	1.8	4.8	1.7
Total fertility rate (per woman)		3.1	1.6	1.7	1.8	1.9
Life expectancy (years)						
Total	Birth	72.1	75.3	79.0	81.2	83.1
	60	..	..	22.0	23.6	25.2
	65	..	..	18.0	19.5	20.9
	80	..	..	8.3	9.2	10.1
Female	Birth	73.4	78.6	81.6	83.8	85.7
	60	..	..	24.2	25.9	27.4
	65	..	..	19.9	21.5	23.0
	80	..	..	9.1	10.2	11.3
Male	Birth	70.9	72.1	76.3	78.6	80.6
	60	..	..	19.6	21.4	23.0
	65	..	..	15.8	17.4	18.8
	80	..	..	7.0	7.9	8.8
Survival rate (percentage)						
Total	60	..	..	91.9	93.7	94.9
	65	..	..	87.4	90.1	92.0
	80	..	..	55.5	62.2	67.9
Female	60	..	..	93.6	95.1	96.2
	65	..	..	90.4	92.6	94.1
	80	..	..	65.6	71.3	75.9
Male	60	..	..	90.2	92.2	93.7
	65	..	..	84.5	87.6	89.9
	80	..	..	45.2	53.2	59.9

		1980	1990	2007	2010	2020
Labour force participation (percentage)						
Total	65+	3.5	2.8	4.2	4.7	5.9
Female	65+	1.2	0.9	2.8	3.6	5.6
Male	65+	6.7	5.6	6.0	6.1	6.3

Percentage married, age 60+			Percentage living alone, age 60+ (1994)		
Total	Female	Male	Total	Female	Male
60.5	48.0	77.0	34.5	47.4	16.9

Statutory pensionable age (2006)			Percentage illiterate, age 65+		
	Female	Male	Total	Female	Male
	65	65	..	..	..

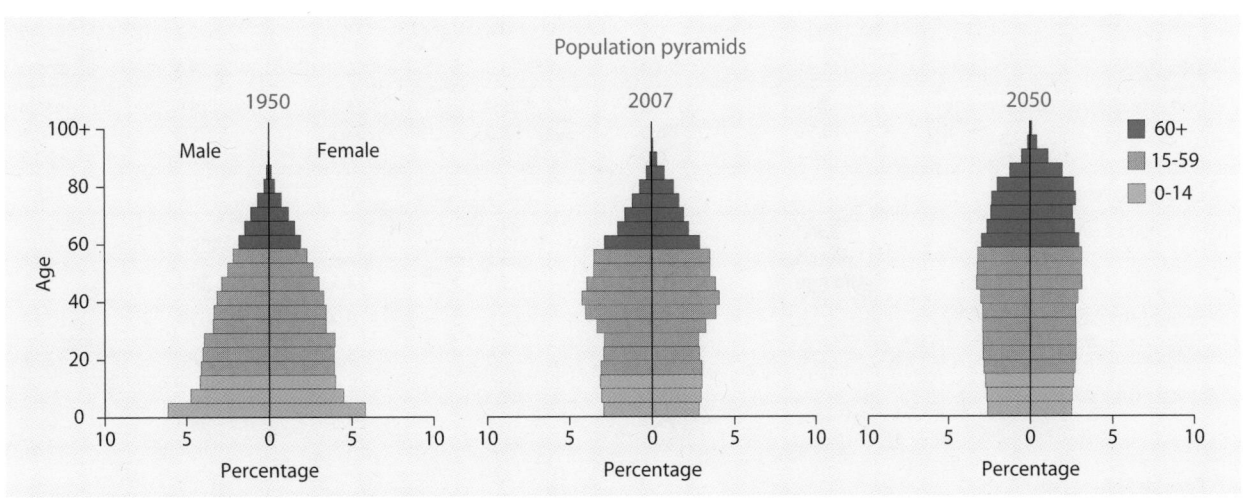

Population pyramids

Netherlands Antilles

Indicator	Age	1950	1975	2007	2025	2050
Population (thousands)						
Total	Total	111.7	166.2	185.3	202.0	202.9
	0-14	39.3	54.6	40.3	37.5	33.2
	15-59	62.6	97.4	117.3	112.6	113.8
	60-64	2.7	4.7	9.2	14.9	13.7
	65-69	2.4	4.1	6.5	13.2	11.0
	70-74	2.2	2.7	5.0	9.8	6.5
	75-79	1.5	1.6	3.4	7.3	7.7
	80-84			2.0	4.0	7.7
	85-89			1.0	1.8	5.7
	90-94	1.0	1.1	0.4	0.7	2.8
	95-99			0.1	0.2	0.8
	100+			0.0	0.0	0.1
Female	Total	57.6	83.9	97.9	106.3	104.8
	0-14	19.5	27.1	19.9	18.3	16.2
	15-59	31.5	49.1	62.2	57.2	56.0
	60-64	1.7	2.4	5.1	8.2	7.0
	65-69	1.6	2.1	3.6	7.6	5.7
	70-74	1.5	1.5	2.8	5.8	3.5
	75-79	1.0	1.0	2.0	4.5	4.6
	80-84			1.2	2.7	4.9
	85-89			0.7	1.3	3.9
	90-94	0.7	0.8	0.3	0.6	2.1
	95-99			0.1	0.1	0.7
	100+			0.0	0.0	0.1
Male	Total	54.1	82.3	87.4	95.7	98.1
	0-14	19.8	27.5	20.5	19.2	17.0
	15-59	31.1	48.2	55.2	55.4	57.8
	60-64	1.0	2.4	4.1	6.7	6.7
	65-69	0.8	2.1	2.9	5.6	5.3
	70-74	0.7	1.2	2.2	4.0	3.0
	75-79	0.4	0.6	1.4	2.8	3.1
	80-84			0.7	1.4	2.8
	85-89			0.3	0.5	1.8
	90-94	0.3	0.3	0.1	0.1	0.6
	95-99			0.0	0.0	0.1
	100+			0.0	0.0	0.0
Percentage in older ages						
Total	60+	8.8	8.6	14.9	25.7	27.5
	65+	6.4	5.7	9.9	18.3	20.8
	80+	0.9	0.7	1.9	3.4	8.4
Female	60+	11.4	9.2	16.2	28.9	31.0
	65+	8.5	6.3	11.0	21.2	24.3
	80+	1.3	0.9	2.4	4.5	11.2
Male	60+	5.9	7.9	13.4	22.1	23.8
	65+	4.1	5.1	8.7	15.2	17.0
	80+	0.5	0.4	1.3	2.2	5.4
Ageing index		24.9	26.0	68.3	138.4	168.0
Broad age groups (percentage)	0-14	35.2	32.9	21.8	18.6	16.4
	15-59	56.0	58.6	63.3	55.7	56.1
	60+	8.8	8.6	14.9	25.7	27.5
Median age (years)		23.3	22.3	36.2*	38.4	42.8
Dependency ratio	Total	71.1	62.8	46.4	58.5	59.1
	Youth	60.2	53.5	31.9	29.4	26.1
	Old Age	10.9	9.3	14.5	29.1	33.1
Potential support ratio		9.2	10.8	6.9	3.4	3.0
Parent support ratio		3.4	2.0	4.3	7.0	22.7
Sex ratio (per 100 women)	60+	48.6	84.6	73.9	68.9	71.8
	65+	45.8	78.4	70.6	64.4	65.2
	80+	35.5	41.6	49.1	43.7	44.7

* *Estimate refers to year 2005.*

Indicator	Age	1950-1955	1975-1980	2005-2010	2025-2030	2045-2050
Growth rate (percentage)	Total	1.9	0.9	0.6	0.3	–0.1
	60+	–0.6	2.6	3.9	1.6	0.8
	65+	–1.6	4.0	3.3	3.1	0.0
	80+	0.8	14.6	2.1	5.7	0.7
Total fertility rate (per woman)		5.7	2.5	2.0	1.9	1.9
Life expectancy (years)						
Total	Birth	60.5	72.1	76.9	79.6	81.7
	60	..	..	20.6	22.5	24.1
	65	..	..	16.6	18.4	19.9
	80	..	..	7.4	8.5	9.5
Female	Birth	61.6	74.8	79.8	82.3	84.4
	60	..	..	22.7	24.6	26.3
	65	..	..	18.5	20.3	21.9
	80	..	..	8.3	9.5	10.6
Male	Birth	59.1	69.5	73.7	76.5	78.8
	60	..	..	18.2	19.8	21.5
	65	..	..	14.5	15.9	17.4
	80	..	..	6.1	6.8	7.8
Survival rate (percentage)						
Total	60	..	..	90.4	92.8	94.2
	65	..	..	85.3	88.7	90.8
	80	..	..	49.2	57.5	63.8
Female	60	..	..	92.9	94.6	95.7
	65	..	..	89.3	91.7	93.4
	80	..	..	59.2	66.5	72.1
Male	60	..	..	87.5	90.9	92.7
	65	..	..	80.7	85.3	88.2
	80	..	..	38.4	46.6	54.3

		1980	1990	2007	2010	2020
Labour force participation (percentage)						
Total	65+	10.7	8.2	8.3	8.5	9.0
Female	65+	4.1	3.6	5.8	6.5	8.1
Male	65+	20.1	14.6	11.8	11.4	10.4

Percentage married, age 60+			Percentage living alone, age 60+ (1992)		
Total	Female	Male	Total	Female	Male
50.1	37.0	67.0	14.8	15.2	14.4

Statutory pensionable age (2006)		Percentage illiterate, age 65+		
Female	Male	Total	Female	Male
..	..	..	..	..

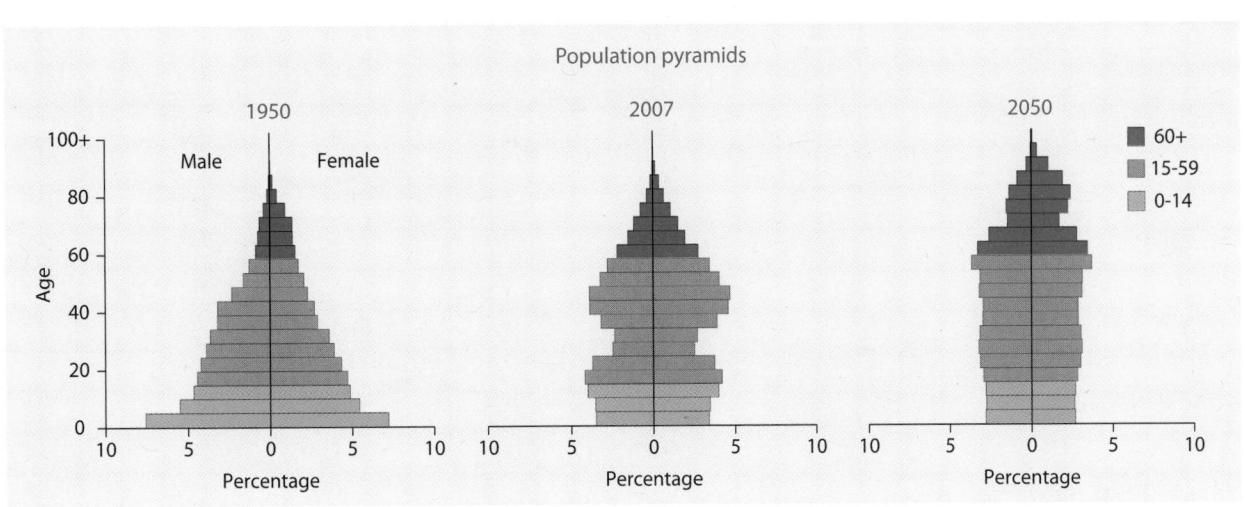

Population pyramids

1950   2007   2050

60+
15-59
0-14

Male   Female

Age — Percentage

New Caledonia

Indicator	Age	1950	1975	2007	2025	2050
Population (thousands)						
Total	Total	64.8	128.9	245.1	314.1	382.1
	0-14	23.6	49.9	67.3	68.4	67.2
	15-59	37.2	71.2	154.0	196.9	222.6
	60-64	1.5	3.0	8.3	15.8	22.3
	65-69	1.1	2.0	6.1	11.8	19.0
	70-74	0.7	1.2	4.3	8.7	16.5
	75-79	0.4	0.7	2.7	6.3	14.5
	80-84			1.5	3.6	10.5
	85-89			0.6	1.8	6.1
	90-94	0.2	0.8	0.2	0.6	2.6
	95-99			0.1	0.1	0.8
	100+			0.0	0.0	0.1
Female	Total	30.7	61.8	119.3	153.3	187.4
	0-14	11.6	24.6	32.6	33.2	32.7
	15-59	17.1	33.4	74.6	94.8	106.7
	60-64	0.7	1.4	3.9	7.8	10.7
	65-69	0.6	1.0	3.0	6.0	9.3
	70-74	0.4	0.6	2.2	4.4	8.4
	75-79	0.2	0.4	1.5	3.3	7.6
	80-84			0.9	2.0	5.9
	85-89			0.4	1.1	3.7
	90-94	0.1	0.4	0.2	0.4	1.8
	95-99			0.0	0.1	0.6
	100+			0.0	0.0	0.1
Male	Total	34.1	67.1	125.8	160.8	194.7
	0-14	12.1	25.3	34.7	35.1	34.5
	15-59	20.1	37.8	79.3	102.1	115.9
	60-64	0.8	1.7	4.4	8.0	11.6
	65-69	0.5	1.0	3.1	5.8	9.7
	70-74	0.4	0.6	2.1	4.3	8.1
	75-79	0.2	0.3	1.3	3.0	7.0
	80-84			0.6	1.6	4.6
	85-89			0.2	0.6	2.4
	90-94	0.1	0.3	0.1	0.2	0.8
	95-99			0.0	0.0	0.2
	100+			0.0	0.0	0.0
Percentage in older ages						
Total	60+	6.1	6.0	9.7	15.5	24.2
	65+	3.8	3.7	6.3	10.5	18.3
	80+	0.3	0.6	1.0	2.0	5.3
Female	60+	6.5	6.2	10.1	16.5	25.6
	65+	4.2	4.0	6.8	11.4	19.9
	80+	0.4	0.7	1.2	2.4	6.4
Male	60+	5.7	5.8	9.4	14.6	22.8
	65+	3.5	3.4	5.9	9.7	16.8
	80+	0.3	0.5	0.8	1.5	4.1
Ageing index		16.7	15.5	35.4	71.4	137.5
Broad age groups (percentage)	0-14	36.5	38.7	27.5	21.8	17.6
	15-59	57.5	55.3	62.8	62.7	58.2
	60+	6.1	6.0	9.7	15.5	24.2
Median age (years)		22.5	20.7	28.4*	34.0	40.5
Dependency ratio	Total	67.4	73.6	51.0	47.6	56.0
	Youth	61.0	67.2	41.5	32.1	27.4
	Old Age	6.4	6.4	9.6	15.5	28.6
Potential support ratio		15.7	15.7	10.4	6.4	3.5
Parent support ratio		1.2	2.4	3.0	4.6	13.2
Sex ratio (per 100 women)	60+	96.4	101.8	98.1	93.3	92.4
	65+	91.8	90.4	91.2	88.9	87.8
	80+	68.0	78.9	65.3	66.4	66.5

* *Estimate refers to year 2005.*

Indicator	Age	1950-1955	1975-1980	2005-2010	2025-2030	2045-2050
Growth rate (percentage)	Total	0.8	2.0	1.7	1.0	0.6
	60+	0.9	2.4	4.4	3.7	1.9
	65+	0.9	3.3	4.4	4.2	1.8
	80+	1.0	−1.2	5.2	5.4	4.2
Total fertility rate (per woman)		5.0	3.9	2.3	1.9	1.9
Life expectancy (years)						
Total	Birth	51.4	65.7	76.0	79.2	81.8
	60	..	..	20.3	22.3	24.2
	65	..	..	16.6	18.3	20.1
	80	..	..	7.7	8.6	9.7
Female	Birth	53.0	69.0	78.8	81.9	84.4
	60	..	..	22.1	24.4	26.4
	65	..	..	18.2	20.2	22.0
	80	..	..	8.5	9.7	10.8
Male	Birth	50.0	63.0	73.6	76.8	79.4
	60	..	..	18.6	20.3	22.2
	65	..	..	15.0	16.5	18.2
	80	..	..	6.6	7.3	8.3
Survival rate (percentage)						
Total	60	..	..	88.0	91.8	93.8
	65	..	..	81.9	87.1	90.3
	80	..	..	46.7	56.1	63.9
Female	60	..	..	91.3	93.9	95.5
	65	..	..	86.6	90.4	92.9
	80	..	..	55.4	64.8	71.8
Male	60	..	..	85.1	89.8	92.3
	65	..	..	77.9	84.1	87.8
	80	..	..	39.1	48.1	56.6

		1980	1990	2007	2010	2020
Labour force participation (percentage)						
Total	65+	8.8	8.5	8.6	8.7	8.7
Female	65+	5.3	5.6	5.4	5.4	5.4
Male	65+	12.7	11.9	12.2	12.3	12.3

Percentage married, age 60+			Percentage living alone, age 60+		
Total	Female	Male	Total	Female	Male
52.1	39.0	66.0	..	..	..

Statutory pensionable age (2006)			Percentage illiterate, age 65+		
	Female	Male	Total	Female	Male
	..	..	..	..	..

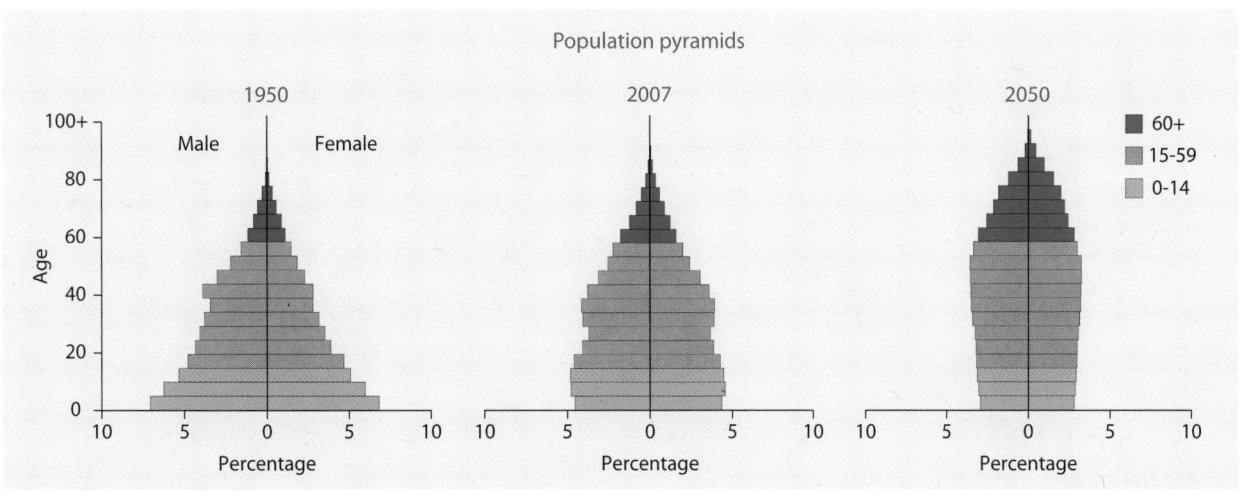

Population pyramids

New Zealand

Indicator	Age	1950	1975	2007	2025	2050
Population (thousands)						
Total	Total	1 908.0	3 083.1	4 092.6	4 539.4	4 789.6
	0-14	555.0	924.8	849.6	810.8	768.5
	15-59	1 103.0	1 766.0	2 529.8	2 577.0	2 582.8
	60-64	79.0	124.2	199.4	296.2	307.3
	65-69	69.0	100.8	152.6	260.5	261.7
	70-74	52.0	75.2	120.0	212.2	221.2
	75-79	29.0	47.6	100.2	174.1	206.3
	80-84			76.2	106.9	187.9
	85-89			42.4	61.6	142.4
	90-94	21.0	44.5	17.4	27.9	76.6
	95-99			4.4	10.2	28.2
	100+			0.6	2.0	6.8
Female	Total	949.0	1 544.8	2 079.7	2 298.2	2 413.7
	0-14	272.0	453.3	412.3	393.7	373.0
	15-59	548.0	872.5	1 283.1	1 283.1	1 257.5
	60-64	40.0	64.6	100.6	154.5	152.0
	65-69	35.0	53.5	78.2	136.5	130.9
	70-74	27.0	42.2	62.6	112.1	116.1
	75-79	15.0	28.9	54.1	93.8	115.2
	80-84			44.8	60.4	108.6
	85-89			27.8	37.3	86.1
	90-94	12.0	29.8	12.4	18.1	49.6
	95-99			3.4	7.2	19.7
	100+			0.5	1.6	5.1
Male	Total	959.0	1 538.3	2 013.0	2 241.2	2 375.8
	0-14	283.0	471.5	437.3	417.1	395.6
	15-59	555.0	893.5	1 246.7	1 293.9	1 325.3
	60-64	39.0	59.5	98.8	141.7	155.3
	65-69	34.0	47.3	74.4	124.0	130.9
	70-74	25.0	33.1	57.4	100.1	105.1
	75-79	14.0	18.7	46.1	80.3	91.1
	80-84			31.5	46.5	79.3
	85-89			14.6	24.3	56.3
	90-94	9.0	14.7	5.0	9.8	27.0
	95-99			1.1	3.0	8.4
	100+			0.1	0.5	1.6
Percentage in older ages						
Total	60+	13.1	12.7	17.4	25.4	30.0
	65+	9.0	8.7	12.6	18.8	23.6
	80+	1.1	1.4	3.4	4.6	9.2
Female	60+	13.6	14.2	18.5	27.0	32.4
	65+	9.4	10.0	13.6	20.3	26.2
	80+	1.3	1.9	4.3	5.4	11.1
Male	60+	12.6	11.3	16.3	23.7	27.6
	65+	8.6	7.4	11.4	17.3	21.0
	80+	0.9	1.0	2.6	3.7	7.3
Ageing index		45.0	42.4	84.0	142.0	187.1
Broad age groups (percentage)	0-14	29.1	30.0	20.8	17.9	16.0
	15-59	57.8	57.3	61.8	56.8	53.9
	60+	13.1	12.7	17.4	25.4	30.0
Median age (years)		29.4	26.3	35.8*	39.6	44.0
Dependency ratio	Total	61.4	63.1	50.0	58.0	65.7
	Youth	47.0	48.9	31.1	28.2	26.6
	Old Age	14.5	14.2	18.8	29.8	39.1
Potential support ratio		6.9	7.1	5.3	3.4	2.6
Parent support ratio		3.3	4.2	9.1	11.9	27.8
Sex ratio (per 100 women)	60+	93.8	79.2	85.6	85.3	83.6
	65+	92.1	73.7	81.2	83.2	79.2
	80+	75.0	49.5	58.9	67.5	64.2

*   *Estimate refers to year 2005.*

Indicator	Age	1950-1955	1975-1980	2005-2010	2025-2030	2045-2050
Growth rate (percentage)	Total	2.3	0.2	0.7	0.4	0.1
	60+	1.5	2.2	2.9	1.7	0.9
	65+	2.3	2.9	2.1	2.6	0.5
	80+	5.0	3.4	2.6	4.6	1.3
Total fertility rate (per woman)		3.7	2.2	2.0	1.9	1.9
Life expectancy (years)						
Total	Birth	69.6	72.4	79.8	82.5	84.4
	60	..	..	23.0	24.8	26.2
	65	..	..	19.0	20.6	21.9
	80	..	..	8.9	9.9	10.8
Female	Birth	71.8	75.9	82.0	84.4	86.3
	60	..	..	24.7	26.5	27.9
	65	..	..	20.5	22.1	23.5
	80	..	..	9.7	10.8	11.7
Male	Birth	67.5	69.3	77.7	80.6	82.4
	60	..	..	21.2	23.0	24.3
	65	..	..	17.3	18.9	20.1
	80	..	..	7.9	8.9	9.6
Survival rate (percentage)						
Total	60	..	..	92.0	94.4	95.8
	65	..	..	87.8	91.2	93.1
	80	..	..	58.9	66.3	71.3
Female	60	..	..	93.4	95.3	96.4
	65	..	..	89.9	92.7	94.3
	80	..	..	66.2	72.5	76.9
Male	60	..	..	90.5	93.6	95.1
	65	..	..	85.6	89.7	91.9
	80	..	..	51.6	59.9	65.2

		1980	1990	2007	2010	2020
Labour force participation (percentage)						
Total	65+	9.5	6.6	12.2	12.9	13.4
Female	65+	4.6	3.7	8.1	8.8	9.3
Male	65+	16.1	10.5	17.2	17.9	18.3

Percentage married, age 60+			Percentage living alone, age 60+ (1991)		
Total	Female	Male	Total	Female	Male
62.3	50.0	77.0	27.6	36.1	17.1

Statutory pensionable age (2006)			Percentage illiterate, age 65+		
	Female	Male	Total	Female	Male
	65	65	..	..	..

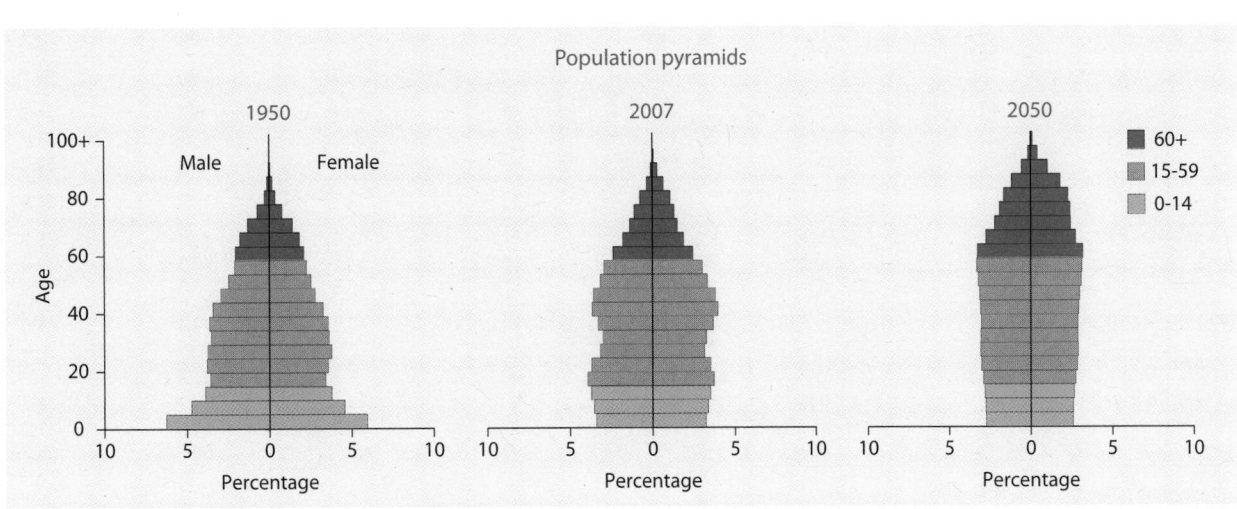

Population pyramids

Nicaragua

Indicator	Age	1950	1975	2007	2025	2050
Population (thousands)						
Total	Total	1 190.3	2 621.8	5 715.2	7 674.3	9 370.8
	0-14	528.1	1 258.7	2 156.4	2 186.6	1 827.2
	15-59	608.4	1 257.3	3 272.6	4 863.8	5 782.3
	60-64	22.6	41.5	92.1	205.0	510.3
	65-69	11.0	27.5	71.3	158.3	435.6
	70-74	9.5	19.0	53.0	116.5	324.9
	75-79	5.7	11.3	36.6	70.0	227.8
	80-84			21.4	42.0	141.8
	85-89			8.9	21.9	78.3
	90-94	5.1	6.6	2.5	8.2	32.9
	95-99			0.3	1.8	8.7
	100+			0.0	0.1	0.9
Female	Total	599.3	1 312.7	2 858.8	3 844.5	4 725.6
	0-14	260.2	619.7	1 057.9	1 070.0	892.4
	15-59	309.7	634.4	1 645.2	2 434.8	2 878.7
	60-64	12.1	22.3	48.1	108.9	263.5
	65-69	6.0	15.1	37.8	84.8	228.8
	70-74	5.3	10.6	29.0	63.3	174.9
	75-79	3.2	6.5	20.8	38.8	126.9
	80-84			12.6	24.0	83.4
	85-89			5.4	13.2	48.5
	90-94	2.9	4.1	1.6	5.3	21.6
	95-99			0.2	1.3	6.1
	100+			0.0	0.1	0.6
Male	Total	591.0	1 309.1	2 856.4	3 829.8	4 645.2
	0-14	267.9	638.9	1 098.5	1 116.6	934.8
	15-59	298.7	622.9	1 627.4	2 429.0	2 903.6
	60-64	10.6	19.2	43.9	96.1	246.8
	65-69	5.0	12.5	33.5	73.5	206.8
	70-74	4.2	8.4	24.0	53.2	150.0
	75-79	2.5	4.8	15.8	31.2	100.9
	80-84			8.8	18.0	58.4
	85-89			3.5	8.7	29.8
	90-94	2.2	2.5	0.9	2.9	11.3
	95-99			0.1	0.5	2.6
	100+			0.0	0.0	0.3
Percentage in older ages						
Total	60+	4.5	4.0	5.0	8.1	18.8
	65+	2.6	2.5	3.4	5.5	13.3
	80+	0.4	0.3	0.6	1.0	2.8
Female	60+	4.9	4.5	5.4	8.8	20.2
	65+	2.9	2.8	3.8	6.0	14.6
	80+	0.5	0.3	0.7	1.1	3.4
Male	60+	4.1	3.6	4.6	7.4	17.4
	65+	2.3	2.1	3.0	4.9	12.1
	80+	0.4	0.2	0.5	0.8	2.2
Ageing index		10.2	8.4	13.3	28.5	96.4
Broad age groups (percentage)	0-14	44.4	48.0	37.7	28.5	19.5
	15-59	51.1	48.0	57.3	63.4	61.7
	60+	4.5	4.0	5.0	8.1	18.8
Median age (years)		17.7	15.9	19.7*	26.7	36.8
Dependency ratio	Total	88.6	101.9	69.9	51.4	48.9
	Youth	83.7	96.9	64.1	43.1	29.0
	Old Age	5.0	5.0	5.8	8.3	19.9
Potential support ratio		20.2	20.2	17.3	12.1	5.0
Parent support ratio		1.5	1.4	3.0	4.0	7.1
Sex ratio (per 100 women)	60+	82.7	80.7	83.8	83.7	84.5
	65+	79.4	77.5	80.5	81.5	81.0
	80+	74.7	60.7	66.7	68.7	63.8

* Estimate refers to year 2005.

Indicator	Age	1950-1955	1975-1980	2005-2010	2025-2030	2045-2050
Growth rate (percentage)	Total	3.0	3.1	2.0	1.1	0.5
	60+	0.6	3.3	3.6	4.2	3.6
	65+	2.4	4.3	3.5	4.4	4.3
	80+	–4.9	6.0	5.7	4.6	4.4
Total fertility rate (per woman)		7.3	6.4	2.9	2.0	1.9
Life expectancy (years)						
Total	Birth	42.3	57.5	71.1	75.6	78.6
	60	..	..	20.1	22.2	23.5
	65	..	..	16.6	18.4	19.6
	80	..	..	7.7	8.7	9.5
Female	Birth	43.8	59.8	73.5	78.1	81.2
	60	..	..	21.0	23.5	25.2
	65	..	..	17.4	19.6	21.1
	80	..	..	8.1	9.3	10.1
Male	Birth	40.9	55.2	68.6	73.0	75.9
	60	..	..	19.1	20.7	21.8
	65	..	..	15.7	17.1	18.0
	80	..	..	7.2	8.0	8.5
Survival rate (percentage)						
Total	60	..	..	79.0	84.8	88.4
	65	..	..	72.9	79.8	84.1
	80	..	..	41.9	51.6	58.3
Female	60	..	..	82.8	88.0	91.1
	65	..	..	77.2	83.8	87.7
	80	..	..	47.1	58.3	65.8
Male	60	..	..	75.2	81.6	85.7
	65	..	..	68.6	75.8	80.5
	80	..	..	36.7	44.9	50.7

		1980	1990	2007	2010	2020
Labour force participation (percentage)						
Total	65+	33.6	35.9	38.6	38.7	38.8
Female	65+	14.8	15.4	16.5	16.3	16.1
Male	65+	57.9	62.6	66.1	66.2	66.4

Percentage married, age 60+			Percentage living alone, age 60+ (1998)		
Total	Female	Male	Total	Female	Male
52.6	35.0	74.0	5.2	4.6	5.8

Statutory pensionable age (2006)			Percentage illiterate, age 65+ (2001)		
	Female	Male	Total	Female	Male
	60	60	54.0	56.4	51.4

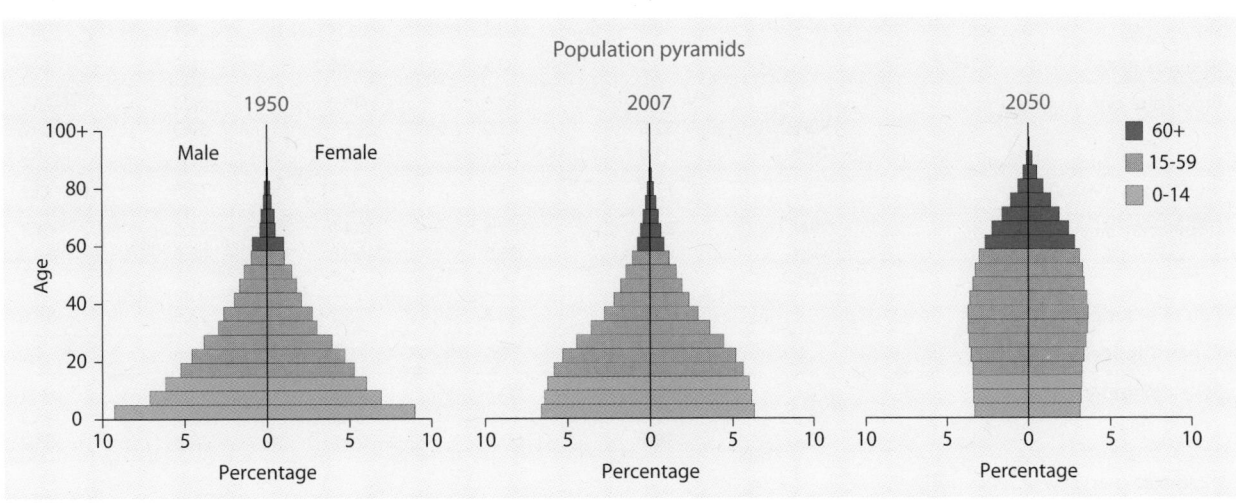

Population pyramids

Niger

Indicator	Age	1950	1975	2007	2025	2050
Population (thousands)						
Total	Total	2 612.5	5 325.4	14 907.2	26 376.1	50 156.4
	0-14	1 149.4	2 554.4	7 309.2	12 140.8	18 156.9
	15-59	1 357.8	2 552.9	7 114.9	13 265.1	29 392.1
	60-64	44.9	90.7	192.7	385.2	988.7
	65-69	30.5	63.7	137.5	275.4	713.9
	70-74	17.8	38.3	86.5	179.3	475.6
	75-79	8.4	18.3	45.1	86.6	273.2
	80-84			17.0	34.1	117.5
	85-89			3.9	8.5	33.0
	90-94	3.6	7.0	0.5	1.2	5.1
	95-99			0.0	0.1	0.4
	100+			0.0	0.0	0.0
Female	Total	1 348.5	2 652.5	7 280.0	12 823.8	24 382.1
	0-14	586.2	1 246.0	3 555.9	5 901.4	8 816.5
	15-59	702.8	1 288.5	3 460.4	6 417.4	14 242.8
	60-64	24.8	48.6	103.5	195.0	489.5
	65-69	17.1	34.4	75.1	142.2	358.9
	70-74	10.2	21.0	47.8	94.3	244.0
	75-79	5.0	10.2	25.1	48.2	144.1
	80-84			9.6	19.5	64.1
	85-89			2.3	5.0	18.8
	90-94	2.3	3.9	0.3	0.7	3.1
	95-99			0.0	0.1	0.3
	100+			0.0	0.0	0.0
Male	Total	1 264.0	2 672.9	7 627.2	13 552.3	25 774.3
	0-14	563.2	1 308.4	3 753.3	6 239.3	9 340.4
	15-59	655.0	1 264.5	3 654.5	6 847.7	15 149.2
	60-64	20.1	42.1	89.1	190.2	499.2
	65-69	13.4	29.3	62.4	133.2	355.0
	70-74	7.6	17.4	38.6	85.0	231.5
	75-79	3.4	8.2	19.9	38.5	129.1
	80-84			7.4	14.5	53.5
	85-89			1.7	3.5	14.3
	90-94	1.3	3.1	0.2	0.5	2.0
	95-99			0.0	0.0	0.1
	100+			0.0	0.0	0.0
Percentage in older ages						
Total	60+	4.0	4.1	3.2	3.7	5.2
	65+	2.3	2.4	1.9	2.2	3.2
	80+	0.1	0.1	0.1	0.2	0.3
Female	60+	4.4	4.5	3.6	3.9	5.4
	65+	2.6	2.6	2.2	2.4	3.4
	80+	0.2	0.1	0.2	0.2	0.4
Male	60+	3.6	3.7	2.9	3.4	5.0
	65+	2.0	2.2	1.7	2.0	3.0
	80+	0.1	0.1	0.1	0.1	0.3
Ageing index		9.2	8.5	6.6	8.0	14.4
Broad age groups (percentage)	0-14	44.0	48.0	49.0	46.0	36.2
	15-59	52.0	47.9	47.7	50.3	58.6
	60+	4.0	4.1	3.2	3.7	5.2
Median age (years)		17.9	16.0	15.5*	16.8	21.5
Dependency ratio	Total	86.2	101.4	104.0	93.2	65.1
	Youth	81.9	96.6	100.0	88.9	59.8
	Old Age	4.3	4.8	4.0	4.3	5.3
Potential support ratio		23.3	20.8	25.2	23.3	18.8
Parent support ratio		0.4	0.3	0.5	0.6	1.0
Sex ratio (per 100 women)	60+	76.9	84.6	83.2	92.1	97.1
	65+	74.0	83.3	81.3	88.7	94.3
	80+	55.1	77.9	76.5	72.9	81.0

* *Estimate refers to year 2005.*

Indicator	Age	1950-1955	1975-1980	2005-2010	2025-2030	2045-2050
Growth rate (percentage)	Total	2.9	3.1	3.3	3.0	2.1
	60+	2.8	2.6	3.1	3.8	4.2
	65+	2.7	2.8	3.1	4.1	4.2
	80+	1.2	3.4	3.8	4.6	4.9
Total fertility rate (per woman)		7.7	8.2	7.5	5.9	3.6
Life expectancy (years)						
Total	Birth	36.2	38.9	45.4	52.7	61.4
	60	..	..	14.6	15.8	17.1
	65	..	..	11.4	12.4	13.5
	80	..	..	4.5	4.9	5.3
Female	Birth	36.4	38.9	45.4	52.8	61.9
	60	..	..	15.0	16.3	17.8
	65	..	..	11.6	12.7	14.0
	80	..	..	4.6	5.1	5.5
Male	Birth	35.9	38.8	45.4	52.7	61.0
	60	..	..	14.2	15.2	16.5
	65	..	..	11.1	12.0	13.0
	80	..	..	4.4	4.8	5.1
Survival rate (percentage)						
Total	60	..	..	46.1	56.1	69.5
	65	..	..	40.2	49.9	63.4
	80	..	..	12.1	17.9	26.9
Female	60	..	..	46.8	56.6	70.6
	65	..	..	41.2	51.1	65.3
	80	..	..	12.9	19.3	29.4
Male	60	..	..	45.5	55.5	68.4
	65	..	..	39.1	48.8	61.6
	80	..	..	11.2	16.5	24.5

		1980	1990	2007	2010	2020
Labour force participation (percentage)						
Total	65+	53.9	56.5	57.0	57.0	57.8
Female	65+	33.2	34.2	34.1	34.1	34.1
Male	65+	78.6	83.2	85.2	85.2	85.3

Percentage married, age 60+				Percentage living alone, age 60+ (1998)		
Total	Female	Male		Total	Female	Male
55.5	25.0	92.0		3.5	6.0	1.5

Statutory pensionable age (2006)				Percentage illiterate, age 65+ (2005)		
	Female	Male		Total	Female	Male
	60	60		84.6	98.9	76.3

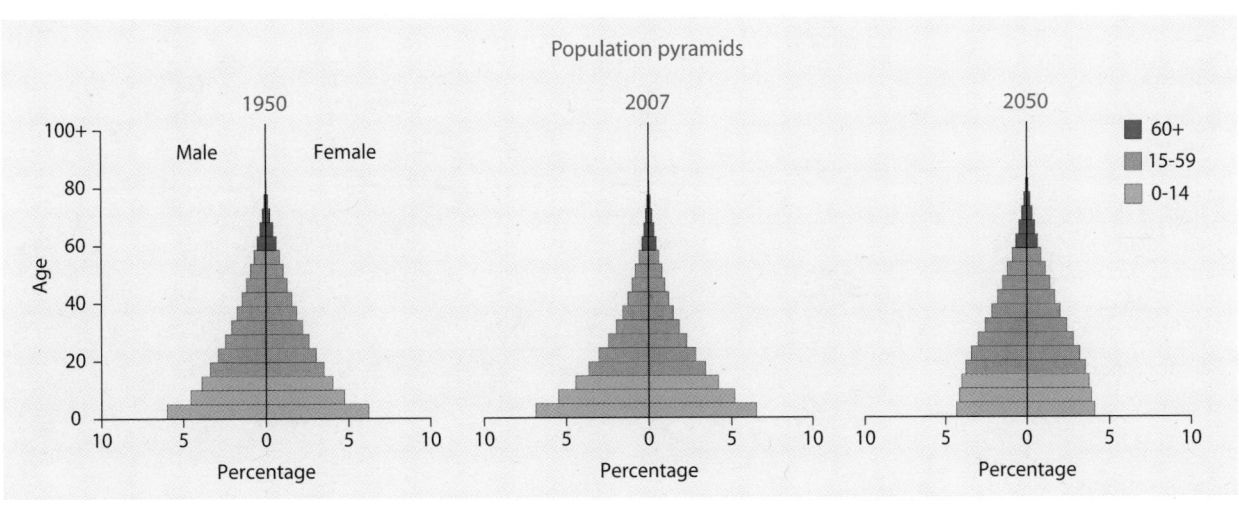

Population pyramids

Nigeria

Indicator	Age	1950	1975	2007	2025	2050
Population (thousands)						
Total	Total	32 768.7	58 949.7	137 243.3	190 286.7	258 108.4
	0-14	13 669.6	26 233.6	60 024.1	70 559.9	70 599.2
	15-59	17 423.8	29 858.0	70 644.5	109 421.9	164 314.0
	60-64	695.7	1 092.2	2 376.5	3 540.5	8 468.8
	65-69	478.2	793.3	1 811.2	2 792.0	6 265.1
	70-74	291.6	518.1	1 218.5	1 996.8	4 103.0
	75-79	145.5	302.5	710.8	1 148.7	2 448.6
	80-84			327.3	575.7	1 258.6
	85-89			106.8	200.4	498.7
	90-94	64.3	152.1	21.1	44.7	131.2
	95-99			2.4	5.8	19.7
	100+			0.2	0.4	1.4
Female	Total	16 699.5	29 592.3	67 696.0	93 052.0	125 771.0
	0-14	6 830.9	12 930.0	29 248.5	34 355.2	34 328.7
	15-59	8 907.4	15 075.3	34 910.3	53 231.7	79 808.0
	60-64	385.4	588.4	1 249.0	1 819.1	4 147.6
	65-69	272.9	436.7	965.6	1 468.2	3 113.2
	70-74	172.1	292.3	661.4	1 072.6	2 068.3
	75-79	89.1	175.2	393.7	631.5	1 260.1
	80-84			187.1	323.7	673.3
	85-89			64.6	117.7	279.8
	90-94	41.8	94.5	13.9	28.0	78.2
	95-99			1.7	4.0	12.8
	100+			0.1	0.3	1.0
Male	Total	16 069.2	29 357.4	69 547.3	97 234.7	132 337.4
	0-14	6 838.7	13 303.6	30 775.7	36 204.8	36 270.5
	15-59	8 516.4	14 782.7	35 734.2	56 190.2	84 506.1
	60-64	310.4	503.8	1 127.4	1 721.3	4 321.3
	65-69	205.3	356.6	845.6	1 323.7	3 151.8
	70-74	119.5	225.8	557.1	924.3	2 034.7
	75-79	56.4	127.3	317.1	517.2	1 188.5
	80-84			140.2	251.9	585.3
	85-89			42.2	82.7	218.9
	90-94	22.5	57.6	7.2	16.6	53.0
	95-99			0.6	1.8	6.9
	100+			0.0	0.1	0.4
Percentage in older ages						
Total	60+	5.1	4.8	4.8	5.4	9.0
	65+	3.0	3.0	3.1	3.6	5.7
	80+	0.2	0.3	0.3	0.4	0.7
Female	60+	5.8	5.4	5.2	5.9	9.3
	65+	3.4	3.4	3.4	3.9	6.0
	80+	0.3	0.3	0.4	0.5	0.8
Male	60+	4.4	4.3	4.4	5.0	8.7
	65+	2.5	2.6	2.7	3.2	5.5
	80+	0.1	0.2	0.3	0.4	0.7
Ageing index		12.3	10.9	11.0	14.6	32.9
Broad age groups (percentage)	0-14	41.7	44.5	43.7	37.1	27.4
	15-59	53.2	50.6	51.5	57.5	63.7
	60+	5.1	4.8	4.8	5.4	9.0
Median age (years)		19.1	17.7	17.5*	20.9	27.9
Dependency ratio	Total	80.8	90.5	88.0	68.5	49.4
	Youth	75.4	84.8	82.2	62.5	40.9
	Old Age	5.4	5.7	5.7	6.0	8.5
Potential support ratio		18.5	17.5	17.4	16.7	11.7
Parent support ratio		0.6	0.8	1.4	1.9	2.0
Sex ratio (per 100 women)	60+	74.3	80.1	85.9	88.6	99.4
	65+	70.1	76.8	83.5	85.5	96.7
	80+	53.9	61.0	71.2	74.5	82.7

* *Estimate refers to year 2005.*

Indicator	Age	1950-1955	1975-1980	2005-2010	2025-2030	2045-2050
Growth rate (percentage)	Total	2.2	3.0	2.1	1.4	1.0
	60+	2.4	2.6	2.2	2.3	4.0
	65+	2.5	2.5	2.6	2.5	4.2
	80+	2.9	3.7	3.2	3.1	3.1
Total fertility rate (per woman)		6.9	6.9	5.3	3.2	2.4
Life expectancy (years)						
Total	Birth	36.3	44.5	44.2	52.8	61.7
	60	..	..	15.4	16.6	17.9
	65	..	..	12.4	13.3	14.4
	80	..	..	5.4	5.9	6.3
Female	Birth	37.9	46.1	44.3	53.0	62.4
	60	..	..	15.9	17.1	18.5
	65	..	..	12.7	13.7	14.9
	80	..	..	5.6	6.0	6.5
Male	Birth	34.8	42.8	44.1	52.6	61.0
	60	..	..	14.9	16.1	17.4
	65	..	..	11.9	12.9	14.0
	80	..	..	5.2	5.7	6.1
Survival rate (percentage)						
Total	60	..	..	38.2	50.6	64.8
	65	..	..	33.2	45.0	59.1
	80	..	..	11.9	18.5	27.7
Female	60	..	..	38.3	50.8	65.7
	65	..	..	33.6	45.6	60.5
	80	..	..	12.7	19.6	29.8
Male	60	..	..	38.1	50.4	64.0
	65	..	..	32.6	44.4	57.7
	80	..	..	11.0	17.3	25.8

		1980	1990	2007	2010	2020
Labour force participation (percentage)						
Total	65+	46.2	48.0	46.2	46.0	45.7
Female	65+	29.9	30.3	26.9	26.6	26.4
Male	65+	67.0	70.1	69.3	69.1	68.5

Percentage married, age 60+			Percentage living alone, age 60+ (1999)		
Total	Female	Male	Total	Female	Male
64.1	43.0	89.0	6.4	10.7	3.3

Statutory pensionable age (2006)			Percentage illiterate, age 65+		
	Female	Male	Total	Female	Male
	60	60	..	..	..

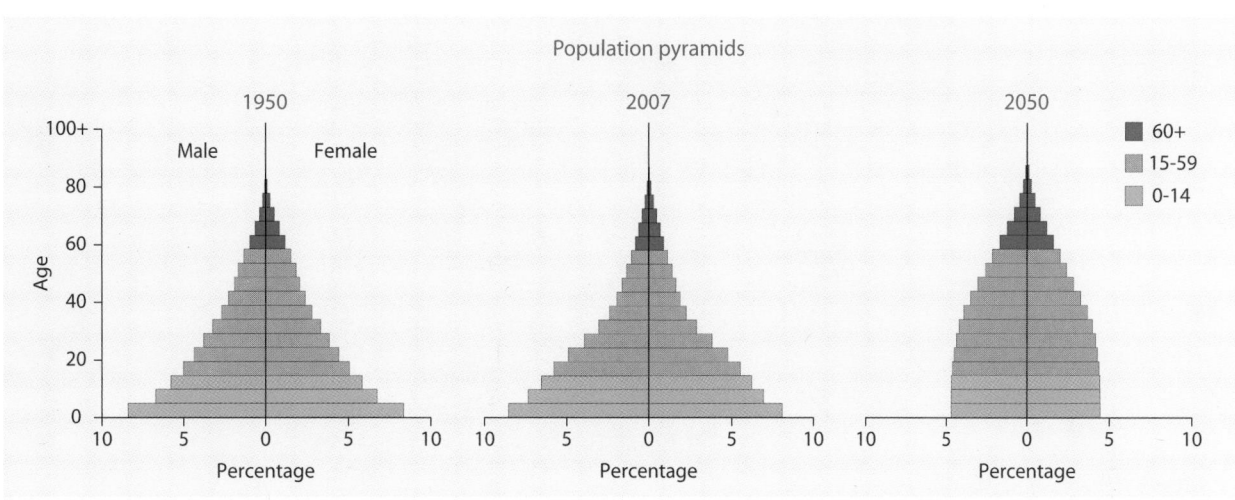

Population pyramids

Norway

Indicator	Age	1950	1975	2007	2025	2050
Population (thousands)						
Total	Total	3 265.0	4 007.3	4 664.6	5 080.2	5 434.9
	0-14	798.0	953.5	893.7	872.7	887.0
	15-59	2 014.0	2 287.2	2 805.9	2 849.3	2 918.2
	60-64	137.0	218.1	259.9	315.6	309.0
	65-69	110.0	187.3	190.0	289.4	272.9
	70-74	89.0	151.9	153.7	255.5	260.3
	75-79	61.0	109.7	137.9	228.4	269.0
	80-84			119.1	144.1	233.5
	85-89			71.9	76.1	156.7
	90-94	56.0	99.5	26.5	35.3	86.7
	95-99			5.4	11.7	33.4
	100+			0.6	2.2	8.2
Female	Total	1 647.0	2 016.8	2 345.8	2 549.8	2 745.9
	0-14	389.0	464.7	435.5	424.9	431.7
	15-59	1 010.0	1 125.9	1 380.6	1 407.2	1 436.3
	60-64	73.0	113.0	129.0	156.7	154.5
	65-69	60.0	101.0	97.2	145.9	138.0
	70-74	48.0	86.1	81.9	131.2	134.1
	75-79	34.0	64.6	76.9	120.7	142.7
	80-84			71.9	81.1	128.6
	85-89			48.2	47.0	92.5
	90-94	33.0	61.4	19.7	24.3	56.4
	95-99			4.4	9.0	24.4
	100+			0.5	1.8	6.7
Male	Total	1 618.0	1 990.5	2 318.8	2 530.4	2 689.0
	0-14	409.0	488.8	458.2	447.8	455.3
	15-59	1 004.0	1 161.3	1 425.2	1 442.1	1 481.9
	60-64	64.0	105.1	130.9	158.9	154.5
	65-69	50.0	86.3	92.8	143.5	135.0
	70-74	41.0	65.8	71.9	124.3	126.2
	75-79	27.0	45.1	61.0	107.7	126.3
	80-84			47.2	63.0	104.9
	85-89			23.7	29.0	64.3
	90-94	23.0	38.1	6.8	11.1	30.2
	95-99			1.0	2.7	9.0
	100+			0.1	0.3	1.5
Percentage in older ages						
Total	60+	13.9	19.1	20.7	26.7	30.0
	65+	9.7	13.7	15.1	20.5	24.3
	80+	1.7	2.5	4.8	5.3	9.5
Female	60+	15.1	21.1	22.6	28.1	32.0
	65+	10.6	15.5	17.1	22.0	26.3
	80+	2.0	3.0	6.2	6.4	11.2
Male	60+	12.7	17.1	18.8	25.3	28.0
	65+	8.7	11.8	13.1	19.0	22.2
	80+	1.4	1.9	3.4	4.2	7.8
Ageing index		56.8	80.4	108.0	155.6	183.7
Broad age groups (percentage)	0-14	24.4	23.8	19.2	17.2	16.3
	15-59	61.7	57.1	60.2	56.1	53.7
	60+	13.9	19.1	20.7	26.7	30.0
Median age (years)		32.7	32.5	38.2*	41.6	43.8
Dependency ratio	Total	51.8	60.0	52.2	60.5	68.4
	Youth	37.1	38.1	29.2	27.6	27.5
	Old Age	14.7	21.9	23.0	32.9	40.9
Potential support ratio		6.8	4.6	4.3	3.0	2.4
Parent support ratio		4.3	5.1	12.0	12.5	28.7
Sex ratio (per 100 women)	60+	82.7	79.9	82.2	89.2	85.6
	65+	80.6	75.2	76.0	85.9	82.6
	80+	69.7	62.0	54.4	65.0	68.0

* *Estimate refers to year 2005.*

Indicator	Age	1950-1955	1975-1980	2005-2010	2025-2030	2045-2050
Growth rate (percentage)	Total	1.0	0.4	0.5	0.4	0.2
	60+	2.1	1.5	2.2	1.7	0.4
	65+	1.9	1.9	1.4	1.8	0.0
	80+	1.7	4.0	0.5	4.6	2.0
Total fertility rate (per woman)		2.6	1.8	1.8	1.9	1.9
Life expectancy (years)						
Total	Birth	72.7	75.3	80.2	82.7	84.9
	60	..	..	23.0	24.8	26.5
	65	..	..	18.9	20.5	22.1
	80	..	..	8.5	9.6	10.8
Female	Birth	74.5	78.6	82.5	85.0	87.2
	60	..	..	24.8	26.7	28.5
	65	..	..	20.5	22.3	24.0
	80	..	..	9.3	10.6	12.0
Male	Birth	70.9	72.6	77.8	80.5	82.7
	60	..	..	21.1	22.8	24.4
	65	..	..	17.1	18.7	20.1
	80	..	..	7.4	8.4	9.4
Survival rate (percentage)						
Total	60	..	..	92.6	94.8	96.2
	65	..	..	88.8	91.8	93.9
	80	..	..	60.7	67.3	73.0
Female	60	..	..	94.3	95.9	97.0
	65	..	..	91.4	93.6	95.2
	80	..	..	68.7	74.6	79.4
Male	60	..	..	90.9	93.7	95.5
	65	..	..	86.3	90.0	92.5
	80	..	..	52.7	60.3	66.6

		1980	1990	2007	2010	2020
Labour force participation (percentage)						
Total	65+	21.9	17.4	13.1	13.4	14.0
Female	65+	12.7	12.0	11.2	11.6	12.0
Male	65+	34.3	25.0	15.6	15.8	16.3

Percentage married, age 60+				Percentage living alone, age 60+ (1990)		
Total	Female	Male		Total	Female	Male
55.3	44.0	70.0		32.7	42.5	20.1

Statutory pensionable age (2006)				Percentage illiterate, age 65+		
	Female	Male		Total	Female	Male
	67	67		..	..	..

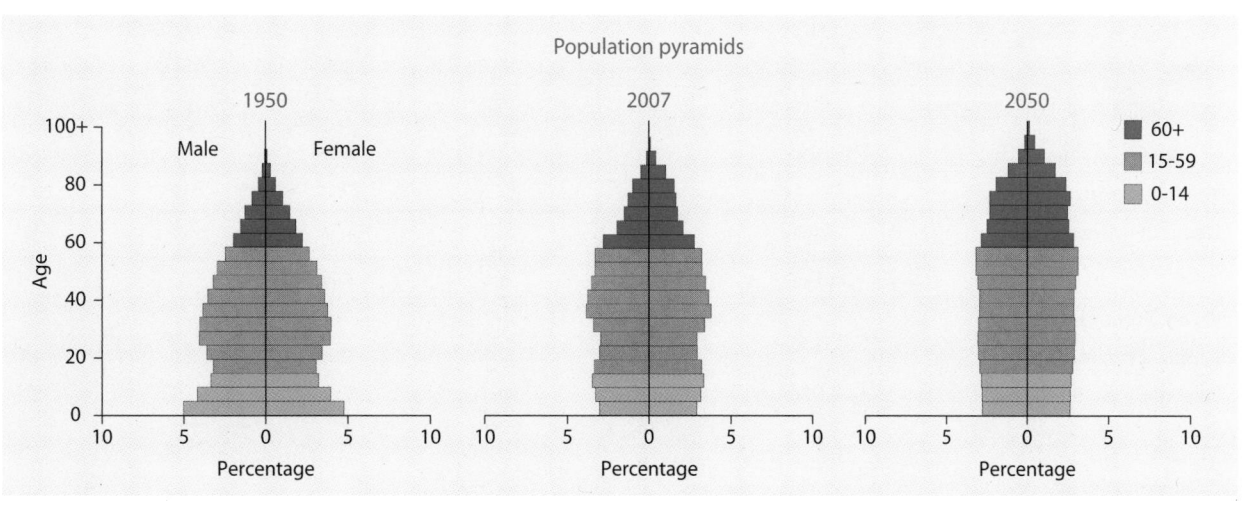

Population pyramids

Occupied Palestinian Territory

Indicator	Age	1950	1975	2007	2025	2050
Population (thousands)						
Total	Total	1 004.8	1 255.1	3 945.1	6 421.7	10 058.3
	0-14	459.3	578.4	1 779.2	2 332.6	2 644.2
	15-59	470.9	614.9	1 991.1	3 705.8	6 296.3
	60-64	26.0	21.3	57.2	144.1	365.7
	65-69	20.2	16.1	40.8	101.2	263.1
	70-74	15.6	11.9	32.7	64.9	201.5
	75-79	8.4	7.5	24.4	40.0	144.6
	80-84			13.5	21.3	84.2
	85-89			4.6	8.5	42.3
	90-94	4.3	4.9	1.4	2.8	13.5
	95-99			0.2	0.5	2.7
	100+			0.0	0.0	0.3
Female	Total	483.4	614.0	1 937.6	3 151.2	4 953.0
	0-14	219.1	284.1	870.2	1 139.3	1 290.1
	15-59	229.7	298.2	968.6	1 811.8	3 082.3
	60-64	11.9	10.9	29.8	70.9	181.7
	65-69	9.4	8.3	23.6	50.9	132.3
	70-74	7.3	6.0	19.1	34.9	103.7
	75-79	3.9	3.8	14.4	22.0	77.2
	80-84			8.1	13.2	47.7
	85-89			2.7	5.9	26.1
	90-94	2.0	2.7	0.9	2.0	9.4
	95-99			0.1	0.4	2.2
	100+			0.0	0.0	0.3
Male	Total	521.4	641.0	2 007.6	3 270.5	5 105.4
	0-14	240.1	294.3	909.1	1 193.3	1 354.1
	15-59	241.2	316.7	1 022.4	1 894.0	3 214.0
	60-64	14.1	10.3	27.4	73.2	184.0
	65-69	10.9	7.8	17.2	50.2	130.8
	70-74	8.3	6.0	13.7	30.1	97.8
	75-79	4.5	3.7	10.0	18.1	67.4
	80-84			5.3	8.2	36.5
	85-89			1.8	2.6	16.2
	90-94	2.3	2.2	0.6	0.8	4.1
	95-99			0.1	0.1	0.5
	100+			0.0	0.0	0.0
Percentage in older ages						
Total	60+	7.4	4.9	4.4	6.0	11.1
	65+	4.8	3.2	3.0	3.7	7.5
	80+	0.4	0.4	0.5	0.5	1.4
Female	60+	7.1	5.2	5.1	6.4	11.7
	65+	4.7	3.4	3.6	4.1	8.1
	80+	0.4	0.4	0.6	0.7	1.7
Male	60+	7.7	4.7	3.8	5.6	10.5
	65+	5.0	3.1	2.4	3.4	6.9
	80+	0.4	0.3	0.4	0.4	1.1
Ageing index		16.3	10.7	9.8	16.4	42.3
Broad age groups (percentage)	0-14	45.7	46.1	45.1	36.3	26.3
	15-59	46.9	49.0	50.5	57.7	62.6
	60+	7.4	4.9	4.4	6.0	11.1
Median age (years)		17.2	17.0	17.1*	21.5	29.1
Dependency ratio	Total	102.2	97.3	92.6	66.8	51.0
	Youth	92.4	90.9	86.9	60.6	39.7
	Old Age	9.8	6.4	5.7	6.2	11.3
Potential support ratio		10.2	15.7	17.4	16.1	8.9
Parent support ratio		1.4	2.1	2.7	2.2	4.4
Sex ratio (per 100 women)	60+	116.2	94.6	77.0	91.5	92.6
	65+	114.7	94.7	70.6	85.1	88.6
	80+	116.7	80.8	66.1	54.1	67.1

* *Estimate refers to year 2005.*

Indicator	Age	1950-1955	1975-1980	2005-2010	2025-2030	2045-2050
Growth rate (percentage)	Total	0.7	3.2	3.1	2.2	1.4
	60+	−1.0	3.6	2.8	4.6	4.3
	65+	−1.2	4.6	2.2	5.6	3.8
	80+	−2.3	6.7	2.9	5.0	5.1
Total fertility rate (per woman)		7.4	7.4	5.0	3.1	2.3
Life expectancy (years)						
Total	Birth	43.2	60.8	73.4	76.9	79.5
	60	..	..	18.6	20.4	22.3
	65	..	..	14.8	16.4	18.2
	80	..	..	6.2	7.2	8.3
Female	Birth	44.3	62.6	75.0	78.8	81.5
	60	..	..	19.4	22.0	24.0
	65	..	..	15.5	17.9	19.7
	80	..	..	6.4	7.9	9.1
Male	Birth	42.2	59.0	71.8	75.1	77.5
	60	..	..	17.5	18.7	20.5
	65	..	..	14.0	14.9	16.6
	80	..	..	5.9	6.3	7.2
Survival rate (percentage)						
Total	60	..	..	86.4	90.8	92.9
	65	..	..	80.1	85.7	88.8
	80	..	..	39.6	48.7	57.0
Female	60	..	..	88.6	92.2	94.1
	65	..	..	83.4	88.2	91.0
	80	..	..	44.1	56.1	64.2
Male	60	..	..	84.4	89.5	91.8
	65	..	..	77.0	83.2	86.7
	80	..	..	34.4	41.5	50.2

		1980	1990	2007	2010	2020
Labour force participation (percentage)						
Total	65+	10.4	11.1	8.8	8.9	9.2
Female	65+	3.0	5.2	2.3	2.3	2.2
Male	65+	18.1	17.4	18.0	18.0	17.9

Percentage married, age 60+			Percentage living alone, age 60+ (1997)		
Total	Female	Male	Total	Female	Male
73.4	61.0	90.0	6.0	9.4	1.8

Statutory pensionable age (2006)			Percentage illiterate, age 65+		
	Female	Male	Total	Female	Male
	..	..	..	..	..

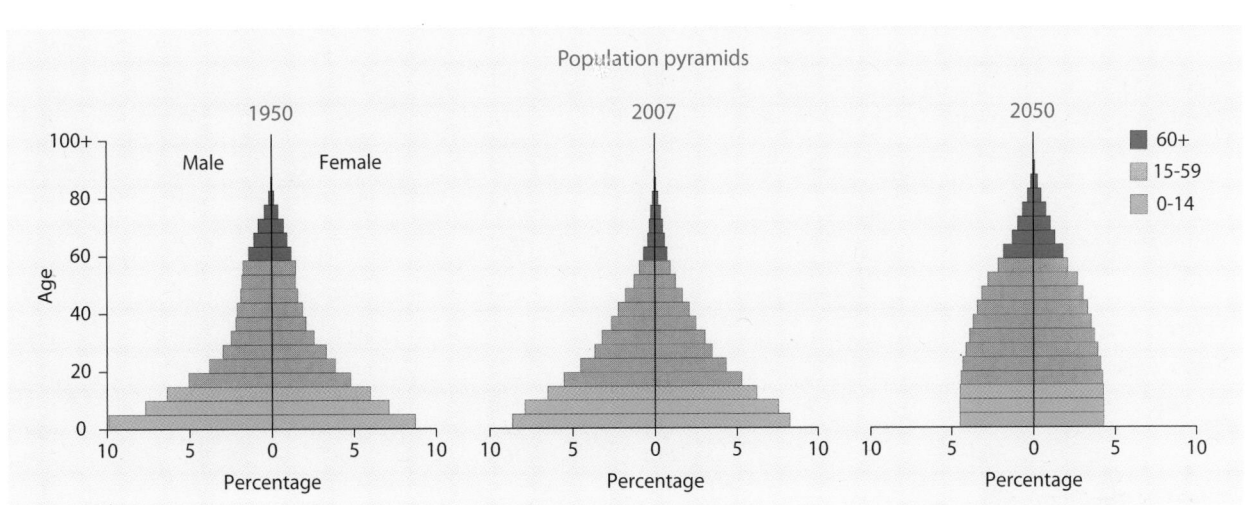

Population pyramids

1950   2007   2050

Male   Female

60+
15-59
0-14

Age

Percentage

Oman

Indicator	Age	1950	1975	2007	2025	2050
Population (thousands)						
Total	Total	456.4	917.0	2 668.3	3 776.0	4 957.7
	0-14	193.2	431.8	895.3	1 046.1	1 022.2
	15-59	240.5	446.1	1 656.8	2 400.9	2 959.5
	60-64	8.8	14.6	42.8	127.4	270.8
	65-69	6.4	10.9	32.1	87.7	234.9
	70-74	4.2	7.3	20.5	56.2	198.9
	75-79	2.2	4.1	12.3	30.5	135.3
	80-84			5.7	18.0	79.7
	85-89			2.3	7.0	40.2
	90-94	1.0	2.2	0.6	1.9	13.2
	95-99			0.1	0.3	2.8
	100+			0.0	0.0	0.3
Female	Total	224.7	454.7	1 178.4	1 728.3	2 372.2
	0-14	94.9	212.4	436.6	510.3	498.7
	15-59	118.4	221.1	686.8	1 086.1	1 425.9
	60-64	4.4	7.8	19.2	45.1	127.7
	65-69	3.2	5.9	15.0	34.1	113.3
	70-74	2.1	4.0	9.6	23.4	90.2
	75-79	1.1	2.2	6.0	14.1	55.7
	80-84			3.2	9.7	33.0
	85-89			1.5	4.0	18.4
	90-94	0.6	1.2	0.4	1.2	7.4
	95-99			0.1	0.2	1.9
	100+			0.0	0.0	0.2
Male	Total	231.7	462.3	1 489.9	2 047.7	2 585.5
	0-14	98.3	219.4	458.7	535.8	523.5
	15-59	122.1	225.0	970.0	1 314.8	1 533.5
	60-64	4.4	6.7	23.5	82.3	143.1
	65-69	3.2	5.0	17.1	53.6	121.6
	70-74	2.1	3.4	11.0	32.8	108.8
	75-79	1.1	1.9	6.2	16.4	79.6
	80-84			2.5	8.3	46.7
	85-89			0.8	3.0	21.8
	90-94	0.4	0.9	0.2	0.7	5.9
	95-99			0.0	0.1	0.9
	100+			0.0	0.0	0.1
Percentage in older ages						
Total	60+	5.0	4.3	4.4	8.7	19.7
	65+	3.0	2.7	2.8	5.3	14.2
	80+	0.2	0.2	0.3	0.7	2.7
Female	60+	5.1	4.6	4.7	7.6	18.9
	65+	3.1	2.9	3.0	5.0	13.5
	80+	0.2	0.3	0.4	0.9	2.6
Male	60+	4.9	3.9	4.1	9.6	20.4
	65+	3.0	2.4	2.5	5.6	14.9
	80+	0.2	0.2	0.2	0.6	2.9
Ageing index		11.7	9.0	13.0	31.5	95.5
Broad age groups (percentage)	0-14	42.3	47.1	33.6	27.7	20.6
	15-59	52.7	48.7	62.1	63.6	59.7
	60+	5.0	4.3	4.4	8.7	19.7
Median age (years)		18.8	16.4	22.3*	28.5	35.9
Dependency ratio	Total	83.0	99.1	57.0	49.4	53.5
	Youth	77.5	93.7	52.7	41.4	31.6
	Old Age	5.5	5.3	4.3	8.0	21.8
Potential support ratio		18.1	18.8	23.1	12.5	4.6
Parent support ratio		0.8	1.1	1.6	1.9	6.6
Sex ratio (per 100 women)	60+	99.0	84.9	111.6	149.3	118.1
	65+	98.4	84.0	105.8	132.2	120.5
	80+	79.8	76.6	67.7	79.0	124.0

* *Estimate refers to year 2005.*

Indicator	Age	1950-1955	1975-1980	2005-2010	2025-2030	2045-2050
Growth rate (percentage)	Total	2.0	5.2	2.2	1.4	0.8
	60+	1.3	2.1	4.5	5.3	3.1
	65+	1.3	2.5	5.5	6.4	3.6
	80+	3.4	4.8	5.7	5.0	5.4
Total fertility rate (per woman)		7.2	7.2	3.2	2.4	2.0
Life expectancy (years)						
Total	Birth	37.6	57.4	75.0	77.9	80.3
	60	..	..	19.3	21.0	22.8
	65	..	..	15.5	17.0	18.6
	80	..	..	6.6	7.6	8.5
Female	Birth	38.3	58.7	76.8	80.1	82.5
	60	..	..	20.6	22.9	24.7
	65	..	..	16.6	18.7	20.4
	80	..	..	7.1	8.4	9.6
Male	Birth	36.9	55.9	73.7	76.5	78.8
	60	..	..	18.2	19.8	21.5
	65	..	..	14.5	15.9	17.4
	80	..	..	6.1	6.8	7.8
Survival rate (percentage)						
Total	60	..	..	88.6	91.8	93.6
	65	..	..	82.8	86.9	90.0
	80	..	..	43.3	51.8	59.5
Female	60	..	..	90.4	93.1	94.7
	65	..	..	85.8	89.6	91.9
	80	..	..	49.7	60.0	67.0
Male	60	..	..	87.4	90.9	92.7
	65	..	..	80.6	85.3	88.2
	80	..	..	38.3	46.6	54.4

		1980	1990	2007	2010	2020
Labour force participation (percentage)						
Total	65+	13.7	13.8	17.3	17.4	18.3
Female	65+	4.1	3.2	3.6	3.7	3.7
Male	65+	25.9	29.2	30.2	30.3	30.3

Percentage married, age 60+			Percentage living alone, age 60+		
Total	Female	Male	Total	Female	Male
57.1	31.0	81.0	..	..	..

Statutory pensionable age (2006)			Percentage illiterate, age 65+ (2003)		
	Female	Male	Total	Female	Male
	55	60	83.7	93.3	75.4

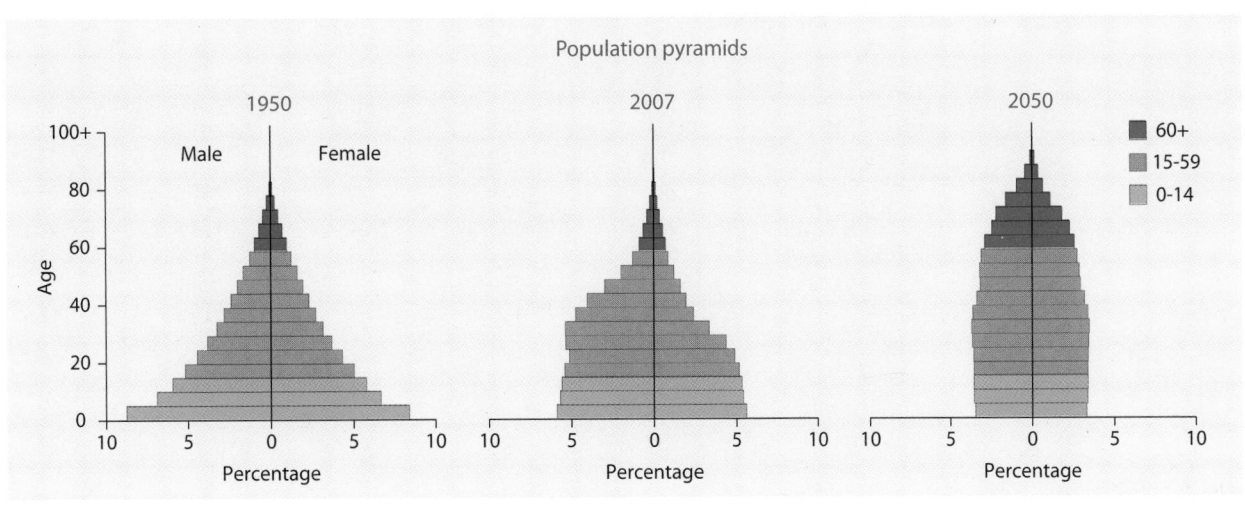

Population pyramids

Pakistan

Indicator	Age	1950	1975	2007	2025	2050
Population (thousands)						
Total	Total	36 943.8	68 293.8	164 593.8	229 353.4	304 700.4
	0-14	14 015.7	29 052.1	61 196.4	70 209.2	68 330.5
	15-59	19 888.4	35 459.9	93 698.7	140 284.0	189 625.2
	60-64	1 064.9	1 433.3	3 285.0	6 578.9	15 625.3
	65-69	912.5	1 020.0	2 552.8	5 051.5	11 921.1
	70-74	557.2	624.6	1 819.1	3 459.1	8 241.2
	75-79	330.0	394.3	1 159.9	1 998.6	5 306.1
	80-84			582.1	1 086.8	3 251.2
	85-89			223.6	491.7	1 661.0
	90-94	174.8	309.6	63.7	157.4	593.5
	95-99			11.3	32.8	130.7
	100+			1.1	3.3	14.7
Female	Total	17 579.0	32 889.5	79 886.9	111 444.5	149 241.7
	0-14	6 947.1	14 043.7	29 730.4	34 059.4	33 316.2
	15-59	9 333.3	17 126.5	45 222.5	68 011.3	92 247.3
	60-64	479.6	661.0	1 643.7	3 224.3	7 723.6
	65-69	370.3	470.7	1 305.2	2 486.8	5 970.9
	70-74	236.6	281.6	931.2	1 718.1	4 200.9
	75-79	139.3	171.4	610.1	1 020.9	2 762.6
	80-84			301.6	572.4	1 728.4
	85-89			108.4	254.6	893.1
	90-94	72.9	134.6	28.6	78.7	319.7
	95-99			4.7	16.3	70.7
	100+			0.4	1.6	8.3
Male	Total	19 364.7	35 404.4	84 706.8	117 908.9	155 458.7
	0-14	7 068.6	15 008.5	31 466.1	36 149.8	35 014.3
	15-59	10 555.2	18 333.4	48 476.1	72 272.6	97 377.9
	60-64	585.3	772.3	1 641.3	3 354.6	7 901.6
	65-69	542.3	549.2	1 247.5	2 564.7	5 950.2
	70-74	320.7	343.1	887.9	1 741.0	4 040.3
	75-79	190.7	222.9	549.8	977.7	2 543.5
	80-84			280.5	514.4	1 522.8
	85-89			115.3	237.1	767.9
	90-94	101.9	175.0	35.1	78.7	273.8
	95-99			6.7	16.5	60.0
	100+			0.7	1.8	6.4
Percentage in older ages						
Total	60+	8.2	5.5	5.9	8.2	15.3
	65+	5.3	3.4	3.9	5.4	10.2
	80+	0.5	0.5	0.5	0.8	1.9
Female	60+	7.4	5.2	6.2	8.4	15.9
	65+	4.7	3.2	4.1	5.5	10.7
	80+	0.4	0.4	0.6	0.8	2.0
Male	60+	9.0	5.8	5.6	8.0	14.8
	65+	6.0	3.6	3.7	5.2	9.8
	80+	0.5	0.5	0.5	0.7	1.7
Ageing index		21.7	13.0	15.8	26.9	68.4
Broad age groups (percentage)	0-14	37.9	42.5	37.2	30.6	22.4
	15-59	53.8	51.9	56.9	61.2	62.2
	60+	8.2	5.5	5.9	8.2	15.3
Median age (years)		21.2	18.6	20.0*	25.7	33.3
Dependency ratio	Total	76.3	85.1	69.7	56.2	48.5
	Youth	66.9	78.7	63.1	47.8	33.3
	Old Age	9.4	6.4	6.6	8.4	15.2
Potential support ratio		10.6	15.7	15.1	12.0	6.6
Parent support ratio		1.7	2.1	2.2	2.9	4.7
Sex ratio (per 100 women)	60+	134.1	120.0	96.6	101.2	97.4
	65+	141.1	121.9	94.9	99.7	95.1
	80+	139.7	130.1	98.7	91.9	87.1

* Estimate refers to year 2005.

Indicator	Age	1950-1955	1975-1980	2005-2010	2025-2030	2045-2050
Growth rate (percentage)	Total	2.1	3.0	2.1	1.4	0.8
	60+	0.0	2.6	2.8	3.3	4.1
	65+	0.6	2.8	2.7	4.0	4.2
	80+	4.6	1.4	5.0	4.0	3.7
Total fertility rate (per woman)		6.6	6.6	3.7	2.6	2.1
Life expectancy (years)						
Total	Birth	43.4	54.0	64.8	70.9	75.4
	60	..	..	17.5	19.2	20.9
	65	..	..	14.1	15.6	17.0
	80	..	..	6.7	7.4	8.1
Female	Birth	42.1	53.7	64.9	71.5	76.7
	60	..	..	17.8	19.8	21.9
	65	..	..	14.4	16.0	17.8
	80	..	..	6.6	7.4	8.3
Male	Birth	44.8	54.4	64.6	70.4	74.1
	60	..	..	17.1	18.7	20.0
	65	..	..	13.8	15.2	16.3
	80	..	..	6.8	7.3	7.8
Survival rate (percentage)						
Total	60	..	..	74.5	83.0	88.4
	65	..	..	67.0	76.6	83.1
	80	..	..	29.6	39.5	48.6
Female	60	..	..	75.2	84.0	89.9
	65	..	..	68.4	78.3	85.5
	80	..	..	31.3	42.2	53.3
Male	60	..	..	73.8	82.1	87.0
	65	..	..	65.7	75.0	80.8
	80	..	..	28.0	37.0	44.2

		1980	1990	2007	2010	2020
Labour force participation (percentage)						
Total	65+	37.8	34.5	32.2	31.8	30.9
Female	65+	12.0	14.3	18.7	19.6	22.7
Male	65+	59.8	53.3	46.5	44.7	39.2

Percentage married, age 60+			Percentage living alone, age 60+ (1991)		
Total	Female	Male	Total	Female	Male
64.3	50.0	79.0	2.7	2.3	2.9

Statutory pensionable age (2006)			Percentage illiterate, age 65+ (2005)		
	Female	Male	Total	Female	Male
	55	60	78.3	91.7	69.0

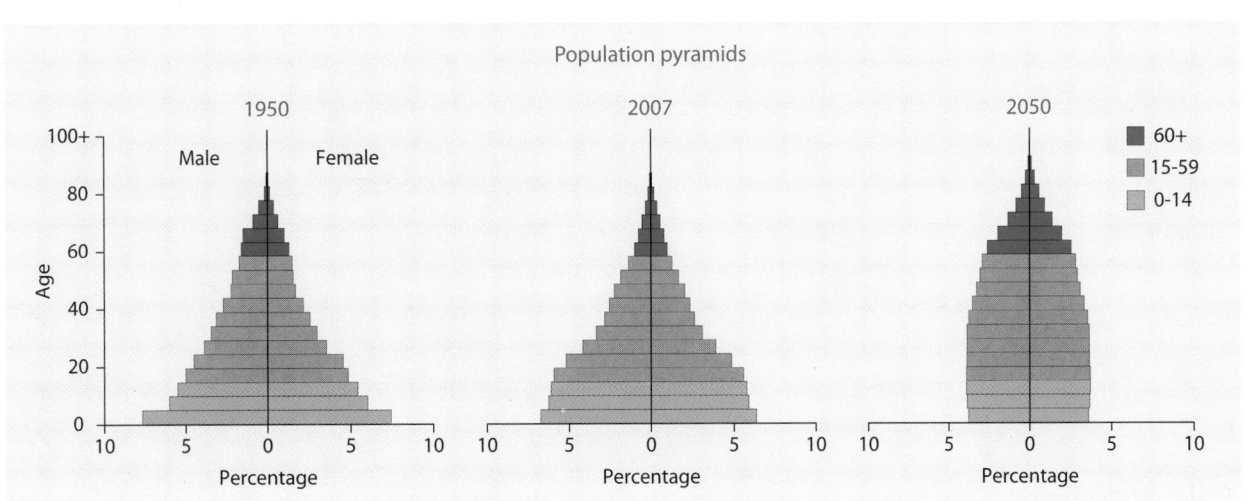

Population pyramids

United Nations Department of Economic and Social Affairs, Population Division

Panama

Indicator	Age	1950	1975	2007	2025	2050
Population (thousands)						
Total	Total	860.1	1 723.2	3 343.4	4 267.1	5 092.7
	0-14	346.2	738.6	996.9	1 026.5	942.1
	15-59	458.1	872.5	2 041.4	2 630.8	2 986.9
	60-64	20.8	38.4	96.4	187.1	274.2
	65-69	15.1	28.1	73.6	147.0	242.1
	70-74	10.1	20.1	54.7	111.0	211.7
	75-79	6.1	14.3	39.4	78.3	182.7
	80-84			24.5	49.8	132.9
	85-89			12.0	24.8	77.1
	90-94	3.8	11.1	3.8	9.4	32.7
	95-99			0.6	2.2	8.8
	100+			0.0	0.2	1.2
Female	Total	419.4	845.3	1 657.4	2 123.4	2 554.5
	0-14	170.4	362.8	487.8	501.4	459.6
	15-59	220.6	427.5	1 012.9	1 300.5	1 468.6
	60-64	10.2	18.3	48.3	95.7	138.9
	65-69	7.7	13.7	37.2	76.3	124.7
	70-74	5.2	9.9	28.0	58.4	111.8
	75-79	3.2	7.3	20.6	41.8	100.1
	80-84			13.3	27.6	76.0
	85-89			6.6	14.3	46.7
	90-94	2.1	5.9	2.2	5.8	21.2
	95-99			0.4	1.4	6.1
	100+			0.0	0.1	0.8
Male	Total	440.6	877.9	1 686.0	2 143.7	2 538.2
	0-14	175.7	375.8	509.0	525.1	482.6
	15-59	237.5	445.1	1 028.6	1 330.3	1 518.3
	60-64	10.5	20.2	48.1	91.4	135.3
	65-69	7.4	14.4	36.4	70.6	117.5
	70-74	4.9	10.2	26.7	52.5	99.9
	75-79	2.9	7.1	18.8	36.5	82.7
	80-84			11.2	22.3	56.9
	85-89			5.3	10.5	30.4
	90-94	1.7	5.2	1.6	3.7	11.5
	95-99			0.2	0.8	2.8
	100+			0.0	0.1	0.4
Percentage in older ages						
Total	60+	6.5	6.5	9.1	14.3	22.8
	65+	4.1	4.3	6.2	9.9	17.5
	80+	0.4	0.6	1.2	2.0	5.0
Female	60+	6.8	6.5	9.5	15.1	24.5
	65+	4.3	4.3	6.5	10.6	19.1
	80+	0.5	0.7	1.4	2.3	5.9
Male	60+	6.2	6.5	8.8	13.5	21.2
	65+	3.8	4.2	5.9	9.2	15.8
	80+	0.4	0.6	1.1	1.7	4.0
Ageing index		16.1	15.2	30.6	59.4	123.5
Broad age groups (percentage)	0-14	40.2	42.9	29.8	24.1	18.5
	15-59	53.3	50.6	61.1	61.7	58.7
	60+	6.5	6.5	9.1	14.3	22.8
Median age (years)		20.2	18.4	26.1*	31.5	38.6
Dependency ratio	Total	79.6	89.2	56.4	51.4	56.2
	Youth	72.3	81.1	46.6	36.4	28.9
	Old Age	7.3	8.1	9.8	15.0	27.3
Potential support ratio		13.7	12.4	10.2	6.7	3.7
Parent support ratio		1.7	2.6	4.5	5.5	13.5
Sex ratio (per 100 women)	60+	96.5	103.7	94.7	89.7	85.8
	65+	93.0	100.4	92.5	87.2	82.5
	80+	84.3	87.5	81.6	75.7	67.6

* *Estimate refers to year 2005.*

Indicator	Age	1950-1955	1975-1980	2005-2010	2025-2030	2045-2050
Growth rate (percentage)	Total	2.6	2.5	1.6	1.0	0.4
	60+	3.0	3.0	3.7	3.7	1.8
	65+	2.9	3.6	3.8	4.0	1.8
	80+	4.0	4.2	4.0	4.5	3.9
Total fertility rate (per woman)		5.7	4.1	2.6	2.1	1.9
Life expectancy (years)						
Total	Birth	55.2	68.7	75.5	78.4	80.4
	60	..	..	21.9	23.2	24.3
	65	..	..	17.9	19.2	20.2
	80	..	..	8.0	8.9	9.6
Female	Birth	56.2	70.8	78.2	81.3	83.5
	60	..	..	23.0	24.8	26.2
	65	..	..	18.9	20.5	21.9
	80	..	..	8.4	9.5	10.3
Male	Birth	54.3	66.8	73.0	75.6	77.5
	60	..	..	20.8	21.7	22.3
	65	..	..	17.0	17.8	18.4
	80	..	..	7.6	8.2	8.6
Survival rate (percentage)						
Total	60	..	..	85.9	88.9	91.0
	65	..	..	81.6	85.0	87.5
	80	..	..	52.3	58.3	62.9
Female	60	..	..	89.7	92.3	94.1
	65	..	..	86.1	89.3	91.6
	80	..	..	59.0	66.2	71.8
Male	60	..	..	82.3	85.7	88.1
	65	..	..	77.3	80.9	83.6
	80	..	..	46.1	50.6	54.3

		1980	1990	2007	2010	2020
Labour force participation (percentage)						
Total	65+	22.1	20.5	24.1	24.2	24.0
Female	65+	7.3	6.0	9.3	9.4	9.4
Male	65+	36.8	35.5	40.0	40.2	40.3

Percentage married, age 60+			Percentage living alone, age 60+ (2000)		
Total	Female	Male	Total	Female	Male
54.7	43.0	67.0	11.3	8.5	14.1

Statutory pensionable age (2006)			Percentage illiterate, age 65+ (2000)		
	Female	Male	Total	Female	Male
	57	62	24.4	24.5	24.3

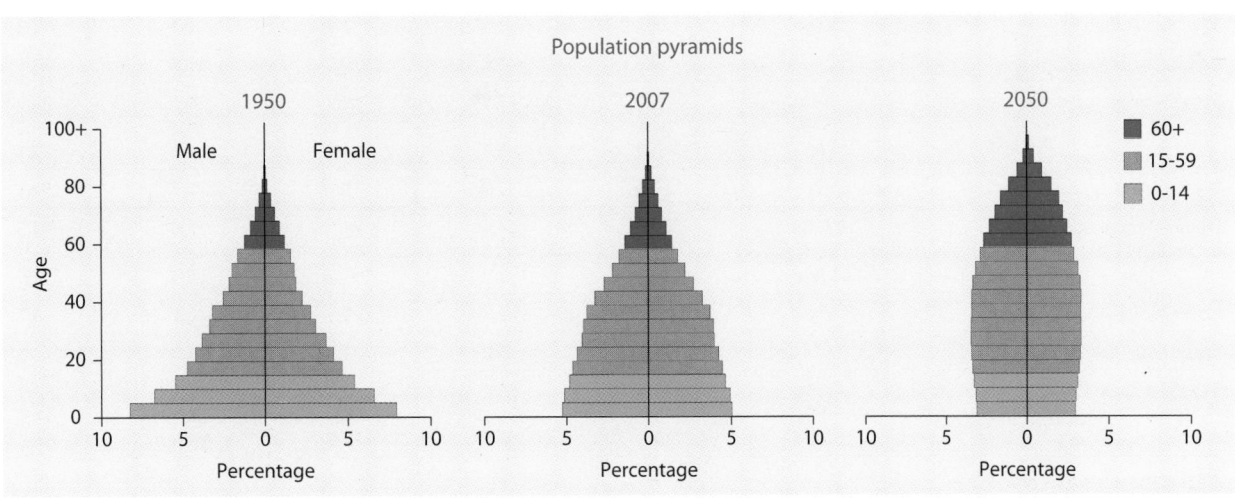

Population pyramids

Papua New Guinea

Indicator	Age	1950	1975	2007	2025	2050
Population (thousands)						
Total	Total	1 798.1	2 866.1	6 114.2	8 205.2	10 619.0
	0-14	707.1	1 251.7	2 395.3	2 502.7	2 427.2
	15-59	982.5	1 507.9	3 473.7	5 182.3	6 902.0
	60-64	34.1	46.0	97.0	222.3	448.0
	65-69	32.7	30.0	69.2	141.2	339.4
	70-74	22.7	17.4	42.9	84.8	229.0
	75-79	12.6	8.6	21.6	44.1	153.5
	80-84			9.9	18.6	78.8
	85-89			3.5	7.2	31.5
	90-94	6.3	4.5	0.9	1.7	8.1
	95-99			0.1	0.3	1.4
	100+			0.0	0.0	0.1
Female	Total	850.6	1 397.8	2 964.9	3 992.5	5 194.4
	0-14	339.1	613.4	1 159.6	1 208.0	1 173.6
	15-59	460.2	726.3	1 687.1	2 507.9	3 341.5
	60-64	16.0	23.7	46.2	114.8	215.8
	65-69	15.5	16.3	33.3	74.7	170.0
	70-74	10.8	10.0	21.2	45.6	125.4
	75-79	6.1	5.2	10.7	25.0	91.3
	80-84			4.7	10.8	49.2
	85-89			1.6	4.4	20.8
	90-94	2.9	2.9	0.4	1.0	5.7
	95-99			0.1	0.2	1.0
	100+			0.0	0.0	0.1
Male	Total	947.5	1 468.3	3 149.4	4 212.6	5 424.5
	0-14	368.0	638.4	1 235.7	1 294.6	1 253.6
	15-59	522.3	781.6	1 786.7	2 674.3	3 560.5
	60-64	18.1	22.3	50.8	107.5	232.2
	65-69	17.2	13.7	35.9	66.5	169.3
	70-74	11.9	7.3	21.7	39.2	103.6
	75-79	6.6	3.3	10.9	19.1	62.2
	80-84			5.2	7.8	29.6
	85-89			1.9	2.8	10.7
	90-94	3.4	1.6	0.5	0.6	2.4
	95-99			0.1	0.1	0.4
	100+			0.0	0.0	0.0
Percentage in older ages						
Total	60+	6.0	3.7	4.0	6.3	12.1
	65+	4.1	2.1	2.4	3.6	7.9
	80+	0.4	0.2	0.2	0.3	1.1
Female	60+	6.0	4.2	4.0	6.9	13.1
	65+	4.1	2.5	2.4	4.1	8.9
	80+	0.3	0.2	0.2	0.4	1.5
Male	60+	6.0	3.3	4.0	5.8	11.3
	65+	4.1	1.8	2.4	3.2	7.0
	80+	0.4	0.1	0.2	0.3	0.8
Ageing index		15.3	8.5	10.2	20.8	53.1
Broad age groups (percentage)	0-14	39.3	43.7	39.2	30.5	22.9
	15-59	54.6	52.6	56.8	63.2	65.0
	60+	6.0	3.7	4.0	6.3	12.1
Median age (years)		20.3	17.9	19.7*	25.3	32.1
Dependency ratio	Total	76.9	84.4	71.2	51.8	44.5
	Youth	69.6	80.5	67.1	46.3	33.0
	Old Age	7.3	3.9	4.1	5.5	11.5
Potential support ratio		13.7	25.7	24.1	18.1	8.7
Parent support ratio		1.3	0.8	1.0	1.0	2.3
Sex ratio (per 100 women)	60+	111.3	83.1	107.4	88.1	89.9
	65+	110.7	75.5	105.8	84.2	81.6
	80+	114.2	56.5	111.2	68.9	56.0

* Estimate refers to year 2005.

Indicator	Age	1950-1955	1975-1980	2005-2010	2025-2030	2045-2050
Growth rate (percentage)	Total	1.3	2.5	1.8	1.4	0.8
	60+	−4.0	2.4	3.1	4.3	3.2
	65+	−4.5	2.5	2.3	5.2	3.5
	80+	1.0	3.2	1.9	5.4	5.3
Total fertility rate (per woman)		6.2	5.9	3.6	2.5	2.1
Life expectancy (years)						
Total	Birth	34.7	47.2	57.1	64.4	70.0
	60	..	..	13.6	15.5	17.4
	65	..	..	11.0	12.6	14.1
	80	..	..	5.4	6.1	6.8
Female	Birth	35.7	48.2	57.8	65.4	71.5
	60	..	..	14.9	16.8	19.0
	65	..	..	12.1	13.7	15.5
	80	..	..	5.8	6.5	7.2
Male	Birth	33.8	46.3	56.6	63.5	68.5
	60	..	..	12.6	14.2	15.8
	65	..	..	10.1	11.4	12.7
	80	..	..	5.1	5.6	6.1
Survival rate (percentage)						
Total	60	..	..	57.6	70.6	80.1
	65	..	..	47.3	61.0	71.6
	80	..	..	13.4	22.3	32.1
Female	60	..	..	59.0	72.0	81.8
	65	..	..	50.0	63.8	75.0
	80	..	..	17.2	27.1	38.6
Male	60	..	..	56.3	69.2	78.5
	65	..	..	44.9	58.2	68.6
	80	..	..	10.6	17.7	25.6

		1980	1990	2007	2010	2020
Labour force participation (percentage)						
Total	65+	53.2	56.1	54.1	54.0	53.6
Female	65+	48.1	47.7	48.2	48.2	48.2
Male	65+	60.0	60.6	59.7	59.7	59.7

Percentage married, age 60+			Percentage living alone, age 60+		
Total	Female	Male	Total	Female	Male
64.7	52.0	75.0	..	..	..

Statutory pensionable age (2006)			Percentage illiterate, age 65+		
Female	Male		Total	Female	Male
55	55		..	..	..

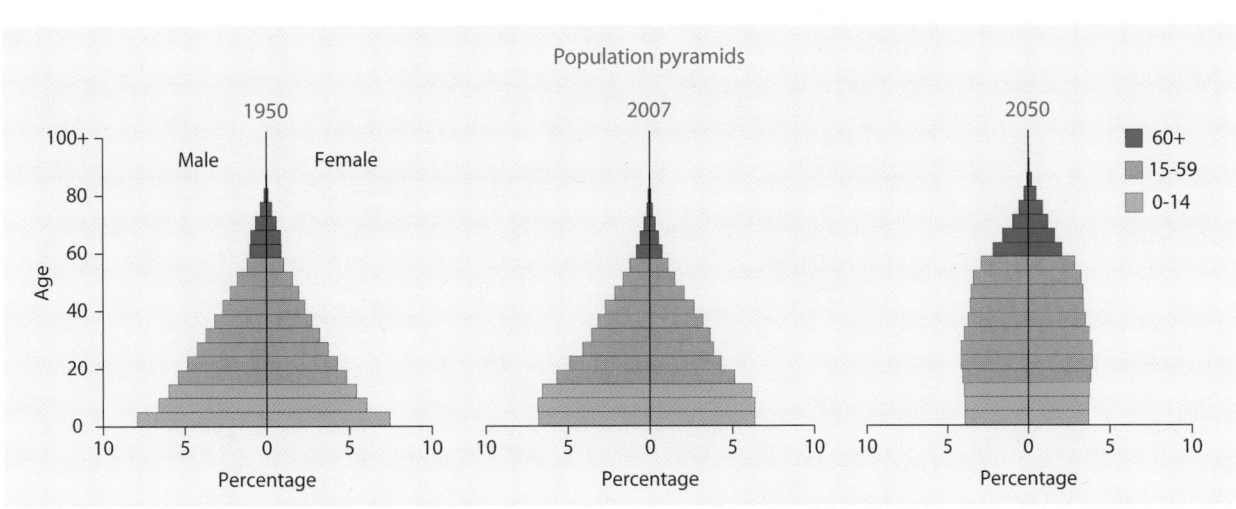

Population pyramids

Paraguay

Indicator	Age	1950	1975	2007	2025	2050
Population (thousands)						
Total	Total	1 488.1	2 658.9	6 444.8	9 055.2	12 094.9
	0-14	579.6	1 159.3	2 371.7	2 716.9	2 711.9
	15-59	775.6	1 308.6	3 705.5	5 479.7	7 419.3
	60-64	46.6	56.1	119.1	281.9	569.2
	65-69	35.8	46.1	98.4	226.8	476.2
	70-74	25.1	38.9	66.9	174.0	341.8
	75-79	15.5	29.0	43.7	87.1	252.7
	80-84			25.0	53.2	173.9
	85-89			10.9	25.7	97.7
	90-94	9.9	20.9	3.2	8.0	40.3
	95-99			0.5	1.8	10.8
	100+			0.0	0.2	1.2
Female	Total	765.3	1 331.9	3 198.7	4 504.7	6 052.8
	0-14	285.0	569.5	1 164.2	1 331.7	1 327.3
	15-59	407.4	653.9	1 834.2	2 718.1	3 670.7
	60-64	24.3	30.8	60.5	144.7	291.4
	65-69	18.9	26.1	51.2	118.0	248.1
	70-74	13.8	22.2	37.3	91.6	182.5
	75-79	9.2	16.8	26.2	47.8	139.3
	80-84			15.4	30.2	99.8
	85-89			7.0	15.7	59.2
	90-94	6.6	12.6	2.2	5.5	26.1
	95-99			0.4	1.3	7.6
	100+			0.0	0.2	0.9
Male	Total	722.8	1 326.9	3 246.2	4 550.5	6 042.1
	0-14	294.6	589.8	1 207.5	1 385.1	1 384.6
	15-59	368.1	654.6	1 871.3	2 761.6	3 748.6
	60-64	22.3	25.3	58.6	137.2	277.9
	65-69	16.8	20.0	47.2	108.8	228.0
	70-74	11.3	16.7	29.6	82.4	159.3
	75-79	6.3	12.2	17.5	39.4	113.3
	80-84			9.6	23.0	74.2
	85-89			3.9	10.0	38.6
	90-94	3.3	8.3	1.0	2.5	14.2
	95-99			0.1	0.4	3.2
	100+			0.0	0.0	0.3
Percentage in older ages						
Total	60+	8.9	7.2	5.7	9.5	16.2
	65+	5.8	5.1	3.9	6.4	11.5
	80+	0.7	0.8	0.6	1.0	2.7
Female	60+	9.5	8.1	6.3	10.1	17.4
	65+	6.3	5.8	4.4	6.9	12.6
	80+	0.9	0.9	0.8	1.2	3.2
Male	60+	8.3	6.2	5.2	8.9	15.0
	65+	5.2	4.3	3.4	5.9	10.4
	80+	0.5	0.6	0.4	0.8	2.2
Ageing index		22.9	16.5	15.5	31.6	72.4
Broad age groups (percentage)	0-14	39.0	43.6	36.8	30.0	22.4
	15-59	52.1	49.2	57.5	60.5	61.3
	60+	8.9	7.2	5.7	9.5	16.2
Median age (years)		20.9	17.8	20.8*	26.0	33.4
Dependency ratio	Total	81.0	94.8	68.5	57.2	51.4
	Youth	70.5	84.9	62.0	47.2	33.9
	Old Age	10.5	9.9	6.5	10.0	17.5
Potential support ratio		9.5	10.1	15.4	10.0	5.7
Parent support ratio		2.1	3.4	2.7	3.6	7.8
Sex ratio (per 100 women)	60+	82.6	76.1	83.6	88.8	86.2
	65+	77.8	73.6	77.8	86.0	82.7
	80+	50.4	66.2	58.1	68.1	67.4

* Estimate refers to year 2005.

Indicator	Age	1950-1955	1975-1980	2005-2010	2025-2030	2045-2050
Growth rate (percentage)	Total	2.2	3.2	2.2	1.5	0.9
	60+	2.5	1.0	3.4	3.7	3.2
	65+	2.7	0.9	3.7	4.3	3.5
	80+	4.1	2.6	4.1	4.2	3.6
Total fertility rate (per woman)		6.5	5.2	3.5	2.5	2.1
Life expectancy (years)						
Total	Birth	62.6	66.5	71.9	75.6	78.5
	60	..	..	19.5	21.4	23.0
	65	..	..	15.8	17.6	19.0
	80	..	..	7.1	8.2	9.0
Female	Birth	64.6	68.6	74.2	78.0	81.0
	60	..	..	20.7	22.9	24.7
	65	..	..	16.8	18.8	20.4
	80	..	..	7.5	8.7	9.7
Male	Birth	60.6	64.3	69.7	73.3	76.0
	60	..	..	18.2	19.9	21.2
	65	..	..	14.7	16.3	17.4
	80	..	..	6.6	7.5	8.2
Survival rate (percentage)						
Total	60	..	..	82.9	87.0	89.7
	65	..	..	77.0	82.0	85.5
	80	..	..	41.5	50.2	57.3
Female	60	..	..	86.0	89.7	92.2
	65	..	..	81.2	85.8	89.0
	80	..	..	47.4	57.1	64.9
Male	60	..	..	80.0	84.4	87.3
	65	..	..	73.0	78.3	82.1
	80	..	..	35.5	43.6	49.9

		1980	1990	2007	2010	2020
Labour force participation (percentage)						
Total	65+	31.6	25.2	28.0	28.6	30.3
Female	65+	15.8	17.9	18.6	19.7	23.5
Male	65+	53.2	35.3	40.0	39.6	38.2

Percentage married, age 60+			Percentage living alone, age 60+ (1990)		
Total	Female	Male	Total	Female	Male
59.1	45.0	77.0	5.4	5.1	5.8

Statutory pensionable age (2006)			Percentage illiterate, age 65+		
	Female	Male	Total	Female	Male
	60	60	..	..	..

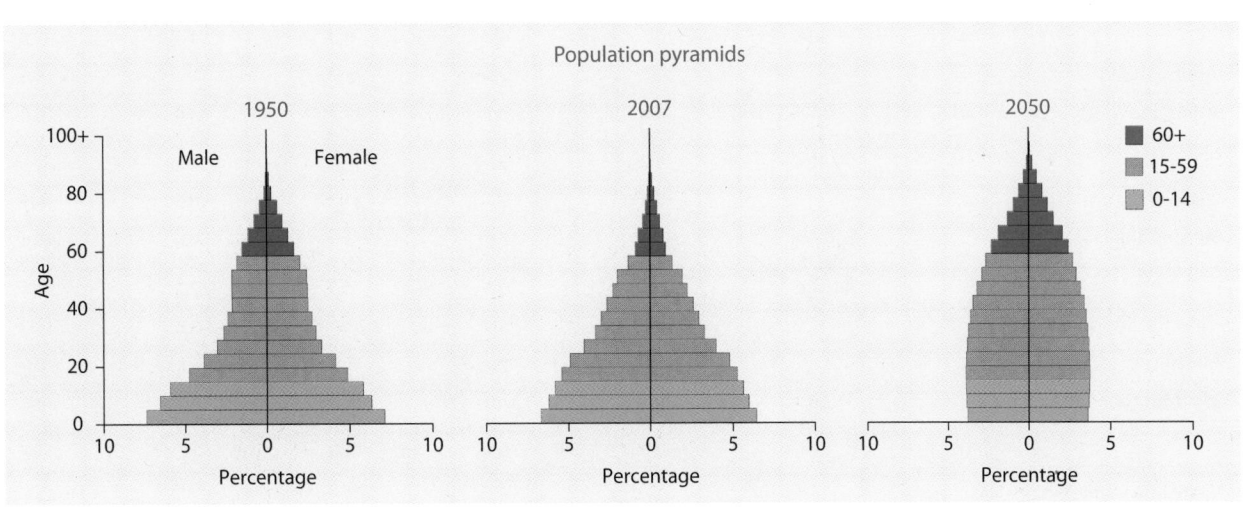

Population pyramids

United Nations Department of Economic and Social Affairs, Population Division

Peru

Indicator	Age	1950	1975	2007	2025	2050
Population (thousands)						
Total	Total	7 632.5	15 161.1	28 797.3	36 191.1	42 551.9
	0-14	3 172.5	6 556.1	8 998.5	9 064.6	7 990.9
	15-59	4 026.8	7 761.8	17 485.3	22 643.8	25 329.8
	60-64	169.5	306.7	738.2	1 412.2	2 368.5
	65-69	113.8	236.4	579.7	1 097.2	2 047.9
	70-74	81.2	157.1	434.7	812.5	1 748.2
	75-79	43.8	94.0	287.1	547.3	1 319.9
	80-84			163.2	336.3	906.2
	85-89			77.0	181.8	531.7
	90-94	24.9	49.1	26.9	73.4	230.7
	95-99			5.9	19.1	67.5
	100+			0.7	2.8	10.5
Female	Total	3 790.3	7 521.0	14 325.8	18 080.5	21 426.6
	0-14	1 563.5	3 225.0	4 417.6	4 438.8	3 905.7
	15-59	1 995.8	3 846.4	8 683.1	11 236.9	12 516.2
	60-64	87.9	159.0	377.0	725.4	1 211.8
	65-69	60.1	124.9	300.5	574.6	1 067.1
	70-74	43.9	84.9	230.4	435.4	934.8
	75-79	24.4	52.3	157.1	302.6	730.8
	80-84			92.8	193.8	526.3
	85-89			45.8	110.3	326.9
	90-94	14.6	28.4	17.0	47.4	151.9
	95-99			4.0	13.1	47.5
	100+			0.5	2.0	7.4
Male	Total	3 842.2	7 640.1	14 471.5	18 110.6	21 125.3
	0-14	1 609.0	3 331.1	4 580.9	4 625.8	4 085.1
	15-59	2 031.0	3 915.4	8 802.3	11 406.8	12 813.7
	60-64	81.6	147.7	361.2	686.8	1 156.7
	65-69	53.6	111.4	279.2	522.6	980.8
	70-74	37.3	72.2	204.3	377.1	813.4
	75-79	19.4	41.7	130.0	244.7	589.1
	80-84			70.4	142.5	379.9
	85-89			31.2	71.5	204.8
	90-94	10.2	20.7	9.9	26.0	78.8
	95-99			1.9	5.9	20.0
	100+			0.2	0.8	3.1
Percentage in older ages						
Total	60+	5.7	5.6	8.0	12.4	21.7
	65+	3.5	3.5	5.5	8.5	16.1
	80+	0.3	0.3	1.0	1.7	4.1
Female	60+	6.1	6.0	8.6	13.3	23.4
	65+	3.8	3.9	5.9	9.3	17.7
	80+	0.4	0.4	1.1	2.0	4.9
Male	60+	5.3	5.2	7.5	11.5	20.0
	65+	3.1	3.2	5.0	7.7	14.5
	80+	0.3	0.3	0.8	1.4	3.3
Ageing index		13.7	12.9	25.7	49.5	115.5
Broad age groups (percentage)	0-14	41.6	43.2	31.2	25.0	18.8
	15-59	52.8	51.2	60.7	62.6	59.5
	60+	5.7	5.6	8.0	12.4	21.7
Median age (years)		19.1	18.2	24.2*	30.5	38.1
Dependency ratio	Total	81.9	87.9	58.0	50.4	53.6
	Youth	75.6	81.3	49.4	37.7	28.8
	Old Age	6.3	6.6	8.6	12.8	24.8
Potential support ratio		15.9	15.0	11.6	7.8	4.0
Parent support ratio		0.9	1.0	3.8	5.5	10.9
Sex ratio (per 100 women)	60+	87.5	87.6	88.8	86.4	84.5
	65+	84.3	84.7	85.7	82.8	80.9
	80+	69.8	73.0	70.9	67.3	64.8

* Estimate refers to year 2005.

Indicator	Age	1950-1955	1975-1980	2005-2010	2025-2030	2045-2050
Growth rate (percentage)	Total	2.6	2.7	1.4	0.9	0.4
	60+	2.4	2.6	3.3	3.4	2.3
	65+	2.3	3.1	3.3	3.9	2.5
	80+	0.4	4.6	4.8	4.2	3.6
Total fertility rate (per woman)		6.9	5.4	2.7	2.1	1.9
Life expectancy (years)						
Total	Birth	43.9	58.4	71.2	75.6	78.2
	60	..	..	20.3	22.3	23.5
	65	..	..	16.7	18.4	19.5
	80	..	..	8.1	9.0	9.5
Female	Birth	45.0	60.0	73.9	78.5	81.0
	60	..	..	21.6	24.0	25.4
	65	..	..	17.8	19.9	21.2
	80	..	..	8.6	9.7	10.3
Male	Birth	42.9	56.3	68.7	72.9	75.4
	60	..	..	18.9	20.5	21.5
	65	..	..	15.5	16.9	17.8
	80	..	..	7.5	8.1	8.5
Survival rate (percentage)						
Total	60	..	..	80.4	85.6	88.4
	65	..	..	74.5	80.7	84.2
	80	..	..	42.0	51.7	57.8
Female	60	..	..	84.1	88.8	91.2
	65	..	..	79.1	85.0	88.1
	80	..	..	48.6	59.6	66.1
Male	60	..	..	76.9	82.5	85.7
	65	..	..	70.1	76.6	80.5
	80	..	..	35.7	44.0	49.6

		1980	1990	2007	2010	2020
Labour force participation (percentage)						
Total	65+	37.0	32.6	48.0	50.3	56.8
Female	65+	14.8	22.6	37.7	40.9	49.4
Male	65+	63.4	44.5	60.1	61.4	65.7

Percentage married, age 60+			Percentage living alone, age 60+ (2000)		
Total	Female	Male	Total	Female	Male
59.2	45.0	75.0	8.7	9.2	8.1

Statutory pensionable age (2006)			Percentage illiterate, age 65+ (2004)		
	Female	Male	Total	Female	Male
	65	65	38.2	51.5	23.6

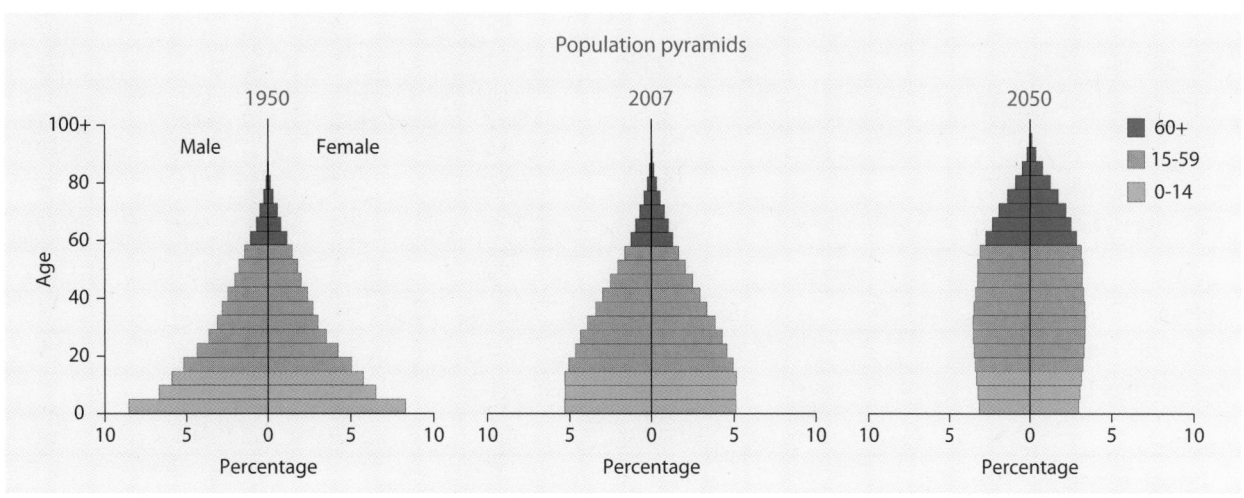

Population pyramids

Philippines

Indicator	Age	1950	1975	2007	2025	2050
Population (thousands)						
Total	Total	19 996.2	42 018.7	85 884.0	109 084.2	127 068.2
	0-14	8 716.7	18 574.8	29 254.4	28 367.3	24 111.1
	15-59	10 175.3	21 364.4	51 223.4	69 448.6	77 570.4
	60-64	386.5	789.0	1 920.1	3 830.9	7 299.3
	65-69	302.4	594.1	1 455.5	2 984.0	6 130.4
	70-74	212.9	360.9	1 018.7	2 171.0	4 903.5
	75-79	129.8	206.4	585.5	1 265.6	3 459.8
	80-84			291.0	678.5	2 133.1
	85-89			108.2	263.3	1 027.9
	90-94	72.7	129.1	24.2	65.9	350.3
	95-99			3.0	8.5	75.1
	100+			0.2	0.6	7.4
Female	Total	10 052.7	20 846.7	42 652.7	54 341.0	63 688.9
	0-14	4 242.0	9 111.3	14 294.0	13 827.3	11 709.9
	15-59	5 128.8	10 610.4	25 443.8	34 392.9	38 163.5
	60-64	232.3	420.7	983.5	1 988.5	3 709.5
	65-69	186.8	312.0	775.0	1 589.7	3 187.5
	70-74	132.1	190.9	554.7	1 197.2	2 636.2
	75-79	82.6	115.9	334.8	713.7	1 955.1
	80-84			178.9	407.5	1 297.4
	85-89			69.6	171.1	692.3
	90-94	48.2	85.6	16.2	45.9	266.5
	95-99			2.1	6.6	64.1
	100+			0.1	0.5	6.8
Male	Total	9 943.5	21 172.0	43 231.4	54 743.2	63 379.4
	0-14	4 474.6	9 463.5	14 960.4	14 540.0	12 401.1
	15-59	5 046.6	10 754.0	25 779.5	35 055.7	39 406.9
	60-64	154.1	368.3	936.7	1 842.4	3 589.8
	65-69	115.6	282.1	680.4	1 394.3	2 942.9
	70-74	80.8	170.1	464.0	973.7	2 267.3
	75-79	47.2	90.5	250.7	551.8	1 504.7
	80-84			112.1	271.0	835.6
	85-89			38.6	92.2	335.6
	90-94	24.6	43.5	8.0	20.0	83.8
	95-99			0.9	1.9	11.0
	100+			0.0	0.1	0.6
Percentage in older ages						
Total	60+	5.5	4.9	6.3	10.3	20.0
	65+	3.6	3.1	4.1	6.8	14.2
	80+	0.4	0.3	0.5	0.9	2.8
Female	60+	6.8	5.4	6.8	11.3	21.7
	65+	4.5	3.4	4.5	7.6	15.9
	80+	0.5	0.4	0.6	1.2	3.7
Male	60+	4.2	4.5	5.8	9.4	18.3
	65+	2.7	2.8	3.6	6.0	12.6
	80+	0.2	0.2	0.4	0.7	2.0
Ageing index		12.7	11.2	18.5	39.7	105.3
Broad age groups (percentage)	0-14	43.6	44.2	34.1	26.0	19.0
	15-59	50.9	50.8	59.6	63.7	61.0
	60+	5.5	4.9	6.3	10.3	20.0
Median age (years)		18.2	17.6	22.2*	28.8	37.9
Dependency ratio	Total	89.3	89.7	61.6	48.9	49.7
	Youth	82.5	83.8	55.0	38.7	28.4
	Old Age	6.8	5.8	6.6	10.1	21.3
Potential support ratio		14.7	17.2	15.2	9.9	4.7
Parent support ratio		1.5	1.3	1.7	2.4	6.1
Sex ratio (per 100 women)	60+	61.9	84.8	85.5	84.1	83.8
	65+	59.6	83.2	80.5	80.0	79.0
	80+	51.0	50.9	59.9	61.0	54.4

*   *Estimate refers to year 2005.*

Indicator	Age	1950-1955	1975-1980	2005-2010	2025-2030	2045-2050
Growth rate (percentage)	Total	3.0	2.7	1.6	0.9	0.4
	60+	1.2	2.5	3.6	3.7	2.8
	65+	1.1	3.4	3.9	4.1	3.1
	80+	3.0	3.0	3.0	4.9	4.4
Total fertility rate (per woman)		7.3	5.5	2.8	2.0	1.9
Life expectancy (years)						
Total	Birth	47.8	60.1	71.6	75.8	78.6
	60	..	..	18.0	19.8	21.6
	65	..	..	14.4	16.0	17.6
	80	..	..	6.1	7.0	8.0
Female	Birth	49.5	61.9	73.8	78.1	81.0
	60	..	..	19.1	21.5	23.6
	65	..	..	15.2	17.4	19.3
	80	..	..	6.3	7.6	8.9
Male	Birth	46.0	58.2	69.5	73.4	76.3
	60	..	..	16.9	18.1	19.6
	65	..	..	13.4	14.4	15.7
	80	..	..	5.7	6.1	6.7
Survival rate (percentage)						
Total	60	..	..	83.6	89.3	92.2
	65	..	..	76.8	83.8	87.7
	80	..	..	36.0	45.9	54.3
Female	60	..	..	86.8	91.6	93.7
	65	..	..	81.3	87.4	90.5
	80	..	..	41.7	53.9	62.6
Male	60	..	..	80.5	87.0	90.7
	65	..	..	72.5	80.2	85.0
	80	..	..	30.3	37.8	45.8

		1980	1990	2007	2010	2020
Labour force participation (percentage)						
Total	65+	42.4	41.0	39.6	38.9	36.1
Female	65+	27.9	27.2	28.8	28.7	28.6
Male	65+	60.3	59.3	53.1	51.4	45.3

Percentage married, age 60+			Percentage living alone, age 60+ (1998)		
Total	Female	Male	Total	Female	Male
65.6	52.0	82.0	5.3	6.4	4.0

Statutory pensionable age (2006)			Percentage illiterate, age 65+ (2000)		
	Female	Male	Total	Female	Male
	60	60	21.6	22.7	20.1

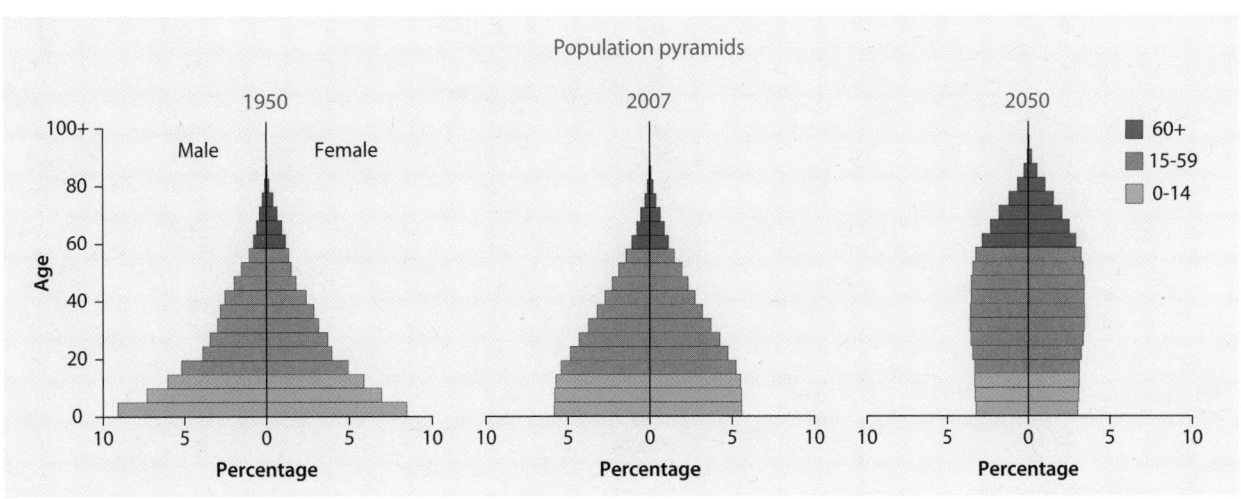

Population pyramids

Poland

Indicator	Age	1950	1975	2007	2025	2050
Population (thousands)						
Total	Total	24 824.0	34 015.2	38 466.7	37 095.5	31 916.1
	0-14	7 295.0	8 174.0	5 973.6	5 152.5	4 237.2
	15-59	15 484.0	21 159.3	25 783.5	22 070.8	15 595.4
	60-64	747.0	1 437.9	1 731.1	2 268.3	2 587.5
	65-69	531.0	1 313.8	1 428.3	2 535.9	2 786.0
	70-74	354.0	957.5	1 380.9	2 196.4	2 377.2
	75-79	230.0	571.4	1 093.1	1 465.2	1 753.1
	80-84			700.9	693.1	1 139.8
	85-89			260.9	454.9	786.3
	90-94	183.0	401.2	91.1	199.9	472.3
	95-99			21.5	52.4	157.0
	100+			1.7	6.1	24.1
Female	Total	12 994.0	17 466.5	19 822.6	19 179.9	16 543.4
	0-14	3 602.0	3 988.0	2 907.1	2 504.1	2 058.8
	15-59	8 172.0	10 699.6	12 868.7	10 902.1	7 636.4
	60-64	435.0	808.2	942.4	1 192.6	1 313.1
	65-69	313.0	746.6	817.2	1 389.1	1 457.4
	70-74	214.0	574.8	827.5	1 271.9	1 294.2
	75-79	140.0	369.1	698.1	906.6	1 010.9
	80-84			483.6	467.0	708.4
	85-89			190.8	335.6	542.7
	90-94	118.0	280.2	69.1	160.1	364.7
	95-99			16.8	45.3	134.5
	100+			1.4	5.5	22.3
Male	Total	11 830.0	16 548.7	18 644.0	17 915.6	15 372.7
	0-14	3 693.0	4 185.9	3 066.5	2 648.4	2 178.5
	15-59	7 312.0	10 459.7	12 914.9	11 168.8	7 959.1
	60-64	312.0	629.7	788.7	1 075.7	1 274.4
	65-69	218.0	567.2	611.1	1 146.8	1 328.6
	70-74	140.0	382.7	553.4	924.4	1 083.0
	75-79	90.0	202.4	395.1	558.7	742.2
	80-84			217.3	226.1	431.4
	85-89			70.1	119.2	243.6
	90-94	65.0	121.0	22.0	39.7	107.6
	95-99			4.6	7.2	22.5
	100+			0.4	0.6	1.8
Percentage in older ages						
Total	60+	8.2	13.8	17.4	26.6	37.9
	65+	5.2	9.5	12.9	20.5	29.8
	80+	0.7	1.2	2.8	3.8	8.1
Female	60+	9.4	15.9	20.4	30.1	41.4
	65+	6.0	11.3	15.7	23.9	33.5
	80+	0.9	1.6	3.8	5.3	10.7
Male	60+	7.0	11.5	14.3	22.9	34.1
	65+	4.3	7.7	10.1	16.9	25.8
	80+	0.5	0.7	1.7	2.2	5.2
Ageing index		28.0	57.3	112.3	191.6	285.2
Broad age groups (percentage)	0-14	29.4	24.0	15.5	13.9	13.3
	15-59	62.4	62.2	67.0	59.5	48.9
	60+	8.2	13.8	17.4	26.6	37.9
Median age (years)		25.8	28.6	36.5*	43.8	50.8
Dependency ratio	Total	52.9	50.5	39.8	52.4	75.5
	Youth	44.9	36.2	21.7	21.2	23.3
	Old Age	8.0	14.4	18.1	31.2	52.2
Potential support ratio		12.5	7.0	5.5	3.2	1.9
Parent support ratio		2.3	2.6	5.0	10.0	21.3
Sex ratio (per 100 women)	60+	67.6	68.5	65.8	71.0	76.4
	65+	65.4	64.6	60.4	66.0	71.6
	80+	55.1	43.2	41.3	38.8	45.5

* Estimate refers to year 2005.

Indicator	Age	1950-1955	1975-1980	2005-2010	2025-2030	2045-2050
Growth rate (percentage)	Total	1.9	0.9	−0.1	−0.5	−0.7
	60+	2.4	0.1	2.2	0.3	0.5
	65+	2.9	2.1	0.1	0.8	1.5
	80+	0.5	6.0	4.3	4.6	−0.6
Total fertility rate (per woman)		3.6	2.3	1.2	1.5	1.8
Life expectancy (years)						
Total	Birth	61.5	71.0	75.1	78.2	80.5
	60	..	..	19.9	21.5	23.2
	65	..	..	16.2	17.6	19.2
	80	..	..	7.5	8.3	9.2
Female	Birth	64.2	75.0	79.0	81.6	83.8
	60	..	..	22.2	24.1	25.8
	65	..	..	18.1	19.9	21.5
	80	..	..	8.1	9.2	10.3
Male	Birth	58.6	67.0	71.2	74.6	77.2
	60	..	..	17.1	18.5	20.4
	65	..	..	13.9	14.9	16.6
	80	..	..	6.4	6.6	7.5
Survival rate (percentage)						
Total	60	..	..	86.3	90.7	92.8
	65	..	..	80.0	85.5	88.7
	80	..	..	44.4	52.4	59.6
Female	60	..	..	91.7	93.9	95.3
	65	..	..	87.8	90.7	92.7
	80	..	..	56.7	64.6	70.6
Male	60	..	..	80.9	87.6	90.4
	65	..	..	72.2	80.3	84.7
	80	..	..	31.5	39.7	48.5

		1980	1990	2007	2010	2020
Labour force participation (percentage)						
Total	65+	22.3	20.2	5.0	4.3	3.4
Female	65+	17.5	17.2	3.6	3.3	3.1
Male	65+	30.0	25.1	7.3	6.0	3.8

Percentage married, age 60+			Percentage living alone, age 60+ (1988)		
Total	Female	Male	Total	Female	Male
57.2	46.0	74.0	20.7	27.5	10.4

Statutory pensionable age (2006)			Percentage illiterate, age 65+		
	Female	Male	Total	Female	Male
	60	65	..	..	..

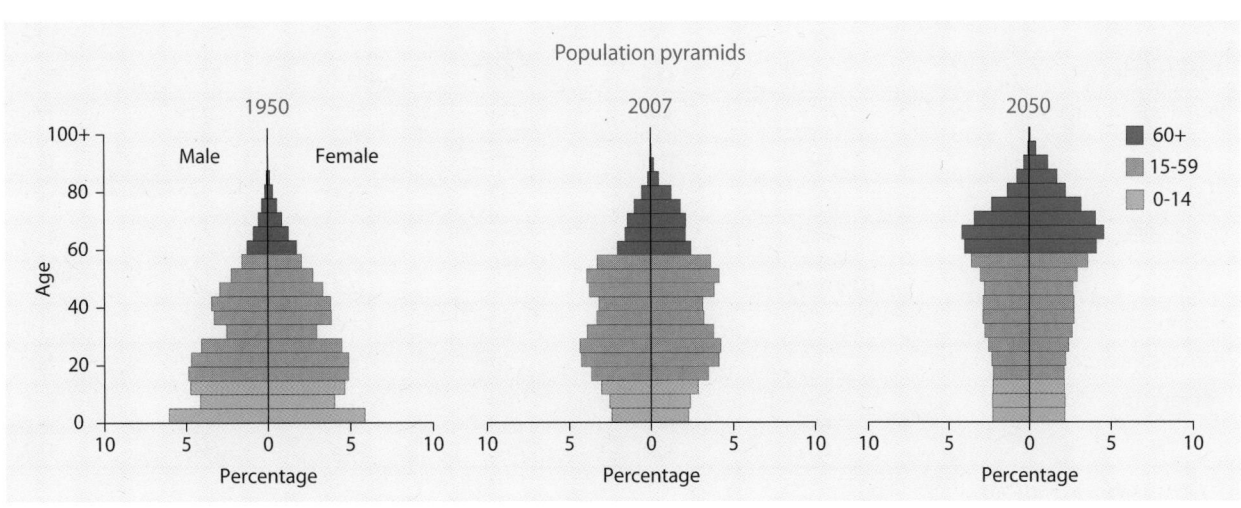

Population pyramids

United Nations Department of Economic and Social Affairs, Population Division

Portugal

Indicator	Age	1950	1975	2007	2025	2050
Population (thousands)						
Total	Total	8 405.0	9 093.4	10 592.7	10 924.0	10 722.6
	0-14	2 477.0	2 539.4	1 672.8	1 519.9	1 542.1
	15-59	5 048.0	5 249.9	6 506.6	6 226.9	5 285.8
	60-64	293.0	406.4	575.7	776.4	652.0
	65-69	228.0	355.7	527.8	699.6	729.8
	70-74	169.0	264.6	490.1	602.0	764.7
	75-79	107.0	147.6	392.6	480.7	682.6
	80-84			261.4	322.3	507.5
	85-89			119.6	191.5	333.6
	90-94	83.0	129.7	38.3	81.2	160.6
	95-99			7.1	20.7	53.1
	100+			0.6	2.8	10.8
Female	Total	4 362.0	4 794.5	5 469.2	5 612.1	5 487.4
	0-14	1 216.0	1 239.3	812.9	738.0	748.9
	15-59	2 622.0	2 790.0	3 273.6	3 088.4	2 596.5
	60-64	168.0	221.5	306.3	400.6	326.0
	65-69	134.0	201.9	286.8	368.0	369.9
	70-74	100.0	159.2	274.5	327.3	398.0
	75-79	66.0	94.9	231.1	274.8	370.1
	80-84			164.9	198.9	293.2
	85-89			83.0	131.8	214.3
	90-94	56.0	87.8	29.5	63.5	116.8
	95-99			6.1	18.1	43.9
	100+			0.5	2.6	9.8
Male	Total	4 043.0	4 298.9	5 123.5	5 312.0	5 235.2
	0-14	1 261.0	1 300.1	859.9	781.9	793.2
	15-59	2 426.0	2 459.9	3 233.0	3 138.5	2 689.3
	60-64	125.0	184.9	269.4	375.8	326.0
	65-69	94.0	153.9	241.0	331.6	359.9
	70-74	69.0	105.4	215.6	274.8	366.7
	75-79	41.0	52.8	161.6	206.0	312.5
	80-84			96.5	123.4	214.3
	85-89			36.6	59.7	119.3
	90-94	27.0	41.9	8.8	17.7	43.8
	95-99			1.1	2.6	9.3
	100+			0.1	0.2	1.0
Percentage in older ages						
Total	60+	10.5	14.3	22.8	29.1	36.3
	65+	7.0	9.9	17.3	22.0	30.2
	80+	1.0	1.4	4.0	5.7	9.9
Female	60+	12.0	16.0	25.3	31.8	39.0
	65+	8.2	11.3	19.7	24.7	33.1
	80+	1.3	1.8	5.2	7.4	12.4
Male	60+	8.8	12.5	20.1	26.2	33.5
	65+	5.7	8.2	14.9	19.1	27.3
	80+	0.7	1.0	2.8	3.8	7.4
Ageing index		35.5	51.4	144.3	209.0	252.6
Broad age groups (percentage)	0-14	29.5	27.9	15.8	13.9	14.4
	15-59	60.1	57.7	61.4	57.0	49.3
	60+	10.5	14.3	22.8	29.1	36.3
Median age (years)		26.2	28.7	39.5*	46.4	48.7
Dependency ratio	Total	57.4	60.8	49.6	56.0	80.6
	Youth	46.4	44.9	23.6	21.7	26.0
	Old Age	11.0	15.9	25.9	34.3	54.6
Potential support ratio		9.1	6.3	3.9	2.9	1.8
Parent support ratio		2.6	2.7	8.5	12.1	28.6
Sex ratio (per 100 women)	60+	67.9	70.4	74.5	77.9	81.8
	65+	64.9	65.1	70.7	73.3	78.6
	80+	48.2	47.7	50.4	49.0	57.2

* Estimate refers to year 2005.

Indicator	Age	1950-1955	1975-1980	2005-2010	2025-2030	2045-2050
Growth rate (percentage)	Total	0.5	1.4	0.4	0.0	−0.2
	60+	1.0	1.7	1.5	1.4	−0.2
	65+	1.3	2.6	1.2	1.7	0.3
	80+	2.5	0.7	3.2	2.3	1.7
Total fertility rate (per woman)		3.0	2.4	1.5	1.7	1.9
Life expectancy (years)						
Total	Birth	59.4	70.3	77.9	80.3	82.3
	60	..	..	21.5	23.1	24.6
	65	..	..	17.4	18.9	20.4
	80	..	..	7.6	8.6	9.6
Female	Birth	61.9	73.8	81.2	83.4	85.4
	60	..	..	23.8	25.5	27.1
	65	..	..	19.5	21.1	22.6
	80	..	..	8.5	9.7	10.9
Male	Birth	56.9	66.7	74.6	77.2	79.4
	60	..	..	18.9	20.5	22.1
	65	..	..	15.1	16.5	18.0
	80	..	..	6.2	7.1	8.0
Survival rate (percentage)						
Total	60	..	..	90.7	92.9	94.4
	65	..	..	86.2	89.2	91.3
	80	..	..	53.8	60.5	66.2
Female	60	..	..	93.7	95.2	96.2
	65	..	..	90.8	92.8	94.2
	80	..	..	65.1	70.9	75.5
Male	60	..	..	87.6	90.7	92.6
	65	..	..	81.5	85.7	88.5
	80	..	..	42.1	50.0	57.1

		1980	1990	2007	2010	2020
Labour force participation (percentage)						
Total	65+	16.8	12.8	19.9	20.4	21.1
Female	65+	8.6	7.7	15.1	15.6	16.1
Male	65+	28.1	19.9	26.8	27.2	28.0

Percentage married, age 60+			Percentage living alone, age 60+ (1994)		
Total	Female	Male	Total	Female	Male
62.7	49.0	81.0	15.8	20.6	9.2

Statutory pensionable age (2006)		Percentage illiterate, age 65+		
Female	Male	Total	Female	Male
65	65	..	..	..

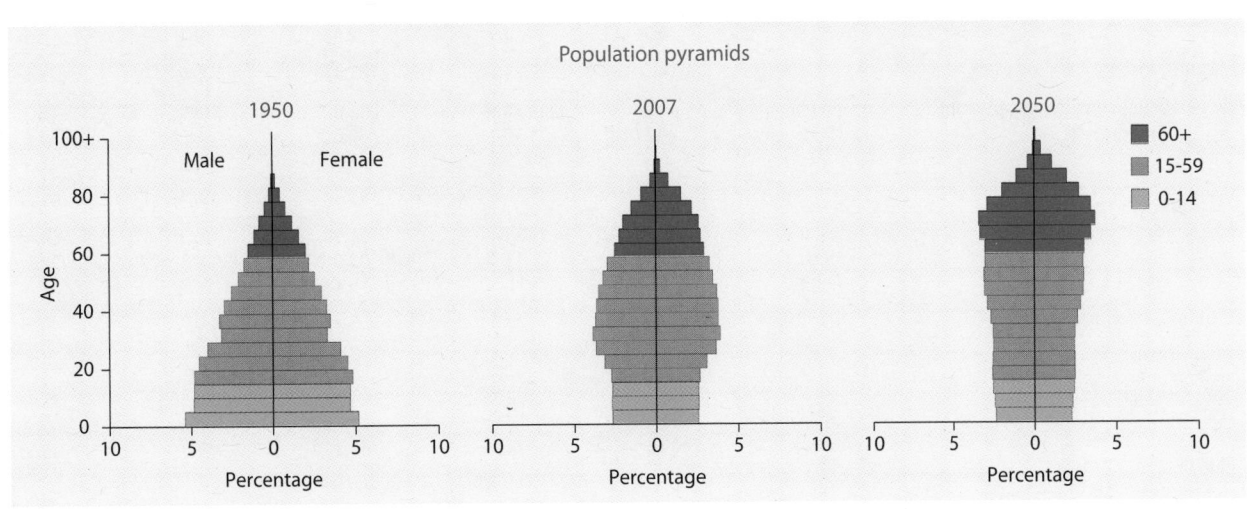

Population pyramids

United Nations Department of Economic and Social Affairs, Population Division

Puerto Rico

Indicator	Age	1950	1975	2007	2025	2050
Population (thousands)						
Total	Total	2 218.0	2 938.8	3 998.0	4 310.7	4 404.6
	0-14	958.3	987.9	864.8	813.0	725.8
	15-59	1 124.1	1 679.2	2 432.0	2 522.3	2 406.3
	60-64	49.5	87.1	199.4	237.2	272.2
	65-69	33.4	70.1	159.8	210.6	267.6
	70-74	21.9	53.0	124.6	180.7	232.6
	75-79	19.9	30.3	94.0	150.8	183.6
	80-84			65.8	102.7	138.8
	85-89			36.4	56.7	98.9
	90-94	10.9	31.2	15.4	25.8	52.3
	95-99			4.8	8.8	20.6
	100+			1.0	2.2	5.8
Female	Total	1 103.8	1 501.3	2 081.4	2 249.3	2 274.9
	0-14	471.8	487.7	422.0	396.3	353.7
	15-59	563.7	872.3	1 258.0	1 267.7	1 184.8
	60-64	23.5	43.6	109.9	131.8	139.7
	65-69	16.7	36.0	88.8	120.6	140.4
	70-74	10.9	27.5	70.7	107.0	128.1
	75-79	12.0	16.2	55.0	92.7	107.7
	80-84			39.9	66.0	88.5
	85-89			23.0	39.1	69.0
	90-94	5.2	18.0	10.1	19.2	40.4
	95-99			3.3	7.0	17.4
	100+			0.7	1.8	5.2
Male	Total	1 114.2	1 437.5	1 916.6	2 061.4	2 129.6
	0-14	486.5	500.2	442.8	416.7	372.1
	15-59	560.4	806.9	1 173.9	1 254.6	1 221.5
	60-64	26.0	43.5	89.5	105.4	132.5
	65-69	16.7	34.1	71.0	89.9	127.1
	70-74	11.0	25.5	53.9	73.8	104.5
	75-79	7.9	14.1	39.0	58.0	75.9
	80-84			25.9	36.7	50.3
	85-89			13.4	17.6	29.9
	90-94	5.7	13.2	5.3	6.5	11.9
	95-99			1.5	1.8	3.2
	100+			0.3	0.4	0.6
Percentage in older ages						
Total	60+	6.1	9.2	17.5	22.6	28.9
	65+	3.9	6.3	12.6	17.1	22.7
	80+	0.5	1.1	3.1	4.5	7.2
Female	60+	6.2	9.4	19.3	26.0	32.4
	65+	4.1	6.5	14.0	20.2	26.2
	80+	0.5	1.2	3.7	5.9	9.7
Male	60+	6.0	9.1	15.6	18.9	25.2
	65+	3.7	6.0	11.0	13.8	18.9
	80+	0.5	0.9	2.4	3.1	4.5
Ageing index		14.2	27.5	81.1	120.0	175.3
Broad age groups (percentage)	0-14	43.2	33.6	21.6	18.9	16.5
	15-59	50.7	57.1	60.8	58.5	54.6
	60+	6.1	9.2	17.5	22.6	28.9
Median age (years)		18.4	22.6	33.3*	38.4	43.1
Dependency ratio	Total	89.0	66.4	51.9	56.2	64.4
	Youth	81.7	55.9	32.9	29.5	27.1
	Old Age	7.3	10.5	19.1	26.7	37.3
Potential support ratio		13.6	9.6	5.2	3.7	2.7
Parent support ratio		2.8	5.1	8.8	12.7	21.2
Sex ratio (per 100 women)	60+	98.5	92.3	74.7	66.6	72.8
	65+	92.2	88.9	72.2	62.8	67.6
	80+	109.6	73.3	60.3	47.3	43.5

* *Estimate refers to year 2005.*

Indicator	Age	1950-1955	1975-1980	2005-2010	2025-2030	2045-2050
Growth rate (percentage)	Total	0.3	1.7	0.5	0.2	0.0
	60+	2.8	5.5	2.4	1.0	0.9
	65+	3.6	6.3	2.5	1.5	1.3
	80+	12.0	8.3	2.4	3.0	0.9
Total fertility rate (per woman)		5.0	2.8	1.9	1.9	1.9
Life expectancy (years)						
Total	Birth	64.3	73.6	76.8	79.6	81.8
	60	..	..	22.1	23.3	24.7
	65	..	..	18.3	19.3	20.6
	80	..	..	8.8	9.4	10.2
Female	Birth	66.0	77.0	81.1	83.4	85.3
	60	..	..	24.4	25.9	27.3
	65	..	..	20.2	21.6	22.9
	80	..	..	9.7	10.5	11.4
Male	Birth	62.7	70.2	72.6	75.6	78.0
	60	..	..	19.6	20.2	21.7
	65	..	..	16.1	16.5	17.7
	80	..	..	7.7	7.6	8.2
Survival rate (percentage)						
Total	60	..	..	86.8	90.8	92.9
	65	..	..	82.0	86.6	89.4
	80	..	..	52.1	58.5	64.1
Female	60	..	..	92.3	94.3	95.7
	65	..	..	88.9	91.5	93.4
	80	..	..	63.6	69.5	74.4
Male	60	..	..	81.0	87.1	90.1
	65	..	..	74.5	81.3	85.3
	80	..	..	40.4	45.9	52.9

		1980	1990	2007	2010	2020
Labour force participation (percentage)						
Total	65+	8.0	8.5	7.0	6.7	6.6
Female	65+	2.2	3.4	4.9	5.2	6.0
Male	65+	14.4	14.5	9.8	8.9	7.5

Percentage married, age 60+				Percentage living alone, age 60+		
Total	Female	Male		Total	Female	Male
55.4	43.0	71.0		..	..	..

Statutory pensionable age (2006)				Percentage illiterate, age 65+		
	Female	Male		Total	Female	Male
	65	65		..	..	..

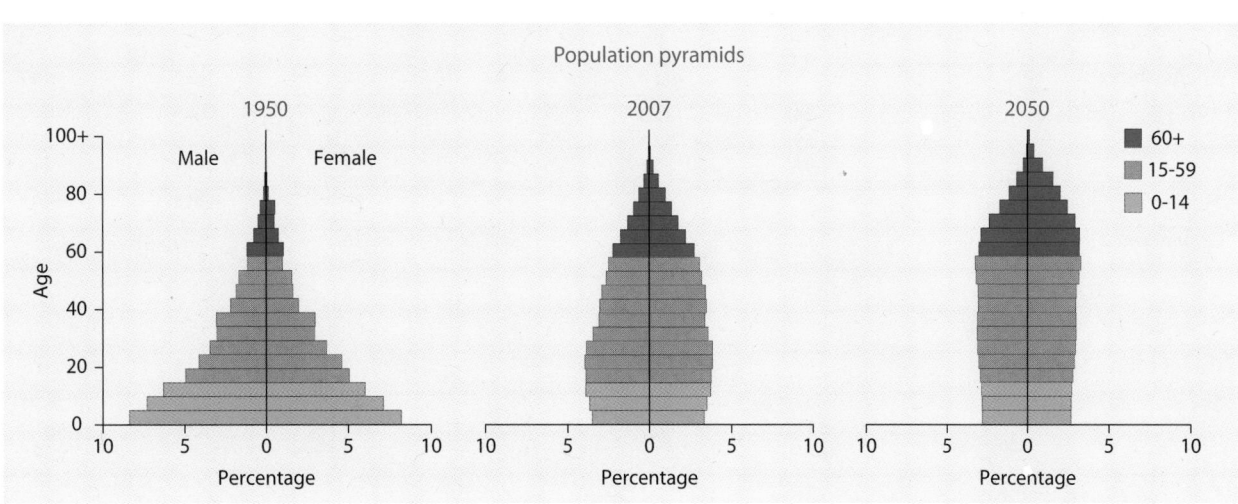

Population pyramids

Qatar

Indicator	Age	1950	1975	2007	2025	2050
Population (thousands)						
Total	Total	25.0	171.2	857.5	1 098.0	1 329.8
	0-14	10.6	57.1	186.1	211.1	219.4
	15-59	13.0	108.8	648.0	797.4	784.3
	60-64	0.6	1.8	11.4	37.0	72.9
	65-69	0.4	1.5	6.0	28.1	81.1
	70-74	0.3	0.9	3.2	14.0	78.6
	75-79	0.1	0.7	1.6	5.3	52.3
	80-84			0.7	3.3	24.5
	85-89			0.3	1.3	11.4
	90-94	0.1	0.4	0.1	0.4	4.5
	95-99			0.0	0.1	0.8
	100+			0.0	0.0	0.1
Female	Total	12.3	56.3	282.2	410.2	551.9
	0-14	5.2	27.6	91.1	103.1	107.0
	15-59	6.4	26.6	184.0	273.1	328.4
	60-64	0.3	0.6	2.9	15.1	26.4
	65-69	0.2	0.7	1.8	9.8	22.3
	70-74	0.1	0.4	1.2	4.7	23.2
	75-79	0.1	0.3	0.6	2.3	22.2
	80-84			0.3	1.2	12.9
	85-89			0.2	0.6	6.4
	90-94	0.0	0.2	0.1	0.2	2.5
	95-99			0.0	0.0	0.5
	100+			0.0	0.0	0.1
Male	Total	12.7	114.9	575.3	687.8	777.9
	0-14	5.4	29.6	95.0	108.0	112.4
	15-59	6.6	82.2	464.0	524.3	455.9
	60-64	0.3	1.2	8.5	21.9	46.5
	65-69	0.2	0.9	4.2	18.3	58.8
	70-74	0.1	0.5	2.0	9.2	55.4
	75-79	0.1	0.3	1.0	3.0	30.1
	80-84			0.4	2.1	11.6
	85-89			0.2	0.7	5.0
	90-94	0.0	0.2	0.0	0.1	2.0
	95-99			0.0	0.0	0.3
	100+			0.0	0.0	0.0
Percentage in older ages						
Total	60+	5.7	3.1	2.7	8.1	24.5
	65+	3.4	2.0	1.4	4.8	19.0
	80+	0.2	0.2	0.1	0.5	3.1
Female	60+	5.9	3.9	2.5	8.3	21.1
	65+	3.6	2.8	1.5	4.6	16.3
	80+	0.3	0.3	0.2	0.5	4.1
Male	60+	5.4	2.7	2.8	8.1	27.0
	65+	3.2	1.7	1.4	4.9	21.0
	80+	0.2	0.2	0.1	0.4	2.4
Ageing index		13.4	9.2	12.6	42.4	148.7
Broad age groups (percentage)	0-14	42.3	33.4	21.7	19.2	16.5
	15-59	52.1	63.5	75.6	72.6	59.0
	60+	5.7	3.1	2.7	8.1	24.5
Median age (years)		18.9	23.4	30.9*	36.4	40.4
Dependency ratio	Total	84.1	54.8	30.0	31.6	55.1
	Youth	77.8	51.7	28.2	25.3	25.6
	Old Age	6.3	3.1	1.8	6.3	29.6
Potential support ratio		15.8	31.8	55.0	15.9	3.4
Parent support ratio		1.0	1.0	0.5	0.9	7.5
Sex ratio (per 100 women)	60+	92.9	143.1	228.4	162.9	180.1
	65+	90.9	120.4	184.7	177.1	181.3
	80+	87.1	102.2	123.3	139.0	84.6

* *Estimate refers to year 2005.*

Qatar

Indicator	Age	1950-1955	1975-1980	2005-2010	2025-2030	2045-2050
Growth rate (percentage)	Total	6.7	5.8	1.9	1.1	0.4
	60+	3.8	−0.3	4.4	6.4	1.6
	65+	3.9	−5.9	7.6	7.0	3.6
	80+	4.9	−7.6	6.6	4.8	6.7
Total fertility rate (per woman)		7.0	6.1	2.8	2.2	1.9
Life expectancy (years)						
Total	Birth	47.9	65.0	73.7	77.1	79.6
	60	..	..	19.0	20.6	22.4
	65	..	..	15.4	16.7	18.4
	80	..	..	7.3	7.9	8.9
Female	Birth	49.3	67.6	77.1	80.3	82.6
	60	..	..	21.2	23.3	25.1
	65	..	..	17.5	19.3	20.9
	80	..	..	8.4	9.3	10.2
Male	Birth	46.7	63.5	72.2	75.4	77.9
	60	..	..	17.9	19.2	20.9
	65	..	..	14.4	15.4	17.0
	80	..	..	6.6	6.9	7.8
Survival rate (percentage)						
Total	60	..	..	85.3	90.2	92.5
	65	..	..	78.2	84.8	88.0
	80	..	..	40.0	48.6	56.6
Female	60	..	..	88.9	92.3	94.2
	65	..	..	83.2	88.0	90.9
	80	..	..	50.1	59.7	66.7
Male	60	..	..	83.8	89.1	91.5
	65	..	..	76.4	82.8	86.4
	80	..	..	35.4	42.8	51.0

		1980	1990	2007	2010	2020
Labour force participation (percentage)						
Total	65+	34.8	36.2	34.6	34.6	32.6
Female	65+	2.4	2.8	3.7	4.0	4.9
Male	65+	61.3	56.9	51.3	50.5	48.0

Percentage married, age 60+				Percentage living alone, age 60+		
Total	Female	Male		Total	Female	Male
70.4	36.0	89.0		..	..	..

Statutory pensionable age (2006)				Percentage illiterate, age 65+ (2004)		
	Female	Male		Total	Female	Male
	..	..		59.0	80.4	46.3

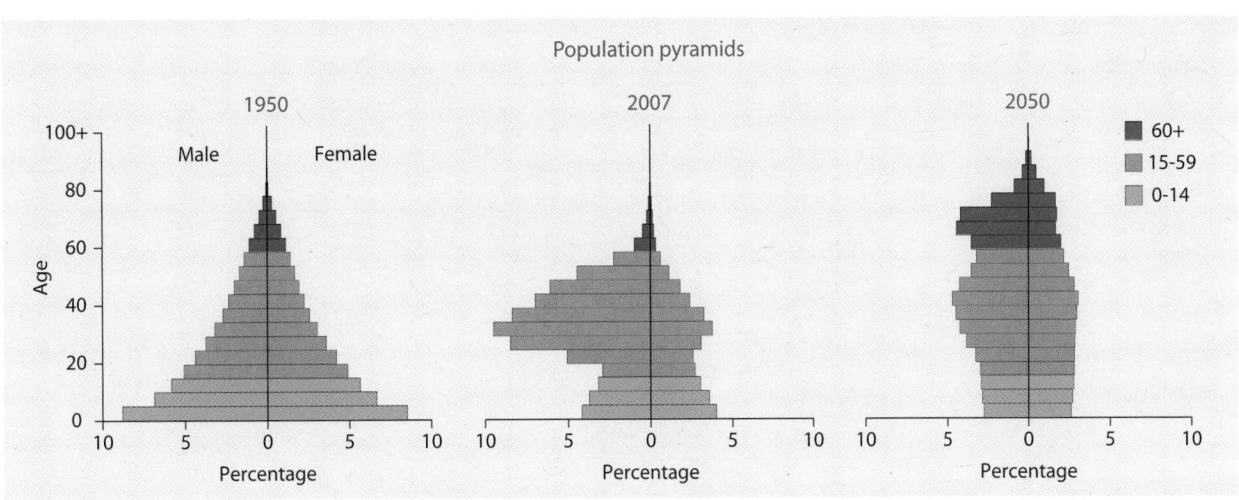

Population pyramids

United Nations Department of Economic and Social Affairs, Population Division

411

Republic of Korea

Indicator	Age	1950	1975	2007	2025	2050
Population (thousands)						
Total	Total	18 858.7	35 280.9	48 141.6	49 456.7	44 628.6
	0-14	7 856.1	13 318.1	8 426.3	6 415.5	5 354.0
	15-59	9 975.2	19 907.8	32 686.1	29 555.1	20 873.8
	60-64	453.0	781.7	2 115.7	3 810.6	2 988.3
	65-69	310.3	577.1	1 864.3	3 464.5	3 329.9
	70-74	141.6	347.1	1 425.5	2 325.4	3 157.8
	75-79	80.7	219.8	869.2	1 665.0	3 133.3
	80-84			480.0	1 150.0	2 481.6
	85-89			206.1	698.3	1 822.5
	90-94	41.8	129.3	57.0	285.4	1 051.2
	95-99			10.3	75.3	347.5
	100+			0.9	11.6	88.6
Female	Total	9 330.3	17 505.7	24 040.1	25 065.2	23 161.5
	0-14	3 854.4	6 467.2	4 024.4	3 130.1	2 612.7
	15-59	4 907.1	9 867.0	16 039.6	14 397.8	10 167.1
	60-64	233.5	415.3	1 093.2	1 961.6	1 462.6
	65-69	176.9	321.6	992.9	1 828.8	1 699.0
	70-74	83.9	206.6	813.7	1 264.4	1 663.7
	75-79	48.4	139.4	547.8	962.5	1 733.6
	80-84			325.3	722.8	1 473.8
	85-89			149.2	490.4	1 199.9
	90-94	26.1	88.6	44.8	229.2	779.2
	95-99			8.5	66.8	288.8
	100+			0.8	10.8	81.0
Male	Total	9 528.4	17 775.2	24 101.4	24 391.5	21 467.1
	0-14	4 001.7	6 850.9	4 402.0	3 285.3	2 741.2
	15-59	5 068.2	10 040.8	16 646.5	15 157.2	10 706.7
	60-64	219.6	366.4	1 022.5	1 849.1	1 525.7
	65-69	133.4	255.5	871.4	1 635.7	1 630.9
	70-74	57.6	140.5	611.7	1 061.0	1 494.1
	75-79	32.3	80.4	321.5	702.5	1 399.7
	80-84			154.8	427.2	1 007.8
	85-89			56.9	207.9	622.6
	90-94	15.7	40.7	12.3	56.2	272.0
	95-99			1.7	8.5	58.7
	100+			0.1	0.8	7.6
Percentage in older ages						
Total	60+	5.4	5.8	14.6	27.3	41.2
	65+	3.0	3.6	10.2	19.6	34.5
	80+	0.2	0.4	1.6	4.5	13.0
Female	60+	6.1	6.7	16.5	30.1	44.8
	65+	3.6	4.3	12.0	22.2	38.5
	80+	0.3	0.5	2.2	6.1	16.5
Male	60+	4.8	5.0	12.7	24.4	37.4
	65+	2.5	2.9	8.4	16.8	30.2
	80+	0.2	0.2	0.9	2.9	9.2
Ageing index		13.1	15.4	83.4	210.2	343.7
Broad age groups (percentage)	0-14	41.7	37.7	17.5	13.0	12.0
	15-59	52.9	56.4	67.9	59.8	46.8
	60+	5.4	5.8	14.6	27.3	41.2
Median age (years)		19.1	19.9	35.1*	45.6	53.9
Dependency ratio	Total	80.8	70.5	38.3	48.2	87.0
	Youth	75.3	64.4	24.2	19.2	22.4
	Old Age	5.5	6.2	14.1	29.0	64.6
Potential support ratio		18.2	16.2	7.1	3.4	1.5
Parent support ratio		0.8	1.3	3.5	9.1	36.0
Sex ratio (per 100 women)	60+	80.6	75.4	76.8	78.9	77.2
	65+	71.3	68.4	70.4	73.5	72.8
	80+	59.9	45.9	42.7	46.1	51.5

* Estimate refers to year 2005.

Indicator	Age	1950-1955	1975-1980	2005-2010	2025-2030	2045-2050
Growth rate (percentage)	Total	2.5	1.6	0.3	−0.1	−0.7
	60+	3.0	2.1	3.3	2.5	−0.1
	65+	6.3	2.6	3.9	3.5	0.5
	80+	14.6	3.2	6.3	3.7	2.2
Total fertility rate (per woman)		5.4	2.9	1.2	1.5	1.8
Life expectancy (years)						
Total	Birth	47.4	64.7	78.2	82.2	84.4
	60	..	..	21.6	24.6	26.4
	65	..	..	17.7	20.4	22.1
	80	..	..	8.1	10.0	11.1
Female	Birth	49.0	68.4	81.9	86.2	88.3
	60	..	..	24.2	27.7	29.6
	65	..	..	19.8	23.2	25.0
	80	..	..	9.0	11.5	12.8
Male	Birth	46.0	61.3	74.5	78.2	80.6
	60	..	..	18.7	21.3	23.1
	65	..	..	15.1	17.3	19.0
	80	..	..	6.6	7.8	8.8
Survival rate (percentage)						
Total	60	..	..	90.4	93.8	95.3
	65	..	..	85.6	90.4	92.6
	80	..	..	53.0	64.5	70.8
Female	60	..	..	94.4	96.6	97.4
	65	..	..	91.5	94.7	95.9
	80	..	..	65.5	76.7	81.4
Male	60	..	..	86.6	91.1	93.2
	65	..	..	79.9	86.2	89.4
	80	..	..	40.1	52.2	60.1

		1980	1990	2007	2010	2020
Labour force participation (percentage)						
Total	65+	28.6	26.3	32.7	34.2	38.9
Female	65+	16.9	18.4	26.4	28.8	36.4
Male	65+	45.2	39.3	41.7	41.9	42.3

Percentage married, age 60+				Percentage living alone, age 60+ (1988)		
Total	Female	Male		Total	Female	Male
58.3	37.0	87.0		7.7	..	..

Statutory pensionable age (2006)				Percentage illiterate, age 65+		
	Female	Male		Total	Female	Male
	60	60		..	..	..

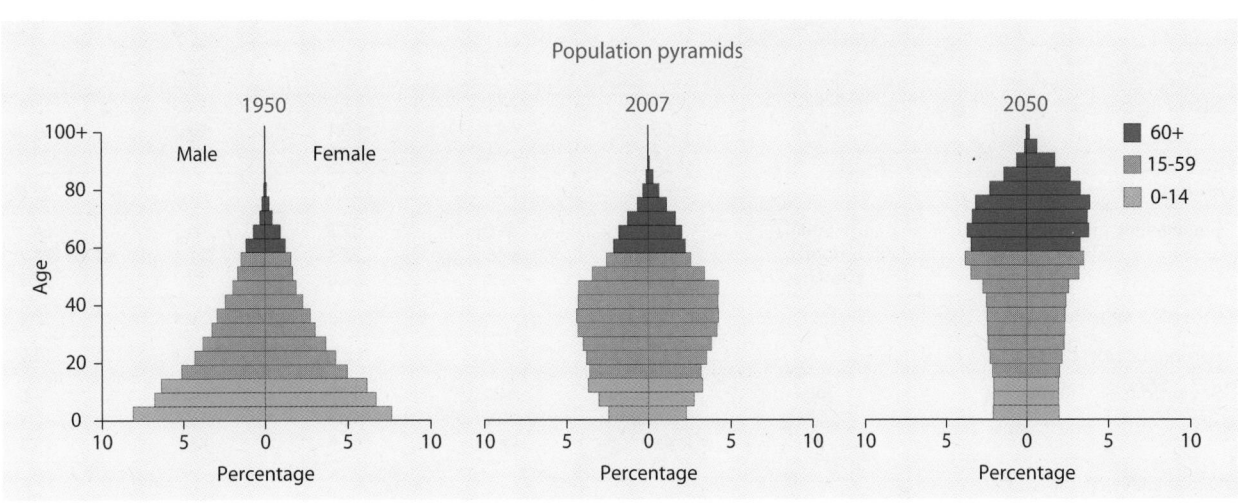

Population pyramids

Republic of Moldova

Indicator	Age	1950	1975	2007	2025	2050
Population (thousands)						
Total	Total	2 341.0	3 839.0	4 185.6	3 967.4	3 312.0
	0-14	657.4	1 108.4	712.6	589.5	447.9
	15-59	1 420.4	2 316.6	2 891.7	2 506.6	1 695.2
	60-64	82.5	152.9	155.8	246.9	318.9
	65-69	68.0	106.1	147.8	241.2	282.0
	70-74	51.8	75.8	121.1	183.6	218.2
	75-79	35.3	42.6	85.9	101.5	152.7
	80-84			49.9	53.0	92.6
	85-89			15.4	32.0	64.4
	90-94	25.6	36.6	4.5	10.2	30.8
	95-99			0.8	2.5	8.4
	100+			0.1	0.3	1.1
Female	Total	1 247.6	2 035.3	2 184.3	2 065.2	1 717.6
	0-14	323.4	547.9	347.2	286.6	217.7
	15-59	759.8	1 235.1	1 480.6	1 258.0	835.4
	60-64	48.6	89.2	88.8	138.7	165.5
	65-69	41.1	63.6	87.9	138.9	151.6
	70-74	32.9	46.8	74.5	109.9	122.1
	75-79	23.9	27.6	55.4	63.9	90.8
	80-84			34.6	35.8	58.1
	85-89			11.2	23.1	45.1
	90-94	18.0	25.1	3.4	7.9	23.5
	95-99			0.7	2.1	6.9
	100+			0.1	0.3	1.0
Male	Total	1 093.5	1 803.7	2 001.2	1 902.2	1 594.4
	0-14	334.1	560.5	365.4	302.9	230.1
	15-59	660.6	1 081.5	1 411.2	1 248.6	859.8
	60-64	33.9	63.6	67.0	108.2	153.3
	65-69	26.9	42.5	59.8	102.3	130.4
	70-74	18.9	29.0	46.6	73.7	96.1
	75-79	11.5	15.0	30.4	37.6	61.9
	80-84			15.3	17.2	34.5
	85-89			4.2	8.9	19.4
	90-94	7.6	11.5	1.1	2.3	7.4
	95-99			0.2	0.4	1.4
	100+			0.0	0.0	0.1
Percentage in older ages						
Total	60+	11.2	10.8	13.9	22.0	35.3
	65+	7.7	6.8	10.2	15.7	25.7
	80+	1.1	1.0	1.7	2.5	6.0
Female	60+	13.2	12.4	16.3	25.2	38.7
	65+	9.3	8.0	12.3	18.5	29.1
	80+	1.4	1.2	2.3	3.4	7.8
Male	60+	9.0	9.0	11.2	18.4	31.6
	65+	5.9	5.4	7.9	12.7	22.0
	80+	0.7	0.6	1.0	1.5	3.9
Ageing index		40.0	37.4	81.6	147.8	261.0
Broad age groups (percentage)	0-14	28.1	28.9	17.0	14.9	13.5
	15-59	60.7	60.3	69.1	63.2	51.2
	60+	11.2	10.8	13.9	22.0	35.3
Median age (years)		26.6	26.2	33.0*	41.0	49.6
Dependency ratio	Total	55.8	55.5	37.3	44.1	64.4
	Youth	43.7	44.9	23.4	21.4	22.2
	Old Age	12.0	10.6	14.0	22.7	42.2
Potential support ratio		8.3	9.5	7.2	4.4	2.4
Parent support ratio		3.2	2.8	3.0	6.1	13.2
Sex ratio (per 100 women)	60+	60.1	64.0	63.0	67.4	75.9
	65+	56.0	60.0	58.9	63.5	70.4
	80+	42.1	45.8	41.6	41.7	46.6

* *Estimate refers to year 2005.*

Indicator	Age	1950-1955	1975-1980	2005-2010	2025-2030	2045-2050
Growth rate (percentage)	Total	2.3	0.9	−0.2	−0.6	−0.9
	60+	−0.3	1.0	1.0	0.4	1.6
	65+	0.8	3.5	−0.1	1.7	1.9
	80+	1.1	2.0	4.6	2.8	−0.7
Total fertility rate (per woman)		3.5	2.4	1.2	1.5	1.7
Life expectancy (years)						
Total	Birth	59.0	65.2	69.6	73.7	77.1
	60	..	..	17.4	19.4	21.3
	65	..	..	14.1	15.9	17.5
	80	..	..	6.4	7.4	8.4
Female	Birth	63.0	68.5	73.1	76.8	80.0
	60	..	..	18.9	21.1	23.3
	65	..	..	15.3	17.3	19.2
	80	..	..	6.8	8.0	9.1
Male	Birth	55.0	61.6	66.0	70.4	74.1
	60	..	..	15.4	17.3	19.1
	65	..	..	12.4	14.0	15.5
	80	..	..	5.7	6.4	7.1
Survival rate (percentage)						
Total	60	..	..	78.4	84.6	89.1
	65	..	..	70.2	77.9	83.6
	80	..	..	31.4	41.6	50.6
Female	60	..	..	84.9	89.3	92.3
	65	..	..	78.3	84.2	88.4
	80	..	..	39.8	50.5	59.7
Male	60	..	..	71.6	80.0	85.9
	65	..	..	61.7	71.5	78.9
	80	..	..	22.4	31.9	41.1

		1980	1990	2007	2010	2020
Labour force participation (percentage)						
Total	65+	7.2	5.4	8.2	8.2	8.5
Female	65+	4.2	3.1	5.3	5.3	5.4
Male	65+	12.2	9.3	13.2	13.3	13.5

Percentage married, age 60+				Percentage living alone, age 60+		
Total	Female	Male		Total	Female	Male
56.0	40.0	81.0		..	..	..

Statutory pensionable age (2006)				Percentage illiterate, age 65+ (2004)		
	Female	Male		Total	Female	Male
	57	62		10.5	13.7	5.3

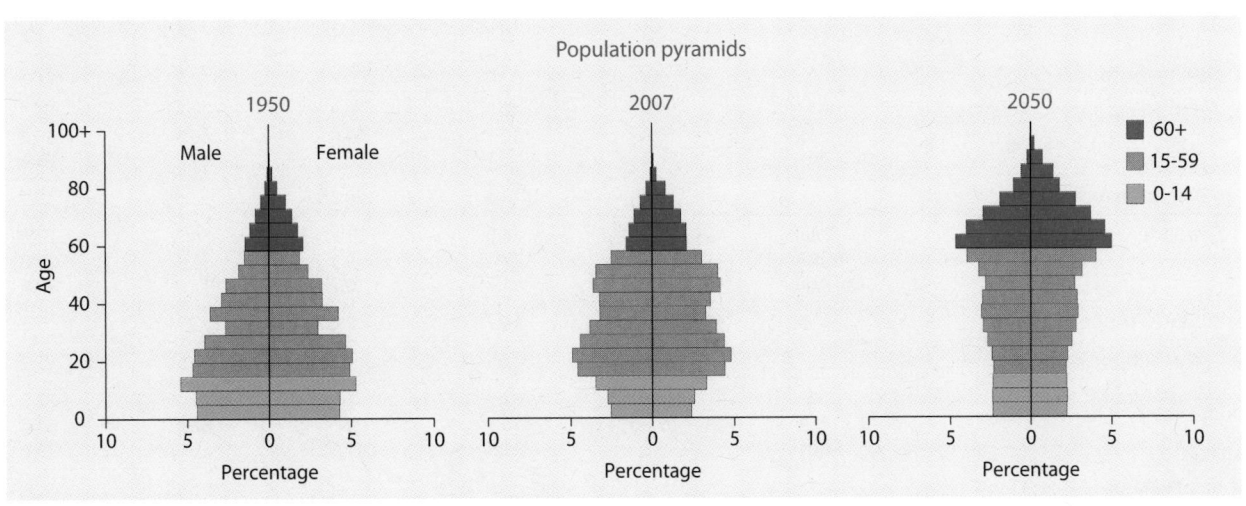

Population pyramids

Réunion

Indicator	Age	1950	1975	2007	2025	2050
Population (thousands)						
Total	Total	248.1	482.9	807.2	971.6	1 091.8
	0-14	98.4	202.0	216.4	217.3	200.2
	15-59	134.7	251.6	508.7	587.4	635.7
	60-64	5.4	10.9	25.0	57.3	61.4
	65-69	3.8	7.6	20.3	39.9	52.2
	70-74	2.9	5.0	15.0	29.9	41.9
	75-79	1.8	3.1	10.3	18.8	37.7
	80-84			6.6	11.3	31.9
	85-89			3.2	6.3	20.1
	90-94	1.2	2.9	1.2	2.5	7.8
	95-99			0.3	0.7	2.5
	100+			0.0	0.1	0.4
Female	Total	129.2	248.2	413.0	499.8	565.0
	0-14	50.1	100.9	107.3	107.8	99.3
	15-59	68.8	129.7	257.8	296.6	317.0
	60-64	3.4	5.8	13.4	29.8	31.4
	65-69	2.6	4.4	11.2	21.5	27.6
	70-74	2.1	3.1	8.8	17.4	23.6
	75-79	1.3	2.1	6.5	11.7	22.9
	80-84			4.5	7.6	20.8
	85-89			2.4	4.6	13.9
	90-94	0.8	2.2	0.9	2.0	6.0
	95-99			0.2	0.6	2.1
	100+			0.0	0.1	0.4
Male	Total	118.9	234.8	394.1	471.9	526.9
	0-14	48.3	101.1	109.1	109.5	100.9
	15-59	65.8	121.9	250.9	290.9	318.7
	60-64	2.0	5.0	11.6	27.5	30.0
	65-69	1.2	3.2	9.1	18.3	24.7
	70-74	0.8	1.9	6.2	12.5	18.4
	75-79	0.5	1.0	3.8	7.1	14.8
	80-84			2.2	3.8	11.1
	85-89			0.8	1.7	6.2
	90-94	0.3	0.7	0.3	0.5	1.8
	95-99			0.1	0.1	0.4
	100+			0.0	0.0	0.1
Percentage in older ages						
Total	60+	6.1	6.1	10.2	17.2	23.4
	65+	3.9	3.8	7.1	11.3	17.8
	80+	0.5	0.6	1.4	2.2	5.7
Female	60+	7.9	7.1	11.6	19.1	26.3
	65+	5.3	4.7	8.4	13.1	20.8
	80+	0.6	0.9	1.9	3.0	7.6
Male	60+	4.0	5.0	8.7	15.2	20.4
	65+	2.4	2.9	5.7	9.3	14.7
	80+	0.3	0.3	0.9	1.3	3.7
Ageing index		15.3	14.6	37.9	76.8	127.9
Broad age groups (percentage)	0-14	39.7	41.8	26.8	22.4	18.3
	15-59	54.3	52.1	63.0	60.5	58.2
	60+	6.1	6.1	10.2	17.2	23.4
Median age (years)		20.3	18.5	29.3*	33.6	39.2
Dependency ratio	Total	77.2	84.0	51.2	50.7	56.6
	Youth	70.3	77.0	40.5	33.7	28.7
	Old Age	6.9	7.1	10.7	17.0	27.9
Potential support ratio		14.5	14.2	9.4	5.9	3.6
Parent support ratio		2.3	2.6	4.7	5.5	15.9
Sex ratio (per 100 women)	60+	46.8	67.3	71.1	75.0	72.2
	65+	41.6	58.1	65.1	67.2	66.0
	80+	40.6	31.5	41.8	41.0	45.2

* Estimate refers to year 2005.

Indicator	Age	1950-1955	1975-1980	2005-2010	2025-2030	2045-2050
Growth rate (percentage)	Total	3.2	0.9	1.3	0.7	0.2
	60+	1.6	2.8	3.2	3.3	1.2
	65+	1.6	3.6	3.0	4.7	1.0
	80+	−0.3	3.0	3.7	3.8	3.3
Total fertility rate (per woman)		5.7	3.3	2.4	2.0	1.9
Life expectancy (years)						
Total	Birth	52.7	67.0	76.1	78.4	80.2
	60	..	..	20.6	21.8	23.1
	65	..	..	17.0	17.9	19.1
	80	..	..	8.3	8.7	9.4
Female	Birth	55.6	71.3	80.1	81.9	83.5
	60	..	..	23.4	24.7	25.8
	65	..	..	19.3	20.4	21.5
	80	..	..	9.1	9.8	10.4
Male	Birth	49.7	62.9	72.0	74.6	76.7
	60	..	..	17.5	18.5	20.1
	65	..	..	14.2	15.0	16.3
	80	..	..	6.8	7.0	7.6
Survival rate (percentage)						
Total	60	..	..	87.4	90.7	92.3
	65	..	..	81.4	85.5	87.9
	80	..	..	47.0	52.8	58.5
Female	60	..	..	91.9	93.5	94.7
	65	..	..	88.1	90.3	92.0
	80	..	..	60.4	65.4	69.8
Male	60	..	..	82.8	87.6	89.9
	65	..	..	74.5	80.4	83.9
	80	..	..	33.1	39.3	46.3

	Age	1980	1990	2007	2010	2020
Labour force participation (percentage)						
Total	65+	1.2	1.0	0.8	0.7	0.7
Female	65+	1.0	0.6	0.4	0.3	0.3
Male	65+	1.6	1.6	1.4	1.4	1.4

Percentage married, age 60+			Percentage living alone, age 60+ (1982)		
Total	Female	Male	Total	Female	Male
52.4	37.0	74.0	14.8	18.3	10.0

Statutory pensionable age (2006)			Percentage illiterate, age 65+		
	Female	Male	Total	Female	Male
	..	..	..	..	..

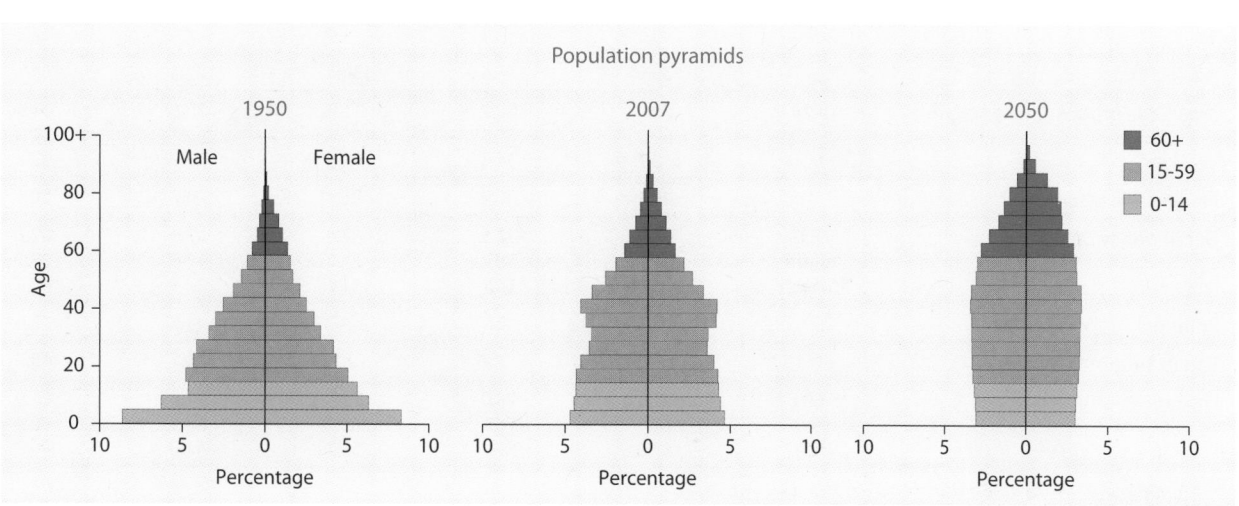

Population pyramids

1950   2007   2050

■ 60+
■ 15-59
■ 0-14

Romania

Indicator	Age	1950	1975	2007	2025	2050
Population (thousands)						
Total	Total	16 311.0	21 245.1	21 544.2	19 858.4	16 757.4
	0-14	4 634.0	5 360.8	3 223.3	2 675.3	2 242.5
	15-59	10 261.0	12 853.9	14 122.2	12 441.8	8 218.8
	60-64	547.0	990.8	1 004.6	1 042.0	1 485.7
	65-69	313.0	832.8	1 007.2	1 207.9	1 287.3
	70-74	296.0	606.3	937.7	1 058.0	1 319.8
	75-79	166.4	352.1	679.1	702.4	988.3
	80-84			403.6	388.9	724.0
	85-89			122.1	244.8	289.2
	90-94	93.5	248.3	37.0	81.1	154.3
	95-99			7.0	15.1	42.1
	100+			0.5	1.3	5.1
Female	Total	8 444.0	10 785.0	11 054.7	10 242.9	8 698.4
	0-14	2 300.0	2 616.4	1 570.3	1 301.8	1 088.8
	15-59	5 318.0	6 466.3	7 058.5	6 182.0	4 030.9
	60-64	312.0	544.1	544.2	555.1	763.8
	65-69	181.0	453.7	566.4	669.8	680.3
	70-74	173.3	337.8	543.8	612.4	726.8
	75-79	100.1	209.2	405.2	426.9	579.2
	80-84			253.8	251.7	459.5
	85-89			82.0	169.9	204.3
	90-94	59.5	157.5	25.3	60.2	122.6
	95-99			4.8	11.9	37.0
	100+			0.3	1.1	4.8
Male	Total	7 867.0	10 460.1	10 489.5	9 615.5	8 059.1
	0-14	2 334.0	2 744.4	1 653.0	1 373.5	1 153.7
	15-59	4 943.0	6 387.6	7 063.7	6 259.7	4 187.9
	60-64	235.0	446.7	460.4	486.8	721.9
	65-69	132.0	379.1	440.8	538.1	607.0
	70-74	122.7	268.6	393.9	445.5	593.0
	75-79	66.3	142.9	273.9	275.5	409.1
	80-84			149.8	137.2	264.5
	85-89			40.1	74.9	84.9
	90-94	34.0	90.9	11.6	21.0	31.7
	95-99			2.2	3.1	5.1
	100+			0.2	0.2	0.3
Percentage in older ages						
Total	60+	8.7	14.3	19.5	23.9	37.6
	65+	5.3	9.6	14.8	18.6	28.7
	80+	0.6	1.2	2.6	3.7	7.2
Female	60+	9.8	15.8	21.9	26.9	41.1
	65+	6.1	10.7	17.0	21.5	32.4
	80+	0.7	1.5	3.3	4.8	9.5
Male	60+	7.5	12.7	16.9	20.6	33.7
	65+	4.5	8.4	12.5	15.6	24.8
	80+	0.4	0.9	1.9	2.5	4.8
Ageing index		30.6	56.5	130.3	177.2	280.8
Broad age groups (percentage)	0-14	28.4	25.2	15.0	13.5	13.4
	15-59	62.9	60.5	65.6	62.7	49.0
	60+	8.7	14.3	19.5	23.9	37.6
Median age (years)		26.1	30.8	36.7*	44.2	50.1
Dependency ratio	Total	50.9	53.5	42.4	47.3	72.7
	Youth	42.9	38.7	21.3	19.8	23.1
	Old Age	8.0	14.7	21.1	27.4	49.6
Potential support ratio		12.4	6.8	4.7	3.6	2.0
Parent support ratio		1.6	2.7	4.3	8.1	13.7
Sex ratio (per 100 women)	60+	71.4	78.0	73.1	71.8	75.9
	65+	69.1	76.1	69.7	67.9	70.9
	80+	57.2	57.7	55.7	47.8	46.7

* Estimate refers to year 2005.

Indicator	Age	1950-1955	1975-1980	2005-2010	2025-2030	2045-2050
Growth rate (percentage)	Total	1.4	0.9	−0.4	−0.6	−0.8
	60+	3.9	−0.6	0.5	1.6	0.8
	65+	5.1	2.2	−0.4	−0.3	0.6
	80+	3.8	3.2	4.1	1.8	3.8
Total fertility rate (per woman)		2.9	2.5	1.3	1.5	1.8
Life expectancy (years)						
Total	Birth	61.2	69.5	72.1	75.4	78.4
	60	..	..	18.5	20.0	21.6
	65	..	..	14.9	16.2	17.7
	80	..	..	6.5	7.2	8.2
Female	Birth	62.8	72.0	75.7	78.6	81.3
	60	..	..	20.1	22.0	23.9
	65	..	..	16.1	17.8	19.7
	80	..	..	6.8	7.9	9.1
Male	Birth	59.4	67.0	68.7	72.2	75.4
	60	..	..	16.6	17.7	19.1
	65	..	..	13.4	14.2	15.4
	80	..	..	6.0	6.2	6.7
Survival rate (percentage)						
Total	60	..	..	82.4	87.4	91.2
	65	..	..	75.6	81.6	86.4
	80	..	..	37.4	45.4	53.5
Female	60	..	..	88.9	91.7	93.8
	65	..	..	84.0	87.7	90.7
	80	..	..	46.9	55.7	63.8
Male	60	..	..	76.2	83.3	88.6
	65	..	..	67.4	75.5	82.2
	80	..	..	28.1	34.8	42.9

		1980	1990	2007	2010	2020
Labour force participation (percentage)						
Total	65+	5.0	15.3	31.3	31.0	30.8
Female	65+	4.7	12.0	30.5	30.6	30.7
Male	65+	5.5	19.9	32.5	31.7	31.0

Percentage married, age 60+			Percentage living alone, age 60+ (1992)		
Total	Female	Male	Total	Female	Male
66.3	50.0	88.0	20.3	27.7	10.6

Statutory pensionable age (2006)			Percentage illiterate, age 65+ (2002)		
	Female	Male	Total	Female	Male
	60	65	8.1	11.6	3.1

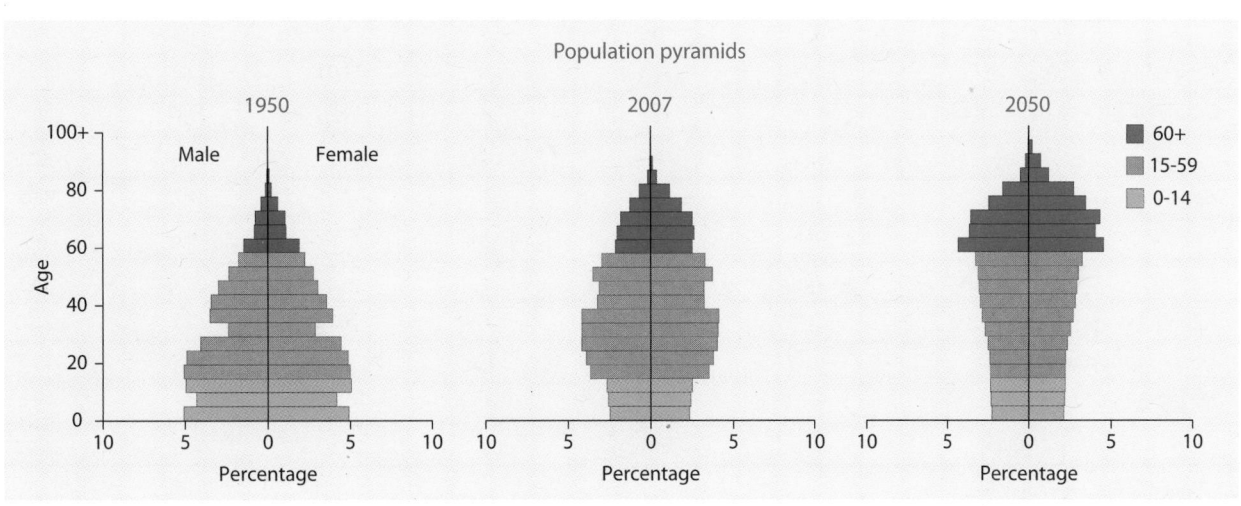

Population pyramids

Russian Federation

Indicator	Age	1950	1975	2007	2025	2050
Population (thousands)						
Total	Total	102 702.5	134 232.5	141 900.4	129 230.4	111 752.2
	0-14	29 689.2	31 280.2	21 293.0	20 448.1	18 538.0
	15-59	63 573.4	84 699.7	96 325.2	77 370.4	58 459.6
	60-64	3 086.3	6 369.3	5 230.9	8 681.1	9 007.5
	65-69	2 421.9	4 886.8	6 243.7	8 419.2	8 224.9
	70-74	1 781.9	3 428.4	5 241.6	6 450.8	6 254.3
	75-79	1 183.1	1 904.1	4 014.7	4 000.1	4 679.7
	80-84			2 342.7	1 649.0	3 046.4
	85-89			781.2	1 573.5	2 153.6
	90-94	966.6	1 664.0	335.0	471.0	1 053.7
	95-99			83.0	151.0	293.4
	100+			9.4	16.3	41.1
Female	Total	58 624.4	72 870.5	76 180.3	70 102.0	59 849.4
	0-14	14 608.8	15 368.7	10 384.3	9 954.6	9 010.8
	15-59	37 409.0	44 565.2	49 758.8	39 929.1	29 085.7
	60-64	2 027.6	4 245.6	3 092.2	5 082.0	4 971.8
	65-69	1 657.6	3 401.3	3 902.4	5 184.5	4 797.2
	70-74	1 272.3	2 550.1	3 448.5	4 212.3	3 901.7
	75-79	884.4	1 442.7	2 799.1	2 768.8	3 107.9
	80-84			1 803.7	1 225.0	2 171.4
	85-89			639.9	1 227.9	1 653.0
	90-94	764.6	1 296.8	275.9	379.7	861.8
	95-99			68.1	124.4	252.0
	100+			7.4	13.7	36.0
Male	Total	44 078.1	61 362.0	65 720.1	59 128.4	51 902.8
	0-14	15 080.4	15 911.4	10 908.7	10 493.5	9 527.2
	15-59	26 164.4	40 134.4	46 566.5	37 441.3	29 373.9
	60-64	1 058.6	2 123.7	2 138.7	3 599.0	4 035.6
	65-69	764.3	1 485.6	2 341.3	3 234.7	3 427.7
	70-74	509.6	878.3	1 793.1	2 238.5	2 352.6
	75-79	298.7	461.4	1 215.6	1 231.2	1 571.8
	80-84			539.0	424.0	875.0
	85-89			141.3	345.6	500.6
	90-94	202.1	367.3	59.1	91.3	191.9
	95-99			14.8	26.6	41.4
	100+			2.0	2.6	5.1
Percentage in older ages						
Total	60+	9.2	13.6	17.1	24.3	31.1
	65+	6.2	8.9	13.4	17.6	23.0
	80+	0.9	1.2	2.5	3.0	5.9
Female	60+	11.3	17.8	21.1	28.8	36.3
	65+	7.8	11.9	17.0	21.6	28.0
	80+	1.3	1.8	3.7	4.2	8.3
Male	60+	6.4	8.7	12.5	18.9	25.1
	65+	4.0	5.2	9.3	12.8	17.3
	80+	0.5	0.6	1.2	1.5	3.1
Ageing index		31.8	58.4	114.0	153.6	187.5
Broad age groups (percentage)	0-14	28.9	23.3	15.0	15.8	16.6
	15-59	61.9	63.1	67.9	59.9	52.3
	60+	9.2	13.6	17.1	24.3	31.1
Median age (years)		25.0	30.8	37.3*	41.7	43.5
Dependency ratio	Total	54.1	47.4	39.7	50.2	65.6
	Youth	44.5	34.3	21.0	23.8	27.5
	Old Age	9.5	13.0	18.8	26.4	38.2
Potential support ratio		10.5	7.7	5.3	3.8	2.6
Parent support ratio		3.6	3.6	4.8	8.8	16.5
Sex ratio (per 100 women)	60+	42.9	41.1	51.4	55.4	59.8
	65+	38.8	36.7	47.2	50.2	53.4
	80+	26.4	28.3	27.1	30.0	32.4

* Estimate refers to year 2005.

Indicator	Age	1950-1955	1975-1980	2005-2010	2025-2030	2045-2050
Growth rate (percentage)	Total	1.6	0.6	−0.4	−0.6	−0.6
	60+	1.5	0.5	0.4	−0.1	0.8
	65+	2.1	3.5	−2.3	1.2	1.1
	80+	2.1	2.6	5.1	2.8	−1.2
Total fertility rate (per woman)		2.9	1.9	1.4	1.6	1.9
Life expectancy (years)						
Total	Birth	64.5	69.0	65.0	69.2	72.9
	60	..	..	16.9	18.7	20.2
	65	..	..	13.9	15.4	16.7
	80	..	..	6.8	7.5	8.2
Female	Birth	67.3	74.1	71.8	73.9	76.5
	60	..	..	19.2	21.1	22.7
	65	..	..	15.5	17.2	18.6
	80	..	..	7.1	8.0	8.8
Male	Birth	60.5	62.7	58.7	64.3	68.9
	60	..	..	13.9	15.5	17.0
	65	..	..	11.4	12.7	13.9
	80	..	..	5.9	6.3	6.7
Survival rate (percentage)						
Total	60	..	..	67.4	74.5	80.6
	65	..	..	59.4	67.4	74.4
	80	..	..	25.7	34.2	41.9
Female	60	..	..	81.5	82.7	85.6
	65	..	..	75.5	77.9	81.6
	80	..	..	39.0	46.5	53.4
Male	60	..	..	54.4	66.0	75.6
	65	..	..	44.5	56.5	66.9
	80	..	..	13.5	20.9	29.0

		1980	1990	2007	2010	2020
Labour force participation (percentage)						
Total	65+	6.6	7.8	5.2	4.8	3.6
Female	65+	3.4	5.9	3.9	3.7	3.1
Male	65+	15.1	13.2	8.1	7.1	4.7

Percentage married, age 60+				Percentage living alone, age 60+ (1989)		
Total	Female	Male		Total	Female	Male
64.7	53.0	87.0		24.8	31.3	10.1

Statutory pensionable age (2006)				Percentage illiterate, age 65+ (2002)		
	Female	Male		Total	Female	Male
	55	60		2.4	3.1	0.9

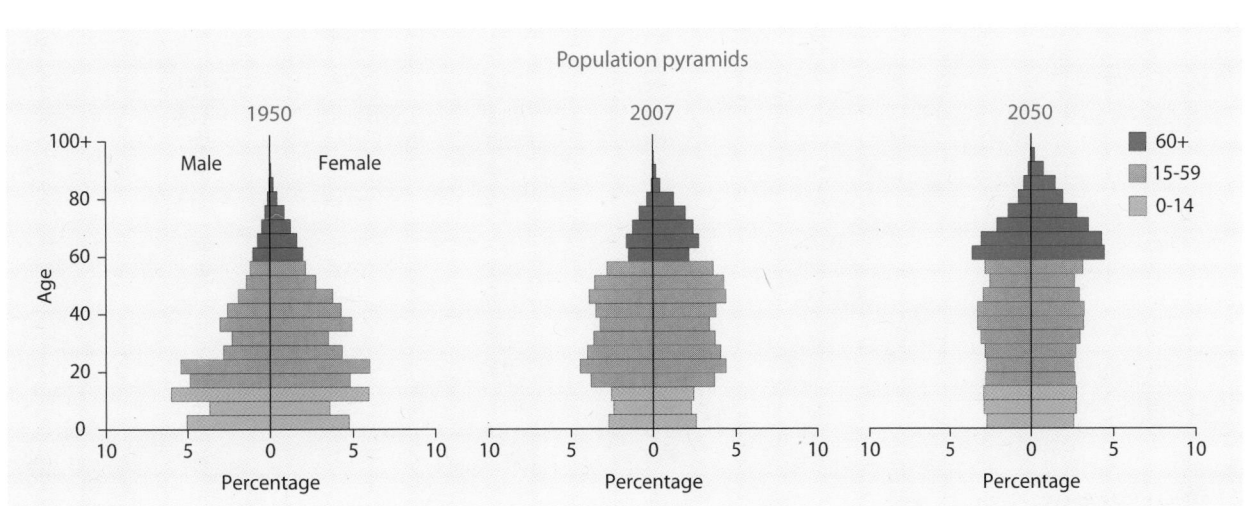

Population pyramids

Rwanda

Indicator	Age	1950	1975	2007	2025	2050
Population (thousands)						
Total	Total	2 162.3	4 410.0	9 441.8	13 373.8	18 153.1
	0-14	1 002.5	2 138.9	4 039.6	5 016.1	5 128.4
	15-59	1 077.3	2 104.8	5 026.2	7 722.0	11 298.6
	60-64	33.4	65.9	140.0	233.2	676.0
	65-69	23.3	46.5	103.2	175.1	475.2
	70-74	14.4	29.5	68.7	112.8	288.6
	75-79	7.5	15.9	39.0	67.4	160.7
	80-84			17.5	32.5	81.9
	85-89			5.8	11.6	33.2
	90-94	3.9	8.5	1.4	2.7	9.0
	95-99			0.2	0.4	1.4
	100+			0.0	0.0	0.1
Female	Total	1 093.4	2 232.2	4 861.3	6 844.8	9 254.4
	0-14	502.3	1 073.5	2 035.3	2 534.8	2 580.5
	15-59	546.1	1 068.2	2 615.6	3 948.7	5 738.2
	60-64	17.8	35.0	76.3	129.3	352.3
	65-69	12.6	25.1	56.8	99.1	252.5
	70-74	8.0	16.3	38.5	65.0	159.3
	75-79	4.3	9.0	22.7	39.2	94.5
	80-84			11.0	19.4	49.7
	85-89			4.0	7.1	20.6
	90-94	2.4	5.1	1.0	1.8	5.8
	95-99			0.2	0.3	1.0
	100+			0.0	0.0	0.1
Male	Total	1 068.9	2 177.9	4 580.4	6 529.0	8 898.7
	0-14	500.2	1 065.4	2 004.3	2 481.2	2 547.9
	15-59	531.2	1 036.6	2 410.6	3 773.3	5 560.4
	60-64	15.6	30.9	63.7	103.9	323.7
	65-69	10.7	21.4	46.4	75.9	222.7
	70-74	6.5	13.3	30.3	47.8	129.3
	75-79	3.2	6.9	16.2	28.2	66.2
	80-84			6.5	13.2	32.2
	85-89			1.8	4.4	12.7
	90-94	1.6	3.4	0.4	0.9	3.1
	95-99			0.1	0.1	0.4
	100+			0.0	0.0	0.0
Percentage in older ages						
Total	60+	3.8	3.8	4.0	4.8	9.5
	65+	2.3	2.3	2.5	3.0	5.8
	80+	0.2	0.2	0.3	0.4	0.7
Female	60+	4.1	4.1	4.3	5.3	10.1
	65+	2.5	2.5	2.8	3.4	6.3
	80+	0.2	0.2	0.3	0.4	0.8
Male	60+	3.5	3.5	3.6	4.2	8.9
	65+	2.0	2.1	2.2	2.6	5.2
	80+	0.1	0.2	0.2	0.3	0.5
Ageing index		8.2	7.8	9.3	12.7	33.7
Broad age groups (percentage)	0-14	46.4	48.5	42.8	37.5	28.3
	15-59	49.8	47.7	53.2	57.7	62.2
	60+	3.8	3.8	4.0	4.8	9.5
Median age (years)		16.7	15.7	17.5*	20.7	27.4
Dependency ratio	Total	94.7	103.2	82.8	68.1	51.6
	Youth	90.3	98.5	78.2	63.1	42.8
	Old Age	4.4	4.6	4.6	5.1	8.8
Potential support ratio		22.6	21.6	21.9	19.8	11.4
Parent support ratio		0.7	0.8	1.4	1.7	2.0
Sex ratio (per 100 women)	60+	83.3	83.9	78.6	76.0	84.5
	65+	80.5	81.1	75.8	73.5	80.0
	80+	65.3	66.8	54.1	64.9	62.8

* *Estimate refers to year 2005.*

Indicator	Age	1950-1955	1975-1980	2005-2010	2025-2030	2045-2050
Growth rate (percentage)	Total	2.8	3.3	2.3	1.4	1.0
	60+	2.7	2.9	2.7	2.9	5.0
	65+	2.7	3.0	2.9	3.3	5.3
	80+	2.3	3.4	3.4	3.6	3.6
Total fertility rate (per woman)		7.8	8.5	5.2	3.2	2.4
Life expectancy (years)						
Total	Birth	40.0	44.8	44.6	52.1	59.5
	60	..	..	15.4	16.5	17.8
	65	..	..	12.3	13.3	14.4
	80	..	..	5.6	6.0	6.5
Female	Birth	41.6	46.4	46.0	53.7	61.1
	60	..	..	16.0	17.1	18.5
	65	..	..	12.8	13.8	14.9
	80	..	..	5.8	6.2	6.7
Male	Birth	38.4	43.2	43.1	50.5	57.9
	60	..	..	14.7	15.7	17.0
	65	..	..	11.8	12.6	13.7
	80	..	..	5.3	5.7	6.2
Survival rate (percentage)						
Total	60	..	..	39.7	49.9	60.4
	65	..	..	34.4	44.2	54.7
	80	..	..	12.2	17.8	25.3
Female	60	..	..	42.0	52.1	62.6
	65	..	..	36.9	46.8	57.5
	80	..	..	13.9	20.1	28.2
Male	60	..	..	37.3	47.5	58.2
	65	..	..	31.8	41.4	52.0
	80	..	..	10.3	15.3	22.3

		1980	1990	2007	2010	2020
Labour force participation (percentage)						
Total	65+	55.0	57.7	47.7	47.4	47.3
Female	65+	50.7	54.3	37.5	37.1	37.1
Male	65+	60.2	62.0	61.2	61.0	60.9

Percentage married, age 60+			Percentage living alone, age 60+ (2000)		
Total	Female	Male	Total	Female	Male
61.7	44.0	85.0	6.5	8.1	4.4

Statutory pensionable age (2006)			Percentage illiterate, age 65+ (2000)		
	Female	Male	Total	Female	Male
	55	55	79.6	94.1	65.4

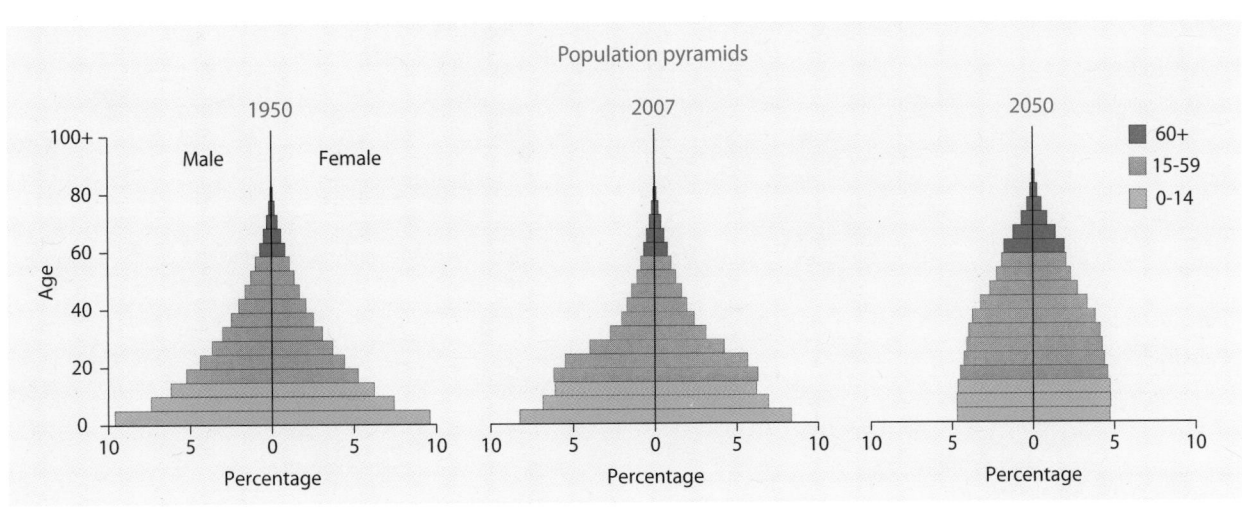

Population pyramids

Saint Lucia

Indicator	Age	1950	1975	2007	2025	2050
Population (thousands)						
Total	Total	82.8	109.9	163.4	183.8	188.4
	0-14	32.4	51.2	45.0	42.2	33.8
	15-59	45.6	50.5	102.5	115.8	108.1
	60-64	1.6	2.8	4.3	8.8	12.3
	65-69	1.1	2.1	3.6	6.4	11.3
	70-74	0.9	1.5	3.0	4.5	8.1
	75-79	0.5	1.1	2.0	2.9	6.4
	80-84			1.6	1.7	4.5
	85-89			0.9	1.0	2.6
	90-94	0.7	0.7	0.3	0.4	1.0
	95-99			0.1	0.1	0.3
	100+			0.0	0.0	0.0
Female	Total	42.0	56.7	82.9	92.7	95.0
	0-14	15.7	25.1	22.2	20.8	16.6
	15-59	23.3	26.9	51.9	57.9	53.1
	60-64	1.0	1.5	2.2	4.6	6.2
	65-69	0.7	1.2	2.0	3.5	5.9
	70-74	0.6	0.9	1.6	2.4	4.3
	75-79	0.3	0.7	1.1	1.6	3.6
	80-84			0.9	1.0	2.6
	85-89			0.6	0.7	1.7
	90-94	0.5	0.4	0.2	0.2	0.7
	95-99			0.1	0.1	0.2
	100+			0.0	0.0	0.0
Male	Total	40.8	53.2	80.6	91.1	93.4
	0-14	16.7	26.1	22.8	21.4	17.1
	15-59	22.3	23.6	50.6	57.9	55.1
	60-64	0.6	1.3	2.1	4.2	6.1
	65-69	0.4	1.0	1.6	2.9	5.4
	70-74	0.3	0.6	1.4	2.1	3.8
	75-79	0.2	0.4	0.9	1.3	2.8
	80-84			0.7	0.7	1.8
	85-89			0.3	0.3	1.0
	90-94	0.2	0.2	0.1	0.1	0.3
	95-99			0.0	0.0	0.1
	100+			0.0	0.0	0.0
Percentage in older ages						
Total	60+	5.8	7.4	9.7	14.0	24.7
	65+	3.8	4.9	7.1	9.3	18.2
	80+	0.8	0.6	1.8	1.8	4.5
Female	60+	7.3	8.3	10.6	15.1	26.6
	65+	4.9	5.6	7.9	10.2	20.1
	80+	1.1	0.8	2.2	2.2	5.5
Male	60+	4.2	6.5	8.9	12.9	22.7
	65+	2.8	4.2	6.3	8.3	16.2
	80+	0.5	0.4	1.4	1.3	3.4
Ageing index		14.8	15.9	35.4	61.1	137.7
Broad age groups (percentage)	0-14	39.1	46.6	27.5	23.0	17.9
	15-59	55.1	45.9	62.7	63.0	57.4
	60+	5.8	7.4	9.7	14.0	24.7
Median age (years)		20.7	16.5	25.6*	32.8	40.3
Dependency ratio	Total	75.4	106.3	53.0	47.6	56.5
	Youth	68.6	96.2	42.1	33.9	28.0
	Old Age	6.7	10.1	10.9	13.7	28.4
Potential support ratio		14.9	9.9	9.2	7.3	3.5
Parent support ratio		4.2	2.3	8.1	5.2	10.6
Sex ratio (per 100 women)	60+	56.5	74.2	82.1	83.6	83.9
	65+	55.6	70.2	78.1	79.4	79.1
	80+	46.0	51.7	63.4	60.5	60.6

* *Estimate refers to year 2005.*

Indicator	Age	1950-1955	1975-1980	2005-2010	2025-2030	2045-2050
Growth rate (percentage)	Total	0.9	1.4	0.8	0.3	−0.1
	60+	−2.9	2.2	1.2	2.8	2.0
	65+	−1.5	2.2	0.5	4.0	2.7
	80+	−0.9	1.8	−1.1	2.5	3.1
Total fertility rate (per woman)		6.0	5.2	2.2	1.9	1.9
Life expectancy (years)						
Total	Birth	54.1	68.0	73.1	75.8	78.7
	60	..	..	19.3	20.4	22.1
	65	..	..	16.0	16.8	18.2
	80	..	..	7.7	8.0	8.7
Female	Birth	55.3	71.0	74.6	77.2	80.3
	60	..	..	20.6	21.7	23.6
	65	..	..	17.1	18.0	19.6
	80	..	..	8.3	8.6	9.4
Male	Birth	52.7	64.8	71.6	74.3	77.0
	60	..	..	18.0	18.9	20.5
	65	..	..	14.8	15.4	16.7
	80	..	..	7.0	7.1	7.7
Survival rate (percentage)						
Total	60	..	..	83.4	87.8	91.1
	65	..	..	75.8	81.3	86.0
	80	..	..	40.4	46.5	54.8
Female	60	..	..	85.1	88.8	92.1
	65	..	..	78.5	83.3	87.9
	80	..	..	45.6	52.0	60.6
Male	60	..	..	81.7	86.7	90.1
	65	..	..	73.1	79.2	84.1
	80	..	..	35.2	40.8	48.5

		1980	1990	2007	2010	2020
Labour force participation (percentage)						
Total	65+	24.4	23.2	20.7	20.8	21.1
Female	65+	6.3	11.2	7.0	6.9	6.9
Male	65+	48.1	38.7	38.3	38.4	38.6

Percentage married, age 60+			Percentage living alone, age 60+ (1980)		
Total	Female	Male	Total	Female	Male
50.9	40.0	64.0	17.8	16.7	19.4

Statutory pensionable age (2006)			Percentage illiterate, age 65+		
	Female	Male	Total	Female	Male
	61	61	..	..	..

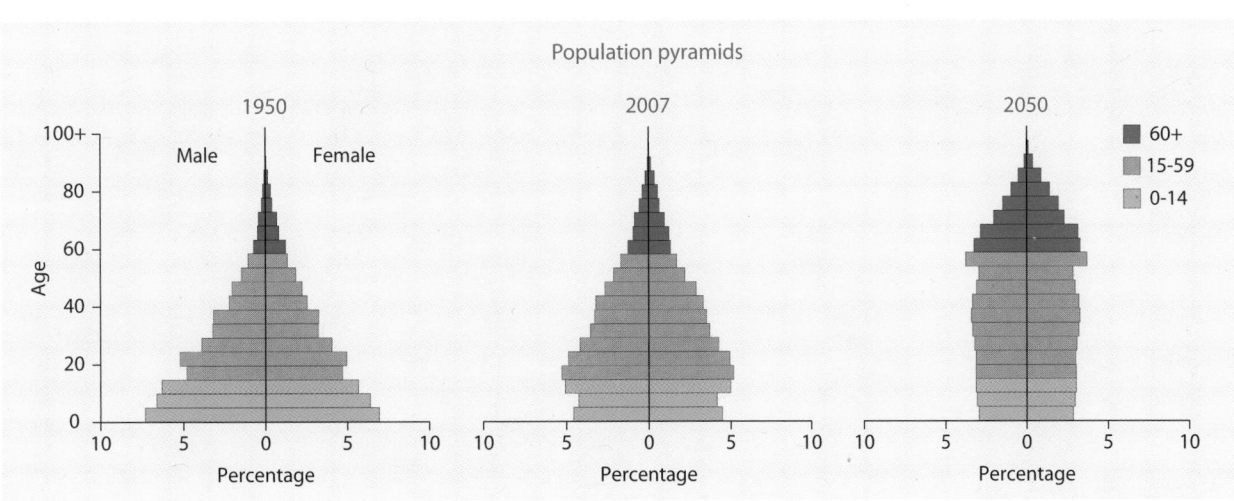

Population pyramids

Saint Vincent and the Grenadines

Indicator	Age	1950	1975	2007	2025	2050
Population (thousands)						
Total	Total	67.0	95.6	120.3	124.8	105.4
	0-14	33.1	45.4	34.0	28.4	17.7
	15-59	29.9	42.4	75.3	78.4	54.2
	60-64	1.5	2.7	3.1	6.8	8.6
	65-69	0.9	2.2	2.6	4.3	8.2
	70-74	0.8	1.5	2.2	2.7	6.8
	75-79	0.5	0.9	1.7	2.2	4.7
	80-84			0.9	1.1	3.0
	85-89			0.3	0.5	1.7
	90-94	0.3	0.5	0.1	0.2	0.4
	95-99			0.0	0.0	0.1
	100+			0.0	0.0	0.0
Female	Total	35.5	50.0	60.4	62.9	54.2
	0-14	16.3	22.4	16.9	14.1	8.7
	15-59	16.5	22.9	37.4	39.2	27.1
	60-64	0.9	1.5	1.6	3.4	4.4
	65-69	0.6	1.3	1.5	2.2	4.3
	70-74	0.5	0.9	1.2	1.5	3.7
	75-79	0.4	0.6	1.0	1.3	2.6
	80-84			0.6	0.7	1.8
	85-89			0.2	0.4	1.1
	90-94	0.2	0.4	0.1	0.1	0.3
	95-99			0.0	0.0	0.1
	100+			0.0	0.0	0.0
Male	Total	31.5	45.6	59.9	61.9	51.2
	0-14	16.8	23.0	17.1	14.4	9.0
	15-59	13.4	19.4	38.0	39.2	27.0
	60-64	0.5	1.1	1.4	3.4	4.2
	65-69	0.3	1.0	1.2	2.1	3.9
	70-74	0.3	0.6	1.0	1.2	3.2
	75-79	0.2	0.3	0.7	0.9	2.1
	80-84			0.3	0.4	1.2
	85-89			0.1	0.2	0.6
	90-94	0.1	0.1	0.0	0.0	0.1
	95-99			0.0	0.0	0.0
	100+			0.0	0.0	0.0
Percentage in older ages						
Total	60+	6.0	8.2	9.1	14.4	31.9
	65+	3.9	5.4	6.6	8.9	23.7
	80+	0.5	0.6	1.2	1.5	5.0
Female	60+	7.5	9.3	10.2	15.3	33.9
	65+	4.9	6.2	7.5	9.9	25.7
	80+	0.7	0.8	1.5	1.9	6.2
Male	60+	4.4	7.0	8.0	13.4	29.7
	65+	2.7	4.5	5.6	7.9	21.5
	80+	0.4	0.3	0.8	1.1	3.6
Ageing index		12.2	17.3	32.1	63.0	189.8
Broad age groups (percentage)	0-14	49.3	47.5	28.3	22.8	16.8
	15-59	44.6	44.3	62.6	62.8	51.4
	60+	6.0	8.2	9.1	14.4	31.9
Median age (years)		15.4	16.0	24.6*	34.0	44.8
Dependency ratio	Total	113.7	112.3	53.5	46.4	67.9
	Youth	105.5	100.8	43.4	33.4	28.2
	Old Age	8.3	11.5	10.1	13.0	39.8
Potential support ratio		12.1	8.7	9.9	7.7	2.5
Parent support ratio		2.1	2.3	4.4	3.5	10.2
Sex ratio (per 100 women)	60+	51.5	69.1	78.1	86.7	82.8
	65+	49.8	66.7	74.0	78.7	79.0
	80+	47.6	38.6	56.1	54.7	55.7

* Estimate refers to year 2005.

Indicator	Age	1950-1955	1975-1980	2005-2010	2025-2030	2045-2050
Growth rate (percentage)	Total	1.9	1.0	0.5	−0.3	−1.2
	60+	1.6	0.8	1.6	3.3	1.6
	65+	2.1	2.0	0.7	5.4	2.2
	80+	1.6	6.0	3.0	3.5	3.0
Total fertility rate (per woman)		7.3	4.4	2.2	1.9	1.9
Life expectancy (years)						
Total	Birth	51.1	64.6	72.0	75.1	77.4
	60	..	..	18.2	19.5	20.7
	65	..	..	14.5	15.7	16.8
	80	..	..	6.1	6.9	7.5
Female	Birth	52.2	65.9	74.8	77.7	80.0
	60	..	..	19.4	21.2	22.8
	65	..	..	15.4	17.2	18.6
	80	..	..	6.4	7.5	8.4
Male	Birth	49.8	63.0	69.3	72.5	75.0
	60	..	..	16.8	17.8	18.7
	65	..	..	13.4	14.1	14.9
	80	..	..	5.7	6.0	6.2
Survival rate (percentage)						
Total	60	..	..	84.1	88.3	91.2
	65	..	..	77.4	82.5	86.3
	80	..	..	36.8	44.2	50.4
Female	60	..	..	88.2	91.3	93.1
	65	..	..	82.9	87.0	89.5
	80	..	..	43.6	52.8	59.7
Male	60	..	..	80.1	85.6	89.4
	65	..	..	72.2	78.4	83.1
	80	..	..	30.0	35.8	41.3

		1980	1990	2007	2010	2020
Labour force participation (percentage)						
Total	65+	19.5	17.6	14.0	13.3	10.9
Female	65+	6.0	8.3	7.0	7.0	6.9
Male	65+	38.3	30.5	23.4	21.7	16.2

Percentage married, age 60+				Percentage living alone, age 60+		
Total	Female	Male		Total	Female	Male
41.4	30.0	56.0		..	..	..

Statutory pensionable age (2006)				Percentage illiterate, age 65+		
	Female	Male		Total	Female	Male
	60	60		..	..	..

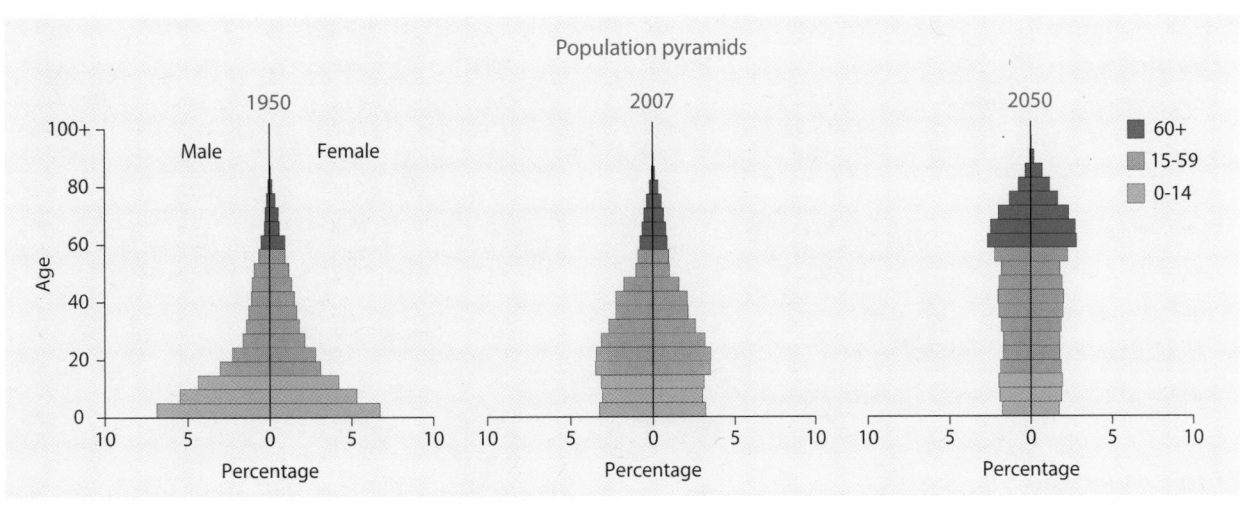

Population pyramids

Samoa

Indicator	Age	1950	1975	2007	2025	2050
Population (thousands)						
Total	Total	82.1	150.4	187.0	189.8	156.7
	0-14	38.5	68.1	75.0	54.3	30.7
	15-59	40.4	77.5	99.7	114.5	94.1
	60-64	1.4	2.0	3.6	8.0	8.1
	65-69	0.8	1.3	3.1	5.3	5.6
	70-74	0.5	0.8	2.3	3.3	5.4
	75-79	0.3	0.4	1.6	2.0	5.6
	80-84			1.1	1.3	4.0
	85-89			0.4	0.7	2.2
	90-94	0.3	0.2	0.1	0.3	0.8
	95-99			0.0	0.1	0.2
	100+			0.0	0.0	0.0
Female	Total	39.8	74.0	89.7	91.1	75.9
	0-14	18.1	33.3	36.0	26.0	14.6
	15-59	20.1	38.0	47.1	54.6	45.0
	60-64	0.7	1.1	1.8	3.7	3.8
	65-69	0.3	0.7	1.6	2.5	2.5
	70-74	0.2	0.4	1.2	1.7	2.7
	75-79	0.1	0.3	0.9	1.1	2.9
	80-84			0.7	0.8	2.2
	85-89			0.3	0.5	1.4
	90-94	0.1	0.2	0.1	0.2	0.5
	95-99			0.0	0.1	0.2
	100+			0.0	0.0	0.0
Male	Total	42.3	76.4	97.3	98.7	80.8
	0-14	20.4	34.7	39.0	28.3	16.1
	15-59	20.2	39.5	52.6	59.9	49.1
	60-64	0.7	1.0	1.8	4.3	4.3
	65-69	0.4	0.6	1.5	2.9	3.1
	70-74	0.3	0.3	1.1	1.6	2.7
	75-79	0.2	0.1	0.7	0.9	2.7
	80-84			0.4	0.5	1.8
	85-89			0.1	0.2	0.8
	90-94	0.2	0.1	0.0	0.1	0.2
	95-99			0.0	0.0	0.0
	100+			0.0	0.0	0.0
Percentage in older ages						
Total	60+	4.0	3.2	6.6	11.1	20.4
	65+	2.3	1.8	4.6	6.9	15.2
	80+	0.4	0.2	0.9	1.3	4.6
Female	60+	3.9	3.6	7.3	11.6	21.5
	65+	2.1	2.1	5.3	7.5	16.4
	80+	0.3	0.2	1.2	1.7	5.7
Male	60+	4.0	2.8	5.8	10.6	19.3
	65+	2.5	1.5	4.0	6.3	14.0
	80+	0.4	0.1	0.6	0.8	3.5
Ageing index		8.4	7.0	16.3	38.7	103.8
Broad age groups (percentage)	0-14	46.9	45.3	40.1	28.6	19.6
	15-59	49.2	51.5	53.3	60.3	60.0
	60+	4.0	3.2	6.6	11.1	20.4
Median age (years)		16.6	16.9	19.4*	25.8	39.5
Dependency ratio	Total	96.7	89.0	81.0	55.0	53.3
	Youth	92.2	85.6	72.6	44.4	30.1
	Old Age	4.5	3.5	8.4	10.7	23.3
Potential support ratio		22.2	29.0	11.9	9.4	4.3
Parent support ratio		1.9	1.1	4.0	4.0	10.1
Sex ratio (per 100 women)	60+	111.0	81.2	86.0	99.7	95.6
	65+	124.3	73.7	80.6	91.7	90.5
	80+	115.6	47.9	55.4	52.3	65.4

* *Estimate refers to year 2005.*

Indicator	Age	1950-1955	1975-1980	2005-2010	2025-2030	2045-2050
Growth rate (percentage)	Total	2.7	0.6	0.4	−0.1	−1.5
	60+	−2.0	2.7	1.0	3.8	1.0
	65+	1.1	3.8	1.1	5.0	−0.3
	80+	−4.6	5.2	3.0	1.7	4.2
Total fertility rate (per woman)		7.3	4.9	3.9	2.7	2.1
Life expectancy (years)						
Total	Birth	45.9	58.7	71.5	75.5	78.4
	60	..	..	18.0	19.9	21.6
	65	..	..	14.7	16.3	17.8
	80	..	..	7.1	7.9	8.6
Female	Birth	49.6	62.1	74.8	78.7	81.4
	60	..	..	20.4	22.6	24.4
	65	..	..	16.6	18.6	20.2
	80	..	..	7.8	8.9	9.8
Male	Birth	43.0	55.5	68.5	72.9	75.8
	60	..	..	15.8	17.6	19.3
	65	..	..	12.7	14.2	15.7
	80	..	..	6.1	6.7	7.3
Survival rate (percentage)						
Total	60	..	..	82.2	88.0	91.4
	65	..	..	74.3	81.5	86.1
	80	..	..	35.1	44.6	52.8
Female	60	..	..	86.5	90.8	93.2
	65	..	..	80.7	86.4	89.7
	80	..	..	46.2	56.5	64.0
Male	60	..	..	78.5	85.7	89.7
	65	..	..	68.6	77.4	83.0
	80	..	..	25.7	35.1	43.6

		1980	1990	2007	2010	2020
Labour force participation (percentage)						
Total	65+	28.6	15.5	12.6	12.4	12.4
Female	65+	10.5	1.5	1.4	1.4	1.7
Male	65+	52.9	30.4	26.4	26.1	25.0

Percentage married, age 60+				Percentage living alone, age 60+		
Total	Female	Male		Total	Female	Male
62.4	46.0	81.0		..	..	..

Statutory pensionable age (2006)				Percentage illiterate, age 65+		
	Female	Male		Total	Female	Male
	55	55		..	..	..

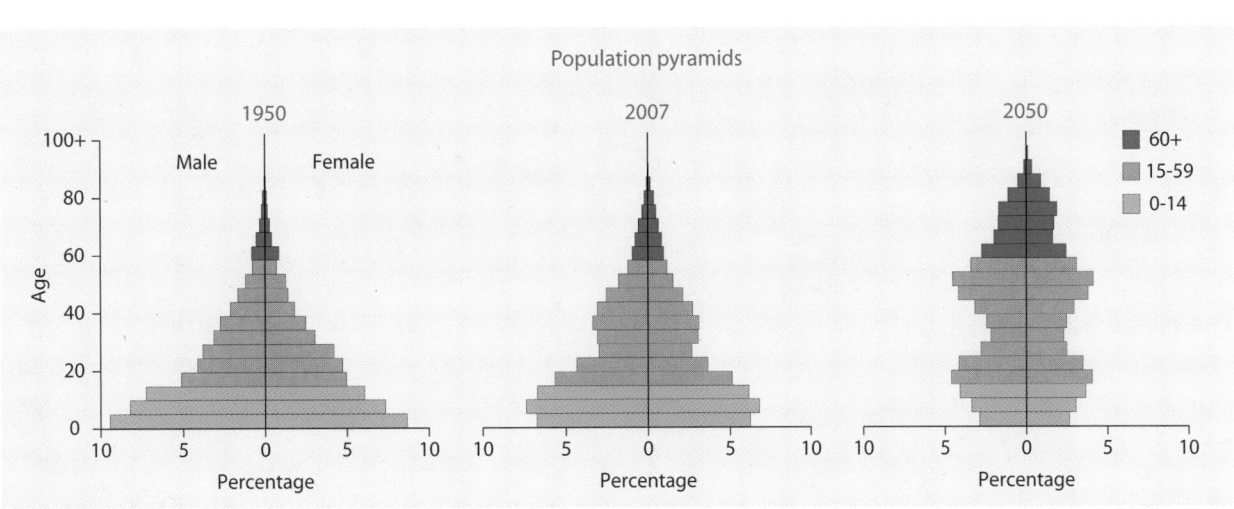

Population pyramids

Sao Tome and Principe

Indicator	Age	1950	1975	2007	2025	2050
Population (thousands)						
Total	Total	60.2	82.1	163.7	225.1	295.3
	0-14	19.8	38.6	63.8	69.3	66.1
	15-59	36.8	38.6	91.0	142.2	182.9
	60-64	3.5	1.8	2.2	5.1	14.2
	65-69	0.1	1.4	2.4	3.5	14.0
	70-74	0.1	0.9	2.1	2.5	9.7
	75-79	0.0	0.5	1.3	1.4	4.9
	80-84			0.7	0.7	2.4
	85-89			0.2	0.4	0.9
	90-94	0.0	0.3	0.0	0.1	0.2
	95-99			0.0	0.0	0.0
	100+			0.0	0.0	0.0
Female	Total	26.8	40.8	82.4	112.9	148.4
	0-14	9.8	18.7	31.4	34.2	32.6
	15-59	15.0	19.4	46.1	70.8	90.9
	60-64	1.9	0.9	1.2	2.8	7.3
	65-69	0.0	0.7	1.3	2.0	7.4
	70-74	0.0	0.5	1.1	1.5	5.3
	75-79	0.0	0.3	0.7	0.8	2.7
	80-84			0.4	0.4	1.5
	85-89			0.1	0.2	0.6
	90-94	0.0	0.2	0.0	0.0	0.1
	95-99			0.0	0.0	0.0
	100+			0.0	0.0	0.0
Male	Total	33.4	41.3	81.3	112.2	146.8
	0-14	10.0	20.0	32.4	35.1	33.4
	15-59	21.7	19.2	44.9	71.4	91.9
	60-64	1.6	0.9	0.9	2.3	6.9
	65-69	0.1	0.7	1.1	1.4	6.7
	70-74	0.0	0.3	1.0	1.0	4.4
	75-79	0.0	0.2	0.6	0.5	2.2
	80-84			0.3	0.3	1.0
	85-89			0.1	0.1	0.3
	90-94	0.0	0.1	0.0	0.0	0.0
	95-99			0.0	0.0	0.0
	100+			0.0	0.0	0.0
Percentage in older ages						
Total	60+	6.1	6.0	5.4	6.0	15.7
	65+	0.3	3.8	4.1	3.8	10.9
	80+	0.0	0.4	0.6	0.5	1.2
Female	60+	7.5	6.7	5.9	7.0	16.7
	65+	0.4	4.4	4.4	4.5	11.8
	80+	0.1	0.5	0.6	0.6	1.5
Male	60+	5.0	5.4	4.9	5.1	14.7
	65+	0.3	3.3	3.8	3.0	10.0
	80+	0.0	0.3	0.5	0.4	0.9
Ageing index		18.6	12.8	13.9	19.6	70.2
Broad age groups (percentage)	0-14	32.8	47.0	39.0	30.8	22.4
	15-59	61.1	46.9	55.6	63.2	61.9
	60+	6.1	6.0	5.4	6.0	15.7
Median age (years)		24.6	16.3	19.6*	24.6	33.6
Dependency ratio	Total	49.6	103.6	75.6	52.7	49.9
	Youth	49.1	95.8	68.4	47.0	33.5
	Old Age	0.5	7.8	7.2	5.7	16.3
Potential support ratio		196.3	12.8	14.0	17.4	6.1
Parent support ratio		0.1	1.3	2.5	2.1	2.3
Sex ratio (per 100 women)	60+	83.6	81.4	82.3	72.2	86.6
	65+	84.7	75.0	84.4	66.6	83.4
	80+	42.9	55.1	76.3	61.6	62.0

* *Estimate refers to year 2005.*

Indicator	Age	1950-1955	1975-1980	2005-2010	2025-2030	2045-2050
Growth rate (percentage)	Total	−0.4	2.8	2.2	1.4	0.7
	60+	−0.2	5.9	0.1	4.2	3.6
	65+	2.9	7.4	−0.6	4.8	6.1
	80+	4.5	18.1	3.0	1.2	4.8
Total fertility rate (per woman)		6.2	6.5	3.6	2.5	2.1
Life expectancy (years)						
Total	Birth	46.4	58.5	64.0	69.2	73.2
	60	..	..	17.5	18.9	20.0
	65	..	..	13.8	15.0	16.0
	80	..	..	5.4	5.8	6.3
Female	Birth	48.0	60.0	65.1	70.8	75.1
	60	..	..	18.2	19.7	21.2
	65	..	..	14.4	15.6	16.9
	80	..	..	5.7	6.1	6.6
Male	Birth	43.6	57.0	62.8	67.5	71.3
	60	..	..	16.7	17.7	18.8
	65	..	..	13.2	14.1	15.0
	80	..	..	5.1	5.5	5.9
Survival rate (percentage)						
Total	60	..	..	73.8	80.9	86.3
	65	..	..	67.8	75.7	81.9
	80	..	..	29.9	38.5	46.2
Female	60	..	..	75.7	83.4	88.8
	65	..	..	70.5	79.2	85.5
	80	..	..	33.3	43.2	52.4
Male	60	..	..	71.5	78.4	83.8
	65	..	..	64.6	72.1	78.2
	80	..	..	26.3	33.1	39.9

		1980	1990	2007	2010	2020
Labour force participation (percentage)						
Total	65+	32.0	24.6	20.7	20.1	18.6
Female	65+	10.2	10.1	4.0	3.9	3.8
Male	65+	60.8	41.5	40.4	40.3	40.1

Percentage married, age 60+				Percentage living alone, age 60+		
Total	Female	Male		Total	Female	Male
39.9	29.0	52.0		..	..	..

Statutory pensionable age (2006)				Percentage illiterate, age 65+		
	Female	Male		Total	Female	Male
	57	62		..	..	..

Population pyramids

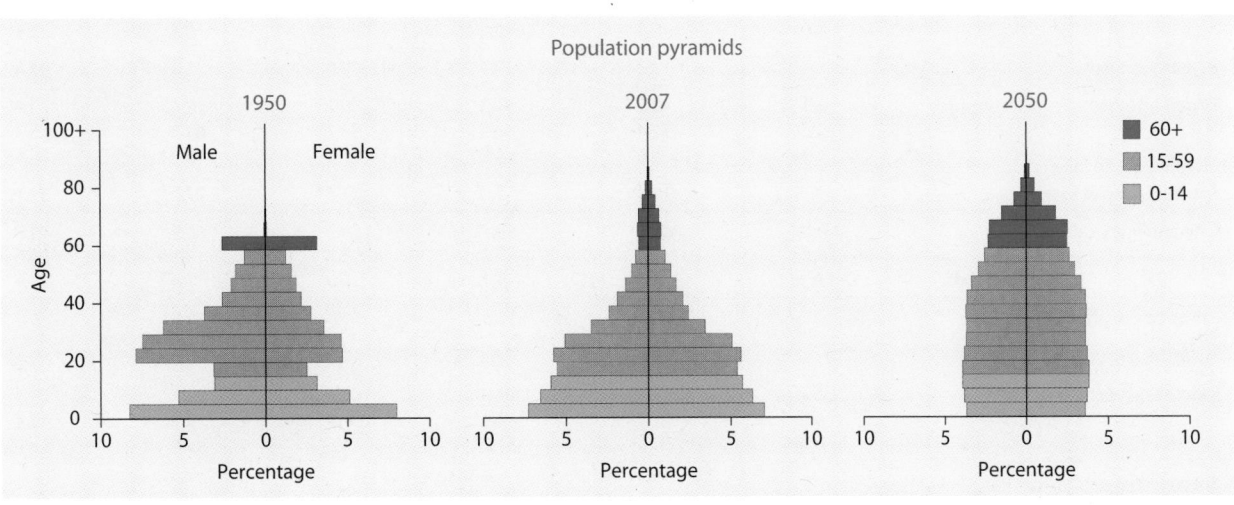

Saudi Arabia

Indicator	Age	1950	1975	2007	2025	2050
Population (thousands)						
Total	Total	3 201.4	7 251.4	25 809.2	37 159.9	49 463.9
	0-14	1 344.9	3 211.5	9 351.7	10 632.3	9 833.8
	15-59	1 677.0	3 689.6	15 252.5	23 538.4	31 523.8
	60-64	72.6	132.4	415.6	1 154.8	2 407.7
	65-69	52.1	96.3	346.3	795.5	1 873.5
	70-74	32.4	65.7	218.6	501.5	1 547.6
	75-79	15.9	37.2	127.1	285.1	1 113.3
	80-84			69.0	167.2	714.0
	85-89			23.0	68.0	331.2
	90-94	6.5	18.7	4.8	14.6	98.8
	95-99			0.6	2.4	18.2
	100+			0.0	0.2	2.0
Female	Total	1 576.6	3 443.7	11 924.4	17 629.5	24 070.4
	0-14	661.4	1 574.0	4 583.3	5 198.3	4 798.7
	15-59	822.4	1 688.1	6 765.1	11 064.4	15 152.0
	60-64	37.0	66.8	196.2	517.1	1 193.7
	65-69	26.9	49.8	164.1	343.5	940.5
	70-74	17.0	34.6	99.7	217.5	799.0
	75-79	8.4	20.0	61.7	144.1	548.5
	80-84			37.6	93.5	362.3
	85-89			13.3	40.0	195.5
	90-94	3.5	10.4	2.9	9.2	64.7
	95-99			0.4	1.8	13.7
	100+			0.0	0.1	1.8
Male	Total	1 624.8	3 807.7	13 884.8	19 530.4	25 393.6
	0-14	683.5	1 637.5	4 768.4	5 434.0	5 035.1
	15-59	854.6	2 001.5	8 487.4	12 474.0	16 371.9
	60-64	35.6	65.6	219.3	637.7	1 214.0
	65-69	25.1	46.5	182.2	452.0	933.0
	70-74	15.4	31.1	119.0	284.0	748.7
	75-79	7.5	17.2	65.4	141.1	564.8
	80-84			31.4	73.7	351.7
	85-89			9.7	27.9	135.7
	90-94	3.0	8.3	1.8	5.4	34.1
	95-99			0.2	0.6	4.4
	100+			0.0	0.0	0.2
Percentage in older ages						
Total	60+	5.6	4.8	4.7	8.0	16.4
	65+	3.3	3.0	3.1	4.9	11.5
	80+	0.2	0.3	0.4	0.7	2.4
Female	60+	5.9	5.3	4.8	7.8	17.1
	65+	3.5	3.3	3.2	4.8	12.2
	80+	0.2	0.3	0.5	0.8	2.7
Male	60+	5.3	4.4	4.5	8.3	15.7
	65+	3.1	2.7	3.0	5.0	10.9
	80+	0.2	0.2	0.3	0.6	2.1
Ageing index		13.3	10.9	12.9	28.1	82.4
Broad age groups (percentage)	0-14	42.0	44.3	36.2	28.6	19.9
	15-59	52.4	50.9	59.1	63.3	63.7
	60+	5.6	4.8	4.7	8.0	16.4
Median age (years)		19.0	17.9	21.6*	27.2	35.1
Dependency ratio	Total	83.0	89.7	64.7	50.5	45.8
	Youth	76.9	84.0	59.7	43.1	29.0
	Old Age	6.1	5.7	5.0	7.4	16.8
Potential support ratio		16.4	17.5	19.8	13.5	6.0
Parent support ratio		0.6	0.9	1.7	2.0	5.4
Sex ratio (per 100 women)	60+	93.5	92.9	109.2	118.7	96.8
	65+	91.7	89.8	107.9	115.9	94.8
	80+	86.6	79.8	79.5	74.4	82.4

* *Estimate refers to year 2005.*

Indicator	Age	1950-1955	1975-1980	2005-2010	2025-2030	2045-2050
Growth rate (percentage)	Total	2.3	5.6	2.4	1.5	0.8
	60+	2.2	3.6	3.7	5.4	3.3
	65+	2.4	4.1	4.5	6.0	3.1
	80+	3.4	6.2	4.5	4.0	6.1
Total fertility rate (per woman)		7.2	7.3	3.6	2.3	1.9
Life expectancy (years)						
Total	Birth	39.9	58.7	72.9	76.4	79.2
	60	..	..	18.3	20.0	22.0
	65	..	..	14.6	16.1	17.9
	80	..	..	6.2	7.1	8.1
Female	Birth	40.7	59.9	75.1	78.9	81.6
	60	..	..	19.5	22.1	24.0
	65	..	..	15.6	17.9	19.8
	80	..	..	6.4	7.9	9.2
Male	Birth	39.1	57.6	71.1	74.6	77.1
	60	..	..	17.3	18.5	20.2
	65	..	..	13.8	14.7	16.3
	80	..	..	5.9	6.2	7.1
Survival rate (percentage)						
Total	60	..	..	85.5	90.3	92.7
	65	..	..	79.1	84.9	88.6
	80	..	..	38.0	47.0	56.0
Female	60	..	..	88.7	92.2	94.1
	65	..	..	83.5	88.3	91.1
	80	..	..	44.5	56.4	64.4
Male	60	..	..	83.3	88.8	91.4
	65	..	..	75.7	82.3	86.2
	80	..	..	33.2	40.3	48.8

		1980	1990	2007	2010	2020
Labour force participation (percentage)						
Total	65+	18.4	15.9	17.4	17.2	17.9
Female	65+	0.9	0.8	1.0	1.1	1.8
Male	65+	37.9	32.4	32.6	32.5	32.2

Percentage married, age 60+			Percentage living alone, age 60+		
Total	Female	Male	Total	Female	Male
..	..	..	..	..	..

Statutory pensionable age (2006)			Percentage illiterate, age 65+ (2000)		
	Female	Male	Total	Female	Male
	55	60	79.3	94.5	68.1

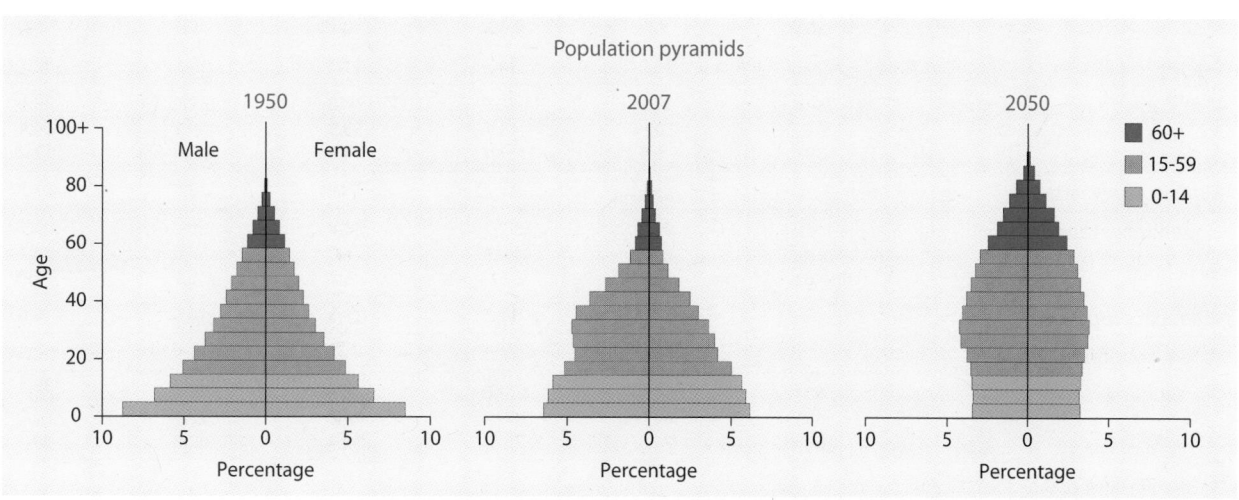

Population pyramids

Senegal

Indicator	Age	1950	1975	2007	2025	2050
Population (thousands)						
Total	Total	2 749.7	5 262.2	12 217.7	17 347.9	23 108.2
	0-14	1 143.6	2 361.0	5 109.1	5 899.1	5 410.8
	15-59	1 454.8	2 563.7	6 508.2	10 418.7	14 871.9
	60-64	56.6	104.8	215.3	377.8	991.3
	65-69	43.2	82.5	158.2	264.2	751.6
	70-74	28.7	59.2	110.8	182.6	513.6
	75-79	15.3	50.4	69.3	117.8	314.5
	80-84			32.5	60.0	169.1
	85-89			11.2	21.5	66.4
	90-94	7.5	40.7	2.6	5.4	16.4
	95-99			0.4	0.8	2.5
	100+			0.0	0.1	0.2
Female	Total	1 374.1	2 677.2	6 205.1	8 782.7	11 733.6
	0-14	564.6	1 184.4	2 529.1	2 923.9	2 685.7
	15-59	728.4	1 331.8	3 336.5	5 272.3	7 521.7
	60-64	29.9	49.5	123.2	207.5	518.7
	65-69	23.3	38.8	89.5	148.8	400.6
	70-74	15.3	28.1	62.4	105.7	280.2
	75-79	8.4	24.3	38.5	71.0	175.6
	80-84			17.8	36.3	98.5
	85-89			6.3	13.2	40.3
	90-94	4.3	20.4	1.5	3.5	10.5
	95-99			0.2	0.5	1.7
	100+			0.0	0.0	0.2
Male	Total	1 375.6	2 585.0	6 012.6	8 565.2	11 374.6
	0-14	579.0	1 176.6	2 580.0	2 975.2	2 725.1
	15-59	726.5	1 231.9	3 171.7	5 146.4	7 350.2
	60-64	26.7	55.3	92.1	170.3	472.6
	65-69	19.9	43.7	68.7	115.4	351.0
	70-74	13.4	31.0	48.4	76.9	233.4
	75-79	6.9	26.2	30.8	46.9	138.9
	80-84			14.7	23.6	70.6
	85-89			4.9	8.3	26.2
	90-94	3.2	20.4	1.1	2.0	5.9
	95-99			0.1	0.3	0.8
	100+			0.0	0.0	0.1
Percentage in older ages						
Total	60+	5.5	6.4	4.9	5.9	12.2
	65+	3.4	4.4	3.2	3.8	7.9
	80+	0.3	0.8	0.4	0.5	1.1
Female	60+	5.9	6.0	5.5	6.7	13.0
	65+	3.7	4.2	3.5	4.3	8.6
	80+	0.3	0.8	0.4	0.6	1.3
Male	60+	5.1	6.8	4.3	5.2	11.4
	65+	3.2	4.7	2.8	3.2	7.3
	80+	0.2	0.8	0.3	0.4	0.9
Ageing index		13.2	14.3	11.8	17.5	52.2
Broad age groups (percentage)	0-14	41.6	44.9	41.8	34.0	23.4
	15-59	52.9	48.7	53.3	60.1	64.4
	60+	5.5	6.4	4.9	5.9	12.2
Median age (years)		19.2	17.7	18.2*	22.8	31.3
Dependency ratio	Total	81.9	97.2	81.7	60.7	45.7
	Youth	75.7	88.5	76.0	54.6	34.1
	Old Age	6.3	8.7	5.7	6.0	11.6
Potential support ratio		16.0	11.5	17.5	16.6	8.6
Parent support ratio		0.8	2.5	1.8	1.9	2.5
Sex ratio (per 100 women)	60+	86.5	109.6	76.8	75.6	85.1
	65+	84.8	108.7	78.0	72.1	82.0
	80+	75.8	100.0	80.3	63.8	68.5

*   *Estimate refers to year 2005.*

Indicator	Age	1950-1955	1975-1980	2005-2010	2025-2030	2045-2050
Growth rate (percentage)	Total	2.3	2.5	2.3	1.5	0.8
	60+	1.0	−0.5	2.8	3.8	4.2
	65+	1.0	−1.1	2.9	3.9	4.5
	80+	1.5	−1.8	3.9	3.7	4.9
Total fertility rate (per woman)		6.7	7.0	4.5	2.7	1.9
Life expectancy (years)						
Total	Birth	34.4	44.3	57.1	63.1	70.6
	60	..	..	16.6	17.7	19.2
	65	..	..	13.2	14.2	15.4
	80	..	..	5.8	6.2	6.7
Female	Birth	35.4	45.3	58.4	64.9	72.8
	60	..	..	17.1	18.3	19.9
	65	..	..	13.6	14.6	16.0
	80	..	..	6.0	6.4	6.9
Male	Birth	33.4	43.2	55.8	61.3	68.3
	60	..	..	16.0	17.0	18.4
	65	..	..	12.8	13.6	14.8
	80	..	..	5.5	5.9	6.4
Survival rate (percentage)						
Total	60	..	..	61.0	69.6	80.7
	65	..	..	54.4	63.3	75.0
	80	..	..	22.0	28.8	39.1
Female	60	..	..	63.2	72.6	84.2
	65	..	..	57.0	66.7	79.1
	80	..	..	24.3	32.0	43.5
Male	60	..	..	58.6	66.7	77.3
	65	..	..	51.6	59.9	71.0
	80	..	..	19.6	25.4	34.6

		1980	1990	2007	2010	2020
Labour force participation (percentage)						
Total	65+	45.1	45.0	33.0	29.4	24.6
Female	65+	26.3	28.3	20.9	20.5	20.2
Male	65+	62.8	62.1	48.5	41.1	30.8

Percentage married, age 60+			Percentage living alone, age 60+ (1997)		
Total	Female	Male	Total	Female	Male
61.7	38.0	90.0	1.3	1.1	1.5

Statutory pensionable age (2006)			Percentage illiterate, age 65+ (2002)		
	Female	Male	Total	Female	Male
	55	55	85.7	96.4	75.6

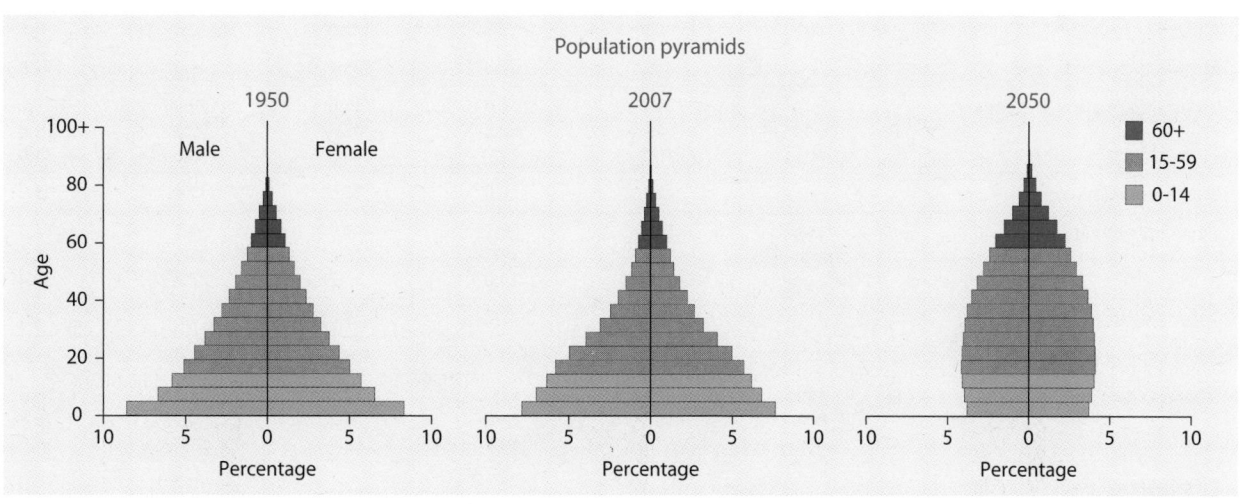

Population pyramids

Serbia and Montenegro

Indicator	Age	1950	1975	2007	2025	2050
Population (thousands)						
Total	Total	7 130.8	9 085.3	10 493.3	10 233.7	9 426.1
	0-14	2 037.2	2 235.6	1 868.6	1 675.3	1 475.0
	15-59	4 317.3	5 674.9	6 655.4	6 120.4	5 031.9
	60-64	233.9	335.7	489.6	609.4	670.7
	65-69	183.8	344.1	448.8	573.1	652.4
	70-74	157.4	249.0	435.5	544.6	564.5
	75-79	118.2	156.0	333.0	354.5	443.1
	80-84			191.5	191.1	307.6
	85-89			53.3	114.4	177.3
	90-94	83.0	90.0	14.5	42.2	77.8
	95-99			2.8	7.9	23.1
	100+			0.2	0.6	2.7
Female	Total	3 671.1	4 586.6	5 271.4	5 130.2	4 735.5
	0-14	1 005.5	1 083.1	900.3	805.6	708.9
	15-59	2 211.2	2 856.1	3 264.3	2 979.1	2 433.8
	60-64	131.8	184.3	257.5	311.8	335.2
	65-69	101.5	182.4	246.4	303.0	334.7
	70-74	94.8	134.8	246.3	300.8	300.5
	75-79	73.6	89.9	195.7	204.8	247.7
	80-84			117.9	117.3	184.4
	85-89			33.2	74.0	114.9
	90-94	52.7	56.0	8.4	28.1	55.2
	95-99			1.4	5.3	17.9
	100+			0.1	0.4	2.2
Male	Total	3 459.7	4 498.7	5 222.0	5 103.5	4 690.6
	0-14	1 031.7	1 152.5	968.3	869.7	766.1
	15-59	2 106.1	2 818.8	3 391.0	3 141.4	2 598.1
	60-64	102.1	151.4	232.1	297.6	335.5
	65-69	82.3	161.7	202.4	270.2	317.7
	70-74	62.6	114.2	189.2	243.8	264.0
	75-79	44.6	66.1	137.3	149.7	195.3
	80-84			73.6	73.8	123.2
	85-89			20.2	40.4	62.5
	90-94	30.3	34.0	6.1	14.1	22.6
	95-99			1.4	2.6	5.2
	100+			0.1	0.2	0.5
Percentage in older ages						
Total	60+	10.9	12.9	18.8	23.8	31.0
	65+	7.6	9.2	14.1	17.9	23.9
	80+	1.2	1.0	2.5	3.5	6.2
Female	60+	12.4	14.1	21.0	26.2	33.6
	65+	8.8	10.1	16.1	20.1	26.6
	80+	1.4	1.2	3.1	4.4	7.9
Male	60+	9.3	11.7	16.5	21.4	28.3
	65+	6.4	8.4	12.1	15.6	21.1
	80+	0.9	0.8	1.9	2.6	4.6
Ageing index		38.1	52.5	105.4	145.5	197.9
Broad age groups (percentage)	0-14	28.6	24.6	17.8	16.4	15.6
	15-59	60.5	62.5	63.4	59.8	53.4
	60+	10.9	12.9	18.8	23.8	31.0
Median age (years)		25.6	30.0	36.5*	41.4	45.0
Dependency ratio	Total	56.7	51.2	46.9	52.1	65.3
	Youth	44.8	37.2	26.2	24.9	25.9
	Old Age	11.9	14.0	20.7	27.2	39.4
Potential support ratio		8.4	7.2	4.8	3.7	2.5
Parent support ratio		3.1	2.8	3.7	8.4	14.9
Sex ratio (per 100 women)	60+	70.8	81.5	77.9	81.2	83.3
	65+	68.1	81.2	74.2	76.9	78.8
	80+	57.5	60.7	63.1	58.3	57.1

* *Estimate refers to year 2005.*

Indicator	Age	1950-1955	1975-1980	2005-2010	2025-2030	2045-2050
Growth rate (percentage)	Total	1.4	0.9	0.0	–0.2	–0.4
	60+	–0.7	0.2	1.1	0.6	0.5
	65+	–0.6	2.1	–0.1	0.7	1.0
	80+	–1.3	6.2	5.9	2.5	1.0
Total fertility rate (per woman)		3.2	2.4	1.6	1.8	1.9
Life expectancy (years)						
Total	Birth	58.0	70.3	74.0	76.6	79.0
	60	..	..	18.8	20.2	21.9
	65	..	..	15.2	16.5	18.0
	80	..	..	6.7	7.4	8.4
Female	Birth	58.8	72.5	76.4	79.0	81.6
	60	..	..	20.1	22.0	24.0
	65	..	..	16.2	17.9	19.8
	80	..	..	6.8	7.9	9.1
Male	Birth	57.1	68.1	71.7	74.3	76.4
	60	..	..	17.3	18.4	19.8
	65	..	..	14.0	14.9	16.1
	80	..	..	6.5	6.7	7.3
Survival rate (percentage)						
Total	60	..	..	86.3	89.7	92.0
	65	..	..	79.3	83.9	87.2
	80	..	..	40.6	47.9	55.3
Female	60	..	..	90.0	92.4	94.2
	65	..	..	85.0	88.3	91.1
	80	..	..	48.1	56.6	64.7
Male	60	..	..	82.7	87.2	89.8
	65	..	..	73.9	79.6	83.5
	80	..	..	33.2	39.4	46.2

		1980	1990	2007	2010	2020
Labour force participation (percentage)						
Total	65+	23.1	23.5	31.1	30.1	28.8
Female	65+	18.6	18.4	28.8	28.7	28.7
Male	65+	28.9	30.6	34.1	32.1	29.0

Percentage married, age 60+			Percentage living alone, age 60+ (1991)		
Total	Female	Male	Total	Female	Male
64.2	51.0	81.0	14.8	20.1	7.9

Statutory pensionable age (2006)			Percentage illiterate, age 65+ (2003)		
	Female	Male	Total	Female	Male
	58	63	13.9	21.7	3.3

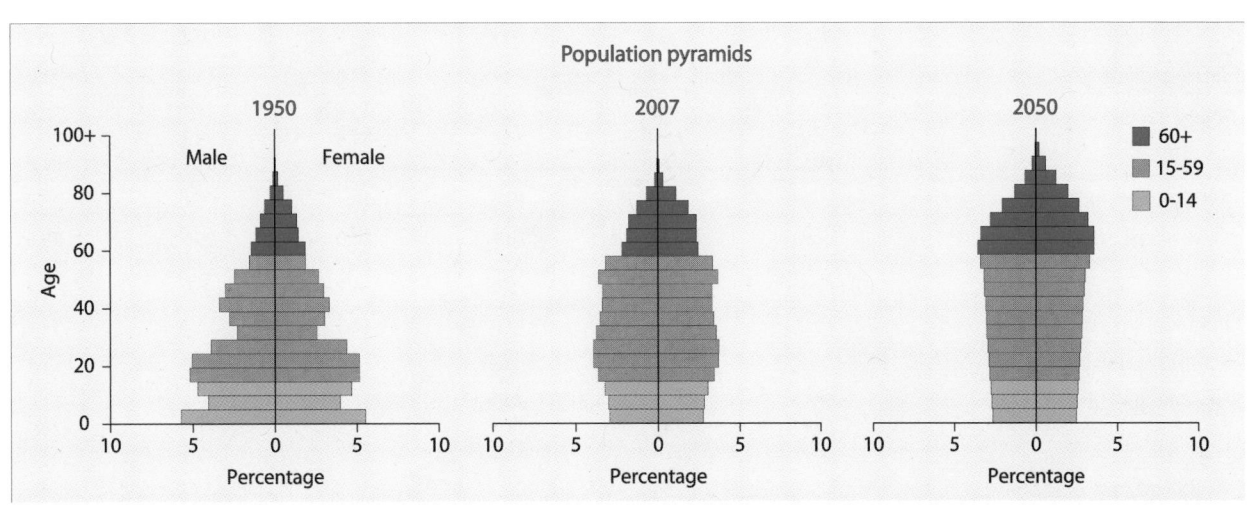

Population pyramids

1950 · Male · Female · 2007 · 2050

Legend: 60+ · 15-59 · 0-14

Sierra Leone

Indicator	Age	1950	1975	2007	2025	2050
Population (thousands)						
Total	Total	1 944.0	2 944.6	5 802.2	8 662.6	13 786.4
	0-14	766.1	1 194.1	2 489.5	3 577.9	4 475.4
	15-59	1 076.3	1 583.9	2 995.1	4 620.6	8 370.5
	60-64	42.9	69.3	123.9	176.2	356.7
	65-69	29.7	48.9	91.0	130.7	255.8
	70-74	17.5	29.5	58.2	85.4	170.9
	75-79	8.3	13.9	30.2	47.3	97.5
	80-84			11.4	19.2	44.9
	85-89			2.6	4.7	12.7
	90-94	3.2	5.0	0.3	0.7	2.0
	95-99			0.0	0.0	0.2
	100+			0.0	0.0	0.0
Female	Total	991.9	1 500.2	2 940.0	4 380.6	6 974.3
	0-14	384.8	601.5	1 246.8	1 792.0	2 233.3
	15-59	550.0	806.6	1 518.8	2 331.4	4 227.0
	60-64	23.5	37.6	66.3	94.8	188.1
	65-69	16.6	27.0	49.7	72.0	138.0
	70-74	10.0	16.6	32.5	48.2	95.0
	75-79	4.9	8.0	17.3	27.3	56.2
	80-84			6.7	11.4	27.2
	85-89			1.6	3.0	8.1
	90-94	2.1	3.0	0.2	0.4	1.3
	95-99			0.0	0.0	0.1
	100+			0.0	0.0	0.0
Male	Total	952.1	1 444.3	2 862.2	4 282.0	6 812.2
	0-14	381.3	592.6	1 242.7	1 785.9	2 242.2
	15-59	526.3	777.3	1 476.3	2 289.2	4 143.5
	60-64	19.4	31.7	57.5	81.4	168.6
	65-69	13.1	21.9	41.3	58.7	117.8
	70-74	7.5	12.9	25.7	37.1	75.9
	75-79	3.4	5.9	12.9	20.0	41.2
	80-84			4.6	7.7	17.7
	85-89			1.0	1.8	4.6
	90-94	1.1	2.0	0.1	0.2	0.6
	95-99			0.0	0.0	0.0
	100+			0.0	0.0	0.0
Percentage in older ages						
Total	60+	5.2	5.7	5.5	5.4	6.8
	65+	3.0	3.3	3.3	3.3	4.2
	80+	0.2	0.2	0.2	0.3	0.4
Female	60+	5.8	6.1	5.9	5.9	7.4
	65+	3.4	3.6	3.7	3.7	4.7
	80+	0.2	0.2	0.3	0.3	0.5
Male	60+	4.7	5.2	5.0	4.8	6.3
	65+	2.6	3.0	3.0	2.9	3.8
	80+	0.1	0.1	0.2	0.2	0.3
Ageing index		13.3	14.0	12.8	13.0	21.0
Broad age groups (percentage)	0-14	39.4	40.6	42.9	41.3	32.5
	15-59	55.4	53.8	51.6	53.3	60.7
	60+	5.2	5.7	5.5	5.4	6.8
Median age (years)		20.4	19.8	18.4*	19.1	23.9
Dependency ratio	Total	73.7	78.1	86.0	80.6	58.0
	Youth	68.5	72.2	79.8	74.6	51.3
	Old Age	5.2	5.9	6.2	6.0	6.7
Potential support ratio		19.1	17.0	16.1	16.7	14.9
Parent support ratio		0.3	0.3	0.6	0.8	1.1
Sex ratio (per 100 women)	60+	77.9	80.8	82.1	80.5	83.0
	65+	74.7	78.3	79.3	77.3	79.1
	80+	52.4	67.9	67.3	65.4	62.7

*   *Estimate refers to year 2005.*

Indicator	Age	1950-1955	1975-1980	2005-2010	2025-2030	2045-2050
Growth rate (percentage)	Total	1.4	1.9	2.1	2.2	1.6
	60+	1.5	2.2	1.8	2.6	3.5
	65+	1.3	2.4	2.1	2.7	3.3
	80+	−0.1	3.5	2.7	3.2	3.8
Total fertility rate (per woman)		6.1	6.5	6.5	4.8	3.1
Life expectancy (years)						
Total	Birth	30.3	36.8	41.9	48.5	56.7
	60	..	..	14.1	15.1	16.4
	65	..	..	11.0	11.8	12.9
	80	..	..	4.4	4.7	5.1
Female	Birth	31.7	38.2	43.3	50.3	58.8
	60	..	..	14.7	15.8	17.3
	65	..	..	11.4	12.3	13.6
	80	..	..	4.5	4.9	5.3
Male	Birth	29.0	35.4	40.5	46.7	54.7
	60	..	..	13.6	14.3	15.4
	65	..	..	10.6	11.2	12.1
	80	..	..	4.3	4.5	4.8
Survival rate (percentage)						
Total	60	..	..	40.8	50.0	62.1
	65	..	..	35.1	43.9	56.0
	80	..	..	9.8	14.3	21.6
Female	60	..	..	43.3	53.1	65.7
	65	..	..	37.9	47.6	60.3
	80	..	..	11.3	16.8	25.6
Male	60	..	..	38.3	46.9	58.7
	65	..	..	32.3	40.4	51.8
	80	..	..	8.3	11.8	17.9

		1980	1990	2007	2010	2020
Labour force participation (percentage)						
Total	65+	43.3	44.4	50.9	51.1	51.0
Female	65+	18.6	20.0	22.0	22.2	22.4
Male	65+	74.9	75.5	87.4	87.6	87.8

Percentage married, age 60+			Percentage living alone, age 60+		
Total	Female	Male	Total	Female	Male
..	..	..	..	..	..

Statutory pensionable age (2006)			Percentage illiterate, age 65+ (2004)		
	Female	Male	Total	Female	Male
	60	60	86.2	94.7	77.1

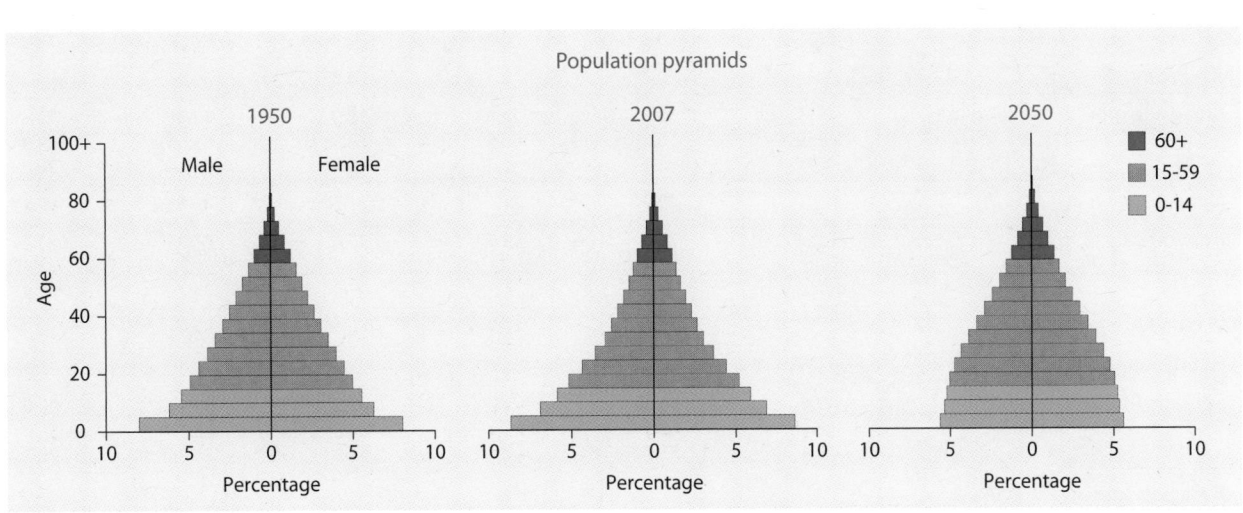

Population pyramids

1950 · 2007 · 2050

Male · Female

- 60+
- 15-59
- 0-14

Singapore

Indicator	Age	1950	1975	2007	2025	2050
Population (thousands)						
Total	Total	1 022.1	2 262.6	4 433.8	5 144.3	5 212.8
	0-14	413.6	742.9	798.9	685.3	658.0
	15-59	570.3	1 367.9	3 037.7	2 859.0	2 572.2
	60-64	13.7	58.7	198.7	451.1	350.2
	65-69	10.4	43.5	139.4	417.9	309.9
	70-74	5.5	26.2	110.4	321.1	287.5
	75-79	4.4	14.1	76.5	214.2	304.9
	80-84			43.3	105.5	301.7
	85-89			20.0	58.2	238.1
	90-94	4.2	9.3	7.1	24.2	134.3
	95-99			1.7	6.8	46.8
	100+			0.2	1.0	9.0
Female	Total	492.8	1 106.4	2 202.8	2 566.2	2 611.6
	0-14	203.9	361.0	385.6	330.5	317.4
	15-59	266.0	666.2	1 501.5	1 397.4	1 245.0
	60-64	7.8	28.9	100.1	229.5	171.3
	65-69	6.2	21.8	71.7	214.1	152.8
	70-74	3.5	14.1	58.7	167.1	144.2
	75-79	2.7	8.3	42.3	114.5	159.2
	80-84			24.9	58.7	167.1
	85-89			12.2	34.1	136.6
	90-94	2.7	6.1	4.6	15.1	81.3
	95-99			1.1	4.4	30.3
	100+			0.1	0.7	6.2
Male	Total	529.3	1 156.2	2 231.0	2 578.1	2 601.1
	0-14	209.7	381.9	413.3	354.7	340.6
	15-59	304.3	701.7	1 536.1	1 461.5	1 327.1
	60-64	5.9	29.8	98.7	221.6	178.9
	65-69	4.2	21.7	67.8	203.7	157.1
	70-74	2.0	12.1	51.7	154.1	143.2
	75-79	1.7	5.8	34.1	99.7	145.7
	80-84			18.5	46.9	134.6
	85-89			7.8	24.1	101.5
	90-94	1.5	3.2	2.5	9.2	53.0
	95-99			0.6	2.3	16.5
	100+			0.1	0.3	2.8
Percentage in older ages						
Total	60+	3.7	6.7	13.5	31.1	38.0
	65+	2.4	4.1	9.0	22.3	31.3
	80+	0.4	0.4	1.6	3.8	14.0
Female	60+	4.6	7.2	14.3	32.7	40.2
	65+	3.1	4.5	9.8	23.7	33.6
	80+	0.5	0.6	1.9	4.4	16.1
Male	60+	2.9	6.3	12.6	29.6	35.9
	65+	1.8	3.7	8.2	21.0	29.0
	80+	0.3	0.3	1.3	3.2	11.9
Ageing index		9.2	20.4	74.8	233.5	301.3
Broad age groups (percentage)	0-14	40.5	32.8	18.0	13.3	12.6
	15-59	55.8	60.5	68.5	55.6	49.3
	60+	3.7	6.7	13.5	31.1	38.0
Median age (years)		20.0	21.9	37.5*	46.6	52.1
Dependency ratio	Total	75.0	58.6	37.0	55.4	78.4
	Youth	70.8	52.1	24.7	20.7	22.5
	Old Age	4.2	6.5	12.3	34.7	55.9
Potential support ratio		23.8	15.3	8.1	2.9	1.8
Parent support ratio		2.3	1.4	3.3	7.4	38.0
Sex ratio (per 100 women)	60+	66.8	91.7	89.2	90.9	89.0
	65+	62.3	85.1	84.8	88.8	85.9
	80+	55.7	52.4	68.3	73.3	73.2

* *Estimate refers to year 2005.*

Indicator	Age	1950-1955	1975-1980	2005-2010	2025-2030	2045-2050
Growth rate (percentage)	Total	4.9	1.3	1.2	0.5	−0.2
	60+	3.2	2.7	6.3	2.7	0.1
	65+	3.4	4.0	4.6	4.1	−0.3
	80+	2.7	5.6	6.6	7.9	1.6
Total fertility rate (per woman)		6.4	1.9	1.3	1.6	1.8
Life expectancy (years)						
Total	Birth	60.4	70.7	79.4	82.2	84.5
	60	..	..	22.0	24.3	26.2
	65	..	..	17.9	20.1	21.8
	80	..	..	8.3	9.6	10.8
Female	Birth	62.0	73.1	81.3	83.9	86.2
	60	..	..	23.3	25.6	27.6
	65	..	..	19.1	21.2	23.2
	80	..	..	8.7	10.2	11.5
Male	Birth	58.8	68.6	77.6	80.5	82.8
	60	..	..	20.5	22.9	24.7
	65	..	..	16.7	18.8	20.5
	80	..	..	7.8	9.0	9.9
Survival rate (percentage)						
Total	60	..	..	92.9	94.7	95.8
	65	..	..	88.6	91.5	93.3
	80	..	..	55.5	64.7	71.2
Female	60	..	..	94.6	95.9	96.8
	65	..	..	91.4	93.4	94.8
	80	..	..	62.2	70.2	76.4
Male	60	..	..	91.3	93.6	94.9
	65	..	..	85.8	89.6	91.8
	80	..	..	48.8	59.1	66.2

		1980	1990	2007	2010	2020
Labour force participation (percentage)						
Total	65+	17.4	12.2	7.9	7.0	4.8
Female	65+	7.2	4.9	3.2	3.1	3.0
Male	65+	29.8	21.3	13.5	11.6	6.8

Percentage married, age 60+			Percentage living alone, age 60+ (1995)		
Total	Female	Male	Total	Female	Male
64.9	49.0	83.0	3.3	2.7	1.6

Statutory pensionable age (2006)			Percentage illiterate, age 65+ (2000)		
	Female	Male	Total	Female	Male
	55	55	39.7	58.8	15.5

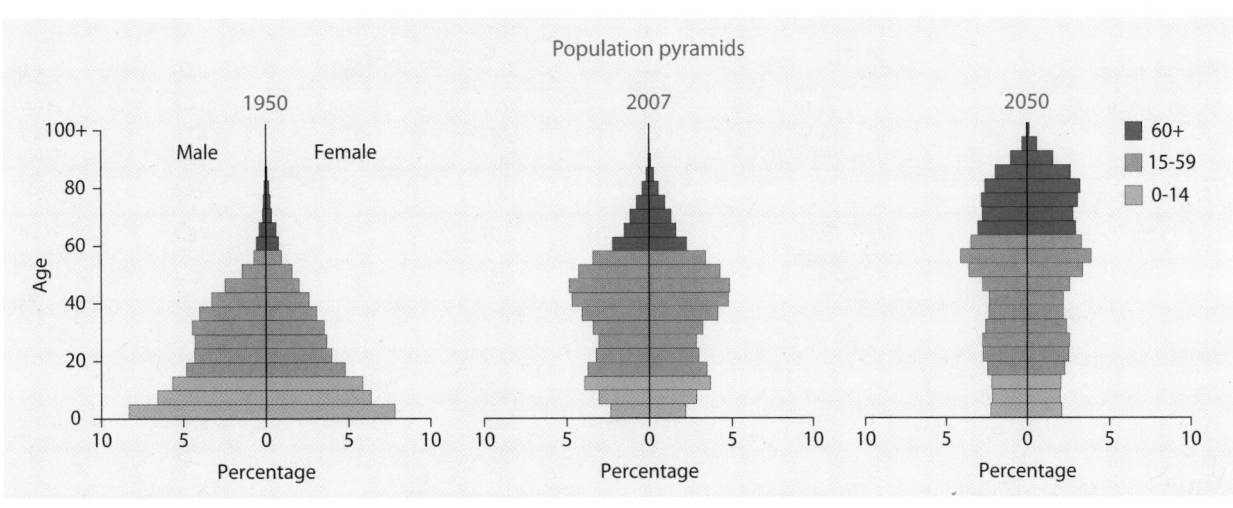

Population pyramids

Slovakia

Indicator	Age	1950	1975	2007	2025	2050
Population (thousands)						
Total	Total	3 463.4	4 735.5	5 400.7	5 286.1	4 612.3
	0-14	1 002.0	1 239.3	853.2	706.7	584.1
	15-59	2 116.8	2 841.1	3 642.4	3 223.0	2 247.6
	60-64	113.5	201.8	256.1	344.3	374.8
	65-69	90.4	181.7	199.7	334.4	384.2
	70-74	67.1	130.7	170.3	293.1	365.9
	75-79	43.6	82.2	135.3	190.1	275.4
	80-84			95.7	108.3	177.5
	85-89			34.2	56.3	119.1
	90-94	30.1	58.7	11.0	23.5	61.0
	95-99			2.4	5.7	19.8
	100+			0.2	0.7	2.8
Female	Total	1 782.0	2 399.8	2 782.5	2 733.7	2 399.5
	0-14	494.2	606.2	416.8	345.1	285.2
	15-59	1 092.8	1 429.4	1 816.4	1 595.6	1 104.9
	60-64	64.0	106.9	141.3	181.0	190.7
	65-69	51.4	98.0	116.5	182.8	200.7
	70-74	37.9	73.1	104.4	170.0	199.7
	75-79	24.5	47.4	88.0	119.2	159.8
	80-84			65.8	74.5	111.4
	85-89			24.2	41.9	82.0
	90-94	17.2	38.8	7.4	18.5	46.2
	95-99			1.5	4.6	16.3
	100+			0.1	0.5	2.4
Male	Total	1 681.4	2 335.7	2 618.2	2 552.5	2 212.8
	0-14	507.9	633.1	436.4	361.6	298.9
	15-59	1 024.0	1 411.7	1 826.0	1 627.4	1 142.7
	60-64	49.5	94.9	114.8	163.4	184.1
	65-69	38.9	83.7	83.2	151.7	183.5
	70-74	29.2	57.6	65.9	123.1	166.2
	75-79	19.1	34.8	47.3	70.9	115.6
	80-84			29.9	33.8	66.1
	85-89			10.0	14.3	37.1
	90-94	12.8	19.9	3.6	5.0	14.8
	95-99			0.9	1.1	3.5
	100+			0.1	0.2	0.4
Percentage in older ages						
Total	60+	9.9	13.8	16.8	25.7	38.6
	65+	6.7	9.6	12.0	19.1	30.5
	80+	0.9	1.2	2.7	3.7	8.2
Female	60+	10.9	15.2	19.7	29.0	42.1
	65+	7.4	10.7	14.7	22.4	34.1
	80+	1.0	1.6	3.6	5.1	10.8
Male	60+	8.9	12.5	13.6	22.1	34.9
	65+	6.0	8.4	9.2	15.7	26.5
	80+	0.8	0.9	1.7	2.1	5.5
Ageing index		34.4	52.9	106.1	192.0	304.8
Broad age groups (percentage)	0-14	28.9	26.2	15.8	13.4	12.7
	15-59	61.1	60.0	67.4	61.0	48.7
	60+	9.9	13.8	16.8	25.7	38.6
Median age (years)		27.3	28.1	35.6*	44.2	51.8
Dependency ratio	Total	55.3	55.6	38.5	48.2	75.9
	Youth	44.9	40.7	21.9	19.8	22.3
	Old Age	10.4	14.9	16.6	28.4	53.6
Potential support ratio		9.7	6.7	6.0	3.5	1.9
Parent support ratio		2.5	2.8	4.7	7.8	20.2
Sex ratio (per 100 women)	60+	76.7	79.9	64.8	71.1	76.4
	65+	76.4	76.2	59.1	65.4	71.7
	80+	74.4	51.3	45.0	38.9	47.1

* *Estimate refers to year 2005.*

Indicator	Age	1950-1955	1975-1980	2005-2010	2025-2030	2045-2050
Growth rate (percentage)	Total	1.8	1.0	0.0	–0.4	–0.7
	60+	1.6	0.3	2.0	0.9	0.5
	65+	1.7	2.7	1.1	1.5	1.1
	80+	3.0	5.3	3.1	3.9	0.5
Total fertility rate (per woman)		3.5	2.5	1.2	1.4	1.7
Life expectancy (years)						
Total	Birth	64.3	70.4	75.0	78.0	80.4
	60	..	..	19.5	21.2	23.0
	65	..	..	15.8	17.3	19.0
	80	..	..	7.2	8.2	9.1
Female	Birth	66.2	74.2	78.7	81.4	83.6
	60	..	..	21.7	23.7	25.5
	65	..	..	17.6	19.5	21.2
	80	..	..	7.7	8.9	10.1
Male	Birth	62.3	66.9	71.1	74.6	77.2
	60	..	..	16.7	18.3	20.3
	65	..	..	13.5	14.7	16.5
	80	..	..	6.4	6.7	7.6
Survival rate (percentage)						
Total	60	..	..	86.6	90.9	92.9
	65	..	..	80.0	85.6	88.7
	80	..	..	43.0	51.4	58.9
Female	60	..	..	92.0	94.1	95.4
	65	..	..	87.8	90.8	92.7
	80	..	..	55.4	63.7	70.0
Male	60	..	..	81.3	87.8	90.6
	65	..	..	72.2	80.4	84.8
	80	..	..	29.8	38.4	47.6

		1980	1990	2007	2010	2020
Labour force participation (percentage)						
Total	65+	11.0	6.3	0.8	0.8	0.5
Female	65+	4.5	2.0	0.5	0.5	0.4
Male	65+	20.0	12.8	1.4	1.2	0.7

Percentage married, age 60+			Percentage living alone, age 60+		
Total	Female	Male	Total	Female	Male
53.9	38.0	78.0	..	..	..

Statutory pensionable age (2006)			Percentage illiterate, age 65+		
	Female	Male	Total	Female	Male
	62	62	..	..	..

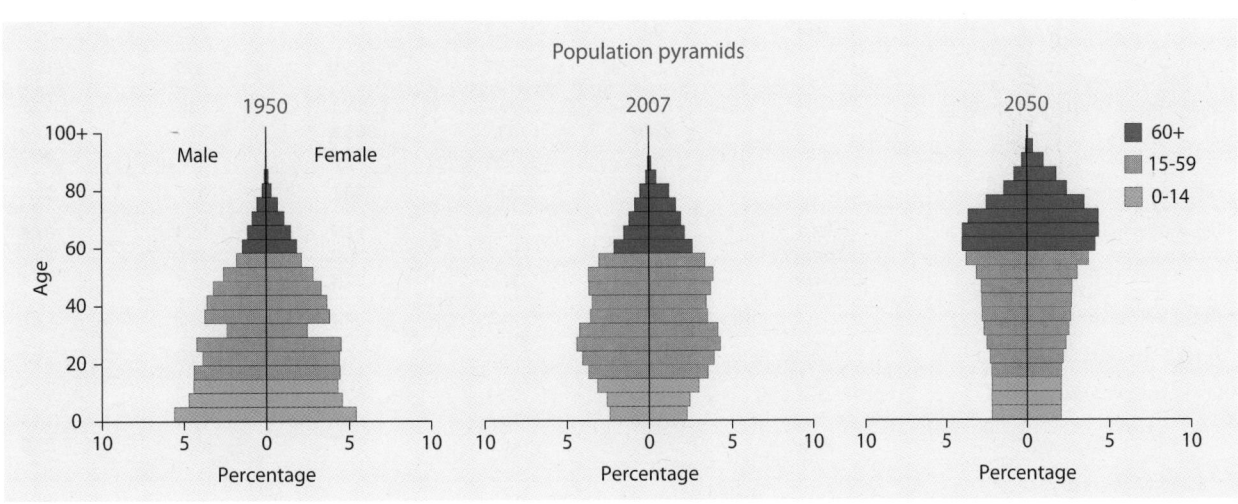

Population pyramids

Slovenia

Indicator	Age	1950	1975	2007	2025	2050
Population (thousands)						
Total	Total	1 473.1	1 742.0	1 964.7	1 883.2	1 630.5
	0-14	405.1	413.0	266.5	231.0	206.6
	15-59	912.8	1 061.6	1 282.6	1 074.4	769.2
	60-64	51.9	76.1	103.9	139.5	120.0
	65-69	41.0	74.7	91.3	132.4	127.0
	70-74	27.7	56.6	84.6	120.1	125.7
	75-79	19.7	37.3	67.6	85.0	103.9
	80-84			44.2	49.1	79.3
	85-89			16.7	32.0	55.8
	90-94	14.9	22.7	5.8	14.7	29.9
	95-99			1.5	4.4	11.0
	100+			0.1	0.6	2.1
Female	Total	768.9	898.7	1 005.1	960.1	831.7
	0-14	198.9	201.8	129.8	112.4	100.6
	15-59	483.7	536.5	629.1	521.6	368.9
	60-64	29.3	43.5	53.8	71.3	59.1
	65-69	22.4	43.0	49.7	70.0	64.2
	70-74	14.8	34.2	49.4	64.5	65.0
	75-79	11.1	24.2	42.7	49.2	56.9
	80-84			31.5	31.4	46.9
	85-89			13.1	23.0	36.7
	90-94	8.7	15.5	4.7	12.1	22.3
	95-99			1.3	4.0	9.2
	100+			0.1	0.6	1.9
Male	Total	704.2	843.3	959.6	923.1	798.8
	0-14	206.2	211.2	136.7	118.5	106.0
	15-59	429.1	525.1	653.5	552.8	400.2
	60-64	22.6	32.6	50.1	68.1	60.9
	65-69	18.6	31.7	41.5	62.4	62.8
	70-74	12.9	22.4	35.2	55.6	60.7
	75-79	8.6	13.1	24.9	35.8	47.0
	80-84			12.8	17.8	32.5
	85-89			3.6	9.0	19.1
	90-94	6.2	7.2	1.0	2.7	7.6
	95-99			0.2	0.4	1.8
	100+			0.0	0.0	0.2
Percentage in older ages						
Total	60+	10.5	15.4	21.2	30.7	40.2
	65+	7.0	11.0	15.9	23.3	32.8
	80+	1.0	1.3	3.5	5.4	10.9
Female	60+	11.2	17.8	24.5	34.0	43.5
	65+	7.4	13.0	19.1	26.5	36.4
	80+	1.1	1.7	5.0	7.4	14.1
Male	60+	9.8	12.7	17.7	27.3	36.6
	65+	6.6	8.8	12.4	19.9	29.0
	80+	0.9	0.9	1.8	3.2	7.7
Ageing index		38.3	64.7	155.9	250.2	317.0
Broad age groups (percentage)	0-14	27.5	23.7	13.6	12.3	12.7
	15-59	62.0	60.9	65.3	57.1	47.2
	60+	10.5	15.4	21.2	30.7	40.2
Median age (years)		27.7	31.4	40.2*	47.4	51.9
Dependency ratio	Total	52.7	53.1	41.7	55.1	83.4
	Youth	42.0	36.3	19.2	19.0	23.2
	Old Age	10.7	16.8	22.5	36.1	60.1
Potential support ratio		9.3	5.9	4.4	2.8	1.7
Parent support ratio		2.6	3.1	6.0	12.2	31.1
Sex ratio (per 100 women)	60+	79.8	66.7	68.8	77.2	80.8
	65+	81.2	63.6	62.0	72.1	76.4
	80+	71.3	46.5	34.7	42.0	52.2

* Estimate refers to year 2005.

Indicator	Age	1950-1955	1975-1980	2005-2010	2025-2030	2045-2050
Growth rate (percentage)	Total	0.8	1.0	−0.1	−0.4	−0.7
	60+	1.6	−0.1	1.9	0.9	−0.2
	65+	1.6	1.8	0.9	1.4	0.2
	80+	1.0	7.7	5.0	3.1	0.6
Total fertility rate (per woman)		2.8	2.2	1.2	1.5	1.7
Life expectancy (years)						
Total	Birth	65.6	71.0	77.2	80.0	82.1
	60	..	..	20.9	22.8	24.4
	65	..	..	17.1	18.7	20.2
	80	..	..	7.9	8.9	9.8
Female	Birth	68.1	74.8	80.7	83.4	85.4
	60	..	..	23.4	25.5	27.1
	65	..	..	19.2	21.1	22.6
	80	..	..	8.7	10.0	11.1
Male	Birth	63.0	67.0	73.5	76.7	78.9
	60	..	..	18.0	19.9	21.7
	65	..	..	14.4	16.1	17.7
	80	..	..	6.3	7.1	8.0
Survival rate (percentage)						
Total	60	..	..	89.5	92.6	94.1
	65	..	..	84.0	88.3	90.7
	80	..	..	49.8	58.1	64.4
Female	60	..	..	93.2	95.0	96.1
	65	..	..	89.8	92.4	93.9
	80	..	..	62.0	69.5	74.6
Male	60	..	..	85.9	90.2	92.2
	65	..	..	78.4	84.4	87.6
	80	..	..	37.0	46.8	54.6

		1980	1990	2007	2010	2020
Labour force participation (percentage)						
Total	65+	13.4	11.0	9.9	10.2	11.0
Female	65+	9.8	9.1	7.3	7.5	7.9
Male	65+	19.3	14.5	14.1	14.6	15.4

Percentage married, age 60+				Percentage living alone, age 60+ (1991)		
Total	Female	Male		Total	Female	Male
59.7	47.0	79.0		20.4	27.4	9.0

Statutory pensionable age (2006)				Percentage illiterate, age 65+		
	Female	Male		Total	Female	Male
	59	63		..	..	..

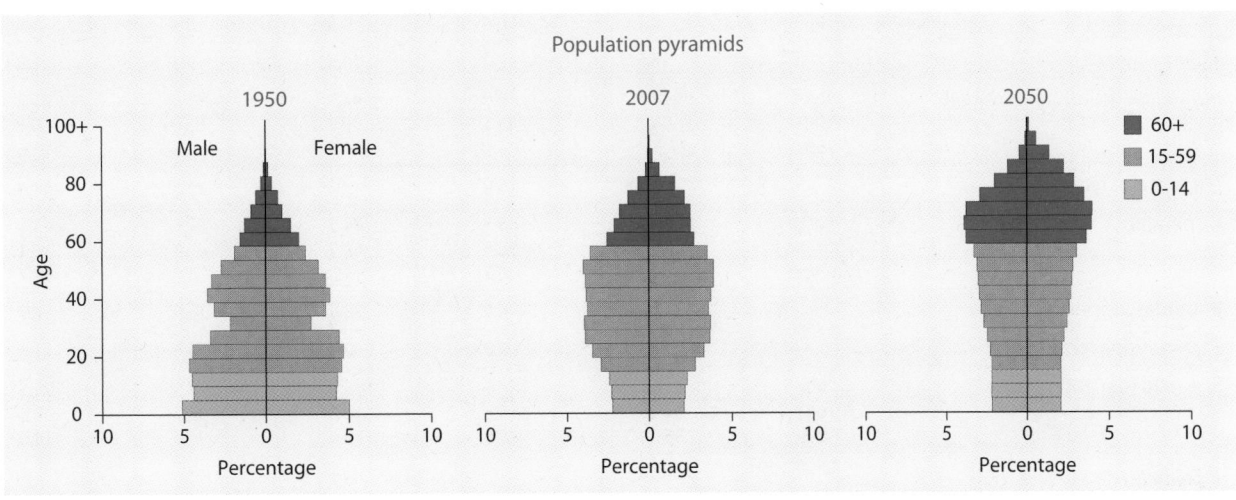

Population pyramids

United Nations Department of Economic and Social Affairs, Population Division

Solomon Islands

Indicator	Age	1950	1975	2007	2025	2050
Population (thousands)						
Total	Total	89.8	192.8	501.7	709.1	920.7
	0-14	38.2	92.5	200.9	220.1	195.4
	15-59	48.7	90.9	279.6	446.9	600.5
	60-64	1.1	3.1	8.7	16.9	43.1
	65-69	0.8	2.7	6.1	11.9	33.8
	70-74	0.5	1.8	3.6	7.4	24.1
	75-79	0.4	1.1	1.9	3.8	15.0
	80-84			0.7	1.6	6.3
	85-89			0.2	0.4	2.0
	90-94	0.1	0.7	0.0	0.1	0.4
	95-99			0.0	0.0	0.0
	100+			0.0	0.0	0.0
Female	Total	40.3	92.0	242.8	343.8	448.9
	0-14	18.8	44.4	96.4	105.7	93.8
	15-59	20.8	44.1	136.2	216.2	291.2
	60-64	0.3	1.2	4.2	8.8	21.4
	65-69	0.2	1.0	2.9	6.2	17.1
	70-74	0.1	0.7	1.7	3.8	12.4
	75-79	0.1	0.4	0.9	2.0	7.9
	80-84			0.3	0.8	3.6
	85-89			0.1	0.2	1.2
	90-94	0.0	0.2	0.0	0.0	0.2
	95-99			0.0	0.0	0.0
	100+			0.0	0.0	0.0
Male	Total	49.5	100.7	258.9	365.3	471.8
	0-14	19.4	48.0	104.5	114.4	101.6
	15-59	27.9	46.8	143.4	230.7	309.3
	60-64	0.8	1.9	4.5	8.1	21.7
	65-69	0.6	1.7	3.2	5.7	16.7
	70-74	0.4	1.2	1.9	3.6	11.7
	75-79	0.3	0.7	1.0	1.8	7.1
	80-84			0.4	0.8	2.8
	85-89			0.1	0.2	0.8
	90-94	0.1	0.4	0.0	0.0	0.2
	95-99			0.0	0.0	0.0
	100+			0.0	0.0	0.0
Percentage in older ages						
Total	60+	3.2	4.9	4.2	5.9	13.6
	65+	2.0	3.3	2.5	3.5	8.9
	80+	0.1	0.4	0.2	0.3	1.0
Female	60+	1.7	3.8	4.2	6.4	14.2
	65+	1.0	2.5	2.5	3.8	9.5
	80+	0.1	0.3	0.2	0.3	1.1
Male	60+	4.4	5.9	4.3	5.5	12.9
	65+	2.8	3.9	2.5	3.3	8.3
	80+	0.2	0.4	0.2	0.3	0.8
Ageing index		7.6	10.2	10.5	19.1	63.9
Broad age groups (percentage)	0-14	42.5	48.0	40.1	31.0	21.2
	15-59	54.2	47.1	55.7	63.0	65.2
	60+	3.2	4.9	4.2	5.9	13.6
Median age (years)		18.3	16.0	19.2*	24.5	33.4
Dependency ratio	Total	80.3	105.1	74.1	52.9	43.1
	Youth	76.7	98.4	69.7	47.5	30.4
	Old Age	3.6	6.7	4.3	5.4	12.7
Potential support ratio		27.7	14.9	23.0	18.4	7.9
Parent support ratio		0.3	0.8	0.5	0.6	1.6
Sex ratio (per 100 women)	60+	313.1	167.6	108.7	92.5	95.5
	65+	347.8	169.0	110.1	92.7	92.5
	80+	363.0	188.6	126.6	94.7	74.0

* *Estimate refers to year 2005.*

Indicator	Age	1950-1955	1975-1980	2005-2010	2025-2030	2045-2050
Growth rate (percentage)	Total	2.6	3.4	2.4	1.4	0.7
	60+	8.3	3.5	3.2	4.5	3.6
	65+	4.4	3.4	3.8	4.5	4.1
	80+	13.7	4.0	5.6	4.7	6.5
Total fertility rate (per woman)		6.4	7.0	3.8	2.4	1.9
Life expectancy (years)						
Total	Birth	45.5	58.1	63.4	67.8	72.3
	60	..	..	14.4	16.0	17.9
	65	..	..	11.0	12.4	14.1
	80	..	..	4.3	5.1	6.0
Female	Birth	46.4	58.9	64.3	69.4	74.2
	60	..	..	14.6	16.5	18.8
	65	..	..	11.2	12.9	14.9
	80	..	..	4.4	5.2	6.3
Male	Birth	44.9	57.4	62.6	66.4	70.6
	60	..	..	14.1	15.4	17.0
	65	..	..	10.9	12.0	13.4
	80	..	..	4.3	4.9	5.6
Survival rate (percentage)						
Total	60	..	..	71.7	78.7	85.1
	65	..	..	62.8	70.9	78.7
	80	..	..	17.2	25.1	35.4
Female	60	..	..	73.4	81.3	87.9
	65	..	..	64.7	74.0	82.3
	80	..	..	18.4	28.0	40.4
Male	60	..	..	70.2	76.4	82.6
	65	..	..	61.0	68.0	75.4
	80	..	..	16.1	22.3	30.9

		1980	1990	2007	2010	2020
Labour force participation (percentage)						
Total	65+	52.9	40.7	40.5	40.6	40.6
Female	65+	34.2	19.0	24.2	24.9	27.3
Male	65+	64.4	55.4	55.4	55.1	54.2

Percentage married, age 60+			Percentage living alone, age 60+		
Total	Female	Male	Total	Female	Male
63.3	51.0	74.0	..	..	..

Statutory pensionable age (2006)			Percentage illiterate, age 65+		
	Female	Male	Total	Female	Male
	50	50	..	..	..

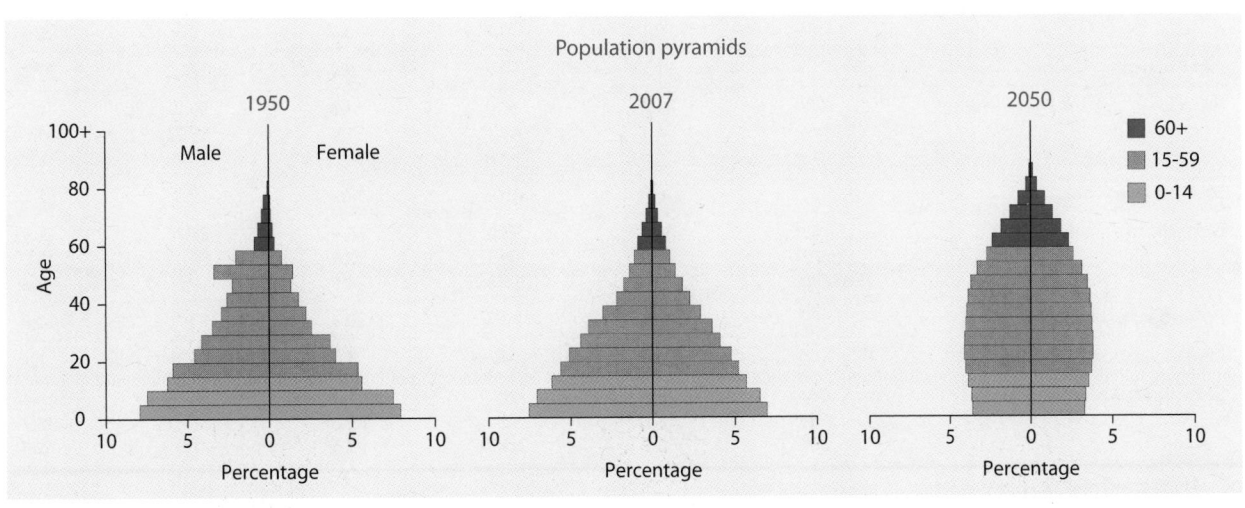

Population pyramids

Somalia

Indicator	Age	1950	1975	2007	2025	2050
Population (thousands)						
Total	Total	2 264.1	4 134.1	8 766.3	13 787.4	21 329.1
	0-14	933.8	1 903.7	3 882.6	5 448.7	6 443.9
	15-59	1 225.3	2 030.2	4 519.1	7 622.1	13 123.4
	60-64	46.3	78.6	135.1	269.8	599.7
	65-69	31.1	56.7	101.9	197.7	449.6
	70-74	17.5	36.4	67.0	133.1	354.4
	75-79	7.6	19.2	37.3	70.4	209.1
	80-84			16.9	31.7	101.7
	85-89			5.3	11.2	37.0
	90-94	2.6	9.3	1.0	2.3	8.9
	95-99			0.1	0.3	1.3
	100+			0.0	0.0	0.1
Female	Total	1 140.2	2 091.1	4 415.7	6 925.0	10 707.4
	0-14	468.1	954.7	1 931.5	2 704.2	3 192.3
	15-59	612.9	1 027.7	2 287.4	3 835.6	6 579.9
	60-64	25.4	41.4	71.4	141.7	310.9
	65-69	17.5	30.6	55.1	105.6	236.2
	70-74	10.1	20.1	36.3	72.4	189.3
	75-79	4.6	11.0	20.5	38.8	114.0
	80-84			9.6	18.1	56.9
	85-89			3.2	6.8	21.4
	90-94	1.6	5.7	0.7	1.5	5.5
	95-99			0.1	0.2	0.8
	100+			0.0	0.0	0.1
Male	Total	1 123.8	2 042.9	4 350.6	6 862.4	10 621.7
	0-14	465.8	949.0	1 951.1	2 744.5	3 251.5
	15-59	612.3	1 002.5	2 231.7	3 786.5	6 543.5
	60-64	20.9	37.2	63.8	128.1	288.8
	65-69	13.5	26.1	46.7	92.2	213.3
	70-74	7.3	16.3	30.7	60.6	165.1
	75-79	3.1	8.3	16.9	31.6	95.1
	80-84			7.3	13.6	44.8
	85-89			2.1	4.5	15.5
	90-94	1.0	3.6	0.4	0.9	3.5
	95-99			0.0	0.1	0.4
	100+			0.0	0.0	0.0
Percentage in older ages						
Total	60+	4.6	4.8	4.2	5.2	8.3
	65+	2.6	2.9	2.6	3.2	5.4
	80+	0.1	0.2	0.3	0.3	0.7
Female	60+	5.2	5.2	4.5	5.6	8.7
	65+	3.0	3.2	2.8	3.5	5.8
	80+	0.1	0.3	0.3	0.4	0.8
Male	60+	4.1	4.5	3.9	4.8	7.8
	65+	2.2	2.7	2.4	3.0	5.1
	80+	0.1	0.2	0.2	0.3	0.6
Ageing index		11.2	10.5	9.4	13.2	27.3
Broad age groups (percentage)	0-14	41.2	46.0	44.3	39.5	30.2
	15-59	54.1	49.1	51.6	55.3	61.5
	60+	4.6	4.8	4.2	5.2	8.3
Median age (years)		19.5	16.9	17.9*	19.8	25.6
Dependency ratio	Total	78.1	96.0	88.4	74.7	55.4
	Youth	73.4	90.3	83.4	69.0	47.0
	Old Age	4.6	5.8	4.9	5.7	8.5
Potential support ratio		21.6	17.3	20.3	17.7	11.8
Parent support ratio		0.3	0.7	1.1	1.3	2.1
Sex ratio (per 100 women)	60+	77.3	84.0	85.2	86.1	88.4
	65+	73.5	80.4	82.8	83.6	86.2
	80+	58.9	62.9	71.5	71.6	75.9

* *Estimate refers to year 2005.*

Indicator	Age	1950-1955	1975-1980	2005-2010	2025-2030	2045-2050
Growth rate (percentage)	Total	2.2	9.0	3.1	2.1	1.4
	60+	2.8	8.4	3.4	3.7	3.2
	65+	3.0	8.7	3.0	3.8	3.1
	80+	5.6	10.1	3.8	4.3	4.6
Total fertility rate (per woman)		7.3	7.3	6.0	4.1	2.7
Life expectancy (years)						
Total	Birth	33.0	42.0	48.8	56.9	64.3
	60	..	..	15.2	16.5	17.9
	65	..	..	12.1	13.2	14.3
	80	..	..	5.3	5.8	6.3
Female	Birth	34.5	43.6	50.1	58.4	65.9
	60	..	..	15.7	17.1	18.5
	65	..	..	12.5	13.6	14.8
	80	..	..	5.5	6.0	6.5
Male	Birth	31.5	40.4	47.6	55.5	62.6
	60	..	..	14.6	15.9	17.2
	65	..	..	11.6	12.7	13.8
	80	..	..	5.0	5.5	6.0
Survival rate (percentage)						
Total	60	..	..	49.0	60.6	71.4
	65	..	..	42.5	54.0	65.2
	80	..	..	14.6	21.8	30.2
Female	60	..	..	51.4	63.2	74.2
	65	..	..	45.1	57.0	68.4
	80	..	..	16.5	24.3	33.4
Male	60	..	..	46.6	58.1	68.7
	65	..	..	39.9	51.1	62.0
	80	..	..	12.7	19.3	27.1

		1980	1990	2007	2010	2020
Labour force participation (percentage)						
Total	65+	55.3	54.7	52.7	52.8	53.8
Female	65+	28.7	26.0	24.1	24.5	26.7
Male	65+	88.0	89.3	87.2	87.0	86.3

Percentage married, age 60+			Percentage living alone, age 60+		
Total	Female	Male	Total	Female	Male
..	..	..	..	..	..

Statutory pensionable age (2006)			Percentage illiterate, age 65+		
	Female	Male	Total	Female	Male
	..	..	..	..	..

Population pyramids

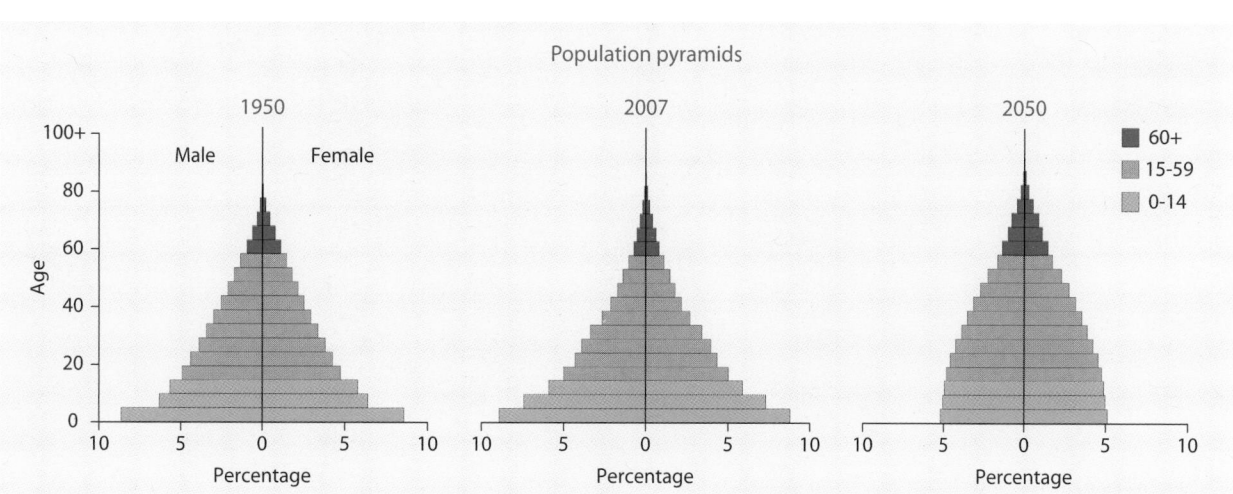

South Africa

Indicator	Age	1950	1975	2007	2025	2050
Population (thousands)						
Total	Total	13 683.2	25 853.5	47 698.7	48 297.2	48 659.9
	0-14	5 279.6	10 920.6	15 359.3	13 719.9	11 500.6
	15-59	7 589.0	13 601.4	28 898.6	29 018.2	30 807.2
	60-64	324.2	503.0	1 263.5	1 628.3	1 832.9
	65-69	228.0	367.2	921.8	1 438.7	1 455.8
	70-74	147.9	227.1	612.9	1 120.6	1 017.4
	75-79	77.0	133.7	361.7	719.8	807.9
	80-84			181.8	408.0	626.0
	85-89			74.6	176.1	387.4
	90-94	37.5	100.5	20.6	55.3	170.7
	95-99			3.5	11.0	47.1
	100+			0.4	1.3	6.8
Female	Total	6 867.6	12 968.9	24 236.7	23 949.9	23 862.1
	0-14	2 636.2	5 426.0	7 608.1	6 775.2	5 666.4
	15-59	3 774.4	6 765.1	14 600.4	13 818.1	14 788.3
	60-64	177.3	271.7	696.1	903.4	854.0
	65-69	126.7	212.3	532.0	838.8	691.0
	70-74	84.1	139.1	370.7	683.2	514.6
	75-79	45.6	86.2	229.7	464.5	467.6
	80-84			124.5	282.0	413.7
	85-89			55.5	130.4	283.3
	90-94	23.3	68.6	16.4	43.7	136.5
	95-99			3.0	9.2	40.6
	100+			0.3	1.2	6.2
Male	Total	6 815.6	12 884.6	23 462.0	24 347.4	24 797.8
	0-14	2 643.4	5 494.6	7 751.2	6 944.7	5 834.3
	15-59	3 814.6	6 836.3	14 298.2	15 200.1	16 018.9
	60-64	146.9	231.3	567.3	724.9	978.9
	65-69	101.3	154.9	389.8	599.8	764.8
	70-74	63.8	88.1	242.2	437.4	502.8
	75-79	31.4	47.5	132.0	255.3	340.3
	80-84			57.3	126.0	212.3
	85-89			19.1	45.7	104.1
	90-94	14.2	31.9	4.2	11.6	34.2
	95-99			0.5	1.8	6.5
	100+			0.0	0.1	0.6
Percentage in older ages						
Total	60+	6.0	5.2	7.2	11.5	13.1
	65+	3.6	3.2	4.6	8.1	9.3
	80+	0.3	0.4	0.6	1.3	2.5
Female	60+	6.7	6.0	8.4	14.0	14.3
	65+	4.1	3.9	5.5	10.2	10.7
	80+	0.3	0.5	0.8	1.9	3.7
Male	60+	5.2	4.3	6.0	9.0	11.9
	65+	3.1	2.5	3.6	6.1	7.9
	80+	0.2	0.2	0.3	0.8	1.4
Ageing index		15.4	12.2	22.4	40.5	55.2
Broad age groups (percentage)	0-14	38.6	42.2	32.2	28.4	23.6
	15-59	55.5	52.6	60.6	60.1	63.3
	60+	6.0	5.2	7.2	11.5	13.1
Median age (years)		20.9	18.7	23.5*	26.0	30.2
Dependency ratio	Total	72.9	83.3	58.1	57.6	49.1
	Youth	66.7	77.4	50.9	44.8	35.2
	Old Age	6.2	5.9	7.2	12.8	13.8
Potential support ratio		16.1	17.0	13.9	7.8	7.2
Parent support ratio		0.9	1.7	2.0	4.9	9.3
Sex ratio (per 100 women)	60+	78.3	71.2	69.6	65.6	86.4
	65+	75.4	63.7	63.5	60.2	77.0
	80+	60.9	46.5	40.7	39.7	40.6

* Estimate refers to year 2005.

Indicator	Age	1950-1955	1975-1980	2005-2010	2025-2030	2045-2050
Growth rate (percentage)	Total	2.3	2.5	0.2	0.0	0.1
	60+	2.8	1.9	3.4	0.8	1.3
	65+	3.4	1.7	3.8	1.7	0.9
	80+	8.2	0.6	4.5	4.1	0.3
Total fertility rate (per woman)		6.5	5.0	2.6	2.1	1.9
Life expectancy (years)						
Total	Birth	45.0	55.5	44.1	51.3	59.4
	60	..	..	16.5	18.2	19.5
	65	..	..	13.7	15.1	16.2
	80	..	..	6.7	7.4	8.0
Female	Birth	46.0	58.8	43.8	50.6	60.4
	60	..	..	18.7	20.3	22.0
	65	..	..	15.4	16.9	18.3
	80	..	..	7.3	8.0	8.8
Male	Birth	44.0	52.5	44.2	51.7	58.6
	60	..	..	14.1	15.6	17.1
	65	..	..	11.5	12.8	14.0
	80	..	..	5.7	6.2	6.6
Survival rate (percentage)						
Total	60	..	..	27.4	37.0	51.8
	65	..	..	23.8	32.9	47.1
	80	..	..	10.1	16.3	25.4
Female	60	..	..	26.7	34.6	52.0
	65	..	..	24.1	31.8	48.8
	80	..	..	12.4	18.5	31.2
Male	60	..	..	27.8	39.0	51.7
	65	..	..	23.0	33.4	45.7
	80	..	..	7.2	12.7	20.1

		1980	1990	2007	2010	2020
Labour force participation (percentage)						
Total	65+	13.8	13.3	11.3	11.1	10.8
Female	65+	9.7	7.5	4.1	3.9	3.7
Male	65+	20.2	22.3	22.7	22.5	22.4

Percentage married, age 60+			Percentage living alone, age 60+ (1998)		
Total	Female	Male	Total	Female	Male
59.9	47.0	78.0	8.1	8.2	8.0

Statutory pensionable age (2006)			Percentage illiterate, age 65+ (1996)		
Female	Male		Total	Female	Male
60	65		50.9	52.9	47.8

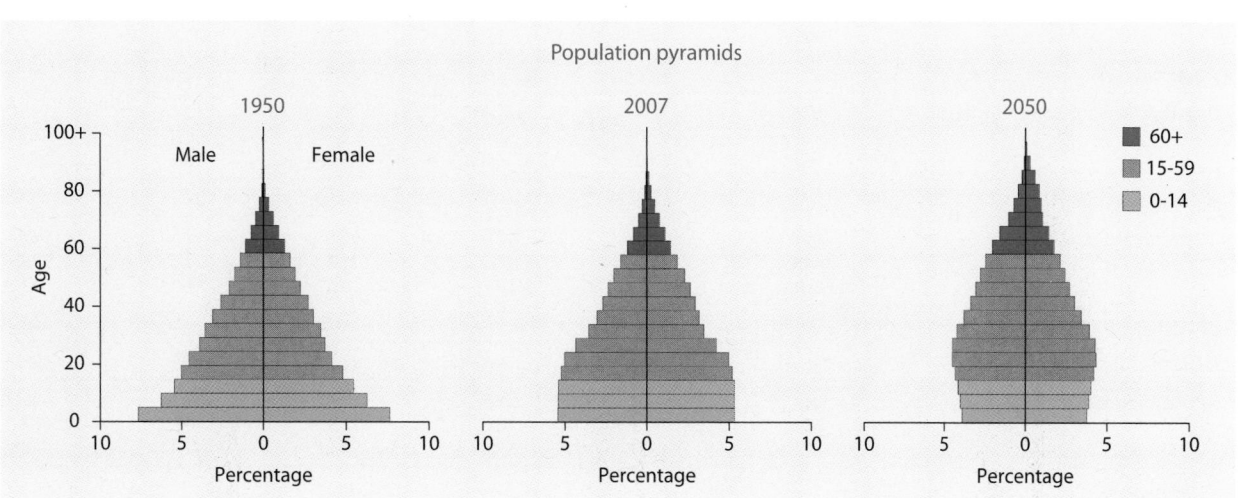

Population pyramids

1950   2007   2050

Male   Female

■ 60+
■ 15-59
■ 0-14

Spain

Indicator	Age	1950	1975	2007	2025	2050
Population (thousands)						
Total	Total	28 008.8	35 596.0	43 604.3	44 244.4	42 541.3
	0-14	7 587.1	9 828.5	6 342.3	5 946.8	6 070.1
	15-59	17 358.2	20 646.5	27 797.0	25 665.7	19 595.3
	60-64	1 019.1	1 550.0	2 219.4	3 188.0	2 372.3
	65-69	743.7	1 325.6	1 789.3	2 783.3	2 872.6
	70-74	627.2	1 010.3	1 797.6	2 154.4	3 326.8
	75-79	380.9	633.8	1 696.1	1 788.7	3 091.5
	80-84			1 150.2	1 312.8	2 319.0
	85-89			568.0	761.8	1 611.6
	90-94	292.5	601.3	202.7	477.3	886.9
	95-99			40.2	149.0	318.5
	100+			1.6	16.7	76.6
Female	Total	14 482.8	18 234.3	22 191.0	22 543.8	21 824.0
	0-14	3 736.8	4 795.8	3 078.9	2 872.8	2 932.2
	15-59	8 945.0	10 489.6	13 743.3	12 622.6	9 552.8
	60-64	555.8	852.6	1 148.7	1 629.5	1 189.2
	65-69	420.1	739.2	953.2	1 460.1	1 461.0
	70-74	381.9	587.4	992.4	1 162.3	1 733.7
	75-79	243.2	382.2	986.0	1 013.0	1 671.6
	80-84			714.7	794.2	1 329.7
	85-89			389.1	503.8	1 010.5
	90-94	200.0	387.5	151.4	348.9	621.7
	95-99			31.8	121.3	252.4
	100+			1.5	15.3	69.2
Male	Total	13 526.0	17 361.7	21 413.4	21 700.6	20 717.2
	0-14	3 850.3	5 032.7	3 263.3	3 073.9	3 137.9
	15-59	8 413.2	10 156.9	14 053.7	13 043.1	10 042.5
	60-64	463.3	697.4	1 070.7	1 558.5	1 183.1
	65-69	323.6	586.4	836.1	1 323.2	1 411.7
	70-74	245.2	422.9	805.2	992.1	1 593.1
	75-79	137.7	251.6	710.1	775.8	1 419.9
	80-84			435.5	518.6	989.3
	85-89			178.9	258.0	601.1
	90-94	92.5	213.8	51.2	128.4	265.2
	95-99			8.4	27.7	66.2
	100+			0.2	1.3	7.3
Percentage in older ages						
Total	60+	10.9	14.4	21.7	28.6	39.7
	65+	7.3	10.0	16.6	21.3	34.1
	80+	1.0	1.7	4.5	6.1	12.3
Female	60+	12.4	16.2	24.2	31.3	42.8
	65+	8.6	11.5	19.0	24.0	37.3
	80+	1.4	2.1	5.8	7.9	15.0
Male	60+	9.3	12.5	19.1	25.7	36.4
	65+	5.9	8.5	14.1	18.5	30.7
	80+	0.7	1.2	3.1	4.3	9.3
Ageing index		40.4	52.1	149.2	212.4	278.0
Broad age groups (percentage)	0-14	27.1	27.6	14.5	13.4	14.3
	15-59	62.0	58.0	63.7	58.0	46.1
	60+	10.9	14.4	21.7	28.6	39.7
Median age (years)		27.7	29.7	38.6*	47.2	49.9
Dependency ratio	Total	52.4	60.4	45.3	53.3	93.7
	Youth	41.3	44.3	21.1	20.6	27.6
	Old Age	11.1	16.1	24.1	32.7	66.0
Potential support ratio		9.0	6.2	4.1	3.1	1.5
Parent support ratio		2.7	4.1	11.1	13.3	43.0
Sex ratio (per 100 women)	60+	70.1	73.7	76.3	79.2	80.7
	65+	64.2	70.3	71.7	74.3	78.0
	80+	46.2	55.2	52.3	52.4	58.8

* *Estimate refers to year 2005.*

Indicator	Age	1950-1955	1975-1980	2005-2010	2025-2030	2045-2050
Growth rate (percentage)	Total	0.8	1.1	0.4	–0.1	–0.3
	60+	1.9	1.7	1.3	2.0	–0.4
	65+	2.3	2.3	1.2	2.3	0.3
	80+	1.5	0.9	4.5	2.0	2.6
Total fertility rate (per woman)		2.6	2.6	1.3	1.6	1.9
Life expectancy (years)						
Total	Birth	64.0	74.4	80.1	82.6	84.8
	60	..	..	23.3	25.1	26.8
	65	..	..	19.2	20.8	22.4
	80	..	..	8.7	10.0	11.1
Female	Birth	65.2	76.9	83.8	86.1	88.3
	60	..	..	25.8	27.7	29.5
	65	..	..	21.3	23.1	24.9
	80	..	..	9.6	11.1	12.6
Male	Birth	61.6	71.4	76.5	79.1	81.4
	60	..	..	20.7	22.4	24.0
	65	..	..	16.8	18.3	19.8
	80	..	..	7.5	8.4	9.3
Survival rate (percentage)						
Total	60	..	..	91.9	93.9	95.4
	65	..	..	88.2	90.9	93.0
	80	..	..	61.0	67.3	72.8
Female	60	..	..	95.4	96.6	97.4
	65	..	..	93.3	94.8	95.9
	80	..	..	73.0	77.8	81.9
Male	60	..	..	88.5	91.4	93.4
	65	..	..	83.3	87.2	90.1
	80	..	..	49.0	56.9	63.7

		1980	1990	2007	2010	2020
Labour force participation (percentage)						
Total	65+	7.6	2.6	1.4	1.4	1.3
Female	65+	4.0	1.7	0.8	0.8	0.7
Male	65+	12.7	3.8	2.3	2.3	2.2

Percentage married, age 60+			Percentage living alone, age 60+ (1994)		
Total	Female	Male	Total	Female	Male
62.4	49.0	80.0	14.0	19.2	7.4

Statutory pensionable age (2006)			Percentage illiterate, age 65+		
	Female	Male	Total	Female	Male
	65	65	..	..	..

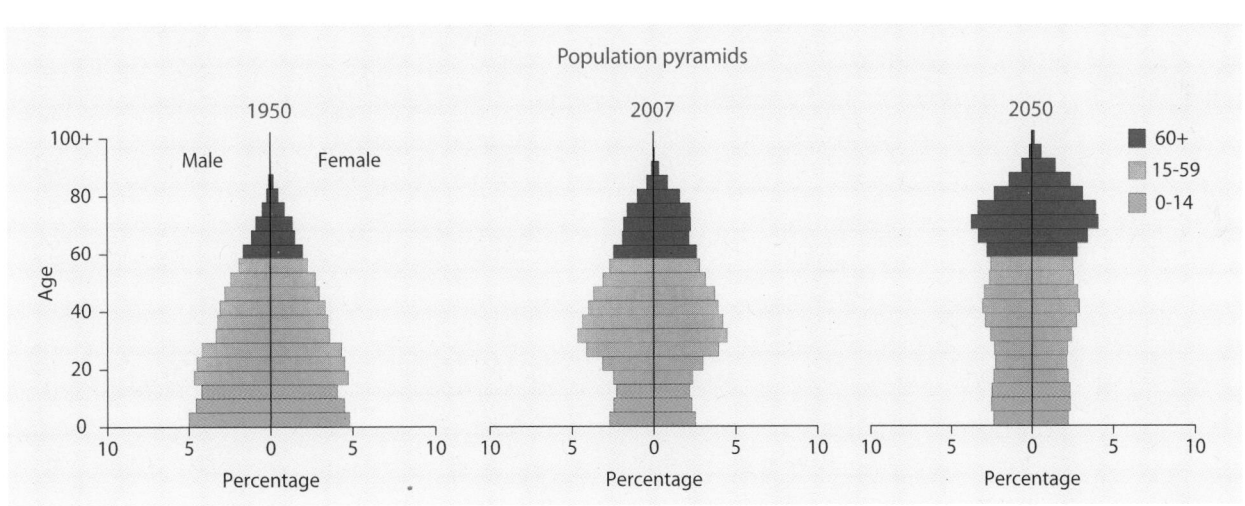

Population pyramids

1950   2007   2050

■ 60+
■ 15-59
□ 0-14

Sri Lanka

Indicator	Age	1950	1975	2007	2025	2050
Population (thousands)						
Total	Total	7 782.1	14 041.8	21 077.9	23 358.4	23 553.6
	0-14	3 126.1	5 283.7	4 926.0	4 536.5	3 861.8
	15-59	4 083.5	7 898.2	13 794.8	14 529.5	12 773.2
	60-64	143.7	322.6	759.3	1 302.7	1 523.0
	65-69	134.1	223.8	586.6	1 117.6	1 580.2
	70-74	131.2	161.0	428.7	813.8	1 345.3
	75-79	92.0	94.6	318.0	545.4	1 034.0
	80-84			179.3	313.1	772.3
	85-89			66.8	142.0	429.9
	90-94	71.3	57.9	16.4	46.1	181.6
	95-99			2.0	10.8	45.8
	100+			0.1	0.9	6.4
Female	Total	3 688.2	6 793.7	10 376.1	11 589.8	11 834.0
	0-14	1 523.2	2 593.4	2 428.6	2 227.5	1 894.0
	15-59	1 881.3	3 810.2	6 699.0	7 122.9	6 221.6
	60-64	61.0	142.9	372.1	643.5	757.4
	65-69	77.2	98.8	306.9	557.8	801.0
	70-74	63.7	78.6	229.8	418.2	700.3
	75-79	45.3	40.1	185.5	285.6	562.2
	80-84			101.5	192.2	449.2
	85-89			40.2	96.4	274.2
	90-94	36.5	29.7	10.9	35.6	130.7
	95-99			1.3	9.3	37.5
	100+			0.1	0.8	5.8
Male	Total	4 093.9	7 248.1	10 701.9	11 768.6	11 719.6
	0-14	1 603.0	2 690.3	2 497.4	2 309.0	1 967.7
	15-59	2 202.3	4 088.0	7 095.8	7 406.6	6 551.6
	60-64	82.7	179.7	387.2	659.2	765.6
	65-69	56.9	124.9	279.7	559.8	779.2
	70-74	67.5	82.4	198.9	395.6	645.0
	75-79	46.7	54.5	132.5	259.8	471.8
	80-84			77.8	120.9	323.1
	85-89			26.5	45.6	155.8
	90-94	34.9	28.3	5.5	10.5	50.9
	95-99			0.6	1.4	8.2
	100+			0.0	0.1	0.6
Percentage in older ages						
Total	60+	7.4	6.1	11.2	18.4	29.4
	65+	5.5	3.8	7.6	12.8	22.9
	80+	0.9	0.4	1.3	2.2	6.1
Female	60+	7.7	5.7	12.0	19.3	31.4
	65+	6.0	3.6	8.4	13.8	25.0
	80+	1.0	0.4	1.5	2.9	7.6
Male	60+	7.1	6.5	10.4	17.4	27.3
	65+	5.0	4.0	6.7	11.8	20.8
	80+	0.9	0.4	1.0	1.5	4.6
Ageing index		18.3	16.3	47.9	94.6	179.2
Broad age groups (percentage)	0-14	40.2	37.6	23.4	19.4	16.4
	15-59	52.5	56.2	65.4	62.2	54.2
	60+	7.4	6.1	11.2	18.4	29.4
Median age (years)		20.2	20.5	29.6*	37.5	43.5
Dependency ratio	Total	84.1	70.8	44.8	47.5	64.8
	Youth	74.0	64.3	33.8	28.7	27.0
	Old Age	10.1	6.5	11.0	18.9	37.7
Potential support ratio		9.9	15.3	9.1	5.3	2.6
Parent support ratio		3.8	1.5	2.9	4.6	14.8
Sex ratio (per 100 women)	60+	101.7	120.4	88.8	91.7	86.1
	65+	92.5	117.4	82.3	87.3	82.2
	80+	95.6	95.3	71.7	53.4	60.0

* *Estimate refers to year 2005.*

Indicator	Age	1950-1955	1975-1980	2005-2010	2025-2030	2045-2050
Growth rate (percentage)	Total	2.5	1.6	0.8	0.3	−0.2
	60+	−1.1	3.4	3.2	2.8	0.9
	65+	−2.6	3.8	3.0	3.2	1.8
	80+	−0.4	4.1	5.5	4.4	3.2
Total fertility rate (per woman)		5.7	3.8	1.9	1.9	1.9
Life expectancy (years)						
Total	Birth	53.2	65.8	75.1	78.0	80.5
	60	..	..	19.5	21.2	23.0
	65	..	..	15.7	17.2	18.9
	80	..	..	6.8	7.8	8.8
Female	Birth	52.3	67.7	77.9	80.7	83.0
	60	..	..	21.3	23.4	25.2
	65	..	..	17.2	19.2	20.8
	80	..	..	7.5	8.8	9.9
Male	Birth	54.2	64.2	72.6	75.6	78.0
	60	..	..	17.8	19.1	20.9
	65	..	..	14.2	15.2	16.9
	80	..	..	6.0	6.5	7.4
Survival rate (percentage)						
Total	60	..	..	88.3	91.8	93.5
	65	..	..	82.6	87.0	89.8
	80	..	..	44.4	52.1	60.0
Female	60	..	..	91.4	93.6	95.0
	65	..	..	87.2	90.2	92.3
	80	..	..	53.2	61.9	68.5
Male	60	..	..	85.7	90.0	92.1
	65	..	..	78.5	84.0	87.3
	80	..	..	36.0	43.3	51.6

		1980	1990	2007	2010	2020
Labour force participation (percentage)						
Total	65+	32.0	24.8	13.1	11.7	8.3
Female	65+	13.2	8.5	4.7	4.6	4.6
Male	65+	48.5	40.3	23.4	20.4	12.5

Percentage married, age 60+			Percentage living alone, age 60+ (1990)		
Total	Female	Male	Total	Female	Male
65.3	51.0	81.0	2.9	4.6	1.4

Statutory pensionable age (2006)			Percentage illiterate, age 65+		
	Female	Male	Total	Female	Male
	50	55	..	..	..

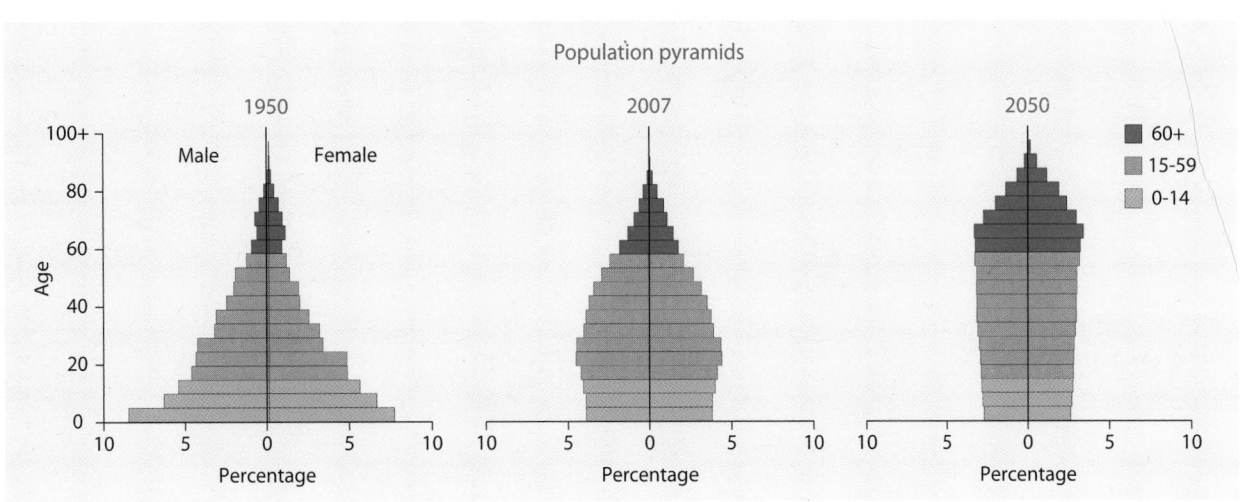

Population pyramids

Sudan

Indicator	Age	1950	1975	2007	2025	2050
Population (thousands)						
Total	Total	9 190.0	17 055.6	37 793.0	51 031.5	66 705.0
	0-14	4 024.6	7 642.6	14 608.4	16 065.7	16 035.3
	15-59	4 673.5	8 631.9	20 987.2	31 016.7	41 970.5
	60-64	185.9	304.2	793.6	1 346.5	2 721.5
	65-69	138.2	218.4	588.8	1 027.6	2 233.9
	70-74	92.4	138.9	403.9	729.7	1 666.3
	75-79	50.3	76.0	242.7	478.3	1 119.9
	80-84			117.5	246.8	618.2
	85-89			41.1	93.5	256.7
	90-94	25.1	43.6	8.7	23.2	70.7
	95-99			1.0	3.3	11.3
	100+			0.1	0.2	1.0
Female	Total	4 607.6	8 520.8	18 766.8	25 270.2	33 099.9
	0-14	2 001.6	3 769.4	7 167.6	7 880.4	7 862.3
	15-59	2 349.7	4 332.2	10 429.6	15 300.8	20 739.5
	60-64	95.2	159.7	412.6	693.4	1 364.5
	65-69	71.7	116.6	310.4	537.9	1 134.6
	70-74	49.0	75.5	216.6	388.4	864.0
	75-79	26.9	41.9	133.0	260.7	597.4
	80-84			66.3	137.9	340.7
	85-89			24.3	54.1	146.7
	90-94	13.5	25.4	5.5	14.2	42.3
	95-99			0.7	2.2	7.2
	100+			0.1	0.2	0.7
Male	Total	4 582.4	8 534.9	19 026.2	25 761.2	33 605.1
	0-14	2 023.0	3 873.2	7 440.7	8 185.3	8 173.1
	15-59	2 323.8	4 299.7	10 557.6	15 715.9	21 231.0
	60-64	90.7	144.5	381.0	653.1	1 357.0
	65-69	66.5	101.8	278.4	489.7	1 099.2
	70-74	43.4	63.4	187.3	341.2	802.2
	75-79	23.4	34.1	109.8	217.6	522.5
	80-84			51.2	108.9	277.5
	85-89			16.8	39.4	110.0
	90-94	11.6	18.2	3.2	9.0	28.3
	95-99			0.3	1.1	4.0
	100+			0.0	0.1	0.3
Percentage in older ages						
Total	60+	5.4	4.6	5.8	7.7	13.0
	65+	3.3	2.8	3.7	5.1	9.0
	80+	0.3	0.3	0.4	0.7	1.4
Female	60+	5.6	4.9	6.2	8.3	13.6
	65+	3.5	3.0	4.0	5.5	9.5
	80+	0.3	0.3	0.5	0.8	1.6
Male	60+	5.1	4.2	5.4	7.2	12.5
	65+	3.2	2.5	3.4	4.7	8.5
	80+	0.3	0.2	0.4	0.6	1.3
Ageing index		12.2	10.2	15.0	24.6	54.3
Broad age groups (percentage)	0-14	43.8	44.8	38.7	31.5	24.0
	15-59	50.9	50.6	55.5	60.8	62.9
	60+	5.4	4.6	5.8	7.7	13.0
Median age (years)		18.1	17.6	20.1*	24.4	31.2
Dependency ratio	Total	89.1	90.9	73.5	57.7	49.3
	Youth	82.8	85.5	67.1	49.6	35.9
	Old Age	6.3	5.3	6.4	8.0	13.4
Potential support ratio		15.9	18.7	15.5	12.4	7.5
Parent support ratio		1.0	0.9	1.7	2.3	3.4
Sex ratio (per 100 women)	60+	91.9	86.4	87.9	89.0	93.4
	65+	89.9	83.8	85.5	86.5	90.8
	80+	85.9	71.6	73.8	75.9	78.1

* *Estimate refers to year 2005.*

Indicator	Age	1950-1955	1975-1980	2005-2010	2025-2030	2045-2050
Growth rate (percentage)	Total	2.2	3.2	2.1	1.3	0.8
	60+	1.1	3.4	3.6	3.3	2.9
	65+	1.3	3.6	3.7	3.3	3.2
	80+	2.0	3.2	4.6	4.1	3.9
Total fertility rate (per woman)		6.7	6.5	4.0	2.7	2.2
Life expectancy (years)						
Total	Birth	38.6	47.8	56.9	63.7	70.1
	60	..	..	17.2	18.4	19.5
	65	..	..	13.8	14.8	15.7
	80	..	..	6.1	6.5	6.8
Female	Birth	40.1	49.2	58.2	65.2	72.0
	60	..	..	17.8	19.1	20.3
	65	..	..	14.3	15.4	16.3
	80	..	..	6.3	6.7	7.0
Male	Birth	37.3	46.5	55.6	62.4	68.3
	60	..	..	16.5	17.7	18.6
	65	..	..	13.3	14.3	15.0
	80	..	..	5.8	6.2	6.5
Survival rate (percentage)						
Total	60	..	..	58.4	67.9	78.5
	65	..	..	52.6	62.4	73.2
	80	..	..	22.9	30.6	39.1
Female	60	..	..	60.5	69.8	81.1
	65	..	..	55.1	64.9	76.5
	80	..	..	25.3	33.6	43.4
Male	60	..	..	56.4	66.1	76.0
	65	..	..	50.2	60.0	70.0
	80	..	..	20.5	27.7	35.1

		1980	1990	2007	2010	2020
Labour force participation (percentage)						
Total	65+	50.8	45.0	36.9	35.6	31.0
Female	65+	25.8	21.6	16.3	16.2	16.2
Male	65+	80.6	72.9	61.0	58.3	48.2

Percentage married, age 60+			Percentage living alone, age 60+ (1979)		
Total	Female	Male	Total	Female	Male
61.8	38.0	89.0	9.8	15.4	5.6

Statutory pensionable age (2006)			Percentage illiterate, age 65+ (2000)		
	Female	Male	Total	Female	Male
	60	60	72.1	91.8	61.3

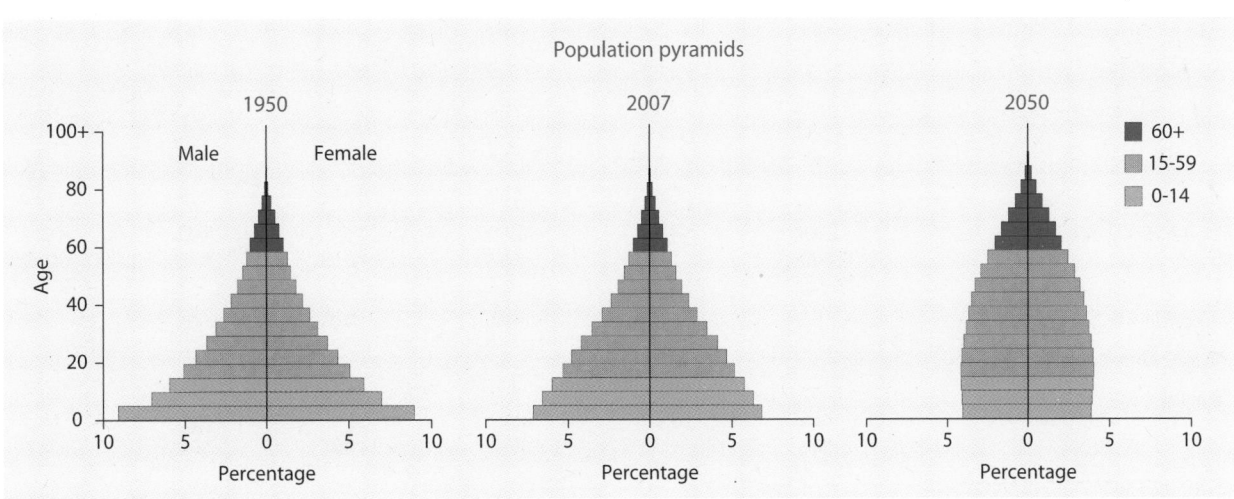

Population pyramids

Suriname

Indicator	Age	1950	1975	2007	2025	2050
Population (thousands)						
Total	Total	215.0	364.5	454.6	480.1	429.3
	0-14	86.0	173.7	134.2	111.6	71.8
	15-59	111.0	169.7	278.7	294.7	239.0
	60-64	5.0	7.0	12.0	26.9	29.6
	65-69	4.0	5.4	10.5	18.3	29.4
	70-74	4.0	4.5	8.7	12.7	19.6
	75-79	3.0	3.0	5.7	7.7	16.8
	80-84			3.0	4.6	12.4
	85-89			1.2	2.5	7.5
	90-94	2.0	1.3	0.4	0.9	2.5
	95-99			0.1	0.2	0.6
	100+			0.0	0.0	0.1
Female	Total	108.0	181.7	227.7	240.3	215.2
	0-14	43.0	85.8	64.9	53.9	34.5
	15-59	56.0	85.2	139.8	145.6	115.4
	60-64	2.0	3.5	6.6	13.8	14.6
	65-69	2.0	2.8	5.8	9.9	15.4
	70-74	2.0	2.2	4.8	7.3	10.7
	75-79	2.0	1.5	3.1	4.6	9.7
	80-84			1.7	2.9	7.6
	85-89			0.7	1.6	4.9
	90-94	1.0	0.7	0.2	0.6	1.8
	95-99			0.1	0.1	0.5
	100+			0.0	0.0	0.1
Male	Total	107.0	182.8	226.9	239.8	214.1
	0-14	43.0	87.9	69.3	57.7	37.2
	15-59	55.0	84.4	138.9	149.0	123.6
	60-64	3.0	3.5	5.4	13.0	15.0
	65-69	2.0	2.6	4.6	8.4	13.9
	70-74	2.0	2.2	3.9	5.4	9.0
	75-79	1.0	1.5	2.6	3.1	7.1
	80-84			1.3	1.7	4.8
	85-89			0.5	0.9	2.6
	90-94	1.0	0.6	0.2	0.4	0.7
	95-99			0.1	0.1	0.1
	100+			0.0	0.0	0.0
Percentage in older ages						
Total	60+	8.4	5.8	9.2	15.4	27.6
	65+	6.0	3.9	6.5	9.8	20.7
	80+	0.9	0.4	1.0	1.7	5.4
Female	60+	8.3	5.9	10.1	17.0	30.3
	65+	6.5	4.0	7.2	11.2	23.5
	80+	0.9	0.4	1.2	2.2	6.9
Male	60+	8.4	5.7	8.2	13.8	24.9
	65+	5.6	3.8	5.8	8.3	17.9
	80+	0.9	0.3	0.9	1.3	3.9
Ageing index		20.9	12.2	31.0	66.1	165.1
Broad age groups (percentage)	0-14	40.0	47.6	29.5	23.3	16.7
	15-59	51.6	46.5	61.3	61.4	55.7
	60+	8.4	5.8	9.2	15.4	27.6
Median age (years)		20.1	16.0	25.1*	32.8	43.3
Dependency ratio	Total	85.3	106.3	56.4	49.3	59.8
	Youth	74.1	98.3	46.2	34.7	26.7
	Old Age	11.2	8.0	10.2	14.6	33.1
Potential support ratio		8.9	12.5	9.8	6.9	3.0
Parent support ratio		3.4	1.7	3.6	4.5	12.2
Sex ratio (per 100 women)	60+	100.0	97.1	81.2	81.0	81.7
	65+	85.7	95.4	80.7	74.2	75.7
	80+	100.0	75.2	78.4	59.2	55.7

* *Estimate refers to year 2005.*

Indicator	Age	1950-1955	1975-1980	2005-2010	2025-2030	2045-2050
Growth rate (percentage)	Total	3.0	−0.5	0.6	−0.1	−0.8
	60+	0.0	1.2	1.8	3.0	1.3
	65+	−1.6	2.7	1.7	4.7	2.2
	80+	0.0	20.1	4.5	2.3	2.9
Total fertility rate (per woman)		6.6	4.2	2.4	2.0	1.9
Life expectancy (years)						
Total	Birth	56.0	65.1	70.2	74.7	78.1
	60	..	..	18.5	19.9	21.5
	65	..	..	15.0	16.2	17.6
	80	..	..	7.1	7.7	8.4
Female	Birth	57.7	67.7	73.3	77.1	80.6
	60	..	..	19.6	21.5	23.5
	65	..	..	15.8	17.5	19.4
	80	..	..	7.2	8.1	9.2
Male	Birth	54.4	62.8	67.1	72.3	75.7
	60	..	..	17.2	18.2	19.4
	65	..	..	14.0	14.7	15.7
	80	..	..	6.9	7.0	7.3
Survival rate (percentage)						
Total	60	..	..	79.0	86.5	91.0
	65	..	..	72.1	80.4	85.9
	80	..	..	35.0	43.9	52.3
Female	60	..	..	84.5	89.3	92.9
	65	..	..	78.7	84.6	89.2
	80	..	..	41.7	51.5	61.0
Male	60	..	..	73.8	83.8	89.2
	65	..	..	65.6	76.2	82.8
	80	..	..	28.4	35.9	43.4

		1980	1990	2007	2010	2020
Labour force participation (percentage)						
Total	65+	12.9	3.9	2.8	2.9	2.9
Female	65+	4.7	3.5	3.9	4.0	4.1
Male	65+	22.0	4.4	1.5	1.4	1.3

Percentage married, age 60+				Percentage living alone, age 60+		
Total	Female	Male		Total	Female	Male
52.1	39.0	67.0		..	..	..

Statutory pensionable age (2006)				Percentage illiterate, age 65+ (2004)		
	Female	Male		Total	Female	Male
	..	..		37.1	44.3	28.9

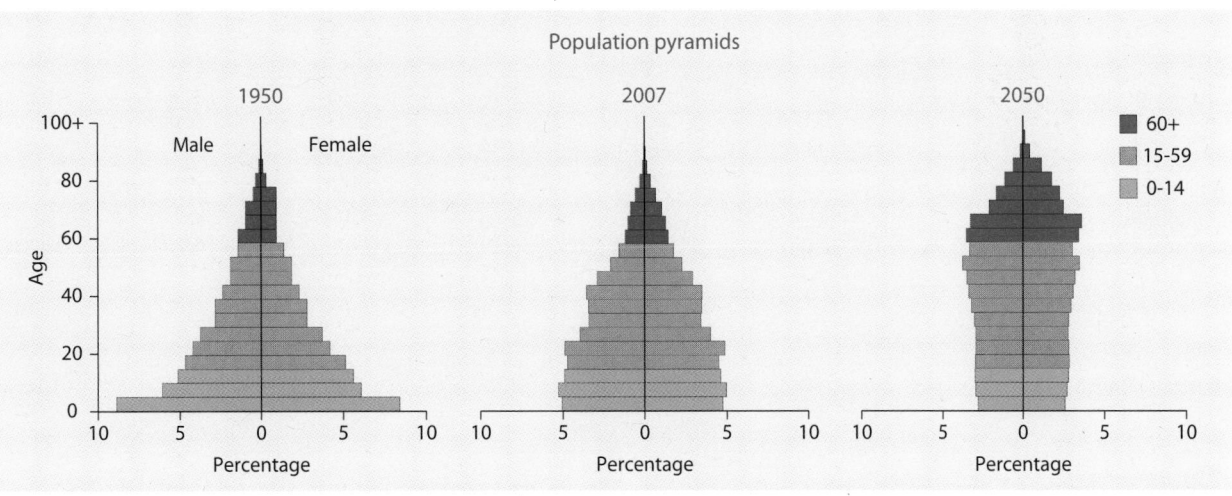

Population pyramids

Swaziland

Indicator	Age	1950	1975	2007	2025	2050
Population (thousands)						
Total	Total	273.0	528.1	1 025.2	975.0	1 026.0
	0-14	117.4	255.6	407.7	368.5	319.4
	15-59	143.2	249.5	559.1	546.2	658.3
	60-64	5.1	9.1	19.9	12.5	21.7
	65-69	3.7	6.4	15.9	14.9	12.0
	70-74	2.2	4.1	11.3	14.4	5.3
	75-79	1.0	2.2	6.7	10.3	3.3
	80-84			3.2	5.5	2.8
	85-89			1.1	2.2	2.0
	90-94	0.5	1.2	0.2	0.5	0.9
	95-99			0.0	0.1	0.2
	100+			0.0	0.0	0.0
Female	Total	140.3	277.0	528.3	476.7	496.4
	0-14	59.5	128.1	203.0	183.2	158.3
	15-59	73.6	135.5	292.7	256.2	319.1
	60-64	2.9	5.1	11.0	7.5	7.6
	65-69	2.1	3.7	8.5	9.3	4.0
	70-74	1.3	2.4	6.2	9.0	1.9
	75-79	0.6	1.3	4.0	6.4	1.6
	80-84			2.0	3.4	1.8
	85-89			0.7	1.3	1.5
	90-94	0.3	0.8	0.2	0.3	0.7
	95-99			0.0	0.0	0.1
	100+			0.0	0.0	0.0
Male	Total	132.7	251.1	496.9	498.3	529.5
	0-14	57.9	127.4	204.7	185.3	161.2
	15-59	69.6	114.0	266.4	290.0	339.1
	60-64	2.3	4.0	8.9	4.9	14.1
	65-69	1.6	2.7	7.4	5.6	8.1
	70-74	0.9	1.6	5.1	5.4	3.5
	75-79	0.4	0.9	2.7	3.9	1.7
	80-84			1.2	2.1	1.1
	85-89			0.4	0.8	0.6
	90-94	0.2	0.4	0.1	0.2	0.2
	95-99			0.0	0.0	0.0
	100+			0.0	0.0	0.0
Percentage in older ages						
Total	60+	4.6	4.4	5.7	6.2	4.7
	65+	2.7	2.6	3.8	4.9	2.6
	80+	0.2	0.2	0.4	0.8	0.6
Female	60+	5.1	4.8	6.2	7.8	3.8
	65+	3.0	3.0	4.1	6.2	2.3
	80+	0.2	0.3	0.6	1.1	0.8
Male	60+	4.0	3.9	5.2	4.6	5.5
	65+	2.3	2.3	3.4	3.6	2.9
	80+	0.1	0.2	0.3	0.6	0.4
Ageing index		10.6	9.0	14.3	16.3	15.1
Broad age groups (percentage)	0-14	43.0	48.4	39.8	37.8	31.1
	15-59	52.4	47.2	54.5	56.0	64.2
	60+	4.6	4.4	5.7	6.2	4.7
Median age (years)		18.4	15.7	18.1*	20.3	24.0
Dependency ratio	Total	84.1	104.2	77.1	74.5	50.9
	Youth	79.2	98.8	70.4	66.0	47.0
	Old Age	4.9	5.4	6.7	8.5	3.9
Potential support ratio		20.3	18.6	15.0	11.7	25.6
Parent support ratio		0.7	0.9	1.9	9.0	3.4
Sex ratio (per 100 women)	60+	74.2	72.9	79.2	61.6	153.8
	65+	71.3	68.6	77.9	60.6	131.8
	80+	65.1	56.1	57.7	62.0	46.5

* Estimate refers to year 2005.

Indicator	Age	1950-1955	1975-1980	2005-2010	2025-2030	2045-2050
Growth rate (percentage)	Total	2.5	3.1	−0.4	0.0	0.5
	60+	2.3	3.0	2.0	−3.2	5.4
	65+	2.9	3.2	2.3	−2.1	2.7
	80+	2.8	3.0	3.3	2.3	−5.7
Total fertility rate (per woman)		6.7	6.7	3.5	2.5	2.1
Life expectancy (years)						
Total	Birth	41.4	52.6	29.7	41.4	51.9
	60	..	..	15.6	17.1	17.8
	65	..	..	12.9	14.1	14.5
	80	..	..	5.7	6.1	6.5
Female	Birth	43.4	54.4	29.2	38.9	51.7
	60	..	..	16.8	17.9	19.4
	65	..	..	13.8	14.8	15.7
	80	..	..	5.9	6.3	6.9
Male	Birth	39.4	50.6	30.8	43.5	52.3
	60	..	..	14.5	15.8	16.7
	65	..	..	12.1	13.0	13.6
	80	..	..	5.4	5.7	5.9
Survival rate (percentage)						
Total	60	..	..	6.4	16.4	35.5
	65	..	..	5.5	14.4	31.8
	80	..	..	2.2	6.6	15.0
Female	60	..	..	5.6	11.2	34.5
	65	..	..	4.9	10.0	32.0
	80	..	..	2.2	4.9	17.0
Male	60	..	..	7.7	21.0	36.9
	65	..	..	6.4	17.9	32.5
	80	..	..	2.2	7.1	13.9

		1980	1990	2007	2010	2020
Labour force participation (percentage)						
Total	65+	23.8	21.0	19.3	19.1	17.8
Female	65+	10.1	8.8	5.1	4.9	4.8
Male	65+	43.6	38.0	37.6	37.6	37.7

Percentage married, age 60+				Percentage living alone, age 60+		
Total	Female	Male		Total	Female	Male
78.3	68.0	91.0		..	..	..

Statutory pensionable age (2006)				Percentage illiterate, age 65+ (2000)		
	Female	Male		Total	Female	Male
	50	50		64.1	70.9	56.6

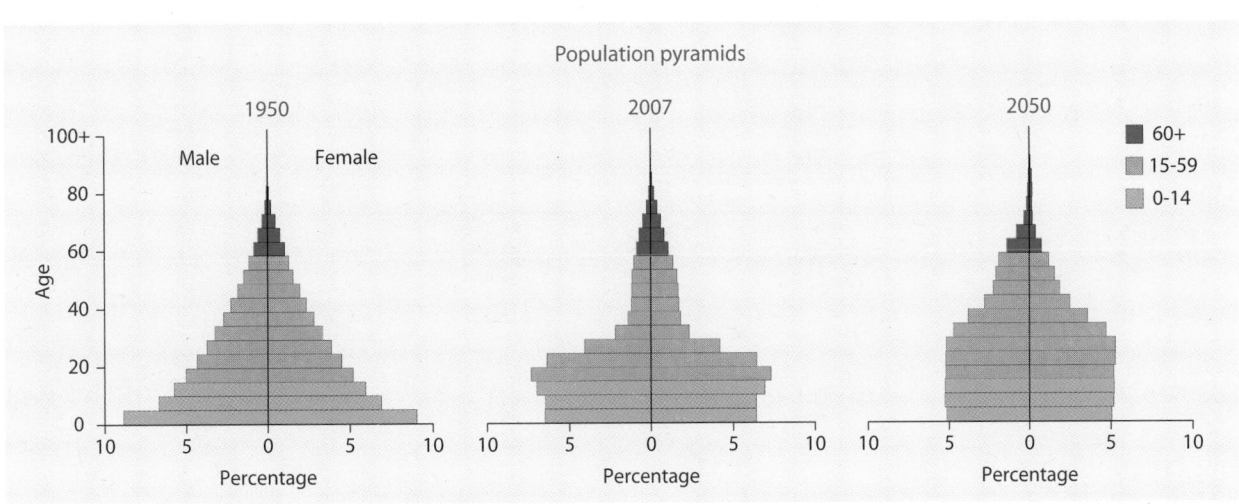

Population pyramids

Sweden

Indicator	Age	1950	1975	2007	2025	2050
Population (thousands)						
Total	Total	7 014.0	8 192.6	9 095.4	9 649.6	10 054.4
	0-14	1 644.0	1 695.3	1 536.2	1 644.7	1 619.8
	15-59	4 322.0	4 775.5	5 365.6	5 278.7	5 328.5
	60-64	329.0	483.8	592.6	589.9	618.4
	65-69	269.0	435.6	456.7	529.1	527.9
	70-74	210.0	342.6	354.0	491.9	497.1
	75-79	134.0	238.7	305.7	481.8	491.8
	80-84			256.4	342.7	423.4
	85-89			153.3	178.0	296.6
	90-94	106.0	221.0	60.0	80.9	163.3
	95-99			13.5	26.9	68.3
	100+			1.4	5.0	19.3
Female	Total	3 521.0	4 118.0	4 577.3	4 831.9	5 024.2
	0-14	803.0	825.7	745.1	796.2	783.8
	15-59	2 160.0	2 352.0	2 636.3	2 574.9	2 574.9
	60-64	173.0	247.3	296.4	296.2	306.1
	65-69	142.0	229.4	232.0	269.8	265.2
	70-74	111.0	189.0	188.1	256.2	255.3
	75-79	72.0	137.8	171.4	258.6	260.3
	80-84			153.3	191.7	233.2
	85-89			99.7	108.5	174.6
	90-94	60.0	136.9	43.2	55.1	105.7
	95-99			10.7	20.4	49.4
	100+			1.2	4.2	15.6
Male	Total	3 493.0	4 074.5	4 518.1	4 817.7	5 030.1
	0-14	841.0	869.6	791.1	848.5	835.9
	15-59	2 162.0	2 423.5	2 729.3	2 703.8	2 753.6
	60-64	156.0	236.6	296.2	293.7	312.4
	65-69	127.0	206.2	224.7	259.2	262.6
	70-74	99.0	153.6	165.9	235.7	241.8
	75-79	62.0	100.9	134.3	223.3	231.6
	80-84			103.2	151.0	190.1
	85-89			53.6	69.5	121.9
	90-94	46.0	84.2	16.8	25.8	57.6
	95-99			2.8	6.4	18.9
	100+			0.2	0.8	3.7
Percentage in older ages						
Total	60+	14.9	21.0	24.1	28.3	30.9
	65+	10.3	15.1	17.6	22.1	24.7
	80+	1.5	2.7	5.3	6.6	9.7
Female	60+	15.8	22.8	26.1	30.2	33.1
	65+	10.9	16.8	19.7	24.1	27.1
	80+	1.7	3.3	6.7	7.9	11.5
Male	60+	14.0	19.2	22.1	26.3	28.6
	65+	9.6	13.4	15.5	20.2	22.4
	80+	1.3	2.1	3.9	5.3	7.8
Ageing index		63.7	101.6	142.8	165.8	191.8
Broad age groups (percentage)	0-14	23.4	20.7	16.9	17.0	16.1
	15-59	61.6	58.3	59.0	54.7	53.0
	60+	14.9	21.0	24.1	28.3	30.9
Median age (years)		34.3	35.3	40.1*	42.5	43.9
Dependency ratio	Total	50.8	55.8	52.7	64.4	69.1
	Youth	35.3	32.2	25.8	28.0	27.2
	Old Age	15.5	23.5	26.9	36.4	41.8
Potential support ratio		6.5	4.2	3.7	2.7	2.4
Parent support ratio		3.5	5.2	12.9	15.8	29.9
Sex ratio (per 100 women)	60+	87.8	83.1	83.4	86.6	86.5
	65+	86.8	78.6	78.0	83.4	83.0
	80+	76.7	61.5	57.3	66.7	67.8

* Estimate refers to year 2005.

Indicator	Age	1950-1955	1975-1980	2005-2010	2025-2030	2045-2050
Growth rate (percentage)	Total	0.7	0.3	0.3	0.2	0.2
	60+	1.8	1.1	1.9	1.0	0.6
	65+	1.9	1.8	1.8	1.1	0.1
	80+	2.1	3.6	0.5	3.6	1.5
Total fertility rate (per woman)		2.2	1.7	1.7	1.9	1.9
Life expectancy (years)						
Total	Birth	71.8	75.2	80.8	83.3	85.5
	60	..	..	23.3	25.1	26.9
	65	..	..	19.1	20.8	22.5
	80	..	..	8.6	9.8	11.0
Female	Birth	73.3	78.3	83.0	85.4	87.6
	60	..	..	25.0	27.0	28.8
	65	..	..	20.7	22.5	24.3
	80	..	..	9.4	10.8	12.2
Male	Birth	70.4	72.3	78.6	81.2	83.4
	60	..	..	21.5	23.3	24.9
	65	..	..	17.4	19.0	20.6
	80	..	..	7.6	8.7	9.7
Survival rate (percentage)						
Total	60	..	..	93.4	95.3	96.6
	65	..	..	89.9	92.5	94.4
	80	..	..	62.3	68.9	74.4
Female	60	..	..	94.9	96.3	97.2
	65	..	..	92.2	94.1	95.6
	80	..	..	69.8	75.5	80.2
Male	60	..	..	92.0	94.4	96.0
	65	..	..	87.6	90.9	93.2
	80	..	..	54.6	62.2	68.5

		1980	1990	2007	2010	2020
Labour force participation (percentage)						
Total	65+	8.3	8.2	9.8	10.2	10.9
Female	65+	3.7	5.1	5.8	6.2	6.9
Male	65+	14.2	12.4	14.9	15.2	15.8

Percentage married, age 60+			Percentage living alone, age 60+ (1990)		
Total	Female	Male	Total	Female	Male
53.7	44.0	66.0	37.1	47.3	24.3

Statutory pensionable age (2006)			Percentage illiterate, age 65+		
	Female	Male	Total	Female	Male
	65	65	..	..	..

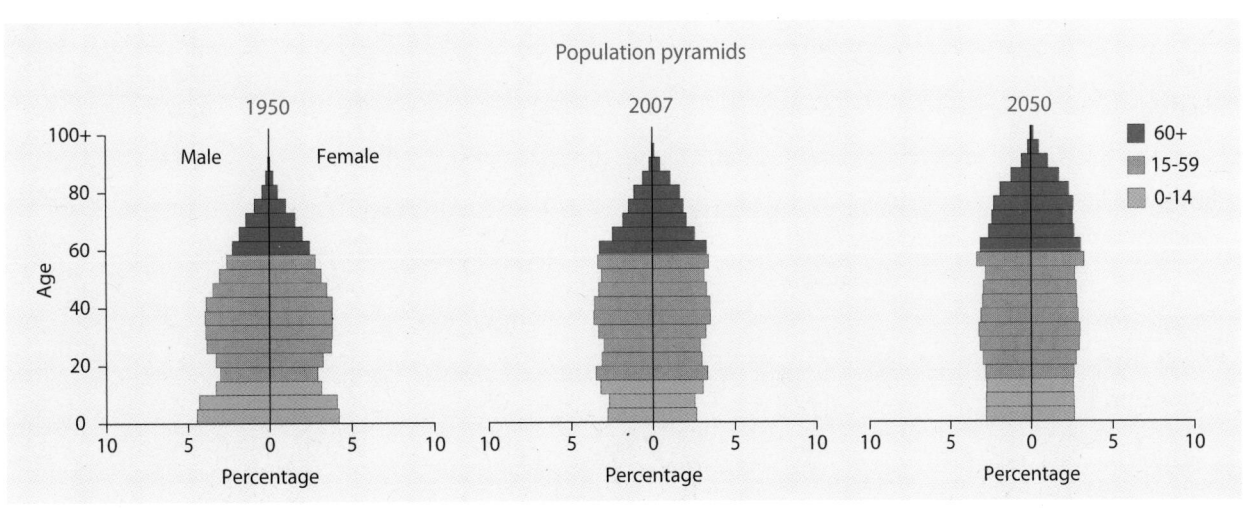

Population pyramids

Switzerland

Indicator	Age	1950	1975	2007	2025	2050
Population (thousands)						
Total	Total	4 694.0	6 338.7	7 274.5	7 398.3	7 252.5
	0-14	1 105.0	1 422.0	1 156.5	1 064.5	1 123.4
	15-59	2 930.0	3 809.5	4 464.9	4 007.1	3 686.6
	60-64	208.0	310.1	444.8	567.8	433.1
	65-69	176.0	283.1	355.1	490.4	393.7
	70-74	138.0	226.7	283.5	399.4	356.2
	75-79	82.0	155.3	231.0	351.2	356.7
	80-84			176.8	263.2	362.3
	85-89			101.9	148.9	291.9
	90-94	55.0	132.0	44.8	74.4	163.7
	95-99			13.3	25.9	65.6
	100+			1.9	5.5	19.3
Female	Total	2 432.0	3 248.9	3 755.7	3 869.6	3 860.7
	0-14	541.0	694.0	563.8	518.9	547.6
	15-59	1 519.0	1 914.1	2 255.2	2 064.2	1 895.2
	60-64	114.0	165.7	232.8	291.7	234.4
	65-69	97.0	158.4	190.4	255.3	217.3
	70-74	79.0	133.3	157.1	216.2	201.9
	75-79	48.0	96.5	133.5	197.1	205.8
	80-84			110.0	154.8	210.4
	85-89			68.3	95.2	175.9
	90-94	34.0	86.9	32.6	51.8	107.9
	95-99			10.5	19.8	48.5
	100+			1.6	4.6	15.8
Male	Total	2 262.0	3 089.8	3 518.8	3 528.7	3 391.8
	0-14	564.0	728.0	592.8	545.6	575.8
	15-59	1 411.0	1 895.5	2 209.7	1 943.0	1 791.3
	60-64	94.0	144.4	212.0	276.1	198.7
	65-69	79.0	124.7	164.7	235.1	176.4
	70-74	59.0	93.4	126.4	183.1	154.3
	75-79	34.0	58.8	97.5	154.1	150.9
	80-84			66.8	108.5	151.9
	85-89			33.6	53.7	115.9
	90-94	21.0	45.0	12.2	22.6	55.8
	95-99			2.8	6.1	17.1
	100+			0.3	0.9	3.5
Percentage in older ages						
Total	60+	14.0	17.5	22.7	31.4	33.7
	65+	9.6	12.6	16.6	23.8	27.7
	80+	1.2	2.1	4.7	7.0	12.4
Female	60+	15.3	19.7	24.9	33.2	36.7
	65+	10.6	14.6	18.7	25.7	30.7
	80+	1.4	2.7	5.9	8.4	14.5
Male	60+	12.7	15.1	20.4	29.5	30.2
	65+	8.5	10.4	14.3	21.7	24.4
	80+	0.9	1.5	3.3	5.4	10.2
Ageing index		59.6	77.9	142.9	218.6	217.4
Broad age groups (percentage)	0-14	23.5	22.4	15.9	14.4	15.5
	15-59	62.4	60.1	61.4	54.2	50.8
	60+	14.0	17.5	22.7	31.4	33.7
Median age (years)		33.3	33.1	40.8*	45.7	46.5
Dependency ratio	Total	49.6	53.9	48.2	61.7	76.0
	Youth	35.2	34.5	23.6	23.3	27.3
	Old Age	14.4	19.3	24.6	38.4	48.8
Potential support ratio		7.0	5.2	4.1	2.6	2.1
Parent support ratio		2.7	4.7	11.4	16.2	40.5
Sex ratio (per 100 women)	60+	77.2	72.8	76.5	80.9	72.3
	65+	74.8	67.8	71.6	76.8	69.8
	80+	61.8	51.8	51.9	58.8	61.6

* *Estimate refers to year 2005.*

Indicator	Age	1950-1955	1975-1980	2005-2010	2025-2030	2045-2050
Growth rate (percentage)	Total	1.2	−0.1	0.1	0.0	−0.1
	60+	1.8	0.8	2.1	1.3	−0.1
	65+	1.7	1.9	2.3	2.1	−0.4
	80+	3.6	5.6	2.0	3.0	1.2
Total fertility rate (per woman)		2.3	1.5	1.4	1.6	1.9
Life expectancy (years)						
Total	Birth	69.3	75.3	81.1	83.4	85.7
	60	..	..	24.0	25.7	27.5
	65	..	..	19.8	21.4	23.0
	80	..	..	9.3	10.3	11.5
Female	Birth	71.6	78.6	83.8	86.1	88.3
	60	..	..	26.0	27.8	29.6
	65	..	..	21.6	23.3	25.0
	80	..	..	10.0	11.4	12.7
Male	Birth	67.0	72.0	78.2	80.6	82.8
	60	..	..	21.8	23.4	25.1
	65	..	..	17.7	19.3	20.8
	80	..	..	8.1	9.0	9.9
Survival rate (percentage)						
Total	60	..	..	92.8	94.7	96.0
	65	..	..	89.4	92.0	93.8
	80	..	..	63.5	69.5	75.2
Female	60	..	..	94.9	96.3	97.3
	65	..	..	92.5	94.4	95.7
	80	..	..	72.2	77.3	81.6
Male	60	..	..	90.7	92.9	94.6
	65	..	..	86.3	89.4	91.7
	80	..	..	54.1	61.3	67.6

		1980	1990	2007	2010	2020
Labour force participation (percentage)						
Total	65+	8.9	14.1	8.1	7.7	6.5
Female	65+	4.8	10.5	5.8	5.8	5.7
Male	65+	15.1	19.6	11.4	10.3	7.6

Percentage married, age 60+			Percentage living alone, age 60+ (1990)		
Total	Female	Male	Total	Female	Male
59.7	47.0	77.0	29.8	40.9	14.9

Statutory pensionable age (2006)			Percentage illiterate, age 65+		
	Female	Male	Total	Female	Male
	64	65	..	..	..

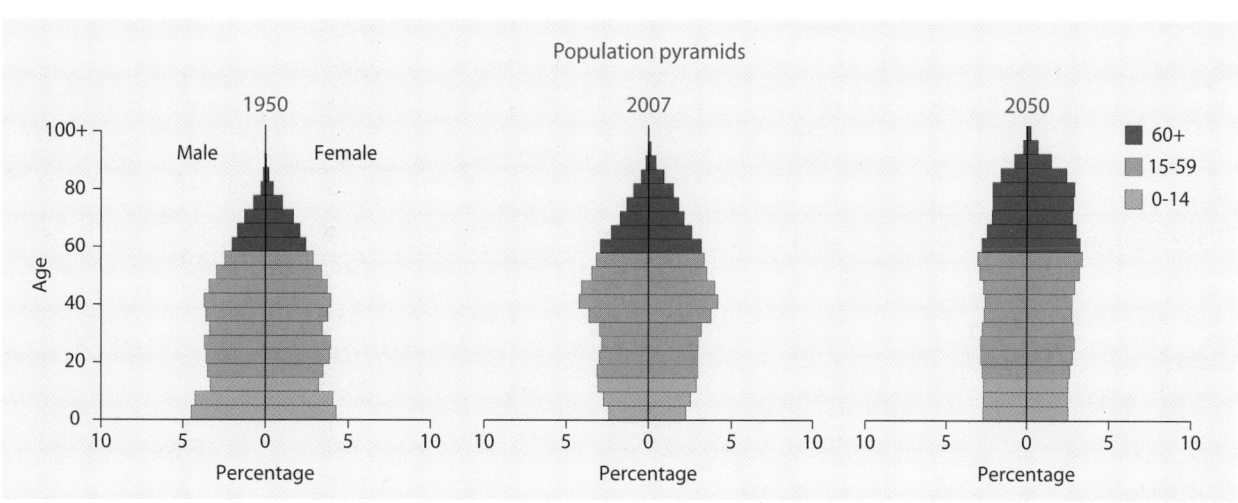

Population pyramids

United Nations Department of Economic and Social Affairs, Population Division

Syrian Arab Republic

Indicator	Age	1950	1975	2007	2025	2050
Population (thousands)						
Total	Total	3 495.1	7 537.6	19 988.0	28 081.1	35 935.0
	0-14	1 448.5	3 656.4	7 205.3	7 841.9	6 975.6
	15-59	1 808.6	3 549.3	11 821.6	17 991.7	21 956.6
	60-64	84.9	118.9	320.6	812.0	2 060.0
	65-69	64.8	89.0	250.5	587.1	1 814.9
	70-74	49.4	61.1	184.0	409.5	1 334.3
	75-79	26.1	37.4	118.3	235.3	893.2
	80-84			60.6	127.9	532.2
	85-89			21.9	56.3	257.3
	90-94	12.8	25.4	4.7	16.4	88.5
	95-99			0.6	2.8	20.1
	100+			0.0	0.2	2.2
Female	Total	1 689.5	3 738.8	9 923.6	13 917.6	17 869.7
	0-14	702.3	1 801.0	3 526.2	3 829.3	3 403.8
	15-59	879.9	1 763.7	5 877.6	8 870.1	10 767.2
	60-64	38.4	61.9	166.7	417.9	1 031.4
	65-69	29.2	46.8	133.5	311.1	924.0
	70-74	22.4	32.2	100.7	225.9	699.3
	75-79	11.7	19.7	66.8	133.9	488.4
	80-84			35.4	77.6	309.8
	85-89			13.3	37.3	164.1
	90-94	5.5	13.5	3.0	12.0	63.5
	95-99			0.4	2.2	16.3
	100+			0.0	0.2	2.0
Male	Total	1 805.6	3 798.8	10 064.5	14 163.6	18 065.3
	0-14	746.2	1 855.4	3 679.1	4 012.6	3 571.8
	15-59	928.6	1 785.6	5 944.0	9 121.7	11 189.5
	60-64	46.5	57.0	153.9	394.1	1 028.7
	65-69	35.6	42.2	117.0	276.0	890.9
	70-74	27.0	28.9	83.4	183.5	635.0
	75-79	14.5	17.7	51.5	101.4	404.8
	80-84			25.2	50.3	222.4
	85-89			8.6	19.0	93.2
	90-94	7.3	11.9	1.7	4.4	25.0
	95-99			0.2	0.5	3.8
	100+			0.0	0.0	0.2
Percentage in older ages						
Total	60+	6.8	4.4	4.8	8.0	19.5
	65+	4.4	2.8	3.2	5.1	13.8
	80+	0.4	0.3	0.4	0.7	2.5
Female	60+	6.3	4.7	5.2	8.8	20.7
	65+	4.1	3.0	3.6	5.8	14.9
	80+	0.3	0.4	0.5	0.9	3.1
Male	60+	7.2	4.2	4.4	7.3	18.3
	65+	4.7	2.7	2.9	4.5	12.6
	80+	0.4	0.3	0.4	0.5	1.9
Ageing index		16.4	9.1	13.3	28.7	100.4
Broad age groups (percentage)	0-14	41.4	48.5	36.0	27.9	19.4
	15-59	51.7	47.1	59.1	64.1	61.1
	60+	6.8	4.4	4.8	8.0	19.5
Median age (years)		19.2	15.7	20.6*	27.2	37.0
Dependency ratio	Total	84.6	105.5	64.6	49.3	49.6
	Youth	76.5	99.7	59.3	41.7	29.0
	Old Age	8.1	5.8	5.3	7.6	20.6
Potential support ratio		12.4	17.2	19.0	13.1	4.9
Parent support ratio		1.2	1.5	2.0	2.4	5.8
Sex ratio (per 100 women)	60+	122.0	90.6	84.9	84.5	89.3
	65+	122.6	89.7	81.4	79.4	85.3
	80+	131.4	88.7	68.5	57.4	62.0

* *Estimate refers to year 2005.*

Indicator	Age	1950-1955	1975-1980	2005-2010	2025-2030	2045-2050
Growth rate (percentage)	Total	2.7	3.5	2.4	1.3	0.7
	60+	1.1	2.9	3.7	4.9	3.6
	65+	1.0	2.6	3.5	5.3	4.7
	80+	4.1	2.2	5.2	5.0	5.6
Total fertility rate (per woman)		7.2	7.5	3.1	2.1	1.9
Life expectancy (years)						
Total	Birth	45.9	61.3	74.3	77.6	80.0
	60	..	..	19.0	20.9	22.7
	65	..	..	15.2	16.9	18.6
	80	..	..	6.5	7.5	8.6
Female	Birth	47.2	63.3	76.2	79.6	82.1
	60	..	..	20.2	22.6	24.5
	65	..	..	16.2	18.4	20.2
	80	..	..	6.9	8.2	9.4
Male	Birth	44.8	59.5	72.5	75.5	78.0
	60	..	..	17.7	19.1	20.9
	65	..	..	14.1	15.2	16.9
	80	..	..	6.0	6.5	7.4
Survival rate (percentage)						
Total	60	..	..	87.6	91.4	93.3
	65	..	..	81.6	86.5	89.4
	80	..	..	41.8	51.0	58.8
Female	60	..	..	89.8	92.8	94.5
	65	..	..	85.0	89.1	91.5
	80	..	..	47.8	58.5	66.0
Male	60	..	..	85.5	90.0	92.1
	65	..	..	78.3	83.9	87.2
	80	..	..	35.7	43.2	51.6

		1980	1990	2007	2010	2020
Labour force participation (percentage)						
Total	65+	22.8	27.4	32.4	32.3	31.3
Female	65+	9.3	10.8	16.2	17.3	20.8
Male	65+	38.6	47.4	52.4	50.8	44.5

Percentage married, age 60+			Percentage living alone, age 60+ (1978)		
Total	Female	Male	Total	Female	Male
67.9	50.0	89.0	4.2	6.8	1.9

Statutory pensionable age (2006)		Percentage illiterate, age 65+ (2004)		
Female	Male	Total	Female	Male
55	60	65.5	77.0	54.1

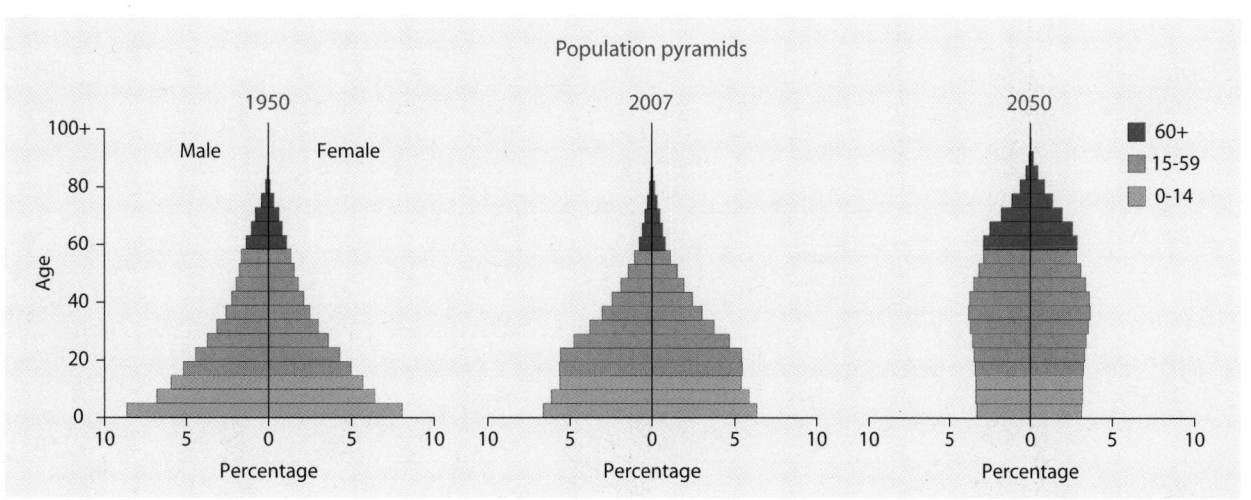

Population pyramids

Tajikistan

Indicator	Age	1950	1975	2007	2025	2050
Population (thousands)						
Total	Total	1 531.5	3 442.0	6 681.5	8 769.5	10 422.5
	0-14	517.7	1 562.9	2 506.7	2 603.1	2 074.4
	15-59	899.5	1 647.1	3 839.2	5 451.3	6 638.5
	60-64	47.5	71.2	81.5	282.5	616.7
	65-69	31.1	58.6	92.5	200.0	411.7
	70-74	19.0	48.4	73.3	114.2	265.1
	75-79	10.3	26.8	48.1	56.5	190.6
	80-84			26.8	28.3	122.0
	85-89			8.6	23.3	71.5
	90-94	6.4	26.9	3.1	7.4	25.5
	95-99			1.2	2.4	5.7
	100+			0.5	0.5	0.9
Female	Total	790.3	1 742.6	3 373.7	4 452.6	5 328.0
	0-14	259.8	770.6	1 231.5	1 278.2	1 015.5
	15-59	473.8	837.8	1 960.6	2 770.8	3 333.3
	60-64	23.5	41.6	40.2	153.2	328.5
	65-69	15.3	34.7	47.7	111.0	228.4
	70-74	9.4	27.1	41.0	66.6	155.4
	75-79	5.2	14.9	26.6	33.8	116.5
	80-84			16.7	16.3	78.8
	85-89			6.0	15.2	47.8
	90-94	3.2	15.9	2.1	5.2	18.4
	95-99			0.9	1.8	4.5
	100+			0.4	0.4	0.8
Male	Total	741.2	1 699.3	3 307.8	4 316.9	5 094.6
	0-14	257.9	792.4	1 275.3	1 324.9	1 058.9
	15-59	425.7	809.3	1 878.6	2 680.5	3 305.2
	60-64	24.0	29.6	41.3	129.3	288.3
	65-69	15.7	24.0	44.9	89.0	183.3
	70-74	9.5	21.2	32.3	47.6	109.7
	75-79	5.1	11.9	21.5	22.8	74.1
	80-84			10.1	12.0	43.1
	85-89			2.5	8.1	23.7
	90-94	3.1	11.0	1.0	2.1	7.1
	95-99			0.3	0.6	1.1
	100+			0.1	0.1	0.1
Percentage in older ages						
Total	60+	7.5	6.7	5.0	8.2	16.4
	65+	4.4	4.7	3.8	4.9	10.5
	80+	0.4	0.8	0.6	0.7	2.2
Female	60+	7.2	7.7	5.4	9.1	18.4
	65+	4.2	5.3	4.2	5.6	12.2
	80+	0.4	0.9	0.8	0.9	2.8
Male	60+	7.8	5.8	4.7	7.2	14.3
	65+	4.5	4.0	3.4	4.2	8.7
	80+	0.4	0.6	0.4	0.5	1.5
Ageing index		22.1	14.8	13.4	27.5	82.4
Broad age groups (percentage)	0-14	33.8	45.4	37.5	29.7	19.9
	15-59	58.7	47.9	57.5	62.2	63.7
	60+	7.5	6.7	5.0	8.2	16.4
Median age (years)		22.3	17.2	19.3*	26.2	35.4
Dependency ratio	Total	61.7	100.3	70.4	52.9	43.7
	Youth	54.7	91.0	63.9	45.4	28.6
	Old Age	7.0	9.4	6.5	7.5	15.1
Potential support ratio		14.2	10.7	15.4	13.3	6.6
Parent support ratio		1.6	4.7	3.2	3.6	5.2
Sex ratio (per 100 women)	60+	101.4	72.8	84.8	77.2	74.6
	65+	100.9	73.5	79.7	72.8	67.9
	80+	97.0	69.2	53.5	58.7	50.0

* Estimate refers to year 2005.

Indicator	Age	1950-1955	1975-1980	2005-2010	2025-2030	2045-2050
Growth rate (percentage)	Total	3.0	2.8	1.4	1.0	0.4
	60+	3.1	1.0	1.1	3.6	4.6
	65+	5.9	2.2	−0.2	5.8	3.7
	80+	7.0	4.1	6.4	1.7	3.0
Total fertility rate (per woman)		6.0	5.9	3.3	2.2	1.9
Life expectancy (years)						
Total	Birth	53.1	61.9	64.3	68.6	72.9
	60	..	..	18.4	19.5	20.7
	65	..	..	15.1	15.9	17.0
	80	..	..	7.4	7.7	8.2
Female	Birth	55.7	64.2	67.1	71.4	75.5
	60	..	..	20.1	21.1	22.4
	65	..	..	16.4	17.3	18.4
	80	..	..	8.0	8.4	8.9
Male	Birth	50.7	59.5	61.7	65.7	70.1
	60	..	..	16.8	17.5	18.7
	65	..	..	13.6	14.3	15.2
	80	..	..	6.6	6.8	7.2
Survival rate (percentage)						
Total	60	..	..	72.3	78.2	83.8
	65	..	..	65.4	71.9	78.2
	80	..	..	31.7	38.0	45.1
Female	60	..	..	76.1	81.9	87.0
	65	..	..	70.6	76.9	82.6
	80	..	..	38.7	45.3	52.8
Male	60	..	..	68.4	74.3	80.6
	65	..	..	60.4	66.6	73.5
	80	..	..	25.2	30.0	36.7

		1980	1990	2007	2010	2020
Labour force participation (percentage)						
Total	65+	6.0	7.8	4.4	4.0	3.4
Female	65+	3.3	5.1	3.4	3.3	3.2
Male	65+	9.7	12.2	5.6	4.9	3.6

Percentage married, age 60+			Percentage living alone, age 60+		
Total	Female	Male	Total	Female	Male
58.8	38.0	83.0	..	..	..

Statutory pensionable age (2006)			Percentage illiterate, age 65+ (2000)		
	Female	Male	Total	Female	Male
	..	..	4.9	7.0	2.4

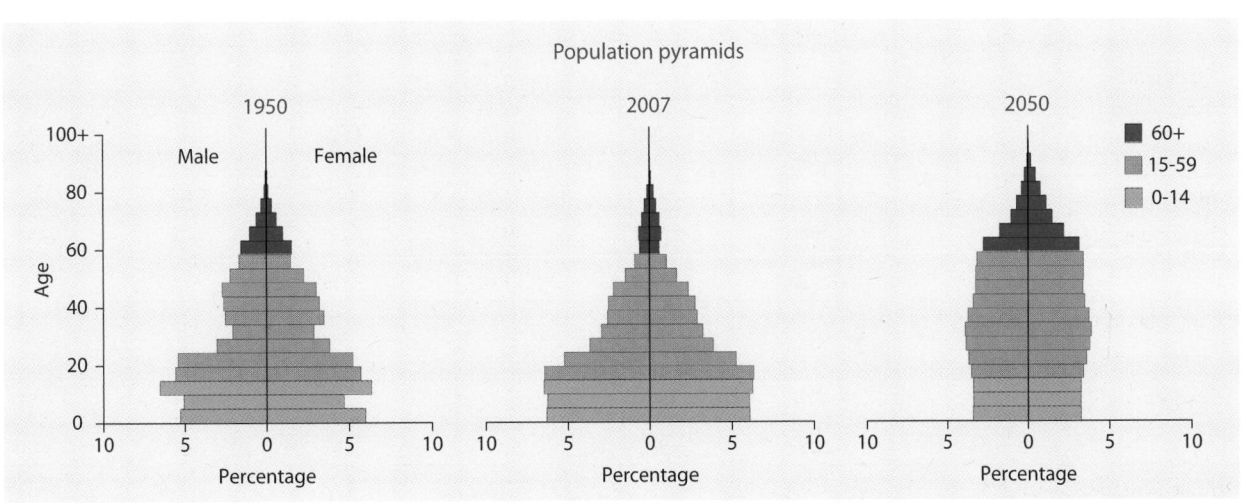

Population pyramids

1950   2007   2050

Male   Female

60+
15-59
0-14

Thailand

Indicator	Age	1950	1975	2007	2025	2050
Population (thousands)						
Total	Total	19 626.0	41 291.9	65 283.0	72 635.1	74 594.3
	0-14	8 269.2	17 658.4	15 117.8	14 005.8	12 511.3
	15-59	10 365.8	21 561.5	42 978.0	44 671.5	41 380.7
	60-64	354.1	760.1	2 342.0	4 317.8	4 746.9
	65-69	281.0	579.4	1 894.5	3 615.4	4 521.9
	70-74	165.1	388.7	1 432.9	2 766.7	3 981.0
	75-79	110.2	225.5	898.4	1 720.8	3 098.4
	80-84			433.8	932.6	2 313.2
	85-89			149.9	447.2	1 353.4
	90-94	80.6	118.3	31.8	133.2	536.6
	95-99			3.5	22.4	134.4
	100+			0.2	1.7	16.6
Female	Total	9 781.2	20 675.2	33 264.5	37 264.6	38 288.3
	0-14	4 075.2	8 771.9	7 460.5	6 884.7	6 137.3
	15-59	5 156.5	10 786.8	21 868.4	22 535.1	20 509.3
	60-64	192.7	392.7	1 218.2	2 344.8	2 429.2
	65-69	154.5	311.5	1 024.0	1 964.9	2 361.8
	70-74	90.8	212.7	804.9	1 529.4	2 151.7
	75-79	62.7	128.0	515.7	993.7	1 784.8
	80-84			256.1	580.4	1 449.2
	85-89			93.3	309.1	928.6
	90-94	48.9	71.5	21.0	102.2	407.4
	95-99			2.5	18.8	113.7
	100+			0.1	1.5	15.4
Male	Total	9 844.8	20 616.8	32 018.5	35 370.5	36 306.0
	0-14	4 194.0	8 886.5	7 657.4	7 121.1	6 374.0
	15-59	5 209.3	10 774.8	21 109.7	22 136.5	20 871.5
	60-64	161.5	367.4	1 123.8	1 973.0	2 317.7
	65-69	126.5	267.8	870.6	1 650.5	2 160.1
	70-74	74.3	176.0	628.1	1 237.4	1 829.3
	75-79	47.5	97.5	382.7	727.1	1 313.6
	80-84			177.7	352.2	864.0
	85-89			56.7	138.2	424.8
	90-94	31.7	46.8	10.8	31.0	129.2
	95-99			1.0	3.6	20.6
	100+			0.0	0.2	1.3
Percentage in older ages						
Total	60+	5.0	5.0	11.0	19.2	27.8
	65+	3.2	3.2	7.4	13.3	21.4
	80+	0.4	0.3	0.9	2.1	5.8
Female	60+	5.6	5.4	11.8	21.1	30.4
	65+	3.6	3.5	8.2	14.8	24.1
	80+	0.5	0.3	1.1	2.7	7.6
Male	60+	4.5	4.6	10.2	17.3	25.0
	65+	2.8	2.9	6.6	11.7	18.6
	80+	0.3	0.2	0.8	1.5	4.0
Ageing index		12.0	11.7	47.5	99.7	165.5
Broad age groups (percentage)	0-14	42.1	42.8	23.2	19.3	16.8
	15-59	52.8	52.2	65.8	61.5	55.5
	60+	5.0	5.0	11.0	19.2	27.8
Median age (years)		18.6	18.2	30.5*	37.4	42.5
Dependency ratio	Total	83.1	85.0	44.0	48.3	61.7
	Youth	77.1	79.1	33.4	28.6	27.1
	Old Age	5.9	5.9	10.7	19.7	34.6
Potential support ratio		16.8	17.0	9.4	5.1	2.9
Parent support ratio		1.8	1.1	2.0	4.4	14.3
Sex ratio (per 100 women)	60+	80.3	85.6	82.6	77.9	77.8
	65+	78.5	81.3	78.3	75.3	73.2
	80+	64.8	65.5	66.0	51.9	49.4

Estimate refers to year 2005.

Indicator	Age	1950-1955	1975-1980	2005-2010	2025-2030	2045-2050
Growth rate (percentage)	Total	3.0	2.3	0.8	0.3	−0.1
	60+	1.8	3.0	3.6	2.5	0.8
	65+	1.7	3.2	3.3	3.3	1.2
	80+	0.2	4.3	6.5	4.6	2.4
Total fertility rate (per woman)		6.4	4.0	1.9	1.9	1.9
Life expectancy (years)						
Total	Birth	52.0	63.1	71.7	76.4	79.1
	60	..	..	19.0	20.9	22.5
	65	..	..	15.2	16.9	18.4
	80	..	..	6.5	7.5	8.5
Female	Birth	54.3	65.7	75.0	79.1	81.5
	60	..	..	20.4	22.9	24.3
	65	..	..	16.4	18.7	20.0
	80	..	..	7.0	8.5	9.4
Male	Birth	49.8	60.6	68.5	73.6	76.5
	60	..	..	17.4	18.6	20.3
	65	..	..	13.9	14.9	16.3
	80	..	..	5.9	6.2	7.1
Survival rate (percentage)						
Total	60	..	..	81.7	88.6	91.6
	65	..	..	75.9	83.8	87.6
	80	..	..	38.9	49.3	56.8
Female	60	..	..	86.9	91.1	93.3
	65	..	..	82.4	87.5	90.3
	80	..	..	47.1	58.6	64.8
Male	60	..	..	76.7	86.1	89.9
	65	..	..	69.6	79.8	84.7
	80	..	..	30.9	39.6	48.1

		1980	1990	2007	2010	2020
Labour force participation (percentage)						
Total	65+	30.9	31.0	26.1	24.4	19.4
Female	65+	15.7	17.8	16.8	16.7	16.7
Male	65+	49.5	47.0	38.0	34.2	23.0

Percentage married, age 60+				Percentage living alone, age 60+ (1995)		
Total	Female	Male		Total	Female	Male
64.5	49.0	83.0		4.3	5.5	2.9

Statutory pensionable age (2006)				Percentage illiterate, age 65+ (2000)		
	Female	Male		Total	Female	Male
	55	55		31.5	40.1	20.8

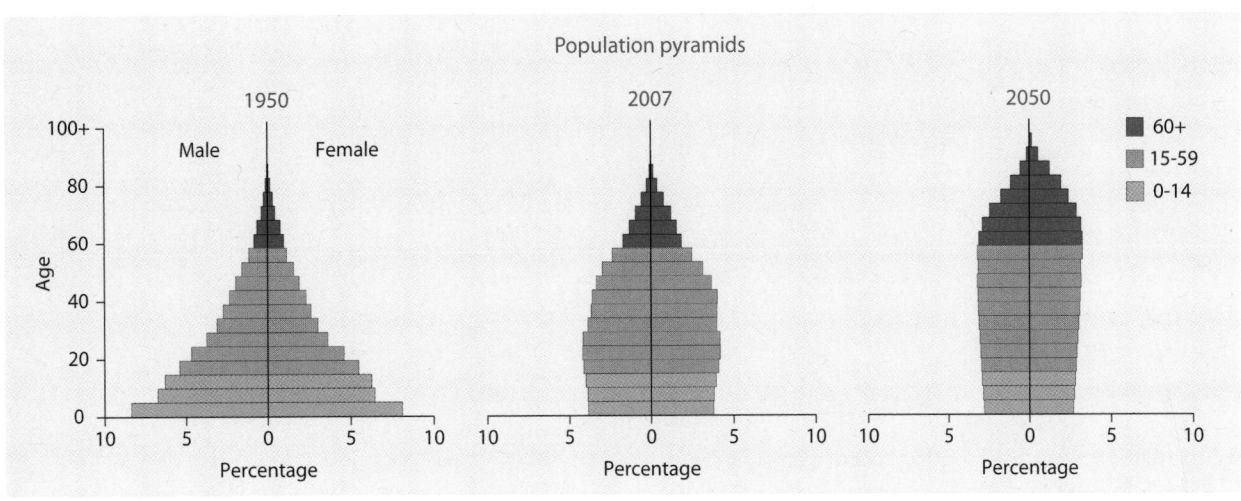

Population pyramids

The former Yugoslav Republic of Macedonia

Indicator	Age	1950	1975	2007	2025	2050
Population (thousands)						
Total	Total	1 229.7	1 675.6	2 039.8	2 047.5	1 884.4
	0-14	436.2	515.1	380.2	333.1	285.4
	15-59	655.5	1 005.8	1 334.6	1 251.5	991.5
	60-64	33.2	51.4	92.4	127.8	138.6
	65-69	28.3	42.6	79.8	115.1	135.3
	70-74	35.8	29.3	68.3	95.5	118.1
	75-79	24.0	17.8	46.7	61.3	91.5
	80-84			26.5	36.4	65.0
	85-89			8.8	18.7	37.9
	90-94	16.7	13.6	2.2	6.7	16.2
	95-99			0.4	1.2	4.4
	100+			0.0	0.1	0.5
Female	Total	613.4	826.5	1 022.7	1 028.2	947.6
	0-14	215.0	250.1	183.2	160.1	137.1
	15-59	325.4	498.5	658.3	611.9	479.1
	60-64	17.9	25.6	48.5	65.5	69.0
	65-69	14.4	20.8	42.8	59.8	68.8
	70-74	18.5	14.7	38.0	52.1	62.3
	75-79	12.9	9.6	27.4	36.0	50.7
	80-84			16.7	23.2	39.0
	85-89			5.9	13.2	25.2
	90-94	9.3	7.2	1.6	5.3	12.2
	95-99			0.3	1.1	3.7
	100+			0.0	0.1	0.5
Male	Total	616.3	849.1	1 017.1	1 019.3	936.8
	0-14	221.2	265.0	196.9	173.0	148.3
	15-59	330.1	507.3	676.3	639.5	512.5
	60-64	15.3	25.8	43.9	62.4	69.5
	65-69	13.9	21.8	37.0	55.3	66.5
	70-74	17.3	14.6	30.3	43.5	55.8
	75-79	11.1	8.2	19.3	25.4	40.8
	80-84			9.8	13.3	26.0
	85-89			2.9	5.5	12.7
	90-94	7.4	6.4	0.7	1.4	4.1
	95-99			0.1	0.2	0.7
	100+			0.0	0.0	0.0
Percentage in older ages						
Total	60+	11.2	9.2	15.9	22.6	32.2
	65+	8.5	6.2	11.4	16.4	24.9
	80+	1.4	0.8	1.9	3.1	6.6
Female	60+	11.9	9.4	17.7	24.9	35.0
	65+	9.0	6.3	13.0	18.5	27.7
	80+	1.5	0.9	2.4	4.2	8.5
Male	60+	10.5	9.0	14.1	20.3	29.5
	65+	8.1	6.0	9.8	14.2	22.0
	80+	1.2	0.8	1.3	2.0	4.6
Ageing index		31.6	30.0	85.5	139.0	212.8
Broad age groups (percentage)	0-14	35.5	30.7	18.6	16.3	15.1
	15-59	53.3	60.0	65.4	61.1	52.6
	60+	11.2	9.2	15.9	22.6	32.2
Median age (years)		22.3	24.8	34.2*	41.2	46.5
Dependency ratio	Total	78.6	58.5	42.9	48.4	66.8
	Youth	63.3	48.7	26.6	24.2	25.3
	Old Age	15.2	9.8	16.3	24.3	41.5
Potential support ratio		6.6	10.2	6.1	4.1	2.4
Parent support ratio		4.8	3.4	3.3	6.5	14.9
Sex ratio (per 100 women)	60+	89.0	98.6	79.4	80.7	83.3
	65+	90.2	97.5	75.4	75.7	78.7
	80+	79.6	88.9	55.1	47.5	53.9

Estimate refers to year 2005.

Indicator	Age	1950-1955	1975-1980	2005-2010	2025-2030	2045-2050
Growth rate (percentage)	Total	1.9	1.4	0.1	–0.2	–0.5
	60+	–2.9	1.3	1.7	1.3	0.7
	65+	–2.8	3.6	1.5	1.7	1.1
	80+	0.4	1.9	4.6	2.5	1.7
Total fertility rate (per woman)		5.3	2.7	1.4	1.7	1.9
Life expectancy (years)						
Total	Birth	55.0	69.6	74.5	77.1	79.6
	60	..	..	18.9	20.4	22.3
	65	..	..	15.2	16.5	18.3
	80	..	..	6.7	7.5	8.5
Female	Birth	55.0	71.4	77.0	79.5	82.0
	60	..	..	20.7	22.4	24.4
	65	..	..	16.7	18.3	20.1
	80	..	..	7.4	8.3	9.5
Male	Birth	54.9	67.9	72.0	74.7	77.2
	60	..	..	17.0	18.2	20.2
	65	..	..	13.5	14.5	16.3
	80	..	..	5.7	6.1	7.1
Survival rate (percentage)						
Total	60	..	..	87.7	90.9	92.9
	65	..	..	81.3	85.4	88.7
	80	..	..	41.2	48.5	56.9
Female	60	..	..	90.6	92.8	94.5
	65	..	..	85.6	88.7	91.3
	80	..	..	50.0	57.6	65.4
Male	60	..	..	84.8	89.0	91.5
	65	..	..	76.9	82.2	86.2
	80	..	..	32.3	39.2	48.4

		1980	1990	2007	2010	2020
Labour force participation (percentage)						
Total	65+	25.6	17.2	3.6	3.2	2.5
Female	65+	12.2	10.0	2.4	2.3	2.1
Male	65+	39.5	25.6	5.2	4.5	3.1

Percentage married, age 60+				Percentage living alone, age 60+		
Total	Female	Male		Total	Female	Male
70.0	60.0	82.0		..	..	..

Statutory pensionable age (2006)				Percentage illiterate, age 65+ (2002)		
	Female	Male		Total	Female	Male
	..	..		17.5	25.6	7.6

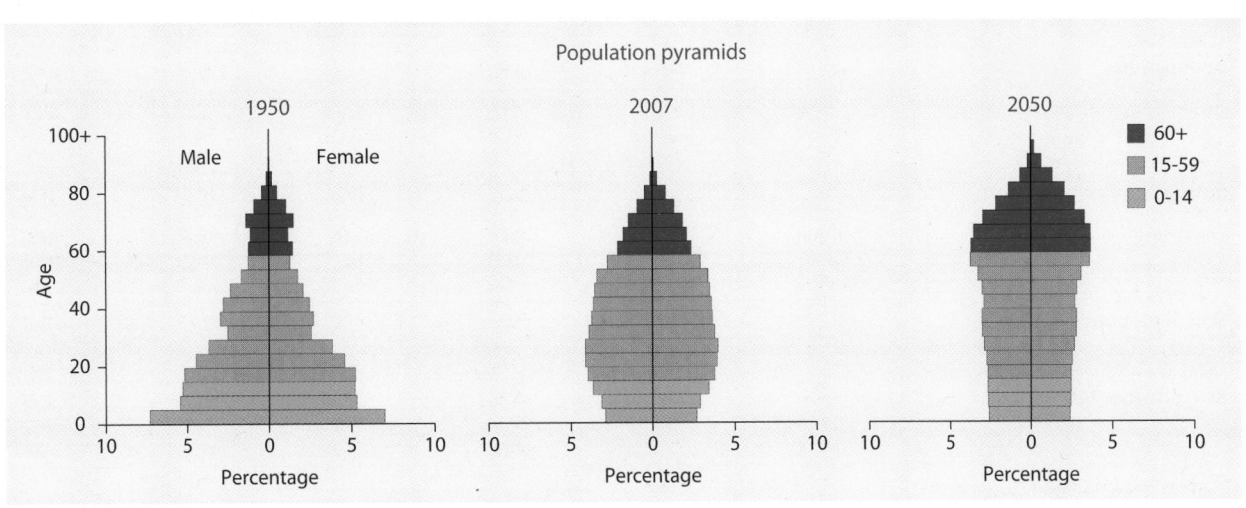

Population pyramids

Togo

Indicator	Age	1950	1975	2007	2025	2050
Population (thousands)						
Total	Total	1 329.0	2 446.3	6 470.2	9 613.3	13 543.9
	0-14	548.7	1 114.3	2 779.3	3 418.2	3 330.5
	15-59	690.1	1 210.0	3 374.6	5 617.3	8 736.1
	60-64	32.7	47.7	112.1	197.5	501.7
	65-69	25.5	34.2	85.8	155.5	391.9
	70-74	17.4	21.9	60.0	112.0	281.7
	75-79	9.7	12.0	36.1	67.3	171.7
	80-84			16.5	32.9	89.5
	85-89			4.9	10.5	33.2
	90-94	4.9	6.2	0.8	1.9	7.0
	95-99			0.1	0.2	0.7
	100+			0.0	0.0	0.0
Female	Total	674.0	1 242.5	3 274.2	4 850.7	6 832.5
	0-14	276.4	559.2	1 390.3	1 709.1	1 661.8
	15-59	353.0	615.6	1 709.3	2 819.0	4 374.3
	60-64	16.3	25.9	59.8	106.1	258.0
	65-69	12.4	18.9	46.7	85.7	206.0
	70-74	8.6	12.3	33.6	63.3	152.9
	75-79	4.8	6.9	20.9	39.3	97.9
	80-84			10.0	19.9	54.5
	85-89			3.1	6.7	21.6
	90-94	2.5	3.5	0.5	1.3	4.9
	95-99			0.0	0.1	0.5
	100+			0.0	0.0	0.0
Male	Total	655.0	1 203.8	3 196.1	4 762.6	6 711.4
	0-14	272.3	555.0	1 389.0	1 709.1	1 668.6
	15-59	337.1	594.3	1 665.4	2 798.3	4 361.8
	60-64	16.4	21.8	52.3	91.4	243.7
	65-69	13.1	15.3	39.1	69.9	185.9
	70-74	8.8	9.6	26.4	48.7	128.8
	75-79	4.9	5.1	15.2	28.0	73.9
	80-84			6.5	12.9	35.0
	85-89			1.8	3.7	11.5
	90-94	2.4	2.6	0.3	0.6	2.1
	95-99			0.0	0.0	0.2
	100+			0.0	0.0	0.0
Percentage in older ages						
Total	60+	6.8	5.0	4.9	6.0	10.9
	65+	4.3	3.0	3.2	4.0	7.2
	80+	0.4	0.3	0.3	0.5	1.0
Female	60+	6.6	5.4	5.3	6.6	11.7
	65+	4.2	3.4	3.5	4.5	7.9
	80+	0.4	0.3	0.4	0.6	1.2
Male	60+	7.0	4.5	4.4	5.4	10.1
	65+	4.5	2.7	2.8	3.4	6.5
	80+	0.4	0.2	0.3	0.4	0.7
Ageing index		16.4	11.0	11.4	16.9	44.4
Broad age groups (percentage)	0-14	41.3	45.5	43.0	35.6	24.6
	15-59	51.9	49.5	52.2	58.4	64.5
	60+	6.8	5.0	4.9	6.0	10.9
Median age (years)		19.4	17.2	17.9*	21.8	29.9
Dependency ratio	Total	83.9	94.5	85.6	65.3	46.6
	Youth	75.9	88.6	79.7	58.8	36.1
	Old Age	8.0	5.9	5.9	6.5	10.6
Potential support ratio		12.6	16.9	17.1	15.3	9.5
Parent support ratio		0.9	0.8	1.3	1.7	2.2
Sex ratio (per 100 women)	60+	102.3	80.5	81.1	79.1	85.5
	65+	103.0	78.4	77.7	75.7	81.2
	80+	97.3	74.8	62.9	61.5	59.8

* *Estimate refers to year 2005.*

Indicator	Age	1950-1955	1975-1980	2005-2010	2025-2030	2045-2050
Growth rate (percentage)	Total	1.6	2.6	2.5	1.7	1.0
	60+	−0.7	2.4	3.0	3.2	4.0
	65+	−0.4	2.8	3.2	3.5	4.3
	80+	−0.7	2.0	3.7	4.1	3.7
Total fertility rate (per woman)		6.8	7.1	4.8	2.9	2.0
Life expectancy (years)						
Total	Birth	38.6	52.9	55.8	63.4	69.7
	60	..	..	17.1	18.5	19.8
	65	..	..	13.5	14.7	15.8
	80	..	..	5.3	5.8	6.2
Female	Birth	40.0	54.6	57.5	65.1	71.7
	60	..	..	18.0	19.6	21.1
	65	..	..	14.2	15.6	16.8
	80	..	..	5.6	6.1	6.6
Male	Birth	37.2	51.2	54.0	61.7	67.7
	60	..	..	16.0	17.2	18.4
	65	..	..	12.7	13.7	14.6
	80	..	..	5.0	5.4	5.7
Survival rate (percentage)						
Total	60	..	..	57.0	68.4	78.8
	65	..	..	51.7	63.5	74.3
	80	..	..	22.0	31.3	41.2
Female	60	..	..	59.8	70.5	81.1
	65	..	..	55.4	66.6	77.9
	80	..	..	25.7	36.1	47.6
Male	60	..	..	54.1	66.3	76.5
	65	..	..	48.0	60.2	70.9
	80	..	..	18.0	26.2	34.7

		1980	1990	2007	2010	2020
Labour force participation (percentage)						
Total	65+	51.2	53.3	50.5	50.2	49.2
Female	65+	34.1	34.6	28.7	28.5	28.4
Male	65+	73.3	77.3	78.6	78.1	76.5

Percentage married, age 60+			Percentage living alone, age 60+ (1998)		
Total	Female	Male	Total	Female	Male
54.6	34.0	80.0	8.0	9.0	6.9

Statutory pensionable age (2006)			Percentage illiterate, age 65+ (2000)		
	Female	Male	Total	Female	Male
	55	55	86.1	93.7	77.3

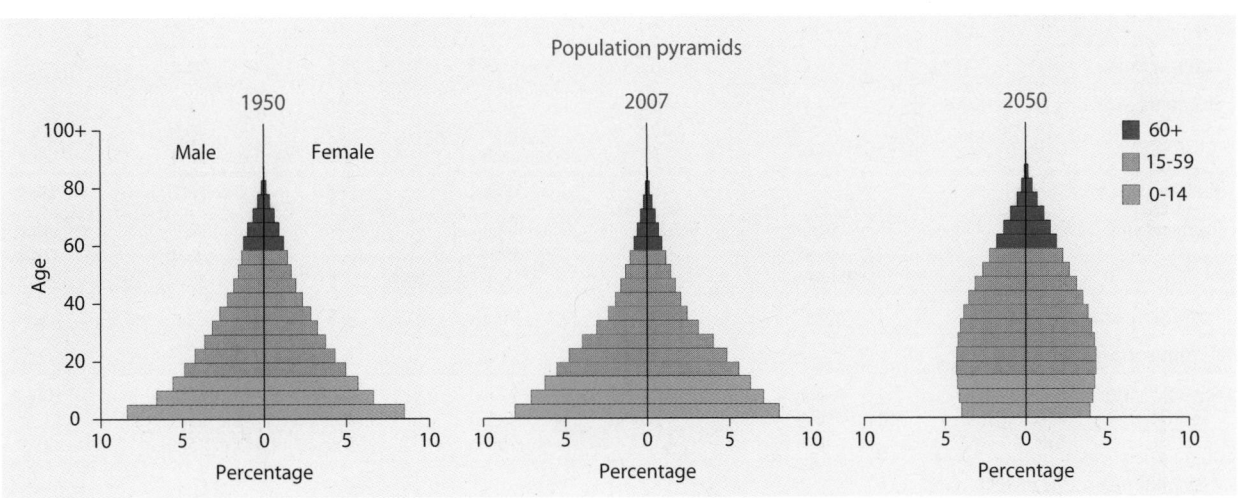

Population pyramids

Tonga

Indicator	Age	1950	1975	2007	2025	2050
Population (thousands)						
Total	Total	47.2	92.0	102.8	101.0	75.0
	0-14	23.1	42.8	36.0	27.0	13.1
	15-59	22.7	45.5	57.7	61.4	41.1
	60-64	0.6	1.4	2.8	3.9	5.0
	65-69	0.4	1.0	2.1	2.7	5.4
	70-74	0.3	0.6	1.8	2.5	3.8
	75-79	0.1	0.4	1.3	1.6	2.7
	80-84			0.7	1.1	2.3
	85-89			0.4	0.5	1.0
	90-94	0.1	0.3	0.1	0.2	0.4
	95-99			0.0	0.1	0.1
	100+			0.0	0.0	0.0
Female	Total	23.2	44.7	50.4	49.2	36.5
	0-14	11.2	20.3	17.5	13.2	6.4
	15-59	11.2	22.5	28.3	29.8	20.1
	60-64	0.3	0.7	1.5	1.9	2.2
	65-69	0.2	0.4	0.9	1.2	2.5
	70-74	0.1	0.3	0.8	1.2	1.8
	75-79	0.1	0.3	0.7	0.9	1.3
	80-84			0.4	0.6	1.2
	85-89			0.2	0.3	0.6
	90-94	0.0	0.2	0.1	0.1	0.3
	95-99			0.0	0.0	0.1
	100+			0.0	0.0	0.0
Male	Total	24.0	47.3	52.5	51.8	38.5
	0-14	11.9	22.5	18.5	13.8	6.7
	15-59	11.5	23.0	29.4	31.7	20.9
	60-64	0.3	0.7	1.3	2.0	2.9
	65-69	0.2	0.5	1.2	1.5	2.9
	70-74	0.1	0.3	0.9	1.3	2.0
	75-79	0.1	0.2	0.6	0.8	1.4
	80-84			0.3	0.5	1.1
	85-89			0.2	0.2	0.4
	90-94	0.0	0.1	0.0	0.1	0.1
	95-99			0.0	0.0	0.0
	100+			0.0	0.0	0.0
Percentage in older ages						
Total	60+	3.1	4.0	8.9	12.4	27.8
	65+	1.8	2.5	6.2	8.6	21.1
	80+	0.1	0.3	1.1	1.8	5.2
Female	60+	3.5	4.2	9.1	12.7	27.3
	65+	2.1	2.7	6.2	8.9	21.3
	80+	0.2	0.4	1.3	2.2	5.9
Male	60+	2.7	3.9	8.8	12.2	28.3
	65+	1.5	2.3	6.2	8.4	20.8
	80+	0.1	0.2	0.9	1.5	4.5
Ageing index		6.3	8.6	25.6	46.5	159.1
Broad age groups (percentage)	0-14	48.8	46.6	35.0	26.7	17.5
	15-59	48.1	49.4	56.1	60.8	54.8
	60+	3.1	4.0	8.9	12.4	27.8
Median age (years)		15.5	16.5	21.8*	28.7	44.7
Dependency ratio	Total	102.7	96.3	69.9	54.7	62.7
	Youth	99.0	91.4	59.4	41.4	28.4
	Old Age	3.7	4.9	10.5	13.3	34.3
Potential support ratio		27.1	20.3	9.5	7.5	2.9
Parent support ratio		1.0	1.2	5.0	5.8	9.4
Sex ratio (per 100 women)	60+	78.5	97.4	99.9	101.7	109.3
	65+	73.7	91.7	104.7	99.2	103.1
	80+	51.1	73.9	71.9	75.0	79.3

* *Estimate refers to year 2005.*

Indicator	Age	1950-1955	1975-1980	2005-2010	2025-2030	2045-2050
Growth rate (percentage)	Total	3.7	1.0	0.2	−0.5	−2.0
	60+	3.5	4.1	1.4	3.2	0.9
	65+	3.5	3.4	1.7	2.1	3.0
	80+	5.8	5.1	4.6	1.8	4.9
Total fertility rate (per woman)		7.3	5.5	3.2	2.4	2.0
Life expectancy (years)						
Total	Birth	58.6	66.7	73.0	75.8	77.9
	60	..	..	18.5	20.0	21.4
	65	..	..	15.0	16.3	17.5
	80	..	..	7.1	7.7	8.3
Female	Birth	58.7	67.8	74.4	77.5	79.8
	60	..	..	20.2	21.8	23.3
	65	..	..	16.5	17.9	19.2
	80	..	..	7.7	8.5	9.2
Male	Birth	58.5	65.8	71.7	74.3	76.5
	60	..	..	17.1	18.4	19.8
	65	..	..	13.8	14.9	16.1
	80	..	..	6.4	6.9	7.5
Survival rate (percentage)						
Total	60	..	..	84.9	88.7	91.0
	65	..	..	77.7	82.4	85.7
	80	..	..	38.2	45.4	51.9
Female	60	..	..	85.9	89.5	91.8
	65	..	..	79.9	84.7	87.7
	80	..	..	45.1	53.1	59.3
Male	60	..	..	83.9	87.9	90.3
	65	..	..	75.1	80.3	84.0
	80	..	..	32.4	39.0	45.8

		1980	1990	2007	2010	2020
Labour force participation (percentage)						
Total	65+	35.8	35.6	43.3	43.1	41.9
Female	65+	15.1	15.5	26.9	27.5	29.6
Male	65+	58.2	57.1	58.9	58.2	54.1

Percentage married, age 60+			Percentage living alone, age 60+		
Total	Female	Male	Total	Female	Male
66.5	55.0	78.0	..	..	..

Statutory pensionable age (2006)		Percentage illiterate, age 65+ (1996)		
Female	Male	Total	Female	Male
..	..	3.0	3.3	2.7

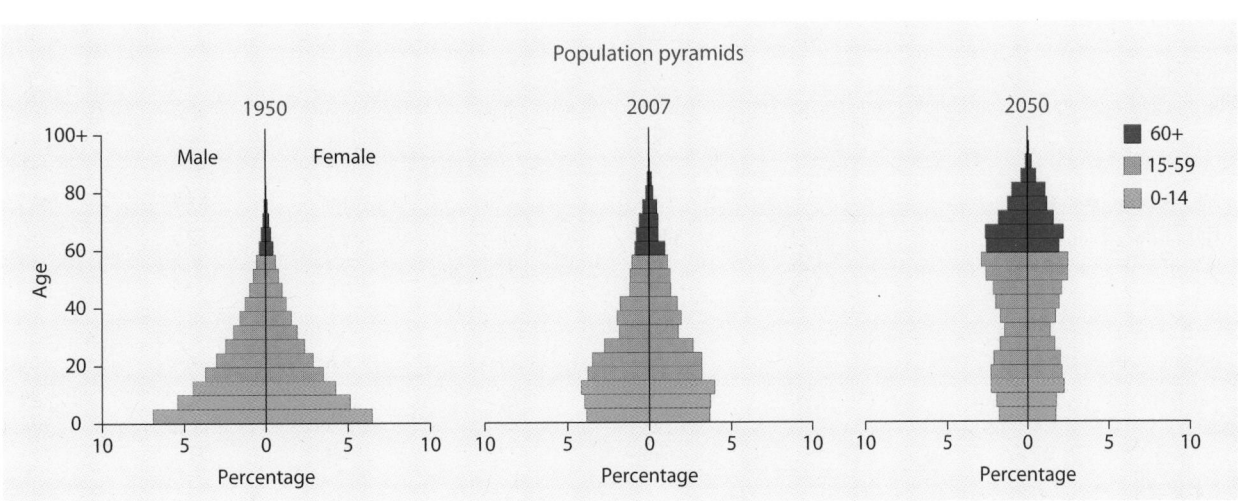

Population pyramids

United Nations Department of Economic and Social Affairs, Population Division

Trinidad and Tobago

Indicator	Age	1950	1975	2007	2025	2050
Population (thousands)						
Total	Total	636.0	1 011.9	1 312.9	1 343.2	1 229.6
	0-14	257.0	385.0	271.9	257.4	203.9
	15-59	340.0	549.8	891.8	814.1	626.1
	60-64	14.0	27.3	47.8	81.0	91.0
	65-69	10.0	19.4	36.3	68.2	95.8
	70-74	7.0	14.7	26.0	51.3	72.2
	75-79	5.0	8.9	17.9	35.4	54.1
	80-84			12.3	20.5	39.0
	85-89			6.2	10.2	29.3
	90-94	3.0	6.8	2.1	3.7	13.5
	95-99			0.5	1.0	4.0
	100+			0.1	0.2	0.7
Female	Total	319.0	509.1	666.4	687.9	634.9
	0-14	128.0	191.3	133.8	126.5	100.1
	15-59	170.0	276.3	451.2	409.4	312.8
	60-64	7.0	13.8	24.9	43.3	46.8
	65-69	5.0	9.9	19.3	37.2	49.9
	70-74	4.0	8.2	14.2	28.4	38.7
	75-79	3.0	5.3	10.1	20.1	30.4
	80-84			7.2	12.5	23.7
	85-89			3.8	6.7	19.1
	90-94	2.0	4.3	1.4	2.7	9.7
	95-99			0.4	0.8	3.2
	100+			0.1	0.2	0.6
Male	Total	317.0	502.8	646.5	655.3	594.7
	0-14	129.0	193.7	138.0	131.0	103.8
	15-59	170.0	273.5	440.6	404.7	313.3
	60-64	7.0	13.5	22.9	37.7	44.3
	65-69	5.0	9.5	16.9	31.0	45.9
	70-74	3.0	6.5	11.8	22.9	33.4
	75-79	2.0	3.6	7.9	15.3	23.7
	80-84			5.1	8.0	15.3
	85-89			2.4	3.5	10.2
	90-94	1.0	2.5	0.7	1.0	3.8
	95-99			0.1	0.2	0.8
	100+			0.0	0.0	0.1
Percentage in older ages						
Total	60+	6.1	7.6	11.4	20.2	32.5
	65+	3.9	4.9	7.7	14.2	25.1
	80+	0.5	0.7	1.6	2.6	7.0
Female	60+	6.6	8.2	12.2	22.1	35.0
	65+	4.4	5.4	8.5	15.8	27.6
	80+	0.6	0.8	1.9	3.3	8.9
Male	60+	5.7	7.1	10.5	18.3	29.9
	65+	3.5	4.4	6.9	12.5	22.4
	80+	0.3	0.5	1.3	1.9	5.1
Ageing index		15.2	20.0	54.9	105.5	196.0
Broad age groups (percentage)	0-14	40.4	38.0	20.7	19.2	16.6
	15-59	53.5	54.3	67.9	60.6	50.9
	60+	6.1	7.6	11.4	20.2	32.5
Median age (years)		20.7	20.0	29.4*	38.5	43.9
Dependency ratio	Total	79.7	75.3	39.7	50.0	71.5
	Youth	72.6	66.7	28.9	28.8	28.4
	Old Age	7.1	8.6	10.8	21.3	43.0
Potential support ratio		14.2	11.6	9.3	4.7	2.3
Parent support ratio		1.9	3.0	4.8	6.4	21.0
Sex ratio (per 100 women)	60+	85.7	85.7	83.4	78.7	80.0
	65+	78.6	79.7	79.6	75.4	76.0
	80+	50.0	57.9	65.2	55.2	53.7

* *Estimate refers to year 2005.*

Indicator	Age	1950-1955	1975-1980	2005-2010	2025-2030	2045-2050
Growth rate (percentage)	Total	2.5	1.3	0.3	−0.2	−0.5
	60+	2.4	2.6	3.2	1.6	1.1
	65+	2.3	3.8	2.8	3.2	2.2
	80+	2.5	4.4	1.8	4.8	0.7
Total fertility rate (per woman)		5.3	3.4	1.6	1.8	1.9
Life expectancy (years)						
Total	Birth	59.0	68.3	70.1	74.1	78.5
	60	..	..	20.1	21.9	23.5
	65	..	..	16.4	18.0	19.4
	80	..	..	7.7	8.5	9.4
Female	Birth	59.9	70.9	72.5	75.9	80.6
	60	..	..	21.7	23.7	25.3
	65	..	..	17.9	19.6	21.1
	80	..	..	8.4	9.4	10.3
Male	Birth	58.2	65.9	67.7	72.0	76.4
	60	..	..	18.4	19.8	21.4
	65	..	..	14.9	16.1	17.5
	80	..	..	6.8	7.3	8.1
Survival rate (percentage)						
Total	60	..	..	75.8	81.4	88.2
	65	..	..	70.3	76.9	84.3
	80	..	..	39.3	48.1	57.4
Female	60	..	..	78.9	82.6	89.3
	65	..	..	74.5	79.2	86.4
	80	..	..	46.3	54.8	64.1
Male	60	..	..	72.6	80.1	87.1
	65	..	..	66.0	74.4	82.2
	80	..	..	32.4	40.8	50.3

		1980	1990	2007	2010	2020
Labour force participation (percentage)						
Total	65+	18.4	11.8	8.1	7.9	7.7
Female	65+	8.0	4.3	4.5	4.2	4.0
Male	65+	31.2	20.5	12.7	12.6	12.4

Percentage married, age 60+			Percentage living alone, age 60+ (1980)		
Total	Female	Male	Total	Female	Male
48.5	37.0	62.0	14.9	14.4	15.6

Statutory pensionable age (2006)			Percentage illiterate, age 65+		
	Female	Male	Total	Female	Male
	65	65	..	..	..

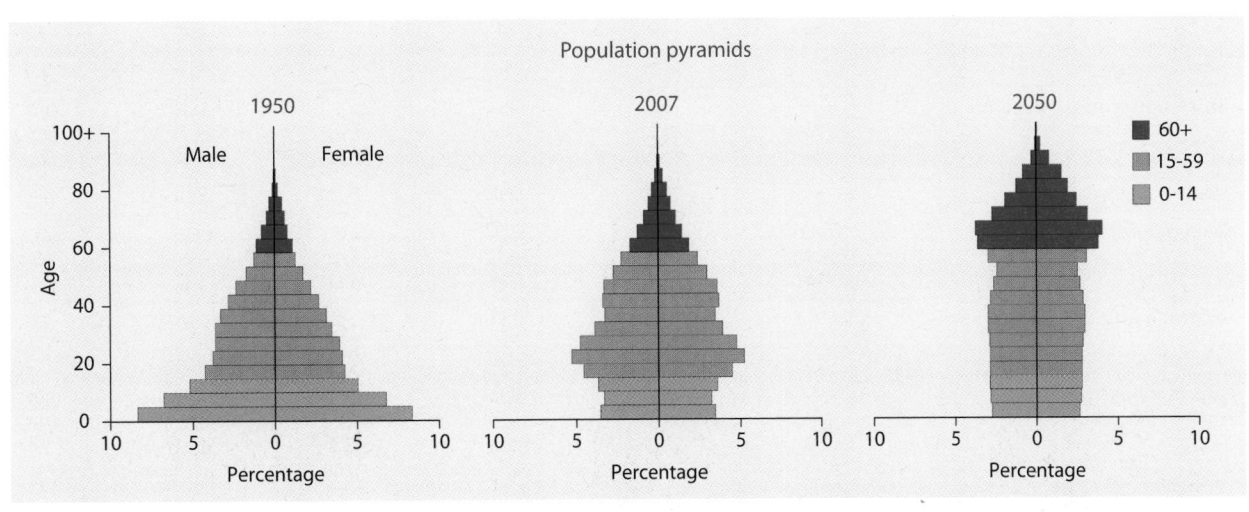

Population pyramids

United Nations Department of Economic and Social Affairs, Population Division

Tunisia

Indicator	Age	1950	1975	2007	2025	2050
Population (thousands)						
Total	Total	3 529.6	5 667.5	10 318.6	12 028.0	12 926.7
	0-14	1 372.3	2 482.8	2 538.5	2 402.1	2 102.1
	15-59	1 873.8	2 854.7	6 877.2	7 850.0	7 099.0
	60-64	81.7	131.4	251.6	595.2	963.4
	65-69	68.9	87.9	226.9	477.9	875.9
	70-74	48.5	59.2	195.4	338.1	726.8
	75-79	52.5	25.8	133.9	189.9	533.6
	80-84			67.2	102.2	354.5
	85-89			22.3	54.1	186.4
	90-94	31.9	25.9	5.0	16.0	68.6
	95-99			0.6	2.5	14.8
	100+			0.0	0.2	1.5
Female	Total	1 770.8	2 794.4	5 122.0	5 982.7	6 461.9
	0-14	680.0	1 212.1	1 229.9	1 160.5	1 015.2
	15-59	929.8	1 436.3	3 407.8	3 856.9	3 445.2
	60-64	43.2	56.6	131.0	310.6	481.9
	65-69	38.4	39.4	123.4	251.4	446.5
	70-74	26.8	25.5	105.5	182.4	380.4
	75-79	32.2	12.1	72.2	107.9	296.0
	80-84			37.1	63.0	212.2
	85-89			12.2	36.4	121.6
	90-94	20.4	12.4	2.6	11.4	49.6
	95-99			0.3	2.0	12.0
	100+			0.0	0.1	1.3
Male	Total	1 758.8	2 873.1	5 196.6	6 045.4	6 464.9
	0-14	692.3	1 270.7	1 308.6	1 241.6	1 086.9
	15-59	944.0	1 418.3	3 469.4	3 993.1	3 653.8
	60-64	38.5	74.8	120.6	284.6	481.5
	65-69	30.5	48.5	103.6	226.5	429.5
	70-74	21.7	33.7	89.9	155.7	346.4
	75-79	20.3	13.6	61.7	81.9	237.7
	80-84			30.1	39.2	142.3
	85-89			10.1	17.7	64.7
	90-94	11.5	13.4	2.4	4.5	19.0
	95-99			0.3	0.5	2.8
	100+			0.0	0.0	0.2
Percentage in older ages						
Total	60+	8.0	5.8	8.8	14.8	28.8
	65+	5.7	3.5	6.3	9.8	21.4
	80+	0.9	0.5	0.9	1.5	4.8
Female	60+	9.1	5.2	9.5	16.1	31.0
	65+	6.7	3.2	6.9	10.9	23.5
	80+	1.2	0.4	1.0	1.9	6.1
Male	60+	7.0	6.4	8.1	13.4	26.7
	65+	4.8	3.8	5.7	8.7	19.2
	80+	0.7	0.5	0.8	1.0	3.5
Ageing index		20.7	13.3	35.6	73.9	177.2
Broad age groups (percentage)	0-14	38.9	43.8	24.6	20.0	16.3
	15-59	53.1	50.4	66.6	65.3	54.9
	60+	8.0	5.8	8.8	14.8	28.8
Median age (years)		20.9	17.7	26.8*	36.0	43.3
Dependency ratio	Total	80.5	89.8	44.7	42.4	60.3
	Youth	70.2	83.1	35.6	28.4	26.1
	Old Age	10.3	6.7	9.1	14.0	34.3
Potential support ratio		9.7	15.0	10.9	7.2	2.9
Parent support ratio		2.8	1.1	2.5	3.5	10.2
Sex ratio (per 100 women)	60+	76.1	126.2	86.4	84.0	86.1
	65+	71.3	122.3	84.3	80.3	81.8
	80+	56.4	108.1	82.0	54.9	57.7

* *Estimate refers to year 2005.*

Indicator	Age	1950-1955	1975-1980	2005-2010	2025-2030	2045-2050
Growth rate (percentage)	Total	1.8	2.6	1.0	0.6	0.0
	60+	−1.4	2.8	2.2	3.7	2.2
	65+	−2.5	4.0	1.3	4.3	2.7
	80+	−0.3	−3.4	5.4	3.7	4.0
Total fertility rate (per woman)		6.9	5.7	1.9	1.8	1.9
Life expectancy (years)						
Total	Birth	44.6	59.8	74.2	77.5	80.0
	60	..	..	19.0	20.8	22.6
	65	..	..	15.1	16.8	18.5
	80	..	..	6.2	7.3	8.4
Female	Birth	45.1	61.0	76.3	79.7	82.1
	60	..	..	20.3	22.6	24.4
	65	..	..	16.2	18.4	20.1
	80	..	..	6.6	8.0	9.2
Male	Birth	44.1	58.8	72.1	75.3	77.7
	60	..	..	17.6	18.9	20.7
	65	..	..	14.0	15.1	16.7
	80	..	..	5.8	6.3	7.3
Survival rate (percentage)						
Total	60	..	..	87.6	91.4	93.3
	65	..	..	81.8	86.6	89.4
	80	..	..	41.9	50.9	58.8
Female	60	..	..	90.5	93.2	94.7
	65	..	..	86.3	89.9	91.9
	80	..	..	49.0	59.4	66.4
Male	60	..	..	84.8	89.5	91.8
	65	..	..	77.5	83.2	86.8
	80	..	..	35.0	42.4	50.9

		1980	1990	2007	2010	2020
Labour force participation (percentage)						
Total	65+	19.8	19.0	18.0	17.7	17.6
Female	65+	4.1	3.2	2.9	2.9	2.9
Male	65+	32.5	33.0	35.8	35.8	35.9

Percentage married, age 60+			Percentage living alone, age 60+ (1991)		
Total	Female	Male	Total	Female	Male
68.2	48.0	90.0	2.7	3.7	1.9

Statutory pensionable age (2006)			Percentage illiterate, age 65+ (2004)		
	Female	Male	Total	Female	Male
	60	60	80.3	94.3	66.6

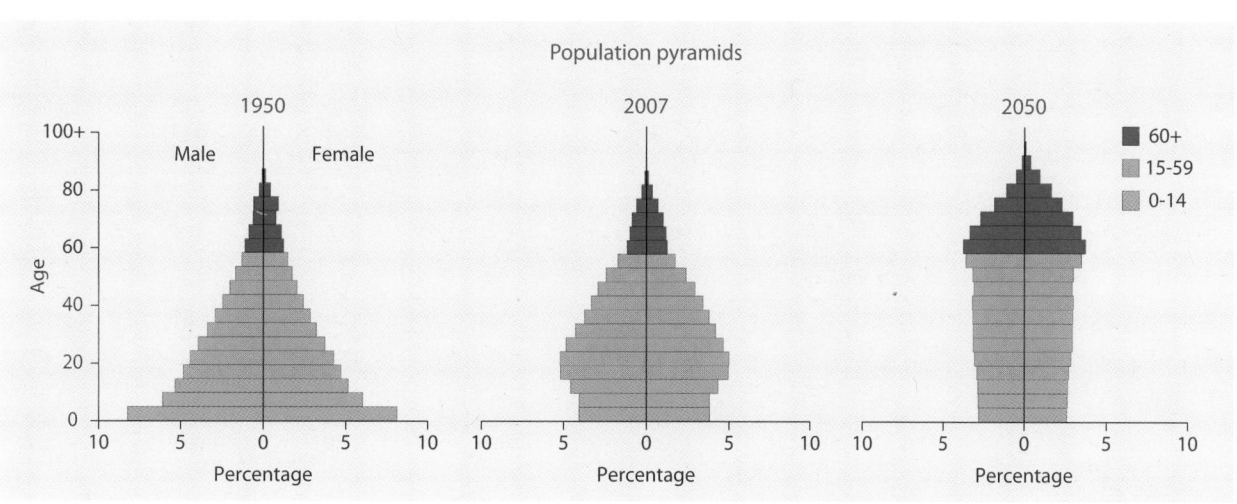

Population pyramids

Turkey

Indicator	Age	1950	1975	2007	2025	2050
Population (thousands)						
Total	Total	21 484.0	41 210.5	75 160.7	90 565.2	101 208.4
	0-14	8 600.0	17 059.0	21 480.1	20 613.8	18 274.6
	15-59	11 644.0	21 406.5	47 531.4	58 077.2	59 877.3
	60-64	553.0	937.0	1 997.7	4 176.0	5 826.5
	65-69	267.0	831.0	1 568.9	3 184.1	5 576.0
	70-74	241.0	532.0	1 265.1	2 234.6	4 736.8
	75-79	123.0	303.0	844.9	1 322.6	3 506.3
	80-84			356.5	640.9	2 083.5
	85-89			91.6	250.2	983.5
	90-94	56.0	142.0	21.6	59.1	290.1
	95-99			2.6	6.6	49.8
	100+			0.1	0.3	3.9
Female	Total	10 762.0	20 162.7	37 312.4	45 212.2	51 130.3
	0-14	4 175.0	8 308.0	10 541.5	10 097.0	8 915.0
	15-59	5 814.0	10 439.7	23 419.7	28 755.0	29 541.5
	60-64	357.0	459.0	1 043.4	2 133.9	2 985.7
	65-69	153.0	433.0	875.0	1 669.1	2 931.7
	70-74	147.0	273.0	688.0	1 216.1	2 556.3
	75-79	78.0	163.0	471.0	746.6	1 995.1
	80-84			204.2	391.7	1 274.0
	85-89			54.4	161.2	664.7
	90-94	38.0	87.0	13.3	37.1	220.5
	95-99			1.7	4.4	42.2
	100+			0.1	0.2	3.5
Male	Total	10 722.0	21 047.8	37 848.3	45 353.0	50 078.0
	0-14	4 425.0	8 751.0	10 938.7	10 516.8	9 359.6
	15-59	5 830.0	10 966.8	24 111.7	29 322.2	30 335.8
	60-64	196.0	478.0	954.3	2 042.1	2 840.8
	65-69	114.0	398.0	693.9	1 515.0	2 644.3
	70-74	94.0	259.0	577.1	1 018.6	2 180.5
	75-79	45.0	140.0	373.9	576.0	1 511.2
	80-84			152.3	249.2	809.5
	85-89			37.2	89.0	318.8
	90-94	18.0	55.0	8.3	21.9	69.7
	95-99			0.9	2.2	7.6
	100+			0.0	0.1	0.3
Percentage in older ages						
Total	60+	5.8	6.7	8.2	13.1	22.8
	65+	3.2	4.4	5.5	8.5	17.0
	80+	0.3	0.3	0.6	1.1	3.4
Female	60+	7.2	7.0	9.0	14.1	24.8
	65+	3.9	4.7	6.2	9.3	18.9
	80+	0.4	0.4	0.7	1.3	4.3
Male	60+	4.4	6.3	7.4	12.2	20.7
	65+	2.5	4.0	4.9	7.7	15.1
	80+	0.2	0.3	0.5	0.8	2.4
Ageing index		14.4	16.1	28.6	57.6	126.2
Broad age groups (percentage)	0-14	40.0	41.4	28.6	22.8	18.1
	15-59	54.2	51.9	63.2	64.1	59.2
	60+	5.8	6.7	8.2	13.1	22.8
Median age (years)		19.4	19.0	26.3*	32.5	39.5
Dependency ratio	Total	76.1	84.4	51.8	45.5	54.0
	Youth	70.5	76.3	43.4	33.1	27.8
	Old Age	5.6	8.1	8.4	12.4	26.2
Potential support ratio		17.8	12.4	11.9	8.1	3.8
Parent support ratio		0.8	1.2	1.4	2.1	7.0
Sex ratio (per 100 women)	60+	60.4	94.0	83.5	86.7	81.9
	65+	65.1	89.1	79.9	82.1	77.8
	80+	47.4	63.2	72.6	60.9	54.7

* Estimate refers to year 2005.

Indicator	Age	1950-1955	1975-1980	2005-2010	2025-2030	2045-2050
Growth rate (percentage)	Total	2.7	2.3	1.3	0.7	0.2
	60+	3.0	1.2	2.8	3.5	1.5
	65+	3.5	3.1	2.1	4.2	2.2
	80+	5.3	15.5	7.3	5.0	3.9
Total fertility rate (per woman)		6.9	4.7	2.3	2.0	1.9
Life expectancy (years)						
Total	Birth	43.6	59.5	69.7	74.5	77.7
	60	..	..	17.5	19.2	20.9
	65	..	..	13.9	15.3	16.9
	80	..	..	5.6	6.4	7.4
Female	Birth	45.2	61.7	72.1	76.9	80.1
	60	..	..	18.6	20.7	22.9
	65	..	..	14.6	16.6	18.7
	80	..	..	5.8	6.9	8.3
Male	Birth	42.0	57.5	67.5	72.1	75.2
	60	..	..	16.3	17.6	18.8
	65	..	..	13.0	14.0	15.1
	80	..	..	5.4	5.8	6.3
Survival rate (percentage)						
Total	60	..	..	81.3	87.9	91.5
	65	..	..	74.4	82.1	86.7
	80	..	..	33.0	42.8	51.5
Female	60	..	..	85.3	91.1	93.5
	65	..	..	79.8	87.0	90.3
	80	..	..	38.9	51.0	60.8
Male	60	..	..	77.6	84.8	89.5
	65	..	..	69.3	77.5	83.2
	80	..	..	27.2	35.0	42.4

		1980	1990	2007	2010	2020
Labour force participation (percentage)						
	65+	33.0	19.2	21.6	21.9	21.7
	65+	23.8	9.3	16.6	17.8	19.3
	65+	44.3	30.9	27.8	27.0	24.6

Percentage married, age 60+				Percentage living alone, age 60+ (1998)		
Total	Female	Male		Total	Female	Male
68.3	53.0	86.0		8.5	12.5	4.4

Statutory pensionable age (2006)				Percentage illiterate, age 65+ (2004)		
	Female	Male		Total	Female	Male
	58	60		46.9	65.1	25.0

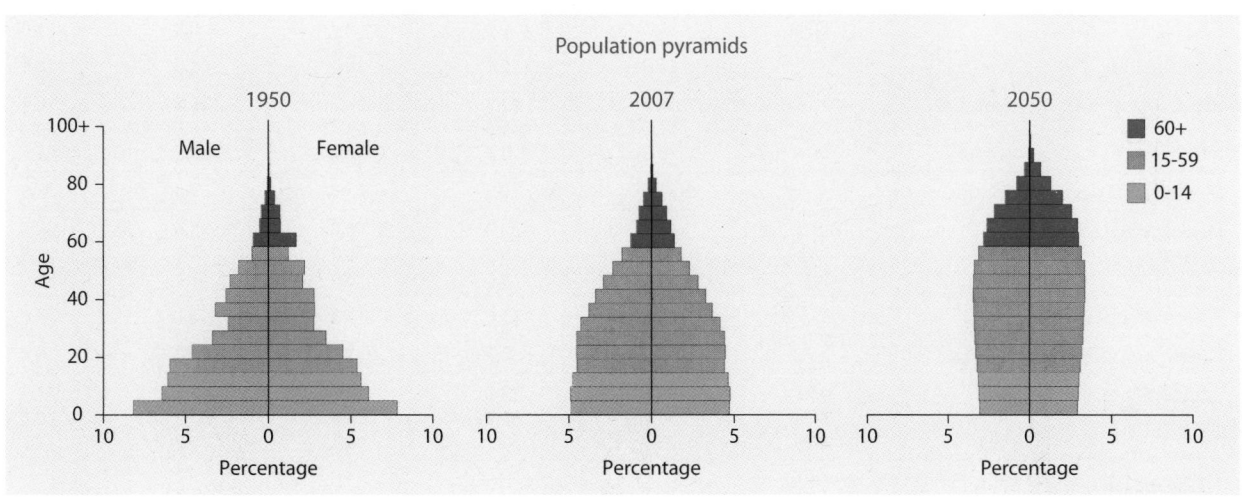

Population pyramids

Turkmenistan

Indicator	Age	1950	1975	2007	2025	2050
Population (thousands)						
Total	Total	1 211.0	2 520.0	4 965.3	6 067.7	6 779.8
	0-14	397.5	1 095.1	1 494.2	1 463.8	1 250.4
	15-59	698.1	1 254.4	3 166.3	3 948.4	4 092.0
	60-64	44.5	57.9	79.3	247.6	456.0
	65-69	31.5	44.6	80.1	187.4	348.5
	70-74	20.5	32.5	66.1	113.9	258.6
	75-79	11.7	17.9	45.1	57.6	180.0
	80-84			23.6	25.5	110.7
	85-89			7.8	17.5	59.5
	90-94	7.3	17.6	2.4	4.8	20.2
	95-99			0.4	1.0	3.7
	100+			0.0	0.1	0.3
Female	Total	617.4	1 279.1	2 521.5	3 101.5	3 492.5
	0-14	192.1	541.2	738.5	721.6	613.8
	15-59	366.6	635.0	1 604.0	1 993.6	2 053.0
	60-64	21.6	35.2	42.9	139.5	242.5
	65-69	15.6	27.0	44.6	108.0	192.1
	70-74	10.9	19.1	38.7	68.8	149.2
	75-79	6.4	10.8	28.3	36.6	109.9
	80-84			16.6	16.9	71.5
	85-89			6.0	12.3	42.3
	90-94	4.2	10.8	1.8	3.5	15.1
	95-99			0.3	0.7	2.9
	100+			0.0	0.0	0.2
Male	Total	593.6	1 240.9	2 443.7	2 966.1	3 287.2
	0-14	205.3	553.9	755.7	742.2	636.6
	15-59	331.5	619.4	1 562.4	1 954.8	2 039.0
	60-64	22.9	22.6	36.4	108.1	213.5
	65-69	15.9	17.6	35.5	79.4	156.4
	70-74	9.6	13.4	27.4	45.1	109.3
	75-79	5.3	7.1	16.9	21.1	70.0
	80-84			7.0	8.6	39.1
	85-89			1.8	5.2	17.3
	90-94	3.1	6.9	0.6	1.3	5.1
	95-99			0.1	0.3	0.8
	100+			0.0	0.0	0.1
Percentage in older ages						
Total	60+	9.5	6.8	6.1	10.8	21.2
	65+	5.9	4.5	4.5	6.7	14.5
	80+	0.6	0.7	0.7	0.8	2.9
Female	60+	9.5	8.0	7.1	12.5	23.6
	65+	6.0	5.3	5.4	8.0	16.7
	80+	0.7	0.8	1.0	1.1	3.8
Male	60+	9.6	5.4	5.1	9.1	18.6
	65+	5.7	3.6	3.7	5.4	12.1
	80+	0.5	0.6	0.4	0.5	1.9
Ageing index		29.0	15.6	20.4	44.8	115.0
Broad age groups (percentage)	0-14	32.8	43.5	30.1	24.1	18.4
	15-59	57.6	49.8	63.8	65.1	60.4
	60+	9.5	6.8	6.1	10.8	21.2
Median age (years)		23.5	17.9	23.3*	31.3	38.8
Dependency ratio	Total	63.1	92.0	53.0	44.6	49.1
	Youth	53.5	83.5	46.0	34.9	27.5
	Old Age	9.6	8.6	6.9	9.7	21.6
Potential support ratio		10.5	11.6	14.4	10.3	4.6
Parent support ratio		1.9	3.7	2.5	2.7	6.1
Sex ratio (per 100 women)	60+	96.8	65.7	70.2	69.7	74.1
	65+	91.4	66.4	65.5	65.2	68.3
	80+	73.8	64.0	38.4	46.1	47.3

* *Estimate refers to year 2005.*

Indicator	Age	1950-1955	1975-1980	2005-2010	2025-2030	2045-2050
Growth rate (percentage)	Total	2.3	2.5	1.3	0.7	0.2
	60+	0.2	0.2	1.7	3.6	3.1
	65+	2.8	1.7	−0.4	5.1	2.9
	80+	3.7	1.4	5.7	3.9	3.0
Total fertility rate (per woman)		6.0	5.3	2.5	1.9	1.9
Life expectancy (years)						
Total	Birth	51.3	60.2	63.2	69.0	73.1
	60	..	..	17.3	19.0	20.3
	65	..	..	14.0	15.5	16.6
	80	..	..	6.5	7.1	7.8
Female	Birth	55.1	63.7	67.5	72.8	76.4
	60	..	..	19.2	20.9	22.2
	65	..	..	15.5	17.0	18.2
	80	..	..	6.8	7.6	8.3
Male	Birth	47.9	56.6	59.0	65.1	69.6
	60	..	..	15.3	16.7	18.1
	65	..	..	12.3	13.5	14.7
	80	..	..	5.8	6.4	6.9
Survival rate (percentage)						
Total	60	..	..	69.3	78.1	83.9
	65	..	..	62.1	71.6	78.1
	80	..	..	27.6	37.0	44.5
Female	60	..	..	76.9	84.1	88.4
	65	..	..	71.1	79.2	84.2
	80	..	..	37.6	47.3	54.4
Male	60	..	..	61.9	72.1	79.4
	65	..	..	53.4	64.0	72.1
	80	..	..	18.5	26.4	34.2

		1980	1990	2007	2010	2020
Labour force participation (percentage)						
Total	65+	10.6	9.9	10.1	9.5	8.5
Female	65+	7.0	6.7	7.3	6.6	5.2
Male	65+	16.5	16.0	14.3	13.9	13.7

Percentage married, age 60+				Percentage living alone, age 60+		
Total	Female	Male		Total	Female	Male
51.9	35.0	76.0		..	..	..

Statutory pensionable age (2006)				Percentage illiterate, age 65+ (1995)		
	Female	Male		Total	Female	Male
	57	62		11.9	14.6	7.5

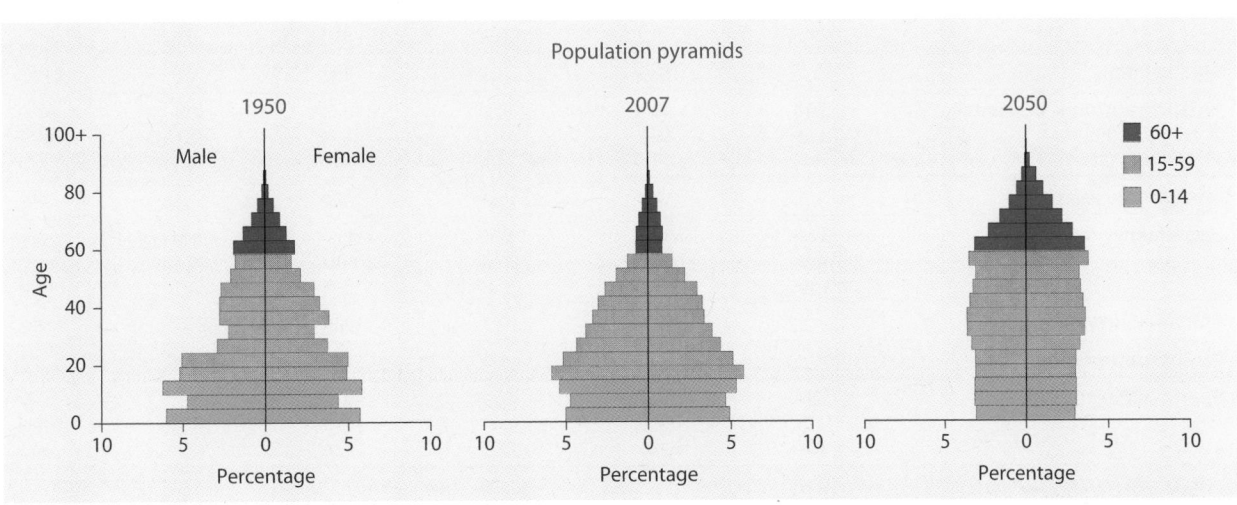

Population pyramids

Uganda

Indicator	Age	1950	1975	2007	2025	2050
Population (thousands)						
Total	Total	5 054.2	10 765.8	30 945.5	60 601.1	126 949.7
	0-14	2 242.3	5 171.1	15 639.0	29 674.7	48 052.5
	15-59	2 569.2	5 148.1	14 144.6	29 139.8	72 528.0
	60-64	90.0	170.7	417.0	581.8	2 338.8
	65-69	67.6	122.7	296.3	455.2	1 728.6
	70-74	45.9	81.2	214.3	344.2	1 167.5
	75-79	25.9	46.4	139.2	229.4	691.5
	80-84			66.7	120.8	299.5
	85-89			23.1	41.8	107.6
	90-94	13.3	25.7	4.8	11.6	30.1
	95-99			0.6	1.7	5.1
	100+			0.0	0.1	0.4
Female	Total	2 527.5	5 405.6	15 454.2	30 190.1	63 228.0
	0-14	1 115.9	2 575.8	7 759.5	14 713.9	23 766.2
	15-59	1 283.1	2 592.9	7 064.3	14 513.9	36 173.2
	60-64	46.7	88.3	223.0	297.5	1 192.9
	65-69	35.8	64.4	159.6	243.8	890.1
	70-74	24.8	43.7	116.4	190.2	605.8
	75-79	13.9	25.6	76.8	128.8	360.6
	80-84			37.7	69.1	157.6
	85-89			13.6	24.6	59.9
	90-94	7.4	14.9	3.0	7.2	18.0
	95-99			0.4	1.1	3.3
	100+			0.0	0.1	0.3
Male	Total	2 526.7	5 360.2	15 491.2	30 411.0	63 721.7
	0-14	1 126.4	2 595.3	7 879.5	14 960.8	24 286.3
	15-59	1 286.1	2 555.2	7 080.3	14 625.9	36 354.8
	60-64	43.3	82.4	194.0	284.3	1 145.9
	65-69	31.8	58.3	136.7	211.5	838.5
	70-74	21.2	37.4	97.8	154.0	561.6
	75-79	11.9	20.8	62.5	100.6	330.9
	80-84			29.0	51.8	141.9
	85-89			9.5	17.2	47.7
	90-94	5.9	10.8	1.8	4.4	12.1
	95-99			0.2	0.5	1.8
	100+			0.0	0.0	0.1
Percentage in older ages						
Total	60+	4.8	4.1	3.8	2.9	5.0
	65+	3.0	2.6	2.4	2.0	3.2
	80+	0.3	0.2	0.3	0.3	0.3
Female	60+	5.1	4.4	4.1	3.2	5.2
	65+	3.2	2.8	2.6	2.2	3.3
	80+	0.3	0.3	0.4	0.3	0.4
Male	60+	4.5	3.9	3.4	2.7	4.8
	65+	2.8	2.4	2.2	1.8	3.0
	80+	0.2	0.2	0.3	0.2	0.3
Ageing index		10.8	8.6	7.4	6.0	13.3
Broad age groups (percentage)	0-14	44.4	48.0	50.5	49.0	37.9
	15-59	50.8	47.8	45.7	48.1	57.1
	60+	4.8	4.1	3.8	2.9	5.0
Median age (years)		17.7	16.0	14.8*	15.5	20.5
Dependency ratio	Total	90.1	102.4	112.5	103.9	69.6
	Youth	84.3	97.2	107.4	99.8	64.2
	Old Age	5.7	5.2	5.1	4.1	5.4
Potential support ratio		17.4	19.3	19.5	24.7	18.6
Parent support ratio		1.0	1.0	1.9	2.0	1.6
Sex ratio (per 100 women)	60+	88.9	88.5	84.3	85.7	93.7
	65+	86.6	85.7	82.8	81.2	92.3
	80+	80.0	72.3	74.0	72.5	85.2

* *Estimate refers to year 2005.*

Indicator	Age	1950-1955	1975-1980	2005-2010	2025-2030	2045-2050
Growth rate (percentage)	Total	2.6	3.1	3.6	3.5	2.4
	60+	1.2	3.0	2.5	3.7	5.1
	65+	1.2	2.9	2.8	2.6	5.6
	80+	2.2	3.4	3.7	3.8	5.4
Total fertility rate (per woman)		6.9	7.1	7.1	5.5	3.4
Life expectancy (years)						
Total	Birth	40.0	50.4	52.1	63.6	69.6
	60	..	..	16.6	18.1	19.3
	65	..	..	13.4	14.6	15.6
	80	..	..	5.9	6.4	6.8
Female	Birth	41.6	51.9	53.0	65.0	70.9
	60	..	..	17.2	18.7	19.9
	65	..	..	13.8	15.0	16.1
	80	..	..	6.1	6.6	6.9
Male	Birth	38.5	48.5	51.2	62.2	68.2
	60	..	..	16.0	17.5	18.7
	65	..	..	12.9	14.1	15.1
	80	..	..	5.6	6.1	6.6
Survival rate (percentage)						
Total	60	..	..	49.5	68.9	77.7
	65	..	..	44.0	63.0	72.3
	80	..	..	18.2	30.1	38.2
Female	60	..	..	50.8	71.0	79.6
	65	..	..	45.7	65.6	74.8
	80	..	..	19.9	32.8	41.4
Male	60	..	..	48.2	66.8	75.8
	65	..	..	42.2	60.5	69.8
	80	..	..	16.3	27.3	35.1

		1980	1990	2007	2010	2020
Labour force participation (percentage)						
Total	65+	59.6	61.9	59.5	59.1	58.8
Female	65+	47.7	48.0	54.2	55.2	57.6
Male	65+	73.4	78.2	65.9	63.8	60.2

Percentage married, age 60+			Percentage living alone, age 60+ (1995)		
Total	Female	Male	Total	Female	Male
50.6	33.0	71.0	12.1	12.2	11.9

Statutory pensionable age (2006)			Percentage illiterate, age 65+		
	Female	Male	Total	Female	Male
	55	55	..	..	..

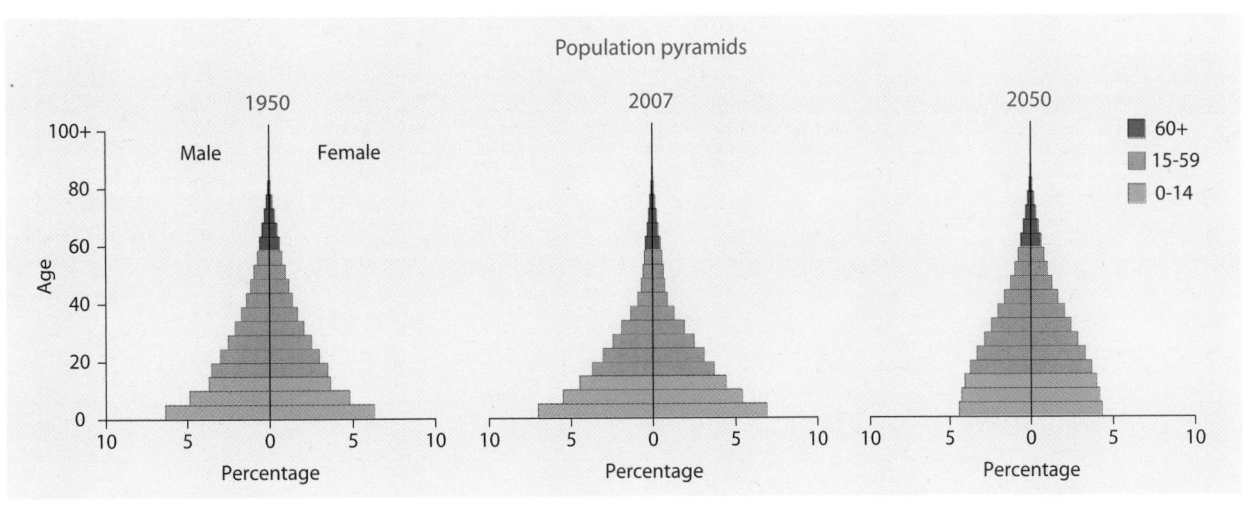

Population pyramids

Ukraine

Indicator	Age	1950	1975	2007	2025	2050
Population (thousands)						
Total	Total	37 297.7	49 016.0	45 509.2	37 334.8	26 392.6
	0-14	10 159.7	11 272.5	6 387.8	4 993.7	3 476.2
	15-59	23 055.3	30 005.5	29 573.3	22 105.4	12 692.6
	60-64	1 244.4	2 611.4	2 101.2	2 725.1	2 535.2
	65-69	1 023.3	2 047.4	2 598.8	2 533.1	2 279.4
	70-74	798.3	1 452.0	1 940.0	2 059.5	1 840.5
	75-79	571.5	857.6	1 521.5	1 293.0	1 493.5
	80-84			979.3	823.9	997.8
	85-89			298.3	617.7	699.5
	90-94	445.1	769.6	95.1	146.7	298.1
	95-99			13.4	34.6	72.4
	100+			0.6	2.0	7.5
Female	Total	21 288.9	26 759.5	24 705.7	20 569.4	14 620.4
	0-14	5 187.1	5 518.4	3 107.2	2 425.5	1 686.3
	15-59	13 399.0	16 032.7	15 435.9	11 568.3	6 523.8
	60-64	774.3	1 711.0	1 242.2	1 600.9	1 404.0
	65-69	660.8	1 348.4	1 592.6	1 551.7	1 329.5
	70-74	538.0	990.8	1 235.7	1 323.7	1 146.4
	75-79	403.4	598.4	1 034.2	880.2	977.2
	80-84			729.2	595.3	701.7
	85-89			237.6	471.5	532.1
	90-94	326.3	559.8	78.9	119.7	247.1
	95-99			11.7	30.7	65.1
	100+			0.5	1.9	7.1
Male	Total	16 008.8	22 256.5	20 803.4	16 765.4	11 772.2
	0-14	4 972.6	5 754.2	3 280.6	2 568.2	1 789.9
	15-59	9 656.3	13 972.8	14 137.4	10 537.1	6 168.7
	60-64	470.1	900.4	859.0	1 124.2	1 131.2
	65-69	362.5	699.0	1 006.2	981.4	949.9
	70-74	260.3	461.3	704.4	735.7	694.1
	75-79	168.1	259.2	487.2	412.8	516.3
	80-84			250.1	228.6	296.1
	85-89			60.6	146.3	167.4
	90-94	118.8	209.8	16.2	27.1	51.0
	95-99			1.7	3.9	7.3
	100+			0.0	0.1	0.3
Percentage in older ages						
Total	60+	10.9	15.8	21.0	27.4	38.7
	65+	7.6	10.5	16.4	20.1	29.1
	80+	1.2	1.6	3.0	4.4	7.9
Female	60+	12.7	19.5	24.9	32.0	43.8
	65+	9.1	13.1	19.9	24.2	34.2
	80+	1.5	2.1	4.3	5.9	10.6
Male	60+	8.6	11.4	16.3	21.8	32.4
	65+	5.7	7.3	12.1	15.1	22.8
	80+	0.7	0.9	1.6	2.4	4.4
Ageing index		40.2	68.6	149.5	205.0	294.1
Broad age groups (percentage)	0-14	27.2	23.0	14.0	13.4	13.2
	15-59	61.8	61.2	65.0	59.2	48.1
	60+	10.9	15.8	21.0	27.4	38.7
Median age (years)		27.6	33.6	39.0*	44.1	51.9
Dependency ratio	Total	53.5	50.3	43.7	50.4	73.3
	Youth	41.8	34.6	20.2	20.1	22.8
	Old Age	11.7	15.7	23.5	30.2	50.5
Potential support ratio		8.6	6.4	4.3	3.3	2.0
Parent support ratio		4.1	3.9	5.0	10.2	17.8
Sex ratio (per 100 women)	60+	51.1	48.6	54.9	55.7	59.5
	65+	47.2	46.6	51.3	51.0	53.6
	80+	36.4	37.5	31.1	33.3	33.6

*   Estimate refers to year 2005.

Indicator	Age	1950-1955	1975-1980	2005-2010	2025-2030	2045-2050
Growth rate (percentage)	Total	1.4	0.4	–1.0	–1.3	–1.5
	60+	1.3	0.0	–0.7	–0.4	0.3
	65+	1.2	3.1	–1.0	0.8	0.4
	80+	1.8	2.3	4.8	–0.3	–1.2
Total fertility rate (per woman)		2.8	2.0	1.1	1.4	1.7
Life expectancy (years)						
Total	Birth	65.9	69.4	66.5	71.1	74.7
	60	..	..	17.5	19.3	20.7
	65	..	..	14.3	15.8	17.0
	80	..	..	6.4	7.3	8.0
Female	Birth	69.7	73.7	72.5	75.3	78.0
	60	..	..	19.6	21.5	23.0
	65	..	..	15.8	17.5	18.9
	80	..	..	6.8	7.8	8.7
Male	Birth	61.3	64.2	60.7	66.5	70.8
	60	..	..	14.6	16.2	17.6
	65	..	..	12.0	13.3	14.3
	80	..	..	5.6	6.1	6.6
Survival rate (percentage)						
Total	60	..	..	69.4	77.7	83.8
	65	..	..	61.8	71.1	77.9
	80	..	..	28.9	38.2	45.9
Female	60	..	..	81.8	84.8	88.1
	65	..	..	76.3	80.3	84.4
	80	..	..	41.8	49.9	56.9
Male	60	..	..	57.4	70.2	79.2
	65	..	..	47.9	61.1	70.9
	80	..	..	16.7	25.2	33.1

		1980	1990	2007	2010	2020
Labour force participation (percentage)						
Total	65+	7.1	6.3	5.4	5.3	5.3
Female	65+	4.1	4.5	4.1	4.0	4.0
Male	65+	14.0	10.5	7.8	7.8	7.8

Percentage married, age 60+				Percentage living alone, age 60+		
Total	Female	Male		Total	Female	Male
52.2	35.0	83.0		..	..	..

Statutory pensionable age (2006)				Percentage illiterate, age 65+ (2001)		
	Female	Male		Total	Female	Male
	55	60		2.5	3.3	0.8

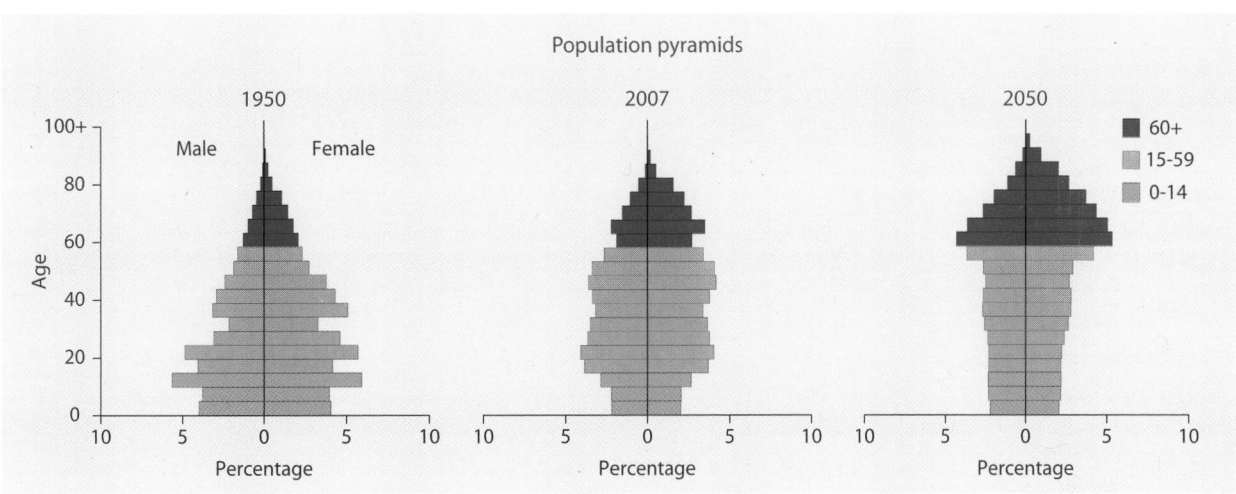

Population pyramids

United Nations Department of Economic and Social Affairs, Population Division

United Arab Emirates

Indicator	Age	1950	1975	2007	2025	2050
Population (thousands)						
Total	Total	69.6	530.0	4 775.3	6 692.8	9 056.2
	0-14	29.4	149.5	1 019.6	1 209.1	1 314.3
	15-59	36.3	362.3	3 675.0	5 062.9	5 627.4
	60-64	1.6	7.5	28.5	222.0	482.2
	65-69	1.1	3.9	20.7	109.8	448.5
	70-74	0.7	3.6	15.2	43.6	460.8
	75-79	0.4	2.1	8.1	22.4	376.7
	80-84			5.0	11.9	218.2
	85-89			2.3	7.9	95.4
	90-94	0.2	1.1	0.7	2.6	27.6
	95-99			0.1	0.6	4.5
	100+			0.0	0.1	0.7
Female	Total	34.3	162.9	1 535.9	2 352.9	3 463.3
	0-14	14.5	71.4	499.7	590.2	641.5
	15-59	17.8	83.8	1 003.8	1 640.5	2 087.9
	60-64	0.8	2.9	9.8	61.8	183.9
	65-69	0.6	1.5	8.1	29.8	154.3
	70-74	0.4	1.6	6.3	11.7	151.7
	75-79	0.2	1.0	3.7	7.4	123.0
	80-84			2.6	5.3	72.1
	85-89			1.4	4.0	34.6
	90-94	0.1	0.6	0.4	1.6	11.5
	95-99			0.1	0.4	2.3
	100+			0.0	0.1	0.5
Male	Total	35.3	367.2	3 239.4	4 339.9	5 592.9
	0-14	14.9	78.1	520.0	618.9	672.9
	15-59	18.4	278.5	2 671.2	3 422.3	3 539.5
	60-64	0.8	4.6	18.7	160.2	298.3
	65-69	0.5	2.4	12.6	79.9	294.2
	70-74	0.3	1.9	8.9	31.9	309.0
	75-79	0.2	1.1	4.4	15.0	253.6
	80-84			2.4	6.6	146.1
	85-89			1.0	3.9	60.8
	90-94	0.1	0.5	0.2	1.0	16.2
	95-99			0.0	0.2	2.3
	100+			0.0	0.0	0.2
Percentage in older ages						
Total	60+	5.7	3.4	1.7	6.3	23.3
	65+	3.4	2.0	1.1	3.0	18.0
	80+	0.2	0.2	0.2	0.3	3.8
Female	60+	5.9	4.7	2.1	5.2	21.2
	65+	3.6	2.9	1.5	2.6	15.9
	80+	0.3	0.4	0.3	0.5	3.5
Male	60+	5.4	2.9	1.5	6.9	24.7
	65+	3.2	1.6	0.9	3.2	19.4
	80+	0.2	0.1	0.1	0.3	4.0
Ageing index		13.4	12.2	7.9	34.8	160.9
Broad age groups (percentage)	0-14	42.3	28.2	21.4	18.1	14.5
	15-59	52.1	68.4	77.0	75.6	62.1
	60+	5.7	3.4	1.7	6.3	23.3
Median age (years)		18.9	25.4	29.0*	34.8	40.0
Dependency ratio	Total	84.1	43.3	28.9	26.6	48.2
	Youth	77.8	40.4	27.5	22.9	21.5
	Old Age	6.3	2.9	1.4	3.8	26.7
Potential support ratio		15.9	34.5	71.1	26.6	3.7
Parent support ratio		0.8	1.2	1.4	1.0	8.2
Sex ratio (per 100 women)	60+	92.7	137.7	148.7	244.5	188.1
	65+	90.6	126.6	130.7	229.7	196.8
	80+	81.6	93.5	81.2	102.4	186.5

* *Estimate refers to year 2005.*

Indicator	Age	1950-1955	1975-1980	2005-2010	2025-2030	2045-2050
Growth rate (percentage)	Total	2.5	13.0	2.3	1.5	0.9
	60+	2.2	2.1	4.8	10.9	2.7
	65+	2.4	3.2	4.0	12.7	3.3
	80+	3.6	12.4	4.9	5.6	11.3
Total fertility rate (per woman)		7.0	5.7	2.4	2.0	1.9
Life expectancy (years)						
Total	Birth	48.0	66.2	79.1	81.5	83.7
	60	..	..	22.0	23.8	25.5
	65	..	..	18.0	19.6	21.2
	80	..	..	8.3	9.4	10.2
Female	Birth	49.3	68.9	82.2	85.0	87.2
	60	..	..	24.5	26.7	28.6
	65	..	..	20.2	22.3	24.1
	80	..	..	9.5	10.9	12.1
Male	Birth	46.7	64.7	77.4	79.9	82.2
	60	..	..	20.4	22.4	24.2
	65	..	..	16.5	18.3	20.0
	80	..	..	7.2	8.3	9.4
Survival rate (percentage)						
Total	60	..	..	92.3	94.3	95.7
	65	..	..	88.0	90.8	93.0
	80	..	..	55.7	62.5	69.6
Female	60	..	..	94.5	96.0	97.0
	65	..	..	91.6	93.8	95.2
	80	..	..	66.2	73.6	78.9
Male	60	..	..	91.6	93.5	94.9
	65	..	..	86.5	89.6	91.7
	80	..	..	49.5	58.3	65.3

		1980	1990	2007	2010	2020
Labour force participation (percentage)						
Total	65+	37.4	23.8	18.6	18.5	19.9
Female	65+	2.8	1.6	1.3	1.4	1.4
Male	65+	64.2	43.1	31.8	31.2	29.3

Percentage married, age 60+				Percentage living alone, age 60+		
Total	Female	Male		Total	Female	Male
60.7	29.0	82.0		..	..	..

Statutory pensionable age (2006)				Percentage illiterate, age 65+		
	Female	Male		Total	Female	Male
	..	..		..	..	..

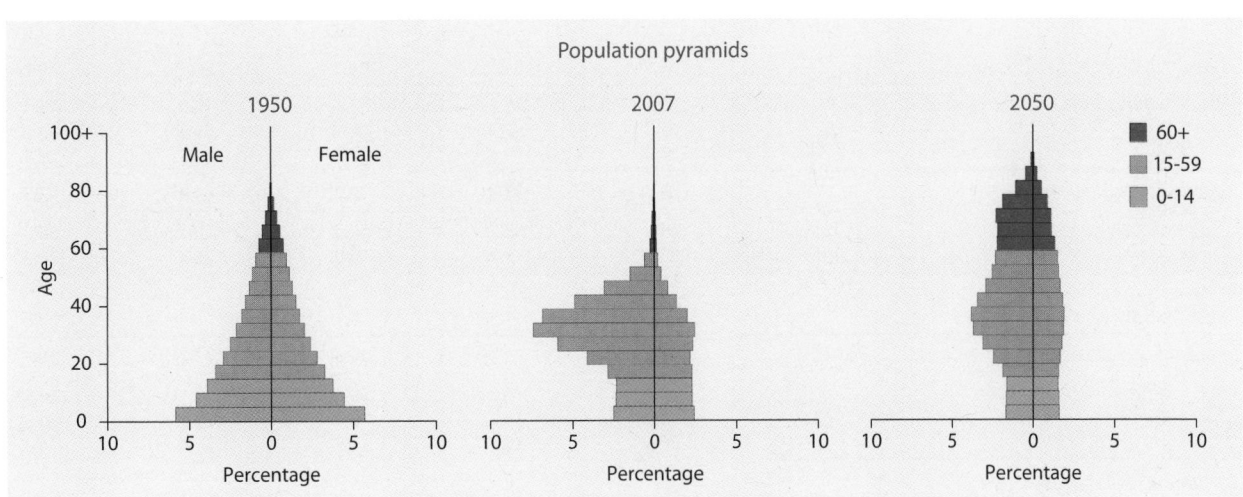

Population pyramids

United Kingdom of Great Britain and Northern Ireland

Indicator	Age	1950	1975	2007	2025	2050
Population (thousands)						
Total	Total	49 816.0	55 426.0	60 018.3	63 662.9	67 143.4
	0-14	11 127.3	12 934.9	10 491.4	10 788.1	11 021.4
	15-59	30 958.8	31 615.6	36 443.3	35 973.5	36 381.0
	60-64	2 386.7	3 143.5	3 438.3	4 281.4	4 182.6
	65-69	2 024.5	2 800.2	2 696.0	3 554.7	3 633.2
	70-74	1 566.8	2 188.0	2 305.7	2 931.2	3 132.6
	75-79	1 015.7	1 430.3	1 917.5	2 779.3	2 907.6
	80-84			1 449.7	1 701.5	2 681.5
	85-89			820.2	985.2	1 872.1
	90-94	736.2	1 313.6	343.6	472.9	916.0
	95-99			98.1	162.4	328.8
	100+			14.5	32.8	86.6
Female	Total	25 629.4	28 412.8	30 664.3	32 430.2	34 106.1
	0-14	5 448.5	6 290.9	5 119.9	5 276.8	5 388.3
	15-59	15 746.1	15 717.3	18 290.0	17 924.7	18 035.6
	60-64	1 325.7	1 671.6	1 755.1	2 210.2	2 075.7
	65-69	1 144.6	1 551.9	1 395.8	1 847.8	1 820.4
	70-74	899.6	1 298.7	1 231.1	1 562.5	1 621.0
	75-79	594.5	939.7	1 086.6	1 529.4	1 583.4
	80-84			889.2	989.4	1 540.7
	85-89			550.7	615.5	1 137.0
	90-94	470.4	942.6	254.2	323.4	599.2
	95-99			79.0	122.9	236.1
	100+			12.6	27.5	68.7
Male	Total	24 186.6	27 013.2	29 354.0	31 232.7	33 037.2
	0-14	5 678.8	6 644.0	5 371.5	5 511.3	5 633.1
	15-59	15 212.7	15 898.3	18 153.3	18 048.8	18 345.3
	60-64	1 061.0	1 471.8	1 683.1	2 071.2	2 106.8
	65-69	879.9	1 248.3	1 300.2	1 706.9	1 812.8
	70-74	667.3	889.2	1 074.6	1 368.7	1 511.6
	75-79	421.2	490.6	830.9	1 249.9	1 324.3
	80-84			560.5	712.1	1 140.8
	85-89			269.5	369.6	735.2
	90-94	265.7	370.9	89.4	149.4	316.8
	95-99			19.1	39.4	92.7
	100+			1.9	5.3	17.9
Percentage in older ages						
	60+	15.5	19.6	21.8	26.5	29.4
	65+	10.7	14.0	16.1	19.8	23.2
	80+	1.5	2.4	4.5	5.3	8.8
Female	60+	17.3	22.5	23.7	28.5	31.3
	65+	12.1	16.7	17.9	21.6	25.2
	80+	1.8	3.3	5.8	6.4	10.5
Male	60+	13.6	16.6	19.9	24.6	27.4
	65+	9.2	11.1	14.1	17.9	21.0
	80+	1.1	1.4	3.2	4.1	7.0
Ageing index		69.5	84.1	124.7	156.7	179.1
Broad age groups (percentage)	0-14	22.3	23.3	17.5	16.9	16.4
	15-59	62.1	57.0	60.7	56.5	54.2
	60+	15.5	19.6	21.8	26.5	29.4
Median age (years)		34.6	33.9	39.0*	41.4	42.9
Dependency ratio	Total	49.4	59.5	50.5	58.1	65.5
	Youth	33.4	37.2	26.3	26.8	27.2
	Old Age	16.0	22.2	24.2	31.4	38.4
Potential support ratio		6.2	4.5	4.1	3.2	2.6
Parent support ratio		3.6	5.3	11.6	13.1	25.7
Sex ratio (per 100 women)	60+	74.3	69.8	80.4	83.1	84.8
	65+	71.9	63.4	75.4	79.8	80.8
	80+	56.5	39.3	52.7	61.4	64.3

* *Estimate refers to year 2005.*

United Kingdom of Great Britain and Northern Ireland

Indicator	Age	1950-1955	1975-1980	2005-2010	2025-2030	2045-2050
Growth rate (percentage)	Total	0.2	0.0	0.3	0.3	0.2
	60+	1.1	0.6	1.8	1.4	0.6
	65+	1.2	1.6	0.9	1.9	0.3
	80+	2.8	3.1	1.2	3.7	1.8
Total fertility rate (per woman)		2.2	1.7	1.7	1.9	1.9
Life expectancy (years)						
Total	Birth	69.3	73.0	79.0	81.4	83.5
	60	..	..	22.0	23.7	25.3
	65	..	..	17.9	19.5	21.0
	80	..	..	8.5	9.4	10.3
Female	Birth	71.8	75.9	81.2	83.5	85.4
	60	..	..	23.7	25.5	27.1
	65	..	..	19.6	21.2	22.6
	80	..	..	9.2	10.2	11.2
Male	Birth	66.7	70.1	76.6	79.2	81.5
	60	..	..	20.0	21.8	23.5
	65	..	..	16.2	17.7	19.3
	80	..	..	7.4	8.3	9.2
Survival rate (percentage)						
Total	60	..	..	92.0	94.0	95.5
	65	..	..	87.4	90.4	92.6
	80	..	..	54.6	62.0	68.2
Female	60	..	..	93.6	95.1	96.2
	65	..	..	90.1	92.3	93.9
	80	..	..	62.6	69.1	74.3
Male	60	..	..	90.3	92.9	94.8
	65	..	..	84.7	88.5	91.2
	80	..	..	46.5	54.7	61.9

		1980	1990	2007	2010	2020
Labour force participation (percentage)						
Total	65+	5.8	5.6	5.7	5.9	6.2
Female	65+	3.5	3.4	3.6	3.7	4.0
Male	65+	9.3	8.8	8.5	8.7	9.0

Percentage married, age 60+			Percentage living alone, age 60+ (1994)		
Total	Female	Male	Total	Female	Male
64.0	54.0	77.0	34.7	44.7	21.5

Statutory pensionable age (2006)			Percentage illiterate, age 65+		
	Female	Male	Total	Female	Male
	60	65	..	..	..

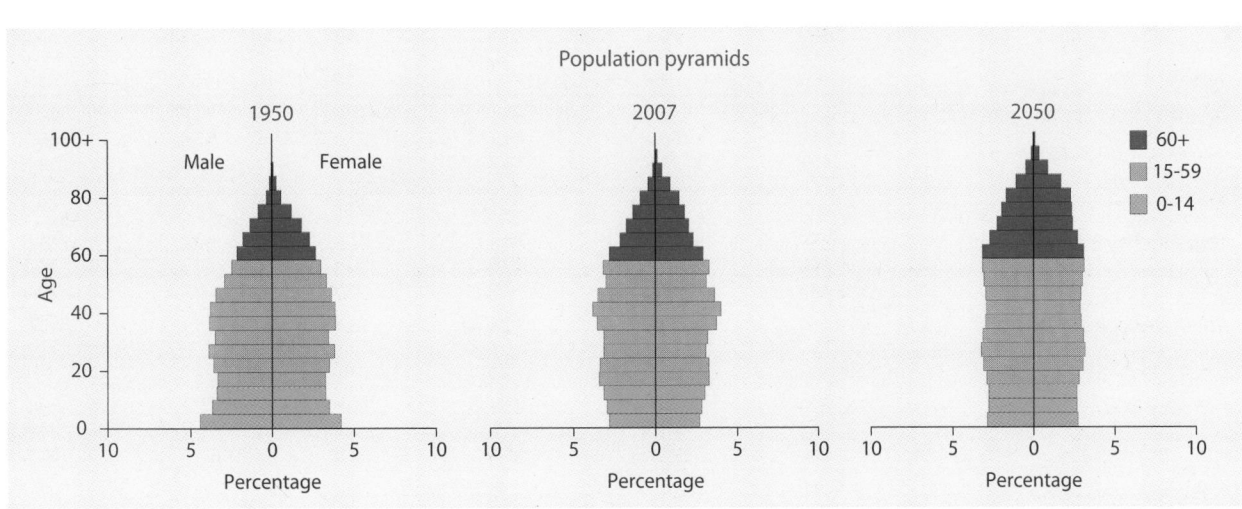

Population pyramids

United Republic of Tanzania

Indicator	Age	1950	1975	2007	2025	2050
Population (thousands)						
Total	Total	7 649.8	16 043.5	39 718.0	52 806.5	66 844.9
	0-14	3 515.7	7 398.4	16 653.9	18 260.0	16 063.9
	15-59	3 846.2	7 973.2	20 996.2	31 372.3	43 622.9
	60-64	119.5	265.5	755.4	1 035.8	2 526.5
	65-69	82.0	189.4	564.6	844.5	1 902.4
	70-74	49.9	121.1	388.7	620.4	1 336.2
	75-79	24.9	64.6	225.2	408.2	795.5
	80-84			99.2	191.1	403.7
	85-89			29.5	61.4	154.2
	90-94	11.5	31.4	4.9	11.5	35.2
	95-99			0.4	1.1	4.0
	100+			0.0	0.1	0.3
Female	Total	3 918.3	8 132.1	19 930.7	26 245.4	33 068.8
	0-14	1 782.1	3 693.7	8 280.6	9 065.7	7 963.8
	15-59	1 976.0	4 066.0	10 492.7	15 419.2	21 401.1
	60-64	65.0	143.3	411.0	543.5	1 252.2
	65-69	45.5	104.3	312.6	461.5	963.8
	70-74	28.2	68.2	220.2	350.4	697.3
	75-79	14.5	37.5	131.3	240.5	431.7
	80-84			59.9	116.7	234.6
	85-89			18.7	39.1	97.1
	90-94	7.1	19.1	3.3	7.8	24.0
	95-99			0.3	0.8	2.9
	100+			0.0	0.1	0.2
Male	Total	3 731.4	7 911.4	19 787.3	26 561.1	33 776.1
	0-14	1 733.6	3 704.6	8 373.3	9 194.3	8 100.1
	15-59	1 870.2	3 907.2	10 503.6	15 953.1	22 221.8
	60-64	54.5	122.2	344.3	492.3	1 274.2
	65-69	36.6	85.1	252.0	382.9	938.6
	70-74	21.6	53.0	168.5	270.0	638.9
	75-79	10.4	27.1	93.9	167.7	363.8
	80-84			39.2	74.3	169.1
	85-89			10.9	22.3	57.1
	90-94	4.5	12.3	1.6	3.7	11.2
	95-99			0.1	0.3	1.1
	100+			0.0	0.0	0.1
Percentage in older ages						
Total	60+	3.8	4.2	5.2	6.0	10.7
	65+	2.2	2.5	3.3	4.0	6.9
	80+	0.2	0.2	0.3	0.5	0.9
Female	60+	4.1	4.6	5.8	6.7	11.2
	65+	2.4	2.8	3.7	4.6	7.4
	80+	0.2	0.2	0.4	0.6	1.1
Male	60+	3.4	3.8	4.6	5.3	10.2
	65+	2.0	2.2	2.9	3.5	6.5
	80+	0.1	0.2	0.3	0.4	0.7
Ageing index		8.2	9.1	12.4	17.4	44.6
Broad age groups (percentage)	0-14	46.0	46.1	41.9	34.6	24.0
	15-59	50.3	49.7	52.9	59.4	65.3
	60+	3.8	4.2	5.2	6.0	10.7
Median age (years)		16.9	16.9	18.2*	22.2	29.9
Dependency ratio	Total	92.9	94.7	82.6	62.9	44.8
	Youth	88.7	89.8	76.6	56.3	34.8
	Old Age	4.2	4.9	6.0	6.6	10.0
Potential support ratio		23.6	20.3	16.6	15.2	10.0
Parent support ratio		0.7	0.7	1.3	1.9	2.1
Sex ratio (per 100 women)	60+	79.6	80.5	78.7	80.3	93.3
	65+	76.8	77.5	75.9	75.7	88.9
	80+	63.5	64.1	63.0	61.2	66.5

* Estimate refers to year 2005.

Indicator	Age	1950-1955	1975-1980	2005-2010	2025-2030	2045-2050
Growth rate (percentage)	Total	2.6	3.2	1.8	1.2	0.7
	60+	3.2	3.6	2.8	2.2	4.1
	65+	3.3	3.7	2.9	2.3	4.2
	80+	4.0	4.1	3.8	4.1	3.0
Total fertility rate (per woman)		6.7	6.7	4.4	2.7	1.9
Life expectancy (years)						
Total	Birth	40.5	52.1	46.6	54.9	62.8
	60	..	..	16.2	17.5	18.9
	65	..	..	12.9	13.9	15.2
	80	..	..	5.3	5.7	6.1
Female	Birth	42.0	54.0	46.8	55.3	63.6
	60	..	..	17.0	18.5	20.2
	65	..	..	13.5	14.7	16.1
	80	..	..	5.5	5.9	6.5
Male	Birth	39.0	50.3	46.2	54.5	61.8
	60	..	..	15.3	16.4	17.6
	65	..	..	12.1	13.1	14.1
	80	..	..	5.0	5.3	5.7
Survival rate (percentage)						
Total	60	..	..	39.9	52.2	65.1
	65	..	..	35.5	47.5	60.6
	80	..	..	13.7	21.2	31.1
Female	60	..	..	39.9	52.2	65.4
	65	..	..	36.2	48.5	62.0
	80	..	..	15.2	23.6	35.2
Male	60	..	..	39.7	52.2	64.5
	65	..	..	34.6	46.6	58.9
	80	..	..	11.9	18.5	26.8

		1980	1990	2007	2010	2020
Labour force participation (percentage)						
Total	65+	66.9	65.9	61.3	60.7	60.2
Female	65+	57.3	56.1	49.5	49.0	48.5
Male	65+	79.3	78.5	76.8	76.3	75.8

Percentage married, age 60+			Percentage living alone, age 60+ (1999)		
Total	Female	Male	Total	Female	Male
59.2	41.0	82.0	7.5	7.8	7.3

Statutory pensionable age (2006)			Percentage illiterate, age 65+ (2002)		
	Female	Male	Total	Female	Male
	60	60	72.2	86.2	57.1

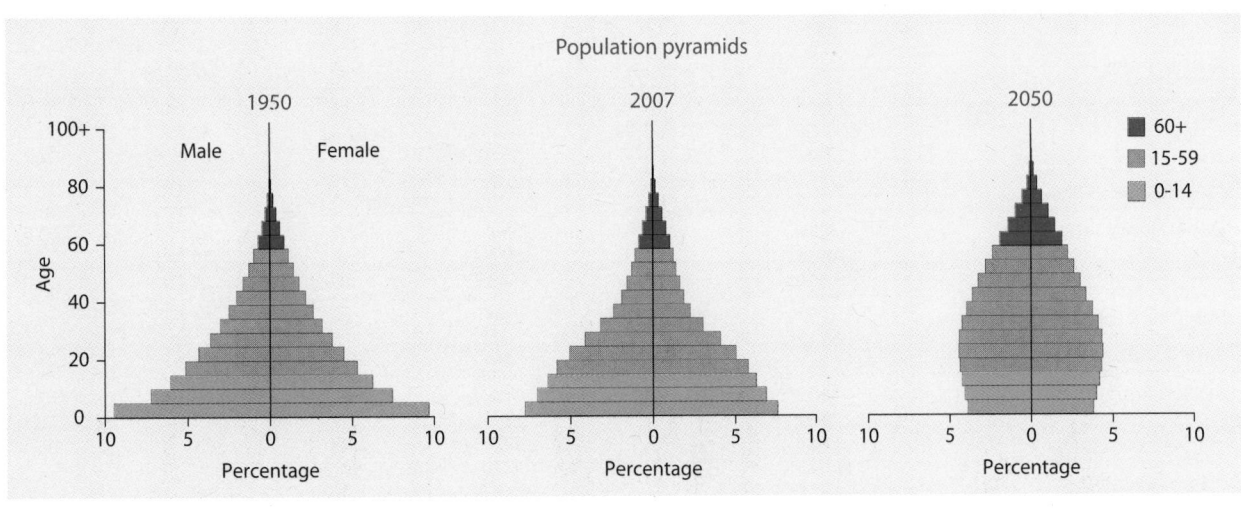

Population pyramids

United States of America

Indicator	Age	1950	1975	2007	2025	2050
Population (thousands)						
Total	Total	157 813.0	220 165.0	303 851.2	350 102.6	394 976.5
	0-14	42 595.7	55 424.0	62 135.8	65 249.2	68 187.2
	15-59	95 489.3	132 140.1	189 572.2	201 679.9	222 356.5
	60-64	6 685.3	9 566.1	14 426.7	21 104.2	22 886.2
	65-69	5 485.4	8 134.6	10 793.0	19 712.3	20 474.0
	70-74	3 540.7	5 832.4	8 595.3	16 148.6	17 442.6
	75-79	2 216.0	4 377.9	7 296.6	11 995.9	14 904.7
	80-84			5 661.9	7 316.6	12 178.8
	85-89			3 384.8	3 992.1	9 134.6
	90-94	1 800.6	4 689.9	1 465.1	1 949.4	5 104.8
	95-99			434.5	760.3	1 875.0
	100+			85.4	194.1	432.2
Female	Total	78 982.6	112 025.0	154 348.1	177 631.0	200 329.5
	0-14	20 849.7	27 108.1	30 301.2	31 814.9	33 254.2
	15-59	47 792.6	66 142.5	94 698.6	99 955.1	109 756.0
	60-64	3 381.5	5 089.5	7 536.8	10 916.5	11 600.6
	65-69	2 872.0	4 521.1	5 750.5	10 420.5	10 536.9
	70-74	1 867.6	3 381.9	4 716.1	8 744.6	9 178.3
	75-79	1 193.2	2 689.8	4 177.3	6 749.8	8 109.5
	80-84			3 449.0	4 349.2	6 989.8
	85-89			2 230.4	2 551.2	5 644.1
	90-94	1 026.1	3 092.1	1 064.8	1 370.1	3 475.6
	95-99			349.1	592.8	1 421.2
	100+			74.2	166.4	363.1
Male	Total	78 830.4	108 140.0	149 503.1	172 471.6	194 647.0
	0-14	21 746.0	28 315.8	31 834.6	33 434.3	34 933.0
	15-59	47 696.7	65 997.6	94 873.6	101 724.8	112 600.6
	60-64	3 303.8	4 476.6	6 889.9	10 187.7	11 285.6
	65-69	2 613.5	3 613.5	5 042.4	9 291.9	9 937.0
	70-74	1 673.1	2 450.6	3 879.2	7 404.0	8 264.2
	75-79	1 022.8	1 688.1	3 119.3	5 246.1	6 795.1
	80-84			2 213.0	2 967.4	5 189.0
	85-89			1 154.4	1 440.9	3 490.4
	90-94	774.5	1 597.8	400.2	579.4	1 629.2
	95-99			85.4	167.5	453.8
	100+			11.2	27.7	69.1
Percentage in older ages						
Total	60+	12.5	14.8	17.2	23.8	26.4
	65+	8.3	10.5	12.4	17.7	20.6
	80+	1.1	2.1	3.6	4.1	7.3
Female	60+	13.1	16.8	19.0	25.8	28.6
	65+	8.8	12.2	14.1	19.7	22.8
	80+	1.3	2.8	4.6	5.1	8.9
Male	60+	11.9	12.8	15.2	21.6	24.2
	65+	7.7	8.6	10.6	15.7	18.4
	80+	1.0	1.5	2.6	3.0	5.6
Ageing index		46.3	58.8	83.9	127.5	153.2
Broad age groups (percentage)	0-14	27.0	25.2	20.4	18.6	17.3
	15-59	60.5	60.0	62.4	57.6	56.3
	60+	12.5	14.8	17.2	23.8	26.4
Median age (years)		30.0	28.8	36.1*	38.3	41.1
Dependency ratio	Total	54.5	55.4	48.9	57.1	61.1
	Youth	41.7	39.1	30.5	29.3	27.8
	Old Age	12.8	16.3	18.5	27.9	33.3
Potential support ratio		7.8	6.2	5.4	3.6	3.0
Parent support ratio		3.2	5.7	10.0	11.2	23.2
Sex ratio (per 100 women)	60+	90.8	73.6	77.7	81.4	82.2
	65+	87.4	68.3	72.9	77.6	78.4
	80+	75.5	51.7	53.9	57.4	60.5

*   Estimate refers to year 2005.

Indicator	Age	1950-1955	1975-1980	2005-2010	2025-2030	2045-2050
Growth rate (percentage)	Total	1.6	1.0	0.9	0.6	0.4
	60+	2.6	2.0	2.5	1.4	0.9
	65+	2.9	2.3	1.7	2.3	0.7
	80+	4.2	3.0	1.6	4.2	0.6
Total fertility rate (per woman)		3.4	1.8	2.0	1.9	1.9
Life expectancy (years)						
Total	Birth	68.8	73.3	77.9	80.2	82.4
	60	..	..	22.2	23.7	25.1
	65	..	..	18.4	19.7	20.9
	80	..	..	9.0	9.6	10.2
Female	Birth	72.0	77.2	80.6	82.8	85.0
	60	..	..	24.1	25.6	27.0
	65	..	..	20.1	21.4	22.7
	80	..	..	9.8	10.6	11.3
Male	Birth	66.1	69.5	75.2	77.5	79.9
	60	..	..	20.1	21.6	23.0
	65	..	..	16.4	17.7	18.9
	80	..	..	7.7	8.3	8.9
Survival rate (percentage)						
Total	60	..	..	88.9	91.3	93.6
	65	..	..	83.9	87.2	90.4
	80	..	..	53.4	60.0	66.2
Female	60	..	..	91.4	93.5	95.3
	65	..	..	87.5	90.3	92.8
	80	..	..	61.6	67.7	73.2
Male	60	..	..	86.3	89.2	92.0
	65	..	..	80.2	84.1	87.9
	80	..	..	45.0	52.0	59.0

		1980	1990	2007	2010	2020
Labour force participation (percentage)						
Total	65+	12.5	11.8	14.4	14.9	15.6
Female	65+	8.1	8.6	10.7	11.2	12.0
Male	65+	19.0	16.3	19.5	19.9	20.2

Percentage married, age 60+			Percentage living alone, age 60+ (2000)		
Total	Female	Male	Total	Female	Male
59.7	48.0	75.0	25.9	34.5	14.9

Statutory pensionable age (2006)			Percentage illiterate, age 65+		
	Female	Male	Total	Female	Male
	65	65	..	..	..

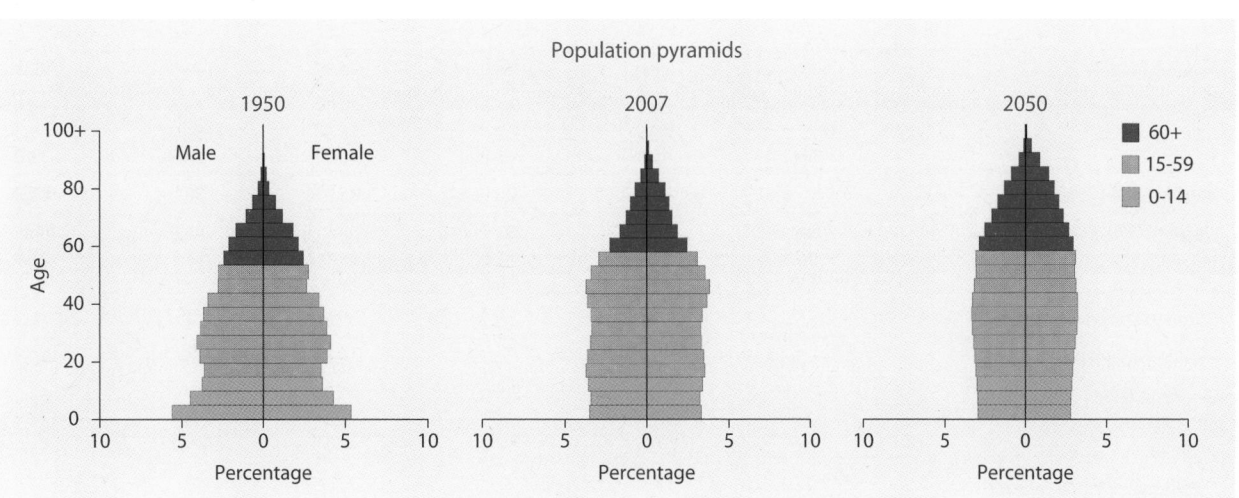

Population pyramids

United States Virgin Islands

Indicator	Age	1950	1975	2007	2025	2050
Population (thousands)						
Total	Total	26.8	86.0	111.8	107.2	82.3
	0-14	10.5	35.9	25.6	20.7	12.2
	15-59	13.4	45.0	65.8	55.6	43.1
	60-64	0.9	1.9	7.1	6.8	5.9
	65-69	0.8	1.3	5.1	6.5	5.1
	70-74	0.6	0.8	3.5	5.8	2.7
	75-79	0.4	0.5	2.3	5.4	3.5
	80-84			1.3	3.7	3.6
	85-89			0.7	1.8	3.2
	90-94	0.3	0.5	0.3	0.8	1.9
	95-99			0.1	0.2	0.9
	100+			0.0	0.0	0.3
Female	Total	13.7	43.9	58.7	56.9	43.2
	0-14	5.2	17.8	12.5	10.0	5.9
	15-59	6.7	23.4	34.9	28.4	20.6
	60-64	0.5	0.9	3.7	3.8	3.1
	65-69	0.5	0.7	2.7	3.6	2.7
	70-74	0.4	0.5	2.0	3.5	1.6
	75-79	0.2	0.3	1.3	3.3	2.2
	80-84			0.8	2.3	2.3
	85-89			0.5	1.2	2.2
	90-94	0.2	0.3	0.2	0.6	1.5
	95-99			0.0	0.2	0.7
	100+			0.0	0.0	0.2
Male	Total	13.1	42.0	53.1	50.3	39.1
	0-14	5.3	18.1	13.1	10.6	6.3
	15-59	6.6	21.6	30.9	27.2	22.4
	60-64	0.4	1.0	3.4	3.0	2.8
	65-69	0.3	0.6	2.4	2.9	2.4
	70-74	0.2	0.4	1.6	2.3	1.1
	75-79	0.1	0.2	0.9	2.2	1.3
	80-84			0.5	1.4	1.3
	85-89			0.2	0.5	1.0
	90-94	0.1	0.2	0.1	0.2	0.5
	95-99			0.0	0.0	0.1
	100+			0.0	0.0	0.0
Percentage in older ages						
Total	60+	10.9	5.8	18.2	28.9	32.8
	65+	7.5	3.6	11.8	22.6	25.6
	80+	1.0	0.6	2.1	6.1	12.0
Female	60+	12.5	6.2	19.2	32.5	38.5
	65+	8.8	4.0	12.9	25.8	31.3
	80+	1.3	0.7	2.7	7.7	16.2
Male	60+	9.3	5.4	17.1	24.7	26.5
	65+	6.2	3.2	10.6	18.9	19.4
	80+	0.8	0.4	1.5	4.2	7.3
Ageing index		28.0	13.9	79.5	149.8	220.9
Broad age groups (percentage)	0-14	39.1	41.8	22.9	19.3	14.9
	15-59	49.9	52.4	58.9	51.9	52.3
	60+	10.9	5.8	18.2	28.9	32.8
Median age (years)		22.0	20.0	35.0*	38.2	47.2
Dependency ratio	Total	87.4	83.2	53.3	71.9	68.1
	Youth	73.3	76.6	35.1	33.1	25.0
	Old Age	14.1	6.6	18.2	38.8	43.1
Potential support ratio		7.1	15.1	5.5	2.6	2.3
Parent support ratio		3.4	2.6	4.9	16.5	35.4
Sex ratio (per 100 women)	60+	72.0	83.8	80.3	67.2	62.4
	65+	67.2	75.1	74.4	64.5	55.9
	80+	59.4	54.8	48.3	48.7	41.0

* *Estimate refers to year 2005.*

Indicator	Age	1950-1955	1975-1980	2005-2010	2025-2030	2045-2050
Growth rate (percentage)	Total	1.9	2.8	0.0	–0.6	–1.3
	60+	0.1	6.5	4.3	0.2	0.2
	65+	0.8	7.2	5.3	1.2	–0.3
	80+	1.7	3.3	4.4	4.9	–0.8
Total fertility rate (per woman)		5.7	4.3	2.1	1.9	1.9
Life expectancy (years)						
Total	Birth	59.2	70.5	79.3	82.0	84.5
	60	..	..	22.4	24.4	26.4
	65	..	..	18.5	20.2	22.1
	80	..	..	9.1	9.9	11.0
Female	Birth	60.7	73.8	83.2	85.6	87.8
	60	..	..	25.6	27.4	29.1
	65	..	..	21.3	22.9	24.5
	80	..	..	10.4	11.4	12.5
Male	Birth	57.7	67.5	75.4	78.2	80.6
	60	..	..	19.0	21.1	23.0
	65	..	..	15.4	17.2	18.9
	80	..	..	7.2	8.0	8.8
Survival rate (percentage)						
Total	60	..	..	92.1	94.1	95.5
	65	..	..	87.2	90.5	92.8
	80	..	..	55.6	64.0	71.4
Female	60	..	..	94.6	96.1	97.2
	65	..	..	91.7	93.9	95.6
	80	..	..	68.7	74.9	80.2
Male	60	..	..	89.3	91.9	93.8
	65	..	..	82.3	86.8	89.9
	80	..	..	42.3	51.9	60.1

		1980	1990	2007	2010	2020
Labour force participation (percentage)						
Total	65+	16.8	15.7	18.8	19.0	19.0
Female	65+	10.4	9.8	17.6	18.3	18.9
Male	65+	24.8	23.1	20.4	19.9	19.2

Percentage married, age 60+			Percentage living alone, age 60+ (1990)		
Total	Female	Male	Total	Female	Male
55.0	41.0	72.0	23.5	25.3	21.2

Statutory pensionable age (2006)			Percentage illiterate, age 65+		
Female	Male		Total	Female	Male
65	65		..	..	..

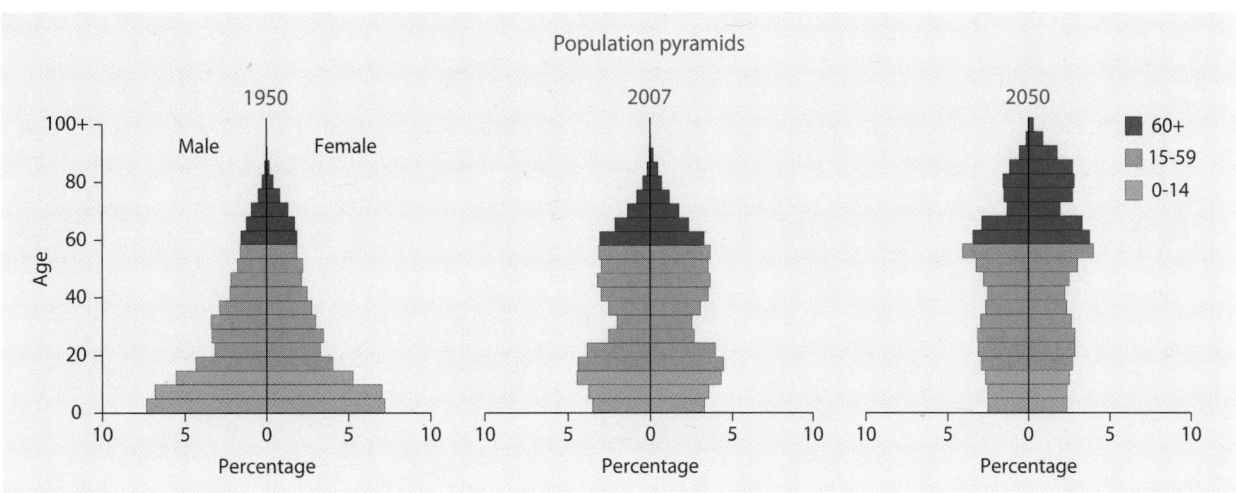

Population pyramids

1950 2007 2050

Male Female

60+
15-59
0-14

Age

Percentage

Uruguay

Indicator	Age	1950	1975	2007	2025	2050
Population (thousands)						
Total	Total	2 238.5	2 828.6	3 509.4	3 848.1	4 043.3
	0-14	624.0	783.3	840.4	785.0	687.2
	15-59	1 350.5	1 645.8	2 053.4	2 287.3	2 278.4
	60-64	79.7	127.3	148.9	193.0	231.8
	65-69	66.3	99.1	130.3	171.3	210.5
	70-74	51.2	76.2	117.9	138.2	206.7
	75-79	35.0	50.9	98.9	109.7	168.6
	80-84			67.0	78.9	119.3
	85-89			34.6	49.7	82.4
	90-94	31.8	45.9	14.2	25.6	42.4
	95-99			3.4	8.2	13.7
	100+			0.4	1.2	2.3
Female	Total	1 106.2	1 427.1	1 805.8	1 966.7	2 059.4
	0-14	310.0	384.0	411.2	383.6	335.4
	15-59	659.2	823.8	1 032.0	1 132.8	1 122.4
	60-64	39.7	66.6	80.3	102.8	118.1
	65-69	33.5	52.2	73.0	94.2	109.7
	70-74	26.4	41.7	68.4	78.2	111.4
	75-79	18.9	29.6	60.3	65.7	94.9
	80-84			43.3	50.0	72.1
	85-89			23.8	33.8	53.7
	90-94	18.6	29.2	10.4	18.5	29.7
	95-99			2.6	6.3	10.1
	100+			0.3	1.0	1.7
Male	Total	1 132.3	1 401.4	1 703.6	1 881.4	1 983.9
	0-14	314.0	399.3	429.2	401.4	351.9
	15-59	691.3	822.0	1 021.4	1 154.5	1 156.0
	60-64	40.0	60.7	68.6	90.2	113.7
	65-69	32.8	46.9	57.2	77.1	100.8
	70-74	24.8	34.5	49.5	60.0	95.3
	75-79	16.1	21.3	38.6	44.0	73.6
	80-84			23.6	29.0	47.2
	85-89			10.8	15.8	28.7
	90-94	13.2	16.7	3.8	7.2	12.7
	95-99			0.8	1.9	3.5
	100+			0.1	0.3	0.6
Percentage in older ages						
Total	60+	11.8	14.1	17.5	20.2	26.7
	65+	8.2	9.6	13.3	15.1	20.9
	80+	1.4	1.6	3.4	4.3	6.4
Female	60+	12.4	15.4	20.1	22.9	29.2
	65+	8.8	10.7	15.6	17.7	23.5
	80+	1.7	2.0	4.5	5.6	8.1
Male	60+	11.2	12.9	14.8	17.3	24.0
	65+	7.7	8.5	10.8	12.5	18.3
	80+	1.2	1.2	2.3	2.9	4.7
Ageing index		42.3	51.0	73.2	98.8	156.8
Broad age groups (percentage)	0-14	27.9	27.7	23.9	20.4	17.0
	15-59	60.3	58.2	58.5	59.4	56.4
	60+	11.8	14.1	17.5	20.2	26.7
Median age (years)		27.8	30.0	32.1*	36.0	41.8
Dependency ratio	Total	56.5	59.5	59.3	55.1	61.1
	Youth	43.6	44.2	38.2	31.7	27.4
	Old Age	12.9	15.4	21.2	23.5	33.7
Potential support ratio		7.8	6.5	4.7	4.3	3.0
Parent support ratio		4.5	4.1	10.5	13.4	18.9
Sex ratio (per 100 women)	60+	92.6	82.2	69.8	72.3	79.1
	65+	89.3	78.3	65.3	67.7	74.9
	80+	71.1	57.1	48.5	49.5	55.3

* *Estimate refers to year 2005.*

Indicator	Age	1950-1955	1975-1980	2005-2010	2025-2030	2045-2050
Growth rate (percentage)	Total	1.2	0.6	0.6	0.3	0.0
	60+	1.1	1.4	1.0	1.3	0.9
	65+	0.9	2.3	0.9	1.6	1.0
	80+	1.1	2.0	3.4	1.6	1.4
Total fertility rate (per woman)		2.7	2.9	2.2	1.9	1.9
Life expectancy (years)						
Total	Birth	66.1	69.5	76.3	79.4	81.3
	60	..	..	21.5	23.4	24.5
	65	..	..	17.8	19.5	20.5
	80	..	..	8.6	9.5	10.0
Female	Birth	69.3	73.0	79.8	82.7	84.6
	60	..	..	23.7	25.6	26.9
	65	..	..	19.7	21.4	22.6
	80	..	..	9.3	10.2	10.9
Male	Birth	63.3	66.3	72.6	76.0	78.1
	60	..	..	18.8	20.8	22.0
	65	..	..	15.5	17.1	18.2
	80	..	..	7.5	8.3	8.8
Survival rate (percentage)						
Total	60	..	..	86.8	90.0	92.0
	65	..	..	81.2	85.5	88.2
	80	..	..	49.9	58.5	63.7
Female	60	..	..	90.8	93.2	94.7
	65	..	..	87.0	90.3	92.3
	80	..	..	60.9	68.9	74.0
Male	60	..	..	82.8	86.9	89.4
	65	..	..	75.2	80.8	84.1
	80	..	..	38.4	47.5	53.3

		1980	1990	2007	2010	2020
Labour force participation (percentage)						
Total	65+	10.5	7.4	24.4	26.4	30.7
Female	65+	3.6	5.5	19.5	22.8	29.7
Male	65+	19.5	10.0	31.8	32.0	32.2

Percentage married, age 60+				Percentage living alone, age 60+ (1996)		
Total	Female	Male		Total	Female	Male
53.3	40.0	72.0		15.6	17.9	12.4

Statutory pensionable age (2006)				Percentage illiterate, age 65+		
	Female	Male		Total	Female	Male
	60	60		..	..	..

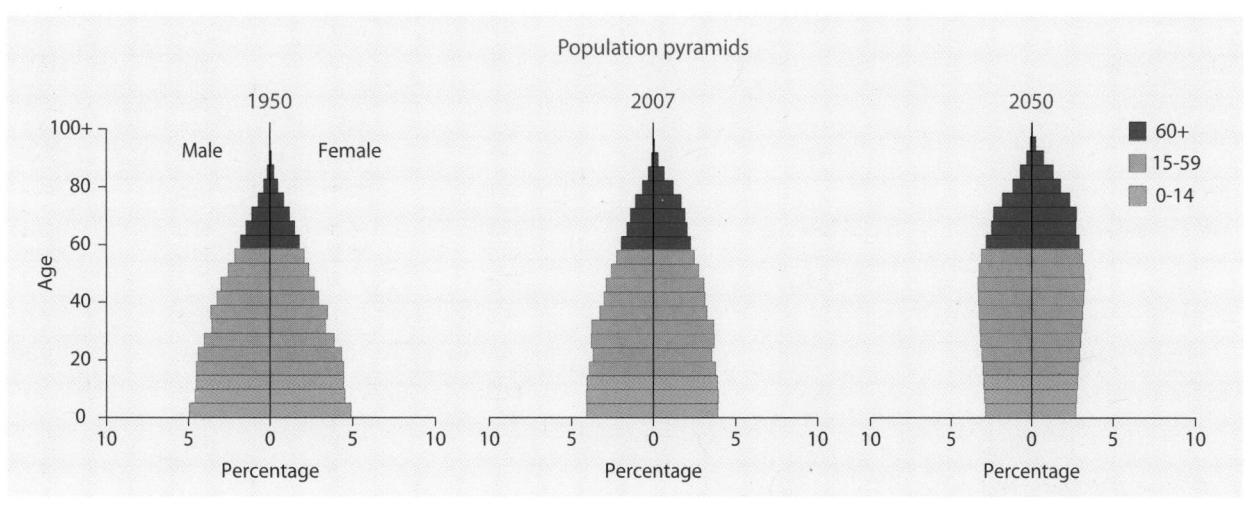

Population pyramids

Uzbekistan

Indicator	Age	1950	1975	2007	2025	2050
Population (thousands)						
Total	Total	6 314.0	13 981.0	27 371.3	34 041.8	38 665.3
	0-14	2 000.5	6 059.9	8 642.1	8 337.0	7 081.0
	15-59	3 737.5	6 837.1	17 057.7	22 073.1	23 431.7
	60-64	223.6	309.3	403.2	1 349.5	2 545.3
	65-69	158.1	281.4	434.8	1 021.7	1 959.5
	70-74	100.6	240.4	365.4	621.2	1 420.1
	75-79	57.2	132.5	251.9	311.9	1 024.7
	80-84			139.1	147.8	636.9
	85-89			48.7	121.2	376.7
	90-94	36.4	120.4	19.6	42.3	148.4
	95-99			6.8	13.7	35.6
	100+			2.0	2.4	5.5
Female	Total	3 257.3	7 117.5	13 760.4	17 154.5	19 606.8
	0-14	999.7	2 987.6	4 247.1	4 089.7	3 466.5
	15-59	1 975.9	3 480.9	8 569.2	11 023.8	11 616.1
	60-64	104.9	194.9	210.0	729.6	1 319.3
	65-69	77.3	169.3	232.2	562.0	1 047.3
	70-74	50.3	139.7	205.4	354.3	785.0
	75-79	29.7	74.9	147.6	185.9	594.6
	80-84			91.8	89.5	394.9
	85-89			36.4	79.1	248.7
	90-94	19.4	70.3	14.6	29.1	103.8
	95-99			4.9	9.8	26.4
	100+			1.3	1.8	4.1
Male	Total	3 056.7	6 863.5	13 610.9	16 887.3	19 058.5
	0-14	1 000.7	3 072.3	4 395.0	4 247.3	3 614.5
	15-59	1 761.6	3 356.2	8 488.5	11 049.3	11 815.5
	60-64	118.7	114.5	193.3	620.0	1 226.0
	65-69	80.7	112.1	202.6	459.7	912.1
	70-74	50.3	100.7	160.0	267.0	635.0
	75-79	27.5	57.5	104.3	126.0	430.1
	80-84			47.3	58.4	242.0
	85-89			12.3	42.0	128.0
	90-94	17.0	50.1	5.0	13.2	44.6
	95-99			1.9	3.9	9.2
	100+			0.7	0.6	1.4
Percentage in older ages						
Total	60+	9.1	7.8	6.1	10.7	21.1
	65+	5.6	5.5	4.6	6.7	14.5
	80+	0.6	0.9	0.8	1.0	3.1
Female	60+	8.6	9.1	6.9	11.9	23.1
	65+	5.4	6.4	5.3	7.6	16.3
	80+	0.6	1.0	1.1	1.2	4.0
Male	60+	9.6	6.3	5.3	9.4	19.0
	65+	5.7	4.7	3.9	5.7	12.6
	80+	0.6	0.7	0.5	0.7	2.2
Ageing index		28.8	17.9	19.3	43.6	115.1
Broad age groups (percentage)	0-14	31.7	43.3	31.6	24.5	18.3
	15-59	59.2	48.9	62.3	64.8	60.6
	60+	9.1	7.8	6.1	10.7	21.1
Median age (years)		24.1	17.9	22.6*	30.6	38.9
Dependency ratio	Total	59.4	95.6	56.8	45.3	48.8
	Youth	50.5	84.8	49.5	35.6	27.3
	Old Age	8.9	10.8	7.3	9.7	21.6
Potential support ratio		11.2	9.2	13.8	10.3	4.6
Parent support ratio		1.9	5.0	3.5	3.9	7.2
Sex ratio (per 100 women)	60+	104.5	67.0	77.0	77.9	80.2
	65+	99.3	70.6	72.8	74.0	75.0
	80+	87.7	71.2	45.1	56.4	54.7

*   *Estimate refers to year 2005.*

Indicator	Age	1950-1955	1975-1980	2005-2010	2025-2030	2045-2050
Growth rate (percentage)	Total	2.8	2.6	1.4	0.7	0.2
	60+	2.3	−0.2	1.6	3.5	3.3
	65+	4.3	0.9	−0.2	5.2	3.1
	80+	5.5	3.3	6.2	2.8	2.9
Total fertility rate (per woman)		6.0	5.6	2.5	1.9	1.9
Life expectancy (years)						
Total	Birth	55.8	64.7	67.1	71.7	74.9
	60	..	..	18.4	19.9	21.1
	65	..	..	15.1	16.4	17.4
	80	..	..	7.5	8.0	8.5
Female	Birth	59.4	68.1	70.4	74.7	77.7
	60	..	..	20.0	21.6	22.9
	65	..	..	16.4	17.8	18.9
	80	..	..	7.9	8.5	9.1
Male	Birth	52.4	61.1	64.0	68.7	72.1
	60	..	..	16.7	18.0	19.2
	65	..	..	13.6	14.7	15.7
	80	..	..	6.7	7.2	7.6
Survival rate (percentage)						
Total	60	..	..	74.7	81.5	85.8
	65	..	..	67.4	75.1	80.2
	80	..	..	32.8	41.2	47.7
Female	60	..	..	80.0	85.8	89.2
	65	..	..	73.9	80.8	84.9
	80	..	..	40.8	49.6	56.1
Male	60	..	..	69.4	77.2	82.6
	65	..	..	61.0	69.5	75.7
	80	..	..	25.1	32.6	39.3

		1980	1990	2007	2010	2020
Labour force participation (percentage)						
Total	65+	11.7	11.5	16.8	16.6	15.3
Female	65+	7.5	7.6	12.1	12.1	12.0
Male	65+	18.5	18.6	23.3	22.8	19.7

Percentage married, age 60+			Percentage living alone, age 60+ (1996)		
Total	Female	Male	Total	Female	Male
55.8	36.0	82.0	7.6	10.8	3.6

Statutory pensionable age (2006)			Percentage illiterate, age 65+		
	Female	Male	Total	Female	Male
	55	60	..	..	..

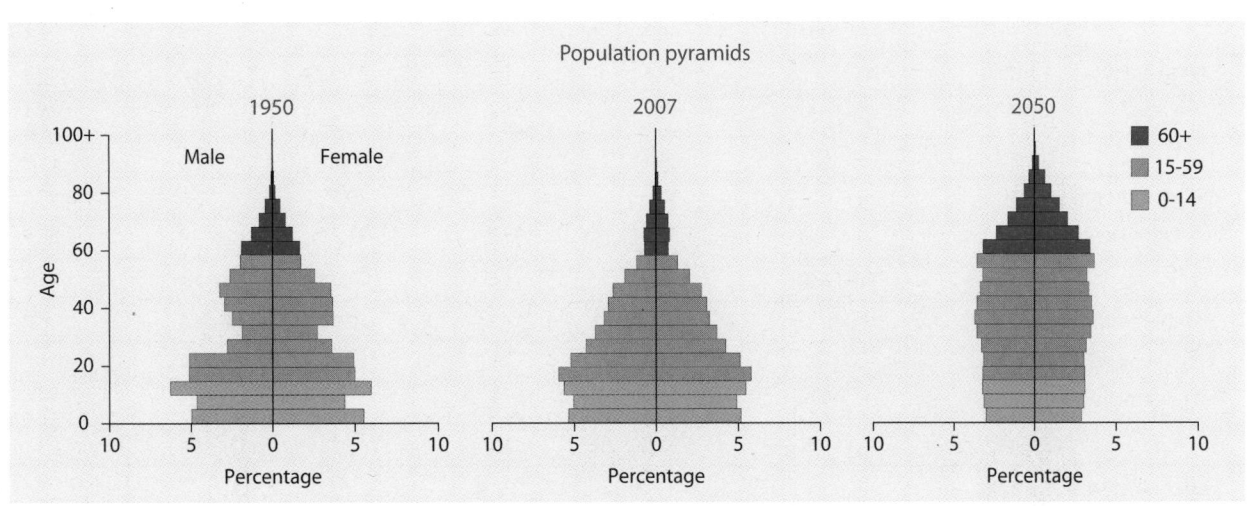

Population pyramids

United Nations Department of Economic and Social Affairs, Population Division

Vanuatu

Indicator	Age	1950	1975	2007	2025	2050
Population (thousands)						
Total	Total	47.7	101.0	219.5	293.7	375.0
	0-14	22.1	45.9	85.7	92.5	86.7
	15-59	23.6	50.6	122.1	178.8	232.0
	60-64	0.7	1.5	4.3	7.8	18.1
	65-69	0.6	1.2	3.0	6.1	14.2
	70-74	0.4	0.8	2.1	3.9	9.8
	75-79	0.2	0.6	1.4	2.7	7.4
	80-84			0.6	1.3	4.4
	85-89			0.3	0.5	1.9
	90-94	0.1	0.3	0.1	0.1	0.6
	95-99			0.0	0.0	0.1
	100+			0.0	0.0	0.0
Female	Total	22.8	47.4	107.7	145.5	187.4
	0-14	10.5	21.8	41.7	45.0	42.0
	15-59	11.2	23.8	60.6	89.1	115.6
	60-64	0.4	0.6	2.0	4.0	9.1
	65-69	0.3	0.5	1.4	3.1	7.1
	70-74	0.2	0.3	0.9	2.0	5.1
	75-79	0.1	0.2	0.6	1.4	4.1
	80-84			0.3	0.7	2.6
	85-89			0.1	0.3	1.2
	90-94	0.1	0.1	0.0	0.1	0.4
	95-99			0.0	0.0	0.1
	100+			0.0	0.0	0.0
Male	Total	24.9	53.6	111.7	148.2	187.6
	0-14	11.6	24.2	44.0	47.5	44.7
	15-59	12.4	26.8	61.5	89.6	116.4
	60-64	0.4	0.9	2.2	3.8	9.0
	65-69	0.3	0.7	1.6	3.1	7.0
	70-74	0.2	0.5	1.1	1.9	4.7
	75-79	0.1	0.4	0.7	1.4	3.3
	80-84			0.3	0.6	1.8
	85-89			0.1	0.2	0.6
	90-94	0.1	0.2	0.0	0.0	0.2
	95-99			0.0	0.0	0.0
	100+			0.0	0.0	0.0
Percentage in older ages						
Total	60+	4.3	4.4	5.3	7.6	15.0
	65+	2.7	2.9	3.4	5.0	10.2
	80+	0.2	0.3	0.4	0.6	1.9
Female	60+	4.6	3.7	5.0	7.8	15.9
	65+	3.0	2.4	3.2	5.1	11.0
	80+	0.3	0.3	0.4	0.7	2.3
Male	60+	4.0	5.0	5.6	7.5	14.2
	65+	2.5	3.3	3.6	4.9	9.4
	80+	0.2	0.4	0.5	0.6	1.4
Ageing index		9.3	9.7	13.6	24.2	64.9
Broad age groups (percentage)	0-14	46.3	45.5	39.0	31.5	23.1
	15-59	49.5	50.1	55.6	60.9	61.9
	60+	4.3	4.4	5.3	7.6	15.0
Median age (years)		16.8	17.1	19.6*	25.2	33.0
Dependency ratio	Total	96.0	93.7	73.7	57.4	50.0
	Youth	90.7	88.1	67.8	49.6	34.7
	Old Age	5.4	5.6	5.9	7.8	15.3
Potential support ratio		18.7	17.7	17.0	12.8	6.5
Parent support ratio		1.0	1.3	2.1	2.0	4.2
Sex ratio (per 100 women)	60+	95.8	151.7	114.7	97.3	89.4
	65+	93.8	153.7	117.5	97.5	84.9
	80+	93.1	169.7	107.0	88.5	60.3

* *Estimate refers to year 2005.*

Vanuatu

Indicator	Age	1950-1955	1975-1980	2005-2010	2025-2030	2045-2050
Growth rate (percentage)	Total	2.8	3.0	1.8	1.3	0.7
	60+	1.3	3.6	3.7	4.1	3.7
	65+	0.6	3.6	2.7	3.9	3.9
	80+	1.2	7.4	3.1	6.2	5.4
Total fertility rate (per woman)		7.6	5.8	3.7	2.6	2.1
Life expectancy (years)						
Total	Birth	42.0	56.8	70.0	74.8	77.9
	60	..	..	17.5	19.2	21.1
	65	..	..	13.9	15.4	17.1
	80	..	..	5.9	6.6	7.6
Female	Birth	43.5	58.8	72.1	77.1	80.2
	60	..	..	18.6	20.8	23.0
	65	..	..	14.8	16.7	18.8
	80	..	..	6.2	7.2	8.5
Male	Birth	40.6	55.3	68.2	72.7	75.7
	60	..	..	16.6	17.8	19.2
	65	..	..	13.2	14.2	15.3
	80	..	..	5.6	6.0	6.5
Survival rate (percentage)						
Total	60	..	..	81.2	88.2	91.7
	65	..	..	74.1	82.3	86.9
	80	..	..	32.8	43.0	52.0
Female	60	..	..	84.2	90.7	93.2
	65	..	..	78.2	86.2	89.8
	80	..	..	38.3	50.7	60.5
Male	60	..	..	78.5	85.8	90.1
	65	..	..	70.3	78.6	84.2
	80	..	..	28.5	36.1	43.7

		1980	1990	2007	2010	2020
Labour force participation (percentage)						
Total	65+	69.9	69.8	69.5	69.4	69.2
Female	65+	64.7	63.9	64.3	64.3	64.3
Male	65+	73.4	74.4	73.9	73.9	73.9

Percentage married, age 60+			Percentage living alone, age 60+		
Total	Female	Male	Total	Female	Male
68.0	57.0	77.0	..	..	..

Statutory pensionable age (2006)			Percentage illiterate, age 65+		
	Female	Male	Total	Female	Male
	55	55	..	..	..

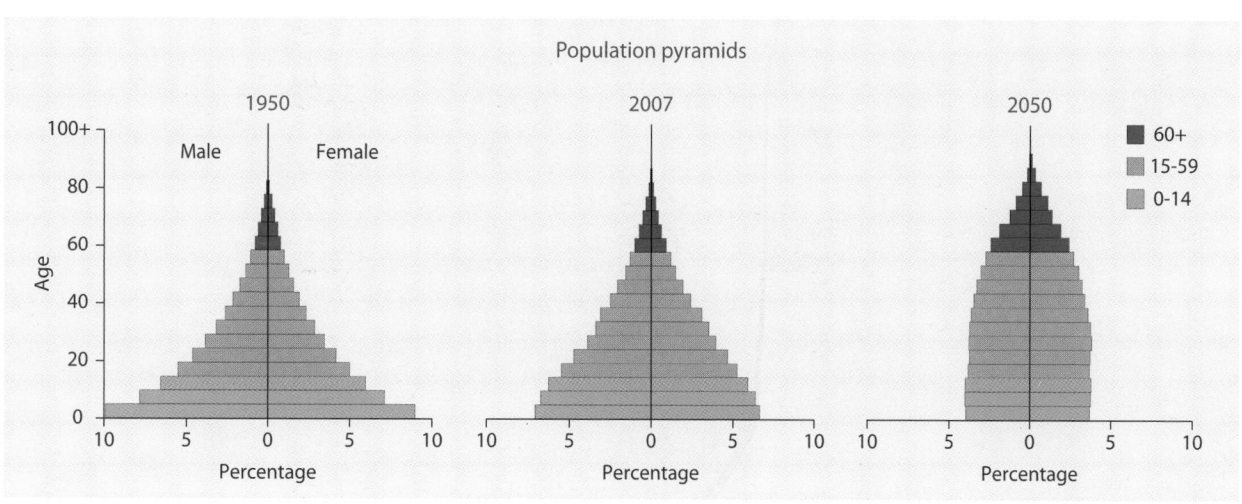

Population pyramids

United Nations Department of Economic and Social Affairs, Population Division

505

Venezuela

Indicator	Age	1950	1975	2007	2025	2050
Population (thousands)						
Total	Total	5 093.7	12 734.3	27 683.6	35 406.3	41 991.2
	0-14	2 213.8	5 513.7	8 412.7	8 671.2	7 761.4
	15-59	2 706.1	6 593.6	17 045.7	21 913.0	24 808.8
	60-64	76.8	226.7	757.4	1 510.7	2 404.5
	65-69	48.4	172.1	536.8	1 168.7	2 081.5
	70-74	26.9	113.9	394.7	910.8	1 738.2
	75-79	13.9	64.8	290.6	636.5	1 315.5
	80-84			168.7	369.3	995.1
	85-89			65.2	169.5	605.2
	90-94	7.9	49.6	11.4	50.6	230.2
	95-99			0.5	5.8	48.1
	100+			0.0	0.1	2.6
Female	Total	2 514.4	6 289.6	13 780.9	17 738.0	21 233.3
	0-14	1 084.5	2 704.3	4 115.4	4 236.6	3 790.0
	15-59	1 340.5	3 254.3	8 488.0	10 924.9	12 303.0
	60-64	38.9	115.3	386.9	780.6	1 240.1
	65-69	24.8	90.0	280.2	613.1	1 094.7
	70-74	14.0	61.2	211.1	487.7	937.8
	75-79	7.4	35.8	159.3	349.2	733.7
	80-84			95.2	210.2	579.1
	85-89			37.9	100.9	371.0
	90-94	4.4	28.7	6.7	31.2	149.5
	95-99			0.3	3.6	32.8
	100+			0.0	0.1	1.7
Male	Total	2 579.3	6 444.7	13 902.7	17 668.2	20 757.9
	0-14	1 129.3	2 809.3	4 297.3	4 434.6	3 971.4
	15-59	1 365.7	3 339.3	8 557.6	10 988.2	12 505.8
	60-64	37.9	111.3	370.5	730.2	1 164.4
	65-69	23.6	82.1	256.7	555.6	986.9
	70-74	12.9	52.7	183.6	423.1	800.4
	75-79	6.5	29.0	131.3	287.3	581.8
	80-84			73.5	159.1	416.0
	85-89			27.2	68.6	234.2
	90-94	3.5	21.0	4.7	19.4	80.7
	95-99			0.2	2.2	15.3
	100+			0.0	0.0	0.9
Percentage in older ages						
Total	60+	3.4	4.9	8.0	13.6	22.4
	65+	1.9	3.1	5.3	9.4	16.7
	80+	0.2	0.4	0.9	1.7	4.5
Female	60+	3.6	5.3	8.5	14.5	24.2
	65+	2.0	3.4	5.7	10.1	18.4
	80+	0.2	0.5	1.0	2.0	5.3
Male	60+	3.3	4.6	7.5	12.7	20.6
	65+	1.8	2.9	4.9	8.6	15.0
	80+	0.1	0.3	0.8	1.4	3.6
Ageing index		7.9	11.4	26.5	55.6	121.4
Broad age groups (percentage)	0-14	43.5	43.3	30.4	24.5	18.5
	15-59	53.1	51.8	61.6	61.9	59.1
	60+	3.4	4.9	8.0	13.6	22.4
Median age (years)		18.3	18.1	24.7*	31.1	38.5
Dependency ratio	Total	83.0	86.7	55.5	51.2	54.3
	Youth	79.5	80.8	47.3	37.0	28.5
	Old Age	3.5	5.9	8.2	14.1	25.8
Potential support ratio		28.7	17.0	12.1	7.1	3.9
Parent support ratio		1.0	1.6	2.6	4.5	11.8
Sex ratio (per 100 women)	60+	94.3	89.5	89.0	87.2	83.3
	65+	92.0	85.7	85.7	84.4	79.9
	80+	81.0	73.1	75.5	72.1	65.9

*   *Estimate refers to year 2005.*

Indicator	Age	1950-1955	1975-1980	2005-2010	2025-2030	2045-2050
Growth rate (percentage)	Total	4.0	3.4	1.7	1.0	0.4
	60+	7.2	3.8	4.6	3.4	2.2
	65+	5.9	4.0	4.3	4.1	2.4
	80+	7.7	3.5	6.2	5.9	3.2
Total fertility rate (per woman)		6.5	4.5	2.5	2.1	1.9
Life expectancy (years)						
Total	Birth	55.1	67.5	73.7	77.1	79.6
	60	..	..	21.0	22.6	23.9
	65	..	..	17.2	18.7	19.8
	80	..	..	7.2	8.3	9.2
Female	Birth	56.5	70.4	76.8	80.2	82.7
	60	..	..	22.1	24.1	25.7
	65	..	..	18.0	19.9	21.4
	80	..	..	7.3	8.7	9.8
Male	Birth	53.8	64.7	70.9	74.1	76.5
	60	..	..	19.9	21.1	22.0
	65	..	..	16.3	17.3	18.1
	80	..	..	6.9	7.7	8.3
Survival rate (percentage)						
Total	60	..	..	83.8	87.5	90.1
	65	..	..	78.7	83.2	86.3
	80	..	..	49.8	56.9	61.9
Female	60	..	..	88.5	91.5	93.5
	65	..	..	84.4	88.2	90.8
	80	..	..	57.4	65.6	71.1
Male	60	..	..	79.3	83.7	86.8
	65	..	..	73.4	78.4	81.9
	80	..	..	42.7	48.5	52.9

		1980	1990	2007	2010	2020
Labour force participation (percentage)						
Total	65+	27.4	27.3	26.3	26.5	27.1
Female	65+	6.5	9.2	5.3	4.9	4.5
Male	65+	52.1	49.1	50.8	51.6	53.5

Percentage married, age 60+			Percentage living alone, age 60+ (1990)		
Total	Female	Male	Total	Female	Male
49.4	34.0	67.0	6.4	5.4	7.6

Statutory pensionable age (2006)			Percentage illiterate, age 65+		
	Female	Male	Total	Female	Male
	55	60	..	..	..

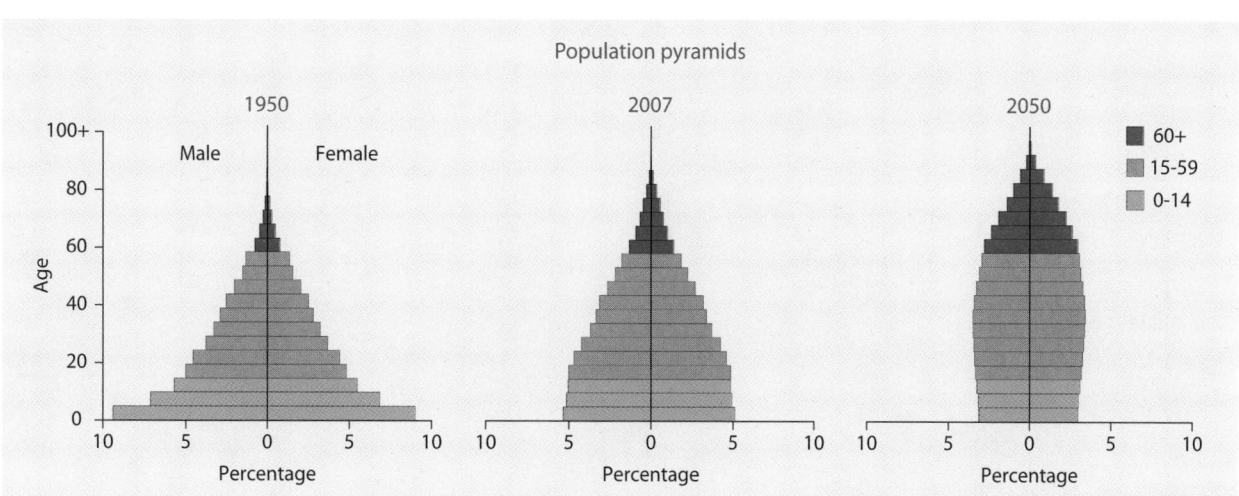

Population pyramids

United Nations Department of Economic and Social Affairs, Population Division

507

Viet Nam

Indicator	Age	1950	1975	2007	2025	2050
Population (thousands)						
Total	Total	27 366.7	47 974.3	86 444.7	104 343.1	116 654.2
	0-14	8 688.1	20 682.5	24 258.2	22 924.2	20 263.2
	15-59	16 759.8	23 699.6	55 750.2	67 839.0	66 623.3
	60-64	767.1	1 263.5	1 741.3	4 809.5	8 055.5
	65-69	536.4	951.8	1 502.7	3 653.1	6 783.3
	70-74	342.7	737.4	1 362.0	2 508.8	5 595.1
	75-79	179.0	403.7	972.0	1 292.6	4 251.6
	80-84			548.7	754.7	2 859.2
	85-89			234.5	386.6	1 540.0
	90-94	93.6	235.8	64.6	146.1	552.0
	95-99			9.7	25.8	119.5
	100+			0.8	2.5	11.3
Female	Total	13 756.9	24 149.8	43 271.2	52 247.1	58 668.6
	0-14	4 314.4	10 300.6	11 908.5	11 225.7	9 901.3
	15-59	8 387.3	11 910.0	27 943.7	33 834.9	32 943.2
	60-64	408.9	659.3	900.8	2 486.9	4 076.9
	65-69	292.7	507.4	784.7	1 910.8	3 488.5
	70-74	191.9	402.6	723.1	1 330.9	2 938.1
	75-79	103.6	228.1	526.6	702.5	2 310.6
	80-84			304.1	421.4	1 621.8
	85-89			134.0	224.8	928.6
	90-94	58.0	141.9	38.9	90.1	362.9
	95-99			6.3	17.2	87.4
	100+			0.6	1.8	9.3
Male	Total	13 609.8	23 824.5	43 173.5	52 096.0	57 985.6
	0-14	4 373.7	10 381.9	12 349.7	11 698.5	10 361.9
	15-59	8 372.5	11 789.7	27 806.5	34 004.1	33 680.1
	60-64	358.2	604.2	840.5	2 322.6	3 978.6
	65-69	243.7	444.5	718.0	1 742.3	3 294.8
	70-74	150.7	334.8	638.9	1 177.9	2 657.0
	75-79	75.4	175.6	445.4	590.0	1 941.0
	80-84			244.7	333.3	1 237.3
	85-89			100.5	161.8	611.5
	90-94	35.6	93.9	25.8	56.0	189.1
	95-99			3.4	8.6	32.2
	100+			0.2	0.7	2.1
Percentage in older ages						
Total	60+	7.0	7.5	7.4	13.0	25.5
	65+	4.2	4.9	5.4	8.4	18.6
	80+	0.3	0.5	1.0	1.3	4.4
Female	60+	7.7	8.0	7.9	13.8	27.0
	65+	4.7	5.3	5.8	9.0	20.0
	80+	0.4	0.6	1.1	1.4	5.1
Male	60+	6.3	6.9	7.0	12.3	24.0
	65+	3.7	4.4	5.0	7.8	17.2
	80+	0.3	0.4	0.9	1.1	3.6
Ageing index		22.1	17.4	26.5	59.2	146.9
Broad age groups (percentage)	0-14	31.7	43.1	28.1	22.0	17.4
	15-59	61.2	49.4	64.5	65.0	57.1
	60+	7.0	7.5	7.4	13.0	25.5
Median age (years)		24.6	18.2	24.9*	33.4	41.3
Dependency ratio	Total	56.1	92.2	50.4	43.6	56.2
	Youth	49.6	82.9	42.2	31.6	27.1
	Old Age	6.6	9.3	8.2	12.1	29.1
Potential support ratio		15.2	10.7	12.2	8.3	3.4
Parent support ratio		0.9	1.4	3.9	3.3	9.5
Sex ratio (per 100 women)	60+	81.8	85.2	88.3	89.0	88.1
	65+	78.2	81.9	86.4	86.6	84.8
	80+	61.4	66.2	77.4	74.2	68.8

* *Estimate refers to year 2005.*

Viet Nam

Indicator	Age	1950-1955	1975-1980	2005-2010	2025-2030	2045-2050
Growth rate (percentage)	Total	1.9	2.0	1.3	0.7	0.2
	60+	2.5	1.7	1.7	4.1	2.5
	65+	2.6	2.4	1.2	5.1	2.5
	80+	2.5	4.3	2.9	3.1	4.1
Total fertility rate (per woman)		5.7	5.9	2.1	1.9	1.9
Life expectancy (years)						
Total	Birth	40.4	55.8	71.9	76.2	78.9
	60	..	..	19.5	21.2	22.6
	65	..	..	15.7	17.2	18.5
	80	..	..	6.8	7.6	8.5
Female	Birth	41.8	58.0	73.9	78.1	81.0
	60	..	..	20.2	22.2	24.0
	65	..	..	16.2	18.1	19.7
	80	..	..	7.0	8.1	9.2
Male	Birth	39.1	53.6	69.9	74.2	76.9
	60	..	..	18.7	20.1	21.2
	65	..	..	15.0	16.3	17.2
	80	..	..	6.5	7.1	7.7
Survival rate (percentage)						
Total	60	..	..	82.6	88.3	91.3
	65	..	..	77.1	83.7	87.4
	80	..	..	41.2	50.7	57.5
Female	60	..	..	85.6	90.6	93.1
	65	..	..	80.8	86.7	90.0
	80	..	..	45.5	55.9	63.5
Male	60	..	..	79.7	85.9	89.4
	65	..	..	73.5	80.7	84.8
	80	..	..	37.0	45.5	51.6

		1980	1990	2007	2010	2020
Labour force participation (percentage)						
Total	65+	19.8	19.5	18.7	18.6	18.4
Female	65+	12.7	13.3	15.1	15.5	16.8
Male	65+	28.4	26.7	22.8	22.1	20.2

Percentage married, age 60+			Percentage living alone, age 60+		
Total	Female	Male	Total	Female	Male
63.3	45.0	84.0	..	..	..

Statutory pensionable age (2006)			Percentage illiterate, age 65+		
Female	Male		Total	Female	Male
55	60		..	..	..

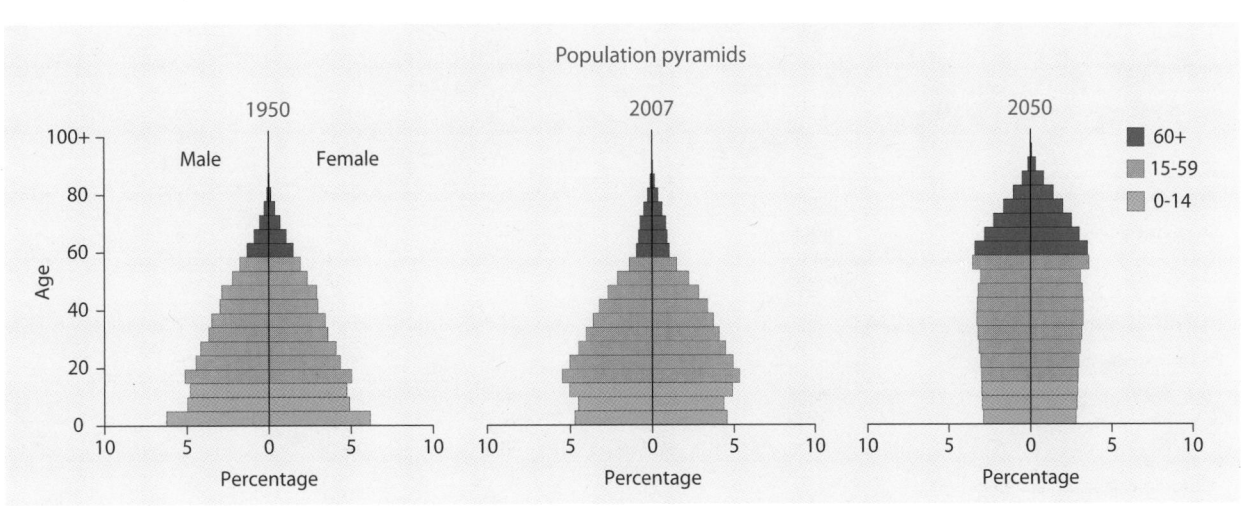

Population pyramids

Western Sahara

Indicator	Age	1950	1975	2007	2025	2050
Population (thousands)						
Total	Total	13.8	75.3	372.4	680.5	895.8
	0-14	5.9	33.3	122.7	196.9	195.6
	15-59	7.3	39.0	226.2	420.7	538.1
	60-64	0.3	1.1	9.7	21.3	53.7
	65-69	0.2	0.8	6.4	17.9	45.5
	70-74	0.1	0.6	3.9	12.6	29.8
	75-79	0.1	0.3	2.1	6.9	17.5
	80-84			1.0	2.9	9.8
	85-89			0.3	1.0	4.3
	90-94	0.0	0.1	0.1	0.2	1.3
	95-99			0.0	0.0	0.2
	100+			0.0	0.0	0.0
Female	Total	7.0	34.3	179.8	330.2	444.5
	0-14	2.9	16.5	60.6	97.2	96.1
	15-59	3.7	16.5	108.8	202.7	265.1
	60-64	0.1	0.5	4.4	10.2	26.4
	65-69	0.1	0.4	2.9	8.7	22.8
	70-74	0.1	0.3	1.7	6.1	15.3
	75-79	0.0	0.2	0.9	3.3	9.4
	80-84			0.4	1.5	5.6
	85-89			0.1	0.5	2.7
	90-94	0.0	0.1	0.0	0.1	0.9
	95-99			0.0	0.0	0.2
	100+			0.0	0.0	0.0
Male	Total	6.8	41.0	192.5	350.3	451.3
	0-14	2.9	16.8	62.1	99.8	99.5
	15-59	3.6	22.5	117.4	218.1	273.0
	60-64	0.1	0.7	5.3	11.1	27.3
	65-69	0.1	0.5	3.5	9.2	22.7
	70-74	0.1	0.3	2.2	6.6	14.5
	75-79	0.0	0.2	1.2	3.5	8.2
	80-84			0.5	1.5	4.2
	85-89			0.2	0.5	1.6
	90-94	0.0	0.1	0.0	0.1	0.4
	95-99			0.0	0.0	0.0
	100+			0.0	0.0	0.0
Percentage in older ages						
Total	60+	4.7	4.0	6.3	9.2	18.1
	65+	2.8	2.5	3.7	6.1	12.1
	80+	0.2	0.2	0.4	0.6	1.7
Female	60+	5.1	3.8	5.8	9.2	18.7
	65+	3.1	2.4	3.4	6.1	12.8
	80+	0.2	0.2	0.3	0.6	2.1
Male	60+	4.3	4.1	6.7	9.3	17.5
	65+	2.5	2.5	4.0	6.1	11.4
	80+	0.1	0.2	0.4	0.6	1.4
Ageing index		11.1	9.0	19.1	31.9	82.9
Broad age groups (percentage)	0-14	42.5	44.2	32.9	28.9	21.8
	15-59	52.8	51.8	60.8	61.8	60.1
	60+	4.7	4.0	6.3	9.2	18.1
Median age (years)		18.7	17.7	22.7*	29.1	34.2
Dependency ratio	Total	83.0	87.6	57.9	53.9	51.4
	Youth	77.8	82.9	52.0	44.6	33.1
	Old Age	5.1	4.6	5.9	9.4	18.3
Potential support ratio		19.5	21.6	17.1	10.7	5.5
Parent support ratio		0.7	0.5	0.9	1.5	3.7
Sex ratio (per 100 women)	60+	82.0	130.7	123.8	107.2	94.8
	65+	78.7	122.5	125.4	105.9	90.8
	80+	58.8	98.6	125.7	97.8	66.4

* *Estimate refers to year 2005.*

Indicator	Age	1950-1955	1975-1980	2005-2010	2025-2030	2045-2050
Growth rate (percentage)	Total	8.5	13.8	4.6	1.3	0.9
	60+	7.5	18.7	6.7	3.1	3.9
	65+	7.7	19.4	6.3	3.5	5.1
	80+	2.8	27.0	6.0	6.8	3.6
Total fertility rate (per woman)		6.5	6.1	3.4	2.5	2.0
Life expectancy (years)						
Total	Birth	35.5	47.5	65.9	72.3	76.2
	60	..	..	16.6	18.1	20.0
	65	..	..	13.2	14.4	16.1
	80	..	..	5.6	6.1	7.0
Female	Birth	37.1	49.4	68.0	74.7	78.6
	60	..	..	17.7	19.3	21.9
	65	..	..	14.1	15.4	17.8
	80	..	..	5.9	6.4	7.8
Male	Birth	34.0	46.1	64.2	70.2	73.9
	60	..	..	15.8	17.1	18.3
	65	..	..	12.6	13.6	14.6
	80	..	..	5.4	5.8	6.1
Survival rate (percentage)						
Total	60	..	..	74.5	84.7	89.8
	65	..	..	66.8	78.1	84.4
	80	..	..	27.1	36.9	46.8
Female	60	..	..	77.7	88.2	92.0
	65	..	..	71.1	82.9	88.1
	80	..	..	32.0	43.5	55.6
Male	60	..	..	71.8	81.7	87.8
	65	..	..	63.2	73.9	81.1
	80	..	..	23.5	31.5	38.9

		1980	1990	2007	2010	2020
Labour force participation (percentage)						
Total	65+	51.6	57.6	50.7	49.8	48.1
Female	65+	11.6	18.1	10.4	10.2	10.1
Male	65+	88.1	86.6	82.9	82.5	81.8

Percentage married, age 60+			Percentage living alone, age 60+		
Total	Female	Male	Total	Female	Male
71.3	54.0	84.0	..	..	..

Statutory pensionable age (2006)		Percentage illiterate, age 65+		
Female	Male	Total	Female	Male
..	..	..	..	..

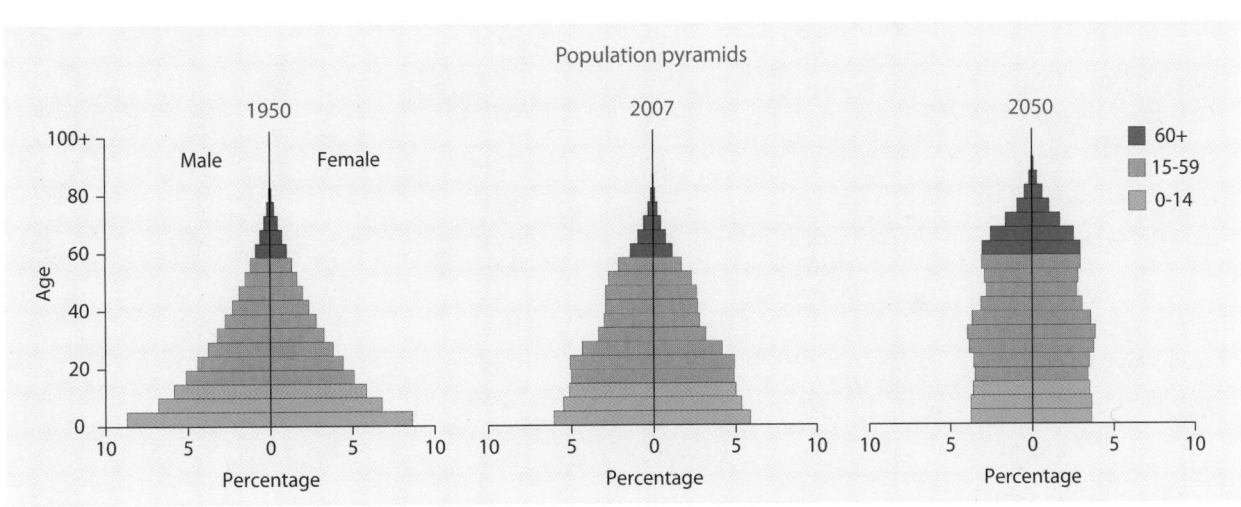

Population pyramids

United Nations Department of Economic and Social Affairs, Population Division

Yemen

Indicator	Age	1950	1975	2007	2025	2050
Population (thousands)						
Total	Total	4 316.0	6 968.2	22 325.0	37 094.1	59 453.8
	0-14	1 825.3	3 478.6	10 194.4	14 636.1	17 030.2
	15-59	2 223.1	3 220.1	11 315.3	20 690.3	37 174.6
	60-64	97.4	105.5	305.3	659.9	1 964.6
	65-69	75.8	75.9	218.0	497.1	1 455.9
	70-74	52.4	48.3	142.8	323.1	912.6
	75-79	28.3	26.0	86.3	173.7	519.1
	80-84			43.6	80.8	262.6
	85-89			15.2	26.7	105.8
	90-94	13.7	13.8	3.6	5.7	25.3
	95-99			0.4	0.7	3.1
	100+			0.0	0.1	0.2
Female	Total	2 136.8	3 499.1	11 009.9	18 349.0	29 533.0
	0-14	898.4	1 699.1	4 996.0	7 178.7	8 345.2
	15-59	1 096.2	1 650.2	5 588.9	10 213.8	18 409.1
	60-64	51.1	57.5	156.3	351.7	1 003.3
	65-69	40.2	41.8	112.0	265.2	756.7
	70-74	27.8	27.1	74.5	176.2	486.7
	75-79	15.5	14.9	46.3	97.6	288.9
	80-84			24.5	46.0	156.8
	85-89			9.0	15.7	67.2
	90-94	7.6	8.4	2.2	3.5	16.8
	95-99			0.3	0.5	2.2
	100+			0.0	0.0	0.1
Male	Total	2 179.2	3 469.1	11 315.1	18 745.1	29 920.8
	0-14	926.9	1 779.5	5 198.4	7 457.3	8 685.0
	15-59	1 126.9	1 569.8	5 726.4	10 476.6	18 765.5
	60-64	46.3	48.0	149.0	308.2	961.3
	65-69	35.6	34.1	106.0	231.9	699.2
	70-74	24.6	21.2	68.4	146.9	425.9
	75-79	12.8	11.0	40.0	76.0	230.2
	80-84			19.2	34.7	105.7
	85-89			6.2	10.9	38.5
	90-94	6.1	5.4	1.4	2.2	8.5
	95-99			0.1	0.2	0.9
	100+			0.0	0.0	0.0
Percentage in older ages						
Total	60+	6.2	3.9	3.7	4.8	8.8
	65+	3.9	2.4	2.3	3.0	5.5
	80+	0.3	0.2	0.3	0.3	0.7
Female	60+	6.7	4.3	3.9	5.2	9.4
	65+	4.3	2.6	2.4	3.3	6.0
	80+	0.4	0.2	0.3	0.4	0.8
Male	60+	5.8	3.5	3.4	4.3	8.3
	65+	3.6	2.1	2.1	2.7	5.0
	80+	0.3	0.2	0.2	0.3	0.5
Ageing index		14.7	7.7	8.0	12.1	30.8
Broad age groups (percentage)	0-14	42.3	49.9	45.7	39.5	28.6
	15-59	51.5	46.2	50.7	55.8	62.5
	60+	6.2	3.9	3.7	4.8	8.8
Median age (years)		18.9	15.0	16.5*	19.8	27.2
Dependency ratio	Total	86.0	109.5	92.1	73.7	51.9
	Youth	78.7	104.6	87.7	68.6	43.5
	Old Age	7.3	4.9	4.4	5.2	8.4
Potential support ratio		13.6	20.3	22.8	19.3	11.9
Parent support ratio		0.9	0.9	1.5	1.3	1.9
Sex ratio (per 100 women)	60+	88.2	79.9	91.8	84.8	88.9
	65+	86.8	77.7	89.8	83.2	85.0
	80+	80.3	64.1	74.7	73.2	63.2

* *Estimate refers to year 2005.*

Indicator	Age	1950-1955	1975-1980	2005-2010	2025-2030	2045-2050
Growth rate (percentage)	Total	1.8	3.2	3.1	2.2	1.5
	60+	–1.1	2.0	3.4	3.6	5.0
	65+	–1.0	2.1	3.2	4.4	5.5
	80+	0.7	2.6	2.0	4.9	3.7
Total fertility rate (per woman)		8.2	8.5	5.7	3.5	2.5
Life expectancy (years)						
Total	Birth	32.5	44.2	62.7	70.1	73.8
	60	..	..	16.2	17.6	18.8
	65	..	..	12.9	14.0	15.1
	80	..	..	5.6	5.9	6.4
Female	Birth	32.7	44.4	64.1	72.2	76.0
	60	..	..	17.1	18.6	20.1
	65	..	..	13.6	14.8	16.1
	80	..	..	5.8	6.2	6.8
Male	Birth	32.4	43.9	61.3	68.2	71.8
	60	..	..	15.4	16.6	17.5
	65	..	..	12.3	13.2	14.0
	80	..	..	5.3	5.6	5.9
Survival rate (percentage)						
Total	60	..	..	69.4	81.2	86.9
	65	..	..	61.6	74.2	80.8
	80	..	..	24.0	33.4	40.7
Female	60	..	..	71.8	84.3	89.6
	65	..	..	64.9	78.3	84.7
	80	..	..	27.5	38.4	47.3
Male	60	..	..	67.0	78.3	84.3
	65	..	..	58.4	70.2	76.9
	80	..	..	20.7	28.4	34.4

		1980	1990	2007	2010	2020
Labour force participation (percentage)						
Total	65+	15.2	14.8	16.4	16.4	16.2
Female	65+	7.1	7.4	6.8	6.8	6.8
Male	65+	25.8	24.9	27.1	27.2	27.3

Percentage married, age 60+			Percentage living alone, age 60+ (1992)		
Total	Female	Male	Total	Female	Male
66.4	47.0	87.0	4.0	6.0	2.3

Statutory pensionable age (2006)			Percentage illiterate, age 65+		
	Female	Male	Total	Female	Male
	55	60	..	..	..

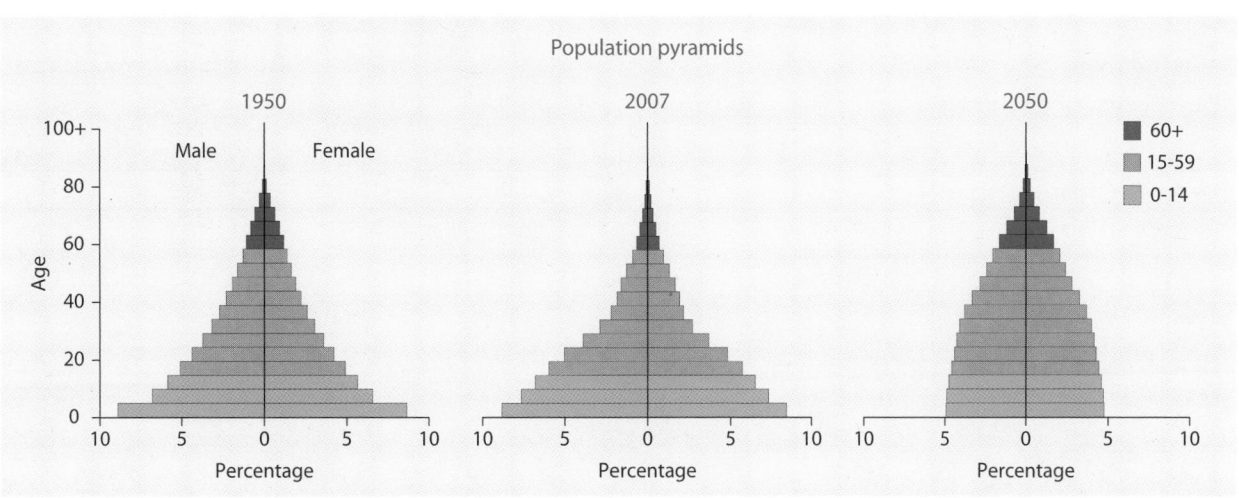

Population pyramids

Zambia

Indicator	Age	1950	1975	2007	2025	2050
Population (thousands)						
Total	Total	2 440.4	5 151.5	12 056.0	16 418.9	22 781.0
	0-14	1 096.0	2 463.4	5 476.9	6 702.0	7 104.9
	15-59	1 238.6	2 472.8	6 014.3	8 998.1	14 212.9
	60-64	39.5	84.7	196.4	208.5	546.6
	65-69	29.9	60.3	152.9	185.9	378.7
	70-74	20.0	38.7	107.3	144.2	254.2
	75-79	11.0	21.1	64.5	99.9	159.0
	80-84			30.8	53.9	77.9
	85-89			10.5	20.7	34.0
	90-94	5.4	10.5	2.2	5.0	10.8
	95-99			0.3	0.7	1.9
	100+			0.0	0.1	0.2
Female	Total	1 234.6	2 591.8	6 009.5	8 097.4	11 315.0
	0-14	547.2	1 224.4	2 724.4	3 330.6	3 528.2
	15-59	632.6	1 251.1	2 974.4	4 379.5	7 072.9
	60-64	20.2	44.6	105.7	103.7	263.9
	65-69	15.6	32.3	83.2	99.2	181.8
	70-74	10.3	21.5	59.3	80.0	123.0
	75-79	5.8	11.8	36.5	56.8	78.0
	80-84			18.0	31.5	40.2
	85-89			6.4	12.5	19.0
	90-94	2.9	6.1	1.4	3.2	6.6
	95-99			0.2	0.5	1.2
	100+			0.0	0.0	0.1
Male	Total	1 205.8	2 559.7	6 046.6	8 321.5	11 466.0
	0-14	548.8	1 239.0	2 752.4	3 371.4	3 576.7
	15-59	606.0	1 221.7	3 039.9	4 618.6	7 140.0
	60-64	19.3	40.2	90.7	104.8	282.8
	65-69	14.3	28.0	69.7	86.8	196.9
	70-74	9.7	17.2	48.0	64.2	131.2
	75-79	5.1	9.3	28.0	43.1	81.0
	80-84			12.8	22.4	37.6
	85-89			4.1	8.2	15.0
	90-94	2.5	4.4	0.8	1.8	4.2
	95-99			0.1	0.2	0.6
	100+			0.0	0.0	0.0
Percentage in older ages						
Total	60+	4.3	4.2	4.7	4.4	6.4
	65+	2.7	2.5	3.1	3.1	4.0
	80+	0.2	0.2	0.4	0.5	0.5
Female	60+	4.4	4.5	5.2	4.8	6.3
	65+	2.8	2.8	3.4	3.5	4.0
	80+	0.2	0.2	0.4	0.6	0.6
Male	60+	4.2	3.9	4.2	4.0	6.5
	65+	2.6	2.3	2.7	2.7	4.1
	80+	0.2	0.2	0.3	0.4	0.5
Ageing index		9.7	8.7	10.3	10.7	20.6
Broad age groups (percentage)	0-14	44.9	47.8	45.4	40.8	31.2
	15-59	50.8	48.0	49.9	54.8	62.4
	60+	4.3	4.2	4.7	4.4	6.4
Median age (years)		17.5	16.1	16.7*	18.9	24.4
Dependency ratio	Total	90.9	101.4	94.1	78.3	54.3
	Youth	85.8	96.3	88.2	72.8	48.1
	Old Age	5.2	5.1	5.9	5.5	6.2
Potential support ratio		19.3	19.6	16.9	18.0	16.1
Parent support ratio		0.9	0.8	1.9	3.3	2.2
Sex ratio (per 100 women)	60+	93.0	85.1	81.8	85.6	105.0
	65+	91.4	82.0	79.8	80.0	103.7
	80+	87.1	72.7	68.7	68.6	85.5

*   Estimate refers to year 2005.

Indicator	Age	1950-1955	1975-1980	2005-2010	2025-2030	2045-2050
Growth rate (percentage)	Total	2.4	3.2	1.7	1.5	1.1
	60+	0.9	3.5	2.0	0.9	4.5
	65+	0.9	3.8	2.4	0.8	4.1
	80+	1.6	5.1	3.5	2.7	1.6
Total fertility rate (per woman)		6.6	7.2	5.2	3.3	2.4
Life expectancy (years)						
Total	Birth	38.3	51.7	39.1	49.0	57.5
	60	..	..	16.0	17.2	18.4
	65	..	..	13.0	14.0	15.0
	80	..	..	5.8	6.2	6.6
Female	Birth	39.9	53.3	38.6	49.2	59.1
	60	..	..	16.6	17.9	19.3
	65	..	..	13.4	14.5	15.6
	80	..	..	6.0	6.4	6.8
Male	Birth	36.7	50.0	39.6	48.8	56.2
	60	..	..	15.3	16.4	17.6
	65	..	..	12.4	13.4	14.4
	80	..	..	5.5	5.9	6.3
Survival rate (percentage)						
Total	60	..	..	24.8	37.4	51.6
	65	..	..	21.6	33.2	47.0
	80	..	..	8.5	14.9	23.4
Female	60	..	..	23.3	36.9	53.9
	65	..	..	20.6	33.3	49.9
	80	..	..	8.6	15.8	26.6
Male	60	..	..	26.1	37.8	49.5
	65	..	..	22.3	33.2	44.4
	80	..	..	8.1	13.8	20.8

		1980	1990	2007	2010	2020
Labour force participation (percentage)						
Total	65+	49.8	49.8	50.7	50.5	50.4
Female	65+	35.7	32.6	31.6	31.4	31.2
Male	65+	66.8	70.8	74.7	74.7	74.9

Percentage married, age 60+			Percentage living alone, age 60+ (2002)		
Total	Female	Male	Total	Female	Male
64.6	46.0	87.0	8.8	12.3	5.5

Statutory pensionable age (2006)			Percentage illiterate, age 65+ (1999)		
	Female	Male	Total	Female	Male
	55	55	61.4	82.7	43.2

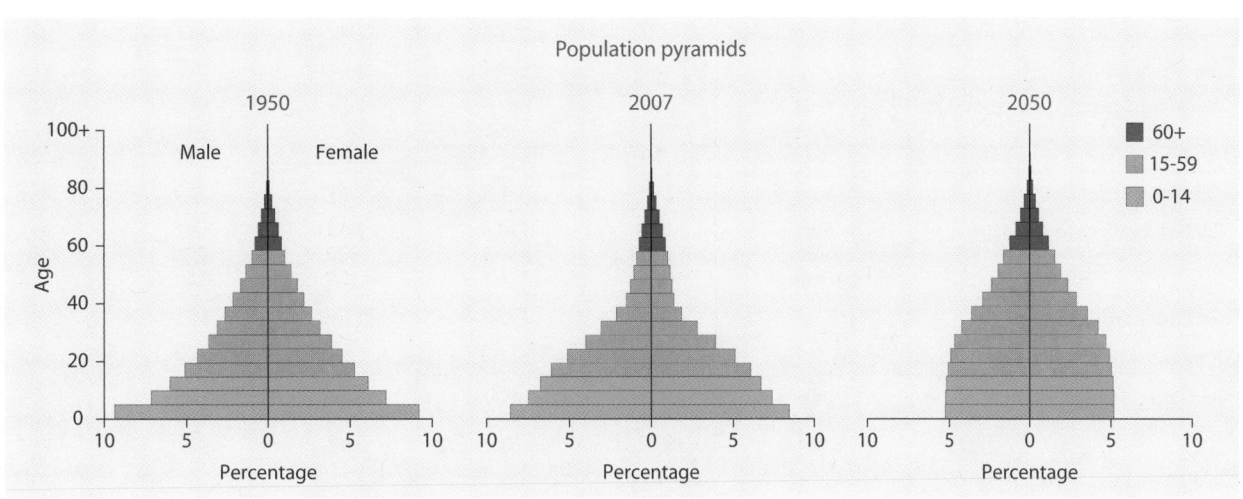

Population pyramids

United Nations Department of Economic and Social Affairs, Population Division   515

Zimbabwe

Indicator	Age	1950	1975	2007	2025	2050
Population (thousands)						
Total	Total	2 743.7	6 212.5	13 162.1	14 430.1	15 804.6
	0-14	1 149.8	3 041.4	5 129.8	5 009.3	4 363.3
	15-59	1 447.2	2 881.7	7 304.6	8 491.0	9 987.7
	60-64	57.7	103.4	229.3	238.5	516.9
	65-69	41.4	77.0	192.0	236.2	387.3
	70-74	26.6	54.8	138.5	205.4	249.5
	75-79	14.2	33.6	93.4	124.5	141.3
	80-84			48.6	80.8	86.1
	85-89			20.3	33.6	49.3
	90-94	6.8	20.6	4.9	9.3	19.0
	95-99			0.6	1.5	4.0
	100+			0.0	0.1	0.3
Female	Total	1 377.3	3 125.8	6 614.7	7 073.3	7 764.1
	0-14	567.7	1 519.5	2 559.9	2 500.8	2 173.7
	15-59	728.1	1 450.9	3 658.0	4 049.4	4 913.7
	60-64	31.4	53.7	123.7	126.3	233.0
	65-69	22.6	40.9	103.2	132.5	173.2
	70-74	15.1	29.8	75.3	118.3	112.8
	75-79	8.4	18.8	51.8	72.3	66.8
	80-84			27.5	47.0	46.1
	85-89			11.8	19.8	29.6
	90-94	4.1	12.2	3.0	5.8	12.4
	95-99			0.4	1.0	2.8
	100+			0.0	0.1	0.2
Male	Total	1 366.4	3 086.7	6 547.3	7 356.8	8 040.6
	0-14	582.1	1 521.9	2 569.9	2 508.4	2 189.6
	15-59	719.1	1 430.8	3 646.6	4 441.6	5 074.1
	60-64	26.4	49.7	105.7	112.1	283.9
	65-69	18.8	36.1	88.8	103.7	214.1
	70-74	11.5	25.0	63.3	87.1	136.7
	75-79	5.8	14.7	41.6	52.2	74.6
	80-84			21.1	33.8	40.1
	85-89			8.4	13.7	19.7
	90-94	2.6	8.4	1.9	3.6	6.6
	95-99			0.2	0.5	1.2
	100+			0.0	0.0	0.1
Percentage in older ages						
Total	60+	5.3	4.7	5.5	6.4	9.2
	65+	3.2	3.0	3.8	4.8	5.9
	80+	0.2	0.3	0.6	0.9	1.0
Female	60+	5.9	5.0	6.0	7.4	8.7
	65+	3.6	3.3	4.1	5.6	5.7
	80+	0.3	0.4	0.6	1.0	1.2
Male	60+	4.8	4.3	5.1	5.5	9.7
	65+	2.8	2.7	3.4	4.0	6.1
	80+	0.2	0.3	0.5	0.7	0.8
Ageing index		12.8	9.5	14.2	18.6	33.3
Broad age groups (percentage)	0-14	41.9	49.0	39.0	34.7	27.6
	15-59	52.7	46.4	55.5	58.8	63.2
	60+	5.3	4.7	5.5	6.4	9.2
Median age (years)		19.0	15.5	18.7*	22.0	26.7
Dependency ratio	Total	82.3	108.1	74.7	65.3	50.5
	Youth	76.4	101.9	68.1	57.4	41.5
	Old Age	5.9	6.2	6.6	7.9	8.9
Potential support ratio		16.9	16.0	15.1	12.6	11.2
Parent support ratio		1.0	1.4	3.0	5.9	4.0
Sex ratio (per 100 women)	60+	79.8	86.2	83.4	77.8	114.8
	65+	77.3	82.9	82.5	74.3	111.1
	80+	63.7	68.9	73.8	70.1	74.3

* Estimate refers to year 2005.

Indicator	Age	1950-1955	1975-1980	2005-2010	2025-2030	2045-2050
Growth rate (percentage)	Total	3.1	3.3	0.6	0.4	0.4
	60+	3.2	3.3	1.3	−0.3	4.0
	65+	3.5	2.7	2.3	0.3	4.2
	80+	5.1	3.3	3.3	1.2	−1.0
Total fertility rate (per woman)		6.8	7.3	3.2	2.4	2.0
Life expectancy (years)						
Total	Birth	48.5	57.7	37.3	46.8	54.8
	60	..	..	17.2	18.4	19.5
	65	..	..	14.1	15.1	16.0
	80	..	..	6.3	6.7	7.1
Female	Birth	50.0	59.4	36.3	45.9	55.7
	60	..	..	18.0	19.2	20.7
	65	..	..	14.7	15.7	16.9
	80	..	..	6.5	6.9	7.4
Male	Birth	46.9	56.0	38.2	47.5	54.1
	60	..	..	16.3	17.4	18.5
	65	..	..	13.5	14.4	15.2
	80	..	..	6.0	6.4	6.7
Survival rate (percentage)						
Total	60	..	..	17.2	29.6	43.0
	65	..	..	15.2	26.7	39.4
	80	..	..	6.9	13.5	21.6
Female	60	..	..	15.3	27.3	44.0
	65	..	..	13.8	25.0	41.2
	80	..	..	6.7	13.4	24.5
Male	60	..	..	19.1	31.7	42.2
	65	..	..	16.5	28.1	38.1
	80	..	..	6.9	13.2	19.5

		1980	1990	2007	2010	2020
Labour force participation (percentage)						
Total	65+	66.2	61.8	58.6	58.2	57.3
Female	65+	70.2	63.6	55.4	54.6	53.2
Male	65+	61.5	59.7	62.4	62.6	62.8

Percentage married, age 60+				Percentage living alone, age 60+ (1999)		
Total	Female	Male		Total	Female	Male
60.3	39.0	85.0		8.8	9.4	8.1

Statutory pensionable age (2006)				Percentage illiterate, age 65+		
	Female	Male		Total	Female	Male
	60	60		..	..	..

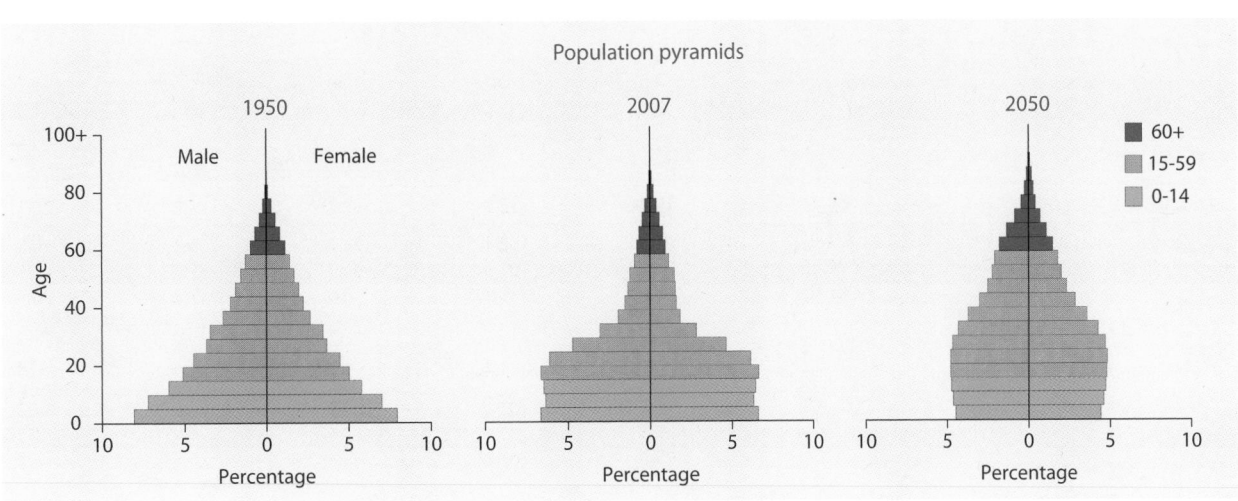

Population pyramids

Litho in United Nations, New York
07-23042—March 2007—6,535
ISBN 978-92-1-151432-2

United Nations publication
Sales No. E.07.XIII.5
ST/ESA/SER.A/260